한국의 토익 수험자 여러분께,

토익 시험은 세계적인 직무 영어능력 평가 시험으로, 지난 40여 년간 비즈니스 현장에서 필요한 영어능력 평가의 기준을 제시해 왔습니다. 토익 시험 및 토익스피킹, 토익라이팅 시험은 세계에서 가장 널리 통용되는 영어능력 검증 시험으로, 160여 개국 14,000여 기관이 토익 성적을 의사결정에 활용하고 있습니다.

YBM은 한국의 토익 시험을 주관하는 ETS 독점 계약사입니다.

ETS는 한국 수험자들의 효과적인 토익 학습을 돕고자 YBM을 통하여 'ETS 토익 공식 교재'를 독점 출간하고 있습니다. 또한 'ETS 토익 공식 교재' 시리즈에 기출문항을 제공해 한국의 다른 교재들에 수록된 기출을 복제하거나 변형한 문항으로 인하여 발생할 수 있는 수험자들의 혼동을 방지하고 있습니다.

복제 및 변형 문항들은 토익 시험의 출제의도를 벗어날 수 있기 때문에 기출문항을 수록한 'ETS 토익 공식 교재'만큼 시험에 잘 대비할 수 없습니다.

'ETS 토익 공식 교재'를 통하여 수험자 여러분의 영어 소통을 위한 노력에 큰 성취가 있기를 바랍니다.

감사합니다.

Dear TOEIC Test Takers in Korea,

The TOEIC program is the global leader in English-language assessment for the workplace. It has set the standard for assessing English-language skills needed in the workplace for more than 40 years. The TOEIC tests are the most widely used English language assessments around the world, with 14,000+ organizations across more than 160 countries trusting TOEIC scores to make decisions.

YBM is the ETS Country Master Distributor for the TOEIC program in Korea and so is the exclusive distributor for TOEIC Korea.

To support effective learning for TOEIC test-takers in Korea, ETS has authorized YBM to publish the only Official TOEIC prep books in Korea. These books contain actual TOEIC items to help prevent confusion among Korean test-takers that might be caused by other prep book publishers' use of reproduced or paraphrased items.

Reproduced or paraphrased items may fail to reflect the intent of actual TOEIC items and so will not prepare test-takers as well as the actual items contained in the ETS TOEIC Official prep books published by YBM.

We hope that these ETS TOEIC Official prep books enable you, as test-takers, to achieve great success in your efforts to communicate effectively in English.

Thank you.

입문부터 실전까지 수준별 학습을 통해 최단기 목표점수 달성!

ETS TOEIC® 공식수험서
스마트 학습 지원

www.ybmbooks.com에서도 무료 MP3를 다운로드 받을 수 있습니다.

ETS 토익 모바일 학습 플랫폼!
ETS 토익기출 수험서 앱

구글플레이　앱스토어

교재 학습 지원
- LC 음원 MP3
- 교재 해설 동영상 강의
- 교재/부록 모의고사 채점 분석
- 단어 암기장

부가 서비스
- 데일리 학습(토익 기출문제 풀이)
- 토익 최신 경향 무료 특강
- 토익 타이머

모의고사 결과 분석
- 파트별/문항별 정답률
- 파트별/유형별 취약점 리포트
- 전체 응시자 점수 분포도

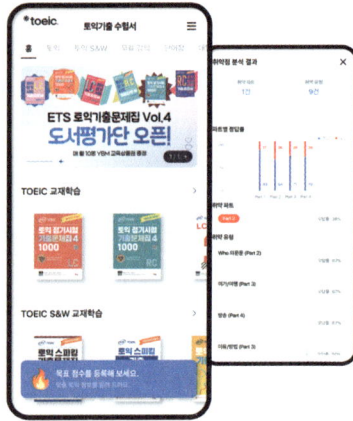

ETS 토익 학습 전용 온라인 커뮤니티!
ETS TOEIC® Book 공식카페

etstoeicbook.co.kr

강사진의 학습 지원　토익 대표강사들의 학습 지원과 멘토링

교재 학습관 운영　교재별 학습게시판을 통해 무료 동영상 강의 등 학습 지원

학습 콘텐츠 제공　토익 학습 콘텐츠와 정기시험 예비특강 업데이트

ETS 토익 단기공략 750+

최신 개정판
무료 동영상 강의

LC
RC

ETS 토익 단기공략 750⁺

발행인	허문호
발행처	YBM
편집	이태경, 정유상, 김유나, 김현식
디자인	김현경, 김희원, 정규리
마케팅	고영노, 김한석, 김동진, 박찬경, 문근호
	장은선, 하재희, 임재민, 류혜윤, 김예린
초판발행	2025년 7월 1일
3쇄발행	2025년 9월 15일
신고일자	1964년 3월 28일
신고번호	제1964-000003호
주소	서울시 종로구 종로 104
전화	(02) 2000-0515 [구입문의] / (02) 2000-0304 [내용문의]
팩스	(02) 2285-1523
홈페이지	www.ybmbooks.com
ISBN	978-89-17-24378-9

ETS, TOEIC and 토익 are registered trademarks of Educational Testing Service, Princeton, New Jersey, U.S.A., used in the Republic of Korea under license. Copyright © 2025 by Educational Testing Service, Princeton, New Jersey, U.S.A. All rights reserved. Reproduced under license for limited use by YBM. These materials are protected by United States Laws, International Copyright Laws and International Treaties. In the event of any discrepancy between this translation and official ETS materials, the terms of the official ETS materials will prevail. All items were created or reviewed by ETS. All item annotations and test-taking tips were reviewed by ETS.

서면에 의한 저자와 출판사의 허락 없이 내용의 일부 혹은 전부를 인용 및 복제하거나 발췌하는 것을 금합니다.
낙장 및 파본은 교환해 드립니다.
구입 철회는 구매처 규정에 따라 교환 및 환불 처리됩니다.

ETS 토익 단기공략 750+

최신 개정판

무료 동영상 강의

LC

RC

PREFACE

Dear test taker,

The purpose of this book is to help you prepare for success on the TOEIC® Listening and Reading Test. A good TOEIC score is a valuable asset for demonstrating your English communication proficiency to colleagues and clients in Korea and globally.

This book provides practical steps that you can follow during a two-week or four-week program of study to help you in your preparation for the TOEIC test. Use your TOEIC test score as a respected professional credential and a sign that you are ready to take your career to the next level. Your TOEIC score is recognized globally as evidence of your English-language proficiency.

With 〈ETS 토익 단기공략 750+〉, you will have the tools you need to ensure you are thoroughly prepared for the TOEIC test. This book contains key study points that will familiarize you with the test format and content, and you will be able to practice at your own pace. The test questions are created by the same test specialists who develop the TOEIC test itself, and the book contains questions taken from actual TOEIC tests.

Here are some features of 〈ETS 토익 단기공략 750+〉.

- This newly revised edition, reflecting the latest TOEIC questions, features carefully selected items from actual TOEIC tests.
- All TOEIC Listening and Reading content is included in a single book designed for short-term study plans of two or four weeks.
- You will hear the same ETS voice actors that you will hear in an actual TOEIC test.
- Key study points will help you to achieve your target score efficiently, with minimal time and effort.
- Enhanced analyses and explanations are based on the latest TOEIC test research.

In preparing for the test with 〈ETS 토익 단기공략 750+〉, you can be confident that you are taking the best approach to maximizing your TOEIC test score.
Use 〈ETS 토익 단기공략 750+〉 to become familiar with the test, including actual test tasks, content, and format. You will be well prepared to demonstrate to the world your proficiency in English communication by taking the TOEIC test and receiving your score report.

We hope that you will find this high-quality resource to be of the utmost use, and we wish you all the very best success.

출제기관이 만든 점수대별 단기 완성 전략서!

최신 기출 문항으로 보강된 단기 완성 시리즈
풍부한 최신 기출 문항과 최신 출제 경향을 반영한 ETS의 체계적인 공략법으로 구성된 고품질의 단기 완성 전략서이다.

단기 목표 달성에 최적화된 구성
LC와 RC를 한 권으로 구성하여 학습 부담은 줄이고, 목표 점수 달성에 필요한 핵심 내용만을 수록하여 학습 효율은 높였다.

정기시험과 동일한 성우 음원
토익 정기시험 성우가 실제 시험과 동일한 속도와 발음으로 녹음한 음원으로 실전에 완벽하게 대비할 수 있다.

토익 최신 경향을 반영한 명쾌한 분석과 해설
최신 출제 경향을 완벽하게 분석하고 반영하여 목표 점수를 달성하게 해줄 해법을 낱낱이 제시하고 있다.

점수 상승을 돕는 다양한 부가 학습자료 제공
실전에 보다 완벽하게 대비할 수 있도록 실전 모의고사 1회분을 추가로 제공하며, 이해를 돕는 동영상 강의와 기출어휘 PDF, APP을 무료로 제공한다.

CONTENTS

LC

PART 1

INTRO	018
UNIT 01 인물 등장 사진	020
UNIT 02 사물/풍경 사진	024
ETS ACTUAL TEST	028
PART 1 빈출 표현	031

PART 2

INTRO	036
UNIT 03 Who/When/Where 의문문	038
UNIT 04 What·Which/Why/How 의문문	044
UNIT 05 일반/부정/부가 의문문	050
UNIT 06 선택/요청·제안 의문문/평서문	056
ETS ACTUAL TEST	062
PART 2 빈출 표현	063

PART 3

INTRO	068
UNIT 07 주제·목적/화자·장소 문제	070
UNIT 08 세부 사항/문제점·걱정거리 문제	076
UNIT 09 요청·제안/다음에 할 일 문제	082
UNIT 10 의도 파악/시각 정보 연계 문제	088
ETS ACTUAL TEST	095
PART 3 빈출 표현	099

PART 4

INTRO	104
UNIT 11 전화 메시지	106
UNIT 12 공지/회의	110
UNIT 13 설명/소개	114
UNIT 14 광고/방송	118
ETS ACTUAL TEST	122
PART 4 빈출 표현	125

PART 5&6		
INTRO		130
UNIT 01	품사와 문장 구조	134
UNIT 02	명사	140
UNIT 03	대명사	146
UNIT 04	형용사	152
UNIT 05	부사	158
UNIT 06	동사의 형태와 종류	164
UNIT 07	수 일치와 태	170
UNIT 08	시제	176
UNIT 09	to부정사와 동명사	182
UNIT 10	분사와 분사구문	188
UNIT 11	전치사와 접속사	194
UNIT 12	부사절 접속사	200
UNIT 13	관계대명사	204
UNIT 14	명사절 접속사	210
UNIT 15	비교/도치 구문	216
UNIT 16	어휘	222
ETS ACTUAL TEST		244

PART 7		
INTRO		252
UNIT 17	편지/이메일	254
UNIT 18	회람/공지/광고/기사	264
UNIT 19	메시지/웹페이지/기타	272
UNIT 20	복수 지문	280
ETS ACTUAL TEST		294
PART 7 빈출 표현		314

정답과 해설 (책 속의 책)
실전 모의고사 (별책)

무료 동영상 강의
기출 포인트를 짚는 핵심 강의로 토익 단기완성!

TOEIC 소개

» TOEIC

Test of English for International Communication(국제적 의사소통을 위한 영어 시험)의 약자로서, 영어가 모국어가 아닌 사람들을 대상으로 일상생활 또는 비즈니스 상황에서 필요한 실용영어 능력을 갖추었는지 평가하는 시험이다.

» 시험 구성

구성	PART	유형		문항 수	시간	배점
Listening	Part 1	사진 묘사		6	45분	495점
	Part 2	질의 응답		25		
	Part 3	짧은 대화		39		
	Part 4	짧은 담화		30		
Reading	Part 5	단문 빈칸 채우기		30	75분	495점
	Part 6	장문 빈칸 채우기		16		
	Part 7	독해	단일 지문	29		
			이중 지문	10		
			삼중 지문	15		
Total		7 Parts		200문항	120분	990점

» 평가 항목

LC	RC
사진 묘사 문장을 듣고 이해하는 능력	문장 구조를 파악해 문장에서 필요한 품사, 어휘 등을 찾는 능력
질의/응답하는 문장을 듣고 이해하는 능력	글의 목적, 주제, 의도 등을 파악하는 능력
짧은 대화에서 주고받은 내용을 파악할 수 있는 능력	장문에서 특정한 정보를 찾을 수 있는 능력
담화에서 핵심이 되는 정보를 파악할 수 있는 능력	글의 내용에서 추론할 수 있는 능력
화자의 의도나 함축된 의미를 이해하는 능력	뜻이 유사한 단어의 정확한 용례를 파악하는 능력

※ 성적표에는 전체 수험자의 평균과 해당 수험자가 받은 성적이 백분율로 표기되어 있다.

수험 정보

» 시험 접수

시험 약 2개월 전부터 아래와 같은 방법으로 접수할 수 있다.
인터넷 접수: TOEIC위원회 공식 홈페이지(https://exam.toeic.co.kr)를 통해 접수
모바일 접수: TOEIC위원회 공식 어플리케이션 또는 모바일 웹사이트
 (https://m.exam.toeic.co.kr)를 통해 접수

» 시험장 준비물

신분증	규정 신분증만 가능 (주민등록증, 운전면허증, 기간 만료 전의 여권, 공무원증 등)
필기구	연필, 지우개 (볼펜이나 사인펜은 사용 금지)

» 시험 진행 시간

09:20	입실 (9:50 이후 입실 불가)
09:30 ~ 09:45	답안지 작성에 관한 오리엔테이션
09:45 ~ 09:50	휴식
09:50 ~ 10:05	신분증 확인
10:05 ~ 10:10	문제지 배부 및 파본 확인
10:10 ~ 10:55	듣기 평가 (LISTENING TEST)
10:55 ~ 12:10	독해 평가 (READING TEST)

» 성적 확인

성적은 TOEIC 홈페이지에 안내된 성적 발표일에 인터넷 홈페이지, 어플리케이션을 통해 확인 가능하다. 최초 성적표 발급은 우편 또는 온라인을 통해 수령 가능하며, 재발급은 성적 유효기간(시험 시행일로부터 2년) 내에만 가능하다. 단, 유효기간은 공공기관에 한하여 2023년 4월부터 5년으로 연장되었다.

» 토익 점수

TOEIC 점수는 듣기 영역(LC) 점수와 읽기 영역(RC) 점수, 그리고 두 영역을 합계한 전체 점수로 구성된다. 각 영역의 점수는 5점 단위로 5점에서 495점까지 주어지고, 두 영역을 합계한 전체 점수는 10점에서 990점까지 주어진다. TOEIC 성적은 각 문제 유형의 난이도에 따른 점수 환산표에 의해 결정된다.

LC 출제 유형 및 경향 분석

PART 1
문제 유형 및 출제 비율

사람을 주어로 행동이나 상태를 묘사하는 문제의 비중이 가장 높다. 최근 주어가 다양하고 보기가 긴 문제들이 출제되고 있다.

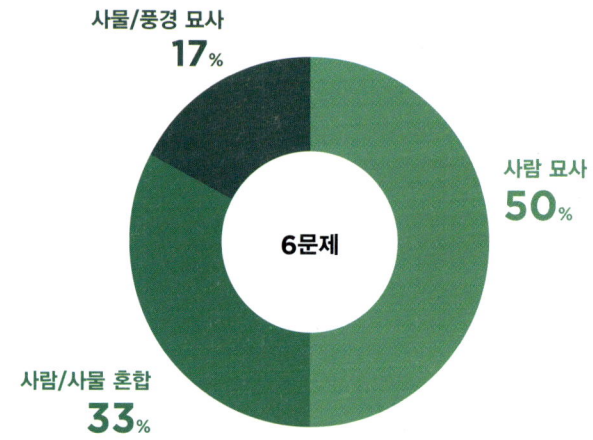

PART 2
문제 유형 및 출제 비율

의문사 의문문이 거의 절반을 차지하며 일반 의문문과 평서문도 비중 있게 출제된다. 질문에 대해 우회적으로 응답하는 문제 비중이 높아지고 있다.

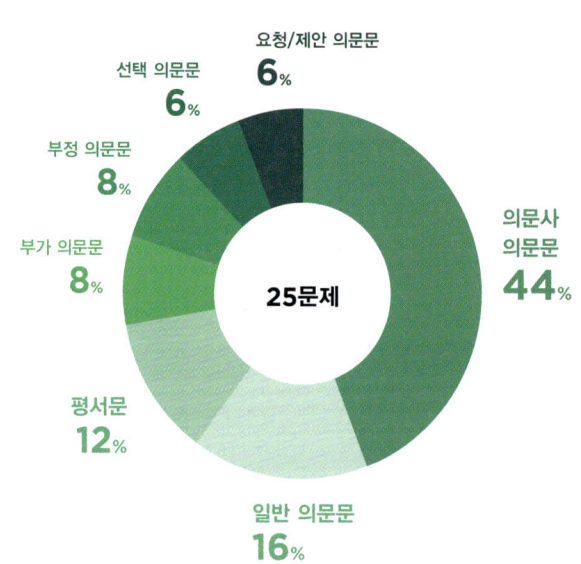

PART 3

문제 유형 및 출제 비율

세부 사항을 물어보는 문제가 가장 많이 출제되며, 의도 파악 문제와 시각 정보 문제가 각각 2문항과 3문항씩 고정적으로 출제된다. 대화에서 사용된 표현을 다른 말로 paraphrasing한 보기가 정답으로 자주 출제된다.

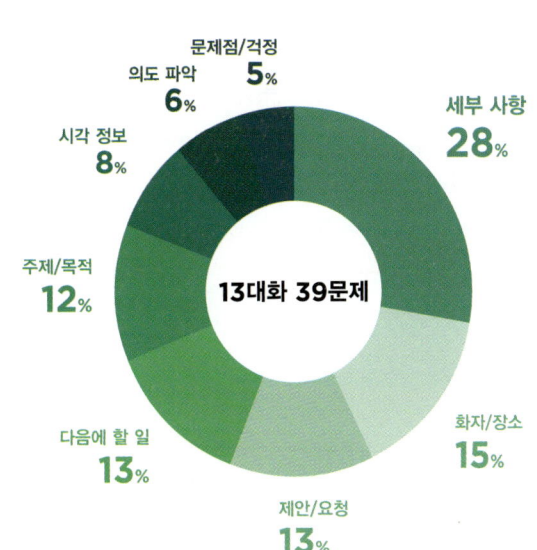

PART 4

담화 유형 및 출제 비율

전화 메시지와 공지/안내/회의의 발췌록 등의 출제 빈도가 가장 높다. 담화 곳곳에 흩어져 있는 단서들로 정답을 유추해야 하는 문제가 고난도로 출제된다.

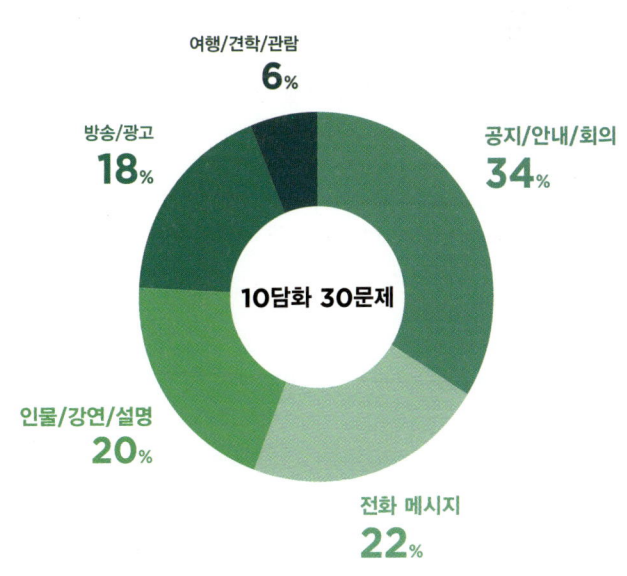

RC 출제 유형 및 경향 분석

PART 5
문법 문제 유형 및 출제 비율

주요 품사 자리를 판단하는 문제와 전치사와 접속사/부사를 구별하는 문제가 주로 출제된다. 그 외 준동사, 관계사, 명사절 접속사 관련 문제가 고난도로 출제된다.

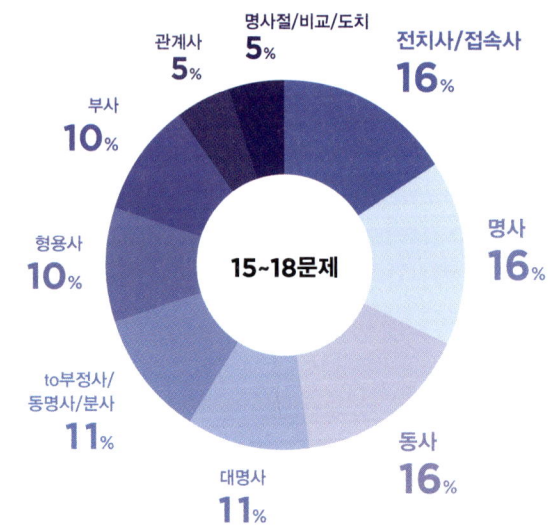

PART 5
어휘 문제 유형 및 출제 비율

명사, 동사, 형용사, 부사 등 주요 품사 어휘 문제가 골고루 출제된다. 최근 어휘의 의미뿐 아니라 문법적인 구조를 알아야 해결할 수 있는 문제들도 출제되고 있다.

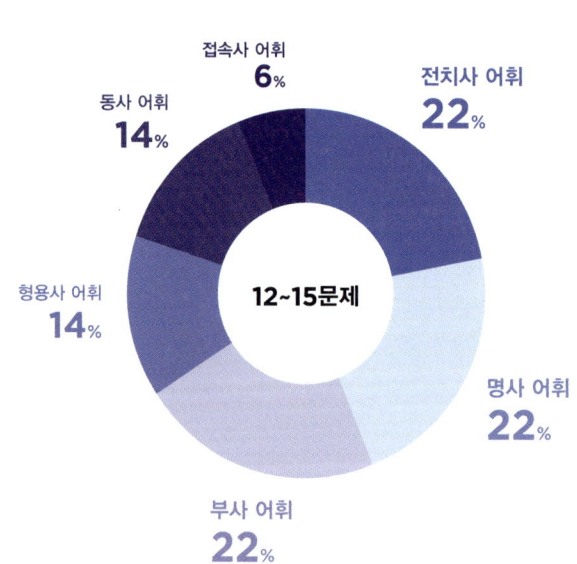

PART 6
문제 유형 및 출제 비율

문법과 어휘 문제가 비슷한 비중으로 골고루 나오며, 빈칸에 알맞은 문장을 고르는 문제가 매 지문마다 1문항 출제된다. PART 5와 달리 문맥과 전체 흐름을 파악해야 풀 수 있는 문제들이 출제된다.

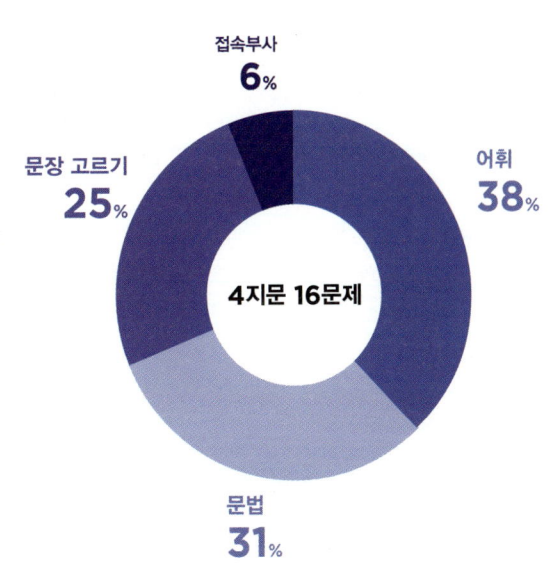

PART 7
지문 유형 및 출제 비율

이메일/편지, 기사, 공지/안내문, 광고, 메시지 대화 지문은 거의 항상 나오는 유형이다. 문제 유형으로는 세부 사항, 주제/목적, 추론 등이 있으며 문장 삽입, 의도 파악 문제가 각 2문항씩 고정적으로 출제된다. 복수 지문에서는 연계 문제가 항상 출제된다.

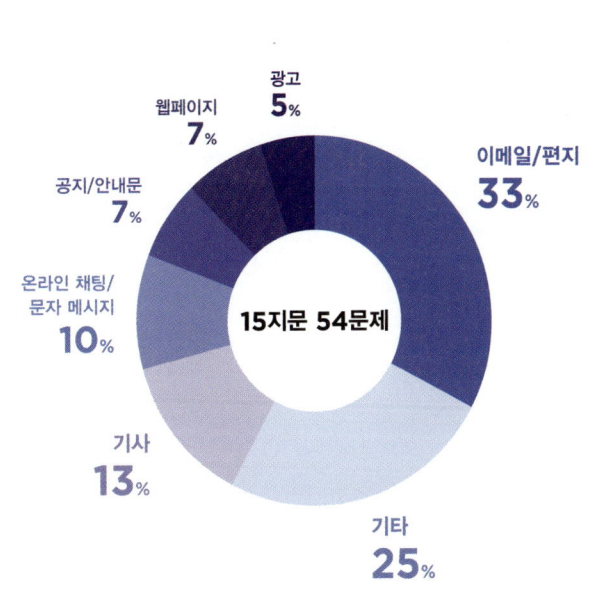

2주 완성 플랜

초단기에 토익 750점 이상을 달성하고자 하는 중·고급 수험생을 위한 2주 완성 플랜

	DAY 1	DAY 2	DAY 3	DAY 4	DAY 5
LC	PART 1 UNIT 1~2 ETS ACTUAL TEST	PART 2 UNIT 3~4	PART 2 UNIT 5~6	PART 2 ETS ACTUAL TEST	PART 3 UNIT 7~8
RC	PART 5&6 UNIT 1~3	PART 5&6 UNIT 4~6	PART 5&6 UNIT 7~9	PART 5&6 UNIT 10~12	PART 5&6 UNIT 13~15

	DAY 6	DAY 7	DAY 8	DAY 9	DAY 10
LC	PART 3 UNIT 9~10	PART 3 ETS ACTUAL TEST	PART 4 UNIT 11~12	PART 4 UNIT 13~14	PART 4 ETS ACTUAL TEST
RC	PART 5&6 UNIT 16	PART 5&6 ETS ACTUAL TEST	PART 7 UNIT 17~18	PART 7 UNIT 19~20	PART 7 ETS ACTUAL TEST

4주 완성 플랜

단기에 차근차근 토익 750점 이상을 달성하고자 하는 중·고급 수험생을 위한 4주 완성 플랜

	DAY 1	DAY 2	DAY 3	DAY 4	DAY 5
LC	PART 1 UNIT 1	PART 1 UNIT 2	PART 1 ETS ACTUAL TEST	PART 2 UNIT 3	PART 2 UNIT 4
RC	PART 5&6 UNIT 1	PART 5&6 UNIT 2~3	PART 5&6 UNIT 4~5	PART 5&6 UNIT 6	PART 5&6 UNIT 7~8

	DAY 6	DAY 7	DAY 8	DAY 9	DAY 10
LC	PART 2 UNIT 5	PART 2 UNIT 6	PART 2 ETS ACTUAL TEST	PART 3 UNIT 7	PART 3 UNIT 8
RC	PART 5&6 UNIT 9~10	PART 5&6 UNIT 11~12	PART 5&6 UNIT 13	PART 5&6 UNIT 14~15	PART 5&6 UNIT 16(1)

	DAY 11	DAY 12	DAY 13	DAY 14	DAY 15
LC	PART 3 UNIT 9	PART 3 UNIT 10	PART 3 ETS ACTUAL TEST	PART 4 UNIT 11	PART 4 UNIT 12
RC	PART 5&6 UNIT 16(2)	PART 5&6 ETS ACTUAL TEST	PART 7 UNIT 17	PART 7 UNIT 18	PART 7 UNIT 19

	DAY 16	DAY 17	DAY 18	DAY 19	DAY 20
LC	PART 4 UNIT 13	PART 4 UNIT 14	PART 4 ETS ACTUAL TEST	PART 1&2 복습	PART 3&4 복습
RC	PART 7 UNIT 20	PART 7 ETS ACTUAL TEST	PART 5&6 복습	PART 5&6 복습	PART 7 복습

LC LISTENING COMPREHENSION

PART 1

사진 묘사

INTRO

UNIT 01 인물 등장 사진
UNIT 02 사물/풍경 사진

ETS ACTUAL TEST
PART 1 빈출 표현

 무료 강의

INTRO PART 1 사진 묘사 총 6문항

주어진 사진을 가장 잘 설명한 보기를 선택하는 유형으로, 사람 및 사물의 동작이나 상태, 배경 등을 묘사하는 문장이 나온다.

ETS 예제

문제지

음원

Number 1.
Look at the picture marked number 1 in your test book.
(A) The man is cleaning a vehicle.
(B) The man is getting out of a car.
(C) The man is putting on a hat.
(D) The man is changing a tire.

풀이 전략

❶ 보기를 듣기 전에 사진을 잘 살핀다.

사진에 등장하는 사람의 동작이나 상태, 사물의 상태나 위치, 배경 등을 파악하고 표현을 예상한다.

> **예제** 1인 등장 사진
> • 남자의 동작 및 자세 cleaning, standing, holding, washing
> • 주변 사물 car, vehicle, tire, hose, hat
> • 배경 mountain, building, outdoor

❷ 보기를 들으면서 오답을 소거한다.

동작/상태를 다르게 묘사하거나, 사진에 없는 사물을 언급하거나, 위치를 잘못 묘사한 오답이 자주 등장한다.

(A) **The man is cleaning a vehicle.** ○
   정답 | 세차하고 있는 모습을 적절히 묘사함

(B) The man is getting out of a car. ✗
   오답 | 차에서 내리고 있는 모습이 아님

(C) The man is putting on a hat. ✗
   오답 | 이미 모자를 쓴 상태로 착용하고 있는 모습이 아님

(D) The man is changing a tire. ✗
   오답 | 타이어를 교체하고 있는 모습이 아님

빈출구문

❶ 동작이나 상태를 묘사하는 be+-ing

Some people are stocking shelves.
사람들이 선반에 물건을 채우고 있다.

The man is handing merchandise to the woman.
남자가 여자에게 상품을 건네고 있다.

❷ 상태를 묘사하는 be+p.p.와 have been+p.p.

Overhead wires are suspended near an unfinished structure.
고가선이 아직 완공되지 않은 건축물 가까이에 늘어져 있다.

Some vehicles have been parked near a construction site.
공사장 옆에 차들이 주차되어 있다.

❸ 동작의 대상을 묘사하는 be+being+p.p.

Glass panels are being washed. 유리판이 닦이고 있다.

Some cleaning work is being done.
청소 작업이 진행되고 있다.

be+being+p.p.는 사진에 그 동작을 행하는 주체(사람)가 있어야 한다.

❹ 위치나 구도를 묘사하는 전치사구와 There is/are

Some people are standing on the bridge.
사람 몇 명이 다리 위에 서 있다.

There is a bridge over the water.
물 위에 다리가 있다.

UNIT 01 인물 등장 사진

출제 포인트

1. 출제 비중이 높으며, be+-ing 구조를 사용해 사람의 동작이나 상태를 묘사하는 문제가 주를 이룬다. have+p.p., be+p.p., be+being+p.p.도 간혹 출제된다.
2. 사람을 묘사하는 보기와 사물을 묘사하는 보기가 함께 제시될 수 있다.
3. worker, cashier, diner, driver 등 특정 사람을 나타내는 명사가 등장하기도 한다.

▶ 1인 등장 사진

🔊 750_P1_01

한 사람의 주요 동작이나 상태, 동작의 대상 파악

<u>A man</u> **is playing** an instrument. 남자가 악기를 연주하고 있다.
<u>A man</u> **is looking down** at his guitar. 남자가 기타를 내려다보고 있다.
<u>He</u> **is wearing** headphones. 남자가 헤드폰을 쓰고 있다.

고득점 TIP 착용한 상태(wearing)와 착용하고 있는 동작(putting on, trying on)을 구분한다.

▶ 2인 이상 등장 사진

사람들의 개별 행동, 공통 행동, 상호 동작 파악

<u>One of the people</u> **is standing** near a screen.
사람들 중 한 명이 스크린 근처에 서 있다.
<u>Some people</u> **are attending** a presentation. 사람들이 발표에 참석하고 있다.
<u>A presentation</u> **is being given** in a meeting room.
회의실에서 발표가 진행되고 있다.

고득점 TIP presentation, construction work 등 진행 중인 작업도 주어가 될 수 있다.

▶ 사람 · 사물 혼합 사진

눈에 띄는 사람 및 사물의 동작이나 상태 파악

<u>A person</u> **is seated** in a **vehicle**. 한 사람이 차량에 앉아 있다.
<u>A driver</u> **has opened** a **car door**. / <u>A car door</u> **has been left open**.
운전자가 차 문을 열어 두었다. / 차 문이 열려 있다.
<u>Some bags</u> **have been loaded** onto a truck. 봉지들이 트럭에 실려 있다.

고득점 TIP be sitting과 be seated 모두 앉아 있는 상태를 나타낸다.

ETS 유형연습

음원을 듣고 사진을 가장 잘 묘사한 문장을 고르세요.
다시 들으면서 빈칸을 채우세요.

🎧 750_P1_02

정답과 해설 p.002

1.

   (A) A man is _____ for a meal.
   (B) A man is _____ dishes.
   (C) A man is _____ for a coat on a hook.
   (D) A man is _____ some food from a buffet.

2.

   (A) A man is _____ some handouts.
   (B) A woman is _____ at a computer screen.
   (C) Some people are _____ from a table.
   (D) Some people are _____ documents.

3.

   (A) She's _____ a potted plant.
   (B) Some vegetables _____ in a bucket.
   (C) She's _____ some leaves.
   (D) Some stones _____ a walkway.

4.

   (A) Some people are _____ on a bench.
   (B) Some people are _____ in line.
   (C) Some lights are _____.
   (D) Some people are _____ at artwork.

UNIT 01 인물 등장 사진

ETS 실전문제

1.

(A) (B) (C) (D)

2.

(A) (B) (C) (D)

3.

(A) (B) (C) (D)

4.

(A) (B) (C) (D)

5.

(A) (B) (C) (D)

6.

(A) (B) (C) (D)

7.

(A)　(B)　(C)　(D)

8.

(A)　(B)　(C)　(D)

9.

(A)　(B)　(C)　(D)

10.

(A)　(B)　(C)　(D)

11.

(A)　(B)　(C)　(D)

12.

(A)　(B)　(C)　(D)

UNIT 02 사물 / 풍경 사진

출제 포인트
1. 매회 1~2문항 정도 출제되며, 보기 문장이 길어 상대적으로 난이도가 높은 편이다.
2. 다양한 주어와 동사 형태로 사물의 상태 및 위치, 풍경의 일부를 묘사하는 문제가 출제된다.
3. 사람이 등장하지 않는 사진에 사람의 동작을 묘사하는 be+being+p.p.가 오답 보기로 자주 출제된다.
   단, 몇몇 예외적인 경우에 유의한다.

◆ 실내 사물 사진

실내 주요 사물의 상태 및 위치 파악

Bowls **have been stacked** on shelves. 그릇들이 선반 위에 쌓여 있다.

Some dishes **are on display**. 식기들이 진열되어 있다.

Some items **are being displayed** on shelves. 상품들이 선반에 진열되어 있다.

고득점 TIP be displayed, be on display, be being displayed 모두 진열된 상태를 나타낸다.

◆ 실외 사물 사진

눈에 띄는 사물 및 장소, 상황 파악

Vehicles **are positioned** next to each other. 차량들이 나란히 배치되어 있다.

A truck **is full** of **construction materials**. 트럭에 건설 자재가 가득 실려 있다.

Heavy machinery **is being operated** at a work site.
중장비가 작업 현장에서 작동되고 있다.

고득점 TIP 중장비 운전처럼 사람이 잘 보이지 않아도 관여하는 것이 확실한 상황은 be being p.p.로 묘사될 수 있다.

◆ 풍경 사진

전체적인 풍경 및 사물의 구도 파악

Some trees **are reflected** in the pond.
몇몇 나무들이 연못에 비치고 있다.

A building **is overlooking** the water. 건물이 물을 내려다보고 있다.

A stone wall **separates** the walkway from the water.
돌담이 산책로와 물을 구분하고 있다.

고득점 TIP overlook, face 등의 동사는 be -ing 형태로 상태를 나타낼 수도 있다.

ETS 유형연습

음원을 듣고 사진을 가장 잘 묘사한 문장을 고르세요.
다시 들으면서 빈칸을 채우세요.

🎧 750_P1_05
정답과 해설 p.006

1.

(A) Some books _____ on a cart.

(B) A librarian _____ a sign near an entrance.

(C) Some bookshelves _____ .

(D) The doors to a hallway _____ open.

2.

(A) All of the seats _____ .

(B) The railing is _____ .

(C) A dining room _____ for a meal.

(D) _____ a large plant _____ two tables.

3.

(A) Some scarves _____ on a table.

(B) Some merchandise _____ outside a store.

(C) Leaves _____ a walkway.

(D) A sign _____ from an awning.

4.

(A) People _____ a boat from a pier.

(B) _____ a parking area _____ .

(C) Ships _____ under a bridge.

(D) Trees _____ along the shore.

ETS 실전문제

1.

(A) (B) (C) (D)

2.

(A) (B) (C) (D)

3.

(A) (B) (C) (D)

4.

(A) (B) (C) (D)

5.

(A) (B) (C) (D)

6.

(A) (B) (C) (D)

7.

(A) (B) (C) (D)

8.

(A) (B) (C) (D)

9.

(A) (B) (C) (D)

10.

(A) (B) (C) (D)

11.

(A) (B) (C) (D)

12.

(A) (B) (C) (D)

ETS ACTUAL TEST 750_P1_07

1.

2.

3.

4.

5.

6.

PART 1 빈출 표현

손 동작 묘사

reaching into a drawer 서랍 안으로 손을 뻗고 있다
extending one's arm 팔을 뻗고 있다
loading a cart 카트에 짐을 싣고 있다
unloading some items 물품을 내리고 있다
handing papers 서류를 전달하고 있다
carrying some boxes 상자들을 나르고 있다
folding some clothing 옷을 접고 있다
stapling a document 서류를 철하고 있다
pointing at a screen 스크린을 가리키고 있다
adjusting the glasses 안경을 고쳐 쓰고 있다
hanging a picture on the wall 벽에 사진을 걸고 있다

발 동작 묘사

going up/down some stairs
계단을 올라가고/내려가고 있다
boarding a train 기차에 승차하고 있다
stepping down from a bus 버스에서 내리고 있다
strolling on a beach 해변을 거닐고 있다
passing through a doorway 출입문을 통과하고 있다
jogging on a walkway 산책로에서 조깅을 하고 있다
crossing over a stream 개울을 건너고 있다
entering a hallway 현관으로 들어가고 있다

올라타는 동작 vs. 타고 있는 상태

getting on a bicycle 자전거에 올라타고 있다 (동작)
riding a motorbike 오토바이를 타고 있다 (상태)

착용하는 동작 vs. 착용한 상태

putting[trying] on a jacket 재킷을 입고 있다 (동작)
removing[taking off] one's hat
모자를 벗고 있다 (동작)
wearing sunglasses 선글라스를 쓰고 있다 (상태)

시선

looking into the refrigerator
냉장고 안을 살펴보고 있다
facing a board 칠판을 마주보고 있다
examining a document 서류를 살펴보고 있다
reviewing the contents 내용을 검토하고 있다
inspecting the back of the car
차의 뒷부분을 살피고 있다
studying a drawing 그림을 살펴보고 있다
checking one's phone 휴대전화를 확인하고 있다

자세

holding onto a handrail 난간을 잡고 있다
kneeling in the garden 정원에서 무릎을 꿇고 앉아 있다
relaxing outdoors 야외에서 쉬고 있다
resting in a waiting area 대합실에서 쉬고 있다
sitting on a bench 벤치에 앉아 있다
lying on the grass 잔디 위에 누워 있다
leaning against a wall 벽에 기대어 있다
standing at a counter 카운터에 서 있다
bending over a bicycle
자전거 위로 몸을 구부리고 있다

상태

be lined up at the side of a road
도로 옆에 줄지어 늘어서 있다
be gathered around a table 탁자 주위에 모여 있다
be crowded with pedestrians 보행자들로 붐비고 있다
be filled with people 사람들로 가득 차 있다
be placed on the floor 바닥에 놓여 있다
be cut down 베어져 있다
be covered with leaves 나뭇잎으로 덮여 있다
be on the path 오솔길 위에 있다
be scattered on the floor 바닥에 흩어져 있다

사무실

working at a computer 컴퓨터로 작업하고 있다
typing on a keyboard 키보드를 치고 있다
using some office equipment
사무기기를 사용하고 있다
putting paper in a copy machine
복사기에 종이를 넣고 있다
arranging materials on the table
테이블 위 자료를 정리하고 있다
posting a notice on a bulletin board
게시판에 공지를 붙이고 있다
A cord is being plugged in.
코드가 전원에 연결되고 있다.
Some drawers have been left open.
서랍들이 열려 있다.
Some binders have been stacked on shelves.
바인더들이 선반 위에 쌓여 있다.
Some chairs have been folded up.
의자들이 접혀 있다.
The books have been arranged in piles.
책들이 수북이 쌓여 있다.

회의실

attending a meeting 회의에 참석하고 있다
greeting each other 서로 인사하고 있다
exchanging business cards 명함을 교환하고 있다
be seated in a circle 둥글게 앉아 있다
facing each other 서로 마주하고 있다
distributing papers 서류를 나눠주고 있다
taking notes 메모하고 있다
writing on a board 칠판에 적고 있다
cleaning[erasing] a whiteboard
화이트보드를 닦고 있다
giving[delivering] a presentation 발표하고 있다
listening to a speaker 발표자의 말을 경청하고 있다
chatting in a conference room
회의실에서 이야기하고 있다

작업실 / 실험실

inspecting some power lines 전선을 점검하고 있다
wiping a counter 작업대를 닦고 있다
unplugging a power cord 전기선을 뽑고 있다
securing a box with tape
테이프로 상자를 단단히 봉하고 있다
operating a machine 기계를 작동하고 있다
packing items into boxes
물품을 상자에 포장하고 있다
taking measurements 치수를 재고 있다
pressing a button on a device
장치의 버튼을 누르고 있다
looking into a microscope
현미경을 들여다보고 있다
working with some laboratory equipment
실험 장비를 가지고 일하고 있다
lying on a counter 작업대에 놓여 있다
be spread out on a table 테이블 위에 널려 있다

강의실 / 강당

entering an auditorium 강당에 들어가고 있다
setting up a podium 연단을 설치하고 있다
lining up chairs 의자를 일렬로 배열하고 있다
sitting in rows 여러 줄로 앉아 있다
attending a presentation
프레젠테이션에 참석하고 있다
giving a lecture 강의를 하고 있다
passing around some documents
서류를 나눠주고 있다
addressing an audience 청중에게 연설하고 있다
speaking to a microphone
마이크에 대고 말하고 있다
adjusting a microphone 마이크를 조정하고 있다
raising their hands 손을 들고 있다
Some seats are unoccupied.
몇몇 좌석들이 비어 있다.

실외 작업

be under construction 공사 중이다
be closed for construction 공사로 폐쇄되다
be stacked in a pile 무더기로 쌓여 있다
wearing a safety helmet 안전모를 쓰고 있다
fastening a helmet 헬멧을 조이고 있다
erecting[setting up] scaffolding 비계를 세우고 있다
drilling a hole 드릴로 구멍을 내고 있다
hammering a nail 망치로 못을 박고 있다
standing on a ladder 사다리에 올라 서 있다
lifting bricks and planks of wood
벽돌과 나무판자를 들어올리고 있다
pouring cement into a container
시멘트를 용기에 붓고 있다
repairing[fixing] the roof of the house
집의 지붕을 수리하고 있다
replacing some tiles 타일을 교체하고 있다
pushing a wheelbarrow 수레를 밀고 있다
working on the power lines 전선 작업을 하고 있다
adjusting a wire 전선을 조정하고 있다
paving a walkway 보도를 포장하고 있다
painting lines on a road 도로에 선을 그리고 있다
trimming some trees 나무를 다듬고 있다
mowing the lawn 잔디를 깎고 있다
watering some plants 식물에 물을 주고 있다
using[working with] a shovel 삽으로 작업하고 있다
A ladder is propped against the building.
사다리가 건물에 기대어져 있다.
The signs are being painted.
표지판이 칠해지고 있다.
A road is being resurfaced. 도로가 재포장되고 있다.
A construction work is being carried out.
공사 작업이 진행되고 있다.
Fences are being constructed around a building. 건물 둘레에 울타리가 세워지고 있다.
There is heavy machinery at a construction site. 공사장에 중장비가 있다.

교통/차량 관련 작업

be stuck in traffic 교통체증에 갇히다
be stopped at an intersection 교차로에 멈춰 서 있다
waiting at a traffic light 신호가 바뀌기를 기다리고 있다
driving down the road 도로에서 운전하고 있다
driving across the bridge 다리를 건너고 있다
be being towed 견인되고 있다
crossing the road[street] 길을 건너고 있다
traveling in opposite directions
반대 방향으로 이동하고 있다
backing a car into a garage
차를 후진해서 차고에 넣고 있다
crossing at a crosswalk 횡단보도를 건너고 있다
directing traffic 교통정리를 하고 있다
disembarking from a bus 버스에서 내리고 있다
storing luggage above one's seats
좌석 위에 짐을 보관하고 있다
approaching the platform 승강장으로 들어오고 있다
departing from a station 역에서 출발하고 있다
working on a vehicle 차를 수리하고 있다
transporting a load of bricks
벽돌을 한 짐 운반하고 있다
be parked side by side 나란히 주차되어 있다
A bicycle is chained to a pole.
자전거가 기둥에 체인으로 묶여 있다.
There is a railing beside the railroad tracks.
철로 옆에 난간이 있다.
The vehicles are all traveling in the same direction. 차량들이 모두 같은 방향으로 가고 있다.
Traffic lanes are separated by fences.
차선이 펜스로 분리되어 있다.
The truck is parked next to containers.
트럭이 컨테이너 옆에 주차되어 있다.
The vehicle is pulling into a garage.
차가 차고 안으로 들어오고 있다.

상점

stocking shelves 선반에 물건을 채우고 있다
hanging a jacket on a rack 옷걸이에 재킷을 걸고 있다
shopping in an outdoor market
야외 시장에서 쇼핑하고 있다
examining goods on display
진열된 상품을 살펴보고 있다
browsing in a store 가게 안을 둘러보고 있다
reaching for some merchandise
상품을 집으려고 손을 뻗고 있다
selecting some groceries 식료품을 고르고 있다
showing customers an item
손님들에게 물건을 보여주고 있다
wrapping a product 상품을 포장하고 있다
waiting in line 줄을 서서 기다리고 있다
be stocked with supplies 물품으로 차 있다
be piled near the entrance 입구 근처에 쌓여 있다
be lined up in a display case
진열장 안에 줄지어 놓여 있다

식당

having a meal 식사하고 있다
eating[dining] by the water 물가에서 식사하고 있다
drinking from a cup 컵으로 물을 마시고 있다
reading[studying] the menu 메뉴를 보고 있다
pointing at a menu 메뉴를 가리키고 있다
taking an order 주문을 받고 있다
pouring a beverage into a glass
음료를 유리잔에 붓고 있다
filling a cup 컵을 채우고 있다
wiping[cleaning] the table 식탁을 닦고 있다
holding a serving tray 쟁반을 들고 있다
putting plates away 접시를 치우고 있다
serving a meal to some customers
손님에게 식사를 서빙하고 있다
be set[prepared] for a meal
식사 준비가 되어 있다

여가 / 취미

walking toward a park 공원을 향해 걷고 있다
hiking on a path 길을 따라 하이킹을 하고 있다
rowing a boat 노를 젓고 있다
sailing on the water 항해하고 있다
holding an oar 노를 잡고 있다
running up a ramp 경사로를 뛰어 올라가고 있다
stepping onto a stage 무대에 오르고 있다
playing musical instruments 악기를 연주하고 있다
performing outdoors 야외에서 공연하고 있다
looking at some artwork 미술품을 감상하고 있다
fishing from a dock 부두에서 낚시를 하고 있다
arranging flowers in a vase
꽃병에 꽃꽂이를 하고 있다
drawing on a canvas 캔버스에 그림을 그리고 있다
taking a photograph 사진을 찍고 있다

사물 / 배경

hanging from the ceiling 천장에 매달려 있다
be hung next to the door 문 옆에 걸려 있다
be decorated with plants 식물로 장식되어 있다
be pulled closed 당겨서 닫혀 있다
be laid out on the floor 바닥에 깔려 있다
be reflected in the water 물에 비치고 있다
be shaded by 그늘이 드리워져 있다
casting shadows 그림자를 드리우고 있다
be planted along a path 길을 따라 심어져 있다
be bordered by a fence 울타리가 경계를 이루고 있다
overlooking the water 강을 내려다보고 있다
line the street 길을 따라 늘어서 있다
run alongside a shoreline
(길이) 해안을 따라 나 있다

PART 2

질의 응답

INTRO

UNIT 03 Who/When/Where 의문문
UNIT 04 What·Which/Why/How 의문문
UNIT 05 일반/부정/부가 의문문
UNIT 06 선택/요청·제안 의문문/평서문

ETS ACTUAL TEST
PART 2 빈출 표현

 무료 강의

INTRO PART 2 질의 응답 총 25문항

질문 혹은 서술문과 3개의 보기를 들은 후 가장 적절한 응답을 선택하는 유형으로, 다양한 종류의 의문문과 평서문이 출제된다.

ETS 예제

문제지
7. Mark your answer on your answer sheet.

음원
Number 7.
M Why are you traveling to Denver?
W (A) Only for a few days.
　　(B) To spend time with my relatives.
　　(C) I'm planning to drive there.

풀이 전략

❶ 질문을 듣고 가능한 답변을 예상한다.
의문사 의문문인지 비의문사 의문문인지 재빨리 파악하고 각 질문의 키워드에 집중한다. 질문을 듣고 가능한 답변을 예상하며 보기를 듣는다.

> **예제** 의문사 Why로 시작하는 의문문
> • 이유　Because
> • 목적　to부정사
> • 기타 가능 응답　Because가 생략/함축된 응답

❷ 보기를 들으며 오답을 소거한다.
정답에 확신이 없을 경우 확실한 오답을 소거한 후 남은 보기를 선택하는 것도 한 방법이다.

(A) Only for a few days. ✗
　　오답 | 기간을 묻는 How long 의문문에 적합한 응답

(B) To spend time with my relatives. ○
　　정답 | 덴버에 가는 목적

(C) I'm planning to drive there. ✗
　　오답 | 방법을 묻는 How 의문문에 적합한 응답

다양한 응답 방식

질문에 직접적으로 답하지 않고 우회적으로 표현하거나, 답변할 수 없음을 나타내는 등 다양한 형태의 응답이 정답으로 출제된다. 아래 예시를 참고하여 응답 패턴을 익혀 두자.

질문	What time does the workshop begin? 워크숍이 몇 시에 시작하죠?
직접 응답	At two o'clock. 2시예요. After the lunch break. 점심시간 후예요. As soon as the trainer arrives. 교육 강사가 도착하면 바로요.
간접 응답	You should ask Sam. 샘에게 물어보세요. Oh, I thought you were not coming. 아, 안 오시는 줄 알았는데요. Didn't your manager tell you? 매니저가 말해주지 않았나요?

빈출 오답 유형

❶ 유사 발음, 반복 어휘, 파생어 활용

Who's scheduled to clean the break room? 누가 휴게실을 청소하기로 되어 있죠?

오답 I could use a break. 좀 쉬었다가 하면 좋겠어요.
정답 Sarah is. 사라요.

❷ 연상 가능한 어휘 활용

Have you had your laptop fixed yet? 노트북 수리 받았나요?

오답 Yes, my new computer. 네, 제 새 컴퓨터요.
정답 I'll get a new one. 새로 살 거예요.

❸ 의문사 의문문에 Yes/No로 답변

Why did you cancel tomorrow's meeting? 왜 내일 회의를 취소하셨나요?

오답 No, it didn't last long. 아니요, 오래 걸리진 않았어요.
정답 I have an appointment with my client. 고객과 약속이 있어요.

❹ 다른 의문사에 적합한 답변

Where will the orientation be held this year? 올해에는 오리엔테이션이 어디에서 열리죠?

오답 On September third. 9월 3일이요. (시점을 묻는 When 의문문에 적합한 응답)
정답 In conference room A. A 회의실이요.

UNIT 03 Who / When / Where 의문문

무료 강의

1 Who 의문문

출제 포인트
1 특정 행위를 하는 사람이나 업무 담당자를 묻는 문제가 출제된다.
2 사람 이름, 직위, 직업과 같은 직접적인 대답이 주를 이루지만, 다양한 간접 응답 표현도 등장한다.

◆ 빈출 질문 & 응답 패턴

🎧 750_P2_01

사람 이름	Q	**Who** will replace Mr. Fernandez when he retires?	페르난데즈 씨가 퇴직하면 누가 그 자리를 대신하나요?
	정답	I heard that **Maria Ortega** will.	마리아 오테가 씨가 대신할 거라고 들었어요.
	오답	No, I'm not tired.	아니요, 전 피곤하지 않아요.
		→ 유사 발음 [retires / tired]	
직위/ 직업	Q	**Who** is the woman in the black suit?	검은색 정장을 입은 여자는 누구인가요?
	정답	She is the new **marketing manager**.	그녀는 새로운 마케팅 매니저입니다.
	오답	Everyone has to be formally dressed.	모두 정장을 입어야 해요.
		→ 연상 어휘 [suit / formally dressed]	
부정 대명사	Q	**Who** attended the awards ceremony?	누가 시상식에 참석했죠?
	정답	**No one** in my office.	제 사무실에서는 아무도 안 했어요.
	오답	Attendance is mandatory.	의무적으로 참석해야 해요.
		→ 파생어 [attend / attendance]	
여러 사람	Q	**Who** conducts the quality control test on the brand-new products?	누가 신제품 품질 검사를 하죠?
	정답	**Several people** do.	여러 명이 합니다.
	오답	The testing begins next week.	테스트는 다음 주에 시작해요.
간접 응답	Q	**Who** do you want to recommend for the job?	그 일에 누구를 추천하고 싶으세요?
	정답	Well, **why don't you ask your supervisor**?	글쎄요, 당신의 상관에게 물어보는 게 어때요?
	오답	The job is still available. → 단어 반복 [job]	그 자리는 여전히 비어 있어요.

ETS Check-Up

🎧 750_P2_02   정답과 해설 p.012

음원을 듣고 적절한 응답을 고르세요.

1 (A) (B) (C)   4 (A) (B) (C)
2 (A) (B) (C)   5 (A) (B) (C)
3 (A) (B) (C)   6 (A) (B) (C)

2 When 의문문

출제 포인트
1. 여러 가지 시제를 사용해 특정 시점을 묻는 문제가 출제된다.
2. 시간과 관련된 다양한 표현(at, on, by, ago, before, later 등)이 포함된 보기가 정답일 확률이 높다.

◆ 빈출 질문 & 응답 패턴

🎧 750_P2_03

구체적 시점

Q: **When** is the financial report due?
정답: Not until **next Friday**.
오답: I'll do it.

재무 보고서 제출 기한이 언제죠?
다음 주 금요일까지는 아니에요.
제가 그걸 할게요.

Q: **When** are we interviewing the next job candidate?
정답: In about **fifteen minutes**.
오답: As part of the hiring process.
→ 연상 어휘 [interviewing / hiring process]

다음 입사 지원자는 언제 면접할 건가요?
15분 정도 후에요.
채용 과정의 일환으로요.

모호한 시점

Q: **When** can I expect your final decision?
정답: **After** I speak to regional headquarters.
오답: An increased project budget.

최종 결정이 언제쯤 내려진다고 생각하면 될까요?
제가 지역 본부에 이야기한 다음에요.
인상된 프로젝트 예산이에요.

Q: **When** will the concert start?
정답: **As soon as** everyone is seated.
오답: It was first performed ten years ago.
→ 연상 어휘 [concert / performed]

음악회는 언제 시작하나요?
사람들이 모두 착석하는 대로요.
10년 전에 처음 연주되었어요.

간접 응답

Q: **When** would you like to schedule your next checkup?
정답: **I'll be out of town** until August.
오답: He checks his e-mail daily.
→ 유사 발음 [checkup / checks]

다음 검진을 언제로 예약하시겠어요?
제가 8월까지는 다른 지역에 있어서요.
그는 이메일을 매일 확인해요.

Q: **When** will we hire someone to fill the open position?
정답: **Ms. Watson is handling that.**
오답: I think I left my office window open.
→ 단어 반복 [open]

공석을 채울 사람을 언제 고용할 예정인가요?
그 일은 왓슨 씨가 담당하고 있습니다.
제 사무실 창문을 열어둔 것 같아요.

ETS Check-Up

🎧 750_P2_04 정답과 해설 p.013

음원을 듣고 적절한 응답을 고르세요.

1. (A) (B) (C)
2. (A) (B) (C)
3. (A) (B) (C)
4. (A) (B) (C)
5. (A) (B) (C)
6. (A) (B) (C)

3 Where 의문문

출제 포인트
1 장소 및 위치 관련 정보를 묻는 질문이 주를 이루며, 간혹 출처나 특정 정보를 찾을 수 있는 곳을 묻는 질문이 출제되기도 한다.
2 장소 관련 어휘와 위치를 나타내는 표현(in, on, next to 등)이 있는 응답이 정답일 가능성이 높다.

◆ 빈출 질문 & 응답 패턴

🎧 750_P2_05

장소/위치			
	Q	**Where** are you holding the staff meeting?	직원회의를 어디에서 하나요?
	정답	**In the conference room.**	회의실에서요.
	오답	Because our deadline's changed.	마감일이 바뀌었기 때문이에요.
	Q	**Where** did you put your expense report?	당신의 비용 보고서를 어디에 두셨죠?
	정답	I left it **in your mailbox**.	당신의 우편함에 넣어놨어요.
	오답	It wasn't expensive at all.	그건 전혀 비싸지 않았어요.
		→ 파생어 [expense / expensive]	

담당자			
	Q	**Where** should I submit the application form?	지원서를 어디에 제출해야 하죠?
	정답	The **personnel manager** takes care of it.	인사부장이 그걸 담당해요.
	오답	You should fill it out.	그것을 작성하셔야 합니다.
		→ 연상 어휘 [application form / fill out]	

출처			
	Q	**Where** can I get a copy of the workshop schedule?	어디에서 워크숍 일정표를 얻을 수 있죠?
	정답	**On our Web site.**	저희 웹사이트에서요.
	오답	We're right on schedule.	예정대로 하고 있어요.
		→ 단어 반복 [schedule]	

간접 응답			
	Q	**Where**'s the company retreat being held this year?	올해 회사 야유회는 어디에서 열리나요?
	정답	**Didn't you get the memo?**	메모 못 받으셨어요?
	오답	In the middle of April.	4월 중순이에요.
	Q	**Where** should we store these extra supplies?	여분의 물품을 어디에 보관해야 하나요?
	정답	Well, **the supply room is full.**	음, 비품실은 꽉 찼어요.
	오답	The store will be closed for a holiday.	그 가게는 휴일 동안 문을 닫을 예정이에요.
		→ 다의어 [store]	

ETS Check-Up

🎧 750_P2_06   정답과 해설 p.014

음원을 듣고 적절한 응답을 고르세요.

1 (A) (B) (C)   4 (A) (B) (C)
2 (A) (B) (C)   5 (A) (B) (C)
3 (A) (B) (C)   6 (A) (B) (C)

ETS 유형연습

음원을 듣고 적절한 응답을 고르세요.
다시 들으면서 빈칸을 채우세요.

🎧 750_P2_07
정답과 해설 p.015

1. Mark your answer.
   (A)   (B)   (C)

   _____ does the promotional _____?
   (A) For _____.
   (B) It _____.
   (C) She's the _____.

2. Mark your answer.
   (A)   (B)   (C)

   _____ send me the _____?
   (A) On the _____.
   (B) As soon as _____.
   (C) A new _____.

3. Mark your answer.
   (A)   (B)   (C)

   _____ while you're away?
   (A) _____, please.
   (B) _____ the end of the month.
   (C) I _____ to do it.

4. Mark your answer.
   (A)   (B)   (C)

   _____ I stay in Shanghai?
   (A) I strongly _____.
   (B) One hundred _____.
   (C) I know a _____.

5. Mark your answer.
   (A)   (B)   (C)

   _____ the company-wide _____?
   (A) In the _____.
   (B) _____ real oak paneling.
   (C) They've hired _____.

ETS 실전문제

1. Mark your answer. (A) (B) (C)

2. Mark your answer. (A) (B) (C)

3. Mark your answer. (A) (B) (C)

4. Mark your answer. (A) (B) (C)

5. Mark your answer. (A) (B) (C)

6. Mark your answer. (A) (B) (C)

7. Mark your answer. (A) (B) (C)

8. Mark your answer. (A) (B) (C)

9. Mark your answer. (A) (B) (C)

10. Mark your answer. (A) (B) (C)

11. Mark your answer. (A) (B) (C)

12. Mark your answer. (A) (B) (C)

13. Mark your answer. (A) (B) (C)

14. Mark your answer. (A) (B) (C)

15. Mark your answer. (A) (B) (C)

16. Mark your answer. (A) (B) (C)

17. Mark your answer. (A) (B) (C)

18. Mark your answer. (A) (B) (C)

19. Mark your answer. (A) (B) (C)

20. Mark your answer. (A) (B) (C)

21. Mark your answer. (A) (B) (C)

22. Mark your answer. (A) (B) (C)

23. Mark your answer. (A) (B) (C)

24. Mark your answer. (A) (B) (C)

25. Mark your answer. (A) (B) (C)

UNIT 04 What · Which / Why / How 의문문

무료 강의

1 What · Which 의문문

출제 포인트
1 What 의문문은 시간/종류/의견 등 다양한 내용을 묻기 때문에 What 뒤에 오는 부분을 집중해서 들어야 한다.
2 Which 다음에 오는 명사가 질문의 핵심 포인트가 된다. 이 명사의 하위어나 대명사 one이 들어간 보기가 정답일 가능성이 높다.

◆ 빈출 질문 & 응답 패턴

 750_P2_09

시간	Q	**What time** does the presentation begin?	발표가 몇 시에 시작하죠?
	정답	It starts **at 10 o'clock**.	10시에 시작합니다.
	오답	I was present there.	저는 거기 참석했어요.
종류	Q	**What** would you like for dessert?	디저트로 무엇을 드시겠어요?
	정답	I'll have **ice cream**.	아이스크림으로 할게요.
	오답	Yes, it will arrive soon. → Yes/No 불가 [의문사 의문문]	네, 곧 도착할 겁니다.
의견	Q	**What do you think** of the new Web site?	새 웹사이트에 대해 어떻게 생각하세요?
	정답	I think **it's well-designed**.	잘 설계된 것 같아요.
	오답	It will be provided on-site.	그건 현장에서 제공될 겁니다.
한 가지 선택	Q	**Which paint color** did you choose for the kitchen?	주방에 칠할 페인트를 무슨 색으로 선택했나요?
	정답	A bright shade of **pink**.	밝은 분홍색이요.
	오답	On the stove. → 연상 어휘 [kitchen/stove]	가스레인지 위예요.
상관 없음	Q	**Which restaurant** should we eat dinner at?	어느 식당에서 저녁을 먹을까요?
	정답	**Either one** is fine.	어느 곳이든 괜찮습니다.
	오답	Dinner is at seven P.M. → 단어 반복 [dinner]	저녁 식사는 오후 7시예요.
선택 안 함	Q	**Which of these ties** will look better with this suit?	이 넥타이들 중 어떤 게 이 정장과 더 잘 어울리나요?
	정답	Actually, **neither**.	사실 다 안 어울려요.
	오답	You should wear them.	그것들을 착용해야 해요.

ETS Check-Up

 750_P2_10 정답과 해설 p.021

음원을 듣고 적절한 응답을 고르세요.

1 (A) (B) (C)
2 (A) (B) (C)
3 (A) (B) (C)
4 (A) (B) (C)
5 (A) (B) (C)
6 (A) (B) (C)

2 Why 의문문

출제 포인트
1. 이유/원인/목적을 묻는 Why 의문문 문제에서는 Because나 To부정사로 시작하는 응답이 정답일 확률이 높다. 하지만 Because가 생략된 정답도 자주 나오므로, 반드시 질문의 요지가 무엇인지 파악해야 한다.
2. 다른 의문사와 달리 종종 부정 의문문(Why isn't / Why hasn't 등) 형태로도 출제된다.

◆ 빈출 질문 & 응답 패턴

🎧 750_P2_11

이유	Q	**Why** did you stop using that insurance company?	왜 그 보험회사와 계약을 중단하셨죠?
	정답	**Because** the rates were too high.	왜냐하면 보험료가 너무 비쌌기 때문이에요.
	오답	Yes, I'm sure. → Yes/No 불가 [의문사 의문문]	네, 확신합니다.

목적	Q	**Why** did you decide to advertise on social media?	왜 소셜 미디어에 광고하기로 결정하신 건가요?
	정답	**To attract** more customers.	더 많은 고객을 유치하기 위해서요.
	오답	At least one post per day. → 연상 어휘 [social media / post]	적어도 하루에 게시물 한 개요.

부정 의문문	Q	**Why** hasn't the launch date been finalized?	출시 날짜가 왜 확정되지 않았죠?
	정답	The product is still being tested.	제품이 여전히 테스트 중입니다.
	오답	They haven't visited before.	그들은 전에 방문한 적이 없어요.

제안	Q	**Why don't you** join Mary and me for a walk?	나와 메리랑 같이 산책하러 갈래요?
	정답	Some fresh air would be lovely.	신선한 공기를 좀 마시는 게 좋겠네요.
	오답	It's a great organization.	그곳은 훌륭한 조직이에요.

※ "Why don't you ~?"는 제안이 아닌 이유를 묻는 질문으로 출제되기도 하므로 주의가 필요하다. 맥락을 파악하기 어려운 경우에는 소거법을 활용해 정답을 추론하는 것이 좋다.

	Q	**Why don't you** ask Ms. Taylor for help?	왜 테일러 씨에게 도움을 요청하지 않으세요?
	정답	**Because** she's on a conference call.	전화 회의 중이시라서요.

간접 응답	Q	**Why** did they postpone the departmental meeting?	그들이 왜 부서 회의를 연기했죠?
	정답	I haven't heard anything about that.	그것에 대해 아무것도 들은 게 없어요.
	오답	There is a post office on the corner. → 유사 발음 [postpone / post]	모퉁이에 우체국이 있어요.

ETS Check-Up

🎧 750_P2_12 정답과 해설 p.022

음원을 듣고 적절한 응답을 고르세요.

1 (A) (B) (C)   4 (A) (B) (C)
2 (A) (B) (C)   5 (A) (B) (C)
3 (A) (B) (C)   6 (A) (B) (C)

3 How 의문문

출제 포인트
1. 의문사 How는 형용사나 부사와 함께 쓰여 빈도, 수량, 기간, 가격 등의 정보를 묻거나, 단독으로 사용되어 방법이나 의견을 묻는 형태로 출제된다.
2. 직접적으로 정보를 제공하는 응답이 많지만, 방법이나 의견을 우회적으로 표현한 보기도 정답이 될 수 있다.

▶ 빈출 질문 & 응답 패턴

🎧 750_P2_13

빈도
- Q: **How often** do employees at your company have performance reviews?
  당신 회사 직원들은 얼마나 자주 업무 평가를 받나요?
- 정답: We have them **twice a year**.
  일 년에 두 번 받아요.
- 오답: My manager's Ms. Aweel.
  제 부서장님은 아웰 씨예요.
  → 연상 어휘 [performance reviews / manager]

수량
- Q: **How many** people are coming to the reception?
  그 환영회에 사람들이 얼마나 올까요?
- 정답: There could be **several hundred**.
  수백 명은 될 겁니다.
- 오답: I don't have time tonight.
  저는 오늘 밤에 시간이 없어요.

기간
- Q: **How long** did you work for your previous employer?
  이전 회사에서 얼마나 근무했나요?
- 정답: **For seven years**.
  7년간요.
- 오답: Yes, I liked my employer.
  네, 저는 고용주가 마음에 들었습니다.
  → Yes/No 불가 [의문사 의문문]

방법
- Q: **How** will the new equipment be delivered to the factory?
  새 장비는 공장에 어떻게 배달될 건가요?
- 정답: I think it'll come **by truck**.
  아마 트럭으로 올 거예요.
- 오답: On this delivery form.
  이 인수증이에요.
  → 파생어 [deliver / delivery]

의견
- Q: **How** do you like your new computer?
  새 컴퓨터 어때요?
- 정답: **It's much faster than the old one.**
  이전 것보다 훨씬 빨라요.
- 오답: It's a long way to travel.
  이동하기 먼 거리예요.

ETS Check-Up

🎧 750_P2_14 정답과 해설 p.023

음원을 듣고 적절한 응답을 고르세요.

1 (A) (B) (C)   4 (A) (B) (C)
2 (A) (B) (C)   5 (A) (B) (C)
3 (A) (B) (C)   6 (A) (B) (C)

ETS 유형연습

음원을 듣고 적절한 응답을 고르세요.
다시 들으면서 빈칸을 채우세요.

🎧 750_P2_15
정답과 해설 p.024

1. Mark your answer.
   (A) (B) (C)

   _____ about our progress?
   (A) She _____ on Wednesday.
   (B) Mostly _____.
   (C) Yes, she did.

2. Mark your answer.
   (A) (B) (C)

   _____ should I take _____?
   (A) _____.
   (B) An _____.
   (C) Take _____.

3. Mark your answer.
   (A) (B) (C)

   _____ can I _____ with Doctor Feinstein?
   (A) She's _____.
   (B) Just _____.
   (C) It _____.

4. Mark your answer.
   (A) (B) (C)

   _____ the market intelligence data?
   (A) Just _____.
   (B) Because it's _____.
   (C) No, I think _____.

5. Mark your answer.
   (A) (B) (C)

   _____ at the workshop this morning?
   (A) I'll _____.
   (B) It's expected to _____.
   (C) _____ for about 25.

ETS 실전문제

1. Mark your answer. (A) (B) (C)

2. Mark your answer. (A) (B) (C)

3. Mark your answer. (A) (B) (C)

4. Mark your answer. (A) (B) (C)

5. Mark your answer. (A) (B) (C)

6. Mark your answer. (A) (B) (C)

7. Mark your answer. (A) (B) (C)

8. Mark your answer. (A) (B) (C)

9. Mark your answer. (A) (B) (C)

10. Mark your answer. (A) (B) (C)

11. Mark your answer. (A) (B) (C)

12. Mark your answer. (A) (B) (C)

13. Mark your answer. (A) (B) (C)

14. Mark your answer. (A) (B) (C)

15. Mark your answer. (A) (B) (C)

16. Mark your answer. (A) (B) (C)

17. Mark your answer. (A) (B) (C)

18. Mark your answer. (A) (B) (C)

19. Mark your answer. (A) (B) (C)

20. Mark your answer. (A) (B) (C)

21. Mark your answer. (A) (B) (C)

22. Mark your answer. (A) (B) (C)

23. Mark your answer. (A) (B) (C)

24. Mark your answer. (A) (B) (C)

25. Mark your answer. (A) (B) (C)

UNIT 05 일반/부정/부가 의문문

1 일반 의문문

출제 포인트

1. Be/Do/Have/조동사로 시작하는 일반 의문문은 사실, 계획, 경험 등을 확인하는 용도로 쓰인다. 따라서 본동사를 정확히 확인하여 질문 전체의 요지를 파악하는 것이 중요하다.
2. Yes/No 답변이 기본이지만 Sure/Sorry와 같은 대체 표현이 쓰일 수도 있다. 보기에 Yes와 No가 둘 다 등장하는 경우가 있으므로 뒤따르는 내용을 반드시 들어야 하고, 최근에는 Yes/No를 생략한 함축적인 답변도 자주 출제된다는 점에 유의한다.

▶ 빈출 질문 & 응답 패턴

750_P2_17

Be동사 (사실 확인)	Q	**Is** this the newest type of battery?	이것이 최신형 배터리인가요?
	정답	I think **it is**.	그런 것 같군요.
	오답	No, I'm not. → 대명사 오류 [Is this/I'm]	아니요, 전 아닙니다.
Do동사 (행위)	Q	**Did** Mark call someone to fix the refrigerator?	마크가 냉장고 수리를 위해 누군가에게 전화를 걸었나요?
	정답	**Yes**, a repair person will be here soon.	네, 수리 기사가 곧 여기 올 거예요.
	오답	To maintain accurate records.	정확한 기록을 유지하려고요.
간접 의문문	Q	**Do you know** where I can check the schedule?	일정표를 어디에서 확인할 수 있는지 아세요?
	정답	**Yes**, it's over there on the wall.	네, 저쪽 벽에 붙어 있어요.
	오답	Can I have the check please? → 다의어 [check]	계산서 좀 주시겠어요?
조동사 Will (계획)	Q	**Will** you be attending the trade fair next Monday?	다음 주 월요일에 무역 박람회에 참가하실 건가요?
	정답	**I'm still thinking** about it.	여전히 생각 중이에요.
	오답	I went to Hawaii.	저는 하와이에 갔었어요.
Have 동사 (경험, 완료)	Q	**Have** they set up the equipment yet?	그들이 장비를 설치했죠?
	정답	**No**, they'll do it tomorrow.	아니요, 그들은 내일 할 겁니다.
	오답	You can sit over there. → 유사 발음 [set/sit]	저쪽에 앉으셔도 됩니다.

ETS Check-Up

750_P2_18 정답과 해설 p.031

음원을 듣고 적절한 응답을 고르세요.

1 (A) (B) (C)
2 (A) (B) (C)
3 (A) (B) (C)
4 (A) (B) (C)
5 (A) (B) (C)
6 (A) (B) (C)

2 부정 의문문

출제 포인트

1. Aren't, Didn't, Haven't 등의 부정어로 시작하는 부정 의문문은 사실을 확인할 때 자주 쓰이며, 간혹 동의를 구하거나 제안(Shouldn't, Wouldn't)을 할 때도 쓰인다.
2. 긍정의 답변은 Yes로, 부정의 답변은 No로 시작하는 경우가 많지만 이를 생략한 채 우회적으로 표현한 응답도 간혹 등장한다. 따라서 부정어 뒤에 나오는 내용과 질문의 목적을 파악한 후 정답을 선택해야 한다.

◆ 빈출 질문 & 응답 패턴

🎧 750_P2_19

Be동사 부정
Q **Isn't** the special exhibit at the museum closing soon?
박물관 내 특별 전시가 곧 끝나지 않나요?
정답 **Yes**, it's only open for two more weeks.
네, 2주간만 더 공개됩니다.
오답 It's pretty close to here.
거긴 이곳과 매우 가까워요.
→ 다의어 [closing / close]

Do동사 부정
Q **Don't** we have a conference call at ten?
10시에 전화 회의가 있지 않나요?
정답 It's been **canceled**.
취소되었어요.
오답 No, only four.
아니요, 네 명뿐이에요.

Have동사 부정
Q **Haven't** you filled the secretarial position yet?
이미 비서직 인원을 충원하지 않았나요?
정답 **We finally hired someone** yesterday.
마침내 어제 사람을 채용했어요.
오답 I've been a secretary for nine years.
저는 9년간 비서를 하고 있어요.
→ 파생어 [secretarial / secretary]

조동사 부정
Q **Shouldn't** we print the brochure in color?
브로셔를 컬러로 인쇄해야 하지 않을까요?
정답 **I thought so, too.**
저도 그렇게 생각했어요.
오답 Twenty pages at a time.
한 번에 20페이지씩요.
→ 연상 어휘 [print / pages]

의문사 부정
Q **Why didn't** the flight to Dublin depart on schedule?
왜 더블린행 항공편이 제시간에 출발하지 않았나요?
정답 **Bad weather caused a delay.**
악천후로 인해 지연되었어요.
오답 No, it's a direct flight.
아니요, 직항편입니다.
→ 단어 반복 [flight]

ETS Check-Up

🎧 750_P2_20   정답과 해설 p.032

음원을 듣고 적절한 응답을 고르세요.

1 (A) (B) (C)   4 (A) (B) (C)
2 (A) (B) (C)   5 (A) (B) (C)
3 (A) (B) (C)   6 (A) (B) (C)

3 부가 의문문

출제 포인트
1. 동사+주어가 덧붙여진 형태가 일반적이나, right/correct/don't you think 등을 사용한 유형도 종종 출제된다. 사실을 확인하거나 동의를 구하는 내용이 대부분이므로 앞에 나온 평서문의 내용에 집중해야 한다.
2. Yes/No로 응답하는 경우, 답변을 기준으로 질문 내용에 긍정이면 Yes, 부정이면 No를 사용해야 한다. 우회적으로 동의/반대하거나 질문자에게 추가 정보를 제공/요청하는 대답이 정답이 되기도 한다.

◆ 빈출 질문 & 응답 패턴

🎧 750_P2_21

Be동사	Q	This package was damaged during delivery, **wasn't it**?	이 소포는 배송 도중에 손상되었죠, 그렇지 않나요?
	정답	**Yes**, you'll need to fill out a claim form.	네, 배상 청구서를 작성하셔야 할 거예요.
	오답	No, the mail comes in the afternoon. → 연상 어휘 [package/mail]	아니요, 우편물은 오후에 와요.
Do동사	Q	We ordered a cabinet yesterday, **didn't we**?	우리가 어제 수납장 하나를 주문했죠, 그렇지 않나요?
	정답	**Yes**, it'll be delivered this morning.	네, 그것은 오늘 오전에 배달될 거예요.
	오답	Sorry, they're out of order. → 다의어 [order]	미안하지만, 그것들은 고장이에요.
Have 동사	Q	Ms. Yansky's entered the lab results, **hasn't she**?	얀스키 씨가 실험 결과를 입력했죠, 그렇지 않나요?
	정답	**No**, she's been busy ordering supplies.	아니요, 그녀는 물품을 주문하느라 바빴어요.
	오답	She entered the contest and won. → 단어 반복 [entered]	그녀는 경연대회에 참가해 우승했어요.
조동사	Q	You'd prefer a seat by the window, **wouldn't you**?	창가 쪽 좌석을 선호하시죠, 그렇지 않나요?
	정답	**Yes**, I would.	네, 그렇습니다.
	오답	No, I don't see it. → 유사 발음 [seat/see it]	아니요, 안 보입니다.
특수 형태	Q	This train runs every hour, **right**?	이 기차는 매 시간 운행되죠, 그렇죠?
	정답	**Here's the schedule.**	여기 시간표가 있어요.
	오답	No, we went there by bus.	아니요, 거기에 버스를 타고 갔어요.

ETS Check-Up

🎧 750_P2_22 정답과 해설 p.033

음원을 듣고 적절한 응답을 고르세요.

1 (A) (B) (C)
2 (A) (B) (C)
3 (A) (B) (C)
4 (A) (B) (C)
5 (A) (B) (C)
6 (A) (B) (C)

ETS 유형연습

음원을 듣고 적절한 응답을 고르세요.
다시 들으면서 빈칸을 채우세요.

🎧 750_P2_23
정답과 해설 p.034

1. Mark your answer.
   (A)   (B)   (C)

   Are those shoes _____?
   (A) _____ of shoes.
   (B) Please _____ at the next light.
   (C) No, I _____.

2. Mark your answer.
   (A)   (B)   (C)

   Do you know why I need to _____?
   (A) I don't believe _____.
   (B) No, I _____.
   (C) Maybe you need to _____.

3. Mark your answer.
   (A)   (B)   (C)

   Have you finished _____?
   (A) Just _____.
   (B) He _____ Mr. Garcia.
   (C) Yes, the apartment _____.

4. Mark your answer.
   (A)   (B)   (C)

   _____ in the shipping department?
   (A) Please send it _____.
   (B) Yes, but he _____.
   (C) _____ today.

5. Mark your answer.
   (A)   (B)   (C)

   Ms. Park will be _____, won't she?
   (A) It's a _____.
   (B) _____ on a business trip.
   (C) _____ are on my desk.

UNIT 05 일반/부정/부가 의문문

ETS 실전문제

1. Mark your answer. (A) (B) (C)

2. Mark your answer. (A) (B) (C)

3. Mark your answer. (A) (B) (C)

4. Mark your answer. (A) (B) (C)

5. Mark your answer. (A) (B) (C)

6. Mark your answer. (A) (B) (C)

7. Mark your answer. (A) (B) (C)

8. Mark your answer. (A) (B) (C)

9. Mark your answer. (A) (B) (C)

10. Mark your answer. (A) (B) (C)

11. Mark your answer. (A) (B) (C)

12. Mark your answer. (A) (B) (C)

13. Mark your answer. (A) (B) (C)

14. Mark your answer. (A) (B) (C)

15. Mark your answer. (A) (B) (C)

16. Mark your answer. (A) (B) (C)

17. Mark your answer. (A) (B) (C)

18. Mark your answer. (A) (B) (C)

19. Mark your answer. (A) (B) (C)

20. Mark your answer. (A) (B) (C)

21. Mark your answer. (A) (B) (C)

22. Mark your answer. (A) (B) (C)

23. Mark your answer. (A) (B) (C)

24. Mark your answer. (A) (B) (C)

25. Mark your answer. (A) (B) (C)

UNIT 06 선택/요청·제안 의문문/평서문

무료 강의

1 선택 의문문

출제 포인트
1. A or B 구조로 두 가지 선택 사항이 주어지며, A와 B는 구 혹은 문장의 형태를 띤다.
2. 둘 중 하나를 직접적으로 선택하거나 이를 우회적으로 드러내는 응답이 보편적이다. 선택을 회피하는 답변이 출제되기도 하며, Either/Neither/Whichever 등의 표현이 있는 보기가 정답일 확률이 높다.

◆ 빈출 질문 & 응답 패턴

🎧 750_P2_25

한 가지 선택	Q	Will the construction be completed **this year or next year**?	공사는 올해 끝나요, 아니면 내년에 끝나요?
	정답	It will be done **by the end of the year**.	연말까지는 끝날 거예요.
	오답	I've already read the instructions.	저는 이미 설명서를 읽었어요.
상관 없음	Q	Martin, would you rather **complete the data entry or start the filing project**?	마틴 씨, 데이터 입력을 마무리하실래요, 아니면 서류 정리를 시작하실래요?
	정답	**Either is fine** with me.	어느 것이든 좋아요.
	오답	It is still on file. → 파생어 [filing/file]	아직 보관되어 있어요.
제3의 선택	Q	**Can you fix this computer, or should I call the service center?**	이 컴퓨터를 고칠 수 있겠어요, 아니면 서비스 센터에 전화할까요?
	정답	**I don't think it can be repaired.**	그건 수리가 안 될 거 같은데요.
	오답	Usually between ten and six.	대개 10시에서 6시 사이에요.
선택 안 함	Q	Will you watch **the movie or the game**?	영화를 볼 건가요, 경기를 볼 건가요?
	정답	**Neither**; I'm too tired.	둘 다 안 봐요. 너무 피곤하거든요.
	오답	There was a movie premiere yesterday. → 단어 반복 [movie]	어제 영화 시사회가 있었어요.
간접 응답	Q	**Should we walk or take a taxi to the train station?**	기차역까지 걸어갈까요, 아니면 택시를 탈까요?
	정답	Well, **the train leaves in thirty minutes.**	음, 기차가 30분 후에 출발해요.
	오답	No, I went to a training session. → 유사 발음 [train/training]	아니요, 저는 연수에 다녀왔어요.

ETS Check-Up

🎧 750_P2_26 정답과 해설 p.040

음원을 듣고 적절한 응답을 고르세요.

1. (A) (B) (C)
2. (A) (B) (C)
3. (A) (B) (C)
4. (A) (B) (C)
5. (A) (B) (C)
6. (A) (B) (C)

2 요청·제안 의문문

출제 포인트
1. Can/Could, Would you like/mind, Why don't we, How about 등 요청이나 제안을 나타내는 다양한 표현의 질문이 출제된다.
2. Yes/Sure나 Sorry처럼 직접적으로 수락이나 거절을 나타내는 응답이 대부분이다. 간혹 이를 생략하고 수락/거절의 이유만 언급하거나 결정을 보류하는 답변도 등장하므로 유의한다.

▶ 빈출 질문 & 응답 패턴

🎧 750_P2_27

부탁/요청			
	Q	**Could you** make twenty copies of this report?	이 보고서를 20부 복사해 주시겠어요?
	정답	**Sure**, I'll do it right now.	네, 지금 당장 할게요.
	오답	Yes, he's a news reporter.	네, 그는 기자예요.
		→ 파생어 [report/reporter]	
	Q	**Would you mind** interviewing a job applicant on Thursday?	목요일에 입사 지원자를 면접하는 게 괜찮으세요?
	정답	**Sorry**, I'll be away on holiday.	죄송해요, 저는 휴가라 자리를 비울 거예요.
	오답	Three open positions.	세 개의 공석이요.
		→ 연상 어휘 [job applicant/positions]	

제안/권유			
	Q	**Why don't you** sign the contract?	그 계약에 서명하는 게 어떠세요?
	정답	**I need some more time** to review it.	저는 좀 더 검토할 시간이 필요해요.
	오답	You can contact me by phone anytime.	언제든지 제게 전화로 연락하시면 됩니다.
		→ 유사 발음 [contract/contact]	
	Q	**How about** sending Jeremy a thank-you card for his help?	제레미에게 도와줘서 고맙다는 카드를 보내는 게 어떨까요?
	정답	**Yes, that's a nice idea.**	네, 좋은 생각이에요.
	오답	They came this morning.	그들은 오늘 아침에 왔어요.
	Q	**Would you like** some help organizing the conference?	회의 준비하는 걸 도와드릴까요?
	정답	I think **I can manage by myself**.	저 혼자 할 수 있을 것 같아요.
	오답	To the conference center.	회의장으로요.
		→ 단어 반복 [conference]	

ETS Check-Up

🎧 750_P2_28 정답과 해설 p.042

음원을 듣고 적절한 응답을 고르세요.

1. (A) (B) (C)
2. (A) (B) (C)
3. (A) (B) (C)
4. (A) (B) (C)
5. (A) (B) (C)
6. (A) (B) (C)

3 평서문

출제 포인트

1 평서문은 정보/상황/의견/제안 사항 등을 진술하는 문장이다. 정해진 응답 패턴이 없어 문장 전체를 이해해야 하며, 때로는 어조까지 파악해야 정답을 고를 수 있다.

2 정보/의견을 수용하는 응답, 상황/문제점에 대한 방안을 제시하는 응답, 제안을 수락/거절하는 응답 이외에, 질문을 하는 응답도 종종 정답으로 출제된다.

◆ 빈출 평서문 & 응답 패턴

🎧 750_P2_29

사실/정보	Q	They won't bill us for their consulting service.	그들은 우리에게 컨설팅 서비스에 대한 비용을 청구하지 않을 거예요.
	정답	Yes, I saw their advertisement.	네, 저도 광고 봤어요.
	오답	I have change for a 10 dollar bill. → 다의어 [bill]	제게 10달러 지폐를 바꿀 잔돈이 있어요.
의견/바람	Q	I hope the articles affect our business positively.	그 기사들이 우리 사업에 긍정적인 영향을 미치면 좋겠어요.
	정답	Our products are already selling well.	우리 상품들은 이미 잘 팔리고 있어요.
	오답	The policy will go into effect next month. → 유사 발음 [affect/effect]	그 정책은 다음 달에 실시될 겁니다.
문제점	Q	I'm afraid the address you entered is incorrect.	죄송하지만 입력하신 주소가 올바르지 않네요.
	정답	Oh, let me check it.	아, 확인해볼게요.
	오답	By express mail, please. → 연상 어휘 [address/mail]	빠른 우편으로 보내주세요.
제안/명령	Q	Let's put the new merchandise in the front of the store.	신제품을 상점 전면에 진열합시다.
	정답	That's a good idea.	좋은 생각이에요.
	오답	Yes, everything was half off.	네, 모든 게 반값이었어요.
	Q	Please take a copy of our new catalogue.	새로 나온 카탈로그 한 부 가져가세요.
	정답	I already have one.	전 이미 한 부 있어요.
	오답	I'll take notes. → 단어 반복 [take]	제가 필기를 할게요.
질문하는 응답	Q	I can't make it to the party tonight.	저는 오늘 밤 파티에 못 가요.
	정답	Do you have other plans?	다른 약속이 있나요?
	오답	She will come, too. → 연상 어휘 [make it/come]	그녀도 올 겁니다.

ETS Check-Up

🎧 750_P2_30 정답과 해설 p.043

음원을 듣고 적절한 응답을 고르세요.

1 (A) (B) (C)   4 (A) (B) (C)
2 (A) (B) (C)   5 (A) (B) (C)
3 (A) (B) (C)   6 (A) (B) (C)

ETS 유형연습

음원을 듣고 적절한 응답을 고르세요.
다시 들으면서 빈칸을 채우세요.

🔊 750_P2_31
정답과 해설 p.044

---

1. Mark your answer.
   (A)   (B)   (C)

Should I _____ for _____ in the day?

(A) _____ on Twelfth Street.

(B) Just _____.

(C) I'm usually _____.

---

2. Mark your answer.
   (A)   (B)   (C)

Could you _____, please?

(A) The contract _____.

(B) Sorry, _____.

(C) _____.

---

3. Mark your answer.
   (A)   (B)   (C)

I'd like to _____.

(A) What's _____?

(B) Yes, in the _____.

(C) _____ turkey sandwich.

---

4. Mark your answer.
   (A)   (B)   (C)

We can't _____ until three P.M. tomorrow.

(A) It's _____.

(B) _____ to Denver for two.

(C) _____ and look at the Web site.

---

5. Mark your answer.
   (A)   (B)   (C)

_____ that tomorrow when you're not so tired?

(A) He _____ this time.

(B) Whenever you _____.

(C) That's _____.

UNIT 06 선택/요청·제안 의문문/평서문

ETS 실전문제

1. Mark your answer. (A) (B) (C)

2. Mark your answer. (A) (B) (C)

3. Mark your answer. (A) (B) (C)

4. Mark your answer. (A) (B) (C)

5. Mark your answer. (A) (B) (C)

6. Mark your answer. (A) (B) (C)

7. Mark your answer. (A) (B) (C)

8. Mark your answer. (A) (B) (C)

9. Mark your answer. (A) (B) (C)

10. Mark your answer. (A) (B) (C)

11. Mark your answer. (A) (B) (C)

12. Mark your answer. (A) (B) (C)

13. Mark your answer. (A) (B) (C)

14. Mark your answer.   (A)   (B)   (C)

15. Mark your answer.   (A)   (B)   (C)

16. Mark your answer.   (A)   (B)   (C)

17. Mark your answer.   (A)   (B)   (C)

18. Mark your answer.   (A)   (B)   (C)

19. Mark your answer.   (A)   (B)   (C)

20. Mark your answer.   (A)   (B)   (C)

21. Mark your answer.   (A)   (B)   (C)

22. Mark your answer.   (A)   (B)   (C)

23. Mark your answer.   (A)   (B)   (C)

24. Mark your answer.   (A)   (B)   (C)

25. Mark your answer.   (A)   (B)   (C)

ETS ACTUAL TEST 750_P2_33

7. Mark your answer on your answer sheet.
8. Mark your answer on your answer sheet.
9. Mark your answer on your answer sheet.
10. Mark your answer on your answer sheet.
11. Mark your answer on your answer sheet.
12. Mark your answer on your answer sheet.
13. Mark your answer on your answer sheet.
14. Mark your answer on your answer sheet.
15. Mark your answer on your answer sheet.
16. Mark your answer on your answer sheet.
17. Mark your answer on your answer sheet.
18. Mark your answer on your answer sheet.
19. Mark your answer on your answer sheet.
20. Mark your answer on your answer sheet.
21. Mark your answer on your answer sheet.
22. Mark your answer on your answer sheet.
23. Mark your answer on your answer sheet.
24. Mark your answer on your answer sheet.
25. Mark your answer on your answer sheet.
26. Mark your answer on your answer sheet.
27. Mark your answer on your answer sheet.
28. Mark your answer on your answer sheet.
29. Mark your answer on your answer sheet.
30. Mark your answer on your answer sheet.
31. Mark your answer on your answer sheet.

PART 2 빈출 표현

신분/직업

assistant 비서, 부하 직원
receptionist 접수 담당자, 안내 데스크 직원
director 감독, 국장, 이사
board members 임원, 이사진
chairperson 회장 (= president)
vice president 부회장, 부사장
colleague 동료 (= coworker)
supervisor 관리자, 상사
entrepreneur 기업가
proprietor 소유자, 소유주
tenant 세입자
real estate agent 부동산 중개인
property manager 부동산 관리인
financial consultant 재무 상담가
program coordinator 프로그램 진행자
inspector 검사관, 조사관
contractor 계약자, 도급업자
client 고객, 의뢰인

시간/시점

a few months ago 몇 달 전에
since last summer 지난여름 이후로
the day before yesterday 그저께
at the beginning of August 8월 초에
recently 최근에
any minute now 지금 당장에라도
earlier today 오늘 아까
shortly 곧
on October fifteenth 10월 15일에
within the next few days 며칠 이내로
sometime next spring 내년 봄쯤

in about a year or so 대략 1년쯤 후에
at the end of the month 이달 말에
by the end of the day 오늘까지, 오늘 안으로
no later than Thursday 늦어도 목요일까지
not until June 6월 이후에야
by six o'clock at the latest 늦어도 6시까지
at the next staff meeting 다음 직원회의에서
as soon as it's ready 준비가 되자마자
once the plan is finalized 계획이 확정되면

장소/위치

in the front/back row 앞/뒷줄에
in the cabinet 수납장 안에
in the tenth floor meeting room 10층 회의실에서
across the street 길 건너편에
at the end of the hall 복도 끝에
at the corner of the street 길 모퉁이에
at the customer service desk 고객 서비스 창구에서
on the ceiling 천장에
on the left side 왼쪽에
on the second floor 2층에
on the Web site 웹사이트에
on the bottom shelf 맨 아래 선반에
to the address below 아래에 있는 주소로
to the supply room 비품실로
from the printing company 인쇄소로부터
from the city center 시내 중심가에서
next to the movie theater 영화관 옆에
near Fourth Avenue 4번 가 근처에
directly across from the old one 예전 것 바로 맞은편에
down the hall and to the left 복도 끝에서 왼쪽으로
just past the exit 출구를 지나자마자

방법/수단

in writing 서면으로
in person 직접, 손수 (= personally)
in alphabetical order 알파벳순으로
by courier 택배로
by credit card 신용 카드로
by bus/plane/subway 버스/비행기/지하철로
by express mail 속달[특급] 우편으로
by overnight delivery 익일 배송으로
by searching on the Internet 인터넷 검색으로
through fund-raising events 모금 행사를 통해서
You can register online. 온라인으로 등록할 수 있어요.
You'll need your ID card. 신분증이 필요해요.
Push the button on the side.
측면에 있는 버튼을 누르세요.

기간/빈도/가격/수량

for more than 5 years 5년 이상
every ten minutes 10분마다
every other week/month 격주/격월로
on a regular basis 정기적으로 (= regularly)
at least once a month 최소한 한 달에 한 번
the rest of the month 이번 달 남은 기간 (동안)
once in a while 가끔
twice a day 하루에 두 번
on Saturdays 토요일마다
twenty dollars each 각각 20달러
about a dozen 열두 명[개] 정도
50 euros a month 한 달에 50유로
by 10 percent 10퍼센트
probably around fifty 아마 50 정도
It's almost doubled. 거의 두 배입니다.
Your total is 75 dollars. 총 75달러입니다.
within/over budget 예산 내의/초과의

이유/목적

Because he had an appointment.
그가 약속이 있었기 때문이에요.
Because we are understaffed.
우리가 일손이 부족하기 때문이에요.
probably because of the rain 아마도 비 때문에
due to bad[inclement] weather 악천후 때문에
for personal business 개인적인 용무 때문에
for a dentist appointment 치과 예약 때문에
to shorten the commute 통근 시간을 줄이기 위해서
to accommodate more customers
더 많은 고객을 수용하기 위해
to match the new curtain
새 커튼과 어울리게 하기 위해
to increase efficiency 효율을 높이기 위해
to discuss a new project
새 프로젝트에 관해 논의하기 위해
So that more people can attend.
더 많은 사람들이 참석할 수 있도록요.

상태/의견

I enjoyed it. 즐거웠어요.
It couldn't have been better. 정말 최고였어요.
It was helpful. 도움이 되었어요.
It was very informative. 굉장히 유익했어요.
It went very well. 잘 (진행)되었어요.
It has a great view. 전망이 아주 좋아요.
Better than I expected. 기대 이상이에요.
Well, I was disappointed. 음, 실망했어요.
It should be here soon. 그건 곧 올 겁니다.
It's an impressive design. 인상적인 디자인이군요.
It rained all day. 하루 종일 비가 왔어요.
It was too busy[crowded]. 굉장히 붐볐어요.
We may want to consult some experts.
아마 몇몇 전문가들과 상담을 해야 할 겁니다.

잘 모른다/듣지 못했다

I wish I knew. 저도 알았으면 좋겠어요.
Nobody knows. 아무도 모르죠.
I have no idea. 몰라요.
We're not sure yet. 아직 잘 모르겠어요.
I don't know anything about it.
그것에 대해선 전혀 몰라요.
I'm not certain. 잘 모르겠어요.
Who knows? 누가 알겠어요?
We won't know until March.
3월이나 되어야 알게 될 거예요.
He hasn't told us yet.
그가 아직 우리에게 말하지 않았어요.
I haven't been told[informed] yet.
아직 듣지(안내받지) 못했어요.
I still haven't heard from them.
그들에게서 아직 소식을 듣지 못했어요.

결정되지 않았다

I'm still considering it. 아직 고려 중이에요.
It's still up in the air. 아직 결정 난 게 아니에요.
I'm still thinking about it.
아직 그것에 대해 생각 중이에요.
They're still deciding. 그들은 아직 결정 중이에요.
The manager is reviewing it. 매니저가 검토 중입니다.
I haven't made up my mind. 아직 결정하지 못했어요.
It hasn't been decided yet. 아직 결정되지 않았어요.
It hasn't been discussed yet.
아직 논의되지 않았어요.
It hasn't been finalized yet. 아직 마무리되지 않았어요.
We're waiting for the confirmation.
확정을 기다리는 중이에요.
It depends on the traffic. 교통 상황에 따라 달라요.
It depends on the design. 디자인에 따라 달라요.
It depends on when it is.
그때가 언제인지에 달려 있어요.

확인해 보다/문의해 보다

Let me check that for you. 확인해 볼게요.
Let me ask someone. 다른 사람에게 물어볼게요.
Let me call the supplier. 납품업체에 전화해 볼게요.
I'll find out. 제가 알아볼게요.
I'll let you know soon. 곧 알려 드릴게요.
I'll check the schedule. 제가 일정을 확인해 볼게요.
I will take care of it. 제가 처리할게요.
I'll get back to you. 다시 연락드릴게요.
Try asking Mr. Taylor. 테일러 씨에게 문의해 보세요.
Refer to your manual. 설명서를 참고해 주세요.
John knows better than I do.
존이 저보다 더 잘 알아요.
I'll have to ask Chris about that.
크리스에게 물어봐야 해요.
The manager has a floor plan.
매니저가 층 배치도를 가지고 있어요.
Why don't you ask your supervisor?
관리자에게 문의하는 게 어때요?

하나 선택

I prefer green. 초록색이 더 좋아요.
I'll go with the red one. 붉은 것으로 할게요.
I like the grey ones better. 회색인 것이 더 좋아요.
The one with the yellow tag.
노란 꼬리표가 달린 거요.
I'd rather leave early. 저는 빨리 출발하는 게 좋겠어요.
The soup sounds good. 수프가 좋을 것 같아요.
Now would be fine. 지금이 좋겠어요.
Monday is best for me. 월요일이 저한테는 제일 좋아요.
Late afternoon, if possible. 가능하면 늦은 오후로요.
Any time in the morning. 오전이면 언제든요.
Let's try the new restaurant. 새 식당에 가보죠.
Let's order in, since it's raining.
비가 오니 배달시켜 먹어요.

모두 선택/반대

I like both. / I like both of them. 둘 다 좋아요.
Both of them would be fine. 둘 다 좋을 것 같아요.
I like all of them. 모두 좋아요.
He did both. 그는 둘 다 했어요.
We can afford to do both. 둘 다 할 수 있어요.
Actually, neither of them.
사실 그중 아무것도 아니에요.
I prefer neither. 둘 다 별로예요.
I like neither of them. 둘 다 싫어요.
Neither, thanks. 고맙지만 둘 다 됐어요.

제3의 선택

Just some water, please. 그냥 물 좀 부탁할게요.
Can we do it tomorrow instead?
내일 하면 안 될까요?

상관없다

I don't care. 상관없어요.
Whatever you prefer. 당신이 더 선호하시는 걸로요.
Whichever you like. 좋아하시는 대로요.
Anywhere is fine. 어디라도 좋아요.
Either (one) is fine (with me).
저는 어느 쪽이든 괜찮아요.
Whichever we can get faster.
어떤 것이든 더 빠른 것으로요.
Any day except Monday.
월요일을 제외하고 언제라도요.
It doesn't matter (to me). 저는 상관없어요.
It doesn't make any difference.
(어떤 것이든) 별로 차이가 없어요.
I'll leave it to you. 당신에게 맡길게요.
It's up to you. 당신이 원하는 대로 해요.
I don't have a preference. 선호하는 게 없어요.

수락/동의

Suit yourself. 좋을 대로 하세요.
No problem. 문제없어요.
Not at all. 전혀요.
OK, I'll be sure to do that. 네, 꼭 그렇게 할게요.
**You bet. / Certainly. / Absolutely. / Definitely. /
Why not?** 물론이죠.
Be my guest. / Go ahead. / By all means.
그렇게 하세요.
I'd love to. / I'd be happy to. 그러고 싶어요.
It certainly was. 정말 그랬어요.
That's a good idea. 좋은 생각이네요.
Yes, that would be great. 네, 그럼 아주 좋겠네요.
If you're not too busy. 당신이 많이 바쁘지 않다면요.
If it's not too much trouble.
그게 너무 수고스럽지 않다면요.

거절/부정

I can manage[handle] that, thanks.
내가 혼자 할 수 있어요, 고마워요.
Actually, I already have. 실은 벌써 했습니다.
I'm almost done, thanks. 고맙지만, 거의 다 했어요.
I decided not to go. 저는 가지 않기로 했어요.
**Oh, I can't make it because of a scheduling
conflict.** 오, 일정이 겹쳐서 참석을 못 해요.
Thanks, but I have other plans.
고맙지만, 다른 계획이 있어요.
Sorry, I have an appointment then.
미안하지만 그때 약속이 있어요.
I wish I could, but I'm very busy.
그러고 싶지만 너무 바빠요.
I don't have time right now. 지금은 시간이 없어요.
Well, I'm about to leave. 음, 막 퇴근하려던 참이에요.
I have to return to the office right now.
저는 지금 바로 사무실로 돌아가야 해요.
No, it's much too cold. 아니요, 너무 추워요.

짧은 대화

INTRO

UNIT 07 주제·목적/화자·장소 문제
UNIT 08 세부 사항/문제점·걱정거리 문제
UNIT 09 요청·제안/다음에 할 일 문제
UNIT 10 의도 파악/시각 정보 연계 문제

ETS ACTUAL TEST
PART 3 빈출 표현

무료 강의

PART 3

짧은 대화 총 13세트 39문항

대화를 듣고 이와 관련된 세 개의 문제를 푸는 유형으로, 업무와 일상생활 관련 대화문이 출제된다. 매회 3인 대화가 2개씩 포함되며, 문제 유형은 다음과 같이 크게 두 가지로 나눌 수 있다.

전체 내용 관련 문제	주제/목적, 대화가 이루어지는 장소, 화자들의 직업/업종/근무지
세부 사항 관련 문제	화자의 요청/제안/추천 사항, 화자의 의도 파악, 다음에 할 일/일어날 일, 이유/원인, 방법, 문제점, 세부 사항, 시각 정보 연계

ETS 예제 및 풀이 전략

① 대화를 듣기 전에 문제와 보기를 읽고, 키워드에 표시해 둔다.

② 문제의 키워드가 등장하면 집중해서 듣고, 대화를 듣는 동시에 답을 찾는다.

각 문제 및 보기의 키워드를 파악한 후, 단서가 나올 부분을 노려 듣는다. 관련 내용을 확인하는 즉시 답을 체크하고 다음 문제로 넘어가야 한다. 문제 순서에 맞춰 단서가 주어지는 경우가 많다.

문제지

32. Why is the man surprised?
    (A) The woman has not finished a report.
    (B) The woman knows Sarah.
    (C) The woman is still at the office.
    (D) The woman lives near him.

33. What is Sarah's problem?
    (A) Her car is not working.
    (B) The store will close soon.
    (C) Her home needs some repairs.
    (D) She forgot an appointment.

34. What is the woman planning to do tonight?
    (A) Visit her parents' home
    (B) Look for a new house
    (C) Work on a report
    (D) Go to dinner with Sarah

음원

Questions 32 through 34 refer to the following conversation.

M **32** I didn't expect to see you still here. Are you staying late to work on the Billows report?

W No, actually, **33** I'm just waiting for Sarah. Her car broke down; it's in the shop for repairs, so I'm giving her a ride home.

M I didn't know you two lived near each other.

W Oh, we don't—but **34** I'm having dinner at my parents' house tonight, and Sarah lives near them.

※ 이후 문제만 읽어주며, 문제 사이에 8초가 주어진다.

32. 남자가 놀란 이유: 여자가 아직 사무실에 있어서 정답 (C) The woman is still at the office.
33. 사라의 문제: 차 고장 정답 (A) Her car is not working.
34. 오늘 밤 여자의 계획: 부모님 댁에서 저녁 식사 정답 (A) Visit her parents' home

패러프레이징(Paraphrasing)

패러프레이징이란 '다른 말로 바꾸어 표현하는 것'을 뜻한다. 대화 내의 단서가 보기에 그대로 나오는 경우도 있지만, 패러프레이징되어 제시되는 경우가 많으므로 유형을 미리 파악해 두면 실전에 도움이 된다. 자주 나오는 대표적인 표현들을 암기해 두는 것도 좋은 방법이다.

❶ 동의어, 유의어, 사전적 의미 활용

W I bought this mobile phone yesterday, but it seems to be defective.
여 어제 이 휴대폰을 구매했는데, 결함이 있는 것 같아요.

Q What problem does the woman have?
A Her phone is not working properly.
질문 여자는 어떤 문제가 있는가?
정답 전화기가 제대로 작동하지 않는다.

→ defective의 사전적 의미에 가까운 not working properly로 표현

❷ 포괄적 개념을 지닌 상위어 활용

M I'm calling to ask you about the upcoming conference.
남 곧 있을 학회와 관련해서 문의하려고 전화했어요.

Q Why is the man calling?
A To inquire about an event
질문 남자는 왜 전화하고 있는가?
정답 행사에 관해 문의하려고

→ conference를 더 포괄적인 개념인 event로 표현

❸ 품사 변경

W I'll order a replacement later. Don't worry.
여 제가 이따가 대체품을 주문할게요. 걱정 마세요.

Q What does the woman offer to do?
A Place an order
질문 여자는 무엇을 하겠다고 제안하는가?
정답 주문 넣기

→ 동사 order를 명사로 바꾼 뒤 place와 함께 사용

❹ 내용 축약

M I own a small store that sells furniture such as tables and chairs.
남 탁자나 의자 같은 가구를 판매하는 작은 가게를 소유하고 있어요.

Q What kind of business does the man own?
A A furniture store
질문 남자는 어떤 종류의 업체를 소유하는가?
정답 가구점

→ a small store that sells furniture를 furniture store로 줄여서 표현

UNIT 07 주제·목적/화자·장소 문제

무료 강의

1 주제 · 목적 문제

출제 포인트 대화 주제나 전화/방문의 목적을 묻는 질문은 주로 첫 번째 문제로 출제된다. 보통 대화 초반에 단서가 등장하지만, 간혹 중반까지 들어야 확인이 가능한 경우도 있다.

주제 질문
What are the speakers **discussing**?
What is the conversation mainly **about**?
What is the (main) **topic** of the conversation?

목적 질문
What is the purpose of the **call/visit**?
Why is the man **calling**?
Why does the woman **call** the business?

▶ **기출 공략 포인트** | 대화 초반부에서 주제와 목적을 나타내는 단서를 포착한다.   🔊 750_P3_01

W I can't believe the trouble we had coming up with **the design for our new logo**. It seems to have taken forever. → 대화 주제 등장 M Yes, but the results are worthwhile, don't you think? **It sums up exactly what our company stands for**: it looks both sporty and dependable. W Yes, and it comes out well both small on our letterhead and large on our store signs and products.	문제 **What** are the speakers **discussing**? (A) A new kind of bicycle (B) A company logo (C) A letter (D) A new store 단서 회사를 잘 표현하는 새 로고 정답 **(B) A company logo**

정답과 해설 p. 055

정답으로 이어지는 단서 표현

전화나 방문의 목적을 묻는 질문이 있을 경우, 대화 초반에 다음 표현들이 등장할 가능성이 높다. 이 뒤에 이어지는 부분에 집중해야 한다.

I'm here to interview Mr. Park for an article.
기사 작성을 위해 박 씨를 인터뷰하러 왔습니다.

I need[want, would like] to change my hotel reservation.
제 호텔 예약을 변경해야 합니다[하고 싶습니다].

I'm calling to confirm my attendance at the meeting on Friday.
금요일 회의 참석을 확정하려고 전화했어요.

I'm calling because there seems to be a problem with the heating system.
난방 시스템에 문제가 있는 것 같아서 전화했어요.

ETS 유형연습

다음 대화를 듣고 문제를 풀어보세요.
다시 들으면서 빈칸을 채우세요.

750_P3_02
정답과 해설 p. 055

1. What are the speakers discussing?
   (A) A real estate loan
   (B) A ride-sharing initiative
   (C) A company budget
   (D) A hiring plan

   M Thanks for meeting with me to _____ _____, Georgia.
   W No problem.
   M With the _____ for office space this year, we're definitely _____ right now.
   W Yes, we'll have to find areas to _____.

2. Why is the man calling?
   (A) To make a cancellation
   (B) To change a delivery request
   (C) To request extra preparation time
   (D) To check on ticket sales

   M Hi. This is Yun Wei, the manager for the Enzo Jazz Band.
   W Oh, hi. Are you calling about _____ on the thirtieth?
   M Yes. Would it be possible for my crew _____ _____ to the venue _____ we'd agreed upon? They'd like some _____ _____.
   W No problem. We don't have _____ for the day before.

3. What is the conversation mainly about?
   (A) Organizing a meeting
   (B) Redecorating an office
   (C) Stopping mail delivery
   (D) Finding a lost package

   W I'm going to be out of town starting Monday, August first, and I'd like to _____ _____, please.
   M Certainly. We can _____ at the post office while you're away. Incidentally, did you know that you could _____ _____ to another address instead?
   W Well, I'm actually going to be _____, so I don't think that'd be possible.

4. What is the main purpose of the man's visit?
   (A) To tour a facility
   (B) To renew a contract
   (C) To deliver some materials
   (D) To interview job candidates

   W Welcome, Mr. Molina. I'm glad you have time to _____.
   M Glad to be here. My car company's been looking for _____ our electric automobile motors. It'll save us a lot of money to work with you since you're _____. We wouldn't have to pay as much _____ _____.

UNIT 07 주제·목적/화자·장소 문제 **71**

2 화자·장소 문제

출제 포인트 화자(들)의 신분/직업/업계, 혹은 근무지/대화 장소를 묻는 질문도 첫 번째 문제로 자주 출제된다. 대화 초반부에 특정 직업이나 업체명이 명시되는 경우가 많지만 대화 곳곳에 있는 단서를 조합하여 답을 찾아야 할 수도 있으므로, 직업/업계 관련 표현은 암기해 두는 것이 좋다.

신분/직업/업계 질문
Who (most likely) is the **woman**?
What is the **man's job[occupation, profession]**?
What industry[field] do the speakers most likely **work** in?

근무지/장소 질문
Where does the woman **work**?
Where most likely **are** the speakers?
Where does this conversation most likely **take place**?

◆ **기출 공략 포인트** | 대화 초반부의 직업/업체명, 혹은 대화 곳곳에 있는 관련 표현에 주목한다. 🔊 750_P3_03

W Hi, Gerhard. You wanted to talk to me about **the strawberries that we're growing**?
→ 화자들이 하는 일 언급

M Yes. This year, **our farm's** doing better than last year. I'm glad we tried something different by using another brand of fertilizer on the strawberries. Amazing results!
→ 구체적인 근무 장소 등장

W That's great! Then we should use that brand on the blueberries, too.

문제 **Where** do the **speakers** most likely **work**?
(A) At a park
(B) At a farm
(C) At a garden supply store
(D) At a landscaping company

단서 우리가 재배하는 딸기, 우리 농장

정답 **(B) At a farm**

정답과 해설 p.057

정답으로 이어지는 단서 표현

화자/장소 문제의 단서가 제시되는 대표적인 방식을 파악해 둔다.

화자 본인 소개	Hello, **this** is Lewis **calling from** Sunville <u>Marketing</u>. → 마케팅 회사 안녕하세요, 저는 선빌 마케팅의 루이스입니다.	
환영 인사	**Welcome to** the Chester <u>Art Museum</u>. → 미술관 체스터 미술관에 오신 걸 환영합니다.	
상대방 회사 언급	I heard that you've started **your own** <u>advertising company</u>. → 광고 회사 당신이 직접 광고 회사를 설립했다고 들었어요.	
관련 표현 사용	I'm **writing an** <u>article</u> about your company for **our** <u>magazine</u>. → 기자/언론인 저희 잡지에 실을 귀사 관련 기사를 작성 중입니다.	

ETS 유형연습

다음 대화를 듣고 문제를 풀어보세요.
다시 들으면서 빈칸을 채우세요.

750_P3_04
정답과 해설 p.057

1. Who most likely is the woman?
   (A) A store owner
   (B) A ticket agent
   (C) A city official
   (D) A maintenance worker

M Excuse me, when is the _____ up the canal?

W It's at noon, but _____. There's another one at two. Would you like to buy _____ now? That tour is likely to sell out too.

M Yes, I'll _____, please.

2. Where does the conversation most likely take place?
   (A) At a factory
   (B) At a construction site
   (C) At a home furnishings store
   (D) At a real estate agency

W Good morning. Are you _____ today?

M Actually, I'm _____ for some friends who just _____. Something decorative, maybe.

W Over here we have a _____ _____—pitchers and vases and even some sculptures—if you think they'd enjoy that.

3. Who most likely are the speakers?
   (A) Advertising executives
   (B) Apparel salespeople
   (C) Fashion designers
   (D) Magazine editors

M Lucy, have you _____ any ideas for _____ for The Sawgrass Company's _____?

W Well, from the samples the _____, I think what really stands out is the fabric. The material is _____. Plus, it's washable and wrinkle-resistant.

M Then why don't we _____?

4. Where does the man most likely work?
   (A) At a travel agency
   (B) At a computer repair shop
   (C) At an automobile manufacturer
   (D) At a movie theater

M Welcome to Z Tech Solutions. How can I help you?

W The screen's _____. I'm hoping _____.

M Let's take a look. I should be able to _____ _____. But I'll have to _____.

W Oh, I was hoping it'd be ready _____.

UNIT 07 주제·목적/화자·장소 문제

ETS 실전문제

1. What is the topic of an interview?
   (A) Manufacturing
   (B) Budgeting
   (C) Marketing strategies
   (D) Art restoration

2. What does the woman say she recently did?
   (A) She moved to a new city.
   (B) She started a new job.
   (C) She renewed a certification.
   (D) She attended a seminar.

3. What will the woman do next?
   (A) Read an excerpt from her book
   (B) Share her contact information
   (C) Explain some contest rules
   (D) Discuss some survey results

4. Where do the speakers most likely work?
   (A) At a real estate office
   (B) At a video arcade
   (C) At a sporting goods store
   (D) At a ticketing agency

5. Why has the woman postponed a plan?
   (A) She does not have enough employees.
   (B) She is waiting for a permit to be granted.
   (C) A building needs repairs.
   (D) Rents are too expensive.

6. What does the woman ask the man to do?
   (A) Submit an advertisement
   (B) Survey customers
   (C) Tour a facility
   (D) Contact a supplier

7. Who most likely is the man?
   (A) A car rental agent
   (B) A department store manager
   (C) A hotel receptionist
   (D) A restaurant employee

8. Why is Ms. Klein calling?
   (A) To change a reservation
   (B) To ask about a missing item
   (C) To report a mistaken charge
   (D) To inquire about a policy

9. What will Ms. Klein most likely do next?
   (A) Provide an address
   (B) Check a calendar
   (C) Speak to a colleague
   (D) Go to a bank

10. Where do the speakers work?
    (A) At a botanical garden
    (B) At a museum
    (C) At a sports stadium
    (D) At a theater

11. According to the man, what will happen at 5:00 P.M.?
    (A) A video will be shown.
    (B) A facility will be cleaned.
    (C) A tour will begin.
    (D) A ticket office will open.

12. What information does the woman need about an event?
    (A) The number of people attending
    (B) The cost of a catering service
    (C) The type of equipment required
    (D) The name of a keynote speaker

13. What are the speakers mainly discussing?
    (A) A play
    (B) A sports match
    (C) A movie premiere
    (D) A concert

14. Why was the woman disappointed?
    (A) She could not get a ticket.
    (B) She missed the beginning of the event.
    (C) The sound system was not working well.
    (D) Some people were blocking her view.

15. What does the man think the woman should do?
    (A) Ask for a refund
    (B) Attend a different performance
    (C) Watch a television program
    (D) Write a review

16. What department do the speakers most likely work in?
    (A) Accounting
    (B) Sales
    (C) Legal
    (D) Human resources

17. Why does a celebration have to be postponed?
    (A) A project deadline cannot be changed.
    (B) A company executive is visiting the office.
    (C) A venue is unavailable.
    (D) A client meeting is scheduled.

18. What will the man do next?
    (A) Sign some documents
    (B) Update a Web site
    (C) Make a reservation
    (D) Review some job applications

19. Where does the conversation take place?
    (A) At a fitness center
    (B) At a furniture store
    (C) At a medical clinic
    (D) At a farmers market

20. What does the woman apologize for?
    (A) Some construction
    (B) Some noise
    (C) An extra charge
    (D) A staff shortage

21. What will the man do later today?
    (A) Renew a membership
    (B) Pick up a prescription
    (C) Make a bank deposit
    (D) Take a tour

22. Who most likely is the woman?
    (A) A building inspector
    (B) A management consultant
    (C) An architect
    (D) A reporter

23. What is the goal of Mr. Howard's firm?
    (A) Using recycled materials
    (B) Building affordable homes
    (C) Preserving historic structures
    (D) Increasing energy efficiency

24. What does Mr. Howard plan to do in the future?
    (A) Speak at universities
    (B) Publish a book
    (C) Lead a volunteer project
    (D) Open an overseas office

UNIT 08 세부 사항 / 문제점·걱정거리 문제

무료 강의

1 세부 사항 문제

출제 포인트 What, How, Why 등 다양한 의문사를 사용하여 특정 정보나 화자가 언급한 내용을 묻는 문제가 출제된다. 문제 및 보기의 키워드가 대화에 그대로 혹은 패러프레이징되어 나타나므로, 문제를 먼저 읽어서 키워드를 파악한 후 해당 부분을 노려 들어야 한다.

특정 정보를 묻는 질문
What is/are ~?
What does[did] the woman ~?
How/Why/When/Where did the man ~?

언급한 내용을 묻는 질문
What does the man **say** ~?
What does the woman **mention about** ~?
According to the man, **what** ~?

▶ **기출 공략 포인트** | 문제 및 보기의 키워드를 파악한 후 해당 부분을 노려 듣는다.   🎧 750_P3_06

W Hi, Ken. How are the preparations for the conference going? M Good. I just finished writing a draft of the **information packet describing the products we'll showcase** at our booth. → 키워드 information packet 등장 W That's great. Can you e-mail me a copy? I'd like to proofread it.	**문제** **What** is in the information packet? (A) Company descriptions (B) Booth regulations (C) Conference schedules (D) Product details **단서** 제품을 설명하는 자료집 **정답** (D) Product details

정답과 해설 p.064

정답으로 이어지는 단서 표현

정답의 단서는 키워드 뒤에 등장할 수도 있고, 키워드보다 앞서 등장할 수도 있다. 문제를 보고 단서의 대략적인 위치를 예상해 두고, 주요 내용을 간략히 메모하며 듣는 것이 좋다.

How do the speakers hope to **increase sales**? 매출 증대 방식: 키워드가 들리면 집중
We could **increase our sales** by offering a free delivery service.   → By offering a new service
무료 배달 서비스를 제공하면 매출을 올릴 수 있을 거예요.   새로운 서비스를 제공함으로써

What does the woman say she **did last week**? 지난주에 한 일: 과거 시제가 들리면 집중
I e-mailed him the contract **last week**, but I haven't heard from him yet.   → She sent some document.
지난주에 그에게 이메일로 계약서를 보냈는데, 아직도 소식이 없네요.   서류를 보냈다.

ETS 유형연습

다음 대화를 듣고 문제를 풀어보세요.
다시 들으면서 빈칸을 채우세요.

750_P3_07
정답과 해설 p.064

1. What most likely started last week?
(A) An internship program
(B) An art exhibit
(C) A science experiment
(D) A remodeling project

W Hi, Hongtai. How has your _____ been _____?
M Very interesting! I've _____ at an aquarium.
W That's great. Today I'll show you how to perform the _____ in the freshwater habitats.

2. Why is the woman in Sydney?
(A) To audition for a theater production
(B) To take a dance class
(C) To perform at a friend's party
(D) To participate in a dance competition

M Welcome to Marley's Dance Shop.
W Hi. I'm here _____ in the All-Star _____, and I need _____ right away.
M Oh, did something happen to yours?
W Well, _____ was put _____ and ended up in Melbourne.

3. How did the woman learn about the man's agency?
(A) From a neighbor
(B) From a magazine
(C) From a coworker
(D) From the Internet

W Hello, my name is Melissa Stein. I'm calling because I'm _____. I was _____ to you _____. You helped her sell her house a while ago, and she was very _____.
M I'd be happy to help you with that, Ms. Stein. Are you ready to _____ immediately?

4. What does the woman say she likes about her job?
(A) Using her creativity
(B) Specializing in one area
(C) Earning bonus pay
(D) Having the chance to travel

M Hi, Barbara. Nice to run into you! We've missed you _____ Allen Real Estate.
W Kevin! Yes, it's been a while. That was a big decision, to change companies. But I _____ _____ a lot.
M That's great. How's _____ what you did with us?
W Well—I only _____ now. But I like being able to _____.

UNIT 08 세부 사항/문제점·걱정거리 문제 77

2 문제점 · 걱정거리 문제

출제 포인트 화자가 언급한 문제점이나 걱정거리를 묻는 질문이 출제되며, 주로 대화의 초 · 중반에 단서가 제시된다.
부정적인 표현이 등장하면 집중해서 청취해야 한다.

문제점 질문
What is the woman's **problem**?
What **problem** does the man **mention**?
What **problem** are the speakers **discussing**?

걱정거리 질문
What is the man **worried about**?
What is the woman **concerned about**?
Why is the man **concerned**?

▶ **기출 공략 포인트** | 부정적인 표현 뒤에 등장하는 단서를 포착한다.   🎧 750_P3_08

> W Is there any way I can get on the next flight to Los Angeles? **My flight from New York didn't arrive on time so I missed my connection.**
> → 부정어(didn't) 등장
>
> M Let's see, I don't have any direct flights, but if you're willing to connect in San Francisco, there is a flight leaving in twenty minutes.
>
> W As long as it takes me to Los Angeles, I'll take it.

문제 What is the woman's **problem**?
　(A) She lost her luggage.
　(B) She missed a flight.
　(C) She forgot her airplane ticket.
　(D) She does not know where the gate is.

단서 비행기 연착으로 연결편 놓침

정답 **(B) She missed a flight.**

정답과 해설 p.065

정답으로 이어지는 단서 표현

문제점/걱정거리 문제의 단서는 아래와 같은 표현과 함께 등장한다.

Not이 포함된 부정어: can't, wasn't, didn't, won't, haven't 등
I **won't** be able to make it to the meeting. 회의에 못 갈 것 같아요.

부정적인 의미를 나타내는 표현: unfortunately, mistake, problem, miss, delay 등
I noticed **a mistake** in one of the presentation slides. 프레젠테이션 슬라이드 중 하나에서 오류를 발견했어요.

대조/반전의 뜻을 지닌 표현: but, however, though, actually 등
I bought this camera yesterday, **but** I think it may be defective. 어제 이 카메라를 샀는데, 결함이 있는 것 같아요.

걱정의 표현: concern, worried, afraid 등
I'm **worried** that we might arrive late. 늦게 도착할까 봐 걱정이 돼요.

ETS 유형연습

다음 대화를 듣고 문제를 풀어보세요.
다시 들으면서 빈칸을 채우세요.

🎧 750_P3_09
정답과 해설 p.065

---

1. What is the woman worried about?
(A) Missing a deadline
(B) Disappointing a client
(C) Wasting time
(D) Encountering technical difficulties

M Hey, Narumi. There's a _____ happening downtown this weekend. Maybe we can _____ our entry-level graphic _____.

W I don't know. I'm _____ that we'll _____ on this and _____ any suitable candidates.

---

2. What problem are the speakers discussing?
(A) A piece of art has not arrived.
(B) A magazine is not available.
(C) A library card has expired.
(D) A store is closing.

W I'm looking for the current issue of *Crafts Magazine*. Do you know if the library _____ _____? It wasn't _____ where I usually find it.

M Oh, yes, I'm sorry. The library _____ _____ from last year, so you _____ _____ on the shelves.

---

3. Why is the woman concerned?
(A) She does not have transportation.
(B) She forgot to make a reservation.
(C) She lacks the appropriate skills.
(D) She does not have some equipment.

M Sabine, did you _____ our department is organizing this weekend?

W Yes. I'm really excited, but I'm _____ that I don't have all the _____.

M Well, our department is providing tents. And there's a camping _____ in the Sunnydale Shopping Center.

---

4. What issue does the man describe?
(A) Inadequate floor space
(B) Poor quality control
(C) High repair costs
(D) Production delays

M Thanks for coming to the factory today. We've been _____. Maybe it's our Internet connection.

W Our firm _____. We help businesses improve their internal wireless signals so that all connections _____ _____.

M That would be great.

UNIT 08 세부 사항/문제점·걱정거리 문제 **79**

ETS 실전문제

1. What problem does the woman mention?
   (A) Her schedule is very busy.
   (B) A fee has increased.
   (C) A fitness center is closing.
   (D) A building is under construction.

2. What does the man say about the swimming pool?
   (A) It will not be open next month.
   (B) It has swim instructors available.
   (C) Its hours were recently extended.
   (D) It is not used a lot in the morning.

3. How can the woman obtain a discount?
   (A) By presenting a coupon
   (B) By providing a friend's name
   (C) By going to a facility on weekdays only
   (D) By paying for several months in advance

4. What has the man been contracted to do?
   (A) Build a Web site
   (B) Create a restaurant menu
   (C) Design product packaging
   (D) Advertise a business

5. What will happen next week?
   (A) A business will open a new location.
   (B) A receipt will be sent.
   (C) An episode will have a guest speaker.
   (D) A video will be posted online.

6. What does the woman remind the man to do?
   (A) Call her with an update
   (B) Make sure a logo is easy to see
   (C) Read some market research
   (D) Use a specific color palette

7. What did the woman recently do?
   (A) She published an article.
   (B) She completed a research project.
   (C) She appeared in a documentary film.
   (D) She returned from a lecture tour.

8. What field does the woman work in?
   (A) Robotics
   (B) Mechanical engineering
   (C) Plant biology
   (D) Software development

9. What will the woman do next?
   (A) Talk to a colleague
   (B) Accept an award
   (C) Discuss a book
   (D) Explain a future project

10. Who is the woman?
    (A) A chef
    (B) A corporate executive
    (C) A salesperson
    (D) An event organizer

11. How does the man hope to attract more customers?
    (A) By improving some packaging
    (B) By lowering prices
    (C) By offering new items
    (D) By renovating a location

12. What does the man say he can do?
    (A) Hire additional staff
    (B) Redesign some uniforms
    (C) Provide employee discounts
    (D) Order specialized equipment

13. What is causing a problem?
    (A) Bad weather
    (B) Heavy traffic
    (C) A train cancellation
    (D) A broken-down vehicle

14. Why is the man worried?
    (A) He has paid for some tickets already.
    (B) He needs to go to another appointment.
    (C) He wants enough time to conduct a demonstration.
    (D) He will not have Internet access.

15. What do the women agree about?
    (A) Taking an alternate route
    (B) Training an assistant
    (C) Sending a presentation by e-mail
    (D) Consulting a manual

16. What does the man say he did last month?
    (A) He moved to a new town.
    (B) He started a new job.
    (C) He took a science class.
    (D) He visited a park.

17. What task does the woman ask the man to help with?
    (A) Leading hikes
    (B) Counting birds
    (C) Planting trees
    (D) Cleaning parks

18. What is the man concerned about?
    (A) His busy schedule
    (B) His lack of experience
    (C) The distance to a work site
    (D) The cost to participate

19. According to the woman, what did the company recently do?
    (A) Announce a merger
    (B) Hire an editor
    (C) Launch a Web site
    (D) Host a workshop

20. What problem does the man mention?
    (A) Content is not displayed correctly.
    (B) A deadline was missed.
    (C) Sales are lower than expected.
    (D) Equipment is outdated.

21. What does the woman say is a growing trend?
    (A) Listening to audiobooks
    (B) Holding training sessions online
    (C) Signing contracts electronically
    (D) Reading news on mobile devices

22. What are the speakers discussing?
    (A) A software training session
    (B) An investment opportunity
    (C) A recording session
    (D) A marketing plan

23. What did Andrew think was problematic?
    (A) The lack of technical support
    (B) The excessive amount of repetition
    (C) The complicated registration process
    (D) The high subscription fee

24. What does Lola suggest Andrew do?
    (A) Read a magazine article
    (B) Test some equipment
    (C) Review an official document
    (D) Distribute customer surveys

UNIT 09 요청·제안/다음에 할 일 문제

1 요청 · 제안 문제

출제 포인트 화자가 요청하거나 제안하는 것이 무엇인지 묻는 질문은 두 번째, 세 번째 문제로 출제되는 경우가 많다. 단서는 주로 대화 중·후반에 등장한다.

요청 사항을 묻는 질문
What does the man **request**?
What does the woman **ask** the man **to do**?

제안 사항을 묻는 질문
What does the man **suggest**?
What does the woman **offer to do**?

▶ **기출 공략 포인트** | 요청/제안의 표현이 등장하면 집중해서 청취한다.   🎧 750_P3_11

> W Jeff, I'm wondering who are these plastic desk covers for?
>
> M They're for us—remember? The contractor starts work on upgrading our office area next Tuesday. There'll be a lot of dust, so…
>
> W Ah, I didn't realize it's starting so soon. Will we need to work elsewhere then?
>
> M We'll stay here. Here's a **timeline** showing which areas the crews will work in each day. Take a look.
>
> W Oh, good. **I can post this on our staff bulletin board.** → 제안의 표현(I can) 등장

문제 **What does the woman offer to do?**
(A) Adjust her work hours
(B) Order office supplies
(C) Post a schedule
(D) Expand a training program

단서 일정표를 게시판에 붙이겠다

정답 **(C) Post a schedule**

정답과 해설 p.073

정답으로 이어지는 단서 표현

요청이나 제안할 때 자주 쓰이는 표현은 암기해 두도록 한다.

요청: Can/Could you, Please, I'd like you to, Would you mind, I was wondering if 등
Could you tell me what you think of the video? 그 동영상에 대해 어떻게 생각하는지 말해줄래요?

제안: You could, You might want to, Why don't you, I recommend, I can, Let me 등
You might want to join our membership program. 저희 멤버십 프로그램에 가입하시는 게 좋을 것 같아요.
Let me send you the instructions via e-mail. 설명서를 이메일로 보내드릴게요.

ETS 유형연습

다음 대화를 듣고 문제를 풀어보세요.
다시 들으면서 빈칸을 채우세요.

750_P3_12
정답과 해설 p.073

1. What does the woman request?
   (A) A signature
   (B) Another work shift
   (C) A supply list
   (D) Another uniform

M You've had a great first week. We're _____ _____ for lunch today, and I'd like you _____.

W Sure. But before I start my shift, can I _____ _____? The medium one I have is too big.

M Of course. I'll _____ right now.

2. What is the man asking the woman to do?
   (A) Take charge of a new project
   (B) Recruit a consultant
   (C) Attend a management meeting
   (D) Report on a sales promotion

M Andrea, can I talk to you about a _____ _____? Management would like to see _____ between the sales department and the marketing department. We'd like you to _____.

W That _____, Mark. But, what exactly would this _____?

3. What does the man recommend that the woman do?
   (A) Come back the following day
   (B) Place an order in advance
   (C) Park in a nearby garage
   (D) Register for a membership card

M Before I start scanning your items, did you _____ for me to put your groceries in?

W Oh, no—I didn't. Was I supposed to _____ _____?

M It is our store policy, but you could _____ one of our _____. You'd receive a reusable bag for free _____, and it only takes _____.

4. What does the man offer to do?
   (A) Cancel an order
   (B) Hire a technician
   (C) Provide a refund
   (D) Arrange a delivery

W I bought a chair from your store, and I was _____ it, but I don't think I have all of the parts I need.

M Oh, I'm sorry to hear that. Do you know _____ _____?

W Well, I have all the long bolts for the legs but none of the other bolts for the seat.

M OK, I have _____ here at the store, and I can have the _____ _____ at your house this afternoon.

UNIT 09 요청·제안/다음에 할 일 문제 **83**

2 다음에 할 일 문제

출제 포인트 화자가 할 일이나 미래에 일어날 일을 묻는 질문도 두 번째, 세 번째 문제로 자주 출제되며, 요청/제안 문제와 함께 나오는 경우가 많다. 미래를 나타내는 다양한 시제뿐만 아니라 화자의 의지/결심이 드러나는 표현이나 제안·청유의 표현에도 주목해야 한다.

할 일을 묻는 질문
What will the woman **do next**?
What does the man say he **will do**?

일어날 일을 묻는 질문
What will happen ~?
What will take place ~?

◆ **기출 공략 포인트** | 미래를 나타내는 시제와 의지/결심이 드러나는 표현에 주목한다. 🎧 750_P3_13

W Excuse me, I'm planning to paint the walls of my kitchen white, but there are so many different paint types that I'm not sure which one to buy.

M Well, I'd suggest getting a high gloss paint, since it's going to be in your kitchen and it's easier to wash.

W Great—thanks! I'll need two cans of that, then. Also, **can you show me where the paintbrushes are?**

M Sure—**those are in aisle ten. Let me take you there.**
→ 의지/결심이 드러나는 표현(Let me) 등장

문제 What will the speakers most likely do next?
(A) Review a purchase order
(B) Go to a different part of the store
(C) Discuss hiring professional painters
(D) Try out a product

단서 그곳으로 안내해 드리겠다

정답 **(B) Go to a different part of the store**

정답과 해설 p.074

정답으로 이어지는 단서 표현

미래를 나타내는 다양한 시제를 알아두고, 해당 표현이 나오면 집중해서 단서를 포착한다.

미래/계획: Will, be going to, be planning to
I'll ask Danna if we can meet next Thursday. 다음 주 목요일에 만날 수 있는지 다나에게 물어볼게요.
I'm going to call my supervisor and ask about that. 제 상사에게 전화해서 여쭤볼게요.

예정된 가까운 미래: 단순 현재형, be+ing
I have an appointment with a client **this afternoon**. 오늘 오후에 고객과 약속이 있어요.
I'm meeting with Dr. Ray **tomorrow** to discuss the results of the product testing.
제품 시험 결과를 논의하기 위해 내일 레이 박사와 만날 예정이에요.

ETS 유형연습

다음 대화를 듣고 문제를 풀어보세요.
다시 들으면서 빈칸을 채우세요.

750_P3_14
정답과 해설 p.074

1. What will the man do next?
   (A) Conduct an inspection
   (B) Print some paperwork
   (C) Issue a refund
   (D) Ask a coworker for help

M Welcome to Starlay Used Vehicles. _____ _____ today?
W Hi. I have a car that's only a few years old, and I was wondering _____ _____ me for it. Since I _____, I decided that I don't really need a car.
M I see. Well, _____, and then I can make you an offer.

2. What will happen in March?
   (A) A product will be discounted.
   (B) A building will be closed for renovations.
   (C) A marketing campaign will launch.
   (D) A training course for students will take place.

W Langfield Museum of Art. This is Karima speaking. How can I help you?
M Hi, I heard that the museum will be _____ _____ in March. Will it still be _____?
W The museum _____ for the _____, but the outdoor garden will still be open.

3. What does the man say he will do this afternoon?
   (A) Place an order
   (B) Meet with a supervisor
   (C) Update a database
   (D) Call a customer

W Amit, a new _____ came in, so I have to put price tags on them, but I don't think we have any more.
M I'm _____ this afternoon so I'll _____ to the list. They should arrive by tomorrow.

4. What will take place next Wednesday?
   (A) A dinner with a client
   (B) A farewell party for a coworker
   (C) A reception for new employees
   (D) A lunch with some friends

M Julie, when are you coming back from London?
W Well, if my meetings go really well, I could be _____, but I may _____ Friday. Why do you ask?
M Stephanie announced that she's _____ _____. So I'm _____ at Vega's Restaurant next Wednesday, and I was hoping you'd be able to come.

UNIT 09 요청·제안/다음에 할 일 문제 **85**

ETS 실전문제

1. What will happen on Monday?
   (A) A staff party will be held.
   (B) A new director will be announced.
   (C) A parking area will be repaved.
   (D) A safety demonstration will take place.

2. What will the hospital provide?
   (A) Travel reimbursement
   (B) Free refreshments
   (C) A shuttle service
   (D) Additional training

3. What will the man send?
   (A) A map
   (B) A newsletter
   (C) An identification card
   (D) A registration form

4. What does the woman mention about the Selwin 6?
   (A) It is easy to use.
   (B) It is an earlier model.
   (C) It is well designed.
   (D) It is very popular.

5. What does the man request?
   (A) A warranty
   (B) A reimbursement
   (C) A replacement part
   (D) An instruction manual

6. What does the woman offer to do?
   (A) Reset a password
   (B) Explain a policy
   (C) Check part of an order
   (D) Send a link to a Web site

7. What is the conversation about?
   (A) A contract
   (B) An event location
   (C) A plan of action
   (D) A security risk

8. What does the woman say about her book?
   (A) It was made into a movie.
   (B) It was reviewed in a magazine.
   (C) It was nominated for an award.
   (D) It was translated into another language.

9. What does Roberto offer to do?
   (A) Contact some podcast producers
   (B) Volunteer for an industry trade show
   (C) Organize a book-signing event
   (D) Design some cover art

10. Where do the speakers most likely work?
    (A) At a medical-supply store
    (B) At a research institute
    (C) At a security firm
    (D) At a community hospital

11. What will the man ask the security office to give the woman?
    (A) A storage-room key
    (B) A parking permit
    (C) A tour of the building
    (D) A list of safety procedures

12. What does the woman say she will do in the afternoon?
    (A) Make copies of a report
    (B) Conduct an experiment
    (C) Obtain an identification card
    (D) Pick up some work supplies

13. What does the man want to know?
    (A) An arrival time
    (B) A boarding location
    (C) An expiration date
    (D) A round-trip price

14. What does the woman recommend that the man do?
    (A) Call an information line
    (B) Speak with a conductor
    (C) Save a ticket receipt
    (D) Check a display monitor

15. What will the man probably do next?
    (A) Buy something to drink
    (B) Use a ticket machine
    (C) Send a text message
    (D) Pick up a schedule

16. Why is the man going to Madrid?
    (A) To report on an event
    (B) To visit relatives
    (C) To buy some artwork
    (D) To study at a university

17. What does the man say he wants to do before he travels?
    (A) Register for a course
    (B) Book a hotel
    (C) Research some artists
    (D) Purchase a guidebook

18. What does the woman offer to do?
    (A) Check her calendar
    (B) Find some contact information
    (C) Make a telephone call
    (D) Consult a price list

19. According to the woman, why are the solar panels popular?
    (A) They are small.
    (B) They are easy to install.
    (C) They are attractive.
    (D) They are inexpensive.

20. What will take place in September?
    (A) A factory tour
    (B) An employee training
    (C) A trade show
    (D) A company merger

21. What will the man most likely do next?
    (A) Make a phone call
    (B) Read a report
    (C) Review a procedure
    (D) Send a payment

22. Where do the speakers most likely work?
    (A) At a farm
    (B) At a restaurant
    (C) At an airport
    (D) At a concert hall

23. According to Viktoriya, what will Penn Food Service do?
    (A) Train some employees
    (B) Reduce some prices
    (C) Replace an order
    (D) Provide a parking permit

24. What will Ilya most likely do next?
    (A) Create some displays
    (B) Modify a contract
    (C) Drive to a vendor's location
    (D) Contact a senior manager

UNIT 10 의도 파악 / 시각 정보 연계 문제

1 의도 파악 문제

출제 포인트 화자의 의도를 묻는 문제는 매회 2문항씩 출제된다. 앞뒤 문맥을 파악하는 것이 중요하므로 주요 내용은 메모하며 듣고, 제시문 앞뒤 문장이나 상대 화자의 반응에서 단서를 잡아야 한다.

의미/암시하는 바를 묻는 질문
What does the man **mean[imply]** when he says, "~"?

목적을 묻는 질문
Why does the woman **say**, "~"?

▶ **기출 공략 포인트** | 제시문 앞뒤 문장이나 상대 화자의 반응에서 단서를 포착한다.

M Hi, Gabriella. **I wanted to talk to you about using the new online time reporting system...** A lot of people have been asking about it.
→ 새로운 시스템에 대해 대화 시도: 문제 상황 언급

W Yes, well, I've been very busy. **But I am planning the training session for early next week.** That should make it quite clear to everyone.
→ 직원 교육이 예정되어 있다고 안내: 해결책 제시

M OK.

문제 **What** does the man **imply** when he says, "A lot of people have been asking about it"?
(A) Staff are confused about a procedure.
(B) People have heard that a workshop is interesting.
(C) Staff are waiting for a new assignment.
(D) A vacation calendar has not been posted yet.

단서 새로운 시스템에 대한 사람들의 많은 문의

정답 **(A) Staff are confused about a procedure.**

정답과 해설 p.081

정답으로 이어지는 단서 표현

제시문 앞에 나온 내용을 놓쳤다면 바로 뒤에 오는 문장이나 상대 화자의 반응에 집중한다.

바로 뒤에 오는 문장: 단서가 될 말을 덧붙이는 경우가 있다.
W Did you contact Norwood? 노우드에 연락했나요?
M **The office closed at four o'clock.** I'll check again tomorrow. 사무실이 4시에 닫아요. 내일 다시 확인할게요.
→ 다시 확인하겠다는 말로 미루어 보아 연락하지 못했음을 알 수 있다.

상대 화자의 반응: 제시문을 어떻게 받아들였는지가 드러난다.
M **Some of us are going to see a movie tonight.** 우리 중 몇 명이서 오늘 밤에 영화를 보러 갈 예정이야.
W That sounds great, but I can't come with you. 재미있을 거 같은데, 나는 같이 갈 수 없어.
→ 제시문을 '초대'로 받아들여 거절했음을 알 수 있다.

ETS 유형연습

다음 대화를 듣고 문제를 풀어보세요.
다시 들으면서 빈칸을 채우세요.

750_P3_17
정답과 해설 p.081

1. Why does the man say, "On digital billboards, you can display video clips"?
   (A) To request technical support
   (B) To correct a mistaken assumption
   (C) To explain a local regulation
   (D) To propose a research project

M I recommend that you consider billboard ads. They're a _____ your athletic shoe brand _____.
W But what makes our athletic shoes special is _____. I doubt we can convey that through a billboard.
M On digital billboards, you can display video clips.
W Oh. Then I'd be open to that as long as it's _____.

2. What does the woman imply when she says, "we have twenty people signed up"?
   (A) A Web site should be updated.
   (B) Some people are late.
   (C) Additional volunteers are unnecessary.
   (D) Some tasks have not been assigned.

W I'm happy our _____ so well for the _____ next month, Tae-Joon.
M Yes. But do you think _____ _____ to help out on the day of the event?
W Well, we have twenty people signed up.
M Oh, OK. Great.

3. Why does the woman say, "I have three payroll checks left to process"?
   (A) To complain about some software
   (B) To reject an invitation
   (C) To ask for a volunteer
   (D) To reassure a colleague

M Hi, Elaine. It's almost twelve-thirty. I'm _____ _____ with Sam if you'd like to _____.
W I have three payroll checks left to process.
M Oh, OK. I'll see you at the _____ _____.

4. What does the man mean when he says, "Most of the content will be rather technical"?
   (A) He wants to revise the content of a workshop.
   (B) He is looking forward to attending a workshop.
   (C) He thinks presenting a workshop will be challenging.
   (D) He thinks a workshop may not benefit all the staff.

W Fred, the Regional Library Association is _____ _____ in town called Managing Digital Content. It looks useful. I think our _____ _____ should attend, don't you?
M Oh, I've already inquired about that workshop. Uh… Most of the content will be rather technical.
W I see. OK. Then I should have only the _____ _____?
M That sounds like a _____.

UNIT 10 의도 파악/시각 정보 연계 문제 89

2 시각 정보 연계 문제

출제 포인트 대화를 들으면서 표, 그래프, 약도 등 다양한 시각 정보의 내용을 파악해야 하는 문제가 매회 3문항 출제된다. 대화 중에는 문제 및 보기 단어가 그대로 언급되기보다, 시각 정보에 제시된 추가 정보가 키워드로 등장할 가능성이 높다.

시각 정보 연계: 세부 사항을 묻는 질문
Look at the **graphic**. **What / Which / Where** ~?

▶ **기출 공략 포인트** | 시각 정보의 키워드를 포착하고, 보기와 연결고리를 파악한다. 🎧 750_P3_18

M Mona, I just got an e-mail from someone who'd like to donate some pottery to our museum collection. These are the pieces she's interested in donating.

W Oh, it would be wonderful to display them all. But **we can only add items to our collection of Egyptian artifacts** at this time.
→ 시각 정보의 키워드 중 Egyptian (artifacts) 등장

M OK. I'll contact the donor and let her know **we'd be happy to accept the Egyptian piece**. It's too bad we can't take all four of them though.
→ 다시 한번 Egyptian (piece)에 대해 언급

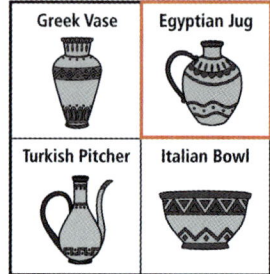

문제 Look at the **graphic. Which item do the speakers select**?
(A) The vase
(B) The jug
(C) The pitcher
(D) The bowl

단서 이집트 유물, 이집트 작품
→ 시각 정보의 이집트 물병

정답 **(B) The jug**

정답과 해설 p.082

정답으로 이어지는 단서 표현

시각 정보에 제시된 추가 정보가 키워드로 등장하지 않는 경우에는 비교급 및 최상급 표현에 귀를 기울인다. 지도나 평면도에서는 위치 관련 표현에 주목한다.

We'd like to limit our cost to **no more than** $400. → 400달러 이하에 해당하는 금액 선택
400달러 이하로 비용을 제한하고 싶습니다.

We've booked tickets for **the second most popular** play instead. → 2위에 해당하는 연극 선택
대신 두 번째로 인기 있는 연극을 예매했어요.

I moved to the office right **next to** the kitchen. → 탕비실 바로 옆 사무실 번호 선택
탕비실 바로 옆에 있는 사무실로 옮겼어요

ETS 유형연습

다음 대화를 듣고 문제를 풀어보세요.
다시 들으면서 빈칸을 채우세요.

🎧 750_P3_19
정답과 해설 p.083

Instrument	Case Size (in centimeters)
Bass	195
Cello	131
Guitar	107
Violin	82

1. Look at the graphic. Which instrument does the man play?

   (A) A bass   (B) A cello
   (C) A guitar   (D) A violin

W Thanks for calling Mahady Air. How can I help you?
M I'll be traveling with _____.
   Can I bring it _____?
W If it's small, it will fit in the overhead compartment. But if _____ 82 centimeters, you'll need to buy a second seat or put it in the cargo hold.
M It's _____. Since the instrument is fragile, I'd prefer to _____.

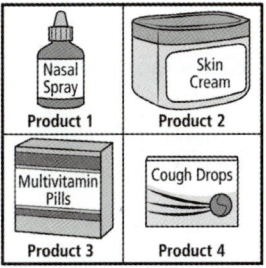

2. Look at the graphic. Which product will the woman buy?

   (A) Product 1   (B) Product 2
   (C) Product 3   (D) Product 4

M So, Ms. Becker, I recall that you _____ in the community footrace in the park last weekend. How did it go?
W Not so good, doctor. My _____ acting up, and I _____.
M I'm sorry to hear that. I _____ that will help with that.
W That's great, doctor.

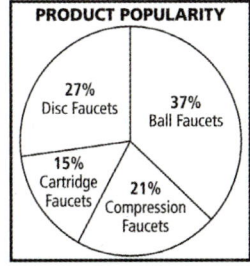

3. Look at the graphic. Which percentage of total sales does the man find surprising?

   (A) 27%   (B) 37%
   (C) 21%   (D) 15%

M Lolade, did you _____ the quarterly report? I e-mailed it to you this morning.
W I did. Thanks for sending it. The results were quite promising.
M Yes! I was surprised to see _____ have become. Our ball faucets are _____, of course, but the disc faucets _____ last quarter.

ETS 실전문제

1. What industry does the woman most likely work in?
   (A) Communications
   (B) Roofing
   (C) Manufacturing
   (D) Retail sales

2. What does the woman imply when she says, "We have most of the supplies in our warehouse"?
   (A) Some items have been moved to another location.
   (B) An inventory list contains an error.
   (C) A project can be finished quickly.
   (D) A delivery was completed successfully.

3. What will the woman most likely do next?
   (A) Retrieve a camera
   (B) Contact a colleague
   (C) Prepare an invoice
   (D) Post a sign

4. Why does the woman say, "this counter is for domestic services only"?
   (A) To criticize a rule
   (B) To express confusion
   (C) To reject a request
   (D) To verify a fact

5. What does the customer decide to do?
   (A) Cancel a shipment
   (B) Exchange a product
   (C) Buy special packaging
   (D) Pay for faster delivery

6. What will the customer probably pay an extra fee for?
   (A) Damage insurance
   (B) Overnight shipping
   (C) Delivery confirmation
   (D) Oversized parcels

7. Why does the woman call the man?
   (A) To report a problem
   (B) To request vacation time
   (C) To arrange for an inspection
   (D) To suggest a policy change

8. Who is Chen?
   (A) A company spokesperson
   (B) A salesclerk
   (C) A machinist
   (D) A security guard

9. What does the man mean when he says, "we have to keep the equipment running"?
   (A) His workload is too heavy.
   (B) A night shift should be added.
   (C) Production needs to be increased.
   (D) An expense is acceptable.

10. What problem does the woman mention?
    (A) She cannot find some data.
    (B) She is unable to use a computer program.
    (C) A customer is unhappy.
    (D) A timeline has been shortened.

11. What does the man suggest?
    (A) Visiting a Web site
    (B) Contacting a technician
    (C) Obtaining a supervisor's approval
    (D) Postponing a decision

12. What does the man imply when he says, "I have a client meeting this morning"?
    (A) He is pleased to have a new client.
    (B) He had been confused about his schedule.
    (C) He needs some additional materials.
    (D) He is not available to provide help.

Powell Hardware Company		
Item Number	Product	Quantity
7055	Wire fencing roll	1
9021	Plywood panel	4
3022	Sandbag	10
8106	Chainsaw	1

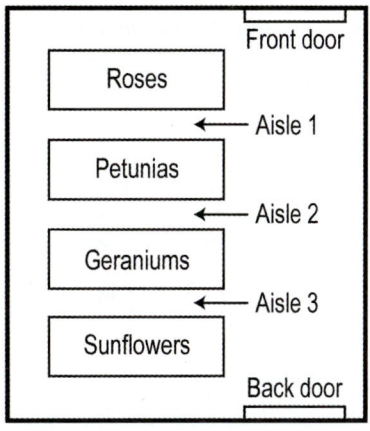

13. Look at the graphic. What item number is the man looking for?

    (A) 7055
    (B) 9021
    (C) 3022
    (D) 8106

14. What does the woman say the man will need?

    (A) A piece of equipment
    (B) A printed map
    (C) A manager's signature
    (D) A catalog

15. Why will the man speak to a customer?

    (A) To confirm the spelling of a name
    (B) To indicate that there will be a delay
    (C) To give an update on pricing
    (D) To recommend an additional product

16. What does the woman compliment the man on?

    (A) His attention to detail
    (B) His knowledge of plants
    (C) His customer service skills
    (D) His time management skills

17. Look at the graphic. Which type of flowers does the woman ask the man to water?

    (A) Roses
    (B) Petunias
    (C) Geraniums
    (D) Sunflowers

18. What does the woman say she is doing in the afternoon?

    (A) Ordering supplies
    (B) Meeting with a landscaper
    (C) Setting up a display
    (D) Planning a special event

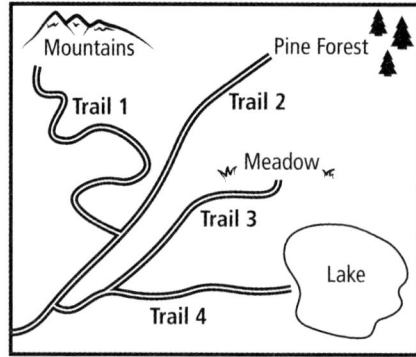

19. How did the woman learn about a product?
    (A) From her hairdresser
    (B) From a social media site
    (C) From a magazine advertisement
    (D) From a coworker

20. Look at the graphic. What is the price of the shampoo that the woman wants?
    (A) $5.00
    (B) $8.00
    (C) $10.00
    (D) $12.00

21. What does the man say the woman can do on a Web site?
    (A) Complete a survey
    (B) Sign up for a loyalty program
    (C) Read customer reviews
    (D) Apply for a job

22. What are the speakers discussing?
    (A) An environmental project
    (B) A government regulation
    (C) A bridge repair
    (D) A job posting

23. Look at the graphic. Which trail will the woman take?
    (A) Trail 1
    (B) Trail 2
    (C) Trail 3
    (D) Trail 4

24. What does the woman suggest posting on a Web site?
    (A) Tour leaders' names
    (B) Photographs
    (C) Research results
    (D) Driving directions

ETS ACTUAL TEST

32. Where are the speakers?
(A) At a print shop
(B) At a library
(C) At a bookstore
(D) At an electronics store

33. Why does the woman apologize?
(A) The man had to wait a long time.
(B) The business will be closing early.
(C) An order was incorrect.
(D) A device is not working.

34. What will the man most likely do next?
(A) Make a phone call
(B) Go to a bank
(C) Download a mobile application
(D) Use a coupon

35. What problem is the woman calling about?
(A) A pipe is leaking.
(B) A door will not open.
(C) A washing machine is not functioning properly.
(D) A heating unit is broken.

36. Who most likely is the man?
(A) A plumber
(B) A safety inspector
(C) A property manager
(D) A real estate agent

37. What does the man say he will do?
(A) Consult a manual
(B) Contact a repair service
(C) Fill out some paperwork
(D) Find a replacement part

38. What kind of event is being planned?
(A) A birthday party
(B) A company picnic
(C) A soccer game
(D) A charity fund-raiser

39. Why does the woman say she is relieved?
(A) A weather report is good.
(B) A caterer is available.
(C) A covered area was reserved.
(D) A product launch was successful.

40. What will Lorenzo contribute to an event?
(A) Some lawn furniture
(B) Some sports equipment
(C) Some beverages
(D) Some food

41. What event are the speakers discussing?
(A) A press conference
(B) A health fair
(C) A celebration
(D) A workshop

42. What does the woman imply when she says, "Thirty people plan to attend"?
(A) A caterer should be contacted.
(B) A guest list should be updated.
(C) A time frame is too short.
(D) A room is not big enough.

43. What does the woman say she will do this afternoon?
(A) Visit a hotel
(B) Review a budget
(C) Prepare a presentation
(D) Pick up some invitations

44. Where do the speakers most likely work?

(A) At an apartment complex
(B) At a software company
(C) At an architecture firm
(D) At an employment agency

45. What does the man recommend doing?

(A) Proposing a change of venue
(B) Using information from an earlier project
(C) Hiring a professional photographer
(D) Purchasing some new machinery

46. What will the woman most likely do next?

(A) Contact her coworker
(B) Check her calendar
(C) Take her lunch break
(D) Practice her presentation

47. Where is the conversation most likely taking place?

(A) At a flour processing plant
(B) At a bakery
(C) At a cooking school
(D) At a food festival

48. Why was a recipe modified?

(A) To create a better product
(B) To address customer complaints
(C) To lower production costs
(D) To compensate for a supply shortage

49. What will the woman do next?

(A) Sample a new product
(B) Contact a customer
(C) Schedule an employee party
(D) Review some records

50. What news does the man share?

(A) A rail line has been expanded.
(B) Some training events have been scheduled.
(C) A new director has been appointed.
(D) A special election will be held soon.

51. What improvement do the speakers hope to see?

(A) Better equipment
(B) Faster service
(C) Higher salaries
(D) Longer hours of operation

52. What is scheduled for this afternoon?

(A) An investors' meeting
(B) A facility tour
(C) A press conference
(D) A job interview

53. What are the speakers discussing?

(A) A hiring decision
(B) A budget request
(C) Some computer software
(D) Some sales tactics

54. What are some staff now allowed to do?

(A) Decorate their offices
(B) Attend a conference
(C) Work from home
(D) Wear casual clothes

55. What will the woman do this afternoon?

(A) Conduct some research
(B) Meet with a client
(C) Repair some equipment
(D) Update a calendar

56. Why is the woman calling?
 (A) To discuss a research project
 (B) To inquire about a product order
 (C) To ask about an employee benefit
 (D) To confirm a meeting time

57. What information does the man ask for?
 (A) An identification number
 (B) An e-mail address
 (C) An office location
 (D) A telephone number

58. What does the man say the woman needs?
 (A) Management approval
 (B) Advanced computer skills
 (C) A signed application form
 (D) An updated agenda

59. What will the man do tomorrow?
 (A) Conduct a training
 (B) Finalize a budget
 (C) Meet with a client
 (D) Submit a report

60. Why does the woman say, "the project I'm working on isn't due until next week"?
 (A) To indicate her availability
 (B) To correct a mistake
 (C) To decline an offer
 (D) To propose a new deadline

61. What does the man suggest changing?
 (A) The size of a diagram
 (B) The location of a logo
 (C) The length of a list
 (D) The order of some information

62. Where most likely are the speakers?
 (A) At a coffee shop
 (B) At a theater
 (C) At a fitness center
 (D) At an electronics store

63. What does the woman offer to help the man with?
 (A) Recycling some materials
 (B) Setting up some equipment
 (C) Posting some signs
 (D) Sweeping the floor

64. Look at the graphic. Which song should be moved to the end of the playlist?
 (A) "Long Ocean"
 (B) "Not in Flux"
 (C) "Opal Field"
 (D) "Fancy Heart"

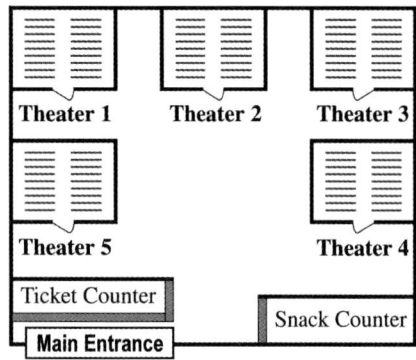

Hotels	Location	Fitness Center	Breakfast
The Parkview	✓		✓
The Ridgemore	✓	✓	
The Granville		✓	✓
The Marlington			✓

65. What does the man ask the woman about?

   (A) Free parking
   (B) Seating options
   (C) A student discount
   (D) A payment method

66. Why does the man decline an offer?

   (A) He rarely goes to the theater.
   (B) He is meeting a friend.
   (C) He buys tickets online.
   (D) He just ate a meal.

67. Look at the graphic. Where will the man go next?

   (A) To Theater 1
   (B) To Theater 2
   (C) To Theater 3
   (D) To Theater 4

68. What are the speakers organizing?

   (A) A hiring event
   (B) A family reunion
   (C) A marketing conference
   (D) An employee retreat

69. Look at the graphic. Which hotel do the speakers prefer?

   (A) The Parkview
   (B) The Ridgemore
   (C) The Granville
   (D) The Marlington

70. What does the man say he is working on?

   (A) Renting some equipment
   (B) Getting official permits
   (C) Updating a Web site
   (D) Finalizing a menu

PART 3 빈출 표현

🎧 750_P3_22

회의/일정

participant 참석자
agenda 안건
top priority 최우선 사항[과제]
sales meeting 영업 회의
videoconferencing 화상 회의
conference call 전화 회의
conference organizer 회의 기획자
handout 유인물, 인쇄물
submit a proposal 제안서를 제출하다
last-minute change 막판 변경
ahead of/behind schedule 일정보다 빠른/늦은
a change in policy 정책 변경
come up with (아이디어 등을) 내놓다, 고안하다
interoffice (조직 내에서) 부서 간의, 사내의
reschedule 일정을 조정하다
adjust the work schedule 업무 시간을 조정하다
scheduling conflict 일정 충돌
attend the meeting 회의에 참석하다
meet the deadline 마감일을 맞추다
move up the deadline 마감일을 당기다
push back the deadline 마감일을 미루다
expedite the process 과정을 신속하게 처리하다
scheduled 예정된
set up an appointment 약속을 잡다
postpone 미루다, 연기하다
available (만날 수 있는) 시간이 되는
board of directors 이사회
progress report 경과 보고서

출장/출근

be out of town (출장 등으로) 도시를 떠나 있다
on a business trip 출장 중인
on assignment 업무차
report to work 출근하다
commute 통근하다
security badge 보안 카드, 출입증
swipe (신용카드 등을) 판독기에 통과시키다
call in sick 아파서 결근하겠다고 전화하다
take a day off 월차/하루 휴가를 내다
medical leave 병가 (= sick leave)
maternity leave 출산 휴가, 육아 휴직
reimbursement 사용 경비 정산, 환급
paid/unpaid leave 유급/무급 휴가

인사/평가

performance 업무 실적
advancement 승진
benefits (급여 이외의) 혜택, 수당
nomination 지명, 추천
transfer 인사이동하다
understaffed 인원 부족의, 손이 모자라는
personnel department 인사부
performance evaluation/appraisal/review 업무 평가, 인사 고과
hands-on 실제로 참가하는, 실무의
lay off 정리해고하다
get a promotion 승진하다
have a lot of connections 인맥이 넓다

계약

contract 계약(서)
contractor 도급업자, 시공업체
estimate 견적
negotiation 협상, 교섭
term 조건, 임기, 기한
expense report 지출 보고서, 경비 내역서
specifications 세부 내역서, 사양
statement 명세서, (사업) 보고서, 계산서
association 협회
manufacture 제조하다
budget 예산
confidentiality 기밀성, 비밀성
reimburse 상환하다, 변제하다
permit 허가하다; 허가서

마케팅

public relations 홍보
findings 조사 결과, 연구 결과
survey results 설문조사 결과
advertising agency 광고 대행사
draft 밑그림, 초안
revision 수정, 개정
expand 확대하다
sales figures 판매 수치, 매출액
product launch 제품 출시
demonstration 시연, 설명
make revisions 수정하다, 개정하다
marketing strategy 마케팅 전략
place an advertisement 광고를 하다
target audience 대상 고객층

사무기기/시설

office supplies 사무용품
supplier 납품업체
run out of ~이 떨어지다
stockroom 비품 저장실
copy machine 복사기 (= photocopier)
computer components 컴퓨터 부품
installation 설치
malfunctioning 고장 난, 오작동하는
out of service 운행이 중단된, 사용이 불가한
maintenance 유지, 정비
crew 작업자들
floor plan 평면도
break room 휴게실

사내 행사

upcoming 다가오는, 곧 있을
company retreat 회사 야유회
retirement party 은퇴 기념 파티
corporate event 기업 행사
awards banquet 시상식 연회
turnout 참가자 수
extend an invitation 초대하다, 초대장을 보내다
enroll 등록하다
new employee orientation 신입 직원 오리엔테이션
recruitment fair 채용 박람회
shareholders' meeting 주주총회
company newsletter 사보
attend a training session 교육 과정에 참석하다

교통

driveway 진입로, (사설) 차도
compartment 구획, 칸막이
transportation 운송, 교통편
fare (교통) 요금
photo identification 사진이 부착된 신분증
luggage 수하물
return flight 돌아오는 비행편, 귀국 항공편
directions 길 안내
get to ~에 도착하다 (= reach)
congestion 교통 혼잡
make it 제시간에 도착하다, 장소에 나타나다
be scheduled to do ~하기로 예정되다
run late (도착 등이) 늦다

여가

amenities 오락시설, 편의시설
accommodation 숙박 시설
single room 1인실
one-way/round trip 편도/왕복 여행
time slot 시간대
exhibition 전시회
performance 공연, 연주
ticket agent 발권 담당 직원
fully booked 전석 매진의
annual fee 연회비
fill out a form 서식을 작성하다, 기입하다
register for ~에 등록하다
hold an event 행사를 열다, 개최하다

쇼핑

representative 담당 직원, 대표
sales associate 영업 사원
flyer 전단, 광고지
instruction manual 사용 설명서
user-friendly 사용하기 쉬운
warranty (품질) 보증
full refund 전액 환불
appliance (가정용) 기구, 전기 제품
subscription 가입, 구독
gift certificate 상품권
store credit 상점 포인트, 적립금
release 출시하다
have ~ in stock ~의 재고가 있다, 물품을 보유하고 있다
total comes to 합이 ~이 되다

식당

vegetarian 채식주의자를 위한
nutritional 영양의
cuisine 요리
culinary 요리의, 음식의
ingredient 요리 재료
seasoning 양념, 조미료
assorted 여러 가지의, 갖은
caterer 출장 연회업체
catering service 출장 연회 서비스
diner 식사하는 사람
gourmet 미식가; (음식이) 고급인
order a meal 음식을 주문하다
complimentary 무료 제공의
outdoor seating 야외 좌석

부동산

real estate 부동산
property 부동산, 건물
deposit 보증금
utility bill 공과금
monthly rent 월세
renovation 개보수
spacious 널찍한
storage space 수납 공간
residential area 주거지역
relocate to ~로 옮기다
suburb 교외
fully furnished 가구가 모두 갖춰진
have a nice view 전망이 좋다
within walking distance 걸어갈 수 있는 거리 내에

병원

diagnose 진단하다
prescription 처방전
eye exam 눈 검사
sneeze 재채기를 하다
bother 괴롭히다
remedy 치료법
medication 약
get a shot[an injection] 주사 맞다
get some vaccinations 예방 접종하다
take medicine 약을 복용하다
have a high fever 열이 높다
act up (몸에) 문제가 생기다
medical checkup 건강 검진
health insurance 건강 보험

은행

account number 계좌 번호
deposit 예금하다
withdraw 인출하다
deposit/withdrawal slip 입금/출금 전표
transfer 송금하다(= remit)
set up a savings account 보통예금 계좌를 개설하다
apply for a loan 대출을 신청하다
endorse (수표에) 이서하다
transaction 거래, 처리
bank statement 은행 입출금 내역서
balance 잔고, 잔액
exchange rate 환율
bank teller 은행 창구 직원

우체국 및 기타 장소

parcel 소포
regular delivery 일반 배송
express mail service 속달 우편 서비스
overnight delivery 익일 배송
by courier 택배로
track (우편물을) 추적하다
pick up a package 소포를 찾아가다
box[ticket] office 매표소
admission fee 입장료
hair salon 미용실
have the hair trimmed 머리를 다듬다
check out (책을) 대출하다, (호텔에서) 퇴실하다

PART 4

짧은 담화

INTRO

UNIT 11 전화 메세지
UNIT 12 공지/회의
UNIT 13 설명/소개
UNIT 14 광고/방송

ETS ACTUAL TEST
PART 4 빈출 표현

무료 강의

INTRO PART 4 · 짧은 담화 총 10세트 30문항

화자 한 명의 담화를 듣고 이와 관련된 세 개의 문제를 푸는 유형으로, 전화 메시지, 회의 발췌, 안내 방송 등이 다양한 내용으로 출제된다. 문제 유형은 다음과 같이 크게 두 가지로 나눌 수 있다.

| 전체 내용 관련 문제 | 주제/목적, 담화가 나오는 장소, 화자·청자의 직업/업종/근무지 |
| 세부 사항 관련 문제 | 화자의 요청/제안/추천 사항, 화자의 의도 파악, 화자·청자가 다음에 할 일, 앞으로 일어날 일, 이유/원인, 방법, 문제점, 세부 사항, 시각 정보 연계 |

ETS 예제 및 풀이 전략

❶ 담화를 듣기 전에 문제와 보기를 읽고, 키워드에 표시해 둔다.
Part 4에서는 화자에 관한 문제인지 청자에 관한 문제인지 정확히 파악해야 한다.

❷ 단서가 나올 부분을 노려 듣고, 듣는 동시에 답을 선택한다.

문제지

71. What is the [purpose] of the [message]?
 (A) To book a business trip
 (B) To confirm attendance at a meeting
 (C) To cancel a telephone conference
 (D) To discuss an e-mail message

72. What did Mr. Patel's [assistant] tell Mr. Walsh?
 (A) Mr. Patel's plans are uncertain.
 (B) Mr. Patel will attend a meeting.
 (C) Mr. Patel is on vacation.
 (D) Mr. Patel's e-mail address has changed.

73. What does [Jack Walsh] say he [will do]?
 (A) Visit Mr. Patel's office
 (B) Inform the board of Mr. Patel's schedule
 (C) Send an e-mail message to Mr. Patel
 (D) Telephone Mr. Patel again

음원

Questions 71 through 73 refer to the following telephone message.

Mr. Patel, this is Jack Walsh from the Dublin office. **71** I'm calling to confirm your attendance at the board meeting here in July. The meeting is scheduled for July third. **72** Last week your assistant said you weren't certain if you could attend. Is this still true? If you won't be able to travel here, please let me know whether you could participate in a conference call meeting by phone. **73** I'll send you an e-mail message with possible meeting times for a conference call. I'll also send the meeting agenda in the e-mail. I hope to hear back from you soon.

※ 이후 문제만 읽어주며, 문제 사이에 8초가 주어진다.

71. 메시지의 목적: 이사회 참석 여부 확인 정답 **(B) To confirm attendance at a meeting**
72. 파텔 씨의 비서가 한 말: 참석 여부 불확실 정답 **(A) Mr. Patel's plans are uncertain.**
73. 잭 월시 씨가 할 일: 이메일 발송 정답 **(C) Send an e-mail message to Mr. Patel**

담화 유형별 빈출 내용

담화별로 자주 출제되는 내용을 알아두면, 단서를 노려 듣는 데 도움이 된다.

- 전화 메시지   정보 전달, 문의, 업무 관련 요청, 예약 확인/변경 등
- ARS 메시지   업체/조직 소개, 운영/휴무 시간 안내, 내선 번호 안내 등
- 공지/회의   고객 대상 안내/당부, 회사 정책 공지, 시스템 도입/변경 공지, 기타 업무 관련 공지 등
- 설명/소개   행사/견학/오리엔테이션 관련 안내, 회사/제품 소개, 인물과 그의 업적 소개 등
- 광고   상품/서비스 광고, 개점 광고, 할인/구매 혜택 소개 등
- 방송   프로그램 내용/인터뷰 소개, 지역/비즈니스 뉴스 보도, 날씨/교통 안내 등

패러프레이징(Paraphrasing)

Part 4는 한 사람이 계속해서 말하기 때문에 상대적으로 긴 문장이 등장하기도 하며, 패러프레이징 방식이 복잡한 양상을 띠는 경우가 있다.

❶ 한 문장에 두 개가 등장하는 경우

W The new intern hasn't learned how to use the database software yet, so I'd like you to work with him tomorrow.

Q What does the speaker say about the new intern?
A He is not familiar with a procedure.

여 새 인턴이 아직 데이터베이스 소프트웨어 사용법을 배우지 않아서, 내일 당신이 함께 작업해 주었으면 해요.

질문 화자는 새 인턴에 대해 무엇이라고 말하는가?
정답 절차에 익숙하지 않다.

→ 배우지 않았다는 것을 not familiar with로, 데이터베이스 소프트웨어 사용법을 procedure로 표현

❷ 두 문장에 있는 단서를 조합해야 하는 경우

M As you all know, we were planning to start work on the camera advertisement this week. But the client called and said the camera won't be ready until the end of this month.

Q What is the speaker mainly talking about?
A A delay in the project

질문 화자는 주로 무엇에 대해 이야기하고 있는가?
정답 프로젝트 지연

남 모두 아시다시피, 이번 주에 카메라 광고 작업에 착수할 계획이었습니다. 하지만 고객사에서 전화해서 말하길, 카메라가 이번 달 말에나 준비될 거랍니다.

→ 광고 작업을 project로, 문제가 생겨 이번 달 말이나 되어야 작업이 가능하다는 것을 delay로 표현

UNIT 11 전화 메시지

출제 포인트: 발신자가 남기는 음성 메시지나 회사 자동 응답을 통한 정보 전달, 문의, 요청 내용이 주를 이룬다. 메시지의 주제는 다양하며 화자의 신분/근무지, 전화 목적, 요청/제안 사항을 묻는 문제가 자주 출제된다.

▶ 담화 구성과 단서 파악

750_P4_01

인사/소개	Hi Rose, it's Jennifer.
목적/용건	❶ I just found out that I can't attend the information technology job fair, so I won't be able to drive you there on Monday morning.
세부 내용	But I think José Morales is planning on going.
요청/제안	❷ Why don't you give him a call to see whether he has space in his car for you?
세부 내용	And since I'm not going, ❸ I'll drop off the company brochures we were planning to hand out at the fair. May I stop by your office tomorrow to give them to you?

1 전화 목적: 박람회 참석 불가로 차로 데려다 주지 못함

2 제안 사항: 동료에게 전화해보기

3 내일 할 일: 안내 책자 가져다 주기

정답과 해설 p.100

1. Why is the speaker **calling**?
   (A) To explain an office procedure
   (B) To cancel some travel plans

   주제/목적 문제 | 초반부 확인하기
   화자가 전화한 목적
   정답 (B) 출장 계획을 취소하려고

2. What does the speaker **suggest**?
   (A) Calling a coworker
   (B) Leaving at an earlier time

   제안 사항 문제 | 중반부 확인하기
   화자가 제안하는 것
   정답 (A) 동료에게 전화하기

3. What does the speaker **plan to do tomorrow**?
   (A) Register for an event
   (B) Deliver some brochures

   세부 사항 문제 | 후반부 확인하기
   화자가 내일 할 일
   정답 (B) 안내 책자 가져다 주기

상황별 빈출 표현

수신자 정보	**Hello, this message is for** Lynn Taylor in the maintenance department. 안녕하세요. 이 메시지는 관리부의 린 테일러 씨에게 남기는 것입니다.
발신자 정보	Hi, Mr. Brown. **This is** Stacy Jackson **from** MacDougall's Bookstore. 안녕하세요, 브라운 씨. 맥두걸 서점의 스테이시 잭슨입니다.
전화 목적	**I'm calling to** confirm your appointment for Friday. 귀하의 금요일 예약을 확인하고자 전화 드립니다.
요청 사항/연락 방법	**Please call me back** at your earliest convenience. **My number is** 555-0112. 가능한 한 빨리 저에게 전화 주십시오. 제 번호는 555-0112입니다.

ETS 유형연습

다음 담화를 듣고 문제를 풀어보세요.
다시 들으면서 빈칸을 채우세요.

🔊 750_P4_02
정답과 해설 p.100

1. What is the purpose of the voice-mail message?
   (A) To request some information
   (B) To report an accident

2. What is the caller waiting for?
   (A) Insurance papers
   (B) X-rays

Hello, this message is for Robert Costa _____ _____. This is Dr. Mina Wilson from the Rosemont Medical Group. My patient, Sara Santos, _____ of her foot at your office last week. It's been six days, and I'm still waiting for the _____ to me. Could you please give me a call to let me know _____? My direct number is 555-3156. Thank you.

3. Where does the speaker most likely work?
   (A) At a flower shop
   (B) At a bakery

4. Why does the speaker say, "April is a very busy month for us"?
   (A) To apologize for a misunderstanding
   (B) To encourage the listener to act quickly

Hello, Mr. Gupta. I'm responding to your message _____ for your company's event in April. I suggest we meet at the venue so I can see the size of the room and _____ _____. Please _____ _____. April is a very busy month for us. In the meantime, make sure to visit our Web site to _____ for ideas and prices.

5. What type of business does the speaker work for?
   (A) A landscaping service
   (B) A solar energy company

6. Why are some services being canceled today?
   (A) Some workers are out sick.
   (B) The weather is bad.

You've reached SunMerc Incorporated, the region's leading supplier and installer of _____ _____. We apologize for this inconvenience. But because of _____, we're canceling all service appointments for today. We are _____ all of today's appointments to another date. If you are a customer with work that _____, please press 1 to speak with a representative.

ETS 실전문제

1. Where does the speaker most likely work?
   (A) At a lawyer's office
   (B) At a hardware store
   (C) At an electronics store
   (D) At a shipping company

2. What does the speaker say about this weekend?
   (A) A business will be closed.
   (B) An appointment will be required.
   (C) A sale will begin.
   (D) An order will arrive.

3. According to the speaker, what is the business offering?
   (A) A consultation by telephone
   (B) A personalized gift
   (C) A discount coupon
   (D) An extended warranty

4. What is the purpose of the message?
   (A) To invite the listener to an event
   (B) To follow up on a job application
   (C) To discuss an upcoming publication
   (D) To advertise a professional organization

5. What is Lisa Cheng's area of expertise?
   (A) Social media marketing
   (B) Diet and nutrition
   (C) Hospital management
   (D) Urban planning

6. What does the speaker offer to do?
   (A) Share some research data
   (B) Create an advertisement
   (C) Contact a colleague
   (D) Pay for travel costs

7. What type of business is Starry Ways?
   (A) A tour company
   (B) A car service
   (C) A bus line
   (D) An airline

8. According to the speaker, what new benefit is available with the mobile app?
   (A) Early boarding
   (B) Luggage tracking
   (C) Lounge access
   (D) Travel advice

9. According to the speaker, what information should the listener be ready to provide?
   (A) A confirmation number
   (B) A credit card number
   (C) The name of a traveler
   (D) The name of a destination

10. Who most likely is the listener?
    (A) A photographer
    (B) A chef
    (C) A food critic
    (D) A musician

11. What is the purpose of the speaker's call?
    (A) To offer the listener a magazine subscription
    (B) To invite the listener to participate in a competition
    (C) To schedule an interview for an article
    (D) To request a donation for an event

12. What does the speaker say will happen until May 1?
    (A) A Web site will be under construction.
    (B) A venue will be available.
    (C) A fee will be waived.
    (D) An employee will be out of the office.

13. Where does the speaker work?

(A) At a cooking school
(B) At a university
(C) At a botanical garden
(D) At a community center

14. What does the speaker imply when she says, "The instructor closes the doors at six o'clock"?

(A) It is important to arrive to class on time.
(B) It is safe to store personal items in the classroom.
(C) A passcode is required for entry to the class.
(D) A class is very popular.

15. Who is eligible for free classes?

(A) Guests of a local hotel
(B) Children under the age of ten
(C) Volunteers
(D) City residents

16. What did the speaker discuss with Janet Lin?

(A) A hiring plan
(B) A product design
(C) A supply order
(D) A travel itinerary

17. What does the speaker imply when he says, "she's the head of the department"?

(A) He wants to introduce a staff member.
(B) He cannot make the final decision.
(C) A job title is incorrect.
(D) A colleague is very successful.

18. What will the speaker most likely do next?

(A) Set up a meeting
(B) Check a catalog
(C) Complete a form
(D) Call a client

Kumar Tower Directory	
Floor	Business
1	Olson and Liu Associates
2	Naftig Brothers Limited
3	Five Peaks Consulting
4	Pantrel Solutions Incorporated

19. What position did the listener most likely apply for?

(A) Computer technician
(B) Sales representative
(C) Journalist
(D) Lawyer

20. Look at the graphic. Which company does the speaker represent?

(A) Olson and Liu Associates
(B) Naftig Brothers Limited
(C) Five Peaks Consulting
(D) Pantrel Solutions Incorporated

21. Why does the speaker want the listener to return the call?

(A) To negotiate a salary
(B) To verify a graduation date
(C) To provide additional references
(D) To confirm an appointment time

UNIT 12 공지/회의

출제 포인트 공공장소 또는 사내 공지와 업무 관련 회의 발췌도 출제 빈도가 높은 편이다. 새로운 시스템 도입과 변경 사항이 언급되는 경우가 많고, 주제나 목적, 청자들(listeners)과 관련된 요청/제안 사항 문제가 자주 출제된다.

◆ 담화 구성과 단서 파악

🔊 750_P4_04

인사/소개	Hi, everyone. A quick announcement before we start the day.	
주요 내용	❶ **While our sales of outerwear here at the store are doing well**, our Web site is having some issues. Namely, ❷ **the link to view men's jackets isn't working**. IT is looking into this, but we don't know when it will be fixed.	❶ 근무지 암시: 매장의 겉옷 판매 실적 우수 ❷ 문제점 언급: 웹사이트 링크 오류
요청/당부	So, ❸ **if any customers come in looking to find the jackets that are online, please send them to our customer service manager.**	❸ 요청 사항: 온라인 제품을 찾는 고객은 고객 서비스 매니저에게 보내라고 당부
마무리	She'll be able to help them. Thanks!	

정답과 해설 p.105

1. **Where** do the listeners most likely **work**?
   (A) At a clothing store
   (B) At an electronics store

   근무지 문제 | 초반부 확인하기
   청자들의 근무지
   정답 (A) 의류 매장

2. **What problem** does the speaker **mention**?
   (A) Some photographs are not clear.
   (B) A link is not working.

   문제점 문제 | 중반부 확인하기
   화자가 언급한 문제점
   정답 (B) 링크가 작동하지 않는다.

3. **What** does the speaker **ask the listeners to do**?
   (A) Give refunds to some customers
   (B) Send some customers to a manager

   요청 사항 문제 | 후반부 확인하기
   청자들에게 요청한 일
   정답 (B) 고객을 매니저에게 보내기

상황별 빈출 표현

개요/주제	**The last item on the meeting agenda** is a new system for entering customer orders. 회의의 마지막 안건은 고객 주문을 입력하는 새로운 시스템에 관한 것입니다.
요청/당부	**Please** write your name and e-mail address clearly on the sheet. 종이에 성함과 이메일 주소를 깔끔하게 적어주시기 바랍니다.
주의 환기	**Attention**, passengers flying to London. 런던행 승객 여러분께 알려드립니다.
공지/발표	**I'm happy[pleased] to announce** that we will be opening a new store in July. 7월에 새 지점을 연다는 것을 알리게 되어 기쁩니다.

ETS 유형연습

다음 담화를 듣고 문제를 풀어보세요.
다시 들으면서 빈칸을 채우세요.

750_P4_05

정답과 해설 p.106

1. Where is the announcement being made?
   (A) In a movie theater
   (B) In a library

2. What can listeners do at the service desk?
   (A) Check out materials
   (B) Sign up to use computers

Good evening, _____. We'll be closing in 30 minutes. If you're working on _____, we ask that you shut it down before you leave. If you would like to _____, please _____ near the front entrance. Also, we'd like to remind you that we will be _____ tomorrow evening at six o'clock called *Life in Tuscany*. Please join us for this wonderful film.

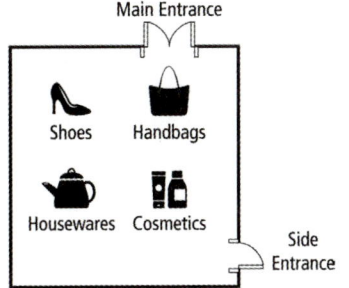

3. Look at the graphic. Which products will be moved on Friday?
   (A) Handbags
   (B) Cosmetics

4. What does the speaker say he will do?
   (A) Meet with a designer
   (B) Provide some food

In just a few days, we'll be receiving a line of _____ here in the store. We've never sold candles before. The manufacturer has sent us the materials we need _____. I expect the candles to attract many customers into our store. I'd like to put them up front—_____. We'll need to move the display that's currently there. If anyone can work a few hours after closing on Friday to help set up, _____.

5. What does the speaker update the listeners about?
   (A) Weather conditions will be clear.
   (B) Refreshments will be complimentary.

6. What does the speaker tell the listeners to do?
   (A) Move their belongings
   (B) Fasten their seat belts

Welcome aboard, passengers! My name is Myung Hwa, and I'll be your guide _____ this afternoon. The estimated trip time is 90 minutes. And I have an _____. It's predicted _____, with calm waters throughout the trip. Also, in accordance with guidelines, the crew asks that all passengers _____ out of the aisles and put them below the seats.

ETS 실전문제

1. Where is the announcement being made?
   (A) At a museum
   (B) At a university
   (C) At a furniture store
   (D) At a library

2. What are the listeners waiting to attend?
   (A) A lecture
   (B) A film
   (C) An exhibition
   (D) A concert

3. What does the speaker say about the 5 o'clock event?
   (A) It is less expensive.
   (B) It is shorter.
   (C) It will be less crowded.
   (D) It will include refreshments.

4. Where are the listeners?
   (A) At an airport
   (B) At a train station
   (C) At a boat harbor
   (D) At a bus station

5. What is causing a delay?
   (A) Lost luggage
   (B) Bad weather
   (C) A late passenger
   (D) A maintenance check

6. According to the speaker, which item was found?
   (A) A wallet
   (B) A mobile phone
   (C) A pair of glasses
   (D) A book

7. How does the speaker start the meeting?
   (A) By playing a video
   (B) By announcing some poll results
   (C) By showing some slides
   (D) By congratulating a team

8. What is the main purpose of the meeting?
   (A) To lower production costs
   (B) To evaluate potential projects
   (C) To choose new suppliers
   (D) To assess the competition

9. Why does the speaker say, "change is not easy"?
   (A) To recommend extending a timeline
   (B) To explain why a proposal was not approved
   (C) To express surprise
   (D) To address the listeners' doubts

10. What have the listeners volunteered to do?
    (A) Direct traffic
    (B) Set up camping sites
    (C) Lead bird-watching tours
    (D) Perform maintenance tasks

11. What does the speaker want to do with some photographs?
    (A) Make identification badges
    (B) Post them on a Web site
    (C) Display them at a ceremony
    (D) Include them in a handbook

12. What will the speaker do next?
    (A) Unlock a storage area
    (B) Take attendance
    (C) Provide some refreshments
    (D) Pass out some forms

13. Who most likely are the listeners?

    (A) Politicians
    (B) Accountants
    (C) Investors
    (D) Scientists

14. According to the speaker, how did a company survive?

    (A) By reducing a workforce
    (B) By adjusting product formulas
    (C) By lowering prices
    (D) By renting a less expensive space

15. What will the speaker do next?

    (A) Pass out copies of a report
    (B) Check attendance
    (C) Give a presentation
    (D) Introduce a guest speaker

16. What kind of event is taking place?

    (A) An awards banquet
    (B) A trade show
    (C) A product launch
    (D) A grand opening

17. Why did a company make a change?

    (A) To cut costs
    (B) To improve productivity
    (C) To attract new customers
    (D) To comply with new regulations

18. Why should the listeners speak to an associate?

    (A) To submit an application
    (B) To try on some merchandise
    (C) To sign up for some training
    (D) To get a discount coupon

Cloud Storage Options	Option 1	Option 2	Option 3	Option 4
Storage Capacity	5 GB	2 TB	6 TB	10 TB
Monthly Fee per User	Free	$8	$20	$35

19. Where do the listeners most likely work?

    (A) At a graphic design firm
    (B) At a bank
    (C) At a technical school
    (D) At an electronics store

20. Look at the graphic. Which option does the speaker recommend?

    (A) Option 1
    (B) Option 2
    (C) Option 3
    (D) Option 4

21. What will Scott do at a meeting tomorrow?

    (A) Confirm available funds
    (B) Prepare for an audit
    (C) Demonstrate some software
    (D) Review some sales results

UNIT 13 설명 / 소개

무료 강의

출제 포인트 견학, 대회 등 다양한 행사 안내, 업무 개요 설명, 특정 인물 소개, 혹은 제품의 특징을 설명하는 담화가 주를 이룬다. 소개 대상에 관해 묻는 세부 사항 문제와 다음에 할 일/일어날 일을 묻는 문제가 자주 출제된다.

◆ 담화 구성과 단서 파악

750_P4_07

인사/소개	Welcome, everyone. My name is Isobel, and ❶ I'll be your instructor for this evening's cooking class.	❶ 진행 중인 행사: 요리 교실 강사가 본인 및 수업 소개
행사 개요	Tonight, I'm going to teach you how to bake some artisanal bread.	
진행 상황/요청 사항	Now, I've already set the ingredients you'll need on the counter, but ❷ could you please come to the front of the room and get one large bowl and a loaf pan?	❷ 요청 사항: 수강생들에게 앞으로 나와 조리도구를 가져갈 것을 요청
할 일/일어날 일	Oh, by the way, ❸ in about half an hour, a photographer will be stopping by to take some pictures for our new promotional brochure. If you'd prefer not to be in the photos, please just let him know.	❸ 30분 후에 일어날 일: 사진 기사가 방문할 예정

정답과 해설 p.112

1. **What** are listeners **attending**?
   (A) A dinner party
   (B) A cooking class

   세부 사항 문제 | 초반부 확인하기
   행사 종류
   정답 (B) 요리 교실

2. **What** does the speaker **ask** the **listeners to do**?
   (A) Read some instructions
   (B) Gather supplies

   요청 사항 문제 | 중반부 확인하기
   청자들에게 요청한 일
   정답 (B) 도구 가져가기

3. **What** does the woman say **will happen** in **half an hour**?
   (A) Photographs will be taken.
   (B) An artist will give a speech.

   일어날 일 문제 | 후반부 확인하기
   30분 후에 일어날 일
   정답 (A) 사진 촬영이 있을 것이다.

상황별 빈출 표현

행사 소개	**Thank you for** attending the 5th Creative Art Awards. 제5회 창의적 예술 시상식에 참석해 주셔서 감사합니다.
목적	**I am here to** tell you about the features of our new monitor. 저희가 새롭게 출시한 모니터의 특징을 설명드리러 왔습니다.
할 일	**Now, I'm going to show you** how to use the company's accounting software. 이제, 회사의 회계 소프트웨어 사용법을 보여드리겠습니다.
소개	**I'd like to introduce** our keynote speaker, Dr. Cindy Lowe. 기조 연설자인 신디 로우 박사를 소개하겠습니다.

ETS 유형연습

다음 담화를 듣고 문제를 풀어보세요.
다시 들으면서 빈칸을 채우세요.

750_P4_08
정답과 해설 p.112

1. Where is the speaker?
   (A) At a computer store
   (B) At a technology convention

2. What new feature is mentioned by the speaker?
   (A) Rooms with Internet access
   (B) A special price on software

Welcome to the sixth annual Corzell _____ _____. I know you're looking forward to a weekend filled with _____, workshops, and some fantastic exhibits of _____ _____. Those of you who participated in previous conventions will notice something new this year—we now have _____ _____. One final note: if you're planning to attend _____, there's been a change. It will be held in the Hudson Room, not the Bayside Center.

3. Why does the speaker say, "make sure you leave some room on those walls"?
   (A) To show admiration
   (B) To give a warning

4. What will Dr. Trevor do today?
   (A) Fly to the Galapagos Islands
   (B) Share part of her book

Our next speaker is Dr. Clarissa Trevor, a _____ _____ who has greatly impacted the scientific world. The evidence is on the walls of her office, which are lined with numerous _____. This past year, Dr. Trevor found _____ in the Galapagos Islands. So I think it's safe to tell her—make sure you leave some room on those walls. Her findings are documented in her new book, *The Unknown Turtle*. Today, she will be _____ her amazing discovery. Please join me in welcoming Dr. Clarissa Trevor.

5. Which part of the museum will the tour start with?
   (A) The landscape painting exhibits
   (B) The conservation department

6. According to the speaker, how can the listeners learn more about a topic?
   (A) By listening to an audio guide
   (B) By reading a recent publication

On this tour of the Klauston Art Museum, I'm going to take you behind the scenes to see _____ _____ where _____ before it goes on display. As you can see, we have an _____ historic pigments here. We use them _____ when we're researching the material composition of older paintings. We _____ on the subject if you want to learn more about it.

ETS 실전문제

1. Who most likely is the speaker?
   (A) The head of a theater crew
   (B) A costume designer
   (C) An actor
   (D) A sound technician

2. What does the speaker say needs to be increased?
   (A) The length of a script
   (B) The level of teamwork
   (C) The number of props
   (D) The amount of funding

3. What is Klaus asked to check?
   (A) The security system
   (B) The lighting
   (C) A supply list
   (D) A lunch delivery

4. What is the purpose of the speech?
   (A) To honor a retiring employee
   (B) To explain administrative changes
   (C) To announce a new advertising campaign
   (D) To present an award winner

5. What does the speaker say she appreciates about Nathan Milo?
   (A) His artistic talent
   (B) His financial experience
   (C) His technical skills
   (D) His leadership ability

6. What does the speaker say about the company?
   (A) It is well-known throughout the country.
   (B) It will relocate next year.
   (C) It plans to hire more employees.
   (D) It was featured in a newspaper article.

7. What does the speaker say is special about a material?
   (A) It is inexpensive to make.
   (B) It resembles natural wood.
   (C) It is environmentally friendly.
   (D) It comes in a variety of colors.

8. Why does the speaker say, "we've already partnered with several other instrument makers"?
   (A) To encourage the listeners to do business with them
   (B) To provide a reason for a delay
   (C) To invite the listeners to an event
   (D) To reject a colleague's suggestion

9. What will the speaker do next?
   (A) Give a demonstration
   (B) Conduct a survey
   (C) Describe a process
   (D) Distribute some brochures

10. What is the purpose of the event?
    (A) To honor new graduates
    (B) To dedicate a building
    (C) To celebrate an employee's retirement
    (D) To raise funds for an organization

11. What is the video about?
    (A) A new charity
    (B) A company's development
    (C) A historical landmark
    (D) A training program

12. What will take place after the meal?
    (A) A building tour
    (B) A dance party
    (C) A president's speech
    (D) A group photo

13. Where most likely are the listeners?

    (A) At an awards ceremony
    (B) At a home-repair workshop
    (C) At a sales meeting
    (D) At an employee training session

14. What does the speaker say buyers will appreciate about a product?

    (A) It is available in many colors.
    (B) It is simple to operate.
    (C) It needs no electrical outlet.
    (D) It requires no regular maintenance.

15. According to the speaker, what will happen in March?

    (A) An interview will take place.
    (B) A product will be featured in a magazine.
    (C) A product will be available for purchase.
    (D) A home-improvement store will open.

16. What industry do the listeners most likely work in?

    (A) Hospitality
    (B) Entertainment
    (C) Agriculture
    (D) Manufacturing

17. What will the speaker do next?

    (A) Give a tour
    (B) Show a video
    (C) Collect contact information
    (D) Hand out business cards

18. Why does the speaker say, "I'll be at booth 40 for the rest of the day"?

    (A) To complain about a location
    (B) To request assistance with a task
    (C) To apologize for declining an invitation
    (D) To explain how the listeners can get more information

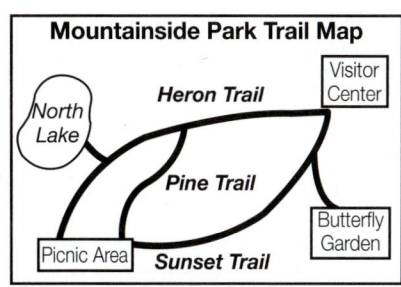

Mountainside Park Trail Map

19. Who most likely are the listeners?

    (A) Maintenance workers
    (B) Bus drivers
    (C) Tourists
    (D) Park rangers

20. Look at the graphic. Where will the listeners be unable to go today?

    (A) The North Lake
    (B) The Picnic Area
    (C) The Butterfly Garden
    (D) The Visitor Center

21. What does the woman encourage the listeners to do?

    (A) Bring a map
    (B) Check the weather forecast
    (C) Store their belongings
    (D) Use sun protection

UNIT 14 광고/방송

무료 강의

| 출제 포인트 | 상품/서비스/사업체 광고와 라디오 방송 및 뉴스 보도가 자주 출제된다. 광고되는 대상, 방송/뉴스의 주제, 그리고 관련 세부 사항을 묻는 경우가 많다. |

◆ 담화 구성과 단서 파악

🎧 750_P4_10

광고 대상 및 특징 소개	❶ City Instruments has opened a new store! For over ten years, City Instruments has been proud to offer musical instruments at fantastic low prices. Now, in addition to our city-center location, we've opened a new store in the Skylarville Shopping Center.	❶ 광고 대상: 새 악기점 개점 소식 및 상점의 특징 소개
혜택	To welcome our customers to the new location, ❷ for a limited time we'll be offering one month of free music lessons for any instrument that you purchase.	❷ 특별 혜택: 기간 한정 이벤트로 악기를 구매하면 한 달 무료 수업 제공
추가 정보	❸ And this Saturday only, we'll stay open late for your shopping convenience.	❸ 토요일에 일어날 일: 영업 시간 연장

정답과 해설 p.118

1. **What** is **being advertised**?
   (A) A radio program
   (B) The opening of a store

   광고 대상 문제 | 초반부 확인하기
   광고되는 대상
   정답 (B) 상점 개점

2. **What special offer** is being made?
   (A) Preferred seating
   (B) Free music instruction

   세부 사항 문제 | 중반부 확인하기
   특별 혜택
   정답 (B) 무료 음악 강좌

3. **What will happen** on **Saturday**?
   (A) Shopping hours will be extended.
   (B) A band will perform.

   일어날 일 문제 | 후반부 확인하기
   토요일에 일어날 일
   정답 (A) 영업 시간이 연장된다.

상황별 빈출 표현

광고 멘트	**Do you want** to stay updated on fashion trends? Subscribe to our magazine, *Fashion Plus*. 최신 패션 트렌드를 계속 확인하고 싶으신가요? 저희 잡지 〈패션 플러스〉를 구독해 보세요.
특별 혜택	**For a limited time only, we offer** free delivery on any orders over $30. 한시적으로, 30달러 이상 주문 시 무료 배송을 제공합니다.
프로그램 소개	**You're listening to** *Breakfast with Tim Smith*. **Today, we'll be talking about** your eating habits. 〈팀 스미스와 함께하는 아침〉을 듣고 계십니다. 오늘은 식습관에 대해서 이야기해 보겠습니다.
채널 고정	**Stay tuned** for our traffic report. **We will be back after** a short commercial break. 교통 방송을 들으시려면 채널을 고정해 주세요. 잠시 광고 듣고 오겠습니다.

ETS 유형연습

다음 담화를 듣고 문제를 풀어보세요.
다시 들으면서 빈칸을 채우세요.

750_P4_11
정답과 해설 p.118

1. Who is this report for?
   (A) Traffic police
   (B) Car drivers

2. What caused the problem?
   (A) A defective traffic light
   (B) A broken water pipe

This is Ken Harrison with a _____. If you are driving southbound on Clover Street, you should be ready for delays. There is a _____ _____ between Morris Boulevard and Ridge Avenue, which has caused the right lane _____. The police are now on the scene directing traffic, but things are still moving quite slowly on Clover. We recommend avoiding Clover Street altogether and _____ _____. Our next traffic report will be in fifteen minutes, so keep listening.

3. What is the focus of the podcast?
   (A) Book reviews
   (B) Unusual jobs

4. What does the speaker say has happened in recent years?
   (A) Podcast episodes have increased in length.
   (B) Audiobooks have become more popular.

Welcome back to *Odd Job Journeys*, the podcast where we interview people who've _____ _____ quirky and _____. Now, it may seem like everyone's reading fewer books nowadays, but _____ in popularity in recent years. I like them myself because _____. And today's guest, Pablo Espinoza, has a lot to say about this trend.

5. What did style experts say about Ella Bancroft's products?
   (A) They are popular this season.
   (B) They are made from natural materials.

6. When will the promotion end?
   (A) On Saturday
   (B) On Sunday

Come to Endwell Shoes this weekend for our annual winter sale! _____, we're _____ our entire inventory as we make room for our new styles. The discount even applies to Ella Bancroft designer boots, which style experts on the Forward Fashion television network say are _____ of footwear. You'll be sure to find something you like—and at a price that can't be beat. Remember, _____, so come take advantage of these great deals while they last!

ETS 실전문제

1. What is the purpose of the broadcast?
   (A) To advertise a store's grand opening
   (B) To announce a business merger
   (C) To discuss a new product
   (D) To report on a change in regulations

2. What type of business is Ashton Holt?
   (A) A construction company
   (B) An interior design firm
   (C) An advertising agency
   (D) A clothing company

3. What does the speaker encourage listeners to do?
   (A) Listen to an interview
   (B) Visit a Web site
   (C) Apply for a job
   (D) Enter a contest

4. What is being advertised?
   (A) A computer accessory
   (B) An exercise machine
   (C) A kitchen appliance
   (D) A sewing machine

5. According to the speaker, how has the product changed?
   (A) It weighs less.
   (B) It has a larger capacity.
   (C) It is available in a new color.
   (D) Its settings are easier to adjust.

6. What does the speaker tell the listeners to remember?
   (A) A return policy
   (B) A release date
   (C) A store location
   (D) A discount offer

7. Where is the speaker?
   (A) At an airport
   (B) At a museum
   (C) At a public library
   (D) At a subway station

8. According to the speaker, how will customers benefit from an upgrade?
   (A) Memberships will be renewed automatically.
   (B) Customers will be notified about schedule changes.
   (C) Wireless Internet coverage will improve.
   (D) Customer wait times will decrease.

9. What are some listeners encouraged to do?
   (A) Attend board meetings
   (B) Respond to a survey
   (C) Read a report
   (D) Reserve tickets

10. What does the speaker say he does for a living?
    (A) He leads workshops.
    (B) He coaches sports.
    (C) He designs buildings.
    (D) He illustrates books.

11. What does the speaker imply when he says, "we went seriously overtime"?
    (A) He had been forced to start late.
    (B) He should have practiced more.
    (C) He made a planning mistake.
    (D) He received some negative feedback.

12. What will the listeners most likely hear next?
    (A) A listener's question
    (B) An advertisement
    (C) An interview
    (D) A preview of the next episode

13. What does the speaker suggest about today's weather?

    (A) It will be unusually warm.
    (B) It will rain all day.
    (C) It will cause traffic problems.
    (D) It will change later today.

14. What will likely happen next week?

    (A) Spring will begin.
    (B) Temperatures will decrease.
    (C) The weather center will close.
    (D) The days will be very sunny.

15. When will the next weather report take place?

    (A) In twelve minutes
    (B) In twenty minutes
    (C) In a half hour
    (D) In an hour

16. What type of business is being advertised?

    (A) A Web-design firm
    (B) A hardware store
    (C) A real estate agency
    (D) A remodeling company

17. What special service does the business offer?

    (A) Free installation
    (B) A flexible payment plan
    (C) A follow-up inspection
    (D) Emergency repairs

18. What does the speaker suggest listeners do online?

    (A) View work samples
    (B) Leave comments
    (C) Request a consultation
    (D) Find a business location

Airline Name	Number of Stops	Ticket Price
Pinyon Airlines	0	$450
Rondo Air	1	$400
Blaze Airways	2	$350
Vela Air	0	$375

19. What is the main topic of the broadcast segment?

    (A) Inexpensive summer activities
    (B) Popular tourist destinations
    (C) Helpful purchasing tips
    (D) Unknown local restaurants

20. Look at the graphic. Which airline does the speaker point out?

    (A) Pinyon Airlines
    (B) Rondo Air
    (C) Blaze Airways
    (D) Vela Air

21. According to the speaker, how can the listeners receive free meals?

    (A) By redeeming an online coupon
    (B) By joining a frequent-fliers club
    (C) By applying for a travel rewards credit card
    (D) By booking travel using a mobile application

ETS ACTUAL TEST 750_P4_13

71. What is the talk mainly about?
    (A) A construction project
    (B) A fund-raising event
    (C) A grant proposal
    (D) An anniversary party

72. Who most likely are the listeners?
    (A) Maintenance workers
    (B) Medical staff
    (C) Patients
    (D) Journalists

73. According to the speaker, what will be provided at no cost?
    (A) Professional development
    (B) Internet access
    (C) Cafeteria lunches
    (D) Shuttle bus service

74. Who most likely is the speaker?
    (A) A building inspector
    (B) A store employee
    (C) A factory worker
    (D) A truck driver

75. What information from the manager does the speaker share?
    (A) A product is unavailable.
    (B) Some repairs are needed.
    (C) Invoices will be mailed.
    (D) Rain is expected.

76. What does the speaker remind the listeners about?
    (A) Business hours have changed.
    (B) Job applications are accepted on Saturdays.
    (C) Tomorrow is the last day of an event.
    (D) Deliveries take one week.

77. Who most likely is the speaker?
    (A) A painter
    (B) A hotel manager
    (C) A computer technician
    (D) An event organizer

78. What does the speaker want to buy?
    (A) Artwork
    (B) Furniture
    (C) Snacks
    (D) Tools

79. What does the speaker mean when she says, "My shift ends at four o'clock"?
    (A) She does not have time for a task.
    (B) She would like to meet today.
    (C) She would like to work an extra shift.
    (D) She thinks a schedule is wrong.

80. What is being advertised?
    (A) A concert series
    (B) A science museum
    (C) A pet store
    (D) A monthly publication

81. What will new customers receive for a limited time?
    (A) Free food samples
    (B) Invitations to lectures
    (C) Entry tickets to parks
    (D) Souvenir T-shirts

82. What are listeners asked to do on a Web site?
    (A) Use a promotional code
    (B) Look at some photos
    (C) Join a mailing list
    (D) Enter a contest

83. What type of business does the speaker work for?

    (A) A moving company
    (B) A landscaping service
    (C) A manufacturing firm
    (D) A food supplier

84. What problem does the speaker mention?

    (A) A price list contained an error.
    (B) A payment could not be processed.
    (C) A business is short-staffed.
    (D) A product had a defect.

85. What does the speaker say about tomorrow's delivery?

    (A) It will contain substitute items.
    (B) It can go to a different location.
    (C) It will arrive as scheduled.
    (D) It may be postponed.

86. What type of construction project is the speaker discussing?

    (A) Building a shopping mall
    (B) Expanding a public transportation system
    (C) Renovating a local history museum
    (D) Adding on to a city hospital

87. Why does the speaker say, "the proposal hasn't been approved yet"?

    (A) To complain about a delay
    (B) To urge an immediate response
    (C) To provide reassurance
    (D) To justify a decision

88. What will be broadcast later?

    (A) An interview
    (B) A debate
    (C) A sports event
    (D) A concert

89. Where do the listeners work?

    (A) At a technology company
    (B) At a medical clinic
    (C) At an accounting firm
    (D) At a manufacturing plant

90. What does the speaker imply when he says, "it's not software you're familiar with"?

    (A) A company announcement was incorrect.
    (B) A project proposal will not work.
    (C) Some software is still being developed.
    (D) Some training will be necessary.

91. What will the listeners most likely do next?

    (A) Indicate their availability
    (B) Call their managers
    (C) Analyze some data
    (D) Confirm some appointments

92. What is the purpose of the talk?

    (A) To introduce a guest speaker
    (B) To provide a tour schedule
    (C) To promote a new exhibit
    (D) To explain a museum's history

93. What does the speaker say about the gift shop?

    (A) It will be closing for renovations.
    (B) It will be selling special merchandise.
    (C) It has free maps.
    (D) It is offering a discount today.

94. What does the speaker encourage the listeners to do?

    (A) Volunteer at the museum
    (B) Purchase advance tickets
    (C) Register for an annual membership
    (D) Meet some visiting artists

Flooring Type	Materials Cost per Square Foot
Carpeting	$2.50
Finished wood	$6.00
Tile	$8.50
Vinyl	$3.00

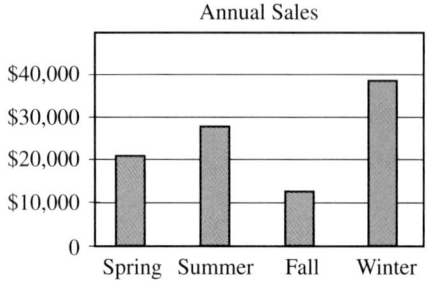

95. Who most likely are the listeners?

    (A) Real estate agents
    (B) Construction workers
    (C) Architects
    (D) Salespeople

96. What does the speaker say the listeners can do tomorrow?

    (A) Get their paychecks
    (B) Attend a training session
    (C) Tour a building
    (D) Take the day off

97. Look at the graphic. Which type of flooring does the speaker refer to?

    (A) Carpeting
    (B) Finished wood
    (C) Tile
    (D) Vinyl

98. What type of product does the business sell?

    (A) Clothing
    (B) Footwear
    (C) Appliances
    (D) Software

99. Look at the graphic. In what season did the business relocate?

    (A) Spring
    (B) Summer
    (C) Fall
    (D) Winter

100. What did the business do after it relocated?

    (A) It expanded its inventory.
    (B) It hired additional staff.
    (C) It placed some advertisements.
    (D) It organized an inauguration event.

PART 4 빈출 표현

🎧 750_P4_14

제품/서비스 관련 메시지

inquiry about ~에 대한 문의
service representative 고객 상담원
replacement 대체품, 교환품
out of stock 재고가 없는
inventory 재고 조사, 재고품, 재고 목록
place an order 주문하다
hold until ~까지 보관해 두다
warranty 품질 보증서
waive a fee 수수료를 면제해 주다
frequent customer 단골 고객
confirm a reservation 예약을 확정하다
compensate 보상하다
issue a refund 환불해 주다

기업/기관 ARS 메시지

extension 내선, 구내전화
office[business] hours 업무 시간
pound key (전화기의) 우물 정자(#)
after the tone[beep] 삐 소리가 난 후
You have reached ~로 전화하셨습니다
stay on the line 전화를 끊지 않고 기다리다
in the meantime 그동안, 그 사이에
You will be connected to ~로 연결될 겁니다
relay a message 메시지를 전달하다
I apologize for any inconvenience 불편을 드려 죄송합니다
I'm currently attending 현재 ~에 참석 중입니다
Please feel free to 편하게 ~하세요

사내 공지사항

identification badge 사원증
efficiency of the work 작업·업무의 효율성
company-wide 전사적인, 회사 전체의
receive a reimbursement 비용을 돌려받다
on[at] short notice 갑작스런 통지에도
be sure to check for updates 추가 공지사항을 꼭 확인하세요
share some good news 몇 가지 좋은 소식을 나누다
Employees are encouraged to 직원 여러분들께 ~하시길 권장합니다
according to the recent market surveys 최근 시장 설문조사에 따르면
This policy will be in effect until 이 방침은 ~까지 유효할 것이다.
adopt a new policy 새로운 정책을 채택하다
how the system works 시스템 작동 방식

업무/회의

upcoming 다가오는, 곧 있을
reschedule 일정을 변경하다
sales fluctuations 매출 변동
potential client 잠재 고객
annual report 연례 보고서
out of town on business 업무차 타 지역에 있는
confirm one's attendance 참석 여부를 확인하다
meeting agenda 회의 안건
call a meeting 회의를 소집하다
wrap up the meeting 회의를 마무리하다
give a quick overview 간략하게 설명하다
familiarize oneself with ~을 숙지하다
make up for the extra cost 추가 비용을 만회하다
follow up on ~에 대해 후속조치를 취하다
won't be ready until ~이 되어야 준비될 것이다
at the latest 늦어도

건물 내 안내 방송

attention 안내 말씀드립니다
patron 고객, 후원자
voucher 상품권, 쿠폰
checkout counter 계산대
special offer 특가품, 특별 할인 행사
sign-up sheet 가입 신청서
extend hours of operation 운영 시간을 늘리다
proceed to ~로 가다
bulletin board 게시판
designated area 지정 구역
in order to serve you better 여러분들을 더 잘 모시기 위해
Please be advised that ~임을 알려 드립니다
I'd like to remind you that ~임을 알려 드립니다

교통 수단 안내 방송

delayed 지연된
departure gate 탑승구
personal belongings 개인 소지품
carry-on baggage 기내 휴대용 수하물
check in 탑승 수속하다
security check point 보안 검색대
boarding pass 보딩패스, 탑승권
have the ticket and identification ready 표와 신분증을 준비하다
connection 연결 항공편
cabin 선실, 기내
inbound/outbound 귀항하는/출항하는
cargo hold 화물 적재실
Welcome aboard ~에 탑승하신 것을 환영합니다

발표/연설/소개

press conference 기자회견
conference organizer 회의 주관자
keynote speaker 기조 연설자
opening/closing remarks 개회사, 폐회사
on behalf of ~를 대신하여, 대표하여
make an appearance 출연하다
give[make] a presentation on ~에 관해 발표하다
insightful 통찰력 있는
contribute 공헌하다
reputation 명성, 권위
leading expert on ~분야의 뛰어난 전문가
dedicated to ~에 헌신하는, 전념하는
the prestigious award 권위 있는 상
give a round of applause for ~에게 큰 박수를 보내다
let's welcome ~ to the front ~를 앞으로 모시겠습니다

관광/견학

landmark 주요 지형 지물
observatory 전망대
guided tour 해설 관광, (가이드 동반) 견학
itinerary 일정(표)
excursion 소풍, (단체) 여행
featured exhibition 특별 전시회
admission fee 입장료
register in advance 사전에 등록하다
display area 전시장
plant 공장, 시설 (= factory, facility)
state-of-the-art 최첨단의
refrain from ~을 삼가다
demonstrate 시연하다
inspection 점검, 검사
safety gear 안전 장비

광고

a large[wide] selection of 많은, 다양한
complimentary 무료로 제공되는
feature ~을 특징으로 하다
authentic 정통의, 진짜의
promotion 홍보, 판촉 행사
guarantee 보장하다
customized 맞춤식의
trial period 무료 체험 기간
affordable (가격이) 적당한 (= reasonable)
half off 50퍼센트 할인
discount code 할인 코드
for a limited time only 제한된 기간에만, 한시적으로
clearance sale 재고 정리 세일
Don't miss out ~을 놓치지 마십시오

뉴스/라디오 방송

host (TV·라디오 프로그램의) 사회자, 진행자
news flash 뉴스 속보
commercial break 광고 방송을 위한 프로그램 중단 시간
segment 방송의 일부, 코너
tune in 주파수를 맞추다, 방송을 보다, 청취하다
stay tuned 채널을 고정하다
exclusive interview with ~와의 독점 인터뷰
keep ~ posted ~에게 계속 알려주다
local residents 지역 주민들
city council 시 의회
market share 시장 점유율
drop in profits 수익 하락
merge with ~와 합병하다
reveal a plan 계획을 공개하다

교통 방송

commuter 통근자
renovation 보수 공사
ongoing 현재 진행 중인, 계속되는
real time 실시간
traffic jam[congestion] 교통 체증
be stuck in traffic 교통 체증에 걸리다
time-consuming 시간이 걸리는
expect delays on ~에서의 정체가 예상되다
expressway 고속도로 (= motorway)
transportation network 교통망
bottleneck 좁은 도로, 병목 지역
road closure 도로 폐쇄
complimentary shuttle bus 무료 셔틀버스
make[take] a detour 우회하다
take an alternative route 다른 길로 가다, 우회하다

일기 예보

inclement weather 악천후
high pressure 고기압
degree (온도 단위) 도
temperature 온도
precipitation 강수량
average 평균
humid 습기가 많은
heat wave 폭염
snowstorm 눈보라
gusty wind 돌풍
thunderstorm (강풍이 따르는) 뇌우
hail 우박
unseasonably 철에 맞지 않게
scattered 간헐적인
clear up (날씨가) 맑아지다, 개다

RC READING COMPREHENSION

PART 5 & 6

단문/장문 채우기

INTRO

UNIT 01 품사와 문장 구조
UNIT 02 명사
UNIT 03 대명사
UNIT 04 형용사
UNIT 05 부사
UNIT 06 동사의 형태와 종류
UNIT 07 수 일치와 태
UNIT 08 시제
UNIT 09 to부정사와 동명사
UNIT 10 분사와 분사구문
UNIT 11 전치사와 접속사
UNIT 12 부사절 접속사
UNIT 13 관계대명사
UNIT 14 명사절 접속사
UNIT 15 비교/도치 구문
UNIT 16 어휘

ETS ACTUAL TEST

 무료 강의

INTRO PART 5·6 기본 다지기

문장 형식

PART 5에서는 기본적인 문장 형식을 알아야 문장 구조를 분석하여 문제를 풀 수 있다. 문장 형식은 PART 5뿐만 아니라 PART 6, 7에서도 필요한 기본 지식이므로 확실히 짚고 넘어가도록 한다.

1형식 주어 + 동사

주어와 동사로만 이루어진 구조이다. 목적어를 취하지 않는 자동사가 쓰인다.

The cost of a room at the River Hotel varies according to size.
　　　　주어　　　　　　　　　　　　　　동사
리버 호텔의 객실 요금은 크기에 따라 다르다.

2형식 주어 + 동사 + 주격 보어

주어와 동사만으로는 의미가 완성되지 않으므로, 주어를 보충 설명하는 주격 보어가 필요한 구조이다. 주로 명사와 형용사가 주격 보어 역할을 한다.

The contract will remain valid for 3 months.
　　주어　　　　동사　　주격 보어
계약은 3개월간 유효할 것이다.

3형식 주어 + 동사 + 목적어

가장 많이 쓰이는 문장 형태로, 목적어를 필요로 하는 타동사가 쓰인다.

Ms. Carson submitted her expense report right after she returned from the trip.
　　주어　　　　동사　　　　목적어
카슨 씨는 출장을 다녀온 직후에 지출 품의서를 제출했다.

4형식 주어 + 동사 + 간접 목적어 + 직접 목적어

동사 뒤에 간접 목적어(~에게)와 직접 목적어(~을)가 순서대로 오는 구조이다.

Rowell Enterprises offers employees excellent benefits.
　　주어　　　　　　동사　　간접 목적어　　직접 목적어
로웰 엔터프라이지즈는 직원들에게 탁월한 복지 혜택을 제공한다.

5형식 주어 + 동사 + 목적어 + 목적격 보어

3형식 문장 뒤에 목적어를 보충 설명하는 목적격 보어가 추가된 구조이다. 명사, 형용사, 동사원형, to부정사, 분사가 목적격 보어로 쓰일 수 있으며, 동사에 따라 다른 형태가 온다.

Many readers found Mr. Tsang's article in the second issue very interesting.
　　주어　　　　동사　　　　목적어　　　　　　　　　　　　　　목적격 보어
많은 독자들이 2호에 실린 창 씨의 기사가 굉장히 흥미롭다고 생각했다.

INTRO PART 5 단문 빈칸 채우기 총 30문항

단문의 빈칸을 채우는 문제로, 총 30문항이 출제된다. 문제 유형은 다음과 같이 크게 두 가지로 나눌 수 있다. 문법 문제와 어휘 문제가 비슷한 비중으로 출제되며, 간혹 문법과 어휘가 혼합된 유형이 등장하기도 한다.

> **문법 문제** 명사/동사/형용사/부사/전치사/접속사 자리 문제, 인칭대명사의 격/재귀대명사 문제,
> 동사의 태/시제/수 일치 문제, 비교급 및 최상급 문제, 관계대명사 문제 등
> **어휘 문제** 의미상 빈칸에 알맞은 명사/동사/형용사/부사/전치사/접속사 선택 문제

ETS 예제 및 풀이 전략

❶ 문제 유형을 먼저 파악한다.

PART 5는 문제당 권장 풀이 시간이 20~30초로 굉장히 짧기 때문에, 읽는 순간 바로 정답을 선택하고 다음 문제로 넘어가야 한다. 문장 전체를 읽기 전에, 문제의 보기를 보고 유형을 먼저 파악하는 것이 좋다.

문법 문제 빈칸과 주변의 관계를 살핀다.

어근이 같지만 품사가 다른 단어들, 혹은 다양한 동사 형태로 보기가 구성되어 있다면, 우선 빈칸과 주변 구성 요소 간의 관계를 살핀 후 정답을 찾아본다. 문장 해석은 필요할 때만 한다.

101. Ms. Seo has ------- experience in community planning and development.
 (A) extent 명사
 (B) extensive 형용사
 (C) extensively 부사
 (D) extensiveness 명사

뒤에 오는 명사를 수식하는 형용사 자리

정답 **(B)**

어휘 문제 문장의 핵심 구성 요소를 중심으로 해석한다.

어휘 문제라도 기본적으로 문장 구조는 파악해야 한다. 가령 목적어 역할을 하는 명사 어휘를 선택하는 문제라면, 동사와 수식어구를 확인하고 문맥상 가장 어울리는 보기를 선택해야 한다.

102. The marketing team must submit its quarterly progress ------- for analysis by June 1.
 (A) signature 서명
 (B) report 보고서
 (C) payment 지불금
 (D) hold 잡기

분석(analysis)을 위해 제출(submit)해야 하는 것

정답 **(B)**

❷ 권장 풀이 시간 내에 정답을 찾을 수 없다면 표시한 후 다음 문제로 넘어간다.

풀리지 않는 문제에 너무 많은 시간을 투자해서는 안 된다. 권장 풀이 시간 내에 문제를 해결하려면, 학습 시 문법 포인트를 정확히 이해하고 Collocation 위주로 어휘를 암기해 두도록 한다.

※ Collocation이란? 자주 함께 쓰이는 단어들의 결합 ⓔ renew the contract 계약을 갱신하다

INTRO PART 6 장문 빈칸 채우기 총 4지문 16문항

총 4지문이 출제되고 각 지문당 4개의 문제가 있다. 문법/어휘 문제 3문항과 문장 고르기 문제 1문항으로 구성되어 있는데, 문장 고르기 문제를 제외한 3문항의 구성은 지문별로 다르다. 문법과 어휘 문제가 주를 이루며, 앞뒤 내용을 자연스럽게 연결하는 연결어를 선택하는 문제도 종종 출제된다.

ETS 예제

Questions 131-134 refer to the following e-mail.

To: Douglas Lovato, Floor Manager
From: Jessa Nicols, Production Manager
Subject: Thursday Client Meeting
Date: August 3

Hi Douglas,

Our clients called this morning to inform us that one more person will be joining our meeting at our glass factory this Thursday. This ------- change won't affect us in any major way. The
                                                                              131.
clients will still arrive at 10 A.M. to discuss technical matters. That afternoon, we will still take them on an ------- and informative tour of the factory. -------, before we start the tour,
                       132.   133.
please have safety equipment ready for four, not three, people. -------.
                                                                134.
Call me if you have any questions.

Jessa

어휘 문제

131. (A) doubtful
(B) seasonal
(C) continuous
(D) unforeseen

문법 문제

132. (A) interesting
(B) interestingly
(C) interested
(D) interests

연결어 문제

133. (A) Instead
(B) However
(C) Besides
(D) Similarly

문장 고르기 문제

134. (A) Now we will look at the tools used to shape that glass.
(B) I hope this time change isn't an inconvenience.
(C) This includes an extra hard hat, earplugs, and boots.
(D) They asked questions about our safety standards during the tour.

풀이 전략

❶ 지문을 처음부터 읽는다.
PART 6에서는 문맥을 파악해야 풀 수 있는 문제가 대부분이므로, 지문을 처음부터 읽어야 한다. 시간을 절약해 보려고 빈칸이 있는 문장만 읽는 것은 위험하다.

❷ 순서대로 한 문제씩 해결해 나간다.
문법 문제는 해당 문장만 보고 풀 수 있는 경우가 간혹 있지만, 시제/지시어/대명사 문제는 앞뒤 문장과 내용의 흐름을 파악하고 풀어야 한다. 따라서 문제 유형에 상관없이, 반드시 순서대로 해결해 나가도록 한다.

어휘 문제 문장의 핵심 구성 요소를 중심으로 해석한 후, 빈칸 주변 단어를 확인한다.

131. 고객이 아침에 전화해 회의 참석 인원 추가(one more person)
  이(This) 변동 사항(change)과 가장 어울리는 형용사 선택

  정답 **(D) unforeseen**(예기치 못한)

문법 문제 문장의 구조를 분석한다. 시제/지시어/대명사 문제는 앞뒤 문장과 내용의 흐름을 살핀다.

132. 빈칸 앞 | 관사 an
  빈칸 뒤 | 등위접속사 and + 형용사 informative + 명사 tour (of the factory)
    informative와 함께 tour를 수식할 형용사 선택

  정답 **(A) interesting**(흥미로운)

연결어 문제 빈칸 앞뒤 문장의 내용 관계(대조, 인과, 첨언, 예시, 시간 흐름, 감정 표현)를 파악한다.

133. 빈칸 앞 | 고객들이 여전히(still) 10시에 도착, 오후에 공장 견학 예정 → 일정 변동 X
  빈칸 뒤 | 세 명이 아닌 네 명(four, not three)을 위한 안전 장비 준비 → 준비 사항 변동 O
    서로 대조적인 내용을 연결해 주는 접속부사 선택

  정답 **(B) However**(그러나)

문장 고르기 문제 빈칸 앞뒤 내용을 보고 오답을 소거한 후, 전체 흐름상 가장 적절한 문장을 선택한다.
  보기에 지시어, 대명사 등이 있을 경우, 가리키는 대상을 앞 문장에서 찾아야 한다.

134. 빈칸 앞 | 세 명이 아닌 네 명을 위한 안전 장비(safety equipment) 준비 당부
  빈칸 뒤 | 질문 있으면 전화 요망

  (A) 오답 유리 형태를 잡는 데 쓰는 도구를 관찰할 예정 → 견학 중 나올 법한 대사
  (B) 오답 시간 변경 양해 → 앞서 일정은 변동이 없다고 고지
  (C) 정답 이것은 추가 안전모, 귀마개, 부츠 포함 → this = safety equipment
  (D) 오답 견학 동안 안전 기준에 관해 질문 → 견학 후 언급될 만한 내용

UNIT 01 품사와 문장 구조

1 주어와 동사

출제 포인트 일반적으로 문장에는 주어와 동사가 있어야 한다. 문장에 동사가 없다면 빈칸은 동사 자리이다.

▶ 주어 자리

주어는 보통 동사 앞에 쓴다. 주어 자리에는 (대)명사와 to부정사구, 동명사구, 명사절 접속사가 이끄는 명사절이 올 수 있다. 주어와 동사는 수가 일치하고 자연스럽게 해석되어야 한다.

명사	Many [**investors** / ~~invests~~] **have** concerns about the recent decline in the stock market. 많은 투자자들이 최근 주식 시장 하락을 염려하고 있다.
동명사구	[**Correcting** / ~~Correct~~] errors in the reports **is** one of your main responsibilities. 보고서에 있는 오류를 바로잡는 것이 당신의 주요 업무 중 하나이다. → 주어 자리에 동명사를 쓸 수 있다. 타동사의 동명사는 목적어(errors)를 동반한다.
명사절	[**What** / ~~Because~~] the builder likes about this contract **is** the early completion bonus. 건축업자가 이 계약에서 마음에 들어 한 것은 조기 완공에 대한 보너스다. → 명사절을 이끄는 접속사 What이 쓰여야 한다.

▶ 동사 자리

완전한 문장에는 반드시 동사가 있어야 한다. 동사 자리에는 to부정사, 분사, 동명사 등의 준동사를 쓸 수 없다. 만약 문장에 절을 이끄는 접속사가 있으면 주어와 동사가 추가된다.

The current board members at Ampifay, Inc., [**started** / ~~to start~~] their term two months ago.
엠피파이 주식회사의 현 이사진은 두 달 전 임기를 시작했다.

[**Complete** / ~~Completing~~] the online form if you are interested in the sculpture competition.
조각 대회에 관심이 있으시면 온라인 서식을 작성하세요.
→ 접속사 if가 이끄는 부사절을 생략하고 나면 문장에 동사가 없다. 명령문은 주어를 생략하고 동사원형으로 시작한다.

Once the subscription [**begins** / ~~to begin~~], it will continue throughout the year.
일단 구독이 시작되면, 그것은 일 년 동안 지속될 것이다.
→ 접속사 Once가 두 절을 이어주고 있기 때문에 주어와 동사가 두 개씩 있어야 한다.

ETS 유형연습

정답과 해설 p.131

1. Passengers arriving at Gate H had to walk up the stairs to the main terminal because the ------- was temporarily out of order.
   (A) escalate
   (B) escalator
   (C) escalation
   (D) escalating

2. At Kaylee Knitwear, associates ------- a 15 percent discount on any merchandise in the store.
   (A) receiving
   (B) to receive
   (C) receive
   (D) to be received

3. New software that should reduce employee training time -------.
   (A) to develop
   (B) developing
   (C) is being developed
   (D) to be developed

2 목적어

출제 포인트 타동사 뒤에는 목적어가 필요하고, 목적어 자리에는 주로 명사가 쓰인다. 전치사는 명사와 함께 수식어구를 형성하는데, 이때 전치사 뒤의 명사를 '전치사의 목적어'라고 부른다.

◆ 동사의 목적어 자리

동사 뒤에는 목적어, 보어, 수식어가 나올 수 있지만, 동사 뒤에 빈칸이 나오면 목적어 자리인지 아닌지 먼저 확인하는 것이 효율적이다. 목적어 자리에는 (대)명사, to부정사구, 동명사구, 명사절이 온다.

명사 Improved working conditions **can increase** [productivity / ~~productively~~].
개선된 근무 환경은 생산성을 높일 수 있다.
→ 동사 뒤에 목적어 역할을 하는 명사가 나와서 '~을'이라고 자연스럽게 해석된다.

to부정사구 The management team **is planning** [to transfer / ~~transfers~~] the plant to South America.
경영진은 공장을 남미로 이전할 계획이다.
→ 동사 plan의 목적어 자리에는 명사나 to부정사를 쓸 수 있다. 명사 뒤에는 목적어가 올 수 없지만, to부정사 뒤에는 목적어(the plant)가 올 수 있다.

명사절 The survey **indicates** [that / ~~while~~] the MCN Hotel provides the highest-quality service.
조사는 MCN 호텔이 가장 높은 수준의 서비스를 제공한다는 것을 보여준다.
→ 동사 뒤 목적어 자리이므로 명사절 접속사를 선택한다. that은 명사절 접속사, while은 부사절 접속사이다.

◆ 전치사의 목적어 자리

전치사의 목적어 자리에는 (대)명사, 동명사구, 명사절이 온다. '전치사+목적어'는 주로 수식어로 사용된다.

명사 According to the supply contract, the payment should be made **upon** [delivery / ~~deliver~~].
납품 계약에 따르면, 배송 즉시 지불이 되어야 한다.

동명사구 We can improve customer service **by** [reading / ~~reads~~] many complaint letters.
우리는 많은 불만 서신을 읽음으로써 고객 서비스를 개선할 수 있다.
→ 전치사 뒤에 동명사를 쓸 수 있지만, 동사는 올 수 없다.

ETS 유형연습

정답과 해설 p.131

1 The director of marketing got ------- to hire additional staff for the upcoming advertising campaign.

(A) approval
(B) approving
(C) approve
(D) approves

2 Most government and commercial establishments will be closed on Monday in ------- of Independence Day.

(A) observe
(B) observing
(C) observance
(D) observant

3 Mr. Song's promotion to the position of division ------- was announced at this morning's staff meeting.

(A) manage
(B) manager
(C) managed
(D) manageable

3 보어

출제 포인트 보어에는 주어를 보충 설명하는 주격 보어와 목적어를 보충 설명하는 목적격 보어가 있다. 주격 보어를 취하는 동사와 목적격 보어를 취하는 동사를 기억하자.

◆ 주격 보어 자리

주격 보어 자리에는 주로 형용사나 명사가 온다. 형용사 보어는 주어를 보충 설명하고, 명사 보어는 주어와 동격 관계이다.

형용사	Online shopping **has become** more [**popular** / ~~popularly~~] around the world. 온라인 쇼핑은 세계적으로 더 인기 있게 되었다. (온라인 쇼핑 → 인기 있는)
명사	Rural areas with traditional houses **have become** tourist [**attractions** / ~~attractive~~]. 전통 가옥들이 있는 시골 지역들이 관광 명소가 되었다. (시골 지역들 = 관광 명소)

주격 보어를 취하는 동사

be ~이다	become ~이 되다	remain/stay ~인 채로 있다	seem/appear ~인 듯하다
look ~처럼 보이다	sound ~하게 들리다	feel ~하게 느끼다	turn ~이 되다
			taste ~한 맛이 나다

> **고득점 TIP**
> 주격 보어 자리에 명사, 형용사가 아닌 전치사구가 올 수도 있다.
> The hospital is [**currently** / ~~current~~] **under construction**. 그 병원은 현재 건설 중이다.

◆ 목적격 보어 자리

목적격 보어의 형태는 동사에 따라 다양하므로 각 동사가 이끄는 구조를 기억하도록 한다.

목적격 보어를 취하는 동사	목적어	목적격 보어의 형태
make 만들다 keep 유지하다 find/consider/deem 여기다	the seminar	helpful 〔형용사〕
ask/request/invite 요청하다 encourage 격려하다	more people	to attend 〔to부정사〕
make 만들다 have 하게 하다 let 허락하다	more people	attend 〔동사원형〕
have 되게 하다	the computer	fixed 〔과거분사〕

Many nutritionists **found** the results [**fascinating** / ~~fascinatingly~~].
많은 영양학자들은 결과가 흥미롭다고 생각했다.

ETS 유형연습

1 Our home repair workshop is ------- to the public every first Saturday of the month.
(A) open
(B) openly
(C) opener
(D) be opened

2 The Ashford Chamber of Commerce invites visitors ------- the restaurants and theaters on the city's waterfront.
(A) patronize
(B) patronized
(C) to patronize
(D) be patronizing

3 Changes to financial markets have made investors even more ------- on quality advice and information.
(A) depends
(B) dependent
(C) to depend
(D) dependency

4 수식어

출제 포인트 수식어는 완전한 문장에 의미를 더하기 위해 쓰는 말로, 다른 요소를 꾸며주는 역할을 한다. 따라서 생략해도 문장 구조에 영향을 미치지 않는다. 수식어 자리에는 부사, 전치사구, 접속사절이 올 수 있다.

◆ 부사

부사는 명사를 제외한 모든 품사를 수식할 수 있으며, 문장에서 다양한 위치에 올 수 있다. 수식어인 부사는 생략 가능하며, 생략해도 문장 구조에 영향을 미치지 않는다. 동사구 사이와 자동사 뒤는 대표적인 부사 자리이다.

At Correia Electronics, we **are** [**continually** / continues] **researching** appliance technology.
코레이아 전자에서 우리는 가전제품 기술을 끊임없이 연구하고 있다.

→ 동사구 be+-ing, be+p.p., have+p.p. 사이와 '조동사+일반동사' 사이에 부사가 들어갈 수 있다.

◆ 전치사+명사

전치사는 전치사의 목적어 역할을 하는 명사와 결합하여 '전치사+명사'의 전치사구를 형성한다. 전치사구가 수식어 역할을 할 때는 생략해도 문장 구조에 영향을 미치지 않는다.

The construction project was completed on time [**despite** / although] **the inclement weather**.
건설 프로젝트는 궂은 날씨에도 불구하고 제때 끝났다.

→ despite와 although는 둘 다 양보의 의미를 지니지만 despite는 전치사, although는 접속사이다.

◆ 접속사+주어+동사

접속사가 뒤에 주어와 동사를 이끌어 수식어 역할을 할 수 있다. 문제의 보기에 접속사가 있으면 빈칸 뒤 동사의 개수를 먼저 확인해 접속사절인지 아닌지 판단하도록 한다.

[**Before** / Prior to] we **had** interviews with qualified applicants, we **read** their résumés thoroughly.
자격 있는 지원자들과 면접을 하기 전에, 우리는 그들의 이력서를 꼼꼼하게 읽어보았다.

The company **needs** Middle East specialists [**because** / due to] it **plans** to expand into Egypt.
회사는 이집트로 사업을 확장할 계획이기 때문에 중동 전문가들을 필요로 한다.

ETS 유형연습

정답과 해설 p.132

1 The keypad should be pressed ------- to ensure that all the digits of the code are transmitted.
   (A) firmly
   (B) firmness
   (C) firm
   (D) firmest

2 Chairperson Darlene Kay will honor board member Elena Costas ------- tonight's award ceremony.
   (A) during
   (B) herself
   (C) then
   (D) because

3 ------- money has been budgeted for the staff professional development program, the director is reluctant to proceed.
   (A) In spite of
   (B) Therefore
   (C) Because of
   (D) Although

ETS 실전문제

1. Nallot Computers' marketing team ------- a new television promotional campaign.
   (A) to plan
   (B) is planning
   (C) planning
   (D) planner

2. After your ------- is finalized, please notify Ms. Tang in human resources of your new home address.
   (A) relocate
   (B) relocates
   (C) relocated
   (D) relocation

3. At the annual meeting, management will ------- employees who have done outstanding work.
   (A) recognize
   (B) recognizing
   (C) recognition
   (D) to recognize

4. Orchestra patrons who are not interested in this evening's auction may register for the dinner event -------.
   (A) separates
   (B) separated
   (C) separation
   (D) separately

5. The ------- advertised in yesterday's *Shifnal Daily Echo* do not apply to kitchen appliances.
   (A) discounts
   (B) discounted
   (C) discounting
   (D) discount

6. Some proposed models of the new building will be on display in the lobby for the ------- of the week.
   (A) remainder
   (B) remaining
   (C) remained
   (D) remain

7. You will find the manual very helpful ------- any problems you encounter when you first use the software.
   (A) must solve
   (B) be solved
   (C) will solve
   (D) in solving

8. To encourage ------- from respondents, Geojedo Women's Club is offering a 25,000 won gift card to everyone who completes the survey.
   (A) participate
   (B) participation
   (C) participatory
   (D) participates

9. A recent study has shown that assembly-line workers are likely to be much less ------- during overtime shifts.
   (A) attentively
   (B) attention
   (C) attentive
   (D) attentiveness

10. Team members are being asked to postpone any vacations ------- the entire project has been completed.
    (A) while
    (B) during
    (C) upon
    (D) until

11. The editors consider several factors when selecting papers for ------- in the *Bainbridge Psychology Journal*.
    (A) includes
    (B) included
    (C) inclusion
    (D) inclusive

12. Fleet Hotel guarantees the lowest rates to guests who book rooms ------- through its Web site.
    (A) directness
    (B) directing
    (C) directly
    (D) directed

13. If you move, ------- your contact information in the company directory as soon as possible.
    (A) updating
    (B) updated
    (C) updates
    (D) update

14. Solar power is rapidly becoming an important ------- throughout the world.
    (A) industrial
    (B) industrious
    (C) industries
    (D) industry

Questions 15-18 refer to the following job advertisement.

Educational Business Seeks Social Media Assistance

Ghee Tree Games is a small company that sells ---15--- educational board games for young adults. We are seeking an individual to create five engaging posts for our social media accounts each week. Since we started our business one year ago, we have been doing our own advertising on the most popular platforms. ---16--- . In addition, because we have been so busy with other aspects of the business, we have been unable to devote adequate time to ---17--- it online. We are now ready to hand the responsibility to someone new. This ---18--- is best suited to an educator with marketing skills who understands our unique audience. If you are interested, please contact us at jobs@gheetreegames.ca.

15. (A) innovation
    (B) innovative
    (C) innovator
    (D) to innovate

16. (A) However, marketing is not our strength.
    (B) We are discontinuing our product line.
    (C) Nevertheless, we appreciate the power of social media.
    (D) They recently launched a new campaign for us.

17. (A) enlarging
    (B) promoting
    (C) evaluating
    (D) acquiring

18. (A) class
    (B) location
    (C) program
    (D) opportunity

UNIT 02 명사

1 명사의 자리 1

출제 포인트 명사는 주어 자리, 목적어 자리, 보어 자리에 쓸 수 있다. 특히 목적어 자리에 명사를 넣는 문제가 자주 출제된다.

◆ 주어 자리

문장에서 동사 앞에 등장하는 명사는 주어 역할을 할 수 있다.

[**Improvements** / ~~Improved~~] in the way we work **proved** effective in meeting increased demands.
우리 업무 방식의 개선이 늘어난 수요를 충족하는 데 효과가 있는 것으로 드러났다.

→ 동사 **proved**의 주어 역할을 하는 명사가 필요하다. **in the way we work**는 앞에 있는 명사를 수식한다.

◆ 목적어 자리

명사는 타동사의 목적어와 전치사의 목적어 역할을 한다. 또한 to부정사나 동명사 등 준동사의 목적어 역할도 할 수 있다.

동사의 목적어	If you **have** [**suggestions** / ~~suggest~~] for future workshops, please write them down. 향후 워크숍에 대해 제안할 것이 있으면 적어 주세요.
전치사의 목적어	Remember the security code **for** [**entrance** / ~~enters~~] into the research facility. 연구 시설 입장을 위한 보안 코드를 기억하세요.
준동사의 목적어	Some exercise during work helps **to increase** [**productivity** / ~~productively~~]. 근무 중에 하는 약간의 운동은 생산성을 높이는 데 도움이 된다.

◆ 보어 자리

명사는 주격 보어와 목적격 보어 자리에 올 수 있다. 명사 보어는 주어 또는 목적어와 동격 관계를 이룬다.

주격 보어	Ms. Montgomery **is** an outstanding [**expert** / ~~expertise~~] in the stock market. 몽고메리 씨는 주식 시장의 뛰어난 전문가이다. → be동사 뒤 주격 보어 자리이다. Ms. Montgomery = an expert
목적격 보어	Mr. Kim **considers** himself the best [**negotiator** / ~~negotiation~~] on his team. 김 씨는 팀에서 가장 능숙한 협상가라고 자처한다. → 동사 **consider**의 목적어 뒤 목적격 보어 자리이다. himself = the negotiator

ETS 유형연습

정답과 해설 p.134

1 ------- of homegrown and organic fruits and vegetables, as well as handmade crafts and jewelry, are available for purchase at the Springdale community market.

(A) Varies
(B) Variant
(C) Varieties
(D) Various

2 Naomi Takeda was not able to attend the meeting last Tuesday, but Claire Marsters gave her a ------- of the discussion.

(A) summarily
(B) summarizer
(C) summarized
(D) summary

3 The Burlington Book Club will choose titles from a list of ------- by local booksellers.

(A) recommends
(B) recommending
(C) recommendations
(D) recommended

2 명사의 자리 2

출제포인트 관사, 소유격, 형용사 뒤는 명사 자리이다. 또한, 명사 앞이나 뒤에 빈칸이 있으면 복합명사가 될 수 있는지 확인한다.

◆ 관사, 소유격, 형용사 뒤

관사(a, an, the), 소유격(my, your, his, her, its, our, their, Mr. Kim's), 형용사 뒤에는 명사가 온다. 관사 a(n) 뒤에는 셀 수 있는 명사의 단수형만 쓸 수 있다.

관사 뒤   All workers greeted the [**arrival** / arrive] of the new president with excitement.
모든 직원들이 들뜬 마음으로 신임 사장의 등장을 환영했다.

형용사 뒤   The manual provides comprehensive [**instructions** / instructed] for the maintenance.
설명서는 관리를 위한 포괄적인 설명을 제공한다.

> **고득점 TIP**
> '관사/소유격+형용사+명사' 덩어리를 기억하자. 관사나 소유격 뒤에 명사를 수식하는 형용사가 올 수 있다.
> The CEO will announce his [**strategic** / strategy] investment plans soon.
> CEO는 곧 그의 전략적인 투자 계획안을 발표할 것이다.

◆ 복합명사

복합명사는 한 단어로 취급된다. 복합명사에서 앞 명사는 주로 뒤 명사의 종류나 목적을 나타내는 역할을 하고, 뒤의 명사는 가산/불가산 또는 단수/복수를 표현한다.

It is common for the application [**process** / to process] of foreign students to take a long time.
외국 학생들의 신청 절차에 시간이 많이 소요되는 것은 흔한 일이다.

account information 계좌 정보	office supplies 사무용품	deadline extension 기한 연장
product availability 상품 입수가능성	workplace safety 작업장 안전	job description 직무 소개
job responsibilities 직무, 책무	staff productivity 직원 생산성	employee performance 직원 성과
travel arrangements 여행 준비	travel expenses 여행 경비	investment decision 투자 의사 결정
consumer preference(s) 소비자 선호	customer satisfaction 고객 만족	expense report 경비 보고서
safety standards 안전 기준	safety precautions 안전 예방책	product launch 제품 출시
awards ceremony 시상식	customs clearance 세관 통관	earnings figures 수익 금액

*복합명사의 앞 명사는 대부분 단수이지만, 복수형을 쓰는 경우도 있다.

ETS 유형연습
정답과 해설 p.134

1 According to *Star Watch* magazine, singer-songwriter Kylie Norton has announced her upcoming ------- in a charity concert.

(A) participate
(B) participated
(C) participating
(D) participation

2 Leroy-Bontemps researched consumer ------- around the nation as part of the development of its low-calorie beverage products.

(A) preferred
(B) preferable
(C) preferences
(D) preferring

3 The executive team has delayed the product ------- of the new smartphone for six months.

(A) launch
(B) launched
(C) to launch
(D) launchable

3 명사의 종류

출제 포인트 명사는 가산명사 단수, 가산명사 복수, 불가산명사로 나뉜다. 명사의 자리를 묻는 문제와 더불어 가산명사와 불가산명사를 구분하는 문제가 자주 출제된다.

◆ 가산명사(셀 수 있는 명사)의 단수형

가산명사는 기본적으로 셀 수 있는 명사를 뜻한다. 가산명사의 단수형은 앞에 한정사, 즉 관사, 소유격, 지시/수량형용사 등을 반드시 동반하며, 절대 단독으로 쓰지 않는다.

가산명사의 **단수형** 앞에 쓸 수 있는 한정사
- ❶ 관사 a(n), the
- ❷ 소유격
- ❸ 지시형용사 this, that
- ❹ 수량형용사 each, another, every, either

A more detailed [**description** / descriptions] will be available on the company Web site.
더 상세한 설명은 회사 웹사이트에서 볼 수 있습니다.

◆ 가산명사(셀 수 있는 명사)의 복수형

가산명사의 복수형은 주로 뒤에 -(e)s를 붙인다. 앞에 한정사가 올 수도 있고 단독으로 사용할 수도 있지만, '하나의'라는 뜻의 a(n) 뒤에는 쓸 수 없다.

가산명사의 **복수형** 앞에 쓸 수 있는 한정사
- ❶ 관사 the
- ❷ 소유격
- ❸ 지시형용사 these, those
- ❹ 수량형용사 both, (a) few, various, many

These [**surveys** / research] indicate that many residents are dissatisfied with the government policy. 이 조사는 많은 주민들이 정부 정책에 불만족한다는 것을 보여준다.

◆ 불가산명사(셀 수 없는 명사)

불가산명사는 앞에 부정관사 a(n)이 올 수 없고, 뒤에 -(e)s를 붙일 수도 없다. 불가산명사는 단수 취급한다.

information 정보	negligence 부주의	consent 동의, 허락	advice 조언	equipment 장비
machinery 기계류	access 접근, 이용	permission 허락	luggage 수하물	clothing 의류
furniture 가구	merchandise 상품	research 연구	employment 고용	manufacture 제조, 생산

Only a few manufacturing plants have [**access** / accesses] to new computer technologies.
단지 몇몇 제조 공장들만 새로운 컴퓨터 기술을 이용할 수 있다.

고득점 TIP
일부 불가산명사는 다른 의미로 쓰일 때 가산명사가 되기도 하므로 주의한다.
work 일, 직장 – works 작품   condition 상태 – conditions 조건   receipt 수령 – receipts 영수증

ETS 유형연습

1 The final day to submit an application for a ------- in the finance department will be next Tuesday.
(A) position
(B) positions
(C) positioning
(D) positioned

2 Mr. Ono asked for ------- of all the documents that were passed out during the presentation.
(A) duplicate
(B) duplicates
(C) duplicated
(D) duplicative

3 The Zirko 5000 bottling machine is a feat of ------- that has revolutionized the beverage industry.
(A) engineer
(B) engineered
(C) engineering
(D) to be engineered

4 명사의 형태

출제포인트 품사나 의미, 단/복수가 헷갈리는 명사들이 종종 문제로 출제된다. 형태가 특이한 명사는 따로 외워 두자.

▶ 품사가 혼동되는 명사

형용사 혹은 동사와 형태가 동일한 명사가 있다. 또한, 형용사처럼 보이는 명사도 있으니 주의해야 한다.

alternative 명 대안 형 대안의	adhesive 명 접착제 형 들러붙는	objective 명 목적 형 객관적인
directive 명 지시 형 지시하는	perspective 명 관점	initiative 명 계획, 주도권
original 명 원본 형 원래의	characteristic 명 특징 형 특유의	estimate 명 견적서 동 견적 내다
increase 명 증가 동 증가하다	decline 명 감소 동 감소하다	visit 명 방문 동 방문하다
permit 명 허가증 동 허가하다	measure 명 수단, 조치 동 측정하다	delay 명 지연 동 지연시키다

▶ 주의해야 할 사람 명사

사람 명사는 가산명사이므로, 단수형일 경우 앞에 한정사 없이 단독으로 쓸 수 없다.

executive 명 중역 형 경영의	representative 명 대표, 직원 형 대표하는	candidate 명 지원자, 후보자
applicant 명 지원자	delegate 명 대표자 동 파견하다	critic 명 비평가
associate 명 동료 동 연관 짓다	graduate 명 졸업생 동 졸업하다	acquaintance 명 지인
resident 명 주민, 거주자	authority 명 권위자	attendant 명 참석자, 승무원

I need to have a meeting with account [**executives** / ~~executive~~] at our advertising agency.
저는 광고 대행사의 광고 기획자(AE)들과 회의를 해야 합니다.

▶ 동명사와 혼동되는 -ing형 명사

-ing형 명사는 동명사와 형태는 같지만 뒤에 목적어가 올 수 없다. 대개 불가산명사이며 앞에 관사나 형용사가 올 수 있다.

seating 명 좌석 배치	ticketing 명 티켓 발급	processing 명 처리	funding 명 재정 지원, 자금
accounting 명 회계	planning 명 계획 수립, 기획	pricing 명 가격 책정	housing 명 주택, 주택 공급

The project was successfully finished thanks to careful [**planning** / ~~plan~~].
프로젝트는 신중한 기획 덕분에 성공적으로 완료되었다.

→ plan은 가산명사로 단수형인 경우 앞에 관사가 필요하다.

고득점 TIP
가산명사로 쓰이는 -ing형 명사도 있다.

openings 명 공석, 개막식	findings 명 발견한 사항	writings 명 저작물, 글	settings 명 장소, 환경

ETS 유형연습

1. Mr. Rouja would like to see all employees take more ------ and develop contacts with potential clients.
   (A) initiative
   (B) initiated
   (C) initiate
   (D) initiating

2. Drevno flooring products are designed for ------ in industrial settings.
   (A) user
   (B) used
   (C) useful
   (D) use

3. The Manila Wellness Center has part-time and temporary employment ------ for certified nursing attendants in our Makati branch.
   (A) opens
   (B) openings
   (C) openness
   (D) opener

ETS 실전문제

1. Recent ------- can learn about employment opportunities in a wide range of industries by attending a career fair.
   (A) graduating
   (B) graduated
   (C) graduates
   (D) graduation

2. The lightbulbs on the Werriver Building's second ------- are scheduled to be replaced this week.
   (A) floor
   (B) floors
   (C) floored
   (D) flooring

3. Parnpradub Graphic Design requires that employees possess advanced technical -------, including proficiency in numerous computer programs.
   (A) expert
   (B) experts
   (C) expertly
   (D) expertise

4. The president announced that a bonus will be awarded to the factory division that has demonstrated the highest ------- over the past year.
   (A) product
   (B) productive
   (C) produce
   (D) productivity

5. A job candidate's interview ------- must be submitted by December 15.
   (A) request
   (B) requested
   (C) requesting
   (D) requesters

6. ------- from the International Society of Engineers met last week to plan next year's conference.
   (A) Representatives
   (B) Representing
   (C) Represented
   (D) Represents

7. The mayor of Brightwood issued a ------- about the city's plans for growth and development.
   (A) declare
   (B) declares
   (C) declared
   (D) declaration

8. To support the school's library, please donate books appropriate for children between the ------- of five and twelve.
   (A) aged
   (B) ages
   (C) agedly
   (D) aging

9. The updated patient portal Web site includes a ------- for communicating with healthcare providers.
   (A) mechanism
   (B) mechanize
   (C) mechanic
   (D) mechanical

10. The fund-raising campaign will help small businesses win cash prizes of up to $1,000 for office -------.
    (A) supply
    (B) supplier
    (C) supplied
    (D) supplies

11. Decide which technology ------- are most important to you before searching for a new automobile.
    (A) optionally
    (B) optional
    (C) option
    (D) options

12. We expect that an ------- search for a new human resources director will begin in September.
    (A) actively
    (B) active
    (C) activate
    (D) activity

13. The company's list of job openings shows several ------- that may appeal to you.

(A) numbers
(B) systems
(C) positions
(D) deadlines

14. Arturo's shoes and belts are made with the highest-quality synthetic -------.

(A) versions
(B) materials
(C) portions
(D) models

Questions 15-18 refer to the following press release.

FOR IMMEDIATE RELEASE

Contact: Jin-Ho Chung, jhchung@elbasinaproperties.com.sg

SINGAPORE (3 June)—This month, Elbasina Properties welcomes Mindy Liu to its executive team. Ms. Liu, who until last month was head of advertising at Iotasoft Technologies, ---15.--- the recently created position of digital media director. Her official start date is 17 June.

"Advertising through social media and other digital outlets is crucial to businesses today," said Elbasina Properties CEO Quiang He. " ---16.--- . Ms. Liu brings an essential skill set we need."

Ms. Liu studied at the Salina Business Academy, where she earned a degree ---17.--- digital advertising. Upon graduating, she secured a position at Iotasoft Technologies. Ms. Liu draws on her ---18.--- crafting major advertising campaigns.

---

15. (A) will assume
(B) had assumed
(C) could assume
(D) was assuming

16. (A) That is why the new role at our company is so important.
(B) Few people can do what she has in a short time.
(C) There are many reasons to use social media.
(D) We have always appreciated Iotasoft's products.

17. (A) onto
(B) to
(C) over
(D) in

18. (A) experiencing
(B) to experience
(C) experienced
(D) experience

UNIT 03 대명사

무료 강의

1 인칭대명사와 소유대명사

출제 포인트 인칭대명사의 격을 구별하는 문제는 거의 매회 출제되며, 인칭대명사가 지칭하는 대상을 확인해야 하는 문제도 간혹 출제된다. 소유대명사는 '소유격+명사' 역할을 한다.

◆ 인칭대명사의 종류

수	인칭/성		인칭대명사			소유대명사
			주격(~은)	소유격(의)	목적격(~을)	(~의 것)
			동사 앞 주어 자리	명사 앞 명사 수식	동사 뒤, 전치사 뒤	주어, 목적어, 보어 자리
단수	1인칭		I	my	me	mine
	2인칭		you	your	you	yours
	3인칭	남성	he	his	him	his
		여성	she	her	her	hers
		사물	it	its	it	-
복수	1인칭		we	our	us	ours
	2인칭		you	your	you	yours
	3인칭(사람/사물)		they	their	them	theirs

The already established companies will be reducing [**their** / ~~them~~] advertising costs.
이미 기반을 잡은 회사들은 그들의 광고 비용을 줄일 것이다.

◆ 소유대명사

소유대명사는 명사 앞에서 명사를 수식할 수 없다. '~의 것'이라고 해석하며, 주어, 목적어, 보어 자리에 두루 사용된다.

Though the president gathered different opinions, the final choice was [**hers** / her].
대표가 다양한 의견을 모았지만, 최종 선택은 그녀의 몫이었다.
→ be동사 뒤 주격 보어 자리에 소유대명사 hers(= her choice)가 사용되었다.

◆ 소유의 의미를 강조하는 one's own

one's own은 '자신만의'라는 의미로 소유격 자리에서 소유격을 대신하거나, 전치사 of 또는 on 뒤에 쓰여 '자기 자신(의 것)' 혹은 '스스로'라는 의미를 나타낸다.

Ms. Lynne decided to quit the job for reasons of [**her own** / ~~herself~~].
린 씨는 자신만의 이유로 일을 그만두기로 결정했다.
→ of와 함께 '그녀 자신의 것(이유)'을 강조하는 her own이 쓰여야 한다.

ETS 유형연습

정답과 해설 p.137

1. Please type your notes from the meeting and distribute ------- to everyone by Friday.
   (A) them
   (B) their
   (C) ourselves
   (D) us

2. As a newly hired accounting associate, Ms. Gu meets with ------- assigned mentor weekly.
   (A) she
   (B) her
   (C) hers
   (D) herself

3. The fast-food giant NuTru claims that our logo is a poorly disguised version of ------- own.
   (A) them
   (B) their
   (C) theirs
   (D) themselves

2 재귀대명사

출제포인트 재귀대명사는 동사의 목적어 자리와 부사 자리에 쓰일 수 있다. 목적격 대명사와 재귀대명사를 구별하는 문제가 자주 출제된다.

◆ 재귀대명사의 종류
재귀대명사는 -self/-selves 형태를 가지며 '(자기) 자신, 직접'을 의미한다. 주어 자리에는 재귀대명사를 쓸 수 없다.

단수					복수		
1인칭	2인칭	3인칭			1인칭	2인칭	3인칭
myself	yourself	himself	herself	itself	ourselves	yourselves	themselves

◆ 재귀적 용법: 동사의 목적어 자리
주어와 목적어가 동일할 때 목적어 자리에 재귀대명사를 쓴다. 인칭대명사의 목적격과 재귀대명사를 구별해야 한다.

Painting is an effective way for **artists** to express [**themselves** / ~~them~~].
그림은 예술가들이 자신을 표현할 수 있는 효과적인 방법이다.
→ to express의 의미상 주어 artists와 목적어 themselves의 지칭 대상이 일치한다.

◆ 강조적 용법: 부사 자리
재귀대명사는 '직접'이라는 의미로 주어나 목적어를 강조한다. 부사 역할을 하는 강조적 용법의 재귀대명사는 생략 가능하다.

Jason Miller conducted the survey and analyzed the results [**himself** / ~~themselves~~].
제이슨 밀러 씨는 직접 설문조사를 시행하고 결과를 분석했다.
→ 재귀대명사 himself가 주어인 Jason Miller를 강조하고 있다.

◆ 관용적 용법: 전치사의 목적어 자리

전치사+재귀대명사

by oneself 혼자서(= alone)	for oneself 혼자 힘으로	in itself 본래	of itself 저절로
to oneself 혼자서만	in spite of oneself 자신도 모르게	between ourselves (우리끼리) 비밀인데	

Dr. Edwards is unable to conduct his studies **by** [**himself** / ~~his own~~] and needs some assistance.
에드워드 박사는 혼자서 연구할 수 없고 도움이 필요하다.

ETS 유형연습
정답과 해설 p.137

1 The laboratory technicians decided to perform the statistical analysis ------- because hiring outside analysts would be too costly.

(A) myself
(B) herself
(C) yourselves
(D) themselves

2 The guests seemed very happy with the meal Chef Mirabel served ------- at the holiday banquet.

(A) they
(B) themselves
(C) their
(D) them

3 Mr. Shin updated the company's Web site by ------- because the other programmer had a problem with her password.

(A) itself
(B) herself
(C) themselves
(D) himself

3 지시대명사

출제포인트 지시대명사에는 this(이것), that(저것), these(이것들), those(저것들)가 있는데, 각 대명사가 지칭하는 대상의 단수/복수를 구별해야 한다. 또한 that, those의 고유한 용법을 기억해야 한다.

◆ those '~하는 사람들'

대명사 those는 뒤에 who, -ing, -ed, 전치사구 등의 수식어구/절을 동반하여 '~하는 사람들'이라는 의미를 나타낼 수 있다.

[**Those** / ~~They~~] **who** are interested in attending the charity event are welcome to e-mail us.
자선 행사 참석에 관심 있는 분들은 저희에게 이메일을 보내 주세요.

[**Those** / ~~They~~] **remaining** in the office are required to leave the building in a few minutes.
사무실에 남아 있는 사람들은 잠시 후 건물을 나가야 한다.

◆ 비교 대상을 지칭하는 that / those

두 대상을 비교하는 문장에서 앞에 언급된 명사를 지칭할 때 단수일 경우에는 that을, 복수일 경우에는 those를 쓴다. that과 those 뒤에는 대체로 수식어가 동반된다.

My relationship with my colleagues is similar to [**that** / ~~it~~] with my classmates at school.
나와 내 동료들과의 관계는 나와 학교 친구들과의 관계와 비슷하다.
→ My relationship을 지칭하는 지시대명사 that을 써야 한다.

The paintings in the room look much better than [**those** / ~~that~~] in the lobby.
방에 있는 그림들이 로비에 있는 그림들보다 훨씬 좋아 보인다.
→ The paintings를 지칭하므로 복수형 those를 써야 한다.

◆ 앞서 언급된 내용을 지칭하는 this / these

this와 these는 앞서 언급된 명사를 대신하는 대명사와 형용사로 쓰일 수 있다. this는 단수형, these는 복수형이다.

The seminar includes group discussions and [**these** / ~~this~~] discussions will be led by the organizer.
세미나는 집단 토론을 포함하며 이 토론들은 주최 측에 의해 진행될 것이다.

ETS 유형연습

정답과 해설 p.138

1. ------ who have not received the conference housing form should report to the registration desk as soon as possible.

   (A) These
   (B) This
   (C) Those
   (D) That

2. Those employees ------ in an assembly area must wear protective gear at all times.

   (A) are working
   (B) have worked
   (C) working
   (D) worked

3. This year's revenue figures from major auto rental agencies are remarkably similar to ------ of the preceding four years.

   (A) those
   (B) that
   (C) them
   (D) this

4 부정대명사

출제포인트 '부정'이란 정해지지 않았다는 뜻으로, 부정대명사는 지칭하는 대상을 명확히 밝히지 않을 때 쓰는 대명사이다. 부정대명사는 수 일치에 주의해야 한다.

▶ 부정대명사

부정대명사는 우리말 의미뿐 아니라 품사와 수 일치를 함께 기억해야 한다.

종류	우리말 의미	품사 대명사	품사 형용사	수 일치 대명사일 때	수 일치 형용사일 때
one	(막연한) 하나(의)	O	O	The new one is different. 단수	one reason 단수
another	(막연한) 또 하나(의)	O	O	Another is expensive. 단수	another reason 단수
other	(막연한) 다른	X	O	X	other reasons 복수 other equipment 불가산명사
the other	(특정 범위의) 나머지(의)	O	O	The other looks good. 단수	the other reason(s) 단수/복수 the other equipment 불가산명사
some	(막연한) 몇몇(의)/약간(의)	O	O	Some are from Europe. 복수	some reasons 복수 some equipment 불가산명사
others	(막연한) 다른 것/사람들	O	X	Others are from America. 복수	X
the others	(특정 범위의) 나머지들	O	X	The others are correct. 복수	X
each other one another	서로	O	X	They helped each other. (주어 자리에 못 씀)	X

▶ 부분을 나타내는 부정대명사

'부정대명사+of+the/소유격+명사' 형태로 사용된다. of the 뒤에 나오는 명사의 종류와 동사의 수가 중요하다.

one ~ 중 하나 either 둘 중 하나	each 각각 *neither 둘 다 (아니다)	of the candidates 복수	is qualified. 3인칭 단수
several ~ 중 몇몇 a few/few ~ 중 몇몇/거의 (아니다)	both 둘 다 many ~ 중 다수	of the candidates 복수	are qualified. 복수
much ~ 중 많은 부분	a little/little ~ 중 약간/거의 (아니다)	of the information 불가산명사	is useful. 3인칭 단수
all ~의 전부 some ~ 중 일부 none ~ 중 아무(것)도 (아니다)	most ~의 대부분 half ~의 절반 any ~ 중 무엇이든지/누구든지	of the candidates 복수	are qualified. 복수
		of the information 불가산명사	is useful. 3인칭 단수

*neither는 단수 주어 취급하지만 비격식 상황에서는 복수 동사와 쓰이기도 한다.

ETS 유형연습

1. ------- of the people involved in developing this software imagined it would become so popular.
   (A) None
   (B) Anybody
   (C) Whoever
   (D) Something

2. Construction of the carpet showroom will be finished by the end of the week, but operations will not begin for ------- month.
   (A) other
   (B) another
   (C) one another
   (D) some other

3. Dr. Hemana and Dr. Wareham, the joint recipients of the Cobalt Research Prize, have known ------- since they were university students in Auckland.
   (A) other one
   (B) another one
   (C) any other
   (D) each other

ETS 실전문제

1. At Stanwick and Associates, we pride ourselves on giving ------- of our clients a personalized wealth-management plan.
   (A) each
   (B) whose
   (C) whatever
   (D) every

2. The Biomedics podcast will cover health-care topics, and ------- first episode will be available on Monday.
   (A) it
   (B) its
   (C) who
   (D) whose

3. Education coordinators at the Parla Museum dedicate ------- to offering stimulating learning opportunities to all visitors.
   (A) themselves
   (B) them
   (C) their
   (D) their own

4. Now that the store manager position is open, Ms. Kim says ------- would like to apply for it.
   (A) she
   (B) her
   (C) hers
   (D) herself

5. Steven Brad, the office manager, requests that all staff communicate directly with ------- about new supply orders.
   (A) he
   (B) his
   (C) him
   (D) his own

6. Although the team worked together to develop the graphics for this report, the text is primarily -------.
   (A) myself
   (B) mine
   (C) me
   (D) my

7. Employees traveling next month must submit ------- itineraries to Ms. Havanian's office by next Friday.
   (A) them
   (B) theirs
   (C) themselves
   (D) their

8. For ------- who want to rest during the flight, our airline provides sleep masks and blankets.
   (A) either
   (B) whichever
   (C) those
   (D) one another

9. The home sales and rental markets should strengthen soon, as ------- usually benefit when the local economy improves.
   (A) it
   (B) both
   (C) that
   (D) which

10. Although Mr. Kim and Ms. Novak have very different skills, ------- would be an asset to the company.
    (A) other
    (B) either
    (C) anybody
    (D) whoever

11. Although he performed the experiment several times, Professor Katakura's results differed from ------- of his colleagues.
    (A) it
    (B) them
    (C) theirs
    (D) those

12. Staff members should work in pairs during the training workshop to help ------- master the procedure for handling customer service inquiries.
    (A) one such
    (B) each other
    (C) yourself
    (D) everything

13. The last customer survey indicated that ------- were dissatisfied with their hotel dining experience.

    (A) much
    (B) many
    (C) somebody
    (D) anybody

14. Instead of sending the entire staff to an outside course to learn the new software, the director decided to train ------- himself.

    (A) ourselves
    (B) anyone
    (C) themselves
    (D) everyone

Questions 15-18 refer to the following e-mail.

To: Nils McCallister <nmccallister@coralmail.com>
From: Tricia Spatz <tspatz@mulltonartscouncil.org>
Date: March 1
Subject: Arts Council board

Dear Mr. McCallister,

It is my pleasure to notify you that you --15.-- for membership on the Board of Trustees of the Mullton Arts Council. For your information, the board is tasked with overseeing the financial operations of the council and organizing important fund-raising events. Board members, of which there are six, decide among --16.-- who will take on key leadership responsibilities. --17.--, board members serve a six-year term and communicate regularly with the executive director, the position I currently hold.

The present board members and I will be meeting on Thursday, March 8, to vote on new members. --18.--.

Many thanks for your consideration,

Tricia Spatz, Executive Director, Mullton Arts Council

---

15. (A) have been nominated
    (B) to be nominated
    (C) has nominated
    (D) are nominating

16. (A) oneself   (B) itself
    (C) yourselves   (D) themselves

17. (A) In other words   (B) Nevertheless
    (C) Furthermore   (D) Likewise

18. (A) We often arrange a catered lunch for this purpose.
    (B) Please reply to this e-mail to indicate acceptance of this offer.
    (C) The Mullton Arts Council has been operating for two decades.
    (D) Meetings are usually held on Mondays, but we will reschedule this.

UNIT 04 형용사

1 형용사의 자리

출제 포인트 명사 앞은 대표적인 형용사 자리이다. 명사를 수식하는 형용사는 2개 이상 연달아 사용할 수 있다. 형용사를 주격 보어, 목적격 보어로 취하는 동사를 외워 두자.

◆ 명사 앞, 명사 뒤

형용사는 명사의 앞이나 뒤에서 수식할 수 있다. 형용사는 2개 이상 연달아 사용할 수 있지만, 관사 앞에는 형용사를 쓸 수 없다.

Thanks to the [**massive** / massively] public **campaign**, more commuters started to use public transportation.
대대적인 공공 캠페인 덕분에, 보다 많은 통근자들이 대중교통을 이용하기 시작했다.
→ 형용사인 massive와 public 둘 다 명사를 수식하고 있다.

Fen Jiang's first attempt at directing a film was [**clearly** / clear] **a** success.
펜 장의 첫 영화 연출 시도는 분명 성공적이었다.
→ 관사 앞에는 형용사를 쓸 수 없다.

◆ 주격 보어

be동사 등 2형식 동사 뒤에는 주어를 보충 설명하는 주격 보어가 나온다. 형용사는 주격 보어 역할을 하며 주어의 상태를 설명한다. (주격 보어를 취하는 동사 목록은 UNIT 01 품사와 문장 구조 참고)

The idea of seeking sponsorship rather than laying off workers **seems** [**persuasive** / persuasively].
직원들을 해고하는 대신 후원을 받아보자는 아이디어가 설득력 있어 보인다.
→ seems는 2형식 동사로 보어 자리에 형용사는 올 수 있지만 부사는 올 수 없다.

◆ 목적격 보어

make 등 5형식 동사의 목적어 뒤에는 목적어를 보충 설명하는 목적격 보어가 나온다. 형용사는 목적격 보어로서 목적어의 상태를 설명할 수 있다. (목적격 보어를 취하는 동사 목록은 UNIT 01 품사와 문장 구조 참고)

Residents **have found** the new recycling program [**convenient** / conveniently].
주민들은 새로운 재활용 프로그램이 편리하다고 생각했다.
→ 동사 have found의 목적격 보어로 the new recycling program의 특징을 설명하는 형용사가 알맞다.

ETS 유형연습

1 Our applicant screening tool matches companies with ------- employees.
   (A) qualified
   (B) qualification
   (C) qualify
   (D) qualifier

2 The architects at Brightman Partners, Inc., design buildings that are elegant as well as -------.
   (A) function
   (B) functioned
   (C) functionality
   (D) functional

3 Critics of the recent movie with Michelle Zhao have called the plot too -------.
   (A) predicting
   (B) predicted
   (C) predictable
   (D) predictably

2 수량/부정형용사

출제 포인트: 수와 양을 나타내는 수량형용사, 정해지지 않은 범위를 지칭하는 부정형용사는 수식하는 명사와 수가 일치되어야 한다. 각각의 형용사에 어울리는 명사형을 외워 두자.

◆ 가산명사의 단수형과 어울리는 형용사

	가산명사의 단수형 (O)	가산명사의 복수형 (×)	불가산명사 (×)
a(n) 하나의 another 또 하나의 each 각각의 every 모든 either 둘 중 하나의	each team	each ~~teams~~	each ~~equipment~~
a/the single 하나의 *앞에 관사 필요 the entire/the whole 전체의 *앞에 관사 필요	the whole team	the whole ~~teams~~	the whole ~~equipment~~

> **고득점 TIP**
> 'every+숫자+복수명사'는 '~마다', 'another+숫자+복수명사'는 '추가적인'이라는 뜻이다.
> every three months 세 달마다   another three months 추가 세 달

◆ 가산명사의 복수형과 어울리는 형용사

	가산명사의 단수형 (×)	가산명사의 복수형 (O)	불가산명사 (×)
many 많은 numerous 많은 several 몇몇의 various 다양한 a few 몇몇의 few 거의 없는 both 둘 다 these 이 those 저 multiple 많은 a couple of 두서넛의 a number of 많은 a series of 일련의 a selection/variety of 다양한	several ~~product~~	several products	several ~~advice~~

◆ 불가산명사와 어울리는 형용사

	가산명사의 단수형 (×)	가산명사의 복수형 (×)	불가산명사 (O)
much 많은 a little 약간의 less 더 적은 little 거의 없는 a great amount/deal of 많은	little ~~question~~	little ~~questions~~	little information

◆ 복수명사, 불가산명사와 어울리는 형용사

	가산명사의 단수형 (×)	가산명사의 복수형 (O)	불가산명사 (O)
all 모든 most 대부분의 other 다른 some 몇몇의 more 더 많은 a lot/plenty of 많은	more ~~survey~~	more surveys	more research

---

ETS 유형연습

정답과 해설 p.141

1. ------- sample from Ando Biology Labs must be kept at the correct temperature.
   (A) All
   (B) Most
   (C) Other
   (D) Every

2. Despite the cost, ------- staff members were in favor of renovating the auditorium.
   (A) mass
   (B) many
   (C) much
   (D) plenty

3. Delmoor Corporation is not responsible for damage caused by misuse, improper care, or ------- consumer negligence.
   (A) another
   (B) the other
   (C) others
   (D) other

3 혼동하기 쉬운 형용사

출제 포인트 끝말의 형태가 특이해 다른 품사로 오해하기 쉬운 형용사를 주의해야 한다. 또한, 같은 어원을 가져 형태는 유사하지만 의미가 다른 형용사를 정확히 구별하여 외워 두자.

◆ 끝말의 형태가 특이한 형용사

형용사는 보통 -ous, -ical, -ful, -able, -ish 등과 같은 끝말이 오지만, 이 밖에도 다양한 형태의 형용사들이 있다.

timely 시기적절한	costly 비용이 많이 드는	likely ~할 것 같은	orderly 질서 정연한	wide 넓은
broad 폭넓은	thorough 철저한	diverse 다양한	distinct 뚜렷한	definite 명확한
adequate 충분한	accurate 정확한	complete 완전한	deliberate 의도적인	delicate 섬세한, 민감한

◆ 형태는 유사하지만 의미가 다른 형용사

respectful attitude 존중하는 태도	informative lecture 유익한 강연	competitive salary 경쟁력 있는 급여
respective rooms 각각의 방들	informed decision 정보에 입각한 결정	competent person 유능한 사람
successful products 성공적인 제품	favorite sport 좋아하는 운동	reliant on exports 수출에 의존하는
successive years 계속되는 해	favorable response 호의적인 반응	reliable source 믿을 만한 소식통
considerate of others 타인을 배려하는	be confident of ~을 믿다, 자신하다	complimentary mug 무료 머그잔
considerable loss 상당한 손해	confidential document 기밀 문서	complementary role 상호보완적 역할
advisory committee 자문 위원회	economic issue 경제 문제	be responsible for ~을 책임지다
It is advisable to ~하는 것이 바람직하다	economical use 경제적인 사용	be responsive to ~에 대응하다

◆ -ing/-ed로 끝나는 형용사

동사에 -ing, -ed를 붙인 분사 형태가 형용사로 굳어져 사용되는 경우가 있다. 감정과 관련된 의미의 -ed 형용사는 보통 사람 명사를 수식한다.

lasting 지속되는	remaining 남아 있는	missing 분실된	rewarding 보람 있는
encouraging 고무적인	deteriorating 악화되는	outstanding 뛰어난	fascinating 매력적인
motivated 의욕적인	distinguished 뛰어난, 유명한	impressed 감동받은	satisfied 만족하는
qualified 자격을 갖춘	limited 제한된	unprecedented 유례없는	repeated 반복적인

ETS 유형연습

1 The ------- attractions of the Hale Valley continue to delight visitors and residents.
   (A) diversification
   (B) diversifying
   (C) diverse
   (D) diversity

2 All passengers should be ------- of others by speaking softly when talking on mobile phones.
   (A) considerable
   (B) considering
   (C) considerate
   (D) consideration

3 Enclosed is the latest listing of the ------- companies and institutions that use our firm's specialized consulting services.
   (A) distinguishably
   (B) distinguishability
   (C) distinguished
   (D) distinguish

4 형용사 빈출 표현

출제 포인트 시험에 자주 나오는 'be+형용사+전치사', 'be+형용사+to부정사' 표현을 외워 두자.

◆ 'be+형용사+전치사' 빈출 표현

be responsible for ~에 책임이 있다	be eligible for ~ 자격이 있다 (= be entitled to 명사)	be related to 명사 ~와 관련되다 (= be associated with)
be notable for ~로 유명하다 (= be renowned for)	be accustomed/used to 명사 ~에 익숙하다 (= be familiar with)	be aware of ~을 알고 있다 (= be conscious of)
be compliant with ~을 따르다	be appreciative of ~을 감사하다	be accessible to 명사 ~에 접근 가능하다
be open to 명사 ~에 열려 있다	be comparable to 명사 ~에 필적하다	be compared with ~와 비교되다
be compatible with ~와 호환 가능하다	be indicative of ~을 나타내다	be exempt from ~을 면제받다
be representative of ~을 대표하다	be contingent on ~에 달려 있다	be consistent with ~와 일치하다

◆ 'be+형용사+to부정사' 빈출 표현

be reluctant to do ~하기를 꺼리다	be eager to do ~하기를 열망하다	be pleased to do ~해서 기쁘다
be hesitant to do ~하기를 주저하다	be eligible to do ~할 자격이 있다	be entitled to do ~할 자격이 있다

We are [**pleased** / ~~indicative~~] **to introduce** the new marketing director.
우리는 신임 마케팅 이사를 소개하게 되어 기쁩니다.

◆ 기타 주의해야 할 형용사의 용법

형용사	특징	예
possible 가능한	사람을 수식할 수 없다.	a **possible** [merger / ~~supervisor~~]
following 다음의	앞에 반드시 the를 써야 한다.	the **following** year
upcoming 다가오는	명사는 미래에 일어날 일이다.	the **upcoming** election
sincere 진실한	감정과 관련된 명사와 쓴다.	our **sincere** apologies
diverse 다양한	단수 명사와 함께 쓸 수 있다.	a **diverse** world

Ron Wiseman was invited to speak at a conference [**next** / ~~following~~] Monday.
론 와이즈먼은 다음 월요일 회의에서 연설하도록 요청받았다.
→ 앞에 the가 없으므로 following은 쓸 수 없다.

ETS 유형연습

1 According to company guidelines, new employees are ------- to receive vacation benefits after three months of full-time employment.
(A) capable
(B) variable
(C) flexible
(D) eligible

2 All passengers are responsible ------- obtaining proper travel documents before departure.
(A) for
(B) to
(C) in
(D) with

3 Please accept our ------- thanks for the fine work you are doing in our sales department.
(A) original
(B) estimated
(C) sincere
(D) completed

1. Employees should keep the keys to the file cabinets in a ------- location at all times.
   (A) safe
   (B) safety
   (C) safest
   (D) safely

2. Local manufacturers have been ------- to hire additional employees until productivity improves.
   (A) hesitate
   (B) hesitation
   (C) hesitated
   (D) hesitant

3. The next payment for your subscription is scheduled for ------- withdrawal from your bank account on June 15.
   (A) automatically
   (B) automation
   (C) automatic
   (D) automate

4. The candidate for the administrative assistant position must have strong ------- skills.
   (A) organizational
   (B) organizationally
   (C) organizes
   (D) organize

5. Luben's Business Central sells a ------- range of attractive yet functional office furniture.
   (A) comprehensive
   (B) comprehensively
   (C) comprehend
   (D) comprehension

6. The loan application process at Palau Bay Bank is very -------.
   (A) efficient
   (B) efficiency
   (C) efficiently
   (D) efficiencies

7. ------- employees who wish to volunteer for the book-sale event should sign up by Friday.
   (A) Everyone
   (B) Which
   (C) Those
   (D) Whoever

8. A new version of the program is now readily ------- at the Reyan Software download site.
   (A) accessibility
   (B) accesses
   (C) access
   (D) accessible

9. Several supervisors have complained that the unscheduled maintenance has been ------- to vehicle assembly.
   (A) disruptive
   (B) disruptions
   (C) disrupt
   (D) disrupted

10. In order to keep prices -------, Kim's Bakery will begin making its breads and cakes on the premises.
    (A) reasonable
    (B) reasonably
    (C) reasoning
    (D) reason

11. Third-party inspection of Accuceutical Corporation's clinical laboratory takes place ------- three months.
    (A) enough
    (B) every
    (C) several
    (D) some

12. *Desk Job*, which opened last night at Roundel Theater, tells a ------- story about an office worker whose daydreams come to life.
    (A) mover
    (B) movement
    (C) movingly
    (D) moving

13. Passengers are asked to form an ------- line at the gate ten minutes before boarding begins.

(A) orderly (B) excessive
(C) opposite (D) accidental

14. Last week's ------- weather interfered with MacMillan Florist's home deliveries.

(A) severe (B) strategic
(C) full (D) detailed

Questions 15-18 refer to the following posting.

Bus drivers wanted!

The Bartley School District is currently hiring bus drivers. Only part-time positions --15-- available. We are seeking both new and experienced bus drivers. As long as you have held a driver's license for at least three years, you are encouraged to apply. --16-- .

Bartley School District offers --17-- wages for all our employees. --18-- , we extend an option to drivers to earn extra money by taking extra bus routes throughout the school year. If you have an interest in joining our team, please call Soo-Min Lim at 904-555-0125 for more details.

---

15. (A) are
(B) were
(C) have been
(D) will have been

16. (A) Applications are due today.
(B) Opportunities for promotions are available.
(C) We will provide any necessary training.
(D) Bus drivers are a necessary part of our school community.

17. (A) compete
(B) competing
(C) competition
(D) competitive

18. (A) If not
(B) In addition
(C) Above all
(D) Once again

UNIT 05 부사

1 부사의 자리

출제 포인트 부사는 동사, 형용사, 부사, 전치사구 등을 수식하며, 수식어이기 때문에 생략해도 문장 구조가 달라지지 않는다.
부사 자리를 찾는 문제는 출제 빈도가 높고 난도가 낮은 편이므로 반드시 다 맞힐 수 있도록 하자.

◆ 주어와 동사 사이
빈칸 앞이 주어, 뒤가 동사이면 빈칸에는 부사가 들어갈 수 있다.

A travel agent [**mistakenly** / ~~mistakes~~] **cancelled** my flight and hotel reservation.
여행사 직원이 나의 항공권 예약과 호텔 예약을 실수로 취소했다.

◆ 동사구 사이
동사가 두 단어 이상으로 이루어져 있는 경우, 동사구 사이에 빈칸이 있으면 부사 자리이다.

All public facilities **must be** [**fully** / ~~full~~] **equipped** for convenience of the disabled.
모든 공공시설은 장애인의 편의를 위한 시설을 완비해야 한다.

◆ 자동사 뒤
부사는 자동사 뒤에서 동사를 수식할 수 있고, 'be+p.p.' 형태의 수동태 뒤에서도 동사를 수식할 수 있다.

Sales of the latest computer game **rose** [**significantly** / ~~significance~~] last week.
최근 발매된 컴퓨터 게임의 매출액이 지난주에 눈에 띄게 증가했다.

◆ 형용사, 부사, 전치사, 접속사 앞
부사는 형용사, 부사, 전치사, 접속사 앞에 올 수 있다.

The two opposing parties have not found a [**mutually** / ~~mutual~~] **agreeable** solution yet.
반대 의견을 가진 양측은 서로 동의할 만한 해결책을 아직 찾아내지 못했다.
→ 부사 mutually가 형용사 agreeable을 앞에서 수식하고 있다.

◆ 준동사 앞
부사는 준동사인 to부정사, 동명사, 분사를 수식할 수 있다.

Mr. Oman is responsible for [**regularly** / ~~regular~~] **checking** the medical equipment in the clinic.
오만 씨는 병원 내 의료 장비를 정기적으로 점검하는 일을 담당하고 있다.
→ 동명사를 수식할 수 있는 것은 부사이다.

ETS 유형연습

정답과 해설 p.144

1. Ms. Sato ------- monitors the newspapers for reviews of her new play.
   (A) close
   (B) closer
   (C) closest
   (D) closely

2. The mayor's office will be ------- closed for a few hours on Monday for a special event.
   (A) briefer
   (B) briefest
   (C) briefly
   (D) brief

3. To prevent overheating, avoid running your spice grinder ------- for more than two minutes.
   (A) continues
   (B) continuing
   (C) continuous
   (D) continuously

2 시간부사와 빈도부사

출제 포인트 시간을 나타내는 시간부사는 동사 시제와 어울리는지가 중요하고, 빈도를 나타내는 빈도부사는 위치가 중요하다.

▶ 시간부사

시간을 의미하는 부사는 해석하기 전에 동사의 시제가 부사의 시간 표현과 어울리는지 먼저 확인해야 한다.

❶ already 이미 / **still** 여전히 / **yet** 아직 (~ 않다)

already는 주로 현재완료형(have p.p.) 동사와 쓰인다. still은 부정문일 때 'still+not'의 어순으로 사용된다.
yet은 'have not p.p. ~ yet' 또는 'have[be] yet to(아직 ~하지 않았다)' 구문으로 출제된다.

The office furniture arrived this morning, but it **has not been assembled** [**yet** / already / still].
사무용 가구는 오늘 아침에 도착했지만, 아직 조립되지는 않았다.

The maintenance workers **have** [**already** / still / yet] **inspected** the security system.
관리 직원들은 보안 시스템을 이미 점검했다.

❷ now / currently / presently 지금, 현재

'현재'를 의미하는 부사는 현재, 현재진행(is/are -ing) 동사와 함께 쓴다.

The analysts **are** [**currently** / previously] **reviewing** the data gathered by surveillance cameras.
분석가들은 현재 감시 카메라가 수집한 정보를 검토하고 있다.

❸ ago 전에(과거) / **recently**(= lately) 최근에(과거, 현재완료)

ago는 과거 동사와 어울리며 '기간+ago' 형태로 쓰인다. recently는 과거, 현재완료 동사와 모두 어울린다.

Five new interns **were hired** by the advertising agency **some time** [**ago** / recently].
얼마 전에 광고회사에 다섯 명의 새 인턴사원이 채용되었다.

▶ 빈도부사

빈도부사는 be동사나 조동사 뒤, 일반동사 앞에 온다. 이 중 일부는 문장 앞이나 끝에 올 수 있다.

0%						100%
never 결코 ~ 않다	**hardly / rarely / scarcely / seldom** 거의 ~ 않다	**sometimes** 가끔	**usually / regularly** 보통	**often** 자주	**always** 항상	

Visitors [**always** / even] **express** their amazement at how sophisticated the ancient temple is.
방문객들은 고대 사원이 얼마나 정교한지에 대해 언제나 놀라움을 표현한다.

ETS 유형연습

정답과 해설 p.144

1 The central accounting office has ------- not released the annual spending figures for last year.

(A) once
(B) soon
(C) almost
(D) still

2 Due to technical problems, Nelson's Electronic Auctions is ------- not accepting any picture submissions via e-mail.

(A) quickly
(B) currently
(C) precisely
(D) temperately

3 With panels of sheer blue fabric hanging from its ceiling, the Nordaris Café is ------- mistaken for an art gallery.

(A) often
(B) prior to
(C) usual
(D) if only

3 주의해야 할 부사 1

출제 포인트 형태는 비슷하지만 의미가 전혀 다른 부사, 명사구 앞에서 의미를 강조하는 부사, 특정 수식 대상과 함께 쓰는 부사 등 주의해야 할 부사들이 있다.

◆ 형태는 비슷하지만 의미가 다른 부사

| even 심지어 – evenly 공평하게 | hard 열심히 – hardly 거의 ~ 않다 | close 가까이에 – closely 자세히 |
| high 높이 – highly 매우 | late 늦게 – lately 최근에 | |

Many of the manufacturing staff have worked overtime to meet the demand [**lately** / ~~late~~].
많은 제조 직원들이 수요를 맞추기 위해 최근 초과 근무를 했다.

◆ 명사구를 강조하는 부사

| only 오직 | just 단지 | quite 완전히 | even 심지어 |

The directions for Masuda's do-it-yourself projects are comprehensive enough for [**even** / ~~right~~] **a novice builder**.
마스다의 DIY 프로젝트 설명서는 초보 건축가조차 이해할 수 있을 만큼 충분히 자세하다.

◆ 숫자, 수량을 수식하는 부사

| approximately / roughly / around / about / almost / nearly 거의, 대략 | over / more than ~ 이상 |
| barely / only / just / at (the) most / no more than 겨우 | at (the very) least 최소한, 적어도 |

[**About** / ~~By~~] 50 percent of the participants gave positive reviews to our product demonstration.
약 50퍼센트의 참가자들이 우리의 제품 시연에 대해 긍정적인 평가를 해주었다.
→ about은 숫자를 수식하는 부사로 쓸 수 있다.

◆ 증가, 감소, 변화의 동사를 수식하는 부사

| considerably / significantly / substantially 상당히 | steadily 꾸준히 | gradually 점차적으로 |
| sharply / noticeably / remarkably / dramatically 급격하게, 두드러지게 | greatly 크게 | slightly 약간 |

The sales of organic foods **increased** [**remarkably** / ~~nearly~~] with rising health care demand.
건강 관리 수요가 증가함에 따라 유기농 식품 판매량이 눈에 띄게 증가했다.
→ nearly는 '거의'라는 뜻의 부사로 숫자 등의 수식 대상이 뒤에 나온다.

ETS 유형연습

정답과 해설 p.144

1 The X200's crisp, film-like images prove that it is the most ------- advanced digital camera on the market.

(A) high (B) higher
(C) highly (D) highest

2 There are currently ------- two Ian's Tool Shed stores in County Cork.

(A) only (B) including
(C) might (D) else

3 If companies standardize their products instead of offering different versions of the same product, they will be able to reduce their expenses ------- .

(A) signify (B) to signify
(C) significantly (D) significant

4 주의해야 할 부사 2

출제포인트 특별한 쓰임새가 있는 부사들이 있다. 각 부사의 대표적인 용례를 기억해 두자. 접속부사는 접속사가 아닌 부사인 점에 유의한다.

◆ 형용사, 부사를 수식하는 부사

| very / fairly / quite / highly 매우 |
| extremely / incredibly / overly / exceptionally 극도로 | *형용사, 부사를 수식할 수 있지만 동사를 수식할 수 없다. |

The recent presentation on sales strategies was [**quite** / ~~well~~] **informative**.
영업 전략에 대한 최근의 발표는 상당히 유익했다.

| much / still / even / far / a lot 훨씬 | *비교급 표현 앞에서 형용사, 부사를 수식하며 '훨씬'이라고 해석한다. |

The fact that the prices are very unstable makes the study [**much** / ~~very~~] **harder**.
가격이 매우 불안정하다는 사실은 연구를 훨씬 더 어렵게 만든다.

| too 너무 | too ~ to ... 너무 ~해서 …할 수 없다 | far/much too 너무, 지나치게 | |
| so 매우 | so ~ that ... 너무 ~해서 …하다 | enough 충분히 | enough to ~할 만큼 충분히 |

Some models are [**so** / ~~too~~] popular **that** manufacturers are unable to keep up with the demand.
몇몇 제품은 너무 인기가 많아서 제조업체가 수요를 따라잡을 수 없다.

◆ 기타 주의해야 할 부사

| ever (부정문, 조건문, 비교 구문) 한 번이라도, 여태까지 | hardly ever 좀처럼 ~ 않다 | ever since ~ 이후로 지금까지 |
| well (분사 수식) 잘, (전치사구 수식) 훨씬 | well ahead of schedule 일정보다 훨씬 앞서 | |

The relations between management and employees are now stronger **than** [**ever** / ~~then~~].
경영진과 직원 사이의 관계가 어느 때보다 더 굳건하다.

◆ 접속부사

| however 그러나 | meanwhile 한편, 그동안 | besides 게다가 | moreover / furthermore 게다가 |
| therefore 그러므로 | then 그러고 나서 | likewise 마찬가지로 | nevertheless / nonetheless 그럼에도 불구하고 |

The director is eager to expand into China, [**but** / ~~however~~] **he doesn't have** any specific plans.
이사는 중국으로 확장하기를 원하지만, 구체적인 계획을 가지고 있지 않다.

→ 접속부사는 문법적으로 부사이기 때문에 뒤에 '주어+동사'를 포함하는 절을 이끌 수 없다.

ETS 유형연습

1. Market research results for Thermabrite's new handheld thermometer prototype were ------- encouraging.
   (A) well
   (B) near
   (C) freely
   (D) very

2. For the period ending June 30, the Horizon Stadium Corporation recorded unprecedented revenues from ticket sales, and ------- more from advertising.
   (A) all
   (B) very
   (C) any
   (D) even

3. Nonaka Consultancy's strength lies in its accomplished team of data analysts, and ------- the company highlights its analytic services when seeking new clients.
   (A) therefore
   (B) now that
   (C) in case
   (D) otherwise

ETS 실전문제

1. Volunteers should arrive ------- for the event and use the parking area behind the building.
   (A) prompt
   (B) prompted
   (C) promptly
   (D) promptness

2. All interns are expected to complete daily tasks -------.
   (A) effective
   (B) effectively
   (C) effectual
   (D) effects

3. Groford Corporation's regulations mandate that ------- licensed and insured contractors be hired.
   (A) much
   (B) only
   (C) whose
   (D) unless

4. Mr. Kwon ------- suggests hiring a second engineer for the research and development team.
   (A) strength
   (B) strengthen
   (C) strongly
   (D) stronger

5. ------- after graduating from Pellenem University, classmates Trevor Thorsen and Heidi Smith cofounded a consulting firm.
   (A) As soon as
   (B) Provided that
   (C) Shortly
   (D) Despite

6. Exploring the caves along the coast has become an ------- popular recreational pursuit.
   (A) increases
   (B) increased
   (C) increasingly
   (D) increase

7. The Queensland Transport Authority urges all motorists to obey the rules of the road and always drive -------.
   (A) safest
   (B) safety
   (C) safely
   (D) safeness

8. Mr. Vance is an excellent supervisor, and the staff members appreciate how ------- he reacts in an emergency.
   (A) calmed
   (B) calmly
   (C) calmer
   (D) calmest

9. This bus stop will be closed for ------- one year during construction at the Juring Medical Center.
   (A) approximate
   (B) approximated
   (C) approximation
   (D) approximately

10. To apply for membership, ------- complete the form on the society's Web site.
    (A) simple
    (B) simply
    (C) simplify
    (D) simplicity

11. ------- demonstrating an impressive work ethic, Ms. Hyun often takes on extra projects in addition to her regular workload.
    (A) Consistently
    (B) Consistency
    (C) Consisted
    (D) Consistent

12. The statistics on library visitors are now robust ------- to forecast library usage on a seasonal basis.
    (A) enough
    (B) much
    (C) as well as
    (D) between

13. The CEO of Oshida Tech, Mr. Ignacio, tends to avoid publicity and is ------- seen in public.
    (A) evenly
    (B) rarely
    (C) nicely
    (D) already

14. The dishwasher dispenser should be filled with Kleen Choice detergent ------- for spot-free dishes.
    (A) comparably
    (B) regularly
    (C) strongly
    (D) wetly

Questions 15-18 refer to the following advertisement.

Is It Time for Your Business to Rebrand?

With styles and products constantly changing, a business must reinvent ---15.--- from time to time. To keep up with current business trends, your brand must appear modern and relevant. For over twenty years, Tradaelia has helped companies develop a new ---16.--- . From beginning to end, we help companies analyze the steps needed to change their company's image ---17.--- .

---18.--- . For a free initial assessment, contact us at 713-555-0172.

---

15. (A) it
    (B) some
    (C) itself
    (D) ourselves

16. (A) staff
    (B) identity
    (C) offering
    (D) process

17. (A) succeed
    (B) successful
    (C) succeeding
    (D) successfully

18. (A) Strong brands were difficult to develop and maintain.
    (B) Joe Tradaelia started the company in his garage.
    (C) Let Tradaelia help you stand out from the competition.
    (D) Note that not all rebranding efforts end favorably.

UNIT 06 동사의 형태와 종류

무료 강의

1 동사의 형태

출제포인트 동사는 문장의 필수 구성 성분일 뿐 아니라 문장 구조를 만드는 데 가장 중요한 역할을 한다. 동사의 형태와 형태별 쓰임을 알아야 문장을 정확히 파악할 수 있다.

◆ 동사원형

주어가 3인칭 단수가 아닌 경우, 즉 1, 2인칭이거나 3인칭 복수일 때 현재 시제는 동사원형을 쓴다. 이 밖에 동사원형을 쓰는 대표적인 경우는 명령문, 조동사 뒤, 주장/요구/명령/제안의 동사 뒤 that절, 사역동사의 목적격 보어 자리이다.

The wedding and reception **will** [**take place** / ~~taking place~~] in the Grand Hall at Shelton Hotel.
결혼식과 피로연은 셸턴 호텔의 대연회장에서 열릴 것이다.
→ 조동사 will 뒤에 동사원형이 나와야 한다.

The president firmly **requested that** the authorities [**regulate** / ~~regulated~~] its copyright laws.
사장은 당국이 저작권법을 규제해야 한다고 강력하게 요구했다.
→ request, suggest 같은 요청, 제안의 동사 뒤에 오는 that절에는 'should+동사원형'이나 '동사원형'을 쓴다.

◆ 완료형

완료형은 'have+과거분사(p.p.)' 형태이며 타동사의 완료형은 뒤에 목적어가 필요하다. have 뒤에 빈칸을 두고 p.p. 형태를 채우는 문제가 종종 출제된다.

The snow sculptures **have** [**attracted** / ~~attractions~~] many tourists throughout the winter.
눈 조각품들이 겨울 내내 많은 관광객들을 끌어모았다.
→ 완료형 동사 have attracted 뒤에 목적어인 many tourists가 왔다. have attractions 뒤에는 목적어가 올 수 없다.

◆ 진행형

진행형은 'be+현재분사(-ing)' 형태이며 타동사의 진행형은 뒤에 목적어가 필요하다.

The director **is** [**producing** / ~~productive~~] an independent film about small business owners.
그 영화감독은 소상공인에 관한 독립 영화를 제작 중이다.
→ 진행형 동사 is producing 뒤에 목적어인 an independent film이 왔다. is productive 뒤에는 목적어가 올 수 없다.

ETS 유형연습

정답과 해설 p.147

1. Many companies have strongly ------- several provisions in the new government tax plan.
   (A) critical
   (B) criticism
   (C) criticizing
   (D) criticized

2. The senior project manager will be on-site next Thursday and has requested that the editors ------- him in his office at 9:30 A.M.
   (A) meet
   (B) met
   (C) have met
   (D) will meet

3. The Desorbo Company will be ------- its new leather boots in the fall catalog.
   (A) introduce
   (B) introducing
   (C) introduces
   (D) introduced

2 자동사와 타동사

> **출제포인트** 자동사는 목적어를 바로 취할 수 없고, 타동사는 목적어가 필요하다. 자동사는 함께 쓰이는 전치사를 알아야 한다. 또한, 의미가 비슷한 자동사와 타동사에 주의한다.

◆ 자동사

자동사 뒤에는 목적어 역할을 하는 명사가 바로 나올 수 없다. 자동사 뒤에 목적어가 오려면 전치사가 필요하다.

rise 오르다	appear 나타나다	exist 존재하다
vary 다양하다	expire 만료되다	participate in ~에 참가하다
specialize in ~을 전문으로 하다	apply for ~에 지원하다	commute to ~로 통근하다
subscribe to ~을 구독하다	adhere to ~을 고수하다	depart from ~에서 출발하다
benefit from ~로부터 혜택을 얻다	belong to ~에 속하다	make up for ~을 보상하다
refrain from ~을 삼가다	qualify for ~의 자격이 있다	coincide with ~와 동시에 일어나다
depend/rely on ~에 의존하다	focus on ~에 집중하다	comply with ~을 따르다
refer to ~을 참조하다	conform to ~을 따르다	consent to ~에 동의하다
succeed in ~에서 성공하다	result in/from ~하게 되다/~ 때문이다	agree with/on ~에 동의하다
cooperate with ~와 협력하다	compete with ~와 경쟁하다	enroll (in)/register for ~에 등록하다

◆ 타동사

타동사는 뒤에 목적어가 필요하고, 전치사구는 목적어를 대신할 수 없다.

discuss ~을 토론하다	attend ~에 참석하다	adopt ~을 채택하다	accompany ~와 동반하다
answer ~에 답하다	access ~에 접근하다	exceed ~을 초과하다	comprise ~로 구성되다

Business leaders gathered to [**discuss** / ~~talk~~] **the main issues** related to a new business.
경영진은 새로운 사업에 관련된 주요 쟁점을 논의하기 위해 모였다.

→ 자동사 talk은 바로 뒤에 목적어를 쓸 수 없고 to, with, about 등의 전치사와 함께 쓴다.

◆ 혼동하기 쉬운 자동사와 타동사

~을 기다리다 ㉧ await ㉨ wait for	~을 매료시키다 ㉧ attract ㉨ appeal to	~에 도착하다 ㉧ reach ㉨ arrive at/in
~을 야기하다 ㉧ cause ㉨ lead to	~에 반대하다 ㉧ oppose ㉨ object to	~로 구성되다 ㉧ comprise ㉨ consist of
~을 처리하다 ㉧ handle ㉨ deal with	~을 방해하다 ㉧ interrupt ㉨ interfere with	~을 설명하다 ㉧ explain ㉨ account for

Local people [**object** / ~~oppose~~] **to** building a shopping center near the national park.
지역 주민들은 국립 공원 근처에 쇼핑센터를 짓는 것에 반대한다.

→ 뒤에 전치사 to가 있으므로 자동사 object가 와야 한다.

ETS 유형연습

정답과 해설 p.147

1 Preparing a budget encourages an executive to ------- several options before deciding on a course of action.
(A) think
(B) reply
(C) inquire
(D) examine

2 To ------- for the local-shopper discount, customers must show proof of residency.
(A) qualify
(B) award
(C) experience
(D) certify

3 All new employees are required to ------- in the three-day orientation.
(A) attend
(B) take
(C) inquire
(D) participate

3 4형식 동사와 5형식 동사

출제 포인트 4형식 동사는 목적어를 두 개 취하고, 5형식 동사는 목적어 뒤에 목적격 보어가 온다. 4형식 동사와 5형식 동사의 특징을 알아 두자.

◆ 목적어를 두 개 가지는 4형식 동사

4형식 동사는 2개의 목적어를 가진다. '~에게'에 해당하는 간접 목적어 뒤에 '~을/를'에 해당하는 직접 목적어가 온다.

give 주다   offer 제공하다   send 보내다   bring 가져다주다   award 수여하다   grant 허가하다   show 보여주다

Mr. Wilson has [**offered** / ~~provided~~] investors reliable investment advice.
윌슨 씨는 투자자들에게 믿을 만한 투자 조언을 제공해 왔다.
→ offer 뒤에 간접 목적어(investors)와 직접 목적어(investment advice)가 왔다. provide A with B: A에게 B를 제공하다

사람 목적어를 취하는 동사

| inform 알리다 | notify 알리다 | remind 상기시키다 | convince 설득하다 |
| assure 확신시키다 | brief 간략히 말하다 | tell 말해주다 | warn 경고하다 |

The manager [**notified** / ~~said~~] the team that the meeting was canceled.
관리자는 팀에게 회의가 취소되었음을 알렸다.
→ 사람 목적어를 취하고 뒤에 that절이나 전치사구를 동반하는 동사들에 유의한다.

◆ 목적격 보어를 취하는 5형식 동사

대표적인 5형식 동사들은 목적어 뒤에 목적격 보어로 to부정사를 취할 수 있다. 수동태가 되면 수동태 동사 뒤에 to부정사가 온다.

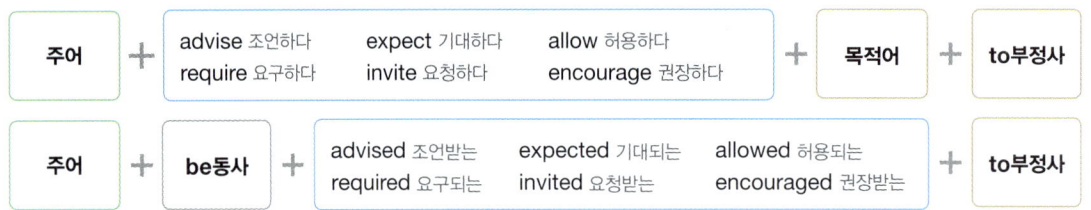

목적격 보어는 동사와 목적어에 따라 다양한 형태가 있다.

동사	목적어	목적격 보어
keep, find, consider, make make, have, let get, have, keep, leave	the presentation 명사 patients 사람 명사 the door 사물 명사	impressive 형용사 take a short walk 동사원형 locked 과거분사

ETS 유형연습
정답과 해설 p.147

1 To avoid leaving anyone behind, the tour operator ------ all the visitors to be in the front lobby by 7 A.M.

(A) recalled
(B) memorized
(C) reminded
(D) identified

2 Mr. Kawano wants the staff to ------ him of any flaws that they see in the store's display furniture.

(A) supply
(B) inform
(C) reply
(D) notice

3 All employees working in the assembly area will be ------ to take a course on machine operation.

(A) recognized
(B) required
(C) given
(D) grown

4 주의해야 할 동사

> **출제포인트** 명사로도 쓰이는 동사, 감정 유발 동사와 더불어 '타동사+목적어+전치사' 관용 표현을 알아 두자.

◆ 명사로도 쓰이는 동사

review	통 검토하다	review the decision	명 검토, 평가	an annual review
permit	통 허가하다	permit us to build	명 허가증	a building permit
access	통 접근하다	access the data	명 (불가산) 접근	access to the Internet
influence	통 영향을 미치다	influence the results	명 영향	have an influence on the results
manufacture	통 제조하다	manufacture products	명 제조(품)	car manufacture

Plastic is widely used in the [**manufacture** / ~~manufacturer~~] of the kitchen utensils.
플라스틱은 주방 용품의 제조에 폭넓게 사용된다.
→ manufacture가 '제조'라는 의미의 명사로도 쓰일 수 있음을 유념한다. manufacturer는 '제조업체'를 뜻하는 명사이다.

◆ 감정 유발 동사

감정 유발 동사는 '(감정을 느끼게) 만들다'라고 해석한다. 주어가 감정을 유발하면 능동태, 감정을 느끼면 수동태로 쓴다. 따라서 주로 사물 주어일 때는 능동태가, 사람 주어일 때는 수동태가 쓰인다.

surprise ~을 놀라게 하다	impress ~을 감동시키다	delight ~을 기쁘게 하다	fascinate ~을 매혹시키다
satisfy ~을 만족시키다	interest ~에게 흥미를 갖게 하다	please ~을 기쁘게 하다	depress ~을 낙담시키다
frustrate ~을 좌절시키다	disappoint ~을 실망시키다	confuse ~을 혼란스럽게 하다	worry ~을 걱정시키다

Most customers that we surveyed were [**satisfied** / ~~satisfying~~] with Barlow's Window Designs.
우리가 조사한 대부분의 고객은 바로우 윈도우 디자인에 만족했다.

◆ '타동사+목적어+전치사' 관용 표현

clear/deprive A of B A에게서 B를 치우다/빼앗다	inform/notify A of/about B A에게 B에 대해 알려주다	acquaint A with B A가 B를 잘 알게 하다
prevent/stop/keep A from B A가 B하지 못하게 하다	distinguish/tell A from B A와 B를 구별하다	provide/supply A with B A에게 B를 제공하다
charge A for B B에 대해 A를 부과하다	honor/recognize/blame A for B B에 대해 A를 칭찬하다/인정하다/비난하다	replace A with B A를 B로 교체하다
contribute A to B B에 A를 기여하다	attribute A to B A를 B 때문이라고 여기다	associate A with B A와 B를 결부하다

ETS 유형연습

1. Please be aware that annual ------- of job performance will take place during the third week of January.
   (A) reviews
   (B) reviewed
   (C) reviewer
   (D) reviewers

2. Our chief operating officer was very ------- by the latest sales figures.
   (A) impress
   (B) impressing
   (C) impressed
   (D) impressive

3. All commercial catering businesses refrigerate perishable food to ------- it from spoiling.
   (A) remove
   (B) oppose
   (C) prevent
   (D) forbid

ETS 실전문제

1. With the Alli-Tekk software package, files can ------- easily among several users.
   (A) sharing
   (B) to share
   (C) be shared
   (D) being shared

2. Although we have ------- not to offer you a position at this time, we will keep your résumé on file for future openings.
   (A) decided
   (B) deciding
   (C) decision
   (D) decidedly

3. Mr. Osaki would like the entire staff ------- together and complete the task by the deadline.
   (A) works
   (B) be working
   (C) to work
   (D) will work

4. To celebrate World Health Day, all employees are ------- to replace their sugary snacks with fruits and vegetables.
   (A) encourage
   (B) encouraging
   (C) encouragement
   (D) encouraged

5. Because small businesses can ------- from working with each other, many owners find it helpful to join local business associations.
   (A) benefit
   (B) serve
   (C) assist
   (D) help

6. For a limited time, Becker Street Electronics will ------- shipping costs on all TX266 cameras as part of the July sale.
   (A) proceed
   (B) hesitate
   (C) displace
   (D) waive

7. Textile products shipped overseas must ------- with all international labeling requirements.
   (A) comply
   (B) confront
   (C) update
   (D) assign

8. Employees of Osijek Systems were ------- at the board of directors' decision to make Sasha Vasilev the new vice president.
   (A) surprise
   (B) surprising
   (C) surprised
   (D) surprises

9. Judith Cooke, the manager of the sales department, will inform you ------- the exact shipment date by tomorrow morning.
   (A) of
   (B) along
   (C) over
   (D) through

10. Ms. Rafferty's references noted her strong work ethic, but directors feel she ------- the skills for the position.
    (A) lacks
    (B) pretends
    (C) removes
    (D) vacates

11. Marburg Electro Company is ------- to report a significant increase in profits for the year.
    (A) earned
    (B) outgrown
    (C) expected
    (D) risen

12. An article in *Business Epoch* magazine ------- that textile prices will stabilize within two years.
    (A) waits
    (B) issues
    (C) results
    (D) predicts

13. From among 25 nominated bank managers, the awards committee ------- Mr. Arjun Patel as manager of the year.

(A) began
(B) explained
(C) chose
(D) left

14. Although the new design is highly innovative, it would be too costly for us to ------- with development at this time.

(A) examine
(B) treat
(C) urge
(D) proceed

Questions 15-18 refer to the following e-mail.

To: info@kathyscaterers.com
From: jberthel@bertheltech.com
Date: December 1
Subject: Event catering inquiry

To whom it may concern,

I am currently planning my company's annual holiday party. All of the reviews that I have ------- about your catering company are very positive. However, before I make a final decision, I have a few ------- .
15.
16.

Are you available to cater for 25 people on Friday, December 16? The event will take place in my company's building at 138 Larrington Avenue. Would you be able to deliver the refreshments by 2:00 p.m. on that day? I think that your Small Bites menu would work perfectly for the party. ------- . This would be the easiest way to satisfy everyone's food preferences.
17.

------- , many people are concerned about wasting any leftover food. Can you provide carryout boxes for people to take any leftovers home with them?
18.

Thank you,

James Berthel, Berthel Technologies

15.
(A) seen
(B) saw
(C) sees
(D) seeing

16.
(A) numbers
(B) problems
(C) services
(D) questions

17.
(A) We use environmentally friendly cups, plates, and utensils.
(B) I like that it offers a variety of delicious options.
(C) Please send only experienced serving staff.
(D) The final cost needs to include beverages.

18.
(A) Although
(B) Meanwhile
(C) Finally
(D) Otherwise

UNIT 07 수 일치와 태

1 주어와 동사의 수 일치

출제 포인트 보기에 동사만 있어 동사의 적절한 어형을 골라야 할 때, 우선 주어와 동사의 수 일치를 확인한다.
주어가 3인칭 단수일 때 현재 시제 동사 뒤에는 -(e)s를 붙여야 한다.

◆ be동사의 수 일치
be동사는 주어의 인칭과 단수/복수, 동사의 시제에 따라 다양한 형태가 있다.

The construction project of the public library [**was** / ~~were~~] approved by the city council.
공공 도서관 건설 프로젝트는 시 의회에 의해 승인되었다.
→ 주어(The construction project)가 3인칭 단수이므로 was를 쓴다.

◆ 조동사, 과거 시제 동사의 수 일치
조동사와 일반동사의 과거형은 주어의 수에 영향을 받지 않는다.

The mayor [**announced** / ~~announce~~] the extension of subway hours starting January 3.
시장은 1월 3일부터 지하철 운행 시간 연장을 발표했다.
→ 주어(The mayor)가 3인칭 단수이므로 동사가 현재 시제라면 동사 뒤에 -(e)s를 붙여야 한다.

◆ 수식어가 붙은 긴 주어
주어 뒤에 전치사구, 분사구, 관계대명사절 등의 수식어가 올 수 있다. 수식어는 동사의 수 일치에 영향을 미치지 않는다.

The courses the intern will take [**focus** / ~~focuses~~] on the basic concepts of security programs.
그 인턴이 받게 될 수업들은 보안 프로그램의 기본 개념에 초점을 맞춘다.
→ 목적격 관계대명사 that이 생략된 관계대명사절(the intern will take)이 주어를 수식하고 있다. 따라서 주어 The courses와 수 일치가 되어야 한다.

◆ There+be동사+명사
'There+be동사+명사' 구문은 뒤에 나오는 명사가 주어 역할을 한다. 따라서 be동사와 이 명사의 수를 일치시킨다.

There are still unfinished business [**transactions** / ~~transaction~~] involving a huge amount of money.
막대한 금액이 관련된 미완료 거래들이 아직 남아 있다.
→ There 뒤 복수형 be동사 are에 수 일치되도록 복수 명사가 나와야 한다.

ETS 유형연습

정답과 해설 p.150

1 We hope that you ------- to use Docuprint Services for all your printing and office needs.
(A) continue
(B) continues
(C) continuation
(D) continuing

2 Please use the color printer sparingly, since the ink cartridges it requires ------- currently unavailable.
(A) are
(B) is
(C) been
(D) being

3 The coffee makers we compared ------- in terms of price, size, and durability.
(A) varies
(B) vary
(C) variable
(D) varying

2 단수주어 vs. 복수주어

출제 포인트 주어와 동사의 수 일치를 확인할 때, 주어의 단/복수를 구별하기 어려운 경우가 있다. 특히 주어에 수량 표현이 있다면 UNIT 03의 부정대명사와 UNIT 04의 수량형용사를 기억하여 적용해 보자.

▶ 수량 표현이 있는 주어의 수

one of the / each of the / either of the / the number of the	+ 복수명사	+ 단수동사
a couple of / a number of / a majority of	+ 복수명사	+ 복수동사
some (of the) / most (of the) / half (of the) / many (of the) / few (of the)	+ 복수명사	+ 복수동사
some (of the) / most (of the) / half (of the) / much (of the) / little (of the)	+ 불가산명사	+ 단수동사

Each of the trainers [**has** / ~~have~~] a master's degree as well as years of teaching experience.
각 교육관들은 석사 학위뿐 아니라 수년의 교습 경력도 가지고 있다.

A number of large shopping centers positively [**affect** / ~~affects~~] the local economy.
많은 대형 쇼핑센터들은 지역 경제에 긍정적으로 영향을 미친다.

▶ 주어 자리의 to부정사, 동명사, 명사절은 단수

동명사 주어 [**Addressing** / ~~Addressed~~] problems with the heating system **takes** time and effort.
난방 시스템의 문제를 해결하는 것은 시간과 노력이 든다.
→ Addressed가 오면 problems가 주어가 되는데 문장의 동사인 takes와 수 일치가 되지 않는다.

명사절 주어 **Whether** the broken machine will be replaced [**has** / ~~have~~] not been decided yet.
고장 난 기계가 교체될지는 아직 결정되지 않았다.
→ Whether가 이끄는 명사절 주어는 단수 취급한다.

▶ 주의해야 할 주어의 수

복합명사 **The job opportunities** [**are** / ~~is~~] available for temporary employment.
이 취업 기회는 임시직에 대해 유효하다.
→ 주어가 복합명사일 때 동사의 수는 뒤의 명사에 일치시킨다.

or로 연결된 경우 The sales manager **or his team members** [**are** / ~~is~~] invited to deliver several presentations. 영업부장 또는 그의 팀원들은 몇 차례 프레젠테이션을 진행해야 한다.
→ 주어가 or로 연결된 경우 동사는 동사와 가까운 뒤쪽 명사와 수를 일치시킨다.

ETS 유형연습

정답과 해설 p.151

1 While performing my preliminary research, I learned that very ------- has been written about the poetry of Miho Aoki in the past decade.
(A) some
(B) few
(C) other
(D) little

2 Roughly half of the employees at Century Photo Labs ------- to work by bus.
(A) commutes
(B) commute
(C) is commuting
(D) has commuted

3 The Stellen Museum's extensive ------- consist of a mix of ancient artifacts and paintings from various cultures.
(A) holds
(B) holder
(C) holding
(D) holdings

3 동사의 수동태

출제 포인트 수동태는 능동태 문장의 목적어를 주어로 바꾸어 주어가 동작을 당하고 있음을 표현하는 방법이다. 문제에서 동사가 능동태가 되어야 하는지 수동태가 되어야 하는지 판단할 수 있어야 한다.

◆ 수동태의 개념

능동태 문장의 목적어가 수동태 문장의 주어가 되어 '~되다, 당하다'라고 해석한다. 수동태 동사는 'be+p.p.' 형태로 사용된다. 대부분의 수동태 동사 뒤에는 목적어가 없고, 전치사 등의 수식어를 동반한다.

능동태 The executives will [**discuss** / be discussed] practical ways to promote profit growth.
경영진은 수익 성장을 촉진할 현실적인 방법을 논의할 것이다.

수동태 Practical ways to promote profit growth will [**be discussed** / discuss] by the executives.
수익 성장을 촉진하기 위한 현실적인 방법이 경영진에 의해 논의될 것이다.
→ 수동태 동사 'be+p.p.' 뒤에는 목적어가 없고, 주로 전치사구가 나온다.

◆ 수동태로 쓸 수 없는 자동사

목적어를 취하지 않는 자동사는 수동태(be+p.p.)가 될 수 없다.

Car accidents [**occur** / are occurred] more often because of careless driving rather than bad weather. 자동차 사고는 나쁜 날씨보다는 부주의한 운전 때문에 더 자주 일어난다.

◆ 목적어가 2개인 동사의 수동태

4형식 동사는 목적어가 두 개이므로, 간접 목적어(사람)가 주어로 쓰인 수동태 동사 뒤에 여전히 목적어가 남는다. 'be given+명사(~을 받다)' 형식으로 익혀 두도록 한다.

be offered+명사 ~을 제공받다   be granted+명사 ~을 받다   be awarded+명사 ~을 수여받다
be charged+명사 ~을 청구받다   be issued+명사 ~을 발급받다

Only those with a visitor pass [**are given** / give] **access** to the university's museums.
방문증을 가진 사람만 그 대학의 박물관에 입장할 수 있다.

◆ 5형식 동사의 수동태

5형식 동사는 목적어와 목적격 보어를 가지며, 목적격 보어 자리에는 명사, 형용사, to부정사 등 다양한 형태가 올 수 있다. 따라서 5형식 문장의 수동태는 동사 뒤에 다양한 형태가 올 수 있다.

The movie [**is considered** / consider] **one of the 100 most influential films** of the century.
그 영화는 세기의 가장 영향력 있는 영화 100선 중 하나로 여겨진다.

ETS 유형연습

정답과 해설 p.151

1 Due to new restrictions on international travelers, certain types of plants cannot ------ into most countries without a permit.

(A) bring
(B) be brought
(C) brought
(D) bringing

2 Library patrons who fail to return an item by the due date ------ a fee.

(A) charge
(B) will be charged
(C) have charged
(D) are charging

3 The delegation will depart from the embassy at 9 A.M. and ------ to the airport by the Minister of Sports.

(A) will accompany
(B) accompanied
(C) will be accompanied
(D) being accompanied

4 여러 가지 수동태

출제포인트 특정 전치사와 결합하는 수동태 동사들이 있다. 행위 주체를 표현할 때에는 주로 by를 쓰지만, 동사의 의미에 따라 다양한 전치사가 나올 수 있다.

◆ be p.p. + 전치사

with	be associated with ~와 연관되어 있다 be satisfied with ~에 만족하다 be faced with ~에 직면하다	be acquainted with ~을 알고 있다 be disappointed with ~에 실망하다 be concerned with ~와 관련이 있다	be equipped with ~을 갖추고 있다 be provided with ~을 제공받다
to	be accustomed/used to ~에 익숙하다 be exposed to ~에 노출되다 be dedicated to ~에 헌신하다	be limited to ~로 제한되다 be attributed/ascribed to ~ 때문이다 be devoted to ~에 헌신하다	be related to ~와 관련이 있다 be committed to ~에 헌신하다 be assigned to ~에 배정되다
in	be interested in ~에 관심을 갖다	be engaged in ~에 종사하다	be involved in ~에 연관되어 있다
for	be known for ~로 알려져 있다 (업적)	be honored for ~로 표창을 받다	be blamed for ~로 비난받다
기타	be based on ~에 기초해 있다 be concerned about ~에 대해 걱정하다	be accused of ~에 대해 비난받다	be divided into ~으로 나누어지다

◆ '자동사 + 전치사'의 수동태

'자동사 + 전치사'가 결합하여 마치 타동사처럼 수동태로 쓸 수 있다. 이때 수동태 동사 뒤에는 여전히 전치사가 결합되어 있다.

- account for ~을 설명하다 / be accounted for 설명되다
- deal with ~을 다루다 / be dealt with 다루어지다
- take care of ~을 처리하다 / be taken care of 처리되다
- refer to ~을 언급하다 / be referred to 언급되다
- carry out ~을 수행하다 / be carried out 수행되다
- dispose of ~을 처분하다 / be disposed of 처분되다

Safety issues should **be [dealt / ~~dealing~~] with** immediately.
안전 문제는 즉시 처리되어야 한다.
→ **deal with**는 하나의 동사 덩어리이다. 뒤에 목적어가 없고 수식어인 부사가 있으므로 수동태 동사를 써야 한다.

ETS 유형연습

정답과 해설 p.151

1 Each month, we will select five outstanding employees to be honored ------- their exceptional contributions to the company's performance.

(A) for
(B) at
(C) across
(D) over

2 Sleeping-car passengers will be provided ------- the bedding they need for the journey.

(A) with
(B) for
(C) to
(D) of

3 The apartments on the lower floors cost less because they are more exposed ------- dust and the noise of traffic.

(A) to
(B) without
(C) from
(D) against

ETS 실전문제

1. Mr. Rosen ------- that there are still spaces open for vendors at February's auto show.
   (A) report
   (B) reported
   (C) reporter
   (D) reporting

2. The customer's loan application documents ------- to her for her signature.
   (A) returning
   (B) has returned
   (C) is returning
   (D) have been returned

3. Because the boardroom is being painted, the meeting this afternoon will ------- in the conference room on the fourth floor.
   (A) have held
   (B) be holding
   (C) hold
   (D) be held

4. Employees who would like to contribute to the company charity drive ------- to place their donations in the box in Jack Elliott's office.
   (A) will invite
   (B) are inviting
   (C) can invite
   (D) are invited

5. Comco, Inc., became the leading supplier of computer parts last year, less than ten years after it -------.
   (A) was founded
   (B) founds
   (C) have founded
   (D) founded

6. ------- hundreds of technical specialists at the convention in Zurich last month.
   (A) Several
   (B) Many of the
   (C) Having had
   (D) There were

7. New shipments from our factory ------- because of a production shortage.
   (A) delay
   (B) have been delayed
   (C) have delayed
   (D) are delaying

8. Full-time ------- of Hauto Production Plant are entitled to take a fifteen-minute break for each four-hour shift.
   (A) employment
   (B) employees
   (C) employs
   (D) employ

9. The weekly financial records ------- that profits have begun to rise again.
   (A) indicate
   (B) indicates
   (C) indicating
   (D) to indicate

10. Inclement weather and a reduced workforce ------- the greatest challenges to the renovation of the Kern Science Center.
    (A) have posed
    (B) is posing
    (C) does pose
    (D) will have been posed

11. The fabric used in Alpinta nursing uniforms ------- to withstand the wear and tear of daily use.
    (A) is confirming
    (B) has been confirmed
    (C) will confirm
    (D) confirm

12. Six highly qualified candidates ------- to become CEO of Noank Medical Center.
    (A) applied
    (B) applying
    (C) were applied
    (D) applies

13. Shoppers at the Woodfield Discount Store may ------- their phone numbers at checkout to qualify for special offers.

(A) answer
(B) provide
(C) accept
(D) purchase

14. Mayor Williams proudly described the city as a place where the citizens are ------- for their hospitality.

(A) returned
(B) known
(C) taken
(D) held

Questions 15-18 refer to the following article.

Auction House to Celebrate Hundredth Birthday

ATHLONE (5 September) — Today McShane Farm Machinery Auction House, one of Ireland's longest-running auction businesses, ---15.--- an upcoming hundredth birthday celebration. Multiple ---16.--- have participated in McShane's auctions. These farming families have long relied on McShane's to supply a range of used farm equipment. McShane's will be holding the birthday celebration at ---17.--- auction facilities on Cornamagh Road in Athlone on Sunday, 16 September. Vintage tractors and antique equipment will be displayed at the event. ---18.--- . As a bonus, the celebration will feature the Ballymahon Family Band.

---

15. (A) announce
(B) announced
(C) announcing
(D) announcement

16. (A) generations
(B) manufacturers
(C) engineers
(D) salespeople

17. (A) his
(B) its
(C) whose
(D) your

18. (A) You can send in your photos online.
(B) The store will be closed on Saturdays.
(C) Light refreshments will also be served.
(D) There is a back order on certain items.

UNIT 08 시제

1 단순 시제

출제 포인트 시제 문제는 시간 표현을 먼저 단서로 활용하고, 별다른 단서가 없는 경우 해석으로 풀어야 한다. 시간 표현에는 부사, 전치사구, 부사절(접속사+주어+동사), 주변 동사의 시제가 있다.

◆ 현재 시제
현재 시제는 주로 현재의 상황, 반복적인 일, 일반적인 사실 등을 표현한다.

현재 시제와 잘 어울리는 시간 표현

| every week 매주 | usually 보통 | regularly 정기적으로 | routinely 일상적으로 |
| always 항상 | generally 일반적으로 | often 자주 | frequently 자주 |

Online shopping malls [**offer** / ~~are offering~~] special discounts <u>usually on weekends</u>.
온라인 쇼핑몰은 보통 주말에 특별 할인을 제공한다.

◆ 과거 시제
과거 시제는 과거의 상태 또는 과거 시점에 발생한 일을 나타낸다. 빈도부사와 함께 쓰여 과거의 습관을 표현하기도 한다.

과거 시제와 잘 어울리는 시간 표현

| yesterday 어제 | two days ago 이틀 전에 | last Friday 지난주 금요일에 | in 2010 2010년에 |
| recently/lately 최근에 | when+주어+과거 동사 ~했을 때 | the other day 며칠 전에 | once 한때 |

Colin Phillips [**was** / ~~has been~~] awarded the World's Best Architect Award <u>four years ago</u>.
콜린 필립스 씨는 4년 전 세계 최고의 건축가 상을 받았다.

◆ 미래 시제
미래 시제는 미래 시점에 발생할 일을 나타낸다. 미래를 나타내는 동사는 'will+동사원형', 'is/are -ing' 등으로 다양하다.

미래 시제와 잘 어울리는 시간 표현

| tomorrow 내일 | next week 다음 주 | this coming Sunday 다가오는 일요일에 | soon/shortly 곧 |
| as of/effective/starting May 10 5월 10일부터 | | anticipate/predict that ~일 것으로 예상하다 | |

Registration for the public relations conference [**will open** / ~~has opened~~] <u>shortly</u>.
홍보 컨퍼런스의 등록이 곧 시작될 것이다.

ETS 유형연습

정답과 해설 p.153

1 Seating in the Bogor Stadium completely ------- the field so that all visitors are afforded excellent views of events.
(A) surround
(B) surrounds
(C) surrounded
(D) surrounding

2 The engineers had only begun analyzing the problem when a new discovery ------- their working model obsolete.
(A) rendering
(B) rendered
(C) renders
(D) will render

3 Agnes Hanady ------- her latest album at the Morgantown Music Festival tomorrow.
(A) debuting
(B) debuted
(C) has debuted
(D) will debut

2 진행 시제

> **출제포인트** 진행 시제는 be동사 뒤에 -ing를 붙여 특정 시점에 일어나고 있는 동작을 표현한다. 현재진행 시제와 단순 현재 시제를 잘 구별하도록 하자.

▶ 현재진행 (is/are -ing)

❶ 현재진행은 현재의 한 시점에 진행되고 있는 일을 나타내며 '~하는 중이다'라고 해석한다.

현재진행 시제와 잘 어울리는 시간 표현

| now 지금 | currently 현재 | presently 현재 | at the moment 지금 |

The development team [**is discussing** / ~~discusses~~] the feasibility of new ideas at the moment.
개발팀은 현재 새로운 아이디어들의 실현 가능성에 대해 논의하고 있다.

❷ 현재진행 시제는 가까운 미래를 나타낼 수 있다.
Train EXP101 **is arriving** in approximately 20 minutes. EXP101 열차는 약 20분 후에 도착할 것이다.

▶ 과거진행 (was/were -ing)

과거진행 시제는 과거의 한 시점에 진행되었던 일을 표현한다.

He gained valuable experience while he [**was working** / ~~works~~] on the team a few years ago.
그는 몇 년 전에 그 팀에서 일하면서 소중한 경험을 얻었다.

▶ 미래진행 (will be -ing)

미래진행 시제는 미래의 한 시점에 진행될 일을 표현한다.

The vice president [**will be delivering** / ~~was delivered~~] a speech at the annual meeting next Monday.
다음 주 월요일에 열릴 연례 회의에서 부사장님이 연설하고 있을 것이다.

ETS 유형연습

정답과 해설 p.154

1. LTD Enterprises is currently ------- an accomplished individual to replace the current director, who will be retiring at the end of the month.
   (A) seeking
   (B) seeks
   (C) being sought
   (D) having sought

2. Ms. Yoon ------- from jet lag when she returned on Thursday, so the meeting has been postponed until next week.
   (A) will suffer
   (B) suffers
   (C) will have suffered
   (D) was suffering

3. While Ms. Atitam is on vacation next June, Mr. Al-Jamri ------- over the contract negotiations with our Mumbai vendor.
   (A) takes
   (B) have taken
   (C) had taken
   (D) will be taking

3 완료 시제

출제 포인트 완료 시제는 우리말 해석이 애매해서 특히 함정에 빠지기 쉽다. 빈출 시간 표현과 우리말 해석을 통해 현재완료 시제와 과거 시제, 현재완료 시제와 과거완료 시제를 구별해야 한다.

◆ 현재완료 (have/has p.p.)

현재완료 시제는 과거의 불특정 시점에 일어난 사건이 현재까지 지속되거나 영향을 미치고 있음을 나타낸다. 따라서 특정 과거 시점을 나타내는 부사와 함께 쓸 수 없다.

현재완료 시제와 잘 어울리는 시간 표현

since 2010 2010년 이후	since+주어+과거 동사 ~한 이후로	already 이미 (not) yet 아직 (~ 안 했다)
for the last decade 지난 10년 동안	over the past few years 지난 몇 년에 걸쳐서	

Since the bridge [**was built** / has built] in 2005, it [**has become** / became] a popular attraction in the city. 다리가 2005년에 세워진 이후로, 그것은 도시에서 인기 있는 명소가 되었다.

◆ 과거완료 (had p.p.)

과거완료 시제는 주로 '~했었다'라고 해석하며, 특정 과거 시점보다 이전에 일어난 일을 표현한다.

과거완료 시제와 잘 어울리는 시간 표현

before+주어+과거 동사 ~하기 전에   by the time+주어+과거 동사 ~했을 즈음에

Ms. Han [**had conducted** / conducts] extensive research **before** she **came** to a conclusion.
한 씨는 결론에 이르기 전에 광범위한 연구를 했었다.

By the time the documents **arrived**, the team [**had** / will have] already **concluded** its meeting.
서류가 도착했을 무렵 그 팀은 이미 회의를 마쳤다.

◆ 미래완료 (will have p.p.)

미래완료 시제는 주로 '~했을 것이다'라고 해석한다. 미래의 어느 시점까지 계속되거나 미래에 완료될 일을 나타낸다.

미래완료 시제와 잘 어울리는 시간 표현

by the time+주어+현재 동사 ~할 즈음에   by next year 내년 즈음에

By the time Ms. Anderson **is promoted** to the vice president, she [**will have worked** / will work] for 10 years at our company.
앤더슨 씨가 부사장으로 승진될 즈음이면, 그녀는 우리 회사에서 10년 동안 일한 것이 될 것이다.

ETS 유형연습

1. For the last fifteen years, Matlock, Inc., has consistently ------- among the nation's ten leading toy manufacturers.
   (A) rank
   (B) ranked
   (C) ranking
   (D) ranks

2. The hiring committee ------- the possibility of interviewing the candidates in person but decided on telephone interviews instead.
   (A) discuss
   (B) had discussed
   (C) will be discussed
   (D) discussing

3. By the time Clear Blaze Technology's word processing program goes on the market, software engineers ------- its remaining flaws.
   (A) will have corrected
   (B) had been correcting
   (C) are correcting
   (D) will correct

4 시제 일치의 예외

> **출제포인트** 시간과 조건의 부사절, 그리고 주장/요구/제안의 동사 뒤 that절은 일반적인 시제의 규칙을 따르지 않는다. when, if, request that 등이 보이면 시제 문제일 가능성이 높다는 것을 기억하자.

◆ 시간, 조건의 부사절에서는 현재(완료) 시제가 미래(완료) 시제를 대신한다.
시간, 조건의 부사절에서는 미래의 일을 이야기하더라도 현재 시제를 쓴다. 그러나 주절의 동사는 그대로 미래 시제를 쓴다.

시간과 조건의 부사절을 이끄는 접속사

| when ~할 때 | until ~할 때까지 | before ~하기 전에 | after ~한 후에 | while ~하는 동안 |
| as soon as ~하자마자 | if ~라면 | unless ~하지 않는다면 | once 일단 ~하면 | |

The hotel **will be** able to accommodate guests **after** the plumbers [**repair** / ~~will repair~~] the pipes tomorrow. 배관공들이 내일 수도관을 수리하고 나면, 호텔은 손님들을 받을 수 있을 것이다.

If you [**sign** / ~~will sign~~] up for a membership, you **will get** 10% discount for any purchases.
만약 당신이 회원권을 신청하시면 어떤 구매에 대해서든 10퍼센트의 할인을 받을 수 있습니다.

> **고득점 TIP**
> if로 시작하는 명사절에서는 현재 시제가 미래를 대신하지 않는다.
> Many customers have asked us if their orders [**will be** / ~~are~~] delivered soon.
> 많은 고객들이 그들의 주문품이 곧 배달될 것인지 우리에게 물었다.

◆ 주장, 요구, 제안의 동사/형용사/명사 뒤 that절에 동사원형을 쓴다.
'주장한다' 다음에는 '~해야 한다'라는 의미의 조동사 should가 나오는 것이 자연스럽다. 하지만 should가 생략되는 경우가 많아 that 다음에는 '주어+동사원형'이 나오게 된다.

주장하다	insist / urge
요구하다	require / request / ask
명령하다	order
제안하다	suggest / recommend
중요한	important / essential / imperative
요청, 제안	request / suggestion / recommendation

+ that + 주어 + (should) 동사원형

Mr. James **insisted that** the new security policy [**be implemented** / ~~is implemented~~] without delay. 제임스 씨는 새로운 보안 정책이 지체 없이 시행되어야 한다고 주장했다.

ETS 유형연습

정답과 해설 p.154

1 When you ------- to access your account, please type your password in the appropriate field.
(A) wanted
(B) want
(C) will want
(D) wanting

2 As soon as the warehouse ------- examined for fire hazards, you may resume your normal business operations.
(A) has been
(B) was
(C) had been
(D) will be

3 Executive Director Rajiv Kutty has complied with shareholders' requests that he ------- quality control procedures at Srinivisan Foods facilities.
(A) review
(B) was reviewing
(C) be reviewed
(D) reviewed

ETS 실전문제

1. Every summer, Brighton store owners ------- unique window displays in an effort to attract more tourists.
   (A) create
   (B) creating
   (C) creates
   (D) were created

2. Magnum Plus cameras ------- very popular right now because they are so easy to use.
   (A) became
   (B) are becoming
   (C) to become
   (D) becomes

3. The number of customers requesting refunds ------- over the last few years due to the improved quality.
   (A) declined
   (B) has declined
   (C) decline
   (D) have declined

4. After Mr. Li ------- some adjustments, the engine worked more smoothly than it had before.
   (A) to make
   (B) made
   (C) is making
   (D) having made

5. Larper Painting ------- a special sale next month to celebrate its new store on Abagael Avenue.
   (A) has run
   (B) will be running
   (C) will be run
   (D) ran

6. Ever since Mr. Derrick joined the staff, Mr. Zapata and Ms. Coleman have ------- the marketing team for its excellent results.
   (A) to be praised
   (B) praise
   (C) been praising
   (D) been praised

7. Ritoc Engineering ------- checked all of the electrical wiring of the building by the time new tenants move in.
   (A) will
   (B) have
   (C) having
   (D) will have

8. To validate today's results, Dr. Lum is requesting that the experiment ------- tomorrow by a second research group.
   (A) be repeated
   (B) is repeating
   (C) will have repeated
   (D) had been repeating

9. If the plumbing problem -------, we recommend that you contact the product manufacturer.
   (A) to persist
   (B) was persisting
   (C) persists
   (D) persistence

10. Until Ms. Yang returns from the international travel conference in Taipei, Mr. Woo ------- all hotel reservations.
    (A) handled
    (B) had been handling
    (C) will be handled
    (D) will handle

11. Because of low enrollment, the workshop scheduled to begin in August ------- until September.
    (A) postponed
    (B) will postpone
    (C) will be postponing
    (D) has been postponed

12. By the time Ms. Okada ------- in Incheon for the sales meeting, she had already completed preliminary negotiations by telephone.
    (A) arrives
    (B) arrived
    (C) has arrived
    (D) will arrive

13. Sylvia Cho ------- her training at Frio County Animal Hospital last week and will begin working as a veterinary technician.

(A) will conclude
(B) to conclude
(C) concludes
(D) concluded

14. It is ------- that the documents be meticulously examined before they are sent out to clients.

(A) immediate
(B) imperative
(C) ultimate
(D) conclusive

Questions 15-18 refer to the following e-mail.

To: Lawrence Mason <l.mason@callastreetbakery.com>
From: Carla Manfred <ms.manfred@colincenterschool.org>
Date: April 16
Subject: Thank you
Attachment: Student artwork

Dear Mr. Mason,

Thank you for allowing my first-grade class to visit your bakery. It was the first trip outside our town for many of our students. ---15--- . And when they saw your operation, they were mesmerized!

I want to commend the floor manager, Ms. Cho, for leading the ---16--- . She did an excellent job of explaining the processes in a way that was easy for the children to understand. She was also very patient in answering all ---17--- questions.

When we ---18--- to the school, the children each drew a picture of the bakery. I have scanned the pictures and attached them for you.

Best regards and thanks again,

Ms. Manfred and the first-grade students at Colin Center School

---

15. (A) We go on field trips twice each month.
(B) For example, the students especially enjoy fresh baked goods.
(C) I am sorry that we were so late in arriving.
(D) The children were excited just to be on the bus for so long.

16. (A) tour
(B) meeting
(C) campaign
(D) performance

17. (A) its
(B) your
(C) their
(D) his

18. (A) returned
(B) returning
(C) will return
(D) to return

UNIT 09 to부정사와 동명사

무료 강의

1 to부정사의 용법

출제포인트 to부정사는 'to+동사원형'의 형태로 명사, 형용사, 부사 역할을 할 수 있지만 동사로는 쓸 수 없는 준동사이다. to부정사 자리 문제에 대비하여 to부정사를 동반하는 동사와 명사, to부정사의 숙어 표현을 외워 두어야 한다.

◆ 명사적 용법(~하는 것): 주어, 목적어, 보어

주어 It is necessary [to make / for making] a reservation in advance to receive a discount.
할인을 받기 위해서는 사전 예약하는 것이 필요하다.
→ It이 가주어, 뒤에 오는 to부정사가 진주어 역할을 하는 가주어 – 진주어 구문이다.

목적어 Ms. Paik plans [to convert / converted] an empty office space into a meeting room.
백 씨는 비어 있는 사무실 공간을 회의실로 바꿀 계획이다.

보어 Those with good communication skills seem [to perform / performing] well in their workplace. 의사소통을 잘하는 사람들이 직장에서 일을 잘하는 것 같다.
→ 주격 보어 자리에 to부정사가 오는 동사에는 remain (to be), seem (to be), appear (to be) 등이 있다.

동사+to부정사

want to do ~하는 것을 원하다	would like to do ~하고 싶다	hesitate to do ~하기를 주저하다
expect to do ~할 것을 기대하다	plan to do ~하는 것을 계획하다	tend to do ~하는 경향이 있다
manage to do 가까스로 ~하다	afford to do ~할 여유가 있다	fail to do ~하지 않다/못하다

◆ 형용사적 용법(~할, ~하기 위한): 명사 뒤에서 명사 수식

명사+to부정사

ability to do ~할 수 있는 능력	right to do ~할 권리	way to do ~할 방법
authority to do ~할 수 있는 권한	opportunity to do ~할 기회	attempt to do ~하기 위한 시도
effort to do ~하기 위한 노력	decision to do ~하겠다는 결정	plan to do ~할 계획

◆ 부사적 용법(~하기 위해서, ~해서): 수식어 역할

Publication should be suspended **in order to** [reflect / reflecting] last-minute changes.
막판 변경사항을 반영하기 위해 출간이 연기되어야 한다.
→ '~하기 위해서'는 to 동사원형, in order to 동사원형, so as to 동사원형으로 표현할 수 있다.

ETS 유형연습

정답과 해설 p.157

1. The purpose of this government program is ------- schools with better access to new learning technologies.
   (A) to provide
   (B) provides
   (C) provided
   (D) to providing

2. Today Tenopy Tech announced its plans ------- with Shaffly Energy Systems to manufacture solar panels in Quito and Caracas.
   (A) to partner
   (B) be partnering
   (C) is partnered
   (D) will partner

3. In order to ------- overseas clients, the Majeski Group will open offices in both Europe and Asia.
   (A) accommodation
   (B) accommodates
   (C) accommodate
   (D) accommodating

2 to부정사의 활용

> **출제포인트** to부정사는 동사는 아니지만, 동사와 마찬가지로 뒤에 목적어, 보어, 수식어가 올 수 있다. to부정사를 목적격 보어로 취하는 동사 관련 문제도 자주 출제되므로 빈출 표현을 외워 두자.

▶ to부정사의 동사적 특징

to부정사는 동사의 성격이 남아 있어 뒤에 목적어를 취하거나 부사의 수식을 받을 수 있다.

The conference organizers need [**to produce** / ~~production~~] **a large number of copies** of the materials for all attendees. 회의 기획자들은 모든 참석자들에게 줄 많은 부수의 자료들을 제작해야 한다.

▶ 목적격 보어 자리에 쓰이는 to부정사

동사 + 목적어 + to부정사

| ask 명사 to do ~하라고 요청하다 | require 명사 to do ~하라고 요구하다 | allow 명사 to do ~할 수 있게 하다 |
| invite 명사 to do ~하도록 요청하다 | instruct 명사 to do ~하라고 지시하다 | encourage 명사 to do ~하도록 독려하다 |

The mass storage devices **allow** users [**to process** / ~~processing~~] much information at a time.
대용량 저장 장치는 사용자들이 많은 정보를 한 번에 처리할 수 있도록 해준다.

빈출 5형식 동사의 수동태

| be required to do ~하도록 요청받다 | be invited to do ~하도록 요청받다 | be encouraged to do ~하도록 독려받다 |
| be reminded to do ~할 것을 주의받다 | be forced to do ~하도록 강요받다 | be advised to do ~하도록 조언받다 |

The mayor [**was invited** / ~~invited~~] **to appear** as a special guest speaker at the conference.
시장은 회의에 특별 초청 연사로 참석해 달라는 요청을 받았다.

▶ 원형부정사

make, have 등의 사역동사는 목적어와 목적격 보어가 능동이면 원형부정사를, 수동이면 과거분사를 쓴다. 동사 help는 목적어와 목적격 보어로 원형부정사 또는 to부정사를 쓸 수 있다.

사역동사 Please make sure to **have** all your mail [**forwarded** / ~~forward~~] to your new address.
반드시 모든 우편물이 새 주소로 전달되도록 하세요.

동사 help The investment guideline **will help** potential buyers [**make** / ~~making~~] an informed decision. 투자 지침서는 잠재적 구매자들이 현명한 결정을 내리도록 도와줄 것이다.

ETS 유형연습

1. Anisk Pharmaceuticals makes every effort ------- the confidentiality of all participants in the clinical study.
   (A) to maintain
   (B) maintains
   (C) will maintain
   (D) is maintaining

2. ------- a discount, enter the code on the purchasing form.
   (A) To receive
   (B) Receiving
   (C) Have received
   (D) Receives

3. The director strongly believes that professional development seminars can help ------- the knowledge and expertise of employees in many areas.
   (A) broaden
   (B) broader
   (C) broadly
   (D) broad

3 동명사

출제 포인트 동명사는 '동사원형+-ing' 형태로 '~하는 것'이라고 해석하는 준동사이다. 명사와 동명사를 구별하는 문제, 동명사를 포함하는 숙어 관련 문제가 자주 출제된다.

◆ 동명사의 자리

동명사는 주어나 보어, 그리고 동사 및 전치사의 목적어로 쓰인다.

주어	[**Advertising** / ~~Advertise~~] on social media **is** the most effective way to attract customers.
	소셜 미디어에 광고하는 것이 고객을 유치하는 가장 효과적인 방법이다.
보어	Our first priority **is** [**making** / ~~made~~] sure that the project is completed on time.
	우리의 최우선 과제는 그 프로젝트가 제시간에 완료되도록 하는 것이다.
동사의 목적어	We decided to **discontinue** [**selling** / ~~to sell~~] shoes and focus on clothes.
	우리는 신발 판매를 중단하고 옷에 집중하기로 결정했다.
전치사의 목적어	Mr. Bradley is responsible **for** [**developing** / ~~develop~~] the company's Web site.
	브래들리 씨는 그 회사의 웹사이트 개발을 담당하고 있다.

동사+동명사(-ing)

consider -ing ~을 고려하다	suggest -ing ~을 제안하다	recommend -ing ~을 추천하다	avoid -ing ~을 피하다
admit -ing ~을 인정하다	deny -ing ~을 부인하다	discontinue -ing ~을 중단하다	quit -ing ~을 중단하다
keep -ing ~을 계속하다	include -ing ~을 포함하다	mind -ing ~을 꺼리다	give up -ing ~을 포기하다

◆ 동명사 vs. 명사

동명사 뒤에는 목적어가 올 수 있지만 명사 뒤에는 목적어가 올 수 없다. 또한 부정관사(a/an) 뒤에는 동명사가 올 수 없다.

We should discuss how to solve the problem after [**analyzing** / ~~analysis~~] **the data**.
우리는 데이터 분석 후 문제를 해결할 방법에 대해 논의해야 한다.
→ 명사 analysis는 목적어를 취할 수 없다.

◆ 동명사 관용 표현

before -ing ~하기 전에	after -ing ~한 후에	on -ing ~하자마자
in -ing ~하는 데 있어서	by -ing ~함으로써	feel like -ing ~하고 싶다
be busy -ing ~하느라 바쁘다	be capable of -ing ~할 수 있다	cannot help -ing ~하지 않을 수 없다
spend 시간/돈 -ing ~하는 데 (시간/돈)을 쓰다	have difficulty -ing ~하는 데 어려움을 겪다	

ETS 유형연습

1. For many years the local government has considered ------- Red Valley as a wilderness park.

   (A) designate
   (B) designates
   (C) designating
   (D) designation

2. To avoid ------- your audience during your presentation, please do not use complex layouts.

   (A) distraction
   (B) distracts
   (C) distracted
   (D) distracting

3. Ms. Baxter would like to meet with all members of the hiring committee again after ------- candidates.

   (A) interview
   (B) interviews
   (C) interviewing
   (D) interviewed

4 to부정사 / 전치사 to

> **출제 포인트**: 'to+동사원형'의 to와 전치사 to를 잘 구별하자. 전치사 to 뒤에는 명사, 동명사가 오고 동사원형은 쓸 수 없다. to부정사는 '~하는 것, ~해야 할' 등으로 해석되고, 전치사 to는 '~에게, ~로'라는 의미로 방향성을 나타낸다.

◆ to부정사 관련 표현

be able to do ~할 수 있다	be pleased to do ~하게 되어 기쁘다	be available to do ~할 시간이 있다
be anxious to do ~하기를 간절히 바라다	be eager to do ~하기를 갈망하다	be willing to do 기꺼이 ~할 것이다
be likely to do ~할 것 같다	be liable to do ~할 것 같다	be apt to do ~하기 쉽다
be about to do 막 ~하려고 하다	be eligible to do ~할 자격이 있다	be free to do 자유롭게 ~하다
be supposed to do ~하기로 되어 있다	be scheduled to do ~할 예정이다	be designed to do ~하도록 고안되다
be hesitant to do ~하기를 망설이다	be reluctant to do ~하기를 꺼리다	be ready to do ~할 준비가 되어 있다

Mr. Smith **will be** [**able** / ~~capable~~] **to** manage hundreds of accounts by himself.
스미스 씨는 혼자서 수백 개의 거래를 관리할 수 있을 것이다.
→ capable은 뒤에 전치사 of를 붙여 'be capable of+(동)명사(~할 수 있다)' 구조로 사용된다.

The planning department **is supposed to** [**arrange** / ~~arranging~~] next week's company meeting.
기획부에서 다음 주 회사 회의를 준비하기로 되어 있다.

◆ 전치사 to 관련 표현

전치사 to는 뒤에 명사 또는 동명사와 결합하여 주로 '~에'라고 해석한다.

be subject to ~에 달려 있다, ~될 수 있다	be accustomed to ~에 익숙하다
be committed/dedicated/devoted to ~에 헌신하다	contribute to ~에 기여하다
look forward to ~을 기대하다	object to ~에 반대하다
come close to 거의 ~할 뻔하다	be opposed to ~에 반대하다
be vulnerable to ~에 취약하다	be resistant to ~에 저항하다, 강하다

This guidebook is sure to **contribute to** [**improving** / ~~improve~~] the experience of travelers.
이 안내서는 분명 여행자들이 더 좋은 경험을 하게 해 줄 것이다.

The new agricultural method made crops more [**resistant** / ~~reluctant~~] **to** specific pests.
새로운 농사법은 작물들이 특정 해충에 더욱 강해지도록 만들었다.
→ reluctant는 to부정사와 쓰인다.

Many civil groups [**objected** / ~~opposed~~] **to** the legislation on a new free trade agreement.
많은 시민 단체가 새 자유무역협정 입법에 반대했다.

ETS 유형연습

정답과 해설 p.158

1 Sweetness Chocolate is pleased ------- that it will be listed on the Public Stock Exchange as of August 1.

(A) to announce
(B) announcement
(C) announced
(D) be announcing

2 The newspaper's circulation department is committed to ------- excellent service.

(A) provision
(B) provided
(C) providing
(D) provides

3 A few of the Fairmont Finance employees object to ------- for parking on the company premises.

(A) charge
(B) have charged
(C) be charged
(D) being charged

ETS 실전문제

1. Editor-in-chief Kyra Daley confirmed plans to expand the distribution area of the *Harnett Times* ------- Wilston County.
   (A) inclusive
   (B) to include
   (C) inclusion
   (D) will include

2. Please note that all outdoor programs are subject to ------- without prior notice.
   (A) cancellation
   (B) canceling
   (C) canceled
   (D) cancel

3. To handle the increase in sales, the human resources department intends ------- a number of new employees.
   (A) recruited
   (B) recruitment
   (C) recruiting
   (D) to recruit

4. ------- an international conference for over 1,000 participants was the most challenging assignment for the team.
   (A) Preparation
   (B) Preparing
   (C) Prepared
   (D) Being prepared

5. The management of Eurosan Enterprises is in the process of ------- a new set of guidelines for customer service.
   (A) establish
   (B) establishes
   (C) established
   (D) establishing

6. Artour Cycling executives cited slow sales as the reason for the decision ------- the Nordique bicycle line.
   (A) have discontinued
   (B) was discontinuing
   (C) will discontinue
   (D) to discontinue

7. At the end of November, author Eunice Kim is scheduled ------- her fifth lecture in Turnham.
   (A) to give
   (B) will be giving
   (C) giving
   (D) may have given

8. The consulting firm is responsible for ------- customized marketing solutions to small businesses.
   (A) offer
   (B) offered
   (C) offering
   (D) offers

9. It is usually most effective ------- a meeting agenda to the attendees in advance.
   (A) to circulate
   (B) circulating
   (C) circulated
   (D) circulation

10. The sales manager spends considerable time ------- his team members and new employees.
    (A) training
    (B) trains
    (C) trained
    (D) trainer

11. The CEO of Vento Cosmetics did not let the recent problems with foreign sales ------- the company's long-term export plans.
    (A) have affected
    (B) to affect
    (C) affect
    (D) affecting

12. Rosewood Library permits patrons ------- up to ten books at a time.
    (A) borrow
    (B) borrowed
    (C) will borrow
    (D) to borrow

13. All dancers should have at least two years of prior experience ------- be considered for the City Ballet.

    (A) likewise
    (B) in order to
    (C) currently
    (D) only if

14. The carpentry firm of Marcello & Buhl is seeking a summer apprentice with a strong interest in ------- the craft.

    (A) to learn
    (B) will learn
    (C) learning
    (D) learns

Questions 15-18 refer to the following e-mail.

To: a.menke@branwinmanufacturing.au
From: nobu.ito@peraltaelectronics.jp
Date: 4 November
Subject: Wholesale account setup
Attachment: Required_documents

Dear Ms. Menke,

Thank you for creating an online profile. We have taken the time to verify that your business meets our wholesale account requirements. Your business appears to be ---15---. There are just a few more steps to complete. ---16---, respond to this e-mail, letting us know that you have received it. Then, submit the documents listed in the attachment. To avoid delays, please be sure they include the same business name and phone number you used to create your online profile. ---17---.

Please note that all documents are examined by our tax department and may take up to fifteen business days ---18--- processed. You will be notified once your wholesale account has been created, and you can proceed to place your orders.

Thank you,

Nobu Ito, Peralta Electronics Wholesale Support

---

15. (A) intact
    (B) eligible
    (C) efficient
    (D) accountable

16. (A) First
    (B) Instead
    (C) Besides
    (D) Conversely

17. (A) Further action is needed.
    (B) We are likely out of stock.
    (C) It is important that they match.
    (D) Several options are still available.

18. (A) are
    (B) to be
    (C) is being
    (D) have been

UNIT 10 분사와 분사구문

무료 강의

1 분사의 자리

출제포인트 분사는 동사에 -ing, -ed가 붙어 형용사 역할을 하는 준동사이다. 문제를 풀 때는 먼저 빈칸이 형용사 자리인지 확인하고, 수식 및 보충하는 명사와 능동 관계인지 수동 관계인지 확인해야 한다.

◆ 명사 앞에서 수식

분사는 형용사처럼 명사 앞에서 명사를 수식할 수 있다.

National Bank will offer business loans at [**reduced** / ~~reduces~~] **interest rates** as of next Monday.
내셔널 은행은 다음 주 월요일부터 할인된 이자율로 기업 대출을 제공할 것이다.

◆ 명사 뒤에서 수식

명사 뒤에 온 '주격 관계대명사+be동사'를 생략하면 분사가 명사 뒤에서 명사를 수식하게 된다.

명사 뒤에서 수식할 때	분사 뒤에 목적어가 있으면 주로 능동 (-ing)	the paper [**detailing** / ~~detailed~~] the requirements 요구사항을 상세히 설명하는 서류
	분사 뒤에 전치사가 있으면 주로 수동 (p.p.)	the report [**written** / ~~writing~~] by a new assistant 새 조수에 의해 쓰인 보고서

Invitations were e-mailed for **a banquet** [**celebrating** / ~~celebrated~~] **the company's 60th anniversary**. 회사 창립 60주년을 기념하는 연회를 위해 이메일로 초대장이 발송되었다.

◆ 주격 보어

be동사와 같은 2형식 동사 뒤 주격 보어 자리에 분사를 쓸 수 있다. 주어와 보어의 능동/수동 관계에 주목한다.

The results of inspections on the food safety and quality in some restaurants **were** [**disappointing** / ~~disappointed~~]. 몇몇 식당의 식품 안전성과 품질에 관한 조사 결과는 실망스러웠다.

◆ 목적격 보어

keep, find, consider와 같은 5형식 동사의 목적어 뒤 목적격 보어 자리에 분사를 쓸 수 있다. 목적어와 목적격 보어의 능동/수동 관계에 주목해야 한다.

Novice readers might not **find** some of **the award-winning books** [**appealing** / ~~appealed~~].
초보 독자들은 수상작들 중 일부가 흥미롭다고 생각하지 않을 수도 있다.

ETS 유형연습

정답과 해설 p.160

1. The laboratory assistant job requires an ------- degree in chemistry or a related field.
   (A) advancement
   (B) advancing
   (C) advances
   (D) advanced

2. Our office secretary had made a backup of the computer files, so the information was ------- successfully after the power failure.
   (A) recovered
   (B) recover
   (C) recovering
   (D) recovery

3. The Bryntown Cobbler is a family-operated shoe repair business ------- in the reconditioning of fine leather footwear.
   (A) specialty
   (B) specializes
   (C) specialists
   (D) specializing

2 분사의 종류

출제포인트 현재분사는 능동, 과거분사는 수동의 의미를 갖는다. 분사와 수식/보충하는 명사의 관계가 능동이면 현재분사(-ing), 수동이면 과거분사(p.p.)를 선택한다.

▶ 현재분사

현재분사는 수식 또는 보충하는 명사와 능동 관계이다.

Some consumers have complained that **the labels** on appliances are [**confusing** / ~~confused~~].
일부 소비자들은 가전제품에 있는 라벨이 혼란스럽다고 불평했다.

→ 빈칸은 주격 보어 자리이다. 주어인 the labels와 보어인 confusing(혼란을 주는)은 능동 관계이다.

▶ 과거분사

과거분사는 수식 또는 보충하는 명사와 수동 관계이다. 완료의 의미를 나타내기도 한다.

The president has approved the [**revised** / ~~revising~~] **proposals** after much consideration.
사장은 많은 고민 끝에 수정된 제안을 승인했다.

→ 수식하는 명사 proposals는 revise(수정하다)와 수동 관계이다.

현재분사, 과거분사 빈출 표현

challenging assignment 힘든 (도전을 주는) 과제	closing ceremony 폐회식
opposing opinions 반대 의견	outstanding debts 미지불 채무
overwhelming demand 압도적인 수요	preceding years 지난 몇 년
distinguished economist 뛰어난 경제학자	confirmed reservation 확인된 예약
dedicated staff 헌신적인 직원	sophisticated system 정교한 시스템
designated area 지정된 장소	written consent 서면 동의

▶ 감정동사의 분사

-ed형(감정을 느끼는)은 주로 사람 명사와, -ing형(감정을 유발하는)은 주로 사물 명사와 어울린다.

사람 명사와 어울리는 과거분사(p.p.)

pleased 기쁜	excited 신난	satisfied 만족하는	amused 즐거운	impressed 감동받은
fascinated 매혹된	overwhelmed 압도된	confused 혼란스러운	frustrated 좌절한	concerned 걱정하는

ETS 유형연습

1. Based on the ------- number of advance ticket sales, we expect to see record attendance levels at this year's festival in Donegal.

   (A) overwhelm
   (B) overwhelms
   (C) overwhelming
   (D) overwhelmingly

2. Our team of ------- insurance specialists is ready to assist with any questions about claims.

   (A) experience
   (B) experienced
   (C) experiencing
   (D) experiences

3. Mr. and Ms. Cooper decided to build their house outside the city limits when the city's rigid building codes became too ------- to accommodate.

   (A) frustrated
   (B) frustration
   (C) frustrate
   (D) frustrating

3 분사의 활용

출제 포인트 분사 자리 찾기 유형 문제는 다른 품사 문제들에 비해 적용 능력, 해석 능력을 많이 요구한다. 분사와 형용사, 동명사, 동사를 구별하는 방법을 익히도록 한다.

▶ 분사 구별하기

현재분사는 동명사와 형태가 같고, 과거분사는 과거 시제 동사와 형태가 같으므로 구별에 유의한다.

[**Satisfying** / Satisfied] regular customers with the best service possible **is** our priority.
가능한 한 최고의 서비스로 단골 고객을 만족시키는 것이 우리가 우선시하는 것이다.
→ 동명사 Satisfying이 주어 역할을 하고 있다. Satisfied를 선택하면 주어(regular customers)와 동사(is)의 수가 불일치한다.

The paper [**included** / including] more details of the contracts with our suppliers.
그 서류에는 우리 공급업체와의 계약에 대한 상세 내용이 들어 있었다.
→ 문장에 동사가 없으므로 빈칸에 과거 시제 동사인 included가 필요하다.

The cost of leasing office equipment would be [**comparable** / comparing] to buying.
사무용 기기 임대 비용은 구매 비용과 맞먹을 수 있다.
→ 형용사와 분사를 구별할 때는 먼저 해석으로 구별하고, 해석상 차이가 없다면 형용사를 우선적으로 선택한다.

▶ 자동사의 분사

자동사는 목적어가 필요 없는 동사이므로, 수동의 의미를 가지는 과거분사(p.p.) 형태로 쓰지 않는다.

-ing 형태로만 쓰는 분사

existing facilities 기존의 시설   emerging market 신흥 시장   rising costs 증가하는 비용
lasting impression 지속되는 인상   missing luggage 분실 수하물   remaining work 남은 업무

Few in the IT industry have reported [**rising** / risen] profits in the past few years.
지난 몇 년간 수익 증가를 보고한 IT 업계 회사들은 거의 없었다.

▶ as p.p./than p.p. 구문

as 바로 뒤에 p.p.를 동반하여 '~했듯이, ~했던 대로'라고 해석한다. than 뒤에 p.p.를 쓰면 '~했던 것보다'라고 해석한다.

as expected 예상했던 대로   as requested 요청했던 대로   than anticipated 예상했던 것보다

As [**discussed** / discusses] before, special group rates will be applied.
전에 논의했던 대로 특별 단체 요금이 적용될 것이다.

ETS 유형연습

정답과 해설 p.161

1. Adequate storage space is very important to companies ------- large quantities of materials.
   (A) produced
   (B) produces
   (C) produce
   (D) producing

2. Patients may enjoy a ------- apple juice or tea while waiting to be seen by the chiropractor.
   (A) compliment
   (B) complimenting
   (C) complimentary
   (D) compliments

3. As ------- in our telephone conversation this morning, Mr. Fox will arrive at your factory at 2 P.M. on Wednesday, March 14.
   (A) discuss
   (B) discussion
   (C) discussing
   (D) discussed

4 분사구문

출제 포인트 분사구문은 수식어 역할을 하는 부사절이 변형된 것으로, 분사 자리의 능동과 수동을 구별하는 문제가 가장 많이 출제된다.

▶ 분사구문 만들기
'접속사+주어+동사'의 부사절에서 접속사와 주어를 생략하면 분사구문을 만들 수 있다.

┌ **Once it hires** a famous chef, the restaurant will make more profits. ❶ 접속사 생략 가능
└ **Hiring** a famous chef, the restaurant will make more profits. ❷ 주어(가 주절의 주어와 같으면) 생략
　유명한 주방장을 고용하면, 그 식당은 더 많은 수익을 낼 것이다. ❸ 동사를 '동사원형+-ing' 형태로 바꾸기

▶ 분사구문의 특징
분사구문은 주로 콤마를 동반하며, 분사 자리에 동사나 명사는 쓸 수 없다. 생략된 주어를 찾아 주어와 동사의 능동/수동 관계를 파악해야 하는데, 타동사인 경우 목적어가 있으면 현재분사(능동), 없으면 과거분사(수동)를 쓰면 된다. 분사구문에서 -ing는 '~하면서, ~하기 때문에' 등으로 다양하게 해석할 수 있다.

[**Posting** / ~~Posted~~] **a comment** on the review page, you will not be able to edit or delete it later.
평가 페이지에 의견을 남기시면, 이후에 그것을 편집 또는 삭제하실 수 없습니다.
→ 빈칸 앞에 생략된 주어와 분사의 관계가 능동 관계이며, 분사 뒤에 목적어가 있으므로 현재분사를 쓴다.

▶ 수동 분사구문
분사구문에서 be동사는 being으로 바뀌는데, being 또는 having been을 생략하면 과거분사로 시작하는 수동 분사구문이 될 수 있다. 과거분사는 주로 뒤에 전치사가 온다.

[**Faced** / ~~Facing~~] **with** problems with some machines, the management decided to extend the deadline for production. 몇몇 기계들에 발생한 문제에 직면하자, 경영진은 생산 마감일을 연장하기로 결정했다.

▶ 완료 분사구문
분사구문의 시제가 주절의 시제보다 앞설 때 쓴다.

[**Having traveled** / ~~Traveled~~] all around the globe, the photographer is having her photo exhibition at London Museum. 세계를 여행한 뒤, 그 사진작가는 런던 박물관에서 사진전을 열고 있다.

ETS 유형연습
정답과 해설 p.161

1 The city has experienced an unusually large amount of rainfall this year, ------- it difficult for road projects to be completed on time.

(A) made
(B) make
(C) makes
(D) making

2 ------- by the product demonstration last week, the operations manager has decided to order several of Handimaid's appliances.

(A) Impressed
(B) Impressive
(C) Impressing
(D) Impression

3 ------- a degree in accounting, Ms. Sakai is considered one of the top candidates for the management position.

(A) Having earned
(B) Earned
(C) Being earned
(D) Earn

1. In accordance with Chandu Museum policy, any personal items left in the building that are not ------- within one week will be discarded.
   (A) claim
   (B) claims
   (C) claimed
   (D) claiming

2. New employees should report to their ------- training locations at 8 A.M. with all necessary paperwork.
   (A) assigned
   (B) assign
   (C) assigns
   (D) assigning

3. Ms. Harrison is a long-time human resources professional ------- in the field for her outstanding achievements.
   (A) recognized
   (B) recognizes
   (C) recognizing
   (D) recognize

4. Most of our clients are ------- about the prospect of our showroom moving to a larger space.
   (A) exciting
   (B) to excite
   (C) excites
   (D) excited

5. Next week, the candidates in the local city council election will be on television ------- their ideas.
   (A) introduction
   (B) introducing
   (C) introduce
   (D) introductory

6. Lavelle Hospital's policy states that patients' personal information may not be released without ------- consent.
   (A) writing
   (B) written
   (C) write
   (D) wrote

7. Ever since the management of Glover Company was restructured, the quality of the company's products has been much -------.
   (A) improved
   (B) improving
   (C) improvement
   (D) improvable

8. Citing a survey ------- by an independent polling firm, *The Town Voice* reported that 70 percent of residents were in favor of constructing a new stadium.
   (A) conduct
   (B) conductor
   (C) conducted
   (D) conducting

9. When ------- your Galaxy glass dishware in boxes, first wrap it in soft tissue paper to protect against scratches.
   (A) stores
   (B) storing
   (C) store
   (D) stored

10. Alinton Hardware's policy is that customers may return any item within 30 days if they are not ------- with their purchase.
    (A) satisfactory
    (B) satisfaction
    (C) satisfied
    (D) satisfy

11. Tinley Typewriter Shop has been serving the Northport region for 25 years, ------- in vintage typewriter sales and repairs.
    (A) specializes
    (B) specializing
    (C) specialist
    (D) specialization

12. Due to the late arrival of his flight, Mr. Medina was unable to speak with reporters as -------.
    (A) scheduled
    (B) scheduling
    (C) schedule
    (D) schedules

13. There are many ------- signs that high-quality job-training programs in the Winton Area are expanding the pool of qualified workers for companies in the area.
    (A) encourage
    (B) encouraged
    (C) encouraging
    (D) encouragement

14. ------- that her order would not arrive on time, Ms. Chang requested the express delivery option.
    (A) Concern
    (B) Concerning
    (C) Concerns
    (D) Concerned

Questions 15-18 refer to the following advertisement.

Apple Picking at Habol Farms

The opportunity to pick your own apples at Habol Farms begins in September. This year we are expecting --15.-- , abundant crops. The variety called Honey Crisps will be ready to pick in early September. --16.-- , you can expect our famous Gala apples in mid-September. From the end of September through early October, you will be able to enjoy our crop of sweet Empire apples. --17.-- .

Of course, you do not have to pick your own apples. Visit our farm market where you can --18.-- apples that we have packaged in small and large baskets. You will also find many treats for sale, including cider donuts and other baked goods.

---

15. (A) amazed
    (B) amazes
    (C) amazement
    (D) amazing

16. (A) Next
    (B) As a result
    (C) For instance
    (D) Consequently

17. (A) Freshly baked apple pies are easy to make.
    (B) The farm hosts a music festival every October.
    (C) The growing season ends with delicious Granny Smith apples.
    (D) Apple trees originated in Central Asia.

18. (A) prefer
    (B) allow
    (C) connect
    (D) purchase

UNIT 11 전치사와 접속사

무료 강의

1 전치사 어휘 1

출제 포인트 전치사 어휘 문제는 매회 3문제 내외로 출제된다. 전치사의 기본 의미 두세 개 정도는 정확하게 외워 두어야 한다. '전치사+명사' 또는 '동사+전치사' 덩어리를 먼저 해석하면 문제 풀이 시간을 단축할 수 있다.

◆ at, on, in, by, until

at + 시점, 지점, 금액, 회사명*	~에(서)	at 9:00, at night, at the station, at a low price, at YBM
on + 날짜, 요일, 주제, 인터넷	~에 (대한)	on March 6, on Saturday, on education, on the Web site
in + 월, 계절, 연도, 아침/오후, 기간, 큰/독립된 공간, 분야	~에, ~ 동안, ~ 안에	in March, in summer, in 2016, in the morning, in a week, in the last ten years, in New York, in a conference room an increase in profits, advances in science
by + 시점, 행위자(수동태 뒤)*	~까지, ~에 의해	should arrive by this Friday, suggested by customers
until + 시점	~까지	not arrive until this weekend

*this/last/next Friday 앞에는 전치사 at, on, in을 쓸 수 없다.
*by, until은 시점 명사와 함께 쓰여 모두 '~까지'라고 해석되지만, 함께 쓰이는 동사 짝이 다르다. 완료를 나타내는 by는 1회성 동사(arrive, submit, complete 등), until은 지속성 동사(postpone, stay 등) 또는 동사의 부정형(not arrive)과 함께 쓴다.

◆ for, during, throughout, within

for + 기간(주로 숫자) 이유, 목적, 교환	~ 동안, ~ 때문에, ~ 대신에	for an hour, for the next five years blame A for B, substitute A for B
during + 기간(주로 명사)	~ 동안	during the presentation
throughout + 기간, 장소	~ 동안, 내내, ~ 도처에	throughout winter, throughout the building
within + 기간, 범위	~ 이내에	within a week, within 10 kilometers, within the budget

◆ around, beside, to, through

around + 장소	~ 근처에	around the office
beside + 장소	~ 옆에	beside(= next to) the escalator
to + 지점, 도착점	~에게	send packages to customers, given to the sales team
through + 장소, 추상 수단, 과정	~을 통하여, 내내	through the tunnel, through the Internet, through the process

ETS 유형연습

정답과 해설 p.164

1. Please label any food placed in the company refrigerator, or it will be thrown away ------- the end of each week.
   (A) at
   (B) into
   (C) plus
   (D) to

2. When preparing ------- a job interview, research your prospective employer's vision and core values.
   (A) of
   (B) to
   (C) for
   (D) among

3. Coffee filters, creamer, and sugar are located ------- the microwave in the break room.
   (A) down
   (B) beside
   (C) from
   (D) between

2 전치사 어휘 2

출제 포인트 전치사 중에는 두세 단어로 이루어진 구 전치사와 동명사와 함께 쓰여 특정한 의미를 나타내는 전치사가 있다. 전치사의 기본 의미와 더불어 빈출 용례를 함께 기억하자.

◆ 다양한 빈출 전치사

of + 소유, 소속 동격, 관련	~의	the films of the famous director, president of the medical clinic the fact of being late, a story of success
with + 동반, 소유	~와 함께, ~을 가지고	bring the notepad with you, with care(= carefully)
without	~ 없이	without previous experiences, without getting enough funds
behind	~ 뒤에, ~에 뒤처져	behind the building, behind schedule
unlike	~와 달리	unlike most other companies
except	~을 제외하고	every day except (on) Sunday
under + 진행, 영향	~ 중인, ~ 아래	under consideration, under control, under the direction of
against	~에 반대하는	compete against, vote against
for	~에 찬성하는	vote for, advocate for
*between	~ 사이에	between A and B, between the (two) options
*among	~ 중에	Among the candidates, Dan is the most qualified.
across	~을 가로질러, ~ 전체에 걸쳐	across the river, all across Canada

*between(둘 사이에)과 among(셋 이상 사이에) 뒤에는 복수명사가 온다.

◆ 구 전치사와 -ing 전치사

prior to ~ 이전에
apart from ~ 이외에
as to ~에 관하여
by means of ~을 이용하여
regarding / concerning ~에 관하여
following ~ 이후에

ahead of ~보다 앞서
because of / due to / owing to ~ 때문에
in addition to ~뿐만 아니라
on behalf of ~을 대신하여
notwithstanding ~에도 불구하고
including ~을 포함하여

regardless of ~와 상관없이
instead of ~ 대신에
on account of ~ 때문에
in spite of ~에도 불구하고
considering / given ~을 고려하여
excluding ~을 배제하고

고득점 TIP

'전치사+-ing' 관용 표현
전치사 뒤에 동명사가 왔을 때 특정한 의미를 나타내는 관용 표현들을 외워 두자.
by -ing ~함으로써   in -ing ~하는 데 있어서   on -ing ~하자마자

ETS 유형연습

정답과 해설 p.164

1 The Grovesburg Historical Society leads tours of local historical sites every day ------- Sunday.

(A) other
(B) except
(C) than
(D) some

2 ------- Ms. Wattanasin, everyone on the team needed additional time to complete the Web design tutorial.

(A) Even
(B) Rather than
(C) Apart from
(D) If not for

3 Please contact Ms. Blackwell in the personnel office if you have not received information ------- company reimbursement procedures.

(A) regard
(B) regards
(C) regarding
(D) regarded

3 전치사와 접속사

출제 포인트: 연결어 문제는 먼저 품사를 구분하는 것이 중요하다. PART 5에서는 접속사와 전치사 중 적절한 품사를 선택하는 문제가 자주 출제되고, PART 6에서는 접속부사를 이용한 어휘 문제가 자주 출제된다.

◆ 접속사와 전치사

접속사는 대개 절과 절을 연결하는 역할을 하며, '접속사+주어+동사'의 덩어리를 만든다. 전치사는 '전치사+명사(구)'의 수식어 덩어리를 만들며, 뒤에 '주어+동사'가 올 수 없다.

의미가 비슷한 접속사와 전치사

	접속사+주어+동사	전치사+명사
시간	when ~할 때 while ~하는 동안 as soon as ~하자마자	during ~ 동안 following ~ 이후에 prior to ~ 전에
조건	if ~라면 unless ~ 않는다면 as long as ~하는 한	in case of ~의 경우에 without ~가 없다면
이유	because ~하기 때문에	because of/due to/owing to ~ 때문에
양보	though/although/even though/even if 비록 ~일지라도	despite/in spite of ~에도 불구하고

Every visitor should not take a photo [**while** / ~~during~~] **they take a tour** of the facility.
모든 방문객은 시설을 둘러보는 동안 사진을 찍으면 안 된다.
→ during은 전치사이고 while은 접속사이다. 접속사 뒤에는 주어와 동사가 뒤따른다.

No matter how attractive, any proposal will not be accepted [**without** / ~~unless~~] **the cost projections**. 얼마나 매력적인지에 상관없이, 어떤 제안도 비용 계획이 없다면 받아들여지지 않을 것이다.
→ unless는 접속사이고 without은 전치사이다. 전치사는 뒤의 명사(구)와 결합한다.

두 가지 이상의 품사를 가지는 연결어

	접속사 (뒤에 절 추가)	전치사 (뒤에 명사 결합)	부사 (생략 가능)
as	~할 때, ~하듯이, ~ 때문에	~로서, ~만큼	–
besides	–	~ 이외에도	게다가
once	일단 ~하면	–	한때, 한 번
since	~ 이후로, ~ 때문에	~ 이후로	그 이후로
however	얼마나 ~든지, 어떻게 ~든지	–	하지만

ETS 유형연습

정답과 해설 p.164

1 Employees may not request a repayment of business travel expenses ------- a detailed itinerary is submitted with the claim.

(A) without
(B) unless
(C) as a result of
(D) while

2 Despite ------- declines in revenue over the past six months, the Mori & McGee firm intends to hire three new patent lawyers next year.

(A) will experience
(B) having experienced
(C) has experienced
(D) have been experiencing

3 ------- company president, Ms. Chen prioritizes balancing the short-term and long-term goals of Hideo Holdings.

(A) For
(B) As
(C) About
(D) Of

4 등위접속사와 상관접속사

출제 포인트: 등위접속사는 앞뒤의 단어, 구, 절 등 동일한 요소를 연결한다. 두 단어가 짝을 이루는 접속사를 상관접속사라고 한다. 상관접속사의 짝이 문제를 푸는 단서가 된다.

◆ 등위접속사의 종류와 병렬 구조

등위접속사는 대등한 단어, 구, 절을 연결한다. 단, so와 for는 절과 절만 연결할 수 있다. 등위접속사는 앞뒤에 있는 동일한 품사를 연결한다.

| and 그리고 | but/yet 그러나 | or 혹은, 그렇지 않으면 | so 그래서 | for 왜냐하면 |

The budget for the new project has been approved, [**so** / ~~therefore~~] renowned architects and designers will be hired. 새 프로젝트를 위한 예산이 승인되어서 유명한 건축가들과 디자이너들이 고용될 것이다.
→ 등위접속사 so가 문장과 문장을 연결하고 있다. therefore는 부사이기 때문에 뒤에 절(문장)을 추가할 수 없다.

The weekly talk show was very informative [**but** / ~~and~~] too long.
주간 토크쇼는 매우 유익했지만 너무 길었다.

The promotional materials should be concise **and** easily [**understandable** / ~~understands~~].
홍보 자료는 간결하고 이해하기 쉬워야 한다.

◆ 상관접속사의 종류와 수 일치

상관접속사는 두 단어가 짝을 이루어 단어와 단어, 구와 구, 절과 절을 연결한다. 상관접속사가 주어 자리에 사용된 경우 주어와 동사의 수 일치에 유의한다.

both A and B A와 B 둘 다		복수동사
either A or B A와 B 둘 중 하나	*neither A nor B A와 B 둘 다 아닌	B에 수 일치
not only A but (also) B/B as well as A A뿐 아니라 B도	not A but B/B but not A A가 아니라 B	

*neither A nor B는 B에 수를 일치시키는 것이 원칙이지만, A, B가 모두 단수 명사일 경우 복수 동사를 쓰기도 한다.

Both the main entrance [**and** / ~~or~~] the elevators **are** not available today for the regular inspection.
정기점검으로 인해 오늘 정문과 엘리베이터 둘 다 이용이 불가하다.

Ms. Patel **not only** graduated from university, majoring in economics, [**but** / ~~and~~] had abundant experience. 파텔 씨는 경제학 전공으로 대학교를 졸업했을 뿐 아니라 풍부한 경험도 가지고 있었다.

Neither the plot **nor** characters in the play [**were** / ~~was~~] very attractive to the kids.
연극의 줄거리나 등장인물 모두 아이들에게 그다지 매력적이지 않았다.

ETS 유형연습

1 The international catalog is comprehensive, ------ certain items may not be available in every country.
   (A) but
   (B) whereas
   (C) how
   (D) whenever

2 Conference participants can get to the Wyatt Hotel ------ by train or by bus.
   (A) unless
   (B) both
   (C) either
   (D) without

3 After discussing the terms of the new health-benefits contract, ------ management and employees were satisfied.
   (A) both
   (B) also
   (C) either
   (D) too

ETS 실전문제

1. The office staff had to be relocated ------- the renovation of the Cooper Street building.
   (A) during
   (B) so
   (C) spans
   (D) concerning

2. Customer inquiries will be responded to ------- one business day.
   (A) into
   (B) within
   (C) outside
   (D) opposite

3. ------- adding your contact information, you agree to allow Pontman Electronics to contact you with special offers.
   (A) By
   (B) To
   (C) Over
   (D) Behind

4. Buyers must pay inspection fees ------- other expenses related to completing a property transaction.
   (A) although
   (B) as well as
   (C) according to
   (D) that is

5. Make sure to dispose of all household waste in the proper containers ------- you are staying in the rental property.
   (A) yet
   (B) however
   (C) due to
   (D) while

6. Mr. Rossi's employment experience makes him a suitable candidate ------- the job.
   (A) on
   (B) by
   (C) per
   (D) for

7. The cancellation of the career fair was ------- a lack of interest among potential sponsors.
   (A) rather than
   (B) at any rate
   (C) due to
   (D) in case

8. The report suggests that neither insufficient advertising ------- a lack of effort were factors in the decreasing sales.
   (A) but
   (B) nor
   (C) so
   (D) yet

9. ------- the equipment did not function according to specifications, it was shipped back to the engineering department.
   (A) In order that
   (B) While
   (C) Because
   (D) Due to

10. Customers who do not wish to receive information ------- sales and promotions from Harmony Home Goods can change their account settings.
    (A) regard
    (B) regards
    (C) regarded
    (D) regarding

11. Because Ms. Min is a very popular salesperson, she is likely to receive a year-end bonus, ------- her actual sales totals.
    (A) regardless of
    (B) against
    (C) nevertheless
    (D) except for

12. Marany Consulting recommends hiring ------- experienced and newly licensed engineers to support the company in the long term.
    (A) whether
    (B) either
    (C) both
    (D) nor

13. ------- offering lightweight clothing, Hurvitz Travel Wear also sells stylish luggage and accessories.

(A) Except
(B) Besides
(C) However
(D) Unless

14. ------- the increase in ticket prices, the number of commuters using the city bus system has not changed.

(A) Despite
(B) Even though
(C) In consequence
(D) Rather

Questions 15-18 refer to the following job advertisement.

Volunteers Needed

Public Health Services (PHS) is seeking twelve employees wishing to volunteer at our information booth ---15.--- Grayerson University's Career Fair Weekend. The event will be held on April 13 and 14 from 10:00 a.m. to 6:00 p.m. Volunteers will work in four-hour shifts and inform ---16.--- about job opportunities, educational requirements, and possibilities for advancement. They will also be expected to discuss PHS's activities and describe a typical day in ---17.--- job. ---18.--- . A one-hour coaching session will be held in advance of the event. Interested employees can fill out a form, available at https://phs.employees.site.com/grayerson_cfw.

15. (A) onto
(B) around
(C) during
(D) towards

16. (A) workers
(B) students
(C) agents
(D) contestants

17. (A) them
(B) her
(C) his
(D) their

18. (A) Volunteers will offer suggestions following the presentation.
(B) Volunteers must indicate that they have read the policy.
(C) Volunteers will receive a complimentary lunch.
(D) Volunteers must re-register online each calendar year.

UNIT 12 부사절 접속사

무료 강의

1 시간, 조건의 부사절

출제포인트 부사절은 '부사절 접속사+주어+동사' 덩어리가 문장에서 부사 역할을 하는 것으로, 수식어이기 때문에 생략해도 전체 문장에 영향을 주지 않는다. 부사절 접속사 뒤에는 보통 주어와 동사를 갖춘 절이 나온다.

◆ 시간을 나타내는 부사절 접속사

| when/as ~할 때 | before ~ 전에 | after ~ 후에 | while ~하는 동안 |
| until ~까지 | since ~ 이후로 | once ~하자마자 | as soon as ~하자마자 |

[**As** / ~~During~~] actors appeared on the stage, the audience applauded enthusiastically.
배우들이 무대에 등장했을 때, 관중들은 열광적으로 박수갈채를 보냈다.
→ 시간의 접속사 as 뒤에는 완전한 절이 뒤따르며, 전치사 during 뒤에는 절이 올 수 없다.

The travel guide book has been translated into multiple languages [**since** / ~~when~~] it was published in 2005. 여행 안내서는 2005년에 출간된 이후로 다양한 언어로 번역되어 왔다.
→ 부사절 접속사 since가 '~ 이후로'라고 해석되는 경우, 부사절의 동사는 과거 시제, 주절의 동사는 현재완료 시제를 쓴다.

◆ 조건을 나타내는 부사절 접속사

| if 만약 ~라면 | unless/if not 만약 ~이 아니라면 | once 일단 ~하면 | as long as ~하는 한 |
| as far as ~하는 한 | considering that ~을 고려하면 | provided that ~라면 | in case ~의 경우에 (대비하여) |

The new business plan will be implemented soon [**unless** / ~~if~~] there is something wrong with it.
문제가 있는 게 아니라면, 새로운 사업 계획은 곧 시행될 것이다.

The client may make suggestions to the design [**as long as** / ~~in case of~~] they are made before work begins. 작업이 시작되기 전에 한다는 전제하에, 고객은 디자인에 대해 제안을 할 수 있다.
→ as long as는 부사절 접속사로서 뒤에 완전한 절을 이끌고, in case of는 전치사로서 뒤에 절이 올 수 없다.

> **고득점 TIP**
> 시간과 조건의 부사절에서는 현재 시제로 미래의 일을 나타낸다.
> Please be reminded that the class will be cancelled if there [**are** / ~~will be~~] less than 4 students.
> 만약 학생이 네 명 미만일 경우 수업이 취소될 것임을 잊지 마세요.

ETS 유형연습

정답과 해설 p.167

1 Please keep this temporary driver's card ------- the permanent card arrives at your address.
(A) and
(B) until
(C) because
(D) so

2 ------- the training period continues, new employees will receive sixty percent of their starting salary.
(A) As long as
(B) At times
(C) In time for
(D) By

3 ------- something is done, traffic congestion on the Winfield Parkway will continue to worsen.
(A) Unless
(B) Also
(C) Except
(D) Therefore

2 양보, 이유, 목적의 부사절

> **출제 포인트** 부사절 접속사를 전치사나 명사절 접속사와 구별하는 문제, 해석상 적절한 부사절 접속사를 선택하는 문제, 문장이 축약됐을 때 접속사 뒤 동사의 -ing/p.p. 형태를 고르는 문제 등이 나온다.

◆ 양보를 나타내는 부사절 접속사

| though/although/even though/even if 비록 ~일지라도 | while/whereas ~인 반면에 |

[**Although** / ~~Despite~~] there is a parking lot, it is not large enough for all employees.
주차장이 있지만, 그것은 모든 직원을 수용할 만큼 크지 않다.

→ although는 부사절 접속사로서 절을 이끌고, despite는 전치사이므로 명사(구)가 온다.

◆ 이유/목적을 나타내는 부사절 접속사

| because/since/as ~ 때문에 | now that 이제 ~하니까 | in that ~라는 점에서, ~ 때문에 |
| so that ~하기 위해서, ~할 수 있도록 | in order that ~하기 위해서 | |

[**Now that** / ~~Even if~~] you have renewed your rental agreement, you can continue to use the office space for a year. 당신이 임대 계약을 갱신했기 때문에, 사무실 공간을 일 년 더 사용할 수 있다.

◆ 부사절 접속사의 축약

❶ 능동태 문장의 축약: 접속사+-ing+목적어

부사절에서 주어는 생략하고 동사를 -ing형으로 바꿀 수 있다.

Mr. Pearson found out that some parts were missing [**while** / ~~during~~] assembling the shelves.
피어슨 씨는 선반을 조립하다가 몇몇 부품이 빠진 것을 발견했다.

→ while he was assembling the shelves에서 주어와 be동사를 생략한 구문이 사용되었다. during 다음에는 명사가 와야 한다.

❷ 수동태 문장의 축약: 접속사+p.p.(+부사(구))

부사절에서 주어와 be동사를 함께 생략한다.

As [**stated** / ~~states~~] in the supply contract, customized items cannot be returned without defects.
공급 계약서에 명시된 대로, 맞춤 제작 제품들은 결함이 없다면 반품될 수 없다.

→ 주어 it과 be동사가 생략된 'as+p.p.' 관용 표현에는 as stated, as requested, as discussed, as mentioned 등이 있다.

ETS 유형연습
정답과 해설 p.167

1 Mr. Sasaki has promised his staff a bonus ------- product sales are less than anticipated.

(A) furthermore
(B) in contrast
(C) as though
(D) even if

2 ------- the band has finally confirmed its availability, the outdoor concert will be scheduled for Sunday, June 11.

(A) In order for
(B) Now that
(C) So that
(D) Regarding

3 In his five years with Techniflex, Inc., Mr. Park has demonstrated repeatedly that he excels when ------- with a challenge.

(A) faces
(B) face
(C) facing
(D) faced

ETS 실전문제

1. Audience handouts can be designed to include relatively large amounts of text ------- the font size is not too small.
   (A) rather than
   (B) likewise
   (C) as long as
   (D) without

2. Empress Shoes is having a sale on summer items ------- it can make room for fall and winter products.
   (A) so that
   (B) which
   (C) in part
   (D) that is

3. This afternoon's flights to Barcelona, London, and Rome have all been delayed ------- inclement weather in the destination cities.
   (A) as for
   (B) due to
   (C) now that
   (D) only if

4. ------- First Regional Bank has done so well in Juniper, it will be opening branches in Pinewood and North Haven.
   (A) Unless
   (B) Since
   (C) Rather
   (D) Therefore

5. ------- receiving notice that the director of the Deerfield Orchestra will retire, the board of directors has been searching for a replacement.
   (A) Since
   (B) While
   (C) Once
   (D) Because

6. ------- the company faced hardships initially, it has now found success as the country's biggest manufacturer of plant-based cosmetics.
   (A) Instead
   (B) Unless
   (C) Whatever
   (D) Although

7. Employees currently working in Ridge Manufacturing's branch offices will move into the new headquarters ------- the building is finished.
   (A) once
   (B) even
   (C) besides
   (D) moreover

8. ------- Barn Owl Furniture is able to get bulk prices on basic components, the shop can afford to sell its chairs at a discount.
   (A) Because
   (B) Than
   (C) Again
   (D) Therefore

9. The deadline to submit vacation requests is January 15, ------- your vacation time is predetermined based on your job classification.
   (A) thus
   (B) unless
   (C) besides
   (D) despite

10. Taking an international trip will be a stress-free experience ------- you book with Fessner Travel.
    (A) yet
    (B) despite
    (C) whereas
    (D) when

11. Although initially ------- to be too heavy, the truck's load was well within state guidelines.
    (A) believed
    (B) believing
    (C) was believed
    (D) had been believed

12. Attendees who arrive ------- the presentation is underway should quietly find a seat and silence their phones.
    (A) while
    (B) as though
    (C) in order for
    (D) unless

13. Passengers must present photo identification ------- boarding trains that cross international borders.

    (A) because
    (B) when
    (C) and
    (D) whether

14. Please note that products ordered from Herb Emporium Online will not be shipped ------- full payment is received.

    (A) within
    (B) until
    (C) during
    (D) inside

Questions 15-18 refer to the following Web page.

Mantokos Supermarket — About Our Aisle Five

Regular shoppers at Mantokos Supermarket know about ---15--- we refer to as "Aisle Five Surprise." Aisle five in each of our stores is restocked weekly with an ever-changing selection of nonfood items, ranging from home decorations to small appliances that are priced to sell quickly. ---16--- . We acquire items from various sources. For instance, ---17--- an appliance manufacturer has a surplus of a specific blender, we will buy them. Accordingly, it is impossible to forecast each week's offerings. Of course, most customers enjoy this ---18--- aspect of our stores. They say the surprise enhances their shopping experience.

---

15. (A) whose
    (B) where
    (C) what
    (D) other

16. (A) We do not charge a restocking fee on unopened returns.
    (B) Follow the instructions carefully when constructing the shelf.
    (C) Locally made desserts have become increasingly popular.
    (D) We purchase these items from our suppliers and give the savings to you.

17. (A) yet
    (B) also
    (C) when
    (D) even so

18. (A) obsolete
    (B) unpredictable
    (C) cautious
    (D) new

UNIT 13 관계대명사

1 관계대명사의 종류

출제 포인트 관계대명사는 '접속사+대명사' 역할을 한다. 관계대명사 자리를 확인하는 문제, 관계대명사의 종류를 묻는 문제가 출제된다.

◆ 관계대명사의 이해
관계대명사는 두 문장을 하나로 이어주는 접속사 역할을 하는 동시에, 관계사절에서 주어, 한정사, 또는 목적어 역할을 한다. 관계사절은 선행사를 수식하거나, 앞서 언급한 것에 대한 부연 설명을 한다.

We received feedback from **the employees**. + **The employees** attended the workshop.
→ We received feedback from **the employees** [who / ~~those~~] attended the workshop.
우리는 워크숍에 참석했던 직원들로부터 피드백을 받았다.
→ 관계대명사 who가 관계사절에서 동사 attended의 주어 역할을 한다.

◆ 관계대명사의 종류
관계대명사의 형태는 선행사가 사람인지 아닌지, 관계대명사절에서 관계대명사의 격이 무엇인지에 따라 결정된다.

선행사(앞 명사)	주격	소유격	목적격
사람	who, that	whose	whom, that
사물	which, that	whose	which, that

❶ **주격 관계대명사**: 바로 뒤에 동사가 나온다.
The novel is based on **the documentary** [which / ~~whom~~] **was produced** in the 1990s.
그 소설은 1990년대에 제작된 다큐멘터리에 기초하고 있다.

❷ **소유격 관계대명사**: 바로 뒤 명사의 소유격 역할을 한다.
The crowds gathered to see **the prime minister** [whose / ~~who~~] **visit** hit the headlines in local papers. 군중들은 총리를 보려고 모여들었고, 그의 방문은 지역 신문에 대서특필되었다.

❸ **목적격 관계대명사**: 뒤에 주어와 동사가 나오며, 관계사절에서 목적어 역할을 하므로 뒤에 목적어가 없다.
The discount coupon [that / ~~whose~~] **purchasers receive** with their first order is valid for a month.
구매자들이 첫 주문과 함께 받게 되는 할인 쿠폰은 한 달 동안 유효하다.

ETS 유형연습

정답과 해설 p.170

1 The furniture store is owned by a talented carpenter ------- sells handmade as well as factory-made products.

(A) who
(B) whom
(C) whose
(D) which

2 Fong & Haas, Inc., has automated its toothpaste mixing processes, ------- used to take up more than half of the production time.

(A) and
(B) which
(C) though
(D) when

3 Metropolitan Artworks is an organization ------- mission is to support public art projects in the Twin Rivers area.

(A) that
(B) what
(C) which
(D) whose

2 관계대명사의 생략

출제포인트 목적격 관계대명사나 '주격 관계대명사+be동사'가 생략될 수 있다. 관계대명사 생략 문제가 나오면 능동, 수동 관계를 구분해야 한다.

◆ 목적격 관계대명사의 생략
목적격 관계대명사는 생략 가능하다.

The architect showed officials a floor plan of the airport he [**designed** / ~~was designed~~].
　　　　　　　　　　　　　　　　　　　　　　　　　　　　　= that he designed
건축가는 관계자들에게 자신이 설계한 공항의 평면도를 보여주었다.

◆ '주격 관계대명사+be동사'의 생략
주격 관계대명사 자체만은 생략할 수 없지만, '주격 관계대명사+be동사'는 생략 가능하다. 이 경우 선행사 뒤에 바로 현재분사 또는 과거분사가 오게 된다. 축약 전 동사가 능동태라면 현재분사가, 수동태라면 과거분사가 온다.

The career coach [**leading** / ~~lead~~] the motivation workshop has recently been awarded a prize.
　　　　　　　　= (who is) **leading** the motivation workshop
동기부여 워크숍을 이끌고 있는 커리어 코치가 최근 상을 받았다.

It will take at least 4 years to restore the historic palace [**damaged** / ~~was damaged~~] by a big fire.
　　　　　　　　　　　　　　　　　　　　　　　　　　　　　　 = (that was) **damaged** by a big fire
큰 화재로 손상된 유서 깊은 궁전을 복구하는 데 최소 4년이 걸릴 것이다.

> **고득점 TIP**
>
> **that의 용법**
> 관계대명사 that은 선행사가 사람일 때와 사물일 때 모두 수식할 수 있으며 뒤에 불완전한 절을 이끈다. 하지만 콤마 뒤, 전치사 뒤에는 관계대명사 that을 쓸 수 없다.
>
> The office is near the subway station, [**which** / ~~that~~] makes daily commutes easy.
> 사무실이 지하철역 근처에 있는데, 이 점이 매일 통근을 쉽게 만들어준다.
> → 여기서 **which**는 앞 문장 전체를 가리킨다. (= and this)
>
> There was a retirement celebration of John Weinstein for [**whom** / ~~that~~] employees have great respect.
> 직원들이 대단히 존경하는 존 와인스타인 씨의 은퇴 기념식이 있었다.
> → 관계대명사 **that**은 전치사 **for**의 목적어 역할을 할 수 없다.

ETS 유형연습

1 Province Bank customers are requested to update annually the passwords ------- use for online banking.

(A) they
(B) them
(C) their
(D) themselves

2 Of all the business plans ------- by the marketing manager, Mr. Martin's idea is the most impressive.

(A) review
(B) reviewed
(C) are reviewed
(D) which reviewed

3 The Springden government has published regulations ------- owners of rental property to provide recycling services for tenants.

(A) required
(B) will require
(C) requiring
(D) are required

3 관계대명사의 활용

출제 포인트 '전치사+관계대명사' 구조도 시험에 자주 출제된다. 선행사가 사람인지 사물인지 구분하여 적절한 목적격 관계대명사를 선택하거나, 어울리는 전치사를 선택할 수 있어야 한다.

◆ 전치사+관계대명사
선행사가 관계대명사절에서 전치사의 목적어로 쓰인 경우 '전치사+관계대명사' 덩어리를 만든다.

The weather is scorching **this week**. + Citizens are advised to stay indoors **during this week**.
→ The weather is scorching this week **during [which / when]** citizens are advised to stay indoors.
이번 주 날씨가 타는 듯이 더우니 (이번 주 동안) 시민 여러분은 실내에 머무는 것이 좋겠습니다.

Ms. Peng, the former HR director, was respected by the people **with [whom / which]** she worked.
전 인사부장이었던 펑 씨는 함께 일했던 사람들의 존경을 받았다.

→ 선행사가 사람이므로 whom이 쓰여야 한다.

◆ 수량 표현+of+관계대명사
수량 표현 뒤에 'of+관계대명사' 형태로 one of whom/which, some of whom/which, all of whom/which, none of whom/which 등이 쓰인다. '수량 표현+of+관계대명사' 뒤에는 불완전한 절이 온다.

The reporter interviewed 10 entrepreneurs, **most of [whom / them]** didn't have enough money in their early stages.
기자는 10명의 사업가들을 인터뷰했는데, 그들 중 다수가 초기에 충분한 자본이 없었다.

→ 두 문장을 연결하는 접속사가 없으므로 them은 쓸 수 없으며, 접속사 역할을 하는 동시에 전치사 of의 목적어 역할을 하는 목적격 관계대명사 whom을 써야 한다.

Students are asked to read reference books, **all of which [are / is]** written in English.
학생들은 참고 도서를 읽어야 하는데, 그것들은 모두 영어로 쓰여 있다.

→ which가 가리키는 대상이 reference books이므로 all of reference books와 어울리는 복수동사를 써야 한다.

The new staff lounge, **half of which [has / have]** been painted, is still under construction.
새 직원 휴게실은 절반만 페인트칠이 되었고 여전히 공사 중이다.

→ which가 가리키는 대상이 The new staff lounge이므로 단수동사를 써야 한다.

ETS 유형연습

정답과 해설 p.170

1. The names of the department heads to ------- the monthly reports should be sent are located on the last page of the manual.

   (A) whoever
   (B) whom
   (C) what
   (D) where

2. Candidates are asked to indicate their research interests by checking the boxes next to the projects on ------- they prefer to work.

   (A) that
   (B) whom
   (C) which
   (D) where

3. VECTO Design Co. has 12 graphic artists, all of ------- are skilled designers with at least 3 years of experience.

   (A) what
   (B) them
   (C) they
   (D) whom

4 관계부사

출제 포인트 관계부사는 '접속사+부사' 역할을 한다. 관계부사의 종류를 선택하는 문제, 관계대명사와 관계부사를 구별하는 문제가 출제된다.

◆ 관계부사의 종류

관계부사는 '접속사+부사' 역할을 한다. 관계부사절은 선행사를 수식하지만, 관계부사의 선행사는 생략되기도 한다.
관계부사는 '전치사+관계대명사'로 대체할 수 있다.

선행사	관계부사	전치사+관계대명사
시간을 나타내는 명사 (time)	when	in which/on which/at which
장소를 나타내는 명사 (place)	where	in which/on which/at which
이유를 나타내는 명사 (reason)	why	for which
방법을 나타내는 명사 (way)	*how	in which

*관계부사 how는 선행사와 함께 쓸 수 없다. 선행사 또는 관계부사 중 하나만 사용해야 한다.

- Welmart will install self-checkout counters. + Customers pay for their items **at the counters**.
→ Welmart will install self-checkout counters at [**which** / ~~where~~] customers pay for their items.
  Welmart will install self-checkout counters [**where** / ~~which~~] customers pay for their items.
  웰마트는 고객이 자신의 물건을 계산하는 셀프계산대를 설치할 예정이다.

We aim to reply to all e-mails within 24 hours, but there may be times [**when** / ~~which~~] we are slow to respond. 모든 이메일에 24시간 이내로 답변하려고 하지만, 대응이 늦어질 때가 있을 수도 있습니다.

◆ 관계부사 vs. 관계대명사

관계부사와 관계대명사는 뒤 문장의 구조를 통해 구별할 수 있다. 소유격을 제외한 주격, 목적격 관계대명사 뒤에는 불완전한 절이 오고, '전치사+관계대명사' 또는 관계부사 뒤에는 완전한 절이 온다.

The strong demand for commercial buildings is one of the reasons [**why** / ~~which~~] the overall price of properties has increased. 상가 건물에 대한 높은 수요는 전반적인 부동산 가격이 증가하는 원인 중 하나이다.
→ 관계부사 why 뒤에 '주어+자동사'의 완전한 절이 왔다.

We should update the directory [**that** / ~~where~~] includes the details about hotel amenities.
우리는 호텔 시설에 대한 세부 사항을 포함하는 안내책자를 갱신해야 한다.
→ 관계대명사 that 뒤에 주어가 없는 불완전한 절이 나왔다. 관계부사 where 뒤에는 완전한 절이 나와야 한다.

ETS 유형연습

정답과 해설 p.171

1 All shipments arrive at the receiving dock, ------- a warehouse worker checks their tracking labels.

(A) who
(B) which
(C) for which
(D) where

2 The facility manager has the key to the storage room ------- the office supplies are kept.

(A) where
(B) how
(C) when
(D) why

3 Dr. Kim's acceptance speech is expected to last about ten minutes, after ------- dessert will be served.

(A) that
(B) whose
(C) whom
(D) which

ETS 실전문제

1. The carpet in the lobby of the Chiang Mai Opera House will be replaced with material ------- is easier to maintain.
   (A) what
   (B) where
   (C) that
   (D) this

2. Central Zoo visitors ------- arrive by bus or train can receive a 10 percent discount on admission.
   (A) who
   (B) when
   (C) but
   (D) how

3. Dr. Thomsen, a leading biologist ------- work has been published in numerous journals, will be the featured speaker at next week's conference.
   (A) whose
   (B) which
   (C) that
   (D) their

4. Dr. Johnson is offering a three-hour workshop during ------- she will share some perspectives on effective time management.
   (A) whose
   (B) while
   (C) whatever
   (D) which

5. The jacket you ordered is currently unavailable in the color you -------, but we will send the rest of your order promptly.
   (A) requests
   (B) requested
   (C) are requested
   (D) requesting

6. Content strategist Lorna Poggioli is an expert on the trends ------- the business world.
   (A) shape
   (B) shaped
   (C) shaping
   (D) shaper

7. Ella Portofino, ------- is known for her motivational speeches, will be the guest speaker at ORIL Leadership Conference in June.
   (A) each
   (B) which
   (C) who
   (D) this

8. All motorists are required to avoid the areas of Fifth Street ------- traffic lanes are being repainted.
   (A) which
   (B) whom
   (C) where
   (D) why

9. Supervisors ------- have questions about the new expense report process should contact the budget office for assistance.
   (A) what
   (B) whose
   (C) which
   (D) who

10. *Red Sand Garden*, ------- was released by Dream Town Studios last week, has been popular with those in their 30s.
    (A) when
    (B) which
    (C) who
    (D) whose

11. The museum's conservation project is made possible by a donation from Mr. Nguyen, ------- family owns the land.
    (A) those
    (B) itself
    (C) whose
    (D) each other

12. To improve efficiency, Boisclair Robotics designed a machine ------- can monitor the entire assembly line in the factory.
    (A) that
    (B) like
    (C) near
    (D) so

13. Managers often have to decide between several courses of action, none of ------- is completely right or wrong.

(A) that
(B) which
(C) when
(D) where

14. ------- for server positions who have not received a response within two weeks should send a follow-up e-mail.

(A) Applications
(B) Applies
(C) Applicants
(D) Applying

Questions 15-18 refer to the following e-mail.

To: Customer Service
From: Eun-Ju Tang
Date: November 14
Subject: Order number 491001

Dear Customer Service Agent,

I have received the two items ---**15.**--- I purchased from your Web site on November 8. ---**16.**--- . Unfortunately, the gray blouse I ordered was supposed to be a medium, but a large one was shipped.

I would like to ---**17.**--- . the blouse. In fact, I would prefer to exchange it by mail for the correct size, but I could not determine from the Web site which ---**18.**--- to use. Sadly, I lost the instructions included with the package. Would you please advise me at your earliest convenience?

Sincerely,

Eun-Ju Tang

---

15. (A) that
(B) what
(C) when
(D) these

16. (A) Both of the items were the wrong size.
(B) I ordered a medium-sized blue sweater.
(C) The blue sweater I received is perfect.
(D) Now I would like to see other styles you offer.

17. (A) return
(B) model
(C) display
(D) examine

18. (A) addressable
(B) addressed
(C) addressing
(D) address

UNIT 14 명사절 접속사

1 명사절 접속사의 이해

출제포인트 명사절 접속사는 주어나 목적어 역할을 하는 명사절을 이끌며, 관계대명사나 다른 접속사와 구별하는 문제가 자주 출제된다. that, whether가 자주 출제되며, 다른 명사절 접속사들의 비중도 높아지고 있다.

◆ 명사절 접속사의 역할

'접속사+주어+동사'로 이루어진 절이 문장에서 주어나 목적어, 또는 보어의 역할을 할 때 명사절이라고 부른다. 명사절 접속사는 다음과 같으며, 명사절 접속사 자리에 although, because, while 등과 같은 부사절 접속사를 쓸 수 없다.

that ~라는 것	whether/if ~인지 아닌지	who 누가	whose 누구의	whom 누구를	
what 무슨, 무엇	which 어느, 어느 것	when 언제	where 어디에	how 어떻게, 얼마나	why 왜

주어 [**Whether** / ~~While~~] we can secure the research funding or not **is** still uncertain.
우리가 연구 자금을 확보할 수 있을지는 아직 미지수다.

목적어 The clinic **decided** [**that** / ~~because~~] it will terminate the contract with the current supplier. 병원은 현재 납품 업체와의 계약을 해지하기로 결정했다.

◆ 명사절 접속사와 관계대명사의 구별

that절이 주어, 목적어, 또는 보어 역할을 하면 명사절이고, 앞 명사를 수식하면 관계사절이다.

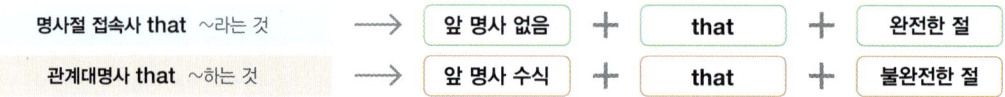

명사절 접속사 The director **asked** [**that** / ~~whereas~~] researchers meet her in person.
　　　　　　　　　　　　동사　　　　　　　　　완전한 절(주어+동사+목적어)

이사는 연구원들이 자신을 직접 만나야 한다고 요청했다.
→ that 명사절이 asked의 목적어 역할을 하고 있다. whereas는 '~인 반면에'라는 의미의 부사절 접속사이다.

관계대명사 The lecturer will answer **inquiries** [**that** / ~~whether~~] you might have.
　　　　　　　　　　　　　　　　　　　　　　　　　불완전한 절(주어+동사+목적어)

강연자는 여러분이 가지고 있을 법한 질문들에 대답해줄 것이다.
→ that 관계대명사절이 앞 명사(선행사 inquiries)를 수식하고 있다. whether 명사절은 앞 명사를 수식할 수 없다.

ETS 유형연습

정답과 해설 p.173

1 Hua Husing's achievements in biochemistry were remarkable, especially considering ------- he was only twenty-six at the time.

(A) that
(B) what
(C) since
(D) whether

2 Given the number of small farms in the region, it is not surprising ------- the Bowe Valley has many organic food shops.

(A) into
(B) that
(C) there
(D) more

3 The policy clearly states ------- food and beverages are not allowed in the museum.

(A) that
(B) what
(C) unless
(D) then

2 명사절 접속사 that/what

출제 포인트 명사절 접속사 that은 뒤에 '주어+동사'와 결합하여 '~라는[하는] 것'이라고 해석하며, 문장에서 주어, 목적어, 보어 역할을 한다. 명사절 접속사 that과 what을 구별하는 문제가 출제된다.

▶ 주어 역할을 하는 that

that이 이끄는 명사절은 It ~ that 구문의 진주어 역할을 한다.

It is obvious [**that** / since] the domestic demand has risen for six months.
국내 수요가 6개월 동안 증가하고 있다는 것은 명백하다.

▶ 목적어 역할을 하는 that

that 명사절을 직접 목적어로 취하는 동사를 기억해야 한다.

agree that ~에 동의하다	indicate that ~을 나타내다	ensure that ~을 보장하다
confirm that ~을 확인하다	announce that ~을 발표하다	note that ~을 유념하다
assure 사람 that ~에게 …라는 것을 장담하다		inform 사람 that ~에게 …라는 것을 알려주다
remind 사람 that ~에게 …라는 것을 상기시키다		notify 사람 that ~에게 …라는 것을 알려주다

We **assure** you [**that** / before] business will continue as usual.
우리는 업무가 평상시와 같이 지속될 것임을 당신에게 장담한다.

▶ that절 관용 표현

형용사+that	be aware that ~을 알다 be afraid that ~을 걱정하다	be certain/sure/confident that ~을 확신하다 be hopeful/optimistic that ~을 희망/낙관하다
명사+that (동격절)	the fact that ~라는 사실 the evidence that ~라는 증거	the news that ~라는 소식 the rumor that ~라는 소문 the idea that ~라는 생각 the opinion that ~라는 의견

▶ 명사절 접속사 that과 what의 구별

명사절 접속사 that 뒤에는 완전한 절이, what 뒤에는 불완전한 절이 온다.

| 명사절 접속사 that | → | 앞 명사 없음 | + | that | + | 완전한 절 |
| 명사절 접속사 what | → | 앞 명사 없음 | + | what | + | 불완전한 절 |

The book talks about [**what** / that] is most important for success.

불완전한 절(주어+be동사+보어)
그 책은 성공을 위해 가장 중요한 것에 대해 이야기한다.

ETS 유형연습

정답과 해설 p.173

1 When you subscribe to *News Update*, you can be confident ------- you will receive a reliable analysis of the latest political and economic trends.

(A) that
(B) whether
(C) which
(D) whoever

2 The administration of Holya Office Park has assured us ------- work will be only minimally impacted while construction continues.

(A) whoever
(B) they
(C) that
(D) because

3 ------- pleased the clients most was the effective customer service provided by Moradon Bank.

(A) Who
(B) That
(C) What
(D) This

3 명사절 접속사 whether/if

출제포인트 명사절 접속사 whether는 주어, 목적어, 보어 자리에 쓸 수 있으며, 동사의 목적어 자리에는 whether 대신 if를 쓸 수 있다.

◆ 명사절 접속사 whether/if

명사절 접속사 whether는 '~인지 아닌지'라고 해석하며 or를 자주 동반한다. if는 동사의 목적어 자리에서만 명사절을 이끌 수 있고, 주어나 보어 자리에 쓸 수 없다.

주어 [**Whether** / If] the gallery will rearrange its displays **has not been approved**.
미술관이 전시품을 재배치할 것인지는 승인되지 않았다.
→ whether절은 not approved와 같이 불확실성을 나타내는 표현과 함께 자주 쓰인다. 주어 자리에 if절은 쓸 수 없다.

목적어 I **wondered** [**if** / about] the university was first founded in Sydney or in Melbourne.
나는 그 대학교가 처음에 시드니에서 설립되었는지 멜버른에서 설립되었는지 궁금했다.
→ about은 전치사이므로 바로 뒤에 '주어+동사'가 올 수 없다.

◆ whether+to부정사

접속사 whether 뒤에 이어지는 주어가 주절의 주어와 같을 경우, 주어를 생략하고 동사를 to부정사로 바꾸어 쓸 수 있다. that과 if를 제외한 모든 명사절 접속사는 '접속사+to부정사' 형태로 쓸 수 있다.

Ms. Jackson is unsure as to **whether** [**to buy** / buy] **or rent a car**. 잭슨 씨는 차를 살지 빌릴지 확신이 없다.
(= Ms. Jackson is unsure as to whether she should buy or rent a car.)

The manager hasn't yet decided [**whether** / while] **to attend** the weeklong seminar series.
부장은 일주일 동안 진행하는 세미나 시리즈에 참석할지 여부를 아직 결정하지 않았다.
→ 부사절 접속사인 while은 뒤에 주어를 생략할 경우 분사(-ing, -ed)가 온다.

고득점 TIP

that과 whether 구별하기

that ~라는 것	확정 사실을 나타내는 동사	뒤에 완전한 문장
whether ~인지 아닌지	미정 사실을 암시하는 동사	뒤에 완전한 문장

One of the largest IT companies concluded [**that** / whether] it would acquire the startup.
가장 큰 IT 회사 중 하나가 그 스타트업 회사를 인수하기로 결정했다.

Our team is wondering [**whether** / that] we will win the contract.
우리 팀은 우리가 계약을 따낼지 아닐지 궁금해하고 있다.

ETS 유형연습

정답과 해설 p.174

1 The fax machine is out of service, and an experienced technician has been called in to see ------- it can be repaired.

(A) if
(B) that
(C) what
(D) though

2 Eun Sung Han, president of Westhaven Glassworks, is considering ------- to renew the contract with Pineford Trucking.

(A) whether
(B) if
(C) what
(D) so

3 Harmony Design consultants can help clients decide whether to use curtains ------- blinds when decorating their windows.

(A) so
(B) but
(C) nor
(D) or

4 의문사와 복합관계대명사

출제 포인트 의문사에는 의문대명사, 의문형용사, 의문부사가 있다. 각각의 의문사가 가지는 우리말 의미뿐 아니라 뒤에 이어지는 문장 구조를 파악해야 한다.

▶ 의문대명사

의문대명사는 명사절을 이끌며, 명사절에서 주어, 목적어 역할을 한다. 뒤에 주어나 목적어가 없는 불완전한 절이 온다.

| who 누가 ~하는지 | whom 누구를 ~하는지 | what 무엇을 ~하는지 | which 어느 것[사람]을 ~하는지 |

The newsletter provides information about [**what** / ~~where~~] employees need to know.
소식지는 직원들이 알아야 할 사항에 대한 정보를 제공한다.

▶ 의문형용사

의문형용사는 명사절을 이끄는 접속사이면서, 명사절에서는 바로 뒤 명사를 수식하는 한정사 역할을 한다.

| which 어느 …가 ~하는지 | what 무슨 …가 ~하는지 | whose 누구의 …가 ~하는지 |

The survey asked [**which** / ~~where~~] **design** for the new product is the best.
설문조사는 어떤 신제품 디자인이 가장 좋은지 물었다.

▶ 의문부사

의문부사는 명사절을 이끌며 명사절에서 부사 역할을 한다. 뒤에 완전한 절이 온다.

| when 언제 ~하는지 | where 어디에서 ~하는지 | how (형용사/부사) 어떻게/얼마나 ~하는지 | why 왜 ~하는지 |

The restaurant should be able to explain [**how** / ~~which~~] **long** it has had each ingredient on shelf.
식당은 각 재료를 얼마나 오랫동안 선반에 놔두었는지를 설명할 수 있어야 한다.

▶ 복합관계대명사

명사절을 이끌어 주어, 목적어 역할을 하거나, 부사절을 이끌어 수식어 역할을 한다. 뒤에 불완전한 절이 온다.

복합관계대명사	명사절	부사절
who(m)ever	anyone who ~하는 사람은[을] 누구든지	no matter who 누가 ~하든 상관없이
whatever	anything that ~하는 것은[을] 무엇이든지	no matter what 무엇이 ~하든 상관없이
whichever	anything that ~하는 것은[을] 어떤 것이든지	no matter which 어느 것이 ~하든 상관없이

*whatever, whichever는 한정사 역할을 할 수도 있다.

[**Whoever** / ~~Who~~] wants to take a paid vacation of more than a week should tell their supervisor.
= **Anyone who** 일주일 이상의 유급 휴가를 받기 원하는 사람은 누구든지 자신의 팀장에게 말해야 한다.

ETS 유형연습

정답과 해설 p.174

1 A good résumé tells employers ------- a candidate's qualifications match the job responsibilities.

(A) how (B) what
(C) which (D) whose

2 Members of the Foster City Historical Society are petitioning to have ------- remains of the courthouse's original architectural elements preserved.

(A) which (B) that
(C) what (D) it

3 ------- acquires the Grotten painting will probably have purchased the most expensive piece of artwork at the auction.

(A) Who (B) Whom
(C) Whose (D) Whoever

ETS 실전문제

1. One frequent complaint air travelers make is ------- the overhead compartments are too small.
   (A) then
   (B) to
   (C) whether
   (D) that

2. Miyo Technologies encourages managers to take responsibility for ------- their teams produce.
   (A) them
   (B) that
   (C) what
   (D) whose

3. ------- should impress passengers most is the comfort of the reupholstered seating at Liverpool Regional Airport.
   (A) Who
   (B) What
   (C) When
   (D) Where

4. Mr. Song has not yet decided ------- of the three candidates is right for the position of lead product developer.
   (A) which
   (B) what
   (C) whom
   (D) whoever

5. The manufacturer guarantees that its cosmetic products are good for three years or until the expiration date on the package, ------- is sooner.
   (A) what
   (B) when
   (C) that
   (D) whichever

6. When asked ------- she will retire soon, Ms. Johannsen said that she will never stop working.
   (A) while
   (B) whereas
   (C) whenever
   (D) whether

7. One recent study published in *Working Trends Today* magazine suggests ------- people who are left-handed are more likely to succeed in business.
   (A) that
   (B) which
   (C) when
   (D) as to

8. The market-research department conducted a survey on ------- often people listen to the radio while driving their cars.
   (A) who
   (B) how
   (C) that
   (D) which

9. The executive team of Trannelin Industries is determining ------- divisions will transfer to the West Coast next year.
   (A) any
   (B) none
   (C) each
   (D) which

10. Today, ------- is known that even moderate exercise is beneficial to the heart.
    (A) which
    (B) that
    (C) what
    (D) it

11. ------- needs assistance is welcome to come to the personnel office for a job application or information on application procedures.
    (A) Whoever
    (B) What
    (C) If
    (D) Since

12. Many readers state that the editorial page of the daily newspaper is more enlightening but admit that ------- they read first is the sports page.
    (A) what
    (B) these
    (C) if
    (D) because

13. Although multiple studies were conducted by market research groups, it is still uncertain ------- customers are ready to purchase their groceries on the Internet.
    (A) who
    (B) so as to
    (C) whether
    (D) whichever

14. Spring Flower Gifts trains every manager in its retail stores in ------- they should deal with customer inquiries.
    (A) which
    (B) who
    (C) what
    (D) how

Questions 15-18 refer to the following Web site.

---

https://www.harrisonbrothersrentals.com

Harrison Brothers Rentals is the leading heavy equipment rental service in Devon. From excavators and cranes to pavers and compactors, Harrison Brothers has ---15.--- you need for commercial and home construction. All of our rentals include delivery of the machinery directly to your ---16.--- .

In addition to our rental service, we also have a repair and resale service. We purchase older equipment that may no longer be working and hand it over to our expert mechanics for repair. ---17.--- . To learn more or to see a catalog of the ---18.--- equipment we have in stock, visit www.harrisonbrothersrentals.com/resale.

---

15. (A) this
    (B) that
    (C) what
    (D) which

16. (A) worksite
    (B) event
    (C) receptacle
    (D) park

17. (A) Casey and Bill Harrison founded the business more than 40 years ago.
    (B) Then we resell it at a significant discount over the cost of new equipment.
    (C) Large companies trust us for their equipment needs.
    (D) Our cranes have been inspected for safety.

18. (A) final
    (B) unusable
    (C) reconditioned
    (D) external

UNIT 15 비교/도치 구문

1 원급 비교

출제 포인트 원급 비교 구문은 두 대상이 서로 동등할 때 쓴다. 시험에는 'as+형용사/부사+as', 'the same+(명사)+as' 구문의 짝 찾기나 원급 비교에서 형용사, 부사의 품사를 판단하는 문제가 자주 출제된다.

◆ as+형용사/부사의 원급+as: ~만큼 …한/하게

The incoming coach will be faced with [**as** / ~~enough~~] many problems **as** other managers have.
새로 취임한 코치는 다른 관리자들이 가지고 있는 것만큼 많은 문제들에 직면할 것이다.
→ 주어진 문장에서 as를 보고 as ~ as 구문을 파악할 수 있다.

The outdoor jacket is made of a new material which is **as** [**light** / ~~lighter~~] **as** a feather.
야외용 재킷은 깃털처럼 가벼운 신소재로 만들어진다.

◆ the same+(명사)+as: ~와 똑같은

The title of the film is actually **the same** [**as** / ~~than~~] the main character's name.
영화의 제목은 사실 주인공의 이름과 똑같다.

The newest computer model has **the same** features [**as** / ~~than~~] the one released three years ago.
최신형 컴퓨터 모델은 3년 전에 출시된 것과 똑같은 특징을 가지고 있다.

◆ 원급 강조

as ~ as 앞에 just(꼭, 똑같이), almost/nearly(거의), twice(두 배로) 등을 써서 원급의 의미를 강조한다.

Investment has risen [**twice** / ~~second~~] **as** fast **as** consumption for the last decade.
지난 10년 간 투자는 소비의 두 배만큼 빠르게 증가했다.

◆ 원급의 품사 판단

원급의 품사를 판단하려면 as ~ as를 빼고 문장 구조를 살핀다.

Houses in New York City **are** almost as [**expensive** / ~~expensively~~] as those in Seoul.
뉴욕시의 주택들은 거의 서울만큼 비싸다.
→ almost as ~ as those in Seoul을 빼고 문장 구조를 살피면 are 뒤에 보어가 없으므로 형용사 expensive가 와야 한다.

In the case of an emergency, please **leave** the building as [**rapidly** / ~~rapid~~] as possible.
응급 상황이 발생할 경우에, 가능한 한 빨리 건물을 떠나십시오.
→ as ~ as possible을 빼고 문장 구조를 살피면 동사 leave를 수식하는 부사 rapidly가 와야 한다.

ETS 유형연습

정답과 해설 p.176

1 The new FRI-25 digital camera model has the same high-tech features ------- many standard models in the market.

(A) as
(B) than
(C) most
(D) more

2 A consumer report has revealed that less expensive laundry detergents can be ------- as effective as the more expensive products.

(A) soon
(B) just
(C) very
(D) so

3 After the disk driver is installed, the protective cover should be replaced as ------- as possible to prevent the accumulation of dust.

(A) quick
(B) quicker
(C) quickest
(D) quickly

216

2 비교급

출제 포인트 비교급 구문은 두 대상 중에서 하나가 우월하거나 열등할 때 쓴다. 시험에는 '비교급+than' 구문에서의 짝 찾기 문제뿐 아니라 비교급 강조 부사 또는 관용 표현과 관련된 문제도 자주 출제된다.

◆ 형용사/부사의 비교급+than: ~보다 더 …한/하게

비교급은 형용사/부사 뒤에 -er을 붙이거나 앞에 more를 붙이고, 주로 than과 함께 쓴다.

Due to rising demand, it is necessary to process orders [**faster** / ~~fast~~] **than** before.
증가하는 수요 때문에, 주문을 전보다 빠르게 처리하는 것이 필요하다.

The new version of the inventory program is [**more** / ~~much~~] difficult **than** the old version.
새로운 버전의 재고 관리 프로그램은 구 버전보다 더 어렵다.

Our mobile phones are guaranteed to require [**fewer** / ~~less~~] repairs **than** competitors' goods.
우리 휴대전화는 경쟁사들 제품보다 수리가 덜 필요할 것임을 보장한다.
→ 'fewer+복수명사'는 '더 적은 수의 ~'를 뜻하며, less 뒤에는 불가산명사가 나와야 한다.

◆ 비교급 강조: much/even/still/far/a lot+비교급 (훨씬 더/덜 ~한)

Most drinks on the market were found to contain [**much** / ~~very~~] more sugar than the stated.
시중에 나와 있는 대부분의 음료들이 명시된 것보다 훨씬 더 많은 설탕을 함유하고 있는 것으로 밝혀졌다.

◆ 비교급의 품사 판단

Dr. Watson's latest economic forecast **is** more [**optimistic** / ~~optimistically~~] than his previous one.
왓슨 박사의 최신 경제 전망은 그의 이전 전망보다 더 낙관적이다.
→ is 뒤 보어 자리이므로, 형용사 optimistic이 와야 한다.

◆ 비교급 관련 표현

more than ~ 이상	less than ~ 이하, ~ 미만	no sooner than ~ 이후에
no later than 늦어도 ~까지	no/not any longer 더 이상 ~ 않다	other than ~ 이외에
rather than ~보다는	the 비교급 of the two 둘 중에서 더 ~한	the 비교급 ~, the 비교급 … ~하면 할수록 더 …하다

The more customers are satisfied, **the** [**more** / ~~most~~] profit the company earns.
고객이 만족할수록 회사는 더 많은 수익을 얻는다.

ETS 유형연습

정답과 해설 p.177

1. In a survey of Office Supply Warehouse's customers, the majority reported that they could order ------- from the Web site than over the phone.
   (A) efficient
   (B) most efficient
   (C) more efficiently
   (D) efficiently

2. In order for Mr. Song's group to complete the data collection project on time, we will need ------- more administrative support.
   (A) so
   (B) even
   (C) too
   (D) very

3. The advertising campaign for the new Cool Fizz soft drink will feature flavor ------- price.
   (A) rather than
   (B) in the event of
   (C) except for
   (D) as for

3 최상급

출제 포인트 최상급 구문은 셋 이상의 대상 중에서 하나가 가장 우월하거나 열등하다는 것을 표현할 때 쓴다. 최상급 앞에 주로 the가 오기 때문에 the 뒤에 빈칸이 있으면 형용사/부사의 최상급이 올 수 있다는 것을 기억해야 한다.

◆ 최상급의 의미와 형태

최상급은 형용사/부사 뒤에 -est를 붙이거나 앞에 most를 써서 나타내고, 앞에 주로 the가 온다. 최상급 뒤에는 'of+복수명사/시간 명사', 'in+장소 명사', 'that 주어 have/has ever p.p.' 등 범위를 나타내는 표현이 자주 붙는다.

What we used for this furniture is the [**most durable** / ~~durability~~] **of all materials** available.
우리가 이 가구에 사용한 것은 이용할 수 있는 모든 소재 중에서 가장 견고한 것이다.

The program is the [**most reliable** / ~~more reliable~~] way to manage network systems **in the industry**.
그 프로그램은 업계 내에서 네트워크 시스템을 관리하기 위한 가장 믿을 만한 방법이다.

The musical performance last night was [**the most** / ~~more~~] impressive **(that) I have ever seen**.
어젯밤에 본 뮤지컬 공연은 내가 여태껏 본 것 중 가장 인상적인 공연이었다.
→ impressive 다음에 one(= musical performance)이 생략된 것으로 볼 수 있다.

◆ 최상급 관련 표현

the+서수+최상급
The taste is **the second** [**most** / ~~more~~] important factor in restaurants after the hygiene. 맛은 식당에서 위생 다음으로 두 번째로 가장 중요한 요소이다.

one of the+최상급+복수명사
Plastic is **one of the most widely used** [**materials** / ~~material~~] in daily goods. 플라스틱은 일상 용품에 가장 널리 사용되는 소재 중 하나이다.

◆ 최상급의 품사 판단

Attendees said the fireworks were the most [**impressive** / ~~impressively~~] **part** of the festival.
참석자들은 축제에서 불꽃놀이가 가장 인상적인 부분이었다고 말했다.
→ 명사 part를 수식하는 자리이므로 형용사 impressive가 와야 한다.

◆ 최상급 강조: much/easily/by far/quite+최상급 (단연코 가장 ~한)

This year's performance is being considered [**by far** / ~~extremely~~] **the most** successful.
올해의 성과는 단연 가장 성공적인 것으로 여겨지고 있다.

ETS 유형연습

1. Of the subway lines that stop in the central business district, the green line is the ------- to walk to from the Franklin Building.
   (A) more easily
   (B) easiest
   (C) most easily
   (D) easy

2. From among the five applicants for the job, naturally we will hire the ------- candidate to fill the position.
   (A) qualified
   (B) most qualified
   (C) qualifying
   (D) most qualifying

3. The funds allocated to new product development in this year's budget are expected to be ------- amount in recent history.
   (A) generously
   (B) more generous
   (C) more generously
   (D) the most generous

4 도치 구문

> **출제 포인트** 강조하려는 말을 앞으로 보냈을 때 주어와 동사의 어순이 바뀌는 경우들이 있다. be동사나 조동사인 경우 주어와 동사의 순서가 바뀌고, 일반동사인 경우 'do/does/did+주어+동사원형'의 순서로 쓰인다.

◆ 보어가 문두에 올 때: 보어+동사+주어

enclosed, attached는 문두에 자주 나오는 보어이다. 보어가 문두에 오면, 주어 자리로 착각하기 쉽다.

[Enclosed / ~~Enclosure~~**] is a copy** of our product catalog with descriptions of the promotional events.
판촉 행사 설명이 포함된 저희 제품 카탈로그 한 부가 동봉되어 있습니다.

→ 주어 자리로 착각해서 Enclosure를 쓰면 a copy가 보어가 되는데, 동격 관계가 아니므로 잘못된 문장이 된다.

Attached [are / ~~is~~**] the minutes** of the all management meetings for the last six months.
지난 6개월 간의 경영진 회의 회의록 전부가 첨부되어 있다.

→ 보어 Attached가 문두에 나와 '주어–동사'가 도치되었으므로, 동사는 뒤에 있는 주어 the minutes와 수를 일치시킨다.

◆ 부정어가 문두에 올 때: 부정어+동사+주어

never / not / hardly / seldom / rarely / little / nothing / nor+조동사+주어+동사원형

[Never / ~~Always~~**] do we start** selling our products without thoroughly inspecting their quality.
우리는 품질을 철저하게 검사하지 않고서 제품 판매를 결코 시작하지 않는다.

→ 여기서 do는 일반동사가 아닌 조동사 역할을 한다.

◆ only가 이끄는 구나 절이 문두에 올 때: only 구/절+동사+주어

only가 부사, 전치사구, 접속사절과 결합하여 문두로 나오는 경우, 문장의 주어와 동사가 도치된다.

부사	**Only recently [has** / ~~have~~**] the marketing team been** able to concentrate fully on the new strategy. 최근에야 비로소 마케팅 팀이 새로운 전략에 온전히 집중할 수 있었다.
접속사절	**[Only** / ~~Soon~~**] after** the inspection is completed **should the plant begin** operations. 점검이 끝나고 나서야 비로소 공장이 운영을 시작할 것이다.

◆ so, neither가 문두에 올 때: so/neither+동사+주어

'so+동사+주어'는 '~도 …하다', 'neither+동사+주어'는 '~도 …하지 않다'라고 해석한다.

Ms. Langton **didn't** like the new shift schedule, and **[neither** / ~~so~~**] did her associates**.
랭튼 씨는 새로운 근무 일정을 좋아하지 않았고, 그녀의 동료들도 마찬가지였다.

→ 'so+동사+주어'는 긍정문 뒤에, 'neither+동사+주어'는 부정문 뒤에 쓰인다.

ETS 유형연습

정답과 해설 p.177

1 Ms. Park will not be able to attend the sales presentation, and ------ will Mr. Jefferson.

(A) also
(B) however
(C) now
(D) neither

2 ------ have market conditions been more ideal for buying a new house.

(A) Seldom
(B) Ever
(C) Appropriately
(D) Moreover

3 As the number of local residents' visits to public swimming facilities climbs, ------ the demand for lifeguards to supervise them.

(A) as long as
(B) whereas
(C) so does
(D) as to

ETS 실전문제

1. After launching a new product line in May, Manzanita Homeware is generating ------- revenue than ever before.
   (A) high
   (B) higher
   (C) highly
   (D) highness

2. Auron Energy, one of the nation's ------- energy suppliers, delivers electricity to nearly twenty million customers.
   (A) largest
   (B) more largely
   (C) largely
   (D) enlarge

3. Candidates for positions at Pereira Consulting should answer the questions on the application form as ------- as possible.
   (A) accurate
   (B) accuracy
   (C) accuracies
   (D) accurately

4. Tough stains can be removed more ------- with Pearl Glow's extra-strength laundry detergent.
   (A) ease
   (B) easier
   (C) easiest
   (D) easily

5. Traffic engineers are working to ease vehicle congestion on Connor Boulevard, the metropolitan area's ------- traveled street.
   (A) heavy
   (B) more heavily
   (C) heaviness
   (D) most heavily

6. Our shop carries as ------- household appliances as our main competitors.
   (A) many
   (B) much
   (C) such
   (D) same

7. Trentelle Business Consulting Ltd. stresses that retaining loyal customers is ------- important than attracting new ones.
   (A) most
   (B) more
   (C) very
   (D) much

8. Farook cream and lotion products promise to leave you with the ------- skin or your money back.
   (A) smoothness
   (B) smoother
   (C) smoothest
   (D) smoothly

9. The merger of Darco Motors and Kessler Automotive has resulted in more production problems ------- analysts predicted.
   (A) while
   (B) whether
   (C) than
   (D) or

10. The engineering department has announced that only at the end of the month ------- a progress report of the project be published.
    (A) is
    (B) has
    (C) will
    (D) does

11. In order for you to receive the early registration rate, your application form must be postmarked ------- Friday, October 28.
    (A) in advance
    (B) beforehand
    (C) previously
    (D) no later than

12. The delivery of flowers for the Hwang wedding reception will be completed by Friday, May 12, -------.
    (A) as late
    (B) later than
    (C) at the latest
    (D) the later

13. Ms. Vialobos has reported that the new mobile telephones are the lightest ------- to be purchased by the department.
(A) ever
(B) before
(C) quite
(D) well

14. Our marketing manager, Hawa Abdella, is away from the office and will not return ------- than January 12.
(A) earlier
(B) more recently
(C) longer
(D) more frequently

Questions 15-18 refer to the following e-mail.

From: deaneckhart@gbhosp.org
To: amanpour@sevcon.org
Subject: Chief of Surgery position
Date: December 10

Dear Mr. Amanpour,

I received your curriculum vitae from a mutual ---15.--- of ours, Gloria Manning. ---16.--- . I am curious if you are aware of the open position at Grace Beth Hospital for Chief of Surgery. We are seeking a talented surgeon like you to fill the position. Because of its size, Grace Beth is an excellent place to enhance your healthcare management career. Actually, Grace Beth Hospital is the ---17.--- of the region's four hospitals. I believe you would find the position to be a very close match to your ---18.--- clinical background. Please review the open position at gbhosp.org/openpositions.htm and contact me if you would like to learn more.

Regards,

Dean Eckhart
Recruitment Manager Grace Beth Hospital

15. (A) acquaint
(B) acquainted
(C) acquainting
(D) acquaintance

16. (A) I was impressed with your extensive experience.
(B) Dr. Manning is currently our Chief of Surgery.
(C) I hope you will carefully consider her application.
(D) We also require letters of recommendation from our applicants.

17. (A) large
(B) larger
(C) largely
(D) largest

18. (A) opaque
(B) particular
(C) forthright
(D) generic

UNIT 16 어휘

1 기출 어휘 – 동사 🔊 750_P5_01

동 동의어 반 반의어

abandon 버리다, 포기하다
the abandoned warehouse 버려진 창고
동 give up v. 포기하다   반 retain v. 유지하다

accommodate (사람을) 수용하다, (의견 등을) 수용하다
accommodate a large tour group 단체 관광객을 수용하다
accommodate your request 당신의 요청 사항을 수용하다

address 연설하다, (일·문제 등을) 처리하다
address the audience 청중에게 연설하다
address customers' complaints 고객들의 불만을 처리하다

adhere to ~을 고수하다, 충실히 지키다
adhere to safety procedures 안전 절차를 고수하다
adhere to the guideline 가이드라인을 준수하다

aim 겨냥하다, 목표로 하다; 목표
aim to provide public transportation for commuters
통근자들에게 대중교통을 제공하는 것을 목표로 하다
동 target v. 겨냥하다

allocate 할당하다, 배정하다
allocate a team to the project 프로젝트에 팀을 배정하다
allocated budget 할당된 예산
동 assign v. 할당하다

appear 나타나다, 나오다, 발생하다
appear on a special broadcast 특별 방송에 출연하다
apparent adj. 분명한   appearance n. 모습
동 emerge v. 나타나다

assume 추정하다, 떠맡다, ~인 체하다
assume that traffic is light 교통량이 적다고 추정하다
assume the responsibility 책임을 맡다
assumption n. 가정   assumably adv. 추측하건대

attribute ~ 탓으로 돌리다, ~ 덕분으로 여기다; 속성, 특질
attribute success to hard work
성공을 열심히 일한 덕분이라고 여기다
동 credit A with B[B to A] B를 A의 공으로 돌리다

boost 북돋우다, 증가시키다; 증가
boost enrollment 등록을 증가시키다
동 increase v. 증가시키다   반 reduce v. 줄이다

charge 청구하다; 충전하다; 요금
charge an additional fee 추가 요금을 청구하다
at no charge 무료로

clarify 명확하게 하다, 설명하다
clarify the new policy 새로운 정책을 설명하다
동 explain v. 설명하다   반 confuse v. 혼란스럽게 하다

comply (법규 등을) 따르다, 지키다
comply with the legal requirements 법적 요구 조건을 따르다
compliance n. 준수   compliant adj. 준수하는

conduct (업무 등을) 행하다; 처신, 행위
conduct market research 시장 조사를 하다
conductor n. 지휘자
동 carry out v. 수행하다

consult 상의하다, 참고하다
consult an expert 전문가와 상의하다
consultant n. 컨설턴트   consultation n. 상의
동 refer to v. ~을 참조하다

contain 포함하다, 담고 있다
contain information 정보를 담고 있다
container n. 용기
동 include v. 포함하다

delegate 위임하다
delegate authority 권한을 위임하다
delegated adj. 위임된
동 assign v. 위임하다

demonstrate 시연하다, 보여 주다
demonstrate admirable skills 감탄할 만한 기술을 보여 주다
demonstration n. 시연회, 설명
동 show v. 보여 주다   반 conceal v. 숨기다

designate 지정하다, 임명하다
designated parking areas 지정된 주차 구역
designation n. 지정   designated adj. 지정된
동 appoint v. 임명하다

determine 결심하다, 밝히다
determine the cause of the delay 지연 이유를 밝히다
determined adj. 결심이 확고한

differ 다르다
differ greatly/significantly 크게 다르다
different adj. 다른   difference n. 다름, 차이
⑤ vary v. 다르다

direct 지시하다, 보내다, 안내하다; 직접적인
Please direct all questions to 모든 질문은 ~로 보내 주세요.
director n. 이사, 감독관   direction n. 지시, 방향
directly adv. 바로, 직접

disclose 밝히다, 공개하다
disclose personal information 개인 정보를 공개하다
disclosure n. 공개
⑤ reveal v. 드러내다   ⑪ conceal v. 숨기다

distinguish 구별하다
distinguish talented sales agents
재능 있는 영업 사원을 구별하다
distinguished adj. 저명한, 뛰어난
⑤ differentiate v. 구별하다

distribute 배포하다, 분배하다
distribute the minutes 회의록을 배포하다
distribution n. 분배, 유통
⑤ hand out v. 나누어 주다

embrace 받아들이다, 수용하다
embrace new trend 새로운 트렌드를 받아들이다
⑤ accept v. 받아들이다   ⑪ reject v. 거부하다

endorse 지지하다, (유명인이) 홍보하다, 보증하다
endorse the makeup line 화장품 라인을 홍보하다
endorsement n. 지지, 이서

enforce 집행하다, 실시하다
enforce new safety regulations 새 안전 규정을 실시하다
enforcement n. 집행, 시행
⑤ carry out v. 수행하다

engage 관여하다, 종사시키다
be engaged in online sales 온라인 판매에 종사하다
engage in volunteer work 자원봉사 업무에 관여하다
engagement n. 관여; 약혼   engaged adj. 관여된

enhance 강화하다, 향상시키다
enhance the customer-service 고객 서비스를 강화하다
enhancement n. 향상
⑤ improve v. 향상시키다   ⑪ diminish v. 약화시키다, 줄이다

ensure 보장하다, 확실하게 하다
ensure stability and safety 안정성과 안전을 보장하다
⑤ guarantee v. 보장하다

establish 실시하다, 설립하다, 확립하다
establish an internship program 인턴 프로그램을 실시하다
establish long-term partnerships
장기적인 협력 관계를 수립하다
establishment n. 기관, 설립   established adj. 확립된, 인정받는

evaluate 평가하다
evaluate their ability 능력을 평가하다
evaluate current and potential investments
현재 및 잠재적 투자를 평가하다
⑤ assess v. 평가하다

excel 능력이 뛰어나다, 탁월하다
excel in the role of organizer 조직자의 역할에서 탁월하다
excellent adj. 우수한
⑤ surpass v. 능가하다, 초과하다

exceed 초과하다
exceed the speed limit 제한 속도를 초과하다
excess n. 초과   excessive adj. 과도한, 지나친
⑤ surpass v. 능가하다, 초과하다

expand 확대하다, 확장하다
expand its production floor 생산 공간을 확장하다
expansion n. 확장
⑤ extend v. 확장하다   ⑪ contract v. 수축하다

expect 예상하다, 기대하다
expect the possibility of last-minute additions
막판에 추가될 가능성을 예상하다
than expected 예상보다
expectation n. 예상, 기대

expire 기한이 되다, 만료하다
food that will expire soon 유통 기한이 곧 만료될 음식
expiration n. 만기   expired adj. 기한이 지난
⑤ run out v. 만기가 되다

extend 연장하다
extend its business hours 영업시간을 연장하다
extension n. 연장; 내선 번호   extensive adj. 광범위한
⑤ prolong v. 연장하다

feature ~을 특징으로 하다, 크게 다루다; 특징, 기능
feature a stylish design 세련된 디자인을 특징으로 하다
featured adj. 특집의, 주연의

forbid 금지하다
phone conversations are forbidden 통화가 금지된다
동 prohibit v. 금지하다 반 permit v. 허락하다

handle 처리하다, 다루다
handle many tasks 많은 일들을 처리하다
handle customer inquiries 고객 문의를 처리하다
동 deal with v. 처리하다

hire 고용하다; 신입 사원
hire a software specialist 소프트웨어 전문가를 고용하다
a temporary worker will be hired 임시 직원이 고용될 것이다
동 employ v. 고용하다 반 dismiss v. 해고하다

honor 기리다, 존경하다; 명예, 존경
honor her 30 years of service 그녀의 30년 근속을 기리다
honorable adj. 명예로운
동 respect v. 존경하다

implement 시행하다, 이행하다; 도구
implement the latest data-analysis methods
최신 데이터 분석 기법을 시행하다
implementation n. 시행, 이행

improvise 즉흥적으로 하다
improvise his speech 그의 연설을 즉석에서 하다
improvisation n. 즉석에서 하기
반 prepare v. 준비하다

inquire 문의하다
inquire about the hiring process 채용 절차에 대해 문의하다
inquiry n. 문의, 조사
동 ask v. 묻다

institute (규칙·제도 등) 마련하다, 실시하다; 협회, 기관
institute a new dress code 새로운 복장 규정을 마련하다
institution n. 기관, 제도

interrupt 방해하다, 중단시키다
The bus service was interrupted. 버스 운행이 중단되었다.
interruption n. 중단, 방해
동 hinder v. 방해가 되다

issue 발급하다, 발행하다, 발표하다; 출판물, 쟁점, 발행
issue a ticket 표를 발권하다
issue a statement officially 공식적으로 성명서를 발표하다
the May issue 5월호

launch 시작하다, 출시하다; 개시
launch a new Web site 새로운 웹사이트를 출시하다
동 initiate v. 시작하다 반 terminate v. 종결하다

lead 이끌다, ~에 이르다
lead the training session 교육을 이끌다
lead to greater opportunities 더 좋은 기회로 이어지다
leading adj. 선도적인

lease 임대하다, 빌리다; 임대차 계약
lease the office space 사무 공간을 임대하다
lease a rental car 렌터카를 임대하다
동 rent v. 임대하다

locate 위치시키다, ~의 위치를 알아내다
The office is located in the city. 사무실은 도시에 위치해 있다.
location n. 위치, 지점   located adj. 위치한

mark 표시하다, 나타내다, 기념하다; 점수
This event marks our 10th anniversary.
이 행사는 10주년을 기념하는 것이다.
동 celebrate v. 기념하다

negotiate 협상하다, 교섭하다
negotiate good deals 좋은 거래를 협상하다
negotiation n. 협상
동 bargain v. 협상하다

notify 통보하다, 통지하다
notify Ms. Suh of her promotion 서 씨에게 승진을 통보하다
notification n. 통지
동 inform v. 알리다

operate 운영하다, 작동하다
operate only in the summer 여름에만 운영한다
operation n. 운영
동 function v. 작동하다

outfit ~을 채비시키다, 착용케 하다; 장비(일체)
should be outfitted with this device
이 장비를 착용해야 한다
동 equip v. 장비를 갖추게 하다

outline 간추려 말하다; 개요
outline the year's budget 그해 예산을 간략히 설명하다
the outline of the contract 계약의 개요
동 brief v. 간략히 설명하다

oversee 감독하다, 지켜보다
be overseen by ~에 의해 감독되다
oversee domestic sales 국내 영업을 감독하다
동 supervise v. 감독하다

permit 허락하다, 허용하다; 허가(증)
be permitted to go home 집에 가는 것이 허용되다
permission n. 허가
동 authorize v. 승인하다   반 forbid v. 금지하다

prohibit ~하지 못하게 하다, 금지하다
prohibit visitors from entering 방문객들의 입장을 금지하다
parking will be prohibited 주차가 금지될 것이다
prohibition n. 금지

recognize 인정하다, 인식하다
recognize Ms. Dale's efforts 데일 씨의 노고를 인정하다
recognition n. 인식, 인지
동 acknowledge v. 인정하다

reduce 줄이다, 감소시키다
reduce production expense 생산 비용을 줄이다
reduction n. 감소
동 decrease v. 감소하다   반 increase v. 증가하다

refer 참조하다, 언급하다, 소개하다, 보내다
refer to the manual first 먼저 설명서를 참조하다
referred me to a specialist 나를 전문의에게 보냈다
reference n. 추천(서); 참고   referral n. 소개, 위탁

reflect 반사하다, 반영하다
reflect the current trend 현재 경향을 반영하다
reflection n. 반사   reflective adj. 반사하는

refund 환불하다; 환불
refund $25 to subscribers 구독자에게 25달러를 환불하다
a full refund 전액 환불
동 reimburse v. 환불하다

remind ~하도록 상기시키다
Please be reminded that ~라는 점을 명심하세요
reminder n. 상기시키는 것

replace 교체하다, 대신하다
replace a defective item 불량품을 교체하다
replacement n. 대체물, 후임자

retain 유지하다, 보유하다
retain loyal customers 단골 고객을 보유하다
retention n. 보유   retained adj. 보유한
동 hold v. 유지하다

secure 확보하다, 고정시키다; 안전한
secure a parking space 주차할 곳을 확보하다
secure the lock on the door 문의 잠금 장치를 고정시키다
security n. 안전, 보안   securely adv. 확실하게

separate 분리하다, 구분하다
separate the participants 참가자들을 분리하다
separately adv. 따로
동 divide v. 나누다   반 combine v. 결합하다

specify 상세히 말하다, 구체화하다
specify the date 날짜를 명확히 하다
specification n. 세부 사항   specific adj. 특정한, 구체적인

sponsor 후원하다, 주최하다; 후원자
be sponsored by ~에 의해 후원되다
sponsorship n. 후원
동 support v. 지원하다   반 oppose v. 반대하다

streamline 간소화하다, 능률적으로 하다
streamline the production process 생산 과정을 간소화하다
streamlined adj. 유선형의, 간결한
동 simplify v. 단순화하다

sustain 지탱하다, 지속하다
sustain strong profits 큰 수익을 유지하다
sustainability n. 지속 가능성   sustainable adj. 지속 가능한

switch 전환하다, 바꾸다; 전환
switch to QH3 from a conventional fuel
전통적인 연료에서 QH3로 전환하다
동 exchange v. 교환하다   반 maintain v. 유지하다

thrive 번창하다, 성장하다
help small businesses thrive 소기업이 번창하도록 돕다
동 flourish v. 번창하다

yield 내다, 생산하다; 양도하다; 산출량
yield higher profits 더 높은 이익을 내다
yield conflicting results 상반된 결과를 내다
동 produce v. 생산하다

2 기출 어휘 - 명사 🎧 750_P5_02

동 동의어   반 반의어

access 접근, 이용 (권한); 접근하다
to get access to the data 자료 이용 권한을 받으려면
accessible adj. 접근 가능한, 이용 가능한
동 approach n. 접근

audit 회계 감사; 회계를 감사하다
after a final audit 최종 감사 후에
auditor n. 회계 감사원
동 inspection n. 조사

advance 발전, 진보; 나아가다; 사전의
advances in mobile phone technology 휴대폰 기술의 발전
advance notice 사전 통지
advanced adj. 최신의, 진보된

authorization 허가(증), 권한 부여
without authorization 허가 없이
authority n. 권한, 허가   authorize v. 허가하다
동 approval n. 승인

affiliation 제휴, 소속 기관
have an affiliation with foreign bank 외국계 은행과 제휴하다
affiliate v. 제휴하다 n. 계열사
동 partnership n. 협력, 제휴

benefit 이익, 혜택; ~에게 도움이 되다
take advantage of membership benefits
회원 혜택을 이용하다
beneficial adj. 혜택이 되는   beneficiary n. 수혜자

agenda 안건, 의제
hand out copies of the agenda 안건의 복사본을 나누어 주다
the agenda for the meeting 회의의 안건

beverage 음료, 마실 것
complimentary snacks and beverages 무료 다과와 음료
동 drink n. 음료

agreement 동의, 계약
reach an agreement 합의에 다다르다, 계약을 체결하다
agree v. 동의하다   agreeable adj. 기분 좋은, 동의하는
반 disagreement n. 불일치

branch 지점, 나뭇가지; 갈라지다
visit a local branch 지역 지점을 방문하다

allowance 용돈, 수당, 허용량
a monthly allowance 월간 허용량
allow v. 허용하다
반 restriction n. 제한

capacity 용량, 수용력, 능력
a seating capacity 좌석 수
at full capacity 최대 능력으로
capacious adj. 용량이 큰, 널찍한

alternative 대안; 대안의
seek an alternative 대안을 찾다
alternation n. 교대, 교체
alternate v. 번갈아 하다 adj. 번갈아 하는, 대안의

committee 위원회
committee's decision 위원회의 결정
동 council n. 위원회   board n. 이사회

analysis 분석
its analysis of the global stock market
세계 주식 시장에 대한 분석
analyze v. 분석하다   analyst n. 분석가

concentration 집중, 밀집, 농도
a concentration of population 인구 집중
concentrate on v. ~에 집중하다
concentrated adj. 밀집된, 농축된

appraisal 평가
performance appraisal 업무 평가
appraise v. 평가하다
동 assessment n. 평가

concern 걱정, 근심, 관심(사)
a matter of little concern 별로 중요하지 않은 문제
concerned adj. 염려하는

attraction 명소, 매력
popular attraction 인기 있는 명소
tourist attraction 관광 명소
attractive adj. 매력적인   attract v. 끌어당기다
동 appeal n. 매력   반 dislikes n. 싫음, 혐오

confidence 확신, 자신, 신뢰
restore confidence in their products
제품에 대한 신뢰를 회복하다
confident adj. 확신하는, 자신 있는   confidential adj. 비밀의

consent 동의; 동의하다
without written consent 서면 동의 없이
mutual consent 상호 합의
give one's consent to ~에 동의하다

contribution 공헌, 기부(금)
contribution to the company 회사에 대한 기여
contributor n. 공헌자, 기고가 contribute v. 기여하다, 기부하다

decline 감소, 쇠퇴; 줄어들다
decline in revenue 수익 감소
declining adj. 쇠퇴하는
동 decrease n. 감소   반 increase n. 증가

defect 결함, 하자
find defects in the product 제품의 하자를 발견하다
defective adj. 결함이 있는
동 flaw n. 결점

delegation 대표단, 위임
Hong Kong delegation 홍콩 대표단
delegate v. 위임하다, 대표자로 보내다

deliberation 숙고, 고려
after much deliberation 심사숙고 후에
deliberate adj. 고의의, 의도적인 v. 숙고하다, 신중히 생각하다
deliberately adv. 고의로, 신중하게

distraction 주의 산만, 방해물, 기분 전환
distractions due to noise 소음으로 인한 주의 산만
distract v. 혼란시키다   distracting adj. 주의를 산만하게 하는

element 요소, 성분
elements for financial success 재정적 성공을 위한 요소
동 component n. 구성 요소

emphasis 강조
put/place an emphasis on quality 품질을 강조하다
emphasize v. 강조하다
동 stress n. 강조

estimate 견적(서); 견적을 내다
get a cost estimate 비용 견적을 받다
estimation n. 추정, 판단   estimated adj. 추정되는
동 quotation n. 견적

exception 예외, 제외
with the exception of personal matters
개인적인 문제들은 제외하고
except prep. ~을 제외하고

expense 지출, 경비
by lowering business expenses 사업비를 낮춤으로써
동 expend v. 소비하다   expenditure n. 소비, 지출

fame 명성
rise to fame 명성을 얻다
famous adj. 유명한
동 reputation n. 평판

figure 수치, 금액
its highest sales figures 최고 매출액
동 number n. 숫자   statistics n. 통계 자료

fluctuation 변동, 불안정
fluctuation in exchange rates 환율의 변동
fluctuate v. 변동하다
반 stability n. 안정

formula 공식, 방식, 제조법
different formula 다른 방식
formulate v. 만들어 내다
동 recipe n. 방안, 요리법

funding 재원, 자금 제공
increase funding for events 행사를 위한 자금을 증원하다
fund v. 자금을 대다   fund-raiser n. 모금 행사
동 financing n. 자금 조달

garment 의류, 옷
production of the garments 의류 생산
동 clothing n. 의류   dress n. 의류

guidance 안내, 조언
provide online guidance 온라인 안내를 제공하다
guide v. 안내하다
동 direction n. 지시

implication 암시, 함축, 영향
have serious implications for ~에 심각한 영향을 끼치다
implicate v. 연루시키다, 암시하다

ingredient 재료, 구성 요소
use fresh ingredients 신선한 재료를 사용하다
동 part n.부품   component n.구성 요소

initiative 새로운 계획, 주도권; 처음의
take the initiative 솔선수범하다, 주도권을 쥐다
initiation n.가입, 개시   initiate v.시작하다
동 plan n.계획

inspection 검사, 점검, 검열
pass a safety inspection 안전 검사를 통과하다
inspect v.점검하다
동 investigation n.조사

interval 간격, 중간 휴식
at regular intervals 일정한 간격을 두고
12-inch interval 12인치 간격
동 gap n.간격   반 continuation n.연속

inventory 재고, 재고 목록
inventory shortages 재고 부족
inventory management software 재고 관리 소프트웨어
동 stock n.재고

investor 투자자
potential investors 잠재적 투자자들
investment n.투자

maintenance 유지 보수, 정비
undergo routine maintenance 정기 점검을 받다
maintenance department 유지 관리 부서
maintain v.유지하다

malfunction 오작동; 오작동하다
a malfunction of the software 소프트웨어의 오작동
동 failure n.고장

means 수단, 방법
various means of payment 다양한 지불 수단
by means of ~에 의하여, ~의 도움으로
동 way n.방법   method n.방법

measure 수단, 조치; 재다
implement cost-cutting measures 비용 삭감 조치를 취하다
measurement n.측정, 치수

merchandise 물품, 상품
returned merchandise 반환된 상품
merchant n.상인
동 product n.제품

merger 합병
after the merger 합병 이후
merger negotiations 합병 협상

obstacle 장애물, 장애
overcome obstacles 장애를 극복하다
obstruct v.방해하다
동 barrier n.장애물

opening 개시, 시작, 공석
the opening ceremony 개막식
the grand opening 개장 행사
job openings 공석

origin 기원, 출처
indicate the place of origin 출처를 표시하다
original adj.원래의 n.원본
동 source n.출처, 기원

outcome 결과
the desirable outcomes 바람직한 결과
동 result n.결과   반 cause n.원인

overview 개요, 개략적인 설명
provide a basic overview 기본적인 개요를 제공하다
동 summary n.요약   반 detail n.세부 사항

panel 위원단, 판(넬); 판으로 덮다
an expert panel 전문가 위원단
install solar panels 태양열 전지판을 설치하다

perspective 관점
from a financial perspective 재정적 관점에서
동 outlook n.관점

pioneer 개척자, 선구자; 개척하다
a brilliant pioneer 뛰어난 선구자
pioneering adj.선구적인
동 developer n.개발자

possession 소유물, 소유
pack one's possessions 소지품을 챙기다
possess v. 소유하다   possessive adj. 소유의
동 belongings n. 소지품

potential 잠재력, 가능성; 잠재력이 있는
employees with potential 잠재력이 있는 직원들
potentially adv. 잠재적으로, 어쩌면

practice 관행, 실행, 연습; 실행하다
common practice 일반적 관행
practical adj. 실제의, 실용적인
동 convention n. 관습   training n. 연습

precaution 예방책
take precautions 예방 조치를 취하다
동 safeguard n. 예방책

preference 선호, 우선권
food preference 음식 선호도
preference will be given to ~에게 우선권이 주어질 것이다
prefer v. 선호하다   preferred adj. 선호되는, 우선시되는

proficiency 능숙함, 숙련도
high level of proficiency 높은 수준의 숙련도
proficient adj. 능숙한
동 skill n. 숙련도

promotion 승진; 홍보, 촉진
be eligible for the promotion 승진할 자격이 있다
promote v. 승진시키다; 홍보하다   promotional adj. 홍보용의

reputation 평판, 명성
maintain a good reputation 좋은 평판을 유지하다
reputable adj. 평판이 좋은

requirement 필요(한 것), 필요 조건
meet the job requirements 직무 필요 조건에 부합하다
require v. 요구하다   required adj. 필수적인
동 demand n. 요구   needs n. 필요, 요구

resource 자원, 재산
natural resources 천연 자원
human resources 인적 자원, 인사부
resourceful adj. 자원이 풍부한

revision 수정, 개정
ask for revisions 수정을 요청하다
revise v. 수정하다
동 modification n. 수정

scale 규모, 등급
a rating scale 평가 척도
on a large scale 대규모로
동 size n. 크기, 규모

schedule 일정; 일정을 정하다
behind schedule 일정에 뒤처진
ahead of schedule 일정보다 앞선
scheduled adj. 예정된

standard 기준, 표준; 일반적인, 보통의
conform to company standards 회사 기준에 따르다
standardize v. 표준화하다
동 criteria n. 기준

tenant 세입자
prospective tenants 예비 세입자

transaction 거래, 처리
online transactions 온라인 거래
each business transaction 각 사업 거래
transact v. 거래하다   transactional adj. 거래의, 업무의

transfer 이체, 이동; 이동하다
electronic transfer 온라인 이체
transferable adj. 양도 가능한
동 relocation n. 이전, 이주

treatment 치료, 대우, 처리
fair treatment 공정한 대우
treat v. 대하다, 치료하다
동 care n. 치료, 돌봄

variety 다양성
a (wide) variety of dishes 각양각색의 요리들
various adj. 다양한
동 diversity n. 다양성

warranty 품질 보증서
come with a warranty 보증서가 포함되다
warrant v. 보증하다
동 guarantee n. 보증

3 기출 어휘 - 형용사 🔊 750_P5_03

동 동의어 반 반의어

abundant 충분한, 넘치는
abundant rainfall 풍부한 강수량
abundance n. 풍부함
동 sufficient adj. 충분한

accomplished 뛰어난, 통달한
an accomplished artist 뛰어난 화가
accomplishment n. 성취   accomplish v. 달성하다, 성취하다
동 distinguished adj. 뛰어난

accustomed 익숙해진, 습관의
get accustomed to an environment 환경에 익숙해지다
accustom v. ~을 익숙하게 하다
동 used adj. 익숙한

adaptable 적응할 수 있는
a recipe adaptable to different styles of cooking
다양한 요리 방식에 맞출 수 있는 조리법
adaptation n. 적응, 각색   adapt v. 적응하다

additional 추가적인
for additional information 추가 정보를 위해서는
addition n. 추가
동 extra adj. 여분의   further adj. 더 많은

affordable 알맞은, 적정한 가격의
at an affordable price/rate 적정한 가격/요금에
afford v. ~할 여유가 있다
동 reasonable adj. 가격이 적정한

appropriate 적절한
appropriate strategies 적절한 전략들
동 suitable adj. 적절한   반 inappropriate adj. 부적절한

aware 알고 있는
be aware of weather changes 날씨 변화를 알다
awareness n. 인식, 앎
동 conscious adj. 인식하고 있는

brief 간략한; 간략히 보고하다
hold a brief meeting 간략한 회의를 하다
briefly adv. 간략하게
동 concise adj. 간결한

capable 할 수 있는
capable of browsing the Internet 인터넷 검색을 할 수 있는
capability n. 능력, 수용력
반 incapable adj. ~할 수 없는

central 중심의, 중추적인, 주된
Online advertising is central to the marketing strategy. 온라인 광고가 마케팅 전략의 중심이다.
centralize v. 중심에 모으다

compatible 호환이 되는, 화합할 수 있는
software compatible with other systems
다른 시스템과 호환 가능한 소프트웨어
compatibility n. 호환성

competitive 경쟁의, 경쟁력이 있는
competitive salary 경쟁력 있는 월급
gain a competitive edge 경쟁력을 얻다
competition n. 경쟁   compete v. 경쟁하다

complimentary 무료의, 칭찬의
a complimentary dinner coupon 무료 저녁 식사 쿠폰
compliment n. 칭찬   v. 칭찬하다

dedicated 헌신적인, 전념하는
The Green Parks Club is dedicated to protecting the environment. 그린 파크 클럽은 환경보호에 헌신적이다.
dedication n. 헌신

deliberate 고의의, 신중한; 숙고하다
in a deliberate way 신중하게
deliberation n. 심사숙고   deliberately adv. 고의로, 신중히
동 prudent adj. 신중한

demanding 지나치게 요구하는, 까다로운
have a demanding job 힘든 직업을 갖고 있다
demand v. 요구하다   n. 수요
동 tricky adj. 까다로운

due 지불해야 하는, 만기인, 적당한
The report is due next Monday.
보고서는 다음 주 월요일까지 제출해야 한다.
overdue adj. (지불) 기한이 지난

eligible 적격의, 적임의, 자격이 있는
eligible to apply for the manager 매니저에 지원할 자격 있는
eligibility n. 적임, 적격
동 qualified adj. 적격의

enclosed 동봉된, 둘러싸인
the enclosed document 동봉된 서류
enclosure n. 동봉, 둘러쌈   enclose v. 동봉하다, 둘러싸다
동 attached adj. 첨부된

exempt 면제되는; 면제하다
be exempt from taxes 세금이 면제되다
exemption n. 면제

experienced 경험이 많은, 능숙한
experienced job candidates 경험이 많은 채용 후보자들
experience n. 경험 v. 경험하다
동 skilled adj. 경험 많은, 숙련된

familiar 익숙한, 잘 알고 있는, 친한
be familiar with the rules 그 규칙들에 익숙하다
familiarize v. 익숙하게 하다
반 unfamiliar adj. 익숙하지 않은

impending 임박한, 곧 일어날
impending issues 임박한 문제들
impend v. 임박하다
동 imminent adj. 임박한   upcoming adj. 곧 있을

outstanding 뛰어난, 훌륭한, 미납의
outstanding service 훌륭한 서비스
outstanding debt 미변제 채무
동 distinguished adj. 뛰어난   unpaid adj. 미납의

preliminary 예비의; 예비 단계
preliminary tests 예비 검사
do preliminary market research 사전 시장 조사를 하다
동 preparatory adj. 예비의

prior ~ 전의, 앞선
prior approval 사전 승인
priority n. 우선순위
반 following adj. 그 다음의

promising 전도유망한, 장래가 밝은
among promising candidates 전도유망한 후보자들 중에서
promised adj. 약속된   promise n. 약속, 가망 v. 약속하다

reliable 믿을 만한, 신뢰할 만한
reliable service 믿을 만한 서비스
reliability n. 믿을 만함   rely on/upon v. ~에 의존하다
reliant adj. 의존하는

remote 거리가 떨어진, 희박한
at a remote distance 멀리 떨어져서
동 distant adj. 멀리 떨어진   반 nearby adj. 가까운

responsible 책임이 있는, 관할하는
be responsible for supervising assemblers 조립자들을 감독할 책임이 있다
responsibility n. 책임

restricted 제한된, 한정된
be restricted to 50 customers 50명의 고객들로 제한되다
restriction n. 규제, 제약, 규정   restrict v. 제한하다
동 limited adj. 제한된

rewarding 가치가 있는, 보람 있는
a rewarding discussion 가치 있는 토론회
reward n. 보상 v. 보상하다
동 worthy adj. 가치 있는

sensitive 민감한, 섬세한
be sensitive to loud noise 큰 소음에 매우 민감하다
sensitivity n. 민감함
동 delicate adj. 섬세한

significant 상당한, 중요한
a significant number of visitors 상당수의 방문객들
significance n. 중요성   significantly adv. 상당히
동 considerable adj. 상당한

similar 유사한, 비슷한
similar to other artist's works 다른 화가의 작품과 유사한
similarity n. 유사성

subject 될 수 있는; 주제, 과목; 복종시키다
The schedule is subject to change without prior notice. 일정은 사전 통보 없이 변경될 수 있습니다.

thorough 철저한, 빈틈없는
undergo a thorough inspection 철저한 검사를 받다
동 rigorous adj. 엄격한

temporary 임시의, 일시적인
a temporary employee 임시 직원
temporarily adv. 임시로
동 provisional adj. 임시 변통의   반 permanent adj. 영구적인

valid 유효한, 타당한
valid identification card 유효한 신분증
validity n. 유효성
반 invalid adj. 효력 없는, 무효한

4 기출 어휘 - 부사 750_P5_04

동 동의어   반 반의어

accordingly 그에 맞게, 따라서
Mr. Kim is a manager, so he should be treated accordingly. 김 씨는 매니저이니까, 그에 맞게 대접받아야 한다.
accord n. 일치 v. 부합하다 (with)

adversely 불리하게, 나쁘게
adversely affect 부정적인 영향을 끼치다
adversity n. 역경, 불운   adverse adj. 반대의, 불리한
동 unfavorably adv. 불리하게

alike 마찬가지로, 똑같은, 비슷한
the performers and the audience alike
연주자들과 청중 모두
alikeness n. 유사함

altogether 아주, 완전히, 전부 합하여
grossed over 1 million dollars altogether
합계 1백만 달러 이상의 수익을 올렸다
동 completely adv. 완전히   반 partially adv. 부분적으로

approximately 대략, 거의
approximately twice a month 대략 한 달에 두 번
approximate adj. 대략의
동 about adv. 거의   around adv. 거의

closely 면밀히, 주의 깊게
closely examine the records 기록을 면밀히 조사하다
closure n. 폐쇄   close adj. 가까운 v. 닫다
동 thoroughly adv. 면밀히, 철저히

collaboratively 합작으로
work collaboratively 협업하다
collaborate v. 협력하다, 공동 작업하다
collaboration n. 협력

completely 완전히
completely free of charge 완전히 무료로
complete adj. 완전한 v. 완료하다

concisely 간결하게
speak clearly and concisely 명료하고 간결하게 말하다
conciseness n. 간결함   concise adj. 간결한
반 lengthily adv. 장황하게

consecutively 연속하여
The two holidays occur consecutively.
휴일이 이틀 연속이다.
consecutive adj. 연속적인
동 successively adv. 연속하여

consistently 지속적으로, 일관되게
consistently happening 꾸준히 발생하는
consist v. 구성되다 (of)   consistent adj. 지속적인, 일관적인
동 constantly adv. 끊임없이

correctly 올바르게, 정확하게
correctly understand the contract's conditions
계약 조건들을 정확히 이해하고 있다
correction n. 수정   correct adj. 올바른 v. 수정하다

definitely 분명히, 반드시, 명확하게
should definitely apply for the internship
인턴십에 반드시 신청해야 한다
definite adj. 명확한, 확정된

diligently 성실히, 열심히
work diligently 성실히 일하다
diligent adj. 근면한, 성실한

dramatically 극적으로
dramatically increase/decrease 극적으로 증가하다/감소하다
dramatic adj. 극적인

efficiently 효율적으로
process orders efficiently 주문을 효율적으로 처리하다
efficiency n. 효율성   efficient adj. 효율적인
동 effectively adv. 효과적으로

exclusively 독점적으로, 전적으로
exclusively available 독점적으로 이용 가능한
exclude v. 제외하다   excluding prep. ~을 제외하고

extremely 몹시, 극도로
extremely successful 매우 성공적인
extremely hot weather 극도로 더운 날씨
동 highly adv. 매우, 몹시   반 moderately adv. 알맞게

generously 관대히, 후하게
donate generously to charities 자선 단체에 후하게 기부하다
generous adj. 관대한
동 leniently adv. 관대하게

gradually 점차로, 서서히
gradually become popular 점차 인기가 높아지다
동 progressively adv. 점진적으로   반 abruptly adv. 갑자기

inadvertently 무심코, 부주의하게
inadvertently made a mistake 무심코 실수를 저질렀다
inadvertent adj. 부주의한
동 negligently adv. 태만하게

independently 독립적으로, 따로
handle the project independently 따로 프로젝트를 처리하다
independence n. 독립   independent adj. 독립적인
동 separately adv. 떨어져서

individually 개별적으로, 개인적으로
be individually interviewed 개별 면접을 보다
individual adj. 개별적인 n. 개인
동 personally adv. 개인적으로

meticulously 꼼꼼하게, 세심하게
a meticulously researched book 꼼꼼하게 연구된 책
meticulous adj. 꼼꼼한
반 carelessly adv. 부주의하게

mutually 서로, 상호간에
be mutually beneficial 상호 이득이 되다
mutual adj. 상호적인, 서로 관계가 있는

nearly 거의
nearly 500 participants 거의 500명의 참석자들
near adj. 가까운
동 approximately adv. 대략   roughly adv. 대략

necessarily 반드시, 어쩔 수 없이
Money does not necessarily bring happiness.
돈이 반드시 행복을 가져다주는 것은 아니다.
necessity n. 필요성, 생필품   necessary adj. 필요한

notably 주목할 만하게, 두드러지게
most notably 가장 주목할 만하게, 특히
note v. 주목하다, 언급하다   notable adj. 주목할 만한, 현저한
동 markedly adv. 두드러지게   noticeably adv. 두드러지게

originally 원래, 독창적으로
was higher than we originally predicted
우리가 원래 예상했던 것보다 높았다
origin n. 기원, 시작   original adj. 원래의, 최초의, 독창적인

otherwise 다르게, 그렇지 않으면
a device otherwise known as "an e-reader"
'이-리더'로도 알려진 기기
unless otherwise indicated 별도의 표시가 없다면

overwhelmingly 압도적으로
overwhelmingly defeat competitors
경쟁자들을 압도적으로 이기다
overwhelm v. 압도하다   overwhelming adj. 압도적인

periodically 주기적으로, 정기적으로
a meeting held periodically 정기적으로 열리는 회의
periodical n. 정기 간행물   adj. 주기적인
동 regularly adv. 정기적으로   routinely adv. 정기적으로

primarily 주로, 무엇보다도 먼저
primarily due to its low cost 무엇보다 저렴한 가격 때문에
primary adj. 주요한
동 mainly adv. 주로

promptly 즉각, 신속히
promptly report to the supervisor 즉시 상관에게 보고하다
prompt adj. 신속한 v. 촉발하다
동 immediately adv. 즉시   instantly adv. 즉각

properly 적절하게, 알맞게
be properly installed 올바르게 설치되어 있다
proper adj. 적절한
동 adequately adv. 적절하게   반 improperly adv. 부적절하게

reasonably 합리적으로, 적당하게
a reasonably-priced compact car 합리적인 가격의 소형차
reason n. 이유, 이성 v. 판단을 내리다
reasonable adj. 합리적인, (가격이) 알맞은

recently 최근에
a recently upgraded building 최근에 보수된 건물
recent adj. 최근의
동 lately adv. 최근에

relatively 상대적으로, 비교적
at a relatively low price 상대적으로 낮은 가격에
relate v. 관련시키다   relative adj. 상대적인 n. 친척
동 comparatively adv. 비교적, 어느 정도

shortly 곧, 즉시
will answer your questions shortly 질문에 곧 답해 줄 것이다
shorten v. 줄이다
동 soon adv. 곧

slightly 약간, 조금
be slightly modified 약간 수정되다
slight adj. 조금의
동 marginally adv. 아주 조금   반 considerably adv. 상당히

ETS 실전문제 1

1. Property taxes in Granville, a relatively new area, are ------- higher than in Powerton.
   (A) considerably
   (B) spaciously
   (C) diligently
   (D) expertly

2. The management appreciates how ------- the company's security officers are.
   (A) best
   (B) helpful
   (C) forward
   (D) promoted

3. Davila's Café is ------- for its desserts made from scratch in the restaurant.
   (A) delicious
   (B) generous
   (C) curious
   (D) famous

4. The registration period for the Vernon Street Marathon has been ------- to March 31.
   (A) extended
   (B) participated
   (C) bought
   (D) claimed

5. After ten years in the marketing department, Ms. Quinn was ------- promoted to director.
   (A) mostly
   (B) thickly
   (C) hardly
   (D) finally

6. Surry Hill Flowers and Gifts is offering special deals on all ------- during November.
   (A) capitals
   (B) ways
   (C) manners
   (D) orders

7. At Monday's meeting, projected sales ------- for next quarter will be discussed.
   (A) figures
   (B) viewpoints
   (C) representatives
   (D) turnouts

8. Market analysts at Fulltrade Financial Services routinely ------- current and potential investments.
   (A) surprise
   (B) evaluate
   (C) participate
   (D) disguise

9. Sun Teng returned to work after retiring, so his pension will be recalculated to reflect the ------- number of his years of service.
   (A) perfect
   (B) total
   (C) main
   (D) wide

10. Small businesses should ------- taking out low-interest loans from Greyhound Bank.
    (A) aim
    (B) observe
    (C) persuade
    (D) consider

11. The evening crew can unload ------- from trucks that arrive after regular business hours.
    (A) transportation
    (B) requests
    (C) power
    (D) cargo

12. Howler monkeys are indigenous to many parts of Central America but are ------- seen by tourists.
    (A) seldom
    (B) ever
    (C) almost
    (D) basically

ETS 실전문제 2

1. Hire the professionals at Glenstone Restoration for your next exterior paint -------.
   (A) project
   (B) flavor
   (C) material
   (D) brush

2. Ecology Soaps produces a broad ------- of all-natural bath products.
   (A) appeal
   (B) variety
   (C) sense
   (D) band

3. The city council of Westlawn has not ------- settled on a name for the new park.
   (A) yet
   (B) later
   (C) rarely
   (D) shortly

4. Pratique Lawn sells top-quality gardening ------- at affordable prices.
   (A) achievements
   (B) associations
   (C) standards
   (D) supplies

5. The Brades Swim Center is ------- closed for renovations.
   (A) greatly
   (B) loosely
   (C) temporarily
   (D) busily

6. Technicians should advise homeowners that the waiting period for window ------- is at least four weeks.
   (A) installation
   (B) organization
   (C) reflection
   (D) connection

7. The audience broke into ------- applause after the inspiring opening remarks by Ms. Heo.
   (A) enthusiastic
   (B) essential
   (C) glamorous
   (D) stolen

8. Many staff members have already made their travel ------- for the conference.
   (A) arrangements
   (B) agencies
   (C) designs
   (D) conditions

9. Ms. Gomez has been ------- to the business office to assist with payroll tasks.
   (A) transformed
   (B) registered
   (C) involved
   (D) transferred

10. City sightseeing tours depart from the West Bay Marina ------- at 10 A.M.
    (A) previously
    (B) very
    (C) slightly
    (D) daily

11. Please be sure to sign in at Haverford Hall before ------- the Shambeck Writer's Convention.
    (A) replacing
    (B) having
    (C) attending
    (D) retreating

12. PL Bicycles has announced plans to open a second factory to meet ------- demand for its electric bikes.
    (A) inspired
    (B) versatile
    (C) common
    (D) heightened

ETS 실전문제 3

1. Fordham Stationers recently decided to switch suppliers because Valley Paper has been ------- late in shipping their orders.
   (A) steadily
   (B) sensibly
   (C) exactly
   (D) consistently

2. After reviewing our corporate policies, please sign the ------- contract and return it before July 1.
   (A) surrounding
   (B) enclosed
   (C) concerned
   (D) accepting

3. The Produce Growers Association has distributed a pamphlet to area supermarkets that lists fruits and vegetables with the highest ------- of vitamins.
   (A) attractions
   (B) concentrations
   (C) beneficiaries
   (D) commands

4. Governor Jayson won the election because she ------- to reduce taxes and allocate more funding to schools.
   (A) followed
   (B) predicted
   (C) invented
   (D) promised

5. Because of the large number of tourists in summer months, travelers should plan ------- and make their reservations early.
   (A) accordingly
   (B) subsequently
   (C) conversely
   (D) assuredly

6. Engineers in the Welber Machine Factory in Cologne work to correct minor flaws in the designs of ------- drilling systems.
   (A) confused
   (B) complex
   (C) informative
   (D) cautious

7. Salesman Carlos Diaz displayed ------- by actively engaging potential customers as they entered the Valley Stream Furniture showroom.
   (A) amount
   (B) objective
   (C) reliance
   (D) initiative

8. Initial projections of quarterly earnings have already been ------- with a month still remaining.
   (A) exceeded
   (B) outdated
   (C) overdrawn
   (D) impressed

9. Sports fans around the world ------- await the results of the annual tennis championship.
   (A) perfectly
   (B) evenly
   (C) rapidly
   (D) eagerly

10. Anwar Badawy was moved to a ------- position with more responsibility.
    (A) slight
    (B) repeating
    (C) probable
    (D) supervisory

11. Hiring a logistics consultant has resulted in faster ------- of goods to our stores.
    (A) founding
    (B) distribution
    (C) treatment
    (D) revision

12. Swabian Motors will ------- its current name even after it merges with a rival company.
    (A) receive
    (B) inquire
    (C) grant
    (D) retain

ETS 실전문제 4

1. The terms and conditions outlined in this document are ------- to change without notice.
   (A) dependent
   (B) subject
   (C) immediate
   (D) final

2. The new plant director, Ha-Jae Cheon, will be ------- for reducing the maintenance costs at the Tamarindo facility.
   (A) fortunate
   (B) possible
   (C) senseless
   (D) responsible

3. The latest microwave oven from Dabato Industries ------- a stainless steel interior and ten different heat settings.
   (A) features
   (B) produces
   (C) implies
   (D) appoints

4. Sign up now for deals available ------- to Platinum members of the Bordner Gym Club.
   (A) exclusively
   (B) financially
   (C) relatively
   (D) productively

5. The CEO has requested our ------- at the award ceremony.
   (A) excuse
   (B) companion
   (C) presence
   (D) training

6. You will receive a ------- e-mail from the Nicoya Hotel verifying your travel plans within two hours of making your reservation.
   (A) sponsor
   (B) confirmation
   (C) margin
   (D) permit

7. A new lighting system has been installed in the administrative offices, ------- the older, less efficient one.
   (A) replacing
   (B) comparing
   (C) brightening
   (D) repairing

8. Dale Department Store will have a special sale on jewelry ------- before the holidays.
   (A) sensitively
   (B) extremely
   (C) immediately
   (D) figuratively

9. The XT1000 is one of the most ------- home-kitchen scales on the market, providing accurate measurement to the milligram.
   (A) tentative
   (B) deliberate
   (C) investigative
   (D) sensitive

10. The Wellborn Science Museum's new astronomy theater has a seating ------- of 250.
    (A) aptitude
    (B) capacity
    (C) demonstration
    (D) compliance

11. Using a mixture of fresh ginger and garlic, chef Gary Peters created an ------- recipe for roasted fish.
    (A) exquisite
    (B) obedient
    (C) enormous
    (D) intentional

12. The impressive floral display at the building entrance is ------- made up of blue flowers, with a few red ones artfully placed throughout.
    (A) enough
    (B) exclusively
    (C) primarily
    (D) everywhere

ETS 실전문제 5

1. During the factory visit, guests will not be permitted to enter the restricted areas, where only ------- employees are allowed.
   (A) successful
   (B) authorized
   (C) concerned
   (D) scattered

2. Wyncote Airlines has announced that it will ------- the £15 baggage fee for members of its Sky Flyer Club.
   (A) prove
   (B) cost
   (C) waive
   (D) align

3. If you no longer wish to receive promotional offers, Heugland's Market will delete your name from the mailing list -------.
   (A) previously
   (B) overall
   (C) neither
   (D) promptly

4. There will be a ------- fifteen-minute intermission between the two performances.
   (A) narrow
   (B) deep
   (C) brief
   (D) sharp

5. Staff must have proper ------- to access the database.
   (A) credentials
   (B) rewards
   (C) consideration
   (D) requirement

6. The accounting department has ------- a new policy in order to decrease paper usage.
   (A) preoccupied
   (B) represented
   (C) characterized
   (D) implemented

7. Guest rooms must be cleaned ------- within two hours after hotel patrons have checked out.
   (A) widely
   (B) highly
   (C) sturdily
   (D) thoroughly

8. Hermann Farm's L10 agricultural tractor is designed to be -------, so it can handle almost any farming task.
   (A) calculating
   (B) receptive
   (C) adaptable
   (D) obligated

9. Employees who cannot attend the training session on March 12 will be scheduled for an ------- date.
   (A) unoccupied
   (B) increased
   (C) irreplaceable
   (D) alternative

10. Fales Bookstores reported a 20 percent decrease in net profit this year, which the company ------- to fierce competition from Yule Booksellers, Inc.
    (A) accused
    (B) presented
    (C) disapproved
    (D) attributed

11. The prevention of environmental pollution has become an important consideration for small and large businesses -------.
    (A) forth
    (B) even
    (C) alike
    (D) beyond

12. Please be ------- that the terms and conditions of the Meyer Company contract are subject to change annually.
    (A) proposed
    (B) known
    (C) aware
    (D) noticed

ETS 실전문제 6

1. With the new Web site enhancements, Hill Street Design customers will be able to view a ------- of recent purchases.
   (A) voucher
   (B) coupon
   (C) summary
   (D) payment

2. In my opinion, the company's stock price is ------- low compared to its annual earnings.
   (A) audibly
   (B) relatively
   (C) plentifully
   (D) anonymously

3. With the forecast of sunny weather, no one ------- that the match would be canceled because of rain.
   (A) permitted
   (B) wondered
   (C) expected
   (D) counted

4. After reviewing the training program for new sales staff, Mr. Vance concluded that more ------- should be placed on networking skills.
   (A) appeal
   (B) analysis
   (C) distinction
   (D) emphasis

5. The Fitzton Gallery has been the ------- promoter of the arts in Worthington, sponsoring numerous public events.
   (A) precise
   (B) separate
   (C) certain
   (D) primary

6. Photos and related documents were supplied by the author, unless ------- noted.
   (A) else
   (B) otherwise
   (C) instead
   (D) rather

7. To best serve its clients, Noguchi Investments regularly conducts ------- analyses of current business trends.
   (A) spacious
   (B) eventual
   (C) thorough
   (D) probable

8. Although our employees did not write the correct address on the shipping form, the machine parts arrived at the dairy farm on -------.
   (A) schedule
   (B) appointment
   (C) authority
   (D) condition

9. Mehri Translations Ltd. suggests that, when ------- with a business associate through an interpreter, you politely focus your attention on the associate.
   (A) regulating
   (B) acquainting
   (C) communicating
   (D) contemplating

10. All new hire paperwork must be filled out ------- and submitted to human resources by the end of the business day.
    (A) lately
    (B) overly
    (C) completely
    (D) hardly

11. The work shifts at Stella's Confectionary are eight hours long and ------- a 30-minute break for lunch.
    (A) prepare
    (B) release
    (C) assemble
    (D) include

12. The Sanulife Web site brings you news of all the latest ------- in medical research.
    (A) novelties
    (B) advances
    (C) elevations
    (D) formations

ETS 실전문제 7

1. The employee handbook clearly ------- the procedure for filing expense reports.
   (A) purchases
   (B) outlines
   (C) rations
   (D) invests

2. When answering calls, telephone representatives are to do what they can, within -------, to address customer concerns.
   (A) return
   (B) reason
   (C) role
   (D) rest

3. Rain fell ------- throughout the night, providing a welcome relief from the recent dry spell.
   (A) continuously
   (B) mutually
   (C) needlessly
   (D) optimistically

4. Employees are ------- to take family and medical leave if they have been employed for at least twelve months.
   (A) eligible
   (B) desirable
   (C) preferred
   (D) suitable

5. To succeed as a store manager, Ms. Sunra must ------- store needs and employee expectations.
   (A) convince
   (B) balance
   (C) gather
   (D) prevent

6. Promotional banners should be ------- visible throughout the store during the sale.
   (A) tightly
   (B) clearly
   (C) eagerly
   (D) commonly

7. The new quality assurance policy requires that all machines be inspected if more than five ------- items are found in a single day.
   (A) collective
   (B) efficient
   (C) immediate
   (D) defective

8. Advertisements placed by merchants in *The Weekly Roundup* do not ------- imply endorsement by the management of the newspaper.
   (A) barely
   (B) highly
   (C) gradually
   (D) necessarily

9. This Saturday, Rose's Fashion Boutique will be ------- a 20 percent discount to all shoppers.
   (A) notifying
   (B) offering
   (C) performing
   (D) joining

10. Department managers must send ------- employee evaluations to Mr. Gang.
    (A) steady
    (B) skillful
    (C) turned
    (D) completed

11. Use of this Web site implies ------- with our terms and conditions.
    (A) contentment
    (B) agreement
    (C) placement
    (D) development

12. When not on display, the rare manuscripts are stored in conditions that are ------- for their preservation.
    (A) attentive
    (B) credible
    (C) optimal
    (D) competent

ETS 실전문제 8

1. Ms. Pattison received an award for ------- missing a deadline in her three years of work at the company.
   (A) even
   (B) quite
   (C) still
   (D) never

2. Home to an extensive collection of Scottish art from the eighteenth century, the Hendron Museum also ------- contemporary works.
   (A) operates
   (B) showcases
   (C) extends
   (D) undergoes

3. Mild weather is ------- to continue throughout the week, with a chance of light rain on Thursday.
   (A) probable
   (B) frequent
   (C) considerable
   (D) likely

4. Lab tests show that a precise combination of the various ------- is necessary for the cleaning compound to be effective.
   (A) divisions
   (B) prospects
   (C) ingredients
   (D) compartments

5. The ------- installed solar array in Amarillo is expected to produce 50,000 kilowatt hours of electricity annually.
   (A) shortly
   (B) recently
   (C) commonly
   (D) increasingly

6. We prefer to ------- our ingredients from local, environmentally friendly companies like Sunrise Farms.
   (A) comprise
   (B) produce
   (C) obtain
   (D) achieve

7. Mello Advertising is known for its brightly colored and eye-catching logos, flyers, and other ------- material.
   (A) conditional
   (B) promotional
   (C) natural
   (D) historical

8. Cross Cove is home to several New Zealand artists, most ------- Francis Seward and Kyle McIntyre.
   (A) easily
   (B) notably
   (C) separately
   (D) commonly

9. Heston Property Management apologizes for any ------- that the current renovation work may cause to our tenants.
   (A) resolution
   (B) inconvenience
   (C) improvement
   (D) distinction

10. If there is time at the end of tomorrow's meeting, Cilla Sampson will speak ------- about the Toronto Arts Festival.
    (A) rarely
    (B) slightly
    (C) recently
    (D) briefly

11. Located far from the stresses of the city, the Cozcal Hotel prides itself on offering guests a ------- vacation experience.
    (A) reclining
    (B) restored
    (C) relaxing
    (D) retired

12. Ms. Atembe of Hartwick Trucking will conduct a workshop on the best ways to ------- customers' concerns about freight delivery.
    (A) inform
    (B) address
    (C) supervise
    (D) promise

ETS 실전문제 9

1. ------- regarding employment at Craddock Surgical Products should be directed to the human resources department.
   (A) Inquiries
   (B) Influences
   (C) Occasions
   (D) Qualifications

2. Business analysts expect the ------- merger decision to be made soon by Jemquist Ltd.
   (A) sparse
   (B) related
   (C) pending
   (D) attentive

3. Customers ------- return to Performance Wireless because of its low fees and excellent customer service.
   (A) greatly
   (B) moderately
   (C) mutually
   (D) frequently

4. Cargo bicycles are designed with ------- in mind, as they are often used to haul heavy loads.
   (A) durability
   (B) freshness
   (C) enthusiasm
   (D) dedication

5. The complicated new time-reporting guidelines at Prindell Communications have caused ------- for employees.
   (A) confusion
   (B) attention
   (C) information
   (D) impression

6. Dr. Okada of Sendai Labs has received the ------- Lowery Award for pharmaceutical research.
   (A) enhanced
   (B) determined
   (C) prestigious
   (D) energetic

7. On August 6, the Oakman Corporation ------- the appointment of its new president.
   (A) informed
   (B) created
   (C) announced
   (D) earned

8. The Wiltshire Orchestra's concert was ------- three hours long, ending just after 11 P.M.
   (A) attentively
   (B) approximately
   (C) endlessly
   (D) comparatively

9. Fischer's Cafeteria is looking for a full-time assistant manager to oversee the evening ------- on weekdays from 3:00 to 10:00 P.M.
   (A) chance
   (B) shift
   (C) practice
   (D) effect

10. Frequent, positive interactions between coworkers have been associated with ------- productivity throughout the year.
    (A) licensed
    (B) gathered
    (C) increased
    (D) presented

11. Because Oswalt International has completed over 200 development projects -------, its services are now in high demand.
    (A) successfully
    (B) instantly
    (C) financially
    (D) hugely

12. It will be difficult to ------- the safety regulations without effective monitoring.
    (A) entrust
    (B) enforce
    (C) imply
    (D) implore

ETS 실전문제 10

1. Personnel who are ------- to attend Thursday's meeting should inform Everett Watson.
   (A) busy
   (B) easy
   (C) unable
   (D) unpleasant

2. The conference offers a variety of options that fit all ------- of interest and expertise.
   (A) sizes
   (B) times
   (C) areas
   (D) designs

3. Construction of the new swimming pool is currently in ------- and is expected to be completed by May 1.
   (A) progress
   (B) place
   (C) use
   (D) demand

4. Danner Corporation met its recruitment goals for the third ------- year.
   (A) following
   (B) consecutive
   (C) approximate
   (D) absolute

5. While some of the trees in Cresson Park were planted ------- by landscaping professionals, most of them have developed naturally from seeds.
   (A) intentionally
   (B) highly
   (C) profoundly
   (D) indefinitely

6. Sondergard heating units are highly -------, resulting in lower heating costs for homeowners.
   (A) produced
   (B) reasonable
   (C) efficient
   (D) preferred

7. Unless customers opt for expedited service, orders ------- take three days to process.
   (A) substantially
   (B) perpetually
   (C) familiarly
   (D) typically

8. When he served as president of Delvan Manufacturing, Pierre Dunn ------- several policies that transformed the company.
   (A) instituted
   (B) relieved
   (C) interviewed
   (D) fabricated

9. The purpose of the WHJ research study was to determine the ------- of adding bicycle lanes throughout the Wilmingdale business district.
   (A) feasibility
   (B) dependency
   (C) intensity
   (D) accuracy

10. Researchers from Wynne University have spent several months ------- the plant species in the Mojowarno Nature Preserve.
    (A) experimenting
    (B) documenting
    (C) commenting
    (D) accomplishing

11. Pineville Library announced that the extensive building renovation is ------- finished.
    (A) nearly
    (B) vaguely
    (C) readily
    (D) previously

12. By ------- the furniture shipping process, we can lower expenses and cut the delivery time in half.
    (A) outpacing
    (B) streamlining
    (C) persevering
    (D) forestalling

ETS ACTUAL TEST

101. Tolo Advertising uses customer data to customize ------- product recommendations.

(A) its
(B) itself
(C) ours
(D) ourselves

102. A ------- list of festival sponsors must be submitted by March 15.

(A) completely
(B) completion
(C) complete
(D) completes

103. Without exception, ------- employees must wear their badge when on company grounds.

(A) whichever
(B) such
(C) either
(D) all

104. The product ------- provides diagrams for assembling the Svetlo floor lamp.

(A) receipt
(B) schedule
(C) record
(D) manual

105. Since Mr. Vos is ------- with the inventory procedure, he will lead today's workshop.

(A) familiar
(B) familiarity
(C) familiarize
(D) familiarization

106. Research assistants should not begin data analysis ------- all results are available.

(A) around
(B) except
(C) despite
(D) until

107. The sofa that Ms. Nakamura requested is ------- still available in green leather.

(A) luck
(B) luckier
(C) luckiest
(D) luckily

108. Ms. Turner was in ------- with the chief operating officer earlier this week.

(A) contacted
(B) contact
(C) contacts
(D) contacting

109. Quan's Donuts sells a variety of breakfast offerings, ranging ------- pastries and scones to bagels and croissants.

(A) like
(B) such
(C) from
(D) with

110. Celia Wu said she is available ------- Monday to paint the cabinets in Mr. Newcombe's kitchen.

(A) done
(B) least
(C) next
(D) several

111. Prices on select sofas will be ------- by up to 50 percent this weekend only.
    (A) softened
    (B) arranged
    (C) reduced
    (D) made

112. If ------- finds a lost item, please give it to Mr. Carines at the security desk.
    (A) it
    (B) anyone
    (C) whichever
    (D) you

113. ------- a birthday or any other special event by booking a private party at Nirmala's Restaurant.
    (A) Celebrated
    (B) Celebrate
    (C) Celebrating
    (D) Celebration

114. Mr. Mendoza is ------- asked to train interns even though he has worked at the firm for less than two years.
    (A) frequent
    (B) frequency
    (C) frequenting
    (D) frequently

115. ------- items left behind on city buses will be held for 30 days at the Transportation Department's main office.
    (A) Personable
    (B) Personally
    (C) Personal
    (D) Person

116. Catering requests for meetings must now be approved by a manager ------- being submitted to Food Services.
    (A) over
    (B) before
    (C) through
    (D) between

117. Despite the stock market's downturn, analysts in the shipping sector speak ------- regarding their next earnings forecast.
    (A) especially
    (B) confidently
    (C) lately
    (D) worriedly

118. Farmer Jake's premier gift box features a delicious ------- of sweet and savory snacks.
    (A) combined
    (B) combination
    (C) combinations
    (D) combine

119. Plexar Industries ------- announced that Ms. Prasad received the Ludwig Award for her work in city transportation.
    (A) evenly
    (B) thoroughly
    (C) recently
    (D) mostly

120. Contact the company's onboarding coordinator ------- any questions about the training videos.
    (A) still
    (B) with
    (C) just
    (D) where

121. There is a one-hour wait for a table inside the restaurant, but seating will be available ------- on the outdoor patio.

(A) short
(B) shortest
(C) shorter
(D) shortly

122. To ensure its ------- growth, McGee Refrigeration, Inc., has added a dedicated phone line for customer service.

(A) continue
(B) continuation
(C) continues
(D) continued

123. The new contract for Barrison factory workers ------- a guarantee of a 6 percent pay raise after two years of employment.

(A) inclusion
(B) includes
(C) inclusive
(D) inclusively

124. Salon Genovia provides ------- services, including haircuts, hair coloring, and manicures.

(A) usual
(B) various
(C) approximate
(D) occasional

125. Interviews for jobs at Jamison's Grocery Store can be ------- by video chat or in person.

(A) honored
(B) spoken
(C) transferred
(D) conducted

126. If anything ------- is missing from the summary page, please let the research manager know.

(A) else
(B) onto
(C) despite
(D) namely

127. ------- John Yakut, two other scientists from IES Biotech will present research results during the seminar.

(A) Except for
(B) Unless
(C) As far as
(D) In addition to

128. The newspaper strives to correct all errors in a timely manner and would never publish erroneous information -------.

(A) knew
(B) knowing
(C) knowingly
(D) knows

129. Although Dr. Wong's fieldwork methods were once considered too demanding, they are now ------- practice on paleontology digs.

(A) accept
(B) acceptance
(C) acceptably
(D) accepted

130. ------- the sales of earlier Lealo Computer models have been weak, this year's LC358 model has been well received.

(A) Consequently
(B) Because
(C) Whereas
(D) Unless

Questions 131-134 refer to the following job posting.

Friendly City Parking is seeking qualified applicants to fill the role of parking attendant. Job candidates must be ------- and attentive. Responsibilities include distributing and collecting receipts, assigning parking spots, and monitoring the facility. Applicants must have a secondary school education with basic math skills. -------. Experience in customer service and operating a cash register is preferred. ------- interested, please send an e-mail to hr@friendlycityparking.com no later than July 18. We ------- competitive pay, a high-energy environment, and flexible schedules.

131. (A) courteously
 (B) courtesy
 (C) courteous
 (D) courtesies

132. (A) Employees work closely with students each day.
 (B) Attendants are required to calculate accurate change for customers.
 (C) Weekends are usually the busiest times.
 (D) The facility remains open 24 hours a day.

133. (A) If
 (B) And
 (C) So
 (D) Still

134. (A) offer
 (B) offered
 (C) offers
 (D) were offering

Questions 135-138 refer to the following e-mail.

To: Catharine Speltz <c.speltz@solariamail.net>
From: Ethan Tsuei <e.tsuei@tsueilearningcentre.org>
Date: 3 April
Subject: Next stage
Attachment: Link

Dear Ms. Speltz,

Thank you for continuing your education at Tsuei Learning Centre. Our records show that you have ------- the first two modules of our course on loans and mortgages. The third module will begin next Monday at 9 A.M. This module contains four classes, all of which ------- must finish to earn full credit for the course. ------- .

The link for your upcoming classes is attached. Be sure to log in ------- the 9 A.M. start time for each class to be granted access.

Best wishes for continued success!

Ethan Tsuei, owner of Tsuei Learning Centre

135. (A) written
(B) misplaced
(C) completed
(D) supervised

136. (A) I
(B) we
(C) you
(D) they

137. (A) The program provides educational opportunities for adults.
(B) The classes will be held in the morning from Monday through Thursday.
(C) The other modules were offered earlier in the year.
(D) This is the third course you have taken at Tsuei Learning Centre.

138. (A) between
(B) without
(C) among
(D) before

Questions 139-142 refer to the following article.

Renowned architect Nicole Barbosa has released images of Catania, the high-rise apartment complex she has planned for Mexico City. When built, the 200-meter tower will be the tallest building ------- by Ms. Barbosa, who is known more for her iconic museums. Danilo Costa, who has partnered with Ms. Barbosa on other -------, will oversee plans for the building's interior.

Though some space will be reserved for offices, the tower will be ------- residential, with full occupancy expected almost immediately upon opening. -------.

139. (A) mapped
(B) purchased
(C) advertised
(D) designed

140. (A) projects
(B) projected
(C) projecting
(D) projectors

141. (A) hastily
(B) primarily
(C) correctly
(D) eagerly

142. (A) The builders acted on the architect's supplemental instructions.
(B) Mexico City is widely known for its distinctive architecture.
(C) Ms. Barbosa's office is located on the top floor of the building.
(D) Prospective renters have already been inquiring about the units.

Questions 143-146 refer to the following e-mail.

To: All Staff <staff@okhosdesign.com>
From: Ruthann Moon <rmoon@okhosdesign.com>
Date: October 12
Subject: Staffing update

Dear Staff,

As was announced last month, Raphael Galli, our art director for the past sixteen years, will soon be relocating to Europe. -----143.----- , he will begin the next chapter of his professional career as an executive director at a German marketing company. Now, after a thorough search for his replacement, I am thrilled to tell you -----144.----- our own Samantha Panayi will be our next art director. -----145.----- . Ms. Panayi has been at Okhos for eight years and has worked closely with Mr. Galli during that time. She will officially step into her new role next week and continue to consult with Mr. Galli until he leaves in November. Please stop by Ms. Panayi's office to -----146.----- her.

Sincerely,

Ruthann Moon

Senior Vice President, Okhos Design Associates

143. (A) Once there
 (B) Instead
 (C) Nevertheless
 (D) For example

144. (A) it
 (B) as
 (C) that
 (D) even

145. (A) The search has begun to fill her old position.
 (B) Okhos has one of the most creative teams in the business.
 (C) Meanwhile, Mr. Galli has been practicing his German.
 (D) We are confident that the transition will be a smooth one.

146. (A) invite
 (B) notify
 (C) interview
 (D) congratulate

PART 7

독해

INTRO

UNIT 17 편지/이메일
UNIT 18 회람/공지/광고/기사
UNIT 19 메시지/웹페이지/기타
UNIT 20 복수 지문

ETS ACTUAL TEST
PART 7 빈출 표현

무료 강의

INTRO PART 7 독해

단일 지문 10개 및 복수 지문 5세트, 총 54문항

지문을 읽고 이와 관련된 문제를 풀어야 하는 파트로, 단일 지문 10개에 29문항, 이중 지문 2세트에 10문항, 삼중 지문 3세트에 15문항으로 구성되어 있다. 이메일, 기사, 회람 등이 주로 나오며, 일정표, 후기, 송장 등 기타 양식도 등장한다.
주제·목적이나 세부 사항을 묻는 문제, Not/True(사실 확인) 문제, 문장 삽입 문제, 추론/암시 문제, 동의어 문제, 의도 파악 문제가 출제된다.

ETS 예제

Questions 147-148 refer to the following **notice**. ● ──── **1** 지문 종류와 제목 읽기

147 Attention Waylon Concert Hall Guests ●

- 147 Ticket holders arriving late will not be admitted to the auditorium until a suitable break during the performance and must be shown to their seats by an usher. ●──── **3** 147번과 관련 내용 확인

- 147 Mobile telephones must be turned off during all performances.

- 148 Cameras and video or audio recorders of any kind are prohibited unless specifically authorized by the **promoter**. ●──── **3** 148번과 관련 내용 확인
Those found during the performance will be held at the box office until the end of the show.

- Standing in the aisles during performances is forbidden by the fire regulations.

- Smoking is prohibited throughout the building.

- Food or beverages may not be brought into the auditorium at any time.

Please be courteous to those around you while you enjoy the show.

147. What does the notice mainly discuss?
(A) Rules for concertgoers
(B) Equipment used by concert-hall staff
(C) Safety procedures
(D) Performance schedules
●──── **2** 문제 유형 및 키워드 파악

148. According to the notice, what might a promoter do?
(A) Distribute concert programs
(B) Escort guests who arrive late to their seats
(C) Approve the use of audio devices
(D) Collect mobile phones

252

풀이 전략

❶ 지문의 종류와 제목을 읽고 내용을 예상한다.

지문 유형마다 자주 다뤄지는 내용이 있다. 지문 유형에 따른 내용 전개 방식을 예상하는 것이 좋다.

Questions 147-148 refer to the following notice.
공지: 정책 / 변경 사항 안내, 당부 사항, 주의 사항 등의 내용 예상

Attention Waylon Concert Hall Guests
웨일런 콘서트 홀 관람객을 대상으로 하는 공지: 홀 이용 관련 안내 사항 열거

❷ 질문을 읽고 문제 유형과 키워드를 파악한다.

147. What does the notice mainly discuss?
주제/목적 | 제목과 초반부에 초점

148. According to the notice, what might a promoter do?
세부 사항 + 추론 | 키워드 'promoter'가 있는 부분에 초점

❸ 지문을 읽으며 주요 내용을 파악하고, 문제와 관련된 내용이 나오면 집중해서 읽는다.

147. 공지에서 주로 다루는 내용은?

Ticket holders arriving late will not be admitted to the auditorium until a suitable break
첫 번째 안내 사항: 늦게 도착하는 사람은 휴식시간 전에는 입장 불가

Mobile telephones must be turned off during all performances
두 번째 안내 사항: 공연 중 휴대전화 전원 OFF

정답 (A) Rules for concertgoers 콘서트 관람객이 지켜야 하는 규정

148. 기획자가 할 것 같은 업무는?

Cameras and ~ audio recorders of any kind are prohibited unless specifically authorized by the promoter.
기획자가 승인하지 않은 카메라나 녹음 장치는 사용 금지 = 기획자가 기기 사용 승인

정답 (C) Approve the use of audio devices 오디오 기기 사용 승인

UNIT 17 편지 / 이메일

무료 강의

출제 포인트
1 이메일 출제 빈도가 높으며, 안내, 요청, 문의, 권고 등의 내용이 자주 등장한다.
2 주제/목적 → 세부 사항 → 추가 안내/당부 사항 순서로 전개되는 것이 일반적이다.

◆ 지문 구성과 독해 전략

정답과 해설 p.196

수신인 발신인 제목 날짜	To: Rachel Morse <rmorse@mailnet.com> From: Frank's Auto Repair <cs@franksautorepair.com> Subject: Vehicle service Date: July 1	**1** 수신인, 발신인 관계 파악 수신인: 레이첼 모스 발신인: 자동차 수리점 **2** 제목에서 내용 예상 자동차 서비스 관련
주제/목적	Dear **Ms. Morse**, **Q1** Based on our records, your vehicle is due for a service appointment. Schedule your appointment in the next 30 days to **Q2** receive a 20% discount on the following inspections.	**3** 메일을 보낸 목적 파악 점검 서비스 시기 안내, 30일 이내 예약 시 일부 점검 20% 할인 혜택
세부 사항	• Engine • Tires • Fluid Levels • Battery	
추가 안내	Just click on the following link, print out the coupon, and when you come in for your appointment, submit it with your payment: www.franksautorepair.com/inspectioncoupon. Call (206) 555-0117 to schedule an appointment. We look forward to seeing you!	**4** 세부 내용 파악 링크 클릭, 쿠폰 출력 후 결제 시 제출 **5** 추가 안내 사항 확인 특정 번호로 전화 예약
발신인 정보	Customer Care Department Frank's Auto Repair	

Q1 What is the **purpose** of the e-mail?

(A) To confirm that a refund has been issued
(B) To request that a customer make a payment
(C) To remind a customer to make an appointment
(D) To confirm that an appointment has been scheduled

주제/목적 문제 | 초반부 확인하기
점검 시기 안내, 서비스 예약 권장
정답 (C) 예약할 것을 상기시키기 위해
※ 초반부에서 주제/목적이 확인되지 않으면 다른 문제를 먼저 푼다.

Q2 What is **indicated** about **Ms. Morse**?

(A) She recently purchased a new vehicle.
(B) Her vehicle is currently being repaired.
(C) Her driver's license is expired.
(D) She is eligible for a discount.

Not/True 문제 | 명확한 근거 찾기
수신자인 모스 씨에 관한 사실:
점검 예약 시 일부 항목 할인
정답 (D) 할인을 받을 자격이 있다.
※ 'NOT'이 포함된 질문은 오답을 소거하며 정답을 찾는다.

E-mail

Dear Colleagues,

I'm pleased to announce that Reyatone Fitness Centers (RFC) has joined our Corporate Discount Program. Beginning on April 1, all staff members who purchase an annual RFC membership will receive 15 percent off the regular price.

Membership forms can be downloaded from the Corporate Partnership page of our company's Web site and must be dropped off in person at an RFC location. The closest RFC facility is located on Stiles Street, just two kilometers from our corporate headquarters; a second location is at 42 West Avenue in Winslow.

I hope you will take advantage of this opportunity.

Jill Kendall
Human Resources Associate

1. Why was the e-mail written?
   (A) To announce the opening of a new fitness club
   (B) To describe an employee benefit

2. What is mentioned about Reyatone Fitness?
   (A) Its fees have recently increased.
   (B) It has more than one location.

Letter

Dear Ms. Kovin,

Our records show that the June issue of *Today's Trends* will be your last and that you have not yet renewed your subscription. To encourage you to renew, we would like to offer you *Today's Trends* at a reduced price. You are currently paying $3.00 per issue. We will offer you the magazine for six months at only $2.25 per monthly issue. That means that you will save a total of $4.50 from July to December if you renew your subscription.

Please contact our business office at 888-555-3214 Monday through Friday from 9 a.m. to 5 p.m. or on Saturday from 10 a.m. to 3 p.m. The business office is closed on Sundays. We look forward to continuing to serve you in the future.

Sincerely,

Marsha Clemmins
Marsha Clemmins
Director of Sales

3. When will Ms. Kovin's current subscription end?
   (A) In June
   (B) In December

4. What is Ms. Kovin currently paying for her subscription per month?
   (A) $2.25
   (B) $3.00

Questions 1-2 refer to the following e-mail.

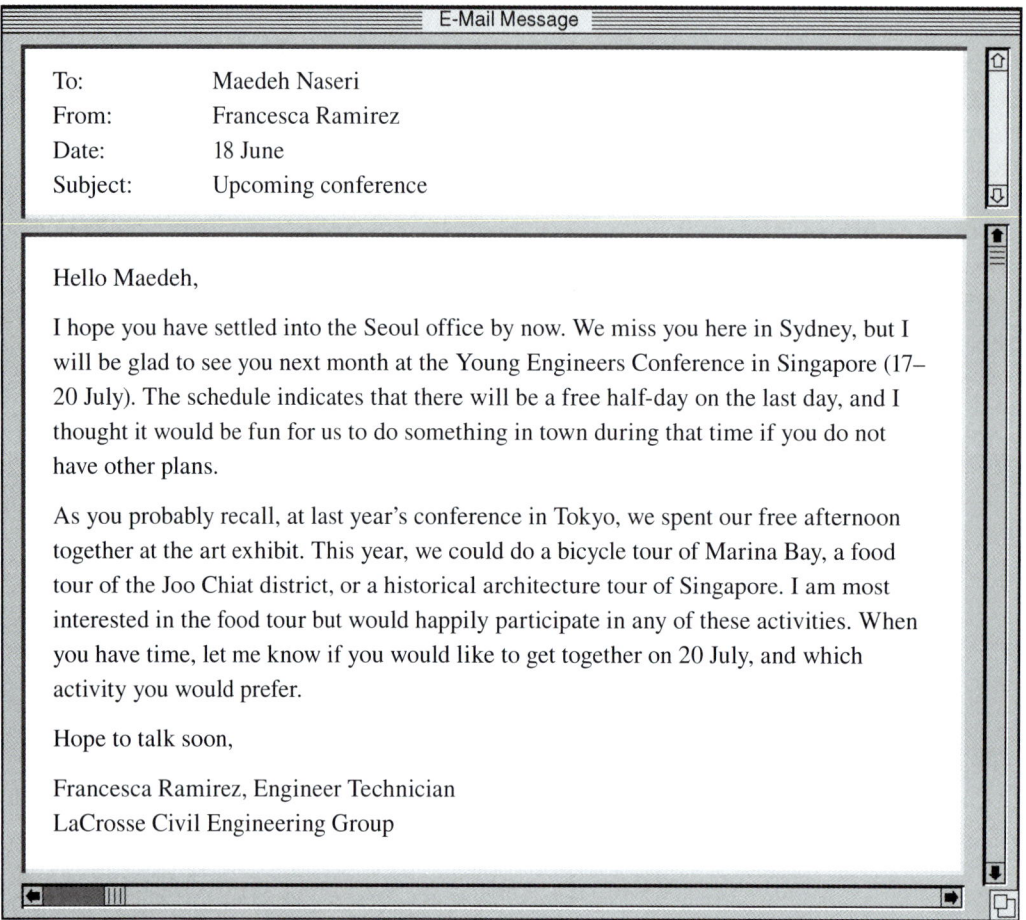

To: Maedeh Naseri
From: Francesca Ramirez
Date: 18 June
Subject: Upcoming conference

Hello Maedeh,

I hope you have settled into the Seoul office by now. We miss you here in Sydney, but I will be glad to see you next month at the Young Engineers Conference in Singapore (17–20 July). The schedule indicates that there will be a free half-day on the last day, and I thought it would be fun for us to do something in town during that time if you do not have other plans.

As you probably recall, at last year's conference in Tokyo, we spent our free afternoon together at the art exhibit. This year, we could do a bicycle tour of Marina Bay, a food tour of the Joo Chiat district, or a historical architecture tour of Singapore. I am most interested in the food tour but would happily participate in any of these activities. When you have time, let me know if you would like to get together on 20 July, and which activity you would prefer.

Hope to talk soon,

Francesca Ramirez, Engineer Technician
LaCrosse Civil Engineering Group

1. What is the purpose of the e-mail?
   (A) To confirm a tour reservation
   (B) To recommend a conference session
   (C) To make plans with a colleague
   (D) To request information about a city

2. What does the e-mail indicate about Ms. Naseri?
   (A) She used to work in Sydney.
   (B) She prefers food tours to bicycle tours.
   (C) She will be attending a conference for the first time.
   (D) She will be going to Seoul on July 17.

Questions 3-4 refer to the following letter.

Forest Living Monthly

Dear Editor,

In the recently published article "A Forgotten Species," the author states that the Nandiimi Fir tree does not grow in North America. However, I want to bring to your readers' attention that the Virginia Heritage Botanical Garden in the United States and the East Sands Preserve in British Columbia, Canada, both contain specimens of this unusual tree. I have dedicated the past twenty years to research initiatives aimed at safeguarding the world's rarest trees—the Nandiimi Fir being one of them—and both of the organizations I have mentioned serve as partners in these efforts. I know the article refers explicitly to trees growing in the wild, but I still think it is important to mention the places where it is being intentionally cultivated so readers are aware.

Kind regards,

Sanjay Rieger
Sanjay Rieger

3. What is the purpose of the letter?
   (A) To encourage readers to plant a particular species of tree
   (B) To explain why a species of tree has become endangered
   (C) To share information about where a species of tree can be found
   (D) To provide advice for identifying trees in the wild

4. What does Mr. Rieger mention about himself?
   (A) He lives in British Columbia.
   (B) He has made an unusual discovery.
   (C) He has changed his research focus.
   (D) He works with conservation groups.

Questions 5-6 refer to the following e-mail.

To:	All Staff
From:	Judd Grodin
Date:	May 30
Subject:	A message from Judd Grodin

Dear Staff,

I want to address some recent reports that have suggested Wiltrout Hardware will offer franchise opportunities this coming autumn. We were indeed considering the possibility of franchising. There are certainly incentives to making that business decision, the main one being that franchising would allow us to attract a more extensive customer base in a much shorter period of time and with fewer operating costs. The idea of expanding our reach in this way is appealing.

That being said, the leadership team has decided that we will remain with our current business model. It is important to maintain consistency in our day-to-day operations and to continue to shape our brand identity in a controlled way. This means that any new Wiltrout Hardware store locations will be wholly owned and managed by our corporation rather than by outside investors.

Please feel free to contact me if you have any questions or concerns.

Sincerely,

Judd Grodin
CEO, Wiltrout Hardware

5. What is the purpose of the e-mail?

(A) To correct misinformation
(B) To praise company leaders
(C) To explain the reason for a poor investment decision
(D) To summarize topics discussed at an all-staff meeting

6. According to the e-mail, what would franchising allow Wiltrout Hardware to do?

(A) Expand its selection of products
(B) Gain more customers quickly
(C) Offer more opportunities for career advancement
(D) Become an industry leader

Questions 7-9 refer to the following e-mail.

To:	board_of_directors@rasp.com
From:	mwatson@eppm.com
Date:	November 21
Subject:	RE: Request for proposal for property management

Dear Board of Directors,

Thank you for allowing East Pacific Property Management (EPPM) to present our proposal on Monday regarding the services we can offer the Residences at Sunrise Pier. — [1] —. As the leading property management firm in this region, EPPM is well equipped to provide the Residences at Sunrise Pier with any support it may require to keep it running smoothly and looking great.

All communities are distinct, and our services can address a wide variety of needs. To provide the highest level of support, we realize that we cannot function using a "one-size-fits-all" management style. — [2] —.

One thing that sets EPPM apart is our use of City Square, a property management mobile app. — [3] —. This app helps us collaborate with your team, connect with neighboring businesses, and stay up-to-date on events in the larger community.

Once again, thank you for the opportunity to present our proposal to you earlier this week. It was a pleasure. — [4] —. Please let us know if you have any further questions about our company.

Sincerely,

Marek Watson, Assistant Director
East Pacific Property Management

7. What is the purpose of the e-mail?

   (A) To promote community events
   (B) To seek a partner for a business
   (C) To offer a vendor a contract extension
   (D) To follow up on a business presentation

8. What is City Square?

   (A) A smartphone application
   (B) A government organization
   (C) A financial software program
   (D) A property management company

9. In which of the positions marked [1], [2], [3], and [4] does the following sentence best belong?

   "For this reason, we customize our service to your property's specific needs."

   (A) [1]
   (B) [2]
   (C) [3]
   (D) [4]

Questions 10-13 refer to the following e-mail.

E-mail

From:	office@chibagrandhotel.com
To:	erik.carlsen@gowmail.com
Subject:	Your recent stay at the Chiba Grand
Date:	April 18

Dear Mr. Carlsen,

At the request of the hotel management, I am writing to ask if you would take a few minutes to share feedback with us regarding your April 8-12 stay at the Chiba Grand Hotel. I would like to know your impressions of our hotel. How happy were you with the amenities? Did you find your stay here enjoyable? Was there anything that was not up to your expectations? If there is room for improvement, let us know. We are one hundred percent committed to total satisfaction for our guests!

Please share your opinions with us directly by going to www.chibagrand.com/yourstay and completing our Total Satisfaction Survey. We ask that you provide responses in all of the listed fields so that we will have a summary of your overall experience. Also, if you provide your feedback by April 30, you will be entered into the $500 Reward Chiba Grand Sweepstakes. Thank you.

Best regards,

Kana Hirota
Chiba Grand Hotel

---

10. Why was the e-mail written?

    (A) To apologize for bad service
    (B) To deliver a payment summary
    (C) To inform a guest about a change
    (D) To inquire about customer satisfaction

11. When did Mr. Carlsen arrive at the hotel?

    (A) On April 8
    (B) On April 12
    (C) On April 18
    (D) On April 30

12. According to the e-mail, what can be found at the online address?

    (A) A questionnaire form
    (B) Directions to the hotel
    (C) A detailed list of expenses
    (D) A description of hotel facilities

13. What does Ms. Hirota offer to Mr. Carlsen?

    (A) A full refund
    (B) A guided tour
    (C) A discount on a future visit
    (D) An opportunity to win a prize

Questions 14-17 refer to the following e-mail.

To:	Zachary Kennedy <zkennedy@sandiahealth.org>
From:	Gina Walker <g.walker@whiteoakmedtechs.com>
Date:	October 29
Subject:	Appointment

Dear Dr. Kennedy,

We at White Oak Medical Technologies are proud to announce the latest addition to our line of medical products. — [1] —. Our recently developed professional thermometer utilizes state-of-the-art technology combining accurate measurement with the convenience of wireless operation. — [2] —. It features a fully digital readout and Bluetooth functionality that connects the thermometer to a medical facility's online recordkeeping system from any location within it. By using the accompanying app, office staff can then copy results directly to a patient's individual chart with a simple click. — [3] —.

Our representative will be in your area next week, and we would be happy to arrange a demonstration for you in your office. — [4] —. If this time frame works for you, please reply to this e-mail with your preferred day and time next week. If you prefer a later date, please call me directly, and I can arrange an appointment that is more convenient for you.

Sincerely,

Gina Walker
White Oak Medical Technologies
863-555-0111

14. What is the purpose of the e-mail?

(A) To promote an innovative device
(B) To request a replacement device
(C) To confirm the order of a product
(D) To advise of a flaw in a product

15. What is indicated about the thermometer?

(A) It requires that data be entered daily.
(B) It is the manufacturer's best-selling product.
(C) It can connect to an online system.
(D) It has an at-home version for patients.

16. According to the e-mail, why might Dr. Kennedy call Ms. Walker?

(A) To request a patient's chart
(B) To schedule a demonstration after next week
(C) To learn more about a discount for bulk orders
(D) To ask questions about a product line

17. In which of the positions marked [1], [2], [3], and [4] does the following sentence best belong?

"This eliminates the possibility of errors that may arise with manual data entry."

(A) [1]
(B) [2]
(C) [3]
(D) [4]

Questions 18-21 refer to the following letter.

Anita Credit Union
528 SE Main Street
Portland, OR 97201

February 1

Dae-Ho Kwon
4246 W Roosevelt Street
Tigard, OR 97224

Dear Mr. Kwon,

At Anita Credit Union, we constantly strive to provide stellar customer service. — [1] —. As part of our commitment to improved banking operations, we are excited to announce new developments that we believe will better serve our members.

After 30 years in a single branch in downtown Portland, we will shift to a new business model incorporating a network of facilities. We believe this decision will benefit our customers as well as our employees. — [2] —. Starting in June, new branches will open in Tigard, Gresham, Beaverton, and Wilsonville. With more locations, Anita Credit Union will be able to serve members directly in their communities, and employees can work closer to their homes. — [3] —. This change will reduce operating costs and improve business operations for the credit union.

In addition to opening new branch offices, we are assessing office spaces to find a new location for our downtown Portland headquarters. — [4] —. Regardless of where the new headquarters is located, it will offer the same convenient hours and excellent services that you expect from Anita Credit Union.

Sincerely,

Priyanka Gupta
Priyanka Gupta
President, Anita Credit Union

18. What is the purpose of the letter?

(A) To confirm the opening of a bank account
(B) To introduce a new bank president
(C) To announce new banking locations
(D) To provide a bank account statement

19. What is NOT mentioned in the letter about Anita Credit Union?

(A) It has been headquartered at its current location for 30 years.
(B) It is now allowing its employees to work from home.
(C) It is keeping the same business operating hours.
(D) It is implementing a new business model.

20. What new branch location would Mr. Kwon most likely visit?

(A) Tigard
(B) Gresham
(C) Beaverton
(D) Wilsonville

21. In which of the positions marked [1], [2], [3], and [4] does the following sentence best belong?

"We will leave the Financial Square complex next year when the current lease ends."

(A) [1]
(B) [2]
(C) [3]
(D) [4]

UNIT 18 회람 / 공지 / 광고 / 기사

무료 강의

출제 포인트
1. 회람/공지는 초반에 주제/목적이 드러나며, 요청, 혹은 당부 사항으로 마무리되는 경우가 많다.
2. 광고는 '제품/서비스/업체 소개 → 특징/장점 → 혜택' 순으로, 구인 광고는 '직책 및 업무 개요 → 자격 요건과 복리후생 → 지원 방법' 순으로 구성된다.
3. 기사에서는 지역 소식부터 인물/사업체 소개, 기업 합병 소식에 이르기까지 다양한 주제가 다뤄진다. 세부 내용이 나온 후 인터뷰 내용이나 향후 전망으로 마무리된다.

◆ 지문 구성과 독해 전략

정답과 해설 p.203

주제	TURNER BAY (July 11)— The Riverrun Complex has received this year's Ribbon of Excellence. **Q1 The Ribbon is awarded each year by Evertrail, a Web site that showcases local firms.** —[1]—.
세부 내용	**To qualify for the award, an enterprise must receive an average of 3.5 stars on a 4-star Q2 rating scale.** —[2]—. Past and present winners include hotels, attractions, and restaurants throughout the Turner Bay area. This marks the third consecutive year that Riverrun has won the award. —[3]—.
인터뷰 내용	"We at Riverrun are thrilled by this honor," said spokesperson Lucia Berrios. "Since we opened six years ago, we have worked hard to provide families with exciting rides and healthy foods. We are especially proud of our Pavilion of the Sciences, which provides games and interactive experiences that educate and delight patrons of all ages." —[4]—.

1 기사 제목이나 초반에서 주제 확인
리버런 콤플렉스의 수상

2 세부 내용 파악
수상 조건: 별 3.5/4개
수상 대상: 호텔, 명소, 식당 등
리버런 3년 연속 수상

3 인터뷰 내용 파악
리버런 대변인의 수상 소감 및 서비스 (놀이기구, 건강에 좋은 음식, 과학 전시장 등) 소개

Q1 According to the article, what does the **Evertrail** Web site do?
(A) It offers discounts on hotel reservations.
(B) It describes scenic train rides.
(C) It sells products made in Turner Bay.
(D) It evaluates local companies.

세부 사항 문제 | 키워드에 주목하기
에버트레일 웹사이트가 하는 일: 지역 사업체 소개, 별점 평가, 시상
정답 (D) 지역 업체들을 평가한다.
※ 세부 사항 문제에서도 약간의 추론이 필요할 수 있다.

Q2 In which of the positions marked [1], [2], [3], and [4] does the following sentence best belong?

"**The ratings** indicate a business's degree of dedication to quality and customer service."

(A) [1]   **(B) [2]**   (C) [3]   (D) [4]

문장 삽입 문제 | 삽입문 분석하기
ratings 앞에 정관사 the가 쓰였으므로 삽입문 앞에 평가 점수와 관련된 내용이 나와야 한다. [2] 앞에서 rating scale(평가 척도)이 언급되었다.
정답 (B)
※ 관사, 지시형용사/대명사, 접속부사, 시간 표현 등이 결정적 단서가 된다.

Advertisement

Spring Fountain Clean
Made with high-quality ingredients for more than 50 years, the soaps from Spring Fountain Clean leave your entire body feeling fresh.

Afternoon Stroll
Feel energized by the fresh scents of lemon and orange.

South Seas
Savor the warm scents of cloves and ginger.

Visit our Web site at www.springfountainclean.com to see our full line of all-natural soaps, shampoos, and moisturizers.

1. What soap variety features the smell of fruit?
   (A) Afternoon Stroll
   (B) South Seas

2. According to the advertisement, what can be found on Spring Fountain Clean's Web site?
   (A) Information about all Spring Fountain Clean products
   (B) Discount coupons for Spring Fountain Clean soaps

Notice

CLUB TEMPORARILY CLOSED

Big Box Fitness will be closed for five days, June 5–9, while we freshen up our appearance. When we reopen on June 10, you can expect to see new paint, plants, and other decorations throughout the gym and locker rooms. We are also refinishing the floor in the dance studio. During this time, club members will have complimentary access to Brigadoon Fitness at 800 Derby Avenue. To use this facility, you will need to show your valid Big Box Fitness membership card upon arrival.

3. What is indicated about Big Box Fitness?
   (A) It is updating its interior.
   (B) It is offering discounts to new members.

4. What are Big Box Fitness members advised to do?
   (A) Visit a different fitness club
   (B) Register for new fitness classes

Questions 1-2 refer to the following article.

EVANBRIDGE (October 27)—On Thursday evening, the Evanbridge City Council voted eight to one to approve an ambitious construction project proposed by the owners of Huston Field that would add 500 seats to the baseball stadium.

While some Evanbridge residents voiced concerns that the project would lead to traffic congestion problems, the council pointed out that increasing the number of seats would encourage more out-of-town sports fans to attend games. The city would see increased tax revenues, which would help fund initiatives like adding new bus routes. The plan will also allow Huston Field to keep ticket prices from rising, the stadium owners claimed.

1. What has the city council allowed the owners of Huston Field to do?

    (A) Raise ticket prices
    (B) Hold more games
    (C) Build a larger parking area
    (D) Expand the seating capacity

2. Why did some people express unhappiness with the plan?

    (A) They thought it would cause property values to fall.
    (B) They thought it would take funds away from public transportation.
    (C) They thought it would create too much traffic.
    (D) They thought it would make the stadium less attractive to visitors.

Questions 3-4 refer to the following notice.

Dear RDX employees,

We are aware that the coffeemaker in our kitchenette is not functioning properly. Our supplier has scheduled a technician to come and repair the machine by the end of the week.

For the time being, please use the electric kettle to boil water and pour it over the grinds to make coffee. We can then pour the coffee into the thermal carafe to keep it warm. It is not the most efficient process, but it will get the job done. I would ask that whoever arrives in the office first make a pot of coffee for everyone. I am happy to see to it this morning, but my hope is that we each will take a turn.

Seema Gupta

3. What is the purpose of the notice?

    (A) To warn employees of a workplace hazard
    (B) To solicit feedback from employees about a new appliance
    (C) To remind employees of a company policy
    (D) To instruct employees on a temporary solution

4. Who most likely is Ms. Gupta?

    (A) An IT specialist
    (B) A coffee supplier
    (C) An office manager
    (D) A repair technician

Questions 5-7 refer to the following advertisement.

Enjoy Two Months of Pueblonet Pro for Half the Price

Reinvigorate your job search by connecting with professionals in your field on Pueblonet Pro and enjoy 50% off the regular price for two months. Join millions of Pueblonet Pro users and create an account that will serve as your pathway to your next dream job. — [1] —.

Enjoy open communication. Set up a profile that outlines your business background, knowledge, and experience. Contact the right people who can help expand your professional network. You can send direct messages to up to twenty other users each month. — [2] —. You can also see all the Pueblonet Pro users who have viewed your profile over the past 30 days.

Get job insights. Stay up-to-date on the companies that are setting trends in your field and see how your skills match up with their needs. As a Pueblonet Pro user, you can receive recommendations for jobs that fit your abilities. You can even learn how your profile compares to those of other applicants. What's more, your information will be noticed by recruiters who can help you get more job interviews. — [3] —.

Grow professionally. Learn up-to-date skills that are most in demand to advance your career. — [4] —. With Pueblonet Pro you have access to over 10,000 courses in the Pueblonet professional library, and you can use these resources to prepare for your next interview.

This limited-time offer ends on January 15. Act now and take advantage of Pueblonet Pro for just $14.99 a month for the next two months! Visit pueblonetpro.com for more information.

---

5. Who is the intended audience for the advertisement?

   (A) Talent recruiters
   (B) Marketing experts
   (C) Employment coaches
   (D) Job seekers

6. What is indicated about Pueblonet Pro?

   (A) It is available at no charge for a limited time.
   (B) It allows users to see who has viewed their profile.
   (C) It lets users contact an unlimited number of people every month.
   (D) It features a listing of universities that offer free courses to users.

7. In which of the positions marked [1], [2], [3], and [4] does the following sentence best belong?

   "But your access to fellow professionals doesn't end there."

   (A) [1]
   (B) [2]
   (C) [3]
   (D) [4]

Questions 8-10 refer to the following memo.

MEMO

To: All staff
From: Ken Nomura
Date: March 18
Subject: Travel policies

FPJ Unlimited recognizes the need for employees to travel in the performance of company business. To ensure employee safety and keep travel costs reasonable, employees must submit a travel authorization form before any trip is undertaken. All fields on the form must be completed. — [1] —.

After the employee's manager has granted travel approval, the employee can then log on to the company's travel portal to select flights and accommodations. — [2] —. Only approved airline and hotel partners appear on the travel portal. — [3] —. Employees traveling on company business may not make travel arrangements with unlisted vendors.

To streamline the booking process, it is recommended that frequent travelers should complete a profile within the portal indicating their preferred travel times and seat selections. — [4] —. Please contact your manager if you have any questions.

---

8. According to the memo, who can approve an employee travel request?

    (A) A travel portal administrator
    (B) A travel partner
    (C) A manager
    (D) A director of human resources

9. What is indicated about travel profiles?

    (A) They should be created by any newly hired employee.
    (B) They can save time when making business trip arrangements.
    (C) They must be created before travel approval can be granted.
    (D) They are a new element of the company's travel portal.

10. In which of the positions marked [1], [2], [3], and [4] does the following sentence best belong?

    "These include the purpose of a trip, dates of travel, and destination."

    (A) [1]
    (B) [2]
    (C) [3]
    (D) [4]

Questions 11-14 refer to the following memo.

> **MEMO**
>
> To: All Staff
> From: Human Resources
> Date: July 2
> Subject: Corporate training program
>
> Employees interested in advancement within our company are encouraged to participate in the corporate training program. Lannone Industries has long prided itself on this initiative. Several updates will take effect on September 1, when a new cycle of the training program will begin.
>
> First, we are excited to announce the following new courses: Improving Written Communication, Innovative Practices in the Steel Industry, and Motivation and Employee Performance.
>
> Furthermore, for the first time, faculty from Brookstone University's School of Business will lead our training courses. Based on employee feedback, these will not take place online; rather, all sessions will occur on-site after regular work hours.
>
> Though courses in the program are open to all staff at Lannone Industries, we recommend that interested employees consult their managers about which course may be best suited to their needs and interests.
>
> Visit www.lannoneindustries.com/training to find all of the offerings for the September cycle, learn more about what each course will cover, and discover how participation in the program will enhance your career.

11. What is the purpose of the memo?
    (A) To encourage employees to obtain a university degree
    (B) To inform employees about a company program
    (C) To specify how employees can receive training program updates
    (D) To remind employees to update their résumés

12. What is most likely true about Lannone Industries?
    (A) It has not been in business very long.
    (B) It is involved in the production of steel.
    (C) It is highly profitable.
    (D) It expects employees to work overtime.

13. What is indicated about courses that begin on September 1 ?
    (A) They will be taught by managers.
    (B) They will be open to nonemployees.
    (C) They will be offered exclusively online.
    (D) They will take place at Lannone Industries.

14. The word "suited" in paragraph 4, line 3, is closest in meaning to
    (A) dressed
    (B) appropriate
    (C) recommended
    (D) prepared

Questions 15-18 refer to the following article.

Seafood Festival Coming Soon

OCEAN CITY (April 7)—The annual OC Seafood Festival will take place from May 10 through May 14 in its usual location at Greenstone Park near the Ocean City Marina. But festival organizer Debbie Hannover says that this year's festival will feature much more than seafood.

"We've invited several artists, who will display and sell their ocean-themed paintings and other works of art," says Ms. Hannover. "Festival attendees will also be able to have their portraits or caricatures drawn for a fee."

Renowned Cajun chef Alex Bourque will be visiting from New Orleans. The chef, who has published two cookbooks, is making his first trip to this part of the country to serve the shrimp and crab dishes that have made his online channel so popular.

Ms. Hannover notes that the advertising budget for this year's event is 20 percent larger than last year's, with positive results. "Many hotels and motels have been reserved for that weekend," she says. "I encourage anyone wanting to attend to plan ahead."

15. What is suggested about Ms. Hannover?

(A) She owns the Ocean City Marina.
(B) She collects ocean-themed artwork.
(C) She has visited New Orleans.
(D) She has added activities to an event.

16. The word "drawn" in paragraph 2, line 6, is closest in meaning to

(A) played
(B) pulled
(C) attracted
(D) sketched

17. According to the article, what will Mr. Bourque do at the festival?

(A) Make a video for his online channel
(B) Sell copies of his cookbooks
(C) Prepare food for attendees
(D) Judge a cooking contest

18. What does Ms. Hannover suggest about advertisements for this year's festival?

(A) They include commercials on television.
(B) They are reaching a wide audience.
(C) Some of them were created by local artists.
(D) Hotel owners are not satisfied with them.

UNIT 19 메시지 / 웹페이지 / 기타

무료 강의

출제 포인트
1. 문자/온라인 채팅에서는 구어체로 정보 및 의견을 주고받는 상황이 주를 이루며, 요청하거나 지시하는 내용도 자주 등장한다.
2. 웹페이지의 내용은 회사, 제품, 서비스 등에 대한 소개 및 사용 방법 안내, 일정표 등 다양하게 출제된다.
3. 주문서, 영수증, 일정표 등의 양식은 날짜, 수량, 가격 등 단편 정보로 구성되는 것이 보편적이다. 별표(*), 비고(Notes), 추가 의견(Comments)에 유의한다.

◆ **지문 구성과 독해 전략**

정답과 해설 p. 208

연락 이유/용건	**Anna Ricci** [9:02 A.M.] **Q1** Where did you get your car fixed last month?	**1** 연락 이유/용건 확인 그린 씨에게 자동차 수리 업체 정보 문의
	Bonnie Green [9:05 A.M.] Mark's Automotive on Linden Avenue. Are you having vehicle trouble?	
세부 내용	**Anna Ricci** [9:06 A.M.] No. I'm at the coffee shop chatting with Kevein Peters from work. **Q1** His car needs to be repaired.	**2** 세부 내용 파악 수리 대상: 리치 씨의 동료인 피터스 씨의 자동차 그린 씨의 업체 추천: 합리적인 비용 언급
	Bonnie Green [9:08 A.M.] **Q1, Q2** Tell him Mark's was great. They found good prices on parts and charged a reasonable amount for labor.	
끝인사	**Anna Ricci** [9:09 A.M.] **Q2** Thanks. I'll pass it on.	**3** 대화의 마무리 확인 감사 인사 후 해당 업체 정보를 피터스 씨에게 전달하겠다고 함

Q1 **Why most likely** does Ms. Ricci **contact** Ms. Green?

(A) She wants a recommendation.
(B) She needs directions to a location.
(C) She wants a cup of coffee.
(D) She needs her car fixed.

추론 문제 | 근거를 바탕으로 추론하기
그린 씨가 자동차를 맡겼던 업체 문의 → 동료가 자동차를 수리해야 한다고 첨언 → 업체를 추천받기 위해 연락
정답 (A) 추천을 원한다.
※ 근거 없는 추측은 지양해야 한다.

Q2 At 9:09 A.M., what does Ms. Ricci most likely mean when she writes, "**I'll pass it on**"?

(A) She will pick up Ms. Green on the way to work.
(B) She will search for a different repair shop.
(C) She will share information with Mr. Peters.
(D) She will bring money to Mr. Peters.

의도 파악 문제 | 앞뒤 문맥 살피기
리치 씨는 그린 씨가 추천한 자동차 수리 업체 정보를 피터스 씨에게 전달하겠다고 한 것이다.
정답 (C) 피터스 씨와 정보를 공유할 것이다.
※ 대화의 주요 흐름을 파악한 후 앞뒤 문장에서 근거를 찾는다.

Web page

https://www.travelwrangler.com/tips-and-advice

Tips and Advice

By Travel Wrangler staff

It is always wise to ensure that you can make last-minute changes or cancellations to your travel plans without paying a fee. Accordingly, when you use our site to book air tickets, hotel reservations, and travel packages, we recommend that you review the change and cancellation policies for each selection you wish to make.

Note that for the month of September, the Suncarr Hotels chain is offering a 10% discount on any room for any length of stay. Discounts are also available for new memberships in Suncarr's loyalty programs.

As always, we thank all our customers for using our services to arrange their future trips.

1. For whom is the Web page information most likely intended?
   (A) An airline official
   (B) A traveler

2. What is mentioned about the Suncarr Hotels chain?
   (A) It is offering room discounts for a limited time.
   (B) It recently made changes to its guest policies.

Label

Samora Masala Mix is an all-purpose, salt-free blend that is perfect for adding flavor to meats, fish, and vegetables. Add a teaspoon to your main dish while cooking, or create a delectable sauce to accompany your meal by adding coconut milk, tomato paste, yogurt, or pureed greens. These are just some of the ways we like to spice things up without adding salt.

We would love to see what you do with Samora Masala Mix. Send your recipe and a picture of your creation to hello@samoramasalamix.com. We will post five of our favorites on social media every month.

3. What information is provided on the label?
   (A) Ideas for using a product
   (B) A listing of the ingredients

4. What will the makers of Samora Masala Mix do every month?
   (A) Release new flavors
   (B) Share customer comments online

Questions 1-2 refer to the following online chat discussion.

Tamara Susilo (9:04 A.M.) Hello. I want to close one of my accounts at the bank and move the funds to my savings account. Can you help me do that?

Greg Hamon (9:05 A.M.) Yes, I can start the process, but first you must complete some documents that our branch manager needs so that she may approve the transfer. Are you still using the same e-mail address you used to set up your account?

Tamara Susilo (9:06 A.M.) Yes.

Greg Hamon (9:07 A.M.) For security reasons, can you please verify the e-mail?

Tamara Susilo (9:07 A.M.) It should be t.susilo24@emailcloud.com.

Greg Hamon (9:09 A.M.) That's it. I can get the documents to you by e-mail as an attachment. Does that work for you?

Tamara Susilo (9:10 A.M.) Yes.

---

1. What does Ms. Susilo want to do?
   (A) Speak to the bank's branch manager
   (B) Report a technical issue
   (C) Open an account
   (D) Transfer money

2. At 9:09 A.M., what does Mr. Hamon most likely mean when he writes, "Does that work for you"?
   (A) He wants to know whether Ms. Susilo's computer is functioning properly.
   (B) He wants Ms. Susilo to confirm a delivery method for some documents.
   (C) He wants to schedule a meeting with Ms. Susilo.
   (D) He wants to verify a street address.

Questions 3-4 refer to the following social media post.

Our team at Luckett Garden Supply has been busy bundling sweet potato seedlings!

If you preordered our sweet potato seedlings and indicated that you would pick up your order locally, you may come to our store starting tomorrow (Sunday, June 5). We recommend picking up the seedlings as soon as possible so that you can get them into the ground quickly. For those who chose to have their orders delivered, note that we will be shipping them out on Monday, June 6. Please check your e-mail for a message from us with a tracking number so that you can plan for your order's arrival. Be sure not to let it sit in your mailbox too long, as it contains live plants. You can watch a clip of us preparing all the orders at www.luckettgardensupply.com/blog/0602.

3. What is the purpose of the post?

    (A) To recruit seasonal farmworkers
    (B) To apologize for a shipping delay
    (C) To announce that a product is available
    (D) To celebrate the opening of a farm store

4. According to the post, what can customers do on a Web page?

    (A) Watch a short video
    (B) Make a special request
    (C) Consult instructions for planting
    (D) View an updated shipping policy

Questions 5-7 refer to the following invitation.

Please join us as we celebrate 25 successful years!

It has been a wonderful journey, and we thank you for being a part of Bakersville Industries.

You and a guest are cordially invited to join colleagues as we celebrate this milestone.

Dinner and dessert will be served.

Saturday, May 8, from 7:00 P.M. to 10:00 P.M.
Fairhampton Resort and Conference Center
8801 Conference Plaza, Redwood Bay

Please respond by April 2 to Madeline Fine at (650) 555-0174 or mfine@bakersvilleindustries.com.

---

5. According to the invitation, what will happen on May 8 ?

    (A) A company will be sold.
    (B) A conference center will expand.
    (C) A business will celebrate an anniversary.
    (D) An executive will have a retirement party.

6. What is NOT included in the invitation?

    (A) The address of a venue
    (B) The date of an event
    (C) The time of an event
    (D) The name of a speaker

7. Who most likely is Ms. Fine?

    (A) A journalist who covers business news
    (B) An employee at Bakersville Industries
    (C) An administrator at a conference center
    (D) A city official of Redwood Bay

Questions 8-11 refer to the following postcard.

Conrad Success Properties
Panita Conrad, Owner
Cheryl Piter, Broker
Jim Tyler, Associate Broker
1178 Wentz Avenue
Saskatoon, Saskatchewan, S7K 1J6
306-880-9339

Your real estate success is our top priority. Let us make buying or selling a home a pleasant experience.
- We have been a family-owned business for 49 years.
- We can provide insights into the community, schools, restaurants, parks, and opportunities where you want to live.
- We handle everything from start to finish.
- We provide a free comparative market analysis.
- We were voted a top-10 business in Saskatchewan.

**Current Resident
21243 Brand Road
Saskatoon, Saskatchewan, S7K 1J6**

8. What is the purpose of the postcard?
   (A) To welcome a new resident to a neighborhood
   (B) To recruit potential salespeople for a growing business
   (C) To announce the opening of a new business
   (D) To promote the services of a real estate company

9. What most likely is true about Mr. Tyler?
   (A) He owns several properties.
   (B) He is employed by Ms. Conrad.
   (C) He is thinking about moving to a new home.
   (D) He lives on Brand Road.

10. What is indicated about Conrad Success Properties?
    (A) It is a family-owned business.
    (B) It is expanding to other cities in Saskatchewan.
    (C) It recently relocated to Saskatoon.
    (D) It was named the number one business in Saskatoon.

11. According to the postcard, what is offered at no charge?
    (A) A detailed map of the area
    (B) An initial consultation
    (C) An invitation to a lecture about operating a small business
    (D) A comparative study of the area's property market

Questions 12-15 refer to the following text-message chain.

Carlo Trujillo (8:19 A.M.)
Good morning. Are you on your way to the office? I just got a call from Sarah Wu at Eco Paints. She wants to meet at 10 A.M. to discuss Eco's fall marketing campaign.

Jane Williams (8:21 A.M.)
That's unexpected! We might have an outline to present to her, though. By the way, I'm already here at the office.

Jeffrey Barnes (8:22 A.M.)
I'm still on the train.

Carlo Trujillo (8:24 A.M.)
We do—I have a full presentation ready to go, actually. Anyway, I'd like to have fresh coffee and healthy snacks for the meeting with her. Jeffrey, could you pick up a fruit platter on the way in?

Jane Williams (8:27 A.M.)
The Morning Delights deli by Winchester Station usually has cut fruit.

Jeffrey Barnes (8:28 A.M.)
You're right, Jane. And my train will be in soon. I'll take care of it.

Carlo Trujillo (8:30 A.M.)
Great! We need to make a good impression on Ms. Wu.

Jeffrey Barnes (8:58 A.M.)
Success! I'll be at the office in ten minutes.

12. What is one reason Mr. Trujillo wrote to his team?

    (A) To ask them to prepare some slides
    (B) To find someone to run an errand
    (C) To request an update on a project
    (D) To apologize for being late for work

13. Who most likely is Ms. Wu?

    (A) A job applicant
    (B) A well-known artist
    (C) A Morning Delights sales associate
    (D) An Eco Paints employee

14. According to the text-message chain, what will likely happen at 10:00 A.M.?

    (A) Mr. Trujillo will pick up a fruit platter.
    (B) Mr. Trujillo will leave for the office.
    (C) A meeting with a client will begin.
    (D) A convenience store will open.

15. At 8:58 A.M., what does Mr. Barnes imply when he writes, "Success"?

    (A) He made a good impression on Ms. Wu.
    (B) He arrived at the office on time.
    (C) He bought some snacks.
    (D) He located a missing campaign outline.

Questions 16-19 refer to the following package insert.

Mumbai Foods Rasmalai—Traditional Indian Dessert

Servings: 12
Net Weight: 850 grams
Keep frozen
Use by 6/10

Delight your family with a unique combination of milk, cream, cottage cheese, sugar, and spices. Rasmalai is a sweet dish that is skillfully prepared and then decorated with sliced pistachios. It makes an elegant addition to any meal and is ideal for holidays and festivals.

Directions:
Remove from the box and place in a serving dish. Microwave on the defrost setting for five minutes. Let sit for ten minutes before serving.
Refrigerate after opening and consume within four days. Do not refreeze.

Ingredients: milk, cream, cottage cheese, sugar, lemon juice, cardamom, rose water, and pistachios

Produced in Aberdeen, Scotland

Distributed by Kolkata Industries, London, England

---

16. According to the package insert, how many dinner guests would one box be suitable for?

(A) Six
(B) Eight
(C) Ten
(D) Twelve

17. What is NOT suggested about the rasmalai from Mumbai Foods?

(A) It can be found in the frozen foods section at stores.
(B) It is an appropriate dish to serve at celebrations.
(C) It won a contest for the best new dessert.
(D) It contains milk products.

18. How soon is the product ready to serve after it is removed from the microwave?

(A) Immediately
(B) After five minutes
(C) After ten minutes
(D) The following day

19. Where is the product manufactured?

(A) In Aberdeen
(B) In Kolkata
(C) In London
(D) In Mumbai

UNIT 20 복수 지문

출제 포인트
1. 복수 지문은 서로 연관이 있는 두 개, 혹은 세 개의 지문과 다섯 문항으로 구성된다. 지문에 이메일이 포함되는 경우가 대다수이며, 반드시 1~2문항이 연계 문제로 출제된다.
2. 보기가 날짜, 시각, 금액 등 단답형으로 구성되어 있거나, 질문이 Not/True 혹은 추론 문제일 경우 연계 문제일 가능성이 높다.

◆ 지문 구성과 독해 전략

정답과 해설 p.213

Important Notice:

Carter's Farm-Fresh has announced that several cases of their canned vegetables (420g/14.5 oz. size) were shipped to area stores last week with incorrect labels. The mislabeled cans are stamped with product codes G7780 or G7781.

To receive a refund, return the product on or before September 12 to the store at which the purchase was made. **Per manufacturer policy, the original receipt must be submitted along with the returned product.**

지문 1 공지
1. 공지 주요 내용 파악
   라벨이 잘못 부착된 제품 반품 및 환불 안내
2. 반품 및 환불 정책 확인
   9월 12일까지 반품 신청
   제조사 카터스 팜 프레쉬의 규정: 반품 시 영수증 제출

Dear Mr. Delgado,

We have received the shipment of canned corn from your store. In two weeks you should receive a check by mail in the amount of $67.50. This should cover the money refunded to your customers when they returned the mislabeled cans. As we discussed, **this includes the $7.50 that you refunded a customer who did not have a receipt.**

We apologize for the inconvenience this has caused you and your patrons.

Sincerely,

Karen Woo
Customer Service Director, Carter's Farm-Fresh

지문 2 이메일
1. 이메일 주요 내용 파악
   제조사 카터스 팜 프레쉬의 직원인 우 씨가 델가도 씨의 가게에서 반품된 제품을 수령한 후 환불 안내
2. 특이 사항에 주목
   델가도 씨가 영수증이 없는 고객에게 환불한 금액까지 환불 수표에 포함

Q What is **suggested** about **Ms. Woo**?

(A) She expects to receive additional canned goods.
(B) She will send a check later than she originally promised.
(C) She made an exception to a policy.
(D) She will meet with Mr. Delgado.

연계 문제 | 지문 간 연결 고리 찾기
우 씨는 델가도 씨가 영수증이 없는 고객에게 환불한 금액까지 포함해 수표를 발행했는데, 이는 공지에 명시된 규정과 다르다.
정답 (C) 정책에 예외를 뒀다.

※ 주요 내용만 파악하면서 속독한 후, 질문의 키워드가 있는 지문과 다른 지문 사이의 연결 고리를 찾는다.

Advertisement + Review

Be There Appliance Repair
839 Saint-Denis Street, Montreal, Quebec, H9R 3J4
514-555-0148

Here are a few great reasons to call us for your appliance repair needs.

Number 1: Affordable prices. We guarantee the lowest prices in town.
Number 2: Friendly, uniformed technicians.
Number 3: We have been a family-owned, local business for three generations.
Number 4: Quick, quality service. We make every effort to provide same-day service.
Number 5: On-site repairs for large appliances and at-store drop-off for small appliances.
Number 6: We keep many items in our large warehouse so there's no waiting for parts.

---

https://www.repairservicesreviews.net

Repair Services Reviews: Be There Appliance Repair

I recently called five different repair services to fix a leaking refrigerator in my home. I left messages with all of them. Only one called me back within ten minutes. That was Be There Appliance Repair. Although I had never heard of the business, I wanted to have the problem attended to right away, so I decided to take the chance. Ms. Kowalczyk, the owner, immediately set the process in motion. A repair professional arrived that afternoon. He was able to diagnose the problem quickly, and he repaired the problem within an hour. I heartily recommend calling Be There Appliance Repair if you need a trusted, reliable service that will not keep you waiting!

—Ralph Duggan, 4 June

---

1. What reason listed in the advertisement was likely the most appealing to Mr. Duggan?

    (A) Number 3
    (B) Number 4

2. What can be concluded about Ms. Kowalczyk?

    (A) She is a third-generation owner of a family business.
    (B) She has lived in Montreal all her life.

ETS 실전문제

Questions 1-5 refer to the following brochure and e-mail.

Colombia Day Trip with Alroy Adventures

Are you searching for a fun and social way to see some of the most beautiful scenery in Colombia? Alroy Adventures offers weekly day trips to the charming small town of Jerico.

Each Saturday, one of our English-speaking local experts leads a busload of day trippers from bustling Medellin to the quaint cobblestone streets of Jerico. After arriving in Jerico, the group will hike to a coffee plantation and enjoy a delicious lunch. The group will then return to Jerico to explore the town's main sites. Details are listed below.

- Departure from terminal bus station in Medellin at 7 A.M.; return at 8 P.M.
- Total walking time: 3 hours; distance: 9 kilometers
- Sturdy hiking shoes, sunscreen, water, and snacks highly recommended
- Lunch included. Choose one of the following options:
  (1) pasta with chicken, (2) beef sandwich, (3) seafood stew, or (4) vegetarian tacos
- Cost (includes transportation): 100,000 Colombian pesos per person

Send an e-mail to Pedro Lara at plara@alroyadventures.com to reserve your spot. Note that the maximum is 20 participants per adventure.

E-mail

To:	Pedro Lara <plara@alroyadventures.com>
From:	Radha Gupta <rgupta@sunmail.com>
Date:	11 March
Subject:	Reservation inquiry

Dear Mr. Lara:

My husband and I would like to join your group hike this Saturday, 15 March. We have wanted to visit Jerico for a while now, and your outing also seems like a great way to meet people!

I have a question about transportation. We have a car and would prefer to drive separately. I know that buses drop passengers at the town's main square. We could meet you there at 10 a.m. After the hike, we would drive ourselves back to Medellin. We are willing to pay the full price. Can you accommodate this request? If so, we would both prefer the vegetarian option for lunch.

Many thanks,

Radha Gupta

1. What is Alroy Adventures?

   (A) A campground
   (B) A tour company
   (C) An amusement park
   (D) A sporting-goods store

2. What is NOT mentioned as part of the advertised event?

   (A) Checking in at a hotel
   (B) Eating a meal
   (C) Walking around a small town
   (D) Visiting a place where coffee is grown

3. Where would Ms. Gupta like to meet the group?

   (A) In Jerico
   (B) In Medellin
   (C) At an airport
   (D) At a plantation

4. In the brochure, the word "leads" in paragraph 2, line 1, is closest in meaning to

   (A) proceeds
   (B) influences
   (C) opens
   (D) guides

5. What do Ms. Gupta and her husband want for lunch on March 15?

   (A) Pasta
   (B) Sandwiches
   (C) Stew
   (D) Tacos

Questions 6-10 refer to the following job posting and memo.

Internship with Exersource LLC

Exersource is a fast-growing company that leads the fitness industry in the design of nutrition programs for both professional and amateur athletes. All programs are scientifically backed. We teach athletes how to use nutrition to improve performance, shorten recovery, and avoid or heal sports-related injuries. Our dedicated marketing team helps our coaches, nutritionists, and medical professionals reach athletes in various arenas, such as skiing, running, bicycling, swimming, and more.

We seek a student currently enrolled in an undergraduate degree program in marketing and interested in an internship in a fast-paced, professional environment. The successful applicant must possess excellent attention to detail, the ability to connect with others, and strong spoken and written communication skills. An ongoing commitment to one or more sports or wellness activities is a definite plus.

To apply, visit https://www.exersource.com/jobs/marketing_internship.

MEMO

To: Human Resources
From: Leanne Townsley
Cc: Evan Peng
Date: May 2
Subject: Update regarding intern position

Two days ago, Evan Peng and I completed interviews with fourteen applicants for the internship position. Yesterday, we compared notes on each candidate and concluded that Sylvia Torres was the best choice for the position. Ms. Torres attends Andon College and meets all the criteria for the internship. She is articulate, agreeable, and well-organized. Her professors submitted enthusiastic recommendations on her behalf. This, in particular, set her apart from the other candidates. Furthermore, Ms. Torres is a member of the school's track team.

Please prepare Ms. Torres' new-employee paperwork. Her orientation with you should be scheduled for the morning of May 9. Mr. Peng and I will be present with the rest of our team to welcome her.

6. In the job posting, the word "backed" in paragraph 1, line 3, is closest in meaning to
   (A) reversed
   (B) supported
   (C) experimented
   (D) delayed

7. What is one goal of Exersource?
   (A) To design exercise equipment
   (B) To help sports teams recruit athletes
   (C) To prepare healthy food to sell
   (D) To help prevent injuries to athletes

8. What is most likely true about Ms. Torres?
   (A) She is studying marketing.
   (B) She is a new manager.
   (C) She is a professional swimmer.
   (D) She is a coach for a bicycling team.

9. According to Ms. Townsley, what was the primary reason Ms. Torres was selected over other candidates?
   (A) She is very organized.
   (B) She attends a local university.
   (C) She was the most skilled candidate.
   (D) She received strong recommendations.

10. What is the Human Resources department expected to do?
    (A) Plan a new-employee orientation
    (B) Contact Andon College
    (C) Transfer Mr. Peng to a new team
    (D) Schedule a second interview

Questions 11-15 refer to the following Web page and review.

---

https://www.bavarianouterwear.com/about

| Home | **About** | Products | Contact Us |

Founder Marvin Prizi was working as a successful accountant when he changed his career path after discovering his true passion was in winter sports like snowboarding and skiing. While visiting a village in the Bavarian mountains, Mr. Prizi noticed a ski sweater that made him wish he could find a sweater with a traditional look but made with a contemporary, eco-friendly fabric. When Mr. Prizi shared his idea with fellow skier Adam Patterson, they decided to launch a sportswear company. The first garment they produced was a modern version of the ski sweater Mr. Prizi had spotted in Germany. It is, in fact, the only model of ski sweater the company has ever manufactured.

Bavarian Outerwear offers apparel for a variety of performance sports that include skiing, hiking, and mountain climbing. Lead designer Kristen Cook carefully researches traditional designs and modern fabrics. Ms. Cook also travels the globe to find inspiration for new products. The company founders have stayed involved in the day-to-day operation of the company for the past ten years, and Mr. Patterson continues to write the product descriptions for our print catalog and Web site.

Review: Bavarian Outerwear Ski Sweater

I have mixed feelings about the ski sweater that I purchased from Bavarian Outerwear one month ago. I appreciate how the sweater fits and keeps me warm as I ski. The stitching and detailed accents on the sweater make it attractive. What disappoints me is the quality of the material. The product description on the Web page led me to believe it would feel soft against the skin. In reality, the material is rather rough and coarse. After a long day of instructing my students, it becomes uncomfortable.

—Amy Schultz

11. What does the Web page mention about Ms. Cook?

(A) She has just been promoted.
(B) She prefers to use traditional fabrics.
(C) She regularly travels in her work.
(D) She has designed a Web site.

12. What does the Web page suggest about Bavarian Outerwear?

(A) Its headquarters are in Germany.
(B) Its products are sold only in physical stores.
(C) It was founded ten years ago.
(D) It is popular with professional athletes.

13. What is most likely true about the product that Ms. Schultz purchased?

(A) It is the same product Bavarian Outerwear has been manufacturing since it started.
(B) It will no longer be manufactured by Bavarian Outerwear.
(C) It is eligible for a discount.
(D) It can be easily damaged.

14. Based on the review, how might a product be improved?

(A) By lowering its price
(B) By offering it in other colors
(C) By making it available in larger sizes
(D) By producing it with a softer material

15. Who most likely is Ms. Schultz?

(A) A clothing importer
(B) A ski instructor
(C) A graphic designer
(D) A fashion magazine writer

Questions 16-20 refer to the following Web page, e-ticket, and e-mail.

https://book-a-train.co.uk/fares

Scheduled Times by Fare Type

Commuter fares apply during traditional commuting hours.
- Monday to Friday from 6:00 A.M. to 9:00 A.M.
- Monday to Friday from 4:00 P.M. to 7:00 P.M.

Off-peak fares apply just during nonpeak commuting hours.
- Monday to Friday from 9:00 A.M. to 11:00 A.M.
- Monday to Friday from 2:00 P.M. to 4:00 P.M.
- Monday to Friday from 7:00 P.M. to 9:00 P.M.

Super off-peak fares apply during the least busy hours of the weekdays.
- Monday to Friday from 11:00 A.M. to 2:00 P.M.
- Monday to Friday from 9:00 P.M. to 6:00 A.M.

Standard fares apply all day on Saturdays, Sundays, and holidays.

Book-a-train.co.uk E-ticket   **Price:** £24.30

Number of passengers: One

Ticket type: Super off-peak—Southbay Line

Date: 17 November   **Valid Until:** 2:00 P.M. on 17 November

Route:

From
NORWALD CENTRAL STATION

To   Via
SCHENCKSVILLE   CLARKSVILLE

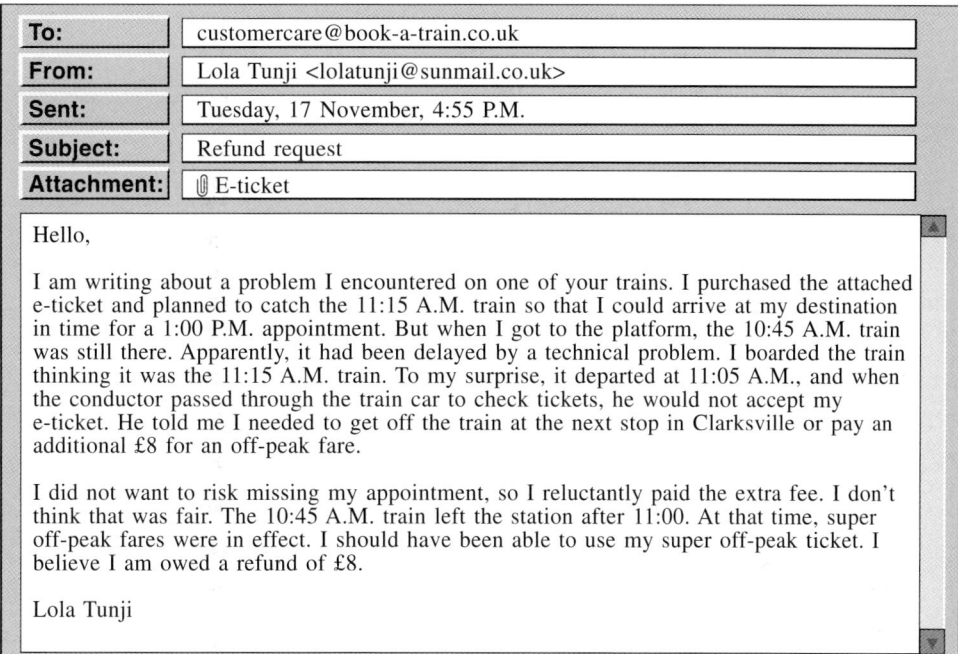

To:	customercare@book-a-train.co.uk
From:	Lola Tunji <lolatunji@sunmail.co.uk>
Sent:	Tuesday, 17 November, 4:55 P.M.
Subject:	Refund request
Attachment:	E-ticket

Hello,

I am writing about a problem I encountered on one of your trains. I purchased the attached e-ticket and planned to catch the 11:15 A.M. train so that I could arrive at my destination in time for a 1:00 P.M. appointment. But when I got to the platform, the 10:45 A.M. train was still there. Apparently, it had been delayed by a technical problem. I boarded the train thinking it was the 11:15 A.M. train. To my surprise, it departed at 11:05 A.M., and when the conductor passed through the train car to check tickets, he would not accept my e-ticket. He told me I needed to get off the train at the next stop in Clarksville or pay an additional £8 for an off-peak fare.

I did not want to risk missing my appointment, so I reluctantly paid the extra fee. I don't think that was fair. The 10:45 A.M. train left the station after 11:00. At that time, super off-peak fares were in effect. I should have been able to use my super off-peak ticket. I believe I am owed a refund of £8.

Lola Tunji

16. According to the Web page, what fare applies for travel on Monday at 2:30 P.M.?
(A) Commuter
(B) Off-peak
(C) Super off-peak
(D) Standard

17. At what time did Ms. Tunji's e-ticket become valid?
(A) 10:00 A.M.
(B) 10:45 A.M.
(C) 11:00 A.M.
(D) 11:05 A.M.

18. According to the e-ticket, what was Ms. Tunji's destination?
(A) Southbay
(B) Norwald
(C) Clarksville
(D) Schencksville

19. When did Ms. Tunji send the e-mail?
(A) Before boarding the train
(B) While aboard the train
(C) Later on the day of her train trip
(D) Several days after her train trip

20. What problem does Ms. Tunji mention?
(A) She purchased the wrong type of ticket.
(B) She took a train trip that was longer than she had expected.
(C) She was late for an appointment.
(D) She mistakenly boarded the wrong train.

Questions 21-25 refer to the following Web page and e-mails.

https://www.leaseallproperties.com/properties/29182

| Home | About | **Properties** | Property Agents |

Property 29182

Just steps away from Surfside Beach, this house is the perfect place for a getaway. The four-bedroom, three-bathroom vacation rental includes a full kitchen, a living room, a sun porch, and a beautiful view of the blue waves. A minimum stay of five nights is required. Guests who stay seven or more nights receive a free night.

Amenities:

- Kitchen: includes oven and stove, silverware, dishes, and cooking supplies

- Bathrooms: include towels and various toiletries

- Laundry: no laundry facilities available

- Parking: free on-site parking; no garage available

- Coupons to local events

To:	<info@leaseallproperties.com>
From:	Natalia Kowalski <kowalskinatalia9@quamail.com>
Date:	Friday, June 9
Subject:	Property 29182

Hello,

I have a reservation to stay in your Surfside Beach rental home beginning in one week.

The amenities list indicates that there will not be a washer and dryer to use, but the photos on the Web site show a washer and dryer. Can you clarify?

My sister and her family will fly into town one day before I arrive. Will there be any problem with them entering the house before my arrival? They were already included in the number of guests I provided when I made the reservation.

I originally booked the house for five nights, but now I would like to take advantage of the offer listed on your Web page. Can we extend our stay to a full week?

Regards,

Natalia Kowalski

```
                              E-Mail Message
To:           Natalia Kowalski <kowalskinatalia9@quamail.com>
From:         <info@leaseallproperties.com>
Date:         Friday, June 9
Subject:      RE: Property 29182
Attachment:   📎 Discount Code
```

Hello Ms. Kowalski,

Thank you for your e-mail. I'm happy to answer your questions.

Unfortunately, the items you mention need to be repaired, so they will be unavailable for use. We were unable to remove the pictures from the Web site. I apologize for any confusion.

You should have already received an introduction e-mail with instructions for entering the house using a door code. It reminds you to call your property agent for the electronic door code the day you arrive. (The code is changed after each reservation.) You can go ahead and forward that e-mail to your sister.

Regrettably, the house is scheduled for renovations immediately after your visit, so we are unable to extend your stay at this time. To show our appreciation for your business, I have attached a discount code for a free night on any weeklong stay you book through us in the future.

Please contact me if you have any further questions.

Best,

Allan Rose
Lease All Properties

---

21. According to the Web page, what is true about the rental property?

    (A) It is next to a restaurant.
    (B) It is near the ocean.
    (C) It can accommodate up to two people.
    (D) It has a parking garage.

22. Why does Ms. Kowalski request to extend her stay at the rental home?

    (A) To take advantage of some event tickets
    (B) To accommodate a visit from her sister
    (C) To get coupons to local events
    (D) To receive a free stay for an extra night

23. According to Mr. Rose, what needs repair?

    (A) The sun porch
    (B) The garage doors
    (C) The washer and dryer
    (D) The oven and stove

24. What is Ms. Kowalski instructed to do?

    (A) Forward an e-mail to her sister
    (B) E-mail the property agent
    (C) Create a door code
    (D) Change her reservation

25. What does Mr. Rose tell Ms. Kowalski about the rental property?

    (A) It was rented to her at a discounted rate.
    (B) It is scheduled to undergo renovations.
    (C) It received a good review from previous guests.
    (D) It is being photographed for the company Web site.

Questions 26-30 refer to the following e-mails and order form.

To:	Tyrone Mackey
From:	Regina Frank
Date:	October 30
Subject:	Order request

Dear Mr. Mackey,

I have been reassigned to the new offices on the third floor of the converted warehouse, and there are very few power outlets in that space. I am unable to plug in my laptop and monitors and charge my phone at the same time. Is there an approved multi-outlet power option that can sit on the top of my desk for easy access? A device with USB ports would be ideal.

Additionally, the cord on the receptionist's desk lamp will not reach any of the outlets in his office. This is a critical issue because of the lack of natural light in the third-floor space—he will need at least one extension cord and possibly two or more of different lengths. Finally, my metalworking team needs three high-amperage power strips to connect their indoor fixed machine tools, and the power-washing team needs one strip suitable for use at their outdoor cleaning station.

Thank you,

Regina Frank, Production Team Management

To:	Regina Frank
From:	Tyrone Mackey
Date:	November 2
Subject:	Re: Order request
Attachment:	📎 Elektro-sell Order Form

Dear Ms. Frank,

I received your e-mail about not having enough power supply outlets for you and your team. Recently, the purchasing department has selected the vendor Elektro-sell for such supplies. Based on the information you provided, I believe their products will serve your needs. Please download their catalog from the purchasing department's page on our company intranet site and choose from the products you find there. Section 1 has all-purpose extension cords. Section 2 lists surge protectors. Section 3 is for industrial power strips. And Section 4 is for desktop power centers.

I've attached an editable order form to this e-mail that you can fill out and return to me with your selections. On the form, make sure to include the product number, product description, price per unit, and number of units of each product ordered. If you send me your completed form by 3:00 P.M. on Wednesday, November 4, your order will go out by the end of the week, and you can expect your shipment of products to arrive by midweek next week.

Please let me know if you have any questions.

Tyrone Mackey, Purchasing Manager

Elektro-sell

Industrial Power Supplies Order Form

Product Number	Product Description	Cost per Unit	Number of Units
APC-114	White single-outlet extension cord, 8-foot cord length	$12	2
APC-116	Black double-outlet extension cord, 12-foot cord length	$15	2
IPS-202	Yellow 4-outlet power strip, high amperage and surge protected, interior use only, 10-foot cord length	$32	3
IPS-198	Black 4-outlet power strip, high amperage and surge protected, waterproof and outdoor rated, 10-foot cord length	$35	1
DPC-45	Gray 3-outlet desktop power center with two USB ports, 12-foot cord length	$41	1

26. What does Ms. Frank suggest in the first e-mail?
    (A) She used to have an office on the second floor.
    (B) She rarely visits the workshop.
    (C) She supervises a manufacturing staff.
    (D) She needs to have her laptop repaired.

27. What is the purpose of the second e-mail?
    (A) To provide information to help in selecting power outlets
    (B) To explain the process for billing a purchase
    (C) To describe a corporate safety policy
    (D) To promote a sale on office equipment

28. What does Mr. Mackey suggest that Ms. Frank do?
    (A) Choose a new electrical supplies vendor
    (B) Make an order within the next two days
    (C) Update the company's intranet site
    (D) Hire additional office employees

29. What section of the Elektro-sell catalog includes products Ms. Frank needs for her office?
    (A) Section 1
    (B) Section 2
    (C) Section 3
    (D) Section 4

30. For whom most likely does Ms. Frank order product IPS-198?
    (A) For herself
    (B) For the receptionist
    (C) For the indoor metalworkers
    (D) For the power washers

ETS ACTUAL TEST

Questions 147-148 refer to the following receipt.

Stanntar Brothers
The region's leading art and hobby supply store

Store number: 7
Customer: Julia Reston

Store location: 6 Main Street, Dover, Ohio
Date/time of sale: July 7, 10:27 A.M.

Quantity: 1   **Description:** Stanntar wooden paintbrush set   **Price:** $40.00

−30% clearance sale

Customer savings: $12.00

Total: $28.00

Cash paid: $28.00

Thank you for shopping at our Dover store. Shop at www.stanntarbrothers.com or any of our ten store locations for all your art and hobby needs. July is paper craft month. Come to a free workshop at any of our stores. Each month features a new type of workshop. Visit our Web site for more information.

---

147. What is indicated about Ms. Reston?

(A) She is a famous artist.
(B) She bought art supplies for a friend.
(C) She paid with a credit card.
(D) She made a purchase at a Dover store.

148. What will likely happen in August?

(A) Ms. Reston will learn about paper crafts.
(B) There will be a new workshop theme.
(C) A clearance sale will end.
(D) Stanntar Brothers will open a new store.

Questions 149-150 refer to the following Web page.

---

https://www.yourprivateguide.co.uk

| Home | Tours | Contact us | Booking |

Millford City Layover Tour

Are you tired of sitting in the airport, waiting for a connecting flight during a long layover?

Your Private Guide can give you and your group a personalized tour of Millford City. Our tours start and end at the airport and last three to eight hours. They are perfect for those who want to enjoy the sights but have limited time. Your itinerary will be designed for you and your party based on your interests and available time. For your tour, choose from popular sites like Iverson Park, the Danforth Museum of Art, Westside Harbour, the historic Emory Jones House, and more. Note that all tours are private; no one else will join your group.

Visit the Booking page for availability and rates.

---

149. What is indicated about the tour?

(A) It has recently grown in popularity.
(B) It begins at the airport.
(C) It is less expensive than similar tours.
(D) It includes a prepared lunch.

150. What is indicated about the Danforth Museum of Art?

(A) It is housed in a historic building.
(B) It is the most visited tourist site in Millford City.
(C) It can be selected as part of a tour.
(D) It takes three hours to visit all parts of the museum.

Questions 151-152 refer to the following text-message chain.

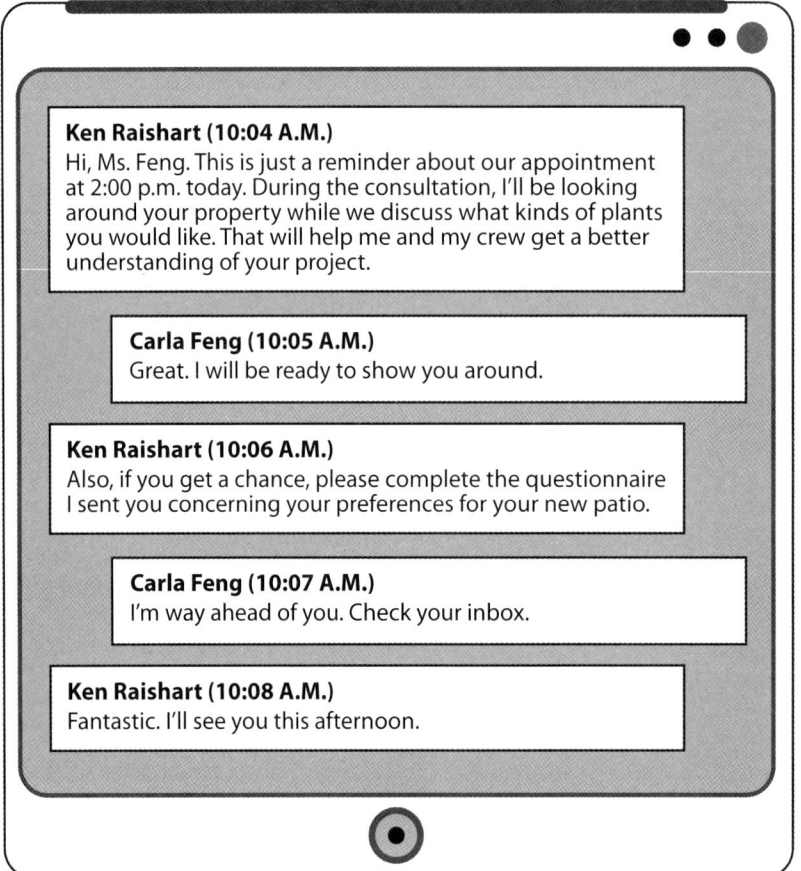

Ken Raishart (10:04 A.M.)
Hi, Ms. Feng. This is just a reminder about our appointment at 2:00 p.m. today. During the consultation, I'll be looking around your property while we discuss what kinds of plants you would like. That will help me and my crew get a better understanding of your project.

Carla Feng (10:05 A.M.)
Great. I will be ready to show you around.

Ken Raishart (10:06 A.M.)
Also, if you get a chance, please complete the questionnaire I sent you concerning your preferences for your new patio.

Carla Feng (10:07 A.M.)
I'm way ahead of you. Check your inbox.

Ken Raishart (10:08 A.M.)
Fantastic. I'll see you this afternoon.

151. Who most likely is Mr. Raishart?

(A) A factory manager
(B) A real estate agent
(C) A professional landscaper
(D) A market research analyst

152. At 10:07 A.M., what does Ms. Feng most likely mean when she writes, "I'm way ahead of you"?

(A) She has already provided some information.
(B) She removed some plants from the patio.
(C) She has already paid Mr. Raishart for the consultation.
(D) She arrived at the site before Mr. Raishart did.

Questions 153-154 refer to the following coupon.

Parri's Plumbing
Water woes? Let us help!

End-of-Year Special: Save $100 on Residential Water-Heater Installation!
- Offer good only on work completed from November 15 through December 31
- Cannot be combined with other special offers
- Installation fee includes removal and disposal of old unit
- Water heaters sold separately
- Valid in Lumberton only

Call 203-555-0129 between November 1 and December 15 to schedule your installation, as it may take up to two weeks before installation work can begin.

153. What is indicated about the coupon?
(A) It cannot be used with other discount offers.
(B) It can be used by all commercial customers.
(C) It is valid in several towns.
(D) It does not cover the cost of disposal of old water heaters.

154. When is the last date that a customer can call to schedule an installation?
(A) November 1
(B) November 15
(C) December 15
(D) December 31

Questions 155-157 refer to the following article.

Energy from Tides to Power Cars

SEASIDE (May 1)—Energy provider Coast Power plans to install automobile charging stations that will use tidal energy as their only power source.

Coast Power recently completed the construction of a group of floating turbines off the coast of Seaside that will convert the energy of the waves into electricity. The turbines were installed primarily to meet the region's rising electrical needs as more drivers switch to electric vehicles.

The first tidal charging stations will be placed in parking lots near Seaside's beaches by the end of the month. By December, the company plans to install additional tidal charging stations throughout Seaside and the surrounding towns. In many locations, these new stations will be built next to existing fuel-powered charging stations, which may be converted to wave power later.

155. According to the article, what led to the decision to build floating turbines?

    (A) The lack of space on land to build turbines
    (B) A need for more jobs in the region
    (C) An increase in the number of cars powered by electricity
    (D) The rapidly growing population along the coast

156. The word "placed" in paragraph 3, line 2, is closest in meaning to

    (A) put
    (B) seen
    (C) ordered
    (D) entered

157. What does Coast Power plan to do by December?

    (A) Install solar panels in parking lots
    (B) Remove all fuel-powered charging stations
    (C) Construct tidal charging stations in towns near Seaside
    (D) Convert charging stations from fuel power to tidal power

Questions 158-160 refer to the following notice.

Kernby Valley Growers Expo

For a fifth year, the Kernby Valley Growers Expo will return to Lewis Conference Center from October 12 to 14. Hundreds of organic-farming enthusiasts of all experience levels are expected to attend the event. Newcomers to the field will appreciate that many sessions will be intentionally geared toward informing and assisting those who are just starting out.

The cost of registration will be $95 for the entire three-day event. Registration will remain open until Friday, October 5. Alternatively, people can arrive at the venue on any day of the expo and pay $45 for a single day's admission. For university students with valid identification, the fees will be $50 for the entire event or $20 for one day.

There will be a very special final session on Sunday afternoon when a panel of top experts will be on hand to respond to live questions from attendees. Snacks will also be provided in the form of a wide variety of locally grown organic fruits and vegetables for attendees to sample.

158. For what group of people will many sessions at the expo be most helpful?

(A) Cooks and food preparation workers
(B) Farmers with limited experience
(C) Manufacturers that develop new farming equipment
(D) Managers of food distribution companies

159. According to the notice, what is true about the expo?

(A) It will be held in a larger venue this year.
(B) It will be run primarily by volunteers.
(C) Students will be able to attend it at a discounted price.
(D) Experts will be available to give individual consultations for a fee.

160. What is indicated about the expo's last event?

(A) It will give attendees a chance to taste different foods.
(B) It will be held in the largest available room.
(C) It will include an awards ceremony.
(D) It will cost an additional $20 to attend.

Questions 161-163 refer to the following Web page.

https://www.homelivingweekly.com

Get Set Up Smoothly

— [1] —. Until recently, when a person moved to a new home, the only way to obtain utility services was to contact each utility company individually. Fortunately, it is now possible for new residents to establish electricity, Internet, gas, and other home services by making just one call to Utili-Connect Solutions. The oldest company in the field of residential services assistance, Utili-Connect has as its motto, "Moving made easier." — [2] —. The company currently covers a larger geographic area than any of its rivals and is most popular in the South and Southwest regions.

A phone conversation with Utili-Connect Solutions typically lasts more than an hour since the representative describes various utility providers to choose from and compares their monthly fees. — [3] —. Also, there is no charge for using the company, and representatives will not order any service without the caller's approval. — [4] —.

Because new residents often find it difficult to schedule dates and times for crews to install needed equipment in a home, Utili-Connect Solutions uses automated planning software to make this process run more smoothly. Centralizing all appointments via this application also makes it easier to track them. As company founder Joe Signorini says, "Our aim at Utili-Connect is above all to save new residents time and effort."

161. What does the Web page indicate about Utili-Connect Solutions?

(A) It is planning to hire new staff.
(B) It serves a larger area than its competitors.
(C) It recently changed ownership.
(D) It is operated by an international shipping company.

162. According to the Web page, what is a problem that new residents often face?

(A) Poorly communicated details about service plans
(B) Unexpected increases in utility fees
(C) Difficulty scheduling installation visits
(D) Long wait times to talk to customer service representatives

163. In which of the positions marked [1], [2], [3], and [4] does the following sentence best belong?

"Establishing utility services for a new residence can sometimes seem overwhelming."

(A) [1]
(B) [2]
(C) [3]
(D) [4]

Questions 164-167 refer to the following article.

Brad Bikes Going Strong

LEXFORD (24 April)—Bicycle riders in the city received good news last week. The city council approved plans to award Brad Bikes, a local bicycle-share operator, a new contract to install an additional twelve docking stations, with 120 bicycles total, around the city.

The programme began three years ago with eight bicycle docking stations. The programme allows residents and tourists to rent a bicycle for an hour or an entire day from various stations. Riders unlock and return the bicycles using an app on their phones.

Brad Bikes offers monthly and annual membership plans for people who use the bicycles daily. It also offers pay-per-ride options for those who are only occasional riders.

"We are just not a large city," said Anita Henderson, the city council chair. "While there were reports of programmes like this gaining popularity in larger cities, we were uncertain it would work here."

In fact, the initial trial programme worked very well. From the outset, residents used the rental bicycles to reach areas of the city that are not well connected to public transportation. From its first to its third year of operation, memberships grew by 250 percent, and one-time rentals have nearly tripled.

The twelve additional docking stations will be distributed throughout the city, bringing bicycle sharing to areas that have not previously been serviced. Increasing the Brad Bikes network will provide access to most neighbourhoods in Lexford.

164. What is the main topic of the article?

(A) Efforts to improve bicycle safety
(B) A new road construction project
(C) The expansion of a popular program
(D) Investments in the city's tourist attractions

165. According to the article, what is needed in order to rent from Brad Bikes?

(A) A credit card
(B) A mobile phone
(C) An activation code
(D) Photo identification

166. Why was Ms. Henderson unsure that Brad Bikes' plan would be successful in Lexford?

(A) Because few tourists visit the city
(B) Because the city is relatively small
(C) Because only a few bicycle docking stations were available
(D) Because many residents prefer to drive their own cars

167. What is suggested in the article about Brad Bikes?

(A) It currently maintains twelve bicycle docking stations in Lexford.
(B) It was founded by Ms. Henderson.
(C) It plans to add services in other cities.
(D) It serves areas that public transportation does not.

Questions 168-171 refer to the following excerpt from a report.

Barriers to Widespread Electric Vehicle Use

Office of Transportation, Special Committee on Energy Efficiency

Abstract

Plug-in electric vehicles (PEVs) offer many benefits, from improved air quality to reduced reliance on fossil fuels. — [1] —. In the United States, PEVs are currently less popular than they are in several countries overseas. Factors that have been shown to discourage some consumers from purchasing PEVs include their high purchase price, their limited driving range, and the scarcity of facilities for charging their batteries. — [2] —.

The Special Committee on Energy Efficiency was tasked with identifying ways to encourage more sales of PEVs. Studies in several states indicate that financial incentives such as rebate offers are an effective way to do this for certain types of PEVs. — [3] —. This report will treat each type in a separate section, as the barriers to vehicle use vary. — [4] —.

168. Who most likely is the author of the report?

(A) A vehicle manufacturing company
(B) A battery manufacturer
(C) An energy-production company
(D) A government agency

169. What is indicated about sales of PEVs in the United States?

(A) They are increasing at a steady rate.
(B) They are generally lower than they are in some other countries.
(C) They have been unaffected by rebate offers.
(D) They now exceed average sales of fossil fuel–powered vehicles.

170. What is NOT mentioned as a factor that discourages consumers from purchasing PEVs?

(A) Their high cost
(B) Their limited driving range
(C) The lack of charging facilities
(D) The frequency of battery malfunctions

171. In which of the positions marked [1], [2], [3], and [4] does the following sentence best belong?

"In fact, there are four types of PEVs currently available."

(A) [1]
(B) [2]
(C) [3]
(D) [4]

Questions 172-175 refer to the following online chat discussion.

Robin Doele (11:00 A.M.) Josie Peters from Sotifo Investments just texted to ask whether we could push today's meeting to 3:00. Does that work for you two?

Andre Oliena (11:02 A.M.) No problem for me. We need to book the Miller Room. Did you check whether it was free then? If not, I can.

Robin Doele (11:03 A.M.) No, I forgot. If you could check, that would be helpful.

Sumata Singh (11:03 A.M.) I have another client meeting starting at 3:30. I could be at the Sotifo meeting for the first half hour. So I should probably do my presentation first, don't you think?

Andre Oliena (11:04 A.M.) Yes, I'll check right now.

Robin Doele (11:05 A.M.) Makes sense. You said you'll need about ten minutes?

Sumata Singh (11:06 A.M.) Yes. Plus, time for questions.

Andre Oliena (11:10 A.M.) The Miller Room is occupied then, but the Benton Room is free. Should I book it?

Robin Doele (11:11 A.M.) Benton will be fine, thanks. I'll let Ms. Peters know.

Andre Oliena (11:12 A.M.) OK. I'll see you there at 3:00.

172. Why does Ms. Doele contact her colleagues initially?

(A) To confirm that a goal has been met
(B) To ask them to summarize a meeting
(C) To confirm the location of a meeting
(D) To ask about their availability to meet

173. Who most likely is Ms. Peters?

(A) Ms. Doele's client
(B) Ms. Doele's friend
(C) Ms. Doele's assistant
(D) Ms. Doele's supervisor

174. At 11:05 A.M., what does Ms. Doele most likely mean when she writes, "Makes sense"?

(A) Ms. Singh's presentation should be shortened.
(B) The Miller Room is appropriate for the meeting.
(C) The meeting room must be equipped with a projector.
(D) Ms. Singh should be the first presenter at the meeting.

175. What will Mr. Oliena most likely do next?

(A) Call Ms. Peters
(B) Reserve the Benton Room
(C) Attend the Sotifo Investments meeting
(D) Find out whether the Miller Room is available

Questions 176-180 refer to the following memo and e-mail.

MEMO

To:	Lylei Restaurant employees
From:	Christopher Delgado
Date:	December 10
Subject:	Extra shifts

The holiday season is coming up, and it is our busiest time of year, so the other managers and I are looking for bussers and servers to work extra hours on December 24 and 26. Let me know whether you can work any of the following shifts.

- Shift 1 (Servers): Saturday, December 24, 10:00 A.M. to 5:00 P.M.
- Shift 2 (Bussers): Saturday, December 24, 11:00 A.M. to 5:00 P.M.
- Shift 3 (Servers): Saturday, December 24, 4:00 P.M. to 11:00 P.M.
- Shift 4 (Bussers): Saturday, December 24, 5:00 P.M. to 10:00 P.M.
- Shift 5 (Servers): Monday, December 26, 4:00 P.M. to 10:00 P.M.

To:	Christopher Delgado
From:	Annalee Browne
Date:	December 11
Subject:	RE: Extra shifts

Christopher,

I am available to work as a busser for the earlier shift on December 24. Since you maintain the weekly schedule, you know I usually do not work on Saturdays, but since Lylei Restaurant will be closed on December 25, I am happy to take on some extra work.

Also, the short-sleeved busser shirt you issued me when I started the job ten months ago is showing signs of wear and tear. Do you have a new uniform shirt for me? I can pick it up during my next shift.

Thank you,

Annalee Browne

176. Why are Lylei Restaurant managers asking employees if they can work additional shifts?
    (A) They need help training new servers.
    (B) It is the restaurant's busy season.
    (C) The restaurant is adding more dining space.
    (D) Some staff members will be on vacation at that time.

177. What does the memo indicate about the servers?
    (A) They will attend a meeting on December 10.
    (B) They will be required to work longer hours every week.
    (C) They will start their shifts one hour earlier than bussers during the holiday hours.
    (D) They earn more per hour during the holiday season.

178. What is indicated about Mr. Delgado?
    (A) He begins his workday at 10:00 A.M.
    (B) He will be working on December 25.
    (C) He is one of several managers at Lylei Restaurant.
    (D) He started his job ten months ago.

179. What extra shift is Ms. Browne available to work?
    (A) Shift 1
    (B) Shift 2
    (C) Shift 3
    (D) Shift 4

180. What is indicated about Ms. Browne?
    (A) She often works on Saturdays.
    (B) She did not read Mr. Delgado's memo.
    (C) She is not sure who makes Lylei Restaurant's work schedule.
    (D) She wants to replace a workplace clothing item.

Questions 181-185 refer to the following e-mail and online form.

To:	Laura Tran <ltran@shorelinehealthcenter.org>
From:	Richard Bonney <rbonney@aventinas.org>
Date:	June 2
Subject:	Reference request

Good afternoon, Ms. Tran.

We recently interviewed Mr. Charles Sanna, and he is under consideration for the position of assistant health education coordinator at Aventinas Health Clinic. He has listed you as his direct supervisor in the Family Fitness Program and as a professional reference. Kindly take a few moments to fill out the questionnaire at www.aventinas.org/hrreference/390B. Your input is greatly appreciated.

Best,

Richard Bonney
Human Resources Director, Aventinas Health Clinic

The following candidate has listed you as a reference: Charles Sanna
Job Listing: Assistant Health Education Coordinator, Aventinas Health Clinic

Please tell us about your experience working with this applicant.

1. In what capacity has the applicant worked for you? For how long?

Mr. Sanna has been working for me at the Shoreline Health Center since January. He currently works twenty-five hours a week as an intern under my direction, counseling clients who were referred by their medical practitioners for lifestyle adjustments.

2. What would you consider the applicant's greatest strengths?

He connects well with clients from every demographic and age group. He is positive and encouraging in his manner and consistently receives high ratings on patient feedback surveys.

3. Were there any issues with this applicant that were of concern to you?

He is not consistently responsive to e-mail messages; however, he answers text messages right away.

4. Would you hire this applicant again if the opportunity arose?

Without question. Unfortunately, there are no open full-time positions at our center. Otherwise, we would hire him. He has broad knowledge in the field of community health, even though he has not yet had much professional experience. I firmly believe he will excel at any task you give him.

181. What is the purpose of the e-mail?

(A) To propose revisions to a questionnaire
(B) To describe the responsibilities of a job
(C) To promote a job opportunity
(D) To request feedback on an employee

182. In the e-mail, the word "listed" in paragraph 1, line 2, is closest in meaning to

(A) identified
(B) inclined
(C) planned
(D) recited

183. What is Mr. Sanna's role in the Family Fitness Program?

(A) He trains new health-care practitioners.
(B) He manages a health center's technology.
(C) He schedules appointments.
(D) He educates clients on health-related issues.

184. What is suggested about Ms. Tran?

(A) She has recently completed an internship.
(B) She works for Shoreline Health Center.
(C) She works in the human resources field.
(D) She has arranged a job interview for Mr. Sanna.

185. What does the online form indicate as one of Mr. Sanna's strengths?

(A) Responding in a timely fashion to e-mails
(B) Interacting positively with clients
(C) Submitting paperwork on time
(D) Taking on additional tasks as needed

Questions 186-190 refer to the following postcard, cost estimate, and Web page.

Light World Windows
81 Fairview Way
Erie, PA 16506

Save Money with Light World Windows

Replacing drafty windows can lower your energy bills, reduce insect problems, and improve your enjoyment of your home. At Light World Windows, our sales staff and certified technicians treat you like family. We're with you every step of the way as we design and install your project. Contact us today for a free cost estimate. Present this postcard to one of our local representatives to receive 20% off your window purchase and installation through the month of November!

Melina Haraway

198 Revels Drive

Erie, PA 16506

COST ESTIMATE
Date: November 10

Owner
Melina Haraway
814-555-0128
melharaway@mailcrate.com

Sales Representative
Jon Lankford
814-555-0155
lankford@lwwindows.com

Light World Windows will provide labor, equipment, materials, and demolition/cleanup service for work on the home located at 198 Revels Drive, Erie, PA 16506. All windows come with a 25-year warranty. Prices are good for 30 days after the date of this estimate.

No.	Window options	Price per item	Totals
6	Series 1500 double-hung windows (price reflects our Price Match Guarantee)	$380	$2,280
2	Slider windows	$350	$700
1	Picture window	$450	$450
	Setup and disposal fee		$175
		Project subtotal	$3,605
		20% discount	- $721
		Total	**$2,884**

If these terms are acceptable to you, please sign below and send this document back to your sales representative. A technician will call you to add you to our installation schedule.

Customer Signature: _____ **Date:** _____

https://www.lwwindows.com/guarantee

Our Price Match Guarantee

At Light World Windows, we are confident that we can deliver the best product at the best price. That's why we offer our special Price Match Guarantee. If you show us a cost estimate from another window company that beats our price, we will match it, provided the project meets the same specifications.

When you shop at Light World Windows, you will always pay the lowest price for windows. Contact your sales representative for more details about this offer.

186. According to the postcard, why should a homeowner consider replacing windows?

   (A) To reduce energy bills
   (B) To create a modern look
   (C) To increase the value of a home
   (D) To allow more light to enter a home

187. What is indicated on the postcard about Light World Windows?

   (A) It can inspect for insect damage.
   (B) It provides estimates at no cost.
   (C) It is a family-owned business.
   (D) It will be closed in November.

188. How did Ms. Haraway receive a 20 percent discount on her cost estimate?

   (A) By asking for a discount as a repeat customer
   (B) By referring a family member as a potential customer
   (C) By giving a postcard to Mr. Lankford
   (D) By downloading a coupon from a Web page

189. What is explained on the Web page?

   (A) How competitive pricing benefits customers
   (B) How to contact a sales representative
   (C) How often windows should be replaced
   (D) How customers can make their windows last longer

190. What can be concluded about Ms. Haraway?

   (A) She owns a small business.
   (B) She is building a new home.
   (C) She revised her order for new windows several times.
   (D) She asked for estimates from more than one company.

Questions 191-195 refer to the following order form and e-mails.

Astor Catering Order Form

Event Date: June 10   **Guests:** 30
Time: 6:30 P.M. to 8:30 P.M.   **Location:** Sunnyview Community Center
Purpose: Trifold Publishers' Annual Employee Appreciation Dinner

Buffet Menu
- **Appetizers:** Barbecue wings, tangy meatballs, and fried zucchini
- **Salad:** Mixed salad with choice of Italian vinaigrette or yogurt herb dressing
- **Choice of Main Course**
  Main Course 1: Garlic chicken with fresh vegetables and brown rice
  Main Course 2: Vegetarian pasta primavera with fresh basil
- **Dessert:** Chocolate chiffon pie
- **Beverages:** Water, sodas, coffee, and assorted teas

Contact: Eun-Mi Pae at Trifold Publishers, Eun-Mi.Pae@trifoldpublishers.com

Note: Simple but tasteful table decorations are available, as are a choice of tablecloths: white linen for long, rectangular tables or light-blue linen tablecloths for circular tables.

To:	Eun-Mi.Pae@trifoldpublishers.com
From:	jim@astorcatering.com
Date:	June 5
Subject:	Attendees and questions

Hi, Eun-Mi,

I just received your voicemail message about the correct number of attendees. We have adjusted the number from 30 to 60 to account for your team members' guests. The cost of the additional meals will be added to the final bill.

The community center has either long, rectangular tables or circular tables. For a group this size, I recommend the circular tables, as they provide a better opportunity for conversation during the meal. Let me know so I can arrange to bring the correct tablecloths. You'll need to inform the community center of your choice.

Also, raspberries are now in season, and we just received a batch from our local fruit supplier. Would you be interested in ice-cream cake with fresh raspberry topping in place of your current dessert selection? The cost will be the same.

Best,

Jim Astor

E-Mail Message

To: jim@astorcatering.com
From: Eun-Mi.Pae@trifoldpublishers.com
Date: June 5
Subject: RE: Attendees and questions

Hi, Jim,

Thank you very much for adjusting the number of diners. I apologize for overlooking the correct total when I placed the order. The additional expense will not be a problem. We have a large budget for this event since it is so important to the company.

Following your suggestion, I will inform the community center this afternoon that we intend to use the circular tables.

Your dessert suggestion sounds refreshing, especially with the recent warm weather we've been having. Let's go with that selection. Thank you for being so flexible.

Yours,

Eun-Mi Pae

---

191. Why is Trifold Publishers planning a dinner event?

(A) To celebrate a retirement
(B) To welcome new employees
(C) To celebrate a recent business success
(D) To thank employees

192. What is NOT included in the buffet menu listed on the order form?

(A) Appetizers
(B) Mixed salad
(C) Bread and butter
(D) A vegetarian meal option

193. According to the first e-mail, why was the number of expected guests adjusted?

(A) Some employees are unable to attend.
(B) The company recently hired additional staff.
(C) The company decided to invite some of its important clients.
(D) Guests of employees had not been counted.

194. What is suggested about the tablecloths Astor Catering will provide for the event?

(A) They are rectangular.
(B) They are light-blue linen.
(C) They will be delivered the day before the event.
(D) They must be cleaned before they are returned.

195. What is indicated about the dessert for the event?

(A) It is a popular choice among clients.
(B) It will feature seasonal fruit.
(C) It will be served warm.
(D) It costs more than other dessert choices.

Questions 196-200 refer to the following schedule, truck panel, and e-mail.

Royland Trucking
March 21 Schedule

Depart	Driver	Vehicle	Route
5:00 A.M.	Bert Pava	Truck 3882	Wichita, Kansas, to Haysville, Kansas (3 round trips)
6:00 A.M.	Rose Macon	Truck 2711	Wichita, Kansas, to Tulsa, Oklahoma (1 round trip)
7:30 A.M.	Emily Choi	Truck 2889	Wichita, Kansas, to South Bend, Indiana (1 round trip)
8:00 A.M.	Ian Ortiz	Truck 6007	Wichita, Kansas, to Springfield, Missouri (1 round trip)

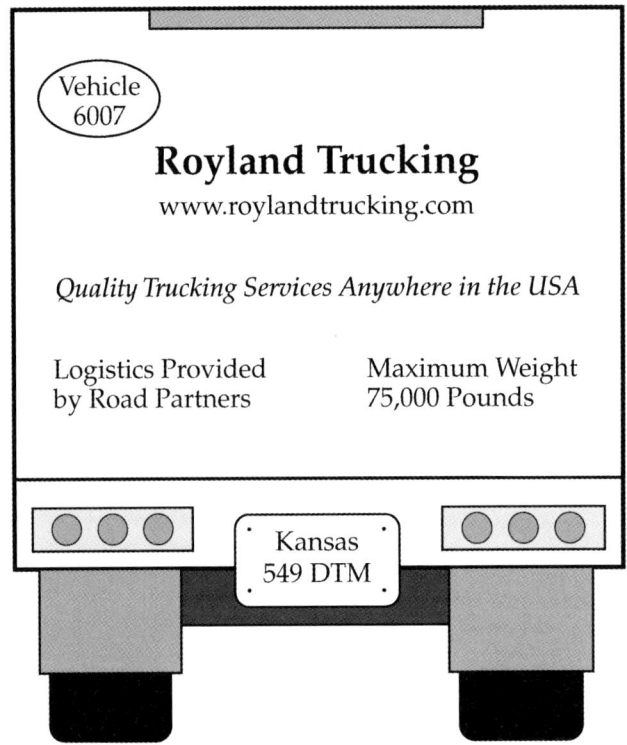

E-mail

To:	Ted Simms <t.simms@roylandtrucking.com>
From:	Kofi Stangel <kofi@amail.com>
Date:	March 22
Subject:	Employment
Attachment:	📎 Stangel_résumé

Dear Mr. Simms,

I met one of your drivers, Rose Macon, early yesterday morning at a highway rest stop just outside Wichita. She spoke highly of your company and suggested that I contact you. I have worked at Pokito Trucking for eight years and have a perfect driving record. Unfortunately, Pokito only has overnight driving opportunities now, and I prefer day shifts.

Attached is my résumé, which includes both personal and professional references. I look forward to speaking with you about opportunities with your company.

Sincerely,

Kofi Stangel

---

196. When did Mr. Pava first leave Wichita, Kansas, on March 21 ?

(A) At 5:00 A.M.
(B) At 6:00 A.M.
(C) At 7:30 A.M.
(D) At 8:00 A.M.

197. What is indicated about the truck that Mr. Ortiz drove on March 21 ?

(A) It is Royland Trucking's newest vehicle.
(B) It can carry loads up to 75,000 pounds.
(C) It recently underwent routine maintenance.
(D) It is used for deliveries in Kansas only.

198. What can be concluded about the driver who spoke with Mr. Stangel at a rest stop?

(A) She lives in Haysville.
(B) She helped train Ms. Choi.
(C) She was traveling to Oklahoma.
(D) She has been a truck driver for eight years.

199. In what department at Royland Trucking does Mr. Simms most likely work?

(A) Scheduling
(B) Purchasing
(C) Human resources
(D) Vehicle maintenance

200. What does Mr. Stangel suggest in the e-mail?

(A) He owns a home near Wichita.
(B) He tried to contact Mr. Simms by phone.
(C) He is satisfied with his schedule at Pokito Trucking.
(D) He has never been fined for driving too fast.

PART 7 빈출 표현

감사

as a token of appreciation 감사의 표시로
be grateful for ~에 감사하다
compensate 보상하다
complimentary 무료의
courteous 공손한, 정중한
delighted 기쁜
on behalf of ~을 대표하여, 대신하여
patronage 애용
recognize 인정하다, 치하하다

초대

banquet 연회
broadcast 방송하다
charity 자선 (단체)
compassionate 인정 많은, 동정적인
cordially 진심으로, 다정하게
credit 칭찬, 인정
decent 괜찮은, 품위 있는
devote 바치다, 헌신하다
donor 기증자
fundraiser 모금 행사

사업

acquire 획득하다, 인수하다
approve 승인하다
asset 재산
bid 입찰에 응하다
endorse 보증하다, 지지하다
establishment 설립, 기관
generate 산출하다, 만들어 내다
patent 특허
profitable 수익성 좋은 (= lucrative)
prototype 원형, 시제품

구매/할인

affordable 가격이 적당한
at no cost 무료로 (= free of charge)
extend 늘이다, 연장하다
voucher 상품권, 쿠폰
giveaway 증정품, 경품
installment 할부
inventory 재고, 재고 목록
markdown 가격 인하
range 범위(가 ~에 이르다)
redeem 현금이나 상품으로 바꾸다

추천

certificate 증명서
considerate 신중한, 사려 깊은
cooperation 협동, 협력
enthusiastic 열성적인
expertise 전문 지식
potential 잠재력 있는
promote 승진시키다, 홍보하다
prospective 장래성 있는, 유망한
qualification 자격 요건
reference 추천서, 추천인

자금

contribution 기부, 공헌
deposit 보증금; 입금하다
exceed 초과하다
financial 금융의, 재무의
generous 후한, 너그러운
monetary donation 금전적 기부
possess 소유하다
property 재산, 부동산
reimburse 상환하다, 변제하다
withdraw 인출하다

축하/기념

anniversary 기념일
cater 음식을 공급하다
celebrate 축하하다
eligible 자격이 있는 (= entitled)
honor 명예; 기리다
in advance 사전에, 미리
plaque 명판, 상패
refreshments 다과
retirement 은퇴
venue 장소

문제/사과

apology 사과
concern 관심사, 우려
defective 결함 있는
delay 지연시키다 (= postpone)
disruption 중단
dissatisfied 불만족스러운
insufficient 불충분한
patience 참을성
regretful 유감스러운
struggle 고군분투하다

경제/경영

aid 원조, 지원; 돕다
aspiring 장차 ~이 되려는
boost 북돋우다
competitor 경쟁업체
enormous 거대한
entrepreneur 기업가
executive 임원; 행정의
expansion 확장
investment 투자
prosperous 번영하는, 번창하는

부동산

- **district** 구역
- **floor plan** 평면도
- **fully-furnished** 내부가 완비된
- **lease** 임대하다
- **real estate agent** 부동산 중개인
- **rent** 임대료; 임대하다
- **residential** 주거용의
- **separate** 분리된
- **tenant** 세입자
- **utilities** 공공요금, 공익사업

서비스 1

- **around the clock** 24시간 내내
- **atmosphere** 분위기
- **exemplary** 본보기가 되는
- **expire** 만료되다
- **hospitality** 서비스업, 환대
- **subscribe** 구독하다
- **substitute** 대체하다; 대체품
- **meet demands** 수요를 충족시키다
- **termination** 종결
- **under the terms of** 조항에 따라

전자제품/가구

- **appliance** 전자제품
- **cutting-edge** 최신식의 (= state-of-the-art)
- **furnishing** 가구
- **light fixture** 조명
- **instructions** 설명서
- **vacuum cleaner** 진공청소기
- **valid** 유효한
- **vendor** 상인
- **warehouse** 창고
- **warranty** 품질보증(서)

커뮤니티

- **grant** 승인하다; 보조금
- **make arrangement** 준비하다
- **make an effort** 노력하다 (= endeavor)
- **mayor** 시장
- **much-anticipated** 매우 기대되는
- **municipal** 시의, 지방 자치의
- **prestigious** 명망 있는
- **proceeds** 수익
- **publicize** 홍보하다
- **town hall** 시청

서비스 2

- **accommodate** 수용하다
- **customized** 맞춤식의
- **exclusively** 독점적으로
- **practical** 실용적인
- **promotional material** 홍보 자료
- **reasonable price** 적당한 가격
- **reliable** 믿을 만한
- **renew** 갱신하다
- **specialize in** ~을 전문으로 하다
- **testimonial** 추천의 글

주문

- **account** 계정, 계좌
- **charge** 요금(을 부과하다)
- **confirm** 확인하다, 확정하다
- **due** 회비; 지불 기일이 된
- **estimate** 견적 (= quote)
- **in stock** 재고가 있는
- **in transit** 수송 중인
- **outstanding balance** 미지불 잔액
- **standing order** 고정 주문, 자동 이체
- **statements** 명세서

식당

- **appetite** 식욕
- **entrée** 주요리
- **assortment** 모음
- **cuisine** 요리(법)
- **culinary** 요리의, 주방의
- **dip** (소스 등에) 담그다
- **family-owned** 가족 소유의
- **ingredient** 재료, 성분
- **platter** 여러 음식을 차려 놓은 요리
- **signature dish** 대표 요리

상품

- **apparel** 옷
- **artifact** 공예품, 인공물
- **bulk order** 대량 주문
- **compact** 소형의
- **craft** 공예
- **durable** 내구성이 좋은
- **exquisite** 정교한, 매우 아름다운
- **portable** 휴대용의
- **versatile** 다재다능한, 다용도의
- **well-suited** 적절한, 잘 어울리는

청구/결제

- **amount** 액수, 금액
- **billing address** 청구 주소
- **deduct** 빼다, 공제하다
- **expedite** 신속히 처리하다
- **incur** 초래하다, 발생시키다
- **measurement** 치수, 측정
- **partial payment** 부분 지불
- **quantity** 수량
- **reduction** 할인, 축소
- **status** 상태

구인 1

- **applicant** 지원자
- **benefits** 복지 혜택
- **candidate** 후보자
- **certified** 공인된
- **cover letter** 자기소개서
- **degree** 학위
- **fluent** 능숙한
- **human resources** 인사부
- **multi-lingual** 여러 언어를 구사하는
- **negotiation** 협상

회의

- **address** 다루다, 취급하다
- **the board of directors** 이사회
- **committee** 위원회
- **make a decision** 결정을 내리다
- **minutes** 회의록 (= proceedings)
- **nomination** 지명, 임명
- **nominee** 후보
- **outline** 약술하다
- **shareholder** 주주 (= stockholder)
- **unanimous** 만장일치의

대회

- **be suitable for** ~에 적합하다
- **competition** 경쟁, 대회
- **content** 내용
- **depict** 묘사하다
- **electronically** 컴퓨터로, 온라인으로
- **foremost** 가장 중요한, 맨 앞의
- **judge** 심사위원
- **on a first-come, first-served basis** 선착순으로
- **participate in** ~에 참가하다
- **precede** ~에 앞서다

구인 2

- **preference** 우대 사항
- **primary duty** 주요 업무
- **proficiency** 능숙함
- **promising** 전도유망한
- **qualified** 자격을 갖춘
- **relevant experience** 관련 경력
- **required** 필수적인
- **responsibilities** 책무
- **salary requirement** 희망 연봉
- **temporary** 임시의, 임시직의

정책/변경

- **activate** 작동시키다, 활성화시키다
- **alternative entrance** 대체 출입구
- **appraisal** 평가
- **compensation** 보상
- **expenditure** 지출
- **immediate supervisor** 직속 상관
- **install** 설치하다
- **mandatory** 의무적인, 필수적인
- **tutorial** 교육 자료
- **violation** 위반

건강/의료

- **antibiotic** 항생제; 항생물질의
- **contagious** 전염성의
- **diagnosis** (병원) 진단, 진찰
- **immune** 면역성이 있는
- **infect** 감염시키다
- **over the counter** 처방전 없이 살 수 있는
- **pharmaceutical** 제약(의)
- **prescription** 처방(전)
- **symptom** 증상
- **vaccinate** 예방 접종을 하다

회사 생활

- **absence** 부재, 결석
- **achieve** 달성하다
- **attendance record** 출근 기록
- **division** 부서
- **duplicate** 복사하다
- **extension** 내선번호
- **job descriptions** 직무 기술서
- **labor** 근로, 노동
- **on duty** 근무 중인
- **performance evaluation** 업무 평가

행사

- **awards ceremony** 시상식
- **drawing** 추첨, 제비뽑기
- **entry** 입장, 출품(작)
- **flat rate** 고정 요금
- **foster** 촉진하다, 조성하다
- **function** 대규모 행사
- **mark** 기념하다 (= celebrate)
- **recognized** 인정받은
- **spectator** 관중
- **tentative** 잠정적인

환경

- **climate change** 기후 변화
- **conservation** 보존, 보호
- **contamination** 오염
- **dispose of** ~을 버리다, 처분하다
- **endangered** 멸종 위기에 처한
- **environmentally friendly** 친환경적인
- **extinction** 멸종, 소멸
- **pollutant** 오염 물질
- **solar power** 태양열
- **species** 종

관광

accommodations 숙소
attraction 명소
excursion 여행
landscape 풍경
lodge 산장
picturesque 그림 같은
scenic 경치가 좋은
spectacular 장관인
stunning 놀랄 만큼 멋진, 훌륭한
vacancy 빈방, 빈자리

공사

aim 목표; 겨냥하다
annex 부속 건물
interrupt 방해하다, 중단시키다
plumbing 배관 (작업)
procedure 절차
put into actions 조치를 취하다
repave 도로를 재포장하다 (= resurface)
resume 재개하다
under construction 공사 중인
upon completion 완공 시에

문화/예술

acclaimed 호평받는
admission 입장
author 작가
award-winning 수상 경력이 있는
critic 비평가
extend an invitation 초대장을 보내다
feature 특집; 포함하다
inspiration 영감
statue 조각상
take place 열리다, 일어나다

여행 1

amenities 생활 편의 시설
botanic garden 식물원
budget 예산; 저렴한
courtesy bus 무료 버스
customs 세관
departure 출발
dining establishment 식당
exotic 이국적인
expedition 탐험
fatigue 피로, 피곤

도로/교통

be advised 권고받다
boulevard 대로
duration 기간
encounter 직면하다, 맞닥뜨리다
fine 벌금, 과태료
intersection 교차로
lane 길, 차선
motorist 운전자
pedestrian 보행자
speed limit 속도 제한

전시

artifact 공예품
artwork 작품
collection 소장품
commemorate 기념하다
contemporary art 현대 예술
exhibition 전시회
existing 현존하는
gathering 모임
host 주최하다
material 재료, 자료

여행 2

house 수용하다
immigration 출입국 관리소
itinerary 여행 일정표
outskirts 변두리, 교외
off season 비수기
ruins 폐허, 유적
rural 시골풍의 (= rustic)
stopover 경유, 단기간 체류
vessel 선박, 배
voyage 항해(하다)

건물/건설

adjacent 인접한
architect 건축가
capacity 수용력, 능력
convert 전환하다
deterioration 악화, 하락
excavation 발굴
insulation 단열
proximity 인접, 근접
refurbish 재단장하다
restoration 복구, 복원

공연

choir 합창단
intermission 중간 휴식 시간
masterpiece 명작, 걸작
overwhelming 압도적인
poet 시인
premiere 개봉, 초연
prohibit 금지하다
remarkable 주목할 만한
star 주연(을 맡다)
usher (극장 등의) 안내인

ANSWER SHEET

ETS ACTUAL TEST

수험번호

응시일자 : 20   년   월   일

성명: 한글 / 한자 / 영자

LISTENING (Part I ~ IV)

READING (Part V ~ VII)

ETS 토익 단기공략 750+

최신 개정판
무료 동영상 강의
LC
RC

정답과 해설

PART 1 LISTENING COMPREHENSION

UNIT 01 인물 등장 사진

ETS 유형연습
본책 p.21

1 (D)　**2** (D)　**3** (A)　**4** (D)

1  W-Am

(A) A man is paying for a meal.
(B) A man is washing dishes.
(C) A man is reaching for a coat on a hook.
(D) A man is selecting some food from a buffet.

(A) 남자가 식사비를 지불하고 있다.
(B) 남자가 설거지를 하고 있다.
(C) 남자가 옷걸이에 걸린 코트를 집으려고 손을 뻗고 있다.
(D) 남자가 뷔페에서 음식을 고르고 있다.

해설 1인 등장 사진 – 식당

(A) 동작 묘사 오답: 남자가 식사비를 지불하고 있는(is paying for) 모습이 아니다.
(B) 동작 묘사 오답: 남자가 설거지하고 있는(is washing) 모습이 아니다.
(C) 상황 묘사 오답: 남자가 손을 뻗고 있는(is reaching for) 쪽은 음식이지 걸이에 걸린 코트(a coat on a hook)가 아니다.
(D) 정답: 남자가 뷔페에서 음식을 고르고 있는(is selecting) 모습이므로 정답이다.

어휘 wash dishes 설거지하다　reach for ~로 손을 뻗다
hook 걸이

2  M-Cn

(A) A man is distributing some handouts.
(B) A woman is pointing at a computer screen.
(C) Some people are getting up from a table.
(D) Some people are reviewing documents.

(A) 남자가 인쇄물을 나누어 주고 있다.
(B) 여자가 컴퓨터 화면을 가리키고 있다.
(C) 사람들이 탁자에서 일어서고 있다.
(D) 사람들이 서류를 검토하고 있다.

해설 2인 이상 등장 사진 – 사무실

(A) 동작 묘사 오답: 남자가 인쇄물을 나누어 주고 있는(is distributing) 모습이 아니다.
(B) 상황 묘사 오답: 여자가 가리키고 있는(is pointing at) 것은 서류이지 컴퓨터 화면(computer screen)이 아니다.
(C) 동작 묘사 오답: 사람들이 탁자에서 일어서고 있는(are getting up) 모습이 아니다.
(D) 정답: 사람들이 서류를 검토하고 있는(are reviewing) 모습이므로 정답이다.

어휘 distribute 나누어 주다　handout 인쇄물, 유인물
review 검토하다　document 서류

3  M-Au

(A) She's watering a potted plant.
(B) Some vegetables have been piled in a bucket.
(C) She's raking some leaves.
(D) Some stones form a walkway.

(A) 여자가 화분에 물을 주고 있다.
(B) 몇몇 채소들이 양동이에 쌓여 있다.
(C) 여자가 나뭇잎을 갈퀴로 긁어모으고 있다.
(D) 돌들이 보도를 형성하고 있다.

해설 사람·사물 혼합 사진 – 화원

(A) 정답: 여자가 화분에 물을 주고 있는(is watering) 모습이므로 정답이다.
(B) 사진에 없는 명사를 이용한 오답: 사진 속 양동이 안에 채소(vegetables)는 보이지 않는다.
(C) 동작 묘사 오답: 여자가 나뭇잎을 갈퀴로 긁어모으고 있는(is raking) 모습이 아니다.
(D) 사진에 없는 명사를 이용한 오답: 사진에 보도(walkway)는 보이지 않는다.

어휘 water 물을 주다　potted plant 화분에 심은 식물
pile 쌓아 올리다　rake 갈퀴로 긁어모으다　form 형성하다

4  M-Au

(A) Some people are resting on a bench.
(B) Some people are waiting in line.
(C) Some lights are being installed.
(D) Some people are looking at artwork.

(A) 몇몇 사람들이 벤치에서 쉬고 있다.
(B) 몇몇 사람들이 줄을 서서 기다리고 있다.
(C) 조명들이 설치되고 있다.
(D) 몇몇 사람들이 미술품을 감상하고 있다.

해설 사람·사물 혼합 사진 – 전시실

(A) 동작 묘사 오답: 사람들이 벤치에서 쉬고 있는(are resting) 모습이 아니다. 사진 속 벤치는 비어 있다.
(B) 동작 묘사 오답: 사람들이 줄을 서서 기다리고 있는(are waiting in line) 모습이 아니다.

(C) 상황 묘사 오답: 조명들이 설치되고 있는(are being installed) 상황이 아니다.
(D) 정답: 사람들이 미술품을 감상하고 있는(are looking at) 모습이므로 정답이다.

어휘 wait in line 줄 서서 기다리다   install 설치하다
artwork 미술품

ETS 실전문제   본책 p.22

| 1 (D) | 2 (C) | 3 (B) | 4 (C) | 5 (B) | 6 (B) |
| 7 (D) | 8 (D) | 9 (A) | 10 (C) | 11 (A) | 12 (C) |

1 M-Au

(A) He's opening up a locker.
(B) He's going up a set of stairs.
(C) He's leaning against a lamppost.
(D) **He's strolling along a walkway.**

(A) 남자가 사물함을 열고 있다.
(B) 남자가 일련의 계단을 올라가고 있다.
(C) 남자가 가로등에 기대어 있다.
(D) **남자가 보도를 따라 걸고 있다.**

해설 1인 등장 사진 – 길거리
(A) 동작 묘사 오답: 남자가 사물함을 열고 있는(is opening up) 모습이 아니다.
(B) 동작 묘사 오답: 남자가 계단을 올라가는(is going up) 모습이 아니다.
(C) 동작 묘사 오답: 남자가 가로등 기둥에 기대어 있는(is leaning against) 모습이 아니다.
(D) 정답: 남자가 보도를 따라 걸고 있는(is strolling) 모습이므로 정답이다.

어휘 a set of 일련의   lean against ~에 기대다
stroll 거닐다, 산책하다   along ~을 따라

2 W-Br

(A) A worker is closing a laptop.
(B) A worker is pouring coffee into a cup.
(C) **Some books are arranged on a shelf.**
(D) Some books are stacked under a window.

(A) 작업자가 노트북 컴퓨터를 닫고 있다.
(B) 작업자가 커피를 컵에 따르고 있다.
(C) **몇몇 책들이 선반에 정리되어 있다.**
(D) 몇몇 책들이 창문 아래 쌓여 있다.

해설 사람 · 사물 혼합 사진 – 작업실
(A) 동작 묘사 오답: 작업자가 노트북 컴퓨터를 닫고 있는(is closing) 모습이 아니다.

(B) 동작 묘사 오답: 작업자가 커피를 컵에 따르고 있는(is pouring) 모습이 아니다.
(C) 정답: 책들이 선반에 정리되어 있는(are arranged) 모습이므로 정답이다.
(D) 위치 묘사 오답: 책들은 선반에 정리되어 있지 창문 아래(under a window)에 쌓여 있지 않다.

어휘 pour (액체를) 따르다, 붓다   arrange 정리하다, 배치하다
stack 쌓다

3 M-Cn

(A) Some people are climbing up a staircase.
(B) **Some diners are eating on a restaurant patio.**
(C) Some umbrellas have been set up on a beach.
(D) Some steps are being swept clean.

(A) 사람들이 계단을 오르고 있다.
(B) **손님들이 식당 테라스에서 식사하고 있다.**
(C) 파라솔이 해변에 설치되어 있다.
(D) 계단이 빗자루로 깨끗이 청소되고 있다.

해설 사람 · 사물 혼합 사진 – 야외 식당
(A) 동작 묘사 오답: 사람들이 계단을 오르고 있는(are climbing up) 모습이 아니다.
(B) 정답: 손님들이 식당 테라스에서 식사하고 있는(are eating) 모습이므로 정답이다.
(C) 사진에 없는 명사를 이용한 오답: 사진에 해변(beach)은 보이지 않는다.
(D) 상황 묘사 오답: 계단이 빗자루로 청소되고 있는(are being swept) 상황이 아니다.

어휘 climb up ~을 오르다   patio 파티오, 야외 테라스
set up ~을 설치하다   sweep 빗자루로 쓸다

4 W-Br

(A) A man is plugging in a fan.
(B) A man is setting some bins on the ground.
(C) **A man is working next to a stack of boxes.**
(D) A man is hanging a safety vest on a hook.

(A) 남자가 선풍기 플러그를 꽂고 있다.
(B) 남자가 바닥에 통들을 내려놓고 있다.
(C) **남자가 상자 더미 옆에서 일하고 있다.**
(D) 남자가 안전 조끼를 걸이에 걸고 있다.

해설 1인 등장 사진 – 공장
(A) 동작 묘사 오답: 남자가 선풍기 플러그를 꽂고 있는(is plugging in) 모습이 아니다.

(B) 동작 묘사 오답: 남자는 통들을 운반하고 있지 바닥에 내려놓고 있는(is setting ~ on the ground) 모습이 아니다.
(C) 정답: 남자가 상자 더미 옆에서 일하고 있는(is working) 모습이므로 정답이다.
(D) 동작 묘사 오답: 남자는 안전 조끼를 입고 있지 걸이에 걸고 있는(is hanging) 모습이 아니다.

어휘 plug in ~의 플러그를 꽂다 set 놓다, 두다 bin 통
next to ~ 옆에 stack 더미, 무더기 hang 걸다, 매달다
safety vest 안전 조끼

5  M-Cn

(A) The women are changing a tire.
(B) **The women are opening the car doors.**
(C) One of the women is washing the car.
(D) One of the women is pushing a shopping cart.

(A) 여자들이 타이어를 교체하고 있다.
(B) **여자들이 자동차 문을 열고 있다.**
(C) 여자들 중 한 명이 세차하고 있다.
(D) 여자들 중 한 명이 쇼핑 카트를 밀고 있다.

해설 2인 이상 등장 사진 – 주차장
(A) 동작 묘사 오답: 여자들이 타이어를 교체하고 있는(are changing) 모습이 아니다.
(B) 정답: 여자들이 자동차 문을 열고 있는(are opening) 모습이므로 정답이다.
(C) 동작 묘사 오답: 여자들 중 한 명이 세차하고 있는(is washing) 모습이 아니다.
(D) 사진에 없는 명사를 이용한 오답: 사진에 쇼핑 카트(shopping cart)는 보이지 않는다

6  W-Am

(A) Some leaves have fallen onto a walkway.
(B) **Some people are relaxing on a bench.**
(C) Some people are swimming in a pool of water.
(D) Some workers are repairing the roof of a building.

(A) 몇몇 나뭇잎들이 보도에 떨어져 있다.
(B) **몇몇 사람들이 벤치에서 쉬고 있다.**
(C) 몇몇 사람들이 물 웅덩이에서 수영하고 있다.
(D) 몇몇 작업자들이 건물 지붕을 수리하고 있다.

해설 사람·사물 혼합 사진 – 공원
(A) 사진에 없는 명사를 이용한 오답: 사진에 보도에 떨어진 나뭇잎들(leaves)은 보이지 않는다.
(B) 정답: 몇몇 사람들이 벤치에서 쉬고 있는(are relaxing) 모습이므로 정답이다.
(C) 동작 묘사 오답: 사람들이 수영하고 있는(are swimming) 모습이 아니다.
(D) 사진에 없는 명사를 이용한 오답: 사진에 지붕을 수리하고 있는 작업자들(workers)은 보이지 않는다.

어휘 relax 쉬다, 휴식하다 repair 수리하다

7  W-Br

(A) He's hiking up a hill in a forest.
(B) He's eating his lunch in a picnic area.
(C) He's cutting a lawn beside a building.
(D) **He's studying a sign next to a walkway.**

(A) 남자가 숲에서 언덕을 오르고 있다.
(B) 남자가 피크닉 구역에서 점심을 먹고 있다.
(C) 남자가 건물 옆에 있는 잔디를 깎고 있다.
(D) **남자가 보도 옆에 있는 표지판을 살펴보고 있다.**

해설 1인 등장 사진 – 안내 구역
(A) 동작 묘사 오답: 남자가 언덕을 오르고 있는(is hiking up) 모습이 아니다.
(B) 동작 묘사 오답: 남자가 점심을 먹고 있는(is eating) 모습이 아니다.
(C) 동작 묘사 오답: 남자가 잔디를 깎고 있는(is cutting) 모습이 아니다.
(D) 정답: 남자가 표지판을 살펴보고 있는(is studying) 모습이므로 정답이다.

어휘 hike up ~을 오르다 lawn 잔디 study 살펴보다

8  M-Cn

(A) One of the women is filling a basket with merchandise.
(B) One of the women is leaning against a lamppost.
(C) The women are getting into a car.
(D) **The women are facing a storefront window.**

(A) 여자들 중 한 명이 바구니에 상품을 담고 있다.
(B) 여자들 중 한 명이 가로등에 기대고 있다.
(C) 여자들이 차에 타고 있다.
(D) **여자들이 가게 진열창을 마주보고 있다.**

해설 2인 이상 등장 사진 – 거리
(A) 동작 묘사 오답: 한 여자가 바구니에 상품을 담고 있는(is filling) 모습이 아니다.
(B) 동작 묘사 오답: 한 여자가 가로등에 기대고 있는(is leaning) 모습이 아니다.
(C) 동작 묘사 오답: 여자들이 차에 타고 있는(are getting into) 모습이 아니다.
(D) 정답: 여자들이 가게 진열창을 마주보고 있는(are facing) 모습이므로 정답이다.

어휘 merchandise 상품, 물품   lamppost 가로등
storefront window 상점 앞 진열창

9

W-Am

(A) One of the women is wearing a backpack.
(B) One of the women is paying for some merchandise.
(C) Some motorized carts have been left near a store entrance.
(D) Some clothing has been arranged on racks.

(A) 여자들 중 한 명이 배낭을 메고 있다.
(B) 여자들 중 한 명이 상품 값을 지불하고 있다.
(C) 몇몇 전동 카트들이 매장 입구 근처에 놓여 있다.
(D) 몇몇 의류들이 옷걸이에 정리되어 있다.

해설 사람·사물 혼합 사진 – 상점
(A) 정답: 여자들 중 한 명이 배낭을 메고 있는(is wearing) 모습이므로 정답이다.
(B) 동작 묘사 오답: 여자들 중 한 명이 상품 값을 지불하고 있는(is paying for) 모습이 아니다.
(C) 상태 묘사 오답: 전동 카트들이 매장 입구에 놓여 있는(have been left) 모습이 아니다.
(D) 사진에 없는 명사를 이용한 오답: 사진에 옷걸이에 정리된 의류(clothing)는 보이지 않는다.

어휘 pay for ~에 대한 값을 지불하다   merchandise 상품
motorized 전동화된   leave 놓다, 두다
arrange 정리하다, 배치하다   rack ~걸이, 거치대

10

W-Br

(A) She's looking in her handbag.
(B) She's standing in line at a store.
(C) She's selecting some items from a display.
(D) She's unloading a shipment of books.

(A) 여자가 핸드백 안을 들여다보고 있다.
(B) 여자가 매장에서 줄을 서 있다.
(C) 여자가 진열대에서 물건을 고르고 있다.
(D) 여자가 도서 배송품을 내리고 있다.

해설 1인 등장 사진 – 서점
(A) 동작 묘사 오답: 여자가 핸드백 안을 들여다보고 있는(is looking in) 모습이 아니다.
(B) 동작 묘사 오답: 여자가 줄을 서 있는(is standing in line) 모습이 아니다.
(C) 정답: 여자가 책 진열대에서 상품을 고르고 있는(is selecting) 모습이므로 정답이다.
(D) 동작 묘사 오답: 여자가 도서 배송품을 내리고 있는(is unloading) 모습이 아니다.

어휘 select 고르다, 선택하다   display 진열(품), 전시(품)
unload (짐 등을) 내리다   shipment 배송(품)

11

W-Br

(A) They're looking in the same direction.
(B) They're climbing over a log.
(C) They're stacking rocks on a beach.
(D) They're preparing to go for a swim.

(A) 사람들이 같은 방향을 바라보고 있다.
(B) 사람들이 통나무 위로 넘어가고 있다.
(C) 사람들이 해변에서 돌을 쌓아 올리고 있다.
(D) 사람들이 수영하러 갈 준비를 하고 있다.

해설 2인 이상 등장 사진 – 해변
(A) 정답: 사람들이 같은 방향을 바라보고 있는(are looking in the same direction) 모습이므로 정답이다.
(B) 동작 묘사 오답: 사람들이 통나무 위로 넘어가고 있는(are climbing over) 모습이 아니다.
(C) 동작 묘사 오답: 사람들이 해변에서 돌을 쌓아 올리고 있는(are stacking) 모습이 아니다.
(D) 동작 묘사 오답: 사람들이 수영하러 갈 준비를 하고 있는(are preparing to go for a swim) 모습이 아니다.

어휘 in the same direction 같은 방향으로   climb over ~ 위로 넘어가다   prepare 준비하다

12

M-Au

(A) Some workers are loading luggage onto a train.
(B) Some workers are repairing a train track.
(C) Some people are waiting at a train stop.
(D) Some people are boarding a train.

(A) 몇몇 작업자들이 기차에 수하물을 싣고 있다.
(B) 몇몇 작업자들이 기차 선로를 수리하고 있다.
(C) 몇몇 사람들이 기차 정거장에서 기다리고 있다.
(D) 몇몇 사람들이 기차에 탑승하고 있다.

해설 2인 이상 등장 사진 – 기차역
(A) 사진에 없는 명사를 이용한 오답: 사진에 수하물을 싣고 있는(are loading) 작업자들은 보이지 않는다.
(B) 사진에 없는 명사를 이용한 오답: 사진에 선로를 수리하고 있는 작업자들(workers)은 보이지 않는다.
(C) 정답: 사람들이 기차 정거장에서 기다리고 있는(are waiting) 모습이므로 정답이다.
(D) 동작 묘사 오답: 사람들이 기차에 탑승하고 있는(are boarding) 모습이 아니다.

어휘 load (짐 등을) 싣다   luggage 수하물, 여행 가방
board 탑승하다

UNIT 02 사물/풍경 사진

ETS 유형연습   본책 p.25

1 (A)   2 (D)   3 (B)   4 (B)

1  M-Cn

(A) Some books have been placed on a cart.
(B) A librarian is posting a sign near an entrance.
(C) Some bookshelves are being installed.
(D) The doors to a hallway have been propped open.

(A) 몇몇 책들이 카트에 놓여 있다.
(B) 사서가 입구 근처에 게시물을 붙이고 있다.
(C) 몇몇 책장들이 설치되고 있다.
(D) 복도로 통하는 문들이 괴어져 열려 있다.

해설 사물 사진 – 도서관
(A) 정답: 몇몇 책들이 카트에 놓여 있는(have been placed) 모습이므로 정답이다.
(B) 사진에 없는 명사를 이용한 오답: 사진에 게시물을 붙이고 있는 사서(librarian)가 보이지 않는다.
(C) 상황 묘사 오답: 몇몇 책장들이 설치되고 있는(are being installed) 상황이 아니다.
(D) 상태 묘사 오답: 문이 무언가에 받쳐져 열려 있는(have been propped open) 상태가 아니다.

어휘 librarian 사서   post a sign 게시물을 붙이다
entrance 입구   install 설치하다   prop 받치다, 괴다

2  M-Cn

(A) All of the seats are occupied.
(B) The railing is being repaired.
(C) A dining room has been prepared for a meal.
(D) There's a large plant between two tables.

(A) 모든 좌석이 차 있다.
(B) 난간이 수리되고 있다.
(C) 식사 공간에 식사가 준비되어 있다.
(D) 두 개의 탁자 사이에 큰 식물이 있다.

해설 사물 사진 – 실내
(A) 상태 묘사 오답: 모든 좌석이 비어 있는(unoccupied) 상태이다.
(B) 상황 묘사 오답: 난간이 수리되고 있는(is being repaired) 상황이 아니다.
(C) 상태 묘사 오답: 식사 공간에 식사가 준비되어 있는(has been prepared) 상태가 아니다.
(D) 정답: 큰 식물이 두 탁자 사이(between two tables)에 있으므로 정답이다.

어휘 occupied 사용 중인   railing 난간   repair 수리하다
prepare for ~을 준비하다

3  W-Br

(A) Some scarves have been arranged on a table.
(B) Some merchandise is on display outside a store.
(C) Leaves have covered a walkway.
(D) A sign is hanging from an awning.

(A) 스카프들이 테이블 위에 정리되어 놓여 있다.
(B) 상품들이 가게 바깥에 진열되어 있다.
(C) 나뭇잎이 보도를 덮고 있다.
(D) 간판이 차양에 매달려 있다.

해설 사물·풍경 사진 – 상점 앞 보도
(A) 사진에 없는 명사를 이용한 오답: 사진에 스카프들이 놓여 있는 테이블(table)이 보이지 않는다.
(B) 정답: 상품이 가게 바깥에(outside a store) 진열되어 있는(is on display) 모습이므로 정답이다.
(C) 상태 묘사 오답: 나뭇잎이 보도를 덮은(have covered) 상태가 아니다.
(D) 상태 묘사 오답: 간판은 바닥에 놓여 있지 차양에 매달려 있는(is hanging) 상태가 아니다.

어휘 be on display 진열 중이다   walkway 보도
awning 차양

4  M-Cn

(A) People are stepping onto a boat from a pier.
(B) There's a parking area near the beach.
(C) Ships are passing under a bridge.
(D) Trees are being planted along the shore.

(A) 사람들이 부두에서 배에 올라타고 있다.
(B) 해변 근처에 주차장이 있다.
(C) 배들이 다리 아래를 지나고 있다.
(D) 나무들이 해변을 따라 심어지고 있다.

해설 사물·풍경 사진 – 해변
(A) 사진에 없는 명사를 이용한 오답: 사진에 배(boat)와 올라타고 있는(are stepping onto) 사람들 모습이 보이지 않는다.
(B) 정답: 해변 근처에 주차장(parking area)이 있으므로 정답이다.
(C) 사진에 없는 명사를 이용한 오답: 사진에 다리 아래를 지나고 있는 배들(Ships)이 보이지 않는다.
(D) 상황 묘사 오답: 나무들이 해변을 따라 심어지고 있는(are being planted) 상황이 아니다.

어휘 pier 부두   plant 심다   shore 물가, 해안

ETS 실전문제   본책 p.26

| 1 (B) | 2 (B) | 3 (C) | 4 (C) | 5 (B) | 6 (C) |
| 7 (C) | 8 (A) | 9 (A) | 10 (A) | 11 (C) | 12 (A) |

1  M-Au

(A) A suitcase has been placed on a bed.
(B) A television has been mounted on a wall.
(C) Some chairs are arranged in a circle.
(D) Some drawers have been left open.

(A) 여행 가방이 침대 위에 놓여 있다.
(B) 텔레비전이 벽에 설치되어 있다.
(C) 몇몇 의자들이 원형으로 배치되어 있다.
(D) 몇몇 서랍들이 열린 채로 있다.

해설 사물 사진 – 거실
(A) 위치 묘사 오답: 여행 가방은 바닥에 놓여 있지 침대 위에(on a bed) 놓여 있지 않다.
(B) 정답: 텔레비전이 벽에 설치되어 있는(has been mounted) 모습이므로 정답이다.
(C) 사진에 없는 명사를 이용한 오답: 사진에 원형으로 배치된 의자들(Some chairs)은 보이지 않는다.
(D) 상태 묘사 오답: 서랍들이 열린 채로 있는(have been left open) 상태가 아니라 닫혀 있다.

어휘 suitcase 여행 가방   place 놓다, 두다
mount (벽 등에) 설치하다, 장착하다   drawer 서랍
be left open 열린 채로 있다

2  M-Cn

(A) A towel is hanging on a fence.
(B) Some plants have been placed in pots.
(C) Some chairs have been set around a table.
(D) The door to a house has been left open.

(A) 수건이 울타리에 걸려 있다.
(B) 몇몇 식물들이 화분에 심어져 있다.
(C) 몇몇 의자들이 탁자 주변에 배치되어 있다.
(D) 집 대문이 열려 있다.

해설 사물 사진 – 실외
(A) 사진에 없는 명사를 이용한 오답: 사진에 울타리에 걸린 수건(towel)은 보이지 않는다.
(B) 정답: 식물들이 화분에 심어져 있는(have been placed in pots) 모습이므로 정답이다.
(C) 사진에 없는 명사를 이용한 오답: 사진에 탁자(table)가 보이지 않는다.
(D) 상태 묘사 오답: 문이 열려 있는(has been left open) 상태가 아니다.

어휘 fence 울타리

3  M-Cn

(A) Some umbrellas are set up on the beach.
(B) Some trees have been cut down.
(C) Some chairs are lined up outside.
(D) Some boats are in the water.

(A) 파라솔들이 해변에 설치되어 있다.
(B) 나무들이 베어져 있다.
(C) 의자들이 바깥에 줄지어 있다.
(D) 배들이 물 위에 있다.

해설 사물·풍경 사진 – 해변
(A) 사진에 없는 명사를 이용한 오답: 사진에 파라솔(umbrellas)이 보이지 않는다.
(B) 상태 묘사 오답: 나무들이 베어져 있는(have been cut down) 상태가 아니다.
(C) 정답: 의자들이 바깥에 줄지어 있는(are lined up) 모습이므로 정답이다.
(D) 위치 묘사 오답: 배들이 해변에 있지만 물 위에(in the water) 떠 있지는 않다.

어휘 cut down (밑부분을 잘라) 넘어뜨리다   be lined up 일렬로 늘어서 있다

4  W-Am

(A) The panels of a glass building are being washed.
(B) An aircraft is lifting off the runway at an airport.
(C) Lane markings have been painted on a roadway.
(D) A passenger bus is exiting a parking garage.

(A) 유리 건물의 유리판들이 세척되고 있다.
(B) 비행기가 공항 활주로에서 이륙하고 있다.

(C) 차선 표시가 도로에 페인트칠되어 있다.
(D) 승객용 버스가 주차장을 빠져나오고 있다.

해설 사물·풍경 사진 – 공항
(A) 상황 묘사 오답: 건물의 유리판들이 세척되고 있는(are being washed) 상황이 아니다.
(B) 동작 묘사 오답: 비행기가 공항 활주로에서 이륙하고 있는(is lifting off) 모습이 아니다.
(C) 정답: 차선 표시가 도로에 페인트칠되어 있는(have been painted) 모습이므로 정답이다.
(D) 동작 묘사 오답: 버스가 주차장에서 빠져나오고 있는(is exiting) 모습이 아니다.

어휘 aircraft 항공기 lift off ~에서 이륙하다 runway 활주로 lane 차선 marking 표시 exit 나가다 parking garage 주차장, 주차 건물

5  W-Am

(A) The chairs are stacked by the wall.
(B) The table has been set for a meal.
(C) Menus have been placed on some chairs.
(D) Some glasses are drying on a rack.

(A) 벽 옆에 의자들이 쌓여 있다.
(B) 탁자에 식사 준비가 되어 있다.
(C) 메뉴가 몇몇 의자들 위에 놓여 있다.
(D) 몇몇 유리잔들이 선반에서 건조되고 있다.

해설 사물 사진 – 식당
(A) 상태 묘사 오답: 의자들이 벽 옆에 쌓여 있는(are stacked) 상태가 아니다.
(B) 정답: 탁자에 식사 준비가 되어 있는(has been set for a meal) 모습이므로 정답이다.
(C) 상태 묘사 오답: 메뉴가 탁자 위에는 있지만 의자 위에는 (on some chairs) 놓여 있지 않다.
(D) 사진에 없는 명사를 이용한 오답: 사진에 선반(rack)은 보이지 않는다.

어휘 dry 마르다, 건조되다

6  M-Au

(A) Some cars have been parked in a parking garage.
(B) Some large tree branches have fallen onto the dirt.
(C) A fence has been erected on the border of a park.
(D) A park bench is covered in leaves.

(A) 몇몇 차들이 주차장에 주차되어 있다.
(B) 몇몇 큰 나뭇가지들이 흙 위에 떨어져 있다.
(C) 울타리가 공원 가장자리에 세워져 있다.
(D) 공원 벤치가 나뭇잎으로 덮여 있다.

해설 사물·풍경 사진 – 공원
(A) 사진에 없는 명사를 이용한 오답: 사진에 주차장(parking garage)이 보이지 않는다.
(B) 사진에 없는 명사를 이용한 오답: 사진에 흙 위에 떨어진 큰 나뭇가지들(large tree branches)이 보이지 않는다.
(C) 정답: 울타리가 공원 가장자리에 세워져 있는(has been erected) 모습이므로 정답이다.
(D) 상태 묘사 오답: 공원 벤치가 나뭇잎으로 덮여 있는(is covered in leaves) 상태가 아니다.

어휘 branch (나무) 가지 dirt 흙, 먼지 erect 세우다 border 가장자리, 경계 be covered in ~로 덮여 있다

7  M-Cn

(A) Some books are stacked on the floor.
(B) Some curtains are being taken down.
(C) One of the walls is lined with shelves.
(D) Chairs have been pushed into a corner.

(A) 책들이 바닥에 쌓여 있다.
(B) 커튼들이 철거되고 있다.
(C) 한쪽 벽면에 선반들이 늘어서 있다.
(D) 의자들이 구석으로 밀려 있다.

해설 사물 사진 – 실내
(A) 위치 묘사 오답: 책들은 선반에 있지 바닥에(on the floor) 쌓여 있지 않다.
(B) 상황 묘사 오답: 커튼이 철거되고 있는(is being taken down) 상황이 아니다.
(C) 정답: 한쪽 벽면에 선반들이 일렬로 늘어서 있는(is lined with shelves) 모습이므로 정답이다.
(D) 위치 묘사 오답: 의자들은 구석으로(into a corner) 밀려 있지 않다.

어휘 take down 치우다, 떼어내다

8  M-Cn

(A) Some flags are waving in the wind.
(B) A plaza is bordered by a fence.
(C) A van is entering a tunnel.
(D) Fountains are on both sides of a park entrance.

(A) 몇몇 깃발들이 바람에 나부끼고 있다.
(B) 광장이 울타리로 둘러싸여 있다.
(C) 승합차가 터널로 진입하고 있다.
(D) 분수대가 공원 입구 양쪽에 있다.

해설 사물·풍경 사진 - 광장 분수대
(A) 정답: 깃발들이 바람에 나부끼고 있는(are waving) 모습이므로 정답이다.
(B) 사진에 없는 명사를 이용한 오답: 사진에 울타리(fence)가 보이지 않는다.
(C) 사진에 없는 명사를 이용한 오답: 사진에 터널(tunnel)이 보이지 않는다.
(D) 상태 묘사 오답: 사진에 분수대는 하나로 공원 입구 양쪽(both sides of a park entrance)에 있지 않다.

어휘 wave 흔들리다, 나부끼다   border 가장자리를 이루다
fountain 분수(대)

9

M-Cn

(A) Some carts have been left unattended.
(B) Customers are sorting clothing into piles.
(C) Some appliances are stacked on top of each other.
(D) Laundry detergent is being poured into a machine.

(A) 몇몇 카트들이 방치되어 있다.
(B) 손님들이 옷을 분류해 쌓고 있다.
(C) 가전제품들이 차곡차곡 쌓여 있다.
(D) 세탁 세제가 세탁기에 부어지고 있다.

해설 사물 사진 - 세탁실
(A) 정답: 카트 몇 개가 방치되어 있는(have been left unattended) 모습이므로 정답이다.
(B) 사진에 없는 명사를 이용한 오답: 사진에 옷을 분류해 쌓고 있는 손님들(Customers)이 보이지 않는다.
(C) 상태 묘사 오답: 가전제품들이 차곡차곡 쌓여 있는(are stacked on top of each other) 상태가 아니다.
(D) 상황 묘사 오답: 세탁 세제가 세탁기에 부어지고 있는(is being poured) 상황이 아니다.

어휘 unattended 방치되어 있는   sort 분류하다
appliance 가전제품   laundry detergent 세탁용 세제

10

M-Au

(A) A pair of matching chairs face each other.
(B) A framed mirror is leaning against a well-lit shelving unit.
(C) A light fixture is suspended from the ceiling.
(D) Objects in a shelving unit are being dusted.

(A) 한 쌍의 똑같은 의자가 서로 마주보고 있다.
(B) 액자형 거울이 조명이 환하게 밝혀진 선반에 기대어져 있다.
(C) 조명 기구가 천장에 매달려 있다.
(D) 선반에 놓인 물건들이 먼지가 털리고 있다.

해설 사물 사진 - 거실
(A) 정답: 똑같이 생긴 의자 한 쌍이 서로 마주보고 있는(face each other) 모습이므로 정답이다.
(B) 상태 묘사 오답: 거울이 선반에 기대어져 있는(is leaning against) 모습이 아니다.
(C) 상태 묘사 오답: 조명 기구가 천장에 매달려 있는(is suspended from) 모습이 아니다.
(D) 상황 묘사 오답: 선반에 놓인 물건의 먼지가 털리고 있는(are being dusted) 상황이 아니다.

어휘 matching 동일한, 일치하는   framed 틀에 끼운
well-lit 환하게 조명이 비춰진   shelving unit 선반   light fixture 조명 기구   be suspended from ~에 매달려 있다
object 물건, 물품   dust 먼지를 털어내다

11

M-Cn

(A) Some mats have been hung over a railing.
(B) Some cleaning supplies have fallen into the plants.
(C) Some steps lead to an entranceway.
(D) Some plants are arranged on a staircase.

(A) 매트들이 난간에 걸려 있다.
(B) 청소용품이 식물들 사이로 떨어져 있다.
(C) 계단이 입구로 이어져 있다.
(D) 식물들이 계단에 배치되어 있다.

해설 사물·풍경 사진 - 건물 앞
(A) 상태 묘사 오답: 매트는 바닥에 놓여 있지 난간에 걸려 있지(have been hung over a railing) 않다.
(B) 사진에 없는 명사를 이용한 오답: 사진에 청소용품(cleaning supplies)이 보이지 않는다.
(C) 정답: 계단이 입구로 이어져 있는(lead to an entranceway) 모습이므로 정답이다.
(D) 위치 묘사 오답: 식물들은 계단에(on a staircase) 배치되어 있지 않다.

어휘 railing 난간   supplies 용품, 물품   fall into ~ 속으로 떨어지다   lead to ~로 이어지다   entranceway 입구 통로
staircase 계단

12

W-Br

(A) There are some mountains in the distance.
(B) There's a restaurant on the roof of the building.
(C) Fences are being constructed around a building.
(D) The residents are leaning out their windows.

(A) 저 멀리 산들이 있다.
(B) 건물 옥상에 식당이 있다.
(C) 울타리들이 건물 주변에 설치되고 있다.
(D) 주민들이 창밖으로 몸을 내밀고 있다.

해설 사물·풍경 사진 – 건물
(A) 정답: 멀리(in the distance) 산들이 보이는 모습이므로 정답이다.
(B) 위치 묘사 오답: 식당으로 보이는 야외 카페는 건물 옥상(roof)이 아닌 지상에 있다.
(C) 상황 묘사 오답: 울타리들이 설치되고 있는(are being constructed) 상황이 아니다.
(D) 사진에 없는 명사를 이용한 오답: 사진에 창밖으로 몸을 내민 주민들(residents)은 보이지 않는다.

어휘 in the distance 저 멀리, 먼 곳에   roof 지붕, 옥상
construct 건설하다, 만들다   resident 주민
lean out ~ 밖으로 몸을 내밀다

ETS ACTUAL TEST   본책 p. 28

1 (B)   2 (D)   3 (D)   4 (C)   5 (D)   6 (B)

1  W-Br

(A) A person is moving a ladder.
(B) A person is reaching for a container on a shelf.
(C) A person is carrying a toolbox.
(D) A person is painting the walls of a utility room.

(A) 한 사람이 사다리를 옮기고 있다.
(B) 한 사람이 선반 위 용기를 잡으려고 손을 뻗고 있다.
(C) 한 사람이 공구상자를 나르고 있다.
(D) 한 사람이 다용도실 벽을 페인트칠하고 있다.

해설 1인 등장 사진 – 다용도실
(A) 동작 묘사 오답: 사람이 사다리를 옮기고 있는(is moving) 모습이 아니다.
(B) 정답: 사람이 선반 위 용기를 잡으려고 손을 뻗고 있는(is reaching for a container) 모습이므로 정답이다.
(C) 동작 묘사 오답: 사람이 공구상자를 나르고 있는(is carrying) 모습이 아니다.
(D) 동작 묘사 오답: 사람이 벽을 페인트칠하고 있는(is painting) 모습이 아니다.

어휘 ladder 사다리   reach for ~을 잡으려고 손을 뻗다
container 용기, 그릇   carry 나르다
utility room 다용도실

2  W-Br

(A) He's assembling a canopy on a lawn.
(B) He's parking a vehicle behind a tent.
(C) He's hanging up some T-shirts.
(D) He's standing behind a merchandise display.

(A) 남자가 잔디밭에서 천막을 조립하고 있다.
(B) 남자가 텐트 뒤쪽에 차량을 주차하고 있다.
(C) 남자가 티셔츠들을 걸고 있다.
(D) 남자가 상품 진열대 뒤에 서 있다.

해설 1인 등장 사진 – 옥외 텐트
(A) 동작 묘사 오답: 남자가 천막을 조립하고 있는(is assembling) 모습이 아니다.
(B) 동작 묘사 오답: 남자가 차량을 주차하고 있는(is parking) 모습이 아니다.
(C) 동작 묘사 오답: 남자가 티셔츠를 걸고 있는(is hanging up) 모습이 아니다.
(D) 정답: 남자가 상품 진열대 뒤에 서 있는(is standing behind) 모습이므로 정답이다.

어휘 assemble 조립하다   canopy (지붕 있는) 천막
lawn 잔디밭   merchandise 상품   display 진열(품)

3  W-Am

(A) A backpack is hanging on the back of a person's chair.
(B) A worker is mopping a walkway.
(C) Some people are boarding a plane.
(D) Some people are walking in a hallway.

(A) 배낭이 한 사람의 의자 등받이에 걸려 있다.
(B) 한 작업자가 통로를 대걸레로 닦고 있다.
(C) 몇몇 사람들이 비행기에 탑승하고 있다.
(D) 몇몇 사람들이 복도에서 걷고 있다.

해설 사람·사물 혼합 사진 – 공항 통로
(A) 사진에 없는 명사를 이용한 오답: 사진에 의자의 등받이(the back of a chair)에 걸려 있는 배낭은 보이지 않는다.
(B) 사진에 없는 명사를 이용한 오답: 사진에 대걸레로 닦고 있는 작업자(worker)는 보이지 않는다.
(C) 동작 묘사 오답: 사람들이 비행기에 탑승하고 있는(are boarding a plane) 모습이 아니다.
(D) 정답: 사람들이 복도에서 걷고 있는(are walking) 모습이므로 정답이다.

어휘 mop 대걸레로 닦다   board 탑승하다   hallway 복도

4  W-Br

(A) A whiteboard has been propped against a doorway.
(B) Some chairs have been arranged in rows.
(C) **A large monitor has been mounted on a wall.**
(D) Some computer equipment has been stacked in a corner.

(A) 화이트보드가 출입문에 기대어져 있다.
(B) 몇몇 의자들이 줄지어 배치되어 있다.
(C) **대형 모니터가 벽에 설치되어 있다.**
(D) 몇몇 컴퓨터 장비들이 구석에 쌓여 있다.

해설 사물 사진 – 회의실
(A) 상태 묘사 오답: 화이트보드가 출입문에 기대어져 있는 (has been propped against) 상태가 아니다.
(B) 상태 묘사 오답: 의자들이 줄지어 배치되어 있는(have been arranged in rows) 상태가 아니다.
(C) 정답: 대형 모니터가 벽에 설치되어 있는(has been mounted) 모습이므로 정답이다.
(D) 상태 묘사 오답: 컴퓨터 장비들이 구석에 쌓여 있는(has been stacked) 상태가 아니다.

어휘 prop against ~에 기대어 세워 놓다 arrange 배치하다 in rows 줄지어 mount (벽 등에) 설치하다 equipment 장비 stack 쌓다

5  M-Cn

(A) One of the workers is directing traffic in the street.
(B) One of the workers is putting on snow boots.
(C) One of the workers is picking up fallen tree branches.
(D) **One of the workers is clearing snow from a roof.**

(A) 작업자들 중 한 명이 거리에서 교통 정리를 하고 있다.
(B) 작업자들 중 한 명이 스노우 부츠를 착용하는 중이다.
(C) 작업자들 중 한 명이 떨어진 나뭇가지들을 줍고 있다.
(D) **작업자들 중 한 명이 지붕에서 눈을 치우고 있다.**

해설 2인 이상 등장 사진 – 거리
(A) 동작 묘사 오답: 작업자들 중 한 명이 교통 정리를 하고 있는(is directing traffic) 모습이 아니다.
(B) 동작 묘사 오답: 작업자들 중 한 명이 스노우 부츠를 착용하고 있는(is putting on) 모습이 아니다.
(C) 동작 묘사 오답: 작업자들 중 한 명이 떨어진 나뭇가지들을 줍고 있는(is picking up) 모습이 아니다.
(D) 정답: 작업자들 중 한 명이 지붕에서 눈을 치우는(is clearing snow) 모습이므로 정답이다.

어휘 direct traffic 교통 정리를 하다 put on (동작) ~을 착용하다 pick up ~을 줍다, ~을 들어올리다 tree branch 나뭇가지

6  W-Br

(A) A wooden fence encloses a construction site.
(B) **Building materials are piled up at a construction site.**
(C) A construction vehicle is lifting bricks and planks of wood.
(D) Some streets are closed because of construction.

(A) 목재 울타리가 공사 현장을 둘러싸고 있다.
(B) **건축 자재들이 공사 현장에 쌓여 있다.**
(C) 건설 차량이 벽돌과 나무 판자들을 들어올리고 있다.
(D) 일부 도로가 공사로 인해 폐쇄되어 있다.

해설 사물·풍경 사진 – 공사장
(A) 사진에 없는 명사를 이용한 오답: 사진에 목재 울타리(A wooden fence)가 보이지 않는다.
(B) 정답: 건축 자재들이 공사 현장에 쌓여 있는(are piled up) 모습이므로 정답이다.
(C) 사진에 없는 명사를 이용한 오답: 사진에 건설 차량(A construction vehicle)이 보이지 않는다.
(D) 사진에 없는 명사를 이용한 오답: 사진에 폐쇄된 도로(streets)가 보이지 않는다.

어휘 enclose 둘러싸다, 에워싸다 construction site 공사 현장 material 자재, 재료 pile 쌓다 lift 들어올리다 brick 벽돌 plank 판자, 널빤지

PART 2　LISTENING COMPREHENSION

UNIT 03　Who / When / Where 의문문

1　Who 의문문

ETS Check-Up　　　　　　　　　　　본책 p.38

1 (B)　**2** (C)　**3** (B)　**4** (B)　**5** (C)　**6** (A)

1　M-Cn / W-Br
Who will be at the opening ceremony?
(A) Yes, ahead of schedule.
(B) The mayor will be, of course.
(C) We'll need a microphone, too.

누가 개막식에 오시나요?
(A) 네, 일정보다 빨리요.
(B) 시장님께서 오실 거예요, 당연히요.
(C) 우리가 마이크도 필요할 겁니다.

해설　개막식 참석자를 묻는 Who 의문문
(A) **Yes/No 불가 오답**: Who 의문문에는 Yes/No로 대답할 수 없다.
(B) **정답**: 누가 개막식에 오는지 묻는 질문에 당연히 시장님께서 오실 것(The mayor will be, of course)이라며 구체적인 인물을 언급하고 있으므로 정답이다.
(C) **연상 어휘 오답**: 질문의 opening ceremony에서 연상 가능한 microphone을 이용한 오답이다.

어휘　ceremony 기념식, 축하 행사　ahead of ~보다 빨리, ~보다 앞서　mayor 시장

2　W-Am / M-Cn
Who's repairing the air conditioner?
(A) OK, I'll prepare 50 copies.
(B) I need some shampoo and conditioner.
(C) Tanya is.

누가 에어컨을 수리하나요?
(A) 좋아요, 50부 준비할게요.
(B) 샴푸와 컨디셔너가 좀 필요해요.
(C) 타냐 씨가요.

해설　에어컨 수리 담당자를 묻는 Who 의문문
(A) **Yes/No 불가 오답**: Who 의문문에는 Yes/No 응답이 불가능한데, OK도 일종의 Yes 응답이라고 볼 수 있으므로 오답이다.
(B) **유사 발음 오답**: 질문의 air conditioner와 부분적으로 발음이 유사한 conditioner를 이용한 오답이다.
(C) **정답**: 에어컨 수리 담당자를 묻는 질문에 구체적인 이름(Tanya)을 제시하고 있으므로 정답이다.

어휘　repair 수리하다　prepare 준비하다

3　M-Cn / W-Am
Who ordered the fish?
(A) It was delivered today.
(B) The customer at table two.
(C) Can we have the bill?

누가 생선을 주문했죠?
(A) 오늘 배달되었어요.
(B) 2번 테이블 손님요.
(C) 계산서 좀 갖다 주시겠어요?

해설　생선을 주문한 사람을 묻는 Who 의문문
(A) 질문과 상관없는 오답
(B) **정답**: 생선을 주문한 사람을 묻는 질문에 2번 테이블 손님(The customer at table two)이라고 구체적으로 대답하고 있으므로 정답이다.
(C) **연상 어휘 오답**: 질문의 ordered에서 연상 가능한 bill을 이용한 오답이다.

어휘　order 주문하다　deliver 배송하다　bill 계산서

4　W-Br / W-Am
Who put the ladder in the hallway?
(A) The letter was mailed.
(B) It was probably the painters.
(C) On the way down.

누가 복도에 사다리를 두었나요?
(A) 편지가 발송되었습니다.
(B) 아마도 페인트칠하는 사람들일 거예요.
(C) 내려가는 길에요.

해설　복도에 사다리를 둔 사람을 묻는 Who 의문문
(A) **유사 발음 오답**: 질문의 ladder와 발음이 유사한 letter를 이용한 오답이다.
(B) **정답**: 누가 복도에 사다리를 두었는지 묻는 질문에 페인트를 칠하고 있는 사람들(the painters)일 것이라고 대답하고 있으므로 정답이다.
(C) **유사 발음 오답**: 질문의 hallway와 부분적으로 발음이 동일한 way를 이용한 오답이다.

어휘　ladder 사다리

5　W-Am / M-Cn
Who booked the airline tickets?
(A) Laura returned the book.
(B) Flights leave every hour.
(C) Someone in the Paris office.

항공권은 누가 예약했나요?
(A) 로라가 책을 반납했어요.
(B) 비행기는 매시간 있어요.
(C) 파리 지점 소속 누군가요.

해설　항공권을 예약한 사람을 묻는 Who 의문문
(A) **다의어 오답**: 질문의 booked는 '예약하다'라는 뜻의 동사이고, 보기의 book은 '책'이라는 뜻의 명사이다.
(B) **연상 어휘 오답**: 질문의 airline tickets에서 연상 가능한 Flights를 이용한 오답이다.

(C) 정답: 누가 예약했는지를 묻는 질문에 파리 지점 소속 누군가(Someone in the Paris office)라고 응답하고 있으므로 정답이다.

어휘 book 예약하다   return 반환하다, 반납하다

6   W-Br / W-Am
Who's going to edit this video?
(A) Do you have experience with that?
(B) My colleague used to live there.
(C) We went for a long walk.

누가 이 동영상을 편집할 예정인가요?
(A) 그 일에 대한 경험이 있으신가요?
(B) 제 동료 직원이 전에 그곳에 살았어요.
(C) 저희는 긴 산책을 했어요.

해설 동영상을 편집할 사람을 묻는 Who 의문문
(A) 정답: 누가 동영상을 편집할 예정인지 묻는 질문에 그에 대한 경험이 있는지 되물으며(Do you have experience with that?) 경험 유무에 따라 상대방에게 맡길 뜻을 나타내고 있으므로 정답이다.
(B) 질문과 상관없는 오답
(C) 연상 어휘 오답: 질문의 going에서 연상 가능한 walk를 이용한 오답이다.

어휘 edit 편집하다   colleague 동료 (직원)   used to do 예전에 ~했다, ~하곤 했다

2 When 의문문

본책 p.39

ETS Check-Up

1 (B)   2 (A)   3 (A)   4 (B)   5 (B)   6 (A)

1   M-Cn / M-Au
When should we schedule the meeting with the investors?
(A) About ten minutes from here.
(B) They'll be in town next week.
(C) The conference room is locked.

투자자들과의 회의를 언제로 잡는 게 좋을까요?
(A) 이곳에서부터 약 10분이요.
(B) 그분들께서 다음 주에 우리 도시로 오실 겁니다.
(C) 회의실이 잠겨 있습니다.

해설 회의 시점을 묻는 When 의문문
(A) 질문과 상관없는 오답
(B) 정답: 투자자들과의 회의를 언제로 잡는 것이 좋을지 묻는 질문에 그 사람들이 다음 주에 올 것(They'll be in town next week)이라며 가능한 시점을 우회적으로 나타내고 있으므로 정답이다.
(C) 연상 어휘 오답: 질문의 meeting에서 연상 가능한 conference room을 이용한 오답이다.

어휘 investor 투자자   about 약, 대략

2   M-Cn / W-Br
When will your book be published?
(A) In January, if all goes well.
(B) A two-hour session.
(C) Online and in bookstores.

당신 책이 언제 출간되나요?
(A) 1월에요, 모든 게 잘 진행되면요.
(B) 2시간짜리 수업입니다.
(C) 온라인과 서점에서요.

해설 출간 시점을 묻는 When 의문문
(A) 정답: 책이 언제 출간되는지 묻는 질문에 1월이라는 구체적인 시점과 함께 모든 게 잘 진행되면(if all goes well)이라는 조건을 덧붙이고 있으므로 정답이다.
(B) 질문과 상관없는 오답
(C) 연상 어휘 오답: 질문의 book에서 연상 가능한 bookstores를 이용한 오답이다.

어휘 publish 출간하다   go well 잘 진행되다   session 수업, (특정 활동을 하는) 시간

3   W-Am / W-Br
When are the conference proposals due?
(A) On January twenty-seventh.
(B) For three days.
(C) He'll do it.

회의 제안서 마감일이 언제예요?
(A) 1월 27일이요.
(B) 3일 동안이요.
(C) 그가 그것을 할 거예요.

해설 제안서 마감 시점을 묻는 When 의문문
(A) 정답: 회의 제안서 마감일을 묻는 질문에 1월 27일(On January twenty-seventh)이라는 구체적인 날짜를 제시하고 있으므로 정답이다.
(B) 질문과 상관없는 오답
(C) 유사 발음 오답: 질문의 due와 발음이 유사한 do를 사용한 오답이다.

어휘 conference 회의   proposal 제안(서)   due 제출 기한이 된

4   M-Cn / W-Br
When does the doctor's office open?
(A) I think there's parking available near the back entrance.
(B) At eight o'clock in the morning.
(C) Just turn left on the next street.

그 병원은 언제 문을 열죠?
(A) 뒷문 근처에 이용 가능한 주차 공간이 있는 것 같아요.
(B) 오전 8시예요.
(C) 다음 거리에서 좌회전하기만 하면 됩니다.

해설 병원이 문을 여는 시점을 묻는 When 의문문
(A) 연상 어휘 오답: 질문의 open에서 연상 가능한 entrance를 이용한 오답이다.

(B) 정답: 병원이 문을 여는 시점을 묻는 질문에 구체적인 시간(At eight o'clock in the morning)을 알려 주고 있으므로 정답이다.
(C) 질문과 상관없는 오답

어휘 parking 주차 (공간) available 이용 가능한 turn left 좌회전하다

5 W-Am / M-Au
When will the next phase of construction begin?
(A) A major improvement.
(B) Once the blueprints are finalized.
(C) In a three-story apartment building.

공사 다음 단계는 언제 시작될 예정인가요?
(A) 주요한 개선이죠.
(B) 설계도가 완성되면요.
(C) 3층짜리 아파트 건물에서요.

해설 공사 다음 단계의 시작 시점을 묻는 When 의문문
(A) 연상 어휘 오답: 질문의 construction에서 연상 가능한 improvement를 이용한 오답이다.
(B) 정답: 공사 다음 단계의 시작 시점을 묻는 질문에 설계도가 완성되면(Once the blueprints are finalized)이라고 대답하고 있으므로 정답이다.
(C) 질문과 상관없는 오답

어휘 phase 단계 construction 공사 improvement 개선
blueprint 설계도, 청사진 finalize 완결하다

6 W-Am / W-Br
When should I send the invitations?
(A) Let me look at the schedule.
(B) Sure, I'll do that.
(C) On the tenth floor.

제가 언제 초대장을 보내야 하나요?
(A) 일정표를 살펴볼게요.
(B) 물론이죠, 제가 할게요.
(C) 10층에서요.

해설 초대장 발송 시점을 묻는 When 의문문
(A) 정답: 언제 초대장을 보내야 하는지 묻는 질문에 일정표를 살펴보겠다(Let me look at the schedule)는 간접 응답으로 해당 정보를 확인하겠다는 의사를 표현하고 있으므로 정답이다.
(B) Yes/No 불가 오답: When 의문문에는 Yes/No 응답이 불가능한데, Sure도 일종의 Yes 응답이라고 볼 수 있으므로 오답이다.
(C) 질문과 상관없는 오답

어휘 invitation 초대(장)

3 Where 의문문

ETS Check-Up ─────────────── 본책 p.40

| 1 (A) | 2 (A) | 3 (C) | 4 (C) | 5 (A) | 6 (B) |

1 W-Am / M-Cn
Where's the new packaging machine?
(A) On the loading dock.
(B) A warranty.
(C) Not really.

새 포장용 기계가 어디 있나요?
(A) 하역장에요.
(B) 품질 보증서요.
(C) 꼭 그렇진 않아요.

해설 기계의 위치를 묻는 Where 의문문
(A) 정답: 새 포장용 기계가 어디 있는지 묻는 질문에 구체적인 장소인 하역장(On the loading dock)을 언급하고 있으므로 정답이다.
(B) 질문과 상관없는 오답
(C) 질문과 상관없는 오답

어휘 packaging 포장(재) loading dock 하역장
warranty 품질 보증(서)

2 M-Cn / W-Am
Where's the international arrival gate?
(A) Follow the yellow signs.
(B) At five o'clock.
(C) Close it behind you.

국제선 도착 게이트가 어디죠?
(A) 노란 표지판을 따라가세요.
(B) 5시에요.
(C) 들어간 후에 닫으세요.

해설 게이트의 위치를 묻는 Where 의문문
(A) 정답: 국제선 도착 게이트의 위치를 묻는 질문에 노란 표지판을 따라가라(Follow the yellow signs)며 게이트가 있는 곳을 안내하고 있으므로 정답이다.
(B) 질문과 상관없는 오답
(C) 연상 어휘 오답: 질문의 gate에서 연상 가능한 문을 닫는 상황(Close it behind you)을 이용한 오답이다.

어휘 international 국제적인 arrival 도착

3 M-Cn / M-Au
Where did you park the rental van?
(A) Yes, I'll be there.
(B) It's a nice day for a walk in the park.
(C) Oh, I used my neighbor's truck.

대여한 승합차를 어디에 주차하셨나요?
(A) 네, 그곳에 갈 겁니다.
(B) 공원에서 산책하기 좋은 날이에요.
(C) 아, 제 이웃의 트럭을 이용했어요.

해설 주차한 장소를 묻는 Where 의문문
(A) Yes/No 불가 오답: Where 의문문에는 Yes/No 응답이 불가능하므로 오답이다.
(B) 다의어 오답: 질문의 park은 '주차하다'를 뜻하는 동사이고, 보기의 park은 '공원'을 의미하는 명사이다.

(C) 정답: 대여한 승합차를 어디에 주차했는지 묻는 질문에 이웃의 트럭을 이용했다(I used my neighbor's truck)며 승합차를 대여하지 않았음을 우회적으로 드러내고 있으므로 정답이다.

어휘 rental 대여, 임대 van 승합차

4 M-Au / W-Br
Where can I read about the organization's history?
(A) Whenever you have time.
(B) He seems very organized.
(C) On the company Web site.

그 조직의 역사는 어디에서 읽어볼 수 있나요?
(A) 시간 되실 때 아무 때나요.
(B) 그는 매우 체계적으로 보여요.
(C) 회사 웹사이트에서요.

해설 조직의 역사를 읽어볼 수 있는 곳을 묻는 Where 의문문
(A) 질문과 상관없는 오답
(B) 파생어 오답: 질문의 organization과 파생어 관계인 organized를 이용한 오답이다.
(C) 정답: 조직의 역사를 읽어볼 수 있는 곳을 묻는 질문에 구체적인 확인처(On the company Web site)를 알려 주고 있으므로 정답이다.

어휘 organization 조직, 단체 organized 정돈된, 체계적인

5 M-Cn / W-Am
Where will the new trainee be assigned to work?
(A) We need staff at the Seventh Street store.
(B) Thanks, I'll be there soon.
(C) Just some change.

신입 수습 직원은 어디에 배정되어 일하게 되나요?
(A) 세븐스 스트리트 매장에 직원이 필요합니다.
(B) 감사합니다, 제가 곧 그곳으로 가겠습니다.
(C) 그저 약간의 변화입니다.

해설 신입 수습 직원의 근무 예정지를 묻는 Where 의문문
(A) 정답: 신입 수습 직원이 어디에 배정되어 일하게 되는지 묻는 질문에 직원이 필요한 매장을 구체적으로(We need staff at the Seventh Street store) 언급하고 있으므로 정답이다.
(B) 질문과 상관없는 오답
(C) 질문과 상관없는 오답

어휘 trainee 수습 직원, 교육생 assign 배정하다, 할당하다

6 W-Am / W-Br
Where did you make the dinner reservation?
(A) Tomorrow at twelve-thirty.
(B) Didn't you make it?
(C) For fourteen people.

저녁 식사 어디로 예약했어요?
(A) 내일 12시 30분에요.
(B) 당신이 한 거 아니에요?
(C) 14명이요.

해설 저녁 식사 예약 장소를 묻는 Where 의문문
(A) 질문과 상관없는 오답
(B) 정답: 저녁 식사를 어디로 예약했는지 묻는 질문에 상대방이 예약한 것이 아닌지(Didn't you make it?) 되물으며 예약을 하지 않았음을 우회적으로 표현하고 있으므로 정답이다.
(C) 질문과 상관없는 오답

어휘 make a reservation 예약하다

ETS 유형연습   본책 p.41

1 (B) **2** (B) **3** (C) **4** (C) **5** (C)

1 M-Cn / M-Au
When does the promotional offer begin?
(A) For large orders.
(B) It starts next week.
(C) She's the assistant editor.

판촉 할인이 언제 시작되나요?
(A) 대량 주문이요.
(B) 다음 주에 시작됩니다.
(C) 그녀는 보조 편집자예요.

해설 판촉 할인 시작 시점을 묻는 When 의문문
(A) 질문과 상관없는 오답
(B) 정답: 판촉 행사가 언제 시작되는지 묻는 질문에 다음 주(next week)라는 구체적인 시점으로 대답하고 있으므로 정답이다.
(C) 질문과 상관없는 오답

어휘 promotional 판촉의, 홍보의 offer 할인 assistant 보조(의)

2 W-Br / M-Cn
When can you send me the inventory report?
(A) On the factory floor.
(B) As soon as it's finished.
(C) A new supplier.

재고 관리 보고서는 언제 제게 보내 주실 수 있으세요?
(A) 공장 작업 현장에서요.
(B) 끝마치는 대로요.
(C) 새로운 공급업체요.

해설 보고서를 보내 줄 수 있는 시점을 묻는 When 의문문
(A) 유사 발음 오답: 질문의 inventory와 부분적으로 발음이 유사한 factory를 이용한 오답이다.
(B) 정답: 재고 관리 보고서를 언제 보내 줄 수 있는지 묻는 질문에 끝마치는 대로(As soon as it's finished)라며 대략적인 시점을 언급하고 있으므로 정답이다.
(C) 연상 어휘 오답: 질문의 inventory에서 연상 가능한 supplier를 이용한 오답이다.

어휘 inventory 재고 (목록) floor 작업 현장 as soon as ~하는 대로, ~하자마자 supplier 공급업체, 공급업자

3 W-Am / M-Cn

Who's watering your plants while you're away?
(A) This way, please.
(B) Not until the end of the month.
(C) I asked my neighbor to do it.

당신이 없는 동안 누가 당신 화초에 물을 주나요?
(A) 이쪽으로 오시죠.
(B) 월말이나 되어서요.
(C) 제 이웃에게 해달라고 부탁했어요.

해설 화초에 물을 줄 사람을 묻는 Who 의문문
(A) 유사 발음 오답: 질문의 away와 부분적으로 발음이 유사한 way를 이용한 오답이다.
(B) 질문과 상관없는 오답
(C) 정답: 화초에 물을 줄 사람이 누구인지 묻는 질문에 이웃에게 부탁했다(I asked my neighbor to do it)며 구체적으로 누구에게 부탁했는지 대답하고 있으므로 정답이다.

어휘 water 물을 주다 away 자리를 비운 neighbor 이웃

4 W-Br / M-Cn

Where do you recommend I stay in Shanghai?
(A) I strongly recommend it.
(B) One hundred pounds a night.
(C) I know a great place downtown.

상하이에서 머물 곳으로 어디를 추천하십니까?
(A) 저는 그것을 강력히 추천해요.
(B) 하루에 100파운드입니다.
(C) 시내에 아주 좋은 곳을 알고 있어요.

해설 숙박 추천 장소를 묻는 Where 의문문
(A) 어휘 반복 오답: 질문에 쓰인 recommend를 반복 사용한 오답이다.
(B) 연상 어휘 오답: stay에서 연상 가능한 one hundred pounds a night을 사용한 오답이다.
(C) 정답: 숙박 장소를 추천해달라는 질문에 좋은 곳을 알고 있다(I know a great place downtown)며 장소를 추천하겠다는 의사를 표현하고 있으므로 정답이다.

어휘 recommend 추천하다 strongly 강력하게 downtown 시내에

5 M-Au / M-Cn

Who will be facilitating the company-wide security training?
(A) In the instruction manual.
(B) Let's use real oak paneling.
(C) They've hired an outside consultant.

누가 전 직원 대상 보안 교육을 진행할 예정인가요?
(A) 사용 설명서예요.
(B) 진짜 오크나무 판재를 사용합시다.
(C) 회사에서 외부 컨설턴트를 고용했어요.

해설 보안 교육을 진행할 사람을 묻는 Who 의문문
(A) 연상 어휘 오답: 질문의 training에서 연상 가능한 manual을 이용한 오답이다.
(B) 질문과 상관없는 오답
(C) 정답: 보안 교육을 진행할 사람을 묻는 질문에 회사에서 외부 컨설턴트를 고용한(They've hired an outside consultant) 사실을 언급하여 우회적으로 담당자를 밝히고 있으므로 정답이다.

어휘 facilitate (원활히) 진행시키다, 용이하게 하다
company-wide 회사 전체적인 training 교육, 훈련
instruction manual 사용 설명서 paneling 판재, 벽판
hire 고용하다

ETS 실전문제 본책 p.42

1 (B)	2 (B)	3 (C)	4 (B)	5 (C)	6 (C)
7 (C)	8 (C)	9 (C)	10 (A)	11 (A)	12 (A)
13 (B)	14 (A)	15 (C)	16 (A)	17 (A)	18 (B)
19 (A)	20 (C)	21 (C)	22 (A)	23 (C)	24 (A)
25 (A)					

1 W-Br / W-Am

Who's being transferred to another branch of the company?
(A) Yes, I have.
(B) Roberto and Ayaka.
(C) The furniture delivery should be here soon.

누가 회사의 다른 지점으로 전근되나요?
(A) 네, 제가 해 본 적 있어요.
(B) 로베르토 씨와 아야카 씨요.
(C) 가구 배송이 곧 도착할 겁니다.

해설 다른 지점으로 전근되는 사람을 묻는 Who 의문문
(A) Yes/No 불가 오답: Who 의문문에는 Yes/No 응답이 불가능하므로 오답이다.
(B) 정답: 누가 회사의 다른 지점으로 전근되는지 묻는 질문에 해당되는 사람의 이름(Roberto and Ayaka)으로 대답하고 있으므로 정답이다.
(C) 질문과 상관없는 오답

어휘 transfer 전근시키다 branch 지점, 지사

2 W-Br / M-Au

When is the construction permit going to be approved?
(A) That's a good idea.
(B) In about a week.
(C) At the library.

공사 허가증이 언제 승인될까요?
(A) 좋은 생각입니다.
(B) 약 일주일 후예요.
(C) 도서관에서요.

해설 공사 허가증의 승인 시점을 묻는 When 의문문
(A) 질문과 상관없는 오답

(B) 정답: 공사 허가증이 언제 승인될지 묻는 질문에 대략적인 미래 시점(In about a week)으로 대답하고 있으므로 정답이다.
(C) 질문과 상관없는 오답

어휘 permit 허가증   approve 승인하다   in (시간) ~후에

3   W-Am / M-Au
Where did you say the research lab is?
(A) At six o'clock in the evening.
(B) They needed more space.
(C) It's behind the library.

연구소가 어디라고 하셨죠?
(A) 저녁 6시에요.
(B) 그들은 공간이 더 필요해요.
(C) 도서관 뒤편이요.

해설 **연구소의 위치를 묻는 Where 의문문**
(A) 질문과 상관없는 오답
(B) 인칭 오류 오답: 보기의 They가 가리키는 대상이 질문에 없다.
(C) 정답: 연구소의 위치를 묻는 질문에 구체적인 위치(behind the library)를 알려 주고 있으므로 정답이다.

어휘 research lab 연구소   space 공간

4   W-Br / M-Cn
Who needs to sign off on the final budget proposal?
(A) You can pay later.
(B) Ms. Perez has the list of names.
(C) On the bottom of the last page, please.

최종 예산 제안서에 누가 승인 서명을 해야 하나요?
(A) 나중에 계산하시면 됩니다.
(B) 페레즈 씨가 명단을 갖고 있어요.
(C) 마지막 페이지 하단에 해 주세요.

해설 **최종 승인 서명자를 묻는 Who 의문문**
(A) 연상 어휘 오답: 질문의 budget에서 연상 가능한 pay를 이용한 오답이다.
(B) 정답: 최종 예산 제안서에 승인 서명을 해야 하는 사람을 묻는 질문에 해당 정보를 제공할 수 있는 특정 인물(Ms. Perez)을 언급하고 있으므로 가장 적절한 응답이다.
(C) 연상 어휘 오답: 질문의 sign에서 연상 가능한 서명 위치(On the bottom of the last page)를 이용한 오답이다.

어휘 sign off (~에 서명하여) 승인하다   budget 예산   proposal 제안   bottom 맨 아래

5   M-Cn / W-Br
When did you purchase your plane tickets?
(A) I like mine with cream and sugar.
(B) More than 200 euros.
(C) About two days ago.

비행기 표를 언제 구입하셨나요?
(A) 저는 크림과 설탕을 넣는 것을 좋아합니다.
(B) 200유로가 넘어요.
(C) 약 이틀 전에요.

해설 **비행기 표의 구입 시점을 묻는 When 의문문**
(A) 질문과 상관없는 오답
(B) 질문과 상관없는 오답
(C) 정답: 비행기 표를 언제 구입했는지 묻는 질문에 구체적으로 약 이틀 전(About two days ago)이라고 답하고 있으므로 정답이다.

어휘 purchase 구입하다; 구입(품)   more than ~ 넘게

6   M-Cn / M-Au
Where did these boxes come from?
(A) No, they were delivered already.
(B) What's your refund policy?
(C) I picked them up from the warehouse.

이 상자들은 어디에서 온 건가요?
(A) 아니요, 그것들은 이미 배송되었습니다.
(B) 환불 정책이 어떻게 되나요?
(C) 제가 창고에서 가져왔습니다.

해설 **상자들의 출처를 묻는 Where 의문문**
(A) Yes/No 불가 오답: Where 의문문에는 Yes/No 응답이 불가능하므로 오답이다.
(B) 질문과 상관없는 오답
(C) 정답: 상자들이 어디에서 온 것인지 묻는 질문에 자신이 창고에서 가져왔다(I picked them up from the warehouse)며 출처를 밝히고 있으므로 정답이다.

어휘 refund 환불(액)   policy 정책, 방침   pick A up A를 가져오다, 가져가다   warehouse 창고

7   W-Br / M-Au
Who should I call about replacing the printer ink cartridge?
(A) On Monday mornings.
(B) Yes, they were delivered yesterday.
(C) Mr. Bauer usually takes care of that.

프린터 잉크 카트리지 교체 건에 대해 누구에게 전화해야 하나요?
(A) 월요일 아침마다요.
(B) 네, 어제 배송됐어요.
(C) 보통 바우어 씨가 맡아서 해요.

해설 **카트리지 교체 담당자를 묻는 Who 의문문**
(A) 질문과 상관없는 오답
(B) Yes/No 불가 오답: Who 의문문에는 Yes/No 응답이 불가능하므로 오답이다.
(C) 정답: 프린터 잉크 카트리지 교체 건에 대해 전화해야 할 대상을 묻는 질문에 보통 바우어 씨가 맡아서 한다(Mr. Bauer usually takes care of that)며 연락할 대상을 특정하고 있으므로 정답이다.

어휘 replace 교체하다   deliver 배송하다

8
M-Au / W-Br

When are we meeting to discuss the project update?

(A) On the second floor.
(B) Yes, I updated my e-mail address.
(C) Do you have time on Monday?

프로젝트 최근 상황을 논의하기 위해 언제 만날까요?
(A) 2층에서요.
(B) 네, 저는 이메일 주소를 변경했어요.
(C) 월요일에 시간 되세요?

해설 만날 시점을 묻는 When 의문문
(A) 질문과 상관없는 오답
(B) Yes/No 불가 오답: When 의문문에는 Yes/No 응답이 불가능하므로 오답이다.
(C) 정답: 언제 만날지 묻는 질문에 월요일에 시간이 되는지 (Do you have time on Monday?) 되물으며 일정을 조율하고 있으므로 정답이다.

어휘 discuss 논의하다

9
M-Cn / W-Br

Where can I book a taxi to take me to the airport?

(A) The in-flight meal.
(B) Three hours long.
(C) There's a taxi stand over there.

저를 공항으로 데려다 줄 택시를 어디서 예약할 수 있나요?
(A) 기내식이요.
(B) 3시간짜리입니다.
(C) 저기 저쪽에 택시 승강장이 있어요.

해설 택시 예약 장소를 묻는 Where 의문문
(A) 연상 어휘 오답: 질문의 airport에서 연상 가능한 flight을 이용한 오답이다.
(B) 질문과 상관없는 오답
(C) 정답: 공항으로 데려다 줄 택시를 어디서 예약할 수 있는지 묻는 질문에 택시 승강장이 있는 위치(There's a taxi stand over there)를 알려 주고 있으므로 정답이다.

어휘 in-flight 기내의

10
W-Br / M-Au

Where do I register for the training course?

(A) You can sign up right here.
(B) Yes, of course I have.
(C) A thirty-dollar registration fee.

교육 과정은 어디에서 등록하나요?
(A) 여기서 신청하시면 됩니다.
(B) 네, 물론 그랬죠.
(C) 등록비 30달러요.

해설 교육 과정의 등록 장소를 묻는 Where 의문문
(A) 정답: 교육 과정의 등록 장소를 묻는 질문에 여기서 신청하면 된다(You can sign up right here)고 대답하고 있으므로 정답이다.
(B) Yes/No 불가 오답: Where 의문문에는 Yes/No 응답이 불가능하므로 오답이다.
(C) 파생어 오답: 질문의 register와 파생어 관계인 registration을 이용한 오답이다.

어휘 register for ~에 등록하다   sign up 등록하다, 신청하다   registration fee 등록비

11
W-Am / M-Cn

When is the new office opening?

(A) The schedule was e-mailed yesterday.
(B) Sure—I'll open the door.
(C) An official letter.

새 사무실이 언제 문을 여나요?
(A) 일정표가 어제 이메일로 발송되었습니다.
(B) 네, 제가 문을 열게요.
(C) 공식적인 편지입니다.

해설 새 사무실이 문을 여는 시점을 묻는 When 의문문
(A) 정답: 새 사무실이 언제 문을 여는지 묻는 질문에 일정표가 어제 이메일로 발송되었다(The schedule was e-mailed yesterday)며 해당 정보를 확인할 수 있는 방법을 알려 주고 있으므로 정답이다.
(B) Yes/No 불가 오답: When 의문문에는 Yes/No 응답이 불가능한데, Sure도 일종의 Yes 응답이라고 볼 수 있으므로 오답이다.
(C) 유사 발음 오답: 질문의 office와 부분적으로 발음이 유사한 official을 이용한 오답이다.

어휘 official 공식적인, 정식의

12
M-Cn / W-Br

Who owns the blue car parked out front?

(A) That sounds like it could be Mr. Hardin's.
(B) It looks much higher.
(C) The park has beautiful trees.

입구 쪽에 주차된 파란색 자동차의 주인이 누구죠?
(A) 그건 하딘 씨의 차 같은데요.
(B) 훨씬 더 높아 보여요.
(C) 그 공원에는 아름다운 나무들이 있어요.

해설 자동차 소유주를 묻는 Who 의문문
(A) 정답: 자동차 소유주를 묻는 질문에 하딘 씨 차인 것 같다(it could be Mr. Hardin's)고 구체적인 인물을 언급하고 있으므로 정답이다.
(B) 질문과 상관없는 오답
(C) 다의어 오답: 질문의 park는 '주차하다'를 뜻하는 동사이고, 보기의 park는 '공원'을 의미하는 명사이다.

어휘 own 소유하다   out front 입구 쪽에

13
W-Br / M-Au

Who can help me update this report?

(A) Not really.
(B) Junko can help.
(C) A savings account.

누가 이 보고서 업데이트를 도와줄 수 있나요?
(A) 꼭 그렇지는 않습니다.
(B) 준코 씨가 도와드릴 수 있어요.
(C) 저축 예금 계좌요.

해설 보고서 업데이트를 도와줄 사람을 묻는 Who 의문문
(A) 질문과 상관없는 오답
(B) 정답: 보고서 업데이트를 도와줄 수 있는 사람을 묻는 질문에 준코 씨가 도울 수 있다(Junko can help)고 구체적인 인물을 언급하고 있으므로 정답이다.
(C) 질문과 상관없는 오답

어휘 savings 저축 예금　account 계좌, 계정

14　W-Am / W-Br
When will the sales report be ready to distribute?
(A) It's almost finished.
(B) There's a special discount today.
(C) To the distribution center.

영업보고서 배포 준비가 언제쯤 될까요?
(A) 거의 완성됐어요.
(B) 오늘 특별 할인이 있어요.
(C) 유통센터로요.

해설 영업보고서의 배포 시점을 묻는 When 의문문
(A) 정답: 영업보고서의 배포 시점을 묻는 질문에 거의 완성됐다(It's almost finished)며 곧 배포될 것임을 우회적으로 드러내고 있으므로 정답이다.
(B) 연상 어휘 오답: 질문의 sales에서 연상 가능한 discount를 이용한 오답이다.
(C) 파생어 오답: 질문의 distribute와 파생어 관계인 distribution을 이용한 오답이다.

어휘 sales report 영업보고서　distribute 분배하다, 배포하다, 나눠주다　discount 할인　distribution 유통, 배포

15　M-Cn / W-Am
Where are the copies of today's schedule?
(A) Just a small cup.
(B) Every Monday and Wednesday.
(C) The printer is still broken.

오늘 일정표 인쇄본은 어디에 있나요?
(A) 그냥 작은 컵이요.
(B) 매주 월요일과 수요일예요.
(C) 프린터가 아직도 고장 난 상태예요.

해설 일정표 인쇄본의 위치를 묻는 Where 의문문
(A) 연상 어휘 오답: 질문의 copies를 coffees로 잘못 들었을 경우 연상 가능한 cup을 이용한 오답이다.
(B) 연상 어휘 오답: 질문의 schedule에서 연상 가능한 Every Monday and Wednesday를 이용한 오답이다.
(C) 정답: 일정표 인쇄본의 위치를 묻는 질문에 프린터가 고장(The printer is still broken)이라며 아직 인쇄가 되지 않았음을 우회적으로 나타내고 있으므로 정답이다.

어휘 copy 인쇄본, 복사본

16　M-Cn / W-Br
Who owns the bakery in Merrittville?
(A) George's family just bought it.
(B) Across from Forrest Avenue.
(C) Because it's near my office.

메릿빌에 있는 제과점은 누가 소유하고 있나요?
(A) 조지네 가족이 막 사들였어요.
(B) 포레스트 애비뉴 맞은편요.
(C) 제 사무실과 가깝거든요.

해설 제과점의 소유자를 묻는 Who 의문문
(A) 정답: 제과점의 소유자를 묻는 질문에 조지네 가족이 막 샀다(George's family just bought it)며 소유주를 특정하고 있으므로 정답이다.
(B) 질문과 상관없는 오답
(C) 질문과 상관없는 오답

어휘 across from ~의 맞은편에 있는

17　W-Br / M-Au
When will we add another science writer to our department?
(A) As soon as we find someone who's qualified.
(B) A three-page article with photographs.
(C) Several years of writing experience.

우리 부서에 과학 부문 저술가를 언제 충원할 예정인가요?
(A) 자격을 갖춘 사람을 찾는 대로요.
(B) 사진이 들어간 3쪽짜리 기사요.
(C) 수년간의 집필 경력요.

해설 충원 예정 시점을 묻는 When 의문문
(A) 정답: 과학 부문 저술가의 충원 예정 시점을 묻는 질문에 자격을 갖춘 사람을 찾는 대로(As soon as we find someone who's qualified)라며 대략적인 시점으로 대답하고 있으므로 정답이다.
(B) 연상 어휘 오답: 질문의 writer에서 연상 가능한 article을 이용한 오답이다.
(C) 파생어 오답: 질문의 writer와 파생어 관계인 writing을 이용한 오답이다.

어휘 department 부서　as soon as ~하자마자　qualified 자격을 갖춘　article 기사　experience 경험, 경력

18　M-Cn / W-Am
Where is the next convention going to be held?
(A) It was too crowded as usual.
(B) I'll find out.
(C) Sooner than we expect.

다음 총회는 어디에서 열리죠?
(A) 평소처럼 매우 붐볐어요.
(B) 알아볼게요.
(C) 예상보다 더 일찍이요.

해설 다음 총회가 열릴 장소를 묻는 Where 의문문
(A) 연상 어휘 오답: 질문의 convention에서 연상 가능한 crowded를 이용한 오답이다.

(B) 정답: 다음 총회가 열릴 장소를 묻는 질문에 알아보겠다(I'll find out)며 아직 모르지만 확인하겠다는 의사를 우회적으로 밝히고 있으므로 정답이다.
(C) 질문과 상관없는 오답

어휘 convention 대회, 총회 crowded 붐비는
as usual 평소대로, 여느 때처럼 expect 예상하다

19 W-Br/W-Am
Who's going to train the new social media coordinator?
(A) Did we hire someone recently?
(B) The train station's on Eleventh Street.
(C) Let's schedule a press conference.

누가 신입 소셜 미디어 담당자를 교육할 예정인가요?
(A) 우리가 최근에 누군가를 고용했나요?
(B) 그 기차역은 11번 가에 있어요.
(C) 기자 회견 일정을 잡읍시다.

해설 신입 교육 담당자를 묻는 Who 의문문
(A) 정답: 누가 신입 소셜 미디어 담당자를 교육하는지 묻는 질문에 최근에 누군가를 고용했는지(Did we hire someone recently?) 되물으며 전혀 아는 바가 없다는 뜻을 나타내고 있으므로 정답이다.
(B) 다의어 오답: 질문의 train은 '교육하다'를 뜻하는 동사이고, 보기의 train은 '기차'를 의미하는 명사이다.
(C) 연상 어휘 오답: 평서문의 media에서 연상 가능한 press conference를 이용한 오답이다.

어휘 train 교육하다, 훈련시키다 coordinator (진행) 담당자
recently 최근에 press conference 기자 회견

20 W-Br/M-Cn
When is the Morrison Bridge going to be repaired?
(A) A pair of them.
(B) He was stuck in traffic.
(C) Sometime next spring.

모리슨 다리가 언제 수리되나요?
(A) 한 쌍이요.
(B) 그가 교통 체증에 꼼짝 못했어요.
(C) 내년 봄쯤에요.

해설 다리가 수리되는 시점을 묻는 When 의문문
(A) 유사 발음 오답: 질문의 repair와 부분적으로 발음이 유사한 pair를 이용한 오답이다.
(B) 인칭 오류 오답: 보기의 He가 가리키는 대상이 질문에 없다.
(C) 정답: 다리가 수리되는 시점을 묻는 질문에 대략적인 시점(Sometime next spring)으로 대답하고 있으므로 정답이다.

어휘 a pair of 한 쌍의 be stuck in traffic 교통 체증에 걸리다

21 W-Am/M-Cn
Where should I send these fabric samples?
(A) It's very durable.
(B) Yes, she did send a gift.
(C) To the fashion designer in New York.

이 원단 샘플들을 어디로 보내야 하나요?
(A) 아주 내구성이 좋습니다.
(B) 네, 그녀가 정말 선물을 보냈어요.
(C) 뉴욕에 있는 패션 디자이너에게요.

해설 원단 샘플의 배송지를 묻는 Where 의문문
(A) 질문과 상관없는 오답
(B) Yes/No 불가 오답: Where 의문문에는 Yes/No 응답이 불가능하므로 오답이다.
(C) 정답: 원단 샘플들을 어디로 보내야 하는지 묻는 질문에 뉴욕에 있는 패션 디자이너에게(To the fashion designer in New York)라며 구체적인 수령인을 언급하고 있으므로 정답이다.

어휘 fabric 원단, 직물, 천 durable 내구성이 좋은

22 M-Au/W-Am
Who's organizing the fund-raiser?
(A) Suki volunteered to do it.
(B) Please rearrange the files.
(C) It's on Friday.

모금 행사는 누가 준비하나요?
(A) 수키가 하겠다고 자원했어요.
(B) 파일들을 재배치해 주세요.
(C) 금요일에요.

해설 모금 행사 담당자를 묻는 Who 의문문
(A) 정답: 모금 행사의 준비 담당자를 묻는 질문에 수키가 하겠다고 자원했다(Suki volunteered to do it)며 담당자를 특정하고 있으므로 정답이다.
(B) 연상 어휘 오답: 질문의 organizing을 '정리하다'라는 뜻으로 잘못 이해했을 경우 연상 가능한 rearrange를 이용한 오답이다.
(C) 질문과 상관없는 오답

어휘 organize 준비하다, 조직하다 fund-raiser 모금 행사
volunteer 자원하다 rearrange 재배열하다, 재배치하다

23 M-Cn/M-Au
When can the building inspector approve the electrical work?
(A) Yes, they do good work.
(B) The building's on Marigold Avenue.
(C) Next week at the earliest.

건물 검사관이 언제 전기 공사를 승인할 수 있을까요?
(A) 네, 그들은 일을 잘해요.
(B) 그 건물은 메리골드 애비뉴에 있어요.
(C) 빨라도 다음 주요.

해설 전기 공사의 승인 시점을 묻는 When 의문문
(A) Yes/No 불가 오답: When 의문문에는 Yes/No 응답이 불가능하므로 오답이다.
(B) 어휘 반복 오답: 질문의 building을 반복 이용한 오답이다.
(C) 정답: 전기 공사의 승인 시점을 묻는 질문에 빨라도 다음 주(Next week at the earliest)라며 가능한 예상 시점을 언급하고 있으므로 정답이다.

어휘 inspector 조사관, 검사관 approve 승인하다
electrical 전기의 at the earliest 빨라도, 일러도

24 M-Au / W-Br
Where do you usually take your dry cleaning?
(A) To Pierre's Cleaners.
(B) It's not dry yet.
(C) All the time.

드라이클리닝할 세탁물을 주로 어디로 가져가나요?
(A) 피에르 세탁소로요.
(B) 그것은 아직 마르지 않았어요.
(C) 언제나요.

해설 세탁물을 맡기는 장소를 묻는 Where 의문문
(A) 정답: 세탁물을 맡기는 장소를 묻는 질문에 피에르 세탁소(To Pierre's Cleaners)라며 구체적으로 업체명을 언급하고 있으므로 정답이다.
(B) 단어 반복 오답: 질문의 dry를 반복 이용한 오답이다.
(C) 질문과 상관없는 오답

어휘 dry cleaning 드라이클리닝(할 세탁물) cleaner 세탁소
all the time 언제나, 줄곧

25 W-Am / M-Au
Who should I speak with about getting a temporary security badge?
(A) The security officer downstairs.
(B) I don't have any batteries.
(C) Three more tickets, please.

임시 보안 출입증을 받는 것과 관련해서 어느 분과 얘기해야 하나요?
(A) 아래층에 계신 경비실 직원이요.
(B) 저는 배터리가 전혀 없어요.
(C) 티켓 세 장 더 부탁합니다.

해설 임시 보안 출입증 담당자를 묻는 Who 의문문
(A) 정답: 임시 보안 출입증을 받는 것과 관련해서 누구와 얘기해야 하는지 묻는 질문에 경비실 직원(The security officer)을 언급해 담당자를 알려 주고 있으므로 정답이다.
(B) 질문과 상관없는 오답
(C) 질문과 상관없는 오답

어휘 temporary 임시의, 일시적인 security badge 보안 출입증 downstairs 아래층에

UNIT 04 What · Which / Why / How 의문문

1 What · Which 의문문

본책 p.44

ETS Check-Up
1 (B) **2** (C) **3** (B) **4** (B) **5** (A) **6** (B)

1 W-Br / W-Am
What time are you serving lunch?
(A) Down at the harbor.
(B) From 11 A.M. to 2 P.M.
(C) Yes, I have time.

몇 시에 점심 식사가 가능한가요?
(A) 항구 아래쪽에서요.
(B) 오전 11시부터 오후 2시까지요.
(C) 네, 저는 시간 있어요.

해설 점심 식사 가능 시간을 묻는 What 의문문
(A) 질문과 상관없는 오답
(B) 정답: 식사 가능 시간을 묻는 질문에 오전 11시부터 오후 2시(From 11 A.M. to 2 P.M.)라는 구체적인 시간대로 대답하고 있으므로 정답이다.
(C) Yes/No 불가 오답: What 의문문에는 Yes/No 응답이 불가능하므로 오답이다.

어휘 serve (음식을) 제공하다 harbor 항구

2 M-Au / M-Cn
Which shipment goes to the Bangkok office?
(A) Because I'm waiting for my manager.
(B) No, I don't mind.
(C) The one from Guangzhou.

어느 배송품이 방콕 사무소로 가는 건가요?
(A) 저희 매니저를 기다리고 있어서요.
(B) 아니요, 저는 상관없어요.
(C) 광저우에서 온 것이요.

해설 방콕 사무소로 가는 배송품을 묻는 Which 의문문
(A) 질문과 상관없는 오답
(B) Yes/No 불가 오답: Which 의문문에는 Yes/No 응답이 불가능하므로 오답이다.
(C) 정답: 어느 배송품이 방콕 사무소로 가는지 묻는 질문에 shipment를 대명사 one으로 지칭하여 광저우에서 온 것(The one from Guangzhou)이라고 알려 주고 있으므로 정답이다.

어휘 shipment 배송(품) mind 상관하다, 신경 쓰다, 유념하다

3 M-Au / W-Am
What's the topic of the workshop?
(A) I already bought a pair.
(B) Leadership skills.
(C) A dozen or so.

워크숍 주제가 뭔가요?
(A) 저는 이미 한 쌍 구입했어요.
(B) 리더십 능력입니다.
(C) 12개 정도요.

해설 워크숍 주제를 묻는 What 의문문
(A) 연상 어휘 오답: 질문에 쓰인 workshop의 shop에서 연상 가능한 bought을 이용한 오답이다.
(B) 정답: 워크숍 주제가 무엇인지 묻는 질문에 리더십 능력(Leadership skills)이라고 주제를 알려 주고 있으므로 정답이다.

(C) 질문과 상관없는 오답

어휘 skill 능력, 기술 dozen 12개의 or so (숫자 표현 뒤에 쓰여) ~ 정도

4 W-Am / M-Cn
Which travel case did you buy for your laptop?
(A) For my trip to Malaysia.
(B) **The brown leather one.**
(C) I bought it yesterday.

노트북용으로 어떤 가방을 샀어요?
(A) 말레이시아 여행을 위해서요.
(B) 갈색 가죽 가방요.
(C) 어제 그걸 샀어요.

해설 구매한 가방을 묻는 Which 의문문
(A) 질문과 상관없는 오답
(B) 정답: 구매한 가방의 종류를 묻는 질문에 travel case를 대명사 one으로 지칭하여 갈색 가죽 가방(The brown leather one)이라고 답하고 있으므로 정답이다.
(C) 어휘 반복 오답: 질문의 buy를 과거형인 bought로 반복 이용한 오답이다.

어휘 laptop 노트북 컴퓨터 leather 가죽

5 W-Am / M-Au
Which packages need to be sent?
(A) **All of them.**
(B) Yes, especially the packages.
(C) Express delivery, please.

어느 소포들이 발송되어야 하나요?
(A) 그것들 모두요.
(B) 네, 특히 그 소포들이요.
(C) 빠른 우편으로 해주세요.

해설 발송되어야 할 소포를 묻는 Which 의문문
(A) 정답: 발송되어야 할 소포를 묻는 질문에 그것들 모두(All of them)라고 답하고 있으므로 정답이다.
(B) Yes/No 불가 오답: 의문사 의문문에는 Yes/No로 응답이 불가능하므로 오답이다.
(C) 연상 어휘 오답: 질문의 package에서 연상 가능한 express delivery를 이용한 오답이다.

어휘 package 소포, (포장용) 봉지 especially 특히
express delivery 속달

6 M-Cn / W-Br
Which route do you usually take to work?
(A) I didn't bring it with me.
(B) **I go down Elm Street.**
(C) Not until Wednesday.

보통 출근할 때 어떤 길로 가세요?
(A) 안 가져왔어요.
(B) 엘름 가를 따라가요.
(C) 수요일이나 되어서요.

해설 출근 경로를 묻는 Which 의문문
(A) 연상 어휘 오답: 질문의 take를 '가져가다'라는 뜻으로 잘못 이해했을 경우 연상 가능한 bring을 이용한 오답이다.
(B) 정답: 출근 경로를 묻는 질문에 구체적인 거리명(Elm Street)을 언급하고 있으므로 정답이다.
(C) 질문과 상관없는 오답

어휘 route 길, 노선 usually 대개, 보통 bring 가져오다
not until ~이후에야 비로소

2 Why 의문문

ETS Check-Up   본책 p.45

| 1 (A) | 2 (B) | 3 (B) | 4 (B) | 5 (C) | 6 (A) |

1 W-Br / M-Au
Why is the office supply store closed today?
(A) **It's a holiday.**
(B) Yes, it's close to our office.
(C) In the supply closet.

오늘 사무용품점이 왜 문을 닫았죠?
(A) 오늘은 공휴일이에요.
(B) 네. 우리 사무실과 가까워요.
(C) 비품 창고예요.

해설 사무용품점이 문을 닫은 이유를 묻는 Why 의문문
(A) 정답: 사무용품점이 문을 닫은 이유를 묻는 질문에 공휴일(a holiday)이기 때문이라는 구체적인 이유를 제시하고 있으므로 정답이다.
(B) Yes/No 불가 오답: Why 의문문에는 Yes/No 응답이 불가능하므로 오답이다.
(C) 어휘 반복 오답: 질문의 supply를 반복 이용한 오답이다.

어휘 office supply 사무용품 holiday 공휴일, 휴일
supply closet 비품 창고

2 M-Cn / W-Br
Why were you late for the meeting?
(A) Yes, it's a big office.
(B) **Because traffic was heavy this morning.**
(C) In the fifth-floor conference room.

회의에 왜 늦으셨나요?
(A) 네, 사무실이 크네요.
(B) 아침에 교통 체증이 심했기 때문에요.
(C) 5층에 있는 회의실에서요.

해설 회의에 늦은 이유를 묻는 Why 의문문
(A) Yes/No 불가 오답: Why 의문문에는 Yes/No 응답이 불가능하므로 오답이다.
(B) 정답: 회의에 왜 늦었는지 묻는 질문에 아침에 교통 체증이 심했기 때문(Because traffic was heavy this morning)이라는 이유를 밝히고 있으므로 정답이다.
(C) 연상 어휘 오답: 질문의 meeting에서 연상 가능한 conference room을 이용한 오답이다.

어휘 traffic 교통(량), 차량들 heavy (수량, 정도 등이) 많은, 심한

3 W-Am / M-Cn

Why isn't Doctor Gutierrez working here anymore?
(A) An appointment tomorrow.
(B) He retired at the end of last year.
(C) Please fill out a patient form.

구티에레즈 의사 선생님은 왜 여기에서 더 이상 일하지 않으시나요?
(A) 내일 약속요.
(B) 작년 말에 은퇴하셨어요.
(C) 진료 신청서를 작성하세요.

해설 의사가 더 이상 일하지 않는 이유를 묻는 Why 의문문
(A) 연상 어휘 오답: 질문의 Doctor에서 연상 가능한 appointment를 이용한 오답이다.
(B) 정답: 의사가 일하지 않는 이유를 묻는 질문에 작년 말에 은퇴했다(He retired at the end of last year)는 이유를 알려 주고 있으므로 정답이다.
(C) 연상 어휘 오답: 질문의 Doctor에서 연상 가능한 patient를 이용한 오답이다.

어휘 appointment 약속, 예약   retire 은퇴하다, 퇴직하다
fill out 작성하다, 기입하다   patient (registration) form 진료 신청서

4 W-Am / M-Au

Why do you have to get certified again?
(A) Please register online.
(B) It's required every five years.
(C) A teaching certificate.

왜 다시 자격증을 취득해야 하죠?
(A) 온라인으로 등록해 주세요.
(B) 5년마다 요구되거든요.
(C) 교사 자격증이요.

해설 자격증 재취득 이유를 묻는 Why 의문문
(A) 질문과 상관없는 오답
(B) 정답: 자격증을 재취득해야 하는 이유를 묻는 질문에 Because를 생략하고 5년마다 요구된다(It's required every five years)며 이유를 제시하고 있으므로 정답이다.
(C) 파생어 오답: 질문에 나오는 certified와 파생어 관계인 certificate를 이용한 오답이다.

어휘 get certified 자격증을 취득하다   register 등록하다
require 필요로 하다   certificate 증명서, 자격증

5 M-Cn / W-Am

Why did Ms. Khan bring an assistant to the trade fair?
(A) I traded it in.
(B) No, not this time.
(C) To help with a demonstration.

칸 씨는 왜 무역박람회에 비서를 데리고 왔나요?
(A) 제가 거래했어요.
(B) 아니요, 이번엔 아닙니다.
(C) 시연을 돕게 하려고요.

해설 비서를 동반한 이유를 묻는 Why 의문문
(A) 다의어 오답: 질문의 trade는 '무역'이라는 뜻의 명사이고, 보기의 traded는 '거래하다'라는 뜻의 동사이다.
(B) Yes/No 불가 오답: Why 의문문에는 Yes/No 응답이 불가능하므로 오답이다.
(C) 정답: 무역박람회에 비서를 동반한 이유를 묻는 질문에 시연을 돕게 하기 위해(To help with a demonstration)라며 구체적인 목적을 밝히고 있으므로 정답이다.

어휘 trade fair 무역박람회   trade in ~을 거래하다, 사고팔다
demonstration 설명, 시연

6 M-Cn / W-Br

Why don't we start interviewing applicants now?
(A) Yes, we have a lot to do.
(B) A long-term contract.
(C) It's supposed to rain the day of the job fair.

지금 지원자들을 면접 보기 시작하는 게 어때요?
(A) 네, 우리가 할 게 많아요.
(B) 장기 계약이요.
(C) 취업 박람회가 있는 날 비가 내릴 예정입니다.

해설 제안·권유의 Why 의문문
(A) 정답: 지금 지원자들을 면접 보기 시작하는 게 어떤지 제안하는 질문에 네(Yes)라고 대답한 뒤, 할 게 많다(we have a lot to do)며 동의를 표하고 있으므로 정답이다.
(B) 연상 어휘 오답: 질문의 applicants에서 연상 가능한 contract를 이용한 오답이다.
(C) 연상 어휘 오답: 질문의 applicants에서 연상 가능한 job fair를 이용한 오답이다.

어휘 Why don't we ~? ~하는 게 어때요?   applicant 지원자, 신청자   long-term 장기적인   contract 계약(서)
be supposed to do ~할 예정이다, ~하기로 되어 있다
job fair 취업 박람회

3 How 의문문

본책 p.46

ETS Check-Up

| 1 (B) | 2 (B) | 3 (A) | 4 (A) | 5 (B) | 6 (C) |

1 M-Cn / W-Br

How much is your gym membership fee?
(A) That's good to know.
(B) It's 65 dollars a month.
(C) I've never met them before.

당신의 헬스클럽 회원권은 얼마인가요?
(A) 알게 되어 다행이네요.
(B) 한 달에 65달러예요.
(C) 전에 그들을 만나본 적이 없어요.

해설 헬스클럽 회원권 가격을 묻는 How 의문문
(A) 질문과 상관없는 오답
(B) 정답: 헬스클럽 회원권의 가격을 묻는 질문에 구체적인 금액(65 dollars a month)을 알려 주고 있으므로 정답이다.

(C) 인칭 오류 오답: 보기의 them이 가리키는 대상이 질문에 없다.

2 W-Am / W-Br
How many copies of the document do you need?
(A) That really wasn't necessary.
(B) Twelve should be enough.
(C) No coffee for me, thanks.

그 서류가 몇 부나 필요하나요?
(A) 그건 정말 필요 없었어요.
(B) 12부면 충분하겠어요.
(C) 저는 커피 안 주셔도 됩니다, 고마워요.

해설 필요한 서류의 수량을 묻는 How 의문문
(A) 연상 어휘 오답: 질문의 need에서 연상 가능한 necessary를 이용한 오답이다.
(B) 정답: 서류가 몇 부나 필요한지 묻는 질문에 12부(Twelve)라는 구체적인 숫자를 제시하고 있으므로 정답이다.
(C) 유사 발음 오답: 질문의 copies와 발음이 비슷한 coffee를 이용한 오답이다.

어휘 copy (책·신문 등) 한 부   document 서류
necessary 필요한

3 W-Am / M-Cn
How's your sales pitch going?
(A) Very well, thank you.
(B) A discount on T-shirts.
(C) That's a fair estimate.

영업 발표는 어떻게 진행되고 있나요?
(A) 아주 잘되고 있어요, 감사합니다.
(B) 티셔츠에 대한 할인이요.
(C) 적당한 견적이네요.

해설 진행 상황을 묻는 How 의문문
(A) 정답: 영업 발표가 어떻게 진행되고 있는지 묻는 질문에 아주 잘되고 있다는 말과 함께 감사의 인사를 덧붙이고 (Very well, thank you) 있으므로 정답이다.
(B) 연상 어휘 오답: 질문의 sales에서 연상 가능한 discount를 이용한 오답이다.
(C) 질문과 상관없는 오답

어휘 sales pitch (고객을 대상으로 판매 권유를 위한) 영업 발표
fair 적당한, 공정한, 타당한   estimate 견적(서)

4 W-Br / M-Au
How do I sign up to attend the workshop?
(A) By responding to the invitation.
(B) About an hour ago.
(C) I prefer that method, too.

워크숍 참가 신청은 어떻게 하나요?
(A) 초대장에 응답하시면 됩니다.
(B) 약 1시간 전에요.
(C) 저도 그 방법을 선호합니다.

해설 워크숍 참가 신청 방법을 묻는 How 의문문
(A) 정답: 워크숍 참가 신청을 어떻게 하는지 묻는 질문에 방법을 나타내는 전치사 by를 이용해 초대장에 응답하라고 (By responding to the invitation) 알려 주고 있으므로 정답이다.
(B) 질문과 상관없는 오답
(C) 질문과 상관없는 오답

어휘 sign up 신청하다, 등록하다   attend 참석하다
respond to ~에 답장하다, ~에 반응하다   invitation 초대(장)   about 약, 대략   prefer 선호하다   method 방법

5 M-Au / W-Br
How often does the number two bus stop here?
(A) She's my neighbor.
(B) Every fifteen minutes.
(C) Twenty-Second Street.

2번 버스가 이곳에 얼마나 자주 정차하나요?
(A) 그녀는 제 이웃입니다.
(B) 15분마다 한 번씩이요.
(C) 22번 가요.

해설 버스가 정차하는 빈도를 묻는 How 의문문
(A) 인칭 오류 오답: 보기의 She가 가리키는 대상이 질문에 없다.
(B) 정답: 2번 버스가 얼마나 자주 정차하는지 묻는 질문에 15분마다 한 번씩(Every fifteen minutes)이라며 구체적인 빈도를 알려 주고 있으므로 정답이다.
(C) 연상 작용 오답: 질문의 bus stop에서 연상 가능한 Twenty-Second Street를 이용한 오답이다.

어휘 every ~마다 (한 번씩)

6 M-Au / M-Cn
How can we reduce our energy costs?
(A) Only twenty percent.
(B) On the hard drive.
(C) By installing better windows.

어떻게 하면 연료비를 줄일 수 있을까요?
(A) 20퍼센트만요.
(B) 하드 드라이브에요.
(C) 더 좋은 창문을 설치해서요.

해설 연료비 절감 방법을 묻는 How 의문문
(A) 질문과 상관없는 오답
(B) 질문과 상관없는 오답
(C) 정답: 연료비를 줄이는 방법을 묻는 질문에 더 좋은 창문을 설치해서(By installing better windows)라는 구체적인 방안을 제시했으므로 정답이다.

어휘 reduce 줄이다   cost 비용   install 설치하다

ETS 유형연습   본책 p.47

1 (B)   **2** (C)   **3** (A)   **4** (B)   **5** (A)

1 M-Cn / M-Au
What did Ms. Newton have to say about our progress?
(A) She stayed on Wednesday.
(B) Mostly positive things.
(C) Yes, she did.

뉴턴 씨는 우리의 진척 상황에 대해 어떤 말씀을 하셨나요?
(A) 그녀는 수요일에 머물렀어요.
(B) 대체로 긍정적인 것들이었어요.
(C) 네, 그녀가 했어요.

해설 진척 상황에 대한 의견을 묻는 What 의문문
(A) 유사 발음 오답: 질문의 say와 발음이 비슷한 stay를 이용한 오답이다.
(B) 정답: 뉴턴 씨의 의견을 묻는 질문에 대체로 긍정적인 것들이었다(Mostly positive things)고 답변하고 있으므로 정답이다.
(C) Yes/No 불가 오답: What 의문문에는 Yes/No 응답이 불가능하므로 오답이다.

어휘 progress 진척 (상황), 진전 positive 긍정적인

2 W-Am / M-Cn
Which route should I take to the stadium?
(A) Twenty dollars each.
(B) An annual event.
(C) Take Highway 23.

경기장까지 어느 경로를 이용해야 하나요?
(A) 각각 20달러입니다.
(B) 연례 행사요.
(C) 23번 고속도로를 이용하세요.

해설 경기장으로 가는 경로를 묻는 Which 의문문
(A) 질문과 상관없는 오답
(B) 질문과 상관없는 오답
(C) 정답: 경기장으로 가는 경로를 묻는 질문에 23번 고속도로를 이용하라(Take Highway 23)며 특정 경로를 추천하고 있으므로 정답이다.

어휘 route 경로, 노선 take (도로, 교통편 등을) 이용하다, 타다 annual 연례적인, 해마다의

3 W-Am / W-Br
How soon can I make an appointment with Doctor Feinstein?
(A) She's available on Thursday.
(B) Just the first part.
(C) It was at 9:30.

파인스타인 박사님과의 예약을 빠르면 언제 잡을 수 있나요?
(A) 그녀는 목요일에 시간이 됩니다.
(B) 첫 부분만요.
(C) 9시 30분이었어요.

해설 예약 가능한 시간을 묻는 How 의문문
(A) 정답: 빠르면 언제 예약을 잡을 수 있는지 묻는 질문에 구체적인 시점(on Thursday)으로 답변하고 있으므로 정답이다.
(B) 질문과 상관없는 오답
(C) 시제 오류 오답: 미래에 가능한 시간을 묻는 질문에 과거로 답하는 것은 어색하다.

어휘 available 시간이 있는, 이용 가능한

4 W-Am / M-Cn
Why can't I find the market intelligence data?
(A) Just past the exit.
(B) Because it's not available yet.
(C) No, I think they'll increase.

왜 시장 정보 데이터를 찾을 수 없는 거죠?
(A) 출구를 조금 지나서요.
(B) 아직 이용할 수 없기 때문입니다.
(C) 아니요, 저는 그것들이 증가할 거라고 생각해요.

해설 시장 정보 자료를 찾을 수 없는 이유를 묻는 Why 의문문
(A) 연상 어휘 오답: 질문의 find에서 연상 가능한 Just past the exit을 이용한 오답이다.
(B) 정답: 시장 정보 자료를 왜 찾을 수 없는지 묻는 질문에 아직 이용할 수 없기 때문(Because it's not available yet)이라는 이유를 밝히고 있으므로 정답이다.
(C) Yes/No 불가 오답: Why 의문문에는 Yes/No 응답이 불가능하므로 오답이다.

어휘 market intelligence data 시장 정보 자료 increase 오르다, 증가하다

5 W-Br / M-Cn
What was covered at the workshop this morning?
(A) I'll lend you my notes.
(B) It's expected to finish early.
(C) There's seating for about 25.

오늘 오전 워크숍에서 어떤 것이 다루어졌나요?
(A) 제가 필기한 것을 빌려드릴게요.
(B) 일찍 끝날 것으로 예상돼요.
(C) 약 25명 분의 좌석이 있어요.

해설 오늘 오전 워크숍의 주제를 묻는 What 의문문
(A) 정답: 오늘 오전 워크숍의 주제를 묻는 질문에 자신이 필기한 것을 빌려주겠다(I'll lend you my notes)며 내용을 공유하겠다고 우회적으로 제안하고 있으므로 정답이다.
(B) 질문과 상관없는 오답
(C) 연상 어휘 오답: 질문의 workshop에서 연상 가능한 seating을 이용한 오답이다.

어휘 cover 다루다, 포함시키다 lend 빌려주다 notes 필기, 기록 expect 기대하다, 예상하다 seating 좌석, 자리

ETS 실전문제

본책 p.48

1 (C)	2 (B)	3 (C)	4 (A)	5 (A)	6 (B)
7 (B)	8 (A)	9 (A)	10 (A)	11 (C)	12 (B)
13 (A)	14 (C)	15 (C)	16 (C)	17 (A)	18 (A)
19 (B)	20 (A)	21 (C)	22 (B)	23 (A)	24 (A)
25 (B)					

1 M-Cn / M-Au
What kind of company does Mr. Perez manage?
(A) For twenty years.
(B) I can manage that.
(C) An advertising agency.

페레즈 씨는 어떤 종류의 회사를 경영하나요?
(A) 20년 동안이요.
(B) 제가 할 수 있어요.
(C) 광고 대행사요.

해설 페레즈 씨의 회사 종류를 묻는 What 의문문
(A) 질문과 상관없는 오답
(B) 어휘 반복 오답: 질문의 manage를 반복 이용한 오답이다.
(C) 정답: 페레즈 씨가 어떤 회사를 경영하고 있는지 묻는 질문에 광고 대행사(An advertising agency)라고 구체적으로 대답하고 있으므로 정답이다.

어휘 manage 관리하다, 경영하다 advertising agency 광고 대행사

2 M-Au / W-Br
What are the dimensions of the apartment on Maple Road?
(A) It's rather far from the city center.
(B) I don't remember the exact measurements.
(C) The real estate agent showed it to us.

메이플 가에 있는 아파트 면적이 어떻게 되나요?
(A) 시내 중심가에서 다소 멀어요.
(B) 정확한 크기는 기억이 안 나네요.
(C) 부동산 중개인이 우리에게 보여 줬어요.

해설 메이플 가에 있는 아파트 면적을 묻는 What 의문문
(A) 질문과 상관없는 오답
(B) 정답: 메이플 가에 있는 아파트 면적이 어떻게 되느냐는 질문에 정확한 크기가 잘 기억나지 않는다(I don't remember the exact measurements)고 대답하고 있으므로 정답이다.
(C) 연상 어휘 오답: 질문의 apartment에서 연상 가능한 real estate agent를 이용한 오답이다.

어휘 dimensions 넓이, 면적   measurements 크기, 면적
real estate agent 부동산 중개업자

3 W-Am / M-Cn
Why is the company moving to a new building?
(A) Next week on Friday.
(B) I have a job interview.
(C) Because the landlord is selling the property.

회사가 왜 새 건물로 이전하는 건가요?
(A) 다음 주 금요일에요.
(B) 제가 구직 면접이 있습니다.
(C) 건물주가 건물을 매각해서요.

해설 회사가 이전하는 이유를 묻는 Why 의문문
(A) 질문과 상관없는 오답
(B) 연상 어휘 오답: 질문의 company에서 연상 가능한 job interview를 이용한 오답이다.
(C) 정답: 회사가 왜 새 건물로 이전하는지 묻는 질문에 건물주가 건물을 매각한다(the landlord is selling the property)는 구체적인 이유를 제시하고 있으므로 정답이다.

어휘 landlord 건물주, 집주인   property 건물, 부동산, 자산

4 M-Cn / W-Br
How's the hiring initiative going so far?
(A) Everything's going smoothly.
(B) The bank is too far from here.
(C) I've read the initial data.

채용 계획은 지금까지 어떻게 되어 가고 있나요?
(A) 모든 일이 순조롭게 진행되고 있어요.
(B) 그 은행은 여기서 너무 멀어요.
(C) 제가 초기 데이터를 읽어 봤어요.

해설 채용 계획의 진행 상황을 묻는 How 의문문
(A) 정답: 채용 계획이 어떻게 되어 가고 있는지 묻는 질문에 모든 일이 순조롭게 진행되고 있다(Everything's going smoothly)며 진행 상황을 설명하고 있으므로 정답이다.
(B) 어휘 반복 오답: 질문의 far를 반복 이용한 오답이다.
(C) 유사 발음 오답: 질문의 initiative와 일부 발음이 유사한 initial을 이용한 오답이다.

어휘 hiring 고용   initiative 계획   so far 지금까지
go smoothly 순조롭게 진행되다   initial 초기의, 처음의

5 M-Cn / M-Au
What answer did you get from the technology department?
(A) Nothing so far.
(B) Did you buy a computer?
(C) Sometimes it does.

기술부서에서 어떤 답을 들었나요?
(A) 아직까지는 답이 없네요.
(B) 컴퓨터 사셨어요?
(C) 가끔 그래요.

해설 기술부서에서 들은 대답의 내용을 묻는 What 의문문
(A) 정답: 기술부서에서 들은 대답의 내용을 묻는 질문에 아직까지 답이 없다(Nothing so far)며 알려 줄 내용이 없음을 우회적으로 드러내고 있으므로 정답이다.
(B) 연상 어휘 오답: 질문의 technology department에서 연상 가능한 computer를 이용한 오답이다.
(C) 질문과 상관없는 오답

어휘 technology 기술

6 W-Am / M-Au
Which stores are open late tonight?
(A) They were delayed by the storm.
(B) None of them except the supermarket.
(C) We store them in plastic containers.

어느 상점들이 오늘 밤 늦게까지 문을 여나요?
(A) 그것들은 폭풍 때문에 지연되었어요.
(B) 그 슈퍼마켓 말고는 없어요.
(C) 저희는 플라스틱 용기에 그것들을 저장해요.

해설 늦게까지 운영하는 상점을 묻는 Which 의문문
(A) 연상 어휘 오답: 의미상 연결이 가능한 두 단어(late 늦게/delayed 지연된)를 이용한 오답이다.
(B) 정답: 어느 상점들이 늦게까지 문을 여는지 묻는 질문에 그 슈퍼마켓을 제외하고는 없다(None of them except the supermarket)고 알려 주고 있으므로 정답이다.
(C) 다의어 오답: 질문의 store는 '상점'을 의미하는 명사이고, 보기의 store는 '저장하다'를 의미하는 동사이다.

어휘 store 상점; 저장하다   delay 지연시키다   except ~을 제외하고   container 그릇, 용기

7 M-Cn / W-Br
Why is our inventory low for that product?
(A) Can you hang the picture higher on the wall?
(B) There are more in the boxes in the storage room.
(C) The corner of Taylor Street.

그 제품 재고가 왜 부족한거죠?
(A) 그 그림을 벽에 더 높게 걸어 주시겠어요?
(B) 창고에 있는 상자에 더 있습니다.
(C) 테일러 가 모퉁이에요.

해설 재고 수준이 낮은 이유를 묻는 Why 의문문
(A) 연상 어휘 오답: 질문의 low에서 연상 가능한 higher를 이용한 오답이다.
(B) 정답: 특정 제품의 재고 수준이 왜 낮은지 묻는 질문에 보관실에 있는 상자에 더 많이 있다(There are more in the boxes in the storage room)고 설명해주고 있으므로 정답이다.
(C) 질문과 상관없는 오답

어휘 inventory 재고 (목록)   hang 걸다, 매달다   storage room 창고, 보관실

8 M-Au / M-Cn
How do you like the new conference room furniture?
(A) It's exactly what we needed.
(B) The conference was very interesting.
(C) Did you try the other one?

새로운 회의실 가구는 어때요?
(A) 딱 필요했던 거예요.
(B) 회의는 매우 흥미로웠어요.
(C) 다른 것 해보셨어요?

해설 새 회의실 가구에 대한 의견을 묻는 How 의문문
(A) 정답: 새로운 회의실 가구에 대한 의견을 묻는 질문에 딱 필요했던 것(It's exactly what we needed)이라며 우회적으로 긍정적인 의견을 표현하고 있으므로 정답이다.
(B) 단어 반복 오답: 질문의 conference를 반복 이용한 오답이다.
(C) 질문과 상관없는 오답

어휘 furniture 가구   exactly 정확히

9 W-Am / M-Cn
Which department is calling this meeting?
(A) The finance department.
(B) No, I don't think so.
(C) An apartment on the third floor.

어느 부서가 이 회의를 소집하는 건가요?
(A) 재무팀이요.
(B) 아니요, 저는 그렇게 생각하지 않아요.
(C) 3층에 위치한 아파트요.

해설 회의를 소집하는 부서를 묻는 Which 의문문
(A) 정답: 어느 부서가 회의를 소집하는지 묻는 질문에 재무팀(The finance department)이라는 특정 부서를 언급하고 있으므로 정답이다.
(B) Yes/No 불가 오답: Which 의문문에는 Yes/No 응답이 불가능하므로 오답이다.
(C) 유사 발음 오답: 질문의 department와 일부 발음이 유사한 apartment를 이용한 오답이다.

어휘 finance 재무, 재정

10 M-Cn / W-Am
Which factory is being turned into apartments?
(A) The one on Greene Street.
(B) No, I didn't see the memo.
(C) Do you need anything from the supply room?

어느 공장이 아파트로 탈바꿈하게 되는 건가요?
(A) 그린 가에 있는 것이요.
(B) 아니요, 저는 그 메모를 보지 못했어요.
(C) 비품 보관실에서 필요하신 게 있나요?

해설 어느 공장이 아파트로 바뀌는지 묻는 Which 의문문
(A) 정답: 어느 공장이 아파트로 탈바꿈하게 되는지 묻는 질문에 factory를 대명사 one으로 지칭해 그린 가에 있는 것(The one on Greene Street)이라고 특정 대상을 밝히고 있으므로 정답이다.
(B) Yes/No 불가 오답: Which 의문문에는 Yes/No 응답이 불가능하므로 오답이다.
(C) 연상 어휘 오답: 질문의 factory에서 연상 가능한 supply를 이용한 오답이다.

어휘 turn A into B A를 B로 탈바꿈시키다   supply room 비품 보관실

11 W-Br / W-Am

What did you think of Lily's suggestions for the package design?
(A) Only recycled materials.
(B) Yes, I thought so.
(C) They were helpful.

릴리의 포장 디자인 제안은 어떠셨어요?
(A) 재활용 소재만요.
(B) 네, 그렇게 생각했어요.
(C) 도움이 되었어요.

해설 디자인 제안에 대한 의견을 묻는 What 의문문
(A) 연상 어휘 오답: 질문의 package design에서 연상 가능한 소재(recycled materials)를 이용한 오답이다.
(B) Yes/No 불가 오답: What 의문문에는 Yes/No 응답이 불가능하므로 오답이다.
(C) 정답: 릴리의 포장 디자인 제안에 대한 의견을 묻는 질문에 도움이 되었다(They were helpful)며 구체적인 의견을 밝히고 있으므로 정답이다.

어휘 suggestion 제안 package 포장 recycled 재활용된 material 소재, 재료 helpful 도움이 되는, 유용한

12 W-Am / M-Cn

How many workstations have lost Internet access?
(A) What's your password?
(B) Seven of them.
(C) In a few minutes.

몇 대의 컴퓨터에서 인터넷 연결이 끊겼나요?
(A) 패스워드가 뭔가요?
(B) 7대요.
(C) 몇 분 후에요.

해설 인터넷이 끊긴 컴퓨터 수를 묻는 How 의문문
(A) 연상 어휘 오답: 질문의 Internet access에서 연상 가능한 password를 이용한 오답이다.
(B) 정답: 인터넷 연결이 끊긴 컴퓨터의 수를 묻는 질문에 구체적인 수량(Seven of them)을 알려 주고 있으므로 정답이다.
(C) 질문과 상관없는 오답

어휘 workstation 다기능 컴퓨터, 단말기 lose 잃다 access 접속, 접근 password 비밀번호, 패스워드

13 M-Cn / W-Br

Why are they raising the toll prices on the Hampton Highway?
(A) To pay for road construction costs.
(B) It's near exit ten.
(C) Up to 75 kilometers an hour.

그들은 왜 햄튼 하이웨이 통행료를 올리는 거죠?
(A) 도로 공사 비용을 지불하려고요.
(B) 10번 출구 근처요.
(C) 시속 75km까지요.

해설 통행료 인상 이유를 묻는 Why 의문문
(A) 정답: 햄튼 하이웨이의 통행료가 인상되는 이유를 묻는 질문에 도로 공사 비용을 지불하기 위해서(To pay for road construction costs)라는 구체적인 목적을 제시하고 있으므로 정답이다.
(B) 연상 어휘 오답: 질문의 the Hampton Highway에서 연상 가능한 exit을 이용한 오답이다.
(C) 연상 어휘 오답: 질문의 the Hampton Highway에서 연상 가능한 제한 속도(Up to 75 kilometers an hour)를 언급한 오답이다.

어휘 raise 올리다 toll 요금, 통행료 construction 공사 cost 비용 up to ~까지

14 M-Au / W-Br

Which application should I fill out to apply for a job in the warehouse?
(A) The contract was for six months.
(B) The first floor staff room.
(C) The one that's in the green box.

창고 업무에 지원하려면 어떤 지원서를 작성해야 합니까?
(A) 계약은 6개월간이었어요.
(B) 1층 직원실요.
(C) 녹색 상자에 있는 거요.

해설 작성할 지원서의 종류를 묻는 Which 의문문
(A) 연상 어휘 오답: 질문의 apply for a job에서 연상 가능한 contract를 이용한 오답이다.
(B) 연상 어휘 오답: 질문의 warehouse에서 연상 가능한 staff room을 이용한 오답이다.
(C) 정답: 창고 업무에 지원하려면 작성해야 하는 지원서의 종류를 묻는 질문에 application을 대명사 one으로 지칭하여 녹색 상자에 있는 것(The one that's in the green box)이라고 알려 주고 있으므로 정답이다.

어휘 application 지원, 지원서 apply for ~에 지원하다 warehouse 창고

15 M-Cn / W-Am

Why weren't you at the training session this morning?
(A) No, maybe next season.
(B) Show your identification card.
(C) My supervisor said it was optional.

왜 오늘 오전에 교육에 참가하지 않았죠?
(A) 아니요, 아마도 다음 시즌이요.
(B) 신분증을 제시해 주세요.
(C) 제 상사가 그건 선택이라고 말했거든요.

해설 오전 교육 불참 이유를 묻는 Why 의문문
(A) Yes/No 불가 오답: Why 의문문에는 Yes/No 응답이 불가능하므로 오답이다.
(B) 질문과 상관없는 오답
(C) 정답: 오전 교육 불참 이유를 묻는 질문에 Because를 생략하고 필수가 아닌 선택이라(it was optional) 교육에 참가하지 않았다는 이유를 밝히고 있으므로 정답이다.

어휘 training session 교육 과정   identification card 신분증
supervisor 감독관, 상사   optional 선택적인

16   M-Cn / M-Au
How can I request more art supplies for the workshop I'm leading?
(A) Yes, in the filing cabinet.
(B) Usually every workshop.
(C) Our budget is limited this year.

제가 진행하는 워크숍에 필요한 미술용품을 어떻게 더 요청할 수 있나요?
(A) 네, 파일 캐비닛 안에요.
(B) 일반적으로 모든 워크숍이요.
(C) 올해 우리 예산이 한정되어 있어요.

해설 미술용품 추가 주문 방법을 묻는 How 의문문
(A) Yes/No 불가 오답: How 의문문에는 Yes/No 응답이 불가능하므로 오답이다.
(B) 단어 반복 오답: 질문의 workshop을 반복 이용한 오답이다.
(C) 정답: 워크숍에 필요한 미술용품을 어떻게 더 요청할 수 있는지 묻는 질문에 올해 예산이 한정되어 있다(Our budget is limited this year)며 추가 주문은 어렵다는 사실을 우회적으로 드러내고 있음으로 정답이다.

어휘 request 요청하다   supplies 용품, 물품   lead 진행하다, 이끌다   budget 예산   limited 제한적인

17   W-Br / W-Am
What did you decide about the marketing plan?
(A) We've hired a consultant to review it.
(B) It just opened for business.
(C) I'm definitely planning on it.

마케팅 계획에 대해 어떤 결정을 하셨나요?
(A) 그것을 검토할 자문위원을 채용했어요.
(B) 그 업체는 막 영업을 시작했어요.
(C) 저는 꼭 그것을 할 계획입니다.

해설 마케팅 계획에 대한 결정 사항을 묻는 What 의문문
(A) 정답: 마케팅 계획에 대한 결정 사항을 묻는 질문에 그것을 검토할 자문위원을 채용했다(We've hired a consultant to review it)고 구체적으로 답했으므로 정답이다.
(B) 연상 어휘 오답: marketing plan에서 연상 가능한 business를 이용한 오답이다.
(C) 다의어 오답: 질문에 나오는 plan은 '계획'을 의미하는 명사이고, 보기의 plan은 '계획하다'를 의미하는 동사이다.

어휘 hire 채용하다   consultant 자문위원   definitely 분명히

18   M-Cn / W-Am
Which parking area is closest to the client's office?
(A) I usually take public transportation.
(B) Maybe around this time tomorrow.
(C) Wow—what a great view!

어느 주차장이 그 고객의 사무실에서 가장 가까운가요?
(A) 저는 보통 대중교통을 이용해요.
(B) 아마도 내일 이 시간쯤이요.
(C) 와, 전망이 훌륭하네요!

해설 가까운 주차장을 묻는 Which 의문문
(A) 정답: 고객의 사무실에서 가장 가까운 주차장을 묻는 질문에 자신은 보통 대중교통을 이용한다(I usually take public transportation)며 모른다는 것을 우회적으로 드러내고 있으므로 정답이다.
(B) 질문과 상관없는 오답
(C) 연상 어휘 오답: 질문의 client's office에서 연상 가능한 사무실 전망에 대한 견해(what a great view)를 언급한 오답이다.

어휘 client 고객   public transportation 대중교통
view 전망

19   W-Br / W-Am
Why don't we all meet in the lobby in five minutes?
(A) She made some excellent points during the meeting.
(B) Matthew promised he'd join a conference call.
(C) That's such an unusual hobby.

우리 모두 5분 후에 로비에서 만나는 게 어때요?
(A) 그녀가 회의 시간에 몇 가지 훌륭한 의견을 냈어요.
(B) 매튜 씨께서 전화 회의에 참여하겠다고 약속하셨어요.
(C) 아주 흔치 않은 취미네요.

해설 제안·권유의 의문문
(A) 인칭 오류 오답: 보기의 She가 가리키는 대상이 질문에 없다.
(B) 정답: 5분 후에 로비에서 만나는 게 어떤지 제안하는 질문에 매튜 씨가 전화 회의에 참여하기로 했다(Matthew promised he'd join a conference call)며 우회적으로 불가능하다는 응답을 하고 있으므로 정답이다.
(C) 유사 발음 오답: 질문의 lobby와 일부 발음이 유사한 hobby를 이용한 오답이다.

어휘 in (시간) ~ 후에   make a point 주장하다, 지적하다   promise 약속하다   conference call 전화 회의   unusual 흔치 않은, 이례적인

20   M-Cn / W-Am
How long is the taxi ride to the train station?
(A) It depends on the traffic.
(B) Around fifty dollars.
(C) The first stop in town.

기차역까지 택시로 얼마나 걸리죠?
(A) 교통 상황에 따라 달라요.
(B) 50달러 정도요.
(C) 시내 첫 번째 정류장요.

해설 기차역까지의 소요 시간을 묻는 How 의문문
(A) 정답: 택시로 기차역까지 가는 데 걸리는 시간을 묻는 질문에 교통 상황에 따라 다르다(It depends on the

traffic)며 정확히 알기 어렵다는 것을 우회적으로 표현하고 있으므로 정답이다.
(B) 질문과 상관없는 오답
(C) 연상 어휘 오답: 질문의 train station에서 연상 가능한 stop(정류장)을 이용한 오답이다.

어휘 depend on ~에 달려 있다

21 M-Au / W-Br
What's on the agenda for the staff meeting?
(A) Next to the lobby.
(B) Attendance was good.
(C) It hasn't been finalized.

직원회의의 안건이 뭐죠?
(A) 로비 옆에서요.
(B) 출석률이 좋았어요.
(C) 확정되지 않았어요.

해설 직원회의 안건을 묻는 What 의문문
(A) 질문과 상관없는 오답
(B) 연상 어휘 오답: 질문의 staff meeting에서 연상할 수 있는 attendance를 이용한 오답이다.
(C) 정답: 직원회의 안건을 묻는 질문에 아직 확정되지 않았다(It hasn't been finalized)며 관련 상황을 언급하고 있으므로 정답이다.

어휘 agenda 안건 staff meeting 직원회의 attendance 출석률 finalize 확정하다, 마무리짓다

22 W-Am / M-Cn
Which route are we going to take to work today?
(A) In the large conference room.
(B) There's a lot of traffic on the highway.
(C) By the end of the day.

오늘은 어떤 경로로 출근할 예정인가요?
(A) 대회의실에서요.
(B) 고속도로에 차량이 많습니다.
(C) 오늘 일과 종료 시점까지요.

해설 출근 경로를 묻는 Which 의문문
(A) 질문과 상관없는 오답
(B) 정답: 어떤 경로로 출근할 예정인지 묻는 질문에 고속도로에 차량이 많다(There's a lot of traffic on the highway)고 답하여 고속도로가 아닌 다른 길로 간다는 것을 우회적으로 나타내고 있으므로 정답이다.
(C) 유사 발음 오답: 질문의 today와 일부 발음이 유사한 day를 이용한 오답이다.

어휘 by (기한) ~까지

23 M-Cn / W-Br
Why do you need to order extra costumes for the play?
(A) Haven't you seen the new script?
(B) A newspaper review.
(C) Put them all in the closet.

왜 연극용 추가 의상을 주문해야 하죠?
(A) 새 대본 못 보셨나요?
(B) 신문 논평이요.
(C) 그것들을 전부 벽장에 넣어 주세요.

해설 의상을 추가 주문하는 이유를 묻는 Why 의문문
(A) 정답: 연극에 필요한 의상을 추가로 주문하는 이유를 묻는 질문에 새 대본을 보지 못했는지(Haven't you seen the new script?) 되물으며 변화가 있었음을 암시하고 있으므로 정답이다.
(B) 질문과 상관없는 오답
(C) 연상 어휘 오답: 질문의 costumes에서 연상 가능한 closet을 이용한 오답이다.

어휘 extra 추가의, 별도의 play 연극 script 대본, 원고 review 논평, 평가, 후기

24 M-Au / M-Cn
How often does the corporate newsletter come out?
(A) Four times a year.
(B) It's longer than usual.
(C) There are no color copies.

회사 소식지는 얼마나 자주 나와요?
(A) 1년에 네 번이요.
(B) 평소보다 더 오래 걸려요.
(C) 컬러 복사본이 없어요.

해설 회사 소식지 발행 빈도를 묻는 How 의문문
(A) 정답: 회사 소식지의 발행 빈도를 묻는 질문에 1년에 네 번(Four times a year)이라는 구체적인 횟수를 알려 주고 있으므로 정답이다.
(B) 질문과 상관없는 오답
(C) 연상 어휘 오답: 질문의 corporate newsletter에서 연상 가능한 color copies를 이용한 오답이다.

어휘 corporate 회사의 newsletter 소식지 come out 나오다 than usual 평소보다 copy 복사(본)

25 W-Br / M-Cn
What should we do to celebrate Ms. Chen's retirement?
(A) Eight years, I think.
(B) Let's go to the High Line Cafe.
(C) She's moving to Australia.

첸 씨의 은퇴를 기념하기 위해 뭘 해야 할까요?
(A) 8년인 것 같아요.
(B) 하이라인 카페에 가죠.
(C) 그녀는 호주로 이사할 거예요.

해설 은퇴 기념 방법 아이디어를 묻는 What 의문문
(A) 질문과 상관없는 오답
(B) 정답: 첸 씨의 은퇴를 기념할 방법에 대한 아이디어를 묻는 질문에 하이라인 카페에 가자(Let's go to the High Line Cafe)고 의견을 제안하고 있으므로 정답이다.
(C) 연상 어휘 오답: 질문의 Ms. Chen's retirement에서 연상 가능한 은퇴 후 계획(She's moving to Australia)을 언급한 오답이다.

어휘 celebrate 기념하다, 축하하다   retirement 은퇴, 퇴직
move 이사하다

UNIT 05 일반 / 부정 / 부가 의문문

1 일반 의문문

본책 p.50

ETS Check-Up

| 1 (C) | 2 (B) | 3 (C) | 4 (A) | 5 (A) | 6 (A) |

1 M-Cn/W-Br
Are you having trouble charging your phone?
(A) At the bottom of my business card.
(B) The product samples are free.
(C) Yes, my charger is broken.

전화기를 충전하는 데 어려움이 있으신가요?
(A) 제 명함 하단에요.
(B) 그 제품 샘플들은 무료입니다.
(C) 네, 제 충전기가 고장 났어요.

해설 **전화기 충전에 어려움이 있는지 묻는 일반 의문문**
(A) 질문과 상관없는 오답
(B) 질문과 상관없는 오답
(C) 정답: 전화기를 충전하는 데 어려움이 있는지 묻는 질문에 네(Yes)라고 대답한 뒤, 충전기가 고장 났다(my charger is broken)며 긍정 답변과 일관된 내용을 덧붙이고 있으므로 정답이다.

어휘 have trouble -ing ~하는 데 어려움을 겪다
charge 충전하다   at the bottom of ~의 하단에, ~의 밑바닥에   free 무료의   broken 고장 난, 망가진, 깨진

2 M-Au/W-Am
Will you arrange the chairs for our staff meeting?
(A) He met some possible vendors.
(B) Certainly—I'll go get them now.
(C) That's a nice floral arrangement.

직원회의를 위해 의자들을 정리해 주시겠어요?
(A) 그가 몇몇 가능성 있는 판매업자들을 만났어요.
(B) 물론이죠, 지금 가서 가져올게요.
(C) 멋진 꽃 장식물이네요.

해설 **부탁·요청의 의문문**
(A) 인칭 오류 오답: 보기의 He가 가리키는 대상이 질문에 없다.
(B) 정답: 직원회의를 위해 의자들을 정리해 달라는 요청에 물론이죠(Certainly)라고 수락한 뒤, 지금 가서 가져오겠다(Certainly—I'll go get them now)고 말하고 있으므로 정답이다.
(C) 파생어 오답: 질문의 arrange와 파생어 관계인 arrangement를 이용한 오답이다.

어휘 arrange 정리하다, 배치하다, 조치하다   vendor 판매업자, 판매업체   floral arrangement 꽃 장식물, 꽃꽂이

3 W-Br/M-Au
Did you purchase the tickets at the theater box office?
(A) Several famous actors.
(B) My car is parked outside.
(C) No, I bought them online.

극장 매표소에서 입장권을 구매하셨나요?
(A) 여러 유명 배우들이요.
(B) 제 차는 밖에 주차되어 있어요.
(C) 아니요, 온라인으로 샀어요.

해설 **입장권을 구매한 방법을 확인하는 일반 의문문**
(A) 연상 어휘 오답: 질문의 theater에서 연상 가능한 actors를 이용한 오답이다.
(B) 질문과 상관없는 오답
(C) 정답: 극장 매표소에서 입장권을 구매했는지 확인하는 질문에 아니요(No)라고 대답한 뒤, 온라인으로 샀다(I bought them online)며 부정 답변과 일관된 내용을 덧붙이고 있으므로 정답이다.

어휘 purchase 구매(품)   several 여럿의, 몇몇의

4 M-Au/W-Am
Have you watched our new promotional video yet?
(A) Yes—it was impressive!
(B) It's fifteen percent off.
(C) I'm not wearing a watch.

저희 새 홍보 동영상을 보셨나요?
(A) 네, 인상 깊었어요!
(B) 15퍼센트 할인입니다.
(C) 저는 시계를 차고 있지 않아요.

해설 **새 홍보 동영상 시청 여부를 확인하는 일반 의문문**
(A) 정답: 새 홍보 동영상을 봤는지 묻는 질문에 네(Yes)라고 대답한 뒤, 인상 깊었다(it was impressive)며 긍정 답변과 일관된 의견을 덧붙이고 있으므로 정답이다.
(B) 연상 어휘 오답: 질문의 promotional에서 연상 가능한 할인율(fifteen percent off)을 언급한 오답이다.
(C) 다의어 오답: 질문의 watched는 '보다'라는 뜻의 동사이고, 보기의 watch는 '시계'라는 뜻의 명사이다.

어휘 promotional 홍보의   impressive 감명 깊은, 인상적인

5 M-Cn/M-Au
Excuse me, do you know where Marie LeDuke's office is?
(A) I'm sorry, I've just started working here.
(B) No, I don't think she is.
(C) That's an official document.

실례지만, 마리 리듀크 씨의 사무실이 어디에 있는지 아세요?
(A) 죄송하지만, 제가 이제 막 이곳에서 근무를 시작했어요.
(B) 아니요, 그녀가 그렇다고 생각하지 않아요.
(C) 그건 공문서입니다.

해설 마리 리듀크 씨의 사무실 위치를 묻는 간접 의문문
(A) 정답: 마리 리듀크 씨의 사무실 위치를 묻는 질문에 먼저 미안하다고 한 뒤, 이곳에서 막 근무를 시작했다(I've just started working here)며 정보를 제공할 수 없는 이유를 덧붙이고 있으므로 정답이다.
(B) 질문과 상관없는 오답
(C) 파생어 오답: 질문에 나오는 office의 파생어 official을 이용한 오답이다.

어휘 official document 공문서

6 M-Cn / W-Am
Ling, do you have time to review this document with me?
(A) Could we go over it tomorrow?
(B) About ten pages long.
(C) Quite a few revisions.

링, 나랑 이 서류 좀 같이 검토할 시간 있어요?
(A) 내일 검토해도 될까요?
(B) 약 10페이지 길이예요.
(C) 꽤 수정이 많군요.

해설 서류를 같이 검토할 시간이 있는지 묻는 일반 의문문
(A) 정답: 서류를 함께 검토할 시간이 있느냐고 묻는 질문에 내일 하면 어떤지(Could we go over it tomorrow?) 되물으며 가능한 일정을 제안하고 있으므로 정답이다.
(B) 연상 어휘 오답: 질문의 document에서 연상 가능한 페이지 수(ten pages)를 언급한 오답이다.
(C) 연상 어휘 오답: 질문의 document에서 연상 가능한 revisions를 이용한 오답이다.

어휘 review 검토하다 go over 검토하다 revision 수정

2 부정 의문문

ETS Check-Up 본책 p.51

| 1 (C) | 2 (A) | 3 (C) | 4 (B) | 5 (A) | 6 (C) |

1 M-Cn / W-Br
Isn't Ms. Lee's speech beginning now?
(A) Ten more copies, please.
(B) Tickets for the evening show.
(C) No, she's speaking later this afternoon.

리 씨의 연설이 지금 시작하지 않나요?
(A) 10부 더 부탁합니다.
(B) 저녁 공연 입장권이요.
(C) 아니요, 그분은 이따 오늘 오후에 연설합니다.

해설 연설이 지금 시작하는지 여부를 확인하는 부정 의문문
(A) 질문과 상관없는 오답
(B) 질문과 상관없는 오답
(C) 정답: 리 씨의 연설이 지금 시작하지 않는지 묻는 질문에 아니요(No)라고 대답한 뒤, 이따 오늘 오후에 연설한다(she's speaking later this afternoon)며 부정 답변과 일관된 내용을 덧붙이고 있으므로 정답이다.

2 W-Am / M-Au
Haven't you already been to that exhibition?
(A) I didn't see everything last time.
(B) No, I put it in the bin.
(C) I'd like to visit Egypt.

그 전시회에 이미 가보지 않았나요?
(A) 지난번에 전부 다 보지 못했어요.
(B) 아니요, 쓰레기통에 그것을 넣었어요.
(C) 저는 이집트를 방문하고 싶어요.

해설 전시회 방문 여부를 확인하는 부정 의문문
(A) 정답: 전시회에 가보지 않았는지 확인하는 질문에 다 관람하지는 못했다(I didn't see everything last time)며 네(Yes)를 생략한 긍정 답변을 하고 있으므로 정답이다.
(B) 유사 발음 오답: 질문의 been과 발음이 유사한 bin을 이용한 오답이다.
(C) 연상 어휘 오답: 의미상 연결이 가능한 두 표현(have been to ~에 가본 적이 있다/visit 방문하다)을 이용한 오답이다.

어휘 exhibition 전시회, 전시 bin 쓰레기통

3 W-Br / M-Cn
Shouldn't we post next month's work schedule?
(A) We can't go then.
(B) There's a letter here for you.
(C) Yes, I'll do it right away.

다음 달 업무 일정을 게시해야 하지 않나요?
(A) 우린 그때 갈 수가 없어요.
(B) 여기 당신에게 온 편지가 있어요.
(C) 네, 지금 바로 할 겁니다.

해설 업무 일정을 게시할지 여부를 확인하는 부정 의문문
(A) 연상 어휘 오답: 질문의 next month에서 연상 가능한 then을 이용한 오답이다.
(B) 연상 어휘 오답: 질문의 post를 '발송하다, 보내다'라는 뜻으로 잘못 이해했을 경우 연상 가능한 letter를 이용한 오답이다.
(C) 정답: 업무 일정을 게시해야 하지 않는지 묻는 질문에 네(Yes)라고 대답한 뒤, 지금 바로 하겠다(I'll do it right away)며 긍정 답변과 일관된 내용을 덧붙이고 있으므로 정답이다.

어휘 post 게시하다 schedule 일정 right away 곧바로

4 M-Cn / M-Au
Didn't you buy a house recently?
(A) Thanks for the recommendation.
(B) We decided to rent for another year.
(C) I'll send it to the manager.

최근에 집을 구입하지 않으셨나요?
(A) 추천 감사합니다.
(B) 1년 더 임대하기로 결정했습니다.
(C) 제가 부장님께 보내 드리겠습니다.

해설 최근에 집을 구입했는지 여부를 확인하는 부정 의문문
(A) 질문과 상관없는 오답

32

(B) 정답: 최근에 집을 구입하지 않았는지 묻는 질문에 1년 더 임대하기로 결정했다(We decided to rent for another year)며 집을 구입하지 않았다는 사실을 우회적으로 나타내고 있으므로 정답이다.
(C) 질문과 상관없는 오답

어휘 recently 최근에 recommendation 추천 rent 임대하다, 대여하다

5 M-Cn / W-Am
Don't you think the Web site needs to be updated?
(A) A new design might attract more customers.
(B) Thanks, but I already have one.
(C) No, only once before.

웹사이트를 업데이트해야 하지 않을까요?
(A) 디자인을 새롭게 하면 고객들이 더 많이 올 거예요.
(B) 고맙지만, 저는 하나 있어요.
(C) 아니요, 전에 한 번만요.

해설 웹사이트 업데이트에 대한 의견을 묻는 부정 의문문
(A) 정답: 웹사이트 업데이트에 대한 의견을 묻는 질문에 새로운 디자인이 더 많은 고객들을 끌어들일 것(A new design might attract more customers)이라며 우회적으로 찬성하고 있으므로 정답이다.
(B) 연상 어휘 오답: needs에서 연상 가능한 already have one을 언급한 오답이다.
(C) 질문과 상관없는 오답

어휘 update 새롭게 하다 attract 끌어들이다

6 W-Br / M-Cn
Why doesn't the bus to the city park ever arrive on time?
(A) Until the next one.
(B) No, you can't park here.
(C) It's frustrating, isn't it?

도심 공원행 버스는 왜 항상 정시에 도착하지 않을까요?
(A) 다음 것이 올 때까지요.
(B) 아니요, 여기에 주차할 수 없어요.
(C) 참 답답해요, 그렇지 않나요?

해설 버스 도착 시간에 대한 불평을 드러내는 부정 의문문
(A) 질문과 상관없는 오답
(B) Yes/No 불가 오답: Why 의문문에는 Yes/No로 응답이 불가능하므로 오답이다.
(C) 정답: 버스가 왜 정시에 도착하지 않느냐고 답답한 심정을 나타낸 질문에 참 답답하다(It's frustrating)며 동감을 표현하고 있으므로 정답이다.

어휘 arrive on time 정시에 도착하다 frustrating 불만스러운, 실망하게 하는

3 부가 의문문

ETS Check-Up   본책 p.52

1 (C)   2 (B)   3 (A)   4 (A)   5 (B)   6 (A)

1 M-Au / W-Am
My dentist appointment is Wednesday, isn't it?
(A) The toothpaste is on sale.
(B) Who was appointed to the board?
(C) Yes, at two o'clock.

제 치과 예약이 수요일에 있죠, 그렇지 않나요?
(A) 그 치약은 할인 중입니다.
(B) 누가 이사회에 선임되었나요?
(C) 네, 2시예요.

해설 치과 예약 요일을 확인하는 부가 의문문
(A) 연상 어휘 오답: 질문의 dentist에서 연상 가능한 toothpaste를 이용한 오답이다.
(B) 파생어 오답: 질문의 appointment와 파생어 관계인 appointed를 이용한 오답이다.
(C) 정답: 치과 예약이 수요일에 있지 않은지 묻는 질문에 네(Yes)라고 대답한 뒤, 2시(at two o'clock)라는 구체적인 시간을 제시하며 긍정 답변과 일관된 내용을 덧붙이고 있으므로 정답이다.

어휘 appointment 예약, 약속 on sale 할인 중인 appoint 선임하다 board 이사회

2 M-Cn / W-Br
I don't have to renew my security badge, do I?
(A) The guard at the front desk.
(B) No, the one you have is still valid.
(C) Tickets are seven dollars each.

제 출입증을 갱신할 필요는 없지요, 그렇죠?
(A) 안내데스크에 있는 경비원이요.
(B) 아니요, 지금 갖고 계신 게 아직 유효해요.
(C) 티켓은 장당 7달러예요.

해설 출입증 갱신 필요 여부를 확인하는 부가 의문문
(A) 연상 어휘 오답: 질문의 security에서 연상 가능한 guard를 이용한 오답이다.
(B) 정답: 출입증 갱신 필요 여부를 묻는 질문에 아니요(No)라고 대답한 뒤, 지금 갖고 있는 것이 아직 유효하다(the one you have is still valid)며 부정 답변과 일관된 내용을 덧붙이고 있으므로 정답이다.
(C) 질문과 상관없는 오답

어휘 renew 갱신하다 security badge 출입증, 보안 명찰 guard 경비원 valid 유효한

3 W-Am / M-Cn
You've operated this equipment before, haven't you?
(A) Yes, many times.
(B) In the training manual.
(C) No, the factory.

이 장비를 전에 다뤄 봤었죠, 그렇지 않나요?
(A) 네, 여러 번이요.
(B) 교육 지침서에서요.
(C) 아니요, 공장이요.

해설 장비를 다루어 본 경험을 확인하는 부가 의문문
(A) 정답: 이 장비를 다루어 본 적이 있는지 묻는 질문에 먼저 네(Yes)라고 대답한 뒤, 여러 번(many times)이며 긍정 답변과 일관된 내용을 덧붙이고 있으므로 정답이다.
(B) 연상 어휘 오답: 질문의 operated this equipment에서 연상 가능한 manual을 이용한 오답이다.
(C) 연상 어휘 오답: 질문의 operated에서 연상 가능한 factory를 이용한 오답이다.

어휘 operate 작동하다 equipment 장비 training manual 교육 지침서 factory 공장

4 M-Cn / M-Au
The software training will end by four, won't it?
(A) It's supposed to.
(B) In the computer lab.
(C) No, I only sent three.

소프트웨어 교육이 4시 전에 끝날 예정이죠, 그렇지 않나요?
(A) 그러기로 되어 있어요.
(B) 컴퓨터실에서요.
(C) 아니요, 저는 세 개만 보냈어요.

해설 교육 종료 예정 시간을 확인하는 부가 의문문
(A) 정답: 소프트웨어 교육이 4시 전에 끝날 예정인지 확인하는 질문에 그러기로 되어 있다(It's supposed to)며 긍정의 응답을 하고 있으므로 정답이다.
(B) 연상 어휘 오답: 질문의 software에서 연상 가능한 computer를 이용한 오답이다.
(C) 연상 어휘 오답: 질문의 four에서 연상 가능한 three를 이용한 오답이다.

어휘 be supposed to ~하기로 되어 있다

5 M-Cn / W-Br
The project proposals are due tomorrow, right?
(A) Yes, I work from home.
(B) No, the deadline was moved.
(C) In conference room B.

프로젝트 제안서 기한이 내일이죠, 그렇죠?
(A) 네, 저는 재택근무를 해요.
(B) 아니요, 기한이 바뀌었어요.
(C) B 회의실에서요.

해설 프로젝트 제안서 기한을 확인하는 부가 의문문
(A) 질문과 상관없는 오답
(B) 정답: 프로젝트 제안서 기한이 내일인지 확인하는 질문에 먼저 아니요(No)라고 대답한 뒤, 기한이 바뀌었다(the deadline was moved)며 부정 답변과 일관된 내용을 덧붙이고 있으므로 정답이다.
(C) 연상 어휘 오답: 질문의 project proposals에서 연상 가능한 제안서 발표 장소(In conference room B)를 언급한 오답이다.

어휘 proposal 제안서 due ~하기로 되어 있는, 예정된 work from home 재택근무하다 deadline 기한

6 M-Cn / M-Au
You wanted these charts copied, didn't you?
(A) And then they should be refiled.
(B) I'll pour the coffee.
(C) At the top of the chart.

이 차트들이 복사되기를 원하셨죠, 그렇지 않나요?
(A) 그러고 나서 그것들을 다시 철해 놓아야 해요.
(B) 제가 커피를 따라 드릴게요.
(C) 차트 맨 위에요.

해설 차트 복사 희망 여부를 확인하는 부가 의문문
(A) 정답: 차트 복사본을 원하지 않았느냐는 질문에 Yes를 생략하고 복사를 원했을 뿐 아니라 그것을 다시 철해놓아야 한다(And then they should be refiled)고 덧붙이고 있으므로 정답이다.
(B) 유사 발음 오답: 질문의 copied와 발음이 유사한 coffee를 이용한 오답이다.
(C) 어휘 반복 오답: 질문의 chart를 반복 이용한 오답이다.

어휘 copy 복사하다 refile (문서 등을) 다시 철하다

ETS 유형연습 본책 p.53

1 (C) **2** (C) **3** (A) **4** (B) **5** (B)

1 M-Cn / W-Br
Are those shoes the right size for you?
(A) Five boxes of shoes.
(B) Please turn left at the next light.
(C) No, I need a smaller size.

그 신발이 당신에게 맞는 사이즈인가요?
(A) 신발 다섯 상자요.
(B) 다음 신호등에서 좌회전해 주세요.
(C) 아니요, 더 작은 사이즈가 필요합니다.

해설 신발 사이즈가 맞는지 여부를 확인하는 일반 의문문
(A) 어휘 반복 오답: 질문의 shoes를 반복 이용한 오답이다.
(B) 연상 어휘 및 유사 발음 오답: 질문의 right에서 연상 가능한 left 및 발음이 유사한 light를 이용한 오답이다.
(C) 정답: 신발이 맞는 사이즈인지 묻는 질문에 아니요(No)라고 대답한 뒤, 더 작은 사이즈가 필요하다(I need a smaller size)며 부정 답변과 일관된 내용을 덧붙이고 있으므로 정답이다.

어휘 turn left 좌회전하다

2 M-Au / W-Am
Do you know why I need to apply in person?
(A) I don't believe we've ever met.
(B) No, I don't need help.
(C) Maybe you need to show identification.

왜 직접 방문해서 지원해야 하는지 아세요?
(A) 제 생각엔 우리가 만난 적이 없어요.
(B) 아니요, 안 도와주셔도 됩니다.
(C) 아마 신분증을 보여줘야 할 거예요.

해설 방문해서 지원해야 하는 이유를 묻는 간접 의문문
(A) 연상 어휘 오답: 질문의 in person에서 연상 가능한 have ever met을 이용한 오답이다.
(B) 어휘 반복 오답: 질문의 need를 반복 이용한 오답이다.
(C) 정답: 직접 방문해서 지원해야 하는 이유를 아는지 묻는 질문에 신분증을 보여줘야 할 것(Maybe you need to show identification)이라고 추측하여 설명하고 있으므로 정답이다.

어휘 in person 손수, 직접 identification 신분증

3 M-Au/M-Cn
Have you finished reading the report?
(A) **Just two more pages.**
(B) He reports to Mr. Garcia.
(C) Yes, the apartment is furnished.

보고서 다 읽었어요?
(A) 두 페이지만 더 읽으면 돼요.
(B) 그는 가르시아 씨에게 업무 보고를 합니다.
(C) 네, 그 아파트에는 가구가 갖춰져 있어요.

해설 보고서를 다 읽었는지 여부를 확인하는 일반 의문문
(A) 정답: 보고서를 다 읽었는지 묻는 질문에 두 페이지만 더 읽으면 된다(Just two more pages)며 다 읽지 못했다는 사실을 우회적으로 드러내고 있으므로 가장 적절한 응답이다.
(B) 다의어 오답: 질문의 report는 '보고서'라는 뜻의 명사이고, 보기의 report는 '보고하다'라는 뜻의 동사이다.
(C) 유사 발음 오답: 질문의 finished와 발음이 유사한 furnished를 이용한 오답이다.

어휘 report to ~에게 보고하다 furnish (가구 등을) 갖추다

4 M-Cn/W-Am
Didn't Joe use to work in the shipping department?
(A) Please send it by overnight mail.
(B) **Yes, but he was transferred.**
(C) A lot of work today.

조가 발송 부서에서 일하지 않았나요?
(A) 그것을 빠른 우편으로 보내주세요.
(B) 네, 그런데 부서를 옮겼어요.
(C) 오늘은 일이 많아요.

해설 조가 발송 부서에서 일하는지 확인하는 부정 의문문
(A) 연상 어휘 오답: 질문의 shipping department에서 연상 가능한 overnight mail을 이용한 오답이다.
(B) 정답: 조가 발송 부서에서 일하지 않았냐는 질문에 네(Yes)라고 대답한 뒤, 그런데 그가 부서를 옮겼다(but he was transferred)며 부연 설명하고 있으므로 정답이다.
(C) 다의어 오답: 질문의 work는 '일하다'라는 뜻의 동사이고, 보기의 work는 '일'이라는 뜻의 명사이다.

어휘 shipping department 발송 부서 overnight mail (다음 날 배달되는) 빠른 우편 transfer 인사 이동하다

5 M-Au/W-Am
Ms. Park will be here to welcome the clients, won't she?
(A) It's a new Web site.
(B) **She's away on a business trip.**
(C) The feedback forms are on my desk.

박 씨가 고객들을 맞이하기 위해 이곳에 오죠, 그렇지 않나요?
(A) 그건 새 웹사이트입니다.
(B) 그분은 출장으로 부재중이세요.
(C) 피드백 양식이 제 책상에 있어요.

해설 박 씨가 고객들을 맞이하러 오는지 확인하는 부가 의문문
(A) 질문과 상관없는 오답
(B) 정답: 박 씨가 고객들을 맞이하기 위해 오는지 확인하는 질문에 출장으로 부재중(She's away on a business trip)이라는 사실을 언급하며 올 수 없음을 우회적으로 나타내고 있으므로 정답이다.
(C) 질문과 상관없는 오답

어휘 away 자리를 비운, 부재중인 form 양식, 서식

ETS 실전문제   본책 p.54

1 (B)	2 (C)	3 (B)	4 (A)	5 (B)	6 (A)
7 (A)	8 (B)	9 (A)	10 (C)	11 (C)	12 (A)
13 (B)	14 (A)	15 (C)	16 (B)	17 (A)	18 (B)
19 (A)	20 (A)	21 (A)	22 (B)	23 (C)	24 (C)
25 (B)					

1 M-Cn/W-Br
Are you coming to the party tonight?
(A) A bottle of orange juice.
(B) **Of course—I've been looking forward to it.**
(C) This is my favorite restaurant in town.

오늘 밤 파티에 오시나요?
(A) 오렌지 주스 한 병이요.
(B) 물론이죠, 저는 계속 고대하고 있었어요.
(C) 이곳이 제가 동네에서 가장 좋아하는 레스토랑이에요.

해설 파티 참석 여부를 확인하는 일반 의문문
(A) 질문과 상관없는 오답
(B) 정답: 오늘 밤 파티에 오는지 묻는 질문에 물론(Of course)라고 수락한 뒤, 계속 고대하고 있었다(I've been looking forward to it)며 긍정 답변과 일관된 내용을 덧붙이고 있으므로 정답이다.
(C) 연상 어휘 오답: 질문의 party에서 연상 가능한 restaurant을 이용한 오답이다.

어휘 look forward to ~을 고대하다 favorite 가장 좋아하는

2 W-Br/M-Cn
Has Mr. Kim's new design been tested?
(A) He used to have one.
(B) Check the signs.
(C) **No, the testing begins next week.**

김 씨의 새 디자인이 테스트를 받았나요?
(A) 그는 예전에 하나를 갖고 있었어요.
(B) 징후들을 확인해 봐요.
(C) 아니요, 테스트는 다음 주에 시작돼요.

해설 새 디자인의 테스트 완료 여부를 확인하는 일반 의문문
(A) 질문과 상관없는 오답
(B) 유사 발음 오답: design과 발음이 비슷한 signs를 사용한 오답이다.
(C) 정답: 새 디자인이 테스트를 받았는지 확인하는 질문에 아니요(No)라고 대답한 뒤, 다음 주에 시작된다(the testing begins next week)며 부정 답변과 일관된 내용을 덧붙이고 있으므로 정답이다.

어휘 used to do 예전에 ~했다 sign 징후, 조짐

3 W-Am / M-Cn
Will you start the training session early tomorrow?
(A) Thanks—I appreciate that.
(B) No, I scheduled it for after lunch.
(C) Yes, I rode the train to work.

내일 일찍 교육을 시작하시나요?
(A) 고맙습니다. 감사드려요.
(B) 아니요, 점심시간 이후로 일정을 잡았습니다.
(C) 네, 저는 기차를 타고 출근했어요.

해설 내일 일찍 교육을 시작하는지 확인하는 일반 의문문
(A) 질문과 상관없는 오답
(B) 정답: 내일 일찍 교육을 시작하는지 묻는 질문에 먼저 아니요(No)라고 대답한 뒤, 점심시간 이후로 일정을 잡았다(I scheduled it for after lunch)며 부정 답변과 일관된 내용을 덧붙이고 있으므로 정답이다.
(C) 유사 발음 오답: 질문의 training과 일부 발음이 유사한 train을 이용한 오답이다.

어휘 training session 교육 (과정) appreciate 감사하다

4 M-Au / W-Am
Isn't meeting room C occupied this morning?
(A) I made our room reservation for the afternoon.
(B) An annual sales conference in Berlin.
(C) Yes, we do offer catered lunch options.

회의실 C가 오늘 아침에 잡혀 있지 않나요?
(A) 제가 오후로 회의실을 예약했어요.
(B) 베를린에서 열리는 연례 영업 콘퍼런스요.
(C) 네, 저희는 케이터링 점심 옵션을 제공합니다.

해설 회의실 예약 여부를 확인하는 부정 의문문
(A) 정답: 회의실 C가 오늘 아침에 잡혀 있지 않은지 묻는 질문에 오후로 회의실을 예약했다(I made our room reservation for the afternoon)며 사실을 확인해 주고 있으므로 정답이다.
(B) 연상 어휘 오답: 질문의 meeting에서 연상 가능한 conference를 이용한 오답이다.
(C) 질문과 상관없는 오답

어휘 occupied (이용하기 위해) 잡아 놓은, 점유된 make one's reservation 예약하다 annual 연례적인, 해마다의 cater 음식을 공급하다

5 M-Cn / M-Au
The number ten bus runs all night, doesn't it?
(A) He left it on the bus.
(B) According to the schedule, yes.
(C) I don't know where the station is.

10번 버스는 밤새도록 운행하죠, 그렇지 않나요?
(A) 그는 그것을 버스에 두고 내렸어요.
(B) 시간표에 따르면 그러네요.
(C) 정류장이 어딘지 모르겠어요.

해설 버스가 밤새도록 운행하는지 여부를 확인하는 부가 의문문
(A) 어휘 반복 오답: 질문의 bus를 반복 이용한 오답이다.
(B) 정답: 버스가 밤새도록 운행하는지 확인하는 질문에 시간표에 따르면 그렇다(According to the schedule, yes)고 확인해 주고 있으므로 정답이다.
(C) 연상 어휘 오답: 질문의 bus에서 연상 가능한 station을 이용한 오답이다.

어휘 leave 남겨두다 according to ~에 따라 station 정류장, 역

6 W-Am / M-Au
Our laboratory supplies were delivered today, weren't they?
(A) The truck broke down.
(B) I'll make a reservation.
(C) A credit card expiration date.

우리 실험실 물품이 오늘 배송되었죠, 그렇지 않나요?
(A) 트럭이 고장 났어요.
(B) 제가 예약할게요.
(C) 신용 카드 만료일이요.

해설 물품 배송 여부를 확인하는 부가 의문문
(A) 정답: 실험실 물품이 오늘 배송되지 않았는지 묻는 질문에 트럭이 고장 났다(The truck broke down)며 배송이 되지 않았다는 사실을 알려 주고 있으므로 정답이다.
(B) 질문과 상관없는 오답
(C) 연상 어휘 오답: 질문의 today에서 연상 가능한 date를 이용한 오답이다.

어휘 laboratory 실험실 supplies 용품, 물품 break down 고장 나다 expiration 만료, 만기

7 W-Am / W-Br
Do you know who's planning Jane's going-away party?
(A) I think it's Tom Shields.
(B) It's on the twenty-third.
(C) No, he can't go.

제인의 송별회를 누가 계획하고 있는지 아세요?
(A) 톰 쉴즈인 것 같아요.
(B) 23일이에요.
(C) 아니요, 그는 못 가요.

해설 **송별회를 계획하고 있는 사람을 묻는 간접 의문문**
(A) 정답: 제인의 송별회를 계획하고 있는 사람이 누구인지 묻는 질문에 구체적인 인물(Tom Shields)을 언급했으므로 정답이다.
(B) 연상 어휘 오답: 질문의 party 날짜로 연상 가능한 twenty-third를 이용한 오답이다.
(C) 파생어 오답: 질문의 going과 파생어 관계인 go를 이용한 오답이다.

어휘 plan 계획하다   going-away party 송별회

8 M-Au / W-Am
Were you able to get in touch with all of the job candidates?
(A) I can get it for you.
(B) I contacted half of them.
(C) An online application.

모든 입사 지원자들과 연락이 됐나요?
(A) 제가 당신을 위해 그것을 구할 수 있어요.
(B) 그들 중 절반과 연락했어요.
(C) 온라인 지원서요.

해설 **연락 여부를 확인하는 일반 의문문**
(A) 다의어 오답: 질문의 get은 in touch와 함께 '연락하다'라는 뜻을 나타내고, 보기의 get은 '얻다, 구하다'라는 뜻이다.
(B) 정답: 모든 입사 지원자들에게 연락했는지 묻는 질문에 그들 중 절반과 연락했다(I contacted half of them)고 답하여 모두와 연락된 것은 아님을 우회적으로 표현하고 있으므로 정답이다.
(C) 연상 어휘 오답: 질문의 job candidates에서 연상 가능한 online application을 이용한 오답이다.

어휘 get in touch with ~와 연락하다   job candidate 입사 지원자   contact 연락하다   half 절반   application 지원서

9 W-Br / M-Au
Don't we have to submit our travel receipts for reimbursement?
(A) Yes, as soon as possible.
(B) South Africa sounds attractive.
(C) A round-trip ticket.

우리 비용 환급을 위해 출장 영수증을 제출해야 하지 않나요?
(A) 네, 가능한 한 빨리요.
(B) 남아프리카 공화국이 매력적인 것 같아요.
(C) 왕복 티켓 한 장이요.

해설 **출장 영수증을 제출해야 하는지 확인하는 부정 의문문**
(A) 정답: 비용 환급을 위해 출장 영수증을 제출해야 하는 것이 아닌지 묻는 질문에 네(Yes)라고 대답한 뒤, 가능한 한 빨리(as soon as possible)라고 덧붙이고 있으므로 정답이다.
(B) 연상 어휘 오답: 질문의 travel에서 연상 가능한 South Africa를 이용한 오답이다.
(C) 연상 어휘 오답: 질문의 travel에서 연상 가능한 round-trip ticket을 이용한 오답이다.

어휘 submit 제출하다   receipt 영수증   reimbursement 비용 환급   as soon as possible 가능한 한 빨리   sound ~한 것 같다, ~한 것처럼 들리다   attractive 매력적인   round-trip 왕복의

10 M-Cn / W-Br
The Human Resources office is on the fourth floor, correct?
(A) I'll call Maintenance.
(B) Actually, we only need three.
(C) The building directory is behind you.

인사부 사무실이 4층에 있죠, 맞나요?
(A) 제가 관리부에 전화할게요.
(B) 사실, 우리는 세 개만 필요해요.
(C) 건물 안내도가 당신 뒤에 있어요.

해설 **인사부 사무실 위치를 확인하는 부가 의문문**
(A) 연상 어휘 오답: 질문의 Human Resources에서 연상 가능한 Maintenance를 이용한 오답이다.
(B) 연상 어휘 오답: 질문의 fourth에서 연상 가능한 three를 이용한 오답이다.
(C) 정답: 인사부 사무실이 4층에 있는지 확인하는 질문에 건물 안내도(building directory)를 언급하며 우회적인 확인 방법을 제시하고 있으므로 정답이다.

어휘 Human Resources 인사부   Maintenance 관리부   actually 사실은   building directory 건물 안내도

11 M-Au / W-Am
Do you know if all employees need to submit a time sheet?
(A) We had a really good time.
(B) In the benefits department.
(C) I'll ask Donna.

모든 직원들이 근무 시간 기록표를 제출해야 하는지 아세요?
(A) 우린 정말 즐겁게 보냈어요.
(B) 복리후생과에서요.
(C) 도나에게 물어봐야겠군요.

해설 **근무 시간 기록표 제출 여부를 확인하는 간접 의문문**
(A) 어휘 반복 오답: 질문에 나온 time을 반복 사용한 오답이다.
(B) 연상 어휘 오답: employees에서 연상 가능한 benefits department를 이용한 오답이다.
(C) 정답: 근무 시간 기록표 제출 관련 질문에 도나에게 물어보겠다(I'll ask Donna)고 답하여 자신이 해당 정보를 알고 있지 않음을 우회적으로 밝히고 있으므로 정답이다.

어휘 employee 직원   time sheet 근무 시간 기록표   benefits (급여 외의) 복리후생   department 과, 부서

12 W-Br / M-Cn
Has the cooling system been checked today?
(A) Miguel has the inspection report.
(B) That tool on the shelf.
(C) I checked in to the hotel.

오늘 냉각 장치 점검을 받았나요?
(A) 미겔이 검사 보고서를 가지고 있어요.
(B) 선반 위에 있는 그 도구요.
(C) 저는 그 호텔에 체크인했어요.

해설 냉각 장치의 점검 여부를 확인하는 일반 의문문
(A) 정답: 냉각 장치의 점검 여부를 묻는 질문에 미겔이 검사 보고서를 가지고 있다(Miguel has the inspection report)며 점검을 받았다는 사실을 우회적으로 드러내고 있으므로 정답이다.
(B) 질문과 상관없는 오답
(C) 어휘 반복 오답: 질문의 checked를 반복 이용한 오답이다.

어휘 cooling system 냉각 장치   inspection 검사, 점검

13 W-Br / M-Au
Is the workshop mandatory for all employees?
(A) Yes, she was hired.
(B) No, only for managers.
(C) It's on Friday.

그 워크숍에 전 직원이 의무적으로 참석해야 하나요?
(A) 네, 그녀는 채용됐어요.
(B) 아니요, 관리자들만요.
(C) 금요일입니다.

해설 워크숍 참석이 의무인지 묻는 일반 의문문
(A) 인칭 오류 오답: 대명사 she가 가리키는 대상이 질문에 없다.
(B) 정답: 워크숍에 전 직원이 참석해야 하는지 묻는 질문에 아니요(No)라고 대답한 뒤, 관리자들만(only for managers)이라며 부정 답변과 일관된 내용을 덧붙이고 있으므로 정답이다.
(C) 연상 어휘 오답: 질문의 workshop에서 연상 가능한 워크숍 일정(It's on Friday)을 언급한 오답이다.

어휘 mandatory 의무적인   hire 채용하다   manager 관리자

14 W-Br / M-Cn
Do you know a good real estate agent?
(A) Jessica just bought a house.
(B) OK, we'll be here!
(C) Each person has a unique password.

좋은 부동산 중개업자를 알고 계신가요?
(A) 제시카 씨가 막 집을 구입했어요.
(B) 좋아요, 저희가 이곳에 와 있을 거예요.
(C) 각자 고유의 비밀번호를 갖고 있습니다.

해설 부동산 중개업자 정보를 묻는 일반 의문문
(A) 정답: 좋은 부동산 중개업자를 알고 있는지 묻는 질문에 제시카 씨가 막 집을 구입했다(Jessica just bought a house)며 그 사람이 알고 있을 것이라는 뜻을 나타내고 있으므로 정답이다.
(B) 질문과 상관없는 오답
(C) 질문과 상관없는 오답

어휘 real estate agent 부동산 중개업자   unique 고유의, 특별한, 독특한

15 M-Au / W-Br
Ms. Ramirez is supposed to be here by now, isn't she?
(A) Here, use this screwdriver.
(B) No, I took the number three bus.
(C) Check your text messages.

라미레즈 씨가 지금쯤 여기 와 계시기로 했죠, 그렇지 않나요?
(A) 여기, 이 드라이버를 이용하세요.
(B) 아니요, 저는 3번 버스를 탔어요.
(C) 문자 메시지를 확인해 보세요.

해설 라미레즈 씨의 도착 여부를 확인하는 부가 의문문
(A) 어휘 반복 오답: 질문의 here를 반복 이용한 오답이다.
(B) 질문과 상관없는 오답
(C) 정답: 라미레즈 씨가 지금쯤 와 있어야 하지 않는지 묻는 질문에 문자 메시지를 확인해 보라(Check your text messages)며 관련 정보를 확인할 수 있는 방법을 알려 주고 있으므로 정답이다.

어휘 by now 지금쯤   take (교통편, 도로 등을) 타다, 이용하다

16 W-Br / W-Am
Did Ms. Patel tell you about her new Web site?
(A) His car is a rental.
(B) I haven't seen her today.
(C) It's down the hall on the right.

파텔 씨가 자신의 새 웹사이트에 관해 얘기해 주셨나요?
(A) 그의 자동차는 대여 차량이에요.
(B) 저는 오늘 그분을 뵙지 못했어요.
(C) 복도를 따라 가시다가 오른편에 있어요.

해설 새 웹사이트에 대해 들었는지 확인하는 일반 의문문
(A) 인칭 오류 오답: 대명사 his가 가리키는 대상이 질문에 없다.
(B) 정답: 파텔 씨가 자신의 새 웹사이트에 관해 얘기해 주었는지 묻는 질문에 그 사람을 오늘 보지 못했다(I haven't seen her today)며 아직 얘기를 듣지 못했음을 우회적으로 표현하고 있으므로 정답이다.
(C) 질문과 상관없는 오답

어휘 rental 대여(한 것)   down (길 등) ~을 따라, ~ 저쪽에

17 W-Am / M-Au
Have you renewed the office lease for another year?
(A) Yes, I signed it today.
(B) A performance review.
(C) A new product release.

사무실 임대차 계약을 한 해 더 갱신하셨나요?
(A) 네, 오늘 서명했어요.
(B) 인사 고과예요.
(C) 신제품 출시입니다.

해설 임대차 계약 갱신 여부를 묻는 일반 의문문
(A) 정답: 사무실 임대차 계약을 갱신했는지 묻는 질문에 네(Yes)라고 대답한 뒤, 오늘 서명했다(I signed it today)며 긍정 답변과 일관된 내용을 덧붙이고 있으므로 정답이다.

(B) 유사 발음 오답: 질문의 renewed와 발음이 유사한 review를 이용한 오답이다.
(C) 유사 발음 오답: 질문의 lease와 일부 발음이 동일한 release를 이용한 오답이다.

어휘 lease 임대차 계약   performance review 인사 고과   release 출시

18 W-Am / M-Cn
Do you think we should take extra product samples to the convention?
(A) I worked with her before.
(B) That's probably a good idea.
(C) It took me all day.

컨벤션에 여분의 제품 샘플을 가져가야 할까요?
(A) 예전에 그녀와 같이 일했어요.
(B) 아마도 그게 좋겠네요.
(C) 그거 하는 데 저는 하루 종일 걸렸어요.

해설 여분의 샘플을 가져가야 하는지 묻는 일반 의문문
(A) 인칭 오류 오답: 보기의 대명사 her가 가리키는 대상이 질문에 없다.
(B) 정답: 여분의 제품 샘플을 가져가야 하는지 의견을 묻는 질문에 대해 좋은 생각(That's probably a good idea)이라며 동의하고 있으므로 정답이다.
(C) 다의어 오답: 서로 다른 의미의 동사 take를 반복 이용한 오답이다. 질문의 take는 '가지고 가다'의 의미이고, 보기의 took은 '시간이 걸리다'라는 의미이다.

어휘 extra 추가의, 여분의

19 M-Cn / W-Am
Aren't we ordering too many supplies?
(A) This is our busiest quarter.
(B) The cabinet in the supply room.
(C) I already tried restarting it.

너무 많은 용품을 주문하는 것 아닌가요?
(A) 지금은 우리가 가장 바쁜 분기예요.
(B) 비품실에 있는 수납장이요.
(C) 이미 한 번 다시 시작해 봤어요.

해설 주문량이 많지 않은지 확인하는 부정 의문문
(A) 정답: 너무 많은 용품을 주문하는 게 아닌지 묻는 질문에 지금이 가장 바쁜 분기(This is our busiest quarter)라며 동의하지 않는 이유를 밝히고 있으므로 정답이다.
(B) 유사 발음 오답: 평서문의 supplies와 일부 발음이 유사한 supply를 이용한 오답이다.
(C) 질문과 상관없는 오답

어휘 supplies 용품, 물품   quarter 분기   supply room 비품실

20 W-Br / M-Au
We'll probably need more chairs in the conference room, won't we?
(A) The entire team will be attending the meeting.
(B) We're trying to buy additional shares of stock.
(C) It wasn't an easy contract negotiation.

아마 회의실에 의자가 더 필요할 것 같아요, 그렇지 않나요?
(A) 팀 전체가 그 회의에 참석할 예정입니다.
(B) 추가 주식을 매입하려 하고 있습니다.
(C) 쉬운 계약 협상은 아니었어요.

해설 동의를 구하는 부가 의문문
(A) 정답: 회의실에 의자가 더 필요하지 않을지 묻는 질문에 팀 전체가 회의에 참석한다(The entire team will be attending the meeting)며 동의를 표현하고 있으므로 정답이다.
(B) 연상 어휘 오답: 질문의 need more에서 연상 가능한 buy additional을 이용한 오답이다.
(C) 질문과 상관없는 오답

어휘 entire 전체의   additional 추가적인   shares of stock 주식   contract 계약(서)   negotiation 협상, 협의

21 M-Au / W-Am
Are the labor-cost projections for the next fiscal year done yet?
(A) Yes, we've just finished them.
(B) Heavy physical work.
(C) I have no objections.

내년 회계연도에 예상되는 인건비 산출이 끝났나요?
(A) 네, 저희가 막 끝냈어요.
(B) 힘든 육체 노동이에요.
(C) 저는 이의가 없습니다.

해설 인건비 산출 완료 여부를 묻는 일반 의문문
(A) 정답: 인건비 산출의 완료 여부를 묻는 질문에 네(Yes)라고 대답한 뒤, 방금 끝냈다(we've just finished them)며 긍정 답변과 일관된 내용을 덧붙이고 있으므로 정답이다.
(B) 연상 어휘 오답: 질문의 labor에서 연상 가능한 work을 이용한 오답이다.
(C) 유사 발음 오답: 질문의 projections와 부분적으로 발음이 유사한 objections를 이용한 오답이다.

어휘 labor cost 인건비   projection 예상, 추정   fiscal year 회계 연도   done 완료된   heavy 힘든   physical work 육체 노동   objection 반대

22 M-Cn / W-Br
Hasn't the outgoing mail been picked up yet?
(A) I can give you a ride.
(B) Not that I know of.
(C) Usually by express mail.

발송 우편물을 아직 수거해 가지 않았나요?
(A) 제가 차로 태워 드릴 수 있어요.
(B) 제가 알기로는 아니에요.
(C) 대개는 빠른 우편으로요.

해설 발송 우편물 수거 여부를 묻는 부정 의문문
(A) 연상 어휘 오답: 질문에 나온 pick up을 '(차로 사람을) 태우러 가다'라는 의미로 이해할 때 연상할 수 있는 give someone a ride를 이용한 오답이다.

(B) 정답: 우편물의 수거 여부를 묻는 질문에 내가 알기로는 아직 안 가져갔다(Not that I know of)고 대답하고 있으므로 정답이다.
(C) 어휘 반복 오답: 질문에 나온 mail을 반복 이용한 오답이다.

어휘 outgoing (우편물이) 발송 준비가 된 pick up 가져가다 give A a ride A에게 차를 태워 주다 express mail 빠른 우편

23 M-Cn / M-Au
Do you have time for a quick football game?
(A) Do you remember that one?
(B) I have seen them play.
(C) Should I bring my ball?

간단하게 축구 한 게임 할 시간 있나요?
(A) 저거 기억나세요?
(B) 그들의 경기를 본 적이 있어요.
(C) 제가 공을 가져올까요?

해설 축구할 시간이 있는지 묻는 일반 의문문
(A) 질문과 상관없는 오답
(B) 연상 어휘 오답: 질문의 game에서 연상 가능한 play를 이용한 오답이다.
(C) 정답: 축구할 시간이 있는지 물어보는 질문에 공을 가져와야 하는지(Should I bring my ball?) 되물으며 관련 내용을 확인하고 있으므로 정답이다.

어휘 quick 잠깐의

24 W-Br / M-Au
Why wasn't a company newsletter published this month?
(A) Yes, I mailed them in advance.
(B) To send to the client.
(C) Because they're redesigning the format.

이번 달에는 왜 회사 소식지가 발행되지 않았나요?
(A) 네, 제가 그것들을 미리 우편으로 보냈어요.
(B) 고객에게 발송하기 위해서요.
(C) 구성을 개편하고 있기 때문입니다.

해설 회사 소식지 미발행 이유를 묻는 부정 의문문
(A) Yes/No 불가 오답: Why 의문문에는 Yes/No 응답이 불가능하므로 오답이다.
(B) 연상 어휘 오답: 질문의 newsletter에서 연상 가능한 send를 이용한 오답이다.
(C) 정답: 이번 달에는 왜 회사 소식지가 발행되지 않았는지 묻는 질문에 구성을 개편하고 있다(they're redesigning the format)는 사실을 이유로 언급하고 있으므로 정답이다.

어휘 mail 우편으로 보내다 in advance 미리, 사전에 format 구성 (방식), 판형

25 M-Cn / M-Au
There's supposed to be a large group coming in for dinner, isn't there?
(A) I prefer yellow.
(B) Yes — 30 people.
(C) What do you want for dinner?

저녁 식사하러 오기로 되어 있는 대규모 단체 손님들이 있죠, 그렇지 않나요?
(A) 저는 노란색을 선호합니다.
(B) 네, 30명이요.
(C) 저녁 식사로 뭘 원하세요?

해설 단체 손님 예정 여부를 확인하는 부가 의문문
(A) 질문과 상관없는 오답
(B) 정답: 저녁 식사하러 오는 대규모 단체 손님들이 있지 않은지 묻는 질문에 네(Yes)라고 대답한 뒤, 30명(30 people)이라는 구체적인 인원수를 밝히고 있으므로 정답이다.
(C) 어휘 반복 오답: 질문의 dinner를 반복 이용한 오답이다.

어휘 prefer 선호하다

UNIT 06 선택 / 요청·제안 의문문 / 평서문

1 선택 의문문

본책 p.56

ETS Check-Up

1 (C)   2 (C)   3 (C)   4 (B)   5 (C)   6 (A)

1 M-Au / W-Am
Will you be using a credit card or cash for your purchase?
(A) At the bank on Main Street.
(B) Thanks, I bought it online.
(C) I'll use my card.

결제를 신용카드로 하시겠어요, 현금으로 하시겠어요?
(A) 메인 가에 있는 은행에서요.
(B) 고마워요, 인터넷으로 샀어요.
(C) 카드로 할게요.

해설 지불 수단을 묻는 선택 의문문
(A) 연상 어휘 오답: 질문의 credit card or cash에서 연상 가능한 bank를 이용한 오답이다.
(B) 연상 어휘 오답: 질문의 purchase에서 연상 가능한 bought를 이용한 오답이다.
(C) 정답: 지불 수단을 묻는 질문에 카드로 하겠다(I'll use my card)며 전자를 선택하여 답하고 있으므로 정답이다.

어휘 credit card 신용카드 cash 현금 purchase 구매(품)

2 M-Cn / M-Au
Can I borrow that book, or are you still reading it?
(A) One of my favorite authors.
(B) They're stored on the bottom shelf.
(C) I'm only halfway through it.

그 책을 빌릴 수 있을까요, 아니면 아직 읽고 계신가요?
(A) 제가 가장 좋아하는 작가들 중 한 명이요.
(B) 그것들은 맨 아래 선반에 보관되어 있어요.
(C) 겨우 반 읽었어요.

해설 **책을 다 읽었는지 묻는 선택 의문문**
(A) 연상 어휘 오답: book에서 연상 가능한 author를 이용한 오답이다.
(B) 연상 어휘 오답: book에서 연상 가능한 bottom shelf를 이용한 오답이다.
(C) 정답: 책을 다 읽었는지 묻는 질문에 반만 읽었다(I'm only halfway through it)며 우회적으로 후자를 선택하여 답하고 있으므로 정답이다.

어휘 author 저자, 작가 store 보관하다, 저장하다 bottom 맨 아래의 shelf 선반 halfway (시간·거리상으로) 중간쯤에

3 W-Am / W-Br
Should we see the new action movie or the comedy?
(A) Popcorn and a beverage.
(B) A five-dollar service fee.
(C) They both have great reviews.

새 액션 영화를 봐야 할까요, 아니면 코미디로 할까요?
(A) 팝콘과 음료요.
(B) 5달러의 서비스 요금이요.
(C) 둘 다 후기가 훌륭해요.

해설 **관람할 영화의 종류를 묻는 선택 의문문**
(A) 연상 어휘 오답: 질문의 movie에서 연상 가능한 Popcorn을 이용한 오답이다.
(B) 질문과 상관없는 오답
(C) 정답: 어떤 영화를 볼지 묻는 질문에 둘 다 후기가 훌륭하다(They both have great reviews)며 어느 쪽이든 상관없다는 뜻을 나타내고 있으므로 정답이다.

어휘 beverage 음료 review 후기, 평가

4 M-Au / W-Br
Are we moving to the new building this month or next?
(A) For the past few months.
(B) We'll find out in today's meeting.
(C) Next to the parking garage.

새 건물로 이번 달에 이사를 가요, 아니면 다음 달에 가요?
(A) 지난 몇 개월간이요.
(B) 오늘 회의에서 알게될 겁니다.
(C) 주차장 옆이요.

해설 **이사 시점을 묻는 선택 의문문**
(A) 어휘 반복 오답: 질문의 month를 반복 이용한 오답이다.
(B) 정답: 이사 시점을 묻는 질문에 어느 것도 선택하지 않고 오늘 회의에서 알게될 것(We'll find out in today's meeting)이라며 관련된 상황을 언급하고 있으므로 정답이다.

(C) 연상 어휘 오답: 질문의 building에서 연상 가능한 parking garage를 언급한 오답이다.

어휘 past 지나간, 지난 find out 알아내다 parking garage 주차장, 주차건물

5 M-Cn / M-Au
Would you like me to order roast beef or pasta for the luncheon?
(A) The keys are on the table by the door.
(B) I'll have a tea with sugar, please.
(C) A couple of our staff members are vegetarians.

오찬 행사에 구운 소고기를 주문해 드릴까요, 아니면 파스타로 할까요?
(A) 열쇠는 문 옆에 있는 탁자에 놓여 있어요.
(B) 설탕을 넣은 차로 한잔할게요.
(C) 우리 직원 두어 명이 채식주의자예요.

해설 **오찬 메뉴를 묻는 선택 의문문**
(A) 연상 어휘 오답: 질문의 beef, pasta, luncheon에서 연상 가능한 table을 이용한 오답이다.
(B) 질문과 상관없는 오답
(C) 정답: 일부 직원이 채식주의자(A couple of our staff members are vegetarians)라며 소고기가 아닌 파스타를 선택하겠다는 뜻을 우회적으로 나타내고 있으므로 정답이다.

어휘 luncheon 오찬

6 M-Au / W-Br
Have you signed the contract, or do you need more time to review it?
(A) I'll need another day or two.
(B) Please address the letter to me.
(C) I didn't see the sign.

계약서에 서명하셨나요, 아니면 계약서를 검토할 시간이 더 필요하세요?
(A) 하루나 이틀 더 필요해요.
(B) 그 편지를 저에게 보내주세요.
(C) 표지판을 못 봤어요.

해설 **계약서 서명 여부를 묻는 선택 의문문**
(A) 정답: 계약서에 서명했는지 아니면 검토할 시간이 더 필요한지 묻는 질문에 하루나 이틀 더 필요하다(I'll need another day or two)며 후자를 선택하여 답했으므로 정답이다.
(B) 질문과 상관없는 오답
(C) 다의어 오답: 질문의 signed는 '서명하다'라는 뜻의 동사이고, 보기의 sign은 '표지판'이라는 뜻의 명사이다.

어휘 sign the contract 계약(서)에 서명하다 address (~앞으로 우편물을) 보내다

2 요청 · 제안 의문문

ETS Check-Up 본책 p.57

1 (B) 2 (A) 3 (B) 4 (B) 5 (C) 6 (B)

1 M-Au / W-Br
Could you give me feedback on my performance?
(A) Thanks for the ride to work.
(B) I'd be happy to.
(C) About an hour ago.

제 성과에 대해 피드백을 주실 수 있나요?
(A) 회사까지 태워 주셔서 감사합니다.
(B) 기꺼이 그렇게 하겠습니다.
(C) 약 1시간 전에요.

해설 부탁 · 요청의 의문문
(A) 질문과 상관없는 오답
(B) 정답: 성과에 대한 피드백을 줄 수 있는지 묻는 질문에 기꺼이 그렇게 하겠다(I'd be happy to)며 수락하고 있으므로 정답이다.
(C) 질문과 상관없는 오답

어휘 feedback 피드백, 의견   performance 성과, 실적

2 M-Cn / W-Am
Can I start setting up the new cosmetics display now?
(A) The order hasn't arrived yet.
(B) Around 25 dollars per hour.
(C) Some brushes and powders.

지금 새 화장품 진열을 시작해도 될까요?
(A) 주문품이 아직 도착하지 않았어요.
(B) 시간당 약 25달러입니다.
(C) 몇몇 브러쉬와 파우더요.

해설 제안 · 권유의 의문문
(A) 정답: 지금 새 화장품 진열을 시작해도 될지 묻는 질문에 주문품이 아직 도착하지 않았다(The order hasn't arrived yet)며 나중에 설치해야 하는 상황임을 나타내고 있으므로 정답이다.
(B) 질문과 상관없는 오답
(C) 연상 어휘 오답: 질문의 cosmetics에서 연상 가능한 brushes and powders를 이용한 오답이다.

어휘 set up 설치하다, 설정하다   cosmetics 화장품   display 진열(품), 전시(품)   arrive 도착하다   around 약, 대략

3 M-Au / W-Br
Why don't we update our corporate Web site?
(A) Up at the top.
(B) I don't have time right now.
(C) Thanks for your cooperation.

회사 웹사이트를 업데이트하는 것이 어때요?
(A) 위쪽 꼭대기에요.
(B) 지금은 시간이 없어요.
(C) 협조해줘서 고마워요.

해설 제안 · 권유의 의문문
(A) 유사 발음 오답: 질문의 update와 발음이 유사한 up at을 이용한 오답이다.
(B) 정답: 회사 웹사이트를 업데이트하는 것이 어떤지 묻는 질문에 지금은 시간이 없다(I don't have time right now)며 우회적으로 거절의 뜻을 밝히고 있으므로 정답이다.
(C) 유사 발음 오답: 질문의 corporate와 발음이 유사한 cooperation을 이용한 오답이다.

어휘 update 최신화하다   corporate 기업의, 회사의   cooperation 협조, 협력

4 M-Au / W-Am
Can you put these books in your office?
(A) I booked a table for four.
(B) Sorry, but I don't have enough space.
(C) About 200 pages.

이 책들을 당신 사무실에 놓아 주시겠어요?
(A) 4인용 테이블로 예약했어요.
(B) 죄송하지만, 공간이 충분하지 않습니다.
(C) 약 200 페이지요.

해설 부탁 · 요청의 의문문
(A) 다의어 오답: 질문의 book은 '책'이라는 뜻의 명사이고, 보기의 book은 '예약하다'라는 뜻의 동사이다.
(B) 정답: 책들을 사무실에 놓아 달라고 부탁하는 질문에 미안하다(Sorry)고 한 뒤, 공간이 충분하지 않다(I don't have enough space)는 이유를 덧붙여 거절의 뜻을 나타내고 있으므로 정답이다.
(C) 연상 어휘 오답: 질문의 book에서 연상 가능한 200 pages를 이용한 오답이다.

어휘 about 약, 대략

5 W-Am / M-Cn
Would you mind updating the meeting notes?
(A) I think the blue one is mine.
(B) We've already picked one out.
(C) Sure, how soon do you need them?

회의록을 업데이트해 줄 수 있나요?
(A) 파란색이 제 것 같아요.
(B) 우리는 벌써 하나를 골랐어요.
(C) 그럼요, 언제까지 필요하세요?

해설 부탁 · 요청의 의문문
(A) 유사 발음 오답: 질문의 mind와 발음이 유사한 mine을 이용한 오답이다.
(B) 질문과 상관없는 오답
(C) 정답: 회의록 업데이트를 부탁하는 요청에 그럼요(Sure)라고 수락한 뒤, 언제까지 필요한지(how soon do you need them?)를 물으며 긍정 답변과 일관된 내용을 덧붙이고 있으므로 정답이다.

어휘 mind 꺼리다

6 M-Cn / M-Au

How about a game of tennis this weekend?
(A) No, I'm afraid I didn't.
(B) Well, I do need the exercise.
(C) I bought ten of them.

이번 주말에 테니스 한 게임 어때요?
(A) 아니요, 유감스럽게도 안 했어요.
(B) 음, 전 정말 운동을 해야 해요.
(C) 제가 그것들 중 열 개를 샀어요.

해설 제안·권유의 의문문
(A) 질문과 상관없는 오답
(B) 정답: 주말에 테니스 한 게임을 치자는 제안에 운동이 정말 필요하다(I do need the exercise)며 긍정적 반응을 보이고 있으므로 정답이다.
(C) 유사 발음 오답: 질문의 tennis와 부분적으로 발음이 유사한 ten을 이용한 오답이다.

어휘 exercise 운동

3 평서문

ETS Check-Up   본책 p.58

1 (C) **2** (A) **3** (B) **4** (A) **5** (A) **6** (B)

1 M-Cn / M-Au

Mr. Cohen has accepted our job offer.
(A) Some new business cards.
(B) The company vacation policy.
(C) I'll start the paperwork.

코헨 씨가 우리의 일자리 제안을 수락하셨습니다.
(A) 몇몇 새 명함들이요.
(B) 회사 휴가 정책이요.
(C) 제가 서류 작업을 시작할게요.

해설 정보를 전달하는 평서문
(A) 연상 어휘 오답: 평서문의 job에서 연상 가능한 business를 이용한 오답이다.
(B) 연상 어휘 오답: 평서문의 job에서 연상 가능한 company를 이용한 오답이다.
(C) 정답: 코헨 씨가 자신들의 일자리 제안을 수락했다는 평서문에 자신이 서류 작업을 시작하겠다(I'll start the paperwork)며 후속 조치에 대해 언급하고 있으므로 정답이다.

어휘 accept 수락하다, 받아들이다   offer 제안, 제공(되는 것)   policy 정책, 방침   paperwork 서류 (작업)

2 M-Au / W-Br

We have a lot more printer paper than I thought.
(A) Let's cancel this month's order.
(B) That desk is heavy.
(C) She works in the office next to me.

제가 생각했던 것보다 프린터 용지가 훨씬 더 많네요.
(A) 이번 달 주문은 취소합시다.
(B) 저 책상은 무거워요.
(C) 그녀는 제 옆 사무실에서 일합니다.

해설 정보를 전달하는 평서문
(A) 정답: 생각했던 것보다 훨씬 더 많은 프린터 용지가 있다는 평서문에 이번 달 주문을 취소하자(Let's cancel this month's order)며 우회적으로 현재 보유 중인 용지를 먼저 사용하자고 제안하고 있으므로 정답이다.
(B) 평서문과 상관없는 오답
(C) 인칭 오류 오답: 대명사 She가 가리키는 대상이 평서문에 없다.

어휘 cancel 취소하다   order 주문(품)   next to ~ 옆에

3 M-Cn / W-Br

You really should try to attend Dr. Wong's talk.
(A) No, she wrote it herself.
(B) OK, but I may have to leave early.
(C) I wonder who the speaker was.

웡 박사님의 강연에 꼭 참석하셔야 해요.
(A) 아니요, 그녀가 직접 그것을 썼어요.
(B) 좋아요, 하지만 저는 아마 일찍 나와야 할 거예요.
(C) 연사가 누구였는지 궁금하네요.

해설 제안하는 평서문
(A) 평서문과 상관없는 오답
(B) 정답: 강연회 참석을 제안하는 평서문에 좋다(OK)고 수락한 뒤, 하지만 아마 일찍 나와야 할 것(but I may have to leave early)이라고 덧붙이고 있으므로 정답이다.
(C) 연상 어휘 오답: 연설을 의미하는 talk에서 연상 가능한 speaker를 이용한 오답이다.

어휘 attend 참석하다   talk 연설, 강연   wonder 궁금해하다   speaker 연설자, 말하는 사람

4 W-Am / M-Cn

I think the vice president should select the location.
(A) But she asked us to.
(B) A wide variety.
(C) We couldn't find them.

부회장님이 장소를 선택하셔야 할 것 같아요.
(A) 그렇지만 그녀가 저희에게 하라고 하셨잖아요.
(B) 아주 다양해요.
(C) 그것들을 찾을 수가 없었어요.

해설 의견을 제시하는 평서문
(A) 정답: 부회장이 장소를 선택해야 할 것 같다는 의견을 제시하는 평서문에 그녀(부회장)가 저희에게 결정하라고 했다(But she asked us to)며 동의하지 않는다는 뜻을 나타내고 있으므로 정답이다.
(B) 연상 어휘 오답: 평서문의 select에서 연상 가능한 variety를 이용한 오답이다.
(C) 인칭 오류 오답: 대명사 them이 가리키는 대상이 평서문에 없다.

어휘 vice president 부회장   location 장소, 위치

5　W-Br / M-Au

Let's have the delivery driver leave our food at the front desk.
(A) That's a good idea.
(B) Just a salad, please.
(C) Thanks, I'll look at it now.

배달 기사에게 우리 음식을 프런트 데스크에 놓아 달라고 합시다.
(A) 좋은 생각이에요.
(B) 샐러드만 부탁합니다.
(C) 감사합니다, 제가 지금 살펴볼게요.

해설　제안하는 평서문
(A) **정답**: 배달 기사에게 음식을 프런트 데스크에 놓아 두게 하자고 제안하는 평서문에 좋은 생각(That's a good idea)이라며 동의하고 있으므로 정답이다.
(B) 연상 어휘 오답: 평서문의 food에서 연상 가능한 salad를 이용한 오답이다.
(C) 평서문과 상관없는 오답

어휘　have A do A에게 ~하게 하다　leave 놓아 두다, 남겨 두다

6　M-Au / M-Cn

I hope this bus stops at Myers Plaza.
(A) No, I haven't.
(B) You should take the number two bus.
(C) A local tour guide.

이 버스가 마이어스 플라자에 정차했으면 좋겠어요.
(A) 아니요, 저는 그러지 않았어요.
(B) 2번 버스를 타셔야 합니다.
(C) 현지 여행 가이드요.

해설　바람을 나타내는 평서문
(A) 평서문과 상관없는 오답
(B) **정답**: 특정 버스가 마이어스 플라자에 서기를 바란다는 평서문에 그곳으로 가기 위해 타야 하는 버스(You should take the number two bus)를 알려 주고 있으므로 정답이다.
(C) 연상 어휘 오답: 평서문의 bus와 Myers Plaza에서 연상 가능한 local tour를 이용한 오답이다.

어휘　local 현지의, 지역의

ETS 유형연습　본책 p.59

1 (C)　2 (B)　3 (A)　4 (C)　5 (C)

1　W-Am / W-Br

Should I make your interview for earlier or later in the day?
(A) The doctor's office on Twelfth Street.
(B) Just once a day.
(C) I'm usually busy in the morning.

그날 인터뷰를 더 일찍 잡을까요, 아니면 늦게 잡을까요?
(A) 12번 가에 있는 병원이요.
(B) 하루에 한 번만이요.
(C) 제가 보통 오전에 바빠요.

해설　인터뷰 시점을 묻는 선택 의문문
(A) 질문과 상관없는 오답
(B) 어휘 반복 오답: 질문의 day를 반복 이용한 오답이다.
(C) **정답**: 인터뷰를 더 일찍 잡을지, 아니면 늦게 잡을지 묻는 질문에 보통 오전에 바쁘다(I'm usually busy in the morning)며 늦은 시간대가 좋다는 의견을 나타내고 있으므로 정답이다.

어휘　usually 보통, 일반적으로

2　M-Cn / M-Au

Could you turn on the air conditioner, please?
(A) The contract was fair.
(B) Sorry, it's not working.
(C) Make the next left.

에어컨 좀 켜 주실래요?
(A) 계약은 공정했어요.
(B) 죄송하지만 작동이 안 돼요.
(C) 다음에 좌회전하세요.

해설　부탁·요청의 의문문
(A) 유사 발음 오답: 질문의 air와 부분적으로 발음이 유사한 fair를 이용한 오답이다.
(B) **정답**: 에어컨을 켜달라는 요청에 미안하지만 작동이 안 된다(Sorry, it's not working)며 우회적으로 거절의 의사를 드러내고 있으므로 정답이다.
(C) 연상 어휘 오답: 질문의 turn을 '방향을 바꾸다, 돌다'라는 뜻으로 잘못 이해했을 경우 연상 가능한 상황(Make the next left)을 이용한 오답이다.

어휘　turn on 켜다　fair 공정한　make a left 좌회전하다

3　M-Au / W-Am

I'd like to order a custom sofa.
(A) What's your budget?
(B) Yes, in the customer waiting room.
(C) Here's your turkey sandwich.

맞춤 제작 소파를 하나 주문하고 싶습니다.
(A) 예산이 어떻게 되시죠?
(B) 네, 고객 대기실에서요.
(C) 여기 주문하신 칠면조 샌드위치입니다.

해설　바람을 나타내는 평서문
(A) **정답**: 맞춤 제작 소파를 하나 주문하고 싶다는 평서문에 예산이 얼마인지(What's your budget?) 되물으며 제품 선택을 위한 조건을 확인하고 있으므로 정답이다.
(B) 유사 발음 오답: 평서문의 custom과 부분적으로 발음이 유사한 customer를 이용한 오답이다.
(C) 연상 어휘 오답: 평서문의 order에서 연상 가능한 상황(Here's your turkey sandwich)을 이용한 오답이다.

어휘　custom 맞춤 제작의　budget 예산

4 W-Br / M-Au

We can't check our flight status until three P.M. tomorrow.
(A) It's a short taxi ride.
(B) A round-trip ticket to Denver for two.
(C) Then let's wait and look at the Web site.

내일 오후 3시까지는 우리 항공편 상태를 확인할 수 없어요.
(A) 택시로 가까운 거리입니다.
(B) 덴버행 2인 왕복 티켓이요.
(C) 그럼 기다리면서 웹사이트를 확인해 봅시다.

해설 문제 상황을 언급하는 평서문
(A) 평서문과 상관없는 오답
(B) 연상 작용 오답: 평서문의 flight에서 연상 가능한 round-trip ticket을 이용한 오답이다.
(C) 정답: 내일 오후 3시까지는 항공편 상태를 확인할 수 없다는 평서문에 기다리면서 웹사이트를 확인해 보자(Then let's wait and look at the Web site)고 제안하고 있으므로 정답이다.

어휘 status 상태, 상황, 현황 ride (차량, 자전거 등) 타고 가기 round-trip 왕복 여행의

5 M-Cn / W-Br

Why don't you finish that tomorrow when you're not so tired?
(A) He wasn't tired this time.
(B) Whenever you have a minute.
(C) That's probably a good idea.

내일 많이 피곤하지 않을 때 그걸 끝내는 게 어때요?
(A) 그는 이번에 피곤하지 않았어요.
(B) 당신이 잠깐 시간이 있을 때면 언제든지요.
(C) 그게 좋은 생각인 것 같아요.

해설 제안·권유의 의문문
(A) 인칭 오류 오답: 보기의 He가 가리키는 대상이 질문에 없다.
(B) 유사 발음 오답: 질문의 when과 부분적으로 발음이 유사한 whenever를 이용한 오답이다.
(C) 정답: 내일 많이 피곤하지 않을 때 일을 끝내는 게 어떻냐는 제안에 좋은 생각인 것 같다(That's probably a good idea)며 동의하고 있으므로 정답이다.

어휘 minute (시간의) 분, 잠깐 동안

ETS 실전문제   본책 p.60

1 (A)	2 (B)	3 (A)	4 (C)	5 (C)	6 (B)
7 (C)	8 (A)	9 (A)	10 (C)	11 (C)	12 (A)
13 (A)	14 (C)	15 (A)	16 (C)	17 (B)	18 (A)
19 (C)	20 (C)	21 (B)	22 (C)	23 (B)	24 (B)
25 (A)					

1 M-Cn / W-Br

Should we mop the floors or just sweep them?
(A) They need to be mopped.
(B) It's on the shelf.
(C) The windows are clean.

대걸레로 바닥을 닦아야 하나요, 아니면 그냥 빗자루로 쓸면 되나요?
(A) 대걸레로 닦아야 합니다.
(B) 선반 위에 있어요.
(C) 창문들이 깨끗해요.

해설 청소 방법을 묻는 선택 의문문
(A) 정답: 대걸레로 바닥을 닦아야 하는지, 아니면 그냥 빗자루로 쓸면 되는지 묻는 질문에 대걸레로 닦아야 한다(They need to be mopped)며 전자를 선택하여 답했으므로 정답이다.
(B) 질문과 상관없는 오답
(C) 연상 어휘 오답: 질문의 mop/sweep에서 연상 가능한 clean을 이용한 오답이다.

어휘 mop 대걸레로 닦다 sweep 빗자루로 쓸다

2 M-Au / W-Am

Could I help you move those file cabinets?
(A) Eight hours a day.
(B) Sure, that'd be great.
(C) At the security desk.

저 파일 캐비닛 옮기는 것을 도와드릴까요?
(A) 하루에 8시간이요.
(B) 네, 그럼 아주 좋죠.
(C) 보안 데스크에서요.

해설 제안·권유의 의문문
(A) 질문과 상관없는 오답
(B) 정답: 파일 캐비닛 옮기는 것을 도와줄지 묻는 질문에 네(Sure)라고 수락한 뒤, 그렇게 하면 아주 좋을 것(that'd be great)이라며 도움이 필요하다는 뜻을 나타내고 있으므로 정답이다.
(C) 연상 어휘 오답: 질문의 file cabinets에서 연상 가능한 desk를 이용한 오답이다.

3 M-Cn / W-Am

Why don't you wait to see the survey results before making a decision?
(A) Oh, we've already taken them into account.
(B) I don't see the waiter anywhere.
(C) A select group of customers.

결정을 내리기 전에 설문 조사 결과를 기다려 보는 게 어때요?
(A) 아, 우리는 이미 그것을 참작했어요.
(B) 웨이터가 어디에도 안 보이네요.
(C) 엄선된 고객 단체요.

해설 제안·권유의 의문문
(A) 정답: 설문 조사 결과를 기다렸다가 결정을 내리라는 제안에 이미 그 결과를 참작했다(We've already taken them into account)고 답하고 있으므로 정답이다.

(B) 파생어 오답: 질문에 나오는 wait의 파생어 waiter를 이용한 오답이다.
(C) 연상 어휘 오답: 질문의 survey에서 연상 가능한 select group을 이용한 오답이다.

어휘 survey 설문 조사　make a decision 결정하다　take A into account A를 고려하다　select 엄선된, 선발된

4 W-Br / M-Cn
I think I'll shop for a new phone this weekend.
(A) Two chairs per table.
(B) My battery needs charging.
(C) The sales event ends today.

이번 주말에 새 전화기를 사러 갈 것 같아요.
(A) 테이블마다 의자 두 개씩이요.
(B) 제 배터리는 충전이 필요해요.
(C) 세일 행사는 오늘 끝나요.

해설 정보를 전달하는 평서문
(A) 평서문과 상관없는 오답
(B) 연상 어휘 오답: 평서문의 phone에서 연상 가능한 battery를 이용한 오답이다.
(C) 정답: 이번 주말에 새 전화기를 사러 갈 것 같다는 평서문에 세일 행사는 오늘 끝난다(The sales event ends today)며 구매 관련 정보를 제공하고 있으므로 정답이다.

어휘 per ~마다, ~당　charge 충전하다

5 M-Au / W-Am
Would you rather see a movie or go to a concert tonight?
(A) Thanks, I had a great seat.
(B) It was interesting.
(C) There is a new film I want to see.

오늘 밤 영화를 보고 싶어요, 아니면 음악회에 가고 싶어요?
(A) 고마워요. 자리가 정말 좋았어요.
(B) 그것은 흥미로웠어요.
(C) 보고 싶은 신작 영화가 있어요.

해설 오늘 밤 계획을 묻는 선택 의문문
(A) 연상 어휘 오답: 질문의 movie 또는 concert에서 연상 가능한 seat를 이용한 오답이다.
(B) 연상 어휘 오답: 질문의 movie 또는 concert에서 연상 가능한 영화 및 음악회에 대한 견해(It was interesting)를 이용한 오답이다.
(C) 정답: 오늘 밤에 영화를 보고 싶은지, 음악회에 가고 싶은지 묻는 질문에 보고 싶은 신작 영화가 있다(There is a new film I want to see)며 우회적으로 전자를 선택하고 있으므로 정답이다.

어휘 seat 자리, 좌석　film 영화

6 W-Am / M-Au
Let's try to use less paper in the office this quarter.
(A) In the supply closet.
(B) OK—do you have a plan?
(C) I think he's arriving soon.

이번 분기에는 사무실에서 종이를 덜 사용하도록 합시다.
(A) 비품 보관함이요.
(B) 알겠어요. 계획이 있으신가요?
(C) 그가 곧 도착하는 것 같아요.

해설 제안하는 평서문
(A) 연상 어휘 오답: 평서문의 paper에서 연상 가능한 supply closet을 이용한 오답이다.
(B) 정답: 이번 분기에 사무실에서 종이를 덜 사용하도록 하자는 평서문에 알겠다(OK)고 대답한 뒤, 그렇게 하기 위한 계획이 있냐며(do you have a plan?) 긍정 답변과 일관된 내용을 덧붙이고 있으므로 정답이다.
(C) 인칭 오류 오답: 대명사 he가 가리키는 대상이 평서문에 없다.

어휘 quarter 분기　supply closet 비품 보관실

7 W-Br / M-Cn
Would you like me to show you the way to the cafeteria?
(A) I did like the show.
(B) I wouldn't throw it away.
(C) Actually, I've been there before.

제가 카페테리아로 가는 길을 알려드릴까요?
(A) 저는 그 공연이 참 좋았어요.
(B) 저는 그걸 버리진 않겠어요.
(C) 사실 전에 거기 가 본 적이 있어요.

해설 제안 · 권유의 의문문
(A) 어휘 반복 및 다의어 오답: 질문의 like 및 show를 반복 이용한 오답이다. 또한 질문의 show는 '알려 주다, 안내하다'라는 뜻의 동사이고, 보기의 show는 '공연, 쇼'라는 뜻의 명사이다.
(B) 유사 발음 오답: 질문의 show you the way와 부분적으로 발음이 유사한 throw it away를 이용한 오답이다.
(C) 정답: 카페테리아로 가는 길을 알려 주겠다는 제안에 전에 거기 가 본 적이 있다(I've been there before)며 우회적으로 거절의 의사를 밝히고 있으므로 정답이다.

어휘 throw away 버리다　actually 사실, 실제로

8 M-Au / W-Am
Would you be willing to lead the new employee orientation?
(A) Well, it depends on when it is.
(B) Around twenty-five people.
(C) No, I didn't read it.

신입사원 오리엔테이션 진행을 해 주시겠어요?
(A) 음, 언제인지에 따라서요.
(B) 약 25명요.
(C) 아니요. 저는 그것을 읽지 않았어요.

해설 부탁 · 요청의 의문문
(A) 정답: 신입사원 오리엔테이션을 진행해달라는 부탁에 언제인지에 달려 있다(it depends on when it is)며 수락 여부를 보류하고 있으므로 가장 적절한 응답이다.

(B) 연상 어휘 오답: 질문의 new employee orientation에서 연상 가능한 참석 인원(Around twenty-five people)을 언급한 오답이다.
(C) 유사 발음 오답: 질문의 lead와 부분적으로 발음이 유사한 read를 이용한 오답이다.

어휘 be willing to 기꺼이 ~하다   lead 이끌다
employee 직원   depend on ~에 달려 있다

9 M-Cn / M-Au
Should I start by cleaning the lab equipment or organizing the new supplies?
(A) Let's see what Mr. Park thinks.
(B) To streamline the process.
(C) Yes, they're much better.

실험 장비 청소부터 해야 할까요, 아니면 새 용품들 정리를 먼저 해야 할까요?
(A) 박 씨의 생각을 알아보죠.
(B) 절차를 간소화하려고요.
(C) 네, 그것들이 훨씬 낫네요.

해설 일의 순서를 묻는 선택 의문문
(A) 정답: 청소와 정리 중 어떤 일을 먼저 해야 할지 묻는 질문에 어느 것도 선택하지 않고 박 씨의 생각을 알아보자(Let's see what Mr. Park thinks)며 결정을 보류하고 있으므로 정답이다.
(B) 연상 어휘 오답: 질문의 organizing을 '체계화하다'라는 뜻으로 잘못 이해했을 경우 연상 가능한 streamline the process를 이용한 오답이다.
(C) Yes/No 불가 오답: 선택 의문문에는 Yes/No 응답이 불가능하므로 오답이다.

어휘 lab 실험실   equipment 장비   organize 정리하다, 배열하다
supply 용품   streamline 간소화하다, 능률화하다
process 절차

10 W-Br / M-Au
I'm planning to work on my tax forms soon.
(A) An online employee survey.
(B) Where can I hang this painting?
(C) I'm almost done with mine.

저는 곧 제 세금 신고서를 작성할 계획이에요.
(A) 온라인 직원 설문 조사요.
(B) 이 그림을 어디에 걸면 되나요?
(C) 저는 제 것을 거의 마쳤어요.

해설 상황을 설명하는 평서문
(A) 평서문과 상관없는 오답
(B) 평서문과 상관없는 오답
(C) 정답: 곧 세금 신고서를 작성할 계획이라는 평서문에 my tax forms를 소유 대명사 mine으로 지칭하여 자신의 것, 즉 세금 신고서 작성을 마친 상황임을 밝히고 있으므로 정답이다.

어휘 tax form 납세 신고서   be done with ~을 끝내다

11 W-Am / W-Br
Will you help me move these chairs?
(A) The fifth-floor conference room.
(B) It's at the information desk.
(C) Where do they need to go?

이 의자들 옮기는 걸 도와주실래요?
(A) 5층 회의실요.
(B) 그건 안내 데스크에 있어요.
(C) 그것들이 어디로 가야 해요?

해설 부탁·요청의 의문문
(A) 연상 어휘 오답: 질문의 move these chairs에서 연상 가능한 옮기는 장소(The fifth-floor conference room)를 언급한 오답이다.
(B) 연상 어휘 오답: 질문의 chairs에서 연상 가능한 desk를 이용한 오답이다.
(C) 정답: 의자 옮기는 걸 도와 달라는 요청에 어디로 옮겨야 하는지(Where do they need to go?) 되물으며 관련 정보를 요청하고 있으므로 정답이다.

어휘 conference 회의   information 정보

12 M-Au / W-Am
We should consider buying new audio equipment.
(A) There is a budget surplus this quarter.
(B) Our post has had lots of views.
(C) Yes, we watched it this morning.

새로운 오디오 장비를 구입하는 것을 고려해야 해요.
(A) 이번 분기에 예산이 남았어요.
(B) 우리 게시물이 조회수가 많았어요.
(C) 네, 저희는 오늘 아침에 시청했어요.

해설 제안하는 평서문
(A) 정답: 새로운 오디오 장비를 구입하는 것을 고려해야 한다고 제안하는 평서문에 이번 분기에 예산이 남았다(There is a budget surplus this quarter)며 가능성을 시사하고 있으므로 정답이다.
(B) 평서문과 상관없는 오답
(C) 평서문과 상관없는 오답

어휘 consider -ing ~하는 것을 고려하다   surplus 여분, 과잉
post 게시물

13 W-Br / M-Au
Did the hiring committee choose Norman, or did they pick Heidi?
(A) Neither of them, actually.
(B) She didn't finish them.
(C) Yes, I'd prefer another date.

채용 위원회는 노먼 씨를 선택했나요, 아니면 하이디 씨를 뽑았나요?
(A) 사실 두 명 다 아니에요.
(B) 그녀는 그것들을 끝내지 않았어요.
(C) 네, 저는 다른 날짜를 원합니다.

해설 **고용 대상을 묻는 선택 의문문**
(A) 정답: 누가 고용되었는지 묻는 질문에 노먼 씨와 하이디 씨 중 어느 누구도 뽑지 않았다(Neither of them)고 답하고 있으므로 정답이다.
(B) 질문과 상관없는 오답
(C) 연상 어휘 오답: 질문의 pick에서 연상 가능한 prefer를 이용한 오답이다.

어휘 hiring committee 채용 위원회   neither (둘 중) 어느 것도 아닌

14 M-Cn/W-Am
Could you give me a detailed list of the supplies we should buy?
(A) At least one hundred euros.
(B) An unlisted phone number.
(C) I have it right here.

구입해야 하는 용품 세부 목록을 주시겠어요?
(A) 적어도 100유로요.
(B) 전화번호부에 없는 번호요.
(C) 지금 저에게 있어요.

해설 **부탁·요청의 의문문**
(A) 유사 발음 오답: 질문의 list와 발음이 유사한 least를 이용한 오답이다.
(B) 파생어 오답: 질문의 list와 파생어 관계인 unlisted를 이용한 오답이다.
(C) 정답: 용품 세부 목록을 달라는 요청에 지금 자신이 가지고 있다(I have it right here)며 바로 제공할 수 있음을 나타내고 있으므로 정답이다.

어휘 detailed 상세한   at least 최소한, 적어도   unlisted 전화번호부에 올라 있지 않은

15 W-Am/M-Au
Shall I show you how to make the font size larger?
(A) It is hard to read at this size.
(B) Sure, I'd love to go.
(C) Thanks for the letter.

글씨 크기를 더 크게 만드는 방법을 알려 드릴까요?
(A) 이 크기로는 읽기가 어렵네요.
(B) 물론이죠, 기꺼이 갈게요.
(C) 편지 주셔서 감사합니다.

해설 **제안·권유의 의문문**
(A) 정답: 글씨 크기 확대 방법을 알려 주겠다는 제안에 이 크기로는 읽기 어렵다(It is hard to read at this size)며 방법을 알려 달라고 우회적으로 요청하고 있으므로 정답이다.
(B) 연상 어휘 오답: 질문의 show를 '공연'으로 잘못 이해했을 때 연상 가능한 상황(I'd love to go)을 이용한 오답이다.
(C) 질문과 상관없는 오답

어휘 font 글씨(체)

16 M-Au/W-Am
These sales figures are really high.
(A) A smaller budget.
(B) No, on the eightieth floor.
(C) Let me check the numbers again.

이 매출액은 정말 높네요.
(A) 규모가 더 작은 예산이요.
(B) 아니요, 8층에 있어요.
(C) 제가 숫자를 다시 확인해 보겠습니다.

해설 **사실을 전달하는 평서문**
(A) 연상 어휘 오답: 평서문의 high에서 연상 가능한 smaller를 이용한 오답이다.
(B) 평서문과 상관없는 오답
(C) 정답: 매출액이 정말 높다는 평서문에 숫자를 다시 확인해 보겠다(Let me check the numbers again)며 정확한 수치인지 알아보겠다는 것을 우회적으로 표현하고 있으므로 정답이다.

어휘 sales 매출, 판매(량), 영업   figure 수치, 숫자

17 W-Br/M-Au
Should we eat at a restaurant or call for delivery?
(A) Yes, last month.
(B) Let's have it delivered.
(C) He arranged the flowers.

레스토랑에 가서 먹을까요, 아니면 배달 주문을 할까요?
(A) 네, 지난달에요.
(B) 배달시킵시다.
(C) 그가 그 꽃들을 정리했어요.

해설 **식사 방법을 묻는 선택 의문문**
(A) Yes/No 불가 오답: 선택 의문문에는 Yes/No 응답이 불가능하므로 오답이다.
(B) 정답: 레스토랑에 가서 먹을지, 아니면 배달 주문을 할지 묻는 질문에 배달시키자(Let's have it delivered)며 후자를 선택하여 답했으므로 정답이다.
(C) 인칭 오류 오답: 보기의 He가 가리키는 대상이 질문에 없다.

어휘 call for 요청하다, 요구하다   arrange 정리하다, 배치하다

18 W-Am/W-Br
Ms. Shimizu is going to be working late tomorrow.
(A) OK—thanks for letting me know.
(B) The training session wasn't hard.
(C) I decided not to go.

시미즈 씨가 내일 늦게까지 근무하실 예정입니다.
(A) 알겠습니다. 알려 주셔서 감사합니다.
(B) 그 교육은 힘들지 않았어요.
(C) 저는 가지 않기로 결정했습니다.

해설 **정보를 전달하는 평서문**
(A) 정답: 시미즈 씨가 내일 늦게까지 근무할 예정이라는 평서문에 정보를 알려 준 것에 대해 감사를 표현(OK—thanks for letting me know)하고 있으므로 정답이다.

(B) 평서문과 상관없는 오답
(C) 유사 발음 오답: 평서문의 going과 부분적으로 발음이 유사한 go를 이용한 오답이다.

어휘 let A know A에게 알리다 training session 교육 (과정) decide not to do ~하지 않기로 결정하다

19 M-Cn / M-Au
Let's schedule the award ceremony for Tuesday.
(A) Yes, I worked at a car repair shop.
(B) It's been broken for a few days.
(C) More people would come on a weekend.

시상식 일정을 화요일로 잡읍시다.
(A) 네, 제가 자동차 수리 전문점에서 근무했습니다.
(B) 며칠 동안 고장 난 상태예요.
(C) 주말에 더 많은 사람들이 올 겁니다.

해설 의견을 제시하는 평서문
(A) 평서문과 상관없는 오답
(B) 평서문과 상관없는 오답
(C) 정답: 시상식 일정을 화요일로 잡자고 제안하는 평서문에 주말에 더 많은 사람들이 올 것(More people would come on a weekend)이라며 다른 의견을 제시하고 있으므로 정답이다.

어휘 award ceremony 시상식 repair 수리 broken 고장 난, 망가진, 깨진

20 W-Am / M-Cn
Could you bring doughnuts to tomorrow's meeting?
(A) Please plug in the projector.
(B) To the grocery store.
(C) I'll be calling in to the meeting.

내일 회의 시간에 도넛 좀 가져올 수 있어요?
(A) 프로젝터 전원 코드를 꽂아 주세요.
(B) 식료품점으로요.
(C) 저는 회의에 전화로 참여할 예정이에요.

해설 부탁·요청의 의문문
(A) 질문과 상관없는 오답
(B) 연상 어휘 오답: 질문의 doughnuts에서 연상 가능한 grocery store를 이용한 오답이다.
(C) 정답: 내일 회의 시간에 도넛을 가져올 수 있는지 묻는 질문에 회의에 전화로 참여할 예정(I'll be calling in to the meeting)이라며 상대방의 요청을 들어줄 수 없다는 뜻을 나타내고 있으므로 정답이다.

어휘 plug in ~의 전원 코드를 꽂다 call in to (전화로) 회의·방송 등에 참여하다

21 M-Au / W-Am
I would like to treat our staff to a nice dinner.
(A) We waited ten minutes for a table.
(B) We do have some money left in the budget.
(C) Just the vegetarian platter.

우리 직원들에게 맛있는 저녁을 대접하고 싶어요.
(A) 우리는 10분 동안 자리가 나기를 기다렸어요.
(B) 예산에 남은 돈이 좀 있긴 해요.
(C) 그냥 채식 요리요.

해설 바람을 나타내는 평서문
(A) 연상 어휘 오답: 평서문의 dinner에서 연상 가능한 table을 이용한 오답이다.
(B) 정답: 직원들에게 저녁을 대접하고 싶다는 평서문에 예산에 남은 돈이 있다(We do have some money left in the budget)며 가능성을 시사하고 있으므로 정답이다.
(C) 연상 어휘 오답: 평서문의 dinner에서 연상 가능한 vegetarian platter를 이용한 오답이다.

어휘 vegetarian 채식의, 채식주의자 platter 모듬 요리, 큰 접시

22 M-Cn / W-Br
Do you mind if I borrow your stapler?
(A) In several different colors.
(B) Yes, last week.
(C) Not at all—here it is.

스테이플러를 빌려주실 수 있나요?
(A) 몇 가지 다양한 색으로요.
(B) 네, 지난주요.
(C) 그럼요. 여기 있어요.

해설 부탁·요청의 의문문
(A) 질문과 상관없는 오답
(B) 연상 어휘 오답: 질문의 borrow에서 연상 가능한 빌린 시점(last week)을 언급한 오답이다.
(C) 정답: 스테이플러를 빌려달라고 요청하는 질문에 꺼리지 않는다(Not at all)며 수락한 후, 여기 있다(here it is)고 덧붙이고 있으므로 정답이다.

어휘 borrow 빌리다 several 몇몇의

23 W-Br / W-Am
Is the conference center on the north side of the highway or on the south side?
(A) I'm attending a two-day seminar.
(B) It's to the south, just past Exit 52.
(C) Within an hour or so.

그 회의장은 고속도로 북쪽에 있나요, 아니면 남쪽에 있나요?
(A) 저는 이틀간 열리는 세미나에 참석하고 있어요.
(B) 남쪽으로 52번 출구를 막 지나서 있어요.
(C) 한 시간 정도 이내에요.

해설 회의장의 위치를 묻는 선택 의문문
(A) 연상 어휘 오답: 질문에 나온 conference center에서 연상 가능한 단어 seminar를 이용한 오답이다.
(B) 정답: 회의장이 어느 방향인지 묻는 질문에 고속도로 남쪽(It's to the south)이라고 답한 뒤, 52번 출구를 막 지나서 있다(just past Exit 52)고 덧붙이고 있으므로 정답이다.
(C) 질문과 상관없는 오답

어휘 conference center (대규모) 회의장 past ~을 지나서 exit 출구 or so ~정도

24 M-Au / W-Am

Mr. Ogawa left his office just a minute ago.
(A) On the left side of the filing cabinet.
(B) Oh, I'll come back later.
(C) A new assistant manager.

오가와 씨는 방금 전에 사무실에서 나가셨어요.
(A) 파일 캐비닛 왼쪽 면에요.
(B) 아, 저는 나중에 다시 올게요.
(C) 새로 오신 대리님이요.

해설 정보를 전달하는 평서문
(A) 연상 어휘 오답: 평서문의 office에서 연상 가능한 filing cabinet을 이용한 오답이다.
(B) 정답: 오가와 씨가 방금 전에 사무실에서 나갔다는 평서문에 자신은 나중에 다시 오겠다(Oh, I'll come back later)고 답하고 있으므로 정답이다.
(C) 연상 어휘 오답: 평서문의 office에서 연상 가능한 manager를 이용한 오답이다.

어휘 filing cabinet 파일 캐비닛, 문서 보관함

25 M-Au / W-Br

Would you like to leave now or wait until the traffic clears up?
(A) I'm still finishing up this report.
(B) Downstairs in the lobby.
(C) That's what Jinyu said as well.

지금 출발하시겠어요, 아니면 교통이 풀릴 때까지 기다리시겠어요?
(A) 저는 아직 이 보고서를 마무리하는 중입니다.
(B) 아래층 로비에요.
(C) 진유 씨도 그렇게 말씀하셨어요.

해설 출발 시점을 묻는 선택 의문문
(A) 정답: 지금 출발하고 싶은지, 아니면 교통이 풀릴 때까지 기다리고 싶은지 묻는 질문에 아직 보고서를 마무리하는 중(I'm still finishing up this report)이라는 말로 나중에 출발하겠다는 뜻을 나타내고 있으므로 정답이다.
(B) 질문과 상관없는 오답
(C) 질문과 상관없는 오답

어휘 traffic 차량들, 교통(량) clear up (깨끗이) 없어지다, 정리되다 finish up 마무리하다 as well ~도, 또한

ETS ACTUAL TEST 본책 p. 62

7 (A)	8 (B)	9 (C)	10 (C)	11 (C)	12 (B)
13 (A)	14 (C)	15 (B)	16 (B)	17 (C)	18 (B)
19 (B)	20 (A)	21 (C)	22 (A)	23 (C)	24 (C)
25 (A)	26 (C)	27 (A)	28 (B)	29 (C)	30 (A)
31 (A)					

---

7 M-Au / W-Am

When would you like me to schedule your haircut?
(A) I have time next Thursday afternoon.
(B) The salon on Marble Street.
(C) It was my manager's.

헤어컷 일정을 언제로 잡아 드릴까요?
(A) 다음 주 목요일 오후에 시간이 있어요.
(B) 마블 가에 있는 미용실이요.
(C) 그건 제 매니저의 것이었어요.

해설 헤어컷 예약 일정을 묻는 When 의문문
(A) 정답: 헤어컷 일정을 언제로 잡을지 묻는 질문에 다음 주 목요일 오후에 시간이 있다(I have time next Thursday afternoon)며 가능한 시간을 밝히고 있으므로 정답이다.
(B) 연상 어휘 오답: 질문의 haircut에서 연상 가능한 salon을 이용한 오답이다.
(C) 질문과 상관없는 오답

어휘 salon 미용실, 고급 의상실 등의 상점

8 W-Am / W-Br

Should I call the clients at noon or at two P.M.?
(A) Lunch at Amy's Café.
(B) I called them already.
(C) Two hundred dollars.

고객들에게 전화 드려야 하나요, 아니면 오후 2시에 해야 하나요?
(A) 에이미스 카페의 점심 식사요.
(B) 제가 이미 그분들께 전화 드렸어요.
(C) 2백 달러요.

해설 고객들에게 전화할 시점을 묻는 선택 의문문
(A) 연상 어휘 오답: 질문의 noon에서 연상 가능한 Lunch를 이용한 오답이다.
(B) 정답: 고객들에게 언제 전화를 하면 좋을지 묻는 질문에 자신이 이미 전화했다(I called them already)고 답하며 할 필요가 없다는 뜻을 나타내고 있으므로 정답이다.
(C) 어휘 반복 오답: 질문의 two를 반복 이용한 오답이다.

어휘 client 고객, 의뢰인

9 W-Am / M-Cn

Wouldn't you rather have a dark color for the carpet?
(A) Yes, it's made of wood.
(B) My car's right over there.
(C) That would look good in this room.

카펫을 어두운 색으로 하시겠어요?
(A) 네, 그건 나무로 만들어졌어요.
(B) 제 차는 바로 저기 있어요.
(C) 그게 이 방에 잘 어울리겠어요.

해설 카펫 색상에 대한 의견을 확인하는 부정 의문문
(A) 질문과 상관없는 오답
(B) 유사 발음 오답: 질문의 carpet과 부분적으로 발음이 유사한 car를 이용한 오답이다.
(C) 정답: 카펫을 어두운 색으로 할지 묻는 질문에 이 방에 잘 어울리겠다(That would look good in this room)며 긍정의 응답을 하고 있으므로 정답이다.

어휘 would rather ~하고 싶다, (차라리) ~하겠다
be made of ~로 만들어지다   over there 저쪽에

10 M-Cn / W-Br
The air conditioner's not working very well, is it?
(A) I need to get shampoo as well.
(B) My car's in pretty good condition.
(C) It is a bit warm in here.

에어컨이 아주 잘 작동되는 것 같지는 않네요, 그렇죠?
(A) 저는 샴푸도 구입해야 해요.
(B) 제 자동차 상태가 꽤 좋습니다.
(C) 여기가 좀 덥네요.

해설 동의를 구하는 부가 의문문
(A) 연상 어휘 오답: 질문의 conditioner에서 연상 가능한 shampoo를 이용한 오답이다.
(B) 유사 발음 오답: 질문의 conditioner와 부분적으로 발음이 유사한 condition을 이용한 오답이다.
(C) 정답: 에어컨이 아주 잘 작동하지는 않는 것 같다며 동의를 구하는 질문에 좀 덥다(It is a bit warm in here)며 동조하고 있으므로 정답이다.

어휘 work (기계 등이) 작동하다   in good condition 상태가 좋은

11 W-Am / M-Cn
Why did you get here so early this morning?
(A) Not until the afternoon.
(B) Yes, I submitted it early.
(C) There was less traffic than usual.

오늘 아침엔 왜 이렇게 일찍 도착했어요?
(A) 오후나 되어서요.
(B) 네, 저는 일찍 제출했어요.
(C) 평소보다 교통량이 적었어요.

해설 일찍 도착한 이유를 묻는 Why 의문문
(A) 연상 어휘 오답: 질문의 morning에서 연상 가능한 afternoon을 이용한 오답이다.
(B) 어휘 반복 오답: 질문의 early를 반복 이용한 오답이다.
(C) 정답: 일찍 도착한 이유를 묻는 질문에 평소보다 교통량이 적었다(There was less traffic than usual)며 구체적인 이유를 제시하고 있으므로 정답이다.

어휘 not until ~이후에야 비로소   submit 제출하다
traffic 교통   than usual 평소보다

12 W-Br / W-Am
You can go to the conference on Monday, can't you?
(A) Every Tuesday morning.
(B) No, I have a project deadline.
(C) On platform six.

월요일 회의에 가실 수 있죠, 그렇지 않나요?
(A) 매주 화요일 오전에요.
(B) 아니요, 프로젝트 마감이 있어요.
(C) 6번 승강장에서요.

해설 회의의 참석 여부를 확인하는 부가 의문문
(A) 연상 작용 오답: 질문의 Monday에서 연상 가능한 Tuesday를 이용한 오답이다.
(B) 정답: 월요일 회의에 갈 수 있는지 확인하는 질문에 아니요(No)라고 대답한 뒤, 프로젝트 마감이 있다(I have a project deadline)며 부정 답변과 일관된 내용을 덧붙이고 있으므로 정답이다.
(C) 질문과 상관없는 오답

어휘 conference (대규모) 회의   deadline 마감일, 마감 기한

13 M-Au / M-Cn
Can we listen to music at our desks while we're working?
(A) As long as you wear headphones.
(B) Yes, a new work desk.
(C) No, we didn't hear it.

일하면서 책상에서 음악을 들어도 되나요?
(A) 헤드폰을 착용하기만 한다면요.
(B) 네, 새 업무 책상이에요.
(C) 아니요, 저희는 못 들었어요.

해설 부탁·요청의 의문문
(A) 정답: 일하면서 책상에서 음악을 들어도 되는지 묻는 질문에 헤드폰을 착용하기만 한다면(As long as you wear headphones)이라는 조건을 제시하여 우회적으로 수락의 의사를 드러내고 있으므로 정답이다.
(B) 어휘 반복 오답: 질문의 desk를 반복 이용한 오답이다.
(C) 연상 어휘 오답: 질문의 listen to에서 연상 가능한 hear를 이용한 오답이다.

어휘 as long as ~하기만 하면, ~하는 한

14 W-Br / W-Am
Where can I buy fresh flowers this time of year?
(A) Ten thirty this morning.
(B) Yes, in July and August.
(C) Try the florist on North Avenue.

연중 이맘때쯤 싱싱한 꽃을 어디에서 살 수 있죠?
(A) 오늘 오전 10시 30분이요.
(B) 네, 7월과 8월이에요.
(C) 노스 가에 있는 꽃집에 가보세요.

해설 꽃 구입 장소를 묻는 Where 의문문
(A) 연상 어휘 오답: 질문의 time에서 연상 가능한 ten thirty를 이용한 오답이다.
(B) Yes/No 불가 오답: Where 의문문에는 Yes/No 응답이 불가능하므로 오답이다.
(C) 정답: 꽃을 살 수 있는 장소를 묻는 질문에 특정 장소(the florist on North Avenue)를 제시했으므로 정답이다.

어휘 florist 꽃집, 꽃집 직원

15 M-Au / W-Am
Who's joining the team for the sales trip?
(A) No, that's not what I meant.
(B) Malik has the list.

(C) No, I'd like to buy three tickets.

누가 영업 출장 팀에 합류하나요?
(A) 아니요, 제 말은 그런 뜻이 아니었어요.
(B) 말릭 씨가 명단을 갖고 계세요.
(C) 아니요, 저는 티켓을 세 장 구입하고 싶습니다.

해설 **출장에 합류하는 사람을 묻는 Who 의문문**
(A) **Yes/No 불가 오답**: Who 의문문에는 Yes/No 응답이 불가능하므로 오답이다.
(B) **정답**: 누가 영업 출장 팀에 합류하는지 묻는 질문에 말릭 씨가 명단을 갖고 있다(Malik has the list)며 정보를 아는 사람을 알려 주고 있으므로 정답이다.
(C) **Yes/No 불가 오답**: Who 의문문에는 Yes/No 응답이 불가능하므로 오답이다.

어휘 join 합류하다, 함께하다   sales 영업, 판매(량), 매출

16 W-Br / W-Am
I just heard a news report on the radio about seasonal farm work.
(A) Some homegrown vegetables.
(B) Which station was it on?
(C) For a music producer.

방금 라디오에서 계절에 따른 농장 일에 대한 뉴스를 들었어요.
(A) 집에서 기른 채소들요.
(B) 어떤 방송에서 나왔어요?
(C) 음악 제작자를 위해서요.

해설 **사실을 전달하는 평서문**
(A) **연상 어휘 오답**: 평서문의 farm에서 연상 가능한 vegetables를 이용한 오답이다.
(B) **정답**: 라디오에서 계절에 따른 농장 일에 대한 뉴스를 들었다는 평서문에 어떤 방송에서 나왔는지(Which station was it on?) 되물으며 관련된 정보를 확인하고 있으므로 정답이다.
(C) **연상 어휘 오답**: 평서문의 heard ~ on the radio에서 연상 가능한 music을 이용한 오답이다.

어휘 news report 뉴스 보도   seasonal 계절의   homegrown 국내산의, 집에서 기른   station 방송국, 방송

17 W-Am / W-Br
What time do you want to conduct the inspection?
(A) Because I forgot my bag.
(B) Let me drive instead.
(C) Well, we'll be in a training session all morning.

몇 시에 점검을 실시하고 싶으신가요?
(A) 가방을 깜빡했기 때문이에요.
(B) 제가 대신 운전할게요.
(C) 음, 저희가 오전 내내 교육에 가 있을 겁니다.

해설 **희망 점검 시간을 묻는 What 의문문**
(A) 질문과 상관없는 오답
(B) 질문과 상관없는 오답
(C) **정답**: 점검을 실시하고 싶은 시간을 묻는 질문에 오전 내내 교육에 가 있을 것(we'll be in a training session all morning)이라고 답하여 그 이후에 가능하다는 것을 우회적으로 나타내고 있으므로 정답이다.

어휘 conduct 실시하다   inspection 점검, 검사   instead 대신

18 M-Au / W-Am
Doesn't the cost of the movie ticket include a beverage?
(A) No, the entrance is around the corner.
(B) Only on weekdays.
(C) You can find one in the brochure.

영화표 값에는 음료가 포함되지 않나요?
(A) 아니요, 입구는 모퉁이를 돌면 있어요.
(B) 평일에만요.
(C) 안내책자에서 볼 수 있어요.

해설 **비용 포함 여부를 확인하는 부정 의문문**
(A) 질문과 상관없는 오답
(B) **정답**: 영화표 값에 음료가 포함되지 않는지 묻는 질문에 평일에만(Only on weekends)이라는 조건을 알려 주고 있으므로 정답이다.
(C) **연상 어휘 오답**: 질문의 movie에서 연상 가능한 brochure를 이용한 오답이다.

어휘 include 포함하다   beverage 음료   entrance 입구   weekday 평일   brochure 안내책자

19 W-Br / W-Am
How often do you have to replace your water heater?
(A) Let's go there for lunch.
(B) My landlord takes care of maintenance.
(C) OK, I'll call to cancel my appointment.

온수기를 얼마나 자주 교체하셔야 하나요?
(A) 그곳에 점심 식사하러 갑시다.
(B) 집주인이 유지 보수를 담당해요.
(C) 좋아요, 전화해서 제 예약을 취소할게요.

해설 **온수기 교체 주기를 묻는 How 의문문**
(A) 질문과 상관없는 오답
(B) **정답**: 온수기를 얼마나 자주 교체해야 하는지 묻는 질문에 집주인이 유지 보수를 담당한다(My landlord takes care of maintenance)며 자신은 잘 알지 못한다는 뜻을 나타내고 있으므로 정답이다.
(C) **Yes/No 불가 오답**: How 의문문에는 Yes/No 응답이 불가능한데, OK도 일종의 Yes 응답이라고 볼 수 있으므로 오답이다.

어휘 replace 교체하다   landlord 집주인   take care of ~을 처리하다, ~을 다루다   maintenance 유지 보수   appointment 예약, 약속

20 M-Cn / W-Br
On which day will the store's return policy change?
(A) Here's your change and receipt.
(B) The manager has that information.
(C) Oh, I can work that day.

상점의 반품 정책이 바뀌는 게 언제인가요?
(A) 여기 거스름돈과 영수증 있습니다.
(B) 그것에 대해서는 관리자가 알아요.
(C) 아, 저는 그날 일할 수 있어요.

해설 반품 정책 변경 시점을 묻는 Which 의문문
(A) 다의어 오답: 질문의 change는 '바뀌다'라는 뜻의 동사이고, 보기의 change는 '거스름돈'이라는 뜻의 명사이다.
(B) 정답: 반품 정책 변경 시점을 묻는 질문에 그것에 대해서는 관리자가 안다(The manager has that information)며 정보를 아는 사람을 알려 주고 있으므로 정답이다.
(C) 어휘 반복 오답: 질문의 day를 반복 이용한 오답이다.

어휘 return 반품 policy 정책 receipt 영수증

21 M-Au / W-Am
How are you getting to the department social event tonight?
(A) I just bought one.
(B) I'll be working until late this evening on an important project.
(C) We brought a copy of the business plan.

오늘 밤에 있을 부서 단합 행사에 어떻게 가시나요?
(A) 방금 하나 구입했어요.
(B) 저는 오늘 저녁 늦게까지 중요한 프로젝트 작업을 할 겁니다.
(C) 사업 계획서를 한 부 가져왔어요.

해설 행사에 어떻게 갈 건지 묻는 How 의문문
(A) 질문과 상관없는 오답
(B) 정답: 행사에 어떻게 갈 건지 묻는 질문에 저녁 늦게까지 중요한 프로젝트 작업을 한다(I'll be working until late this evening on an important project)며 참석할 수 없음을 우회적으로 나타내고 있으므로 정답이다.
(C) 질문과 상관없는 오답

어휘 get to ~로 가다, ~에 도착하다

22 W-Br / M-Au
When will the refrigeration unit be repaired?
(A) On Wednesday afternoon.
(B) The weather will be warmer tomorrow.
(C) Yes, she won last night.

냉장 장치는 언제 수리되나요?
(A) 수요일 오후에요.
(B) 내일은 날씨가 더 따뜻할 겁니다.
(C) 네, 그녀가 어젯밤에 이겼어요.

해설 냉장 장치 수리 시점을 묻는 When 의문문
(A) 정답: 냉장 장치가 언제 수리될지 묻는 질문에 구체적인 시점(On Wednesday afternoon)으로 대답하고 있으므로 정답이다.
(B) 질문과 상관없는 오답
(C) Yes/No 불가 오답: When 의문문에는 Yes/No 응답이 불가능하므로 오답이다.

어휘 refrigeration 냉장 unit 장치, 기기 repair 수리하다

23 M-Au / W-Br
Marcela hasn't heard back from the Canadian distributors, has she?
(A) An equal distribution of funds.
(B) I don't think so, no.
(C) Can you help me move those boxes?

마르셀라는 캐나다의 배급사들로부터 연락을 못 받았죠, 그렇죠?
(A) 자금의 공정한 배분이요.
(B) 아닌 것 같아요, 아니에요.
(C) 저 상자들을 옮기는 것 좀 도와주시겠어요?

해설 연락을 받았는지 여부를 확인하는 부가 의문문
(A) 파생어 오답: 질문에 나오는 distributors와 파생어 관계인 distribution을 이용한 오답이다.
(B) 정답: 연락을 받았는지 확인하는 질문에 아닌 것 같다(I don't think so)고 대답한 뒤, 다시 한 번 아니에요(no)라고 확인해 주고 있으므로 정답이다.
(C) 질문과 상관없는 오답

어휘 distributor 배급사, 배포자 equal 동등한, 공정한 distribution 배분

24 W-Am / W-Br
Let's try to get to the conference early tomorrow.
(A) Because it was removed from the agenda.
(B) They got a free trial for that product.
(C) It would be nice to avoid long lines of attendees.

내일 회의에 일찍 도착하도록 합시다.
(A) 의제에서 제외되었기 때문이에요.
(B) 그들은 그 제품의 무료 체험을 받았어요.
(C) 길게 늘어선 참석자들을 피한다면 아주 좋을 거예요.

해설 제안하는 평서문
(A) 연상 어휘 오답: 평서문의 conference에서 연상 가능한 agenda를 이용한 오답이다.
(B) 인칭 오류 오답: 보기의 They가 가리키는 대상이 평서문에 없다.
(C) 정답: 회의에 일찍 가자는 제안에 길게 늘어선 참석자들을 피한다면 아주 좋을 것(It would be nice to avoid long lines of attendees)이라며 찬성의 뜻을 나타내고 있으므로 정답이다.

어휘 remove 없애다, 제거하다 agenda 의제, 안건, 일정표 free trial 무료 체험 attendee 참석자

25 M-Au / M-Cn
Who does the quality control tests on our company's products?
(A) Several people do them.
(B) Only the highest quality materials.
(C) Before Mr. Keith arrived.

우리 회사 제품의 품질 관리 시험은 누가 하나요?
(A) 여러 명이 해요.
(B) 최고급 소재만요.
(C) 키스 씨가 도착하기 전에요.

해설 **품질 관리 시험 담당자를 묻는 Who 의문문**
(A) 정답: 품질 관리 시험의 담당자를 묻는 질문에 여러 명이 한다(Several people do them)고 대답하고 있으므로 정답이다.
(B) 어휘 반복 오답: 질문의 quality를 반복 이용한 오답이다.
(C) 질문과 상관없는 오답

어휘 quality control 품질 관리 product 제품 several 몇몇의 material 재료, 소재

26 M-Au / W-Am
Can you give me an estimate of how long the flight will be?
(A) At the baggage claim.
(B) That's a good price.
(C) It's about five hours.

비행시간이 얼마나 걸릴지 예상해 주실 수 있나요?
(A) 수하물 찾는 곳에서요.
(B) 좋은 가격이네요.
(C) 약 5시간이요.

해설 **부탁・요청의 의문문**
(A) 연상 어휘 오답: 질문의 flight에서 연상 가능한 baggage claim을 이용한 오답이다.
(B) 연상 어휘 오답: 질문의 estimate에서 연상 가능한 a good price를 이용한 오답이다.
(C) 정답: 예상 비행시간을 묻는 질문에 약 5시간(It's about five hours)이라는 대략적인 소요 시간을 알려 주고 있으므로 정답이다.

어휘 estimate 추정(치), 견적(서) baggage claim (공항의) 수하물 찾는 곳

27 W-Br / M-Cn
This bus line will be adding destinations next month.
(A) I'd love to use public transportation to get to work.
(B) An afternoon flight would be more convenient.
(C) A seat next to the window.

이 버스 노선은 다음 달에 목적지를 추가할 예정입니다.
(A) 저는 출근할 때 대중교통을 이용하고 싶어요.
(B) 오후 항공편이 더 편리할 거예요.
(C) 창문 옆에 있는 좌석이요.

해설 **정보를 전달하는 평서문**
(A) 정답: 특정 버스 노선이 다음 달에 목적지를 추가한다는 평서문에 대중교통을 이용해서 출근하고 싶다(I'd love to use public transportation to get to work)며 반가운 소식이라는 생각을 우회적으로 드러내고 있으므로 정답이다.
(B) 평서문과 상관없는 오답
(C) 연상 어휘 오답: 질문의 bus에서 연상 가능한 seat를 이용한 오답이다.

어휘 destination 목적지, 도착지 public transportation 대중교통 convenient 편리한

28 M-Cn / W-Am
Do you know how many guests are expected on Thursday?
(A) It's on the second floor.
(B) A weekly event.
(C) Definitely more than a hundred.

목요일에 손님이 몇 분 오시는지 알고 있나요?
(A) 그건 2층에 있어요.
(B) 주간 행사요.
(C) 틀림없이 100명이 넘을 거예요.

해설 **방문 예상 인원을 묻는 간접 의문문**
(A) 질문과 상관없는 오답
(B) 연상 어휘 오답: 질문의 guests에서 연상 가능한 event를 이용한 오답이다.
(C) 정답: 방문 예정인 손님의 수를 아는지 묻는 질문에 틀림없이 100명이 넘을 것(Definitely more than a hundred)이라며 인원을 예측하고 있으므로 정답이다.

어휘 expect 예상하다, 기대하다 definitely 분명히, 틀림없이 more than ~이상의

29 M-Cn / W-Br
Are you attending the leadership skills workshop today?
(A) I think she would be a great team leader!
(B) Twenty-five participants so far.
(C) No, I have a conflict at that time.

오늘 리더십 기술 워크숍에 참석하시나요?
(A) 그녀는 훌륭한 팀장이 될 것 같아요.
(B) 지금까지 25명의 참가자들이요.
(C) 아니요, 제가 그때 일정이 겹칩니다.

해설 **워크숍 참석 여부를 묻는 일반 의문문**
(A) 인칭 오류/유사 발음 오답: 보기의 she가 가리키는 대상이 질문에 없고, 질문의 leadership과 부분적으로 발음이 유사한 leader를 이용한 오답이다.
(B) 연상 어휘 오답: 질문의 attending과 workshop에서 연상 가능한 participants를 이용한 오답이다.
(C) 정답: 오늘 리더십 능력 워크숍에 참석하는지 묻는 질문에 아니요(No)라고 대답한 뒤, 그때 일정이 겹친다(I have a conflict at that time)는 구체적인 이유를 들어 부정 답변과 일관된 내용을 덧붙이고 있으므로 정답이다.

어휘 participant 참가자 conflict (일정) 충돌, 겹침, 갈등

30 M-Au / W-Am
Why don't we set up a picnic table next to that fence?
(A) There's more shade under the trees.
(B) Here's a lock for your suitcase.
(C) A couple of picnic baskets.

저 담장 옆에 피크닉 테이블을 설치하면 어떨까요?
(A) 나무 아래에 그늘이 더 많아요.
(B) 여기 여행 가방 잠금 장치입니다.
(C) 피크닉용 바구니 두어 개요.

해설 제안·권유의 Why 의문문
(A) 정답: 담장 옆에 피크닉 테이블을 설치하자는 제안에 나무 아래에 그늘이 더 많다(There's more shade under the trees)며 다른 장소를 제안하고 있으므로 정답이다.
(B) 질문과 상관없는 오답
(C) 어휘 반복 오답: 질문의 picnic를 반복 이용한 오답이다.

어휘 set up 설치하다 shade 그늘 lock 잠금 장치, 자물쇠
suitcase 여행 가방

31 W-Br / M-Au
What do you think about buying another printer?
(A) Why don't we wait until next quarter?
(B) A special type of paper.
(C) I printed plenty of copies.

프린터를 더 사는 걸 어떻게 생각하세요?
(A) 다음 분기까지 기다리면 어때요?
(B) 특수한 종류의 종이요.
(C) 저는 복사를 많이 했어요.

해설 프린터 구입에 대한 의견을 묻는 What 의문문
(A) 정답: 프린터를 더 구매하는 것에 대한 의견을 묻는 질문에 다음 분기까지 기다리면 어떨지(Why don't we wait until next quarter?) 되물으며 반대 의사를 우회적으로 드러내고 있으므로 정답이다.
(B) 연상 어휘 오답: 질문의 printer에서 연상 가능한 paper를 이용한 오답이다.
(C) 파생어 오답: 질문의 printer와 파생어 관계인 printed를 이용한 오답이다.

어휘 quarter 분기 plenty of 많은

PART 3   LISTENING COMPREHENSION

UNIT 07 주제·목적 / 화자·장소 문제

1 주제 · 목적 문제

기출 공략 포인트 ······················· 본책 p.70

여 우리 회사 새 **로고 디자인**이 이렇게 힘들 줄은 몰랐어요. 도대체 끝이 날 것 같지 않아요.
남 그러게요. 그래도 결과는 좋잖아요. 그렇지 않아요? **우리 회사를 정확히 표현하고 있어요.** 활동적이면서도 신뢰를 주는 것 같아요.
여 맞아요, 그리고 회사 편지에 작게 나온 것과 매장 간판과 제품에 크게 나온 것 둘 다 잘된 것 같아요.

어휘 come up with ~을 생각해 내다, 제안하다 take forever 시간이 오래 걸리다 result 결과 worthwhile ~한 보람이 있는 sum up 요약하다 exactly 정확히 stand for ~을 나타내다 sporty 화려한, 민첩한 dependable 믿음직한 come out well (일 등이) 잘되다 letterhead 편지지 위쪽의 인쇄문구, 문구가 적힌 편지지

문제 화자들은 무엇을 논의하고 있는가?
(A) 신형 자전거   (B) 회사 로고
(C) 편지   (D) 새 매장

ETS 유형연습   본책 p.71

1 (C) **2** (C) **3** (C) **4** (A)

[1] M-Cn / W-Br

M Thanks for meeting with me to **revise the company budget**, Georgia.
W No problem.
M With the **increase in rent** for office space this year, we're definitely **over budget** right now.
W Yes, we'll have to find areas to **cut back on**.

남 회사 예산을 수정하기 위해 이렇게 만나 주셔서 고마워요, 조지아.
여 별말씀을요.
남 올해 사무실 임대료가 올라서 우리가 지금 확실히 예산을 초과하고 있거든요.
여 맞아요, 비용을 줄일 수 있는 부분을 찾아야 해요.

어휘 revise 수정하다 budget 예산 rent 임대료
definitely 명백히, 분명히 cut back on ~을 줄이다

1 화자들은 무엇에 대해 논의하고 있는가?
(A) 부동산 대출
(B) 승차 공유 계획
(C) 회사 예산
(D) 채용 계획

해설 전체 내용 – 대화의 주제
남자가 첫 대사에서 여자에게 회사 예산을 수정하기 위해 만나줘서 고맙다(Thanks for meeting with me to revise the company budget)고 했으므로 (C)가 정답이다.

어휘 real estate 부동산   initiative 계획, 발전 방안

[2] M-Cn / W-Am

M Hi. This is Yun Wei, the manager for the Enzo Jazz Band.

W Oh, hi. Are you calling about **your concert** on the thirtieth?

M Yes. **Would it be possible for my crew to have access to the venue earlier than we'd agreed upon? They'd like some extra time to set up.**

W No problem. We don't have **any events booked** for the day before.

남 안녕하세요. 저는 연 웨이고요, 엔조 재즈 밴드의 매니저입니다.

여 아, 안녕하세요. 30일에 있을 콘서트와 관련해서 전화 주신 건가요?

남 네. 저희 작업팀이 합의한 것보다 더 일찍 행사장에 출입하는 것이 가능할까요? 준비하는 데 여분의 시간이 좀 있으면 좋겠습니다.

여 문제없습니다. 저희가 그 전날에 예약된 행사가 전혀 없어서요.

어휘 crew (함께 작업하는) 팀, 조   have access to ~에 출입하다, ~에 접근하다   venue 행사장   agree upon ~에 대해 합의하다   extra 여분의, 추가의   set up 준비하다, 설치하다, 설정하다   book 예약하다

2 남자는 왜 전화하고 있는가?
(A) 취소하기 위해
(B) 배송 요청 사항을 변경하기 위해
(C) 추가 준비 시간을 요청하기 위해
(D) 티켓 판매량을 확인하기 위해

해설 전체 내용 – 남자가 전화하는 이유
남자가 두 번째 대사에서 작업팀이 더 일찍 행사장에 출입하는 것이 가능할지 물으면서 준비하는 데 여분의 시간이 있으면 좋겠다(They'd like some extra time to set up)는 이유를 밝혔으므로 (C)가 정답이다.

어휘 cancellation 취소   request 요청; 요청하다   preparation 준비   check on ~을 확인하다   sales 판매(량), 영업

Paraphrasing 대화의 some extra time to set up →
정답의 extra preparation time

[3] W-Am / M-Au

W I'm going to be out of town starting Monday, August first, and **I'd like to put a hold on my mail, please.**

M Certainly. **We can keep your mail here at the post office** while you're away. Incidentally, did you know that you could have your mail forwarded to another address instead?

W Well, I'm actually going to be traveling overseas, so I don't think that'd be possible.

여 제가 8월 1일 월요일부터 여기 없을 거예요. 그래서 우편물을 보류해 주셨으면 해요.

남 네. 안 계신 동안 이곳 우체국에서 우편물을 보관해 드릴 수 있어요. 그런데 우편물을 대신 다른 주소로 보내게 할 수 있는 건 알고 계세요?

여 음, 저는 사실 해외로 나갈 거라서 그건 불가능할 것 같아요.

어휘 put a hold on ~를 보류하다, 중지하다   incidentally 그런데, 그건 그렇고   forward 전달하다   instead 대신   actually 사실은, 실제로   overseas 해외로

3 주로 무엇에 관한 대화인가?
(A) 회의 준비하기
(B) 사무실 다시 꾸미기
(C) 우편물 배송 중단하기
(D) 분실된 소포 찾기

해설 전체 내용 – 대화의 주제
여자가 첫 대사에서 우편물을 보류해 줄 것(I'd like to put a hold on my mail)을 요청한 뒤, 이에 대해 남자가 우체국에서 우편물을 보관할 수 있다(We can keep your mail here at the post office)며 우편물 배송과 관련된 대화를 이어가고 있으므로 (C)가 정답이다.

어휘 organize 조직하다, 준비하다   redecorate 다시 꾸미다, 실내장식을 새로 하다   delivery 배송

[4] W-Br / M-Cn

W Welcome, Mr. Molina. **I'm glad you have time to tour our manufacturing facility.**

M Glad to be here. My car company's been looking for a factory to produce our electric automobile motors. It'll save us a lot of money to work with you since you're locally based. We wouldn't have to pay as much in shipping costs.

여 환영합니다, 몰리나 씨. 저희 제조 시설을 둘러보실 시간이 있으시다니 기쁩니다.

| 남 | 이곳에 오게 되어 기쁩니다. 저희 자동차 회사가 전기차용 모터를 생산할 공장을 계속 찾고 있어요. 지역적으로 기반을 두고 계시기 때문에 함께 일하는 것이 저희에게 많은 비용을 절약하게 해 줄 겁니다. 저희가 운송비를 그만큼 많이 지불할 필요가 없을 거예요. |

어휘 manufacturing 제조 facility 시설(물) look for ~을 찾다 automobile 자동차 locally based 지역에(현지에) 기반을 둔 as much 그만큼 많이

4 남자가 방문한 주 목적은 무엇인가?
(A) 시설을 견학하려고
(B) 계약을 갱신하려고
(C) 일부 자재를 전달하려고
(D) 입사 지원자들을 면접 보려고

해설 전체 내용 – 남자의 방문 목적
여자가 첫 대사에서 자신이 속한 제조 시설을 남자가 둘러볼 시간이 있어서 기쁘다(I'm glad you have time to tour our manufacturing facility)고 했으므로 (A)가 정답이다.

어휘 renew 갱신하다 contract 계약(서) material 자재, 소재, 재료 candidate 지원자, 후보자

2 화자·장소 문제

기출 공략 포인트 .... 본책 p.72

여	안녕하세요, 거하드. **우리가 재배하는 딸기**에 대해 이야기하고 싶다고 하셨죠?
남	예. 올해 **우리 농장**은 지난해보다 수확이 좋아요. 딸기에 다른 브랜드의 비료를 사용하는 색다른 시도를 했다는 게 기뻐요. 그 결과가 놀랍네요!
여	잘됐어요! 그러면 블루베리에도 그 브랜드의 비료를 사용해야겠네요.

어휘 fertilizer 비료

문제 화자들은 어디에서 일하는 것 같은가?
(A) 공원 (B) 농장
(C) 정원 용품 가게 (D) 조경 회사

ETS 유형연습 .... 본책 p.73

1 (B) **2** (C) **3** (A) **4** (B)

[1] M-Au/W-Am

M	Excuse me, when is the next boat trip up the canal?
W	It's at noon, but it's sold out. There's another one at two. **Would you like to buy a ticket for that trip now?** That tour is likely to sell out too.
M	Yes, I'll take two tickets, please.

남	실례지만, 운하 상류로 향하는 다음 보트 투어가 언제 있나요?
여	정오에 있지만 매진되었어요. 2시에 또 있습니다. **지금 그 투어 티켓을 구입하시겠어요?** 그 투어도 매진될 가능성이 있어서요.
남	네, 두 장 구입할게요.

어휘 up ~의 상류 쪽으로 canal 운하 sold out 매진된 be likely to do ~할 가능성이 있다

1 여자는 누구인 것 같은가?
(A) 매장 소유주 (B) 매표 담당 직원
(C) 시 관계자 (D) 시설 관리 직원

해설 전체 내용 – 여자의 직업
여자가 첫 대사에서 남자에게 지금 티켓을 구입하고 싶은지(Would you like to buy a ticket for that trip now?) 묻는 것으로 보아 여자는 매표 담당 직원임을 알 수 있으므로 (B)가 정답이다.

어휘 official 관계자, 당국자 maintenance 시설 관리, 정비

[2] W-Br/M-Cn

W	Good morning. **Are you shopping for furniture today?**
M	Actually, I'm looking for a gift for some friends who just bought a new house. Something decorative, maybe.
W	Over here we have a large selection of decorative glassware—pitchers and vases and even some sculptures—if you think they'd enjoy that.

여	안녕하세요. **오늘 가구 쇼핑 중이신가요?**
남	실은, 막 새 집을 구입한 몇몇 친구들에게 줄 선물을 찾고 있어요. 아마 장식용 제품이면 될 거예요.
여	이쪽에 아주 다양한 장식용 유리 제품이 있는데, 물병과 꽃병, 그리고 조각품들도 있습니다. 그분들께서 마음에 들어 할 거라고 생각하신다면요.

어휘 decorative 장식용의 pitcher 물병, 주전자 sculpture 조각품 a large selection of 아주 다양한

2 대화는 어디에서 이루어지는 것 같은가?
(A) 공장 (B) 건설 현장
(C) 가정용 가구 매장 (D) 부동산 중개소

해설 전체 내용 – 대화 장소
여자가 첫 대사에서 남자에게 가구를 쇼핑하고 있는지(Are you shopping for furniture today?) 묻고 있으므로 (C)가 정답이다.

Paraphrasing 대화의 furniture → 정답의 furnishings

[3] M-Cn / W-Br

M Lucy, have you come up with any ideas for the print campaign for The Sawgrass Company's new line of spring clothing?

W Well, from the samples the client sent us, I think what really stands out is the fabric. The material is so lightweight. Plus, it's washable and wrinkle-resistant.

M Then why don't we market it as travel clothing?

남 루시, 소그래스 사의 봄 의류 신상품용 인쇄물 광고에 대한 아이디어 좀 생각해 봤나요?

여 음, 고객이 보낸 샘플을 보니까 눈에 확 띄는 게 옷감인 것 같아요. 소재가 아주 가벼워요. 게다가 물세탁도 가능하고 주름도 잘 가지 않아요.

남 그럼 여행용 의류로 마케팅하는 것은 어떨까요?

어휘 line (상품의) 종류, 제품군 stand out 눈에 띄다 fabric 천, 옷감 lightweight 가벼운 washable 물세탁 가능한 wrinkle-resistant 주름이 잘 안 가는

3 화자들은 누구일 것 같은가?
(A) 광고 책임자   (B) 의류 영업직원
(C) 패션 디자이너   (D) 잡지 편집자

해설 전체 내용 – 화자들의 직업
남자가 첫 대사에서 여자에게 봄 의류 신상품용 인쇄물 광고에 대한 아이디어가 있는지(have you come up with any ideas for the print campaign for The Sawgrass Company's new line of spring clothing?) 물었고, 여자의 답변을 들은 후 여행용 의류로 마케팅하자며 의견을 제시했으므로, 화자들이 광고 책임자라는 것을 추론할 수 있다. 따라서 (A)가 정답이다.

[4] M-Cn / W-Am

M Welcome to Z Tech Solutions. How can I help you?

W The screen's broken on my laptop. I'm hoping you can fix it.

M Let's take a look. I should be able to replace the screen. But I'll have to order the part.

W Oh, I was hoping it'd be ready within a few days.

남 Z 테크 솔루션즈에 오신 것을 환영합니다. 무엇을 도와드릴까요?

여 제 노트북 컴퓨터의 화면이 고장 났어요. 고쳐 주실 수 있으면 좋겠습니다.

남 한번 살펴 보겠습니다. 화면을 교체해 드릴 수 있을 거예요. 하지만 부품을 주문해야 할 겁니다.

여 아, 저는 며칠 내로 준비되기를 바라고 있었는데요.

어휘 broken 고장 난, 망가진, 깨진 fix 고치다, 바로잡다 take a look 한번 보다 replace 교체하다 part 부품

4 남자는 어디에서 일하는 것 같은가?
(A) 여행사   (B) 컴퓨터 수리점
(C) 자동차 제조사   (D) 영화관

해설 전체 내용 – 남자의 근무 장소
여자가 첫 대사에서 남자에게 자신의 노트북 컴퓨터 화면이 고장 났다(The screen's broken on my laptop)며 수리를 희망한다(I'm hoping you can fix it)고 했으므로 (B)가 정답이다.

ETS 실전문제

본책 p.74

1 (C)	2 (D)	3 (B)	4 (C)	5 (D)	6 (D)
7 (C)	8 (B)	9 (A)	10 (B)	11 (C)	12 (A)
13 (D)	14 (C)	15 (A)	16 (B)	17 (D)	18 (C)
19 (C)	20 (A)	21 (B)	22 (D)	23 (B)	24 (A)

[1-3] M-Au / W-Br

M Thank you for being on my podcast today, Sara. ¹I'm sure my listeners are looking forward to hearing about how to market products in creative ways.

W I'm happy to be here. ²I recently attended a marketing seminar that focused on engaging potential customers through things like games and contests. I'm looking forward to sharing what I learned at that seminar.

M That's great. Before we get into the details, ³could you please tell our listeners how they can contact you if they have questions? You can share your business e-mail address or Web site.

남 오늘 제 팟캐스트에 나와 주셔서 감사합니다. 새라 씨. ¹분명 저희 청취자들께서 창의적인 방식으로 제품을 마케팅하는 방법에 관해 듣는 걸 기대하고 계실 거예요.

여 이곳에 나오게 되어 기쁩니다. 최근에 게임과 콘테스트 같은 것들을 통해 잠재 고객을 끌어들이는 데 중점을 둔 ²마케팅 세미나에 참석했어요. 제가 그 세미나에서 배운 내용을 여러분과 나눌 수 있기를 고대하고 있습니다.

남 아주 좋아요. 세부적으로 들어가기에 앞서, ³질문이 있을 경우에 저희 청취자들께서 연락 드릴 수 있는 방법을 말씀해 주시겠어요? 업무용 이메일 주소나 웹사이트를 공유해 주시면 됩니다.

어휘 look forward to -ing ~하기를 고대하다 market 마케팅하다 creative 창의적인 recently 최근에 attend 참석하다 engage 참여시키다, 관여시키다 details 세부 사항, 상세 정보 contact 연락하다

1 인터뷰 주제는 무엇인가?
(A) 제조   (B) 예산 책정
(C) 마케팅 전략   (D) 미술품 복원

해설 　전체 내용 – 대화 주제
　　　남자가 첫 대사에서 청취자들이 창의적인 방식으로 제품을 마케팅하는 방법에 대해 듣는 것을 기대하고 있다(my listeners are looking forward to hearing about how to market products in creative ways)며 주제를 소개했으므로 (C)가 정답이다.

어휘 　budget 예산을 책정하다　strategy 전략　restoration 복원, 복구

> Paraphrasing 　대화의 how to market products in creative ways → 정답의 Marketing strategies

2 　여자는 최근에 무엇을 했다고 말하는가?
　　(A) 새로운 도시로 이사했다.
　　(B) 새로운 일을 시작했다.
　　(C) 자격증을 갱신했다.
　　(D) 세미나에 참석했다.

해설 　세부 사항 – 여자가 최근에 한 일
　　　여자가 첫 대사에서 최근에 한 마케팅 세미나에 참석했다(I recently attended a marketing seminar)고 했으므로 (D)가 정답이다.

어휘 　certification 자격증, 수료증

3 　여자는 다음에 무엇을 할 것인가?
　　(A) 자신의 책에서 발췌한 내용 읽어 주기
　　(B) 자신의 연락처 공유하기
　　(C) 콘테스트 규칙 설명하기
　　(D) 설문 조사 결과 이야기하기

해설 　세부 사항 – 여자가 다음에 할 일
　　　남자가 마지막 대사에서 청취자들이 연락할 수 있는 방법을 말해 달라고 요청하면서(could you please tell our listeners how they can contact you if they have questions?) 업무용 이메일 주소나 웹사이트를 공유해 주면 된다(You can share your business e-mail address or Web site)고 했으므로 (B)가 정답이다.

어휘 　excerpt 발췌(한 것)　survey 설문 조사(지)

> Paraphrasing 　대화의 your business e-mail address or Web site → 정답의 her contact information

[4-6] W-Br / M-Cn

W 　⁴**Our sales of hockey gear** are way up from this time last year, Koji. Most of the players from the local youth leagues are shopping here!

M 　Yes, sales have been great. Are you still planning to open another store?

W 　I'd love to, but ⁵**rents on retail spaces are still too high**. I'd like to wait until rents drop.

M 　Well, for now we can focus on improving our inventory. With the youth golf course being built nearby, I'd recommend offering more golf equipment.

W 　Good idea! ⁶**Why don't you contact our supplier about golf equipment that's available for us to stock?**

여 　⁴우리 하키 장비 판매량이 작년 이맘때보다 훨씬 더 높아요, 코지 씨. 지역 청소년 리그에 속한 선수들 대부분이 이곳에서 쇼핑하고 있어요!

남 　네, 판매량이 아주 좋았습니다. 여전히 매장을 하나 더 개장할 계획이신가요?

여 　그렇게 하고 싶긴 한데, ⁵소매 공간에 대한 임대료가 여전히 아주 높아요. 임대료가 떨어질 때까지 기다렸으면 해요.

남 　음, 지금은 우리 재고 수준을 개선하는 데 집중할 수 있겠네요. 근처에 청소년 골프 코스가 지어지고 있으니, 골프 장비를 더 제공하는 것이 좋을 것 같아요.

여 　좋은 생각이에요! ⁶우리가 재고로 갖춰 놓을 수 있는 골프 장비와 관련해 공급업체에 연락해 보는 게 어때요?

어휘 　way (강조 부사) 훨씬　local 지역의, 현지의　retail 소매(업)　improve 개선하다　inventory 재고 (목록)　equipment 장비　supplier 공급업체, 공급자　available 이용할 수 있는　stock 재고로 갖추다

4 　화자들은 어디에서 일하는 것 같은가?
　　(A) 부동산 중개소　　(B) 비디오 게임장
　　(C) 스포츠용품 매장　(D) 매표 대행사

해설 　전체 내용 – 근무 장소
　　　여자가 첫 대사에서 하키 장비의 판매량(Our sales of hockey gear)에 대해 언급한 뒤 관련 매출에 대한 대화가 이어지고 있는 것으로 보아 화자들이 일하는 곳이 스포츠용품 매장임을 알 수 있으므로 (C)가 정답이다.

5 　여자는 왜 계획을 연기했는가?
　　(A) 직원을 충분히 갖추고 있지 않다.
　　(B) 허가서가 승인되기를 기다리고 있다.
　　(C) 건물이 수리를 필요로 한다.
　　(D) 임대료가 너무 비싸다.

해설 　세부 사항 – 여자가 계획을 연기한 이유
　　　여자가 두 번째 대사에서 소매 공간에 대한 임대료가 아주 높다(rents on retail spaces are still too high)는 문제점을 원인으로 언급했으므로 (D)가 정답이다.

어휘 　permit 허가서(증)　grant 승인하다, 주다　repair 수리

> Paraphrasing 　대화의 rents on retail spaces are still too high → 정답의 Rents are too expensive

6 　여자는 남자에게 무엇을 하라고 요청하는가?
　　(A) 광고 제출하기
　　(B) 고객들에게 설문 조사하기
　　(C) 시설 견학하기
　　(D) 공급업체에 연락하기

PART 3
UNIT 07

59

해설 **세부 사항 – 여자의 요청 사항**
여자가 마지막 대사에서 재고로 갖춰 놓을 수 있는 골프 장비와 관련해 공급업체에 연락해 볼 것(Why don't you contact our supplier about golf equipment that's available for us to stock?)을 요청했으므로 (D)가 정답이다.

어휘 submit 제출하다 advertisement 광고 survey 설문 조사하다

[7-9] 3인 대화 M-Au / W-Am / W-Br

M	**7 Hotel Bristol front desk. This is Luca. How can I help you?**
W1	My name's Sabine Klein. I checked out yesterday from room 202, but **8 I think I left my jacket behind. Have you found it?**
M	Let me transfer you to the housekeeping department. Hold on a moment, please.
W2	Hello, Ms. Klein. My colleague told me about your jacket. Could you please describe it for me?
W1	It's blue with a black collar and silver buttons.
W2	I have it here. If you'd like, we could ship it to you and charge the cost of delivery to the credit card we have on file. **9 We'll just need to know where you'd like it sent.**
남	**7 호텔 브리스톨 프런트 데스크입니다. 저는 루카입니다. 무엇을 도와드릴까요?**
여1	제 이름은 사빈 클라인입니다. 제가 어제 202호실에서 체크아웃했는데, **8 재킷을 놓아 두고 온 것 같아요. 혹시 찾으셨나요?**
남	객실 관리팀으로 연결해 드리겠습니다. 잠시만 기다려 주세요.
여2	안녕하세요, 클라인 씨. 동료에게 재킷 이야기를 들었습니다. 어떤 재킷인지 자세히 말씀해 주시겠어요?
여1	파란색이고 검은색 칼라에 은색 단추가 달려 있어요.
여2	여기 있습니다. 원하시면 등록된 신용카드로 배송비를 청구하고 보내 드릴 수 있어요. **9 배송을 원하시는 곳만 알면 됩니다.**

어휘 leave A behind A를 놓아 두고 오다 transfer 연결해주다, 이동시키다 housekeeping 객실 관리(원) colleague 동료 (직원) describe 설명하다, 묘사하다 ship 배송하다 charge 청구하다 on file 등록된, 보관 중인

7 남자는 누구인 것 같은가?
(A) 렌터카 업체 직원   (B) 백화점 관리자
(C) 호텔 접수 담당자   (D) 레스토랑 직원

해설 **전체 내용 – 남자의 직업**
남자가 첫 대사에서 호텔 브리스톨 프런트 데스크라고 언급하면서 무엇을 도와줄지(Hotel Bristol front desk. This is Luca. How can I help you?) 물었으므로 (C)가 정답이다.

어휘 rental 대여, 임대 agent 직원, 대리인 receptionist 접수 담당자, 안내 담당자

8 클라인 씨는 왜 전화를 하고 있는가?
(A) 예약을 변경하기 위해
(B) 분실물에 관해 묻기 위해
(C) 잘못 청구된 요금을 알리기 위해
(D) 정책에 관해 문의하기 위해

해설 **전체 내용 – 클라인 씨가 전화하는 이유**
여자가 첫 대사에서 재킷을 놓아 두고 온 것 같다며 혹시 그것을 찾았는지(I think I left my jacket behind. Have you found it?) 물었으므로 정답은 (B)이다.

어휘 reservation 예약 missing 분실한, 없는, 빠진 inquire 문의하다 policy 정책, 방침

> **Paraphrasing** 대화의 left my jacket behind → 정답의 a missing item

9 클라인 씨는 다음에 무엇을 할 것 같은가?
(A) 주소 제공하기   (B) 일정표 확인하기
(C) 동료와 이야기하기   (D) 은행에 가기

해설 **세부 사항 – 클라인 씨가 다음에 할 일**
두 번째 여자가 마지막 대사에서 클라인 씨에게 배송을 원하는 장소만 알면 된다(We'll just need to know where you'd like it sent)고 한 것으로 보아 클라인 씨는 재킷을 받을 수 있는 주소를 제공할 것으로 예상할 수 있다. 따라서 (A)가 정답이다.

> **Paraphrasing** 대화의 where you'd like it sent → 정답의 an address

[10-12] W-Am / M-Cn

W	OK, **10 we have the dinosaur exhibit opening on Friday**, so let's go over some details about the opening-night activities for our members.
M	Right. **11 Our guides will give a tour of the exhibit from five to six P.M.**, and immediately afterward the reception will begin.
W	Yes. **12 Do you know how many people have reserved a ticket? I need to tell the caterer how many people will be coming.**
여	자, **10 금요일에 시작하는 공룡 전시회가 있으니**, 우리 회원들을 대상으로 하는 개막일 야간 활동에 대한 세부 사항을 살펴보죠.
남	좋습니다. **11 가이드들이 오후 5시부터 6시까지 전시회 투어를 제공할 것이고**, 그 직후에 축하 연회가 시작될 겁니다.
여	네. **12 몇 명이나 입장권을 예매했는지 아시나요? 출장 요리 업체에 얼마나 많은 분들이 오실지 알려 줘야 하거든요.**

어휘 exhibit 전시(회) go over ~을 살펴보다, ~을 검토하다 immediately 즉시 afterward 그 후에, 나중에 reception 축하 연회 reserve 예약하다 caterer 출장 요리 업체

10 화자들은 어디에서 일하는가?
(A) 식물원   (B) 박물관
(C) 스포츠 경기장   (D) 극장

해설 전체 내용 – 화자들의 근무 장소
여자가 첫 대사에서 금요일에 시작하는 공룡 전시회가 있다(we have the dinosaur exhibit opening on Friday)며 세부 사항을 살펴보자(let's go over some details)고 했으므로 (B)가 정답이다.

11 남자에 따르면, 오후 5시에 무슨 일이 있을 것 같은가?
(A) 동영상을 보여 줄 것이다.
(B) 시설이 청소될 것이다.
(C) 투어가 시작할 것이다.
(D) 매표소가 문을 열 것이다.

해설 세부 사항 – 오후 5시에 있을 일
남자가 첫 대사에서 가이드들이 오후 5시부터 6시까지 전시회 투어를 제공할 것(Our guides will give a tour of the exhibit from five to six P.M.)이라고 했으므로 (C)가 정답이다.

> **Paraphrasing** 대화의 will give a tour → 정답의 A tour will begin

12 여자는 행사와 관련해 어떤 정보를 필요로 하는가?
(A) 참석자 수
(B) 출장 요리 서비스 비용
(C) 필요한 장비의 종류
(D) 기조 연설자 이름

해설 세부 사항 – 여자가 필요로 하는 정보
여자가 마지막 대사에서 출장 요리 업체에 알려줘야 한다(I need to tell the caterer)며 몇 명이나 입장권을 예매했는지(Do you know how many people have reserved a ticket?) 물었으므로 (A)가 정답이다.

어휘 required 필요한, 필수의   keynote speaker 기조 연설자

> **Paraphrasing** 대화의 how many people have reserved a ticket → 정답의 The number of people attending

[13-15] M-Au / W-Am

M Hey Mayumi, **13didn't you go see the Johnny Clyde Jazz Trio last night?** I was thinking of seeing them this Saturday—**13how were they**?

W **13Actually, I was pretty disappointed.** The band was really good, but **14it was hard to hear them because the speaker system at the theater wasn't working well.** I think some of the equipment may have been broken. We decided to leave halfway through the show.

M That's too bad. You know, **15you should ask for your money back**. I'm sure the theater doesn't want a lot of negative reviews.

남 마유미, **13어젯밤 조니 클라이드 재즈 트리오 공연 보지 않았어요?** 이번 토요일에 보려고 생각 중이거든요. **13어땠나요?**

여 **13사실 정말 실망했어요.** 밴드는 정말 훌륭했는데 **14공연장 스피커 시스템이 제대로 작동하지 않아서 잘 들리지 않았거든요.** 장비 일부가 고장 났던 것일 수도 있어요. 그래서 공연 중간에 나오기로 결정했죠.

남 유감이네요. **15환불해 달라고 요청하셔야 해요.** 공연장 측에서는 나쁜 후기가 많은 것을 원치 않을 겁니다.

어휘 disappointed 실망한   theater 극장   halfway through ~의 중간쯤   negative 부정적인   review 후기, 평가

13 화자들은 주로 무엇에 대해 이야기하는가?
(A) 연극   (B) 운동 경기
(C) 영화 시사회   (D) 음악회

해설 전체 내용 – 대화의 주제
남자가 첫 대사에서 조니 클라이드 재즈 트리오 공연(the Johnny Clyde Jazz Trio)이 어땠는지(how were they?) 묻자 여자가 정말 실망했다(Actually, I was pretty disappointed)며 공연과 관련된 대화를 이어가고 있으므로 (D)가 정답이다.

> **Paraphrasing** 대화의 the Johnny Clyde Jazz Trio → 정답의 A concert

14 여자는 왜 실망했는가?
(A) 표를 구할 수 없었다.
(B) 행사 시작 부분을 놓쳤다.
(C) 음향 시스템이 제대로 작동하지 않았다.
(D) 사람들 몇 명이 시야를 가렸다.

해설 세부 사항 – 여자가 실망한 이유
여자가 첫 대사에서 공연에 실망했다고 한 뒤, 공연장 스피커 시스템이 제대로 작동하지 않아서 잘 들리지 않았다(it was hard to hear them because the speaker system at the theater wasn't working well)는 이유를 덧붙였으므로 (C)가 정답이다.

어휘 miss 놓치다   block one's view ~의 시야를 가리다

> **Paraphrasing** 대화의 the speaker system → 정답의 The sound system

15 남자는 여자가 무엇을 해야 한다고 생각하는가?
(A) 환불 요청하기
(B) 다른 공연 참석하기
(C) TV 프로그램 시청하기
(D) 후기 쓰기

해설 세부 사항 – 남자의 제안 사항
남자가 마지막 대사에서 환불해 달라고 요청할 것(you should ask for your money back)을 여자에게 제안했으므로 (A)가 정답이다.

어휘 refund 환불   performance 공연

> **Paraphrasing** 대화의 ask for your money back → 정답의 Ask for a refund

[16-18] 3인 대화 M-Au / W-Am / W-Br

M Great job, Susana and Eun-Mi. **16** You were both instrumental in achieving our record-high sales figures this quarter.

W1 Thanks, Mr. Cho. I think advertising on social media for the first time really made a difference.

W2 I agree. **17** I'd suggest we all go out for lunch to celebrate, but Susana and I have a meeting with a new client in twenty minutes.

M Why don't we plan to go tomorrow? There's a new French restaurant in the neighborhood I've been meaning to try.

W1 That would be wonderful.

M Great. **18** I'll make a reservation right away.

남 수고 많으셨습니다. 수잔나 씨 그리고 은미 씨. **16** 두 분 모두 이번 분기에 우리가 사상 최고의 판매 수치를 달성하는 데 중요한 역할을 해 주셨어요.

여1 감사합니다. 조 씨. 처음으로 소셜 미디어에 광고를 해본 게 정말 효과가 있었던 것 같아요.

여2 맞아요. **17** 축하할 겸 다 같이 점심 식사하러 나가는 걸 제안하고 싶지만, 수잔나 씨와 제가 20분 후에 신규 고객과 회의가 있네요.

남 그럼 내일 가는 것으로 계획하면 어떨까요? 근처에 새로 생긴 프랑스 식당이 있는데, 한번 가보고 싶었거든요.

여1 너무 좋네요.

남 좋아요. **18** 제가 지금 바로 예약할게요.

어휘 be instrumental in ~에 있어 중요한 역할을 하다 achieve 달성하다, 성취하다 record-high 사상 최고의 figure 수치, 숫자 quarter 분기 make a difference 효과가 있다, 차이를 만들다 mean to do ~할 생각이다

16 화자들은 어느 부서에서 일하는 것 같은가?
(A) 회계 (B) 영업
(C) 법무 (D) 인사

해설 전체 내용 – 화자들의 근무 부서
남자가 첫 대사에서 여자들에게 이번 분기에 사상 최고의 판매 수치를 달성하는 데 중요한 역할을 했다(You were both instrumental in achieving our record-high sales figures this quarter)고 한 것을 보아 화자들은 판매 업무를 담당하는 영업 부서에서 일할 것임을 알 수 있다. 따라서 (B)가 정답이다.

17 왜 축하를 미루어야 하는가?
(A) 프로젝트 마감 기한이 변경될 수 없다.
(B) 회사 임원이 사무실을 방문한다.
(C) 행사장이 이용할 수 없다.
(D) 고객 회의가 예정되어 있다.

해설 세부 사항 – 축하를 연기하는 이유
두 번째 여자가 첫 대사에서 축하할 겸 다 같이 점심 식사하러 나가는 걸 제안하고 싶지만 수잔나 씨와 자신은 20분 후에 신규 고객과 회의가 있다(I'd suggest we all go out for lunch to celebrate, but Susana and I have a meeting with a new client in twenty minutes)고 말하고 있으므로 (D)가 정답이다.

어휘 celebration 축하, 기념 행사 postpone 미루다, 연기하다 deadline 마감 기한 executive 임원, 이사 unavailable 이용할 수 없는

> **Paraphrasing** 대화의 have a meeting with a new client → 정답의 A client meeting is scheduled

18 남자는 다음에 무엇을 할 것인가?
(A) 문서에 서명하기
(B) 웹사이트 업데이트하기
(C) 예약하기
(D) 입사 지원서 검토하기

해설 세부 사항 – 남자가 다음에 할 일
남자가 마지막 대사에서 지금 바로 예약하겠다(I'll make a reservation right away)고 했으므로 (C)가 정답이다.

어휘 review 검토하다, 살펴보다 application 지원(서), 신청(서)

[19-21] W-Am / M-Cn

W Good afternoon, Mr. Robertson. You didn't have any trouble parking today, did you?

M **19** Well, Doctor, I did, actually. That's why I'm late.

W **20** I'm sorry about that. We're repaving our parking area, and it's a little inconvenient. So, what brings you in today?

M Well, I've been sneezing a lot, and my eyes are itchy. It just started about a week ago.

W That sounds like allergies. It's spring, and you're probably allergic to the pollen in the air. **21** I'll prescribe some medication for you.

M Thanks. **21** I can pick it up at the pharmacy later today.

여 안녕하세요, 로버트슨 씨. 오늘 주차하시는 데 별 문제 없으셨죠, 그렇죠?

남 **19** 저, 의사 선생님, 실은, 있었습니다. 그래서 늦었어요.

여 **20** 죄송합니다. 저희가 주차 구역을 재포장하고 있어서, 좀 불편해요. 자, 오늘은 무슨 일로 오신 건가요?

남	그게, 계속 재채기를 많이 하고 있고, 눈이 가려워서요. 딱 일주일 전쯤 시작됐어요.
여	알레르기인 것 같네요. 봄철인데다, 아마 공기 중의 꽃가루에 알레르기가 있으신 것 같아요. 21약을 좀 처방해 드리겠습니다.
남	감사합니다. 21오늘 이따가 약국에서 찾아갈 수 있어요.

어휘 have trouble -ing ~하는 데 문제를 겪다   park 주차하다   repave (바닥 등을) 재포장하다   inconvenient 불편한   sneeze 재채기하다   itchy 가려운   pollen 꽃가루   prescribe 처방하다   medication 약(물)   pharmacy 약국

19 대화는 어디에서 이루어지는가?
(A) 피트니스 센터   (B) 가구 매장
(C) 병원   (D) 농산물 시장

해설 전체 내용 – 대화 장소
남자가 첫 대사에서 여자를 의사(Doctor)라고 불렀으므로 (C)가 정답이다.

20 여자는 무엇에 대해 사과하는가?
(A) 공사   (B) 소음
(C) 추가 요금   (D) 직원 부족

해설 세부 사항 – 여자가 사과하는 이유
여자가 두 번째 대사에서 사과의 말과 함께 주차 구역을 재포장하고 있다(I'm sorry about that. We're repaving our parking area)며 불편이 초래된 이유를 설명하고 있으므로 (A)가 정답이다.

어휘 apologize for ~에 대해 사과하다   charge (청구하는) 요금   shortage 부족

> **Paraphrasing** 대화의 repaving our parking area → 정답의 construction

21 남자는 오늘 이따가 무엇을 하겠다고 말하는가?
(A) 회원권 갱신하기   **(B) 처방약 찾아가기**
(C) 은행에 예금하기   (D) 견학하기

해설 세부 사항 – 남자가 오늘 할 일
여자가 후반부에서 약을 처방해 주겠다(I'll prescribe some medication for you)고 하자, 남자가 오늘 이따가 약국에서 찾아갈 수 있다(I can pick it up at the pharmacy later today)고 했으므로 (B)가 정답이다.

어휘 prescription 처방약, 처방전   deposit 예금, 보증금

> **Paraphrasing** 대화의 prescribe some medication → 정답의 prescription

[22-24] W-Br / M-Cn

W	Mr. Howard, 22thank you for agreeing to answer a few questions for the article I'm writing. We at *Architectural Art* magazine were surprised to hear that you'll be retiring soon. You've been leading your firm for the last thirty years. How will your decision affect your company?
M	It really won't. 23At our firm, our mission is to build homes that families can afford. The new CEO will continue to be dedicated to the company's goal of building homes that are within the means of most people.
W	Well, I'm sure you're looking forward to having more free time. What are your plans for the future?
M	24I'll continue to pursue my architectural interests by giving lectures at different universities. That way, I can spend all my time doing what I love most—discussing architecture, rather than running a business.
여	하워드 씨, 22제가 쓰고 있는 기사를 위한 몇 가지 질문에 답해 주시기로 한 점 감사드립니다. 저희 〈건축 예술〉 잡지사는 사장님께서 곧 은퇴하신다는 소식을 듣고 놀랐습니다. 지난 30년간 회사를 이끌어 오셨는데요. 사장님의 결정이 회사에 어떤 식으로 영향을 미칠까요?
남	큰 영향이 없을 겁니다. 23저희 회사의 임무는 일반 가정이 감당할 수 있는 집을 짓는 것입니다. 신임 CEO는 대부분의 사람들의 자금 범위 내에 있는 집을 짓겠다는 저희 회사의 목표에 계속해서 헌신할 것입니다.
여	음, 분명히 더 많은 자유 시간을 기대하고 계실텐데요. 앞으로 계획은 어떻게 되나요?
남	24여러 대학에서 강의를 하면서 건축에 대한 관심을 이어갈 겁니다. 그렇게 하면 사업체를 운영하는 대신, 제가 가장 좋아하는 일인 건축에 대해 토론하는 데 온전히 시간을 보낼 수 있을 거예요.

어휘 article 기사   architectural 건축학의   lead 이끌다   affect 영향을 끼치다   mission 임무, 사명   afford ~을 살 여유가 있다   be dedicated to ~에 전념하다   means 자금, 재력   pursue 추구하다   interest 관심   run 운영하다

22 여자는 누구인 것 같은가?
(A) 건축 감리사   (B) 경영 컨설턴트
(C) 건축가   **(D) 기자**

해설 전체 내용 – 여자의 직업
여자가 첫 대사에서 자신이 쓰고 있는 기사를 위한 질문에 답변해 주기로 한 점 고맙다(thank you for agreeing to answer a few questions for the article I'm writing)고 말하는 것을 보아, 여자는 기자임을 알 수 있다. 따라서 (D)가 정답이다.

23 하워드 씨 회사의 목표는 무엇인가?
(A) 재활용 자재 이용
(B) 가격이 적당한 주택 건설
(C) 역사적인 건축물 보존
(D) 에너지 효율성 증대

해설 **세부 사항 – 회사의 목표**
남자가 첫 대사에서 회사의 임무는 일반 가정이 감당할 수 있는 집을 짓는 것(to build homes that families can afford)이라고 했으므로 (B)가 정답이다.

어휘 affordable 가격이 적당한 preserve 보존하다
structure 건축물 efficiency 효율성

> **Paraphrasing** 대화의 build homes that families can afford → 정답의 Building affordable homes

24 하워드 씨는 앞으로 무엇을 할 계획인가?
(A) 대학 강의
(B) 책 출판
(C) 자원봉사 프로젝트 진행
(D) 해외 사무실 개업

해설 **세부 사항 – 미래 계획**
마지막 대사에서 남자가 여러 대학에서 강의를 하면서 건축에 대한 관심을 계속 이어갈 것(I'll continue to pursue my architectural interests by giving lectures at different universities)이라고 했으므로 (A)가 정답이다.

어휘 publish 출판하다 overseas 해외의

> **Paraphrasing** 대화의 giving lectures at different universities → 정답의 Speak at universities

UNIT 08 세부 사항 / 문제점·걱정거리 문제

1 세부 사항 문제

기출 공략 포인트 ················· 본책 p.76

여 안녕하세요, 켄. 회의 준비는 어떻게 진행되고 있죠?
남 잘되고 있어요. **우리가 부스에서 선보일 제품을 설명하는 자료집** 초안 작성을 방금 끝냈어요.
여 좋습니다. 내게 이메일로 한 부 보내 줄래요? 직접 내용을 검수하고 싶어요.

문제 자료집에는 무엇이 들어 있는가?
(A) 회사 소개   (B) 부스 규정
(C) 회의 일정   (D) 제품 상세 설명

어휘 description 설명, 소개 regulation 규정, 규제

ETS 유형연습 ················· 본책 p.77

1 (A)   **2** (D)   **3** (C)   **4** (B)

---

[1] W-Br / M-Au

W Hi, Hongtai. **How has your first week been as an intern?**
M Very interesting! I've always wanted to work at an aquarium.
W That's great. Today I'll show you how to perform the feedings for the fish in the freshwater habitats.

여 안녕하세요, 홍타이 씨. 인턴으로서 보내신 첫 주는 어떠셨나요?
남 아주 흥미로웠습니다! 제가 항상 수족관에서 일해 보고 싶었거든요.
여 잘됐네요. 오늘은 제가 민물 서식지에 사는 물고기에게 먹이를 주는 방법을 보여 드릴 겁니다.

어휘 aquarium 수족관 perform 실시하다, 수행하다
feeding 먹이 주기 habitat 서식지

1 지난주에 무엇이 시작된 것 같은가?
(A) 인턴십 프로그램   (B) 미술 전시회
(C) 과학 실험   (D) 리모델링 프로젝트

해설 **세부 사항 – 지난주에 시작된 것**
여자가 첫 대사에서 남자에게 인턴으로서 보낸 첫 주가 어땠는지(How has your first week been as an intern?) 묻는 것으로 보아 인턴 프로그램이 지난주에 시작되었다는 것을 알 수 있으므로 (A)가 정답이다.

---

[2] M-Au / W-Am

M Welcome to Marley's Dance Shop.
W Hi. **I'm here in Sydney to compete in the All-Star dance competition**, and I need a new pair of dance shoes right away.
M Oh, did something happen to yours?
W Well, my suitcase was put on the wrong flight and ended up in Melbourne.

남 말리스 댄스 매장에 오신 것을 환영합니다.
여 안녕하세요. **올스타 댄스 경연대회에 참가하기 위해 이곳 시드니에 왔는데요.** 새 댄스용 신발 한 켤레가 지금 바로 필요합니다.
남 아, 신발에 무슨 문제라도 생겼나요?
여 그게, 제 여행 가방이 엉뚱한 항공편에 실리면서 결국 멜버른으로 갔어요.

어휘 compete (대회 등에) 참가하다 competition 경연대회
suitcase 여행 가방 end up 결국 ~되다

2 여자는 왜 시드니에 있는가?
(A) 무대 공연 오디션을 보기 위해
(B) 댄스 강좌를 수강하기 위해
(C) 친구의 파티에서 공연하기 위해
(D) 댄스 경연대회에 참가하기 위해

해설 **세부 사항 – 여자가 시드니에 간 이유**
여자가 첫 대사에서 올스타 댄스 경연대회에 참가하기 위해 시드니에 왔다(I'm here in Sydney to compete in the All-Star Dance Competition)고 했으므로 (D)가 정답이다.

어휘 theater production 무대 공연 (작품) participate in ~에 참가하다

> **Paraphrasing** 대화의 compete in the All-Star Dance Competition → 정답의 participate in a dance competition

[3] W-Br / M-Au

W Hello, my name is Melissa Stein. I'm calling because I'm planning to sell my house. **I was referred to you by a coworker.** You helped her sell her house a while ago, and she was very pleased with your agency.

M I'd be happy to help you with that, Ms. Stein. Are you ready to put the house on the market immediately?

여 안녕하세요, 제 이름은 멜리사 스테인입니다. 집을 매매할 계획이라 전화드립니다. 제 동료가 소개해 주었어요. 얼마 전에 제 동료의 집을 팔아주셨다는데 그쪽 부동산이 아주 만족스러웠다고 하네요.

남 기꺼이 도와드리죠, 스테인 씨. 집을 바로 매물로 내놓을 수 있나요?

어휘 refer A to B A한테 B에게 문의하라고 하다 coworker 동료 put A on the market A를 (팔려고) 시장에 내놓다

3 여자는 남자의 부동산 중개소를 어떻게 알았는가?
 (A) 이웃으로부터 (B) 잡지에서
 (C) 동료로부터 (D) 인터넷에서

해설 **세부 사항 – 여자가 남자의 부동산 중개소를 알게 된 방법**
여자가 첫 대사에서 집을 팔 생각인데 직장 동료가 소개를 해줘서(I was referred to you by a coworker) 전화를 한다고 했다. 따라서 (C)가 정답이다.

[4] M-Au / W-Br

M Hi, Barbara. Nice to run into you! We've missed you since you left Allen Real Estate.

W Kevin! Yes, it's been a while. That was a big decision, to change companies. But I like my new job a lot.

M That's great. How's the work different from what you did with us?

W Well—I only handle commercial properties now. **But I like being able to focus on one area.**

남 안녕하세요, 바바라. 이렇게 만나게 돼서 반가워요! 앨런 부동산을 떠난 뒤로 보고 싶었어요.

여 케빈! 네, 오랜만이에요. 회사를 옮긴다는 게 큰 결정이긴 했죠. 하지만 새 직장이 정말 마음에 들어요.

남 잘됐네요. 우리와 일할 때와 업무가 어떻게 다른가요?

여 음, 저는 지금 상업용 부동산만 다뤄요. 그래도 한 분야에 집중할 수 있어서 좋아요.

어휘 commercial 상업용의 property 부동산

4 여자는 자신의 직업에 대해 무엇이 좋다고 말하는가?
 (A) 창의성을 활용하는 것
 (B) 한 분야를 전문으로 다루는 것
 (C) 보너스 급여를 받는 것
 (D) 출장 기회를 갖는 것

해설 **세부 사항 – 여자가 마음에 들어 하는 점**
여자가 두 번째 대사에서 한 분야에 집중할 수 있어서 좋다(I like being able to focus on one area)고 했으므로 (B)가 정답이다.

어휘 creativity 창의성 specialize in ~을 전문으로 하다

2 문제점·걱정거리 문제

기출 공략 포인트   본책 p.78

여 혹시 로스앤젤레스로 가는 다음 비행기를 탈 방법이 있을까요? 뉴욕에서 타고 온 비행기가 정시에 도착하지 못하는 바람에 연결편을 놓쳤어요.
남 잠시만요. 직항편은 없지만 샌프란시스코에서 갈아타도 괜찮으시다면 20분 후에 떠나는 비행기가 하나 있어요.
여 로스앤젤레스로 갈 수만 있다면 탈게요.

문제 여자의 문제는 무엇인가?
 (A) 수하물을 잃어버렸다.
 (B) 비행기를 놓쳤다.
 (C) 항공권을 안 가져왔다.
 (D) 탑승구가 어디인지 모른다.

ETS 유형연습   본책 p.79

1 (C) 2 (B) 3 (D) 4 (D)

[1] M-Cn / W-Am

M Hey, Narumi. There's a college job fair happening downtown this weekend. Maybe we can finally fill our entry-level graphic designer position.

W I don't know. **I'm worried that we'll spend too much time on this and still won't find any suitable candidates.**

남 안녕하세요, 나루미 씨. 이번 주말에 시내에서 열리는 대학 취업 박람회가 있어요. 아마 우리가 드디어 사원급 그래픽 디자이너 직책을 충원할 수 있을 겁니다.

65

여 저는 잘 모르겠어요. 우리가 이 일에 너무 많은 시간을 소비하다가 여전히 어떤 적합한 후보자도 찾지 못할까 봐 걱정돼요.

어휘 job fair 취업 박람회   entry-level 사원급의   position 직책, 일자리   suitable 적합한, 알맞은   candidate 후보자, 지원자

1 여자는 무엇을 걱정하는가?
(A) 마감 기한을 놓치는 것
(B) 고객을 실망시키는 것
(C) 시간을 허비하는 것
(D) 기술적인 문제에 직면하는 것

해설 세부 사항 – 여자가 걱정하는 것
여자가 첫 대사에서 너무 많은 시간을 소비하다가 적합한 후보자를 찾지 못할까 봐 걱정(I'm worried that we'll spend too much time on this and still won't find any suitable candidates)이라고 했으므로 (C)가 정답이다.

어휘 miss 놓치다, 지나치다   disappoint 실망시키다   encounter 직면하다

Paraphrasing 대화의 spend too much time → 정답의 Wasting time

[2] W-Am / M-Cn

W I'm looking for the current issue of *Crafts Magazine*. Do you know if the library stopped subscribing to it? It wasn't in the section where I usually find it.

M Oh, yes, I'm sorry. The library didn't renew its subscription from last year, so you won't see it on the shelves.

여 〈크래프트 매거진〉 이번 호를 찾고 있어요. 도서관에서 구독을 중단했는지 여부를 아세요? 보통 있었던 구역에 없거든요.

남 아, 네. 죄송합니다. 도서관에서 작년부터 구독 갱신을 하지 않았어요. 그래서 책장에 없을 겁니다.

어휘 craft 공예   current 현재의   issue 호   subscribe to ~를 구독하다   renew 갱신하다   subscription 구독

2 화자들은 어떤 문제를 논의하고 있는가?
(A) 작품 한 점이 도착하지 않았다.
(B) 잡지를 이용할 수 없다.
(C) 도서관 카드가 만료됐다.
(D) 매장이 문을 닫는다.

해설 세부 사항 – 화자들이 언급한 문제점
여자가 〈크래프트 매거진〉 이번 호가 보통 있었던 구역에 없다(It wasn't in the section where I usually find it)고 문의하자, 남자가 도서관에서 작년부터 구독 갱신을 하지 않는다(The library didn't renew its subscription from last year)고 응답했으므로, 잡지를 이용할 수 없게 되었음을 알 수 있다. 따라서 (B)가 정답이다.

어휘 arrive 도착하다   expire 만료되다

[3] M-Au / W-Br

M Sabine, did you sign up for the camping trip our department is organizing this weekend?

W Yes. I'm really excited, but I'm concerned that I don't have all the camping gear I need.

M Well, our department is providing tents. And there's a camping store that rents equipment in the Sunnydale Shopping Center.

남 사빈 씨, 우리 부서가 이번 주말에 마련하는 캠핑 여행에 등록하셨나요?

여 네. 정말 기대돼요. 그런데 제가 필요한 모든 캠핑용 장비를 가지고 있지 않아서 걱정이에요.

남 아, 우리 부서에서 텐트를 제공해요. 그리고 써니데일 쇼핑센터에 장비를 대여해 주는 캠핑용품 매장이 있어요.

어휘 sign up for ~에 등록하다, ~을 신청하다   organize 마련하다, 조직하다   concerned 우려되는, 걱정되는   gear 장비   rent 대여하다   equipment 장비

3 여자는 왜 걱정하는가?
(A) 교통편이 없다.   (B) 예약하는 것을 잊었다.
(C) 적절한 능력이 부족하다.   **(D) 장비를 갖고 있지 않다.**

해설 세부 사항 – 여자가 걱정하는 이유
여자가 첫 대사에서 필요한 캠핑용 장비를 갖고 있지 않아서 걱정된다(I'm concerned that I don't have all the camping gear I need)고 했으므로 (D)가 정답이다.

어휘 transportation 교통(편)   make a reservation 예약하다   lack 부족하다   appropriate 적절한

Paraphrasing 대화의 don't have all the camping gear → 정답의 does not have some equipment

[4] M-Cn / W-Am

M Thanks for coming to the factory today. We've been experiencing production delays. Maybe it's our Internet connection.

W Our firm can help with that. We help businesses improve their internal wireless signals so that all connections work without interruptions.

M That would be great.

남 오늘 공장에 와 주셔서 감사합니다. 저희가 생산 지연 문제를 겪고 있거든요. 아마 저희 인터넷 연결 문제일 겁니다.

여 저희 회사가 그런 부분을 도와드릴 수 있습니다. 저희는 모든 연결이 지장 없이 작동하도록 기업들이 내부 무선 신호를 개선하는 데 도움을 드리고 있어요.

남 그럼 아주 좋을 것 같아요.

어휘 experience 겪다, 경험하다   delay 지연, 지체   connection 연결   improve 개선하다, 향상시키다   internal 내부의   interruption 지장, 방해

4 남자는 어떤 문제를 설명하는가?
(A) 불충분한 현장 공간   (B) 좋지 못한 품질 관리
(C) 높은 수리 비용   (D) 생산 지연

해설 세부 사항 – 남자가 설명하는 문제점
남자가 첫 대사에서 생산 지연 문제를 겪고 있다(We've been experiencing production delays)는 사실을 언급하고 있으므로 (D)가 정답이다.

어휘 inadequate 불충분한 floor (작업) 현장 quality control 품질 관리 repair 수리

ETS 실전문제
본책 p.80

1 (C)	2 (D)	3 (B)	4 (D)	5 (D)	6 (B)
7 (B)	8 (C)	9 (A)	10 (A)	11 (C)	12 (D)
13 (B)	14 (C)	15 (A)	16 (A)	17 (B)	18 (B)
19 (C)	20 (A)	21 (D)	22 (D)	23 (B)	24 (A)

[1-3] W-Br / M-Au

W Tim, I'm looking for a new fitness center to join. **1 The one I currently go to is convenient for me, but they just sent out an e-mail saying they're closing down in July.**

M Why don't you join mine? The monthly fee is reasonable, and they just installed some new exercise machines. Personally, I just go there to swim. **2 I usually go first thing in the morning because the pool's practically empty then.**

W Oh, that's good to know. I prefer going to the gym when it's less crowded too. Can I try out the equipment before signing up for a membership?

M Yes, they offer one-day trials. And **3 if you decide to sign up, mention my name, and you'll get a discount on the first month**.

여 팀, 제가 새로 가입할 피트니스 센터를 찾고 있는데요. **1 지금 가는 곳이 편리하긴 한데, 7월에 문을 닫는다는 이메일을 보냈더라고요.**

남 제가 다니는 곳에 가입하지 그래요? 월 이용료도 적당하고 새 운동기구 몇 대를 이제 막 설치했어요. 개인적으로 저는 수영을 하러 가요. **2 보통 아침에 제일 먼저 가죠. 그때는 수영장이 거의 비어 있거든요.**

여 아, 좋은 정보군요. 저도 덜 붐빌 때 체육관에 가는 걸 좋아해요. 회원 등록을 하기 전에 장비를 이용해 볼 수 있나요?

남 네, 하루 시범 이용권을 제공해요. **3 등록하기로 결정하시면 제 이름을 대세요. 그럼 첫 번째 달은 할인을 받게 돼요.**

어휘 look for ~를 찾다 currently 현재 convenient 편리한 reasonable (가격 등이) 적당한, 합리적인 install 설치하다 personally 개인적으로 first thing 제일 먼저 practically 거의, 사실상 crowded 붐비는 trial 시험, 시범 get a discount 할인 받다

1 여자는 어떤 문제를 언급하는가?
(A) 일정이 몹시 바쁘다.
(B) 이용료가 인상됐다.
(C) 피트니스 센터가 문을 닫는다.
(D) 건물이 공사 중이다.

해설 세부 사항 – 여자가 언급한 문제점
여자가 첫 대사에서 지금 가는 피트니스 센터(The one I currently go to)에서 7월에 문을 닫는다는 이메일을 보냈다(they just sent out an e-mail saying they're closing down in July)고 했으므로 (C)가 정답이다.

어휘 increase 증가하다 under construction 공사 중인

2 남자는 수영장에 대해 무엇이라고 말하는가?
(A) 다음 달에는 개장하지 않을 예정이다.
(B) 가르쳐 줄 수영 강사들이 있다.
(C) 최근 운영시간이 연장됐다.
(D) 아침에는 이용이 많지 않다.

해설 세부 사항 – 남자가 수영장에 대해 말한 것
남자가 첫 대사에서 보통 아침에 제일 먼저 수영을 간다(I usually go first thing in the morning)고 한 후, 그때는 수영장이 거의 비어 있다(the pool's practically empty then)고 했으므로, 아침에는 수영장 이용이 많지 않다는 점을 알 수 있다. 따라서 (D)가 정답이다.

어휘 instructor 강사 extend 연장하다

> **Paraphrasing** 대화의 practically empty → 정답의 not used a lot

3 여자는 어떻게 할인을 받을 수 있는가?
(A) 쿠폰을 제시해서
(B) 친구의 이름을 제공해서
(C) 평일에만 시설을 이용해서
(D) 몇 달치 요금을 미리 결제해서

해설 세부 사항 – 여자가 할인을 받을 수 있는 방법
남자가 마지막 대사에서 등록하기로 결정하면 자신의 이름을 댈 것(if you decide to sign up, mention my name)을 제안한 후, 그렇게 하면 첫 번째 달은 할인을 받게 된다(you'll get a discount on the first month)고 했다. 따라서 (B)가 정답이다.

어휘 obtain 얻다 present 제시하다 facility 시설 in advance 미리

> **Paraphrasing** 대화의 mention my name → 정답의 providing a friend's name

[4-6] W-Am / M-Cn

W Hi, Sergey! This is Jessica Murray from Royer's Kebabs. Thanks for signing a contract with us. We enjoy working with social media influencers like yourself.

M ⁴I'm delighted to represent Royer's. Your kebabs are my favorite meal.

W Well, ⁴we're counting on you to share that enthusiasm on your social media sites. As your contract states, you'll film yourself enjoying a Royer's kebab and post it to various sites.

M Yes, ⁵I'll post the video next week.

W Great. ⁶I just wanted to remind you to be sure the logo on our product packaging is clearly visible while you're filming.

여 안녕하세요, 세르게이 씨! 로여스 케밥의 제시카 머레이입니다. 저희와 계약해 주셔서 감사드려요. 저희는 선생님과 같은 소셜 미디어 인플루언서들과 함께 일하는 것을 즐겁게 생각합니다.

남 ⁴로여스를 대표하게 되어 기뻐요. 그곳 케밥은 제가 가장 좋아하는 식사랍니다.

여 네, ⁴그 열정을 소셜 미디어 사이트에 공유해 주실 거라고 기대하고 있어요. 계약서에 명시된 대로, 로여스 케밥을 즐기는 모습을 촬영해 다양한 사이트에 게시해 주시게 될 겁니다.

남 네, ⁵다음 주에 동영상을 올리도록 할게요.

여 좋습니다. ⁶촬영하시는 동안 반드시 저희 제품 포장지의 로고가 명확히 보이도록 해 주시기를 다시 한 번 당부드릴게요.

어휘 sign a contract 계약을 맺다 be delighted to do ~해서 기쁘다 represent 대표하다 count on ~을 기대하다, ~에 의존하다 enthusiasm 열정, 열의 state (문서에) 명시하다 film 촬영하다 post 게시하다 remind A to do A에게 ~하도록 상기시키다 packaging 포장(지) visible 눈에 보이는

4 남자는 무엇을 하기 위한 계약을 맺었는가?
(A) 웹사이트 구축하기   (B) 레스토랑 메뉴 만들기
(C) 제품 포장 디자인하기 **(D) 업체 광고하기**

해설 세부 사항 – 남자가 계약을 맺은 것
남자가 첫 대사에서 로여스를 대표하게 되어 기쁘다(I'm delighted to represent Royer's)며 그곳의 케밥이 가장 좋아하는 식사(Your Kebabs are my favorite meal)라고 하자, 여자가 그 열정을 소셜 미디어 사이트에 공유해 주기를 기대하고 있다(we're counting on you to share that enthusiasm on your social media sites)고 답하고 있다. 이는 여자의 업체를 광고하는 일을 의미한다고 볼 수 있으므로 (D)가 정답이다.

어휘 create 만들어 내다 advertise 광고하다

Paraphrasing 대화의 share that enthusiasm on your social media sites → 정답의 Advertise

5 다음 주에 무슨 일이 일어날 것인가?
(A) 업체가 신규 지점을 열 것이다.
(B) 영수증이 발송될 것이다.
(C) 한 회차에 초대 손님이 있을 것이다.
(D) 동영상이 온라인에 게시될 것이다.

해설 세부 사항 – 다음 주에 있을 일
남자가 두 번째 대사에서 다음 주에 동영상을 게시하겠다(I'll post the video next week)고 했으므로 (D)가 정답이다.

어휘 location 지점, 위치 receipt 영수증 episode 1회 방송분

6 여자는 남자에게 무엇을 하도록 상기시키는가?
(A) 전화로 새로운 소식 알리기
(B) 반드시 로고가 잘 보이게 하기
(C) 시장 조사 내용 읽어 보기
(D) 특정 색조 이용하기

해설 세부 사항 – 여자가 남자에게 상기시키는 것
여자가 마지막 대사에서 반드시 제품 포장지의 로고가 명확히 보이도록 해 주기를 당부드린다(I just wanted to remind you to be sure the logo on our product packaging is clearly visible while you're filming)고 했으므로 (B)가 정답이다.

어휘 make sure 반드시 ~하도록 하다 market research 시장 조사 specific 특정한, 구체적인 color palette 색조, 색채

Paraphrasing 대화의 clearly visible → 정답의 easy to see

[7-9] M-Cn / W-Br

M On today's broadcast, ⁷we talk to Professor Mona Haddad, who just completed her research on the Space Lab. Welcome, Professor Haddad. How exciting to conduct research in space! Please tell us about your research on the Space Lab.

W Sure. ⁸My background is in biology, and my focus was on plants and how low gravity can slow the ripening of fruits and vegetables. This study has many applications in space and on Earth.

M That's so interesting, and we'll definitely return to that. But first, we have a surprise. ⁹A colleague of yours from the Space Lab has just called in and is waiting on the line to talk with you. Let's take that call now.

남 오늘 방송에서는, ⁷모나 하다드 교수님과 이야기를 나눌 텐데요, 이분께서 우주 실험실에 관한 연구를 막 마치셨습니다. 어서 오세요, 하다드 교수님. 우주에서 연구를 하신다니 정말 흥미로운데요! 우주 실험실에 관한 연구에 대해 말씀해 주세요.

여 네. ⁸제 배경은 생물학이고, 연구의 초점은 식물, 그리고 저중력이 과일과 채소의 숙성을 어떻게 늦출 수 있는지에 관한 것이었습니다. 이 연구는 우주와 지구에서 많은 응용 가능성이 있어요.

남 정말 흥미롭네요. 그리고 그 이야기는 분명 다시 다룰 겁니다. 하지만 먼저, 깜짝 소식이 있습니다. ⁹교수님의 우주 실험실 동료 한 분께서 방금 전화를 주셨는데, 교수님과 이야기를 나누기 위해 기다리고 계십니다. 지금 바로 연결해보죠.

어휘 broadcast 방송   complete 완료하다   research 연구   lab 실험실   conduct 실시하다   biology 생물학   focus 초점, 중점   gravity 중력   slow 둔화시키다   ripening 숙성   application 응용 (가능성)   definitely 분명히   surprise 놀라운 소식, 뜻밖의 일

7 여자는 최근에 무엇을 했는가?
(A) 기사를 실었다.
(B) 연구 프로젝트를 완료했다.
(C) 다큐멘터리 영화에 출연했다.
(D) 강연 투어에서 복귀했다.

해설 **세부 사항 – 여자가 최근에 한 일**
남자가 첫 대사에서 여자를 소개하면서 우주 실험실에 관한 연구를 막 완료했다(we talk to Professor Mona Haddad, who just completed her research on the Space Lab)고 언급했으므로 (B)가 정답이다.

어휘 appear 출연하다

8 여자는 어떤 분야에서 일하는가?
(A) 로봇 공학   (B) 기계 공학
(C) 식물 생물학   (D) 소프트웨어 개발

해설 **세부 사항 – 여자가 일하는 분야**
여자가 첫 대사에서 배경이 생물학이라는 점과 자신의 초점이 식물에 맞춰져 있었다(My background is in biology, and my focus was on plants)고 했으므로 (C)가 정답이다.

9 여자는 다음에 무엇을 할 것인가?
(A) 동료와 이야기하기
(B) 상 받기
(C) 책에 관해 이야기하기
(D) 앞으로의 프로젝트 설명하기

해설 **세부 사항 – 여자가 다음에 할 일**
남자가 마지막 대사에서 여자의 동료 한 명이 전화를 걸어와 기다리고 있다며 지금 바로 연결하겠다(A colleague of yours from the Space Lab has just called in and is waiting on the line to talk with you. Let's take that call now)고 했다. 따라서 여자가 전화상으로 동료와 이야기할 것으로 볼 수 있으므로 (A)가 정답이다.

어휘 accept 받아들이다, 수용하다   explain 설명하다

[10-12] M-Au / W-Am

M **10Chef Livingstone**, I'm very glad you chose to accept our offer! The restaurant is lucky to have a chef of your reputation.

W Well, I'm looking forward to working here!

M We're especially pleased that you'll be creating new desserts for our menu. **11Offering new menu items is a top priority so we can attract new customers.**

W Right! I have lots of good recipes that I'll be trying out.

M Great. And **12please don't hesitate to let me know if you need any special equipment we don't already have**.

남 **10리빙스턴 요리사님**, 저희 제안을 수락해 주셔서 정말 기쁩니다! 저희 레스토랑은 셰프님처럼 명성이 높은 분을 모시게 되어 행운이에요.

여 네, 이곳에서 근무하는 것을 기대하고 있습니다!

남 저희 메뉴를 위해 새로운 디저트를 만들어 주신다는 점이 특히 기쁘네요. **11신규 고객들을 끌어들일 수 있도록 새로운 메뉴를 제공하는 것이 최우선 순위거든요.**

여 맞습니다! 제가 시도해 볼 좋은 조리법이 많아요.

남 아주 좋아요. 그리고 **12저희가 아직 보유하고 있지 않은 특별한 장비가 필요하시면 망설이지 마시고 제게 알려 주시기 바랍니다.**

어휘 reputation 명성, 평판   look forward to -ing ~하기를 고대하다   priority 우선 순위   attract 끌어들이다   recipe 조리법   try out 시험해 보다   hesitate 망설이다, 주저하다

10 여자는 누구인가?
(A) 요리사   (B) 기업 임원
(C) 영업사원   (D) 행사 기획자

해설 **전체 내용 – 여자의 직업**
남자가 첫 대사에서 여자를 리빙스턴 요리사(Chef Livingstone)라고 부르고 있으므로 (A)가 정답이다.

11 남자는 어떻게 더 많은 고객을 끌어들이기를 바라는가?
(A) 포장을 개선함으로써
(B) 가격을 내림으로써
(C) 신제품을 제공함으로써
(D) 장소를 개조함으로써

해설 **세부 사항 – 남자가 말하는 신규 고객 유치 방법**
남자가 두 번째 대사에서 신규 고객들을 끌어들일 수 있도록 새로운 메뉴를 제공하는 것이 최우선 순위(Offering new menu items is a top priority so we can attract new customers)라고 했으므로 (C)가 정답이다.

어휘 lower 내리다, 낮추다   renovate 개조하다, 보수하다

12 남자는 자신이 무엇을 할 수 있다고 말하는가?
(A) 추가 직원 고용하기
(B) 유니폼 새디자인하기
(C) 직원 할인 제공하기
(D) 특수 장비 주문하기

해설 **세부 사항 – 남자가 할 수 있다고 말하는 것**
남자가 마지막 대사에서 우리가 아직 보유하고 있지 않은 특별한 장비가 필요하면 주저하지 말고 알려 달라(let me know if you need any special equipment we don't already have)고 당부했다. 이는 필요할 경우 주문해 주겠다는 뜻이므로 (D)가 정답이다.

어휘 hire 고용하다   specialized 특수화된, 전문화된

> **Paraphrasing** 대화의 let me know if you need any special equipment we don't already have → 정답의 Order specialized equipment

[13-15] 3인 대화 W-Am / W-Br / M-Au

W1 Hi, Hend and Kento. We might have a problem getting to the client meeting this afternoon. According to the app on my mobile phone, **13there's heavy traffic because of construction work.**

W2 This is the client in Hamptonville who's interested in our drone equipment, right? We don't want to be late to that.

M Right! We can't be late— **14I want to make sure I have enough time to demonstrate the drone prototypes for everyone.**

W2 Don't worry. **15We can take the Carver Bridge instead.** It would add only another fifteen minutes to our trip.

W1 **15**OK. That route looks good on the app. Let's take that.

여1 안녕하세요. 헨드 씨, 그리고 켄토 씨. 우리가 오늘 오후에 있을 고객 회의에 가는 데 문제가 있을지도 모르겠어요. 제 휴대폰 앱에 따르면, 13공사 작업 때문에 교통량이 극심해요.

여2 그분이 우리 드론 장비에 관심이 있으신 햄튼빌 지역 고객이시죠, 그렇죠? 그 자리에 늦고 싶지 않은데요.

남 맞아요! 늦으면 안 돼요. 14저는 모두에게 드론 시제품을 시연할 충분할 시간을 확보하고 싶어요.

여2 걱정하지 마세요. 15대신 카버 다리를 타고 갈 수 있어요. 이동 시간에 겨우 15분만 더 추가될 겁니다.

여1 15알겠습니다. 앱에서 그 경로가 좋아 보이네요. 그곳을 이용하죠.

어휘 get to ~로 가다, ~에 도착하다 according to ~에 따르면 heavy (수량, 정도 등이) 심한, 많은 traffic 교통(량), 차량들 demonstrate 시연하다 prototype 시제품, 원형 instead 대신 route 경로, 노선

13 무엇이 문제를 초래하고 있는가?
(A) 악천후
(B) 극심한 교통량
(C) 열차 취소
(D) 고장 난 차량

해설 세부 사항 - 문제를 초래하는 원인
첫 번째 여자가 첫 대사에서 문제가 있음을 알리면서 공사 작업 때문에 교통량이 극심하다(there's heavy traffic because of construction work)는 사실을 원인으로 언급했으므로 (B)가 정답이다.

어휘 cause 초래하다 cancellation 취소 broken-down 고장 난 vehicle 차량

14 남자는 왜 걱정하는가?
(A) 이미 티켓 비용을 지불했다.
(B) 다른 약속에 가야 한다.
(C) 시연을 실시하기에 충분한 시간을 원한다.
(D) 인터넷에 접속하지 못할 것이다.

해설 세부 사항 - 남자가 걱정하는 이유
남자가 첫 대사에서 모두에게 드론 시제품을 시연할 충분한 시간을 확보하고 싶다(I want to make sure I have enough time to demonstrate the drone prototypes for everyone)고 했으므로 (C)가 정답이다.

어휘 appointment 약속, 예약 access 접속, 이용

> **Paraphrasing** 대화의 demonstrate → 정답의 conduct a demonstration

15 여자들은 무엇에 대해 동의하는가?
(A) 대체 경로 이용하기
(B) 보조 직원 교육하기
(C) 이메일로 발표 자료 보내기
(D) 설명서 참고하기

해설 세부 사항 - 여자들이 동의하는 것
후반부에서 두 번째 여자가 대신 카버 다리를 타고 갈 수 있다(We can take the Carver Bridge instead)고 하자, 첫 번째 여자가 앱에서 그 경로가 좋아보인다고 동의하며 그곳을 이용하자(That route looks good on the app. Let's take that)고 했으므로 (A)가 정답이다.

어휘 agree 동의하다 alternate 대체의 train 교육하다 assistant 보조, 조수 consult 참고하다 manual 설명서

> **Paraphrasing** 대화의 take the Carver Bridge instead → 정답의 Taking an alternate route

[16-18] W-Br / M-Cn

W You've reached the Parks Department of Monroe City. How can I help you?

M Hello. **16I moved to Monroe last month** and I'm looking for volunteer opportunities. I thought that might help me get to know the area. Do you need any volunteers?

W We do! In fact, right now **17we're conducting a census of native birds in our local parks. We need volunteers to count them so we have an idea of how many there are. Would you like to help with that?**

M Yes. **18My only concern is that I've never done anything like this before.**

W　Don't worry. We'll pair you with a park ranger who'll show you how to identify the birds and count them.

여　먼로시 공원 관리부입니다. 무엇을 도와드릴까요?
남　안녕하세요. **16제가 지난달에 먼로시로 이사 왔는데요**, 자원봉사를 할 기회를 찾고 있습니다. 이 동네를 알아가는 데 도움이 될 것 같아서요. 자원봉사자가 필요하신가요?
여　필요해요! 실은, **17현재 우리 지역 공원에 서식하는 토종 새의 개체 수를 조사하고 있어요**. 그 수가 얼마나 되는지 파악하기 위해 새의 개체 수를 셀 작업을 할 자원봉사자가 필요합니다. 그 일을 도와주시겠어요?
남　네, 그런데 **18한 가지 걱정되는 점은 제가 이런 일을 전에 해 본 적이 없다는 거예요**.
여　걱정 마세요. 토종 새를 구분해서 수를 세는 방법을 알려줄 공원 관리원과 짝을 지어드릴 거예요.

어휘　opportunity 기회　census 개체 수 조사, 인구조사
park ranger 공원 관리원　identify 구분하다, 밝혀내다

16 남자는 지난달에 무엇을 했다고 말하는가?
(A) 새로운 동네로 이사했다.
(B) 새로운 일을 시작했다.
(C) 과학 수업을 수강했다.
(D) 공원을 방문했다.

해설　세부 사항 – 남자가 지난달에 한 일
남자가 첫 대사에서 지난달에 먼로시로 이사 왔다(I moved to Monroe last month)고 했으므로 (A)가 정답이다.

17 여자는 남자에게 어떤 일을 도와달라고 하는가?
(A) 하이킹 인솔　(B) 새의 수 세기
(C) 나무 심기　(D) 공원 청소

해설　세부 사항 – 여자의 요청 사항
여자가 두 번째 대사에서 지역 공원의 토종 새의 개체 수(a census of native birds)를 조사하고 있다고 한 후, 숫자를 셀 작업을 할 자원봉사자가 필요한데(We need volunteers to count them) 도와줄 수 있는지 물었다. 따라서 (B)가 정답이다.

18 남자는 무엇을 걱정하는가?
(A) 바쁜 일정　(B) 경험 부족
(C) 근무지까지의 거리　(D) 참가 비용

해설　세부 사항 – 남자의 우려 사항
남자가 두 번째 대사에서 걱정되는 점이 이런 일을 전에 해 본 적이 없다는 것(My only concern is that I've never done anything like this before)이라고 했으므로 (B)가 정답이다.

Paraphrasing　대화의 I've never done anything like this before → 정답의 His lack of experience

---

[19-21] W-Am / M-Cn

W　John, **19it seems like the launch of our newspaper's new Web site has been a great success**. In just one week the site has already gotten very positive feedback from readers.
M　There do seem to be some issues with the mobile version of the site though—**20people who visit our Web site on their mobile phones are reporting that headlines and text aren't displayed correctly—lines can be completely cut off**.
W　Oh, I wasn't aware of that problem—we'll need to address that right away. **21There's definitely a growing trend of reading news Web sites on a phone instead of on a computer**, so this problem could be affecting a lot of readers.

여　존, **19우리 신문사 신규 웹사이트 개설이 큰 성공을 거둔 것 같아요**. 1주일 만에 사이트가 독자들로부터 아주 긍정적인 평을 받았거든요.
남　그런데 사이트의 모바일 버전은 문제가 있는 듯합니다. **20휴대전화로 웹사이트를 방문하는 사람들이 헤드라인과 본문이 정확하게 표시되지 않는다고 이야기해요. 끝이 완전히 잘리거든요**.
여　아, 그 문제는 몰랐어요. 당장 해결해야겠네요. **21컴퓨터 대신 휴대전화로 뉴스 웹사이트를 보는 추세가 확실히 늘고 있으니** 이 문제가 많은 독자에게 영향을 미칠 수 있어요.

어휘　launch 출시, 시작　positive 긍정적인　correctly 정확하게, 바르게　completely 완전히　be cut off 잘리다
be aware of ~를 알다　address (문제 등을) 해결하다
instead of ~대신에　affect 영향을 미치다

19 여자에 따르면, 회사는 최근에 무엇을 했는가?
(A) 합병 발표　(B) 편집자 채용
(C) 웹사이트 개설　(D) 워크숍 개최

해설　세부 사항 – 회사가 최근에 한 일
여자가 첫 대사에서 신문사 신규 웹사이트 개설이 큰 성공을 거둔 것 같다(it seems like the launch of our newspaper's new Web site has been a great success)고 했으므로 회사가 최근에 웹사이트를 개설했음을 알 수 있다. 따라서 (C)가 정답이다.

어휘　recently 최근에　announce 알리다, 발표하다
merger 합병　host 개최하다

20 남자는 어떤 문제를 언급하는가?
(A) 내용이 정확하게 보이지 않는다.
(B) 마감 시한을 놓쳤다.
(C) 판매량이 예상한 것보다 낮다.
(D) 장비가 구식이다.

해설 **세부 사항 – 남자가 언급한 문제점**
남자가 첫 대사에서 휴대전화로 웹사이트를 방문하는 사람들이 헤드라인과 본문이 정확하게 표시되지 않는다(headlines and text aren't displayed correctly)고 이야기한다며 문제점을 언급한 후, 끝이 완전히 잘린다(lines can be completely cut off)고 덧붙였다. 따라서 (A)가 정답이다.

어휘 than expected 예상보다 outdated 구식인

21 여자는 무엇이 증가 추세라고 말하는가?
(A) 오디오북 청취   (B) 온라인 교육 개최
(C) 계약서 전자 서명   (D) 모바일 기기로 뉴스 읽기

해설 **세부 사항 – 여자가 증가 추세라고 말한 것**
여자가 마지막 대사에서 컴퓨터 대신 휴대전화로 뉴스 웹사이트를 보는 추세가 확실히 늘고 있다(There's definitely a growing trend of reading news Web sites on a phone instead of on a computer)고 했으므로 (D)가 정답이다.

어휘 contract 계약서 electronically 전자적으로, 컴퓨터로

> **Paraphrasing** 대화의 on a phone → 정답의 on mobile devices

[22-24] 3인 대화 M-Cn/M-Au/W-Br

> M1 Hi, Andrew and Lola. So, **22 I hear you have doubts about the new marketing strategy that personalizes commercials in our streaming service**.
> M2 Yes. I used to subscribe to a music streaming service with the same strategy. **23 I kept hearing the same five commercials over and over. It was so annoying!**
> W **24 I agree, Andrew. In fact, I just read an article that explained how personalization can actually reduce subscriptions. You should read it.**
> M2 Thanks, Lola. Can you send it to me?

남1 안녕하세요, 앤드류 씨, 그리고 롤라 씨. 자, **22**제가 듣기로는 두 분께서 우리 스트리밍 서비스 내에서 광고를 개인 맞춤형으로 만드는 새 마케팅 전략에 대해 의문을 갖고 계신다던데요.
남2 네. 제가 전에 같은 전략을 활용하는 음악 스트리밍 서비스를 구독했거든요. **23**같은 광고 다섯 가지를 반복해서 계속 들었어요. 너무 짜증이 났습니다!
여 **24**동의해요, 앤드류 씨. 사실, 제가 방금 개인 맞춤화가 어떻게 실제로 구독자들을 감소시킬 수 있는지 설명하는 기사를 하나 읽었거든요. 이걸 읽어 보셔야 합니다.
남2 감사합니다, 롤라 씨. 그걸 제게 보내 주시겠어요?

어휘 doubt 의문, 의구심 strategy 전략 personalize (개인의 필요에) 맞추다 commercial 광고 (방송) used to do 전에 ~했다, ~하곤 했다 annoying (사람을) 짜증나게 하는 reduce 감소시키다

22 화자들은 무엇을 논의하고 있는가?
(A) 소프트웨어 교육 시간   (B) 투자 기회
(C) 녹화 시간   (D) 마케팅 계획

해설 **전체 내용 – 대화 주제**
첫 번째 남자가 첫 대사에서 나머지 두 사람이 새 마케팅 전략에 대해 의문을 갖고 있다는 얘기가 들린다(I hear you have doubts about the new marketing strategy)고 한 뒤로, 해당 마케팅 전략의 문제와 관련해 이야기하고 있으므로 (D)가 정답이다.

어휘 investment 투자(금)

> **Paraphrasing** 대화의 the new marketing strategy → 정답의 A marketing plan

23 앤드류 씨는 무엇이 문제가 있다고 생각했는가?
(A) 기술 지원의 부족   (B) 과도한 수준의 반복
(C) 복잡한 등록 과정   (D) 높은 구독료

해설 **세부 사항 – 앤드류 씨가 생각한 문제점**
두 번째 남자가 첫 대사에서 같은 광고 다섯 가지를 반복해서 계속 들어 너무 짜증이 났다(I kept hearing the same five commercials over and over. It was so annoying!)고 했으므로 (B)가 정답이다.

어휘 problematic 문제가 있는 excessive 과도한 repetition 반복 complicated 복잡한 registration 등록

> **Paraphrasing** 대화의 so annoying → 질문의 problematic
> 대화의 kept hearing the same five commercials over and over → 정답의 The excessive amount of repetition

24 롤라 씨는 앤드류 씨에게 무엇을 하라고 권하는가?
(A) 잡지 기사 읽어 보기
(B) 장비 테스트하기
(C) 공식 문서 살펴보기
(D) 고객 설문 조사지 배부하기

해설 **세부 사항 – 롤라 씨가 앤드류 씨에게 권하는 것**
여자가 첫 대사에서 앤드류 씨의 생각에 동의한다(I agree, Andrew)고 한 뒤, 특정 기사에 대해 언급하며 그것을 읽어 봐야 한다(I just read an article that explained how personalization can actually reduce subscriptions. You should read it)고 했으므로 (A)가 정답이다.

어휘 review 살펴보다, 검토하다 distribute 배부하다 survey 설문 조사(지)

UNIT 09 요청·제안 / 다음에 할 일 문제

1 요청·제안 문제

기출 공략 포인트 ········· 본책 p.82

여 제프, 이 책상 덮는 비닐은 누구를 위한 건지 궁금해요.
남 우리를 위한 거예요. 기억해요? 건설업체에서 다음 주 화요일에 우리 사무 공간 개선 작업을 시작해요. 먼지가 많이 날 테니…
여 아, 그렇게 빨리 시작하는 줄 미처 몰랐네요. 그럼 우리가 다른 데서 일해야 할까요?
남 우린 여기 그대로 있을 거예요. 이건 작업자들이 일별로 어느 구역을 작업할지 보여 주는 **일정표**예요. 한번 보세요.
여 아, 좋아요. **제가 이것을 직원 게시판에 붙여 놓을게요.**

어휘 contractor 건설업체, 하청업체 timeline 일정표 crew 작업자들 post 게시하다 bulletin board 게시판

문제 여자는 무엇을 하겠다고 제안하는가?
(A) 근무 시간 조정 (B) 사무용품 주문
(C) 일정표 게시 (D) 연수 프로그램 확대

ETS 유형연습 ········· 본책 p.83

1 (D) **2** (A) **3** (D) **4** (D)

[1] M-Au / W-Br

M You've had a great first week. We're expecting a large party for lunch today, and I'd like you to be their server.
W Sure. But before I start my shift, **can I get a different uniform?** The medium one I have is too big.
M Of course. I'll grab you a smaller one right now.

남 첫 주를 아주 잘 보내셨네요. 오늘 점심에 큰 단체 손님이 오는데, 그분들 담당 종업원이 되어 주셨으면 해요.
여 물론입니다. 그런데 근무 시작 전에 **다른 유니폼을 받을 수 있을까요?** 제가 가진 중간 사이즈가 너무 커서요.
남 당연하죠. 지금 바로 더 작은 것으로 가져다 드릴게요.

어휘 expect 기다리다 party 일행 shift (교대) 근무

1 여자는 무엇을 요청하는가?
(A) 서명 (B) 다른 근무 시간
(C) 용품 목록 (D) 다른 유니폼

해설 세부 사항 – 여자가 요청하는 것
여자가 첫 대사에서 다른 유니폼을 받을 수 있는지(can I get a different uniform?) 묻고 있으므로 (D)가 정답이다.

Paraphrasing 대화의 a different uniform → 정답의 Another uniform

[2] M-Cn / W-Am

M Andrea, **can I talk to you about a project we'd like you to work on?** Management would like to see better communication between the sales department and the marketing department. **We'd like you to lead this effort.**
W That sounds really interesting, Mark. But, what exactly would this project involve?

남 안드레아, **당신이 착수해 줬으면 하는 프로젝트에 대해 이야기를 좀 할 수 있을까요?** 경영진은 영업부서와 마케팅부서가 더 원활히 소통하는 것을 원해요. **당신이 이 일을 이끌어 줬으면 해요.**
여 마크, 정말 흥미로운 이야기군요. 하지만 이 프로젝트에 정확히 어떤 일이 포함되는 거죠?

어휘 work on 착수하다 management 경영진, 임원진 department 부서 effort 노력, (특정한 성과를 거두기 위한 집단의 조직적인) 활동 exactly 정확히 involve 포함하다

2 남자는 여자에게 무엇을 해 달라고 요청하는가?
(A) 새 프로젝트 맡기 (B) 자문 위원 뽑기
(C) 임원 회의 참석하기 (D) 판촉 활동 보고하기

해설 세부 사항 – 남자의 요청 사항
남자가 여자에게 착수해 줬으면 하는 프로젝트에 대해 이야기할 수 있는지(can I talk to you about a project we'd like you to work on?) 물어본 뒤, 해당 프로젝트를 이끌어 줄 것(We'd like you to lead this effort)을 요청했으므로 (A)가 정답이다.

어휘 take charge of ~를 맡다, 책임을 지다 recruit 모집하다, 뽑다 attend 참석하다 sales promotion 판촉 활동, 판촉

Paraphrasing 대화의 lead → 정답의 Take charge of

[3] M-Au / W-Br

M Before I start scanning your items, did you bring any reusable bags for me to put your groceries in?
W Oh, no—I didn't. Was I supposed to bring my own bags?
M It is our store policy, but **you could sign up for one of our membership cards.** You'd receive a reusable bag for free with your membership, and it only takes a few minutes to register.

남 상품을 스캔하기 전에 여쭤보는데, 식료품을 담을 장바구니를 가지고 오셨나요?
여 아, 아니요. 가지고 오지 않았어요. 제 개인 가방을 가지고 왔어야 하나요?

남 그게 저희 가게 정책입니다만, **저희 회원 카드 중 하나를 신청하시면 돼요.** 회원 가입을 하시면 장바구니를 무료로 받게 되실 거예요. 그리고 가입하는 데 몇 분밖에 안 걸립니다.

어휘 reusable 재사용할 수 있는 be supposed to ~하기로 되어 있다 register 등록하다, 가입하다

3 남자는 여자에게 무엇을 하라고 추천하는가?
(A) 다음 날 다시 오기
(B) 미리 주문하기
(C) 인근 주차장에 주차하기
(D) 회원 카드 신청하기

해설 세부 사항 – 남자의 권유 사항
남자가 마지막 대사에서 회원 카드 중 하나를 신청하면 장바구니를 무료로 받게 된다(You'd receive a reusable bag for free with your membership)며, 여자에게 회원 카드 신청을 권유하고 있다. 따라서 (D)가 정답이다.

어휘 following 다음의 in advance 미리

Paraphrasing 대화의 sign up for → 정답의 register for

[4] W-Am / M-Cn

W I bought a chair from your store, and I was about to assemble it, but I don't think I have all of the parts I need.

M Oh, I'm sorry to hear that. Do you know what you're missing?

W Well, I have all the long bolts for the legs but none of the other bolts for the seat.

M OK, I have some replacement parts here at the store, and **I can have the delivery driver drop them off at your house this afternoon.**

여 제가 그쪽 가게에서 의자를 하나 사서 막 조립을 하려는데 필요한 부품이 다 있는 것 같지가 않아요.
남 아, 죄송합니다. 뭐가 빠졌는지 아세요?
여 음, 의자 다리용으로 긴 볼트는 전부 있는데 좌석용 볼트는 하나도 없어요.
남 그렇군요. 제가 여기 가게에 교체 부품을 좀 갖고 있으니까, **배달 기사를 통해 오늘 오후에 고객님 댁으로 갖다드리겠습니다.**

어휘 assemble 조립하다 missing 빠진, 없는 replacement part 교체 부품 delivery driver 배달 기사 drop off (물건을) 갖다주다

4 남자는 무엇을 하겠다고 제안하는가?
(A) 주문 취소   (B) 기술자 고용
(C) 환불 제공   **(D) 배달 조치**

해설 세부 사항 – 남자의 제안 사항
남자의 마지막 대사에서 가게에 교체 부품이 있으니 배달 기사를 통해 오늘 오후에 배달해 줄 수 있다(I can have the

delivery driver drop them off at your house this afternoon)고 했으므로 (D)가 정답이다.

2 다음에 할 일 문제

기출 공략 포인트 ················ 본책 p. 84

여 실례합니다. 주방 벽을 흰색으로 칠하려고 하는데 페인트 종류가 너무 많아서 어떤 걸 사야 할지 잘 모르겠어요.
남 음, 고광택 페인트를 추천해 드려요. 왜냐하면 주방용이고 또 씻어 내기도 더 쉽거든요.
여 좋네요, 고맙습니다! 그럼 그걸로 두 통 할게요. 또, **페인트 붓은 어디 있는지 알려주실래요?**
남 네, 그건 10번 통로에 있어요. 제가 거기로 안내해 드릴게요.

어휘 gloss 광택 aisle 통로

문제 화자들은 다음에 무엇을 할 것 같은가?
(A) 구매 주문서 검토하기
(B) 상점 내 다른 곳으로 가기
(C) 전문 페인트공 채용 논의하기
(D) 상품 시험해보기

ETS 유형연습   본책 p. 85

1 (A)   **2** (B)   **3** (A)   **4** (B)

[1] M-Cn / W-Am

M Welcome to Starlay Used Vehicles. What brings you in today?

W Hi. I have a car that's only a few years old, and I was wondering how much you'd give me for it. Since I don't commute to work, I decided that I don't really need a car.

M I see. Well, **let me inspect your vehicle, and then I can make you an offer.**

남 스타레이 중고 자동차에 오신 것을 환영합니다. 오늘은 어떤 일로 오셨나요?
여 안녕하세요. 몇 년밖에 되지 않은 자동차가 한 대 있는데, 그 차에 얼마를 주실 수 있을지 궁금했어요. 통근을 하지 않아서, 차가 꼭 필요하지 않다는 결정을 내렸거든요.
남 알겠습니다. 음, **제가 고객님 자동차를 점검해 드리겠습니다.** 그 후에 가격을 제시해 드릴 수 있어요.

어휘 used 중고 vehicle 차량 wonder 궁금하다 commute to ~로 통근하다 inspect 점검하다

1 남자는 다음에 무엇을 할 것인가?
(A) 점검 실시하기
(B) 문서 출력하기
(C) 환불 금액 지급하기
(D) 동료 직원에게 도움 요청하기

해설 세부 사항 – 남자가 다음에 할 일
남자가 마지막 대사에서 자동차를 점검한 후에 가격을 제시해 줄 수 있다(let me inspect your vehicle, and then I can make you an offer)고 했으므로 (A)가 정답이다.

어휘 conduct 실시하다 paperwork 문서 (작업) issue 지급하다, 발급하다 refund 환불(액)

> **Paraphrasing** 대화의 inspect your vehicle ➔ 정답의 Conduct an inspection

[2] W-Am / M-Cn

W Langfield Museum of Art. This is Karima speaking. How can I help you?

M Hi, I **heard that the museum will be undergoing renovations in March.** Will it still be open for visitors?

W **The museum will be closed for the entire month,** but the outdoor garden will still be open.

여 랭필드 미술관입니다. 저는 카리마라고 합니다. 무엇을 도와드릴까요?
남 안녕하세요. 미술관이 3월에 보수 공사를 할 거라고 들었습니다. 그래도 방문객들에게는 개방되나요?
여 미술관은 한 달 내내 문을 닫지만, 야외 정원은 개방될 겁니다.

어휘 undergo (변화 등을) 겪다 renovation 보수 (공사)

2 3월에 무슨 일이 일어날 것인가?
(A) 제품이 할인될 것이다.
(B) 보수 공사로 건물이 폐쇄될 것이다.
(C) 마케팅 캠페인이 시작될 것이다.
(D) 학생들을 위한 교육 강좌가 열릴 것이다.

해설 세부 사항 – 3월에 있을 일
남자가 첫 대사에서 3월에 있을 미술관 보수 공사(the museum will be undergoing renovations in March)에 대해 문의하자 여자가 두 번째 대사에서 미술관이 한 달 내내 문을 닫는다(The museum will be closed for the entire month)고 안내했으므로 (B)가 정답이다.

[3] W-Am / M-Au

W Amit, a new shipment of shoes came in, so I have to put price tags on them, but I don't think we have any more.

M **I'm placing a supply order this afternoon** so I'll add price tags to the list. They should arrive by tomorrow.

여 아미트, 새 신발 화물이 들어왔어요. 그래서 가격표를 붙여야 하는데 더 이상 없는 것 같아요.
남 오늘 오후에 용품을 주문할 예정이니 목록에 가격표를 추가할 게요. 내일까지 도착할 겁니다.

어휘 shipment 화물, 수송품 price tag 가격표 place an order 주문을 넣다

3 남자는 오늘 오후에 무엇을 할 것이라고 말하는가?
(A) 주문 넣기
(B) 관리자 만나기
(C) 데이터베이스 업데이트하기
(D) 고객에게 전화하기

해설 세부 사항 – 남자가 할 일
남자가 오늘 오후에 용품을 주문할 예정(I'm placing a supply order this afternoon)이라고 했으므로 (A)가 정답이다.

어휘 supervisor 관리자, 감독관

[4] M-Cn / W-Am

M Julie, when are you coming back from London?

W Well, if my meetings go really well, I could be back by next Tuesday, but I may stay through Friday. Why do you ask?

M **Stephanie announced that she's moving to Boston for a new job. So I'm throwing her a party at Vega's Restaurant next Wednesday, and I was hoping you'd be able to come.**

남 줄리, 런던에서 언제 돌아와요?
여 음, 회의가 아주 순조롭게 진행되면 다음 주 화요일쯤에 돌아올 수 있지만, 금요일까지 머물 수도 있어요. 그건 왜 물어요?
남 스테파니가 새 직장 때문에 보스턴으로 이사할 거라고 발표했어요. 그래서 다음 주 수요일 베가스 레스토랑에서 파티를 열어 주려고 하는데 당신도 왔으면 해서요.

어휘 through ~까지 throw A a party A에게 파티를 열어주다

4 다음 주 수요일에 무슨 일이 일어날 것인가?
(A) 고객과의 저녁 식사
(B) 직장 동료를 위한 송별회
(C) 신입 사원들을 위한 환영회
(D) 몇몇 친구들과의 점심 식사

해설 세부 사항 – 다음 주 수요일에 있을 일
남자가 두 번째 대사에서 스테파니가 보스턴으로 이사를 갈 예정이라 그녀를 위해 다음 주 수요일에 파티를 열 것(I'm throwing her a party at Vega's Restaurant next Wednesday)이라고 했으므로 (B)가 정답이다.

어휘 client 고객 farewell party 송별회 reception 환영회

ETS 실전문제

본책 p.86

1 (C)	2 (C)	3 (A)	4 (B)	5 (D)	6 (D)
7 (C)	8 (C)	9 (A)	10 (B)	11 (A)	12 (C)
13 (B)	14 (D)	15 (A)	16 (A)	17 (C)	18 (B)
19 (B)	20 (C)	21 (A)	22 (B)	23 (C)	24 (C)

[1-3] M-Au / W-Am

M Hi, Shushma. **1 Since the hospital's employee parking area is being repaved on Monday**, some of the employees are wondering where they'll be able to park.

W Oh, yes. I talked with the hospital facilities manager yesterday. He says everyone should use the parking garage on Main Street, but **2 a shuttle will be provided between the garage and the hospital**.

M OK. **3 I'll send everyone a map so they know where they can park.**

남 안녕하세요, 슈시마 씨. **1 월요일에 병원 직원용 주차 구역이 재포장될 거라** 일부 직원들이 어디에 주차할 수 있을지를 궁금해하고 있어요.

여 아, 네. 제가 어제 병원 시설 관리 책임자와 이야기했어요. 그분께서 모두 메인 스트리트에 있는 주차장을 이용해야 하지만, **2 그 주차장과 병원 사이에 셔틀 서비스가 제공될 거라고 하더군요**.

남 알겠습니다. **3 어디에 주차할 수 있는지 알 수 있도록 모두에게 안내도를 보내겠습니다.**

어휘 repave (도로 등을) 재포장하다 park 주차하다 facility 시설(물) parking garage 주차장

1 월요일에 무슨 일이 일어날 것인가?
(A) 직원 파티가 개최될 것이다.
(B) 신임 이사가 발표될 것이다.
(C) 주차 구역이 재포장될 것이다.
(D) 안전 시범이 있을 것이다.

해설 세부 사항 – 월요일에 있을 일
남자가 첫 대사에서 월요일에 병원 직원용 주차 구역이 재포장된다(the hospital's employee parking area is being repaved on Monday)고 했으므로 (C)가 정답이다.

어휘 hold 개최하다 demonstration 시연(회) take place 개최되다, 일어나다

2 병원에서 무엇을 제공할 것인가?
(A) 출장 비용 환급   (B) 무료 간식
(C) 셔틀 서비스   (D) 추가 교육

해설 세부 사항 – 병원에서 제공하는 것
여자가 첫 대사에서 주차장과 병원 사이에 셔틀이 제공될 것(a shuttle will be provided between the garage and the hospital)이라고 설명했으므로 (C)가 정답이다.

어휘 reimbursement (비용) 환급 refreshments 간식, 다과

3 남자는 무엇을 보낼 것인가?
(A) 안내도   (B) 소식지
(C) 신분증   (D) 등록 양식

해설 세부 사항 – 남자가 보내는 것
남자가 두 번째 대사에서 어디에 주차할 수 있는지 알도록 모두에게 안내도를 보내겠다(I'll send everyone a map so they know where they can park)고 했으므로 (A)가 정답이다.

어휘 registration 등록 form 양식, 서식

[4-6] W-Br / M-Au

W Hello, Selwin Office Manufacturers. You've reached customer service. How may I help you today?

M Yes, hello. I recently bought a used Selwin 6 label maker. The person I got it from no longer had the instructions, though, and I'm not sure how the machine works.

W **4 Unfortunately, that's an earlier model that we no longer produce.**

M Oh, no. That's a problem.

W No, it's OK, because the Selwin 10 has a similar design, and the instructions should be nearly the same.

M Great! **5 Could you send me the instructions?** My address is...

W Actually, the manual for Selwin 10 is on our Web site. **6 I can send you the link so you can download it.**

여 안녕하세요, 셀윈 오피스 제조사입니다. 귀하께서는 고객 서비스로 연락하셨습니다. 오늘 어떻게 도와드릴까요?

남 네, 안녕하세요. 제가 최근에 중고로 셀윈 6 라벨 제조기를 샀습니다. 그런데 제게 물건을 판매한 분이 더 이상 설명서를 갖고 있지 않아서 기계 작동법을 잘 모르겠습니다.

여 **4 유감스럽게도, 그 제품은 저희가 더 이상 생산하지 않는 초기 모델입니다.**

남 아, 이런. 문제네요.

여 아니에요, 괜찮습니다, 셀윈 10이 비슷한 디자인이라서 설명서가 거의 똑같을 겁니다.

남 다행이네요! **5 제게 설명서를 보내 주실 수 있나요?** 제 주소는…

여 사실 셀윈 10 매뉴얼은 저희 웹사이트에 있습니다. **6 고객님께서 설명서를 다운로드받으실 수 있게 제가 링크를 보내 드리겠습니다.**

어휘 instructions 설명서 though (문장 중간이나 끝에서) 그렇지만 work 작동되다 similar 유사한 nearly 거의

4 여자는 셀윈 6에 대해 무엇이라고 말하는가?
(A) 사용하기 쉽다.   (B) 초기 모델이다.
(C) 잘 만들어졌다.   (D) 매우 인기 있다.

해설 세부 사항 - 셀윈 6에 대한 여자의 언급
여자의 두 번째 대사에서 그 제품은 더 이상 생산하지 않는 초기 모델(Unfortunately, that's an earlier model that we no longer produce)이라고 했으므로 (B)가 정답이다.

5 남자는 무엇을 요청하는가?
(A) 보증서   (B) 상환
(C) 교체 부품   (D) 설명서

해설 세부 사항 - 남자의 요청 사항
후반부에서 남자가 설명서를 보내 달라(Could you send me the instructions?)고 했으므로 (D)가 정답이다.

6 여자는 무엇을 해 주겠다고 제안하는가?
(A) 비밀번호 재설정   (B) 방침 설명
(C) 주문의 일부분 확인   (D) 웹사이트 링크 제공

해설 세부 사항 - 여자의 제안 사항
여자가 마지막 대사에서 설명서를 다운로드받을 수 있게 링크를 보내주겠다(I can send you the link so you can download it)고 했으므로 (D)가 정답이다.

[7-9] 3인 대화 M-Au/W-Am/M-Cn

M1 Mona, I'm delighted your book is shaping up to be a major success. The reviews have been great! But **7 I think we need to consider the next steps we should take**.

W You know, I'm so humbled by all the attention the book's received. **8 I can't believe it's been put up for this year's Watchman Prize.**

M1 It is a big deal. And I'm pleased **9 our in-house publicist, Roberto, was able to join us today**. He has excellent promotional ideas to move us forward.

M2 Thanks. Nowadays, podcasts are where people get information. So, **9 I encourage you to make a guest appearance on one to discuss your book. I'll talk to some producers to make that happen.**

남1 모나 씨, 당신의 책이 큰 성공을 거두고 있어서 정말 기뻐요. 리뷰들도 아주 좋았습니다! 하지만 **7 앞으로 우리가 취해야 할 다음 단계에 대해 고민해봐야 할 것 같아요.**

여 있잖아요, 책이 받은 모든 관심에 정말 겸손해지네요. **8 올해의 와치먼 상 후보작에 올랐다는 게 믿기지 않아요.**

남1 엄청난 사건이죠. 그리고 **9 오늘 우리 내부 홍보 담당자인 로베르토 씨가 함께하실 수 있어서** 기쁩니다. 우리를 앞으로 나아갈 수 있게 해 줄 훌륭한 홍보 아이디어들을 갖고 계세요.

남2 감사합니다. 요즘 사람들은 주로 팟캐스트를 통해 정보를 얻습니다. 그래서, **9 팟캐스트에 초대 손님으로 출연해서 책에 대해 이야기하시는 것을 권해 드려요. 그렇게 될 수 있도록 몇몇 프로듀서들과 이야기해 보겠습니다.**

어휘 shape up (좋은 방향으로) 되어 가다 success 성공(작) be humbled by ~에 겸허한 마음이 들다 attention 관심, 주목 put up ~을 후보로 지명하다 big deal 엄청난 사건 in-house 내부의 publicist 홍보 담당자 promotional 홍보의 move A forward A를 앞으로 나아가게 하다 encourage 권하다 make an appearance 출연하다

7 대화는 무엇에 관한 것인가?
(A) 계약   (B) 행사 장소
(C) 실행 계획   (D) 보안 위험 요소

해설 전체 내용 - 대화 주제
첫 번째 남자가 첫 대사에서 우리가 취해야 할 다음 단계를 고민해봐야 한다(I think we need to consider the next steps we should take)고 한 뒤로, 책을 홍보하는 방안에 대한 이야기를 이어가고 있으므로 (C)가 정답이다.

Paraphrasing 대화의 the next steps we should take → 정답의 A plan of action

8 여자는 자신의 책과 관련해 무슨 말을 하는가?
(A) 영화로 만들어졌다.
(B) 잡지에 서평이 실렸다.
(C) 상의 후보로 지명되었다.
(D) 다른 언어로 번역되었다.

해설 세부 사항 - 여자가 책에 관해 하는 말
여자가 첫 대사에서 올해의 와치먼 상 후보작에 올랐다는 게 믿기지 않는다(I can't believe it's been put up for this year's Watchman Prize)고 했으므로 (C)가 정답이다.

어휘 review 평가하다, 평론을 쓰다 nominate 후보로 지명하다 translate 번역하다

Paraphrasing 대화의 it's been put up for this year's Watchman Prize → 정답의 It was nominated for an award

9 로베르토 씨는 무엇을 하겠다고 제안하는가?
(A) 팟캐스트 프로듀서들에게 연락하는 것
(B) 업계 무역 박람회에서 자원봉사 하는 것
(C) 도서 사인회 행사를 마련하는 것
(D) 표지 그림을 디자인하는 것

해설 세부 사항 - 로베르토 씨가 제안하는 것
첫 번째 남자가 두 번째 남자를 로베르토라고 소개한 뒤, 그가 팟캐스트에 초대 손님으로 출연하는 것을 권한다(I encourage you to make a guest appearance)면서 몇몇 프로듀서와 이야기해 보겠다(I'll talk to some producers to make that happen)고 했으므로 (A)가 정답이다.

어휘 contact 연락하다   volunteer 자원봉사하다   industry 업계   trade show 무역 박람회

> **Paraphrasing** 대화의 talk to → 정답의 Contact

[10-12] M-Cn / W-Am

> M **10**We're so glad you'll be joining the institute's staff of research scientists, Dr. Spencer. This laboratory on the right will be yours — here's the key. It's right next to the equipment storage room.
> W Thank you. Does this key open the storage room, too?
> M Actually, **11**I'll have to ask the security office to have a storage room key made for you, but I'll need a copy of your company identification card to show them. **12**Do you have your card yet?
> W No, but **12**I have an appointment this afternoon to get one.
>
> 남 **10**스펜서 박사님, 박사님께서 연구소의 연구원으로 합류하신다니 아주 기쁩니다. 오른쪽에 있는 실험실이 박사님이 쓰실 곳이고 여기 열쇠가 있습니다. 장비 창고 바로 옆입니다.
> 여 감사합니다. 이 열쇠로 창고도 열 수 있나요?
> 남 실은 **11**박사님께서 사용하실 창고 열쇠를 경비실에 요청해야 하는데, 그들에게 보여줄 박사님의 사원증 복사본이 필요합니다. **12**사원증은 이미 갖고 계신가요?
> 여 아니요, 하지만 **12**오늘 오후에 수령할 예정이에요.
>
> 어휘 institute 협회, 연구소   research scientist 연구원   laboratory 실험실   equipment 장비   storage room 창고   actually 사실   identification card 신분증

10 화자들은 어디에서 일하는 것 같은가?
(A) 의료용품점   (B) 연구소
(C) 보안 회사   (D) 지역 병원

해설 **전체 내용 – 근무 장소**
남자가 첫 대사에서 여자가 연구소의 연구원으로 합류하는 것을 기쁘게 생각한다(We're so glad you'll be joining the institute's staff of research scientists, Dr. Spencer)고 했으므로 (B)가 정답이다.

11 남자는 무엇을 여자에게 주라고 경비실에 요청할 것인가?
(A) 창고 열쇠   (B) 주차증
(C) 건물 견학   (D) 안전 절차 목록

해설 **세부 사항 – 남자가 요청할 것**
남자가 두 번째 대사에서 경비실에 여자가 쓸 창고 열쇠를 요청할 것(I'll have to ask the security office to have a storage room key made for you)이라고 했으므로 (A)가 정답이다.

12 여자는 오후에 무엇을 할 것이라고 말하는가?
(A) 보고서 복사하기   (B) 실험 수행하기
(C) 신분증 수령하기   (D) 업무용품 가지러 가기

해설 **세부 사항 – 여자가 오후에 할 일**
남자가 두 번째 대사에서 여자에게 사원증을 갖고 있는지(Do you have your card yet?)를 묻자, 여자가 아직 없지만 오늘 오후에 수령할 예정(I have an appointment this afternoon to get one)이라고 했으므로 (C)가 정답이다.

[13-15] M-Cn / W-Br

> M Excuse me; I just bought a ticket for the eleven o'clock train to Chicago. **13**But my ticket doesn't show the platform number. How will I know where to go?
> W **14**You can just check the platform number on the display monitor. But it won't be posted until about fifteen minutes before the train is ready to leave.
> M Oh, OK. **15**I guess I still have time to go get a cup of coffee before then.
> W Sure, our food court is right across from the waiting room. And actually, there's a display board over there as well.
>
> 남 실례합니다. 11시 시카고행 기차표를 샀는데요. **13**제 표에는 승강장 번호가 안 나와 있네요. 어디로 가야 하는지 어떻게 알 수 있죠?
> 여 **14**전광판에서 승강장 번호를 확인하실 수 있습니다. 하지만 기차 출발 15분 전이나 되어야 표시될 거예요.
> 남 아, 알겠습니다. **15**그 전에 커피 한 잔 마실 시간은 있을 것 같네요.
> 여 물론이죠. 저희 푸드코트가 대합실 바로 맞은편에 있어요. 사실 거기에도 전광판이 있어요.
>
> 어휘 platform 승강장   display monitor 전광판   as well ~도, 또한

13 남자는 무엇을 알고 싶어 하는가?
(A) 도착 시간   (B) 탑승 장소
(C) 만료일   (D) 왕복 요금

해설 **세부 사항 – 남자가 알고 싶은 것**
남자가 첫 대사에서 자신의 표에는 승강장 번호가 안 나와 있다(my ticket doesn't show the platform number)며 어떻게 알 수 있는지(How will I know where to go?) 문의했으므로, 탑승 장소를 알고 싶어 한다는 것을 알 수 있다. 따라서 (B)가 정답이다.

어휘 arrival 도착   boarding 승차, 탑승   expiration 만료   round-trip 왕복 여행

14 여자는 남자에게 무엇을 하라고 권하는가?
(A) 안내 서비스에 전화하기
(B) 승무원과 이야기하기
(C) 표 영수증 모으기
(D) 전광판 확인하기

해설 세부 사항 – 여자의 제안 사항
남자가 탑승 장소를 어떻게 알 수 있는지 묻자 여자가 전광판에서 승강장 번호를 확인할 수 있다(You can just check the platform number on the display monitor)고 응답했으므로 (D)가 정답이다.

어휘 conductor 승무원, 여행 안내원 receipt 영수증

15 남자는 다음에 무엇을 할 것 같은가?
(A) 마실 것 사기   (B) 매표기 이용하기
(C) 문자 메시지 보내기   (D) 시간표 가져가기

해설 세부 사항 – 남자가 다음에 할 일
남자가 마지막 대사에서 탑승 전에 커피 한 잔 마실 시간은 있을 것 같다(I guess I still have time to go get a cup of coffee before then)고 했으므로 (A)가 정답이다.

> **Paraphrasing** 대화의 go get a cup of coffee → 정답의 Buy something to drink

[16-18] M-Cn / W-Am

M Hi Marta. **16 I'm being sent to Madrid next month to cover an art show at the Ariza Gallery.** I'm supposed to write an article about the show for our magazine. You were there recently, right?

W Yes, and my good friend is actually one of the artists whose work will be shown at that gallery next month. I could put you in touch with her.

M That'd be great. **17 I'd really like to learn as much as I can about the featured artists before attending the event.**

W **18 Her business card is in my office.** If you'll come with me, I can give it to you now.

남 안녕하세요, 마타. **16**제가 다음 달에 아리자 갤러리에서 있을 미술전 취재차 마드리드로 파견될 거예요. 잡지에 미술전 관련 기사를 써야 하거든요. 최근에 거기 다녀오셨죠, 그렇죠?
여 네. 사실 친한 친구가 다음 달 그 미술관에 작품이 전시될 화가 중 한 명이거든요. 그녀와 연락이 닿도록 해 드릴 수 있어요.
남 그래 주시면 좋죠. **17**행사에 참석하기 전에 참여 화가들에 대해 가능한 한 많이 알아두고 싶거든요.
여 **18**그녀의 명함이 제 사무실에 있어요. 저랑 함께 가시면 지금 드릴 수 있어요.

어휘 cover 취재하다 article 기사 put A in touch with B A를 B와 연락이 닿게 하다 feature 특별히 포함하다

16 남자는 왜 마드리드에 가는가?
(A) 행사를 취재하기 위해
(B) 친지를 방문하기 위해
(C) 미술품을 구입하기 위해
(D) 대학교에서 공부하기 위해

해설 세부 사항 – 남자가 마드리드에 가는 이유
남자가 첫 번째 대사에서 다음 달에 아리자 갤러리에서 있을 미술전 취재차 마드리드로 파견될 것(I'm being sent to Madrid next month to cover an art show at the Ariza Gallery)이라고 했으므로 (A)가 정답이다.

> **Paraphrasing** 대화의 cover an art show → 정답의 report on an event

17 남자는 출장 가기 전 무엇을 하고 싶다고 말하는가?
(A) 강좌 등록
(B) 호텔 예약
(C) 화가들에 대해 조사
(D) 안내책자 구입

해설 세부 사항 – 남자가 출장 가기 전에 하고 싶은 일
남자가 두 번째 대사에서 행사에 참석하기 전에 참여 화가들에 대해 가능한 한 많이 알아두고 싶다(I'd really like to learn as much as I can about the featured artists before attending the event)고 했으므로 (C)가 정답이다.

> **Paraphrasing** 대화의 learn as much as I can about the featured artists → 정답의 Research some artists

18 여자는 무엇을 하겠다고 제안하는가?
(A) 일정표 확인하기   **(B) 연락처 찾기**
(C) 전화하기   (D) 가격표 찾아보기

해설 세부 사항 – 여자의 제안 사항
여자가 마지막 대사에서 화가의 명함이 사무실에 있다(Her business card is in my office)며 함께 가면 명함을 주겠다(I can give it to you)고 했으므로 (B)가 정답이다.

> **Paraphrasing** 대화의 Her business card → 정답의 some contact information

[19-21] W-Br / M-Cn

W Hi, Bob. I just got the results back from the market testing on our new solar panels. **19 They were very popular with the technicians— they were very enthusiastic about how easy it was to install them.**

M That's wonderful news! It was a smart idea to mount the solar panels on hinges so that they attach so easily. **20 Do you think they'll be ready for us to present at the Solar Tech Trade Fair in September?**

W   Yes—we still have a few minor issues to fix, but I'm sure they'll be ready to introduce to the market by then. **21 You might want to give the fair's organizers a call right away though, to make sure we can still reserve a booth.**

여   안녕하세요, 밥. 새 태양 전지판에 관한 시장성 조사 결과를 방금 받았어요. **19기술자들에게 굉장히 인기가 많았는데요.** 그들은 설치가 굉장히 쉽다는 점에 아주 열광했습니다.

남   좋은 소식이네요! 태양 전지판을 경첩 위에 설치해서 쉽게 부착되게 한 아이디어가 좋았어요. **20 9월에 있을 솔라 테크 무역 박람회에서 선보일 준비가 될 것 같아요?**

여   네, 아직 해결할 사소한 문제들이 좀 있지만 그때까지는 시장에 내놓을 준비가 될 겁니다. **21박람회 주최측에 바로 전화해서 아직 부스를 예약할 수 있는지 알아보는 게 좋을 거예요.**

어휘 market testing 시장성 조사 solar panel 태양 전지판 technician 기술자 enthusiastic 열광적인 install 설치하다 mount 설치하다, 고정시키다 hinge 경첩 attach 부착하다 minor 작은, 가벼운 fix 고치다 organizer 주최자

19 여자에 따르면, 태양 전지판은 왜 인기가 많은가?
(A) 작다.   (B) 설치하기 쉽다.
(C) 멋지다.   (D) 값이 싸다.

해설 **세부 사항 - 태양 전지판이 인기 있는 이유**
여자가 첫 대사에서 태양 전지판이 기술자들에게 굉장히 인기가 많았다(They were very popular with the technicians)고 한 뒤, 설치가 굉장히 쉽다는 점(how easy it was to install them)에 아주 열광했다고 덧붙였으므로 (B)가 정답이다.

어휘 attractive 멋진, 매력적인   inexpensive 비싸지 않은, 값싼

20 9월에 무엇이 열릴 것 같은가?
(A) 공장 견학   (B) 직원 교육
(C) 무역 박람회   (D) 회사 합병

해설 **세부 사항 - 9월에 열릴 행사**
남자가 첫 대사에서 9월에 있을 솔라 테크 무역 박람회(the Solar Tech Trade Fair in September)에 대해 언급했으므로 (C)가 정답이다.

Paraphrasing 대화의 the Solar Tech Trade Fair → 정답의 A trade show

21 남자는 다음으로 무엇을 할 것 같은가?
(A) 전화하기   (B) 보고서 읽기
(C) 절차 검토하기   (D) 대금 보내기

해설 **세부 사항 - 남자가 다음에 할 일**
여자가 마지막 대사에서 남자에게 박람회 주최측에 바로 전화해서(You might want to give the fair's organizers a call right away though) 아직 부스를 예약할 수 있는지 알아보는 게 좋을 거라고 했으므로, 남자가 이 말을 듣고 전화를 할 것임을 추론할 수 있다. 따라서 (A)가 정답이다.

어휘 review 검토하다   procedure 절차

[22-24] 3인 대화 W-Am / W-Br / M-Au

W1   I'm surprised the new vendor, Penn Food Service, left out the frozen food delivery on the counter instead of placing it in the freezer last night. **22 We'll have to take many breakfast items off the menu this morning because of spoiled food. 23 Did you call them, Viktoriya?**

W2   Yes, I talked to the vendor this morning. They apologized for their mistake. **23 They're sending a replacement order** but **24 won't have a driver available for a few hours. Ilya, are you free to pick it up now?**

M   **24 Yes, I was thinking the same thing.** That way, we can still serve most of our breakfast items.

여1 새로운 납품업체인 펜 푸드 서비스에서 어젯밤에 냉동 식품 배송을 냉동고에 넣지 않고 조리대 위에 그냥 두고 갔다니 놀랍네요. **22상한 식품 때문에 오늘 아침 메뉴에서 많은 아침 식사 품목을 빼야 할 것 같아요. 23그쪽에 전화해 보셨나요, 빅토리야?**

여2 네, 오늘 아침에 업체와 이야기했어요. 그쪽에서 실수에 대해 사과했습니다. **23대체 주문품을 보내 준다는데, 24몇 시간 동안은 가능한 운전 기사가 없을 거예요. 일리야, 지금 가지러 가실 시간이 있으신가요?**

남   **24네, 저도 같은 생각을 하고 있었어요.** 그렇게 하면, 아침 식사 품목 대부분을 여전히 제공할 수 있을 거예요.

어휘 vendor 납품업체, 판매업자   place 놓다, 두다   freezer 냉동실   spoiled 상한   apologize for ~에 대해 사과하다   replacement 대체(품), 교체(품)

22 화자들은 어디에서 일하겠는가?
(A) 농장   (B) 레스토랑
(C) 공항   (D) 콘서트홀

해설 **전체 내용 - 근무 장소**
첫 번째 여자가 첫 대사에서 상한 식품 때문에 오늘 아침 메뉴에서 많은 아침 식사 품목을 빼야 할 것(We'll have to take many breakfast items off the menu this morning because of spoiled food)이라고 한 것을 보아 화자들은 레스토랑에서 근무한다는 것을 알 수 있다. 따라서 (B)가 정답이다.

23 빅토리야에 따르면, 펜 푸드 서비스 사는 무엇을 할 것인가?
(A) 직원들 교육하기   (B) 가격 인하하기
(C) 주문품 대체하기   (D) 주차 허가증 제공하기

해설 **세부 사항 - 펜 푸드 서비스 사가 할 일**
첫 번째 여자가 첫 대사에서 빅토리야에게 펜 푸드 서비스 사에 전화했는지(Did you call them, Viktoriya?) 묻자, 두 번째 여자(빅토리야)가 그곳에서 대체 주문품을 보내 준다(They're sending a replacement order)고 했다고 답했으므로 (C)가 정답이다.

어휘 train 교육하다, 훈련시키다   reduce 인하하다, 감소시키다
replace 대체하다, 교체하다   permit 허가증

> Paraphrasing 대화의 sending a replacement order →
> 정답의 Replace an order

24 일리야는 다음에 무엇을 하겠는가?
(A) 진열품 만들기
(B) 계약서 수정하기
(C) 납품업체 위치로 운전해서 가기
(D) 선임 관리자에게 연락하기

해설 세부 사항 – 일리야가 다음에 할 일
두 번째 여자가 첫 대사에서 몇 시간 동안은 가능한 운전 기사가 없다(won't have a driver available for a few hours)며 일리야에게 지금 가지러 갈 시간이 있는지(Ilya, are you free to pick it up now?) 묻자, 자신도 같은 생각을 하고 있었다(Yes, I was thinking the same thing)고 답했으므로 (C)가 정답이다.

어휘 display 진열(품), 전시(품)   modify 수정하다, 변경하다
contract 계약(서)

UNIT 10 의도 파악 / 시각 정보 연계 문제

1 의도 파악 문제

기출 공략 포인트 ·· 본책 p.88

남 안녕하세요, 가브리엘라. 새로 생긴 온라인 시간 보고 시스템에 대해 얘기하고 싶어요… 많은 사람들이 그것에 대해 물어보고 있거든요.
여 네, 음, 제가 아주 바빴어요. 하지만 다음 주 초에 직원 교육을 계획하고 있어요. 그럼 모든 사람이 명확하게 알 수 있을 겁니다.
남 좋아요.

어휘 training session 교육 (과정)   clear 명료한

문제 남자가 "많은 사람들이 그것에 대해 물어보고 있거든요"라고 말할 때 무엇을 의미하는가?
(A) 직원들이 절차에 대해 혼란스러워 한다.
(B) 사람들이 워크숍이 흥미롭다는 얘기를 들었다.
(C) 직원들이 새로운 업무를 기다리고 있다.
(D) 휴가 일정표가 아직 게시되지 않았다.

ETS 유형연습   본책 p.89

1 (B)   **2** (C)   **3** (B)   **4** (D)

---

[1] M-Cn / W-Br

M I recommend that you consider billboard ads. They're a great way to introduce your athletic shoe brand to a wide audience.
W But what makes our athletic shoes special is the way they move. I doubt we can convey that through a billboard.
M On digital billboards, you can display video clips.
W Oh. Then I'd be open to that as long as it's within our budget.

남 저는 옥외 광고판 광고를 고려해 보시기를 추천합니다. 폭넓은 사람들에게 귀사의 운동화 브랜드를 소개하는 아주 좋은 방법이에요.
여 하지만 저희 운동화들을 특별하게 만들어 주는 것은 움직이는 방식이라서요. 저희가 옥외 광고판을 통해서 그 부분을 전달할 수 있을지가 의문이에요.
남 디지털 옥외 광고판에서는 동영상을 보여줄 수 있어요.
여 아. 그럼 그게 저희 예산 범위 내에서 가능하다면 그렇게 할 의향이 있습니다.

어휘 consider 고려하다   billboard 옥외 광고판
ad 광고   athletic (운동) 경기의   audience 청중   doubt 의문을 갖다   convey 전달하다   display 보여 주다, 진열하다
as long as ~하는 한   budget 예산

1 남자는 왜 "디지털 옥외 광고판에서는 동영상을 보여줄 수 있어요"라고 말하는가?
(A) 기술 지원을 요청하기 위해
(B) 잘못된 생각을 바로잡기 위해
(C) 지역 규정을 설명하기 위해
(D) 연구 프로젝트를 제안하기 위해

해설 화자의 의도 파악
여자가 첫 대사에서 옥외 광고판을 통해서 신발의 특징을 전달할 수 있을지 의문이라고(I doubt we can convey that through a billboard) 말한 뒤 남자가 인용문을 언급한 것으로 보아 여자가 걱정하는 점에 대한 정보를 제공해 생각을 바로잡기 위한 의도임을 알 수 있다. 따라서 (B)가 정답이다.

어휘 correct 바로잡다, 정정하다   mistaken 잘못된
assumption 생각, 추정   regulation 규정, 규제

[2] W-Am / M-Au

W I'm happy our plans are coming along so well for the youth soccer tournament next month, Tae-Joon.
M Yes. But do you think we should find more volunteers to help out on the day of the event?
W Well, we have twenty people signed up.
M Oh, OK. Great.

여 다음 달 유소년 축구 대회 계획이 순조롭게 진행되고 있어서 기뻐요, 태준.
남 네. 그런데 행사 당일에 도와줄 자원봉사자를 더 찾아봐야 할까요?
여 음, 현재 20명이 신청했어요.
남 아, 알겠습니다. 좋네요.

어휘 come along (원하는 대로) 되어 가다, 진행되다
volunteer 자원 봉사자

2 여자가 "현재 20명이 신청했어요"라고 말할 때 무엇을 의미하는가?
(A) 웹사이트가 업데이트되어야 한다.
(B) 몇몇 사람들이 늦었다.
(C) 추가 자원봉사자가 필요하지 않다.
(D) 업무가 배정되지 않았다.

해설 화자의 의도 파악
남자가 첫 대사에서 행사 당일에 도와줄 자원봉사자를 더 찾아봐야 할지(do you think we should find more volunteers to help out on the day of the event?) 의견을 묻자 여자가 인용문을 언급했으므로 자원봉사자가 더 이상 필요하지 않다는 의미임을 알 수 있다. 따라서 (C)가 정답이다.

어휘 additional 추가적인 unnecessary 불필요한 task 업무, 일 assign 배정하다

[3] M-Cn / W-Br

M Hi, Elaine. It's almost twelve-thirty. **I'm on my way to lunch with Sam if you'd like to come with us.**
W **I have three payroll checks left to process.**
M Oh, OK. I'll see you at the department meeting this afternoon then.

남 안녕하세요, 일레인. 거의 12시 30분이네요. 샘하고 점심 먹으러 가는 길인데, 당신도 같이 갈래요?
여 처리해야 할 급여 명세서 세 건이 남아 있어요.
남 아, 알았어요. 그럼 오후에 부서 회의 때 봐요.

어휘 payroll check 급여 명세서 process 처리하다

3 여자는 왜 "처리해야 할 급여 명세서 세 건이 남아 있어요"라고 말하는가?
(A) 소프트웨어에 대해 불평하려고
(B) 초대를 거절하려고
(C) 자원봉사자를 요청하려고
(D) 동료를 안심시키려고

해설 화자의 의도 파악
남자가 점심 먹으러 같이 갈 것(I'm on my way to lunch with Sam if you'd like to come with us)을 제안하자 여자가 인용문을 언급했으므로 점심 초대를 거절하기 위한 의도임을 알 수 있다. 따라서 (B)가 정답이다.

[4] W-Br / M-Au

W Fred, the Regional Library Association is running a workshop in town called Managing Digital Content. It looks useful. **I think our library's whole staff should attend, don't you?**
M Oh, I've already inquired about that workshop. Uh… Most of the content will be rather technical.
W **I see. OK. Then I should have only the data management team attend?**
M That sounds like a much better plan.

여 프레드, 지역 도서관 협회가 우리 시에서 '디지털 콘텐츠 관리'라는 워크숍을 운영한대요. 유용할 것 같아요. 우리 도서관의 모든 직원들이 참석해야 할 것 같아요. 그렇죠?
남 제가 그 워크숍에 대해 이미 물어봤어요. 음… 내용 대부분이 다소 기술적이에요.
여 그렇군요. 알겠어요. 그러면 데이터 관리팀만 참석하도록 해야겠군요?
남 그게 훨씬 더 나은 계획 같아요.

어휘 regional 지역의 association 협회 run 운영하다 content 내용, 주제 inquire 묻다 rather 약간, 다소 technical 기술적인 management 관리

4 남자가 "내용 대부분이 다소 기술적이에요"라고 말할 때 무엇을 의미하는가?
(A) 워크숍의 내용을 수정하기를 원한다.
(B) 워크숍 참석을 고대한다.
(C) 워크숍 발표가 쉽지 않을 거라 생각한다.
(D) 워크숍이 모든 직원들에게 유익하지 않을지도 모른다고 생각한다.

해설 화자의 의도 파악
여자가 첫 대사에서 직원 전체가 워크숍에 참석해야 할 것 같다(I think our library's whole staff should attend)고 말하자 남자가 인용문을 언급했고, 뒤이어 데이터 관리팀만 참석시키겠다(Then I should have only the data management team attend?)는 말에 적극 동의한 것을 보아 남자는 워크숍이 모든 직원에게 유용하지는 않을 거라고 생각한 것임을 알 수 있다. 따라서 (D)가 정답이다.

어휘 revise 수정하다 present 발표하다 challenging 도전적인 benefit 유익하다

2 시각 정보 연계 문제

기출 공략 포인트 ········ 본책 p.90

남 모나, 방금 우리 박물관 컬렉션에 도자기를 기증하고 싶어 하시는 분으로부터 이메일을 받았어요. 이것들이 그분께서 기증을 원하시는 작품들입니다.
여 아, 전부 전시하면 아주 좋을 텐데요. 하지만 현재는 이집트 유물 컬렉션에만 물품을 새로 추가할 수 있어요.

남 알겠습니다. 제가 기증자께 연락드려서 **이집트 작품은 기꺼이 받겠다고** 알려드릴게요. 그래도 네 가지 전부를 받을 수 없어서 아쉽긴 하네요.

어휘 donate 기증하다, 기부하다 pottery 도자기 collection 소장품, 수집품 piece (글, 그림, 음악 등의) 작품 artifact 인공 유물 accept 받아들이다, 수락하다

그리스 꽃병	이집트 물병
터키 주전자	이탈리아 그릇

문제 시각 정보에 따르면, 화자들은 어느 제품을 선택하는가?
(A) 꽃병 **(B) 물병**
(C) 주전자 (D) 그릇

ETS 유형연습 본책 p.91

1 (B) **2** (A) **3** (A)

[1] 대화 + 차트 W-Am / M-Au

W Thanks for calling Mahady Air. How can I help you?

M I'll be traveling with a musical instrument. Can I bring it in the cabin with me?

W If it's small, it will fit in the overhead compartment. But if the case is longer than 82 centimeters, you'll need to buy a second seat or put it in the cargo hold.

M **It's 131 centimeters.** Since the instrument is fragile, I'd prefer to buy an extra seat.

여 마하디 에어에 전화 주셔서 감사합니다. 어떻게 도와드릴까요?

남 악기를 가지고 여행할 예정인데요. 기내에 가져갈 수 있을까요?

여 크기가 작다면, 머리 위쪽의 짐칸에 들어갈 겁니다. 하지만 케이스가 82센티미터보다 더 길다면, 좌석을 하나 더 구입하시거나, 화물 적재칸에 넣으셔야 해요.

남 길이는 131센티미터입니다. 악기가 깨지기 쉬우니, 추가 좌석을 구매하는 게 좋겠네요.

어휘 musical instrument 악기 cabin 객실 fit (크기 등이) 알맞다 overhead compartment 머리 위쪽의 짐칸 cargo hold 화물 적재칸 fragile 깨지기 쉬운

악기	케이스 크기 (센티미터)
베이스	195
첼로	**131**
기타	107
바이올린	82

1 시각 정보에 따르면, 남자는 어느 악기를 연주하는가?
(A) 베이스 **(B) 첼로**
(C) 기타 (D) 바이올린

해설 세부 사항 - 시각 정보 연계

남자가 두 번째 대사에서 길이가 131센티미터(It's 131 centimeters)라며 구체적인 케이스 크기를 언급했다. 표를 보면 케이스 크기가 131센티미터로 표기된 항목의 악기는 첼로이므로 (B)가 정답이다.

[2] 대화 + 상품 목록 M-Cn / W-Br

M So, Ms. Becker, I recall that you had planned to run in the community footrace in the park last weekend. How did it go?

W Not so good, doctor. My seasonal allergies started acting up, and I kept sneezing.

M I'm sorry to hear that. **I can prescribe nasal spray that will help with that.**

W That's great, doctor.

남 자, 베커 씨, 지난 주말에 공원에서 열린 지역 달리기 대회에서 달릴 계획을 세우셨던 것으로 기억합니다. 어떻게 되었나요?

여 그렇게 좋지 않았어요, 선생님. 계절성 알레르기가 말썽을 부리기 시작해서, 계속 재채기를 했거든요.

남 안타깝네요. 도움이 될 만한 비강 스프레이를 처방해 드릴 수 있어요.

여 그거 좋네요, 선생님.

어휘 recall 기억하다, 회상하다 footrace 달리기 경주 act up 말썽을 부리다 sneeze 재채기하다 prescribe 처방하다 nasal 비강의, 코의

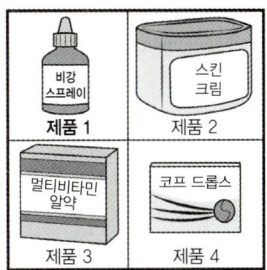

2 시각 정보에 따르면, 여자는 어느 제품을 구입할 것인가?
(A) 제품 1 (B) 제품 2
(C) 제품 3 (D) 제품 4

해설 **세부 사항 – 시각 정보 연계**

남자가 두 번째 대사에서 비강 스프레이를 처방해 줄 수 있다(I can prescribe nasal spray that will help with that)고 했다. 상품 목록을 보면 왼쪽 상단에 Nasal Spray라고 쓰여 있는 제품이 Product 1로 표기되어 있으므로 (A)가 정답이다.

[3] **대화 + 파이 차트** M-Cn / W-Am

> M Lolade, **did you get a chance to read through the quarterly report?** I e-mailed it to you this morning.
>
> W I did. Thanks for sending it. The results were quite promising.
>
> M Yes! **I was surprised to see how popular our disc faucets have become.** Our ball faucets are <u>still our top seller</u>, of course, but the disc faucets <u>really increased in popularity</u> last quarter.
>
> 남 롤라데 씨, 분기 보고서를 읽어 보실 기회가 있으셨나요? 제가 오늘 아침에 이메일로 보내 드렸는데요.
>
> 여 읽어 봤어요. 보내 주셔서 감사합니다. 결과가 꽤 유망하더 군요.
>
> 남 네! 우리 디스크 수도꼭지가 얼마나 인기가 많아졌는지 보고 놀랐어요. 물론 볼 수도꼭지가 여전히 우리의 베스트셀러이긴 하지만, 지난 분기에 디스크 수도꼭지의 인기가 정말 높아졌 어요.

어휘 quarterly 분기의 result 결과 quite 꽤, 상당히 promising 유망한, 촉망받는 faucet 수도꼭지 increase in popularity 인기가 높아지다

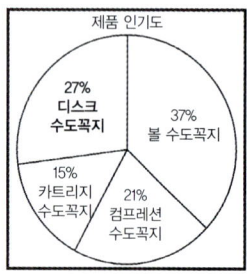

3 시각 정보에 따르면, 남자는 총 판매량의 어느 비율이 놀랍다 고 생각하는가?
(A) 27%   (B) 37%
(C) 21%   (D) 15%

해설 **세부 사항 – 시각 정보 연계**

남자가 두 번째 대사에서 디스크 수도꼭지가 얼마나 인기 가 많아졌는지 보고 놀랐다(I was surprised to see how popular our disc faucets have become)고 했다. 파이 차트를 보면 디스크 수도꼭지(disc faucets)가 27%로 표기되 어 있으므로 (A)가 정답이다.

어휘 find A B A를 B라고 생각하다

ETS 실전문제 본책 p.92

1 (B)	2 (C)	3 (A)	4 (C)	5 (D)	6 (C)
7 (A)	8 (C)	9 (D)	10 (B)	11 (A)	12 (D)
13 (A)	14 (A)	15 (B)	16 (C)	17 (D)	18 (B)
19 (C)	20 (B)	21 (B)	22 (A)	23 (B)	24 (B)

[1-3] M-Cn / W-Am

> M Thanks for meeting with me today, Ms. Salazar. As I mentioned in my call, **¹the roof of my computer store leaks whenever it rains**.
>
> W My company should be able to fix the roof. We just need to replace the area where this occurs. The low-slope roof on this building makes leakage more likely.
>
> M Oh. I didn't know that. **²Will it take long to fix?** The rainy season is coming soon.
>
> W We have most of the supplies in our warehouse.
>
> M Great. So what are the next steps?
>
> W **³I'll need to take some pictures. My camera's in the truck, though.**
>
> 남 오늘 만나 주셔서 감사합니다, 살라자르 씨. 제가 전화상으로 말씀드린 대로, **¹저희 컴퓨터 매장의 지붕이 비가 내릴 때마다 새고 있어요**.
>
> 여 저희 회사가 지붕을 수리할 수 있을 거예요. 문제가 발생하는 부분을 교체하기만 하면 됩니다. 이 건물의 지붕은 경사가 낮 아 누수 가능성이 높아요.
>
> 남 아. 몰랐네요. **²수리하는 데 오래 걸릴까요?** 장마철이 다가오 고 있어서요.
>
> 여 저희 창고에 대부분의 자재가 있어요.
>
> 남 잘됐네요. 그럼 다음 단계는 뭔가요?
>
> 여 **³사진을 좀 촬영해야 합니다. 그런데 제 카메라가 트럭에 있 네요**.

어휘 mention 언급하다 leak (액체, 기체 등이) 새다 replace 교체하다 occur 발생하다 low-slope 낮은 경사면의 leakage 누수 likely 가능성 있는, ~할 것 같은

1 여자는 어떤 업계에서 일할 것 같은가?
(A) 정보 통신   **(B) 지붕 공사**
(C) 제조   (D) 소매 판매

해설 **전체 내용 – 여자가 종사하는 업계**

남자가 첫 대사에서 여자에게 자신이 일하는 컴퓨터 매장의 지붕이 비가 내릴 때마다 샌다(the roof of my computer store leaks whenever it rains)고 말하는 것으로 보아 여 자는 지붕 공사 업체에서 일한다는 것을 알 수 있다. 따라서 (B)가 정답이다.

2 여자가 "저희 창고에 대부분의 자재가 있어요"라고 말할 때 무엇을 의미하는가?
(A) 일부 제품이 다른 장소로 옮겨졌다.
(B) 재고 목록에 오류가 있다.
(C) 프로젝트가 빨리 마무리될 수 있다.
(D) 배송이 성공적으로 완료되었다.

해설 **화자의 의도 파악**
남자가 두 번째 대사에서 고치는 데 오래 걸릴지(Will it take long to fix?) 묻자 여자가 인용문을 언급한 것으로 보아, 이미 필요한 자재를 보유하고 있어 신속하게 작업할 수 있다는 의도로 한 말임을 알 수 있다. 따라서 (C)가 정답이다.

어휘 inventory 재고 (목록) contain 포함하다, 담고 있다
complete 완료하다

3 여자는 다음에 무엇을 할 것 같은가?
(A) 카메라 가져오기
(B) 동료 직원에게 연락하기
(C) 거래 내역서 준비하기
(D) 안내판 게시하기

해설 **세부 사항 – 여자가 다음에 할 일**
여자가 마지막 대사에서 사진을 촬영해야 하는데 카메라가 트럭에 있다(I'll need to take some pictures. My camera's in the truck, though)고 했으므로 카메라를 가지러 가려 한다는 것을 알 수 있다. 따라서 (A)가 정답이다.

어휘 retrieve 가져오다, 되찾아오다 colleague 동료 (직원)
invoice 거래 내역서 post 게시하다

[4-6] 3인 대화 M-Cn / W-Am / M-Au

M1	Hello. ⁴Can I mail a package to Portugal here?
W	I'm sorry, but this counter is for domestic services only.
M1	Oh, OK. So I should go...
M2	I can help you over here.
M1	Yes, hello. I'd like to mail this package.
M2	Of course. Would you like to send it by priority mail or regular mail? ⁵Priority mail takes less time, but it costs more.
M1	⁵I'd prefer priority mail since I want it to get to Lisbon by Friday. ⁶Is there a free tracking service so I can track my package in the delivery process?
M2	Unfortunately, no. ⁶We do, however, offer package delivery notification for an additional fee.
남1	안녕하세요. ⁴여기서 포르투갈로 소포를 부칠 수 있나요?
여	죄송합니다만, 이 창구는 국내 우편 전용입니다.
남1	아, 네. 그럼 제가 가야 할 곳은…
남2	이쪽에서 도와드리겠습니다.
남1	네, 안녕하세요. 이 소포를 부치고 싶습니다.
남2	알겠습니다. 빠른 우편으로 보내시겠습니까, 보통 우편으로 보내시겠습니까? ⁵빠른 우편은 시간은 적게 걸리지만 요금이 더 비쌉니다.
남1	⁵금요일까지 리스본에 도착해야 하니까 빠른 우편으로 하겠어요. ⁶배송 과정에서 제 소포를 추적할 수 있는 무료 추적 서비스가 있나요?
남2	안타깝지만, 없습니다. ⁶하지만 추가 수수료를 내시면 소포 배송 완료 알림을 보내 드립니다.

어휘 package 소포 domestic 국내의 priority mail 빠른 우편 regular mail 보통 우편 track 추적하다 notification 알림, 통지 additional fee 추가 수수료

4 여자는 왜 "이 창구는 국내 우편 전용입니다"라고 말하는가?
(A) 규칙을 비판하려고   (B) 혼동을 표현하려고
(C) 요청을 거절하려고   (D) 사실을 검증하려고

해설 **화자의 의도 파악**
첫 번째 남자가 포르투갈로 소포를 부칠 수 있는지(Can I mail a package to Portugal here?) 묻자 여자가 인용문을 언급하고 있으므로, 포르투갈로 소포를 부칠 수 없다는 의도로 한 말임을 알 수 있다. 따라서 (C)가 정답이다.

어휘 criticize 비판하다 confusion 혼동 verify 검증하다

5 고객은 무엇을 하기로 결정하는가?
(A) 배송 취소하기
(B) 제품 교환하기
(C) 특별 포장재 구매하기
(D) 더 빠른 배송을 위한 요금 지불하기

해설 **세부 사항 – 고객의 결정 사항**
두 번째 남자가 빠른 우편이 시간은 적게 걸리지만 요금이 더 비싸다(Priority mail takes less time, but it costs more)고 하자 고객이 금요일까지 리스본에 도착해야 하니까 빠른 우편으로 하겠다(I'd prefer priority mail since I want it to get to Lisbon by Friday)고 했으므로 (D)가 정답이다.

어휘 cancel 취소하다 shipment 배송 packaging 포장재

6 고객은 무엇을 위해 추가 수수료를 내겠는가?
(A) 파손 보험   (B) 익일 배송
(C) 배송 확인   (D) 규격 초과 소포

해설 **세부 사항 – 추가 수수료를 지불하는 이유**
첫 번째 남자가 배송 과정에서 소포를 추적할 수 있는 무료 추적 서비스가 있는지(Is there a free tracking service so I can track my package in the delivery process?) 묻자, 두 번째 남자가 추가 수수료를 내면 소포 배송 완료 알림을 보내 준다(We do, however, offer package delivery notification for an additional fee)고 했으므로 (C)가 정답이다.

어휘 damage 손상 insurance 보험 overnight shipping 익일 배송 confirmation 확인 oversized 규격이 초과된 parcel 소포

[7-9] W-Br / M-Au

W Hi, Mr. Bora. Sorry to call you so late in the day, but **7 the engineer on the second shift has reported a machinery issue**. One of the centrifuges is not spinning correctly, and a part needs to be replaced.

M I see. **8 The quickest solution would be to have our machinist make the part. Have you called Chen?**

W I wanted to check with you first. **9 If Chen comes in, he'll be working overtime. Do I have your approval for overtime pay?**

M Well, we have to keep the equipment running.

W I'll contact Chen right away.

여 안녕하세요, 보라 씨. 너무 늦은 시간에 전화 드려서 죄송하지만, **7 두 번째 교대 근무조의 엔지니어가 기계 관련 문제를 보고했습니다.** 원심 분리기 중 하나가 제대로 회전하지 않고 있어서, 부품을 교체해야 해요.

남 알겠습니다. **8 가장 빠른 해결책은 우리 기계 기술자에게 그 부품을 만들게 하는 것일 겁니다. 첸 씨에게 전화해 보셨나요?**

여 먼저 당신에게 확인하고 싶었습니다. **9 첸 씨가 오면, 초과 근무를 하게 돼서요. 초과 근무 수당에 대해 승인해 주시는 건가요?**

남 음, 우리는 그 장비를 계속 가동되는 상태로 유지해야 해요.

여 지금 바로 첸 씨에게 연락하겠습니다.

어휘 shift 교대 근무(조) centrifuge 원심 분리기 spin 회전하다 correctly 제대로, 정확히 part 부품 solution 해결책 machinist 기계 (제작 또는 수리) 기술자 work overtime 초과 근무하다 approval 승인

7 여자는 왜 남자에게 전화하는가?
(A) 문제를 보고하기 위해
(B) 휴가를 요청하기 위해
(C) 점검 일정을 잡기 위해
(D) 정책 변경을 제안하기 위해

해설 전체 내용 - 여자가 전화한 목적
여자가 첫 대사에서 두 번째 교대 근무조의 엔지니어가 기계 관련 문제를 보고했다(the engineer on the second shift has reported a machinery issue)고 한 뒤로 해당 문제의 처리와 관련해 대화를 이어가고 있으므로 (A)가 정답이다.

어휘 arrange for ~에 대한 일정을 잡다 inspection 점검 policy 정책, 방침

Paraphrasing 대화의 a machinery issue → 정답의 a problem

8 첸은 누구인가?
(A) 회사 대변인   (B) 영업사원
(C) 기계 기술자   (D) 경비원

해설 세부 사항 - 첸 씨의 직업
남자가 첫 대사에서 우리 기계 기술자에게 부품을 만들어 달라고 하면 된다(The quickest solution would be to have our machinist make the part)며 첸 씨에게 전화해 봤는지(Have you called Chen?) 묻는 것으로 보아, 첸 씨는 기계 기술자임을 알 수 있다. 따라서 (C)가 정답이다.

9 남자가 "우리는 그 장비를 계속 가동되는 상태로 유지해야 해요"라고 말할 때 무엇을 의미하는가?
(A) 자신의 업무량이 너무 많다.
(B) 야간 교대 근무가 추가되어야 한다.
(C) 생산량이 늘어나야 한다.
(D) 비용이 수용 가능하다.

해설 화자의 의도 파악
여자가 두 번째 대사에서 첸 씨가 초과 근무를 하게 될 것이라고 말하면서 초과 근무 수당에 대해 승인해 주는 것인지(If Chen comes in, he'll be working overtime. Do I have your approval for overtime pay?) 묻자 남자가 인용문을 언급했으므로 기계를 계속 가동해야 하니 첸 씨에게 초과 근무 수당을 지급하는 것에 동의한다는 의미임을 알 수 있다. 따라서 (D)가 정답이다.

어휘 workload 업무량 heavy (정도, 양 등이) 많은, 심한 expense (지출) 비용 acceptable 수용 가능한

[10-12] W-Br / M-Cn

W Hector, I'm supposed to prepare a report on our factory inventory, but **10 I'm having trouble with this new spreadsheet program.**

M **11 Have you checked out the company Web site? There's an online tutorial there that's good.**

W I've been through the tutorial. It shows you how to do common spreadsheet functions, but **12 it wasn't helpful for the advanced reports. You've done those, haven't you?**

M Yes, but I have a client meeting this morning.

여 헥터 씨, 제가 우리 공장 재고에 관한 보고서를 준비하기로 되어 있는데, **10 이 새로운 스프레드시트 프로그램 때문에 어려움을 겪고 있어요.**

남 **11 회사 웹사이트는 확인해 보셨어요?** 거기에 좋은 온라인 설명서가 있어요.

여 그 설명서를 죽 살펴봤어요. 일반적인 스프레드시트 기능들을 이용하는 방법은 보여 주는데, **12 고급 보고서에 대해서는 도움이 되지 않았어요.** 당신은 그런 보고서를 작성해 본 적이 있죠, 그렇죠?

남 네, 하지만 제가 오늘 오전에 고객 회의가 있어요.

어휘 be supposed to do ~하기로 되어 있다 spreadsheet 스프레드시트(표 기반의 문서 프로그램) check out 확인하다 tutorial 설명서 common 흔한, 일반적인 function 기능 advanced 고급의, 진보한

10 여자는 어떤 문제점을 언급하는가?
(A) 일부 데이터를 찾을 수 없다.
(B) 컴퓨터 프로그램을 이용할 수 없다.
(C) 고객 한 명이 불만스러워 한다.
(D) 진행 일정이 짧아졌다.

해설 세부 사항 - 여자가 언급하는 문제점
여자가 첫 대사에서 새로운 스프레드시트 프로그램 때문에 어려움을 겪고 있다(I'm having trouble with this new spreadsheet program)고 했으므로 (B)가 정답이다.

어휘 timeline 진행 일정(표)   shorten 짧게 하다, 단축하다

> **Paraphrasing** 대화의 having trouble with this new spreadsheet program → 정답의 unable to use a computer program

11 남자는 무엇을 제안하는가?
(A) 웹사이트 방문하기   (B) 기술자에게 연락하기
(C) 상사의 승인 받기   (D) 결정을 미루기

해설 세부 사항 - 남자가 제안하는 것
남자가 첫 대사에서 회사 웹사이트는 확인해 봤는지(Have you checked out the company Web site?) 물으면서 좋은 온라인 설명서가 있다(There's an online tutorial there that's good)고 조언했으므로 (A)가 정답이다.

어휘 obtain 얻다, 획득하다   supervisor 상사, 책임자, 감독
postpone 미루다, 연기하다

12 남자가 "제가 오늘 오전에 고객 회의가 있어요"라고 말할 때 무엇을 의미하는가?
(A) 신규 고객을 얻게 되어 기쁘다.
(B) 자신의 일정이 헷갈렸다.
(C) 추가 자료가 필요하다.
(D) 도움을 줄 수 없는 상태이다.

해설 화자의 의도 파악
여자가 두 번째 대사에서 설명서가 고급 보고서에 대해서는 도움이 되지 않았다(it wasn't helpful for the advanced reports)면서 그런 보고서를 작성해 본적이 있지 않냐고(You've done those, haven't you?) 묻자 남자가 인용문을 언급했으므로, 고객 회의로 인해 여자를 도울 시간이 없을 것이라는 의미를 나타낸다. 따라서 (D)가 정답이다.

어휘 confused 헷갈린, 혼동하는   material 자료, 재료, 물품

[13-15] 대화 + 거래 내역서 M-Cn/W-Am

M Hi, Sakura. Can you help me for a minute? A customer just pulled up with his truck and **13his invoice shows that he ordered one roll of six-foot fencing. I've looked around the stockyard and I don't see that anywhere.**

W That product's actually on a very high shelf. **14You should use the forklift to reach it**, but I think Alberto is using that equipment right now.

M Thanks. **15I'll go and let the customer know it'll be a few more minutes before I get the fencing.**

남 안녕하세요, 사쿠라 씨. 잠시 저 좀 도와주시겠어요? 손님 한 분이 방금 트럭을 세우고 오셨는데, **13**거래 내역서에 이분께서 6피트짜리 울타리 재료를 한 롤 주문하신 것으로 되어 있어요. 제가 재고품 두는 곳을 둘러봤는데, 어디에도 보이지가 않네요.

여 그 제품은 사실 아주 높은 선반에 있어요. **14**그곳에 닿으려면 지게차를 이용하셔야 하는데, 알베르토 씨가 지금 그 장비를 이용하고 있는 것 같아요.

남 감사합니다. **15**제가 가서 손님에게 해당 울타리 재료를 가져다 드리기까지 몇 분 더 걸릴 거라고 알려 드릴게요.

어휘 pull up (자동차를) 세우다   fencing 울타리 (재료)
stockyard 재고품 두는 곳(일반적으로는 가축 우리를 뜻하나 건설, 유통 등의 업계에서는 야외 재고 보관 구역을 가리키기도 함)
forklift 지게차   reach 닿다, 이르다   equipment 장비

파웰 철물 회사		
품목 번호	제품	수량
7055	**13**철조망 울타리 한 롤	1
9021	합판 판자	4
3022	모래주머니	10
8106	전기톱	1

13 시각 정보에 따르면, 남자는 어떤 품목 번호를 찾고 있는가?
(A) 7055   (B) 9021
(C) 3022   (D) 8106

해설 세부 사항 - 시각 정보 연계
남자가 첫 대사에서 고객의 거래 내역서에 6피트짜리 울타리 재료를 한 롤 주문한 것으로 나온다고 하면서 그것이 보이지 않는다(his invoice shows that he ordered one roll of six-foot fencing. I've looked around the stockyard and I don't see that anywhere)고 했다. 도표를 보면 울타리 재료 한 롤의 품목 번호는 7055로 표기되어 있으므로 (A)가 정답이다.

어휘 look for ~을 찾다

14 여자는 남자가 무엇이 필요할 것이라고 말하는가?
(A) 장비   (B) 인쇄한 지도
(C) 관리자의 서명   (D) 카탈로그

해설 세부 사항 - 남자가 필요한 것
여자가 첫 대사에서 남자가 찾는 것을 꺼내기 위해서는 지게차를 이용해야 한다(You should use the forklift to reach it)고 했으므로 (A)가 정답이다.

> **Paraphrasing** 대화의 forklift → 정답의 A piece of equipment

15 남자는 왜 고객과 이야기할 것인가?
(A) 이름의 철자를 확인하기 위해
(B) 지연이 있을 것임을 알리기 위해
(C) 가격 관련 소식을 전하기 위해
(D) 추가 제품을 추천하기 위해

해설 **세부 사항 – 남자가 고객과 이야기하려는 이유**
남자가 마지막 대사에서 고객에게 가서 울타리 재료를 가져다 주기 전까지 몇 분 더 걸릴 거라고 알리겠다(I'll go and let the customer know it'll be a few more minutes before I get the fencing)고 했으므로 (B)가 정답이다.

어휘 confirm 확인해 주다 spelling 철자 indicate 나타내다, 가리키다 delay 지연, 지체 pricing 가격 (책정)

> **Paraphrasing** 대화의 let the customer know it'll be a few more minutes → 정답의 indicate that there will be a delay

---

[16-18] 대화 + 온실 배치도 W-Br / M-Cn

W Gregor, thanks for coming in early this afternoon. It's been busy here at the nursery today, and **16 you do a great job helping our customers.**
M Thanks. I'm enjoying the work. What can I help you with now that it's slowed down?
W **17 Can you go to the greenhouse and water the flowers between the back door and aisle three?** The irrigation system is broken there.
M Sure. I'll do that right away. And when I finish, I'll start organizing the seeds in the store.
W Great. **18 I'll be assisting a landscaper all afternoon.** Feel free to text me if you have any questions.

여 그레고 씨, 오늘 오후에 일찍 와 주셔서 감사합니다. 오늘 묘목장이 바빴는데, **16 고객들을 돕느라 수고 많으세요.**
남 감사합니다. 일이 즐겁습니다. 이제 여유가 좀 생겼는데 뭘 도와 드리면 될까요?
여 **17 온실로 가서 뒷문과 3번 통로 사이에 있는 꽃에 물 좀 주실 수 있나요?** 그곳 관개 시스템이 고장이 나서요.
남 알겠습니다. 지금 바로 할게요. 그리고 끝나면, 가게에 있는 씨앗들을 정리하겠습니다.
여 좋아요. **18 저는 오후 내내 조경 담당자를 돕고 있을 겁니다.** 질문이 있으시면 언제든지 제게 문자 메시지 보내 주세요.

어휘 nursery 묘목장 now that 이제 ~이므로, ~하기 때문에 slow down 느려지다, 둔화되다 aisle 통로 irrigation 관개(물을 끌어들임) organize 정리하다, 준비하다, 조직하다 seed 씨앗 assist 돕다, 지원하다 landscaper 조경사 text 문자 메시지를 보내다

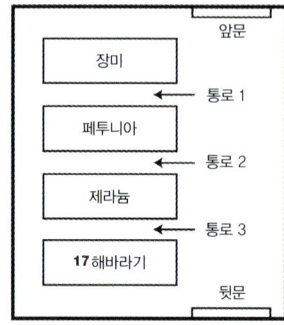

16 여자는 무엇에 대해 남자를 칭찬하는가?
(A) 세부 사항에 대한 주의력
(B) 식물에 대한 지식
(C) 고객 서비스 능력
(D) 시간 관리 능력

해설 **세부 사항 – 여자가 남자를 칭찬하는 이유**
여자가 첫 번째 대사에서 남자에게 고객들을 돕느라 수고가 많다(you do a great job helping our customers)고 했으므로 (C)가 정답이다.

> **Paraphrasing** 대화의 do a great job → 질문의 compliment
> 대화의 helping our customers → 정답의 customer service skills

17 시각 정보에 따르면, 여자는 남자에게 어떤 종류의 꽃에 물을 주라고 요청하는가?
(A) 장비 (B) 페투니아
(C) 제라늄 (D) 해바라기

해설 **세부 사항 – 시각 정보 연계**
여자가 두 번째 대사에서 온실로 가서 뒷문과 3번 통로 사이에 있는 꽃들에게 물을 줄 것을(Can you go to the greenhouse and water the flowers between the back door and aisle three?) 요청하고 있다. 온실 배치도를 보면 뒷문과 3번 통로 사이에 Sunflowers라고 표기되어 있으므로 (D)가 정답이다.

18 여자는 오늘 오후에 무엇을 한다고 말하는가?
(A) 용품 주문하기
(B) 조경 담당자와 만나기
(C) 진열품 설치하기
(D) 특별 행사 계획하기

해설 **세부 사항 – 여자가 오늘 오후에 할 일**
여자가 마지막 대사에서 오후 내내 조경 담당자를 돕고 있을 것(I'll be assisting a landscaper all afternoon)이라고 했으므로 (B)가 정답이다.

[19-21] 대화 + 진열품 W-Am / M-Au

W Hi. **19 I just saw an advertisement in a magazine for a new shampoo.** It's supposed to be good for dry hair.

M Oh, **20 you must mean Sudsy Clean.** It's one of our bestsellers.

W Great. Where are the hair care products?

M They're in aisle five next to the moisturizers.

W OK. By the way, **21 do you have a customer loyalty program**?

M **21 Yes, we do. You can sign up by going to our Web site.**

W OK. Thanks!

여 안녕하세요. 19방금 잡지에서 새로운 샴푸 광고를 봤어요. 건조한 머리결에 좋다고 되어 있어서요.

남 아, 20서드지 클린을 말씀하시는 게 틀림없군요. 저희 베스트셀러 제품 중 하나입니다.

여 잘됐네요. 헤어 케어 제품들은 어디에 있나요?

남 5번 통로의 보습제 옆에 있습니다.

여 알겠습니다. 그건 그렇고, 21고객 우대 프로그램이 있나요?

남 21네, 있습니다. 저희 웹사이트에 가셔서 신청하실 수 있어요.

여 알겠습니다. 감사합니다!

어휘 advertisement 광고 be supposed to do ~하기로 되어 있다, ~해야 하다 aisle 통로 moisturizer 보습제 by the way (화제를 전환할 때) 그런데, 그건 그렇고 customer loyalty program 고객 우대(회원 혜택) 프로그램 sign up 신청하다, 등록하다

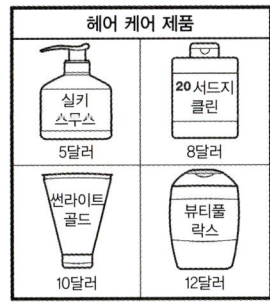

19 여자는 제품에 대해 어떻게 알았는가?
(A) 미용사를 통해서
(B) 소셜 미디어 사이트를 통해서
(C) 잡지 광고를 통해서
(D) 동료 직원을 통해서

해설 세부 사항 - 여자가 제품을 알게 된 방법
여자가 첫 대사에서 잡지에서 새로운 샴푸 광고를 봤다(I just saw an advertisement in a magazine for a new shampoo)면서 해당 제품에 대해 문의했으므로 (C)가 정답이다.

20 시각 정보에 따르면, 여자가 원하는 샴푸의 가격은 얼마인가?
(A) 5달러 (B) 8달러
(C) 10달러 (D) 12달러

해설 세부 사항 - 시각 정보 연계
남자가 첫 대사에서 여자가 원하는 샴푸는 서드지 클린을 말하는 게 틀림없다(you must mean Sudsy Clean)고 했고, 시각 정보에 따르면 Sudsy Clean으로 표기된 제품의 가격은 $8.00이므로 (B)가 정답이다.

21 남자는 여자가 웹사이트에서 무엇을 할 수 있다고 말하는가?
(A) 설문지 작성하기
(B) 고객 보상 프로그램 신청하기
(C) 고객 후기 읽기
(D) 일자리에 지원하기

해설 세부 사항 - 여자가 웹사이트에서 할 수 있는 것
여자가 후반부에서 고객 우대 프로그램이 있는지(do you have a customer loyalty program?) 묻자, 남자가 그렇다(Yes)고 대답한 뒤 자사의 웹사이트에 가서 신청할 수 있다(You can sign up by going to our Web site)고 했으므로 (B)가 정답이다.

어휘 survey 설문 조사(지) apply for ~에 지원하다

[22-24] 대화 + 등산로 안내도 M-Au / W-Am

M Sabine, **22 we need to collect soil samples for the county's annual environmental testing project.** I think it'll be more efficient if we divide up the work. I'll walk to the lake and collect my samples. **23 Can you head to the pine forest to collect yours?** The soil test kits are on that shelf.

W Yes, that works. By the way, while we're working, **24 let's both take some photographs for the city's Web page.** I think the community will find them interesting.

M You're right—let me grab my camera.

남 사빈 씨, 22우리 주의 연례 환경 검사 프로젝트를 위해 토양 샘플을 수집해야 합니다. 우리가 일을 분담한다면 더 효율적일 것 같아요. 저는 호수로 걸어가서 샘플을 채취할게요. 23당신은 소나무 숲으로 가서 샘플을 채취해 주시겠어요? 토양 검사 키트는 저 선반에 있습니다.

여 네, 그러면 되겠네요. 그건 그렇고, 우리가 작업하는 동안, 24우리 둘 다 시 웹페이지를 위해 사진을 좀 찍읍시다. 지역사회에서 흥미롭다고 생각할 것 같아요.

남 맞아요. 제 카메라를 가져올게요.

어휘 collect 수집하다 soil 토양, 흙 annual 연례적인, 해마다의 efficient 효율적인 divide up 분담하다, 나누다 head to ~로 가다, ~로 향하다 kit (용품, 장비 등의) 세트

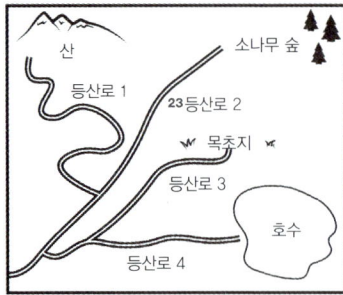

22 화자들은 무엇에 관해 이야기하는가?
(A) 환경 프로젝트 (B) 정부 규제
(C) 다리 수리 (D) 구인 공고

해설 전체 내용 – 대화 주제
남자가 첫 대사에서 연례 환경 검사 프로젝트를 위해 토양 샘플을 수집해야 한다(we need to collect soil samples for the county's annual environmental testing project)고 한 후, 관련 업무 분담에 대해 대화가 이어지고 있으므로 (A)가 정답이다.

어휘 repair 수리 posting 공고, 게시글

23 시각 정보에 따르면, 여자는 어떤 등산로를 이용할 것인가?
(A) 등산로 1 (B) 등산로 2
(C) 등산로 3 (D) 등산로 4

해설 세부 사항 – 시각 정보 연계
남자가 첫 대사에서 여자에게 소나무 숲으로 가서 샘플을 채취해 달라고(Can you head to the pine forest to collect yours?) 요청하고 있다. 등산로 안내도에 따르면, 오른쪽 상단의 소나무 숲(Pine Forest)로 향하는 길은 Trail 2이므로 (B)가 정답이다.

24 여자는 웹사이트에 무엇을 게시하자고 제안하는가?
(A) 투어 진행자 이름 (B) 사진
(C) 연구 결과물 (D) 운전 경로 정보

해설 세부 사항 – 여자가 제안하는 게시물
여자가 첫 대사에서 우리 둘 다 시 웹페이지를 위해 사진을 찍자(let's both take some photographs for the city's Web page)고 제안했으므로 (B)가 정답이다.

어휘 suggest -ing ~하자고 제안하다 directions 길 안내 정보

ETS ACTUAL TEST 본책 p.95

32 (A)	33 (D)	34 (B)	35 (C)	36 (C)	37 (B)
38 (B)	39 (C)	40 (D)	41 (D)	42 (D)	43 (A)
44 (C)	45 (B)	46 (A)	47 (B)	48 (A)	49 (D)
50 (C)	51 (A)	52 (C)	53 (B)	54 (C)	55 (A)
56 (C)	57 (A)	58 (A)	59 (A)	60 (A)	61 (C)
62 (C)	63 (B)	64 (C)	65 (A)	66 (D)	67 (D)
68 (C)	69 (A)	70 (C)			

[32-34] W-Am / M-Au

W **32**Welcome to Casella's for all your printing needs. How can I help you?
M Could you make some photocopies from this book for me? Pages twelve to eighteen, in black and white. And double-sided, if you can.
W Absolutely. **33**Though I should let you know that our credit card reader is broken right now, so you're going to have to pay in cash. Sorry about that.
M Oh, I don't usually carry cash on me. **34**Do you have a cash machine?
W No, but **34**Greenville Bank has a branch just down the street.

여 **32**필요한 모든 인쇄 작업을 제공하는 카셀라스에 오신 것을 환영합니다. 무엇을 도와드릴까요?
남 이 책에서 몇 장 복사해 주실 수 있나요? 12페이지에서 18페이지까지, 흑백으로요. 그리고 가능하시다면 양면으로 해 주세요.
여 물론입니다. **33**다만, 지금 저희 신용 카드 단말기가 고장 나서, 현금으로 결제하셔야 한다는 점 알려드릴게요. 죄송합니다.
남 아, 저는 보통 현금을 가지고 다니지 않는데요. **34**현금 인출기가 있나요?
여 아니요, 하지만 **34**길 바로 아래에 그린빌 은행 지점이 있어요.

어휘 make a photocopy 복사하다 double-sided 양면의 broken 고장 난 in cash 현금으로 carry 휴대하다 branch 지점, 지사

32 화자들은 어디에 있는가?
(A) 인쇄소 (B) 도서관
(C) 서점 (D) 전자제품 매장

해설 전체 내용 – 화자들이 있는 장소
여자가 첫 대사에서 환영 인사를 하면서 필요한 모든 인쇄 작업을 해주는 곳(Welcome to Casella's for all your printing needs)이라고 했으므로 (A)가 정답이다.

33 여자는 왜 사과하는가?
(A) 남자가 오랫동안 대기해야 했다.
(B) 업체가 일찍 문을 닫을 것이다.
(C) 주문이 부정확했다.
(D) 기기가 작동하지 않는다.

해설 세부 사항 – 여자가 사과하는 이유
여자가 두 번째 대사에서 신용 카드 단말기가 고장 나서 현금으로 결제해야 한다는 사실을 알리면서 사과(I should let you know that our credit card reader is broken right now, so you're going to have to pay in cash. Sorry about that)했으므로 (D)가 정답이다.

어휘 order 주문(품) incorrect 부정확한 device 기기, 장치 work (기계 등이) 작동하다

> **Paraphrasing** 대화의 our credit card reader is broken → 정답의 A device is not working

34 남자는 다음으로 무엇을 하겠는가?
(A) 전화 통화하기
(B) 은행으로 가기
(C) 모바일 애플리케이션 다운로드하기
(D) 쿠폰 사용하기

해설 세부 사항 – 남자가 다음에 할 일
남자가 두 번째 대사에서 현금 인출기가 있는지(Do you have a cash machine?) 묻자, 여자가 이용할 수 있는 은행 지점의 위치(Greenville Bank has a branch just down the street)를 알려 주었다. 따라서 남자가 해당 은행 지점으로 갈 것으로 볼 수 있으므로 (B)가 정답이다.

[35-37] W-Am / M-Cn

W Hi, Mr. Reynolds? This is Roberta Heinz from apartment 4B. I'm doing my laundry in the basement right now, and **35 the washing machine doesn't seem to be working properly.** **36 I wanted to make sure building management was aware of the problem.**

M **36 Oh, thanks for letting me know.** I just had that machine installed, so I'm surprised that it's giving you trouble. What's the problem, exactly?

W Well, at the end of the wash cycle, the water doesn't drain out of the machine like it's supposed to. It's still completely full.

M OK—**37 I'll call an appliance repair service now and ask them to come take a look.**

여 안녕하세요, 레이놀즈 씨죠? 저는 아파트 4B에 사는 로버타 하인즈입니다. 지금 지하에서 세탁을 하고 있는데, 35세탁기가 제대로 작동을 하지 않는 것 같아요. 36건물 관리진이 이 문제에 대해 알고 계셨으면 했어요.

남 36오, 알려주셔서 감사해요. 그 기계를 설치한 지 얼마 안 됐는데 애를 먹인다니 놀랍네요. 정확히 뭐가 문제죠?

여 저기, 세탁 마지막 단계에서는 기계에서 물이 빠져야 되는데, 그러질 않네요. 아직도 물이 꽉 차 있어요.

남 알겠어요. 37제가 지금 전자 제품 수리 서비스 센터에 전화해서 와서 점검해달라고 요청할게요.

어휘 do the laundry 빨래하다 basement 지하 properly 제대로, 적절히 be aware of ~을 알다 install 설치하다 give A trouble A를 애먹이다 drain 물이 빠지다 be supposed to do ~하기로 되어 있다 appliance (가정용) 기기, 전자 제품 take a look 점검하다, 보다

35 여자는 어떤 문제로 전화를 하고 있는가?
(A) 파이프가 샌다.
(B) 문이 열리지 않는다.

(C) 세탁기가 제대로 작동하지 않고 있다.
(D) 난방기가 고장이다.

해설 세부 사항 – 문제점
여자가 첫 대사에서 세탁기가 제대로 작동하지 않는 것 같다(the washing machine doesn't seem to be working properly)고 했으므로 (C)가 정답이다.

어휘 leak 새다 function 기능하다, 작용하다

36 남자는 누구일 것 같은가?
(A) 배관공   (B) 안전 검사관
(C) 건물 관리자   (D) 부동산 중개인

해설 전체 내용 – 남자의 직업
여자가 건물 관리진에게 문제를 알리고 싶어 전화했다고 하자, 두 번째 대사에서 남자가 알려줘서 고맙다(thanks for letting me know)고 했으므로 남자는 건물 관리자임을 추론할 수 있다. 따라서 (C)가 정답이다.

37 남자는 무엇을 하겠다고 말하는가?
(A) 설명서를 참고한다.
(B) 수리 서비스 센터에 연락한다.
(C) 서류를 작성한다.
(D) 교체 부품을 찾는다.

해설 세부 사항 – 남자가 할 일
남자가 마지막 대사에서 전자 제품 수리 서비스 센터에 연락할 것(I'll call an appliance repair service now)이라고 했으므로 (B)가 정답이다.

어휘 consult 참고하다, 상담하다 replacement part 교체 부품

[38-40] 3인 대화 W-Br / M-Au / M-Cn

W All right, everyone. To end this meeting, **38 let's discuss the office picnic.** How's the planning going, Hector?

M1 We're all set for Riverside Park. **39 I've booked a picnic pavilion that's got a roof over ten picnic tables.**

W **39 Oh, I'm relieved you were able to get that one.** That'll be perfect, especially if it rains. And what else do we need?

M1 Well, I'll bring plates and cups, and **40 Lorenzo is making his famous pasta salad—right, Lorenzo?**

M2 **40 Yes,** but unfortunately I won't be able to attend. My son's got a soccer game. I'll still drop off the salad, though.

여 좋습니다, 여러분. 회의를 마무리하면서, 38직원 야유회 이야기를 해보죠. 행사 계획은 어떻게 되어 가고 있나요, 헥터 씨?

남1 리버사이드 공원으로 모든 준비가 끝났습니다. 39제가 10개의 피크닉 테이블 위에 지붕이 있는 대형 피크닉 천막을 예약해 두었어요.

여 ³⁹아, 그곳을 구하실 수 있었다니 다행이네요. 그곳이면 완벽할 거예요. 특히 비가 올 경우에요. 그리고 또 뭐가 필요하죠?
남1 저, 제가 접시와 컵을 가져가고, ⁴⁰로렌조 씨가 그의 유명한 파스타 샐러드를 만들 거예요, 그렇죠, 로렌조 씨?
남2 ⁴⁰네, 하지만 안타깝게도 저는 참석할 수 없을 것 같아요. 아들 축구 경기가 있어요. 그래도 샐러드는 가져다 드릴 거예요.

어휘 set 준비된, 예정된 pavilion 대형 천막 relieved 안심인, 다행인 unfortunately 안타깝게도 drop off (사물) 갖다 놓다, (사람) 내려 주다

38 어떤 종류의 행사가 계획되고 있는가?
(A) 생일 파티   (B) 회사 야유회
(C) 축구 경기   (D) 자선 모금 행사

해설 전체 내용 – 계획 중인 행사의 종류
여자가 첫 대사에서 직원 야유회 이야기를 해 보자(let's discuss the office picnic)고 제안한 뒤, 그 행사의 진행 계획에 대한 대화가 이어지고 있으므로 (B)가 정답이다.

어휘 charity 자선 (단체) fund-raiser 모금 행사, 기금 마련 행사

39 여자는 왜 안심이라고 말하는가?
(A) 일기 예보가 좋다.
(B) 출장 요리 업체가 이용 가능하다.
(C) 지붕으로 덮인 공간이 예약되었다.
(D) 제품 출시 행사가 성공적이었다.

해설 세부 사항 – 여자가 안심하는 이유
첫 번째 남자가 첫 대사에서 제가 10개의 피크닉 테이블 위에 지붕이 있는 대형 피크닉 천막을 예약해 두었다(I've booked a picnic pavilion that's got a roof over ten picnic tables)고 하자, 여자가 그곳을 구해서 안심이라고(Oh, I'm relieved you were able to get that one) 했으므로 (C)가 정답이다.

어휘 caterer 출장 요리 업체 covered 지붕으로 덮인 reserve 예약하다 launch 출시 (행사)

> **Paraphrasing** 대화의 booked a picnic pavilion that's got a roof → 정답의 A covered area was reserved

40 로렌조 씨는 무엇을 행사에 제공할 것인가?
(A) 정원용 가구   (B) 스포츠 장비
(C) 음료   (D) 음식

해설 세부 사항 – 로렌조 씨가 제공하는 것
첫 번째 남자가 두 번째 대사에서 로렌조 씨가 파스타 샐러드를 만들 것이라며 맞는지 확인하자(Lorenzo is making his famous pasta salad—right, Lorenzo?) 두 번째 남자가 그렇다(Yes)고 대답하고 있다. 따라서 로렌조 씨가 음식을 제공한다는 것을 알 수 있으므로 (D)가 정답이다.

어휘 contribute 제공하다, 기증하다

> **Paraphrasing** 대화의 pasta salad → 정답의 food

[41-43] M-Au / W-Br

M ⁴¹How are preparations going for the workshop on accounting spreadsheets, Maria? I assume a lot of employees will want to attend since the new software isn't very intuitive.
W ⁴¹There has been a lot of interest in the workshop. Now, I just need to find a place to hold it.
M ⁴²You can't use the meeting room downstairs? It'll hold twenty people.
W Thirty people plan to attend.
M Oh, I see. Well, you could always call the James Hotel—we hosted a training session there a couple of years ago.
W Good idea. ⁴³I'll set aside some time this afternoon to stop by the hotel and see what they have to offer.

남 ⁴¹회계 스프레드시트 워크숍 준비는 어떻게 되어 가나요, 마리아? 새 소프트웨어를 사용하기가 그리 쉽지 않아서 많은 직원들이 참여하고 싶어할 것 같은데요.
여 ⁴¹워크숍에 관심들이 많았어요. 이제 개최할 장소를 찾아야 합니다.
남 ⁴²아래층 회의실은 사용할 수 없나요? 20명을 수용할 수 있을 텐데요.
여 30명이 참석할 계획이에요.
남 아, 알겠어요. 제임스 호텔에 언제든 전화해도 돼요. 2년 전쯤 거기서 교육 강좌를 열었거든요.
여 좋은 생각입니다. ⁴³오늘 오후에 시간을 내서 호텔에 들러 거기서 무엇을 제공하는지 살펴볼게요.

어휘 preparation 준비 accounting 회계 assume 추정하다 intuitive 직관적인, 사용하기에 쉬운 hold 수용할 수 있다 host 개최하다 set aside 확보하다

41 화자들은 어떤 행사에 대해 이야기하는가?
(A) 기자회견   (B) 보건 박람회
(C) 기념 행사   (D) 워크숍

해설 전체 내용 – 화자들이 논의하는 행사
남자가 첫 번째 대사에서 회계 스프레드시트 워크숍(the workshop on accounting spreadsheets) 준비의 진행 상황에 대해 문의한 뒤, 이에 대해 여자가 워크숍에 관심들이 많았다(There has been a lot of interest in the workshop)며 워크숍과 관련된 대화를 이어가고 있으므로 (D)가 정답이다.

42 여자가 "30명이 참석할 계획이에요"라고 말할 때 무엇을 의미하는가?
(A) 케이터링 업체에 연락을 해야 한다.
(B) 참석자 명단을 업데이트해야 한다.
(C) 기간이 너무 짧다.
(D) 회의실 크기가 충분치 않다.

해설 **화자의 의도 파악**
남자가 두 번째 대사에서 아래층 회의실은 사용할 수 없는지(You can't use the meeting room downstairs?) 물으며 그 회의실이 20명을 수용할 수 있다(It'll hold twenty people)고 덧붙이자 여자가 인용문을 언급했다. 이는 수용 가능 인원보다 참석 인원이 많다는 것, 즉 공간이 충분하지 않다는 의미이므로 (D)가 정답이다.

43 여자는 오늘 오후에 무엇을 할 것이라고 말하는가?
(A) 호텔 방문 (B) 예산 검토
(C) 발표 준비 (D) 초대장 찾기

해설 **세부 사항 – 여자가 오후에 할 일**
여자가 마지막 대사에서 오늘 오후에 시간을 내서 호텔에 들러보겠다(I'll set aside some time this afternoon to stop by the hotel)고 했으므로 (A)가 정답이다.

> **Paraphrasing** 대화의 stop by → 정답의 Visit

[44-46] M-Cn / W-Am

M Myung-Hwa, you're in charge of putting together the architectural proposal **44 for our firm to renovate the Olivier Building**, right? How's that coming along?

W I'm nearly finished. I just need to calculate a time estimate for delivering the blueprint designs.

M **45 The scope of work will be similar to the Johnson project that we worked on last year. You could check how long it took to develop those blueprints** and use that as a reference point.

W **46 Kevin led that project, right? I'll give him a call** to see if he can send me the information.

남 명화 씨, 당신이 **44** 우리 회사가 올리비에 빌딩을 개조하기 위한 건축 제안서를 준비하는 일을 담당하고 계시죠, 그렇죠? 어떻게 되어 가고 있나요?

여 거의 끝나갑니다. 설계도면을 완성해서 보내는 데 얼마나 걸릴지만 계산하면 돼요.

남 **45** 작업 범위가 작년에 우리가 작업했던 존슨 프로젝트와 유사할 겁니다. 그 설계도들을 개발하는 데 얼마나 오래 걸렸는지 확인하고 그것을 기준으로 삼을 수 있을 거예요.

여 **46** 케빈 씨가 그 프로젝트를 진행하셨던 게 맞죠? 그분에게 전화해서 관련 정보를 보내 주실 수 있는지 확인해 볼게요.

어휘 in charge of ~을 책임지고 있는 put together ~을 준비하다, ~을 작성하다 architectural 건축(학)의 proposal 제안(서) renovate 개조하다, 보수하다 calculate 계산하다 estimate 추정(치), 견적(서) blueprint 설계도, 청사진 scope 범위, 규모 reference point 기준점 see if ~인지 확인하다

44 화자들은 어디에서 일할 것 같은가?
(A) 아파트 단지 (B) 소프트웨어 회사
(C) 건축 회사 (D) 인력 채용 대행사

해설 **전체 내용 – 화자들의 근무 장소**
남자가 첫 번째 대사에서 소속 회사에서 담당하고 있는 올리비에 빌딩을 개조하는(for our firm to renovate the Olivier Building) 일에 대해 언급했으므로 (C)가 정답이다.

45 남자는 무엇을 하라고 권하는가?
(A) 행사장 변경을 제안하기
(B) 이전 프로젝트 정보 이용하기
(C) 전문 사진가 고용하기
(D) 새 기계 구입하기

해설 **세부 사항 – 남자의 권유 사항**
남자가 두 번째 대사에서 일의 범위가 작년에 작업했던 존슨 프로젝트와 유사하다고 말하면서 그 설계도들을 개발하는 데 얼마나 오래 걸렸는지 확인할 것(The scope of work will be similar to the Johnson project that we worked on last year. You could check how long it took to develop those blueprints)을 권유했으므로 (B)가 정답이다.

어휘 propose 제안하다 venue 행사장, 개최 장소 hire 고용하다 machinery 기계(류)

> **Paraphrasing** 대화의 the Johnson project that we worked on last year / check how long it took to develop those blueprints → 정답의 Using information from an earlier project

46 여자는 다음에 무엇을 하겠는가?
(A) 동료 직원에게 연락하기
(B) 일정표 확인하기
(C) 점심 식사 시간 갖기
(D) 발표 연습하기

해설 **세부 사항 – 여자가 다음에 할 일**
여자가 두 번째 대사에서 케빈 씨가 그 프로젝트를 진행했던 게 맞는지 물으면서 그 사람에게 전화하겠다(Kevin led that project, right? I'll give him a call)고 했으므로 (A)가 정답이다.

어휘 practice 연습하다

> **Paraphrasing** 대화의 Kevin led that project / give him a call → 정답의 Contact her coworker

[47-49] W-Br / M-Au

W **47 I pulled the trays of pastries out of the oven for you. They're cooling.**

M Thanks for doing that.

W	Sure! By the way, this morning I checked our supplies and noticed that **47 we used more bread flour than usual this month**. What's going on?
M	Well, as you know, bread flour makes bread lighter and chewier. **48 To improve the recipe, I've adjusted it to use more bread flour.**
W	OK. I'll consider that when I order supplies.
M	And don't forget to stock up on ingredients for our holiday treats.
W	I appreciate the reminder! **49 I'll check last year's orders now to see what we used previously.**
여	47제가 대신 오븐에서 패스트리 쟁반들을 꺼냈어요. 식히는 중입니다.
남	그렇게 해 주셔서 감사해요.
여	별말씀을요! 그건 그렇고, 오늘 아침에 제가 우리 물품을 확인했는데, 47이번 달에 평소보다 제빵용 밀가루를 더 많이 사용했더라고요. 무슨 일이죠?
남	저, 아시다시피, 제빵용 밀가루는 빵을 더 가볍게, 그리고 더 쫄깃하게 만들어 줘요. 48조리법을 개선하기 위해, 제가 제빵용 밀가루를 더 많이 사용하도록 조정했어요.
여	알겠습니다. 제가 물품을 주문할 때 그 부분을 고려할게요.
남	그리고 우리 연말 특별 선물 제품에 필요한 재료를 비축해 놓는 것도 잊지 마세요.
여	알려줘서 고마워요! 49이전에는 어떤 재료들을 사용했는지 지금 작년 주문 내역을 확인해 볼게요.

어휘 tray 쟁반 notice 알게 되다, 알아차리다 flour 밀가루 chewy 쫄깃한, 쫀득한 adjust 조정하다, 조절하다 consider 고려하다 stock up on ~을 비축하다 ingredient (음식) 재료, 성분 treat 특별 선물, 특별 간식 reminder (메시지 등이) 상기시키는 것 previously 이전에, 과거에

47 대화는 어디에서 이루어지고 있는 것 같은가?
(A) 밀가루 가공 처리 공장   **(B) 제과점**
(C) 요리 학원   (D) 음식 축제

해설 전체 내용 – 대화 장소
여자가 첫 대사에서 오븐에서 패스트리 쟁반들을 꺼내 식히는 중(I pulled the trays of pastries out of the oven for you. They're cooling)이라고 한 뒤, 두 번째 대사에서 이번 달에 평소보다 제빵용 밀가루를 더 많이 사용했다(we used more bread flour than usual this month)고 말하는 것을 보아 화자들이 제과점 직원들임을 알 수 있으므로 (B)가 정답이다.

어휘 processing 가공 처리 plant 공장

48 조리법은 왜 변경되었는가?
(A) 더 나은 제품을 만들기 위해
(B) 고객 불만 사항을 처리하기 위해
(C) 생산비를 낮추기 위해
(D) 공급 부족 문제를 보완하기 위해

해설 세부 사항 – 조리법이 변경된 이유
남자가 두 번째 대사에서 조리법을 개선하기 위해 더 많은 제빵용 밀가루를 사용하도록 조정했다(To improve the recipe, I've adjusted it to use more bread flour)고 설명했다. 이는 더 나은 제품을 만들기 위한 조치에 해당하므로 (A)가 정답이다.

어휘 address (문제 등을) 처리하다, 다루다 complaint 불만 lower 낮추다, 내리다 compensate for ~을 보완하다, ~에 대해 보상하다 supply 공급 shortage 부족

> **Paraphrasing** 대화의 To improve the recipe → 정답의 To create a better product

49 여자는 다음에 무엇을 할 것인가?
(A) 신제품 시식하기   (B) 고객에게 연락하기
(C) 직원 파티 일정 잡기   **(D) 기록 살펴보기**

해설 세부 사항 – 여자가 다음에 할 일
여자가 마지막 대사에서 이전에는 어떤 재료들을 사용했는지 지금 작년 주문 내역을 확인해 보겠다(I'll check last year's orders now to see what we used previously)고 했으므로 (D)가 정답이다.

어휘 sample 시식하다 review 살펴보다, 검토하다

> **Paraphrasing** 대화의 check last year's orders → 정답의 Review some records

[50-52] M-Au / W-Am

M	Hey, Marta. Did you hear the news? **50 The mayor has appointed a new director of city transportation.**
W	That's good news. **51 I hope the new director will make getting some new train cars a priority.**
M	Yes! **51 We've had many customer complaints about our outdated equipment.**
W	Right. People have been unhappy about the old train cars.
M	Well, **52 the mayor is scheduled to hold a press conference this afternoon**. Maybe she'll share some information about plans to solve that problem.
남	있잖아요, 마타 씨. 소식 들으셨어요? 50시장님께서 신임 교통국장님을 선임하셨어요.
여	좋은 소식이네요. 51신임 국장님께서 새로운 열차 차량을 도입하는 일을 우선 순위로 삼아 주셨으면 좋겠어요.
남	네! 51낡은 장비 때문에 고객들의 불만이 많았잖아요.
여	맞아요. 사람들이 오래된 열차에 대해 불편을 호소해오고 있어요.
남	음, 52시장님께서 오늘 오후에 기자 회견을 열 예정이네요. 아마 그 문제를 해결할 계획들을 공유해 주실지도 모르겠네요.

94

어휘 mayor 시장 appoint 선임하다 transportation 교통(편) priority 우선 순위 outdated 낡은, 구식의 equipment 장비 be scheduled to do ~할 예정이다 press conference 기자 회견 share 공유하다 solve 해결하다

50 남자는 어떤 소식을 공유하는가?
(A) 철도 노선이 확대되었다.
(B) 일부 교육 일정이 확정되었다.
(C) 신임 국장이 선임되었다.
(D) 곧 보궐 선거가 개최될 것이다.

해설 세부 사항 - 남자가 공유하는 소식
남자가 첫 대사에서 시장이 신임 교통국장을 선임했다(The mayor has appointed a new director of city transportation)는 소식을 전하고 있으므로 (C)가 정답이다.

어휘 expand 확대하다, 확장하다 election 선거

51 화자들은 어떤 개선 사항을 볼 수 있기를 바라는가?
(A) 더 나은 장비   (B) 더 빠른 서비스
(C) 더 높은 연봉   (D) 더 긴 운영 시간

해설 세부 사항 - 화자들이 바라는 개선 사항
여자가 첫 대사에서 신임 국장이 새로운 열차 차량을 도입하는 것을 우선 순위로 삼기를 바란다(I hope the new director will make getting some new train cars a priority)고 했고, 뒤이어 남자도 낡은 장비 때문에 고객들의 불만이 많았다(We've had many customer complaints about our outdated equipment)고 했으므로 (A)가 정답이다.

어휘 operation 운영, 가동, 영업

52 무엇이 오늘 오후로 예정되어 있는가?
(A) 투자자 회의   (B) 시설 견학
(C) 기자 회견   (D) 구직 면접

해설 세부 사항 - 오늘 오후 예정되어 있는 것
남자가 마지막 대사에서 시장이 오늘 오후에 기자 회견을 열 예정(the mayor is scheduled to hold a press conference this afternoon)이라고 했으므로 (C)가 정답이다.

어휘 investor 투자자 facility 시설(물)

[53-55] 3인 대화 W-Br / M-Cn / M-Au

W OK, **53** the annual budget proposals have to be submitted this week. Is there anything special our sales team needs?

M1 Well, **54** since the company just gave our team permission to work from home twice each week, **53** I think we should consider getting everyone a tablet computer.

M2 **53** Good idea. Then we won't need to use our personal computers when we work at home. Are there enough funds available within the budget?

W I think so, but **55** we might have to do some research to find ones that are reasonably priced. I'll take a look this afternoon and make a list of tablets we can suggest to management.

여 자, **53** 연간 예산 제안서는 이번 주까지 제출해야 해요. 우리 영업팀에 특별히 필요한 것이 있나요?

남1 음, **54** 회사에서 우리 팀이 1주일에 두 번 재택 근무할 수 있도록 허가를 해 줘서, **53** 모두에게 태블릿 컴퓨터를 제공하는 걸 고려해 봐야 할 것 같아요.

남2 **53** 좋은 생각입니다. 그러면 집에서 일할 때는 개인 컴퓨터를 사용할 필요가 없겠군요. 예산 내에서 운용 가능한 자금이 충분히 있나요?

여 그런 것 같은데요. 하지만 **55** 가격이 적당한걸 찾으려면 조사를 좀 해야 할 겁니다. 오늘 오후에 한 번 보고 경영진에게 제안할 만한 태블릿의 목록을 작성할게요.

어휘 annual 연간의 budget 예산 permission 허가 work from home 재택 근무하다 fund 자금 reasonably priced 가격이 적정한 management 경영진, 임원진

53 화자들은 무엇에 관해 이야기하는가?
(A) 채용 결정   (B) 예산 요청
(C) 컴퓨터 소프트웨어 (D) 판매 전략

해설 전체 내용 - 대화의 주제
여자가 첫 대사에서 연간 예산 제안서는 이번 주까지 제출해야 한다(the annual budget proposals have to be submitted this week)며 영업팀에 특별히 필요한 것이 있는지 묻자, 첫 번째 남자가 모두에게 태블릿 컴퓨터를 제공하는 걸 고려해 봐야 한다(we should consider getting everyone a tablet computer)는 의견을 제안했다. 두 번째 남자 또한 좋은 생각(Good idea)이라고 동의하며 대화를 이어가고 있으므로 (B)가 정답이다.

어휘 decision 결정 tactic 전술, 전략

54 직원들은 연새 무엇을 하도록 허가 받았는가?
(A) 사무실 장식   (B) 회의 참석
(C) 재택 근무   (D) 평상복 착용

해설 세부 사항 - 직원들이 허가 받은 사항
첫 번째 남자가 첫 대사에서 회사에서 영업팀이 1주일에 두 번 재택 근무할 수 있도록 허가했다(the company just gave our team permission to work from home twice each week)고 했으므로 (C)가 정답이다.

55 여자는 오늘 오후에 무엇을 할 것인가?
(A) 조사하기   (B) 고객과 만나기
(C) 장비 수리하기   (D) 일정표 업데이트하기

해설 세부 사항 - 여자가 오후에 할 일
여자가 마지막 대사에서 가격이 적당한 태블릿 컴퓨터를 찾으려면 조사를 좀 해야 할 것(we might have to do some research to find ones that are reasonably priced)이라고 한 뒤, 오늘 오후에 한 번 보겠다(I'll take a look this afternoon)고 했으므로 (A)가 정답이다.

어휘 conduct 실시하다   repair 수리하다

[56-58] W-Am / M-Au

W Hello, my name is Rachel Grant. I'm an administrative assistant in the research department. **56 I was hoping someone from Human Resources could answer a question for me about employee benefits.**

M Of course. I'll be happy to help you if I can, Rachel. **57 Why don't you give me your employee ID number,** so I can pull up your file?

W Sure, it's 904376. My question is about the school tuition reimbursement. I heard that our company will pay for full-time employees to attend university classes.

M Yes, it is company policy to pay for university classes for employees. **58 The first thing you'll need to do is talk to your manager and get her approval for the courses you intend to take.**

여 안녕하세요, 저는 레이첼 그랜트입니다. 연구부서의 행정 보조 직원이에요. **56 인사부서의 누군가가 직원 복리후생에 대한 질문에 답변해 주셨으면 하고요.**

남 네, 제가 도움이 되면 좋겠네요, 레이첼. **57 직원 번호를 알려주시면 어떨까요?** 그러면 파일을 찾을 수 있을 텐데요.

여 네, 904376입니다. 제 질문은 학교 수업료 환급에 관한 거예요. 우리 회사에서 풀타임 직원에게 대학 강좌 수업료를 내 준다고 들었거든요.

남 네, 직원의 대학 강좌 비용을 지급하는 것이 회사 정책이에요. **58 가장 먼저 관리자에게 이야기해서 들으려는 강좌에 대해 승인을 받으셔야 해요.**

어휘 administrative assistant 행정 보조 직원   human resources 인사부   employee benefits 직원 복리후생   tuition 수업료   reimbursement 상환   full-time employee 풀타임 직원   policy 정책   approval 승인

56 여자는 왜 전화하고 있는가?
(A) 연구 프로젝트에 대해 논의하려고
(B) 제품 주문에 관해 문의하려고
(C) 직원 복리후생에 대해 물어보려고
(D) 회의 시간을 확정하려고

해설 전체 내용 – 여자가 전화한 이유
여자가 첫 대사에서 인사부서의 누군가가 직원 복리후생에 대한 질문에 답변해 주기를 바란다(I was hoping someone from Human Resources could answer a question for me about employee benefits)고 했으므로, 직원 복리후생에 대해 문의하기 위해 전화했음을 알 수 있다. 따라서 (C)가 정답이다.

어휘 inquire 묻다, 알아보다   confirm 확정하다

57 남자는 어떤 정보를 요청하는가?
(A) 식별 번호   (B) 이메일 주소
(C) 사무실 위치   (D) 전화번호

해설 세부 사항 – 남자가 요청한 정보
남자가 첫 대사에서 여자에게 직원 번호를 알려줄 것(Why don't you give me your employee ID number)을 요청했으므로 (A)가 정답이다.

어휘 identification 신원 확인, 신분 증명

> Paraphrasing 대화의 your employee ID number → 정답의 An identification number

58 남자는 여자에게 무엇이 필요하다고 말하는가?
(A) 관리자 승인   (B) 고급 컴퓨터 능력
(C) 서명한 지원서   (D) 업데이트된 안건

해설 세부 사항 – 여자에게 필요한 것
남자가 마지막 대사에서 가장 먼저 관리자에게 이야기해서 들으려는 강좌에 대해 승인을 받아야 한다(The first thing you'll need to do is talk to your manager and get her approval for the courses you intend to take)고 했으므로 (A)가 정답이다.

어휘 advanced 고급의, 상급의   application form 지원서

[59-61] M-Cn / W-Br

M Amina, **59 I'm training the new sales representatives tomorrow.** It's my first time doing this, and **60 I'd like your input on the materials I'll be using.** Are you busy right now?

W Oh, the project I'm working on isn't due until next week. Have a seat. Did you bring the handout with the sales strategies?

M I've got it right here with me. I like the general outline, but **61 the list of steps for getting to know customers seems too long—I'd recommend shortening it.** What do you think?

남 아미나 씨, **59 제가 내일 신입 영업사원들을 교육해요.** 제가 처음 하는 거라서, **60 사용할 자료와 관련해서 의견을 듣고 싶어요.** 지금 바쁘신가요?

여 아, 제가 작업 중인 프로젝트 기한은 다음 주나 되어야 해요. 앉으세요. 영업 전략이 포함된 유인물을 가져오셨나요?

남 바로 여기 챙겨 왔습니다. 전반적인 개요는 마음에 드는데, **61 고객을 파악하는 단계에 대한 목록이 너무 긴 것 같아서, 그걸 줄이는 게 좋을 것 같아요.** 어떻게 생각하세요?

어휘 representative 직원, 대표자   input 의견 (제공)   not A until B B나 되어야 A하다   due ~가 기한인   handout 유인물   strategy 전략   outline 개요   shorten 줄이다

59 남자는 내일 무엇을 할 것인가?
(A) 교육 실시하기 (B) 예산 최종 확정하기
(C) 고객과 만나기 (D) 보고서 제출하기

해설 **세부 사항 - 남자가 내일 할 일**
남자가 첫 대사에서 내일 신입 영업사원들을 교육한다(I'm training the new sales representatives tomorrow)고 했으므로 (A)가 정답이다.

어휘 finalize 최종 확정하다

Paraphrasing 대화의 training the new sales representatives → 정답의 Conduct a training

60 여자는 왜 "제가 작업 중인 프로젝트 기한은 다음 주나 되어야 해요"라고 말하는가?
(A) 시간이 있음을 나타내려고
(B) 실수를 바로잡아주려고
(C) 제안을 거절하려고
(D) 새로운 마감 기한을 제안하려고

해설 **화자의 의도 파악**
남자가 첫 대사에서 여자의 의견을 원한다는 말과 함께 지금 시간이 있는지(I'd like your input on the materials I'll be using. Are you busy right now?) 묻자 여자가 인용문을 언급했으므로 당장은 바쁘지 않아서 남자와 이야기할 시간이 있다는 뜻으로 한 말임을 알 수 있다. 따라서 (A)가 정답이다.

어휘 indicate 나타내다, 가리키다 availability 이용 가능성, 시간 여유 correct 바로잡다, 정정하다 decline 거절하다

61 남자는 무엇을 변경할 것을 제안하는가?
(A) 도표의 크기 (B) 로고의 위치
(C) 목록의 길이 (D) 일부 정보의 순서

해설 **세부 사항 - 남자가 변경하도록 제안하는 것**
남자가 마지막 대사에서 고객들을 파악하는 단계에 대한 목록이 너무 긴 것 같아서 그걸 줄이는 것을 제안하고 싶다(the list of steps for getting to know customers seems too long—I'd recommend shortening it)고 했으므로 (C)가 정답이다.

어휘 suggest -ing ~하기를 제안하다 diagram 도표

Paraphrasing 대화의 recommend shortening → 질문의 suggest changing
대화의 the list / too long → 정답의 The length of a list

[62-64] 대화 + 재생 목록 W-Br/M-Cn

W I love ⁶²/⁶³**the new yoga mats you bought for the studio,** Ahmed. I can't believe they're made of 100 percent recycled materials.

M Me too! And they're very high quality. I'm excited to use them in ⁶²**today's fitness class.**

W ⁶³**Do you need help setting them up?**

M No, I can do it myself. But can you finish preparing the playlist? It's called Evening Playlist, and it's on my phone.

W OK, I found it. Do you want to add some songs?

M No, just change the order. ⁶⁴**If you move the second song to the end, I think we'll be set for tonight's session.**

여 ⁶²/⁶³당신이 스튜디오를 위해 구입한 새 요가 매트들이 너무 마음에 들어요, 아흐메드 씨. 100퍼센트 재활용 소재로 만들어졌다는 게 믿기지 않네요.

남 저도요! 그리고 품질도 아주 좋아요. ⁶²오늘 있을 피트니스 수업 중에 사용할 거라 기대돼요.

여 ⁶³설치하는 데 도움이 필요하신가요?

남 아니요, 제가 혼자 할 수 있어요. 대신 재생 목록을 준비하는 것을 마무리해 주시겠어요? 제목이 '저녁 재생 목록'이고, 제 휴대폰에 있어요.

여 네, 찾았어요. 노래를 좀 추가하고 싶으세요?

남 아니에요, 순서만 변경해 주세요. ⁶⁴두 번째 곡을 마지막으로 옮기면, 오늘 밤 수업 준비는 끝날 것 같아요.

어휘 be made of ~로 만들어지다 recycled 재활용된 set A up A를 설치하다 session (특정 활동을 하는) 시간

62 화자들은 어디에 있는 것 같은가?
(A) 커피숍 (B) 극장
(C) 피트니스 센터 (D) 전자제품 매장

해설 **전체 내용 - 대화 장소**
여자가 첫 대사에서 언급하는 요가 매트(the new yoga mats you bought for the studio) 및 남자가 첫 대사에서 말하는 피트니스 강좌(today's fitness class)를 통해 화자들이 피트니스 센터에 있다는 것을 알 수 있으므로 (C)가 정답이다.

63 여자는 남자에게 무엇을 돕겠다고 제안하는가?
(A) 물품 재활용하기
(B) 장비 설치하기
(C) 안내 표지 게시하기
(D) 바닥을 빗자루로 쓸기

해설 **세부 사항 - 여자가 도우려는 일**
여자가 새 요가 매트(the new yoga mats)와 관련해 두 번째 대사에서 남자에게 설치하는 데 도움이 필요한지(Do you need help setting them up?) 묻고 있으므로 (B)가 정답이다.

어휘 post 게시하다   sweep 빗자루로 쓸다

> **Paraphrasing** 대화의 new yoga mats / setting them up
> → 정답의 Setting up some equipment

64 시각 정보에 따르면, 어느 곡이 재생 목록의 마지막으로 옮겨져야 하는가?
(A) "롱 오션"   (B) "낫 인 플럭스"
(C) "오팔 필드"   (D) "팬시 하트"

해설 세부 사항 – 시각 정보 연계

남자가 마지막 대사에서 두 번째 곡을 마지막으로 옮겨 달라(If you move the second song to the end, I think we'll be set for tonight's session)고 요청하고 있고, 재생 목록을 보면 2번 노래의 제목은 "Long Ocean"이므로 (A)가 정답이다.

[65-67] 대화 + 지도 M-Cn/W-Am

M Hi, I'd like to buy a ticket for the seven o'clock showing of the nature documentary. **65 Do you offer a student discount?**

W Yes, we do—if you have your student ID, you're eligible for a ten percent discount.

M Great. Here it is.

W Thank you. That'll be twelve dollars. Also, we're running a special at our snack counter today. **66 You'll get a free beverage with the purchase of any food item.**

M That sounds good, **66 but I actually just had dinner, so I'll head directly to the theater.**

W OK. Here's your ticket— **67 the movie is showing in the theater closest to the snack counter.**

남 안녕하세요. 7시에 상영하는 자연 다큐멘터리 영화표를 사려고 합니다. 65학생은 할인되나요?

여 네, 됩니다. 학생증을 지참하시면 10% 할인을 받으실 수 있습니다.

남 잘됐네요. 여기 있습니다.

여 감사합니다. 12달러입니다. 또한, 오늘 스낵 코너에서는 특별 서비스를 제공하고 있습니다. 66어떤 것이든 먹거리를 구매하시면 음료가 무료로 제공됩니다.

남 그렇군요. 66그런데 사실 저는 방금 저녁 식사를 하고 왔습니다. 그래서 상영관으로 바로 가려고요.

여 알겠습니다. 여기 표 있습니다. 67영화는 스낵 코너에서 가장 가까운 상영관에서 상영됩니다.

어휘 eligible ~의 자격이 있는   beverage 음료   directly 바로

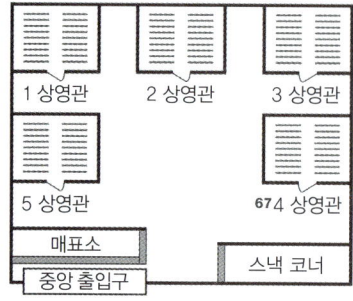

65 남자는 여자에게 무엇에 대해 묻는가?
(A) 무료 주차   (B) 좌석 선택권
(C) 학생 할인   (D) 결제 방법

해설 세부 사항 – 남자의 문의 사항

남자가 첫 대사에서 학생 할인(student discount)을 제공하는지 문의했으므로 (C)가 정답이다.

66 남자는 왜 제안을 거절하는가?
(A) 그는 극장에 거의 가지 않는다.
(B) 그는 친구를 만난다.
(C) 그는 온라인으로 표를 구매한다.
(D) 그는 방금 식사를 했다.

해설 세부 사항 – 남자가 거절한 이유

여자가 두 번째 대사에서 먹거리를 구매하면 음료가 무료로 제공된다(You'll get a free beverage with the purchase of any food item)고 했는데, 남자가 방금 저녁 식사를 하고 와서(but I actually just had dinner) 상영관으로 바로 가겠다(I'll head directly to the theater)고 했으므로 (D)가 정답이다.

> **Paraphrasing** 대화의 had dinner → 정답의 ate a meal

67 시각 정보에 따르면, 남자는 다음에 어디로 갈 것인가?
(A) 1 상영관   (B) 2 상영관
(C) 3 상영관   (D) 4 상영관

해설 세부 사항 – 시각 정보 연계

여자가 마지막 대사에서 남자에게 티켓을 건네며 영화가 스낵 코너에서 가장 가까운 상영관에서 상영된다(the movie is showing in the theater closest to the snack counter)고 했다. 지도를 보면 스낵 코너에서 가장 가까운 상영관은 4 상영관이므로 (D)가 정답이다.

[68-70] 대화 + 도표 W-Br/M-Au

W Fabrice, **68 I've found some excellent venues with enough space to hold our national marketing conference.** Here's a table with the top picks. I've marked the ones that have a fitness center and a complimentary breakfast. I've also noted the ones that are near the train station.

M Well, **⁶⁹the two most important things are that it's located by the train station and that it offers a free breakfast.**

W So, that leaves only one option. I'll reach out to that hotel about our prospective dates.

M Excellent. **⁷⁰I'm working on the conference Web site with information about speaker proposals and registration.** As soon as the venue's confirmed, I'll post the update.

여 파브리스 씨, **⁶⁸**제가 전국 마케팅 콘퍼런스를 열기에 충분한 공간을 갖춘 훌륭한 장소를 몇 군데 찾았어요. 여기 최우선 후보들을 정리한 표입니다. 피트니스 센터와 무료 아침 식사가 있는 곳들은 표시해 두었고요. 기차역 근처에 있는 곳들도 특별히 언급해 두었습니다.

남 음, **⁶⁹**가장 중요한 두 가지는 기차역 근처에 있고 무료 아침 식사를 제공해야 한다는 거예요.

여 그럼, 선택지가 한 곳만 남네요. 제가 예정 날짜에 대해 그 호텔에 연락해 보겠습니다.

남 아주 좋아요. **⁷⁰**저는 연사 제안서 및 등록과 관련된 정보가 포함된 콘퍼런스 웹사이트 작업을 하고 있어요. 장소가 확정되는 대로, 그 소식을 게시할게요.

어휘 table 표 top pick 최우선 후보, 1순위 mark 표기하다 complimentary 무료의 note 특별히 언급하다 be located by ~ 옆에 위치해 있다 reach out to ~에게 연락하다 prospective 잠재적인, 유망한 registration 등록

호텔	위치	피트니스 센터	아침 식사
⁶⁹더 파크뷰	✓		✓
더 리지모어	✓	✓	
더 그랜빌		✓	✓
더 말링턴			✓

68 화자들은 무엇을 준비하고 있는가?
(A) 채용 행사 (B) 가족 모임
(C) 마케팅 콘퍼런스 (D) 직원 야유회

해설 전체 내용 – 화자들이 준비하는 행사
여자가 첫 대사에서 전국 마케팅 콘퍼런스를 개최할 정도로 충분한 공간이 있는 몇몇 훌륭한 행사장을 찾았다(I've found some excellent venues with enough space to hold our national marketing conference)고 했으므로 (C)가 정답이다.

어휘 organize 준비하다, 조직하다 reunion 모임, 친목회, 동창회 retreat 야유회, 짧은 여행

69 시각 정보에 의하면, 화자들은 어느 호텔을 선호하는가?
(A) 더 파크뷰 (B) 더 리지모어
(C) 더 그랜빌 (D) 더 말링턴

해설 세부 사항 – 시각 정보 연계
남자가 첫 대사에서 행사장과 관련해 가장 중요한 두 가지는 기차역 근처에 있고 무료 아침 식사를 제공해야 한다는 것(the two most important things are that it's located by the train station and that it offers a free breakfast)이라고 언급했다. 표를 보면 위치와 아침 식사에 모두 표시되어 있는 곳은 The Parkview이므로 (A)가 정답이다.

70 남자는 어떤 작업을 하고 있다고 말하는가?
(A) 장비 대여하기
(B) 정식 허가증 받기
(C) 웹사이트 업데이트하기
(D) 메뉴 최종 확정하기

해설 세부 사항 – 남자가 작업 중인 것
남자가 마지막 대사에서 연사 제안서 및 등록과 관련된 정보가 포함된 콘퍼런스 웹사이트 작업을 하고 있다(I'm working on the conference Web site with information about speaker proposals and registration)고 했으므로 (C)가 정답이다.

어휘 rent 대여하다 official 정식의, 공식적인 permit 허가증

> **Paraphrasing** 대화의 working on the conference Web site with information about speaker proposals and registration → 정답의 Updating a Web site

PART 4
LISTENING COMPREHENSION

UNIT 11 전화 메세지

담화 구성과 단서 파악 ········· 본책 p.106

안녕하세요, 로즈. 제니퍼예요. 제가 정보통신 기술 취업박람회에 참석할 수 없다는 걸 방금 알게 됐어요. 그래서 월요일 아침에 차로 데려다 주지 못할 거예요. 하지만 호세 모랄레스가 갈 계획인 것 같아요. 그에게 전화해 차에 태워줄 자리가 있는지 확인해 보는 게 어때요? 그리고 제가 가지 않으니, 취업박람회에서 나눠주려고 했던 회사 안내책자를 갖다 줄게요. 그것들을 주러 내일 당신 사무실에 가도 될까요?

어휘 attend 참석하다 job fair 취업박람회 drop off 갖다 놓다, 내려주다 hand out 나눠주다, 배포하다

1 화자는 왜 전화를 걸고 있는가?
(A) 사무 절차를 설명하려고 **(B) 출장 계획을 취소하려고**

2 화자는 무엇을 제안하는가?
(A) 동료에게 전화하기 (B) 더 일찍 출발하기

3 화자는 내일 무엇을 할 계획인가?
(A) 행사에 등록하기 **(B) 안내 책자 가져다 주기**

ETS 유형연습 ········· 본책 p.107

1 (A) **2** (B) **3** (A) **4** (B) **5** (B) **6** (B)

[1-2] 녹음 메시지 W-Br

Hello, this message is for Robert Costa in the radiology department. This is Dr. Mina Wilson from the Rosemont Medical Group. **1/2 My patient, Sara Santos, had some x-rays taken** of her foot at your office last week. It's been six days, and **2 I'm still waiting for the films to be delivered to me. 1 Could you please give me a call to let me know whether they've been sent?** My direct number is 555-3156. Thank you.

안녕하세요, 이것은 방사선과 로버트 코스타 씨께 전하는 메시지입니다. 저는 로즈몬트 메디컬 그룹의 의사 미나 윌슨입니다. 1/2 제 환자 사라 산토스 씨가 지난주 귀하의 진료실에서 발 엑스레이를 몇 장 찍었습니다. 6일이 지났는데, 2 저는 아직도 그 엑스레이 필름이 배달되기를 기다리고 있습니다. 1 필름이 발송되었는지 전화로 제게 알려주시겠습니까? 제 직통 번호는 555-3156입니다. 감사합니다.

어휘 radiology 방사선학 take an X-ray of ~의 엑스레이 촬영을 하다 deliver 배달하다 direct number 직통 번호

1 음성 메시지의 목적은 무엇인가?
(A) 정보를 요청하려고
(B) 사고를 보고하려고

해설 전체 내용 – 전화의 목적
초반부에서 자신의 환자가 상대방(청자)의 방사선과에서 엑스레이를 찍었고 그 엑스레이 필름을 기다리는 중이라고 한 뒤, 후반부에서 필름 발송 여부를 알려달라(Could you please give me a call to let me know whether they've been sent?)고 했으므로 (A)가 정답이다.

2 발신자는 무엇을 기다리고 있는가?
(A) 보험 서류 **(B) 엑스레이 필름**

해설 세부 사항 – 화자가 기다리는 물건
중반부에서 아직도 환자의 엑스레이 필름이 배달되기를 기다리고 있다(I'm still waiting for the films to be delivered to me)고 했으므로 (B)가 정답이다.

[3-4] 전화 메시지 M-Cn

Hello, Mr. Gupta. **3 I'm responding to your message about the flower arrangements for your company's event in April.** I suggest we meet at the venue so I can see the size of the room and discuss your possible flower choices. **4 Please let me know when you can meet.** April is a very busy month for us. In the meantime, make sure to visit our Web site to look at our photo gallery for ideas and prices.

안녕하세요, 굽타 씨. 3 4월에 있을 귀사의 행사용 꽃 장식물에 관한 귀하의 메시지에 답변 드립니다. 제가 해당 공간의 규모를 확인하고 선택하실 가능성이 있는 꽃을 논의할 수 있도록 행사장에서 만나 뵙기를 권해 드려요. 4 언제 만나실 수 있는지 알려 주시기 바랍니다. 4월은 저희에게 아주 바쁜 달입니다. 그 사이에, 반드시 저희 웹사이트를 방문하셔서 아이디어 및 가격에 대해 저희 사진 갤러리를 확인해 보시기 바랍니다.

어휘 flower arrangement 꽃 장식물, 꽃꽂이 venue 행사장, 개최 장소 in the meantime 그 사이에, 그러는 동안 make sure to do 반드시 ~하도록 하다

3 화자는 어디에서 일하는 것 같은가?
(A) 꽃집 (B) 제과점

해설 세부 내용 – 화자의 근무 장소
초반부에서 4월에 있을 행사에 필요한 꽃 장식물과 관련된 상대방의 메시지에 답변한다(I'm responding to your message about the flower arrangements for your company's event in April)고 했으므로 (A)가 정답이다.

4 화자는 왜 "4월은 저희에게 아주 바쁜 달입니다"라고 말하는가?
(A) 오해에 대해 사과하기 위해
(B) 청자에게 신속히 조치하도록 권하기 위해

해설 화자의 의도 파악

중반부에서 언제 만날 수 있는지 알려 달라(Please let me know when you can meet)고 요청하면서 인용문을 언급했으므로 다른 일정이 잡히기 전에 약속을 잡을 수 있도록 빨리 조치하라는 의미이다. 따라서 (B)가 정답이다.

어휘 misunderstanding 오해 encourage A to do A에게 ~하도록 권하다

[5-6] 녹음 메시지 W-Br

You've reached SunMerc Incorporated, **⁵the region's leading supplier and installer of solar panels and batteries**. We apologize for this inconvenience. But **⁶because of current weather conditions, we're canceling all service appointments for today**. We are in the process of rescheduling all of today's appointments to another date. If you are a customer with work that needs to be rescheduled, please press 1 to speak with a representative.

⁵지역에서 손꼽히는 태양열 전지판과 배터리 공급업체이자 설치업체인 선머크 주식회사에 전화 주셨습니다. 불편을 드려 죄송합니다. 하지만 ⁶현재의 날씨 상태로 인해, 오늘로 예정된 모든 서비스 예약을 취소하고 있습니다. 오늘로 예약된 모든 일정을 다른 날짜로 재조정하고 있는 중입니다. 일정을 다시 잡아야 하는 고객이신 경우, 1번을 눌러 담당자와 통화해주시기 바랍니다.

어휘 reach 연락하다 leading 손꼽히는, 선도적인 solar panels 태양열 전지판 inconvenience 불편함 appointment 예약, 약속 reschedule 일정을 재조정하다 representative 직원, 대표자

5 화자는 어떤 종류의 업체에서 일하는가?
(A) 조경 서비스 회사
(B) 태양열 에너지 회사

해설 전체 내용 - 화자의 근무 업체

초반부에서 소속 회사를 지역에서 손꼽히는 태양열 전지판과 배터리 공급업체이자 설치업체(the region's leading supplier and installer of solar panels and batteries)라고 했으므로 (B)가 정답이다.

Paraphrasing 담화의 supplier and installer of solar panels and batteries → 정답의 A solar energy company

6 왜 오늘 일부 서비스가 취소되고 있는가?
(A) 일부 작업자들이 아파서 결근했다.
(B) 날씨가 좋지 못하다.

해설 세부 사항 - 일부 서비스가 오늘 취소되는 이유

중반부에서 현재의 날씨 상태로 인해 오늘로 예정된 모든 서비스 예약을 취소하고 있다(because of current weather conditions, we're canceling all service appointments for today)고 했으므로 (B)가 정답이다.

어휘 be out sick 아파서 결근하다

ETS 실전문제
본책 p.108

1 (C)	2 (A)	3 (D)	4 (A)	5 (B)	6 (D)
7 (D)	8 (C)	9 (A)	10 (B)	11 (B)	12 (C)
13 (D)	14 (A)	15 (D)	16 (B)	17 (B)	18 (A)
19 (D)	20 (C)	21 (D)			

[1-3] 녹음 메시지 M-Cn

Hello, **¹thank you for calling Fellspoint Electronics, the store for all your electronic needs**! The store is now closed. And remember—**²we will be closed this weekend**, October twenty-fifth and twenty-sixth, due to the national holiday. The store will reopen for business on October twenty-seventh. If you're calling about your recent purchase of a Nightingale television set, we are aware that these may be defective. Because of this, the store is offering a five-year warranty on these televisions. **³Just bring in your receipt to register for the extended warranty.**

안녕하세요. ¹전자 제품에 대한 여러분의 모든 필요를 충족시켜 드리는 펠스포인트 전자에 전화해 주셔서 감사합니다. 매장은 현재 문을 닫았습니다. 그리고 기억해 주세요. ²이번 주말인 10월 25일과 26일은 국가 공휴일로 휴무입니다. 매장은 10월 27일에 다시 문을 열 것입니다. 고객님께서 최근에 구입하신 나이팅게일 텔레비전 세트 때문에 전화를 주신 것이라면, 제품의 결함 가능성에 대해 저희도 인지하고 있습니다. 이러한 이유로, 저희 매장에서는 이 텔레비전에 대해 5년 동안의 품질 보증을 제공합니다. ³품질 보증 기간 연장을 신청하시려면 영수증을 지참하여 매장에 방문해 주십시오.

어휘 national holiday 국경일 purchase 구매(품) aware 인지하고 있는 defective 결함이 있는 warranty 품질 보증(서) extended 연장된

1 화자는 어디에서 일할 것 같은가?
(A) 변호사 사무실   (B) 철물점
(C) 전자 제품 매장   (D) 배송 회사

해설 전체 내용 - 화자의 근무 장소

초반부에서 펠스포인트 전자에 전화해 주어 고맙다(thank you for calling Fellspoint Electronics)고 한 뒤, 매장 관련 안내를 이어 가고 있는 것으로 보아 화자는 전자 제품 매장에서 일한다는 것을 알 수 있다. 따라서 (C)가 정답이다.

2 화자는 이번 주말에 대해 무엇이라고 말하는가?
(A) 매장이 문을 닫을 것이다.
(B) 예약이 필요할 것이다.
(C) 할인 판매가 시작될 것이다.
(D) 주문 제품이 도착할 것이다.

해설 세부 사항 - 화자가 주말에 대해 말한 것

초반부에서 매장이 주말에 문을 닫을 것(we will be closed this weekend)이라고 했으므로 (A)가 정답이다.

어휘 require 요구하다, 필요로 하다

3 화자에 따르면, 매장에서는 무엇을 제공하는가?
(A) 전화 상담   (B) 개인 맞춤 선물
(C) 할인 쿠폰   **(D) 품질 보증 기간 연장**

해설 세부 사항 – 매장에서 제공하는 것
후반부에서 품질 보증 기간 연장을 신청하려면 영수증을 지참하여 매장을 방문할 것(Just bring in your receipt to register for the extended warranty)을 권유했으므로 (D)가 정답이다.

[4-6] 전화 메시지 W-Br

Hello, this message is for Lisa Cheng. Ms. Cheng, I'm calling on behalf of the Canadian Association of Nurses. **4/5 We're having our annual conference on November fifteenth in Calgary, and I'd like to invite you to give a lecture about your research on proper nutrition for hospital patients.** I know **5 you've written a book about healthy eating habits,** and I think our audience would benefit a lot from your expertise. **6 We would, of course, be happy to pay for all your transportation expenses for getting to and from the conference.** Please give me a call to discuss the details. Thanks Ms. Cheng, and have a nice day.

안녕하세요. 리사 청 씨께 메시지 남깁니다. 청 씨, 저는 캐나다 간호사협회를 대표해 전화 드립니다. 4/5 11월 15일에 캘거리에서 연례 회의가 열리는데요. 병원 환자에게 적절한 영양에 관해 연구하신 바를 강의해 주셨으면 합니다. 5 건강한 식습관에 대해 책을 쓰신 것도 알고 있으며, 청중들이 당신의 전문 지식에서 많은 것을 얻을 수 있을 거라 생각합니다. 6 물론 회의 장소를 오가는 데 발생하는 여비는 전액 지급해 드릴 것입니다. 전화 주셔서 세부 사항을 논의하시죠. 청 씨, 감사합니다. 좋은 하루 되세요.

어휘 on behalf of ~를 대표하여 association 협회 annual 매년의, 연례의 conference 회의 lecture 강의 research 연구 proper 적절한 nutrition 영양 expertise 전문 지식 transportation expenses 교통비

4 메시지의 목적은 무엇인가?
(A) 청자를 행사에 초청하려고
(B) 입사 지원서에 대한 후속 조치를 취하려고
(C) 곧 있을 출판에 대해 논의하려고
(D) 전문 기관을 광고하려고

해설 전체 내용 – 메시지의 목적
초반부에서 11월 15일에 캘거리에서 연례 회의가 열린다(We're having our annual conference on November fifteenth in Calgary)며 청 씨가 연구한 바에 대해 강의해 줄 것(I'd like to invite you to give a lecture about your research)을 요청했으므로 (A)가 정답이다.

어휘 follow up on ~를 끝맺다, 후속 조치를 하다 upcoming 다가오는 publication 출판

Paraphrasing 담화의 annual conference → 정답의 event

5 리사 청의 전문 영역은 무엇인가?
(A) 소셜 미디어 마케팅   **(B) 식이와 영양**
(C) 병원 관리   (D) 도시 계획

해설 세부 사항 – 리사 청의 전문 영역
중반부에서 병원 환자에게 적절한 영양에 관한 청 씨의 연구에 대해 강의(a lecture about your research on proper nutrition for hospital patients)해줄 것을 부탁한 뒤, 청 씨가 건강한 식습관에 대해 책을 썼다(you've written a book about healthy eating habits)는 사실을 언급했으므로 (B)가 정답이다.

어휘 management 경영, 관리 urban 도시의

6 화자는 무엇을 하겠다고 제안하는가?
(A) 연구 자료 공유   (B) 광고 제작
(C) 동료에게 연락   **(D) 출장비 지급**

해설 세부 사항 – 화자의 제안 사항
후반부에서 회의 장소를 오가는 데 발생하는 여비는 전액 지급할 것(We would ~ pay for all your transportation expenses for getting to and from the conference)이라고 했으므로 (D)가 정답이다.

어휘 travel costs 출장비

Paraphrasing 담화의 transportation expenses → 정답의 travel costs

[7-9] 녹음 메시지 M-Au

Thanks for calling **7 Starry Ways, offering round-trip flights to over 150 destinations worldwide**. Please hold and one of our reservation agents will be with you shortly. And if you haven't already, be sure to download the Starry Ways app to your smartphone. Did you know that Starry Ways has just added a new benefit? **8 The app now lets you access the Starry Ways passenger lounge, for complimentary snacks before your flight.** Thank you for continuing to hold. **9 Make sure to have your confirmation number ready to give to the agent.**

7 전 세계 150곳 이상의 목적지로 향하는 왕복 항공편을 제공하는 스타리 웨이즈에 전화 주셔서 감사합니다. 잠시만 기다려 주시면 곧 예약 담당 직원이 연결됩니다. 아직 하지 않으셨다면, 스마트폰에 스타리 웨이즈 앱을 다운로드하세요. 저희 스타리 웨이즈가 막 새로운 혜택을 추가했다는 사실을 알고 계셨나요? 8 이제 이 앱을 통해 스타리 웨이즈 승객 라운지를 이용하실 수 있으며, 비행 전 무료 간식을 즐기실 수 있습니다. 계속 기다려 주셔서 감사합니다. 9 직원에게 알려주실 예약 확인 번호를 준비해주십시오.

어휘 round-trip 왕복 여행의   destination 목적지, 도착지   hold (전화를 끊지 않고) 대기하다   agent 직원, 대리인   shortly 곧   complimentary 무료의   confirmation number 예약 (확인) 번호

7 스타리 웨이즈는 어떤 종류의 업체인가?
(A) 여행사   (B) 자동차 서비스 회사
(C) 버스 운행 회사   **(D) 항공사**

해설 전체 내용 – 업체의 종류
초반부에서 스타리 웨이즈가 전 세계 150곳 이상의 목적지로 향하는 왕복 항공편을 제공한다(~ Starry Ways, offering round-trip flights to over 150 destinations worldwide)고 했으므로 (D)가 정답이다.

8 화자에 따르면, 모바일 앱에서 이용 가능한 새로운 혜택은 무엇인가?
(A) 조기 탑승   (B) 수하물 추적
(C) 라운지 이용   (D) 여행 관련 조언

해설 세부 사항 – 모바일 앱에서 이용 가능한 혜택
중반부에서 앱을 통해 승객 라운지를 이용할 수 있고, 비행 전 무료 간식을 즐길 수 있다(The app now lets you access the Starry Ways passenger lounge, for complimentary snacks before your flight)고 설명했으므로 (C)가 정답이다.

어휘 available 이용 가능한   boarding 탑승

9 화자에 따르면, 청자는 어떤 정보를 제공할 준비를 해야 하는가?
(A) 예약 확인 번호   (B) 신용카드 번호
(C) 여행자 이름   (D) 목적지 이름

해설 세부 사항 – 청자가 준비해야 하는 정보
후반부에서 직원에게 알려줄 예약 확인 번호를 준비해달라(Make sure to have your confirmation number ready to give to the agent)고 당부하고 있으므로 (A)가 정답이다.

[10-12] 전화 메시지 W-Br

Hi, Ms. Jeong. My name is Maria Casella, and I'm calling from Savor magazine. **10 Yesterday I visited your food truck and had the kimchi tacos you made.** Your recipe is delicious! **11 The reason why I'm calling is to invite you to participate in the Best Food on Wheels competition.** Every year, our magazine hosts this citywide event to recognize and promote food truck operators like yourself. This would be a great opportunity for you to promote your business, as you'll get a lot of great publicity. I've e-mailed you details about the event. And just so you know, **12 the entry fee will be waived if you register by May first**.

안녕하세요, 정 씨. 제 이름은 마리아 카셀라이고, 세이버 잡지에서 전화 드렸습니다. **10** 어제 제가 선생님의 푸드 트럭을 방문해 만들어 주신 김치 타코를 먹었어요. 정말 맛있더라고요! **11** 제가 전화 드리는 이유는 최고의 푸드 트럭 음식 대회 참가를 요청드리기 위해서입니다. 매년 저희 잡지에서 선생님 같은 푸드 트럭 운영자들을 인정하고 홍보해 드리기 위해 이 도시 규모의 행사를 주최합니다. 선생님의 가게를 홍보할 수 있는 아주 좋은 기회가 되실 거예요. 큰 홍보 효과를 얻으실 수 있거든요. 행사에 대한 자세한 내용은 이메일로 보내드렸습니다. 그리고 참고로 말씀드리자면, **12** 5월 1일까지 등록하시는 경우에는 참가비가 면제됩니다.

어휘 citywide 도시 전체의   recognize 인정하다, 표창하다   promote 홍보하다   operator 운영자   publicity 홍보 (효과)   just so you know 참고로 말하자면   entry fee 참가비   waive 면제하다, 포기하다

10 청자는 누구인 것 같은가?
(A) 사진 작가   **(B) 요리사**
(C) 음식 평론가   (D) 음악가

해설 전체 내용 – 청자의 직업
초반부에서 청자의 푸드 트럭을 방문해 그가 만들어준 김치 타코를 먹었다(Yesterday I visited your food truck and had the kimchi tacos you made)고 했으므로 (B)가 정답이다.

11 화자가 전화한 목적은 무엇인가?
(A) 청자에게 잡지 구독을 제안하기 위해
(B) 청자에게 경연대회에 참가하도록 요청하기 위해
(C) 기사에 필요한 인터뷰 일정을 잡기 위해
(D) 행사를 위해 기부를 요청하기 위해

해설 전체 내용 – 화자가 전화한 목적
중반부에서 최고의 푸드 트럭 음식 대회 참가를 요청하기 위해서 전화한다(The reason why I'm calling is to invite you to participate in the Best Food on Wheels competition)고 했으므로 (B)가 정답이다.

어휘 subscription 구독, 서비스 가입   donation 기부(금)

12 화자는 5월 1일까지 무슨 일이 있을 것이라고 말하는가?
(A) 웹사이트가 공사 중일 것이다.
(B) 행사장이 이용 가능할 것이다.
(C) 요금이 면제될 것이다.
(D) 직원이 사무실에 있지 않을 것이다.

해설 세부 사항 – 5월 1일까지 있을 일
후반부에서 5월 1일까지 등록하는 경우에는 참가비가 면제된다(the entry fee will be waived if you register by May first)고 했으므로 (C)가 정답이다.

어휘 under construction 공사 중인, 건설 중인

[13-15] 전화 메시지 W-Am

Hi. **13 This is Magali from Wavedale Community Center,** returning your call about the kickboxing classes that we offer. **14 The classes are held at the community center Monday through Friday at six in the evening.** The instructor closes the doors at six o'clock, so you'll want to keep that in mind. And about pricing: **15 classes are free if you're a resident of the city of Wavedale.** For nonresidents, it's ten dollars per class. Hope to see you there!

안녕하세요. **13** 저는 웨이브데일 커뮤니티 센터의 마갈리이며, 저희가 제공하는 킥복싱 수업과 관련해 회신 드립니다. **14** 이 수업은 저희 커뮤니티 센터에서 월요일부터 금요일까지 저녁 6시에 열립니다. 담당 강사님께서 6시에 문을 닫으시니, 이 점 유념해주세요. 그리고 비용과 관련해서는, **15** 웨이브데일 주민이실 경우에 수업은 무료입니다. 비거주자는 수업 당 10달러입니다. 그럼 그곳에서 뵐 수 있길 바라겠습니다!

어휘 return one's call ~에게 회신하다 hold 열다, 개최하다 keep A in mind A를 명심하다 pricing 가격 (책정)

13 화자는 어디에서 일하는가?
(A) 요리 학원   (B) 대학교
(C) 식물원   **(D) 커뮤니티 센터**

해설 전체 내용 – 화자의 근무 장소
초반부에서 화자가 웨이브데일 커뮤니티 센터의 마갈리(This is Magali from Wavedale Community Center)라고 자신을 소개했으므로 (D)가 정답이다.

14 화자가 "담당 강사님께서 6시에 문을 닫습니다"라고 말할 때 무엇을 의미하는가?
(A) 제때 수업에 도착하는 것이 중요하다.
(B) 강의실에 개인 물품을 보관하는 것이 안전하다.
(C) 수업에 입장하는 데 비밀번호가 필요하다.
(D) 수업이 매우 인기 있다.

해설 화자의 의도 파악
중반부에서 수업이 월요일부터 금요일까지 저녁 6시에 열린다(The classes are held at the community center Monday through Friday at six in the evening)고 한 뒤 인용문을 언급한 것으로 보아 수업 시간에 맞추어 도착하기를 당부하는 것임을 알 수 있다. 따라서 (A)가 정답이다.

어휘 store 보관하다, 저장하다 required 필요한, 필수인

15 무료 수업 대상자는 누구인가?
(A) 지역 호텔 손님들   (B) 10세 미만의 아이들
(C) 자원봉사자들   **(D) 시 주민들**

해설 세부 사항 – 무료 수업 대상자
후반부에서 웨이브데일 주민일 경우에 수업이 무료(classes are free if you're a resident of the city of Wavedale)라고 했으므로 (D)가 정답이다.

어휘 local 지역의, 현지의

[16-18] 녹음 메시지 M-Au

Hi, Aaron. I just got out of my meeting with Janet Lin from product development. **16 She liked our design for the company's new line of raincoats, but unfortunately, she wants us to use different colors than what we proposed.** I tried my best to convince her that a fresh, new look was needed, but she insisted on a more traditional approach. **17 There wasn't much more I could do.** You know... she's the head of the department. Anyway, I'm back at my desk now, so **18 I'm going to find a time on our calendars tomorrow when we can get together and start on these changes.**

안녕하세요, 아론. 제가 방금 제품 개발과의 재닛 린과 회의를 마치고 나왔어요. **16** 재닛이 회사의 새 레인코트에 대한 우리 디자인을 마음에 들어 했지만 아쉽게도 우리가 제안한 것과는 다른 색깔들을 사용하길 원하시네요. 신선하고도 새로운 모습이 필요하다는 점을 설득시키려고 최선을 다했지만 재닛은 좀 더 전통적인 접근을 고집하셨어요. **17** 제가 할 수 있는 게 많지 않았어요. 아시겠지만… 재닛이 부서장이잖아요. 어쨌든 지금 제가 제 자리로 돌아왔으니까 **18** 만나서 이런 변경 작업을 시작할 수 있도록 내일 일정을 한번 잡아 볼게요.

어휘 product development 제품 개발(과) line 종류, 제품 unfortunately 아쉽게도, 불행히도 convince 설득하다 insist on ~을 고집하다 approach 접근 head 책임자, 장 get together 모이다, 만나다

16 화자는 재닛 린과 무엇을 논의했는가?
(A) 채용 계획   **(B) 제품 디자인**
(C) 물품 주문   (D) 여행 일정

해설 세부 사항 – 논의 주제
초반부에서 재닛이 회사의 새 레인코트에 대한 우리 디자인을 마음에 들어 했지만 아쉽게도 우리가 제안한 것과는 다른 색깔들을 사용하길 원한다(She liked our design for the company's new line of raincoats, but unfortunately, she wants us to use different colors than what we proposed)고 했으므로 (B)가 정답이다.

17 화자가 "재닛이 부서장이잖아요"라고 말할 때 무엇을 의미하는가?
(A) 그는 직원을 소개하고 싶어 한다.
(B) 그는 최종 결정을 내릴 수 없다.
(C) 직함이 잘못되었다.
(D) 동료가 큰 성공을 거두었다.

해설 화자의 의도 파악
중반부에서 화자가 자신이 할 수 있는 게 많지 않았다(There wasn't much more I could do)며 인용문을 언급한 것으로 보아 화자 입장에서는 재닛의 최종 결정에 따를 수밖에 없었다는 의미임을 알 수 있다. 따라서 (B)가 정답이다.

18 화자는 다음에 무엇을 할 것 같은가?
(A) 회의 마련   (B) 카탈로그 검토
(C) 양식 작성   (D) 고객에게 전화

해설 **세부 사항 – 화자가 다음에 할 일**
마지막 대사에서 함께 만나서 변경 작업을 시작할 수 있도록 내일 일정을 한번 잡아 보겠다(I'm going to find a time on our calendars tomorrow)고 했으므로 (A)가 정답이다.

[19-21] 전화 메시지 + 건물 안내판 W-Br

Hello, Mr. Park. This is Marcela Lopez. I'm calling to let you know that we've reviewed **19your application materials for the open position on our company's legal team**. We liked what we saw on your résumé. In fact, many of our lawyers have similar backgrounds. Anyway, we'd like you to come in for an interview. **20Our office is located on the third floor of the Kumar Tower. 21The hiring team could meet with you either on Thursday at nine A.M. or at one P.M. on Friday. Could you please call me back to let me know which of those options works best for you?** Thank you.

안녕하세요, 박 씨. 저는 마르셀라 로페즈입니다. 19저희 회사의 법무팀의 공석에 지원하신 서류를 검토했다는 것을 알려 드리기 위해 전화 드립니다. 저희는 선생님의 이력서에서 좋은 인상을 받았습니다. 사실 저희 변호사들 중 많은 분들이 비슷한 경력을 가지고 계세요. 어쨌든, 면접을 보러 와 주셨으면 합니다. 20저희 사무실은 쿠마 타워 3층에 위치해 있습니다. 21채용팀에서 목요일 오전 9시 또는 금요일 오후 1시 중에서 뵐 수 있을 것 같습니다. 이 두 가지 옵션 중 어느 쪽이 괜찮으신지 제게 다시 전화주시겠어요? 감사합니다.

어휘 material 자료, 재료 open position 공석 résumé 이력서 hiring 고용, 채용 work best for (일정, 계획 등이) ~에게 가장 좋다 directory (건물 입구 등에 있는) 안내판, 안내도

쿠마 타워 안내판	
층	업체
1	올슨 앤 리우 어소시에이츠
2	내프틱 브러더스 주식회사
3	20파이브 픽스 컨설팅
4	펜트렐 솔루션즈 주식회사

19 청자는 어느 직책에 지원했을 것 같은가?
(A) 컴퓨터 기술자   (B) 영업사원
(C) 기자   (D) 변호사

해설 **세부 내용 – 청자가 지원한 직책**
초반부에서 청자가 법무팀 공석에 지원한 서류를 검토했다(your application materials for the open position on our company's legal team)고 했으므로 (D)가 정답이다.

20 시각 정보에 따르면, 화자는 어느 회사를 대표하는가?
(A) 올슨 앤 리우 어소시에이츠
(B) 내프틱 브러더스 주식회사
(C) 파이브 픽스 컨설팅
(D) 펜트렐 솔루션즈 주식회사

해설 **세부 사항 – 시각 정보 연계**
중반부에서 화자의 사무실이 쿠마 타워 3층에 위치해 있다(Our office is located on the third floor of the Kumar Tower)고 했다. 건물 안내판에 따르면 3층에 해당하는 업체명은 Five Peaks Consulting이므로 (C)가 정답이다.

어휘 represent 대표하다

21 화자는 왜 청자가 회신하기를 바라는가?
(A) 연봉을 협상하려고
(B) 졸업 날짜를 확인하려고
(C) 추가 추천서를 제공하려고
(D) 약속 시간을 확정하려고

해설 **세부 사항 – 화자가 청자의 회신을 원하는 이유**
후반부에서 채용팀이 만날 수 있는 시간대를 언급하면서 둘 중 어느 쪽이 좋을지 다시 전화해서 알려 달라(The hiring team could meet with you either on Thursday at nine A.M. or at one P.M. on Friday. Could you please call me back to let me know which of those options works best for you?)고 요청하고 있으므로 (D)가 정답이다.

어휘 negotiate 협상하다 verify 확인하다, 인증하다
reference 추천서, 추천인

UNIT 12 공지/회의

담화 구성과 단서 파악 ·············· 본책 p.110

안녕하세요, 여러분. 업무를 시작하기 전에 짧은 공지 사항 전할게요. 이곳 우리 매장에서는 **겉옷 판매가 잘되고 있지만**, 우리 웹사이트에 문제가 몇 가지 있습니다. 자세히 말하자면, **남성용 재킷을 볼 수 있는 링크가 작동하지 않습니다**. IT팀에서 이 문제를 살펴보고 있지만 언제 고쳐질지 모릅니다. 그러니, **온라인상에 있는 재킷을 찾는 고객들이 오시면 그분들을 우리 고객 서비스 관리자에게 보내세요**. 그녀가 그분들을 도와드릴 거예요. 감사합니다!

어휘 outerwear 겉옷 namely 자세히 말하자면, 즉 look into 조사하다

1 청자들은 어디에서 일하는 것 같은가?
(A) 의류 매장   (B) 전자제품 매장

2 화자는 어떤 문제를 언급하는가?
(A) 일부 사진들이 선명하지 않다.
(B) 링크가 작동하지 않는다.

3 화자는 청자들에게 무엇을 해 달라고 요청하는가?
(A) 고객들에게 환불해주기
(B) 고객을 매니저에게 보내기

ETS 유형연습

본책 p.111

1 (B) **2** (A) **3** (A) **4** (B) **5** (A) **6** (A)

[1-2] 공지 W-Br

¹Good evening, library patrons. We'll be closing in 30 minutes. If you're working on a public computer, we ask that you shut it down before you leave. ²If you would like to check out any books, please proceed to the service desk near the front entrance. Also, we'd like to remind you that we will be showing a free movie tomorrow evening at six o'clock called *Life in Tuscany*. Please join us for this wonderful film.

¹안녕하세요, 도서관 이용객 여러분. 저희는 30분 후에 문을 닫습니다. 공용 컴퓨터를 쓰고 계시면 나가시기 전에 전원을 꺼 주세요. ²만약 대출하고 싶은 책이 있으시면 정문 입구 근처의 안내 데스크로 가 주시기 바랍니다. 또한, 내일 저녁 6시에 영화 〈토스카나에서의 삶〉을 무료로 상영할 예정임을 다시 알려 드립니다. 오셔서 이 멋진 영화를 감상하시기 바랍니다.

어휘 patron 고객, 이용객 check out (책을) 대출하다 proceed to ~으로 가다

1 안내 방송은 어디에서 나오고 있는가?
(A) 영화관 (B) 도서관

해설 전체 내용 – 안내 방송의 장소
초반부에서 화자가 청자를 도서관 이용객 여러분(library patrons)이라고 부르며 인사했으므로 (B)가 정답이다.

2 청자들은 안내 데스크에서 무엇을 할 수 있는가?
(A) 자료를 대출한다.
(B) 컴퓨터를 사용하기 위해 등록한다.

해설 세부 사항 – 안내 데스크에서 할 수 있는 일
중반부에서 만약 대출하고 싶은 책이 있으면 입구 근처의 안내 데스크로 가 달라(If you would like to check out any books, please proceed to the service desk near the front entrance)고 했으므로 (A)가 정답이다.

Paraphrasing 담화의 any books → 정답의 materials

[3-4] 회의 발췌 + 매장 진열품 배치도 M-Au

In just a few days, we'll be receiving a line of holiday candles to sell here in the store. We've never sold candles before. The manufacturer has sent us the materials we need to showcase the products. I expect the candles to attract many customers into our store. ³I'd like to put them up front—right inside the main entrance. We'll need to move the display that's currently there. If anyone can work a few hours after closing on Friday to help set up, ⁴I'll bring in pizza.

며칠 후, 이곳 우리 매장에서 판매할 휴일용 양초 제품이 입고될 예정이에요. 우리는 이전에 양초를 판매한 적이 없습니다. 제조사에서 우리가 이 제품을 진열하는 데 필요한 물품을 보내왔습니다. 저는 이 양초가 많은 고객을 우리 매장으로 끌어들일 것으로 기대합니다. ³저는 이것들을 가장 앞쪽, 매장 입구 바로 안쪽에 진열하고 싶어요. 현재 그곳에 있는 진열품을 옮겨야 할 겁니다. 금요일 영업 종료 후에 몇 시간 동안 진열 작업을 도와줄 수 있는 분이 있다면, ⁴제가 피자를 사오겠습니다.

어휘 receive 받다 manufacturer 제조사 up front 가장 앞쪽, 전면에 display 진열(품), 전시(품) currently 현재 set up 설치하다, 준비하다

3 시각 정보에 따르면, 어느 제품이 금요일에 옮겨질 것인가?
(A) 핸드백 (B) 화장품

해설 세부 내용 – 시각 정보 연계
회의의 중반부에서 가장 앞쪽, 매장 입구 바로 안쪽에 진열하고 싶다(I'd like to put them up front—right inside the main entrance)며 현재 그곳에 있는 진열품을 옮겨야 한다(We'll need to move the display that's currently there)고 했다. 매장 진열품 배치도를 보면 정문 바로 안쪽에 위치한 상품은 Handbags이므로 (A)가 정답이다.

4 화자는 자신이 무엇을 할 것이라고 말하는가?
(A) 디자이너와 만나기 (B) 음식 제공하기

해설 세부 내용 – 화자가 하려는 것
회의의 후반부에서 금요일 영업 종료 후에 몇 시간 동안 진열 작업을 도와줄 수 있는 분이 있다면 피자를 사오겠다(If anyone can work a few hours after closing on Friday to help set up, I'll bring in pizza)고 했으므로 (B)가 정답이다.

어휘 applicant 지원자, 신청자

Paraphrasing 담화의 bring in pizza → 정답의 Provide some food

[5-6] 공지 W-Br

Welcome aboard, passengers! My name is Myung Hwa, and I'll be your guide on the river cruise this afternoon. The estimated trip time is 90 minutes. And **5 I have an update about the weather. It's predicted to be clear and sunny,** with calm waters throughout the trip. Also, in accordance with guidelines, **6 the crew asks that all passengers move their personal belongings out of the aisles and put them below the seats.**

탑승을 환영합니다, 승객 여러분! 제 이름은 명화이며, 제가 오늘 오후 여객선에서 여러분의 가이드를 맡게 되었습니다. 예상 여행 시간은 90분입니다. 그리고 5날씨에 관한 소식이 하나 있습니다. 날씨는 맑고 화창하며, 항해 내내 물결도 잔잔할 것으로 예상됩니다. 또한 지침에 따라 6승무원들은 모든 승객 여러분께 개인 소지품을 통로에서 치우고 좌석 아래에 보관해주실 것을 요청드립니다.

어휘 aboard 탑승한 estimated 예상되는, 추정되는 calm (물결이) 잔잔한, 차분한 in accordance with ~에 따라 crew 승무원 belongings 소지품

5 화자는 청자들에게 무엇에 대한 소식을 전하는가?
(A) 기상 상태가 맑을 것이다.
(B) 간식이 무료일 것이다.

해설 세부 사항 – 화자가 전하는 소식
중반부에서 날씨에 관한 소식이 있음을 언급하면서 맑고 화창할 것으로 예측된다(I have an update about the weather. It's predicted to be clear and sunny)고 했으므로 (A)가 정답이다.

어휘 refreshments 간식, 다과

6 화자는 청자들에게 무엇을 하라고 말하는가?
(A) 소지품 옮기기   (B) 안전벨트 착용하기

해설 세부 사항 – 화자가 청자들에게 요청하는 일
후반부에서 개인 소지품을 통로에서 치우고 좌석 아래에 보관해 달라(all passengers move their personal belongings out of the aisles and put them below the seats)는 요청 사항을 전달하고 있으므로 (A)가 정답이다.

어휘 fasten 고정시키다, 단단히 잠그다

ETS 실전문제 본책 p.112

1 (A)	2 (B)	3 (C)	4 (A)	5 (D)	6 (C)
7 (C)	8 (B)	9 (D)	10 (D)	11 (B)	12 (D)
13 (C)	14 (B)	15 (C)	16 (A)	17 (C)	18 (B)
19 (A)	20 (B)	21 (A)			

[1-3] 공지 M-Au

May I have everyone's attention, please? **1 Thank you for coming to the Science Theater at the Brinkley Museum. And 2 thank you all for waiting so patiently in line.** Unfortunately, we have just filled all the seats for the three o'clock showing of today's documentary film. However, **3 there will be another showing at five o'clock, and we usually have fewer attendees at that time.** We hope you'll return then. In the meantime, feel free to continue exploring the museum's exhibits, cafeteria, and gift shop.

모두 주목해 주시겠습니까? 1브링클리 박물관 과학 극장에 와 주셔서 감사합니다. 아울러 2줄을 서서 참을성 있게 기다려 주셔서 감사드립니다. 안타깝게도 오늘 다큐멘터리 영화 3시 상영 좌석이 모두 찼습니다. 하지만 35시 정각에 다시 상영하며, 해당 시간에는 보통 참석자가 더 적습니다. 그때 다시 와 주시기 바랍니다. 그동안 박물관 내 전시실, 카페테리아, 기념품점 등을 자유롭게 계속 둘러보십시오.

어휘 attention 주의, 주목 patiently 참을성 있게, 끈기 있게 attendee 참석자 explore 답사하다

1 안내 방송은 어디에서 나오고 있는가?
(A) 박물관   (B) 대학교
(C) 가구점   (D) 도서관

해설 전체 내용 – 안내 방송 장소
초반부에서 브링클리 박물관의 과학 극장(Science Theater at the Brinkley Museum)에 와주어 감사하다고 했으므로 (A)가 정답이다.

2 청자들은 어디에 참석하려고 기다리는가?
(A) 강의   (B) 영화
(C) 전시회   (D) 음악회

해설 세부 사항 – 청자들이 참석을 기다리는 행사
중반부에서 청자들에게 줄을 서서 참을성 있게 기다려 준 것(waiting so patiently in line)에 감사를 전한 뒤, 오늘 다큐멘터리 영화 3시 상영은 좌석이 모두 찼다(we have just filled all the seats for the three o'clock showing of today's documentary film)고 했으므로, 청자들은 다큐멘터리 영화의 상영을 기다리고 있었음을 알 수 있다. 따라서 (B)가 정답이다.

3 화자는 5시 행사에 대해 무엇이라고 말하는가?
(A) 더 저렴하다.   (B) 더 짧다.
(C) 덜 붐빈다.   (D) 간식이 포함되어 있다.

해설 세부 사항 – 화자가 5시 행사에 대해 언급한 사항
중반부에서 영화는 5시 정각에 다시 상영한다(there will be another showing at five o'clock)고 한 뒤, 해당 시간에는 보통 참석자가 더 적다(we usually have fewer attendees at that time)고 했으므로 (C)가 정답이다.

> **Paraphrasing** 담화의 fewer attendees → 정답의 less crowded

[4-6] 공지 W-Br

Attention, passengers. ⁴**This is your airport gate attendant with some announcements.** First, if you are waiting for flight 421 to Singapore, I'm sorry to inform you that ⁵**departure has been delayed because a routine maintenance check is taking longer than expected.** The good news is that the maintenance team has assured us that we'll be able to begin the boarding process for that flight in twenty minutes. And second, ⁶**if you are missing a pair of reading glasses, please come up to the gate counter to claim them.** Thank you for your attention.

승객 여러분께 알립니다. ⁴몇 가지 안내 말씀을 드릴 공항 탑승구 안내 직원입니다. 먼저 싱가포르행 421 항공편을 기다리시는 승객 여러분, 죄송하지만 ⁵정기 점검 작업이 예상보다 오래 소요되고 있어 출발이 지연되었음을 알려드립니다. 좋은 소식은 정비팀에서 약 20분 후 탑승을 시작할 수 있을 것이라고 알려왔다는 점입니다. 그리고 두 번째로, ⁶돋보기를 분실하신 분은 탑승구 카운터로 오셔서 찾아가시기 바랍니다. 경청해 주셔서 감사합니다.

어휘 attendant 안내원 departure 출발, 떠남 maintenance 정비, 유지 관리 assure 확인하다, 장담하다 reading glasses 돋보기 claim 찾아가다, (소유권 등을) 주장하다

4 청자들은 어디에 있는가?
(A) 공항 (B) 기차역
(C) 보트 항구 (D) 버스 정류장

해설 전체 내용 – 청자들이 있는 장소
초반부에서 화자가 자신을 몇 가지 안내 말씀을 전할 공항 탑승구 안내 직원(This is your airport gate attendant with some announcements)이라고 소개했으므로 (A)가 정답이다.

5 무엇이 지연을 초래하고 있는가?
(A) 분실 수하물 (B) 악천후
(C) 늦은 탑승객 (D) 점검 작업

해설 세부 사항 – 지연을 초래하는 원인
중반부에서 정기 점검 작업이 예상보다 오래 소요되고 있어서 출발이 지연되었다(departure has been delayed because a routine maintenance check is taking longer than expected)고 했으므로 (D)가 정답이다.

6 화자에 따르면, 어느 물품이 발견되었는가?
(A) 지갑 (B) 휴대 전화
(C) 안경 (D) 책

해설 세부 사항 – 발견된 물품
후반부에서 돋보기를 분실한 사람이 있으면 찾아가라(if you are missing a pair of reading glasses, please come up to the gate counter to claim them)고 했으므로 (C)가 정답이다.

[7-9] 회의 발췌 M-Cn

OK, excellent—the projector's working now, so everyone please take a look at the screen. ⁷**I'll start this executive team meeting by presenting some slides on possible future projects.** ⁸**Today we'll assign a priority to each project in order to determine the top three.** Please prioritize using the following criteria: one—how complex the project is and two—whether the project will make us more competitive. Each proposal is a bit unconventional. As CEO, I feel it's important we head in a different direction than in the past. ⁹**This is a pivotal time for us, a time to reassess.** Listen, change is not easy. ⁹**However, our survival depends on adapting and being forward-thinking.**

네, 아주 좋습니다. 이제 프로젝터가 작동하니 모두 스크린을 봐 주시기 바랍니다. ⁷가능성 있는 향후의 프로젝트들에 관한 슬라이드를 보여 드리면서 이번 임원진 회의를 시작하겠습니다. ⁸오늘 우리는 가장 중요한 세 가지를 결정하기 위해 각 프로젝트에 우선순위를 부여할 것입니다. 다음 기준을 이용해 우선순위를 매겨 주시기 바랍니다. 첫째, 프로젝트가 얼마나 복잡한가, 그리고 둘째, 프로젝트가 우리를 더 경쟁력 있게 만들 수 있는가입니다. 각 제안서는 다소 파격적입니다. 대표이사로서, 저는 우리가 과거와는 다른 방향을 향해 나아가는 것이 중요하다고 생각합니다. ⁹지금은 우리에게 중대한 시점, 즉 재평가의 시간입니다. 자, 변화는 쉽지 않습니다. ⁹하지만, 우리의 생존은 적응 및 미래 지향적인 사고에 달려 있습니다.

어휘 executive 임원, 이사 priority 우선순위 prioritize 우선순위를 매기다 following 다음의, 아래의 criteria 기준 competitive 경쟁력의 proposal 제안(서) unconventional 파격적인, 비관습적인 pivotal 중대한, 중추적인 forward-thinking 미래 지향적인, 미래에 대비하는

7 화자는 어떻게 회의를 시작하는가?
(A) 동영상을 재생함으로써
(B) 여론 조사 결과를 발표함으로써
(C) 슬라이드를 보여줌으로써
(D) 한 팀을 축하함으로써

해설 세부 사항 – 화자가 회의를 시작하는 방법
초반부에서 가능성 있는 향후의 프로젝트들에 관한 슬라이드를 보여 주면서 임원진 회의를 시작하겠다(I'll start this executive team meeting by presenting some slides on possible future projects)고 했으므로 (C)가 정답이다.

어휘 poll 여론 조사

> **Paraphrasing** 담화의 presenting → 정답의 showing

8 회의의 주된 목적은 무엇인가?
  (A) 생산비를 낮추는 것
  (B) 잠재 프로젝트를 평가하는 것
  (C) 새로운 공급업체를 선택하는 것
  (D) 경쟁 상대를 평가하는 것

해설 **전체 내용 – 회의의 목적**
중반부에 오늘 가장 중요한 세 가지를 결정하기 위해 각 프로젝트에 우선순위를 부여할 것(Today we'll assign a priority to each project in order to determine the top three)이라며 회의의 목적을 밝히고 있다. 이는 앞에서 언급한 가능성 있는 미래 프로젝트들을 평가하여 우선순위를 정하겠다는 뜻이므로 (B)가 정답이다.

어휘 evaluate 평가하다 potential 잠재적인

> **Paraphrasing** 담화의 assign a priority to each project in order to determine the top three → 정답의 evaluate potential projects

9 화자는 왜 "변화는 쉽지 않습니다"라고 말하는가?
  (A) 진행 일정을 연장하도록 권하기 위해
  (B) 제안이 승인되지 않은 이유를 설명하기 위해
  (C) 놀라움을 표현하기 위해
  (D) 청자들의 의구심을 해결하기 위해

해설 **화자의 의도 파악**
후반부에 지금은 중대한 재평가의 시간(This is a pivotal time for us, a time to reassess)이라고 한 뒤 인용문을 언급했고 뒤이어 자신들의 생존이 적응 및 미래 지향적인 사고에 달려 있다(However, our survival depends on adapting and being forward-thinking)고 덧붙였다. 이는 변화가 필요한 이유를 설명해 청자들을 설득하려는 의도임을 알 수 있다. 따라서 (D)가 정답이다.

어휘 timeline 진행 일정 approve 승인하다 address (문제 등을) 해결하다, 처리하다 doubt 의구심, 의혹

[10-12] 담화 W-Am

> Nearly one hundred thousand campers and hikers visit our park each year. And as a result, many of our trails are overused and eroding. **10 We rely on volunteers like you to help maintain our trails** so they can stay open to the public. **11 I'll be taking photographs during the day to share on the park's social media accounts.** These kinds of publications help us recruit volunteers for future projects. **12 I'll pass out waivers right now.** Please fill one out and return it if you don't mind us sharing your picture on social media.
>
> 매년 거의 10만 명에 달하는 캠핑객들과 등산객들이 저희 공원을 방문합니다. 그리고 그 결과로, 많은 등산로가 과도하게 이용되어 침식되고 있습니다. 저희는 대중에게 계속 개방할 수 있도록 **10 등산로를 유지하는 데 여러분과 같은 자원봉사자의 도움에 의존하고 있습니다**. **11 오늘 활동 중에 공원의 소셜 미디어 계정에 올릴 사진들을 촬영할 예정입니다.** 이런 게시글은 저희가 향후 프로젝트에 자원봉사자들을 모집하는 데 큰 도움이 됩니다. **12 제가 지금 초상권 포기 각서를 나눠 드리겠습니다.** 저희가 여러분의 사진을 소셜 미디어에 공유해도 괜찮으시다면 작성해서 제출해주세요.

어휘 nearly 거의 overuse 과도하게 이용하다 erode 침식되다, 부식되다 publication 공개, 발표 recruit 모집하다 pass out 나눠 주다 waiver 포기 각서 mind A -ing A가 ~하는 것을 상관하다

10 청자들은 무엇을 하겠다고 자원했는가?
  (A) 교통 안내하기
  (B) 캠핑 장소 준비하기
  (C) 새 관찰 투어 진행하기
  (D) 유지 관리 업무 수행하기

해설 **세부 사항 – 청자들이 자원한 일**
초반부에서 등산로를 유지하는 데 청자들과 같은 자원봉사자의 도움에 의존하고 있다(We rely on volunteers like you to help maintain our trails ~)고 감사의 인사를 전했으므로 (D)가 정답이다.

어휘 direct (길 등을) 안내하다 traffic 교통(량), 차량들

> **Paraphrasing** 담화의 maintain our trails → 정답의 Perform maintenance tasks

11 화자는 사진들로 무엇을 하고 싶어 하는가?
  (A) 신분증 만들기
  (B) 웹사이트에 게시하기
  (C) 기념 행사에서 전시하기
  (D) 유인물에 포함하기

해설 **세부 사항 – 화자가 사진으로 하고 싶어 하는 일**
중반부에서 오늘 활동 중에 공원의 소셜 미디어 계정에 올릴 사진을 촬영할 예정(I'll be taking photographs during the day to share on the park's social media accounts)이라고 했으므로 (B)가 정답이다.

어휘 identification badge 신분증 handout 유인물

> **Paraphrasing** 담화의 share on the park's social media accounts → 정답의 Post them on a Web site

12 화자는 다음에 무엇을 할 것인가?
  (A) 보관 구역 잠금 해제하기
  (B) 출석 확인하기
  (C) 간식 제공하기
  (D) 양식 나눠 주기

해설 **세부 사항 – 화자가 다음에 할 일**
후반부에서 지금 초상권 포기 각서를 나눠 주겠다(I'll pass out waivers right now)며 작성해서 제출해 달라고 요청했으므로 (D)가 정답이다.

어휘 storage 보관, 저장

> **Paraphrasing** 담화의 waivers → 정답의 some forms

[13-15] 회의 발췌 M-Cn

At last year's investors' meeting, I had to report some losses. I predicted a difficult year for Richmond Chemical. Rising energy costs and unavailable supplies resulted in **13a negative return on your investments**. However, we found ways to innovate. **14Our research team developed new formulas using different ingredients.** That enabled us to reduce our reliance on costly oil-based chemicals. As a result, the company is stronger than it was two years ago. I think you'll be very pleased with the current profit margins, which **15I'll now outline in my presentation**. Will someone dim the lights?

작년에 열린 투자자 회의에서, 저는 몇 가지 손실을 보고해야 했습니다. 저는 리치먼드 케미컬 사에게 힘든 한 해가 될 것이라고 예상했었죠. 에너지 비용 상승과 공급 부족으로 인해 **13여러분의 투자가 마이너스 수익**을 냈습니다. 하지만, 우리는 혁신할 방법을 찾았습니다. **14우리 연구팀이 여러 다른 재료를 이용해 새로운 공법을 개발했습니다.** 덕분에 우리는 값비싼 석유 기반 화학물질에 대한 의존도를 줄일 수 있었습니다. 그 결과 회사는 2년 전보다 더 강해졌습니다. 여러분께서 현재의 수익 폭에 대해 대단히 만족하시리라 생각하며, **15제가 지금 발표를 통해 간략하게 설명해 드리겠습니다.** 누가 조명을 낮춰 주시겠습니까?

> **어휘** result in ~라는 결과를 낳다 innovative 혁신적인 formula 공법, 제조법 ingredient 재료, 성분 reliance on ~에 대한 의존(도) costly 많은 비용이 드는 profit margins 수익 폭 outline 간략히 설명하다 dim (밝기를) 낮추다, 어둡게 하다

13 청자들은 누구인 것 같은가?
(A) 정치인   (B) 회계사
(C) 투자자   (D) 과학자

> **해설** 전체 내용 – 청자들의 직업
> 초반부에서 청자들의 투자가 마이너스 수익(a negative return on your investments)을 냈다고 언급했으므로 (C)가 정답이다.

14 화자에 따르면, 회사는 어떻게 생존했는가?
(A) 인력을 줄임으로써
(B) 제품 공법을 조정함으로써
(C) 가격을 낮춤으로써
(D) 덜 비싼 공간을 임대함으로써

> **해설** 세부 사항 – 회사가 생존한 방법
> 중반부에서 연구팀이 여러 다른 재료를 이용해 새로운 공법을 개발했다(Our research team developed new formulas using different ingredients)고 했다. 이는 기존의 제품 공법을 조정한 것으로 볼 수 있으므로 (B)가 정답이다.

> **어휘** workforce 인력, 직원들

> **Paraphrasing** 담화의 developed new formulas using different ingredients → 정답의 adjusting product formulas

15 화자는 다음에 무엇을 할 것인가?
(A) 보고서 사본 나눠 주기
(B) 출석 확인하기
(C) 발표하기
(D) 초청 연사 소개하기

> **해설** 세부 사항 – 화자가 다음에 할 일
> 후반부에서 현재의 수익 폭과 관련해 지금 발표를 통해 간략히 설명할 것(I'll now outline in my presentation)이라고 했으므로 (C)가 정답이다.

> **어휘** attendance 출석, 참석

> **Paraphrasing** 담화의 outline in my presentation → 정답의 Give a presentation

[16-18] 연설 W-Br

16Welcome to the grand opening of our very first retail location. Until today, Stanford Hill Clothing only sold products online. While that business model helped us keep prices down, it also meant that customers couldn't walk into a store and feel our cashmere sweaters or try on a linen suit. **17By opening this shop, we hope to bring our clothing to more customers.** We know that online-only retail doesn't work for everyone, especially for shoppers who prefer to try on clothes before purchasing them. Please browse our collections and **18let an associate know if you'd like to try anything on**.

16저희의 첫 번째 매장 개점 행사에 오신 것을 환영합니다. 오늘까지, 스탠포드 힐 의류 회사는 오직 온라인에서만 제품을 판매했습니다. 이 사업 모델이 저희가 가격을 계속 낮게 유지하는 데는 도움이 되었지만, 고객들께서 매장으로 직접 방문해 저희 캐시미어 스웨터를 느껴 보시거나 리넨 정장을 착용해 보실 수 없었다는 뜻이기도 합니다. **17이번에 매장을 열면서, 더 많은 고객께 저희 옷을 선보일 수 있기를 바랍니다.** 온라인 한정 판매가 모든 분께 잘 맞는 것은 아니라는 사실을 저희도 알고 있습니다. 특히 구매하시기 전에 의류를 착용해 보시는 것을 선호하시는 쇼핑객들께는요. 저희 보유 제품들을 둘러보시면서 **18입어보고 싶은 제품이 있으시면 직원에게 말씀해 주세요.**

> **어휘** retail store (소매) 매장 try on ~을 착용해 보다 browse 둘러보다 collection 소장품, 수집품 associate 직원, 동료, 동업자

16 어떤 종류의 행사가 열리고 있는가?
(A) 시상식 연회   (B) 무역 박람회
(C) 제품 출시회   (D) 개점식

해설 **전체 내용 - 개최되는 행사의 종류**
초반부에서 첫 번째 매장 개점 행사에 온 것을 환영한다(Welcome to the grand opening of our very first retail location)고 인사하고 있으므로 (D)가 정답이다.

17 회사는 왜 변화를 단행했는가?
(A) 비용을 절감하기 위해
(B) 생산성을 향상시키기 위해
(C) 신규 고객을 끌어들이기 위해
(D) 새로운 규정을 준수하기 위해

해설 **세부 사항 - 회사가 변화를 단행한 이유**
중반부에서 이번에 매장을 열면서 자사의 의류를 더 많은 고객들께 선보일 수 있기를 바란다(By opening this shop, we hope to bring our clothing to more customers)고 했으므로 (C)가 정답이다.

어휘 productivity 생산성 comply with ~을 준수하다

Paraphrasing 담화의 bring our clothing to more customers → 정답의 attract new customers

18 청자들은 왜 직원에게 이야기해야 하는가?
(A) 지원서를 제출하기 위해
(B) 상품을 착용해 보기 위해
(C) 교육에 등록하기 위해
(D) 할인 쿠폰을 받기 위해

해설 **세부 사항 - 청자들이 직원에게 이야기해야 하는 이유**
후반부에서 입어보고 싶은 제품이 있으면 직원에게 말하라(let an associate know if you'd like to try anything on)고 했으므로 (B)가 정답이다.

어휘 application 지원(서), 신청(서) merchandise 상품
sign up for ~에 등록하다, ~을 신청하다

Paraphrasing 담화의 let an associate know → 질문의 speak to an associate
담화의 try anything on → 정답의 try on some merchandise

[19-21] 회의 발췌 + 도표 M-Cn

I know that we've been talking about how our design firm needs better data storage solutions for **19the logos and graphics we create.** Well, I've done some research, and there's a company that offers a cloud solution that I think would work for our data storage needs. There are several options, but **20I suggest we try the one that will cost eight dollars per month for now.** If our client base continues to grow, we may need to upgrade to the twenty-dollar plan, but **21for now, the less expensive option should be fine. Scott, when you meet with our accountant tomorrow, could you confirm that this is OK?**

우리 디자인 회사가 19우리가 만드는 로고들과 그래픽들을 위한 더 나은 데이터 저장 솔루션이 필요하다는 것에 대해 이야기해 왔다는 것을 알고 있습니다. 음, 제가 조사를 좀 해 봤는데, 우리의 데이터 저장 요구 사항에 맞을 거라고 생각하는 클라우드 솔루션을 제공하는 회사가 한 곳 있어요. 여러 가지 옵션이 있기는 하지만, 20우선은 한 달에 8달러짜리를 사용해 보는 것을 제안해요. 우리 고객층이 지속적으로 늘어난다면, 20달러짜리 플랜으로 업그레이드해야 할 수도 있지만, 21지금으로서는, 더 저렴한 옵션으로 충분할 거예요. 스캇 씨, 내일 우리 회계사와 만날 때 이 부분이 괜찮은지 확인해 주시겠어요?

어휘 solution 솔루션, 해결책 for now 당분간은, 지금으로서는 client base 고객층 accountant 회계사 confirm 확인하다

클라우드 저장 옵션	옵션 1	20옵션 2	옵션 3	옵션4
저장 용량	5 GB	2 TB	6 TB	10 TB
이용자당 월간 요금	무료	20$8	$20	$35

19 청자들은 어디에서 일하는 것 같은가?
(A) 그래픽 디자인 회사 (B) 은행
(C) 기술 학교 (D) 전자제품 매장

해설 **전체 내용 - 청자들의 근무 장소**
도입부에서 우리 디자인 회사가 만들어 내는 로고들과 그래픽들을 위한 더 나은 데이터 저장 솔루션이 필요하다는 것에 대해 이야기해 왔다(we've been talking about how our design firm needs better data storage solutions for the logos and graphics we create)고 했으므로 (A)가 정답이다.

20 시각 정보에 따르면, 화자는 어느 옵션을 추천하는가?
(A) 옵션 1 (B) 옵션 2
(C) 옵션 3 (D) 옵션 4

해설 **세부 사항 - 시각 정보 연계**
중반부에서 한 달에 8달러짜리를 사용해 보자고 제안(I suggest we try the one that will cost eight dollars per month for now)하고 있다. 도표를 보면 월간 요금이 $8로 표기된 제품은 Option 2이므로 (B)가 정답이다.

21 스캇 씨는 내일 회의 시간에 무엇을 할 것인가?
(A) 이용 가능한 자금 확인하기
(B) 회계 감사 준비하기
(C) 소프트웨어 시연하기
(D) 영업 결과물 검토하기

해설 **세부 사항 - 스캇 씨가 내일 회의 시간에 할 일**
후반부에서 지금으로서는 더 저렴한 옵션으로 충분할 것이라며, 스캇 씨에게 내일 회계사와 만날 때 이 부분이 괜찮은지 확인해 달라(for now, the less expensive option should be fine. Scott, when you meet with our accountant tomorrow, could you confirm that this is OK?)고 요청했다. 이는 해당 요금을 지출하는 것과 관련해 자금 이용 가능성을 확인해 달라는 의미이므로 (A)가 정답이다.

어휘 audit 회계 감사   demonstrate 시연하다

UNIT 13 설명 / 소개

담화 구성과 단서 파악 ······ 본책 p.114

환영합니다, 여러분. 제 이름은 이소벨이고, **여러분들과 오늘 저녁 요리 수업을 진행할 강사입니다.** 오늘 밤, 여러분들께 고급 빵 굽는 법을 가르쳐 드릴 텐데요. 자, 필요한 재료는 이미 조리대 위에 놓아드렸지만, **여러분 모두 앞으로 나오셔서 큰 그릇과 빵틀을 하나씩 가져가시겠어요?** 아, 그건 그렇고, 한 30분 후에 사진 작가가 새 홍보 책자용 사진을 찍으러 들를 겁니다. 사진에 찍히고 싶지 않으시다면 그에게 알려주세요.

어휘 instructor 강사   artisanal 고급의   counter 조리대
loaf pan 빵틀   promotional 홍보의

1 청자들은 어디에 참석하고 있는가?
   (A) 저녁 파티   (B) 요리 교실

2 화자는 청자들에게 무엇을 하라고 요청하는가?
   (A) 설명서 읽어보기   (B) 도구 가져가기

3 여자는 30분 뒤에 무슨 일이 일어날 것이라고 말하는가?
   (A) 사진 촬영이 있을 것이다.
   (B) 한 예술가가 연설을 할 것이다.

ETS 유형연습
본책 p.115

1 (B) **2** (A) **3** (A) **4** (B) **5** (B) **6** (B)

[1-2] 설명 W-Br

¹Welcome to the sixth annual Corzell Technology Convention. I know you're looking forward to a weekend filled with software demonstrations, workshops, and some fantastic exhibits of the latest computer technology. **²Those of you who participated in previous conventions will notice something new this year—we now have Internet access in all our meeting rooms.** One final note: if you're planning to attend the computer networking workshop, there's been a change. It will be held in the Hudson Room, not the Bayside Center.

¹제6회 연례 코젤 기술 대회에 오신 것을 환영합니다. 여러분께서는 소프트웨어 시연과 워크숍, 환상적인 최신 컴퓨터 기술 전시로 가득 찬 주말을 고대하고 계실 것입니다. ²이전 대회 참가자분들은 올해 새로워진 점을 알아차리실 텐데요, 이제 모든 회의실에서 인터넷 사용이 가능하다는 겁니다. 마지막으로 컴퓨터 네트워킹 워크숍에 참석하실 분들께 변동사항을 알려 드립니다. 워크숍은 베이사이드 센터가 아니라 허드슨 룸에서 열립니다.

어휘 convention 대회   demonstration 시연   notice 알아차리다

1 화자는 어디에 있는가?
   (A) 컴퓨터 판매점   (B) 기술 대회

해설 **전체 내용 – 담화의 장소**
초반부에서 기술 대회에 온 것을 환영한다(Welcome to the sixth annual Corzell Technology Convention)고 했으므로 (B)가 정답이다.

2 화자에 의해 언급된 새로운 특징은 무엇인가?
   (A) 인터넷 접속이 되는 방
   (B) 특가 소프트웨어

해설 **세부 사항 – 새로운 특징**
중반부에서 올해 새로워진 점으로 모든 회의실에서 인터넷 접속이 가능하다는 것(we now have Internet access in all our meeting rooms)을 언급했으므로 (A)가 정답이다.

[3-4] 소개 M-Au

Our next speaker is Dr. Clarissa Trevor, a marine biologist who has greatly impacted the scientific world. **³The evidence is on the walls of her office, which are lined with numerous awards and plaques.** This past year, Dr. Trevor found a new species of turtle in the Galapagos Islands. So I think it's safe to tell her—make sure you leave some room on those walls. Her findings are documented in her new book, *The Unknown Turtle*. **⁴Today, she will be reading a chapter and discussing her amazing discovery.** Please join me in welcoming Dr. Clarissa Trevor.

다음에 모실 연사는 과학계에 엄청난 영향을 미친 해양 생물학자인 클라리사 트레보 박사입니다. ³증거는 박사님 사무실 벽에 있습니다. 벽에는 수많은 상과 명판이 줄줄이 붙어 있습니다. 작년에 트레보 박사는 갈라파고스 군도에서 새로운 바다거북 종을 발견했습니다. 따라서 저는 그녀에게 그 벽에 공간을 남겨 두라고 말하는 편이 좋을 것 같습니다. 조사 결과는 그녀의 신간 〈알려지지 않은 바다거북〉에 기록되어 있습니다. ⁴오늘 그녀는 책의 한 챕터를 낭독하고 자신의 놀라운 발견에 대해 토론할 예정입니다. 그럼 저와 함께 클라리사 트레보 박사를 환영해 주십시오.

어휘 marine biologist 해양 생물학자   impact 영향을 주다
evidence 증거   be lined with 줄줄이 늘어서 있다
numerous 수많은   plaque 명판   species 종(種)
findings 조사 결과   document 기록하다   unknown 알려지지 않은   discovery 발견

3 화자는 왜 "그 벽에 공간을 남겨 두라"고 말하는가?
   (A) 감탄을 표현하기 위해
   (B) 경고를 해주기 위해

해설 **화자의 의도 파악**

초반부에서 트레보 박사의 사무실 벽에 수많은 상과 명판들이 있다(~ which are lined with numerous awards and plaques)면서 작년에는 갈라파고스 군도에서 새로운 바다 거북 종을 발견했다(This past year, Dr. Trevor found a new species of turtle in the Galapagos Islands)고 했다. 이후에 인용문을 언급했으므로 이는 성과에 대한 감탄을 표현하려는 의도임을 알 수 있다. 따라서 (A)가 정답이다.

어휘 admiration 감탄, 존경 warning 경고

4 트레보 박사는 오늘 무엇을 할 것인가?
(A) 갈라파고스 군도로 날아갈 것이다.
(B) 자신의 책 일부분을 공유할 것이다.

해설 **세부 사항 – 트레보 박사가 오늘 할 일**

후반부에서 트레보 박사가 자신이 저술한 책을 낭독할 것(she will be reading a chapter)이라고 했으므로 (B)가 정답이다.

> Paraphrasing 담화의 reading a chapter → 정답의 share part of her book

[5-6] 설명 M-Cn

On this tour of the Klauston Art Museum, ⁵I'm going to take you behind the scenes to see the conservation center where we repair artwork before it goes on display. As you can see, we have an extensive collection of historic pigments here. We use them as a reference when we're researching the material composition of older paintings. ⁶We recently released a book on the subject if you want to learn more about it.

이번 클라우스톤 미술관 투어에서는, 저희가 미술품이 전시되기 전에 수리하는 곳인 ⁵보존 센터를 보실 수 있도록 이면의 공간으로 여러분을 안내해 드릴 겁니다. 보시다시피, 저희는 이곳에 방대한 양의 역사적인 안료를 보유하고 있습니다. 저희는 오래된 그림들의 소재 구성을 조사할 때 이것들을 참고 자료로 사용합니다. ⁶이 주제에 대해 더 알고 싶으시다면, 저희가 최근 이 주제에 관한 책을 한 권 발간했습니다.

어휘 conservation 보존, 보호 pigment 안료, 색소 composition 구성 (요소) release 발간하다, 공개하다

5 투어는 미술관의 어느 부분에서 시작될 것인가?
(A) 풍경화 전시회
(B) 보존 담당 부서

해설 **세부 사항 – 투어 시작 지점**

초반부에서 보존 센터를 볼 수 있도록 청자들을 안내할 것(I'm going to take you behind the scenes to see the conservation center)이라고 했으므로 (B)가 정답이다.

어휘 landscape painting 풍경화 exhibit 전시(회)

6 화자에 따르면, 청자들은 어떻게 주제에 대해 더 알 수 있는가?
(A) 오디오 가이드를 들음으로써
(B) 최근의 출판물을 읽음으로써

해설 **세부 사항 – 주제에 대해 더 알 수 있는 방법**

후반부에서 이 주제에 대해 더 알아보고 싶으면 최근에 해당 주제에 관한 책을 한 권 발간했다(We recently released a book on the subject if you want to learn more about it)고 했으므로 (B)가 정답이다.

> Paraphrasing 담화의 recently released a book → 정답의 a recent publication

ETS 실전문제   본책 p.116

1 (A)	2 (C)	3 (B)	4 (A)	5 (D)	6 (A)
7 (B)	8 (C)	9 (A)	10 (A)	11 (D)	12 (B)
13 (A)	14 (C)	15 (C)	16 (C)	17 (B)	18 (D)
19 (C)	20 (A)	21 (D)			

[1-3] 담화 M-Au

¹Great job building the set for today's rehearsal, crew. Before the actors get here, there's one more thing we need to do. ²We need more props to fill out the set. Remember, the action takes place in an office that's been used for many years, so it should be full of office supplies like books, binders, and folders. In addition, ³Klaus, can you please check to make sure the stage lighting is adjusted properly? It should look like the Sun is rising.

¹오늘 리허설을 위해 세트를 만드시느라 대단히 수고 많으셨습니다, 팀원 여러분. 배우들이 이곳에 오기 전에, 우리가 해야 할 일이 한 가지 더 있습니다. ²세트를 채울 소품이 더 필요합니다. 기억하세요, 사건이 수년 동안 이용되어 온 사무실에서 발생하기 때문에, 책과 바인더, 그리고 폴더 같은 사무용품으로 가득해야 해요. 추가로, ³클라우스 씨, 무대 조명이 제대로 조정되어 있는지 확인해 주시겠어요? 태양이 떠오르고 있는 것처럼 보여야 합니다.

어휘 rehearsal 리허설, 예행 연습 crew (함께 작업하는) 팀, 조 prop 소품 adjust 조정하다, 조절하다 properly 제대로, 적절히 look like ~하는 것처럼 보이다

1 화자는 누구인 것 같은가?
(A) 연극 스태프 팀장   (B) 의상 디자이너
(C) 배우   (D) 음향 기술자

해설 **전체 내용 – 화자의 직업**

초반부에 청자들에게 리허설을 위해 세트를 만드느라 수고 많았다는 말과 함께 배우들이 오기 전에 해야 할 일이 한 가지 더 있다(Great job building the set for today's rehearsal, crew. Before the actors get here, there's one more thing we need to do)고 한 것으로 보아 화자는 연극 공연을 준비하는 스태프들을 이끄는 역할임을 알 수 있다. 따라서 (A)가 정답이다.

어휘 theater 연극, 무대 공연물

2 화자는 무엇이 늘어나야 한다고 말하는가?
(A) 대본의 길이 (B) 팀워크의 수준
(C) 소품의 숫자 (D) 자금의 액수

해설 세부 사항 – 늘어나야 하는 것
중반부에서 세트를 채울 소품이 더 필요하다(We need more props to fill out the set)고 했으므로 (C)가 정답이다.

어휘 script 대본, 원고 amount 액수, 수량 funding 자금

> **Paraphrasing** 담화의 need more → 질문의 needs to be increased

3 클라우스 씨는 무엇을 확인하도록 요청받는가?
(A) 보안 시스템 (B) 조명
(C) 용품 목록 (D) 점심 식사 배달

해설 세부 사항 – 클라우스 씨가 확인해야 하는 것
후반부에서 클라우스 씨의 이름을 부르면서 무대 조명이 제대로 조정되어 있는지 확인해 달라(Klaus, can you please check to make sure the stage lighting is adjusted properly?)고 요청했으므로 (B)가 정답이다.

[4-6] 연설 발췌 W-Am

> **4 It's great to see such a large crowd gathered at this retirement celebration for our colleague Nathan Milo.** It's not surprising, though, that so many of us want to honor Nathan for his contributions to our company. Although he has many talents, I think **5 what I've appreciated most is Nathan's ability to lead.** When he took over as our chief creative director, our company Main Stay Advertising was a small local business, but due to his leadership, **6 it is now one of the best-known companies in the country.** I think I speak for us all when I say thank you, Nathan. We wish you all the best in your retirement.
>
> **4** 동료인 네이든 마일로의 퇴임식에 이렇게 많은 분들이 모여 주셔서 기쁩니다. 하지만 우리 중 다수가 네이든이 회사에 한 공헌을 기념하고 싶어 한다는 것은 그리 놀라운 일이 아닙니다. 많은 재능을 갖췄지만 **5** 제가 가장 인정하는 부분은 네이든의 통솔력입니다. 그가 광고 제작 수석 감독을 맡았을 때, 우리 메인 스테이 애드버타이징은 소규모 지역 업체였지만 그의 리더십 덕분에 **6** 현재는 국내에서 가장 이름난 회사 중 하나가 됐습니다. 네이든, 제가 감사하다고 이야기하는 것은 우리 모두를 대신해서 하는 말입니다. 은퇴 후 모든 것이 잘되기를 바랍니다.

어휘 crowd 군중 retirement 은퇴, 퇴직 celebration 기념 행사 colleague 동료 contribution 기여, 공헌 appreciate 인정하다, 높이 평가하다 take over as ~를 맡다

4 연설의 목적은 무엇인가?
(A) 은퇴하는 직원을 기념하려고
(B) 행정상의 변동을 설명하려고
(C) 새로운 광고 캠페인을 발표하려고
(D) 수상자를 소개하려고

해설 전체 내용 – 연설의 목적
초반부에서 동료인 네이든 마일로의 퇴임식에 많은 사람들이 모여서 기쁘다(It's great to see such a large crowd gathered at this retirement celebration for our colleague Nathan Milo)고 한 뒤, 그의 헌신에 대해 설명하고 감사를 표현했으므로 (A)가 정답이다.

어휘 administrative 행정상의, 관리상의 present 소개하다

5 화자는 네이든 마일로에 대해 어떤 점을 인정한다고 말하는가?
(A) 예술적인 재능 (B) 재무 경험
(C) 기술적인 역량 (D) 통솔력

해설 세부 사항 – 화자가 네이든 마일로에 대해 인정하는 점
중반부에서 화자가 가장 인정하는 부분은 네이든의 통솔력(what I've appreciated most is Nathan's ability to lead)이라고 했으므로 (D)가 정답이다.

어휘 artistic 예술의 financial 금융의, 재무의

> **Paraphrasing** 담화의 Nathan's ability to lead → 정답의 His leadership Ability

6 화자는 회사에 대해 무엇이라고 말하는가?
(A) 전국적으로 잘 알려져 있다.
(B) 내년에 이전할 예정이다.
(C) 직원을 더 채용할 계획이다.
(D) 신문 기사에 나왔다.

해설 세부 사항 – 화자가 회사에 대해 언급한 사항
후반부에서 회사가 현재는 국내에서 가장 이름난 회사 중 하나가 됐다(it is now one of the best-known companies in the country)고 했으므로 (A)가 정답이다.

어휘 relocate 이전하다, 이동하다

> **Paraphrasing** 담화의 one of the best-known companies in the country → 정답의 well-known throughout the country

[7-9] 담화 W-Br

> Thank you for inviting me to your guitar manufacturing plant. My name is Ingrid Weber, and I'm the president of LVC Materials. **7/8 I'm here to tell you about a new material we produce that can be used to make musical instruments.** LVC has developed an innovative wood-like product made from the materials of linen and resin. **7/8 It looks like real wood but is lighter and more durable.** And just so you know, we've already

partnered with several other instrument makers. **9Now, I'd like to show you one of our musical instruments. I brought a guitar so you can hear its excellent sound quality.**

귀사의 기타 제조 공장에 저를 초대해 주셔서 감사합니다. 저는 LVC 머티리얼의 잉그리드 웨버 회장입니다. 7/8저희가 생산하는 악기 제조가 가능한 새로운 소재에 대해 말씀드리러 왔습니다. LVC는 리넨과 수지 소재로 나무와 같은 혁신적인 제품을 개발했습니다. 7/8진짜 나무처럼 보이지만 더 가볍고 내구성이 더욱 좋습니다. 참고로, 저희는 이미 여러 악기 제조업체와 제휴하고 있습니다. 9이제 여러분께 저희 악기 중 하나를 보여드리고자 합니다. 기타를 가져왔으니 훌륭한 음질을 들어 보실 수 있습니다.

어휘 manufacturing 제조 plant 공장 material 재료, 소재 musical instrument 악기 develop 개발하다 innovative 혁신적인 resin 수지 durable 내구성이 있는 partner with ~와 제휴하다, 협력하다

7 화자는 소재의 어떤 점이 특별하다고 말하는가?
  (A) 제조하는 데 비용이 적게 든다.
  (B) 천연 나무와 비슷하다.
  (C) 환경친화적이다.
  (D) 다양한 색상이 있다.

해설 세부 사항 – 화자가 소재에 대해 특별하다고 언급한 사항
초반부에 화자가 회사가 생산하는 새로운 소재에 대해 알려주기 위해 왔다(I'm here to tell you about a new material we produce)고 한 뒤, 이 소재가 진짜 나무처럼 보이지만 더 가볍고 내구성이 더욱 좋다(It looks like real wood but is lighter and more durable)고 했으므로 (B)가 정답이다.

어휘 inexpensive 저렴한 resemble 닮다, 비슷하다 environmentally friendly 환경친화적인

Paraphrasing 담화의 looks like real wood → 정답의 resembles natural wood

8 화자는 왜 "저희는 이미 여러 악기 제조업체와 제휴하고 있습니다"라고 말하는가?
  (A) 청자들이 자신들과 거래하도록 장려하려고
  (B) 지연되는 이유를 제시하려고
  (C) 청자들을 행사에 초대하려고
  (D) 동료의 제안을 거절하려고

해설 화자의 의도 파악
초반부에 기타 제조 공장을 방문한 목적과 새로운 생산 소재에 대해 설명(I'm here to tell you about a new material we produce ~)한 뒤 인용문을 언급했으므로 청자들이 자신의 회사와 거래하도록 설득하려는 의도임을 알 수 있다. 따라서 (A)가 정답이다.

어휘 encourage 격려하다, 장려하다 do business with ~와 거래하다 delay 지연 reject 거절하다 suggestion 제안

9 화자는 다음에 무엇을 할 것인가?
  (A) 시연하기   (B) 조사하기
  (C) 과정 설명하기   (D) 안내책자 나눠 주기

해설 세부 사항 – 화자가 다음에 할 일
후반부에 악기 하나를 보여주겠다(I'd like to show you one of our musical instruments)며 기타의 훌륭한 음질을 들을 수 있을 것(so you can hear its excellent sound quality)이라고 했으므로 (A)가 정답이다.

[10-12] 담화 M-Au

Good evening, and thank you all for attending this dinner. **10We're here to honor the recent graduates of the Akron carpenters' association apprenticeship program.** It takes years of persistence and hard work for apprentices to graduate from this program and become certified carpenters, so this accomplishment is certainly worth celebrating. I'm sure that **11many of the friends and family who have come tonight are curious about what kind of training the apprentice program involves.** So, before we eat, **11I'll show you a video depicting a typical day in the life of our apprentices.** And **12after dinner, join us for dancing in the ballroom.**

안녕하세요. 오늘 저녁 식사에 와 주셔서 감사합니다. 10오늘은 아크론 목수협회 인턴십 프로그램의 최근 졸업자들을 축하하기 위해 여기 모였습니다. 인턴들이 이 프로그램을 졸업하고 공인된 목수가 되는 데 수년간의 끈기와 노고를 들였으니, 이번 성취는 분명 축하할 만한 가치가 있습니다. 11오늘 오신 많은 친구와 가족 여러분께서는 인턴십 프로그램에 어떤 종류의 교육이 수반되는지 궁금해하실 거라 생각합니다. 그래서 식사에 앞서 11인턴들의 전형적인 하루 일과를 묘사한 동영상을 보여드리려고 합니다. 12저녁 식사 후에는 무도회장에서 함께 춤을 추시죠.

어휘 apprenticeship 수습직, 인턴십 certified 공인된 worth -ing ~할 가치가 있다 depict 그리다, 묘사하다

10 행사의 목적은 무엇인가?
  (A) 새로운 졸업자들을 기념하려고
  (B) 건물을 개관하려고
  (C) 직원의 은퇴를 기념하려고
  (D) 단체 기금을 조성하려고

해설 세부 사항 – 행사의 목적
초반부에서 아크론 목수협회 인턴십 프로그램의 최근 졸업자들을 축하하기 위해 여기 모였다(We're here to honor the recent graduates of the Akron carpenters' association apprenticeship program)고 했으므로 (A)가 정답이다.

어휘 dedicate 바치다, 봉헌하다

Paraphrasing 담화의 the recent graduates → 정답의 new graduates

11 동영상은 무엇에 대한 것인가?
  (A) 새 자선 단체   (B) 회사 발전
  (C) 역사적 장소   **(D) 교육 프로그램**

해설 세부 사항 – 동영상의 내용

중반부에서 참석한 친구와 가족이 인턴십 프로그램에 어떤 종류의 교육이 수반되는지(what kind of training the apprentice program involves) 궁금해할 것이라고 한 뒤, 인턴들의 전형적인 하루 일과를 묘사한 동영상을 보여주겠다(I'll show you a video depicting a typical day in the life of our apprentices)고 했으므로 동영상이 교육 프로그램 관련 내용을 담고 있음을 알 수 있다. 따라서 (D)가 정답이다.

12 식사 후에는 무슨 일이 있을 것인가?
(A) 건물 견학   (B) 댄스 파티
(C) 회장 연설   (D) 단체 사진

해설 세부 사항 – 식사 후에 있을 일

후반부에서 저녁 식사 후에 무도회장에서 함께 춤을 추자(after dinner, join us for dancing in the ballroom)고 했으므로 (B)가 정답이다.

[13-15] 연설 M-Cn

And now, the moment you've all been waiting for. **13 The judges' votes are in, and our Product Designer of the Year Award goes to Yun Hang for his battery-powered light fixture, the Homeglow.** Mr. Hang's fixture requires no electrical wiring, so it's extremely versatile. **14 Buyers will appreciate this because they'll be able to use it during a power failure, or in an older home that lacks conveniently located outlets. 15 Starting in March, the Homeglow will be sold at most major home-improvement stores.** Let's hear it for Yun Hang!

자 이제, 여러분께서 모두 계속 기다리시던 순간입니다. **13** 심사위원단의 투표 결과가 나왔고, 올해의 제품 디자이너 상은 배터리로 작동되는 조명 기구인 홈글로우를 디자인한 윤 항 씨에게 수여됩니다. 항 씨의 조명 기구는 전기 배선이 필요하지 않아 매우 다용도로 쓰일 수 있습니다. **14** 구매자들은 정전 시, 또는 편리한 위치의 콘센트가 부족한 오래된 집에서도 사용할 수 있기 때문에 이 제품을 높이 평가할 것입니다. **15** 3월부터, 홈글로우는 대부분의 주요 주택 개량용품 매장에서 판매될 예정입니다. 윤 항 씨에게 큰 박수 부탁드립니다!

어휘 light fixture 조명 기구   electrical wiring 전기 배선   extremely 대단히, 매우   versatile 다용도의, 다재다능한   power failure 정전   lack 부족하다   outlet (전기) 콘센트   home-improvement store 주택 개량용품 매장   Let's hear it for ~에게 박수를 보냅시다

13 청자들은 어디에 있는 것 같은가?
(A) 시상식   (B) 주택 수리 워크숍
(C) 영업 회의   (D) 직원 교육

해설 전체 내용 – 담화 장소

연설의 초반부에서 심사위원단의 투표 결과가 전달된 사실을 언급하면서 올해의 제품 디자이너 상을 받는 사람의 이름(The judges' votes are in, and our Product Designer of the Year Award goes to Yun Hang ~)을 발표하고 있으므로 (A)가 정답이다.

14 화자는 구매자들이 제품과 관련해 무엇을 높이 평가할 것이라고 말하는가?
(A) 많은 색상으로 구입 가능하다.
(B) 조작하기 간단하다.
(C) 전기 콘센트가 필요하지 않다.
(D) 주기적인 유지 관리가 필요하지 않다.

해설 세부 사항 – 구매자들이 높이 평가할 것으로 예상되는 부분

중반부에서 구매자들이 해당 제품을 높이 평가할 이유로 정전 시, 또는 편리한 위치의 콘센트가 부족한 오래된 집에서도 사용할 수 있다(Buyers will appreciate this because they'll be able to use it during a power failure, or in an older home that lacks conveniently located outlets)는 특징을 언급했으므로 (C)가 정답이다.

Paraphrasing 담화의 be able to use it ~ in an older home that lacks conveniently located outlets → 정답의 needs no electrical outlet

15 화자에 따르면, 3월에 무슨 일이 일어날 것인가?
(A) 인터뷰가 진행될 것이다.
(B) 제품이 잡지에 특집으로 실릴 것이다.
(C) 제품이 구입 가능해질 것이다.
(D) 주택 개량용품 매장이 개장할 것이다.

해설 세부 사항 – 3월에 일어날 일

후반부에서 3월부터 홈글로우가 대부분의 주요 주택 개조용품 매장에서 판매될 것(Starting in March, the Homeglow will be sold at most major home-improvement stores)이라고 했으므로 (C)가 정답이다.

Paraphrasing 담화의 the Homeglow will be sold → 정답의 A product will be available for purchase

[16-18] 담화 W-Am

Good morning, everyone! **16 I'm happy to be giving this presentation here at the Cairo Farming Convention.** This convention always helps me stay up to date with recent innovations in farming equipment. My company, Salazar Manufacturing, builds silos—large storage units for grain, coal, and other agricultural materials. Now, **17 I'm going to play a video** that demonstrates how our proprietary elevator system fills the silos. After the video, **18 I'll only have a few minutes to answer questions,** but I'll be at booth 40 for the rest of the day.

안녕하세요, 여러분! **16**이곳 카이로 농업 박람회에서 발표를 하게 되어 기쁩니다. 이 박람회는 항상 제가 최신 농업 장비 혁신을 파악하는 데 도움을 줍니다. 저희 회사인 살라자르 제조는 사일로, 즉 곡물과 석탄, 그리고 기타 농업용 물품들을 넣어 두는 대형 저장고를 만듭니다. 자, 제가 어떻게 저희 고유의 엘리베이터 시스템이 사일로를 채우는지 보여 주는 **17**동영상을 틀어드리겠습니다. 동영상 이후, **18**제가 질문에 답변해 드릴 시간은 불과 몇 분 밖에 없겠지만, 오늘 남은 시간 동안 40번 부스에 있을 예정입니다.

어휘 up to date 최신의   silo 사일로(타워 모양의 저장고)   storage unit 저장고, 저장 시설   grain 곡물   agricultural 농업의   proprietary 고유의, 독점의

16 청자들은 어떤 업계에서 일하는 것 같은가?
(A) 접객 서비스   (B) 연예
(C) 농업   (D) 제조

해설 **전체 내용 - 청자들의 근무 업계**
초반부에서 화자가 농업 박람회에서 발표를 하게 되어 기쁘다 (I'm happy to be giving this presentation here at the Cairo Farming Convention)고 했으므로 (C)가 정답이다.

17 화자는 다음에 무엇을 할 것인가?
(A) 견학 제공하기
(B) 동영상 보여 주기
(C) 연락처 수집하기
(D) 명함 나눠 주기

해설 **세부 사항 - 화자가 다음에 할 일**
중반부에서 화자가 고유의 엘리베이터 시스템이 어떻게 사일로를 채우는지 보여 주는 동영상을 틀어 드리겠다(I'm going to play a video a video)고 했으므로 (B)가 정답이다.

어휘 collect 수집하다, 모으다

Paraphrasing 담화의 play a video → 정답의 Show a video

18 화자는 왜 "오늘 남은 시간 동안 40번 부스에 있을 예정입니다"라고 말하는가?
(A) 장소와 관련된 불만을 제기하기 위해
(B) 업무에 도움을 요청하기 위해
(C) 초대를 거절한 것을 사과하기 위해
(D) 청자들이 어떻게 추가 정보를 얻을 수 있는지 설명하기 위해

해설 **화자의 의도 파악**
후반부에서 동영상 이후에 질문에 답변할 시간은 불과 몇 분 밖에 없을 것(After the video, I'll only have a few minutes to answer questions)이라고 한 뒤 인용문을 언급했으므로 청자들이 원한다면 추가로 대화를 나눌 수 있는 방법을 알려주는 의도임을 알 수 있다. 따라서 (D)가 정답이다.

[19-21] 담화 + 지도 W-Am

Hello—welcome to the Visitors Center at Mountainside Park. **19**My name's Josephine and I'll be guiding your hike today. **20**Normally we'd be taking the Heron Trail to the Picnic Area, but the second part of that trail is closed for maintenance this week. So instead, we'll be starting out on the Heron Trail and changing over midway to the Pine Trail, as you can see here on the map. We'll break for our lunch at the end of the Pine Trail, and then we'll take the Sunset Trail back to our starting point. **21**It's supposed to be sunny today, so it's a good idea to put on some sunscreen and wear a hat.

안녕하세요, 마운틴사이드 공원 방문자 센터에 오신 것을 환영합니다. **19**제 이름은 조세핀이며 오늘 여러분의 하이킹을 안내해드릴 겁니다. **20**우리는 보통 헤론 길을 이용해 피크닉 구역으로 갑니다만, 그 길의 두 번째 구역이 이번 주 보수 작업 때문에 폐쇄되었습니다. 그래서 대신 여기 지도상에서 보시는 것처럼 우리는 헤론 길에서 출발해 중간쯤에서 파인 길로 빠질 겁니다. 파인 길 끝에서 점심 휴식 시간을 가진 다음 선셋 길을 이용해 다시 출발 지점으로 돌아오겠습니다. **21**오늘은 햇볕이 내리쬘 것이므로 자외선 차단제를 바르고 모자를 쓰는 것이 좋습니다.

어휘 hike 하이킹   midway 중간에, 도중에   put on (화장품 등을) 바르다   sunscreen 자외선 차단제

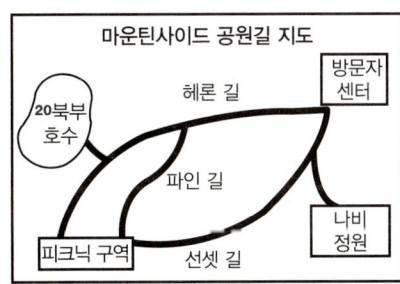

19 청자들은 누구인 것 같은가?
(A) 관리 직원들   (B) 버스 기사들
(C) 관광객들   (D) 공원 경비원들

해설 **전체 내용 - 청자의 직업**
초반부에 화자가 자신을 소개하며 오늘 하이킹을 안내할 것(My name's Josephine and I'll be guiding your hike today)이라고 했으므로 청자들은 관광객임을 추론할 수 있다. 따라서 (C)가 정답이다.

20 시각 정보에 따르면, 청자들은 오늘 어디에 갈 수 없을 것인가?
(A) 북부 호수   (B) 피크닉 구역
(C) 나비 정원   (D) 방문자 센터

해설 **세부 사항 – 시각 정보 연계**
중반부에 보통은 헤론 길을 이용해 피크닉 구역으로 가지만 그 길의 두 번째 구간이 이번 주 정비 작업 때문에 폐쇄되었다(Normally we'd be taking the Heron Trail to the Picnic Area, but the second part of that trail is closed for maintenance this week)고 하며, 헤론 길에서 출발해 중간쯤에서 파인 길로 빠지겠다(So instead, we'll be starting out on the Heron Trail and changing over midway to the Pine Trail)고 했다. 지도를 보면 방문자 센터에서 출발해 파인 길로 빠지게 될 경우 북부 호수에는 갈 수 없다는 것을 알 수 있으므로 (A)가 정답이다.

21 여자는 청자들에게 무엇을 하라고 권하는가?
(A) 지도 지참   (B) 일기예보 확인
(C) 소지품 보관   **(D) 자외선 차단제 사용**

해설 **세부 사항 – 권장 사항**
후반부에 오늘은 햇볕이 내리쬘 것이므로 자외선 차단제를 바르고 모자를 쓰는 것이 좋다(It's supposed to be sunny today, so it's a good idea to put on some sunscreen and wear a hat)고 했으므로 (D)가 정답이다.

> **Paraphrasing** 담화의 put on some sunscreen → 정답의 Use sun protection

UNIT 14 광고/방송

담화 구성과 단서 파악 ················· 본책 p.118

> 시티 악기점이 새 매장을 열었습니다! 십 년 이상 시티 악기점은 굉장히 저렴한 가격에 악기를 제공해 왔으며, 이를 자랑스럽게 생각하고 있습니다. 최근에 저희는 도심에 있는 지점에 이어 스카일러 빌 쇼핑센터에도 새로운 매장을 열었습니다. 새로운 지점에 방문하시는 고객님들을 환영하는 의미에서, **한정된 기간 동안 어떤 악기를 구입하시든 간에 해당 악기에 대한 한 달 무료 음악 수업을 제공해 드리려고 합니다.** 그리고 이번 주 토요일에만, 여러분의 쇼핑 편의를 위해 늦게까지 문을 열어둘 것입니다.

1 무엇이 광고되고 있는가?
(A) 라디오 프로그램   **(B) 상점 개점**

2 어떤 특별 혜택이 있겠는가?
(A) 선호 좌석   **(B) 무료 음악 강좌**

3 토요일에 무슨 일이 일어날 것인가?
(A) 영업 시간이 연장된다.
(B) 밴드가 공연을 한다.

ETS 유형연습   본책 p.119

| **1** (B) | **2** (B) | **3** (B) | **4** (B) | **5** (A) | **6** (B) |

[1-2] 방송 M-Cn

> [1]This is Ken Harrison with a **special traffic report.** If you are driving southbound on Clover Street, you should be ready for delays. [2]**There is a break in a water pipe between Morris Boulevard and Ridge Avenue, which has caused the right lane to be closed down.** The police are now on the scene directing traffic, but things are still moving quite slowly on Clover. We recommend avoiding Clover Street altogether and taking an alternate route. Our next traffic report will be in fifteen minutes, so keep listening.
>
> [1]특별 교통 방송을 보내 드리는 켄 해리슨입니다. 클로버 가 남행 노선에서 운전하고 계시다면, 지체에 대비하셔야겠습니다. [2]모리스 대로와 리지 가 사이에 수도관이 파열되어 오른쪽 차선이 폐쇄되었습니다. 지금 경찰이 현장에서 교통정리를 하고 있지만, 여전히 클로버 가의 진행이 상당히 느립니다. 저희는 클로버 가를 완전히 피하고 우회로로 가실 것을 추천합니다. 저희 다음 교통 방송은 15분 후에 있습니다. 계속 청취해 주십시오.
>
> **어휘** southbound 남행의 delay 지체 water pipe 수도관 lane 차선 close down 폐쇄하다 direct traffic 교통정리를 하다 recommend 추천하다 altogether 완전히, 전적으로 alternate route 우회로

1 이 방송은 누구를 대상으로 하는가?
(A) 교통경찰   **(B) 차량 운전자**

해설 **전체 내용 – 방송 대상**
화자가 자신을 특별 교통 방송을 전하는 켄 해리슨(This is Ken Harrison with a special traffic report)이라고 했으므로 방송 대상은 차량 운전자들이다. 따라서 (B)가 정답이다.

2 무엇이 문제를 일으켰는가?
(A) 고장 난 교통 신호등   **(B) 파열된 수도관**

해설 **세부 사항 – 문제의 원인**
초반부에서 모리스 대로와 리지 가의 수도관이 파열되어 (There is a break in a water pipe between Morris Boulevard and Ridge Avenue) 교통이 정체된다고 했으므로 (B)가 정답이다.

어휘 defective 결함이 있는

[3-4] 방송 W-Br

> Welcome back to *Odd Job Journeys*, [3]**the podcast where we interview people who've found success through quirky and interesting jobs.** Now, it may seem like everyone's reading fewer books nowadays, but [4]**audiobooks have actually grown in popularity in recent years.** I like them myself because they allow me to multitask. And today's guest, Pablo Espinoza, has a lot to say about this trend.

3 독특하고 흥미로운 직업을 통해 성공을 거둔 분들을 인터뷰하는 팟캐스트, 〈기묘한 직업 여행〉을 다시 찾아 주신 것을 환영합니다. 요즘 모두가 책을 덜 읽는 것처럼 보일 수도 있지만, 4실제로는 오디오북의 인기가 최근 몇 년 사이에 크게 늘었습니다. 저도 개인적으로 오디오북을 좋아하는데요, 동시에 여러 일을 할 수 있게 해 주기 때문입니다. 그리고 오늘 초대 손님이신, 파블로 에스피노자 씨께서 이러한 트렌드와 관련해서 해 주실 이야기가 많습니다.

어휘 odd 기묘한, 이상한　find success 성공을 거두다　quirky 기발한, 별난　multitask 동시에 여러 일을 하다　trend 경향, 추세

3 팟캐스트의 주제는 무엇인가?
(A) 도서 평가　　　　**(B) 이색적인 직업**

해설 전체 내용 – 담화의 주제
초반부에서 독특하고 흥미로운 직업을 통해 성공을 거둔 분들을 인터뷰하는 팟캐스트(the podcast where we interview people who've found success through quirky and interesting jobs)라고 소개했으므로 (B)가 정답이다.

4 화자는 최근 몇 년 사이에 무슨 일이 있었다고 말하는가?
(A) 팟캐스트 방송 회차의 길이가 늘어났다.
(B) 오디오북이 더 많은 인기를 얻게 되었다.

해설 세부 사항 – 최근 몇 년 사이에 있었던 일
중반부에서 오디오북의 인기가 최근 몇 년 사이에 크게 늘었다(audiobooks have actually grown in popularity in recent years)고 했으므로 (B)가 정답이다.

어휘 episode 방송 1회분

[5-6] 광고 W-Am

⁶Come to Endwell Shoes this weekend for our annual winter sale! Friday through Sunday, we're taking twenty percent off our entire inventory as we make room for our new styles. ⁵The discount even applies to Ella Bancroft designer boots, which style experts on the Forward Fashion television network say are this season's most popular line of footwear. You'll be sure to find something you like—and at a price that can't be beat. Remember, ⁶the sale ends Sunday, so come take advantage of these great deals while they last!

⁶연례 겨울 할인 행사가 있으니 이번 주말에 엔드웰 슈즈로 오십시오! 신상품을 위한 공간을 마련하기 위해, ⁶금요일부터 일요일까지 전 재고 품목을 20퍼센트 할인해 드립니다. ⁵이 할인 행사는 엘라 밴크로프트 디자이너 부츠에도 적용됩니다. 이 부츠는 포워드 패션 TV 방송에서 스타일 전문가들이 이번 시즌에 가장 인기 있는 신발류로 지목한 품목입니다. 마음에 드는 제품을 꼭 찾으실 수 있을 겁니다. 게다가 가격도 이보다 더 저렴할 수 없습니다. 기억하세요. ⁶할인 행사는 일요일에 끝납니다. 그러니 행사가 끝나기 전에 엄청난 할인 혜택을 누리세요!

어휘 inventory 재고(품)　make room for ~을 위한 공간을 만들다　a line of ~ 상품군　beat 더 낫다, 능가하다　take advantage of ~을 이용하다　deal 흥정, 거래

5 스타일 전문가들은 엘라 밴크로프트 상품에 대해 무엇이라고 말했는가?
(A) 이번 시즌에 인기가 있다.
(B) 천연 재료로 만들어졌다.

해설 세부 사항 – 전문가들의 의견
중반부에서 엘라 밴크로프트 부츠에도 할인이 적용된다고 한 후 스타일 전문가들이 이 부츠를 이번 시즌에 가장 인기 있는 신발류로 지목했다(style experts on the Forward Fashion television network say are this season's most popular line of footwear)고 했으므로 (A)가 정답이다.

6 판촉 행사는 언제 끝나는가?
(A) 토요일　　　　**(B) 일요일**

해설 세부 사항 – 판촉 행사 종료 시점
초반부에서 상품 할인 행사 기간이 금요일부터 일요일까지(Friday through Sunday)라고 했으며, 후반부에서도 할인 행사가 일요일에 끝난다(the sale ends Sunday)고 다시 한 번 강조했으므로 (B)가 정답이다.

어휘 promotion 홍보, 판촉 (행사)

ETS 실전문제　　본책 p.120

1 (B)	2 (D)	3 (A)	4 (C)	5 (B)	6 (A)
7 (D)	8 (C)	9 (A)	10 (A)	11 (C)	12 (C)
13 (A)	14 (B)	15 (D)	16 (D)	17 (C)	18 (A)
19 (C)	20 (D)	21 (D)			

[1-3] 방송 W-Am

Thanks for tuning in for tonight's business report. Today, ¹/²Ashton Holt, a locally based company with over twenty years of experience designing and manufacturing clothing, announced its much-anticipated merger with MW Incorporated. MW Incorporated will provide an online platform for selling Ashton Holt's clothing. ³Make sure to tune in at this time tomorrow for an exclusive interview with the president of Ashton Holt. She'll give us more details about what this merger will mean to the local economy.

오늘 저녁 비즈니스 뉴스를 청취해 주셔서 감사합니다. 오늘, ¹/²20년 이상 의류를 디자인하고 제조해 온 지역 업체 애쉬튼 홀트가 고대해 온 MW 주식회사와의 합병을 발표했습니다. MW 주식회사는 애쉬튼 홀트의 의류 사업에 필요한 온라인 플랫폼을 제공할 것입니다. ³내일 이 시간 애쉬튼 홀트 회장과의 독점 인터뷰가 방송되

니 꼭 청취해 주시기 바랍니다. 애쉬튼 홀트 회장은 이번 합병이 지역 경제에 어떤 의미인지를 더 자세히 설명할 예정입니다.

어휘 tune in 시청하다, 청취하다 locally based 현지에 기반을 둔 manufacture 제조하다 announce 발표하다 incorporated 주식회사의, 유한 책임의 much-anticipated 많이 기다려 온 merger 합병 exclusive 독점적인, 배타적인

1 방송의 목적은 무엇인가?
(A) 매장 개점을 광고하려고
(B) 업체 합병을 발표하려고
(C) 신상품에 대해 이야기하려고
(D) 규정 변경을 보도하려고

해설 전체 내용 – 방송의 목적
초반부에서 지역 업체 애쉬튼 홀트가 MW 주식회사와의 합병을 발표했다(Ashton Holt ~ announced its much-anticipated merger with MW Incorporated)고 했으므로, 두 업체의 합병 소식을 발표하기 위한 방송임을 알 수 있다. 따라서 (B)가 정답이다.

어휘 grand opening 개장, 개점 regulation 규정

2 애쉬튼 홀트는 어떤 종류의 업체인가?
(A) 건설회사   (B) 인테리어 디자인 회사
(C) 광고대행사   (D) 의류업체

해설 세부 사항 – 애쉬튼 홀트의 업종
초반부에서 애쉬튼 홀트를 20년 이상 의류를 디자인하고 제조해 온 지역 업체(a locally based company with over twenty years of experience designing and manufacturing clothing)라고 소개했으므로 (D)가 정답이다.

> **Paraphrasing** 담화의 company with ~ experience designing and manufacturing clothing → 정답의 A clothing company

3 화자는 청자들에게 무엇을 하라고 권하는가?
(A) 인터뷰 청취   (B) 웹사이트 방문
(C) 일자리 지원   (D) 대회 참가

해설 세부 사항 – 화자의 권장 사항
후반부에서 내일 이 시간 애쉬튼 홀트 회장과의 독점 인터뷰가 방송되니 꼭 청취해 주기를 바란다(Make sure to tune in at this time tomorrow for an exclusive interview with the president of Ashton Holt)고 했으므로 (A)가 정답이다.

어휘 apply for ~에 지원하다 enter a contest 대회에 참가하다

> **Paraphrasing** 담화의 tune in ~ for an exclusive interview → 정답의 Listen to an interview

[4-6] 광고 W-Br

Do you love to cook, but find you are missing **4 the appliances you need to prepare larger batches of food?** Consider treating yourself to **4 a new Chef 400 stand mixer.** Just like previous models of our high-quality stand mixer, the Chef 400 comes in six vibrant colors you can choose from to suit your personal style and decor. But in addition to its usual features, **5 this newest model has a larger mixing bowl, almost double the size in volume.** If you try the Chef 400 and decide it's not for you, **6 remember that you can return it to us within 30 days to receive a full refund.** Order yours today!

요리하는 것을 좋아하지만, 4많은 분량의 음식을 준비하는 데 필요한 가전 기기가 부족하다고 느끼시나요? 여러분 자신에게 4새로운 쉐프 400 스탠드 믹서기를 선물하는 것을 고려해 보세요. 이전의 저희 고급형 스탠드 믹서기 모델들과 마찬가지로, 쉐프 400은 여러분의 개인적인 스타일과 실내 장식에 맞게 선택할 수 있는 여섯 가지 생동감 있는 색상으로 출시됩니다. 하지만 기존의 기능들 외에도, 5이 최신 모델은 더 큰 믹싱 볼이 있고 그 용량이 거의 두 배입니다. 쉐프 400을 사용해 보시고 마음에 들지 않으시면, 6저희에게 30일 내로 반품하셔서 전액 환불받으실 수 있다는 점을 기억하시기 바랍니다. 오늘 주문해 보세요!

어휘 appliance 가전 기기 batch (음식 등을 한 번에 만드는) 분량 treat oneself to 자신에게 ~을 선물하다 previous 이전의, 과거의 vibrant 생동감 있는 decor 실내 장식 double the 명사 ~의 두 배 volume 용량, 양

4 무엇이 광고되고 있는가?
(A) 컴퓨터 액세서리   (B) 운동 기계
(C) 주방용 가전 기기   (D) 재봉틀

해설 전체 내용 – 광고 대상
초반부에 많은 분량의 음식 준비에 필요한 가전 기기(the appliances you need to prepare larger batches of food)로써 새로운 쉐프 400 스탠드 믹서기(a new Chef 400 stand mixer)라는 제품을 소개했으므로 (C)가 정답이다.

> **Paraphrasing** 담화의 mixer → 정답의 A kitchen appliance

5 화자에 따르면, 제품은 어떻게 바뀌었는가?
(A) 무게가 덜 나간다.
(B) 용량이 더 크다.
(C) 새로운 색상으로 구입 가능하다.
(D) 설정이 조정하기 더 쉽다.

해설 세부 사항 – 제품의 변경 사항
중반부에 더 큰 믹싱 볼이 있고 그 용량이 거의 두 배(this newest model has a larger mixing bowl, almost double the size in volume)라는 변화를 언급했으므로 (B)가 정답이다.

어휘 capacity 용량, 수용력

> **Paraphrasing** 담화의 almost double the size in volume
> → 정답의 a larger capacity

6 화자는 청자들에게 무엇을 기억하라고 말하는가?
(A) 반품 정책 (B) 출시 날짜
(C) 매장 위치 (D) 할인 제공 혜택

해설 **세부 사항 - 화자가 청자들에게 당부하는 것**
후반부에 30일 내로 반품해 전액 환불받을 수 있다는 점을 기억하라(remember that you can return it to us within 30 days to receive a full refund)고 강조했으므로 (A)가 정답이다.

어휘 release 출시, 발매

> **Paraphrasing** 담화의 return it to us within 30 days to receive a full refund → 정답의 A return policy

[7-9] 방송 M-Au

7 Watcheye News is here on location at the main subway station downtown. We just received details from transit officials about a plan to make a technological improvement to the system's stations. According to officials, **8** five stations will receive updated wireless Internet technology, which will benefit all metro patrons. **8** The new wireless technology will improve coverage throughout the system's stations—as well as in tunnels. For more information on this plan and other improvement efforts, **9** system officials encourage interested citizens to attend monthly board meetings either in person or by joining online.

7〈화치아이 뉴스〉는 현재 시내 주요 지하철역 현장에 나와 있습니다. 저희는 방금 교통 당국으로부터 지하철역 기술 개선 계획에 관한 내용을 전달받았습니다. 관계자들에 따르면, **8**다섯 개 역에 업데이트된 무선 인터넷 기술이 도입될 것이며, 이는 모든 지하철 이용객들에게 혜택을 줄 것입니다. **8**새로운 무선 기술은 지하철역 전역은 물론 터널 내에서도 서비스 범위를 향상시킬 예정입니다. 이 계획 및 기타 개선 노력에 대한 더 많은 정보를 위해, **9**시스템 관계자들은 관심 있는 시민들이 월간 이사회에 직접 참석하거나 온라인으로 참여할 것을 권장하고 있습니다.

어휘 on location 현장에 있는 transit 교통, 수송 official 관계자, 당국자 make an improvement 개선하다 benefit 유익하다 metro 지하철 patron 고객, 손님 improve 개선하다 coverage 서비스 범위, 적용 범위 encourage 권장하다 board 이사회 in person 직접 (가서)

7 화자는 어디에 있는가?
(A) 공항 (B) 박물관
(C) 공공 도서관 **(D) 지하철역**

해설 **전체 내용 - 화자가 있는 장소**
초반부에 현재 시내 주요 지하철역 현장에 나와 있다(Watcheye News is here on location at the main subway station downtown)고 했으므로 (D)가 정답이다.

8 화자에 따르면, 고객들은 업그레이드로부터 어떻게 혜택을 볼 것인가?
(A) 회원 자격이 자동으로 갱신될 것이다.
(B) 고객들이 일정 변경과 관련해 통보받을 것이다.
(C) 무선 인터넷 서비스 범위가 개선될 것이다.
(D) 고객 대기 시간이 줄어들 것이다.

해설 **세부 사항 - 고객들이 받는 혜택**
중반부에서 다섯 개 역에 업데이트된 무선 인터넷 기술이 도입될 것(five stations will receive updated wireless Internet technology)을 언급한 뒤, 그 새로운 무선 기술이 서비스 범위를 개선해 줄 것(The new wireless technology will improve coverage)이라고 했으므로 (C)가 정답이다.

어휘 renew 갱신하다 notify 통보하다, 알리다 decrease 줄어들다, 감소하다

9 일부 청취자들은 무엇을 하도록 권장되는가?
(A) 이사회에 참석하기
(B) 설문 조사에 답하기
(C) 보고서 읽어 보기
(D) 티켓 예매하기

해설 **세부 사항 - 청취자들에게 권장되는 것**
후반부에서 관계자들이 관심 있는 시민들이 월간 이사회에 직접 참석하거나 온라인으로 참여할 것을 권장하고 있다(system officials encourage interested citizens to attend monthly board meetings)고 했으므로 (A)가 정답이다.

어휘 respond to ~에 답변하다, ~에 대응하다 survey 설문 조사(지) reserve 예약하다

[10-12] 팟캐스트 M-Cn

I'd like to start today's podcast with a personal story. As you know, **10** I facilitate workshops for a living. I honed the skill of facilitation over a long period of time. I remember one early workshop I was leading where I had carefully designed every aspect down to the minute. **11** I had planned everything except the question-and-answer session. Then we went seriously overtime. The importance of planning for every aspect of a workshop is the subject of Amanda Ross's brilliant new book. **12** I've invited her on the show today to share her expertise.

개인적인 이야기로 오늘 팟캐스트를 시작하고자 합니다. 아시다시피, **10**저는 워크숍을 원활히 진행하는 일을 업으로 삼고 있어요. 오랜 기간에 걸쳐 원활한 진행의 기술을 연마했죠. 제가 초기에 진행했던 워크숍 중, 모든 부분을 분 단위로 세심하게 설계했던 것 하나

121

가 기억납니다. **11질의응답 시간을 제외하고 모든 것을 계획했었죠. 결국 저희는 심각할 정도로 시간을 초과했습니다.** 워크숍의 모든 측면을 계획하는 것의 중요성은 아만다 로스 씨의 훌륭한 신간에서 다루고 있는 주제입니다. **12이분의 전문 지식을 공유하기 위해 오늘 쇼에 초대했습니다.**

> **어휘** facilitate 원활히 진행하다, 용이하게 하다 | for a living 업으로 삼아, 생계를 위해 | hone (기술 등을) 갈고 닦다, 연마하다 | down to the minute 분 단위로, 아주 세밀하게 | overtime 시간을 초과한, 시간 외의 | brilliant 훌륭한, 뛰어난, 눈부신

10 화자는 생계를 위해 무엇을 한다고 말하는가?
(A) 워크숍을 진행한다.
(B) 스포츠 코치를 한다.
(C) 건물을 디자인한다.
(D) 책에 삽화를 그려 넣는다.

해설 전체 내용 – 화자가 생계를 위해 하는 일
초반부에서 화자가 워크숍을 원활히 진행하는 일을 업으로 삼고 있다(I facilitate workshops for a living)고 했으므로 (A)가 정답이다.

어휘 lead 진행하다, 이끌다 | illustrate 삽화를 넣다

> **Paraphrasing** 담화의 facilitate → 정답의 leads

11 화자가 "저희는 심각할 정도로 시간을 초과했습니다"라고 말할 때 무엇을 의미하는가?
(A) 어쩔 수 없이 늦게 시작해야 했다.
(B) 더 많이 연습했어야 했다.
(C) 계획과 관련된 실수를 했다.
(D) 일부 부정적인 의견을 받았다.

해설 화자의 의도 파악
중반부에서 질의응답 시간을 제외하고 모든 것을 계획했다(I had planned everything except the question-and-answer session)고 한 뒤 인용문을 언급했으므로 잘못된 계획으로 인한 부정적인 결과에 대해 이야기하려는 의도임을 알 수 있다. 따라서 (C)가 정답이다.

어휘 be forced to do 어쩔 수 없이 ~하다

12 청자들은 다음에 무엇을 들을 것 같은가?
(A) 청자의 질문 (B) 광고
(C) 인터뷰 (D) 다음 방송분의 예고편

해설 세부 사항 – 청자들이 다음에 듣는 것
후반부에서 아만다 로스 씨를 언급하면서 이분의 전문 지식을 공유하기 위해 오늘 쇼에 초대했다(I've invited her on the show today to share her expertise)고 했으므로 (C)가 정답이다.

어휘 preview 예고편, 시사회, 미리보기

> **Paraphrasing** 담화의 share her expertise → 정답의 An interview

[13-15] 방송 W-Am

Good morning, this is Rebecca Melaney in the weather room with your hourly weather report. **13We'll have more unseasonably warm weather today.** Although spring is still a month away, we can expect sunny skies and temperatures approaching 20 degrees Celsius in the city today. The National Weather Center reports that a high-pressure system over the western part of the country is keeping the usual winter rains and clouds well to the north of us. **14Things are likely to change early next week, though.** The weather center expects the high-pressure system to begin breaking down on Sunday. **14The clouds will return and high temperatures should drop to around 12 degrees,** which is right around average for this time of the year. It's seven o'clock now; **15we'll have the next weather report in exactly one hour, along with the daily traffic update.**

좋은 아침입니다. 저는 매시간 날씨를 전해드리는 기상 상황실의 레베카 멜라니입니다. **13오늘은 때 아니게 날씨가 덥겠습니다.** 봄이 되려면 아직 한 달이나 더 있어야 하지만, 오늘은 도시의 날씨가 화창하고 기온이 섭씨 20도에 육박할 것으로 예상됩니다. 국립 기상 센터는 나라의 서부 지역에 형성된 고기압이 통상적인 겨울비와 구름을 북쪽 지역에 묶어 두고 있다고 전합니다. **14하지만 다음 주 초에는 이런 상황이 변할 것 같습니다.** 기상 센터는 일요일에 고기압이 약화되기 시작할 것이라고 예상합니다. **14구름이 다시 돌아오고 높은 기온은 약 12도로 떨어질 것으로 보이는데,** 이는 연중 이맘때의 평균 기온에 해당됩니다. 지금 시각은 7시입니다. **15다음 일기 예보는 정확히 한 시간 후에 오늘의 최신 교통 정보와 함께 전해드립니다.**

> **어휘** unseasonably 철에 맞지 않게, 때 아니게 | Celsius 섭씨의 | high-pressure 고기압의 | break down 붕괴하다, 약화되다 | this time of the year 연중 이맘때 | traffic update 최신 교통 정보

13 화자는 오늘의 날씨에 대해 무엇을 시사하는가?
(A) 이례적으로 따뜻할 것이다.
(B) 하루 종일 비가 올 것이다.
(C) 교통 문제를 일으킬 것이다.
(D) 오늘 이따가 변할 것이다.

해설 세부 사항 – 오늘의 날씨 정보
초반부에 오늘은 때 아니게 날씨가 더울 것(We'll have more unseasonably warm weather today)이라고 했으므로 (A)가 정답이다.

어휘 unusually 유별나게, 이례적으로

> **Paraphrasing** 담화의 unseasonably → 정답의 unusually

14 다음 주에 무슨 일이 일어날 것 같은가?
(A) 봄이 시작될 것이다.
(B) 기온이 내려갈 것이다.
(C) 기상 센터가 문을 닫을 것이다.
(D) 날마다 날씨가 매우 화창할 것이다.

해설 **세부 사항 - 다음 주에 일어날 일**
중반부에서 다음 주에 상황이 변할 것이라고 한 뒤, 높은 기온이 약 12도로 떨어질 것(high temperatures should drop to around 12 degrees)이라고 했으므로 (B)가 정답이다.

Paraphrasing 담화의 drop → 정답의 decrease

15 다음 일기 예보는 언제 있겠는가?
(A) 12분 후   (B) 20분 후
(C) 30분 후   **(D) 1시간 후**

해설 **세부 사항 - 다음 일기 예보 시점**
후반부에서 다음 일기 예보는 정확히 한 시간 후에 최신 교통 정보와 함께 전하겠다(we'll have the next weather report in exactly one hour, along with the daily traffic update)고 했으므로 (D)가 정답이다.

[16-18] 광고 W-Br

If your office needs renovating, why not choose a company you trust? **16Yang Brothers is the number-one commercial remodeling contractor in the Springbridge area.** From reception areas to offices, conference rooms and amenities… we do it all! Not only do we offer complete design-and-build services, but we also guarantee long-term quality. **17Unlike our competitors, we offer a free one-year inspection program:** one year after the project is completed, we will come check that everything in your renovated space is working as it should. **18Visit our Web site at www.yangbrothers.com to see pictures of other commercial spaces we've remodeled.** You're sure to be impressed by the creativity and quality of our past projects. No matter the workspace, Yang Brothers has a solution for you.

귀하의 사무실을 보수해야 한다면 신뢰하는 업체를 선택해야 하지 않을까요? **16양 브라더스는 스프링브리지 지역 최고의 상가 리모델링 건설업체입니다.** 안내 구역부터 사무실, 회의실, 편의 시설에 이르기까지 모든 작업을 해 드립니다. 완벽한 설계 및 건축 서비스를 제공할 뿐 아니라 장기적인 품질도 보장합니다. **17경쟁업체와는 달리 1년 점검 프로그램을 무료로 제공합니다.** 작업 완료 1년 후, 저희가 방문해 보수한 공간이 모두 제대로 돌아가고 있는지 확인해 드립니다. **18웹사이트 www.yangbrothers.com을 방문하셔서 저희가 리모델링한 상업 공간의 사진들을 살펴보세요.** 지난 작업들의 창의성과 품질에 감동하실 겁니다. 어떤 업무 공간이든 양 브라더스가 해결책을 제시해 드립니다.

어휘 renovate 보수하다, 수선하다 commercial 상업적인 contractor 건설업체, 도급업체 reception 접수, 안내, 환영 amenities 편의 시설

16 어떤 종류의 업체가 광고되고 있는가?
(A) 웹디자인 회사   (B) 철물점
(C) 부동산 중개업체   **(D) 리모델링 회사**

해설 **전체 내용 - 광고하는 업체의 종류**
초반부에서 양 브라더스는 스프링브리지 지역 최고의 상가 리모델링 건설업체(Yang Brothers is the number-one commercial remodeling contractor in the Springbridge area)라고 소개했으므로 (D)가 정답이다.

17 업체는 어떤 특별 서비스를 제공하는가?
(A) 무료 설치   (B) 융통성 있는 결제 방식
(C) 후속 점검   (D) 긴급 수리

해설 **세부 사항 - 업체가 제공하는 특별 서비스**
중반부에서 경쟁업체와는 달리 1년 점검 프로그램을 무료로 제공한다(Unlike our competitors, we offer a free one-year inspection program)고 했으므로 (C)가 정답이다.

어휘 installation 설치 flexible 융통성 있는, 유연한

18 화자는 청자들에게 온라인에서 무엇을 하라고 제안하는가?
(A) 작업 견본 보기   (B) 의견 남기기
(C) 상담 요청하기   (D) 업체 위치 찾기

해설 **세부 사항 - 화자의 제안 사항**
후반부에서 웹사이트를 방문하여 자신의 회사가 리모델링한 상업 공간의 사진들을 살펴볼 것(Visit our Web site ~ to see pictures of other commercial spaces we've remodeled)을 제안했으므로 (A)가 정답이다.

Paraphrasing 담화의 see pictures of other commercial spaces we've remodeled → 정답의 View work samples

[19-21] 방송 + 도표 M-Cn

Welcome to our "Savvy Consumers" segment, **19where we report on tips our *News 4* viewers can use to make better purchasing decisions.** With summer approaching, many of us have travel in mind, so today we'll share advice for booking flights. Now, when searching for flights online, you might assume that direct, nonstop flights would cost more than flights with layovers. But we compared flights from New York to Los Angeles, and **20one airline's flight was both nonstop and less expensive than most other flights.** Also, be aware that **21some airlines are now offering free meals for flights purchased using the airline's mobile application.**

19저희 〈뉴스 4〉 시청자들께서 더 나은 구매 결정을 내리는 데 이용하실 수 있는 팁을 전해 드리는, "현명한 소비자" 코너에 오신 것

을 환영합니다. 여름철이 다가오면서 많은 분들께서 여행을 염두에 두고 계실 텐데요, 그래서 오늘 저희가 항공편 예약에 필요한 조언을 드리려고 합니다. 자, 온라인으로 항공편을 검색할 때, 직항편이 경유지가 있는 항공편보다 더 비쌀 거라고 생각하실지도 모르겠습니다. 하지만 저희가 뉴욕발 로스엔젤레스행 항공편들을 비교해보니, 20한 항공사의 항공편은 직항이면서 대부분의 다른 항공편보다 저렴했습니다. 또한, 21일부 항공사에서는 현재 자사의 모바일 애플리케이션을 이용해 구매하는 항공편에 대해 무료 식사를 제공하고 있다는 점도 참고하시기 바랍니다.

어휘 savvy 센스 있는, 요령 있는 segment 부분, 단편, 조각 with A -ing A가 ~하면서, A가 ~하는 채로 layover 경유(지)

항공사 이름	경유지 숫자	티켓 가격
피니언 에어라인즈	0	$450
론도 에어	1	$400
블레이즈 에어웨이즈	2	$350
20벨라 에어	0	$375

19 방송 코너의 주요 주제는 무엇인가?
(A) 비싸지 않은 여름 활동
(B) 인기 관광지
(C) 도움이 되는 구매 팁
(D) 알려지지 않은 지역 레스토랑

해설 전체 내용 – 방송 주제
초반부에서 더 나은 구매 결정을 내리는 데 이용할 수 있는 팁을 전하는(~ where we report on tips our News 4 viewers can use to make better purchasing decisions) 코너라고 소개했으므로 (C)가 정답이다.

Paraphrasing 담화의 tips ~ to make better purchasing decisions → 정답의 Helpful purchasing tips

20 시각 정보에 따르면, 화자는 어느 항공사를 가리키는가?
(A) 피니언 에어라인즈 (B) 론도 에어
(C) 블레이즈 에어웨이즈 **(D) 벨라 에어**

해설 세부 사항 – 시각 정보 연계
중반부에서 한 항공사의 항공편은 직항이면서 대부분의 다른 항공편들보다 저렴했다(~ one airline's flight was both nonstop and less expensive than most other flights)고 했다. 도표를 보면 경유지 숫자가 0으로 표기되어 있는 두 곳 중 더 저렴한 항공사는 Vela Air이므로 (D)가 정답이다.

21 화자에 따르면, 청자들은 어떻게 무료 식사를 받을 수 있는가?
(A) 온라인 쿠폰을 교환해서
(B) 항공사 마일리지 프로그램에 가입해서
(C) 여행 보상 신용카드를 신청해서
(D) 모바일 애플리케이션을 이용해 여행을 예약해서

해설 세부 사항 – 무료 식사 서비스를 받는 방법
후반부에서 일부 항공사들이 현재 자사의 모바일 애플리케이션을 이용해 구매하는 항공편에 대해 무료 식사를 제공하고 있다(~ some airlines are now offering free meals for flights purchased using the airline's mobile application)고 했으므로 (D)가 정답이다.

어휘 redeem (쿠폰 등을) 제품으로 교환하다 join 가입하다 frequent-flier club 항공사 마일리지 프로그램

ETS ACTUAL TEST   본책 p.122

71 (A)	72 (B)	73 (D)	74 (B)	75 (A)	76 (C)
77 (B)	78 (A)	79 (B)	80 (D)	81 (C)	82 (A)
83 (D)	84 (B)	85 (C)	86 (B)	87 (C)	88 (A)
89 (B)	90 (D)	91 (A)	92 (C)	93 (B)	94 (B)
95 (B)	96 (D)	97 (C)	98 (B)	99 (C)	100 (C)

[71-73] 회의 발췌 W-Br

As most of you already know, **71we're starting construction next month on a new hospital wing dedicated to pediatric medicine.** It'll include twenty rooms and a teaching center for doctors in training. The board of directors has decided to tear down **72the north parking garage, which has been reserved for the doctors and nurses.** To lessen the burden on you, **73the hospital plans to offer free shuttle service** to and from the garage on Fifteenth Street 24 hours a day.

이미 대부분 알고 계시겠지만, **71저희가 다음 달에 소아과 신축 병동 공사를 시작합니다.** 이 병동은 스무 개의 병실과 수련의들을 위한 교육 센터를 포함할 예정입니다. 이사회에서는 **72의사 및 간호사 전용이던 북쪽 주차장을** 철거하기로 결정했습니다. 여러분의 불편을 덜어드리기 위해, 병원에서는 15번 가에 위치한 주차장을 24시간 오가는 **73무료 셔틀 서비스를 제공할 계획입니다.**

어휘 wing 부속 건물, 동 dedicated to ~에 전념하는, ~에 헌신하는 pediatric medicine 소아과 tear down 철거하다 parking garage 주차장 reserved 지정된, 예약된 lessen 줄이다, 완화하다 burden 불편, 부담

71 담화는 주로 무엇에 관한 것인가?
(A) 공사 프로젝트 (B) 모금 행사
(C) 보조금 제안서 (D) 기념일 파티

해설 전체 내용 – 담화의 주제
초반부에서 다음 달에 신축 병동 공사를 시작한다(we're starting construction next month on a new hospital wing)고 언급한 뒤로 해당 건물 공사에 관해 이야기하고 있으므로 (A)가 정답이다.

어휘 fund-raising 모금, 기금 마련 grant 보조금

72 청자들은 누구인 것 같은가?
(A) 시설 관리 작업자들 **(B) 의료진**
(C) 환자들 (D) 기자들

해설 전체 내용 – 청자들의 직업
중반부에 의사 및 간호사 전용이던 주차장의 철거를 언급하면서 청자들이 겪을 불편을 줄이기 위한(~ which has been reserved for the doctors and nurses. To lessen the burden on you ~) 조치를 설명한 것으로 보아 청자들은 의사 또는 간호사임을 알 수 있으므로 (B)가 정답이다.

> Paraphrasing 담화의 doctors and nurses → 정답의 Medical staff

73 화자에 따르면, 무엇이 무료로 제공될 것인가?
(A) 직업 능력 개발 기회   (B) 인터넷 접속
(C) 구내식당 점심 식사   **(D) 셔틀버스 서비스**

해설 세부 사항 – 무료로 제공되는 것
후반부에 병원에서 무료 셔틀 서비스를 제공할 계획(the hospital plans to offer free shuttle service)이라고 했으므로 (D)가 정답이다.

어휘 at no cost 무료로   access 접속, 접근   cafeteria 구내식당

> Paraphrasing 담화의 free → 질문의 at no cost

[74-76] 공지 M-Cn

74 Attention, customers! Thanks for waiting patiently to take part in our two-day sales event. Please form a line here, by the front door, and then I'll unlock the door so you can start shopping. **75 I have some information from the manager. Because the delivery truck was delayed, we are currently out of the WiredX flat-screen televisions.** All other brands are still available, though. And **76 as a reminder, this sales event lasts until the end of the day tomorrow.**

74고객 여러분, 주목해 주세요! 이틀간 진행되는 저희 할인 행사에 참여하기 위해 인내심 있게 기다려 주셔서 감사합니다. 이쪽, 앞문 옆으로 줄을 서 주시기 바라며, 그런 다음 쇼핑을 시작하실 수 있도록 문을 열어 드리겠습니다. 75저희 점장님께 받은 정보가 있습니다. 배송 트럭이 지연되어 현재 와이어드X 평면 텔레비전은 품절된 상태입니다. 하지만, 다른 모든 브랜드는 여전히 구매하실 수 있습니다. 그리고 76참고로, 이 할인 행사는 내일 영업 종료 시점까지 진행됩니다.

어휘 delayed 지연된, 지체된   out of ~이 품절된   as a reminder 참고로, 상기시켜 드리자면

74 화자는 누구인 것 같은가?
(A) 건물 검사관   **(B) 매장 직원**
(C) 공장 작업자   (D) 트럭 기사

해설 전체 내용 – 화자의 직업
초반부에서 고객들에게 주목해달라(Attention, customers!)며 이틀간 진행되는 할인 행사에 참여하기 위해 인내심 있게 기다려 준 것에 대해 감사하다(Thanks for waiting patiently to take part in our two-day sales event)고 했으므로 (B)가 정답이다.

75 화자는 점장에게서 받은 어떤 정보를 공유하는가?
(A) 한 제품을 구입할 수 없다.
(B) 수리 작업이 필요하다.
(C) 거래 내역서가 우편으로 발송될 것이다.
(D) 비가 예상된다.

해설 세부 사항 – 점장이 전하는 정보
중반부에서 점장에게서 받은 정보가 있다며 배송 트럭 지연으로 인해 현재 와이어드X 평면 텔레비전이 품절된 상태(Because the delivery truck was delayed, we are currently out of the WiredX flat-screen televisions)라고 했으므로 (A)가 정답이다.

어휘 invoice 거래 내역서

> Paraphrasing 담화의 currently out of the WiredX flat-screen televisions → 정답의 A product is unavailable

76 화자는 청자들에게 무엇에 대해 상기시키는가?
(A) 영업 시간이 변경되었다.
(B) 입사 지원서는 매주 토요일에 접수된다.
(C) 내일이 행사 마지막 날이다.
(D) 배송에 일주일이 걸린다.

해설 세부 사항 – 화자가 청자들에게 상기시키는 것
후반부에서 참고로 이 할인 행사는 내일 영업 종료 시점까지 진행된다(as a reminder, this sales event lasts until the end of the day tomorrow)고 했으므로 (C)가 정답이다.

> Paraphrasing 담화의 this sales event lasts until the end of the day tomorrow → 정답의 Tomorrow is the last day of an event

[77-79] 전화 메시지 W-Am

Hi, Tariq. This is Raya. **77 I've been thinking about what you said about making the hotel lobby more appealing, and I have an idea. 78 What do you think about buying some new artwork to hang there?** Some nice paintings or photographs would really improve the hotel's atmosphere. We could hire a local artist or photographer to create something for the space. It might be expensive, though. **79 I'd love to discuss this soon. My shift ends at four o'clock.**

안녕하세요, 타리크 씨. 라야입니다. 77호텔 로비를 더 매력적으로 만들자는 말씀에 대해 생각해 봤는데, 아이디어가 하나 있어요. 78그곳에 걸어 놓을 새 예술 작품을 구입하는 건 어떠세요? 멋진 그림이나 사진들이 호텔 분위기를 한층 향상시켜 줄 거예요. 지역 미술가나 사진 작가를 고용해 그 공간을 위한 뭔가를 제작하는 것도 좋을 것 같아요. 비쌀 수는 있겠지만요. 79이 얘기를 조만간 논의해 보고 싶어요. 제 근무는 4시에 끝납니다.

어휘 appealing 매력적인 atmosphere 분위기 shift (교대) 근무

77 화자는 누구인 것 같은가?
(A) 화가   (B) 호텔 매니저
(C) 컴퓨터 기술자   (D) 행사 주최 담당자

해설 전체 내용 – 화자의 직업
초반부에서 화자가 호텔 로비를 더 매력적으로 만드는 것과 관련해 상대방이 말한 부분에 대해 생각해 봤다는 말과 함께 아이디어가 하나 있다(I've been thinking about what you said about making the hotel lobby more appealing, and I have an idea)고 했으므로 (B)가 정답이다.

78 화자는 무엇을 구입하고 싶어 하는가?
(A) 미술품   (B) 가구
(C) 간식   (D) 도구

해설 세부 사항 – 화자가 구입하고 싶어 하는 것
중반부에서 새 예술 작품을 구입하는 것이 어떤지(What do you think about buying some new artwork to hang there?) 물었으므로 (A)가 정답이다.

79 화자가 "제 근무는 4시에 끝납니다"라고 말할 때 무엇을 의미하는가?
(A) 업무를 할 시간이 없다.
(B) 오늘 만나고 싶어 한다.
(C) 추가 근무를 하고 싶어 한다.
(D) 일정이 잘못되었다고 생각한다.

해설 화자의 의도 파악
후반부에서 이것을 조만간 논의하고 싶다(I'd love to discuss this soon)면서 인용문을 언급했으므로 오늘 내로 논의하고 싶다는 의도임을 알 수 있다. 따라서 (B)가 정답이다.

어휘 task 업무, 일   extra 추가의, 별도의

[80-82] 광고 W-Br

⁸⁰*Natural Earth Magazine* is now offering a year-long subscription for only 15 Euros. When you subscribe to our spectacular magazine, each month you'll receive news of the latest nature discoveries and stories of awe-inspiring locations around the world. And ⁸¹for a limited time only, when you subscribe to *Natural Earth Magazine* you'll receive two free admission tickets to one of the many national parks our magazine supports. You'll be able to see some of the most spectacular plants and animal species the world has to offer. So ⁸²go to our Web site and type in the number 8632 to take advantage of this limited-time offer.

⁸⁰〈내추럴 어스 매거진〉은 현재 단 15유로에 연간 구독권을 제공하고 있습니다. 이 멋진 잡지를 구독하시면, 최신 자연 발견 및 전 세계의 장엄한 장소에 관한 소식을 매월 받으실 수 있습니다. 아울러 ⁸¹한정된 기간 동안 〈내추럴 어스 매거진〉 구독 시, 저희 잡지에서 후원하는 많은 국립공원 중 한 곳의 무료 입장권 2매를 받으시게 됩니다. 지구상에서 가장 인상적인 동식물을 보실 수 있을 겁니다. ⁸²이번 한정 판매 혜택을 받으시려면 웹사이트를 방문하셔서 숫자 8632를 입력하십시오.

어휘 year-long 일 년 내내   awe-inspiring 장엄한   limited 한정된   admission ticket 입장권

80 무엇이 광고되고 있는가?
(A) 음악회 시리즈   (B) 과학관
(C) 반려동물 가게   (D) 월간지

해설 전체 내용 – 광고의 대상
초반부에서 〈내추럴 어스 매거진〉이 단 15유로에 연간 구독권을 제공하고 있다고 한 후, 잡지를 구독하면 매월 소식을 받을 수 있다(When you subscribe to our spectacular magazine, each month you'll receive news)고 했으므로 (D)가 정답이다.

81 신규 고객은 한정 기간 동안 무엇을 받게 되는가?
(A) 무료 견본 식품   (B) 강좌 초청장
(C) 공원 입장권   (D) 기념 티셔츠

해설 세부 사항 – 신규 고객이 한정 기간 동안 받을 것
중반부에서 한정된 기간 동안(for a limited time only) 〈내추럴 어스 매거진〉 구독 시, 여러 국립공원 중 한 곳의 무료 입장권 2매를 받게 된다(you'll receive two free admission tickets to one of the many national parks)고 했으므로 (C)가 정답이다.

어휘 entry ticket 입장권   souvenir 기념품

> Paraphrasing 담화의 admission tickets → 정답의 Entry tickets

82 청자들은 웹사이트에서 무엇을 하라고 요청받는가?
(A) 판촉 번호 사용하기
(B) 사진 보기
(C) 우편물 수신자 목록에 등록하기
(D) 대회 참가하기

해설 세부 사항 – 청자들이 요청받은 사항
후반부에서 한정 판매 혜택을 받으려면 웹사이트를 방문해서 숫자 8632를 입력할 것(go to our Web site and type in the number 8632 to take advantage of this limited-time offer)을 요청했으므로 (A)가 정답이다.

어휘 promotional code 판촉 번호

[83-85] 전화 메시지 M-Cn

This is Rajeev from Sun Mountain Greens. ⁸³We're preparing the usual order of fruits and vegetables for your restaurant. Your order's nearly ready, but there was a problem when I tried to run the credit card that we have on file for you. ⁸⁴I'm afraid the payment was declined and couldn't be processed. Do you have another card that you'd like me to use, or do you want to pay cash on delivery? Please call me back to let me know. Since you've been a customer for such a long time, ⁸⁵**you can still plan on receiving the order tomorrow as scheduled.** I'm sure we'll figure everything out. Talk to you soon.

저는 썬 마운틴 그린즈의 라지브입니다. ⁸³귀하의 레스토랑을 위해 평소와 같이 과일 및 채소 주문을 준비하고 있습니다. 주문은 거의 준비되었는데요, 저희가 등록된 신용카드로 결제를 시도했을 때 문제가 발생해서요. ⁸⁴유감스럽게도 해당 결제가 거절되어 처리되지 못했습니다. 제가 사용하기를 원하시는 다른 카드가 있으신가요, 아니면 배송 시 현금으로 지불하기를 원하시나요? 제게 다시 전화 주셔서 알려 주시기 바랍니다. 아주 오랫동안 고객이셨기 때문에, ⁸⁵주문은 내일 일정대로 받을 것으로 예상하실 수 있습니다. 분명 모든 것이 해결될 것이라고 생각합니다. 곧 연락 드리겠습니다.

어휘 run a card 카드로 결제하다 on file 등록된, 보관 중인 decline 거절하다 process 처리하다 on delivery 배송 시에 figure A out A를 해결하다, A를 알아내다

83 화자는 어떤 종류의 업체에서 일하는가?
(A) 이삿짐 회사
(B) 조경 서비스 회사
(C) 제조 업체
(D) 식품 공급업체

해설 전체 내용 – 화자의 근무 장소
초반부에서 청자의 레스토랑을 위해 평소와 같이 과일 및 채소 주문을 준비하고 있다(We're preparing the usual order of fruits and vegetables for your restaurant)고 했으므로 (D)가 정답이다.

어휘 supplier 공급업체, 공급업자

Paraphrasing 담화의 preparing the usual order of fruits and vegetables → 정답의 A food supplier

84 화자는 어떤 문제를 언급하는가?
(A) 가격표에 오류가 있었다.
(B) 결제가 처리될 수 없었다.
(C) 업체에 직원이 부족하다.
(D) 제품에 결함이 있었다.

해설 세부 사항 – 화자가 언급하는 문제
중반부에서 결제가 거절되어 처리될 수 없었다(I'm afraid the payment was declined and couldn't be processed)고 했으므로 (B)가 정답이다.

어휘 short-staffed 직원이 부족한 defect 결함

85 화자는 내일 배송에 대해 무엇이라고 말하는가?
(A) 대체품을 포함할 것이다.
(B) 다른 장소로 갈 수 있다.
(C) 일정대로 도착할 것이다.
(D) 미뤄질 수 있다.

해설 세부 사항 – 화자가 내일 배송에 대해 하는 말
후반부에서 여전히 주문은 내일 일정대로 받을 것으로 예상하실 수 있다(you can still plan on receiving the order tomorrow as scheduled)고 했으므로 (C)가 정답이다.

어휘 substitute 대체(품) postpone 미루다, 연기하다

Paraphrasing 담화의 receiving the order tomorrow as scheduled → 정답의 will arrive as scheduled

[86-88] 방송 W-Am

⁸⁶**The transportation department is proposing a multiyear plan to add six new stations to the railway system.** ⁸⁷**This plan is causing city residents considerable concern,** because it could entail prolonged disruption to the existing train lines during implementation. It is worth keeping in mind, though, that the proposal hasn't been approved yet. ⁸⁸**Tune in at seven this evening for our exclusive live interview with the director of the transportation department.** I'm sure our reporter will be asking some pointed questions!

⁸⁶교통부는 철도 시스템에 6개의 새로운 역을 추가하는 다년간의 계획을 제안하고 있습니다. ⁸⁷이 계획은 시민들에게 상당한 걱정을 야기하고 있는데요, 시행 기간 동안 기존 열차 노선에 장기간 지장을 줄 수 있기 때문입니다. ⁸⁷하지만 이 제안은 아직 승인되지 않았다는 점을 명심할 필요가 있습니다. ⁸⁸오늘 저녁 7시에 교통부 국장 독점 생방송 인터뷰를 시청하세요. 저희 기자가 분명 날카로운 질문을 던질 것입니다!

어휘 propose 제안하다 multiyear 다년의 considerable 상당한 concern 걱정, 우려 entail 수반하다 prolonged 장기간의 disruption 지장, 방해 implementation 시행 tune in (라디오, TV를) 청취하다, 시청하다 pointed (말 등이) 날카로운

86 화자는 어떤 종류의 공사 프로젝트에 대해 논의하고 있는가?
(A) 쇼핑몰 건설하기
(B) 대중교통 시스템 확대하기
(C) 지역 역사 박물관 개조하기
(D) 시립 병원 증설하기

해설 전체 내용 – 화자가 논의하는 공사 프로젝트의 종류
초반부에서 교통부에서 철도 시스템에 6개의 새로운 역을 추가하는 다년간의 계획을 제안하고 있다(The transportation department is proposing a multiyear plan to add six new stations to the railway system)고 했으므로 (B)가 정답이다.

Paraphrasing 담화의 add six new stations to the railway system → 정답의 Expanding a public transportation system

87 화자는 왜 "이 제안은 아직 승인되지 않았다"라고 말하는가?
(A) 지연 문제에 대해 불만을 제기하기 위해
(B) 즉각적인 대응을 촉구하기 위해
(C) 안심시키기 위해
(D) 결정을 정당화하기 위해

해설	화자의 의도 파악

중반부에서 이 계획이 시민들에게 상당한 걱정을 야기하고 있다(This plan is causing city residents considerable concern ~)고 한 뒤, 하지만 명심해야 할 필요가 있다(It is worth keeping in mind, though ~)면서 인용문을 언급했으므로 당장은 우려할 필요가 없다고 청자를 안심시키기 위한 것임을 알 수 있다. 따라서 (C)가 정답이다.

어휘	urge 촉구하다 immediate 즉각적인 reassurance 안심시키는 말 justify 정당화하다

88 무엇이 나중에 방송될 것인가?
(A) 인터뷰   (B) 토론
(C) 스포츠 행사 (D) 콘서트

해설	세부 사항 – 나중에 방송되는 것

후반부에서 오늘 저녁 7시에 교통부 국장 독점 생방송 인터뷰를 시청해달라(Tune in at seven this evening for our exclusive live interview with the director of the transportation department)고 했으므로 (A)가 정답이다.

> **Paraphrasing** 담화의 at seven this evening → 질문의 later

[89-91] 담화 M-Au

> **89I wanted to give you all an update on the new software program we'll soon begin using here at the clinic.** As you know, we're making this upgrade because our current software takes a long time to load, and that causes delays when we input our patients' information. Well, you'll be happy to know that the new software is very fast. But… it's not software you're familiar with. **90I'd like to find time outside of our regular business hours for you to learn the basics.** I'm passing around a calendar—**91please write down which times you're available to come in.**
>
> **89**우리가 이 병원에서 곧 사용하게 될 새로운 소프트웨어 프로그램에 대한 최신 정보를 여러분 모두에게 알려드리려고 합니다. 여러분도 아시다시피, 이 업그레이드를 하고 있는 이유는 현재 소프트웨어가 로딩하는 데 시간이 오래 걸리고 이로 인해 환자 정보를 입력할 때 시간이 지연되기 때문입니다. 음, 새 소프트웨어가 매우 빠르다는 것을 알면 기쁘실 겁니다. 하지만 여러분들이 잘 아는 소프트웨어가 아니에요. **90**정규 업무 시간 외에 별도로 여러분이 기본기를 배울 수 있는 시간을 가질까 합니다. 지금 달력을 돌리고 있는데요, **91**오실 수 있는 시간을 적어 주세요.

어휘	current 현재의 familiar 익숙한, 잘 아는 regular 정규의 pass around (여러 사람이 보도록) 돌리다

89 청자들은 어디에서 일하는가?
(A) 기술회사   (B) 의료기관
(C) 회계법인   (D) 제조공장

해설	전체 내용 – 청자들의 근무지

초반부에서 청자들에게 우리가 이 병원에서 곧 사용하게 될 새로운 소프트웨어 프로그램(~ the new software program we'll soon begin using here at the clinic)이라고 했으므로 (B)가 정답이다.

90 화자가 "여러분들이 잘 아는 소프트웨어가 아니에요"라고 말할 때 무엇을 의미하는가?
(A) 회사의 발표가 잘못되었다.
(B) 프로젝트 제안서가 성공을 거두지 못할 것이다.
(C) 일부 소프트웨어가 아직 개발 중이다.
(D) 약간의 교육이 필요할 것이다.

해설	화자의 의도 파악

중반부에서 인용문을 언급한 뒤, 정규 업무 시간 외에 청자들이 기본기를 배울 수 있는 시간을 가지려 한다(I'd like to find time outside of our regular business hours for you to learn the basics)고 했으므로 (D)가 정답이다.

어휘	announcement 발표 proposal 제안(서) work 효과가 있다, 성공하다 develop 개발하다

91 청자들은 다음에 무엇을 할 것 같은가?
(A) 가능한 시간 표시하기   (B) 관리자에게 전화하기
(C) 데이터 분석하기   (D) 약속 확인해 주기

해설	세부 사항 – 청자들이 할 일

후반부에서 청자들에게 교육에 올 수 있는 시간을 적어 달라(please write down which times you're available to come in)고 했으므로 (A)가 정답이다.

어휘	indicate 표시하다 availability 가능성 analyze 분석하다

> **Paraphrasing** 담화의 write down which times you're available → 정답의 Indicate their availability

[92-94] 담화 W-Am

> Before we end today's tour of the art museum, **92I'd like to tell you about an upcoming exhibit that will be opening in July.** The exhibit is called International Jewels and it will feature pieces by fifty well-known jewelry artists. This exhibit has already been shown in Rome, Paris, and London, and it has received excellent reviews. Plus, **93our gift shop is going to be selling affordable reproductions of some of the most prominent pieces of jewelry. These replicas have been especially made to be sold during this exhibit.** So if you're interested in this unique exhibit, **94I encourage you to buy your tickets today,** as we're expecting them to sell out quickly.
>
> 오늘 미술관 견학을 마치기 전에 **92**여러분께 곧 7월에 열릴 전시회에 대해 말씀드리고 싶습니다. 전시회 제목은 국제 보석전으로, 유명한 보석 예술가 50인의 작품이 전시될 예정입니다. 본 전시회는 이미 로마, 파리, 런던에서 열렸으며 훌륭한 평을 받았습니다. 아울러 **93**저희 기념품점에서는 가장 인기 있는 보석들의 복제품을 적당

한 가격에 판매할 겁니다. 이 모조품들은 이번 전시회 동안 판매하기 위해 특별히 제작된 것입니다. 이 특별 전시회에 관심이 있으시다면 **94오늘 표를 구입하십시오.** 빠르게 매진될 것으로 예상됩니다.

어휘	affordable 가격이 적당한 reproduction 복제품 prominent 주목을 끄는, 눈에 띄는 replica 복제품, 모조품 sell out 다 팔리다, 매진되다

92 담화의 목적은 무엇인가?
(A) 객원 연설자를 소개하려고
(B) 견학 일정을 제공하려고
(C) 새로운 전시회를 홍보하려고
(D) 미술관 역사를 설명하려고

해설 전체 내용 – 담화의 목적
초반부에서 7월에 열릴 전시회에 대해 말해 주고 싶다(I'd like to tell you about an upcoming exhibit that will be opening in July)고 했으므로 (C)가 정답이다.

Paraphrasing 담화의 tell you about an upcoming exhibit → 정답의 promote a new exhibit

93 화자는 기념품점에 대해 무엇이라고 말하는가?
(A) 보수 공사로 문을 닫을 것이다.
(B) 특별 상품을 판매할 것이다.
(C) 무료 지도를 비치하고 있다.
(D) 오늘 할인을 한다.

해설 세부 사항 – 화자가 기념품점에 대해 언급한 사항
중반부에서 기념품점에서 가장 인기 있는 보석들의 복제품을 판매할 예정(our gift shop is going to be selling affordable reproductions ~)이라며, 이 모조품들은 특별히 제작된 것(These replicas have been especially made ~)이라고 했으므로 (B)가 정답이다.

어휘 renovation 보수, 수리

Paraphrasing 담화의 replicas have been especially made → 정답의 special merchandise

94 화자는 청자들에게 무엇을 하라고 권하는가?
(A) 미술관에서 자원봉사 하기
(B) 예매권 구입하기
(C) 연간 회원 등록하기
(D) 참석하는 예술가 만나보기

해설 세부 사항 – 화자의 권고 사항
후반부에서 오늘 표를 구입할 것(I encourage you to buy your tickets today)을 권고했으므로 (B)가 정답이다.

어휘 advance ticket 예매권

Paraphrasing 담화의 buy your tickets today → 정답의 Purchase advance tickets

[95-97] 담화 + 도표 M-Au

95Now that we've finished putting in the windows and doors, it's time to focus on the interior of the house. **96The electricians and the plumbers will be coming in tomorrow, so you all can have the day off while they get started on their work.** You deserve the break! Once they're finished, we can plaster the walls and lay the flooring. That reminds me—I need to talk to the homeowners about the flooring in the bedrooms—**97they chose the most expensive product,** and I don't think they realize that'll put them over budget.

95이제 우리가 창문과 출입문들을 설치하는 작업을 끝마쳤으므로, 주택 실내에 초점을 맞출 때입니다. **96**전기 기사와 배관 작업자들이 내일 투입될 예정이므로, 이분들이 작업을 시작하는 동안 여러분은 모두 하루 쉬셔도 됩니다. 여러분은 휴식을 누릴 자격이 있어요! 이분들이 끝마치는 대로, 우리는 벽에 석고를 바르고 바닥재를 깔 수 있습니다. 그러고 보니 떠오르는 게 침실 바닥재와 관련해 집 주인들과 이야기를 나눠봐야겠네요. **97**이분들께서 가장 비싼 제품을 선택하셨는데, 그게 예산을 초과하게 만들 거라는 사실을 알고 계시는 것 같지는 않아요.

어휘	now that 이제 ~이므로 electrician 전기 기사 plumber 배관 작업자 have a day off 하루 쉬다 plaster 미장하다, 회반죽을 바르다 lay (바닥에) 깔다, 설치하다 budget 예산 square foot 평방피트

바닥재 유형	1평방피트당 자재비
카페트	$2.50
마감 처리된 목재	$6.00
97타일	$8.50
비닐	$3.00

95 청자들은 누구인 것 같은가?
(A) 부동산 중개업자들   (B) 공사장 인부들
(C) 건축가들   (D) 영업사원들

해설 전체 내용 – 청자들의 직업
초반부에 화자 자신과 청자들이 창문과 출입문들을 설치하는 작업을 끝마쳤다(we've finished putting in the windows and doors)고 했으므로 (B)가 정답이다.

Paraphrasing 담화의 finished putting in the windows and doors → 정답의 Construction workers

96 화자는 청자들이 내일 무엇을 할 수 있다고 말하는가?
(A) 급여 명세서 받기
(B) 교육 시간에 참가하기
(C) 건물 견학하기
(D) 하루 휴식하기

해설 세부 사항 – 청자들이 내일 할 수 있는 일
초반부에 전기 기사와 배관 작업자들이 내일 투입될 예정이라 청자들이 모두 하루 쉴 수 있다(The electricians and the plumbers will be coming in tomorrow, so you all can have the day off)고 했으므로 (D)가 정답이다.

어휘 paycheck 급여 (명세서)

> Paraphrasing 담화의 have the day off → 정답의 Take the day off

97 시각 정보에 따르면, 화자는 어떤 종류의 바닥재를 언급하는가?
(A) 카페트 (B) 마감 처리된 목재
(C) 타일 (D) 비닐

해설 세부 사항 – 시각 정보 연계
후반부에 침실 바닥재를 언급하며, 집주인들이 가장 비싼 제품을 선택했다(they chose the most expensive product)고 했다. 도표를 보면, 1평방피트당 비용이 가장 높은 것은 $8.50로 표기된 Tile이므로 (C)가 정답이다.

어휘 refer to ~을 언급하다

[98-100] 회의 발췌 + 매출 그래프 W-Am

I have one final issue to discuss at today's staff meeting. **98 I just handed out a graph summarizing our shoe store's annual sales data.** And, well…I think this information is particularly interesting since we relocated to a different neighborhood this year. As you might have expected, the relocation decreased our sales significantly at first. **99 During the quarter we moved, we experienced the lowest shoe sales of the entire year.** That was largely because people in the new neighborhood didn't know about us. **100 However, thanks to the newspaper advertisements and radio commercials we put out, business picked up quickly,** and we ended the year by making a record number of sales.

오늘 직원회의에서 마지막으로 논의할 사항이 한 가지 있습니다. **98 제가 방금 우리 신발 가게의 연간 매출 자료를 요약한 그래프를 나눠 드렸습니다.** 그리고 음… 제 생각에 이 정보는 특히 흥미로운데 왜냐하면 우리가 올해 다른 지역으로 이전했기 때문입니다. 예상하셨겠지만 이전하면서 처음에는 매출이 상당히 하락했어요. **99 한 해 전체를 통틀어 우리가 이전한 해당 분기 동안 신발 매출이 가장 저조했습니다.** 대체로 새 주민들이 우리에 관해 몰랐기 때문입니다. **100 하지만 우리가 낸 신문과 라디오 광고로 사업이 빠르게 호전되었고** 기록적인 매출을 달성하며 한 해를 마무리했습니다.

어휘 hand out 나누어 주다 summarize 요약하다 annual sales 연매출 relocate to ~로 이전하다 significantly 상당히 largely 대체로 commercial (TV나 라디오) 광고 put out 내놓다 pick up 개선되다, 회복되다 a record number of 기록적인, 최고치의

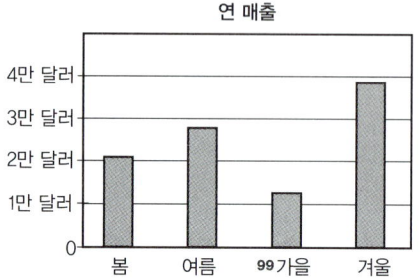

연 매출

98 회사는 어떤 종류의 상품을 판매하는가?
(A) 옷 (B) 신발
(C) 가전기기 (D) 소프트웨어

해설 세부 사항 – 판매 상품
초반부에 신발 가게의 연간 매출 자료(our shoe store's annual sales data)를 요약한 그래프를 나눠주었다고 했으므로 (B)가 정답이다.

> Paraphrasing 담화의 shoe → 정답의 Footwear

99 시각 정보에 따르면, 회사는 어느 계절에 이전했는가?
(A) 봄 (B) 여름
(C) 가을 (D) 겨울

해설 세부 사항 – 시각 정보 연계
중반부에 한 해 전체를 통틀어 이전한 분기에 신발 매출이 가장 저조했다(During the quarter we moved, we experienced the lowest shoe sales of the entire year)고 했다. 표를 보면 매출이 가장 저조한 계절은 가을이므로 (C)가 정답이다.

100 회사는 이전 후 무엇을 했는가?
(A) 물품 목록을 확장했다. (B) 직원을 추가 고용했다.
(C) 광고를 했다. (D) 개업식을 준비했다.

해설 세부 사항 – 이전 후 회사가 한 일
후반부에 이전 후 매출이 저조했지만 신문과 라디오 광고로 (thanks to the newspaper advertisements and radio commercials we put out) 사업이 빠르게 호전되었다고 했으므로 (C)가 정답이다.

어휘 expand 확장하다, 늘리다 inventory 재고품, 물품 목록 additional 추가의 inauguration 개업, 취임

PART 5&6

READING COMPREHENSION

UNIT 01 품사와 문장 구조

1 주어와 동사

ETS 유형연습 본책 p.134

1 (B) 2 (C) 3 (C)

1 (B)

번역 에스컬레이터가 일시 고장이어서 게이트 H에 도착한 승객들은 메인 터미널까지 계단으로 걸어 올라가야 했다.

해설 빈칸은 접속사 because가 이끄는 절의 주어 자리이다. 문맥상 '에스컬레이터가 고장 났다'라는 의미가 적절하므로 (B) escalator가 정답이다.

어휘 passenger 승객, 탑승객 temporarily 일시적으로 out of order 고장인, 작동이 되지 않는 escalate 상승하다 escalation 상승, 확대

2 (C)

번역 케일리 니트웨어의 직원들은 매장 내 모든 상품을 15퍼센트 할인받습니다.

해설 문장에 동사가 없으므로 빈칸은 동사 자리이다. 따라서 (C) receive가 정답이다.

어휘 associate 직원, 동료 merchandise 상품

3 (C)

번역 직원 교육 시간을 줄일 새로운 소프트웨어가 개발되고 있다.

해설 주어 뒤의 수식어구(that ~ time)를 묶어 보면 빈칸은 문장의 동사가 필요한 자리이다. 따라서 문장에서 동사 역할을 할 수 있는 (C) is being developed가 정답이다.

어휘 reduce 줄이다, 감소시키다 develop 개발하다

2 목적어

ETS 유형연습 본책 p.135

1 (A) 2 (C) 3 (B)

1 (A)

번역 마케팅 이사가 다가오는 광고 캠페인을 위해 추가 직원을 고용하도록 승인받았다.

해설 빈칸은 동사 got의 목적어가 들어갈 자리이므로, 명사 (A) approval(승인)이 정답이다.

어휘 upcoming 다가오는, 곧 있을 approve 승인하다

2 (C)

번역 대부분의 정부 기관 및 상업 시설들은 독립기념일을 기념하여 월요일에 문을 닫을 것이다.

해설 빈칸은 전치사 in의 목적어 자리이므로, 전치사의 목적어 역할을 할 수 있는 동명사 (B) observing과 명사 (C) observance 중 하나를 선택해야 한다. 구조상 빈칸 앞의 in과 빈칸 뒤의 of와 결합하여 'in observance of(~을 기념하여, 준수하여)'로 쓰이는 (C) observance가 정답이다. (B) observing은 타동사 observe의 동명사형이므로 빈칸 뒤에 바로 목적어가 있어야 한다.

어휘 commercial 상업의 establishment 기관, 시설 observe 관찰하다, 준수하다 observant 관찰력 있는, 준수하는

3 (B)

번역 송 씨가 부서장으로 승진했다고 오늘 아침 직원회의에서 발표되었다.

해설 division과 결합하여 전치사 of의 목적어 역할을 하는 자리이므로, 명사인 (B) manager가 정답이다. division manager는 '부서장'이라는 뜻의 복합명사이다.

어휘 promotion 진급, 승진 division 부서 staff meeting 직원회의 manageable 처리할 수 있는, 관리할 수 있는

3 보어

ETS 유형연습 본책 p.136

1 (A) 2 (C) 3 (B)

1 (A)

번역 저희 주택 수리 워크숍은 매달 첫 번째 토요일에 일반인들에게 공개됩니다.

해설 주어 Our home repair workshop을 보충 설명하는 주격 보어 자리로, 전치사 to와 함께 '~에게 공개된'이라는 의미가 되어야 자연스러우므로 형용사 (A) open이 정답이다.

2 (C)

번역 애쉬보노 상공회의소에서는 방문객들에게 노시 해변가에 있는 식당과 극장을 애용해 달라고 당부한다.

해설 동사가 invite이고 목적어 visitors 뒤 목적격 보어 자리에 빈칸이 있으므로 to부정사 (C) to patronize가 정답이다. 동사 invite는 5형식일 때 〈invite+목적어+to부정사〉의 구조로 쓰인다.

어휘 Chamber of Commerce 상공회의소 waterfront 강변, 해안가, 부두 patronize 애용하다

3 (B)

번역 금융 시장의 변화는 투자자들이 양질의 조언과 정보에 더욱 의존하도록 만들었다.

해설 동사가 make이고 목적어 investors 뒤 목적격 보어 자리에 빈칸이 있으므로 형용사 (B) dependent(의존하는)가 정답이다. 동사 make는 5형식일 때 목적격 보어 자리에 형용사나 동사원형이 올 수 있다.

어휘 financial market 금융 시장 investor 투자자 quality 고급의, 양질의 dependency 의존, 의지

4 수식어

ETS 유형연습 본책 p.137

1 (A) 2 (A) 3 (D)

1 (A)

번역 모든 코드 숫자가 확실히 전송되게 하려면 키패드를 강하게 눌러야 한다.

해설 빈칸 앞에 있는 수동형 동사 should be pressed를 수식할 수 있는 품사는 부사이므로 (A) firmly가 정답이다.

어휘 keypad 키패드 press 누르다 ensure 확실하게 하다 digit (아라비아) 숫자 transmit 보내다, 전송하다

2 (A)

번역 달린 케이 의장은 오늘 밤 시상식에서 이사회 구성원인 엘레나 코스타스에게 상을 수여할 것이다.

해설 명사구 tonight's award ceremony를 목적어로 취할 수 있는 전치사가 필요하며, '오늘 밤 시상식에서 시상할 것이다'와 같은 의미를 나타내야 자연스러우므로, '~ 중에, ~ 동안'을 뜻하는 (A) during이 정답이다.

어휘 honor (상 등을) 수여하다, 영예를 주다 board 이사회

3 (D)

번역 직원 전문성 개발 프로그램에 예산이 편성되었음에도 불구하고, 이사는 진행하기를 꺼리고 있다.

해설 빈칸 뒤에 〈주어(money)+동사(has been budgeted)〉가 있고, 콤마 뒤에 〈주어(the director)+동사(is)〉가 있으므로 빈칸에는 두 개의 절을 이어주는 부사절 접속사가 필요하다. 따라서 (D) Although(~에도 불구하고)가 정답이다. (A) In spite of(~에도 불구하고)와 (C) Because of(~ 때문에)는 전치사이고, (B) Therefore(그러므로)는 접속부사이다.

어휘 budget 예산을 세우다; 예산 professional 전문(가)의; 전문가, 전문직 종사자 director (회사의) 중역, 이사 be reluctant to ~하기를 꺼리다 proceed 계속하다, 진행하다

ETS 실전문제 본책 p.138

1 (B) 2 (D) 3 (A) 4 (D) 5 (A) 6 (A)
7 (D) 8 (B) 9 (C) 10 (D) 11 (C) 12 (C)
13 (D) 14 (B) 15 (B) 16 (A) 17 (B) 18 (D)

1 (B)

번역 낼럿 컴퓨터즈의 마케팅팀은 새로운 텔레비전 홍보 캠페인을 계획하고 있다.

해설 문장에 동사가 없으므로 빈칸은 동사 자리이다. 따라서 (B) is planning이 정답이다.

어휘 promotional 홍보의, 판촉의

2 (D)

번역 이사가 마무리되면 인사부의 탱 씨에게 새 집주소를 알려주세요.

해설 소유격 your 뒤에 있는 빈칸은 명사 자리로, 해당 절에서 주어 역할을 한다. 따라서 명사인 (D) relocation이 정답이다.

어휘 relocation 이전, 재배치 finalize 마무리짓다 human resources 인사부

3 (A)

번역 연례 회의에서 경영진은 뛰어난 일을 해낸 직원들을 표창할 것이다.

해설 빈칸이 조동사 will과 목적어 역할을 하는 명사 employees 사이에 있으므로, 동사원형인 (A) recognize가 정답이다.

어휘 recognize 인정하다, 표창하다 outstanding 뛰어난

4 (D)

번역 오늘 저녁 경매 행사에 관심이 없는 오케스트라 후원자들은 저녁 만찬 행사에 따로 등록할 수 있다.

해설 자동사 register와 전치사구 for the dinner event 뒤에 위치한 빈칸은 자동사를 뒤에서 수식할 부사가 들어갈 수 있는 자리이므로 (D) separately가 정답이다.

어휘 patron 후원자, 단골 손님 auction 경매 register for ~에 등록하다 separate 별개의; 분리하다 separation 분리

5 (A)

번역 어제 〈시프널 데일리 에코〉에 광고된 할인은 주방 가전에는 적용되지 않는다.

해설 빈칸은 정관사 The 뒤에 오는 명사 자리로, 동사 do not apply의 주어 역할을 한다. 따라서 do와 수가 일치하는 복수 명사 (A) discounts가 정답이다.

어휘 advertise 광고하다 apply to ~에 적용되다 appliance 가전제품

6 (A)

번역 제안된 새 건물의 모형들이 이번 주 남은 기간 동안 로비에 전시될 것이다.

해설 빈칸은 전치사 for의 목적어 역할을 하며 정관사 the의 수식을 받는 명사 자리이므로 (A) remainder가 정답이다.

어휘 proposed 제안된 on display 전시하는, 전시 중인 remainder 잔여 기간, 나머지

7 (D)

번역 사용 설명서는 그 프로그램을 처음 사용할 때 직면하는 문제들을 해결하는 데 아주 도움이 될 것이다.

해설 빈칸 앞에 주어와 동사를 갖춘 절이 왔으므로 빈칸에 동사인 (A), (B), (C)가 올 수 없다. 따라서 '~함에 있어서'라는 의미의 〈in+-ing〉 구문에 해당하는 (D) in solving이 정답이다.

어휘 manual 매뉴얼, 사용 설명서 encounter 우연히 만나다, 직면하다

8 (B)
번역 응답자들의 참여를 독려하기 위해 거제도 여성 클럽은 설문지 작성자 전원에게 25,000원짜리 기프트 카드를 제공하고 있다.

해설 빈칸은 타동사 encourage의 목적어 자리이므로 명사가 필요하다. 따라서 (B) participation이 정답이다.

어휘 respondent 응답자 complete a survey 설문지를 작성하다 participation 참여 participate 참여하다 participatory 참여의

9 (C)
번역 최근 조사에 따르면 조립 공정의 근로자들은 야근하는 동안 집중력이 훨씬 떨어질 가능성이 높은 것으로 밝혀졌다.

해설 빈칸은 주어 assembly-line workers를 설명하는 주격 보어 자리로, much less의 수식을 받는 형용사가 들어가야 한다. 따라서 (C) attentive가 정답이다.

어휘 assembly-line 조립 공정의 be likely to ~할 것 같다, ~할 가능성이 있다 overtime 야근(의), 초과 근무(의) shift 근무조, 교대제 근무시간 attentive 집중하는 attentiveness 조심성

10 (D)
번역 전체 프로젝트가 완료될 때까지 팀원들은 모든 휴가를 연기하라는 요청을 받고 있다.

해설 빈칸 앞뒤에 〈주어+동사〉를 갖춘 완전한 절이 있으므로, 빈칸에는 접속사가 들어가야 한다. 문맥상 '프로젝트가 완료될 때까지'라는 의미가 되어야 자연스러우므로 (D) until이 정답이다.

어휘 postpone 연기하다 vacation 휴가 entire 전체의 complete 완료하다

11 (C)
번역 편집자들은 〈베인브리지 심리학 저널〉에 포함할 논문을 선정할 때 여러 가지 요소를 고려한다.

해설 전치사 for와 in 사이에 위치한 빈칸은 for의 목적어가 들어갈 자리이므로, 명사 (C) inclusion(포함)이 정답이다.

어휘 paper 논문 include 포함하다 inclusive (가격에) 모두 포함된

12 (C)
번역 플리트 호텔은 웹사이트에서 직접 객실을 예약한 고객에게 가장 저렴한 요금을 보장한다.

해설 빈칸은 who가 이끄는 관계사절에서 동사 book을 수식하는 역할을 하므로, 부사인 (C) directly가 정답이다.

어휘 guarantee 보장하다, 약속하다 rate 요금 book 예약하다 directness 단순명쾌함 directly 직접

13 (D)
번역 만약 이사하신다면 회사 안내 책자에 있는 당신의 연락처를 가능한 한 빨리 업데이트하세요.

해설 빈칸은 your contact information을 목적어로 취하는 동사 자리로, 주어 you가 생략된 명령문을 이끈다. 따라서 동사원형인 (D) update가 정답이다.

어휘 directory 안내 책자 as soon as possible 가능한 한 빨리

14 (D)
번역 태양열 발전이 빠르게 전 세계적으로 중요한 산업이 되어 가고 있다.

해설 부정관사 an과 형용사 important 뒤에 빈칸이 있으므로 빈칸은 단수 명사가 들어갈 자리이다. 따라서 (D) industry(산업, 업계)가 정답이다.

어휘 solar power 태양열 발전, 태양열 에너지 industrial 산업의, 공업의 industrious 근면한, 부지런한

[15-18] 구인 광고

> 소셜 미디어 도움을 찾는 교육 업체
>
> 기 트리 게임즈는 청소년을 위한 **15 혁신적인** 교육용 보드 게임을 판매하는 소규모 회사입니다. 저희는 소셜 미디어 계정에 올릴 매력적인 게시물을 매주 5개씩 제작해 주실 분을 찾고 있습니다. 1년 전 사업을 시작한 이후로, 저희는 가장 인기 있는 플랫폼에서 자체적으로 광고를 해 오고 있습니다. **16 하지만, 마케팅은 저희의 강점이 아닙니다.** 게다가, 사업의 다른 측면들로 너무 바빴기 때문에 온라인에서 **17 홍보하는** 데 충분한 시간을 할애할 수 없었습니다. 이제 새로운 사람에게 이 책임을 넘길 준비가 되었습니다. 이 **18 기회는** 저희의 독특한 고객층을 이해하는 마케팅 능력을 갖춘 교육 전문가에게 가장 적합합니다. 관심이 있으시면, jobs@gheetreegames.ca 로 저희에게 연락 주세요.

어휘 seek 찾다, 구하다 individual 사람, 개인 engaging 매력적인 post 게시물 account 계정 advertising 광고 aspect 측면, 양상 devote (시간, 노력 등을) 할애하다, 바치다 adequate 충분한, 적절한 responsibility 책임(감) be suited to ~에 적합하다 unique 고유의, 독특한 audience 고객층, 청중

15 (B)
해설 that절의 동사 sells와 명사구 목적어 educational board games 사이에 위치한 빈칸은 형용사 educational과 함께 board games을 수식할 또 다른 형용사가 쓰일 수 있는 자리이므로 (B) innovative(혁신적인)가 정답이다.

어휘 innovation 혁신(적인 것) innovator 혁신가 innovate 혁신하다

16 (A)
번역 (A) 하지만, 마케팅은 저희의 강점이 아닙니다.
(B) 저희는 저희 제품 라인의 생산을 중단할 것입니다.
(C) 그럼에도 불구하고, 저희는 소셜 미디어의 힘을 높이 평가합니다.
(D) 그들이 최근에 저희를 위해 새로운 캠페인을 시작했습니다.

해설 전체적으로 마케팅 업무를 할 사람을 찾는 글인데, 빈칸 앞에는 자체적으로 광고를 해 오고 있다는 말이 있고, 빈칸 뒤에는 '게다가'라는 말과 함께 마케팅 담당자가 필요한 이유가 덧붙여져 있다. 따라서 빈칸에도 마케팅 담당자가 필요한 이유가 언급된 문장이 들어가는 것이 적절하므로, 마케팅(광고)이 자신들의 강점이 아니라는 사실을 언급하는 (A)가 정답이다.

어휘 strength 강점, 장점 discontinue 생산을 중단하다
appreciate 진가를 인정하다, 감사하다 launch 시작하다, 출시하다

17 (B)

해설 빈칸 뒤에 online이 쓰여 있어 온라인상에서 하는 일과 관련해 충분한 시간을 할애하지 못한 상황을 나타내야 한다. 따라서 앞서 언급한 '광고(advertising)'를 제대로 하지 못했다는 의미를 나타내야 자연스러우므로, 광고와 유사한 의미를 지닌 동사로서 '홍보하다'를 뜻하는 promote의 동명사 (B) promoting이 정답이다.

어휘 enlarge 확대하다 evaluate 평가하다 acquire 얻다, 획득하다

18 (D)

해설 문맥상 빈칸은 광고되고 있는 자리를 나타내야 의미가 자연스러운데, 이는 구직자 입장에서는 기회로 볼 수 있으므로 (D) opportunity(기회)가 정답이다.

어휘 location 지점, 위치

UNIT 02 명사

1 명사의 자리 1

ETS 유형연습   본책 p.140

1 (C)   2 (D)   3 (C)

1 (C)

번역 스프링데일 지역 시장에서는 직접 재배한 다양한 유기농 과일과 채소뿐만 아니라 수공예품과 장신구도 구입할 수 있다.

해설 빈칸은 전치사구 of homegrown and organic fruits and vegetables의 수식을 받으며 주어 역할을 하는 명사 자리이므로, '품종, 종류'라는 의미의 (C) Varieties가 정답이다.

어휘 organic 유기농의 handmade 손으로 만든, 수제의
craft 공예품, 수공예 available 구할 수 있는, 살 수 있는
community 지역사회 variant 다른; 변종
various 다양한, 여러 가지의

2 (D)

번역 나오미 다케다 씨는 지난 화요일 회의에 참석할 수 없었지만, 클레어 마스터스 씨가 그녀에게 논의한 내용을 요약해 주었다.

해설 관사 a 뒤에 빈칸이 있고, 빈칸은 동사 gave의 직접 목적어 자리이므로 명사인 (D) summary가 정답이다.

어휘 attend 참석하다 summarily 간소하게, 간략하게
summarizer 요약하는 사람 summary 요약, 개요

3 (C)

번역 벌링턴 독서 동호회는 지역 도서 판매업자들의 추천 목록에서 책을 선택할 것이다.

해설 전치사 of와 by 사이에 위치한 빈칸은 of의 목적어 역할을 할 명사가 들어갈 자리이므로 (C) recommendations가 정답이다.

어휘 title 서적, 출판물

2 명사의 자리 2

ETS 유형연습   본책 p.141

1 (D)   2 (C)   3 (A)

1 (D)

번역 〈스타 워치〉 매거진에 따르면, 가수 겸 작곡가인 카일리 노턴 씨는 다가오는 자선 음악회에 참가할 것이라고 발표했다.

해설 빈칸은 동사 has announced의 목적어 자리로 소유격 her와 형용사 upcoming의 수식을 받는 명사 자리이다. 따라서 (D) participation이 정답이다.

어휘 upcoming 다가오는 charity 자선 (행위) participate 참가하다, 참여하다 participation 참가, 참석

2 (C)

번역 르로이-봉탕은 저칼로리 음료 제품 개발의 일환으로 전국 소비자들의 기호를 조사했다.

해설 명사 consumer와 복합명사를 이뤄 타동사 researched의 목적어가 될 수 있는 명사가 필요하므로 (C) preferences가 정답이다.

어휘 research 연구(하다), 조사(하다) consumer 소비자, 고객
beverage 음료 preference 기호, 좋아함

3 (A)

번역 임원진은 새로운 스마트폰의 제품 출시를 6개월 연기했다.

해설 명사 product와 복합명사를 이뤄 has delayed의 목적어가 될 수 있는 명사가 필요하므로 (A) launch가 정답이다.

어휘 executive 임원, 이사 launch 출시; 출시하다
launchable 출시할 수 있는, 시작할 수 있는

3 명사의 종류

ETS 유형연습   본책 p.142

1 (A)   2 (B)   3 (C)

1 (A)

번역 재무팀 자리에 대한 지원서 제출 마감일은 다음 주 화요일이다.

해설 부정관사 a 뒤에는 단수 가산명사를 써야 하므로 (A) position이 정답이다.

어휘 submit 제출하다 application 신청(서), 지원(서)
finance 재무, 재정

2 (B)

번역 오노 씨는 프레젠테이션 동안 나눠준 모든 문서의 복사본을 요청했다.

해설 빈칸 앞뒤로 전치사가 있어서 빈칸에는 명사가 들어가야 하는데 빈칸 앞에 관사가 없으므로 복수형인 (B) duplicates가 정답이다.

어휘 document 문서, 서류 pass out ~을 나눠주다 duplicate 사본, 복사; 복사하다; 사본의

3 (C)

번역 지르코 5000 병 포장 기계는 음료 업계에 혁신을 일으킨 공학 기술 업적이다.

해설 전치사 of의 목적어 역할을 하면서 that절의 수식을 받을 명사가 빈칸에 필요하다. 보기에서 명사는 (A) engineer와 (C) engineering인데, 빈칸 앞에 한정사가 없으므로 불가산명사인 (C) engineering이 정답이다. (A) engineer는 가산명사 단수형이므로 한정사가 필요하다.

어휘 feat 업적, 위업 revolutionize 혁신을 일으키다

4 명사의 형태

ETS 유형연습 본책 p.143

1 (A) 2 (D) 3 (B)

1 (A)

번역 로우자 씨는 전 직원들이 더 주도적으로 행동하고 잠재 고객들과 관계를 발전시켜 나가는 것을 보고 싶어 한다.

해설 빈칸에는 타동사 take의 목적어가 필요하므로 명사인 (A) initiative가 정답이다.

어휘 contact 접촉, 교제, 관계 potential client 잠재 고객 initiative 솔선, 주도권 initiate 착수하다, 시작하다

2 (D)

번역 드레브노 바닥재 제품들은 산업 현장에서 사용하기 위해 고안되었다.

해설 전치사 for의 목적어 자리로 '사용을 위해'라는 의미를 나타내는 명사 (D) use가 정답이다. 가산명사의 단수형 (A) user는 관사 없이 쓸 수 없다.

어휘 flooring 마루 (재료), 바닥 industrial 산업의

3 (B)

번역 마닐라 웰니스 센터에는 마카티 지점에서 근무할 시간제 및 임시직 공인 간호 조무사 자리에 공석이 있다.

해설 빈칸에는 앞의 employment와 함께 복합명사를 이루는 명사가 와야 한다. 문맥상 공석이라는 의미가 되는 것이 적절하며 앞에 한정사가 없으므로 복수 명사 (B) openings가 정답이다.

어휘 temporary 임시의, 임시직의 certified 자격증을 가진, 공인된 attendant 간호인, 종업원 opening 공석, 결원 openness 솔직함 opener 개시자, 여는 도구

ETS 실전문제 본책 p.144

1 (C)	2 (A)	3 (D)	4 (D)	5 (A)	6 (A)
7 (D)	8 (B)	9 (A)	10 (D)	11 (D)	12 (B)
13 (C)	14 (B)	15 (A)	16 (A)	17 (D)	18 (D)

1 (C)

번역 최근 졸업생들은 취업 박람회에 참여함으로써 다양한 업계의 취업 기회에 대해 알 수 있다.

해설 빈칸은 형용사 Recent의 수식을 받는 명사 자리로, 동사 can learn의 주어 역할을 한다. learn의 주체는 사람이어야 하므로, '졸업생들'이라는 의미의 (C) graduates가 정답이다.

어휘 employment 취업, 고용 opportunity 기회 a wide range of 다양한 attend 참가하다 career fair 취업 박람회 graduate 졸업하다; 졸업생 graduation 졸업

2 (A)

번역 웨리버 빌딩 2층에 있는 전구들은 이번 주에 교체될 예정이다.

해설 빈칸은 전치사 on의 목적어 역할을 하는 명사 자리로, the Werriver Building's second의 수식을 받는다. 따라서 보기에서 '층'을 뜻하는 (A) floor와 (B) floors 중 하나가 들어가야 하는데, 특정 건물의 2층은 하나이므로, 단수 명사 (A) floor가 정답이다.

어휘 replace 교체하다 flooring 바닥재

3 (D)

번역 판프라덥 그래픽 디자인 사는 직원들에게 수많은 컴퓨터 프로그램에 대한 능숙함을 포함하여 고급 전문 기술을 갖추기를 요구한다.

해설 빈칸은 동사 possess의 목적어 역할을 하며 형용사 technical의 수식을 받는 명사 자리이다. 직원들이 갖추어야 하는 것을 나타내는 명사가 들어가야 하므로, (D) expertise(전문 지식, 전문 기술)가 정답이다.

어휘 advanced 진보된, 첨단의 proficiency 능숙, 노련 numerous 수많은, 다수의 expert 전문가

4 (D)

번역 사장은 작년에 생산성이 가장 높았던 공장 부서에 보너스를 지급할 것이라고 발표했다.

해설 동사 has demonstrated의 목적어 역할을 하는 명사가 필요하다. 문맥상 '가장 높은 생산성'이라는 의미가 되어야 자연스러우므로, (D) productivity(생산성)가 정답이다.

어휘 president 사장 award 주다, 수여하다 demonstrate (능력을) 보여주다, 시연하다 product 상품, 제품 produce 생산하다; 농산물

5 (A)

번역 입사 지원자의 면접 요청서는 반드시 12월 15일까지 제출되어야 한다.

135

해설 　조동사 must 앞에 있는 빈칸에는 소유격 A job candidate's의 수식을 받으면서 interview와 복합명사를 이루는 명사가 들어가야 하며, 제출되는 사물을 나타내야 하므로, '요청서'를 뜻하는 (A) request가 정답이다.

어휘 　candidate 지원자, 후보자 requester 요청자, 청구인

6 (A)

번역 　국제 엔지니어 협회의 위원들은 내년에 열릴 회의를 기획하기 위해 지난주에 모였다.

해설 　빈칸은 동사 met의 주어 역할을 하는 명사 자리이다. 따라서 만남의 주체가 될 수 있는 사람 명사 (A) Representatives가 정답이다.

어휘 　conference 회의, 대회 representative 대표, 위원, 직원
represent 대표하다

7 (D)

번역 　브라이트우드 시장은 시의 성장 및 발전 계획에 관해 공표했다.

해설 　부정관사 a와 전치사 about 사이에 빈칸이 있으므로 단수 명사 (D) declaration(공표, 선언(문))이 정답이다.

어휘 　mayor 시장 issue a declaration 공표하다 declare 선언하다, 선포하다

8 (B)

번역 　학교 도서관을 지원하기 위해, 5세에서 12세 사이의 아이들에게 적합한 도서들을 기증해 주시기 바랍니다.

해설 　정관사 the와 전치사 of 사이에 있는 빈칸은 명사 자리이므로, (B) ages가 정답이다.

어휘 　donate 기증하다, 기부하다 appropriate 적합한, 적절한
agedly 나이가 들어, 노화되어

9 (A)

번역 　업데이트된 환자 포털 웹사이트에는 의료 서비스 제공 기관들과의 소통을 위한 장치가 포함되어 있다.

해설 　빈칸에는 부정관사 a의 수식을 받으면서 타동사 includes의 목적어 역할을 할 명사가 들어가야 하며, 웹사이트에 포함될 수 있는 것으로서 '의료 서비스 제공 기관들과의 소통을 위한 장치'를 의미해야 가장 자연스러우므로, '방법, 장치' 등을 뜻하는 명사 (A) mechanism이 정답이다.

어휘 　patient 환자 mechanize 기계화하다 mechanic 정비사
mechanical 기계적인

10 (D)

번역 　그 모금 운동은 소기업들이 사무용품을 위해 최대 1,000달러의 상금을 탈 수 있게 도와줄 것이다.

해설 　명사 office와 빈칸이 전치사 for의 목적어 역할을 할 복합명사를 구성해야 알맞으며, 상금의 용도와 관련해 '사무용품'을 의미해야 자연스러우므로, '용품, 물품'을 뜻하는 명사 (D) supplies가 정답이다.

어휘 　fund-raising 모금, 기금 마련 supply 공급하다
supplier 공급업체

11 (D)

번역 　새 자동차를 찾아보기 전에 어느 기술 옵션이 가장 중요한지 결정하십시오.

해설 　명사절 접속사 which로 시작하는 명사절에서 명사 technology와 동사 are 사이에 빈칸이 있으므로 빈칸에는 technology와 함께 복합명사를 구성하는 명사가 필요하다. 또한, 복수 동사 are와 수 일치가 되어야 하므로, 복수 명사 (D) options가 정답이다.

어휘 　automobile 자동차 optionally 선택적으로 optional 선택적인

12 (B)

번역 　우리는 9월에 새 인사부 이사를 적극적으로 찾기 시작할 것으로 예상한다.

해설 　빈칸이 관사 an과 명사 search 사이에 있으며 '적극적인 찾기'라는 의미가 적절하므로, 형용사인 (B) active가 정답이다. 명사 (D) activity와 search가 복합명사를 구성하는 것은 어색하다.

어휘 　active 적극적인 activate 활성화하다 activity 활동

13 (C)

번역 　그 회사의 공석 목록은 귀하의 관심을 끌 수 있는 여러 직책을 보여줍니다.

해설 　회사의 공석 목록에서 확인할 수 있는 정보와 관련된 명사가 쓰여야 자연스러우므로, '직책, 일자리'를 의미하는 (C) positions가 정답이다.

어휘 　job opening 공석 appeal to ~의 관심을 끌다
deadline 마감 기한

14 (B)

번역 　아르투로의 신발과 벨트는 최고급 합성 소재로 만들어진다.

해설 　신발과 벨트가 '최고급 합성 소재로 만들어진다'라는 의미를 나타내야 자연스러우므로, '소재, 재료' 등을 뜻하는 (B) materials가 정답이다.

어휘 　synthetic 합성의, 인조의 portion 부분, 일부

[15-18] 보도 자료

즉시 보도용

담당자: 정진호, jhchung@elbasinaproperties.com.sg

싱가포르(6월 3일) — 이번 달에 엘바시나 부동산이 민디 리우를 임원진으로 맞이한다. 리우 씨는 지난달까지 아이오타소프트 테크놀로지의 광고부장이었는데, 최근 신설된 디지털 미디어 이사직을 **15 맡을 것이다.** 공식 업무 시작일은 6월 17일이다.

"소셜 미디어와 다른 디지털 매체들을 통한 광고가 오늘날 업체들에게 아주 중요합니다"라고 엘바시나 부동산의 CEO인 쾅잉 헤가 말했다. "**16 이것이 바로 우리 회사의 새로운 역할이 아주 중요한 이유입니다.** 리우 씨는 우리가 필요로 하는 핵심 역량을 가지고 있습니다."

리우 씨는 샐리나 비즈니스 아카데미에서 공부했고, 그곳에서 디지털 광고 **17 분야** 학위를 취득했다. 졸업 후, 아이오타소프트 테크놀

로지에서 일자리를 얻었다. 리우 씨는 본인의 **18 경험**을 활용해 주요 광고 캠페인을 만들고 있다.

> **어휘** immediate 즉각적인 release 보도, 발표 executive team 임원진 advertising 광고 outlet 매체, 수단 crucial 아주 중요한 essential 필수적인 earn 얻다, 획득하다 degree 학위 graduate 졸업하다 secure 얻다, 확보하다 draw on ~을 활용하다, ~에 의지하다 craft 만들어 내다

15 (A)

해설 보기가 모두 동사이고, 시제만 다르므로 시제 관련 단서를 찾아야 한다. 다음 문장에 공식 업무 시작일이 6월 17일이라고 쓰여 있는데, 이것은 시작 부분에 표시된 6월 3일(3 June)보다 미래이므로 미래 시제인 (A) will assume이 정답이다.

어휘 assume (직책, 책임 등을) 맡다

16 (A)

번역 (A) 이것이 바로 우리 회사의 새로운 역할이 아주 중요한 이유입니다.
(B) 이분께서 보유하고 계신 것을 단기에 할 수 있는 사람은 거의 없습니다.
(C) 소셜 미디어를 이용해야 하는 이유는 많습니다.
(D) 저희는 항상 아이오타소프트 사의 제품을 높이 평가해 왔습니다.

해설 빈칸은 CEO의 말이 이어지는 부분인데, 앞에는 소셜 미디어와 다른 디지털 매체를 통한 광고가 아주 중요하다고 말이 있고, 뒤에는 리우 씨는 회사에서 필요로 하는 핵심 역량을 갖고 있다는 말이 있다. 따라서 이런 경향 및 리우 씨의 역할과 관련된 문장이 쓰여야 흐름상 자연스러우므로, 앞 문장에 언급된 사실을 That으로, 그리고 리우 씨가 맡는 새로운 직책을 the new role로 각각 지칭해 그 역할의 중요성을 말하는 (A)가 정답이다.

어휘 appreciate 높이 평가하다, 감사하다

17 (D)

해설 빈칸 뒤에 있는 digital advertising은 리우 씨가 취득한 학위 종류를 나타내므로 학위 종류를 나타낼 때 사용하는 전치사 (D) in이 정답이다.

18 (D)

해설 빈칸은 소유격 대명사 her의 수식을 받으면서 전치사 on의 목적어 역할을 할 명사가 필요한 자리이므로 (D) experience가 정답이다.

어휘 experience 경험; 경험하다 experienced 경험 많은

UNIT 03 대명사

1 인칭대명사와 소유대명사

ETS 유형연습		본책 p.146
1 (A)	2 (B)	3 (B)

1 (A)

번역 회의에서 메모하신 내용을 타이핑하신 다음, 금요일까지 모두에게 배부해 주시기 바랍니다.

해설 타동사 distribute의 목적어 역할을 할 대명사가 필요하며, 앞에 언급된 notes를 가리켜야 의미가 자연스러우므로 (A) them이 정답이다.

어휘 distribute 배부하다, 나눠 주다

2 (B)

번역 새로 고용된 회계 담당 직원으로서, 구 씨는 배정된 자신의 멘토와 매주 만난다.

해설 전치사 with와 명사구 목적어 assigned mentor 사이에 빈칸이 위치해 있으므로 명사구를 앞에서 수식할 수 있는 소유격 대명사 (B) her가 정답이다.

어휘 associate 직원 assign 배정하다, 할당하다

3 (B)

번역 거대 패스트푸드 기업인 누트루 사는 우리 로고가 그들의 로고를 형편없이 표절한 것이라고 주장한다.

해설 소유의 의미를 강조할 때는 〈one's own+명사〉나 〈명사+of one's own〉을 쓸 수 있으므로 소유격 인칭대명사 (B) their가 정답이다.

어휘 giant 거대 기업, 대가 claim 주장하다 disguised 변장한

2 재귀대명사

ETS 유형연습		본책 p.147
1 (D)	2 (D)	3 (D)

1 (D)

번역 실험실 기술자들은 외부 분석가를 채용하는 것이 비용이 너무 많이 들기 때문에 자신들이 직접 통계를 분석하기로 결정했다.

해설 빈칸이 없어도 완전한 문장이므로 빈칸에는 강조적 용법의 재귀대명사가 들어가야 한다. 따라서 주어인 The laboratory technicians를 강조하는 (D) themselves가 정답이다.

어휘 laboratory 실험실, 연구실 technician 전문가, 기술자 statistical 통계의, 통계(학)상의 analysis 분석 analyst 분석가 costly 비용이 많이 드는

2 (D)

번역 손님들은 미라벨 주방장이 기념일 연회에서 제공한 식사에 아주 만족하는 것처럼 보였다.

해설 동사 served의 목적어 자리로 The guests를 대신하는 목적격 인칭대명사 (D) them이 정답이다.

어휘 chef 주방장 banquet 연회, 축연

3 (D)

번역 다른 프로그래머의 비밀번호에 문제가 있어서 신 씨는 회사 웹사이트를 혼자서 업데이트했다.

해설 by oneself는 '혼자서'라는 뜻으로, 웹사이트를 업데이트하는 주체가 Mr. Shin이므로 (D) himself가 정답이다.

3 지시대명사

ETS 유형연습   본책 p.148

1 (C)   2 (C)   3 (A)

1 (C)

번역 콘퍼런스 숙박 신청서를 받지 못한 분들은 가능한 한 빨리 등록 창구에 알려 주세요.

해설 주격 관계대명사 who가 이끄는 절의 수식을 받으면서 '~하는 사람들'의 의미를 나타내는 지시대명사 (C) Those가 정답이다.

어휘 form 양식, 서식   registration desk 등록 창구

2 (C)

번역 조립 구역에서 근무하는 직원들은 항상 보호 장비를 착용해야 한다.

해설 명사구 Those employees를 수식하는 수식어 자리로 '일을 하는 직원들'이라는 의미를 나타내는 현재분사 (C) working이 정답이다. 문장에 이미 동사(must wear)가 있으므로, (A), (B), (D)는 빈칸에 들어갈 수 없다.

어휘 assembly 조립   protective gear 보호 장비   at all times 항상

3 (A)

번역 주요 자동차 대여 업체들의 올해 수입액은 지난 4년간의 수입액과 매우 비슷하다.

해설 빈칸은 앞에 나온 revenue figures라는 복수 명사를 받아야 하므로 (A) those가 정답이다.

어휘 revenue 수익, 수입   figure 수치   be similar to ~와 비슷하다   remarkably 현저히, 매우   preceding 이전의

4 부정대명사

ETS 유형연습   본책 p.149

1 (A)   2 (B)   3 (D)

1 (A)

번역 이 소프트웨어 개발에 관여한 사람 중 어느 누구도 그것이 아주 인기 있을 것이라고는 짐작하지 못했다.

해설 의미상 '아무도 짐작하지 못했다'라는 뜻의 부정문이 되어야 하므로 (A) None이 정답이다.

어휘 involved in ~에 관련된, 참가한   develop 개발하다

2 (B)

번역 카펫 전시실 공사는 이번 주말까지 완공될 것이지만, 영업은 한 달 더 지난 후에 개시될 것이다.

해설 (A) other 뒤에는 복수 명사와 불가산명사, (B) another 뒤에는 단수 가산명사가 온다. 빈칸 뒤에 단수 가산명사인 month가 있으므로 (B) another가 정답이다.

어휘 construction 건설, 공사   showroom 진열실, 전시실   operation 운영, 조업

3 (D)

번역 코발트 연구상의 공동 수상자인 히마나 박사와 웨어햄 박사는 오클랜드에서 대학생 시절부터 서로 아는 사이였다.

해설 문맥상 '서로 아는 사이였다'라는 의미가 되려면 빈칸에는 (D) each other를 써야 한다. (A) other one은 '다른 것', (B) another one은 '또 다른 것'이라는 의미이므로 적절하지 않다. (C) any other는 '뭔가 다른 (것), 누군가 딴 (사람)'을 지칭하는 형용사나 명사이므로 적절하지 않다.

어휘 joint recipients 공동 수상자

ETS 실전문제   본책 p.150

1 (A)	2 (B)	3 (A)	4 (A)	5 (C)	6 (B)
7 (D)	8 (C)	9 (B)	10 (B)	11 (D)	12 (B)
13 (B)	14 (D)	15 (A)	16 (D)	17 (C)	18 (B)

1 (A)

번역 스탠윅 앤 어소시에이츠에서는 각각의 고객에게 맞춤형 자산 관리 플랜을 제공하는 것을 자랑스럽게 생각합니다.

해설 빈칸은 giving의 간접 목적어 역할을 하는 자리로, 전치사구 of our clients의 수식을 받는다. 따라서 목적어 자리에 들어갈 수 있는 부정대명사 (A) each가 정답이다. (D) every는 바로 뒤에 단수 명사가 와야 한다.

어휘 pride oneself on ~를 자랑하다   personalized 개인 맞춤형의   wealth management 자산 관리

2 (B)

번역 바이오메딕스 팟캐스트는 의료 서비스 관련 주제들을 다룰 것이며, 그 첫 번째 방송분은 월요일에 들을 수 있을 것이다.

해설 빈칸은 명사구 first episode를 수식하는 자리이므로, 소유격 대명사 (B) its가 정답이다.

어휘 cover (주제 등을) 다루다   available 이용할 수 있는

3 (A)

번역 팔라 박물관의 교육 진행 담당자들은 모든 방문객들에게 자극이 되는 학습 기회를 제공하는 데 헌신하고 있다.

해설 빈칸 앞에 있는 동사 dedicate는 '~하는 데 헌신하다' 의미를 나타낼 때 〈dedicate+oneself+to -ing〉 구조로 쓰므로 재귀대명사 (A) themselves가 정답이다.

어휘 coordinator 진행 담당자, 조정 담당자   stimulating 자극이 되는, 활기를 불어넣는   opportunity 기회

4 (A)
번역 그 매장 관리자 직책이 공석이기 때문에, 김 씨는 자신이 그 자리에 지원하고 싶다고 말한다.

해설 동사 would like to 앞에 주어 자리에 빈칸이 있으므로 주격 대명사 (A) she가 정답이다. 소유대명사 (C) hers도 주어 자리에 올 수 있지만, '그녀의 것'이라는 의미로서 지원하는 사람을 나타내지 못하므로, 오답이다.

어휘 position 직책, 자리 apply for ~에 지원하다, ~을 신청하다

5 (C)
번역 사무실 관리자인 스티븐 브래드는 모든 직원에게 새로운 용품 주문에 관련해서는 그와 직접 소통해 달라고 요청한다.

해설 that이 이끄는 명사절에서 전치사 with의 목적어 역할을 하는 자리이다. 문맥상 직원들이 소통할 대상은 앞서 언급된 Steven Brad이므로, 목적격 (C) him이 정답이다.

어휘 request 요청하다 supply 용품

6 (B)
번역 비록 팀에서 협력하여 이 보고서의 그래픽을 개발했지만, 문구는 주로 내가 작업한 것이다.

해설 빈칸은 is의 보어가 되어야 하며 의미상 my text를 줄인 단어가 필요하므로 소유대명사인 (B) mine이 정답이다.

어휘 text 문서, 본문 primarily 주로, 기본적으로

7 (D)
번역 다음 달에 출장을 떠나는 직원들은 반드시 다음 주 금요일까지 하바니언 씨의 사무실로 일정표를 제출해야 한다.

해설 동사 submit과 명사 목적어 itineraries 사이에 빈칸이 위치해 있으므로 명사를 앞에서 수식할 수 있는 소유격 대명사 (D) their가 정답이다.

어휘 itinerary 일정(표)

8 (C)
번역 비행 중 휴식을 원하시는 분들을 위해, 저희 항공사는 수면 마스크와 담요를 제공합니다.

해설 주격 관계대명사 who가 이끄는 절의 수식을 받으면서 '~하는 사람들'이라는 의미를 나타내는 지시대명사 (C) those가 정답이다.

어휘 rest 휴식하다, 쉬다

9 (B)
번역 주택 매매 및 임대 시장은 대개 지역 경제가 호전되면 덕을 보니 곧 활기를 찾을 것이다.

해설 빈칸은 접속사 as가 이끄는 절의 주어가 들어갈 자리인데, 동사가 복수(benefit)이고 문맥상 home sales and rental markets를 가리키므로 '둘 다'를 의미하는 (B) both가 정답이다.

어휘 rental 임대(의), 임대료 strengthen 강화하다, 증강하다 benefit 이익을 얻다, 덕을 보다

10 (B)
번역 김 씨와 노박 씨는 매우 다른 능력을 지니고 있지만, 둘 중 어느 쪽이든 회사에 자산이 될 것이다.

해설 조동사 would 앞에서 주어 역할을 할 대명사가 필요하며, Although절에 언급된 두 사람을 대상으로 해야 하므로 '둘 중 어느 하나'를 뜻하는 (B) either가 정답이다. (C) anybody는 막연한 대상 중 아무나를 뜻하고, (A) other는 형용사이며, (D) whoever는 접속사이다.

어휘 asset (사람, 물건 등) 자산, 재산

11 (D)
번역 카타쿠라 교수는 여러 번 실험을 했지만 그 결과가 동료들의 결과와 달랐다.

해설 빈칸은 전치사 from의 목적어 역할을 하는 자리로, 전치사구 of his colleagues의 수식을 받는다. 문장이 카타쿠라 교수와 동료들의 실험 결과(results)를 비교하고 있으므로, results를 대신하는 지시대명사 (D) those가 정답이다.

어휘 perform 수행하다 experiment 실험 colleague 동료

12 (B)
번역 직원들은 연수 기간 동안 고객의 문의 사항을 처리하는 과정을 완벽하게 숙달하는 데 서로에게 도움이 되도록 2인 1조로 근무해야 한다.

해설 빈칸 앞에는 준동사 to help가, 뒤에는 동사원형 master가 온 〈help+목적어+동사원형〉 구문이므로 빈칸은 목적어 자리이다. 앞에서 둘씩 짝을 지어 활동한다는(work in pairs) 내용이 나오므로 '서로'를 의미하는 부정대명사 (B) each other가 정답이다.

어휘 staff member 직원 master 숙달하다 procedure 절차 handle 처리하다 inquiry 질문, 문의

13 (B)
번역 최근 고객 설문 조사는 많은 사람들이 자신들의 호텔 식사 경험에 대해 불만족했다는 것을 보여준다.

해설 that이 이끄는 명사절에서 동사 were의 주어 역할을 하는 자리이므로, were와 수가 일치하는 부정대명사 (B) many가 정답이다.

어휘 survey 설문 조사 indicate 나타내다, 보여주다 be dissatisfied with ~을 불만스럽게 여기다

14 (D)
번역 이사는 전 직원을 외부 (위탁) 교육 과정에 보내서 새로운 소프트웨어를 배우도록 하는 대신에 자신이 직접 모두를 교육하기로 결정했다.

해설 의미상 the entire staff를 대신하는 단어가 필요하므로 (D) everyone이 정답이다.

어휘 director 이사, 국장

[15-18] 이메일

수신: 닐즈 맥캘리스터 〈nmccallister@coralmail.com〉
발신: 트리샤 스패츠 〈tspatz@mulltonartscouncil.org〉
날짜: 3월 1일
제목: 예술 위원회 이사회

맥캘리스터 씨께,

귀하께서 멀튼 예술 위원회의 이사회 후보로 **15 지명되었다**는 사실을 알려 드리게 되어 기쁩니다. 참고로, 이사회는 예술 위원회의 재정 운영을 감독하고 중요한 기금 마련 행사를 조직하는 일을 맡고 있습니다. 이사진은 총 6명으로, **16 그들** 중에서 누가 핵심적인 리더십 책임을 맡을 것인지 결정합니다. **17 또한**, 이사진은 6년 임기로 재직하며, 사무총장과 주기적으로 소통하는데, 이 직책은 현재 제가 맡고 있습니다.

현 이사진과 제가 3월 8일 목요일에 모여 신임 이사에 대한 투표를 할 것입니다. **18 이 이메일에 답장하셔서 이 제안의 수락 여부를 표명해 주시기 바랍니다.**

고려해 주셔서 대단히 감사합니다.

트리샤 스패츠, 사무총장, 멀튼 예술 위원회

어휘 board 이사회 Board of Trustees 이사회, 평의원회 be tasked with -ing ~하는 일을 맡다 operation 운영, 영업 organize 조직하다, 마련하다 fund-raising 기금 마련, 모금 take on ~을 맡다 responsibility 책임(감) serve 재직하다 term 임기 regularly 주기적으로, 규칙적으로 executive director 사무총장, 전무이사 vote 투표하다 consideration 고려, 숙고

15 (A)
해설 접속사 that과 주어 you 뒤로 빈칸과 전치사구들만 있으므로 빈칸은 that절의 동사 자리이다. 빈칸 바로 뒤에 목적어 없이 for 전치사구가 있으므로 타동사인 nominate는 수동태가 되어야 한다. 따라서 (A) have been nominated가 정답이다.
어휘 nominate 후보로 지명하다

16 (D)
해설 빈칸 앞뒤 부분이 '~ 중에서 누가 핵심적인 리더십 책임을 맡을 것인지 결정한다'는 의미인데, 빈칸에 쓰일 대명사가 주어 Board members(이사진)를 가리켜야 알맞으므로 3인칭 복수 재귀대명사 (D) themselves가 정답이다.

17 (C)
해설 빈칸 앞뒤에 있는 문장들이 모두 board members를 주어로 이사회에서 하는 일을 설명하고 있어 유사 정보가 이어지는 흐름임을 알 수 있다. 따라서 '또한, 더욱이'라는 의미의 접속부사 (C) Furthermore가 정답이다.
어휘 in other words 다시 말해서 nevertheless 그럼에도 불구하고 likewise 마찬가지로

18 (B)
번역 (A) 저희는 흔히 이 목적으로 출장 요리 점심 식사를 마련합니다.
(B) **이 이메일에 답장하셔서 이 제안의 수락 여부를 표명해 주시기 바랍니다.**
(C) 멀튼 예술 위원회는 20년 동안 운영되어 오고 있습니다.
(D) 회의는 보통 매주 월요일에 열리지만, 저희가 이것의 일정을 재조정할 것입니다.

해설 지문 전체적으로 상대방이 이사회 후보로 지명된 사실과 함께 이사회에 대한 간략한 설명이 제시되어 있고, 빈칸 앞에는 신임 이사 투표 일정이 언급되어 있다. 따라서 상대방을 후보로 지명한 것을 this offer로 지칭해 그에 대한 수락 여부를 알려 달라고 부탁하는 (B)가 정답이다.

어휘 arrange 마련하다, 조치하다 catered 출장 요리로 제공되는 indicate (의견 등을) 표명하다, 나타내다 acceptance 수용, 수락 operate 운영되다, 가동되다 decade 10년 reschedule 일정을 재조정하다

UNIT 04 형용사

1 형용사의 자리

ETS 유형연습   본책 p.152

1 (A)   **2** (D)   **3** (C)

1 (A)
번역 저희 지원자 선별 툴은 기업과 자격을 갖춘 직원을 연결해 줍니다.
해설 전치사 with와 명사 목적어 employees 사이에 빈칸이 있으므로 명사를 수식하는 형용사가 들어갈 수 있는 자리이다. 따라서 (A) qualified(자격을 갖춘, 적격인)가 정답이다. 명사 (B) qualification와 (D) qualifier는 employees와 복합명사를 구성하지 않으므로 오답이다.
어휘 applicant 지원자, 신청자 screening 선별, 심사 qualification 자격(증) qualify 자격을 주다 qualifier 예선 경기, 예선 통과자

2 (D)
번역 브라이트먼 파트너스 주식회사의 건축가들은 실용적일 뿐 아니라 우아한 건물을 설계한다.
해설 명사 buildings를 수식하는 관계사(that)절에서 형용사 elegant와 함께(as well as) 건물에 대해 보충 설명하는 주격 보어 자리이다. 따라서 '실용적인'이라는 의미의 형용사 (D) functional이 정답이다.
어휘 architect 건축가 elegant 우아한, 품격 있는 function 기능; 작동하다 functionality 기능성

3 (C)

번역 비평가들은 미셸 자오의 최근 영화 줄거리가 너무 뻔하다고 평했다.

해설 call A B는 'A를 B라고 말하다, 부르다'라는 뜻이다. 빈칸에는 목적격 보어가 필요하므로, 부사 too의 수식을 받으면서 목적어 the plot을 보충 설명하는 형용사 (C) predictable이 정답이다.

어휘 critic 비평가   plot 줄거리, 구상   predictable 예측 가능한, 새로운 게 없는

2 수량/부정형용사

ETS 유형연습 본책 p.153

1 (D)   **2** (B)   **3** (D)

1 (D)

번역 안도 생물학 실험실의 모든 표본은 적정한 온도에서 보관되어야 한다.

해설 빈칸 뒤에 가산명사의 단수형 sample이 있으므로 (D) Every가 정답이다. (A) All, (B) Most, (C) Other 뒤에는 가산명사의 복수형이나 불가산명사가 와야 한다.

어휘 biology 생물학   lab(= laboratory) 실험실   temperature 온도

2 (B)

번역 비용이 듦에도 불구하고, 많은 직원들이 강당을 수리하는 것에 찬성했다.

해설 빈칸이 복수 명사 staff members 앞에 있으므로 (B) many가 정답이다. (A) mass는 '대중의, 대량의'라는 뜻으로 의미상 적합하지 않다. (C) much는 불가산명사 앞에 써야 한다. (D) plenty는 of가 없으므로 정답이 될 수 없다.

어휘 despite ~에도 불구하고   in favor of ~에 찬성하여   renovate 수리하다, 개조하다   auditorium 강당

3 (D)

번역 델무어 사는 오용, 부적절한 관리, 또는 기타 고객 부주의로 인한 파손에 대해서는 책임지지 않습니다.

해설 빈칸이 불가산명사인 consumer negligence 앞에 있으며 의미상 '그 밖의 다른'이라는 뜻이 필요하므로 (D) other가 정답이다. (B) 〈the other+명사〉는 정해진 범위에서 일부를 제외하고 '(남은) 다른 것'이라는 뜻인데 이 문장에서는 consumer negligence의 정해진 범위가 없으므로 의미상 옳지 않다.

어휘 be responsible for ~에 대한 책임이 있다   misuse 오용, 남용   improper 부적절한   consumer 소비자, 고객   negligence 무시, 부주의

3 혼동하기 쉬운 형용사

ETS 유형연습 본책 p.154

1 (C)   **2** (C)   **3** (C)

1 (C)

번역 헤일 밸리의 다양한 명소는 방문객들과 주민들에게 꾸준히 즐거움을 선사한다.

해설 빈칸은 명사 attractions 앞에서 명사를 수식하는 형용사 자리로 (C) diverse가 정답이다. (B) diversifying은 '다양하게 만드는, 다각화하는'이라는 뜻으로 의미상 옳지 않다.

어휘 attraction 인기물, 명소   delight 기쁘게 하다   resident 주민   diverse 다양한   diversity 다양성

2 (C)

번역 모든 승객들은 다른 사람을 배려하여 휴대전화로 통화할 때 작게 말해야 한다.

해설 '모든 승객들은 다른 사람들을 배려해야 한다'라는 의미가 되어야 하므로 '배려하는, 사려 깊은'이라는 뜻의 (C) considerate이 정답이다. 〈be considerate of+사람〉을 '(사람)을 배려하다'라는 뜻으로 기억해두자. (A) considerable은 '상당한'이라는 뜻이므로 의미상 옳지 않다.

어휘 passenger 승객, 탑승객   mobile phone 휴대전화   consideration 고려, 숙고

3 (C)

번역 우리 회사의 전문 컨설팅 서비스를 이용하는 명망 있는 회사 및 단체의 최신 목록을 동봉합니다.

해설 빈칸 뒤의 명사구 companies and institutions를 수식하는 자리이므로 형용사 (C) distinguished가 정답이다.

어휘 enclosed 동봉한   listing 목록   institution 단체, 기관   firm 회사   specialized 전문화된, 전문적인   distinguishably 구별 가능하여   distinguishability 구별 가능성   distinguished 유명한, 뛰어난   distinguish 구별하다, 분간하다

4 형용사 빈출 표현

ETS 유형연습 본책 p.155

1 (D)   **2** (A)   **3** (C)

1 (D)

번역 회사 지침에 따르면, 신입 사원들은 3개월간 풀타임으로 근무한 후에 휴가를 받을 수 있다.

해설 '휴가 혜택을 받을 자격이 있다'가 적합하므로 (D) eligible이 정답이다. eligible은 〈eligible for+명사〉나 〈eligible to+동사원형〉의 형태로 주로 쓰인다. (A) capable(할 수 있는)은 뒤에 〈of+(동)명사〉가 온다.

어휘 guideline 지침   benefits 복리 후생   variable 변하기 쉬운   flexible 유연한, 탄력적인

2 (A)
번역 모든 승객들은 출발 전에 적절한 여행 서류를 구비할 책임이 있다.

해설 빈칸 앞에 있는 형용사 responsible은 전치사 for와 함께 쓰이므로 (A) for가 정답이다.

어휘 passenger 승객 proper 적절한 document 문서, 서류

3 (C)
번역 저희 영업부에서 훌륭히 업무를 수행하고 계신 점 진심으로 감사드립니다.

해설 형용사 어휘 문제이므로, 빈칸 뒤의 명사를 살펴본다. 문맥상 '진심 어린 감사'가 적절하므로 (C) sincere가 정답이다.

어휘 sales department 영업부 sincere 진심에서 우러난 estimated 어림 잡은 completed 완료된

ETS 실전문제
본책 p.156

1 (A)	2 (D)	3 (C)	4 (A)	5 (A)	6 (A)
7 (C)	8 (D)	9 (A)	10 (A)	11 (B)	12 (D)
13 (A)	14 (A)	15 (A)	16 (C)	17 (D)	18 (B)

1 (A)
번역 직원들께서는 파일 캐비닛 열쇠를 항상 안전한 장소에 보관해야 합니다.

해설 부정관사 a와 명사 location 사이에 있는 빈칸은 명사를 수식하는 형용사가 들어갈 수 있는 자리이므로 (A) safe가 정답이다. 최상급 형용사인 (C) safest는 정관사 the와 함께 사용하며, 명사 (B) safety는 location과 복합명사를 구성하지 않으므로 오답이다.

2 (D)
번역 지역 제조업체들은 생산성이 향상될 때까지 직원을 추가로 채용하길 주저했다.

해설 빈칸은 주어 Local manufacturers를 보충 설명하는 주격 보어 자리로, to부정사와 어울려 쓰이는 형용사가 들어가야 한다. 따라서 '~하기를 주저하다'라는 의미를 완성하는 (D) hesitant가 정답이다.

어휘 manufacturer 제조업체, 생산자 additional 추가적인, 부가적인 productivity 생산성

3 (C)
번역 귀하의 다음 번 구독료 결제는 6월 15일에 귀하의 은행 계좌에서 자동 인출될 예정입니다.

해설 전치사 for와 명사 목적어 withdrawal 사이에 있는 빈칸에는 명사를 수식하는 형용사가 들어갈 수 있으므로 (C) automatic이 정답이다. 명사 (B) automation은 withdrawal과 복합명사를 구성하지 않으므로 오답이다.

어휘 subscription 구독 withdrawal 인출, 철회 account 계좌, 계정 automation 자동화 automate 자동화하다

4 (A)
번역 행정 보조직 지원자는 강한 조직력을 보유하고 있어야 한다.

해설 빈칸은 뒤에 있는 명사 skills를 수식하는 자리이므로 형용사 (A) organizational이 정답이다.

어휘 candidate 지원자, 후보자 administrative assistant 행정 보조 organizational 조직적인 organizationally 조직적으로 organize 조직하다, 정리하다

5 (A)
번역 루벤스 비즈니스 센트럴은 매력적이고 실용적인 사무용 가구를 매우 다양하게 판매한다.

해설 부정관사 a와 명사 range 사이에 있는 빈칸은 명사를 수식하는 형용사가 들어갈 수 있는 자리이므로, (A) comprehensive (종합적인)가 정답이다. 명사 (D) comprehension은 range와 복합명사를 구성하지 않는다.

어휘 a comprehensive range of 매우 다양한 attractive 매력적인 functional 실용적인 comprehensively 종합적으로 comprehend 이해하다 comprehension 이해(력)

6 (A)
번역 팔라우 베이 은행의 대출 신청 과정은 아주 효율적이다.

해설 빈칸은 주격 보어 자리로 부사 very의 수식을 받으므로, 형용사인 (A) efficient가 정답이다.

어휘 loan application 대출 신청 process 과정 efficient 효율적인, 효과적인 efficiency 효율성 efficiently 효율적으로

7 (C)
번역 도서 할인 행사에 자원하길 원하는 직원들은 금요일까지 신청해야 한다.

해설 복수 사람 명사 employees를 수식하는 자리에 빈칸이 있으므로 이를 수식할 수 있는 (C) Those가 정답이다. those는 〈those+사람 명사+who절(~하는 사람들)〉 구조로 자주 쓰인다.

어휘 volunteer 자원하다 sign up 신청하다, 등록하다 whoever ~하는 사람은 누구든

8 (D)
번역 그 프로그램의 신규 버전은 현재 리얀 소프트웨어 다운로드 사이트에서 손쉽게 이용할 수 있다.

해설 빈칸은 부사 readily의 수식을 받는 형용사 자리로, 주어 A new version of the program을 보충 설명하는 주격 보어 역할을 한다. 따라서 (D) accessible이 정답이다.

어휘 readily 손쉽게 accessibility 접근하기 쉬움 access 접근, 접속; 접근하다 accessible 접근 가능한, 이용할 수 있는

9 (A)
번역 여러 관리자들은 계획에 없던 유지보수 작업이 차량 조립에 지장을 줬다고 불평했다.

해설 빈칸은 that절의 주어 the unscheduled maintenance를 보충 설명하는 주격 보어 자리로, 계획에 없던 유지보수 작업이 차량 조립에 미치는 영향을 묘사하는 형용사가 빈칸에 들어가야 하므로, '지장을 주는'이라는 의미의 (A) disruptive가 정답이다.

어휘 supervisor 감독관, 관리자 unscheduled 계획에 없던 maintenance 유지 assembly 조립 disruptive 지장을 주는 disruption 중단, 분열 disrupt 지장을 주다, 방해하다

10 (A)

번역 적정 가격을 유지하기 위해 킴스 제과점은 빵과 케이크를 점포에서 만들기 시작할 것이다.

해설 keep은 목적어가 필요한 타동사이므로 빈칸에는 prices와 함께 복합명사를 이루는 명사가 올 수도 있고 〈keep+목적어+목적격 보어〉의 형식으로 쓰여 형용사가 올 수도 있다. 복합명사의 경우 (C) reasoning과 (D) reason을 생각해 볼 수 있는데, 둘 다 prices와 함께 썼을 때 뜻이 통하지 않는다. '가격을 적정하게 유지하기 위해서'라는 의미가 되어야 자연스러우므로, 형용사인 (A) reasonable(합리적인, 비싸지 않은)이 정답이다.

어휘 on the premises 점포 내에서 reasonably 합리적으로 reasoning 추론

11 (B)

번역 제3자에 의해 실시되는 어쿠슈티컬 사의 임상 실험실 검사는 3개월마다 실시된다.

해설 의미상 '3개월마다'라는 뜻이 되어야 하므로 (B) every가 정답이다. 일정한 주기를 나타내는 〈every+기수+복수 명사(~마다)〉를 기억해 두자.

어휘 third-party 제3자의 inspection 점검, 검사 clinical 병상의, 임상의 laboratory 실험실

12 (D)

번역 어젯밤 라운델 극장에서 개막한 〈데스크 잡〉은 공상이 실현되는 한 사무직 근로자에 관한 감동적인 이야기를 전해 준다.

해설 부정관사 a와 명사 story 사이에 있는 빈칸은 명사를 수식하는 형용사가 들어갈 수 있는 자리이므로, (D) moving(감동시키는)이 정답이다. (A) mover와 (B) movement는 story와 복합명사를 이루면 의미가 어색하다.

어휘 daydream 공상 come to life 실현되다 movement 움직임, 이동 movingly 감동적으로

13 (A)

번역 승객들은 탑승이 시작되기 10분 전에 탑승구에서 질서 정연하게 줄을 서도록 요청받는다.

해설 승객들이 줄을 서는 방식과 관련해 '질서 정연한 줄'을 의미해야 자연스러우므로, (A) orderly(질서 정연한)가 정답이다.

어휘 boarding 탑승 excessive 과도한 opposite 반대의 accidental 우연한

14 (A)

번역 지난주 악천후가 맥밀란 플로리스트의 가정 배달 서비스에 지장을 주었다.

해설 배달 서비스에 지장을 준 날씨 상태를 나타낼 형용사가 쓰여야 알맞으므로 '극심한, 혹독한' 등을 뜻하는 (A) severe가 정답이다.

어휘 interfere with ~에 지장을 주다, ~을 방해하다 strategic 전략적인

[15-18] 게시물

버스 기사를 모집합니다!

바틀리 학군에서 현재 버스 기사를 채용 중입니다. 오직 시간제 일자리만 15 **가능합니다**. 신입 및 경력 버스 기사를 모두 찾고 있습니다. 최소 3년 이상 운전면허를 보유하고 계시면, 지원하시기를 권합니다. 16 **저희가 필요한 교육을 제공할 것입니다.**

바틀리 학군은 전 직원에게 17 **경쟁력 있는** 임금을 제공합니다. 18 **게다가,** 기사에게 학기 중에 추가 버스 노선을 맡아서 추가적인 수입을 올릴 수 있는 옵션도 제공합니다. 저희 팀에 합류하시는 데 관심 있으실 경우, 상세 정보는 904-555-0125번으로 임수민에게 전화하시기 바랍니다.

어휘 school district 학군 available 이용 가능한 seek 찾다, 구하다 wage 임금 extend 주다, 전하다 extra 추가의, 별도의 route 노선, 경로

15 (A)

해설 앞 문장에서 현재 버스 기사를 채용 중이라고 했으므로 지원 가능한 일자리에 대해서도 현재를 나타내는 시제여야 한다. 따라서 현재 시제 동사인 (A) are가 정답이다.

16 (C)

번역 (A) 지원은 오늘 마감입니다.
(B) 승진 기회가 있을 수 있습니다.
(C) 저희가 필요한 교육을 제공할 것입니다.
(D) 버스 기사는 저희 학교 커뮤니티에서 필수적인 부분입니다.

해설 앞 문장에 최소 3년 이상 운전면허를 보유한 사람이라면 지원을 권한다는 말이 쓰여 있다. 따라서 그런 조건을 지닌 사람이 근무하는 것과 관련된 내용의 문장이 쓰여야 자연스러우므로, 필요한 모든 교육을 제공하겠다는 의미의 (C)가 정답이다.

어휘 application 지원(서), 신청(서) due 마감 기한인 opportunity 기회 promotion 승진

17 (D)

해설 동사 offers와 명사 목적어 wages 사이에 위치한 빈칸은 명사를 수식하는 형용사가 들어갈 수 있는 자리이므로, (D) competitive가 정답이다. 명사 (C) competition은 wages와 복합명사를 구성하지 않으므로 오답이다.

어휘 compete 경쟁하다 competition 경쟁, 대회

18 (B)

해설 빈칸 앞뒤에 모두 채용된 기사에게 제공하는 혜택을 설명하는 문장이 쓰여 있어 유사 정보를 전달하는 흐름임을 알 수 있다. 따라서 '게다가, 추가로'라는 의미로 유사 정보를 추가해 말할 때 사용하는 (B) In addition이 정답이다.

UNIT 05 부사

1 부사의 자리

ETS 유형연습   본책 p.158

1 (D)   **2** (C)   **3** (D)

1 (D)

번역 사토 씨는 자신의 새 희곡에 대한 평가 때문에 신문을 면밀히 살핀다.

해설 주어와 동사 사이에 위치한 빈칸은 동사를 수식하는 부사가 들어갈 수 있는 자리이므로 (D) closely(면밀히, 밀접하게)가 정답이다.

어휘 monitor 살피다, 감시하다

2 (C)

번역 시장 집무실은 특별 행사를 위해 월요일에 몇 시간 동안 잠시 문을 닫을 것이다.

해설 be동사와 형용사 보어 closed 사이에 위치한 빈칸은 형용사를 앞에서 수식하는 부사 자리이므로 (C) briefly(잠시, 간단히)가 정답이다.

어휘 mayor 시장   brief 잠시 동안의, 짧은

3 (D)

번역 과열을 방지하기 위해, 양념 분쇄기를 2분 넘게 지속적으로 작동하는 것을 피하세요.

해설 동명사 running과 동명사의 목적어 your spice grinder 뒤에 위치한 빈칸은 동명사를 수식하는 부사가 들어갈 수 있는 자리이므로 (D) continuously가 정답이다.

어휘 prevent 방지하다   avoid 피하다   continuous 지속적인, 계속되는

2 시간부사와 빈도부사

ETS 유형연습   본책 p.159

1 (D)   **2** (B)   **3** (A)

1 (D)

번역 본사 경리부에서는 아직도 작년의 연간 지출액을 공개하지 않았다.

해설 '아직도 공개하지 않았다'라는 의미가 가장 적절하므로 부사 (D) still(아직도)이 정답이다. (A) once(한때, 한 번), (B) soon(곧), (C) almost(거의)는 모두 의미상 부적절하다.

어휘 accounting office 경리부   release 발표하다, 공개하다   annual spending figures 연간 지출액

2 (B)

번역 기술적인 문제로 인해, 넬슨스 일렉트로닉 옥션스에서는 현재 이메일로 어떠한 사진 제출도 받지 않습니다.

해설 '기술적인 문제로 인해 지금은 사진 제출을 받고 있지 않다'라는 내용이 되어야 자연스러우므로, 현재진행 동사와 어울리는 (B) currently(지금, 현재)가 정답이다.

어휘 technical 기술상의, 기술적인   submission 제출(물)

3 (A)

번역 투명한 파란색 천이 천장에 매달려 있는, 노르다리스 카페는 흔히 미술관으로 오해를 받는다.

해설 be동사 is와 과거분사 mistaken 사이에 빈칸이 있으므로 빈칸에는 수동태 동사를 수식하는 부사가 들어갈 수 있다. 따라서 (A) often이 정답이다.

어휘 panel 천 조각   sheer (직물 등이) 속이 다 비칠 정도로 얇은   fabric 직물, 천   hang from ~에 매달려 있다

3 주의해야 할 부사 1

ETS 유형연습   본책 p.160

1 (C)   **2** (A)   **3** (C)

1 (C)

번역 X200의 또렷하고 필름 같은 이미지는 그것이 시장에서 가장 발전된 디지털 카메라임을 입증해 준다.

해설 빈칸에는 형용사 advanced를 수식하는 부사가 필요하다. 부사인 (A) high(높이)와 (C) highly(매우, 대단히) 중에서 advanced와 결합해 '대단히 발전된'이라는 뜻이 되어야 하므로 (C) highly가 정답이다.

어휘 crisp 또렷한   film-like 필름과 같은   prove 입증하다   advanced 발전된, 앞선

2 (A)

번역 현재 카운티 코크에는 이언즈 툴 쉐드 매장이 단 두 곳만 있다.

해설 숫자 표현 two를 수식하는 자리에 빈칸이 있으므로 숫자를 강조하는 부사 (A) only가 정답이다.

어휘 currently 현재   including ~을 포함해

3 (C)

번역 만약 회사들이 동일한 제품을 서로 다른 버전으로 제공하지 않고 표준화한다면 회사 비용을 상당히 줄일 수 있을 것이다.

해설 빈칸 앞쪽에 reduce라는 동사가 있으므로 '상당히'라는 뜻으로 증가나 감소의 동사를 수식할 수 있는 부사인 (C) significantly가 정답이다.

어휘 standardize 표준화하다   instead of ~ 대신에, ~하지 않고   reduce 줄이다   expense 비용

4 주의해야 할 부사 2

ETS 유형연습   본책 p.161

1 (D) **2** (D) **3** (A)

1 (D)

번역 서마브라이트의 신형 소형 온도계 시제품에 대한 시장 조사 결과들은 아주 고무적이었다.

해설 형용사 encouraging(고무적인)을 수식하는 부사 자리이므로, 정도를 나타내는 부사가 들어가야 자연스럽다. 따라서 (D) very가 정답이다.

어휘 handheld 손에 쥐고 사용할 수 있는, 포켓용의
thermometer 온도계   prototype 시제품, 모델

2 (D)

번역 6월 30일자로 끝나는 기간 동안 호라이즌 스타디움 사는 티켓 판매로 전례 없는 수익을 기록했는데, 광고로는 훨씬 더 많은 수익을 기록했다.

해설 빈칸 뒤의 비교급 more가 힌트로, 보기들 중 비교급을 강조할 수 있는 부사 (D) even이 정답이다. 이때 even은 '심지어'가 아니라 '훨씬'이라는 의미로 해석된다. 참고로, (B) very는 원급과 쓰인다.

어휘 unprecedented 전례가 없는   revenue 수익

3 (A)

번역 노나카 컨설팅 사의 강점은 뛰어난 데이터 분석가 팀을 갖추고 있다는 것이고, 그러므로 그 회사에서는 신규 고객을 찾을 때 분석적인 서비스를 강조한다.

해설 두 절을 연결하는 접속사 and가 있으므로, 빈칸은 없어도 되는 부사 자리이다. 보기 중 접속사인 (B), (C)를 제외하면 부사는 (A)와 (D)가 남는다. 문맥상 '뛰어난 데이터 분석가 팀이 있어 분석적인 서비스를 강조한다'라는 내용이 되어야 자연스러우므로, (A) therefore(그러므로)가 정답이다.

어휘 consultancy 컨설팅 회사   strength 장점, 강점
accomplished 뛰어난, 우수한   analyst 분석가
highlight 두드러지게 하다, 강조하다   analytic 분석적인

ETS 실전문제   본책 p.162

1 (C)	2 (B)	3 (B)	4 (C)	5 (C)	6 (C)
7 (C)	8 (B)	9 (D)	10 (B)	11 (A)	12 (A)
13 (B)	14 (B)	15 (C)	16 (B)	17 (D)	18 (C)

1 (C)

번역 자원봉사자들은 행사에 정확히 제시간에 도착해야 하며, 건물 뒤쪽에 위치한 주차 구역을 이용해야 한다.

해설 자동사 arrive와 전치사 for 사이에 위치한 빈칸은 자동사를 수식하는 부사가 들어갈 수 있는 자리이므로 (C) promptly (정확히 제시간에, 지체 없이)가 정답이다.

어휘 volunteer 자원봉사자   prompt 즉각적인; 촉발하다
promptness 신속, 민첩함

2 (B)

번역 모든 인턴사원은 일일 업무를 효과적으로 완료해야 한다.

해설 to부정사 to complete와 목적어 daily tasks 뒤에 위치한 빈칸은 to부정사를 수식할 부사가 들어갈 수 있는 자리이므로, (B) effectively가 정답이다.

어휘 effectual 효과가 있는

3 (B)

번역 그로포드 주식회사의 규정은 오직 면허가 있고 보험에 가입된 업체만 고용하도록 요구한다.

해설 that절의 주어 앞에 빈칸이 있는데 '오직 면허가 있고 보험에 가입된 업체만'이라는 의미가 되어야 자연스러우므로 부사 (B) only가 정답이다. 부사 (A) much는 불가산명사를 수식하며, (C) whose와 (D) unless는 접속사이므로 오답이다.

어휘 regulation 규정   mandate 요구하다, 명령하다
licensed 허가를 받은   insured 보험에 가입된
contractor 계약업체, 계약업자

4 (C)

번역 권 씨는 연구 개발팀에 두 번째 엔지니어를 고용할 것을 강력히 제안하고 있다.

해설 주어 Mr. Kwon과 동사 suggests 사이에 빈칸이 있으므로 동사를 앞에서 수식할 부사가 들어갈 수 있는 자리이다. 따라서 (C) strongly(강력히)가 정답이다.

어휘 strength 힘, 강점   strengthen 강화하다

5 (C)

번역 펠레넴 대학교를 졸업한 직후 동급생인 트레버 토슨과 하이디 스미스는 컨설팅 회사를 공동 창립했다.

해설 빈칸은 전치사구 after graduating from Pellenem University를 강조하는 부사 자리로, 전치사 after와 어울려 '바로 직후'라는 의미를 완성하는 (C) Shortly가 정답이다.

어휘 graduate from ~를 졸업하다   cofound 공동 창립하다
provided that ~라면   despite ~에도 불구하고

6 (C)

번역 그 해변을 따라 이어지는 동굴을 탐험하는 것이 점점 더 인기 있는 여가 활동이 되고 있다.

해설 부정관사 an과 형용사 popular 사이에 위치한 빈칸은 형용사를 수식할 부사가 들어갈 수 있는 자리이므로, (C) increasingly(점점 더)가 정답이다.

어휘 explore 탐험하다   cave 동굴   recreational 여가의, 오락의
pursuit (취미) 활동, 추구(하는 것)

7 (C)

번역 퀸즐랜드 교통 당국은 모든 운전자들에게 도로 교통법을 준수하고 항상 안전하게 운전할 것을 촉구한다.

해설 빈칸 앞에 위치한 자동사 drive를 수식할 부사가 빈칸에 쓰여야 알맞으므로 (C) safely가 정답이다.

어휘 urge 촉구하다 obey 준수하다, 지키다

8 (B)
번역 밴스 씨는 훌륭한 상사이며, 직원들은 그가 긴급 상황에서 얼마나 차분하게 반응하는지를 높이 평가한다.

해설 〈how+형용사/부사+주어+동사〉로 이어지는 명사절을 구성해야 하는데, 빈칸은 자동사 reacts를 수식하는 자리이므로, 부사 (B) calmly(차분하게)가 정답이다.

어휘 supervisor 상사, 책임자 appreciate 높이 평가하다, 감사하다 react 반응하다 emergency 긴급 상황

9 (D)
번역 이 버스 정류장은 주링 의료 센터 공사가 진행되는 약 1년 동안 폐쇄될 것이다.

해설 빈칸은 one을 수식하는 자리이므로, '약, 대략'이라는 의미로 숫자를 수식할 수 있는 부사 (D) approximately가 정답이다.

어휘 approximate 근사치인; (수량, 성질 등이) 비슷하다 approximation 근사치

10 (B)
번역 회원 가입을 하시려면 단지 협회 웹사이트에서 양식을 작성하시기만 하면 됩니다.

해설 빈칸 뒤에 동사원형으로 시작하는 명령문이 있고, 빈칸에는 동사를 수식하는 부사가 들어갈 수 있으므로 (B) simply가 정답이다.

어휘 apply for ~을 신청하다, 지원하다 society 협회, 학회 simply 그저, 단지 simplify 단순화하다 simplicity 단순(성)

11 (A)
번역 현 씨는 한결같이 인상 깊은 직업 의식을 보이면서, 종종 자신의 정규 업무 외에도 추가 프로젝트를 맡는다.

해설 빈칸 뒤에 온 분사 demonstrating을 수식하는 자리이므로, 부사 (A) Consistently가 정답이다.

어휘 demonstrate 보여주다 impressive 인상적인, 인상 깊은 work ethic 직업 (윤리) 의식, 직업관 take on ~을 맡다, 책임지다 in addition to ~에 추가로, ~외에도 consistently 한결같이, 일관성 있게 consistency 한결같음, 일관성 consistent 한결같은, 일관된

12 (A)
번역 이제 도서관 방문객 통계는 계절에 따른 도서관 이용량을 예측할 수 있을 만큼 충분히 탄탄하다.

해설 형용사 robust와 to부정사 to forecast 사이에 빈칸이 있는데, '통계 자료가 도서관 이용량을 예측할 수 있을 만큼 충분히 탄탄하다'라는 의미가 되는 것이 자연스러우므로 〈enough+to부정사〉의 형태로 형용사를 뒤에서 수식할 수 있는 (A) enough가 정답이다.

어휘 statistics 통계 (자료) robust 탄탄한, 튼튼한 forecast 예측하다

13 (B)
번역 오시다 테크의 CEO인 이그나시오 씨는 사람들의 이목을 피하는 경향이 있어서 좀처럼 공개 석상에서 보이지 않는다.

해설 사람들의 이목을 피하는 경향이 있다(tends to avoid publicity)는 특징과 어울릴 수 있도록 '공개 석상에서 보이지 않는다'와 같은 의미를 나타내야 자연스러우므로, (B) rarely(좀처럼 ~ 않다)가 정답이다.

어휘 tend 경향이 있다 avoid 피하다 publicity 사람들의 이목, 세상에 알려짐

14 (B)
번역 얼룩 없는 그릇을 위해 식기세척기 세제통에 클린 초이스 세제를 정기적으로 채워야 한다.

해설 식기세척기 세제통에 세제를 채우는 방식과 관련해 '정기적으로 채워야 한다'를 의미해야 자연스러우므로, (B) regularly(정기적으로)가 정답이다.

어휘 dispenser 디스펜서(특정 물품이 나오는 기계나 용기) detergent 세제 spot-free 얼룩 없는 wetly 축축하게

[15-18] 광고

> 업체의 브랜드 이미지를 새롭게 할 시기인가요?
>
> 스타일과 제품이 지속적으로 변하고 있으므로 업체는 때때로 **15 스스로를** 재창조해야 합니다. 현재의 업계 동향에 발맞추기 위해, 여러분의 브랜드는 반드시 현대적이고 적절해 보여야 합니다. 20년 넘게, 저희 트라다일리아는 회사들이 새로운 **16 정체성**을 개발할 수 있게 도움을 주고 있습니다. 처음부터 끝까지, 저희는 회사들이 자사의 이미지를 **17 성공적으로** 변화시키는 데 필요한 조치를 분석하는 것을 도와드립니다.
>
> **18 트라다일리아가 경쟁에서 돋보이도록 도와드리겠습니다.** 무료 초기 평가를 위해, 713-555-0172번으로 저희에게 연락 주시기 바랍니다.

어휘 rebrand 브랜드 이미지를 새롭게 하다 constantly 지속적으로 reinvent 재창조하다 keep up with ~와 발맞춰 가다, ~에 뒤처지지 않다 trend 동향, 추세 appear ~하게 보이다 relevant 관련된, 적절한 analyze 분석하다 initial 초기의, 처음의 assessment 평가

15 (C)
해설 업체가 때때로 스스로를 재창조해야 한다는 의미를 나타내야 하므로, 빈칸에는 주어 a business를 가리킬 대명사가 쓰여야 한다. 따라서 주어와 동사의 목적어가 동일할 때 사용하는 재귀대명사 (C) itself가 정답이다.

16 (B)
해설 리브랜딩 회사의 광고로, 이미지를 새롭게 변화시키는 것에 관해 말하고 있으므로 '회사들이 새로운 정체성을 개발할 수 있게 도움을 주고 있다'와 같은 의미를 나타내야 자연스럽다. 따라서 '정체성'을 뜻하는 (B) identity가 정답이다.

어휘 process 과정

17 (D)

해설 to부정사 to change의 목적어인 명사구 their company's image 뒤에 위치한 빈칸은 to부정사를 수식하는 부사가 들어갈 수 있는 자리이므로, (D) successfully가 정답이다.

어휘 succeed 성공하다, 뒤를 잇다

18 (C)

번역 (A) 강력한 브랜드들을 개발하고 유지하기 어려웠습니다.
(B) 조 트라다일리아는 자신의 차고에서 회사를 시작했습니다.
(C) 트라다일리아가 경쟁에서 돋보이도록 도와드리겠습니다.
(D) 브랜드 이미지를 새롭게 하려는 모든 노력이 좋은 결과를 맺는 것은 아니라는 것을 유의하십시오.

해설 앞 단락에서는 전체적으로 트라다일리아가 제공하는 서비스를 소개하고 있고, 빈칸 뒤에는 서비스를 이용하기 위해 연락을 달라는 말이 쓰여 있다. 따라서 서비스 이용과 관련된 문장이 빈칸에 쓰여야 흐름상 자연스러우므로, 경쟁에서 돋보이도록 도와주겠다는 말로 서비스를 이용하기 위해 연락해야 하는 목적을 나타내는 (C)가 정답이다.

어휘 garage 차고 stand out 돋보이다, 두드러지다
competition 경쟁 effort 노력 favorably 좋게, 호의적으로

UNIT 06 동사의 형태와 종류

1 동사의 형태

ETS 유형연습 본책 p.164

1 (D) 2 (A) 3 (B)

1 (D)

번역 많은 기업들이 새 정부 조세안에 있는 여러 조항을 강력히 비판했다.

해설 빈칸 앞에는 have가, 뒤에는 목적어(several provisions)가 있으므로 완료형을 완성하는 과거분사가 필요하다. 따라서 (D) criticized가 정답이다.

어휘 provision 조항 criticize 비난하다

2 (A)

번역 수석 프로젝트 매니저는 다음 주 목요일에 현장을 방문할 예정인데 편집자들에게 오전 9시 30분에 자신의 사무실에서 만나자고 요청했다.

해설 ask, require, request, insist, suggest, recommend처럼 주장, 제안, 요구의 동사 뒤에 오는 명사절 접속사 that이 이끄는 절에는 〈should+동사원형〉이 오는데, 이때 should는 생략 가능하다. 따라서 동사원형인 (A) meet가 정답이다.

어휘 senior 선임의, 고참의 on-site 현지에, 현장에서
editor 편집자

3 (B)

번역 드소르보 사는 가을 카탈로그에 신상품 가죽 부츠를 소개할 것이다.

해설 동사 will be 뒤에는 현재분사(-ing)와 과거분사(p.p.)가 올 수 있다. 빈칸 뒤에 its new leather boots라는 목적어를 취하면서 '소개하고 있다'는 능동적 의미를 나타내므로 현재분사 (B) introducing이 정답이다. (A) introduce와 (C) introduces는 will be 뒤에 올 수 없고, (D) introduced는 수동적 의미를 나타내므로 정답이 될 수 없다.

어휘 leather 가죽 catalog 카탈로그, 목록

2 자동사와 타동사

ETS 유형연습 본책 p.165

1 (D) 2 (A) 3 (D)

1 (D)

번역 예산안을 준비하는 것은 경영진이 행동 방침을 결정하기 전에 여러 가지 선택지를 검토할 수 있게 한다.

해설 빈칸 뒤에 several options라는 목적어가 왔으며, 문맥상 '여러 선택지를 검토하다'가 적합하므로 타동사 (D) examine이 정답이다.

어휘 budget 예산(안) encourage ~를 하게 하다, 촉진하다
executive 경영진, 임원 option 옵션, 선택지 a course of action 행동 방침

2 (A)

번역 고객들이 지역 쇼핑객 할인을 받기 위해서는 거주 증명서를 제시해야 한다.

해설 뒤의 전치사 for와 함께 쓰여 '~의 자격이 있다'라는 의미를 나타내는 자동사 (A) qualify가 정답이다. '~의 자격이 있다'라는 의미의 표현으로 be eligible for도 함께 알아 두자.

어휘 discount 할인 proof of residency 거주 증명서
award 수여하다 certify 증명하다, 보증하다

3 (D)

번역 신입 사원들은 사흘간 진행되는 오리엔테이션에 전원 참석해야 한다.

해설 빈칸 뒤의 in과 결합하여 '~에 참석하다'라는 뜻을 갖는 자동사 (D) participate가 정답이다. (A) attend 뒤에는 전치사 없이 바로 목적어인 the three-day orientation이 와야 하므로 오답이다.

어휘 be required to (반드시) ~해야 한다

3 4형식 동사와 5형식 동사

ETS 유형연습 본책 p.166

1 (C) 2 (B) 3 (B)

1 (C)

번역 어느 누구도 두고 가지 않도록, 여행 안내원은 모든 방문객들에게 오전 7시까지 정문 로비에 와 있으라고 일러두었다.

해설 〈동사+사람 목적어(all the visitors)+to부정사〉 구조로 쓰일 수 있는 동사를 선택해야 한다. 따라서 '사람들이 ~하도록 일러두다'라는 표현을 완성하는 (C) reminded가 정답이다. 참고로, 〈remind+사람 목적어+that절〉 구조로도 자주 쓰인다.

어휘 leave behind ~을 뒤에 남기다 tour operator 여행 안내원 front lobby 정문 로비 recall 회상하다 memorize 암기하다 remind 일러두다, 상기시키다 identify 확인하다, 알아보다

2 (B)

번역 가와노 씨는 직원들이 매장 전시 가구에서 발견하는 모든 결함을 그에게 알려주기를 바란다.

해설 사람 목적어를 취하고, 전치사 of와 어울려 쓰이는 타동사를 선택해야 한다. 따라서 '알리다, 통지하다'라는 의미의 (B) inform이 정답이다. 참고로 (A) supply는 supply A with B 구조로 쓰인다.

어휘 flaw 결함 display 전시 supply 제공하다 reply 응답하다 notice 주목하다, 알아차리다

3 (B)

번역 조립 구역에서 작업하는 직원들은 모두 기계 조작에 관한 교육을 받아야 할 것이다.

해설 문맥상 주어인 employees가 '교육을 받도록 요구받는다'라는 의미를 나타내므로 (B) required가 정답이다. 참고로 〈be asked/requested/required+to부정사〉는 모두 '~하도록 요구받다'라는 의미로 쓰인다.

어휘 assembly 조립 (부품) operation 조작, 운전

4 주의해야 할 동사

ETS 유형연습   본책 p.167

1 (A) 2 (C) 3 (C)

1 (A)

번역 직무 수행에 대한 연례 평가가 1월 셋째 주에 실시될 예정이니 명심해 주세요.

해설 that절의 주어 자리로, 문맥상 '직무 수행에 대한 연례 평가'가 적합하므로 명사 (A) reviews가 정답이다. review는 동사와 명사로 모두 쓰인다는 사실을 명심한다. (C) reviewer와 (D) reviewers도 명사이지만, '사람'을 나타내는 명사이기 때문에 문맥에 맞지 않다.

어휘 be aware that ~을 알다 annual 연례의, 1년마다 performance 성과, 실적 take place 발생하다, 열리다

2 (C)

번역 우리의 최고 운영 책임자는 최근 매출액에 아주 감명받았다.

해설 사람 주어인 Our chief operating officer는 감동을 받는 대상이므로 수동적 의미를 나타내는 과거분사 (C) impressed가 정답이다.

어휘 chief operating officer 최고 운영 책임자 sales figures 매출 수치, 매출액 impress 깊은 인상을 주다

3 (C)

번역 모든 출장 연회 업체에서는 부패하기 쉬운 음식이 상하지 않도록 냉장 보관한다.

해설 상하기 쉬운 음식을 냉장 보관하는 것은 부패를 방지하기 위함이라고 볼 수 있다. 따라서 〈prevent A from -ing〉 구조로 쓰여 'A가 ~하는 것을 방지하다'라는 의미를 완성하는 (C) prevent가 정답이다.

어휘 commercial 상업상의 catering 출장 연회 refrigerate 냉장 보관하다 perishable 썩기 쉬운, 부패하기 쉬운 spoil (음식이) 상하다 oppose 반대하다 forbid 금지하다

ETS 실전문제   본책 p.168

1 (C) 2 (A) 3 (C) 4 (D) 5 (A) 6 (D)
7 (A) 8 (C) 9 (A) 10 (A) 11 (C) 12 (D)
13 (C) 14 (D) 15 (A) 16 (C) 17 (B) 18 (C)

1 (C)

번역 알리 테크 소프트웨어 패키지를 이용하시면, 파일이 여러 이용자들 사이에서 쉽게 공유될 수 있습니다.

해설 조동사 뒤에는 동사원형이 와야 하므로, 수동태 동사원형인 (C) be shared가 정답이다.

2 (A)

번역 이번에는 귀하에게 일자리를 제안할 수 없게 되었지만, 다음 기회를 위해서 귀하의 이력서를 보관해 두겠습니다.

해설 빈칸은 have와 결합하여 현재완료를 이루는 과거분사 자리이므로, (A) decided가 정답이다. 빈칸 뒤의 not은 to부정사 to offer를 부정하여 '제안하지 않기로'라는 뜻을 나타낸다.

어휘 offer 제안하다 position 직책, 일자리 keep A on file A를 철하다, 보관하다 opening 결원, 공석

3 (C)

번역 오사키 씨는 전 직원이 협력해서 마감일까지 그 업무를 끝내기를 원한다.

해설 동사가 would like이고, 목적어를 보충 설명하는 목적격 보어 자리이므로 (C) to work가 정답이다. 문장에 이미 동사 would like가 있으므로 빈칸에 (A), (D)와 같은 동사는 올 수 없다. 〈would like+목적어+목적격 보어(to부정사)〉의 구조를 기억하자.

어휘 entire staff 전 직원 deadline 마감일

4 (D)

번역 세계 보건의 날을 기념하여 모든 직원들은 설탕이 들어간 간식을 과일과 채소로 대체하라고 권장받는다.

해설 빈칸 앞에 be동사 are가, 뒤에 to부정사가 있으므로 5형식 동사 encourage의 수동태 구문임을 알 수 있다. 따라서 과거분사 (D) encouraged가 정답이다.

어휘 celebrate 기념하다, 축하하다   replace 대체하다, 대신하다
sugary 설탕이 든, 설탕 맛이 나는   encourage 격려하다, 권장하다

5 (A)

번역 소기업들은 협업하는 데서 이득을 볼 수 있기 때문에 많은 소유주들이 지역 사업 조합에 가입하는 것이 도움이 된다고 생각한다.

해설 전치사 from과 어울려 쓰이는 자동사를 선택하는 문제이다. 따라서 from과 함께 '~로부터 이익을 얻다'라는 의미를 완성하는 (A) benefit이 정답이다.

어휘 local 지역의   association 협회   assist 돕다

6 (D)

번역 벡커 스트리트 일렉트로닉스는 7월 할인 행사의 일환으로 모든 TX266 카메라의 배송비를 한시적으로 면제할 것이다.

해설 회사가 할인 행사의 일환으로 배송비(shipping costs)와 관련해 취할 수 있는 조치를 나타내는 타동사가 필요하다. 따라서 '면제하다, (권리 등을) 포기하다'라는 의미의 타동사 (D) waive가 정답이다.

어휘 limited 제한된, 한정된   shipping cost 배송비   proceed 진행하다   hesitate 주저하다   displace 대신하다, 대체하다

7 (A)

번역 해외로 배송되는 섬유 제품은 모든 국제 라벨 표시 요건을 준수해야 한다.

해설 전치사 with와 결합하여 요건(requirements), 규정 등의 명사와 어울려 쓰이는 자동사를 선택해야 한다. 따라서 with와 함께 '~을 준수하다, 지키다'라는 의미를 완성하는 (A) comply가 정답이다.

어휘 textile 직물, 섬유   overseas 해외로   requirement 요건
confront 직면하다   assign 맡기다, 배정하다

8 (C)

번역 오시예크 시스템즈의 직원들은 샤샤 바실레프 씨를 신임 부사장으로 정한 이사진의 결정에 놀랐다.

해설 동사 were의 주어인 Employees를 보충 설명하는 주격 보어 자리로, '직원들은 놀랐다'라는 수동적 의미를 나타내야 한다. 따라서 과거분사 (C) surprised가 정답이다.

어휘 the board of directors 이사진   decision 결정
vice president 부사장   surprise 놀라게 하다

9 (A)

번역 주디스 쿡 영업부장이 내일 아침까지 정확한 발송 날짜를 알려드릴 것입니다.

해설 〈inform+A+of+B(A에게 B를 알리다)〉를 적용시키는 문제이므로 전치사 (A) of가 정답이다. 동사가 특정 전치사와 결합할 때는 동사와 전치사를 함께 기억해 두어야 한다.

어휘 sales department 영업부   shipment 발송, 선적

10 (A)

번역 래퍼티 씨의 추천인들은 그녀의 확고한 직업 의식을 언급했지만, 중역들은 그녀에게 그 직책에 필요한 기술이 부족하다고 여긴다.

해설 but이 앞뒤 절을 연결하고 있으므로, 래퍼티 씨의 추천인(references)과 중역들(directors)의 의견은 상반되는 내용이어야 한다. 따라서 '기술이 부족하다'라는 부정적인 표현을 완성하는 (A) lacks가 정답이다.

어휘 reference 추천서, 추천인   pretend ~인 체하다
remove 제거하다   vacate 비우다

11 (C)

번역 마부르크 일렉트로 사는 올해 상당한 수익 증가를 발표할 것으로 예상된다.

해설 빈칸 앞에 be동사 is가, 뒤에 to부정사가 있으므로 빈칸에는 타동사의 과거분사가 들어가야 한다. 문맥상 '상당한 수익 증가를 발표할 것으로 예상된다'라는 내용이 되어야 자연스러우므로, (C) expected가 정답이다.

어휘 significant 상당한   profit 수익   earn 벌다
outgrow ~보다 커지다   rise 오르다

12 (D)

번역 〈비즈니스 에포크〉 잡지에 실린 한 기사는 직물 가격이 2년 내에 안정될 것으로 예측한다.

해설 빈칸 뒤에 명사절 접속사 that이 이끄는 절이 쓰여 있으므로 that절을 목적어로 취할 수 있는 동사 (D) predicts(예측하다)가 정답이다.

어휘 textile 직물, 섬유   stabilize 안정되다, 안정시키다

13 (C)

번역 후보로 지명된 25명의 은행 지점장 중에서, 시상 위원회는 아르준 파텔 씨를 올해의 지점장으로 선택했다.

해설 '아르준 파텔 씨를 올해의 지점장으로 선택했다'와 같은 의미를 나타내야 자연스러우므로, '선택하다'를 뜻하는 choose의 과거형 (C) chose가 정답이다.

어휘 nominate 후보로 지명하다   committee 위원회

14 (D)

번역 새로운 디자인은 매우 혁신적이지만 이번에 우리가 개발을 진행하기에는 비용이 너무 많이 든다.

해설 전치사 with와 어울려 쓰이는 자동사를 선택하는 문제이다. 따라서 with와 함께 '~을 계속하다, 진행하다'라는 의미를 완성하는 (D) proceed가 정답이다. (A), (B), (C)는 모두 타동사이다.

어휘 innovative 혁신적인   costly 많은 비용이 드는
development 개발   examine 조사하다   treat 대하다
urge 촉구하다

[15-18] 이메일

수신: info@kathyscaterers.com
발신: jberthel@bertheltech.com
날짜: 12월 1일
제목: 행사 케이터링 문의

관계자께,

저는 현재 저희 회사의 연례 연말 파티를 계획하고 있습니다. 케이터링 업체인 귀사에 대해 제가 **15** 본 모든 후기가 매우 긍정적이네요. 하지만 최종 결정을 내리기 전에 몇 가지 **16** 질문이 있습니다.

12월 16일 금요일에 25인분 음식을 제공해 주실 수 있나요? 행사는 래링턴 애비뉴 138번지에 있는 저희 회사 건물에서 개최될 예정입니다. 그날 오후 2시까지 다과를 배달해 주실 수 있습니까? 귀사의 스몰 바이츠 메뉴가 파티에 완벽하게 맞을 것 같아요. **17** 맛있는 음식 종류가 다양하게 제공된다는 점이 좋습니다. 모두의 음식 기호를 만족시킬 가장 쉬운 방법인 것 같네요.

18 마지막으로, 남은 음식을 낭비하는 것에 대해 많은 사람들이 염려하는데요. 남은 음식을 집에 가져갈 사람들을 위해 포장용 상자를 제공해 주실 수 있나요?

감사합니다.

제임스 버텔, 버텔 테크놀로지스

어휘 inquiry 문의 to whom it may concern 관계자에게 currently 현재 annual 연례의, 매년의 positive 긍정적인 make a final decision 최종 결정을 하다 available 이용 가능한, 시간이 되는 take place 개최되다 refreshments 다과 satisfy 만족시키다 preference 선호 be concerned about ~에 대해 우려하다 leftover 남은 음식 carryout 사서 들고 가는, 포장해서 가는

15 (A)
해설 빈칸은 have와 함께 현재완료를 이루는 과거분사 자리이므로, (A) seen이 정답이다.

16 (D)
해설 빈칸 뒤에서 궁금한 점들에 대해 문의하고 있으므로, 해당 문장은 최종 결정 전(before I make a final decision)에 질문을 하고 싶다는 내용이 되어야 문맥상 자연스럽다. 따라서 (D) questions가 정답이다.

17 (B)
번역 (A) 저희는 친환경적인 컵, 접시, 기구를 사용합니다.
(B) 맛있는 음식 종류가 다양하게 제공된다는 점이 좋습니다.
(C) 숙련된 서빙 직원으로만 보내주세요.
(D) 최종 비용은 음료를 포함해야 합니다.

해설 빈칸 뒤에서 모두의 음식 기호를 만족시킬 가장 쉬운 방법인 것 같다(This would ~ satisfy everyone's food preferences)고 했으므로, 빈칸에서 먼저 이 판단의 근거가 제시되어야 문맥상 자연스럽다. 따라서 다양한 음식 종류를 언급한 (B)가 정답이다.

어휘 environmentally friendly 친환경적인 utensil (가정에서 사용하는) 도구, 기구 a variety of 다양한 experienced 숙련된 beverage 음료

18 (C)
해설 콤마 뒤 문장을 수식하는 부사 자리이다. 빈칸 앞에서 몇 가지 문의사항을 나열했고, 빈칸 뒤에서 포장용 상자 제공(provide carryout boxes for people to take any leftovers)이 가능한지 문의하며 끝맺었으므로, '마지막으로'라는 의미의 (C) Finally가 정답이다.

어휘 meanwhile 당분간, 그동안 otherwise 그렇지 않으면

UNIT 07 수 일치와 태

1 주어와 동사의 수 일치

ETS 유형연습 (본책 p.170)

1 (A)   2 (A)   3 (B)

1 (A)
번역 인쇄 및 사무실과 관련해 필요하신 모든 부분에 대해 다큐프린트 서비스를 계속 이용해 주시기 바랍니다.

해설 that절의 주어 you 뒤에 동사가 없으므로 빈칸은 that절의 동사 자리이다. 동사 (A) continue와 (B) continues 중, you와 수 일치가 되는 (A) continue가 정답이다.

어휘 continuation 지속, 연속(되는 것)

2 (A)
번역 현재 프린터에 필요한 잉크 카트리지를 구할 수 없으니, 컬러 프린터를 아껴 사용해 주세요.

해설 since절의 주어는 it requires의 수식을 받는 the ink cartridges이므로 복수 동사 (A) are가 정답이다. 참고로, it requires 앞에는 목적격 관계대명사 that이 생략되어 있다.

어휘 sparingly 절약하여 currently 현재, 지금 unavailable 이용할 수 없는, 구할 수 없는

3 (B)
번역 우리가 비교해 보았던 커피 메이커들은 가격, 크기 및 내구성 면에서 다양하다.

해설 The coffee makers가 주어이고, we compared는 주어를 수식하는 수식어이므로 주어와 수가 일치되는 복수 동사 (B) vary가 정답이다.

어휘 compare 비교하다 in terms of ~에 관하여, ~의 관점에서 durability 튼튼함, 내구성 vary 다양하다, 다르다 variable 변하기 쉬운, 일정치 않은

2 단수주어 vs. 복수주어

ETS 유형연습 본책 p.171

1 (D)　2 (B)　3 (D)

1 (D)

번역 나는 사전 조사를 하면서, 지난 10년간 미호 아오키의 시에 관해 쓰인 글이 거의 없다는 것을 알게 되었다.

해설 빈칸은 that절의 주어 자리로, 단수동사인 has와 수가 일치하는 주어인 부정대명사 (D) little이 정답이다. (B) few는 복수동사와 함께 써야 한다.

어휘 perform 수행하다　preliminary 예비의, 준비의
decade 10년

2 (B)

번역 센트리 사진 현상소 직원들의 절반 가량은 버스로 출퇴근한다.

해설 half of the employees (at Century Photo Labs)가 문장의 주어이고, 빈칸은 문장의 동사 자리이다. half of와 같은 부분을 나타내는 표현은 of 뒤의 명사와 동사의 수를 일치시킨다. 여기서는 복수 명사인 the employees가 왔으므로 복수동사인 (B) commute가 정답이다.

어휘 roughly 대충, 대략　photo lab (사진) 현상소
commute 통근하다

3 (D)

번역 스텔렌 박물관의 폭넓은 소장품은 다양한 문화권에서 온 고대 공예품과 그림으로 어우러져 구성되어 있다.

해설 빈칸은 The Stellen Museum's extensive의 수식을 받는 주어 자리이므로 명사가 들어가야 한다. 따라서 동사 consist와 수가 일치하는 복수 명사 (D) holdings가 정답이다.

어휘 extensive 광대한, 다방면에 걸친　consist of ~으로 구성되다　artifact 공예품　various 다양한　holdings (도서관 등의) 장서, 소장품

3 동사의 수동태

ETS 유형연습 본책 p.172

1 (B)　2 (B)　3 (C)

1 (B)

번역 해외 여행객들에 대한 새로운 규제로 인해, 특정 종류의 식물은 대부분의 국가로 허가 없이 반입될 수 없다.

해설 조동사(cannot) 뒤에는 동사원형이 와야 하며, 주어인 certain types of plants는 bring의 행위자가 아니라 대상이므로 수동태인 (B) be brought가 정답이다. 빈칸 뒤에 목적어가 없으니 수동태로 접근하는 것도 좋다.

어휘 restriction 규제, 제한　plant 식물　permit 허가, 인가

2 (B)

번역 기한 내에 책을 반납하지 않은 도서관 이용객들에게는 연체료가 부과될 것이다.

해설 문장의 동사 자리로 시간상 미래의 일을 나타내고, 의미상 '이 용객이 연체료를 부과받는' 수동의 개념이므로 (B) will be charged가 정답이다.

어휘 patron 이용객, 단골 손님　due date 기한, 지급 기일
fee 요금, 수수료　charge 청구하다

3 (C)

번역 대표단은 오전 9시에 대사관에서 출발할 것이며, 체육부 장관이 공항까지 동행할 것이다.

해설 빈칸은 주어 The delegation의 동사 자리이다. 동사 accompany는 타동사인데, 빈칸 뒤에 목적어 없이 전치사구만 있으므로 수동태가 되어야 한다. 따라서 (C) will be accompanied가 정답이다.

어휘 delegation 대표단　embassy 대사관　minister 장관
accompany 동반하다, 동행하다

4 여러 가지 수동태

ETS 유형연습 본책 p.173

1 (A)　2 (A)　3 (A)

1 (A)

번역 매달 다섯 명의 우수 직원을 선발하여 회사의 성과에 크게 기여한 것에 대해 시상을 할 것이다.

해설 '~에 대한 공로로 표창을 받다'라는 뜻은 be honored for 형태로 써야 하므로 전치사 (A) for가 정답이다. 이때 for는 이유/원인을 나타낸다. at은 보통 장소나 시점에 쓰이고, across는 '(도로가 다리 따위를) 건너서', over는 '(기간에) 걸쳐서', 혹은 '~에 관한'이란 뜻으로 사용된다.

어휘 outstanding 뛰어난, 탁월한　honor 경의를 표하다, 명예를 주다　exceptional 특별한, 예외적인
contribution 공헌, 기여　performance 성과, 실적

2 (A)

번역 침대차 승객들에게는 여정에 필요한 침구류가 제공될 것이다.

해설 동사 provide는 전치사 with와 함께 provide A with B의 형태로 'A에게 B를 제공하다'라는 의미로 자주 쓰이고, 이 문장은 수동태가 되면서 A의 자리에 있어야 할 목적어가 문장의 주어(Sleeping-car passengers)로 문장 맨 앞에 나와 있는 상태이므로 전치사 (A) with가 정답이다.

어휘 sleeping-car 침대차(의)　passenger 승객
bedding 침구류

3 (A)

번역 저층 아파트들은 먼지와 도로의 소음에 더 많이 노출되기 때문에 값이 더 싸다.

해설 be exposed 뒤에 노출되는 대상이 나올 때 전치사 to를 쓰므로 (A) to가 정답이다. 'be exposed to+명사(~에 노출되다)'를 하나의 표현으로 알아 두자.

어휘 dust 먼지　noise 소음

ETS 실전문제

본책 p.174

1 (B)	2 (D)	3 (D)	4 (D)	5 (A)	6 (D)
7 (B)	8 (B)	9 (A)	10 (A)	11 (B)	12 (A)
13 (B)	14 (B)	15 (B)	16 (A)	17 (B)	18 (C)

1 (B)

번역 로젠 씨는 2월 자동차 박람회에 판매업체를 위한 자리가 아직 남아 있다고 보고했다.

해설 빈칸 앞에는 주어 Mr. Rosen이, 뒤에는 명사절인 that절이 있으므로 빈칸은 동사 자리이다. 또한, 주어가 3인칭 단수이므로, 과거시제 동사 (B) reported가 정답이다. (A) report는 주어와 수 일치가 되지 않는다.

어휘 vendor 판매업체, 판매업자

2 (D)

번역 그 고객의 대출 신청 서류가 서명을 위해 그녀에게 반환되었다.

해설 문장에 동사가 없으므로 빈칸은 동사 자리이며, 주어 The customer's loan application documents가 복수이므로 수가 일치되는 복수 동사 (D) have been returned가 정답이다.

어휘 loan 대출 application 신청(서), 지원(서)

3 (D)

번역 중역실에 페인트를 칠하고 있어서 오늘 오후 회의는 4층 회의실에서 열릴 예정이다.

해설 조동사 will의 뒤에는 동사원형이 온다. 문맥상 '회의가 열리다'라는 수동적 의미를 나타내므로 수동태 동사원형인 (D) be held가 정답이다.

어휘 boardroom 중역실, (이사) 회의실 conference room 회의실

4 (D)

번역 회사 자선 모금 운동에 기부하고자 하는 직원들은 잭 엘리엇 씨의 사무실에 있는 상자에 기증품을 넣어 주세요.

해설 관계사절(who ~ charity drive)의 수식을 받는 주어 Employees의 동사 자리이다. 직원들이 '상자에 기증품을 넣어달라'는 요청을 받는 상황이므로, 수동태 동사가 쓰여야 한다. 따라서 (D) are invited가 정답이다. invite는 to부정사를 목적격 보어로 취하는 5형식 동사로, 수동태로 바꾸면 〈be invited to부정사〉의 형태가 된다.

어휘 contribute 기부하다, 기여하다 charity drive 자선 모금 (운동) donation 기부(금), 기증(품)

5 (A)

번역 콤코 사는 지난해 컴퓨터 부품 공급업체 중 선도적인 회사가 되었는데, 당시 그 회사는 설립된 지 10년도 채 되지 않았다.

해설 단수 주어 it(Comco, Inc.)은 설립되는 대상이므로 수동태 단수 동사 (A) was founded가 정답이다. 나머지 (B) founds, (C) have founded, (D) founded는 모두 능동태 동사이다.

어휘 leading 선도하는 supplier 공급업체 found 설립하다

6 (D)

번역 수백 명의 기술 전문가들이 지난달 취리히에서 열렸던 총회에 참석했다.

해설 모든 문장에는 동사가 있어야 하는데 동사가 없는 문장이다. 따라서 동사가 포함된 '~이 있다'라는 의미를 나타내는 (D) There were가 정답이다.

어휘 convention 회의, 총회

7 (B)

번역 저희 공장에서 출발하는 새로운 배송품이 생산량 부족 때문에 지연되었습니다.

해설 delay는 목적어를 필요로 하는 타동사인데, 빈칸 뒤에 목적어 없이 전치사구만 있으므로 수동태로 쓰여야 한다. 따라서 (B) have been delayed가 정답이다.

어휘 shipment 배송(품) shortage 부족 delay 지연시키다

8 (B)

번역 호토 프러덕션 플랜트의 풀타임 직원들은 4시간 근무마다 15분간 휴식을 취할 수 있는 권리가 있다.

해설 빈칸은 주어 자리인데 동사가 are로 복수 동사이므로 복수 명사인 (B) employees(직원들)가 정답이다. of Hauto Production Plant는 빈칸을 수식하는 수식어구이다.

어휘 be entitled to ~할 권리가 있다 shift 교대 근무 (시간) employ 고용하다

9 (A)

번역 주간 재무 기록에 수익이 다시 상승하기 시작한 것으로 나타난다.

해설 빈칸 앞에는 주어 The weekly financial records가, 뒤에는 명사절인 that절이 있으므로 빈칸은 동사 자리이다. 또한 주어가 복수 명사이므로 복수 명사와 수 일치가 되는 (A) indicate가 정답이다.

어휘 financial 재무의, 재정의 profit 수익 rise 상승하다

10 (A)

번역 악천후와 인력 감원으로 인해 컨 사이언스 센터 보수 공사는 가장 큰 어려움을 겪게 되었다.

해설 주어가 'A and B'일 때는 복수 동사를 써야 한다. 또한, 빈칸 뒤에 목적어 the greatest challenges가 있으므로 능동태 복수 동사인 (A) have posed가 정답이다.

어휘 inclement weather 악천후, 나쁜 날씨 reduced 줄어든 workforce 노동 인력, 전직원 challenge 난제, 도전 renovation 수리, 보수 공사 pose 일으키다, 유발하다

11 (B)

번역 앨핀타 간호직 유니폼에 쓰인 천은 일상적인 사용으로 발생하는 마모에 강한 것으로 확인되었다.

해설 빈칸은 used in Alpinta nursing uniforms의 수식을 받는 주어 The fabric의 동사 자리이다. fabric은 확인되는 대상이자 단수 명사이므로, 수동태 단수 동사인 (B) has been confirmed가 정답이다.

어휘 fabric 천, 직물 withstand (잘) 견뎌내다
wear and tear 마모, 손상 confirm 사실임을 보여주다, 확인하다

12 (A)

번역 여섯 명의 뛰어난 자격을 지닌 후보자들이 노앵크 의료 센터의 CEO가 되기 위해 지원했다.

해설 문장에 동사가 없으므로 빈칸은 동사 자리이다. apply가 '지원하다'를 의미할 때 자동사이므로 수동태로 쓰일 수 없으며, 주어가 복수이므로 수 일치 영향을 받지 않는 과거 시제 (A) applied가 정답이다.

어휘 qualified 자격이 있는 candidate 후보자, 지원자

13 (B)

번역 우드필드 할인 매장 쇼핑객들은 계산 시에 자신의 전화번호를 제공하여 특별 혜택 자격을 얻을 수 있다.

해설 쇼핑객들이 특별 혜택 자격을 얻기 위한 방법으로서 '전화번호를 제공하다'와 같은 의미를 나타내야 자연스러우므로, (B) provide(제공하다)가 정답이다.

어휘 checkout 계산, 체크아웃 qualify for ~에 대한 자격이 있다

14 (B)

번역 이 도시는 시민들이 친절하기로 유명한 곳이라고 윌리엄스 시장은 자랑스럽게 말했다.

해설 빈칸 뒤의 전치사 for와 결합하여 '~으로 유명한'이라는 의미를 나타내는 과거분사 (B) known이 정답이다.

어휘 mayor 시장 proudly 자랑스럽게 hospitality 환대, 친절함

[15-18] 기사

창립 100주년을 기념하는 경매 회사

애슬론 (9월 5일) – 오늘 아일랜드에서 가장 오랫동안 운영되어 온 경매 업체 중 하나인, 맥쉐인 농기계 경매 회사가 곧 있을 창립 100주년 기념 행사를 15 **발표했습니다**. 여러 16 **세대**가 맥쉐인의 경매에 참가해 왔습니다. 이 농가들은 다양한 중고 농업용 장비를 공급하는 맥쉐인에 오랫동안 의존해 왔습니다. 맥쉐인은 9월 16일 일요일에 애슬론의 코나마 로에 있는 17 **자사**의 경매 시설에서 창립 기념 행사를 개최할 예정입니다. 빈티지한 트랙터들과 골동품 장비가 행사장에 전시됩니다. 18 **가벼운 다과도 제공될 것입니다.** 보너스로, 이 기념 행사에 밸리마혼 패밀리 밴드가 특별 출연할 것입니다.

어휘 auction 경매 celebrate 기념하다, 축하하다 upcoming 곧 있을, 다가오는 celebration 기념 행사, 축하 행사 participate in ~에 참가하다 rely on ~에 의존하다 supply 공급하다 a range of 다양한 equipment 장비 antique 골동품의 feature 특별히 출연시키다, 특징으로 하다

15 (B)

해설 빈칸 앞에는 부사(Today)와 명사구 주어(McShane Farm Machinery Auction House), 그리고 주어와 동격인 삽입 명사구가 있고, 빈칸 뒤에는 명사구만 있으므로 빈칸이 문장의 동사 자리이다. 동사인 (A) announce와 (B) announced 중에서, 현재 시제인 (A) announce는 3인칭 단수 주어 McShane Farm Machinery Auction House와 수가 일치되지 않으므로 과거 시제인 (B) announced가 정답이다.

16 (A)

해설 다음 문장에 경매에 참가한 사람들을 These farming families로 지칭해 그들이 오랫동안 맥쉐인에 의존해 왔다고 언급하고 있다. 따라서 이 사람들을 대신할 수 있는 명사가 빈칸에 쓰여야 알맞으므로 '세대들'을 의미하는 (A) generations가 정답이다.

어휘 manufacturer 제조사 salespeople 영업사원들

17 (B)

해설 빈칸 뒤에 있는 명사구 auction facilities를 수식하는 말이 들어가야 하는데, '맥쉐인의 경매 시설'이란 의미가 되어야 자연스러우므로 맥쉐인을 가리킬 수 있는 소유격 대명사 (B) its가 정답이다.

18 (C)

번역 (A) 온라인으로 사진들을 발송하실 수 있습니다.
(B) 매장이 매주 토요일에 문을 닫을 것입니다.
(C) 가벼운 다과도 제공될 것입니다.
(D) 특정 제품들에 대한 이월 주문이 있습니다.

해설 빈칸 앞뒤에 기념 행사의 특징을 이루는 전시 물품과 공연이 소개되어 있어 행사의 특징과 관련된 정보를 담은 문장이 빈칸에 들어가야 흐름이 자연스러우므로, 다과가 제공될 것이라는 내용의 (C)가 정답이다.

어휘 refreshments 다과, 간식 serve 제공하다, 내오다 back order 이월 주문

UNIT 08 시제

1 단순 시제

ETS 유형연습 본책 p.176

1 (B) 2 (B) 3 (D)

1 (B)

번역 보고르 스타디움의 좌석은 모든 방문객들이 경기를 잘 관람할 수 있도록 경기장을 완전히 둘러싸고 있다.

해설 문장의 동사가 필요한 자리이고 주어인 Seating이 단수 명사이므로 (B) surrounds, (C) surrounded가 답이 될 수 있는데, 문맥상 일반적인 사실을 나타내므로 현재 시제 동사인 (B) surrounds가 정답이다.

어휘 seating 좌석 completely 완전히 afford ~할 수 있다, (기회를) 주다 view 전망, 경치

2 (B)

번역 새로운 발견이 작동 모델을 구식으로 만들었을 때 기술자들은 겨우 문제를 분석하기 시작했던 참이었다.

해설 접속사 when이 이끄는 부사절의 동사 자리이다. 주절에 과거완료 시제(had begun)가 쓰였으므로, 빈칸에는 과거 시제가 들어가야 한다. 따라서 (B) rendered가 정답이다.

어휘 analyze 분석하다 working model 작동 모델 obsolete 못쓰게 된, 구식의 render ~을 (어떠한 상태가) 되게 하다

3 (D)

번역 아그네스 하나디는 내일 모건타운 뮤직 페스티벌에서 자신의 최신 앨범을 처음 공개할 예정이다.

해설 문장에 동사가 없으므로 빈칸은 동사 자리이며, 미래 시점을 나타내는 tomorrow가 있으므로 미래 시제 (D) will debut가 정답이다.

어휘 debut 처음 공개하다, 데뷔하다

2 진행 시제

ETS 유형연습   본책 p.177

1 (A)   2 (D)   3 (D)

1 (A)

번역 LTD 엔터프라이지스 사에서 현재 이달 말에 퇴직할 현 이사를 대신할 우수한 인재를 찾고 있습니다.

해설 빈칸 앞에 온 is currently가 문제 해결의 단서로, currently는 '현재, 지금'이라는 의미로 현재 시제와 어울리는 부사이다. 따라서 현재진행형 시제를 만들 수 있는 (A) seeking이 정답이다. (B) seeks는 currently 앞에 is가 왔으므로 정답이 될 수 없다는 것에 유의한다.

어휘 accomplished 뛰어난 replace 대신하다, 대체하다 retire 은퇴하다, 퇴직하다

2 (D)

번역 윤 씨는 목요일에 돌아왔을 때 시차로 인해 피곤했고, 그래서 회의는 다음 주로 연기되었다.

해설 when이 이끄는 부사절의 동사 returned가 과거를 나타내고 있다. 따라서 주절 또한 과거 시제가 되어야 하므로 과거진행 시제 동사 (D) was suffering이 정답이다.

어휘 jet lag 시차로 인한 피로 postpone 연기하다, 미루다 suffer 겪다

3 (D)

번역 다음 6월에 아티탬 씨가 휴가를 갈 동안, 알 자므리 씨가 뭄바이 납품업체와의 계약 협상을 맡게 될 것이다.

해설 While Ms. Atitam is on vacation next June이 미래 시점을 나타내므로, 빈칸에도 미래 시제 동사가 들어가야 한다. 따라서 미래진행 동사 (D) will be taking이 정답이다.

어휘 on vacation 휴가 중인 contract 계약(서) negotiation 교섭, 협상 vendor 납품업체 take over 인계 받다, 떠맡다

3 완료 시제

ETS 유형연습   본책 p.178

1 (B)   2 (B)   3 (A)

1 (B)

번역 지난 15년 동안 매틀록 사는 꾸준히 전국 상위 10대 장난감 제조업체에 포함되었다.

해설 앞에 현재완료 시제와 어울리는 시간 표현인 For the last fifteen years가 있으므로 has와 결합하여 현재완료 시제를 나타내는 과거분사 (B) ranked가 정답이다.

어휘 consistently 꾸준히, 끊임없이 leading 일류의, 주도하는 manufacturer 제조업체, 생산자

2 (B)

번역 채용 위원회는 지원자들을 직접 면접하는 가능성에 대해 논의했지만, 그 대신 전화 인터뷰를 하기로 결정했다.

해설 채용 위원회가 전화 인터뷰를 하기로 결정했던 과거 시점 이전에 논의가 이뤄졌으므로 과거완료 (B) had discussed가 정답이다.

어휘 hiring committee 채용 위원회 possibility 가능성 candidate 후보자, 지원자 in person 직접

3 (A)

번역 클리어 블레이즈 테크놀러지 사의 워드 프로세서 프로그램이 시판될 무렵이면, 소프트웨어 엔지니어들은 남아 있는 결함을 수정했을 것이다.

해설 '~할 즈음, ~할 무렵'이라는 의미의 〈By the time+주어+현재 시제〉 표현이 주절을 수식해 주고 있으므로, 빈칸에는 미래완료 시제가 들어가야 자연스럽다. 따라서 (A) will have corrected가 정답이다.

어휘 word processing program 워드 프로세서 프로그램 go on the market 시장에 나오다, 팔리기 시작하다 flaw 결점, 결함

4 시제 일치의 예외

ETS 유형연습   본책 p.179

1 (B)   2 (A)   3 (A)

1 (B)

번역 계정에 접속하길 원하시면 적절한 칸에 비밀번호를 입력하세요.

해설 빈칸은 When이 이끄는 부사절의 동사 자리이다. 시간/조건의 부사절에서는 미래의 일을 나타내더라도 현재 시제를 사용하므로, (B) want가 정답이다.

어휘 access 접속하다 account 계좌, 계정 password 비밀번호 appropriate 적절한, 알맞은 field 영역, 칸

2 (A)
번역 화재 위험에 대비한 창고 조사가 끝나는 대로, 정상적인 영업을 재개할 수 있다.

해설 빈칸은 As soon as가 이끄는 부사절의 동사 자리이다. 시간/조건의 부사절에서는 미래의 일을 나타내더라도 현재 시제를 사용하므로, 현재완료 (A) has been이 정답이다.

어휘 warehouse 창고 hazard 위험, 모험 resume 재개하다 normal 정상적인 operation 운영, 조업

3 (A)
번역 라지브 커티 전무 이사는 스리니바산 푸드 공장의 품질 관리 절차를 검토하라는 주주들의 요청에 응했다.

해설 that이 이끄는 절 앞에 requests(요청)라는 명사가 있으므로, that절의 동사는 《(should)+동사원형》이 되어야 한다. 주어인 he는 절차를 검토하는 주체이므로, 능동태 동사원형인 (A) review가 정답이다.

어휘 executive director 전무 이사 comply with ~의 요구에 응하다 shareholder 주주 quality control 품질 검사, 품질 관리 procedure 절차 facility 시설, 공장

ETS 실전문제   본책 p.180

1 (A)   2 (B)   3 (B)   4 (B)   5 (B)   6 (C)
7 (D)   8 (A)   9 (C)   10 (D) 11 (D) 12 (B)
13 (D) 14 (B) 15 (D) 16 (A) 17 (C) 18 (A)

1 (A)
번역 매년 여름 브라이튼의 상점 주인들은 관광객들을 더 많이 유치하려는 노력의 일환으로 쇼윈도를 독특하게 진열한다.

해설 Brighton store owners가 주어, 빈칸이 동사, unique window displays가 목적어인 문장이다. 따라서 복수 주어와 수가 일치하는 능동 동사가 들어가야 하므로, (A) create가 정답이다.

어휘 owner 소유자, 주인 unique 독특한, 특이한 window display 쇼윈도의 상품 진열 attract 끌다, 유치하다 tourist 관광객 create 만들다

2 (B)
번역 매그넘 플러스 카메라는 아주 사용하기 쉬워서 지금 매우 인기를 끌고 있다.

해설 Magnum Plus cameras가 주어, 빈칸이 동사, very popular가 주격 보어인 문장이다. 뒤에 right now라는 표현이 있으므로, 빈칸에는 현재 시점에 진행되는 일을 나타내는 동사가 들어가야 자연스럽다. 따라서 현재진행형인 (B) are becoming이 정답이다.

어휘 popular 인기 있는

3 (B)
번역 향상된 품질 덕분에 지난 몇 년간 환불을 요청하는 고객들의 수가 감소했다.

해설 단수 주어 The number와 수가 일치하는 (A) declined와 (B) has declined 중 하나를 선택해야 하는데, 뒤에 over the last few years(지난 몇 년간)라는 표현이 있으므로 현재완료 시제가 빈칸에 들어가야 자연스럽다. 따라서 (B) has declined가 정답이다.

4 (B)
번역 리 씨가 조정을 좀 한 후에 엔진은 이전보다 더 부드럽게 작동했다.

해설 빈칸은 After가 이끄는 부사절의 주어인 Mr. Li의 동사 자리이므로, 보기에서 동사 자리에 들어갈 수 있는 (B) made와 (C) is making 중 하나를 선택해야 한다. 조정을 한 후 더 부드럽게 작동했다(worked)고 볼 수 있으므로, 빈칸에는 과거완료 또는 과거 시제가 들어갈 수 있다. 따라서 (B) made가 정답이다.

어휘 adjustment 수정, 조정 smoothly 부드럽게

5 (B)
번역 라퍼 페인팅 사는 아바게일 가에 개장한 새 매장을 축하하기 위해 다음 달에 특별 할인 행사를 할 것이다.

해설 Larper Painting이 주어, 빈칸이 동사, a special sale이 목적어인 문장이다. 라퍼 페인팅 사가 다음 달(next month)에 할인 행사를 진행할 것이라는 내용이므로, 능동태 미래 시제인 (B) will be running이 정답이다.

어휘 celebrate 축하하다

6 (C)
번역 데릭 씨가 팀에 합류한 이후 자파타 씨와 콜먼 씨는 훌륭한 성과를 거둔 마케팅 팀에 찬사를 보내고 있다.

해설 빈칸 앞에 have, 뒤에 목적어 the marketing team이 있으며, 과거부터 현재까지의 기간을 나타내는 since 부사절이 문장 전체를 수식하고 있다. 따라서 '데릭 씨가 합류한 이후로 마케팅 팀을 칭찬해 오고 있다'라는 내용이 되어야 자연스러우므로, have와 결합하여 능동태 현재완료(진행) 동사를 완성하는 (C) been praising이 정답이다.

어휘 join 합류하다 praise 칭찬하다, 찬사를 보내다

7 (D)
번역 리톡 엔지니어링은 새 세입자들이 이사올 때까지 그 건물의 모든 전기 배선 점검을 마칠 것이다.

해설 '~할 즈음, ~할 무렵'이라는 뜻의 《by the time+주어(new tenants)+현재 시제(move in)》 표현이 주절을 수식해 주고 있으므로, 미래의 특정 시점에 완료될 일을 나타내는 미래완료 시제가 쓰여야 자연스럽다. 따라서 과거분사 checked와 결합하여 '점검을 마칠 것이다'라는 의미를 완성하는 (D) will have가 정답이다.

어휘 electrical wiring 전기 배선 tenant 세입자, 임차인

8 (A)

번역 럼 박사는 오늘 나온 결과를 입증하기 위해 내일 두 번째 연구 그룹이 실험을 반복할 것을 요청하고 있다.

해설 요청의 동사 is requesting의 목적어 역할을 하는 that절의 동사 자리로, 〈(should)+동사원형〉이 들어가야 한다. 주어 experiment는 반복되는 대상이므로, 수동태 동사원형 (A) be repeated가 정답이다.

어휘 validate 입증하다 request 요청하다 experiment 실험 research 연구

9 (C)

번역 만약 배관 문제가 지속되면 제품 제조업체에 연락하시길 권해 드립니다.

해설 빈칸은 If가 이끄는 부사절의 동사 자리이다. 조건의 부사절에서는 미래의 일을 나타내더라도 현재 시제를 사용하므로 (C) persists가 정답이다.

어휘 plumbing 배관 recommend 권하다 manufacturer 제조업체 persist 지속되다 persistence 끈기, 고집

10 (D)

번역 양 씨가 타이베이에서 열리는 국제 여행 회의에서 돌아올 때까지 우 씨가 모든 호텔 예약을 처리할 것이다.

해설 Until이 이끄는 시간의 부사절에서 현재 시제(returns)를 사용하여 미래의 상황을 나타내고 있으므로, 주절에 미래 시제가 쓰여야 한다. 주어 Mr. Woo는 호텔 예약을 처리하는 주체이므로, 능동태 미래 시제인 (D) will handle이 정답이다.

어휘 conference 회의, 대회 reservation 예약 handle 다루다, 처리하다

11 (D)

번역 저조한 등록률 때문에, 8월에 시작될 예정이었던 워크숍이 9월로 연기되었다.

해설 postpone은 타동사인데 빈칸 뒤에 목적어 없이 전치사구만 있으므로 수동태로 쓰여야 한다. 따라서 (D) has been postponed가 정답이다.

어휘 enrollment 등록(률) postpone 연기하다, 미루다

12 (B)

번역 오카다 씨가 영업 회의를 위해 인천에 도착했을 무렵, 그녀는 이미 전화상으로 사전 협상을 마친 상태였다.

해설 주절의 동사가 과거 이전의 일을 나타내는 과거완료 시제(had completed)이므로, 빈칸에는 '~했을 즈음에'라는 표현을 완성하는 과거 시제가 들어가야 한다. 따라서 (B) arrived가 정답이다.

어휘 sales meeting 영업 회의 preliminary 예비의, 준비의 negotiation 협상

13 (D)

번역 실비아 조 씨는 지난주에 프리오 카운티 동물병원에서 교육을 마쳤고, 동물병원 간호사로서 일을 시작할 것이다.

해설 Sylvia Cho가 등위접속사 and 앞뒤 절의 공통 주어이다. and 뒤에는 미래 시제가 쓰였지만 and 앞에는 과거를 나타내는 last week가 동사를 수식하므로 과거 시제 동사 (D) concluded가 정답이다.

어휘 training 훈련, 교육 veterinary technician 동물병원 간호사 conclude 끝내다, 마치다

14 (B)

번역 문서를 고객들에게 발송하기 전에 반드시 꼼꼼하게 검토해야 한다.

해설 〈It(가주어) ~ that절(진주어)〉 구문으로, that절이 반드시 해야 하는 일을 나타내면서 동사는 원형(be examined)을 사용했다. 따라서 '필수적인, 중요한'이라는 뜻의 (B) imperative가 정답이다. imperative, important, essential과 같은 형용사 뒤에 오는 that절의 동사는 〈(should)+동사원형〉이 된다.

어휘 meticulously 세심하게, 꼼꼼하게 examine 살펴보다, 검토하다 immediate 즉각적인 ultimate 궁극적인 conclusive 결정적인

[15-18] 이메일

수신: 로렌스 메이슨 〈l.mason@callastreetbakery.com〉
발신: 칼라 맨프레드 〈ms.manfred@colincenterschool.org〉
날짜: 4월 16일
제목: 감사합니다
첨부: 학생 미술 작품

메이슨 씨께,

저희 1학년 학급이 귀하의 제과점을 방문하도록 허락해 주셔서 감사합니다. 이번이 저희 학생들 대부분에게 도시를 벗어난 첫 번째 여행이었습니다. **15 아이들은 그렇게 오랫동안 버스를 탄다는 것만으로도 들떠 있었습니다.** 그리고 귀하의 업체를 봤을 때, 넋을 잃었습니다!

저는 이 **16 견학**을 이끌어 주신 현장 관리자, 조 씨를 칭찬해 드리고 싶습니다. 이분께서 아이들이 이해하기 쉬운 방식으로 그 과정들을 잘 설명해 주셨습니다. 이분께서는 또한 인내심 있게 **17 아이들의** 모든 질문에 답변해 주셨습니다.

저희가 학교로 **18 돌아왔을** 때, 아이들이 각자 그 제과점 그림을 그렸습니다. 제가 이 그림들을 스캔해서 첨부해 드렸습니다.

다시 한번 감사합니다.

맨프레드와 콜린 센터 학교 1학년 학생 일동

어휘 allow 허락하다, 허용하다 operation 사업(체), 운영 mesmerized 넋을 잃은, 매혹된 commend A for B B에 대해 A를 칭찬하다 process 과정 patient 인내심 있는 attach 첨부하다

15 (D)

번역 (A) 저희는 매달 두 번씩 현장 학습을 떠납니다.
(B) 예를 들어, 학생들이 갓 구운 제과제품을 특히 즐겼습니다.
(C) 늦게 도착해서 죄송합니다.
(D) 아이들은 그렇게 오랫동안 버스를 탄다는 것만으로도 들떠 있었습니다.

해설 빈칸 앞에 학생들에게 도시를 벗어난 첫 번째 여행이었다는 말이 있으므로 그런 여행을 떠나는 것에 대한 학생들의 반응을 언급한 (D)가 정답이다.
어휘 field trip 현장 학습

16 (A)

해설 동명사 leading의 목적어로서, 아이들의 제과점 방문과 관련하여 조 씨가 이끈 것을 나타낼 명사가 들어가야 적절하므로, '견학'이라는 의미의 (A) tour가 정답이다.
어휘 campaign 캠페인, (조직적인) 운동   performance 공연, 성과

17 (C)

해설 문장의 주어 She가 Ms. Cho를 가리키므로 조 씨가 인내심 있게 아이들의 모든 질문에 대답했다는 의미를 나타내야 자연스럽다. 따라서 앞선 문장에 언급된 the children을 지칭할 수 있는 소유격 대명사 (C) their가 정답이다.

18 (A)

해설 빈칸 앞에는 접속사 When과 주어 we가, 뒤에는 to 전치사구가 쓰여 있으므로 빈칸은 When절의 동사 자리이다. 또한, When절의 동사는 주절의 동사와 동일 시점을 나타내야 하므로, 주절에 쓰인 동사 drew와 시제가 동일한 과거 시제 동사 (A) returned가 정답이다.

UNIT 09 to부정사와 동명사

1 to부정사의 용법

ETS 유형연습   본책 p.182

1 (A)   **2** (A)   **3** (C)

1 (A)

번역 이 정부 프로그램의 목적은 학교에서 새로운 학습 기술을 더 잘 이용할 수 있도록 하는 것이다.
해설 The purpose (of this government program)가 문장의 주어이고, is가 동사이며, 빈칸은 is의 보어 자리이다. 따라서 '~하는 것'의 의미로 is의 보어 역할을 할 수 있는 to부정사 (A) to provide가 정답이다.
어휘 purpose 목적   access 접근, 이용   provide A with B A에게 B를 제공하다

2 (A)

번역 오늘 테노피 테크는 키토와 카라카스에서 태양 전지판을 제조하기 위해 셰플라이 에너지 시스템즈와의 제휴 계획을 발표했다.
해설 동사 announced의 목적어인 its plans를 수식하는 자리로 '제휴할 계획'이라는 의미를 나타내는 (A) to partner가 정답이다. 문장의 동사인 announced가 있기 때문에 동사인 (C), (D)는 오답이다.

어휘 solar panel 태양 전지판   partner with ~와 제휴하다

3 (C)

번역 해외 고객들의 편의를 도모하기 위해 머제스키 그룹은 유럽과 아시아에 지사를 개설할 것이다.
해설 in order to(~하기 위하여)는 '목적'을 나타내는 to부정사 표현이므로 동사원형 (C) accommodate가 정답이다. 〈so as to 동사원형〉이나 〈to 동사원형〉을 써도 같은 의미이다.
어휘 overseas 해외의   accommodation 숙박 시설, 편의 제공   accommodate ~의 편의를 도모하다

2 to부정사의 활용

ETS 유형연습   본책 p.183

1 (A)   **2** (A)   **3** (A)

1 (A)

번역 애니스크 제약은 임상 연구에 참가한 모든 사람들의 비밀을 유지하고자 모든 노력을 기울인다.
해설 문장의 동사 makes가 있으므로 동사인 (B), (C), (D)는 들어갈 수 없다. 문맥상 '~하기 위해 모든 노력을 한다'가 적합하므로 effort를 뒤에서 수식할 수 있고, 빈칸 뒤에 있는 명사구를 목적어로 받을 수 있는 to부정사 (A) to maintain이 정답이다.
어휘 make every effort to ~하기 위해 온갖 노력을 다하다   confidentiality 기밀성, 비밀성   clinical study 임상 연구   maintain 유지하다

2 (A)

번역 할인을 받으시려면, 구매 양식에 코드를 입력하십시오.
해설 빈칸 뒤에 있는 a discount를 목적어로 받아 '할인을 받기 위해'의 의미가 되어야 자연스러우므로 to부정사 (A) To receive가 정답이다.
어휘 purchasing 구매

3 (A)

번역 그 이사는 전문성 개발 세미나가 다양한 분야에 종사하는 직원들의 견문과 전문 지식을 넓히는 데 도움이 될 수 있다고 확신하고 있다.
해설 동사 help는 목적어로 to부정사 또는 원형부정사를 취할 수 있다. 동사 help의 목적어 역할을 하는 동시에 뒤에 the knowledge and expertise를 목적어로 취할 수 있는 원형부정사 (A) broaden이 정답이다.
어휘 professional 직업의, 전문적인   expertise 전문 지식   area 분야   broaden 넓히다   broadly 대략   broad 넓은

3 동명사

ETS 유형연습   본책 p.184

1 (C)   **2** (D)   **3** (C)

157

1 (C)
번역 여러 해 동안 그 지방 정부는 레드 밸리를 야생 공원으로 지정하는 것을 고려해 왔다.

해설 Red Valley를 목적어로 취하는 동시에 has considered의 목적어가 될 수 있는 동명사 (C) designating이 정답이다. consider(고려하다)는 동명사를 목적어로 취하는 타동사이다.

어휘 consider 고려하다　wilderness 미개지, (자연이 보존된) 야생 지역　designate 지정하다, 선정하다　designation 지정, 지명

2 (D)
번역 발표 중에 청중의 주의력을 흐트러뜨리는 것을 피하기 위해 복잡한 레이아웃을 사용하지 마십시오.

해설 빈칸 뒤에 your audience를 목적어로 취하는 동시에 avoid의 목적어 역할을 할 수 있는 동명사 (D) distracting이 정답이다. avoid는 동명사를 목적어로 취하는 타동사이다.

어휘 avoid 피하다　complex 복잡한　layout 레이아웃, 지면 배정; 배치(도)　distraction 마음이 흐트러짐, 주의 산만　distract (주의력을) 흐트러뜨리다, 산만하게 하다

3 (C)
번역 백스터 씨는 지원자들의 면접을 본 후 고용위원회의 모든 구성원들을 다시 만나고 싶어 한다.

해설 after는 접속사와 전치사로 모두 쓰이지만 빈칸 뒤에 주어가 없으므로 이 문장에서는 전치사로 쓰인 것이다. 따라서 candidates를 목적어로 취하는 동시에 전치사 after의 목적어 역할을 할 수 있는 동명사 (C) interviewing이 정답이다.

어휘 hiring committee 고용위원회　candidate (일자리의) 후보자, 지원자　interview 면접을 보다

4 to부정사 / 전치사 to

ETS 유형연습　본책 p.185
1 (A)　**2** (C)　**3** (D)

1 (A)
번역 스위트니스 초콜릿은 8월 1일자로 공공증권거래소에 상장된다는 사실을 발표하게 되어 기쁩니다.

해설 빈칸 앞에 is pleased가 있고, 문맥상 '발표하게 되어 기쁘다'라는 의미가 적절하므로 (A) to announce가 정답이다. 〈be pleased to 동사원형〉의 형태로 기억하자.

어휘 list (증권거래소에) 상장하다　as of ~일자로

2 (C)
번역 그 신문의 판매국은 훌륭한 서비스를 제공하는 데 전력을 다하고 있다.

해설 be committed to(~에 전념하다)의 to는 전치사이므로 뒤에 명사나 동명사가 올 수 있다. 따라서 뒤에 있는 excellent service를 목적어로 취하는 동시에 전치사 to의 목적어 역할을 할 수 있는 동명사 (C) providing이 정답이다.

어휘 circulation department 판매국　provision 공급, 준비, 예비　provide 제공하다

3 (D)
번역 페어몬트 파이낸스 직원들 몇 명은 회사 구내에서 주차비를 청구하는 것에 반대한다.

해설 object는 전치사 to와 함께 쓰이는 자동사로 to 뒤에 명사나 동명사가 올 수 있다. 문장의 주어인 employees는 청구를 받는 대상이므로 수동태 동명사인 (D) being charged가 정답이다.

어휘 object to ~에 반대하다　parking 주차　premises (토지를 포함한) 건물, 구내　charge (요금을) 청구하다

ETS 실전문제　본책 p.186
1 (B)　**2** (A)　**3** (D)　**4** (B)　**5** (D)　**6** (D)
7 (A)　**8** (C)　**9** (A)　**10** (A)　**11** (C)　**12** (D)
13 (B)　**14** (C)　**15** (B)　**16** (A)　**17** (C)　**18** (B)

1 (B)
번역 편집장 카이라 데일리는 윌스턴 카운티를 포함하도록 〈하넷 타임즈〉의 배포 지역을 확장하는 계획을 확정했다.

해설 빈칸은 명사 Wilston County를 목적어로 취하면서, 수식하는 역할을 한다. 따라서 '포함하도록'이라는 의미를 나타내는 to부정사 (B) to include가 정답이다.

어휘 editor-in-chief 편집장　expand 확장하다, 확대하다　distribution 배포, 보급, 배분　inclusive 포괄적인, 폭넓은　inclusion 포함

2 (A)
번역 모든 야외 프로그램은 사전 통보 없이 취소될 수 있다는 점에 유의하세요.

해설 '~되기 쉽다, ~될 수 있다'라는 의미를 나타내는 be subject to에서 to는 전치사이므로 뒤에 명사나 동명사를 써야 한다. 빈칸 뒤에 목적어가 없으므로 명사 (A) cancellation이 정답이다. (B) canceling은 목적어가 필요한 타동사의 동명사이므로 오답이다.

어휘 prior notice 사전 통보

3 (D)
번역 매출 증가를 처리하고자 인사부는 다수의 신입 사원을 모집할 계획이다.

해설 a number of new employees를 목적어로 취하는 동시에 intends의 목적어 역할을 할 수 있는 to부정사 (D) to recruit가 정답이다.

어휘 handle 다루다, 처리하다　increase in sales 매출 증가　human resources department 인사부　intend to ~할 작정이다　recruit (신입 사원 등을) 모집하다, 뽑다

4 (B)
번역 1,000명 이상의 참가자를 위한 국제 회의를 준비하는 것이 그 팀에게 가장 어려운 임무였다.

해설 빈칸 뒤의 명사구 an international conference를 목적어로 취하면서 동사 was의 주어 역할을 할 수 있는 동명사 (B) Preparing이 정답이다.

어휘 challenging 까다로운, 어려운 assignment 임무, 과제

5 (D)
번역 유로산 엔터프라이지즈의 경영진은 고객 서비스를 위한 일련의 새로운 지침들을 마련하는 중이다.

해설 빈칸 뒤의 a new set of guidelines를 목적어로 취하면서 전치사 of의 목적어 역할을 할 수 있는 동명사 (D) establishing이 정답이다.

어휘 be in the process of ~하는 중이다, ~하는 과정이다 guideline 지침, 정책 establish 제정하다, 확립하다

6 (D)
번역 아투어 사이클링 임원진은 노르딕 자전거 라인을 생산을 중단하기로 결정한 이유로 판매 부진을 들었다.

해설 빈칸은 명사구 the Nordique bicycle line을 목적어로 취하면서, 앞에 있는 명사 decision을 수식하는 역할을 한다. 따라서 '중단하려는 결정'이라는 의미를 완성하는 to부정사 (D) to discontinue가 정답이다.

어휘 executive 경영진, 임원진 cite (이유·예를) 들다 slow sale 판매 부진 decision 결정 discontinue (생산을) 중단하다

7 (A)
번역 작가 유니스 킴은 11월 말에 턴햄에서 다섯 번째 강연을 하기로 예정되어 있다.

해설 빈칸 앞에 동사 is scheduled가 있고, 뒤에 목적어 her fifth lecture가 있다. 따라서 be scheduled와 함께 '~할 예정이다'라는 표현을 완성하는 to부정사 (A) to give가 정답이다.

어휘 author 저자, 작가 give a lecture 강연하다

8 (C)
번역 그 컨설팅 회사는 소규모 회사들에게 맞춤형 마케팅 해결책들을 제공하는 책임을 맡고 있다.

해설 빈칸 뒤의 customized marketing solutions를 목적어로 취하는 동시에 전치사 for의 목적어 역할을 할 수 있는 동명사 (C) offering이 정답이다.

어휘 customized 맞춤형의 solution 해결책

9 (A)
번역 참석자들에게 미리 회의 의제를 배포하는 것이 대체로 가장 효과적이다.

해설 주어인 It은 가짜 주어로 빈칸 이하의 진짜 주어를 대신하고 있으므로 진짜 주어 역할을 할 수 있는 (A) to circulate가 정답이다.

어휘 effective 효과적인 agenda 의제, 안건 attendee 참석자 in advance 미리, 사전에 circulate 배포하다, 배부하다

10 (A)
번역 영업부장은 팀원들과 신입 사원들의 교육에 상당한 시간을 들인다.

해설 spend는 〈spend+시간/돈+(in) 동명사〉의 구조로 쓰이므로, 빈칸은 생략된 전치사 in의 목적어 자리이다. 따라서 목적어 his team members and new employees를 취하면서 전치사의 목적어 역할을 할 수 있는 동명사 (A) training이 정답이다.

어휘 considerable 상당한

11 (C)
번역 벤토 화장품의 CEO는 최근 해외 매출에서 발생한 문제점들이 그 회사의 장기적인 수출 계획에 영향을 미치지 않도록 했다.

해설 사역동사 let의 목적어인 the recent problems with foreign sales를 보충 설명하는 목적격 보어 자리이다. 사역동사는 원형부정사를 목적격 보어로 취하므로 원형부정사 (C) affect가 정답이다.

어휘 cosmetics 화장품 long-term 장기적인 affect 영향을 미치다

12 (D)
번역 로즈우드 도서관은 이용자들에게 한 번에 최대 10권까지 도서를 대출하도록 허용한다.

해설 동사 permit은 〈permit+목적어+to부정사〉의 구조로 쓰여 '~에게 …하도록 허용하다'라는 의미를 나타내므로 to부정사 (D) to borrow가 정답이다.

어휘 borrow 대출하다, 빌리다

13 (B)
번역 모든 무용수는 시립 발레단에 고려되기 위해서 최소 2년의 사전 경력이 있어야 한다.

해설 빈칸 앞에 완전한 절이 왔고, 뒤에는 동사원형이 있으므로, 빈칸에는 to부정사의 to가 들어가야 한다. 따라서 '고려되기 위해서는'이라는 의미를 완성하는 (B) in order to(~하기 위해)가 정답이다. (A) likewise와 (C) currently는 부사, (D) only if는 부사절 접속사이므로 구조상 빈칸에 들어갈 수 없다.

어휘 prior 이전의 consider (채용 등에) 고려하다 currently 현재

14 (C)
번역 마셀로 앤 불 목공사는 공예를 배우는 데 관심이 많은 하계 견습생을 찾고 있다.

해설 빈칸은 명사구 the craft를 목적어로 취하면서, 전치사 in의 목적어 역할을 한다. 따라서 동명사 (C) learning이 정답이다.

어휘 carpentry 목공업 seek 찾다 apprentice 수습생, 도제 craft 공예

[15-18] 이메일

수신: a.menke@branwinmanufacturing.au
발신: nobu.ito@peraltaelectronics.jp
날짜: 11월 4일
제목: 도매용 계정 설정
첨부: 필수_문서

멘크 씨께,

온라인 프로필을 만들어 주셔서 감사합니다. 저희는 시간을 들여 귀하의 업체가 저희 도매용 계정 필수 조건을 충족하는지 확인했습니다. 귀하의 업체는 15 **자격이 있는** 것으로 보입니다. 완료하기 위해서는 몇 가지 단계만 남아 있습니다. 16 **첫 번째로,** 이 이메일에 답장하셔서, 이메일을 받으셨다는 사실을 저희에게 알려 주세요. 그런 다음, 첨부 파일에 기재되어 있는 문서들을 제출해 주세요. 지연을 방지하기 위해, 반드시 온라인 프로필을 만드는 데 사용한 것과 동일한 업체명과 전화번호를 포함해 주세요. 17 **이것들이 일치하는 것이 중요합니다.**

모든 문서가 저희 세무팀에 의해 검토된 후 18 **처리되는 데** 영업일로 최대 15일까지 소요될 수 있다는 점에 유의하시기 바랍니다. 귀하의 도매용 계정이 만들어지는 대로 알림을 받으실 것이며, 주문을 할 수 있을 것입니다.

감사합니다.

노부 이토, 페랄타 전자 도매 지원팀

어휘 wholesale 도매의 account 계정, 계좌 verify 확인하다, 인증하다 requirement 필수 조건, 요건 appear ~하는 것으로 보이다 attachment 첨부 파일 avoid 피하다 delay 지연, 지체 include 포함하다 process 처리하다 proceed 진행하다

15 (B)

해설 빈칸 앞 문장에 시간을 들여 필수 조건을 충족하는지 확인했다는 말이, 빈칸 뒤에는 몇 가지 단계만 남아 있다는 말이 쓰여 있다. 따라서 자격을 갖춘 것은 확인됐고, 몇 가지만 더하면 된다는 의미가 되어야 자연스러우므로 (B) eligible(자격이 있는)이 정답이다.

어휘 intact 온전한, 손상되지 않은 efficient 효율적인 accountable 책임이 있는

16 (A)

해설 앞서 몇 가지 단계만 남아 있다는 말이 있고, 뒤에 있는 문장에는 다음 순서를 말할 때 사용하는 Then(그런 다음)과 함께 해야 하는 일을 설명하고 있으므로 빈칸에는 첫 번째를 뜻하는 말이 들어가야 자연스럽다. 따라서 (A) First가 정답이다.

어휘 instead 대신 besides 게다가, 그뿐만 아니라 conversely 정반대로

17 (C)

번역 (A) 추가적인 조치가 필요합니다.
(B) 저희는 아마 재고가 없을 겁니다.
(C) 이것들이 일치하는 것이 중요합니다.
(D) 여러 선택 사항이 여전히 이용 가능합니다.

해설 빈칸 앞에서 반드시 온라인 프로필을 만드는 데 사용한 것과 동일한 업체명과 전화번호를 포함하라고 알리고 있다. 따라서 이 주의 사항과 관련된 문장이 필요하므로, 업체명과 전화번호를 they로 지칭해 동일하게 하는 것이 중요하다는 의미로 쓰인 (C)가 정답이다.

어휘 further 추가적인, 더 깊이 있는 out of stock 재고가 없는, 품절된 match 일치하다 available 이용 가능한

18 (B)

해설 빈칸 앞에 이미 that절의 동사로 are examined와 may take가 and로 연결된 상태로 제시되어 있으므로 빈칸은 동사 자리가 아니다. 따라서 보기에서 유일하게 동사의 형태가 아닌 to부정사 (B) to be가 정답이다. 〈take+시간+to부정사〉는 '~하는 데 시간이 …가 걸리다'라는 의미이다.

UNIT 10 분사와 분사구문

1 분사의 자리

ETS 유형연습　　　　　　　본책 p.188

1 (D)　　**2** (A)　　**3** (D)

1 (D)

번역 실험실 보조직은 화학 또는 관련 분야의 고급 학위를 필요로 한다.

해설 부정관사 an과 명사 degree 사이에 위치한 빈칸은 명사를 수식하는 형용사가 들어갈 수 있는 자리이므로, (D) advanced (고급의, 상급의)가 정답이다. 명사 (A) advancement는 degree와 복합명사를 구성하지 않으므로 오답이다.

어휘 laboratory 실험실 assistant 보조, 조수 chemistry 화학 advancement 진보, 발전 advance 발전; 발전시키다

2 (A)

번역 우리 사무실 비서가 컴퓨터 파일을 백업해두었기 때문에 정전된 후에도 정보가 성공적으로 복구되었다.

해설 be동사 뒤의 주격 보어 자리로, 주어인 the information은 복구되는 대상이므로 수동의 의미를 나타내는 과거분사 (A) recovered가 정답이다. 뒤에 목적어가 없으니 수동태로 접근하는 것도 좋다. 참고로, 이 문장에서 recover는 '복구하다'라는 타동사로 쓰여 수동태가 가능하지만, 〈recover from+병(~로부터 회복하다)〉과 같은 자동사 용법은 수동태가 불가능하다는 것도 알아두자.

어휘 make a backup of ~을 백업해 두다 power failure 정전 recover 되찾다, 회복하다

3 (D)

번역 브린타운 코블러는 고급 가죽 신발 수선을 전문으로 하는 가족 운영 신발 수리 업체이다.

해설 빈칸 앞에 주어(The Bryntown Cobbler), 동사(is), 명사구 보어(a family-operated shoe repair business)로 구성된 완전한 절이 쓰여 있다. 따라서 동사 specialize의 분사가 빈칸에 쓰여 '~을 전문으로 하는'이라는 의미로 명사구 a family-operated shoe repair business를 뒤에서 수식하는 분사구를 구성해야 알맞으므로 현재분사 (D) specializing이 정답이다.

어휘 family-operated 가족이 운영하는 reconditioning 수선, 수리 specialty 전문 분야, 전공 specialize (in) (~을) 전문으로 하다

2 분사의 종류

ETS 유형연습   본책 p.189

1 (C) **2** (B) **3** (D)

1 (C)

번역 엄청난 수의 티켓 예매에 근거하여, 올해 도니골 축제의 참석자가 기록적인 수치에 이를 것으로 예상된다.

해설 빈칸 뒤의 명사 number를 수식하는 자리로 '압도적인 수치'라는 능동 관계가 성립하므로 현재분사 (C) overwhelming이 정답이다.

어휘 based on ~에 근거하여 advance ticket sales 티켓 예매 record 기록적인 attendance 참석, 참석자 수 overwhelm 압도하다, 제압하다 overwhelming 압도적인, 엄청난 overwhelmingly 압도적으로

2 (B)

번역 경험 많은 보험 전문가들로 구성된 저희 팀은 보험 청구에 관한 어떤 질문에 관해서도 도와드릴 준비가 되어 있습니다.

해설 전치사 of와 명사구 insurance specialists 사이에 있는 빈칸은 명사구를 수식할 형용사 또는 명사구를 목적어로 취할 동명사가 쓰일 수 있는 자리이다. 이 문장에서는 '경험 많은 보험 전문가들로 구성된 팀'이라는 의미로 어떤 전문가들인지 나타낼 형용사가 쓰여야 알맞으므로 (B) experienced(경험 많은)가 정답이다.

어휘 insurance 보험 specialist 전문가 claim (보상 등의) 청구, 주장

3 (D)

번역 쿠퍼 씨 부부는 시의 엄격한 건축 법규가 수용할 수 없을 정도로 좌절감을 주자 시의 경계를 벗어난 곳에 집을 짓기로 결정했다.

해설 빈칸은 2형식 동사 became의 주격 보어 역할을 하는 형용사 자리이다. (A) frustrated와 (D) frustrating이 각각 과거분사, 현재분사로 형용사 역할을 할 수 있지만, 주어인 사물명사 building codes는 감정을 유발하는 주체이므로 현재분사 (D) frustrating이 정답이다.

어휘 city limits 시의 경계 rigid 엄격한 building code 건축 법규 accommodate 수용하다, 받아들이다 frustrate 좌절감을 주다 frustrating 좌절감을 주는, 짜증스럽게 하는

3 분사의 활용

ETS 유형연습   본책 p.190

1 (D) **2** (C) **3** (D)

1 (D)

번역 자재를 대량 생산하는 기업들에게는 충분한 창고 공간이 매우 중요하다.

해설 large quantities of materials를 목적어로 취하는 동시에 빈칸 앞의 명사 companies를 수식할 수 있는 현재분사 (D) producing이 정답이다.

어휘 adequate 충분한, 적당한 storage 저장, 보관, 창고 large quantities of 대량의 material 재료, 소재, 자재 produce 생산하다

2 (C)

번역 환자들이 척추 지압사의 진찰을 받기 위해 대기하는 동안 무료 사과 주스나 차를 즐길 수 있다.

해설 부정관사 a와 명사구 apple juice 사이에 위치한 빈칸은 명사구를 수식할 형용사가 들어갈 수 있는 자리이며, 무료 사과 주스를 의미해야 자연스러우므로 '무료의'라는 의미의 형용사 (C) complimentary가 정답이다. (B) complimenting은 '칭찬하는'이라는 의미이다.

어휘 chiropractor 척추 지압사 compliment 칭찬하다; 칭찬 complimentary 무료의

3 (D)

번역 오늘 오전에 우리가 전화 통화에서 논의했던 바와 같이, 폭스 씨는 3월 14일 수요일 오후 2시에 귀사의 공장에 도착할 것입니다.

해설 부사절 접속사 as가 과거분사와 결합하면 '~된 대로'라는 의미의 관용표현으로 쓰인다. '전화 통화에서 논의된 대로'라는 의미를 완성하는 과거분사 (D) discussed가 정답이다.

어휘 discuss 논의하다, 상의하다 discussion 논의, 상의

4 분사구문

ETS 유형연습   본책 p.191

1 (D) **2** (A) **3** (A)

1 (D)

번역 올해 이 도시에는 이례적으로 많은 양의 비가 내려서 도로공사 계획들이 제때에 완료되기 어려워졌다.

해설 문장의 본동사인 has experienced가 있기 때문에 동사인 (B), (C)는 오답이고, 결국 분사인 (A)와 (D) 중에서 선택해야 하는 분사구문 문제이다. 빈칸 뒤에 목적어 it이 있으므로 능동태 구조의 현재분사인 (D) making이 정답이다.

어휘 unusually 평소와는 달리, 이례적으로 rainfall 강우(량) road project 도로공사 계획 on time 제때에

2 (A)

번역 지난주 제품 설명회에 깊은 인상을 받은 운영부장은 핸디메이드의 가전제품 여러 개를 주문하기로 결정했다.

해설 콤마 앞에서 문장 전체를 수식하는 분사구문의 분사 자리로 주절의 주어인 the operations manager는 감명받는 대상이므로 과거분사 (A) Impressed가 정답이다. 부사절인 〈Because he was impressed by ~〉를 분사구문으로 바꾸면, 〈Being impressed by ~〉의 형태가 되는데, 이때 Being은 생략 가능하다.

어휘 product demonstration 제품 설명회 operations manager 운영부장 several 몇몇, 몇 개 appliance 가전제품 impressed 감명받은, 좋은 인상을 받은 impressive 인상적인 impression 인상, 느낌

3 (A)

번역 회계학 학위를 땄기 때문에 사카이 씨는 관리직의 가장 유력한 후보 중의 한 명으로 여겨진다.

해설 콤마 앞에서 문장 전체를 수식하는 분사구문의 분사 자리다. 빈칸 뒤에 목적어(a degree)가 있으며, 주절의 시제(is considered)보다 한 시제 앞서므로 능동태 완료 분사구문인 (A) Having earned가 정답이다. (C) Being earned는 수동태 분사구문으로 목적어를 취할 수 없다.

어휘 degree 학위 accounting 회계(학) consider A B A를 B로 여기다 candidate (일자리의) 후보자, 지원자 management position 관리직 earn 얻다, 획득하다

ETS 실전문제
본책 p.192

1 (C)	2 (A)	3 (A)	4 (D)	5 (B)	6 (B)
7 (A)	8 (C)	9 (B)	10 (C)	11 (B)	12 (A)
13 (C)	14 (D)	15 (D)	16 (A)	17 (C)	18 (D)

1 (C)

번역 챈두 박물관 정책에 따라, 건물에 두고 가서 1주일 이내에 찾아가지 않은 개인 물품은 모두 폐기될 것이다.

해설 빈칸은 that이 이끄는 관계사절의 주격 보어 자리로, 앞에 나온 선행사 any personal items를 보충 설명한다. 수거되지 않은 개인 물품은 폐기될 것이라는 내용이므로, 수동의 의미를 내포한 과거분사 (C) claimed가 정답이다.

어휘 in accordance with ~에 따라, ~에 부합하여 policy 정책 claim (소유권 등을) 요구하다 discard 폐기하다, 버리다

2 (A)

번역 신입 사원들은 아침 8시에 필요한 모든 서류를 가지고 배정된 교육 장소로 출근해야 한다.

해설 빈칸은 소유격 their와 복합명사 training locations 사이에서 training locations를 수식하는 형용사 자리이다. '교육 장소'는 배정되는 대상이므로, 수동의 의미를 내포한 과거분사 (A) assigned가 정답이다.

어휘 report to ~로 출근하다, ~에 보고하다 necessary 필요한 paperwork 서류 assign 배치하다, 배정하다

3 (A)

번역 해리슨 씨는 그 분야에서 뛰어난 업적으로 인정받은 경력이 오래된 인사 전문가다.

해설 빈칸은 앞에 있는 명사구 a long-time human resources professional을 수식하는 역할을 한다. '인사 전문가'는 인정을 받는 대상이므로, 수동의 의미를 내포한 과거분사 (A) recognized가 정답이다.

어휘 long-time 오랜 professional 전문직 종사자 outstanding 뛰어난, 두드러진 achievement 성취, 업적 recognize 인정하다

4 (D)

번역 고객들 대부분은 우리의 전시실이 더 큰 공간으로 이전한다는 기대감에 들떠 있다.

해설 빈칸은 주어 Most of our clients를 보충 설명하는 보어 자리이다. 전시실 이전으로 고객들이 기대감을 느끼는 것이므로 과거분사 (D) excited가 정답이다.

어휘 prospect 전망, 기대 showroom 전시실

5 (B)

번역 다음 주에 이 지역 시 의회 선거 출마자들이 TV에 출연하여 자신들의 구상을 발표할 것이다.

해설 빈칸 뒤의 their ideas를 목적어로 취하며 수식어 역할을 하는 현재분사 (B) introducing이 정답이다. 명사인 (A)를 쓰면 복합명사가 된다고 생각할 수 있지만, 빈칸 뒤에 소유격 their가 있으므로 어순상 적절하지 않다.

어휘 candidate 출마자, 후보자 local 해당 지역의, 현지의 city council 시 의회 introduce 소개하다, 발표하다

6 (B)

번역 라벨 병원 방침에는 서면 동의 없이 환자의 개인 정보가 공개되지 않는다고 명시되어 있다.

해설 전치사 without의 목적어인 명사 consent를 수식하는 형용사 자리로 '서면으로 된 동의'라는 수동적 의미를 나타내는 과거분사 (B) written이 정답이다.

어휘 state 진술하다, 표명하다 release 공개하다, 발표하다 consent 동의

7 (A)

번역 글로버 사의 경영진이 개편된 이후로 그 회사 제품의 품질이 많이 개선되었다.

해설 동사 has been의 주어인 the quality를 보충 설명하는 주격 보어 자리이다. 품질(quality)은 향상되는 대상이므로 수동적 의미를 나타내는 과거분사 (A) improved가 정답이다.

어휘 restructure (조직·제도 등을) 개편하다, 구조 조정하다 improve 개선하다, 향상시키다 improvement 개선, 향상

8 (C)

번역 한 독자적인 여론조사 회사가 실시한 조사를 인용하며, 〈더 타운 보이스〉는 주민들의 70퍼센트가 새 경기장 건설을 지지했다고 보도했다.

해설 빈칸은 by an independent polling firm과 결합하여 현재분사 Citing의 목적어인 a survey를 수식해주는 자리이다. 설문 조사는 실시되는 대상이므로, 수동의 의미를 내포한 과거분사 (C) conducted가 정답이다.

어휘 cite 인용하다   survey 조사, 설문 조사   polling firm 여론조사 회사   in favor of ~을 찬성하여, 지지하여   stadium 경기장, 스타디움   conduct 실시하다, 수행하다   conductor 안내자, 지휘자

9 (B)

번역 귀하의 갤럭시 유리 접시류를 박스에 담아 보관할 때는 긁힌 자국이 생기지 않도록 먼저 부드러운 화장지로 감싸 주세요.

해설 부사절 접속사 When 다음에 주어가 생략되고 목적어 your Galaxy glass dishware가 왔으므로, 빈칸에는 능동적 의미를 내포한 현재분사가 들어갈 수 있다. 따라서 (B) storing이 정답이다.

어휘 dishware 접시류, 식기류   wrap (포장지 등으로) 싸다, 포장하다   scratch 긁힌 자국   store 보관하다

10 (C)

번역 고객들이 구매한 물건에 만족하지 못하면 30일 이내에 어떤 물품이든 반품할 수 있는 것이 앨린튼 하드웨어 사의 정책이다.

해설 동사 are의 주어인 they(customers)를 보충 설명하는 주격보어 자리로 사람은 주로 감정을 느끼는 대상이므로 과거분사 (C) satisfied(만족한)가 정답이다. (A) satisfactory (만족스러운, 만족시키는)는 주로 감정을 유발하는 주체인 사물 명사와 함께 쓴다.

어휘 satisfaction 만족   satisfy 만족시키다

11 (B)

번역 틴리 타자기 매장은 25년 동안 노스포트 지역에서 서비스를 제공해 오고 있으며, 골동품 타자기의 판매와 수리를 전문으로 한다.

해설 완전한 구조의 주절 뒤에 빈칸과 in 전치사구가 있으므로 분사가 빈칸에 쓰여 분사구문을 구성하는 것이 알맞다. 따라서 현재분사 (B) specializing이 정답이다.

어휘 specialization 전문화, 특수화

12 (A)

번역 비행기가 연착되는 바람에 메디나 씨는 예정대로 기자들과의 간담회를 열 수 없었다.

해설 문맥상 '예정된 대로'라는 내용이 되어야 자연스러우므로, 수동의 의미를 내포한 과거분사 (A) scheduled가 정답이다. as 뒤에 (C), (D)와 같은 명사가 오는 경우에는 '~로서'라고 해석한다.

어휘 due to ~ 때문에   arrival 도착   flight 비행, 항공편   as scheduled 예정대로, 계획대로   schedule 일정; 일정을 잡다

13 (C)

번역 윈튼 지역에서 이뤄지는 양질의 직업 교육 프로그램들이 그 지역 회사들에 자격을 갖춘 인력 풀을 확대하고 있다는 고무적인 신호들이 많이 있다.

해설 사물 명사 signs를 수식하는 자리로, 신호(sings)는 고무적인 느낌을 주는 주체이므로 현재분사 (C) encouraging이 정답이다. 과거분사 (B) encouraged는 격려를 받는 대상인 사람 명사와 함께 쓴다.

어휘 high-quality 양질의   qualified 적격인   encourage 장려하다

14 (D)

번역 주문이 제때에 도착하지 않을 것을 우려해서 장 씨는 속달을 요청했다.

해설 콤마 앞에서 문장 전체를 수식하는 분사구문으로 원래의 부사절인 〈Because she was concerned that ~)을 분사구문으로 바꾼 것이므로 과거분사 (D) Concerned가 정답이다. (C) Concerning은 '걱정을 시키는(형용사)', '~에 관하여(전치사)'라는 뜻으로 빈칸에 적절하지 않다.

어휘 on time 시간에 맞게, 정각에   express delivery 속달

[15-18] 광고

> 하볼 농장에서 사과 수확하기
>
> 하볼 농장에서 직접 사과를 딸 수 있는 기회가 9월에 시작됩니다. 올해, 저희는 **15 놀랍고** 풍성한 수확물을 기대하고 있습니다. 허니크리스프라고 부르는 품종이 9월 초에 수확될 준비가 될 것입니다. **16 다음으로**, 9월 중순에는 유명한 저희 갤러 사과를 예상하실 수 있습니다. 9월 말부터 10월 초까지는, 달콤한 엠파이어 사과 수확물을 즐기실 수 있을 것입니다. **17 재배 기간은 맛있는 그래니 스미스 사과와 함께 종료됩니다.**
>
> 당연히, 직접 사과를 따지 않으셔도 됩니다. 저희 농산물 시장을 방문하셔서 소형 및 대형 바구니에 포장해 놓은 사과를 **18 구입하실** 수 있습니다. 사이다 도넛과 기타 제과제품을 포함해 판매 중인 다양한 간식도 만나보실 수 있습니다.

어휘 pick (과일, 꽃 등을) 따다   opportunity 기회   abundant 풍부한   crop 수확(물)   variety 품종, 종류   treat 특별 선물, 한턱   including ~을 포함해   baked goods 제과제품

15 (D)

해설 빈칸은 바로 뒤에 위치한 abundant와 함께 명사 crops를 수식할 형용사가 들어갈 수 있는 자리이며, crops는 사물 명사로 놀라움을 주는 주체이므로 현재분사인 (D) amazing이 정답이다. (A) amazed(놀란)는 사람 명사를 수식할 때 사용한다.

어휘 amaze 놀라게 하다   amazement 놀라움

16 (A)

해설 빈칸 앞에는 9월 초에 수확되는 사과 품종이 언급되어 있고, 빈칸이 속한 문장에는 9월 중순에 예상할 수 있는 품종이 제시되어 있다. 이는 순서대로 나열한 것이므로, '다음으로'를 뜻하는 (A) Next가 정답이다.

어휘 consequently 결과적으로

17 (C)

번역 (A) 갓 구운 애플파이는 만들기 쉽습니다.
(B) 농장에서 매년 10월에 음악 축제를 주최합니다.
(C) 재배 기간은 맛있는 그래니 스미스 사과와 함께 종료됩니다.
(D) 사과 나무는 중앙아시아에서 유래했습니다.

해설 빈칸 앞에 9월 초에서 10월 초까지 수확되는 사과 품종을 차례대로 소개하는 내용이 제시되어 있어 사과 품종 및 시기와 관련된 문장이 쓰여야 자연스럽다. 따라서 재배 기간에 마지막 순서로 수확되는 품종을 알리는 (C)가 정답이다.

어휘 host 주최하다   growing 재배, 성장   originate 유래하다, 비롯되다

18 (D)

해설 농산물 시장에서 할 수 있는 행동을 나타내는 말이 와야 자연스러우므로, '구입하다'를 뜻하는 동사 (D) purchase가 정답이다.

어휘 prefer 선호하다   allow 할 수 있게 해 주다, 허용하다
connect 연결하다, 교류하다

UNIT 11 전치사와 접속사

1 전치사 어휘 1

ETS 유형연습 본책 p.194

1 (A)   **2** (C)   **3** (B)

1 (A)

번역 회사 냉장고 안에 둔 모든 음식에 라벨로 표기하기 바라며, 그렇지 않으면 매주 주말에 폐기됩니다.

해설 빈칸 뒤에 위치한 명사구 the end of each week를 목적어로 취해 '매주 주말에'라는 의미로 시점을 나타내는 전치사 (A) at이 정답이다.

어휘 label 라벨로 표기하다

2 (C)

번역 구직 면접을 준비할 때, 장래 고용주의 비전과 핵심 가치를 조사하세요.

해설 동사 prepare는 전치사 for와 함께 '~을 준비하다, ~에 대비하다'라는 의미를 나타내므로, (C) for가 정답이다.

어휘 prospective 장래의, 유망한   core 핵심적인   value 가치

3 (B)

번역 커피 필터와 커피 크림, 그리고 설탕은 휴게실 전자레인지 옆에 있다.

해설 커피 필터 등이 있는 위치를 나타낼 전치사가 들어갈 자리로, '휴게실 전자레인지 옆에 있다'와 같은 의미를 나타내야 가장 자연스러우므로, '~ 옆에'를 뜻하는 (B) beside가 정답이다.

어휘 microwave 전자레인지

2 전치사 어휘 2

ETS 유형연습 본책 p.195

1 (B)   **2** (C)   **3** (C)

1 (B)

번역 그로브즈버그 역사 협회는 일요일을 제외하고 매일 현지의 사적지 견학을 실시한다.

해설 빈칸 뒤의 명사 Sunday를 목적어로 취하면서 '일요일을 제외한 매일'이라는 의미를 나타내는 전치사 (B) except가 정답이다.

어휘 historical site 사적지

2 (C)

번역 와타나신 씨를 제외한 그 팀의 모든 팀원들은 웹 디자인 튜토리얼을 완료하기 위해 추가 시간이 필요했다.

해설 Ms. Wattanasin을 목적어로 취하면서 '와타나신 씨를 제외한'이라는 의미를 나타내는 전치사 (C) Apart from이 정답이다. 유사한 뜻의 except도 답이 될 수 있다.

어휘 additional 추가적인   tutorial 튜토리얼, 사용 지침 프로그램

3 (C)

번역 회사 환급 절차에 관한 정보를 받지 못했다면 인사과의 블랙웰 씨에게 연락하세요.

해설 빈칸 앞에 have not received라는 동사가 있기 때문에, 동사로 쓰일 수 있는 (A) regard와 (B) regards는 제외한다. 빈칸 뒤에 company reimbursement procedures를 목적어로 취하면서 '~에 관하여'라는 의미를 나타내는 분사 형태의 전치사인 (C) regarding이 정답이다.

어휘 personnel office 인사과   reimbursement 환급, 상환
procedure 절차, 방법   regard 여기다, 간주하다

3 전치사와 접속사

ETS 유형연습 본책 p.196

1 (B)   **2** (B)   **3** (B)

1 (B)

번역 상세한 여행 일정표가 청구서와 함께 제출되지 않는다면 직원들은 출장 비용의 상환을 요청할 수 없다.

164

해설 빈칸 뒤에 〈주어(a detailed itinerary)+동사(is submitted)〉가 있으므로 접속사인 (B) unless와 (D) while 중 하나를 선택해야 한다. 문맥상 '~하지 않는다면'이라는 뜻의 접속사가 필요하므로, (B) unless가 정답이다.

어휘 repayment 상환(금) detailed 상세한 itinerary 여행 일정표 claim 청구 (신청)

2 (B)

번역 지난 6개월 동안 수익 감소를 겪었음에도 불구하고 모리 앤 맥기 사는 내년에 3명의 특허 전문 변호사를 신규 채용할 계획이다.

해설 전치사인 Despite 뒤에는 명사나 동명사가 올 수 있으므로 동명사 (B) having experienced가 정답이다. 동사인 (A), (C), (D)는 전치사 뒤에 올 수 없다.

어휘 despite ~에도 불구하고 decline 감소, 하락 revenue 수익 intend to ~하려고 의도하다 patent 특허

3 (B)

번역 회사 사장으로서, 첸 씨는 히데오 홀딩스의 단기 목표와 장기 목표의 균형을 맞추는 것을 우선시한다.

해설 명사구 company president를 목적어로 취해 '회사 사장으로서'라는 의미로 주어 Ms. Chen의 신분을 나타내야 알맞으므로 '~로서'라는 뜻으로 신분이나 자격을 나타내는 전치사 (B) As가 정답이다.

어휘 prioritize 우선시하다 balance 균형을 잡다

4 등위접속사와 상관접속사

ETS 유형연습 본책 p.197

1 (A) **2** (C) **3** (A)

1 (A)

번역 해외용 카탈로그는 포괄적이지만, 특정 물품의 경우 모든 나라에서 이용 가능하지는 않을 수도 있다.

해설 절과 절을 연결하는 접속사가 필요한데, 앞뒤 내용이 역접 관계이므로 등위접속사 (A) but이 정답이다.

어휘 comprehensive 종합적인, 포괄적인 available 이용할 수 있는, 얻을 수 있는

2 (C)

번역 회의 참가자들은 기차나 버스로 와이엇 호텔에 갈 수 있다.

해설 or와 호응을 이루는 상관접속사 (C) either가 정답이다. 〈either A or B〉는 'A 또는 B'라는 뜻이다. (B) both는 and와 어울려 쓰인다. (A) unless는 접속사이므로 뒤에 절이 필요하고, (D) without은 전치사이므로 뒤에 명사가 와야 한다.

어휘 conference 회의, 학회 participant 참가자

3 (A)

번역 새로운 의료 보험 계약 조건에 대해 논의한 결과, 경영진과 직원 모두 만족했다.

해설 and와 짝을 이루는 상관접속사 (A) both가 정답이다.

어휘 terms 조건, 조항 health-benefits 의료 혜택(의), 의료 보험(의) contract 계약, 약정 management 경영(진) satisfied 만족한

ETS 실전문제 본책 p.198

1 (A)	**2** (B)	**3** (A)	**4** (B)	**5** (D)	**6** (D)
7 (C)	**8** (B)	**9** (C)	**10** (D)	**11** (A)	**12** (C)
13 (B)	**14** (A)	**15** (C)	**16** (B)	**17** (D)	**18** (C)

1 (A)

번역 그 사무실 직원들은 쿠퍼 스트리트 건물의 개조 공사를 하는 동안 이전되어야 했다.

해설 빈칸 뒤에 위치한 명사구를 목적어로 취할 전치사가 필요하며, '~의 개조 공사를 하는 동안 이전되어야 했다'를 의미해야 자연스러우므로, '~ 중에, ~ 동안'을 뜻하는 (A) during이 정답이다.

어휘 relocate 이전하다 renovation 개조, 보수 span 기간, 범위; (기간, 범위 등에) 걸치다 concerning ~와 관련해

2 (B)

번역 고객 문의는 영업일로 하루 내에 답변될 것이다.

해설 '영업일로 하루 내에 답변될 것이다'와 같이 기간의 의미를 나타내야 알맞으므로 '~ 내에'를 뜻하는 전치사 (B) within이 정답이다.

어휘 inquiry 문의

3 (A)

번역 연락처를 추가함으로써, 폰트만 전자가 특가 제품에 관해 연락하도록 허용하시는 데 동의하게 됩니다.

해설 동명사(adding)를 목적어로 취하는 전치시가 필요하며, 연락하도록 허용하는 데 동의하는 방법의 의미를 나타내야 하므로 '~함으로써, ~해서'를 뜻하는 (A) By가 정답이다.

4 (B)

번역 구매자들은 검사비뿐만 아니라 부동산 거래를 완료하는 데 관련된 다른 비용들도 지불해야 한다.

해설 빈칸은 두 명사구 inspection fees와 other expenses를 연결하는 역할을 하므로, '~뿐만 아니라 ~도'라는 의미의 상관접속사 (B) as well as가 정답이다. (A) although는 부사절 접속사이므로 빈칸에 들어갈 수 없고, (C) according to(~에 따르면)는 문맥상 어색하므로 정답이 될 수 없다. (D) that is를 〈주격 관계대명사+be동사〉로 보더라도 선행사인 fees와 동사 is의 수가 일치하지 않으므로 오답이다.

어휘 inspection 검사 property transaction 부동산 거래

5 (D)

번역 임대 건물에 머무는 동안 반드시 모든 가정 쓰레기를 적절한 용기에 버려 주시기 바랍니다.

해설 빈칸 뒤에 완전한 절이 있으므로 절을 이끌 접속사가 필요하며, 이 절이 '임대 건물에 머무는 동안'을 의미해야 자연스러우므로, '~하는 동안'을 뜻하는 접속사 (D) while이 정답이다.

어휘 dispose of ~을 버리다, 처리하다 household 가정의 proper 적절한 property 건물

6 (D)

번역 로시 씨의 근무 경험이 그를 그 일에 적합한 후보자로 만들어 준다.

해설 candidate 뒤에 대상이 올 때는 전치사 for를 사용하므로 (D) for가 정답이다.

어휘 employment 근무, 고용 suitable 적합한 candidate 후보자

7 (C)

번역 그 취업 박람회의 취소는 잠재 후원사들의 관심 부족 때문이었다.

해설 빈칸 뒤에 위치한 명사구 a lack of interest를 목적어로 취할 전치사가 필요하며, 잠재 후원사들의 관심 부족이 행사 취소의 원인에 해당하므로 '~ 때문에'를 뜻하는 전치사 (C) due to가 정답이다.

어휘 cancellation 취소 career fair 취업 박람회 lack 부족 potential 잠재적인

8 (B)

번역 보고서는 불충분한 광고나 노력 부족 모두 감소하는 판매량의 요인이 아니었음을 나타내고 있다.

해설 앞에 있는 neither와 짝을 이루어 'A와 B 둘 다 아니다'라는 의미를 나타내는 (B) nor가 정답이다.

어휘 insufficient 불충분한 lack 부족 effort 노력 factor 요소

9 (C)

번역 그 장비는 설명서대로 작동하지 않았기 때문에 기술부서로 반송되었다.

해설 콤마 앞의 완전한 절을 이끄는 부사절 접속사 자리로 내용상 '장비가 작동하지 않았기 때문에'라는 이유를 나타내는 부사절 접속사 (C) Because가 정답이다. (D) Due to도 같은 뜻이지만 전치사이므로 뒤에 명사가 와야 한다.

어휘 function 작동하다 specification 설명서 ship 보내다, 배송하다 engineering (공학) 기술

10 (D)

번역 하모니 홈 굿즈의 할인 및 프로모션 관련 정보를 받고 싶지 않은 고객은 계정 설정을 변경하면 된다.

해설 빈칸은 명사구 sales and promotions를 목적어로 취하면서 앞에 나온 명사 information을 수식하는 역할을 하므로, 현재분사 또는 전치사가 들어갈 수 있다. 따라서 '~에 관한'이라는 의미의 분사형 전치사 (D) regarding이 정답이다.

어휘 account 계정

11 (A)

번역 민 씨가 아주 인기 있는 영업사원이기 때문에, 실제 총 판매량과 상관없이, 연말 보너스를 받을 가능성이 있다.

해설 빈칸 뒤에 위치한 명사구 her actual sales totals를 목적어로 취할 전치사가 필요하며, '실제 총 판매량과 상관없이, 연말 보너스를 받을 가능성이 있다'라는 의미를 나타내야 자연스러우므로, '~와 상관없이'를 뜻하는 전치사 (A) regardless of가 정답이다.

12 (C)

번역 머레이니 컨설팅은 장기적으로 회사를 지탱할 수 있도록 경험 많은 엔지니어와 새롭게 자격증을 취득한 엔지니어를 모두 고용할 것을 추천한다.

해설 빈칸 뒤에 위치한 〈A and B〉 구조로 명사구가 쓰여 있으므로 and와 짝을 이뤄 'A와 B 둘 모두'를 의미하는 (C) both가 정답이다.

어휘 licensed 자격증을 취득한 support 지탱하다, 지지하다

13 (B)

번역 후르비츠 여행복은 가벼운 소재의 의류를 제공하는 것 외에도 멋진 여행 가방과 액세서리를 판매한다.

해설 빈칸 뒤의 동명사 구문 offering lightweight clothing을 목적어로 취할 전치사가 필요하며, '가벼운 소재의 의류를 제공하는 것 외에도'라는 의미를 나타내야 자연스러우므로, '~외에도'를 뜻하는 전치사 (B) Besides가 정답이다.

어휘 lightweight 가벼운 stylish 유행을 따르는, 멋진 luggage 여행 가방 accessory 액세서리, 부속물

14 (A)

번역 티켓 가격의 인상에도 불구하고, 시내버스 시스템을 이용하여 통근하는 사람의 수는 바뀌지 않았다.

해설 빈칸 뒤에 있는 명사구 the increase in ticket prices를 목적어로 취하는 전치사가 필요하므로, (A) Despite(~에도 불구하고)이 정답이다.

어휘 commuter 통근하는 사람

[15-18] 구인 공고

자원봉사자 구인

공공보건서비스(PHS)에서는 그레이어슨 대학교 주말 취업박람회 **15 동안** 안내 부스에서 자원봉사를 할 12명의 직원을 구합니다. 행사는 4월 13일과 14일 오전 10시부터 오후 6시까지 열립니다. 자원봉사자들은 4시간 교대 근무로 일하며 **16 학생들에게** 취업 기회, 학력 요건, 승진 기회 등에 관해 알려줄 것입니다. 또한 PHS의 활동에 대해 논의하고 **17 그들의** 일상적인 업무에 관해 설명할 것입니다. **18 자원봉사자는 무료 점심을 제공받게 됩니다.** 행사 전에 1시간의 교육이 있을 겁니다. 관심이 있는 직원은 https://phs.employees.site.com/grayerson_cfw에서 찾을 수 있는 양식을 작성하면 됩니다.

어휘 volunteer 자원봉사자; 자원봉사를 하다 seek 찾다, 구하다 career fair 취업박람회 opportunity 기회 educational 교육의, 교육과 관련된 requirement 요건 possibility 가능성 advancement 발전, 승진 activity 활동 describe 설명하다 typical 일상적인 in advance of ~에 앞서

15 (C)
해설 빈칸 뒤에 있는 행사명을 목적어로 취하는 전치사 자리로, 문맥상 '취업박람회 동안'이라는 내용이 되어야 자연스러우므로, (C) during(~ 동안)이 정답이다.

16 (B)
해설 그레이어슨 대학교 주말 취업박람회에서 자원봉사를 하는 직원들의 역할을 설명하고 있으므로, 정보를 제공받는 대상은 학생들이 되어야 문맥상 자연스럽다. 따라서 (B) students가 정답이다.

어휘 contestant 대회 참가자

17 (D)
해설 자원봉사자들이 자신들의 일상적인 업무를 설명할 것이므로 자원봉사자들을 지칭하는 소유격 대명사인 (D) their가 정답이다.

18 (C)
번역 (A) 자원봉사자는 발표 후에 제안을 할 것입니다.
(B) 자원봉사자는 정책을 읽었음을 명시해야 합니다.
(C) 자원봉사자는 무료 점심을 제공받게 됩니다.
(D) 자원봉사자는 해마다 온라인으로 재등록해야 합니다.

해설 빈칸 앞에서 자원봉사자가 행사에서 할 일을 언급했고, 뒤에서는 전에 자원봉사자를 대상으로 하는 교육(coaching session)이 있을 것이라고 했으므로, 빈칸에도 행사와 관련된 일반적인 공지가 들어가야 문맥상 자연스럽다. 따라서 자원봉사자들에게 제공되는 식사 혜택을 안내한 (C)가 정답이다.

어휘 suggestion 제안 following ~ 후에 presentation 발표 indicate 명시하다 policy 정책 complimentary 무료의 re-register 재등록하다

UNIT 12 부사절 접속사

1 시간, 조건의 부사절

ETS 유형연습 본책 p.200

1 (B) 2 (A) 3 (A)

1 (B)
번역 영구 면허증이 귀하의 주소에 도착할 때까지 이 임시 면허증을 소지하세요.

해설 '영구 면허증이 도착할 때까지 이 임시 면허증을 소지하세요'와 같은 의미를 나타내야 자연스러우므로, '~할 때까지'를 뜻하는 (B) until이 정답이다.

어휘 temporary 임시의, 일시적인 permanent 영구적인

2 (A)
번역 교육 기간이 지속되는 동안 신입 사원들은 초봉의 60퍼센트를 받을 것이다.

해설 빈칸 뒤에 〈주어(the training period)+동사(continues)〉가 나오므로 절을 이끄는 부사절 접속사 (A) As long as(~하는 한)가 정답이다.

어휘 training 교육, 연수 starting salary 초봉

3 (A)
번역 어떤 조치가 취해지지 않는 한, 윈필드 파크웨이의 교통 혼잡은 계속 악화될 것이다.

해설 빈칸 뒤에 〈주어(something)+동사(is done)〉가 나오므로, 절을 이끌 수 있는 부사절 접속사 (A) Unless가 정답이다. (C) Except (that)도 절을 이끌 수 있지만 문맥상 어색하다.

어휘 traffic congestion 교통 혼잡 worsen 악화되다 unless ~하지 않는 한 except ~을 제외하고는 therefore 그러므로

2 양보, 이유, 목적의 부사절

ETS 유형연습 본책 p.201

1 (D) 2 (B) 3 (D)

1 (D)
번역 사사키 씨는 제품 판매량이 예상보다 낮다 하더라도 직원들에게 보너스를 주기로 약속했다.

해설 빈칸 앞뒤에 각각 완전한 절이 있으므로 빈칸에는 두 절을 연결해줄 접속사가 필요하다. 또한, '제품 판매량이 예상보다 낮다 하더라도'와 같은 의미를 나타내야 자연스러우므로, '~한다 하더라도'를 뜻하는 접속사 (D) even if가 정답이다.

어휘 than anticipated 예상보다 furthermore 더욱이 in contrast 그에 반해서

2 (B)
번역 마침내 그 밴드가 가능하다고 확인해 주었으므로 야외 공연은 6월 11일 일요일에 열릴 예정이다.

해설 완전한 절을 이끌면서 '확인해 주었으므로'라는 이유를 나타내는 부사절 접속사 (B) Now that이 정답이다. (C) So that도 부사절 접속사로 사용하지만, 목적을 나타내므로 문맥상 이 문장의 첫머리에서는 사용할 수 없다.

어휘 confirm 확인하다 availability 가용성, 이용할 수 있음

3 (D)
번역 박 씨는 테크니플렉스 사에서 5년간 근무하면서 어려운 일에 직면했을 때 탁월한 능력을 발휘한다는 점을 거듭 보여주었다.

해설 when 뒤에 〈주어(he)+be동사(is)〉가 생략된 구문으로, 전치사 with와 함께 '~에 직면하다'라는 표현을 완성하는 과거분사 (D) faced가 정답이다. 참고로, 타동사 face는 직접 목적어를 취하거나, 〈be faced with〉 구조로 쓰인다.

어휘 demonstrate 입증하다, 보여주다 repeatedly 반복해서, 거듭 excel 능력이 뛰어나다, 탁월하다 challenge 도전, 어려운 일

ETS 실전문제
본책 p.202

1 (C)	2 (A)	3 (B)	4 (B)	5 (A)	6 (D)
7 (A)	8 (A)	9 (B)	10 (D)	11 (A)	12 (A)
13 (B)	14 (B)	15 (C)	16 (D)	17 (C)	18 (B)

1 (C)

번역 청중 유인물은 서체 크기가 너무 작지 않으면 비교적 많은 양의 글을 포함하도록 디자인될 수 있다.

해설 빈칸 앞뒤에 각각 완전한 절이 있으므로 뒤의 절을 이끌 접속사가 필요하다. 따라서 (C) as long as(~하기만 하면, ~하는 한)가 정답이다.

어휘 audience 청중, 관객 handout 유인물 relatively 비교적

2 (A)

번역 엠프레스 슈즈는 가을, 겨울 제품을 위한 공간을 만들기 위해 여름 제품 할인 행사를 하고 있다.

해설 빈칸 앞뒤에 각각 완전한 절이 있으므로 두 절을 연결할 접속사가 필요하며, '가을, 겨울 제품을 위한 공간을 만들기 위해'와 같이 목적을 나타내야 자연스러우므로, '~하기 위해'를 뜻하는 접속사 (A) so that이 정답이다.

어휘 room 공간, 여지 in part 부분적으로

3 (B)

번역 오늘 오후의 바르셀로나행, 런던행, 로마행 비행편은 목적지의 악천후 때문에 모두 연착했다.

해설 빈칸 뒤에 있는 명사 inclement weather를 목적어로 취하는 전치사 자리로, '악천후 때문에'와 같이 이유를 나타내야 자연스러우므로 '~ 때문에'를 뜻하는 전치사 (B) due to가 정답이다. (A) as for(~에 관해서는)는 전치사이지만 의미상 적합하지 않으며, (C) now that(~ 때문에)과 (D) only if(~의 경우에 한해서는)는 부사절 접속사이다.

어휘 flight 비행편 delay 미루다, 연기하다; 지연, 지체 inclement (날씨가) 험한 destination 목적지, 도착지

4 (B)

번역 퍼스트 리저널 은행은 주니퍼에서 아주 좋은 성과를 내었기 때문에 파인우드와 노스 헤이븐에 지점을 열 예정이다.

해설 빈칸은 완전한 절을 이끄는 접속사 자리로, 해당 절은 콤마 뒤 주절을 수식한다. 주니퍼에서 좋은 성과를 낸 것이 원인, 지점을 추가로 여는 것은 결과라고 볼 수 있으므로, '~ 때문에'라는 의미로 쓰일 수 있는 부사절 접속사 (B) Since가 정답이다.

어휘 rather 오히려, 차라리 therefore 그러므로

5 (A)

번역 디어필드 오케스트라 지휘자가 은퇴한다는 공지를 받은 이후로, 이사회에서는 후임자를 찾고 있다.

해설 빈칸 뒤의 분사구문 receiving notice를 이끌면서 콤마 뒤의 완전한 문장을 수식하는 부사절 접속사 자리로 '통지를 받은 이래로'라는 의미를 나타내는 (A) Since가 정답이다. 참고로, 해당 부분은 〈전치사 Since+동명사〉 구문으로 볼 수도 있다.

어휘 notice 공지, 안내문 director 감독, 지휘자 retire 은퇴하다 board of directors 이사회 replacement 대신할 사람, 후임자

6 (D)

번역 회사가 초기에는 난관에 직면했지만 지금은 전국 최대의 식물성 화장품 제조업체로 성공을 거두었다.

해설 완전한 절을 이끌면서 '초기에 난관에 직면했다 하더라도'라는 양보의 의미를 나타내는 부사절 접속사 (D) Although가 정답이다. 부사절 접속사 (B) Unless(~가 아니라면), (C) Whatever(어떤 ~라도)는 의미상 적합하지 않다. 부사인 (A) Instead(대신에)는 주어와 동사가 두 개씩 있는 문장의 맨 앞에는 올 수 없으므로 오답이다.

어휘 face 직면하다 hardship 난관, 곤경 initially 초기에, 처음에 find success 성공을 거두다 manufacturer 제조업체 plant-based 식물성의 cosmetics 화장품

7 (A)

번역 현재 릿지 제조사 지점에서 근무하는 직원들은 일단 건물이 완공되면 새로 지은 본사로 이사할 것이다.

해설 완전한 절을 이끌면서 '건물이 완공되면'이라는 조건의 의미를 나타내는 부사절 접속사 (A) once가 정답이다. (B) even(평평한; 심지어)은 형용사/부사, (C) besides(~ 외에도; 게다가)는 전치사/부사, (D) moreover(더욱이)는 부사로 뒤에 완전한 절을 이끌 수 없다.

어휘 currently 현재 branch 지사 headquarters 본사

8 (A)

번역 반 아울 가구회사는 기본 부품들을 대량 구매가로 구할 수 있기 때문에, 그 매장은 할인가로 의자들을 판매할 여유가 있다.

해설 콤마 앞의 완전한 절을 이끄는 부사절 접속사 자리로, '~ 때문에'라는 의미의 접속사가 들어가야 자연스러우므로 (A) Because가 정답이다.

어휘 bulk 대량의, 대량으로 판매되는 component 부품

9 (B)

번역 휴가 기간이 직무 분류에 따라 미리 결정되지 않는 한, 휴가 요청서 제출 마감 기한은 1월 15일입니다.

해설 빈칸은 완전한 절을 이끄는 접속사 자리로, 해당 절이 콤마 앞 주절을 수식한다. 따라서 빈칸에는 부사절 접속사가 들어가야 하므로, '~하지 않는 한'이라는 의미의 (B) unless가 정답이다.

어휘 submit 제출하다 request 요청 predetermine 미리 결정하다 based on ~에 따라 classification 분류 thus 그러므로 besides 게다가 despite ~에도 불구하고

10 (D)
번역 페스너 트래블에서 예약하시면 해외여행을 떠나는 것이 스트레스 없는 경험이 될 것입니다.

해설 빈칸 앞뒤에 각각 완전한 절이 있으므로 두 절을 연결해줄 접속사가 필요하며, '페스너 트래블에서 예약하면 스트레스 없는 경험이 될 것이다'와 같은 의미가 되는 것이 자연스러우므로, '~하면, ~할 때'를 뜻하는 접속사 (D) when이 정답이다.

어휘 free ~이 없는

11 (A)
번역 트럭 적재량은 처음에 너무 무겁다고 생각됐지만 주 지침에 충분히 부합하고도 남았다.

해설 부사절 접속사 Although 다음에 〈주어(the truck's load) + be동사(was)〉가 생략된 구문으로, 빈칸에는 분사가 들어갈 수 있다. '적재량이 너무 무겁다고 생각됐지만'이라는 내용이 되어야 자연스러우므로, 수동의 의미를 내포한 과거분사 (A) believed가 정답이다.

어휘 state 국가(의), 주(의) guideline 지침

12 (A)
번역 발표가 진행되는 동안 도착하는 참석자들은 조용히 좌석을 찾고, 전화기를 무음으로 바꿔야 한다.

해설 빈칸 뒤에 있는 절(the presentation is underway)을 이끌 접속사가 필요하며, '발표가 진행되는 동안'을 의미해야 자연스러우므로, '~하는 동안'을 뜻하는 접속사 (A) while이 정답이다.

어휘 attendee 참석자 underway 진행 중인 silence 무음으로 바꾸다

13 (B)
번역 탑승객은 국경을 넘는 기차를 탈 때 사진이 부착된 신분증을 제시해야 한다.

해설 빈칸은 분사구문(boarding trains)을 이끄는 부사절 접속사 자리로, 빈칸 뒤에 〈주어(they)+be동사(are)〉가 생략되어 있다. 신분증 제시(present photo identification)는 탑승할 때 행해지는 것이므로, (B) when이 정답이다.

어휘 passenger 승객 present 제시하다, 보여주다 identification 신분증, 신원 증명 board 탑승하다 border 국경

14 (B)
번역 허브 엠포리엄 온라인에서 주문된 상품들은 전액 완납 시까지 운송되지 않는다는 점에 유의하시기 바랍니다.

해설 완전한 절을 이끌면서 '수령될 때까지'라는 시간의 의미를 나타내는 부사절 접속사 (B) until이 정답이다. 〈not ~ until...〉은 '…하고 나서야 ~하다'라는 의미로 주로 쓰이므로 한 덩어리로 외워 두자.

어휘 note 유의하다, 주목하다 payment 지불 (금액)

[15-18] 웹페이지

맨토코스 슈퍼마켓 — 5번 통로 관련

맨토코스 슈퍼마켓 단골 고객들은 "5번 통로 깜짝 판매"라고 부르는 **15 것**에 대해 잘 알고 있습니다. 각 매장의 5번 통로는 계속 변화되는 엄선된 비식품 제품들로 매주 다시 채워지고 있는데, 그 범위는 실내 장식용품에서부터 소형 가전 기기에 이르고 신속히 판매될 수 있는 가격으로 책정됩니다. **16 이런 제품들을 저희 공급업체에서 매입해 절감된 비용을 여러분께 돌려드립니다.** 저희는 다양한 공급원으로부터 제품을 확보합니다. 예를 들어, 한 가전제품 제조사에 특정 믹서기 여분이 **17 있다면**, 저희가 그것들을 구입합니다. 따라서, 매주 제공되는 상품을 예측하는 것은 불가능합니다. 물론, 대부분의 고객들은 저희 매장의 이러한 **18 예측 불가능한** 측면을 즐깁니다. 고객들은 이 이 깜짝 요소가 쇼핑 경험을 향상시켜 준다고 말합니다.

어휘 refer to A as B A를 B라고 일컫다, 언급하다 restock (재고 등을) 다시 채우다 ever-changing 끊임없이 바꾸는 a selection of 엄선된, 다양한 range from A to B 범위가 A에서 B에 이르다 decoration 장식(품) appliance 가전제품 acquire 얻다 source 공급원, 원천 surplus 여분, 과잉 specific 특정한, 구체적인 accordingly 따라서 forecast 예측하다 aspect 측면, 양상 enhance 향상시키다, 강화하다

15 (C)
해설 전치사 about 뒤에 빈칸과 주어(we)와 동사(refer to)가 포함된 절이 있으므로 이 절이 about의 목적어 역할을 하는 명사절이 되어야 한다. 또한, refer to의 목적어가 없는 불완전한 구조이므로 불완전한 명사절을 이끄는 접속사 (C) what이 정답이다. (A) whose와 (B) where는 완전한 절을 이끄는 명사절 접속사이다.

16 (D)
번역 (A) 미개봉 반품에 대해서는 재입고 수수료를 청구하지 않습니다.
(B) 선반을 조립하실 때 지침을 주의 깊게 따르세요.
(C) 현지에서 만든 디저트가 점점 더 많은 인기를 얻고 있습니다.
(D) 이런 제품들을 저희 공급업체에서 매입해 절감된 비용을 여러분께 돌려드립니다.

해설 빈칸 앞에는 5번 통로에서 판매하는 제품의 범위를 알리는 말이, 빈칸 뒤에는 다양한 공급원으로부터 제품을 확보한다는 말이 각각 쓰여 있다. 따라서 제품의 종류나 공급과 관련된 문장이 쓰여야 흐름이 자연스러우므로, 공급 및 판매 방식을 간략히 언급한 (D)가 정답이다.

어휘 charge 청구하다 restocking fee 재입고 수수료 follow 따르다, 따라하다 instructions 설명(서), 안내(서) increasingly 점점 더 savings 절약(된 금액)

17 (C)
해설 빈칸 뒤로 완전한 절 두 개가 콤마(,)로 이어져 있으므로 콤마 앞까지의 절을 이끌 부사절 접속사가 필요하다. 따라서, '~할 때, ~하면'을 뜻하는 부사절 접속사 (C) when이 정답이다.

18 (B)

해설 빈칸 앞뒤에 위치한 this aspect(이러한 측면)는 앞 문장에서 언급한 '매주 제공되는 상품을 예측하는 것은 불가능하다'는 것을 가리키므로 impossible to forecast와 같은 의미에 해당하는 (B) unpredictable(예측 불가능한)이 정답이다.

어휘 obsolete 구식의, 쓸모없는   cautious 조심스러운, 신중한

UNIT 13 관계대명사

1 관계대명사의 종류

ETS 유형연습   본책 p. 204

1 (A)   **2** (B)   **3** (D)

1 (A)

번역 그 가구점은 공장제 제품들뿐만 아니라 수제품도 판매하는 재능 있는 목공이 소유하고 있다.

해설 빈칸은 사람 명사 carpenter를 수식하는 관계사절을 이끄는 동시에, 관계사절에서는 동사 sells의 주어 역할을 한다. 따라서 사람을 수식하는 주격 관계대명사 (A) who가 정답이다.

어휘 own 소유하다   talented 재능 있는   carpenter 목공

2 (B)

번역 풍 앤 하스 사는 생산 시간의 절반 이상을 차지했던 치약 혼합 공정을 자동화했다.

해설 빈칸은 문장의 목적어 its toothpaste mixing processes에 대해 부연 설명하는 관계사절을 이끄는 동시에, 관계사절에서는 동사 used to take up의 주어 역할을 한다. 따라서 사물을 수식하는 주격 관계대명사 (B) which가 정답이다.

어휘 automate 자동화하다   toothpaste 치약   process 공정, 과정

3 (D)

번역 메트로폴리탄 아트웍스는 트윈 강 지역의 공공 미술 프로젝트를 지원하는 것이 임무인 단체이다.

해설 빈칸은 문장의 보어 organization을 수식하는 관계사절을 이끄는 동시에, 관계사절의 주어 mission을 한정 수식하는 역할을 한다. organization과 mission은 '조직의 임무'라는 소유 관계를 나타내므로, 소유격 관계대명사 (D) whose가 정답이다.

어휘 mission 임무, 사명   support 지원하다

2 관계대명사의 생략

ETS 유형연습   본책 p. 205

1 (A)   **2** (B)   **3** (C)

1 (A)

번역 프로빈스 은행 고객들은 온라인 뱅킹 이용에 사용하는 암호를 매년 갱신하시기 바랍니다.

해설 빈칸 앞에 명사, 뒤에는 타동사와 전치사구가 있으므로 빈칸 앞에 목적격 관계대명사가 생략되어 있음을 알 수 있다. 따라서 관계사절에서 동사 use의 주어 역할을 하는 대명사가 빈칸에 들어가야 하므로, (A) they가 정답이다.

어휘 be requested to ~하도록 요청받다   update 업데이트하다, 갱신하다   annually 매년   password 패스워드, 암호

2 (B)

번역 마케팅 부장에 의해 검토된 모든 사업 계획서 중에서 마틴 씨의 안이 가장 인상적이다.

해설 빈칸은 by the marketing manager와 결합해 수동의 의미를 나타내며 명사 plans를 수식해주는 자리이다. 따라서 '검토된'이라는 뜻의 과거분사 (B) reviewed가 정답이다. 참고로, 빈칸 앞에는 〈주격 관계대명사(that/which)+be동사(were)〉가 생략된 것으로 볼 수 있다.

어휘 impressive 인상 깊은

3 (C)

번역 스프링든 정부는 임대 부동산 소유주들이 세입자들에게 재활용 서비스를 제공하도록 요구하는 규정을 공표했다.

해설 빈칸은 owners를 목적어로 취하며, 앞의 명사 regulations를 수식하는 자리이다. 따라서 '소유주들에게 요구하는 규정'이라는 능동적 의미를 나타내는 현재분사 (C) requiring이 정답이다.

어휘 publish 공표하다, 발행하다   regulation 규칙, 규정   rental 임대   property 부동산, 재산   recycling 재활용   tenant 세입자   require 요구하다

3 관계대명사의 활용

ETS 유형연습   본책 p. 206

1 (B)   **2** (C)   **3** (D)

1 (B)

번역 월간 보고서를 받을 부서장들의 이름은 안내서 마지막 페이지에 적혀 있다.

해설 빈칸 앞의 to부터 sent까지가 명사구 department heads를 수식하며 '보고서를 받을 부서장들'이라는 의미를 나타낸다. 따라서 빈칸에는 전치사 to의 목적어 역할을 하며 사람을 수식하는 관계대명사가 들어가야 하므로 (B) whom이 정답이다.

어휘 department head 부서장   be located 위치해 있다

2 (C)

번역 지원자들은 자신이 일하고 싶은 프로젝트 옆에 있는 네모칸에 체크하여 연구 관심사를 표시해 주십시오.

해설 빈칸 앞의 on부터 work까지가 명사 projects를 수식하며 '일하고 싶은 프로젝트'라는 의미를 나타낸다. 따라서 빈칸에는 전치사 on의 목적어 역할을 하며 사물을 수식하는 관계대명사가 들어가야 하므로 (C) which가 정답이다.

어휘 candidate 지원자, 후보자   indicate 나타내다

3 **(D)**

번역 벡토 디자인 회사는 12명의 그래픽 디자이너를 고용하고 있는데, 그들 모두 적어도 3년 이상의 경력이 있는 노련한 디자이너들이다.

해설 문장에 절이 두 개지만 접속사가 없기 때문에, 빈칸을 포함한 절이 콤마 앞의 graphic artists에 대해 부연 설명을 하는 관계절임을 알 수 있다. 따라서 빈칸에는 of의 목적어 역할을 하며 사람을 수식하는 관계대명사가 들어가야 하므로 (D) whom이 정답이다.

어휘 skilled 능숙한, 노련한   at least 적어도

4 관계부사

ETS 유형연습 본책 p.207

1 (D)   2 (A)   3 (D)

1 **(D)**

번역 모든 운송품은 하역장으로 도착하는데, 그곳에서 창고 담당자가 추적 라벨을 확인한다.

해설 빈칸 뒤의 완전한 절을 이끌면서 앞의 장소 명사 the receiving dock을 수식하는 관계부사 (D) where가 정답이다.

어휘 shipment 운송품, 선적물   receiving dock 하역장
warehouse 창고   tracking 추적

2 **(A)**

번역 그 시설 관리자는 사무용품이 보관되어 있는 창고 열쇠를 가지고 있다.

해설 빈칸 뒤의 완전한 절을 이끌면서 앞의 장소 명사 the storage room을 수식하는 관계부사 (A) where가 정답이다. (B) how는 방법, (C) when은 시간, (D) why는 이유를 나타내는 관계부사이므로 적절치 않다.

어휘 facility 시설   storage room 창고, 보관실
office supply 사무용품

3 **(D)**

번역 김 박사의 수상 연설은 대략 10분 정도 지속되리라 예상되며 그 후에 디저트가 제공될 것이다.

해설 연설이 대략 10분 정도 지속될 예정이며, 이후에 디저트가 제공될 예정이라는 내용이 되어야 자연스럽다. 따라서 빈칸에는 after의 목적어 역할을 하며 사물을 수식하는 관계대명사가 들어가야 하므로 (D) which가 정답이다.

어휘 acceptance 수락, 수상   last 지속되다, 계속하다

ETS 실전문제 본책 p.208

1 (C)	2 (A)	3 (A)	4 (D)	5 (B)	6 (C)
7 (C)	8 (C)	9 (D)	10 (B)	11 (C)	12 (A)
13 (B)	14 (C)	15 (A)	16 (C)	17 (A)	18 (D)

1 **(C)**

번역 치앙마이 오페라 하우스의 로비 카펫은 관리하기 더 쉬운 소재로 교체될 것이다.

해설 빈칸은 명사 material을 수식하는 관계사절을 이끄는 동시에, 관계사절에서는 동사 is의 주어 역할을 한다. 따라서 주격 관계대명사로 쓰일 수 있는 (C) that이 정답이다. (A) what은 선행사 뒤에 쓰일 수 없으므로 오답이다.

어휘 be replaced with ~로 교체되다   material 소재, 옷감
maintain 관리하다, 유지하다

2 **(A)**

번역 버스나 기차로 도착하는 센트럴 동물원 방문객들은 입장료를 10퍼센트 할인받을 수 있다.

해설 빈칸은 앞의 사람 명사 Central Zoo visitors를 수식하는 관계사절을 이끄는 동시에, 관계사절에서는 동사 arrive의 주어 역할을 한다. 따라서 주격 관계대명사 (A) who가 정답이다.

어휘 admission 입장(료), 입회, 입학

3 **(A)**

번역 톰슨 박사는 수많은 학술지에 연구가 게재된 선도적인 생물학자로, 다음 주 학회 때 특별 연사로 나올 것이다.

해설 빈칸은 명사구 a leading biologist를 수식하는 관계사절을 이끄는 동시에, 관계사절의 주어 work를 한정 수식하는 역할을 한다. biologist와 work는 '생물학자의 연구'라는 소유 관계를 나타내므로, 소유격 관계대명사 (A) whose가 정답이다.

어휘 leading 선두의, 선도적인   biologist 생물학자
publish 게재하다, 발표하다   numerous 수많은
featured speaker 특별 연사   conference 회의, 학회

4 **(D)**

번역 존슨 박사는 효율적인 시간 관리에 대한 견해를 공유할 세 시간짜리 워크숍을 개최한다.

해설 빈칸 앞에 있는 during부터 management까지가 명사 workshop을 수식하며 '시간 관리에 대한 견해를 공유할 워크숍'이라는 의미를 나타낸다. 따라서 빈칸에는 전치사 during의 목적어 역할을 하며 사물을 수식하는 관계대명사가 들어가야 하므로 (D) which가 정답이다

어휘 offer 제공하다, 개설하다   share 나누다, 공유하다
perspective 견해, 관점   effective 효율적인
time management 시간 관리

5 **(B)**

번역 귀하가 주문하신 재킷의 경우 요청하신 색상으로는 현재 재고가 없지만 나머지 주문품들은 신속히 보내드리겠습니다.

해설 빈칸은 you와 함께 앞에 있는 명사 color를 수식한다. 문맥상 '요청했던 색상'이라는 내용이 되어야 자연스러우므로, 과거 시제인 (B) requested가 정답이다. 참고로, you 앞에는 목적격 관계대명사가 생략되어 있다.

어휘 currently 현재 rest 나머지

6 (C)

번역 콘텐츠 전략가 로나 포지올리는 업계를 형성하는 동향에 박식한 전문가다.

해설 빈칸은 명사구 the business world를 목적어로 취하면서 앞에 있는 trends를 수식하는 역할을 한다. 따라서 능동의 의미를 내포한 현재분사 (C) shaping이 정답이다. 참고로, 빈칸 앞에는 〈주격 관계대명사(that/which)+be동사(are)〉가 생략된 것으로 볼 수 있다.

어휘 strategist 전략가 expert 전문가 shape (어떤) 모양으로 만들다, 형성하다

7 (C)

번역 동기부여 강연으로 유명한 엘라 포르토피노 씨가 6월에 열릴 ORIL 리더십 회의의 초청 연사가 될 예정이다.

해설 빈칸은 사람 명사 Ella Portofino에 대해 부연 설명하는 관계사절을 이끄는 동시에, 관계사절에서는 동사 is의 주어 역할을 한다. 따라서 사람을 수식하는 주격 관계대명사 (C) who가 정답이다.

어휘 motivational speech 동기부여 강연 guest speaker 초청 연사

8 (C)

번역 모든 운전자는 차선이 다시 칠해지고 있는 5번 가 지역을 피해야 한다.

해설 빈칸 뒤의 완전한 절을 이끌면서 앞의 장소 명사 Fifth Street를 수식하는 관계부사 (C) where가 정답이다.

어휘 motorist 운전자 avoid 피하다

9 (D)

번역 새로운 경비 보고 절차에 의문이 있는 관리자들은 예산 담당 사무실에 연락해 도움을 요청해야 한다.

해설 빈칸은 문장의 주어 Supervisors를 수식하는 관계사절을 이끄는 동시에, 관계사절에서는 동사 have의 주어 역할을 한다. 따라서 사람을 수식하는 주격 관계대명사 (D) who가 정답이다.

어휘 supervisor 감독자, 관리자 expense 경비 process 과정, 절차 budget 예산 assistance 지원, 도움

10 (B)

번역 지난주 드림 타운 스튜디오스에서 공개한 〈레드 샌드 가든〉은 30대인 사람들에게 인기가 있었다.

해설 빈칸은 사물 명사 Red Sand Garden에 대해 부연 설명하는 관계사절을 이끄는 동시에, 동사 was released의 주어 역할을 한다. 따라서 사물을 수식하는 주격 관계대명사 (B) which가 정답이다.

어휘 release 공개하다, 출시하다

11 (C)

번역 박물관의 보존 프로젝트는 가족이 그 땅을 소유하고 있는 응우옌 씨의 기부로 가능해졌다.

해설 빈칸은 Mr. Nguyen을 수식하는 관계사절을 이끄는 동시에, 관계사절의 주어 family를 한정 수식하는 역할을 한다. Mr. Nguyen와 family는 '응우옌 씨의 가족'이라는 소유 관계를 나타내므로, 소유격 관계대명사 (C) whose가 정답이다.

어휘 conservation 보존, 보호 donation 기부(금) own 소유하다

12 (A)

번역 부아클레르 로보틱스는 효율성을 향상시키기 위해 공장 내 조립 공정 전체를 감시할 수 있는 기계를 고안했다.

해설 빈칸은 명사 machine을 수식하는 관계사절을 이끄는 동시에, 관계사절에서는 동사 can monitor의 주어 역할을 한다. 따라서 주격 관계대명사로 쓰일 수 있는 (A) that이 정답이다.

어휘 improve 향상시키다, 개선하다 efficiency 효율성 monitor 감시하다, 관찰하다 entire 전체의 assembly 조립

13 (B)

번역 관리자들은 종종 몇 가지 행동 방침들 사이에서 결정을 해야 하는데, 어느 것도 전적으로 옳거나 틀리지 않다.

해설 문장에 절이 두 개지만 접속사가 없기 때문에, 빈칸을 포함한 절이 콤마 앞의 several courses of action에 대해 부연 설명을 하는 관계사절임을 알 수 있다. 따라서 빈칸에는 of의 목적어 역할을 하며 사물을 수식하는 관계대명사가 들어가야 하므로 (B) which가 정답이다.

어휘 course of action 행동 방침

14 (C)

번역 2주 이내에 답신을 받지 못한 서빙 직책 지원자는 후속 이메일을 보내야 한다.

해설 빈칸은 동사 should send의 주어 역할을 하는 명사 자리로, 사람 명사를 수식하는 관계사절(who have not received a response within two weeks)의 수식을 받는다. 따라서 '지원자들'이라는 의미의 명사 (C) Applicants가 정답이다.

어휘 response 대답, 응답 follow-up 후속 조치 application 지원(서)

[15-18] 이메일

수신: 고객 서비스
발신: 은주 탕
날짜: 11월 14일
제목: 주문 번호 491001

고객 서비스 직원께,

귀사의 웹사이트에서 11월 8일에 **15 구입한** 제품 두 가지를 받았습니다. **16 제가 받은 파란색 스웨터는 완벽합니다.** 아쉽게도, 제가 주문한 회색 블라우스는 미디엄이어야 했지만, 라지가 배송되었습니다.

저는 이 블라우스를 17 **반송하고자** 합니다. 사실, 우편을 통해 정확한 사이즈로 교환하고 싶지만, 웹사이트에서 어느 18 **주소**를 이용해야 하는지 알아낼 수 없었습니다. 유감스럽게도, 배송품에 포함된 설명서를 분실했습니다. 가급적 빨리 제게 알려 주시겠습니까?

은주 탕

어휘   agent 직원, 대리인   unfortunately 아쉽게도, 안타깝게도   determine 알아내다, 결정하다   instructions 설명(서), 안내(서)   include 포함하다

15 (A)

해설   빈칸 뒤에 타동사 purchased의 목적어가 빠진 불완전한 절이 있으며, '귀사의 웹사이트에서 11월 8일에 구입한'이라는 의미로 빈칸 앞에 위치한 명사구 the two items를 수식하는 관계대명사절이 되어야 알맞으므로 관계대명사 (A) that이 정답이다.

16 (C)

번역   (A) 두 제품 모두 잘못된 사이즈였습니다.
(B) 저는 미디엄 사이즈의 파란색 스웨터를 주문했습니다.
(C) 제가 받은 파란색 스웨터는 완벽합니다.
(D) 이제 귀사에서 제공하는 다른 스타일들을 확인해 보고 싶습니다.

해설   빈칸 앞에는 두 가지 제품을 받은 사실이, 빈칸 뒤에는 회색 블라우스가 다른 사이즈로 배송된 사실이 각각 쓰여 있다. 따라서 두 가지 제품 중 나머지 하나의 배송 상태와 관련된 문장이 빈칸에 쓰여야 문맥이 자연스러우므로 파란색 스웨터는 완벽하다고 알리는 (C)가 정답이다.

17 (A)

해설   빈칸 뒤에 정확한 사이즈로 교환하기를 원한다는 문장이 쓰여 있으므로 '반송하다'를 의미하는 (A) return이 정답이다.

어휘   model 본받다, 모형을 만들다   display 전시하다, 진열하다   examine 검사하다, 조사하다

18 (D)

해설   빈칸 앞에는 which가 있고, 빈칸 뒤에는 to부정사가 있는데, which가 의문형용사로 쓰이면 뒤에 〈명사+to부정사〉가 올 수 있으며, '어느 주소를 이용해야 하는지'라는 의미가 되는 것이 적절하므로 명사인 (D) address가 정답이다.

어휘   addressable (문제 등) 다룰 수 있는   address 주소; 다루다

UNIT 14 명사절 접속사

1 명사절 접속사의 이해

ETS 유형연습   본책 p.210

1 (A)   2 (B)   3 (A)

1 (A)

번역   특히 당시 겨우 26세였다는 점을 고려하면 생화학 분야에서 후아 허징 씨의 업적은 놀라웠다.

해설   빈칸 이하가 considering의 목적어 역할을 하며, '~라는 점을 고려하면'이라는 의미가 되어야 자연스러우므로, 명사절 접속사 (A) that이 정답이다.

어휘   biochemistry 생화학   remarkable 놀라운, 주목할 만한

2 (B)

번역   지역 내 소규모 농장의 수를 고려해 볼 때, 보우 밸리에 유기농 식품 매장이 많다는 사실은 놀랍지 않다.

해설   빈칸 뒤의 절을 명사절로 바꾸어 줄 수 있는 명사절 접속사가 필요하므로, 명사절 접속사 (B) that이 정답이다. 〈it is not surprising+that절〉은 '~라는 것이 놀랍지 않다'는 의미로 자주 쓰이는 표현으로, that절이 진주어이고, 앞의 it은 가주어이다.

어휘   given ~을 고려해 (볼 때)   organic 유기농의

3 (A)

번역   방침은 박물관 내 식음료 반입이 허용되지 않음을 분명히 명시하고 있다.

해설   빈칸은 states의 목적어 역할을 하는 명사절을 이끈다. 문맥상 '~라고 분명히 명시하다'라는 내용이 되어야 자연스러우므로, (A) that이 정답이다.

어휘   policy 정책, 방침   state 명시하다, 발표하다

2 명사절 접속사 that/what

ETS 유형연습   본책 p.211

1 (A)   2 (C)   3 (C)

1 (A)

번역   〈뉴스 업데이트〉를 구독하시면, 최신 정치와 경제 동향에 대한 신뢰할 만한 분석을 받아 볼 것임을 확신할 수 있습니다.

해설   빈칸 앞에 온 be confident가 문제 해결의 단서로, 뒤의 완전한 절을 이끌면서 be confident와 결합하여 '~에 대해 확신하다'라는 의미를 나타내는 명사절 접속사 (A) that이 정답이다.

어휘   subscribe to ~을 구독하다   reliable 신뢰할 만한

2 (C)

번역   홀리아 오피스 파크 관리소는 공사가 진행되는 동안 업무가 최소한으로만 영향을 받을 것이라고 확인했다.

해설   빈칸은 has assured의 직접 목적어 역할을 하는 명사절을 이끈다. 따라서 '~라는 것을 확언했다'라는 의미를 완성하는 명사절 접속사 (C) that이 정답이다.

어휘   administration 관리, 집행   assure 확실히 하다, 보증하다   minimally 최소한으로   impact 영향을 주다

3 (C)

번역 고객들을 가장 기쁘게 한 것은 모라돈 은행이 제공한 효과적인 고객 서비스였다.

해설 빈칸부터 most까지가 주어, was가 동사인 문장이다. 따라서 빈칸에는 명사절을 이끌면서 pleased의 주어 역할을 하는 명사절 접속사가 들어가야 하므로, '~하는 것'이라는 의미를 나타내는 (C) What이 정답이다.

어휘 effective 효과적인

3 명사절 접속사 whether/if

ETS 유형연습 본책 p.212

1 (A) **2** (A) **3** (D)

1 (A)

번역 팩스가 고장 나서, 수리가 가능한지 여부를 알아보기 위해 숙련된 기술자를 호출했다.

해설 빈칸 이하가 to see의 목적어 역할을 하므로, 빈칸에는 명사절 접속사가 들어가야 한다. 문맥상 '수리가 가능한지 (아닌지) 알아보기 위해'라는 내용이 되어야 자연스러우므로, (A) if(~인지 아닌지)가 정답이다.

어휘 out of service 고장 난 experienced 숙련된 call in 불러들이다

2 (A)

번역 웨스트헤이븐 글래스웍스의 한은성 사장은 파인포드 트럭킹과의 계약을 연장할지 말지를 놓고 숙고하고 있다.

해설 빈칸 이하는 considering의 목적어 역할을 한다. 따라서 빈칸에는 to부정사와 함께 사용될 수 있는 접속사가 필요한데, 문맥상 '계약을 연장할지 (말지) 숙고하다'라는 내용이 되어야 자연스러우므로, (A) whether(~인지 아닌지)가 정답이다. whether는 〈whether+주어+동사〉 또는 〈whether+to부정사〉 구조로 쓰인다.

어휘 glassworks 유리 공장 consider 고려하다, 숙고하다 renew (계약 등을) 갱신하다, 연장하다 trucking 트럭 수송(업)

3 (D)

번역 하모니 디자인 컨설턴트들은 고객들이 창을 장식할 때 커튼을 이용할지 블라인드를 이용할지 결정하는 데 도움을 줄 수 있다.

해설 앞에 있는 명사절 접속사 whether와 어울리는 (D) or가 정답이다. curtains와 blinds가 use의 목적어 역할을 하고 있다.

4 의문사와 복합관계대명사

ETS 유형연습 본책 p.213

1 (A) **2** (C) **3** (D)

1 (A)

번역 좋은 이력서는 지원자의 자격요건이 어떻게 책무에 적합한지를 고용주에게 보여준다.

해설 동사 tells의 직접 목적어 역할을 하는 완전한 절을 이끌면서 '어떻게 적합한지를'이라는 의미를 나타내는 의문부사 (A) how가 정답이다.

어휘 qualification 자격요건 match 어울리다

2 (C)

번역 포스터 시티 역사학회의 회원들은 법원 청사에 남아 있는 원래 건축학적 요소들이 보존되도록 청원하고 있다.

해설 빈칸부터 elements까지가 to have의 목적어 역할을 하며, preserved는 목적격 보어로 쓰였다. 따라서 빈칸에는 불완전한 명사절을 이끌며 remains의 주어 역할을 하는 명사절 접속사가 들어가야 하므로 (C) what이 정답이다.

어휘 historical society 역사학회 petition 탄원하다, 청원하다 remain 남다, 잔존하다 courthouse 법원 청사 original 원래의 architectural 건축학의 preserve 보존하다

3 (D)

번역 누구든 그로튼 그림을 구입하는 사람이 아마도 경매에서 가장 비싼 작품을 구입하는 사람이 될 것이다.

해설 빈칸부터 painting까지가 문장의 주어 역할을 하므로, 빈칸에는 불완전한 절(acquires ~ painting)을 이끄는 명사절 접속사가 들어가야 한다. 문맥상 '~하는 사람은 누구든지'라는 의미가 되어야 자연스러우므로 (D) Whoever가 정답이다. Whoever는 Anyone who로 바꿔 쓸 수 있다.

어휘 artwork 미술품 auction 경매

ETS 실전문제 본책 p.214

1 (D)	2 (C)	3 (B)	4 (A)	5 (D)	6 (D)
7 (A)	8 (B)	9 (D)	10 (D)	11 (A)	12 (A)
13 (C)	14 (D)	15 (C)	16 (A)	17 (B)	18 (C)

1 (D)

번역 비행기 여행객들이 자주 하는 한 가지 불평은 머리 위 짐칸이 너무 작다는 것이다.

해설 빈칸 이하가 동사 is의 주격 보어 역할을 하므로, 빈칸에는 완전한 절을 이끄는 명사절 접속사가 들어가야 한다. 문맥상 '머리 위 짐칸이 작다는 것이다'라는 내용이 되어야 자연스러우므로, (D) that이 정답이다.

어휘 complaint 항의 overhead 머리 위의 compartment 선반, 짐칸

2 (C)

번역 미요 테크놀로지스는 팀이 생산하는 것에 대해 관리자들이 책임지도록 독려한다.

해설 빈칸부터 produce까지가 전치사 for의 목적어 역할을 한다. 따라서 빈칸에는 명사절 접속사가 들어가야 하는데, 뒤에 목적어가 없는 불완전한 절이 왔으므로 (C) what이 정답이다.

어휘 take responsibility for ~에 대해 책임을 지다

3 (B)
번역 리버풀 지역 공항에서 승객들을 가장 감동시키는 것은 천갈이를 한 좌석의 편안함이다.
해설 빈칸부터 most까지가 주어, is가 동사, the comfort 이하가 보어인 문장이다. 따라서 빈칸에는 명사절을 이끌면서 should impress의 주어 역할을 하는 명사절 접속사가 들어가야 한다. 문맥상 '승객들을 가장 감동시키는 것'이라는 내용이 되어야 자연스러우므로, (B) What이 정답이다.
어휘 impress 감동시키다   comfort 편안함   upholster (의자 등의 가구에) 천을 씌우다

4 (A)
번역 송 씨는 3명의 지원자 중 누가 수석 제품 개발자 직책에 적합한지 아직 결정하지 못했다.
해설 빈칸은 decided의 목적어 역할을 하는 명사절을 이끄는 접속사 자리로, 명사절에서는 주어 역할을 한다. 따라서 전치사구 of the three candidates의 수식을 받아 '세 명의 지원자 중 어떤 사람'이라는 의미를 완성하는 (A) which가 정답이다.
어휘 decide 결정하다, 결심하다   candidate 후보자, 지원자   developer 개발자

5 (D)
번역 그 제조업체는 자사에서 제조한 화장품이 3년 또는 제품 용기에 표시된 유효 기간 중 더 빠른 날짜까지 사용 가능하다고 보장한다.
해설 빈칸은 불완전한 절(is sooner)을 이끌어 앞에 있는 절을 수식한다. 따라서 해당 절에서 주어 역할을 하며, 앞서 언급된 for three years or until the expiration date on the package를 가리켜 '둘 중 어느 것이든지'라는 의미를 나타내는 복합관계대명사 (D) whichever가 정답이다.
어휘 manufacturer 제조업체   guarantee 보장하다, 보증하다   cosmetic product 화장품   good 유효한, 사용 가능한   expiration date 유통 기한   package 포장, 용기

6 (D)
번역 요한슨 씨는 곧 은퇴할 것인지 질문받았을 때 자신은 일하는 것을 결코 멈추지 않을 것이라고 말했다.
해설 빈칸 이하는 앞의 과거분사 asked의 직접 목적어 역할을 한다. 따라서 완전한 절을 이끌면서 '~인지 아닌지'라는 의미를 나타내는 명사절 접속사 (D) whether가 정답이다.
어휘 retire 은퇴하다   while ~인 반면에, ~인 한편   whereas ~인 반면에   whenever 언제 ~든지

7 (A)
번역 〈워킹 트렌즈 투데이〉 지에 발표된 한 최근 연구는 왼손잡이인 사람들이 사업에 성공할 가능성이 더 높다는 점을 시사한다.
해설 빈칸 이하는 동사 suggests의 목적어 역할을 한다. 따라서 완전한 절을 이끌면서 '~라는 것'이라는 의미를 나타내는 명사절 접속사 (A) that이 정답이다.

어휘 publish 게재하다, 발표하다   suggest 시사하다   left-handed 왼손잡이인

8 (B)
번역 시장 조사 부서는 사람들이 운전하면서 얼마나 자주 라디오를 듣는지에 관한 조사를 실시했다.
해설 빈칸 이하는 전치사 on의 목적어 역할을 한다. 따라서 빈칸에는 부사 often과 결합하여 '얼마나 자주'라는 의미를 나타내며 완전한 절을 이끄는 명사절 접속사가 들어가야 하므로, 의문부사 (B) how가 정답이다.
어휘 market-research 시장 조사   conduct 실시하다

9 (D)
번역 트래넬린 인더스트리스의 임원진은 어떤 부서들을 내년에 웨스트 코스트로 옮길지 판단하는 중이다.
해설 빈칸은 determining의 목적어 역할을 하는 명사절을 이끄는 접속사 자리로, 명사절에서는 주어 divisions를 수식하는 한정사 역할을 한다. 따라서 '어떤 부서들을 웨스트 코스트로 옮길지(which divisions will transfer to the West Coast)'라는 의미를 완성하는 (D) which가 정답이다.
어휘 executive team 임원진   determine 결정하다, 판단하다   division 부서   transfer 옮기다

10 (D)
번역 오늘날에는 적당한 운동조차도 심장에 도움이 된다고 알려져 있다.
해설 동사 is의 주어 자리로, 진짜 주어인 that이 이끄는 명사절을 대신할 수 있는 가짜 주어 (D) it이 정답이다.
어휘 moderate 보통의, 적당한   beneficial 유익한, 도움이 되는

11 (A)
번역 지원을 하거나 지원 절차 관련 정보를 구하는 데 도움이 필요한 사람은 누구든지 인사부로 오십시오.
해설 빈칸부터 assistance까지가 문장의 주어 역할을 하므로, 빈칸에는 불완전한 절(needs assistance)을 이끄는 명사절 접속사가 들어가야 한다. 문맥상 '~하는 사람은 누구든지'라는 의미가 되어야 자연스러우므로, (A) Whoever가 정답이다.
어휘 assistance 지원, 도움   procedure 절차

12 (A)
번역 많은 독자들이 일간 신문의 사설면이 더 계몽적이라고 말하지만 그들이 처음 읽는 것은 스포츠면이라는 점을 인정한다.
해설 빈칸부터 first까지가 that절의 주어, is가 동사, the sports page가 보어인 절이다. 따라서 빈칸에는 목적어가 없는 불완전한 절(they read first)을 이끄는 명사절 접속사가 들어가야 하므로, '~하는 것'이라는 의미의 (A) what이 정답이다.
어휘 state 말하다   editorial 사설   enlightening 계몽적인, 교육적인

13 (C)
번역 많은 연구가 시장 조사 단체들에 의해 실시되었지만, 고객들이 인터넷에서 식료품을 살 준비가 됐는지는 여전히 불확실하다.

해설 대명사 it은 가짜 주어이고 빈칸 이하가 진짜 주어 자리이다. 따라서 완전한 절을 이끌면서 '~인지 아닌지'라는 의미를 나타내는 명사절 접속사 (C) whether가 정답이다.

어휘 multiple 많은, 다양한 uncertain 불확실한
grocery 식료품

14 (D)

번역 스프링 플라워 기프츠는 모든 소매점 관리자들에게 고객의 문의사항을 어떻게 처리해야 하는지 교육한다.

해설 전치사 in의 목적어 자리로, 빈칸 뒤의 완전한 절을 이끄는 명사절 접속사가 들어가야 한다. 따라서 '~하는 방법, 어떻게'라는 의미를 나타내는 의문부사 (D) how가 정답이다.

어휘 retail store 소매점 deal with ~을 처리하다
inquiry 문의

[15-18] 웹사이트

https://www.harrisonbrothersrentals.com

해리슨 브라더스 렌탈은 데번 지역에서 선두를 달리는 중장비 대여 서비스 업체입니다. 굴착기와 크레인에서부터 도로 포장용 기계와 압착기에 이르기까지, 해리슨 브라더스는 상업 시설 및 주택 공사에 필요한 **15 것**을 갖추고 있습니다. 모든 대여 서비스에는 **16 작업 현장**에 직접 장비를 배송해 드리는 것이 포함됩니다.

대여 서비스뿐만 아니라, 저희는 수리 및 재판매 서비스도 운영하고 있습니다. 저희가 더 이상 작동되지 않는 낡은 장비를 매입하여, 저희 전문 정비사에게 맡겨 수리합니다. **17 그 후 새 장비 가격보다 훨씬 할인된 가격으로 다시 판매합니다.** 자세한 내용을 알아보거나 재고를 보유하고 있는 **18 수리** 장비 카탈로그를 보려면, www.harrisonbrothersrentals.com/resale을 방문하세요.

어휘 leading 선두인, 선도적인 equipment 장비
rental 대여 commercial 상업의 include 포함하다
machinery 기계(류) hand 전달하다, 넘겨 주다 expert 전문적인; 전문가 mechanic 정비사 in stock 재고가 있는

15 (C)

해설 빈칸 앞에는 타동사 has가 있고, 빈칸 뒤에 주어(you)와 동사(need)를 포함한 절이 쓰여 있으므로 빈칸을 포함한 절이 has의 목적어 역할을 하는 명사절이 되어야 한다. 또한, 타동사 need 뒤에 목적어가 빠진 불완전한 구조이므로 '~하는 것'이라는 의미로 불완전한 절을 이끄는 명사절 접속사 (C) what이 정답이다. (B) that은 명사절 접속사일 때 완전한 절을 이끌어야 하며, (D) which도 불완전한 절을 이끄는 명사절 접속사이지만 앞서 언급된 특정 대상에 대해 '어느 것'이라는 선택의 의미를 나타낼 때 사용한다.

16 (A)

해설 전치사 to의 목적어로서 기계가 배송되는 장소를 나타낼 명사가 빈칸에 쓰여야 하며, 앞 문장에 언급된 공사가 진행되는 장소를 의미해야 알맞으므로 (A) worksite(작업 현장)가 정답이다.

어휘 receptacle 용기, 그릇

17 (B)

번역 (A) 케이시와 빌 해리슨이 40년도 더 전에 회사를 설립하였습니다.
(B) 그 후 새 장비 가격보다 훨씬 할인된 가격으로 다시 판매합니다.
(C) 대기업들이 장비가 필요할 때 저희를 신뢰합니다.
(D) 저희 크레인들은 안전 점검을 받았습니다.

해설 앞 문장에 수리 및 재판매 서비스를 위한 첫 단계인 낡은 장비를 매입하는 일이 언급되어 있으므로 다음 순서를 말할 때 사용하는 Then(그 후)과 함께 이후의 단계를 설명하는 내용을 담은 (B)가 정답이다.

어휘 found 설립하다 significant 상당한 inspect 점검하다, 검사하다

18 (C)

해설 앞 문장에 낡은 장비를 수리해 다시 판매하는 과정이 설명되어 있으므로 그러한 종류의 장비를 의미해야 알맞다. 따라서, '수리된'을 뜻하는 (C) reconditioned가 정답이다.

어휘 unusable 사용할 수 없는 recondition 수리하다
external 외부의

UNIT 15 비교/도치 구문

1 원급 비교

ETS 유형연습   본책 p.216

1 (A)   **2** (B)   **3** (D)

1 (A)

번역 신형 FRI-25 디지털 카메라 모델은 시중의 많은 표준 모델들과 동일한 최첨단 기능들을 갖추고 있다.

해설 빈칸 앞에 온 the same이 문제 해결의 단서로, '~와 똑같은'이라는 원급 비교 표현을 완성하는 (A) as가 정답이다.

어휘 feature 특징, 기능

2 (B)

번역 한 소비자 보고서는 저렴한 세탁용 세제가 더 비싼 제품과 똑같이 효과적일 수 있다고 밝혔다.

해설 원급 비교 구문 〈as+원급+as〉를 강조하는 부사 자리로 '꼭 ~만큼 효과적인'이라는 내용이 되는 것이 자연스러우므로 (B) just가 정답이다.

어휘 consumer 소비자 reveal 밝히다 less 덜 laundry detergent 세탁용 세제 effective 효과적인

3 (D)

번역 디스크 드라이버가 설치된 후, 먼지가 쌓이는 것을 막기 위해 보호용 커버는 가능한 한 빨리 원위치에 놓아야 한다.

해설 as 사이에서 동사 should be replaced를 수식하는 원급 부사가 필요하므로, (D) quickly가 정답이다. 참고로 〈as+원급+as possible〉은 '가능한 한 ~하게'라는 의미를 나타낸다.

어휘 replace 원위치에 놓다, 대체하다 prevent 막다, 예방하다
accumulation 축적, 쌓임

2 비교급

ETS 유형연습　　　　　　　　　　　본책 p. 217
1 (C)　　2 (B)　　3 (A)

1 (C)

번역 오피스 서플라이 웨어하우스의 고객 설문 조사에서 대다수 고객들은 전화보다는 웹사이트에서 더 효율적으로 주문할 수 있었다고 응답했다.

해설 앞의 동사 could order를 수식하는 부사 자리로, 빈칸 뒤쪽의 than과 결합하여 '~보다 더 효율적으로'의 의미를 나타내는 비교급 부사 (C) more efficiently가 정답이다.

어휘 survey 설문 조사 majority 대다수 report 응답하다, 보고하다 order 주문하다 over the phone 전화상으로 efficient 효율적인 efficiently 효율적으로

2 (B)

번역 송 씨 그룹이 자료 수집 프로젝트를 제때 완수하려면 우리에게 훨씬 더 많은 행정적인 지원이 필요할 것이다.

해설 빈칸은 비교급을 강조하는 부사 자리이므로, 비교급 강조 부사 (B) even이 정답이다. 비교급 앞에서 '훨씬 더'라는 의미로 비교급을 강조하는 부사에는 even, still, a lot, much, far 등이 있다.

어휘 complete 완수하다 administrative 행정의, 관리의

3 (A)

번역 새로운 음료수 쿨 피즈의 광고 캠페인은 가격보다는 맛을 강조할 것이다.

해설 동사 will feature의 목적어인 flavor와 price를 비교하고 있으므로 '~라기보다는'이라는 의미를 나타내는 (A) rather than이 정답이다.

어휘 advertising campaign 광고 캠페인 flavor 맛 in the event of ~하는 경우에 except for ~을 제외하고는 as for ~에 관해서는

3 최상급

ETS 유형연습　　　　　　　　　　　본책 p. 218
1 (B)　　2 (B)　　3 (D)

1 (B)

번역 중심 상업 지구에 정차하는 지하철 노선들 중에서 초록 노선이 프랭클린 건물에서 걸어가기가 가장 쉽다.

해설 빈칸은 동사 is의 주격 보어 자리이므로, 보기 중 부사는 일단 탈락된다. 이때 비교 대상이 없으면 원급, 비교 대상이 여러 개이면 최상급을 답으로 한다. 맨 앞에 of the subway lines(지하철 노선들 중에서)를 보면 비교 대상이 여러 개이므로 최상급 형용사인 (B) easiest가 정답이다.

어휘 central 중심의, 중앙의 business district 상업 지구

2 (B)

번역 그 일자리에 지원한 5명의 지원자 중에서 우리는 당연히 그 자리를 채울 최적임자를 고용할 것이다.

해설 From among the five applicants를 통해 이야기하는 대상이 셋 이상임을 알 수 있다. 빈칸은 명사 candidate를 수식하는 형용사 자리이므로, 정관사 the와 결합하여 '가장 적격의'라는 의미를 나타내는 최상급 형용사 (B) most qualified가 정답이다.

어휘 applicant 지원자 naturally 당연히 hire 고용하다 candidate 지원자, 후보자 fill a position 자리를 채우다 qualified 자격을 갖춘 qualify 자격을 주다

3 (D)

번역 올해 예산에서 신제품 개발에 할당된 자금은 최근 몇 년 만에 가장 넉넉한 액수가 될 것으로 예상된다.

해설 빈칸은 명사 amount를 수식하는 형용사 자리로, 문장 끝의 in recent history와 결합하여 '최근 몇 년 만에 가장 넉넉한'이라는 의미를 나타내는 최상급 형용사 (D) the most generous가 정답이다.

어휘 funds 자금 allocate 할당하다 budget 예산 in recent history 최근 몇 년 만에, 최근 역사에서 generous 넉넉한, 관대한

4 도치 구문

ETS 유형연습　　　　　　　　　　　본책 p. 219
1 (D)　　2 (A)　　3 (C)

1 (D)

번역 박 씨는 제품 소개 발표에 참석할 수 없는데, 제퍼슨 씨 역시 참석할 수 없을 것이다.

해설 긍정/부정 동의를 나타내는 so/neither 도치 구문은 〈so/neither+동사+주어〉의 어순이 된다. 빈칸 뒤에 동사(will)와 주어(Mr. Jefferson)가 도치되어 있고 앞절에 부정어 not이 있으므로 부정 동의를 나타내는 (D) neither가 정답이다.

어휘 sales presentation 제품 소개 발표

2 (A)

번역 신규 주택을 구매하기에 시장 여건이 이보다 더 이상적이었던 적은 드물었다.

해설 빈칸 뒤 어순이 〈조동사(have)+주어(market conditions)+과거분사(been)〉이므로, 보기 중에서 문장을 도치시킬 수 있는 부정부사 (A) Seldom이 정답이다.

어휘 condition 여건, 상황, 조건 ideal 이상적인

3 (C)

번역 주민들이 공공 수영 시설에 방문하는 횟수가 증가함에 따라, 그들을 감독하는 안전 요원에 대한 수요도 증가한다.

해설 문두에 접속사가 있으므로 빈칸 이하도 절이 되어야 하는데, 동사가 없고 주어만 있다. 따라서 동사를 포함하며 긍정 동의를 나타내는 도치 구문 (C) so does가 정답이다.

어휘 facility 시설, 설비   climb 올라가다, 증가하다
demand 수요

해설 빈칸 뒤에 위치한 형용사 traveled를 수식할 수 있는 것은 부사이며, 빈칸 앞에 위치한 소유격 the metropolitan area's와 어울리는 것은 최상급이므로, 최상급 부사 (D) most heavily가 정답이다.

어휘 traffic 교통(량), 차량들   ease 완화하다   congestion 혼잡
metropolitan area 대도시권

ETS 실전문제   본책 p. 220

1 (B)	2 (A)	3 (D)	4 (D)	5 (D)	6 (A)
7 (B)	8 (C)	9 (C)	10 (C)	11 (D)	12 (C)
13 (A)	14 (A)	15 (D)	16 (A)	17 (D)	18 (B)

1 (B)
번역 5월에 신제품을 출시한 뒤로, 만자니타 홈웨어는 과거 그 어느 때보다 더 높은 수익을 창출하고 있다.

해설 뒤에 위치한 than과 짝을 이뤄 비교를 나타내는 비교급 형용사가 필요하므로, (B) higher가 정답이다.

어휘 launch 출시하다, 시작하다   generate 창출하다, 만들어 내다
revenue 수익, 수입

2 (A)
번역 전국 최대 에너지 공급업체인 오론 에너지는 거의 2천만 고객들에게 전기를 제공한다.

해설 전치사 of의 목적어인 energy suppliers를 수식하는 형용사 자리로, '가장 큰 에너지 공급업체 중 하나'라는 의미를 나타내는 최상급 형용사 (A) largest가 정답이다. 〈one of the+최상급+복수 명사〉 표현을 기억하자.

어휘 electricity 전기

3 (D)
번역 페레이라 컨설팅 사에 지원하는 구직자들은 가능한 한 정확하게 지원서 질문 사항에 답변해야 한다.

해설 동사 should answer를 수식하는 부사 자리로, 앞의 as 및 뒤의 as possible과 결합하여 '가능한 한 정확하게'라는 의미를 나타내는 원급 부사 (D) accurately가 정답이다.

어휘 candidate 후보자, 지원자   position (일)자리
application form 신청서, 지원서

4 (D)
번역 잘 안 빠지는 얼룩은 펄 글로우의 초강력 세탁용 세제를 이용하면 보다 쉽게 제거될 수 있다.

해설 동사 be removed를 수식하는 부사 자리로, more와 결합하여 '더 쉽게'라는 의미를 나타내는 부사 (D) easily가 정답이다.

어휘 tough 힘든, 골치 아픈   stain 얼룩   extra-strength 아주 강력한   laundry detergent 세탁용 세제

5 (D)
번역 교통 공학 전문가들이 그 대도시권에서 가장 통행량이 많은 거리인 코너 대로의 교통 혼잡을 완화하기 위해 노력 중이다.

6 (A)
번역 우리 매장은 주요 경쟁업체들만큼 많은 가전제품을 구비하고 있다.

해설 명사 household appliances를 수식하는 형용사 자리로, 앞뒤에 있는 as와 결합하여 '~만큼 많은 가전제품'이라는 의미를 나타내는 원급 형용사 (A) many가 정답이다. '~만큼이나 많은 ...'이라는 뜻의 〈as many/much+명사+as〉의 원급 구조도 기억하자.

어휘 competitor 경쟁업체, 경쟁자

7 (B)
번역 트렌텔 비즈니스 컨설팅 사는 신규 고객을 유치하는 것보다 충성도 높은 고객을 지키는 것이 더 중요하다고 강조한다.

해설 빈칸 뒤의 than과 어울리는 비교급 형용사가 필요하므로 형용사 important의 비교급을 만드는 (B) more가 정답이다.

어휘 stress 강조하다   retain 간직하다, 보유하다
loyal 충성스러운

8 (C)
번역 파룩 크림과 로션 제품들은 가장 부드러운 피부를 약속드리며, 그렇지 않으면 환불해 드립니다.

해설 명사 skin을 앞에서 수식할 형용사가 빈칸에 필요하며, 정관사 the와 어울리는 최상급 형용사가 쓰여야 알맞으므로 (C) smoothest가 정답이다.

어휘 smoothness 매끄러움, 부드러움

9 (C)
번역 다코 모터스와 케슬러 오토모티브의 합병은 분석가들이 예측한 것보다 더 많은 제조상의 문제를 초래했다.

해설 빈칸 앞의 비교급 표현 more production problems와 어울리는 (C) than이 정답이다. 여기서 more는 형용사 many의 비교급이다.

어휘 merger 합병   automotive 자동차의   result in ~을 초래하다   analyst 분석가   predict 예측하다

10 (C)
번역 기술부는 단지 월말에만 그 프로젝트의 경과 보고서가 발행될 것이라고 발표했다.

해설 that이 이끄는 명사절에서 only at the end of the month가 강조되어 절 앞에 있으므로 주어 a progress report of the project와 동사가 도치되어야 한다. 빈칸은 도치된 주어 앞의 동사 자리로, 뒤의 동사원형 be published와 어울리는 조동사 (C) will이 정답이다.

어휘 engineering department 기술부   progress report 경과 보고서   publish 발행하다

11 (D)

번역 조기 등록 할인을 받으려면 신청서에 10월 28일 금요일자 이전의 소인이 찍혀야 한다.

해설 Friday, October 28를 목적어로 취해 수식어 덩어리를 만들어 동사구 must be postmarked를 수식하는 자리이다. 따라서 전치사를 포함하며 '금요일보다 더 늦지 않게'라는 비교급 표현을 완성하는 (D) no later than이 정답이다. (A) in advance, (B) beforehand, (C) previously는 부사로 품사상 빈칸에 들어갈 수 없다.

어휘 registration 등록, 기재 postmark 소인을 찍다
in advance 사전에 beforehand 미리, 사전에
previously 이전에

12 (C)

번역 황 씨의 결혼식 피로연을 위한 꽃 배달은 늦어도 5월 12일 금요일까지 완료될 것이다.

해설 배달이 완료되는 시점(by Friday, May 12)을 강조하는 부사 자리로, '늦어도'라는 뜻의 최상급 표현인 (C) at the latest가 정답이다.

어휘 delivery 배달 complete 완료하다

13 (A)

번역 비알로보스 씨는 새 휴대폰이 그 부서에서 이제껏 구입한 것들 중 가장 가볍다고 보고했다.

해설 최상급 표현 the lightest를 강조하는 부사 자리로, '이제까지, 지금까지'라는 의미를 나타내는 (A) ever가 정답이다.

14 (A)

번역 마케팅 관리자인 하와 압델라는 사무실을 비워, 1월 12일 전에는 복귀하지 않을 예정이다.

해설 빈칸은 비교급 표현 than January 12와 함께 동사구 will not return을 수식하는 역할을 하므로, 복귀 시간과 어울리는 비교급 부사가 들어가야 한다. 따라서 '1월 12일 전에'라는 내용을 완성하는 (A) earlier(더 일찍)가 정답이다.

어휘 recently 최근에 frequently 자주

[15-18] 이메일

발신: deaneckhart@gbhosp.org
수신: amanpour@sevcon.org
제목: 외과 과장직
날짜: 12월 10일

아만푸어 씨께,

귀하와 저를 함께 아는 **15 지인** 글로리아 매닝 씨를 통해 귀하의 이력서를 받았습니다. **16 귀하의 폭넓은 경험은 참으로 인상적이군요.** 그레이스 베스 병원의 외과 과장직이 공석임을 알고 계시는지 궁금합니다. 저희는 그 자리에 귀하와 같은 실력 있는 외과 의사를 찾고 있습니다. 규모 면에서 그레이스 베스는 의료 경영 경력을 쌓기에 아주 좋은 곳입니다. 사실 그레이스 베스 병원은 지역 내 4개 병원 중에서 **17 가장 규모가 큰** 병원입니다. 저는 이 직책이 귀하의 **18 특유한** 임상 경험에 아주 알맞은 자리임을 알게 되실 거라고 믿습니다. gbhosp.org/openpositions.htm에서 채용 공고를 확인해 보시고, 더 알고 싶은 내용이 있으시면 저에게 연락 주세요.

딘 에크하르트
그레이스 베스 병원 채용 담당자

어휘 chief of surgery 외과 과장 curriculum vitae 이력서
mutual 서로의, 공동의 be aware of ~을 인식하다, 알다
open position 공석 seek 구하다, 찾다 talented 재능이 있는 surgeon 외과 의사 enhance 향상하다 management 경영, 관리 match 아주 잘 어울리는 사람, 물건 clinical 임상의

15 (D)

해설 전치사 from의 목적어 자리로 빈칸 앞의 형용사 mutual의 수식을 받을 수 있는 명사 (D) acquaintance(지인)가 정답이다.

어휘 acquaint 숙지시키다, 알게 하다 acquainted 정통한, 잘 알고 있는

16 (A)

번역 (A) 귀하의 폭넓은 경험은 참으로 인상적이군요.
(B) 매닝 박사가 현재 외과 과장입니다.
(C) 그녀의 지원서를 신중하게 검토해 보시기 바랍니다.
(D) 저희는 또한 지원자들에게 추천서도 요구합니다.

해설 빈칸 앞에서 함께 아는 지인 글로리아 매닝 씨를 통해 이력서를 받았다(I received your curriculum vitae)고 했고, 뒤에서는 공석(open position)을 언급했다. 따라서 빈칸에도 아만 푸어 씨의 이력서와 관련된 내용이 들어가야 자연스러우므로, (A)가 정답이다.

어휘 extensive 폭넓은, 광범위한 currently 현재
application 지원서, 신청서 applicant 지원자

17 (D)

해설 문장의 주어인 Grace Beth Hospital을 보충 설명하는 주격 보어 자리로, 정관사 the 및 전치사구 of the region's four hospitals와 결합하여 '지역 내 4개의 병원 중에 가장 큰 (병원)'을 의미하는 최상급 형용사 (D) largest가 정답이다.

18 (B)

해설 소유격 your와 명사 clinical background 사이에서 명사를 수식하는 형용사 자리로 문맥상 '귀하의 특유한 임상 경험'이라는 의미가 자연스러우므로 (B) particular(특정한, 특유한)가 정답이다.

어휘 opaque 불투명한 forthright 솔직한 generic 일반적인

UNIT 16 어휘

ETS 실전문제 1 본책 p.234

1 (A) 2 (B) 3 (D) 4 (A) 5 (D) 6 (D)
7 (A) 8 (B) 9 (B) 10 (D) 11 (D) 12 (A)

1 (A)
번역 비교적 새로운 지역인 그랜빌의 재산세는 파워튼보다 훨씬 더 높다.
해설 비교급 형용사 higher를 수식하는 자리에 빈칸이 있으므로, '훨씬, 상당히'라는 의미의 (A) considerably가 정답이다.
어휘 property 자산, 건물 relatively 비교적, 상대적으로 spaciously 널찍하게 diligently 부지런히, 성실하게

2 (B)
번역 경영진은 회사의 경비원들이 얼마나 도움이 되는지에 대해 감사한다.
해설 경영진이 감사하는 이유로서 '경비원들이 얼마나 도움이 되는지'라는 의미를 나타내야 자연스러우므로, '도움이 되는'을 뜻하는 (B) helpful이 정답이다.
어휘 management 경영(진), 관리(진) appreciate 감사하다, 진가를 알아보다

3 (D)
번역 다빌라즈 카페는 그 레스토랑에서 처음부터 직접 만든 디저트로 유명하다.
해설 빈칸 앞뒤에 있는 be동사 및 전치사 for와 어울리는 형용사가 필요하므로, 이 둘과 함께 '~로 유명하다'를 뜻하는 (D) famous(유명한)가 정답이다.
어휘 from scratch 맨 처음부터 (직접) generous 관대한, 후한 curious 호기심 많은

4 (A)
번역 버논 거리 마라톤의 등록 기간이 3월 31일로 연장되었다.
해설 특정 시점을 나타내는 전치사구 to March 31과 어울려 '등록 기간이 3월 31일로 연장되었다'와 같이 등록 기간의 변동과 관련된 의미를 나타내야 자연스러우므로, '연장하다'를 뜻하는 동사 extend의 과거분사 (A) extended가 정답이다.
어휘 registration 등록 participate 참가하다 claim 주장하다, 요구하다

5 (D)
번역 마케팅 부서에서 10년간 근무한 후에, 퀸 씨가 마침내 이사로 승진되었다.
해설 마케팅 부서에서 10년간 근무한 것에 따른 결과로서 '마침내 이사로 승진되었다'라는 의미를 나타내야 자연스러우므로, '마침내, 결국'을 뜻하는 (D) finally가 정답이다.
어휘 thickly 두껍게, 빽빽하게

6 (D)
번역 서리 힐 플라워스 앤 기프츠는 11월에 주문하는 모든 품목을 특가로 제공합니다.
해설 빈칸은 전치사 on의 목적어로서 특가로 제공되는 대상을 나타내야 하므로, '주문(품)'을 뜻하는 (D) orders가 정답이다.
어휘 special deal 특가 (상품) capital 자본(금)

7 (A)
번역 월요일 회의에서, 다음 분기 예상 매출 수치가 논의될 것이다.
해설 다음 분기의 매출과 관련해 예상되는 것을 나타낼 명사가 쓰여야 알맞으므로 '수치, 숫자'를 의미하는 (A) figures가 정답이다.
어휘 projected 예상되는 viewpoint 관점, 시각 representative 직원, 대표자 turnout 참가자 수

8 (B)
번역 풀트레이드 파이낸셜 서비스의 시장 분석가들은 일상적으로 현재의 투자와 잠재적인 투자를 평가한다.
해설 분석가들이 일상적으로 하는 일을 나타내는 동사가 빈칸에 들어가야 하며, 목적어인 current and potential investments와 함께 쓰이에 자연스러워야 하므로, '평가하다'를 뜻하는 동사 (B) evaluate이 정답이다.
어휘 analyst 분석가 routinely 일상적으로 potential 잠재적인 investment 투자(금) participate 참가하다 disguise 변장하다

9 (B)
번역 순 텡이 은퇴 후에 직장에 복귀해서, 총 재직 연수를 반영하기 위해 그의 연금이 다시 계산될 것이다.
해설 연금을 다시 계산하는 것과 관련하여 빈칸 뒤에 위치한 명사구 number of his years of service와 함께 '총 재직 연수'를 의미해야 자연스러우므로, '총, 전체의'를 뜻하는 형용사 (B) total이 정답이다.
어휘 pension 연금 recalculate 다시 계산하다 reflect 반영하다

10 (D)
번역 소기업들은 그레이하운드 은행에서 저금리 대출 서비스를 받는 것을 고려해야 한다.
해설 빈칸 뒤에 동명사 taking이 있으므로, 동명사를 목적어로 취하는 동사 (D) consider(고려하다)가 정답이다. (A) aim은 흔히 to부정사와 함께 쓰이며, (C) persuade는 〈persuade+목적어+to부정사(~하도록 …를 설득하다)〉 구조로 자주 쓰인다.
어휘 low-interest 저금리의 loan 대출 observe 관찰하다

11 (D)
번역 저녁 근무조가 정규 영업시간 후에 도착하는 트럭에서 화물을 내릴 수 있다.
해설 트럭에서 내릴 수 있는 것을 나타낼 명사가 빈칸에 쓰여야 알맞으므로, '화물'을 뜻하는 (D) cargo가 정답이다.

어휘 crew (함께 작업하는) 팀, 조   unload (짐 등을) 내리다

12 (A)
번역 짖는원숭이는 중앙 아메리카의 많은 지역에 사는 토종이지만, 관광객들에게 좀처럼 보이지 않는다.
해설 대조를 나타내는 but 뒤에 빈칸이 있으므로, 중앙 아메리카의 많은 지역에 사는 토종이라는 말과 대조되는 '관광객들에게 좀처럼 보이지 않는다'와 같은 의미를 나타내야 자연스럽다. 따라서 '좀처럼 ~ 않다'를 뜻하는 부사 (A) seldom이 정답이다.
어휘 indigenous 토종인   basically 기본적으로

ETS 실전문제 2   본책 p. 235

| 1 (A) | 2 (B) | 3 (A) | 4 (D) | 5 (C) | 6 (A) |
| 7 (A) | 8 (A) | 9 (D) | 10 (D) | 11 (C) | 12 (D) |

1 (A)
번역 다음 외벽 도색 프로젝트를 위해 글렌스톤 레스토레이션에서 전문가를 고용하세요.
해설 전문가를 고용하는 목적으로서 exterior paint와 어울려 '외벽 도색 프로젝트'라는 의미가 되는 것이 자연스러우므로 (A) project가 정답이다.
어휘 restoration 복원, 복구   exterior 외관의   flavor 맛, 풍미   material 재료, 물품

2 (B)
번역 이컬러지 솝스는 아주 다양한 천연 원료 욕실 제품을 생산한다.
해설 형용사 broad의 수식을 받는 자리이고, '아주 다양한 제품을 생산한다'는 의미가 되는 것이 자연스러우므로 '종류, 다양성'을 의미하는 (B) variety가 정답이다. a broad variety of는 '아주 다양한'이라는 의미로 자주 사용되는 표현이다.
어휘 all-natural 천연 원료의   appeal 매력, 호소

3 (A)
번역 웨스트론 시 의회는 새 공원의 이름을 아직 정하지 않았다.
해설 현재완료 시제 동사 has settled와 어울리는 부사로서 not과 함께 '아직 ~하지 않았다'를 의미하는 (A) yet이 정답이다.
어휘 council 의회   settle on ~을 결정하다   rarely 좀처럼 ~ 않다, 드물게

4 (D)
번역 프라티크 론은 최고급 원예 용품을 적정한 가격에 판매한다.
해설 gardening(원예)과 어울리는 명사로서 적정한 가격에 판매될 수 있는 제품을 나타낼 명사가 필요하므로, '용품, 물품'을 뜻하는 (D) supplies가 정답이다.
어휘 top-quality 최고급의   affordable (가격이) 적정한, 알맞은   achievement 성취, 업적   association 협회   standard 기준, 표준

5 (C)
번역 브레이즈 수영 센터는 보수 공사로 인해 일시적으로 문을 닫는다.
해설 '보수 공사로 인해 일시적으로 문을 닫는다'라는 의미가 되는 것이 자연스러우므로 (C) temporarily(일시적으로)'가 정답이다.
어휘 renovation 보수, 개조   loosely 느슨하게, 헐겁게

6 (A)
번역 기술자들은 창문 설치를 위한 대기 기간이 최소 4주라는 것을 집주인에게 알려야 한다.
해설 window와 어울리는 명사가 빈칸에 쓰여야 하며, 창문 설치를 위한 대기 기간이 최소 4주라는 의미가 되는 것이 자연스러우므로 '설치 (작업)'을 뜻하는 (A) installation이 정답이다.
어휘 advise 알리다, 조언하다   organization 기관, 단체   reflection 반영   connection 연결, 접속

7 (A)
번역 청중은 허 씨의 영감을 불어넣는 개회사 후에 열광적인 박수를 터뜨렸다.
해설 박수(applause)를 적절히 묘사하는 형용사가 들어가야 하므로, '열광적인, 열렬한'을 뜻하는 (A) enthusiastic이 정답이다.
어휘 audience 청중, 관객   break into (감정, 행동 등) ~을 터뜨리다   inspiring 영감을 불어넣는   remark 말, 발언   essential 필수적인   glamorous 매혹적인   stolen 도난 당한

8 (A)
번역 많은 직원들이 이미 콘퍼런스를 위한 출장 준비를 해 두었다.
해설 명사 travel과 복합명사를 구성해 콘퍼런스를 위한 '출장 준비'를 의미해야 자연스러우므로, '준비, 채비' 등을 뜻하는 (A) arrangements가 정답이다.
어휘 agency 대행사, 대리점   condition 상태, 조건

9 (D)
번역 급여 업무를 돕기 위해 고메즈 씨가 그 사무소로 보내졌다.
해설 급여 관련 업무를 돕기 위해 특정 근무지로 자리를 옮겼다는 의미를 나타내야 자연스러우므로, '전근시키다, 이동시키다'를 뜻하는 transfer의 과거분사 (D) transferred가 정답이다.
어휘 assist with ~을 돕다   payroll 급여 (지급 명단)   transform 변형시키다   register 등록하다   involve 관련시키다

10 (D)
번역 도시 관광 투어가 매일 오전 10시에 웨스트 베이 마리나에서 출발한다.
해설 동사의 시제가 반복되는 일을 나타내는 현재 시제이고, '매일 오전 10시에 출발한다'는 의미가 되는 것이 자연스러우므로 (D) daily(매일)가 정답이다.
어휘 previously 이전에, 과거에   slightly 약간, 조금

11 (C)

번역 쉠백 작가 컨벤션에 참석하시기 전에 헤이버포드 홀에서 반드시 입장 서명을 해 주시기 바랍니다.

해설 입장 서명을 하도록 요청하는 것은 행사 참석 과정의 하나이므로 '참석하다'를 뜻하는 attend의 동명사 (C) attending이 정답이다.

어휘 sign in 서명하고 들어가다 retreat 후퇴하다, 물러서다

12 (D)

번역 PL 자전거는 자사의 전기 자전거에 대해 높아진 수요를 충족하기 위해 두 번째 공장을 열 계획을 발표했다.

해설 수요(demand)를 수식하는 자리로, '높아진 수요를 충족하기 위해 두 번째 공장을 연다'라는 의미가 되는 것이 자연스러우므로 (D) heightened(높아진)가 정답이다.

어휘 demand 수요, 요구 inspired 영감을 얻은 versatile 다목적의 common 일반적인

ETS 실전문제 3 본책 p.236

| 1 (D) | 2 (B) | 3 (B) | 4 (D) | 5 (A) | 6 (B) |
| 7 (D) | 8 (A) | 9 (D) | 10 (D) | 11 (B) | 12 (D) |

1 (D)

번역 포드햄 문구는 밸리 제지가 지속적으로 주문 배송이 늦어서 최근 공급업체를 교체하기로 결정했다.

해설 late를 수식하는 부사를 선택하는 문제이다. 문맥상 '지속적으로 늦어서 업체를 바꾸었다'는 내용이 되어야 자연스러우므로, '지속적으로'라는 의미의 (D) consistently가 정답이다. (A) steadily는 '꾸준하게, 성실하게'란 좋은 의미이므로 맞지 않다.

어휘 switch 바꾸다 supplier 공급업체 shipping 선적, 배송 sensibly 현저히, 현명하게 exactly 정확하게

2 (B)

번역 회사 정책을 검토한 후 동봉된 계약서에 서명해서 7월 1일 이전에 보내주십시오.

해설 서명해야 하는 계약서(contract)의 상태를 적절히 묘사하는 형용사가 들어가야 하므로, '동봉된'이라는 뜻의 과거분사 (B) enclosed가 정답이다.

어휘 review 검토하다 corporate 회사의 policy 정책 contract 계약서 surrounding 인근의, 주위의 concerned 염려하는 accepting 흔쾌히 받아들이는

3 (B)

번역 농산물 재배자 협회는 비타민이 가장 많이 든 과일과 채소 목록이 있는 소책자를 지역 슈퍼마켓들에 배포했다.

해설 전치사 with의 목적어 자리로 '비타민이 최고로 농축된'이라는 의미가 적합하므로 (B) concentrations(농축, 집중)가 정답이다.

어휘 produce 농작물 grower 재배자 association 협회 distribute 배포하다, 배급하다 list 기록하다, 목록으로 만들다; 목록 attraction 매력 beneficiary 수혜자, 수익자 command 명령, 지휘

4 (D)

번역 제이슨 주지사는 세금을 줄이고 학교들에 더 많은 자금을 할당하겠다고 공약했기 때문에 선거에서 승리했다.

해설 빈칸에는 to부정사구를 목적어로 취하며, 제이슨 주지사(she)가 선거에서 승리한 이유를 나타내는 동사가 들어가야 한다. 따라서 '약속했다'라는 의미의 (D) promised가 정답이다.

어휘 follow 뒤따르다 predict 예측하다 invent 발명하다

5 (A)

번역 여름철에는 관광객이 아주 많으므로 그에 따라 여행객들은 계획을 세우고 일찍 예약해야 한다.

해설 동사 should plan을 수식하는 부사 자리로 문맥상 '(앞에서 언급한 내용)에 따라'라는 의미가 적합하므로 (A) accordingly가 정답이다.

어휘 subsequently 결과적으로 conversely 거꾸로, 반대로 assuredly 확실히, 틀림없이

6 (B)

번역 퀄른의 웰버 기계 공장 엔지니어들은 복잡한 천공 시스템의 설계도에 있는 사소한 결함을 바로잡는 작업을 한다.

해설 천공 시스템의 특성을 설명하는 형용사가 들어가야 자연스러우므로, '복잡한'이라는 뜻의 (B) complex가 정답이다.

어휘 correct 바로잡다, 정정하다 minor flaw 사소한 결함 drilling 구멍 뚫기, 천공 confused 헷갈리는 informative 유익한 cautious 신중한

7 (D)

번역 판매원 카를로스 디아즈는 잠재 고객이 밸리 스트림 가구 전시장에 들어설 때 적극적으로 이끌어 진취성을 보여주었다.

해설 잠재 고객을 적극적으로 이끌며(by actively engaging potential customers) 보여준 태도를 나타내는 명사가 들어가야 자연스러우므로, '진취성, 주도권'이라는 의미의 (D) initiative가 정답이다.

어휘 actively 적극적으로, 활발하게 engage 끌다 potential 잠재적인 showroom 전시실 objective 목적, 목표 reliance 의존, 의지

8 (A)

번역 아직 한 달이 남았는데 애초에 예상했던 분기 예상 수입액이 이미 초과되었다.

해설 주어인 Initial projections와 결합하여 '초기 예상 수입액이 초과되었다'라는 의미를 나타내는 것이 자연스러우므로 '초과했다'를 의미하는 (A) exceeded가 정답이다.

어휘 initial 처음의, 초기의 projection 예상, 예측 quarterly 연 4회의, 분기마다의 outdate 시대에 뒤지게 하다 overdraw (수표나 어음을) 잔액 이상으로 초과 발행하다 impress 깊은 인상을 주다

9 (D)
- 번역: 전 세계 스포츠 팬들은 연례 테니스 선수권 대회의 결과를 간절히 기다린다.
- 해설: 스포츠 팬들이 결과를 기다리는(await the results) 심정을 적절히 묘사하는 부사가 들어가야 하므로, '간절히, 열심히'라는 의미의 (D) eagerly가 정답이다.
- 어휘: perfectly 완벽하게 evenly 균등하게 rapidly 신속히

10 (D)
- 번역: 안와르 배더위는 더 많은 책임이 있는 관리 직책으로 옮겨졌다.
- 해설: 더 많은 책임이 있는 직책의 성격을 나타낼 형용사가 쓰여야 알맞으므로, '관리직의, 감독의'를 의미하는 (D) supervisory가 정답이다.
- 어휘: responsibility 책임(감) slight 약간의, 조금의 repeating 반복되는 probable 가망성 있는

11 (B)
- 번역: 물류 컨설턴트를 고용한 결과 우리 매장들에 상품이 더 빠르게 유통되었다.
- 해설: 물류 컨설턴트의 고용(Hiring a logistics consultant)이 가져올 수 있는 결과를 나타내는 명사가 들어가야 하므로, '유통, 분배' 등을 의미하는 (B) distribution이 정답이다.
- 어휘: founding 설립 treatment 취급, 치료 revision 수정

12 (D)
- 번역: 스와비안 모터스는 경쟁사와 합병한 후에도 현 사명을 그대로 유지할 것이다.
- 해설: 목적어 its current name과 결합하여 '현재의 이름을 계속 유지하다'라는 의미가 되는 것이 자연스러우므로 '유지하다'라는 뜻의 (D) retain이 정답이다.
- 어휘: even 심지어 merge with ~와 합병하다 rival 경쟁하는 inquire 문의하다, 묻다 grant 주다, 수여하다

ETS 실전문제 4 본책 p.237

| 1 (B) | 2 (D) | 3 (A) | 4 (A) | 5 (C) | 6 (B) |
| 7 (A) | 8 (C) | 9 (D) | 10 (B) | 11 (A) | 12 (C) |

1 (B)
- 번역: 이 문서에 기술된 조건들은 사전 공지 없이 변경될 수 있다.
- 해설: 동사 are의 주어인 The terms and conditions를 보충 설명하는 주격 보어 자리로 빈칸 뒤의 to change와 결합하여 '변경될 수 있는'이라는 의미를 나타내는 형용사 (B) subject가 정답이다. 〈be subject to+명사〉 구조는 암기해 두자.
- 어휘: terms and conditions (거래·계약 등의) 조건 outline (개요를) 서술하다, 기술하다 without notice 예고 없이 dependent 의존하는 immediate 즉각적인

2 (D)
- 번역: 신임 공장장인 천하재 씨는 타마린도 시설에서 관리비를 줄이는 업무를 담당할 것이다.
- 해설: '관리비를 줄이는 업무를 담당하다'라는 내용이 되어야 자연스러우므로, 전치사 for와 함께 쓰여 '~을 책임지다, 맡다'라는 뜻을 완성하는 (D) responsible이 정답이다.
- 어휘: plant director 공장장 reduce 줄이다 maintenance cost 관리비, 유지비 fortunate 운이 좋은 senseless 무의미한

3 (A)
- 번역: 다바토 산업에서 나온 최신 전자레인지는 스테인리스강 내부와 10개의 가열 메뉴가 특징이다.
- 해설: 빈칸 뒤의 목적어인 a stainless steel interior and ten different heat settings와 결합하여 '~를 특징으로 하다'라는 의미를 나타내는 (A) features가 정답이다.
- 어휘: microwave oven 전자레인지 imply 암시하다 appoint 임명하다, (시간·장소 등을) 정하다

4 (A)
- 번역: 보드너 체육관 클럽의 플래티넘 회원들만 이용할 수 있는 서비스를 지금 신청하시기 바랍니다.
- 해설: '플래티넘 회원들만 이용할 수 있는'이라는 내용이 되어야 자연스러우므로, '오로지, ~만'이라는 뜻의 (A) exclusively가 정답이다.
- 어휘: deal 거래 (상품, 서비스) available 이용 가능한 platinum 백금 financially 재정적으로 relatively 비교적 productively 생산적으로

5 (C)
- 번역: CEO가 우리에게 시상식 참석을 요청했다.
- 해설: '시상식 참석을 요청했다'와 같은 의미를 나타내야 자연스러우므로, '참석'을 뜻하는 (C) presence가 정답이다.
- 어휘: excuse 변명, 이유 companion 동반자, 동행

6 (B)
- 번역: 예약한 지 2시간 내에 니코야 호텔에서 귀하의 여행 계획을 확정하는 확인 이메일을 받으실 겁니다.
- 해설: '확인 이메일을 받을 것이다'라는 내용이 되어야 자연스러우므로, (B) confirmation(확인)이 정답이다.
- 어휘: sponsor 후원자 margin 여백, 수익 permit 허가증; 허가하다

7 (A)
- 번역: 새로운 조명 시스템이 총무과에 설치되어, 낡고 덜 효율적인 조명을 대체했다.
- 해설: 빈칸 뒤의 목적어인 the older, less efficient one과 결합하여 '낡고 덜 효율적인 것을 대체한다'라는 의미를 나타내는 현재분사 (A) replacing이 정답이다.
- 어휘: compare 비교하다, 비유하다 brighten 밝게 하다

8 (C)

번역 데일 백화점은 연휴 직전에 보석류에 대한 특별 할인에 들어갈 것이다.

해설 before와 결합하여 '~ 직전에'라는 표현을 완성하는 (C) immediately(바로)가 정답이다.

어휘 department store 백화점 holiday 휴가, 공휴일 sensitively 민감하게 extremely 극도로 figuratively 비유적으로

9 (D)

번역 XT1000은 시장에서 가장 민감한 가정용 주방 저울 중 하나로, 밀리그램 단위까지 정확하게 측정한다.

해설 가정용 주방 저울을 수식하는 자리로, '밀리그램 단위까지 정확하게 측정한다'는 말이 있으므로 '민감한'이라는 의미의 (D) sensitive가 정답이다.

어휘 scale 저울 accurate 정확한 tentative 잠정적인, 임시적인 deliberate 신중한 investigative 조사하는, 연구의

10 (B)

번역 웰본 과학박물관의 새로운 천문 극장은 250명을 수용할 수 있는 좌석 규모를 갖추었다.

해설 동사 has의 목적어 자리로 앞의 seating과 결합하여 '좌석 규모'라는 의미를 나타내는 (B) capacity가 정답이다.

어휘 astronomy 천문학 aptitude 소질, 적성 demonstration 시연 compliance 준수, 따름

11 (A)

번역 신선한 생강과 마늘을 혼합한 것을 이용해, 요리사 개리 피터스는 매우 훌륭한 구운 생선 조리법을 만들어 냈다.

해설 명사 recipe를 수식해 어떤 조리법인지를 나타낼 형용사가 쓰여야 알맞으므로, '매우 훌륭한'을 뜻하는 (A) exquisite이 정답이다.

어휘 mixture 혼합(물) recipe 조리법 obedient 순종적인 enormous 거대한, 막대한 intentional 의도적인

12 (C)

번역 건물 입구에 있는 인상적인 꽃 장식은 주로 파란 꽃으로 이루어져 있고, 빨간 꽃 몇 송이가 구석구석에 솜씨 있게 배치되었다.

해설 과거분사 made up of를 수식하는 부사 자리로 '주로 만들어지다, 이루어지다'라는 의미가 적합하므로 (C) primarily(주로)가 정답이다. 동의어인 largely, mostly, mainly도 답이 될 수 있다.

어휘 impressive 인상적인 floral display 꽃 장식 artfully 기교 있게

ETS 실전문제 5   본책 p. 238

1 (B) **2** (C) **3** (D) **4** (C) **5** (A) **6** (D)
7 (D) **8** (C) **9** (D) **10** (D) **11** (C) **12** (C)

1 (B)

번역 공장 방문 중에, 손님들은 제한 구역에 출입하는 것이 허용되지 않을 것이며, 이곳은 오직 승인된 직원만 허용된다.

해설 손님들은 출입이 허용되지 않는다는 말과 대조적으로 '오직 승인된 직원만 허용된다'와 같은 의미를 나타내야 자연스러우므로, '승인된, 권한을 부여 받은'을 뜻하는 (B) authorized가 정답이다.

어휘 permit 허용하다 restricted 제한된 concerned (사람이) 우려하는, 걱정하는 scattered 흩어진, 산발적인

2 (C)

번역 원코트 항공사는 자사의 스카이 플라이어 클럽 회원에게는 15파운드의 수하물 비용을 면제해 줄 것이라고 발표했다.

해설 목적어 the £15 baggage fee와 결합하여 클럽 회원들에게는 '비용을 면제해 준다'는 내용이므로 (C) waive(적용하지 않다)가 정답이다.

어휘 prove 입증되다 cost 비용이 들다 align 정렬하다

3 (D)

번역 더 이상 판촉 할인 광고를 받고 싶지 않으시다면 허글랜드 마켓은 귀하의 이름을 우편물 수신인 목록에서 즉시 삭제할 것입니다.

해설 동사 delete를 수식하는 자리로, '귀하의 이름을 즉시 삭제할 것입니다'라는 내용이 되어야 자연스럽다. 따라서 (D) promptly(즉시, 신속하게)가 정답이다.

어휘 promotional 홍보의, 판촉의 mailing list 우편물 수신인 목록 previously 이전에 overall 전체의; 종합적으로

4 (C)

번역 두 공연 사이에는 15분간의 짧은 중간 휴식 시간이 있을 것이다.

해설 15분간의 중간 휴식 시간(intermission)을 적절히 묘사하는 형용사가 들어가야 하므로, '짧은, 간결한'이라는 의미의 (C) brief가 정답이다.

5 (A)

번역 직원들은 데이터베이스에 접근하려면 반드시 적절한 자격을 지니고 있어야 한다.

해설 직원들이 데이터베이스에 접근하기 위해 지니고 있어야 하는 것을 나타내야 하므로, '자격(증)'을 의미하는 (A) credentials가 정답이다.

어휘 access 접근하다 reward 보상 consideration 고려, 숙고 requirement 필요, 필요 조건

184

6 (D)

번역 회계부는 종이 사용을 줄이기 위해서 새로운 정책을 시행했다.

해설 빈칸은 has와 현재완료 동사를 이루어 명사구 a new policy를 목적어로 취한다. '새로운 정책을 시행했다'라는 내용이 되어야 자연스러우므로, (D) implemented(시행했다)가 정답이다.

어휘 preoccupy 선점하다 represent 나타내다, 대표하다 characterize 특징짓다

7 (D)

번역 객실은 호텔 고객이 체크아웃한 후 2시간 이내에 완전히 청소되어야 한다.

해설 cleaned를 수식하는 자리로, 객실이 청소되는 방식이나 정도를 나타내는 부사가 들어가야 자연스럽다. 따라서 '완전히, 철저히'라는 의미의 (D) thoroughly가 정답이다.

어휘 patron 고객 widely 널리 sturdily 튼튼하게

8 (C)

번역 헤르만 팜의 L10 농업용 트랙터는 적응력이 뛰어나게 만들어져서, 거의 모든 농장 일을 처리할 수 있다.

해설 거의 모든 농장 일을 처리할 수 있다는 말이 쓰여 있어 이러한 특징과 관련된 형용사가 필요하므로, '적응할 수 있는, 적응을 잘하는'을 뜻하는 (C) adaptable이 정답이다.

어휘 agricultural 농업의 be designed to ~하도록 만들어지다 handle 처리하다, 다루다 calculating 계산적인 receptive 수용적인 obligated 의무가 있는

9 (D)

번역 3월 12일 교육에 참석할 수 없는 직원은 대체 가능한 날짜로 편성될 예정이다.

해설 3월 12일 교육에 참석할 수 없는 직원은 다른 날짜에 참석할 수 있게 해 주겠다는 내용이므로, '대체 가능한, 대안적인'이라는 의미의 (D) alternative가 정답이다.

어휘 be scheduled for ~로 예정되다, 편성되다 unoccupied 비어 있는 irreplaceable 대체 불가능한

10 (D)

번역 페일스 북스토어스는 올해 순익이 20퍼센트 하락했다고 발표했는데, 이 회사는 이것을 율 북셀러스 사와의 치열한 경쟁에서 기인한 결과로 보았다.

해설 빈칸은 목적격 관계대명사 which가 이끄는 절의 동사 자리로, which가 가리키는 a 20 percent decrease in net profit이 의미상 직접 목적어 역할을 한다. 따라서 전치사구 to fierce competition과 결합하여 '순익 감소는 치열한 경쟁 때문이다'라는 의미를 완성하는 (D) attributed가 정답이다. 'A를 B의 탓으로 돌리다'라는 뜻의 〈attribute A to B〉 구조를 암기해두자.

어휘 accuse 고발하다, 비난하다 present 증정하다, 제출하다 disapprove 비난하다, 승인하지 않다

11 (C)

번역 환경 오염 예방은 소기업과 대기업 모두에게 중요한 고려 사항이 되었다.

해설 빈칸 앞의 and와 결합하여 '둘 다 똑같이, 모두'의 의미를 나타내는 부사 (C) alike가 정답이다. 〈A and B alike〉는 〈both A and B〉의 형태로도 쓸 수 있다.

어휘 prevention 예방, 방지 environmental 환경의 pollution 오염 forth ~에서 멀리, 밖으로

12 (C)

번역 마이어 컴퍼니의 계약 조건이 매년 변경될 수 있다는 점을 알아 두십시오.

해설 계약 조건(terms and conditions)이 변경될 수 있다는 점을 고지하는 내용이므로, '알아 두십시오'라는 의미를 완성하는 (C) aware(알고 있는)가 정답이다. Please be aware that, Please note that 등과 같은 표현은 암기해두는 것이 좋다.

어휘 terms and conditions 조건, 약관 contract 계약 be subject to ~될 수 있다, ~에 달려 있다 annually 매년, 일 년에 한 번

ETS 실전문제 6   본책 p.239

1 (C)	2 (B)	3 (C)	4 (D)	5 (D)	6 (B)
7 (C)	8 (A)	9 (C)	10 (C)	11 (D)	12 (B)

1 (C)

번역 새롭게 웹사이트를 개선해서, 힐 스트리트 디자인 고객들은 최근 구매품의 간략한 내역을 볼 수 있을 것이다.

해설 빈칸은 동사 view의 목적어 자리로 '최근 구매품들의 내역이 간략하게 정리된 것'을 나타내는 명사가 들어가야 자연스럽다. 따라서 (C) summary(요약, 개요)가 정답이다.

어휘 enhancement 향상, 상승 purchase 구매(품) voucher 상품권, 쿠폰 payment 지불(금)

2 (B)

번역 내 의견으로는, 이 회사의 주가는 연간 수익과 비교해 상대적으로 낮다.

해설 형용사 low를 강조하는 부사 자리로, 뒤의 compared to와 결합하여 '~에 비해서 상대적으로 낮은'이라는 의미를 나타내는 (B) relatively가 정답이다.

어휘 in my opinion 내 의견으로는 stock price 주가 compared to ~와 비교하여 earnings 소득, 이익 audibly 들을 수 있게 plentifully 풍부하게 anonymously 익명으로

3 (C)

번역 화창한 날씨가 예보된 상황에서 그 경기가 비 때문에 취소될 것이라고 예상한 사람은 아무도 없었다.

해설 빈칸 뒤에 접속사 that이 이끄는 절이 쓰여 있으므로 that절을 목적어로 취하는 동사 (C) expected(예상하다)가 정답이다. (B) wondered는 if나 whether, 또는 wh-로 시작하는 접속사가 이끄는 명사절을 목적어로 취한다.

어휘 forecast 예보   match 경기   permit 허용하다
wonder 궁금해하다   count 세다

4 (D)

번역 반스 씨는 신입 영업사원을 위한 교육 프로그램을 검토한 후에, 관계망 형성 기술에 좀 더 주안점을 두어야 한다고 결론 내렸다.

해설 빈칸 뒤 동사 should be placed와 함께 '강조되어야 한다'라는 의미를 완성하는 (D) emphasis가 정답이다. 〈place an emphasis on 명사〉는 '~에 주안점을 두다, ~를 강조하다'라는 의미로 사용된다.

어휘 conclude 결론 내리다   networking 네트워킹, 인맥 형성
appeal 애원, 호소   analysis 분석   distinction 구별

5 (D)

번역 피츠턴 갤러리는 워딩턴에서 주요 예술 기획사였으며 많은 공개 행사를 후원해 왔다.

해설 많은 공개 행사를 후원한 기획사(promoter)를 적절히 수식하는 형용사가 들어가야 하므로, '주요한, 제1의'라는 뜻의 (D) primary가 정답이다.

어휘 sponsor 후원하다   public event 공개 행사   precise 정확한   separate 분리된   certain 확실한, 어떤

6 (B)

번역 달리 명시되어 있지 않다면, 사진과 관련 서류들은 저자에 의해 제공된 것이다.

해설 빈칸 뒤의 과거분사 noted를 수식하는 부사 자리로 unless와 함께 '달리 명시되어 있지 않다면'이라는 의미를 완성하는 (B) otherwise(~와 다르게)가 정답이다. 〈unless otherwise 과거분사〉 구문은 암기해두는 것이 좋다.

어휘 document 문서, 서류

7 (C)

번역 노구치 인베스트먼트는 고객에게 최상의 서비스를 제공하기 위해 정기적으로 철저한 업계 현재 동향 분석을 실시한다.

해설 정기적으로 실시되는 분석(analyses)의 특징을 묘사하는 형용사가 들어가야 하므로, '철저한, 빈틈없는'이라는 의미의 (C) thorough가 정답이다.

어휘 regularly 정기적으로   conduct 실시하다   analysis 분석
current 현재의   spacious 널찍한   eventual 궁극적인, 최종적인   probable 개연성이 있는

8 (A)

번역 우리 직원들이 배송 양식에 정확한 주소를 쓰지 않았지만, 기계 부품들은 예정대로 낙농장에 도착했다.

해설 전치사 on과 결합하여 '일정대로'라는 의미를 나타내는 명사 (A) schedule이 정답이다. '예정보다 늦게'라는 의미의 behind schedule, '예정보다 빨리'라는 의미의 ahead of schedule도 알아두자.

어휘 form 서식, 양식   part 부품   dairy farm 낙농장
appointment 약속   authority 지휘권, 권한
condition 상태

9 (C)

번역 메리 번역회사는 통역사를 통해 사업 관계자와 의사소통할 때 예의 바르게 그 관계자에게 주의를 기울일 것을 제안한다.

해설 빈칸 뒤 전치사 with와 어울려 쓰여 '~와 의사소통하다'라는 의미를 완성하는 (C) communicating이 정답이다.

어휘 suggest 제안하다   associate 동료, 관계자   interpreter 통역사   focus one's attention on ~에 주목하다, 주의를 기울이다   regulate 규제하다, 조정하다   acquaint 숙지시키다   contemplate 고려하다, 생각하다

10 (C)

번역 모든 신규 입사자 서류가 완전히 작성되어 근무 시간 종료 시점까지 인사부로 제출되어야 한다.

해설 서류가 작성되는 방식과 관련해 '완전히 작성되어야 한다'를 의미해야 자연스러우므로, (C) completely(완전히)가 정답이다.

어휘 fill out 작성하다   overly 너무, 몹시   hardly 거의 ~ 아니다

11 (D)

번역 스텔라즈 컨펙셔너리의 교대 근무 시간은 8시간이며, 점심을 위한 30분 휴식이 포함된다.

해설 '근무 시간에는 점심을 위한 30분의 휴식이 포함된다'는 의미를 나타내는 것이 자연스러우므로 '포함하다'를 뜻하는 (D) include가 정답이다.

어휘 shift 교대 근무   release 공개하다   assemble 조립하다

12 (B)

번역 사누라이프 웹사이트는 여러분께 의학 연구 분야의 모든 최신 발전에 대한 소식을 알려 드립니다.

해설 전치사 of의 목적어 자리로, 앞의 all the latest와 결합하여 '최신 발전'이라는 의미를 나타내는 (B) advances가 정답이다. 참고로 명사 advance는 주로 전치사 in과 함께 쓰인다.

어휘 novelty 새로움, 신기함   elevation 격상, 높이   formation 형성, 대형

ETS 실전문제 7   본책 p.240

| 1 (B) | 2 (B) | 3 (A) | 4 (A) | 5 (B) | 6 (B) |
| 7 (D) | 8 (D) | 9 (B) | 10 (D) | 11 (B) | 12 (C) |

1 (B)

번역 직원 편람은 경비 보고서 제출 절차를 명확히 설명한다.

해설 빈칸 뒤의 목적어 the procedure와 결합하여 '절차를 설명하다'라는 의미를 나타내므로 (B) outlines(서술하다, 설명하다)가 정답이다.

어휘 procedure 절차 file (증서나 서류를) 정식으로 제출하다 purchase 구입하다 ration 배급하다 invest 투자하다

2 (B)

번역 전화 상담직원은 전화를 받을 때 합당한 범위 내에서 고객의 우려사항을 처리하기 위해 가능한 것들을 해야 한다.

해설 빈칸 앞 전치사 within과 어울려 쓰이는 명사를 선택하는 문제이다. 고객의 우려사항을 처리하기 위해(to address customer concerns) 하는 일은 합당한 범위 내에서 이루어져야 한다는 내용이므로, '합리적인 범위'를 뜻하는 (B) reason이 정답이다. within reason은 고정된 표현으로 암기해 두는 것이 좋다.

어휘 representative 대리인, 담당자 address 고심하다, 다루다 concern 우려 (사항)

3 (A)

번역 밤새도록 비가 내려 다행히 최근 가뭄을 완화해 주었다.

해설 비가 밤새(throughout the night) 내린 모습을 적절히 묘사하는 부사가 빈칸에 들어가야 하므로, '계속해서, 끊임없이'라는 의미의 (A) continuously가 정답이다.

어휘 relief 안도, 경감 recent 최근의 dry spell 가뭄, 건기 mutually 상호간에, 서로 needlessly 쓸데없이, 불필요하게 optimistically 낙관적으로

4 (A)

번역 직원들은 최소 12개월 이상 근무했다면 육아 휴직과 병가를 낼 자격이 있다.

해설 주어인 Employees를 보충 설명하는 주격 보어 자리로, to 부정사와 결합하여 '~할 자격이 있는'이라는 의미를 나타내는 형용사 (A) eligible이 정답이다.

어휘 leave 휴가 desirable 바람직한, 호감이 가는 preferred 우선의 suitable 적합한

5 (B)

번역 매장 관리자로 성공하려면, 선라 씨는 매장이 필요로 하는 것과 직원 기대치의 균형을 맞춰야 한다.

해설 매장 관리자로 성공하기 위한 조건으로서 '매장이 필요로 하는 것과 직원 기대치 사이에서 반드시 균형을 맞춰야 한다'를 의미해야 자연스러우므로, (B) balance(균형을 맞추다)가 정답이다.

어휘 succeed 성공하다 expectation 기대(치) convince 설득하다 gather 모으다 prevent 예방하다

6 (B)

번역 세일 기간 동안 홍보용 현수막들이 매장 전체에서 명확히 보여야 합니다.

해설 홍보용 현수막들이 어떻게 보여야 하는지를 나타낼 부사가 필요하므로, '명확히, 분명히'를 뜻하는 (B) clearly가 정답이다.

어휘 promotional 홍보의 banner 현수막 visible 눈에 보이는 tightly 꽉 eagerly 간절히 commonly 흔히

7 (D)

번역 새로운 품질보장 정책은 하루에 불량품이 5개 이상 나올 경우 모든 기계를 점검할 것을 요구한다.

해설 기계 점검(all machines be inspected)의 원인이 되는 상품의 상태를 묘사하는 형용사가 들어가야 하므로, '결함이 있는'이라는 의미의 (D) defective가 정답이다.

어휘 quality assurance 품질보장 policy 정책 inspect 점검하다, 검사하다 collective 집단의 efficient 효율적인 immediate 즉각적인

8 (D)

번역 상인들이 〈위클리 라운드업〉에 게재한 광고들이 반드시 해당 신문 경영진의 보증을 받은 것임을 암시하지는 않는다.

해설 imply를 수식하는 부사 자리로, '광고가 해당 신문 경영진의 보증을 받는 것은 아니다'라는 의미가 되는 것이 자연스러우므로 '반드시'를 의미하는 (D) necessarily가 정답이다.

어휘 merchant 상인, 무역상 imply 암시하다 endorsement 지지, (유명인이 광고에 나와 하는 상품에 대한) 보증, 홍보 barely 간신히, 거의 ~ 아니게 gradually 서서히

9 (B)

번역 로즈 패션 부티크는 이번 주 토요일에 모든 고객에게 20퍼센트 할인을 제공할 예정이다.

해설 할인과 관련하여 회사가 고객에게 할 수 있는 행위를 나타내는 동사가 필요하므로, '제공하다'는 의미의 (B) offering이 정답이다.

어휘 notify 알리다 perform 수행하다, 공연하다

10 (D)

번역 부서 관리자는 강 씨에게 완성된 직원 평가서를 보내야 한다.

해설 관리자가 보낼 직원 평가서(employee evaluations)의 상태를 적절히 묘사하는 형용사가 들어가야 하므로, '작성된, 완성된'이라는 뜻의 (D) completed가 정답이다.

어휘 department 부서 evaluation 평가 steady 꾸준한 skillful 숙련된 turned 돌려진

11 (B)

번역 이 웹사이트 이용은 우리의 약관에 동의함을 의미합니다.

해설 동사 implies의 목적어 자리로, 빈칸 뒤 with our terms and conditions와 결합하여 '약관에 대한 동의'라는 의미를 나타내는 (B) agreement가 정답이다.

어휘 imply 의미하다, 암시하다 terms and conditions 약관, 조건 contentment 만족 placement 설치 development 발달

12 (C)

번역 전시 중이 아닐 경우, 희귀 필사본은 보존에 가장 적합한 환경에 보관된다.

해설 원고 보존을 위한 보관 환경의 상태(conditions)를 적절히 묘사하는 형용사가 들어가야 하므로, '최적의, 가장 좋은'이라는 의미의 (C) optimal이 정답이다.

어휘 be on display 전시 중이다   rare 진기한, 드문
manuscript 필사본, 원고   preservation 보존
attentive 주의를 기울이는   credible 믿을 수 있는
competent 능숙한

ETS 실전문제 8   본책 p.241

| 1 (D) | 2 (B) | 3 (D) | 4 (C) | 5 (B) | 6 (C) |
| 7 (B) | 8 (B) | 9 (B) | 10 (D) | 11 (C) | 12 (B) |

1 (D)

번역 패티슨 씨는 그 회사에서 3년간 일하면서 한 번도 마감 기한을 어긴 적이 없는 것으로 상을 받았다.

해설 빈칸 이하는 상을 받은 근거를 나타내므로, '마감 기한을 어긴 적이 없다'는 내용이 되어야 자연스럽다. 따라서 (D) never(결코 ~않는)가 정답이다.

어휘 receive an award 상을 받다   miss a deadline 기한을 놓치다

2 (B)

번역 방대한 18세기 스코틀랜드 미술 소장품의 보금자리인 헨드런 박물관은 현대 작품들도 전시한다.

해설 '헨드런 박물관이 현대 작품들도 전시한다'와 같은 의미를 나타내야 자연스러우므로, '전시하다'를 뜻하는 (B) showcases가 정답이다.

어휘 extensive 방대한, 폭넓은   collection 소장(품), 수집(품)
contemporary 현대의, 동시대의   operate 운영하다
extend 연장하다   undergo 겪다

3 (D)

번역 목요일에 약한 비가 내릴 가능성이 있는 가운데, 이번 주 내내 온화한 날씨가 계속될 것 같다.

해설 be동사 및 to부정사와 어울려 쓰이는 형용사를 선택하는 문제로, '~할 것 같다'는 의미를 완성하는 (D) likely가 정답이다. (A) probable도 비슷한 의미이지만 구조상 빈칸에 들어갈 수 없다. 참고로, likely와 probable은 〈It is probable/likely that절〉의 구조로 가능성 있는 상황을 묘사할 수 있다.

어휘 with a chance of ~할 가능성이 있는   probable 개연성 있는   frequent 빈번한   considerable 상당한, 많은

4 (C)

번역 실험실 테스트는 세정제가 효과적이기 위해서는 다양한 원료들의 정확한 배합이 필요하다는 것을 보여 준다.

해설 전치사 of의 목적어 자리로, 앞의 combination과 결합하여 '다양한 원료들의 배합'이라는 의미를 완성하는 (C) ingredients(재료, 원료)가 정답이다.

어휘 precise 정확한   combination 결합   compound 혼합물, 화합물   effective 효과적인   division 분할, 부문
prospect 가능성   compartment 칸막이, 구획

5 (B)

번역 아마릴로에 최근 설치된 태양열 전지판 시스템이 연간 5만 킬로와트시의 전기를 생산할 것으로 예상된다.

해설 '설치된'을 뜻하는 과거분사 installed를 수식하는 자리로, '최근 설치된 태양열 전지판 시스템'이라는 의미가 자연스러우므로, (B) recently(최근)가 정답이다.

어휘 solar array 태양열 전지판 시스템   commonly 흔히
increasingly 점점 더

6 (C)

번역 우리는 선라이즈 팜즈처럼 현지의 환경친화적 업체로부터 재료를 구하는 것을 선호한다.

해설 현지의 환경친화적인 업체로부터 나온 재료(ingredients)와 관련하여 할 수 있는 행위를 나타내는 동사가 필요하므로, '구하다, 얻다'라는 의미의 (C) obtain이 정답이다.

어휘 environmentally friendly 환경친화적인   comprise 구성하다   achieve 달성하다

7 (B)

번역 멜로 어드버타이징은 색이 밝고 눈길을 끄는 로고, 전단 및 기타 홍보물로 잘 알려져 있다.

해설 광고 회사가 제작하는 자료(material)의 성격을 나타내는 형용사가 들어가야 자연스러우므로, '판촉의, 홍보의'라는 의미의 (B) promotional이 정답이다.

어휘 eye-catching 눈길을 끄는   flyer 전단   conditional 조건부의   promotional material 홍보물

8 (B)

번역 크로스 코브는 많은 뉴질랜드 예술가들의 고향인데, 그중에 특히 프란시스 슈어드 씨와 카일 매킨타이어 씨가 유명하다.

해설 빈칸 뒤의 명사구를 강조하는 자리로, '그중에서도 특히 가장 유명한'이라는 의미를 완성하는 (B) notably(특히)가 정답이다.

어휘 separately 각각, 개별적으로   commonly 공통적으로

9 (B)

번역 헤스턴 부동산 관리는 현재 진행되는 개조 공사가 세입자들에게 줄 수 있는 불편에 대해 사과드립니다.

해설 사과(apologizes)의 이유가 되는 명사가 들어가야 하므로, '불편'이라는 의미의 (B) inconvenience가 정답이다.

어휘 apologize 사과하다   current 현재의   renovation 개조, 수리   tenant 세입자   resolution 해결   improvement 개선, 향상   distinction 차이

10 (D)

번역 내일 회의 말미에 시간이 있으면 실라 샘슨이 토론토 아트 페스티벌에 대해 간략히 이야기할 것이다.

해설 회의 말미에 시간이 있을 경우(If there is time) 특정 주제에 대해 간략하게 이야기할 것이라는 내용이 되어야 자연스러우므로, '간략히'라는 의미의 (D) briefly가 정답이다.

어휘 rarely 드물게 slightly 약간

11 (C)

번역 도시의 스트레스에서 멀리 떨어진 곳에 있는 코즈칼 호텔은 고객에게 편안한 휴가 경험을 제공하는 것에 대해 자부심을 갖고 있습니다.

해설 호텔이 제공하는 휴가 경험(vacation experience)의 특성을 적절히 묘사하는 형용사가 들어가야 하므로, '편안한'이라는 의미의 (C) relaxing이 정답이다.

어휘 pride oneself on ~를 자랑하다 reclining 기대는 restored 회복된 retired 은퇴한

12 (B)

번역 하트웍 운송의 아템브 씨는 화물 운송에 대한 고객들의 우려를 해결해 줄 가장 좋은 방법들에 관한 워크숍을 열 것이다.

해설 목적어인 concerns와 결합하여 '우려를 해결하다'라는 의미를 나타내는 (B) address(처리하다, 해결하다)가 정답이다. 참고로, address는 issue나 problem과도 자주 쓰인다.

어휘 inform 알리다 supervise 관리하다, 감독하다

ETS 실전문제 9 본책 p.242

1 (A) 2 (C) 3 (D) 4 (A) 5 (A) 6 (C)
7 (C) 8 (B) 9 (B) 10 (C) 11 (A) 12 (B)

1 (A)

번역 크래독 서지칼 프로덕트 사에서의 고용 관련 문의는 인사부서로 보내져야 한다.

해설 '고용 관련 문의'라는 의미가 되어야 자연스러우므로, (A) Inquiries(문의, 문의 사항)가 정답이다.

어휘 regarding ~에 관한 employment 고용 direct 보내다 influence 영향 occasion 경우, 때 qualification 자질, 자격

2 (C)

번역 경영 분석가들은 젬퀘스트 주식회사가 보류 중인 합병 결정을 곧 내리기를 기대한다.

해설 합병 결정(merger decision)이 아직 내려지지 않은 상황을 나타내므로, '보류 중인, 미결정인'이라는 의미의 (C) pending이 정답이다.

어휘 analyst 분석가 merger 합병 decision 결정 sparse 드문, 희박한 related 관련된 attentive 주의를 기울이는

3 (D)

번역 고객들은 퍼포먼스 와이어리스의 낮은 요금과 훌륭한 고객 서비스 때문에 흔히 돌아온다.

해설 긍정적인 요인으로 인해 고객들이 돌아오는 경우가 많다는 내용이 되어야 자연스러우므로, '자주, 흔히'라는 의미의 (D) frequently가 정답이다.

어휘 moderately 적당히 mutually 상호간에, 서로

4 (A)

번역 화물 자전거는 내구성을 염두에 두고 디자인되는데, 흔히 무거운 짐을 끄는 데 이용되기 때문이다.

해설 화물 자전거를 디자인할 때 염두에 두어야 하는 특징과 관련된 명사가 필요하므로, '내구성'을 뜻하는 (A) durability가 정답이다.

어휘 haul 끌다 freshness 신선함 enthusiasm 열정 dedication 헌신

5 (A)

번역 프린델 커뮤니케이션즈의 복잡한 신규 시간 보고 지침은 직원들에게 혼란을 야기했다.

해설 복잡한 지침(The complicated new time-reporting guidelines)으로 인해 직원들이 겪게 될 문제점을 나타내는 명사가 들어가야 자연스러우므로, '혼란, 혼동'이라는 의미의 (A) confusion이 정답이다.

어휘 complicated 복잡한 guideline 지침 attention 주의, 주목 impression 인상

6 (C)

번역 센다이 연구소의 오카다 박사는 약학 연구에 대해 권위 있는 로워리 상을 받았다.

해설 상이 지니는 의미나 성격 등과 관련된 의미를 나타낼 형용사가 필요하므로 '권위 있는, 명성 있는'을 뜻하는 (C) prestigious가 정답이다.

어휘 pharmaceutical 약학의, 제약의 enhanced 향상된 determined 단호한

7 (C)

번역 오크만 코퍼레이션은 8월 6일에 신임 회장 임명을 발표했다.

해설 회사에서 신임 회장의 임명을 발표했다는 내용이 되어야 자연스러우므로, '발표했다, 알렸다'라는 의미의 (C) announced가 정답이다. 참고로, (A) informed는 알림의 대상인 사람 명사를 목적어로 취한다.

어휘 appointment 임명 announce 발표하다, 알리다

8 (B)

번역 월트셔 오케스트라의 콘서트는 대략 3시간 길이였고, 밤 11시가 막 지나서 끝났다.

해설 숫자 표현 three (hours)를 수식하는 부사 자리로 '대략'이란 의미의 (B) approximately가 정답이다.

어휘 just after ~ 직후에 attentively 세심하게 endlessly 끝없이 comparatively 비교적

9 (B)

번역 피셔 카페테리아는 평일 오후 3시부터 10시까지 저녁 교대 근무조를 감독할 상근직 부지배인을 찾고 있다.

해설 평일 오후 3시부터 10시까지 부지배인이 감독할 대상을 나타내는 명사가 들어가야 하므로, '교대 근무조'라는 의미의 (B) shift가 정답이다.

어휘 oversee 감독하다 practice 실행, 연습 effect 영향, 효과

10 (C)

번역 동료 간의 빈번하고 긍정적인 상호작용은 연중 생산성 향상과 관련이 있었다.

해설 빈칸 뒤 productivity와 결합하여 '증가된 생산성'이라는 의미를 완성하는 (C) increased가 정답이다.

어휘 frequent 빈번한, 잦은 positive 긍정적인 coworker 동료 be associated with ~와 관련되다 productivity 생산성 licensed 허가를 받은, 면허를 소지한

11 (A)

번역 오스왈트 인터내셔널은 200개가 넘는 개발 프로젝트를 성공적으로 완수했기 때문에 현재 서비스 수요가 높다.

해설 서비스 수요가 높은 이유를 언급한 부분이므로, 개발 프로젝트를 성공적으로 완수했다(has completed)는 내용이 되어야 자연스럽다. 따라서 '성공적으로'라는 의미의 (A) successfully가 정답이다.

어휘 complete 완료하다 development 개발 be in high demand 수요가 높다 instantly 즉각, 즉시 financially 재정적으로

12 (B)

번역 효과적인 감시 없이 안전 규정을 시행하기는 어려울 것이다.

해설 목적어 the safety regulations와 결합하여 '안전 규정을 시행하다'라는 의미를 나타내는 (B) enforce(시행하다)가 정답이다.

어휘 safety regulations 안전 규정 effective 효과적인 monitor 모니터하다, 감시하다 entrust (일을) 맡기다 imply 암시하다, 내포하다 implore 애원하다, 간청하다

ETS 실전문제 10   본책 p.243

| 1 (C) | 2 (C) | 3 (A) | 4 (B) | 5 (A) | 6 (C) |
| 7 (D) | 8 (A) | 9 (A) | 10 (B) | 11 (A) | 12 (B) |

1 (C)

번역 목요일 회의에 참석할 수 없는 직원은 에버렛 왓슨에게 알려야 한다.

해설 be동사 및 to부정사와 함께 쓰여 '~할 수 없다'라는 의미를 완성하는 (C) unable이 정답이다.

어휘 personnel 직원들, 인원 attend 참석하다 unpleasant 불쾌한

2 (C)

번역 그 콘퍼런스는 모든 관심 분야와 전문 분야에 맞는 다양한 옵션을 제공한다.

해설 빈칸이 속한 that절이 '모든 관심 분야와 전문 분야에 맞는'이라는 의미를 나타내야 자연스러우므로, '분야, 영역' 등을 뜻하는 (C) areas가 정답이다.

어휘 fit 맞다, 적합하다 interest 관심(사) expertise 전문 지식

3 (A)

번역 새 수영장 공사는 현재 진행 중으로 5월 1일까지 완료될 것으로 예상된다.

해설 5월 1일 완공 예정인 수영장 공사의 현황을 나타내는 명사가 빈칸에 들어가야 하므로, 전치사 in과 함께 '진행 중인'이라는 의미를 완성하는 (A) progress가 정답이다.

어휘 construction 건설, 공사 currently 현재 complete 완료하다 demand 수요

4 (B)

번역 대너 코퍼레이션은 3년 연속 채용 목표를 달성했다.

해설 명사 year를 수식하는 형용사 자리로, the third 및 year와 결합하여 '3년 연속'이라는 의미를 나타내는 형용사 (B) consecutive(연속적인)가 정답이다.

어휘 meet (기준·목표를) 맞추다, 충족시키다 recruitment 모집, 채용 following 그 다음의 approximate 대략의 absolute 절대적인

5 (A)

번역 크레송 공원의 나무 일부는 조경 전문가들이 의도적으로 심은 반면 대부분은 씨앗에서 자연적으로 성장했다.

해설 '조경 전문가(landscaping professionals)'에 의해 의도적으로 심어진'이라는 내용이 되어야 자연스러우므로, (A) intentionally(의도적으로)가 정답이다.

어휘 plant 심다 landscaping 조경 seed 씨앗 highly 매우 profoundly 완전히, 극심하게 indefinitely 무기한으로

6 (C)

번역 손더가드 난방기기는 매우 효율적이어서 주택 소유자들의 난방비를 줄여준다.

해설 난방비를 줄여주는 기기의 특성을 적절히 묘사한 형용사가 들어가야 하므로, '효율적인'이라는 의미의 (C) efficient가 정답이다.

어휘 result in 그 결과로 ~이 되다 heating cost 난방비 reasonable 합리적인, 가격이 적정한 preferred 우선의

7 (D)

번역 고객이 긴급 서비스를 선택하지 않는 한, 주문은 보통 처리되는 데 사흘이 걸린다.

해설 긴급 서비스가 아닌 일반 주문은 통상 사흘이 걸린다는 내용이 되어야 자연스러우므로, '보통, 통상적으로'라는 의미의 (D) typically가 정답이다.

어휘 opt for ~을 선택하다 expedited 긴급의 process 처리하다 substantially 상당히, 주로 perpetually 영구히 familiarly 스스럼없이, 친근하게

8 (A)

번역 피에르 던 씨는 델번 제조사의 사장으로 근무할 때, 회사를 변화시킨 여러 정책을 실시했다.

해설 목적어 several policies와 결합하여 '여러 정책을 실시하다'라는 의미를 나타내는 (A) instituted(실시했다)가 정답이다.

어휘 transform 바꾸다 relieve 덜어 주다 fabricate 조립하다, 제작하다

9 (A)

번역 WHJ 연구 목적은 윌밍데일 업무지구에 자전거 도로를 추가하는 것의 실행 가능성을 알아내는 것이다.

해설 자전거 도로 추가 계획과 관련하여 연구에서 알아내야 (determine) 하는 사항을 나타내는 명사가 들어가야 하므로, '실행 가능성'이라는 의미의 (A) feasibility가 정답이다.

어휘 purpose 의도, 목적 determine 알아내다, 판단하다 district 지구 dependency 의존, 종속 intensity 강도 accuracy 정확성

10 (B)

번역 윈 대학교 연구원들은 모조와르노 자연보호구역 내 식물 종을 기록하면서 몇 개월을 보냈다.

해설 명사구 the plant species를 목적어로 취하며 '종을 기록하면서'라는 의미를 완성하는 (B) documenting이 정답이다. 참고로, (A) experimenting과 (C) commenting은 자동사로 전치사 on과 함께 쓰인다.

어휘 species 종 nature preserve 자연보호구역 experiment 실험하다 document 기록하다 comment 견해를 밝히다, 논평하다 accomplish 성취하다, 완수하다

11 (A)

번역 파인빌 도서관은 대대적인 건물 개조 공사가 거의 마무리되었다고 발표했다.

해설 finished를 수식해 개조 공사의 마무리 정도를 나타낼 부사가 쓰여야 알맞으므로 '거의'를 뜻하는 (A) nearly가 정답이다.

어휘 extensive 대대적인, 광범위한 renovation 개조, 보수 vaguely 모호하게, 애매하게 previously 이전에, 과거에

12 (B)

번역 가구 운송 절차를 간소화함으로써, 우리는 비용을 낮추고 배송 시간을 절반으로 줄일 수 있다.

해설 목적어인 the furniture shipping process와 결합하여 '절차를 간소화함으로써'라는 의미를 나타내는 동명사 (B) streamlining이 정답이다

어휘 outpace ~을 능가하다 persevere 인내하다 forestall 미연에 방지하다

ETS ACTUAL TEST
본책 p.244

101 (A)	102 (C)	103 (D)	104 (D)	105 (A)
106 (D)	107 (D)	108 (B)	109 (C)	110 (C)
111 (C)	112 (B)	113 (B)	114 (D)	115 (C)
116 (B)	117 (B)	118 (B)	119 (C)	120 (B)
121 (D)	122 (B)	123 (B)	124 (B)	125 (D)
126 (A)	127 (C)	128 (C)	129 (D)	130 (D)
131 (C)	132 (B)	133 (A)	134 (A)	135 (C)
136 (C)	137 (B)	138 (D)	139 (D)	140 (A)
141 (B)	142 (D)	143 (A)	144 (C)	145 (D)
146 (D)				

101 (A)

번역 톨로 광고는 자사의 제품 추천을 맞춤화하기 위해 고객 데이터를 활용한다.

해설 명사 product recommendations 앞에 빈칸이 있으므로, 빈칸은 명사를 수식하는 소유격 인칭대명사가 들어갈 자리이다. 따라서 보기 중 유일한 소유격 인칭대명사인 (A) its가 정답이다.

어휘 customize 맞춤화하다, 고객에게 맞추다

102 (C)

번역 축제 후원사의 전체 목록은 3월 15일까지 제출되어야 한다.

해설 빈칸은 명사 list를 수식하는 형용사 자리이다. 따라서 '완전한, 전부의'라는 의미의 형용사 (C) complete가 정답이다. (B) completion은 list와 복합명사를 구성하지 않는다.

어휘 sponsor 후원업체

103 (D)

번역 예외 없이, 모든 직원은 회사 내에서 반드시 신분증을 착용해야 한다.

해설 빈칸은 복수 명사 employees를 수식하는 형용사 자리이다. 따라서 복수 명사를 수식할 수 있어야 하며, 문맥상 '예외 없이 모든 직원'이라는 의미가 되어야 적절하므로 (D) all이 정답이다.

어휘 exception 예외 badge 신분증, 명찰

104 (D)

번역 제품 설명서에 스베틀로 플로어 램프의 조립도가 제공된다.

해설 빈칸 앞에 있는 명사 product와 복합명사를 이루어 램프의 조립도가 제공되는 곳을 나타내기에 가장 적절한 것은 '제품 설명서'이므로 '설명서'를 의미하는 (D) manual이 정답이다.

어휘 diagram 도표, 도해 assemble 조립하다 receipt 영수증

105 (A)

번역 보스 씨가 재고 관리 절차에 대해 잘 알고 있기 때문에, 그가 오늘 워크숍을 이끌 것이다.

191

해설 be동사 is 뒤에 있는 빈칸은 주어를 보충 설명하는 보어가 들어갈 자리이며, 빈칸 뒤에는 전치사 with가 있으므로, 〈be동사+familiar+with〉 형태로 '~을 잘 알고 있다'는 의미를 나타내는 형용사 (A) familiar가 정답이다. 명사 (B) familiarity와 (D) familiarization은 주어 Mr. Vos와 동격이 아니므로 답이 되지 않는다.

어휘 inventory 재고 procedure 절차 familiarity 익숙함

106 (D)

번역 연구 보조원들은 모든 결과가 준비될 때까지 데이터 분석을 시작해서는 안 된다.

해설 빈칸 앞뒤에 각각 완전한 절이 있으므로 빈칸은 두 절을 연결해 줄 접속사 자리이다. 문맥상 '모든 결과가 준비될 때까지 시작하면 안 된다'라는 의미가 되는 것이 자연스러우므로, '~할 때까지'를 의미하는 접속사 (D) until이 정답이다. (B) except도 접속사로 쓰일 수 있지만 '~ 이외에는'이라는 의미로 문맥상 어울리지 않으며, 보통 that절을 동반한다.

어휘 assistant 보조원 analysis 분석 available 이용 가능한

107 (D)

번역 나카무라 씨가 요청한 소파는 다행히도 녹색 가죽으로 아직 구매 가능하다.

해설 빈칸 앞에는 be동사 is가, 빈칸 뒤에는 부사 still과 형용사 보어 available이 있으므로 빈칸에는 부사만 들어갈 수 있다. 따라서 '다행히'라는 의미의 부사 (D) luckily가 정답이다.

어휘 leather 가죽

108 (B)

번역 터너 씨는 이번 주 초에 최고 운영 책임자와 연락했다.

해설 빈칸 앞뒤에 전치사가 있으므로 빈칸은 명사 자리이다. 따라서 (B) contact가 정답이다. be in contact with를 '~와 연락하다'라는 의미의 덩어리 표현으로 암기해 두자.

어휘 chief operating officer 최고 운영 책임자

109 (C)

번역 퀸스 도넛은 페이스트리와 스콘부터 베이글과 크루아상에 이르기까지 다양한 종류의 아침 식사 제품들을 판매한다.

해설 빈칸은 '(범위가) A에서 B까지 이르다'라는 의미의 표현 'range from A to B'의 from 자리이다. 따라서 정답은 (C) from이다.

110 (C)

번역 셀리아 우는 다음 주 월요일에 뉴컴 씨의 주방에 있는 캐비닛을 페인트칠할 시간이 있다고 말했다.

해설 Monday를 수식하는 자리에 빈칸이 있으며, '다음 주 월요일'이라는 의미가 되는 것이 자연스러우므로 (C) next가 정답이다.

111 (C)

번역 선별된 소파들의 가격이 이번 주말에 한해 최대 50퍼센트까지 인하될 것입니다.

해설 주어가 가격(Prices)이고, 빈칸 뒤에 50퍼센트까지(by up to 50 percent)라는 말이 있으므로, '소파 가격이 인하될 것이다'라는 의미가 되어야 자연스럽다. 따라서 '(가격을) 낮추다, 인하하다'라는 뜻의 동사 reduce의 과거분사형 (C) reduced가 정답이다.

어휘 select 선택된 soften 부드럽게 하다 arrange 준비하다, 마련하다

112 (B)

번역 분실물을 발견하시면, 보안 데스크의 카린스 씨에게 전달해 주세요.

해설 빈칸은 If절의 주어 자리로, 사람을 나타내면서 단수 동사 finds와 수가 일치하는 대명사가 들어가야 한다. 따라서 '누구나'를 뜻하는 (B) anyone이 정답이다. (D) you는 동사 finds와 수 일치가 되지 않으므로 오답이다.

어휘 lost item 분실물 security 보안, 안전

113 (B)

번역 니르말라스 레스토랑에서 개인 파티를 예약해 생일이나 다른 특별한 이벤트를 축하하세요.

해설 문장에 동사가 없으므로 빈칸은 동사 자리이다. 주어 없이 동사원형으로 시작하는 명령문임을 알 수 있다. 따라서 동사원형 (B) Celebrate가 정답이다.

어휘 private 사적인, 개인의

114 (D)

번역 멘도자 씨는 회사에서 근무한 지 2년이 채 되지 않았는데도 불구하고 인턴들을 교육해 달라는 요청을 자주 받는다.

해설 빈칸은 be동사 is와 과거분사 asked 사이에서 수동태 동사를 수식하는 부사 자리이다. 따라서 '자주'라는 의미의 부사 (D) frequently가 정답이다.

어휘 frequent 잦은, 빈번한 frequency 빈도

115 (C)

번역 시내버스에 두고 내린 개인 물품은 교통부 본청에 30일 동안 보관될 것이다.

해설 빈칸은 주어 items를 수식하는 형용사 자리이다. 형용사 (A)와 (C) 중에서 '개인적인'이라는 뜻을 가진 (C) Personal이 정답이다. (A) Personable은 '매력적인'이라는 의미이다.

어휘 Transportation Department 교통부

116 (B)

번역 회의를 위한 케이터링 요청은 이제 음식 서비스 부서에 제출되기 전에 매니저의 승인을 받아야 한다.

해설 빈칸은 동명사구를 이끄는 전치사 자리로, 문맥상 '제출 전에 승인을 받아야 한다'는 내용이 되는 것이 자연스러우므로 '~ 전에'라는 의미의 전치사 (B) before가 정답이다.

어휘 catering 음식 공급 approve 승인하다

117 (B)

번역 주식 시장의 침체에도 불구하고, 해운업계의 분석가들은 다음 수익 예측에 대해 자신 있게 이야기한다.

해설 동사 speak을 수식하는 부사 어휘 문제로, 문맥상 주식 시장 침체와 대조적인 방식으로 이야기한다는 내용이 되어야 하므로 '자신감 있게'라는 의미의 부사 (B) confidently가 정답이다.

어휘 stock market 주식 시장 downturn (경기) 침체
regarding ~에 관하여 earnings 수익 forecast 예측
worriedly 걱정스럽게

118 (B)

번역 파머 제이크의 최고급 선물 상자는 달콤하고 짭짤한 스낵들의 맛있는 조합이 특징이다.

해설 빈칸 앞에 관사 a와 형용사 delicious가 있으므로 빈칸은 단수 명사가 들어갈 자리이다. 따라서 (B) combination이 정답이다.

어휘 premier 최고(급)의 feature 특징을 이루다
savory 맛있는, 짭짤한

119 (C)

번역 플렉사 인더스트리스는 프라사드 씨가 도시 교통 분야에서의 업적으로 루드비히 상을 수상했다고 최근 발표했다.

해설 동사 announced를 수식하는 부사 어휘 문제이다. '최근에 발표했다'라는 의미가 가장 자연스러우므로 '최근에'라는 뜻의 (C) recently가 정답이다.

어휘 evenly 균등하게 thoroughly 철저히 mostly 대부분

120 (B)

번역 교육 영상에 대해 질문이 있으면 회사의 온보딩 담당자에게 문의하세요.

해설 빈칸 앞에 동사 Contact와 목적어 the company's onboarding coordinator가 있고, 빈칸 뒤에는 명사 any questions가 있으므로, 빈칸에는 any questions를 목적어로 취하는 전치사가 들어가야 한다. 따라서 보기 중 유일한 전치사 (B) with가 정답이다.

어휘 onboarding 신입 적응 프로그램 coordinator 진행자, 책임자

121 (D)

번역 레스토랑 내부 테이블은 한 시간 정도 대기해야 하지만, 야외 테라스에 있는 자리는 곧 이용할 수 있을 것입니다.

해설 빈칸이 있는 절이 주어 seating, 동사 will be, 보어 available가 있는 완전한 구조이므로, 빈칸은 부사 자리이다. (A) short도 '짧게; 간략히'라는 의미의 부사로 쓰일 수 있지만, 문맥상 '곧 이용할 수 있을 것이다'라는 의미가 자연스러우므로 '곧'이라는 의미의 (D) shortly가 정답이다.

122 (D)

번역 지속적인 성장을 보장하기 위해 맥기 냉장 주식회사는 고객 서비스 전용 전화선을 추가했다.

해설 소유격 대명사와 명사 사이에 빈칸이 있으므로 빈칸은 명사 growth를 수식하는 형용사가 들어갈 수 있는 자리이다. 따라서 '지속적인'이라는 뜻의 형용사 (D) continued가 정답이다. 명사 (B) continuation은 growth와 복합명사를 구성하지 않는다.

어휘 ensure 보장하다 dedicated 전용의

123 (B)

번역 배리슨 공장 근로자들을 위한 새로운 계약에는 고용 2년 후 6퍼센트의 임금 인상을 보장하는 내용이 포함되어 있다.

해설 문장에 동사가 없으므로 빈칸은 동사 자리이다. 따라서 '~을 포함하다'라는 의미의 동사 (B) includes가 정답이다.

어휘 guarantee 보장 pay raise 급여 인상 employment 고용 inclusion 포함(된 것) inclusive 포함된; 포괄적인 inclusively 포괄적으로

124 (B)

번역 살롱 제노비아는 헤어컷, 염색, 매니큐어를 포함해 다양한 서비스를 제공한다.

해설 형용사 어휘 문제로, 문맥상 including 뒤에 나열된 서비스들을 포함한 '다양한 서비스를 제공한다'라는 의미가 되어야 적절하므로 '다양한'이라는 뜻의 (B) various가 정답이다.

어휘 approximate 대략의 occasional 가끔의

125 (D)

번역 제이미슨 식료품점의 채용 면접은 화상 채팅 또는 대면 방식으로 진행될 수 있다.

해설 알맞은 동사의 과거분사를 고르는 어휘 문제이다. 빈칸은 동사 자리인데, 채용 면접이 주어이고, 빈칸 뒤에는 면접이 진행되는 방식이 있으므로, '면접이 ~ 방식으로 진행될 것이다'라는 의미가 되는 것이 자연스럽다. 따라서 빈칸은 '실시하다, 진행하다'라는 의미의 동사 conduct의 과거분사형 (D) conducted가 정답이다.

어휘 in person 직접 transfer 이동하다, 옮기다

126 (A)

번역 만약 요약 페이지에 누락된 다른 사항이 있으면 연구 관리자에게 알려주세요.

해설 주어 anything과 동사 is missing 사이에 빈칸이 있으므로 빈칸은 anything을 수식하는 자리이다. 따라서 anything과 함께 쓰여 '그 밖에 다른 것'을 나타낼 수 있는 (A) else가 정답이다. (B)와 (C)는 전치사이므로 오답이고, 부사 (D) namely는 '즉, 다시 말해'라는 뜻으로 문맥에 적합하지 않다.

어휘 summary 요약

127 (D)

번역 존 야쿠트뿐 아니라, IES 바이오테크의 다른 두 명의 과학자도 세미나에서 연구 결과를 발표할 것이다.

해설 빈칸 뒤에 고유명사가 있고, 그 뒤로 완전한 절이 있으므로 빈칸은 명사를 목적어로 취하는 전치사 자리이다. 문맥상 '존 야쿠트뿐 아니라 두 명의 과학자가 발표할 것이다'라는 의미가 자연스러우므로 '~에 더하여, ~뿐만 아니라'라는 뜻의 전치사 (D) In addition to가 정답이다.

어휘 except for ~을 제외하고 as far as ~하는 한

128 (C)

번역 그 신문사는 모든 오류를 제시간에 수정하기 위해 노력하며, 잘못된 정보를 절대 의도적으로 게재하지 않는다.

해설 '주어(The newspaper)+동사(would never publish)+목적어(erroneous information)'를 갖춘 완전한 구조의 문장 끝에 빈칸이 있으므로 빈칸은 부사 자리이다. 따라서 '고의로'라는 뜻의 부사 (C) knowingly가 정답이다.

어휘 strive 분투하다, 노력하다   in a timely manner 제시간에   erroneous 잘못된

129 (D)

번역 웡 박사의 현장 조사 방법은 한때 지나치게 까다롭다고 여겨졌지만, 지금은 고생물학 발굴에서 일반적으로 인정되는 관행이다.

해설 빈칸 앞에는 be동사 are와 부사 now가 있고, 빈칸 뒤에는 명사 practice가 있으므로, 빈칸에는 명사 practice를 수식하는 형용사가 들어갈 수 있다. 따라서 '일반적으로 인정된'이라는 의미의 형용사 (D) accepted가 정답이다. 명사 (B) acceptance는 practice와 복합명사를 구성하지 않는다.

어휘 fieldwork 현장 조사   demanding 요구가 지나친   paleontology 고생물학   dig 발굴   acceptance 수용, 수락   acceptably 받아들일 수 있게

130 (C)

번역 이전 리알로 컴퓨터 모델의 판매는 저조한 반면, 올해 출시된 LC358 모델은 호평을 얻고 있다.

해설 빈칸 뒤에 완전한 절이 두 개 있으므로 빈칸에는 접속사가 와야 한다. 또한 이전 모델의 판매 부진과 올해 모델의 호평이라는 대조적인 내용이 이어지고 있으므로, '반면에, 그러나'라는 의미의 부사절 접속사 (C) Whereas가 정답이다.

어휘 weak 약한, 저조한   consequently 결과적으로

[131-134] 구인 공고

프렌들리 시티 파킹에서 주차 안내원 역할을 할 자격을 갖춘 지원자를 찾고 있습니다. 구직 지원자는 반드시 **131 공손하고** 세심해야 합니다. 담당 직무에는 영수증 배부 및 수거, 주차 자리 배정, 그리고 시설물 관찰이 포함됩니다. 지원자는 기본적인 수학 능력을 갖춘 중등 교육을 받은 사람이어야 합니다. **132 안내원은 고객의 거스름돈을 정확히 계산해야 합니다.** 고객 서비스 경험과 금전 등록기 작동 경험이 있으신 분을 선호합니다. 관심이 **133 있으시**면, 늦어도 7월 18일까지 hr@friendlycityparking.com으로 이메일을 보내 주시기 바랍니다. 저희는 경쟁력 있는 급여와 에너지 넘치는 환경, 그리고 탄력적인 일정을 **134 제공합니다.**

어휘 qualified 자격 있는   applicant 지원자, 신청자   attendant 안내원, 수행원   candidate 지원자, 후보자   attentive 세심한, 배려하는   responsibility 담당 직무, 책임(감)   include 포함하다   distribute 배부하다   collect 수거하다, 가져오다   receipt 영수증   assign 배정하다, 할당하다   spot 자리, 장소   monitor 관찰하다, 감시하다   secondary school 중등 학교   operate 작동하다, 운영하다   cash register 금전 등록기   preferred 선호되는   competitive 경쟁력 있는   flexible 탄력적인, 유연한

131 (C)

해설 빈칸은 바로 뒤에 and로 연결된 형용사 attentive와 함께 be동사 뒤에서 보어 역할을 할 또 다른 형용사가 쓰여야 하는 자리이므로 (C) courteous(공손한)가 정답이다.

어휘 courteously 공손하게   courtesy 공손함, 정중함

132 (B)

번역 (A) 직원들은 매일 학생들과 긴밀히 협력합니다.
(B) 안내원은 고객의 거스름돈을 정확히 계산해야 합니다.
(C) 주말이 보통 가장 바쁩니다.
(D) 그 시설은 하루 24시간 문을 엽니다.

해설 빈칸 앞에 지원자가 반드시 기본적인 수학 능력(basic math skills)을 갖추어야 한다고 언급하고 있으므로 그 이유에 해당하는 (B)가 정답이다.

어휘 calculate 계산하다   accurate 정확한   change 거스름돈, 잔돈

133 (A)

해설 빈칸 뒤에 분사 interested가 있고, 그 뒤에 콤마(,)와 완전한 절이 이어지고 있으므로 '빈칸+interested'는 수식어가 되어야 한다. 또한, '관심이 있다면'의 의미로 조건을 나타내야 자연스러우므로, 분사와 결합 가능한 접속사로서 '~한다면'을 뜻하는 (A) If가 정답이다. If는 necessary나 possible, needed 같은 형용사나 분사와 결합한 구조로 사용할 수 있다.

134 (A)

해설 빈칸이 속한 문장은 업체가 현재 제공하는 혜택을 의미해야 알맞으며, 주어가 복수이므로 복수 주어와 수 일치가 되는 (A) offer가 정답이다.

[135-138] 이메일

수신: 캐서린 스펠츠 〈c.speltz@solariamail.net〉
발신: 이선 츠에이 〈e.tsuei@tsueilearningcentre.org〉
날짜: 4월 3일
제목: 다음 단계
첨부: 링크

스펠츠 씨께,

저희 츠에이 교육 센터에서 교육을 계속해 주셔서 감사합니다. 저희 기록에 따르면 귀하께서 대출과 주택 담보 대출에 관한 학업 과정 중에서 첫 두 과정을 **135 이수하신** 것으로 나옵니다. 세 번째 과정은 다음 주 월요일 오전 9시에 시작될 것입니다. 이 과정은 4개의 강좌로 구성되어 있으며, **136 귀하께서** 이 과정의 전체 학점을 취득하시려면 반드시 모두 마치셔야 합니다. **137 이 강좌들은 월요일부터 목요일까지 오전에 열릴 것입니다.**

곧 열릴 강좌들에 대한 링크가 첨부되어 있습니다. 접속 권한을 받기 위해 강좌 시작 시간인 오전 9시 **138 전에** 로그인하시기 바랍니다.

지속적인 성공을 기원합니다!

이선 츠에이, 츠에이 교육 센터 소유주

어휘 module 교과목 단위 loan 대출 mortgage 주택 담보 대출 contain 구성되다, 포함하다 earn 얻다, 획득하다 credit 학점 upcoming 다가오는, 곧 있을 attach 첨부하다 grant 승인하다 access 접속, 이용

135 (C)

해설 뒤이어 세 번째 과정이 곧 시작됨을 알리면서 관련 정보를 제공하고 있으므로 첫 두 과정을 마쳤다는 의미가 되어야 자연스럽다. 따라서 (C) completed(이수하다, 완료하다)가 정답이다.

어휘 misplace 분실하다 supervise 감독하다

136 (C)

해설 학점을 취득하기 위해 모든 강좌를 마쳐야 할 사람은 이 이메일을 받는 상대방이므로 (C) you가 정답이다.

137 (B)

번역 (A) 이 프로그램은 성인들에게 교육 기회를 제공합니다.
(B) 이 강좌들은 월요일부터 목요일까지 오전에 열릴 것입니다.
(C) 다른 과정들은 올해 초에 제공되었습니다.
(D) 이는 귀하께서 초이 교육 센터에서 수강하신 세 번째 학업 과정입니다.

해설 앞서 세 번째 과정이 다음 주 월요일에 시작되고 이는 4개의 강좌로 구성되어 있다는 내용이 제시되어 있다. 따라서 강좌 진행과 관련된 내용을 알리는 문장이 빈칸에 들어가야 흐름이 자연스러우므로, 강좌가 열리는 요일을 알리는 (B)가 정답이다.

어휘 opportunity 기회

138 (D)

해설 빈칸 뒤에 시각을 나타내는 표현이 목적어로 있으며, 접속 권한을 받기 위해 강좌 시작 시간 전에 로그인하라고 당부하는 의미를 나타내야 자연스러우므로, '~ 전에'를 뜻하는 전치사 (D) before가 정답이다.

[139-142] 기사

유명 건축가 니콜 바르보사가 멕시코 시티를 위해 설계한 고층 아파트 복합 건물인 카타니아의 이미지를 공개했다. 200미터 높이의 이 타워는 완공되면, 상징적인 박물관들로 더 잘 알려진 바르보사 씨에 의해 **139 설계된** 가장 높은 건물이 될 것이다. 바르보사 씨와 다른 **140 프로젝트들**을 함께 작업해 온 다닐로 코스타가 이 건물의 인테리어 설계를 감독할 것이다.

일부 공간은 사무실로 사용될 것이지만, 이 타워는 **141 주로** 주거용이 될 것이며, 입주가 시작되자마자 거의 바로 모두 사용될 것으로 예상된다. **142 잠재 세입자들이 이미 이 세대들에 관해 계속 문의하고 있다.**

어휘 renowned 유명한 architect 건축가 release 공개하다, 발매하다 high-rise 고층의 complex 복합 건물, 건물 단지 be known for ~로 알려져 있다 iconic 상징적인 oversee 총괄하다, 감독하다 reserve 지정하다, 예약하다 residential 주거의, 거주지의 occupancy 사용, 점유 immediately 즉시

139 (D)

해설 빈칸 뒤에 언급된 Ms. Barbosa는 첫 문장에 유명 건축가로 소개되어 있으며, '바르보사 씨에 의해 설계된 가장 높은 건물'을 의미해야 자연스러우므로, (D) designed(설계된)가 정답이다.

어휘 map 지도; 지도를 만들다

140 (A)

해설 빈칸에는 형용사 other의 수식을 받으면서 전치사 on의 목적어로 쓰일 명사가 들어가야 하며, 바르보사와 함께 작업해 온 대상이 들어가야 한다. 따라서 '프로젝트'를 의미하는 (A) projects가 정답이다.

어휘 project 프로젝트; 예상하다

141 (B)

해설 일부 공간이 사무실로 사용될 것이라고 언급한 Though절과 대비되어 '주로 주거용이 될 것이다'를 의미해야 자연스러우므로, (B) primarily(주로)가 정답이다.

어휘 hastily 서둘러, 경솔하게 correctly 정확하게, 제대로 eagerly 간절히, 열렬히

142 (D)

번역 (A) 건축 작업자들이 이 건축가의 추가 지침을 따라 행동했다.
(B) 멕시코 시티는 독특한 건축 양식으로 널리 알려져 있다.
(C) 바르보사 씨의 사무실은 이 건물 맨 위층에 위치해 있다.
(D) 잠재 세입자들이 이미 이 세대들에 관해 계속 문의하고 있다.

해설 앞 문장에 건물 입주가 시작되자마자 모두 사용될 것으로 예상된다는 내용이 쓰여 있으므로 입주와 관련된 문장이 빈칸에 쓰여야 문맥이 자연스럽다. 따라서 잠재 세입자들의 문의가 계속 이어지고 있다는 의미의 (D)가 정답이다.

어휘 act on ~에 따라 행동하다 supplemental 보충의, 추가의 instructions 지시, 설명(서) distinctive 독특한 architecture 건축 양식 prospective 잠재적인, 장래의 renter 세입자 inquire 문의하다 unit (아파트 등의) 세대, (상가 등의) 점포

[143-146] 이메일

수신: 전 직원 〈staff@okhosdesign.com〉
발신: 루단 문 〈rmoon@okhosdesign.com〉
날짜: 10월 12일
제목: 인사 관련 소식

직원 여러분께,

지난달에 발표된 대로, 지난 16년 동안 우리의 아트 디렉터였던 라파엘 갈리 씨께서 곧 유럽으로 가실 예정입니다. **143 그곳에 도착하시는 대로**, 독일의 한 마케팅 회사에서 전무로 경력의 다음 장을 시작하실 것입니다. 이제, 이분의 후임자를 철저하게 물색한 끝에, 우리 회사의 사만다 파나이 씨께서 우리의 다음 아트 디렉터가 **144 되신다**는 사실을 전해 드리게 되어 대단히 기쁩니다. **145 우리는 이**

인사 이동이 순조로울 것으로 확신합니다. 파나이 씨께서는 오코스에서 8년간 근무하셨으며, 그 시간 동안 갈리 씨와 긴밀히 작업해 오셨습니다. 파나이 씨께서는 다음 주에 공식적으로 새로운 직책을 맡기 시작할 것이고, 11월에 갈리 씨께서 떠나실 때까지 지속적으로 상의할 것입니다. 파나이 씨의 사무실에 들러 **146 축하해** 주시기 바랍니다.

루단 문
상무, 오코스 디자인 어소시에이츠

> 어휘 staffing 직원 구성, 직원 채용 relocate 이사하다, 이전하다 executive director 전무 이사 thorough 철저한 replacement 후임(자), 대체(품) be thrilled to ~해서 대단히 기쁘다 closely 긴밀히, 면밀히 officially 공식적으로 step into ~을 시작하다 consult with ~와 상의하다

143 (A)

해설 빈칸 앞에는 곧 유럽으로 간다는 말이, 빈칸 뒤에는 독일의 한 마케팅 회사에서 새로운 일을 시작한다는 말이 쓰여 있다. 따라서 앞 문장의 Europe을 there로 지칭하며 '(일단) 그곳에 도착하는 대로'라는 의미로 유럽으로 이주한 후에 있을 일을 언급하는 흐름을 나타낼 수 있는 (A) Once there가 정답이다.

어휘 instead 대신 nevertheless 그럼에도 불구하고
for example 예를 들어

144 (C)

해설 빈칸 뒤에 주어와 동사를 포함한 완전한 절이 쓰여 있어 이 절을 이끌 접속사가 필요하며, 빈칸 앞에 쓰인 동사 tell은 〈tell+A+that절〉의 구조로 'A에게 ~라고 말하다'라는 의미를 나타내므로, 명사절 접속사 (C) that이 정답이다.

145 (D)

번역 (A) 그녀의 기존 직책을 충원하기 위한 조사가 시작되었습니다.
(B) 오코스는 업계에서 가장 창의적인 팀 중 하나를 보유하고 있습니다.
(C) 그동안, 갈리 씨는 독일어를 연습하고 있습니다.
(D) 우리는 이 인사 이동이 순조로울 것으로 확신합니다.

해설 빈칸에 앞서 기존의 디렉터였던 갈리 씨가 유럽으로 가고, 사만다 파나이 씨가 다음 아트 디렉터가 된다는 내용이 쓰여 있다. 따라서 그러한 변화를 The transition으로 표현해 과정이 순조로울 것으로 확신한다는 의미를 나타내는 (D)가 정답이다.

어휘 fill 충원하다, 채우다 creative 창의적인 meanwhile 그동안, 한편 practice 연습하다, 실행하다 confident 확신하는 transition 전환, 변화 smooth 순조로운, 매끈한

146 (D)

해설 앞선 문장에서 파나이 씨가 신임 아트 디렉터로 선임된 사실을 알리고 있어 파나이 씨의 사무실에 들르는 목적과 관련해 '그녀를 축하하다'라는 의미를 나타내야 자연스러우므로, (D) congratulate(축하하다)이 정답이다.

PART 7
READING COMPREHENSION

UNIT 17 편지 / 이메일

지문 구성과 독해 전략 ········· 본책 p.254

수신: 레이첼 모스 〈rmorse@mailnet.com〉
발신: 프랭크스 오토 리페어 〈cs@franksautorepair.com〉
제목: 차량 서비스
날짜: 7월 1일

모스 씨께,

저희 기록에 의하면 귀하의 차량이 점검을 받을 시기가 되었습니다. 앞으로 30일 이내에 예약하셔서 다음 점검 항목들을 20퍼센트 할인받으세요.

- 엔진
- 타이어
- 오일 양
- 배터리

다음의 링크를 클릭해 쿠폰을 출력하시고, 예약에 맞춰 오셔서 비용 지불 시 함께 제출해 주십시오.
www.franksautorepair.com/inspectioncoupon
예약을 하시려면 (206) 555-0117로 전화하세요.
곧 뵙기를 바랍니다!

고객 서비스 부서
프랭크스 오토 리페어

> 어휘 due ~하기로 되어 있는, 예정된 inspection 점검 fluid 유동체, (자동차의) 오일 submit 제출하다

Q1 이메일의 목적은?
(A) 환불되었음을 확인해 주기 위해
(B) 고객에게 지불을 요청하기 위해
(C) 고객에게 예약할 것을 상기시키기 위해
(D) 예약 날짜가 잡혔음을 확인해 주기 위해

어휘 issue a refund 환불해 주다, 환불금을 지불하다 remind 상기시키다 confirm 확인하다, 확정하다

Q2 모스 씨에 대해 명시된 것은?
(A) 최근에 새로 차를 구입했다.
(B) 차가 현재 수리 중이다.
(C) 운전면허증이 만료되었다.
(D) 할인을 받을 자격이 있다.

어휘 recently 최근에 purchase 구입하다 currently 현재 expired 만료된 eligible 자격이 있는

ETS 유형연습
본책 p.255

1 (B) **2** (B) **3** (A) **4** (B)

[1-2] 이메일

동료 여러분께,

레야톤 피트니스 센터스(RFC)가 우리 기업 제휴 할인 프로그램에 추가되었음을 알리게 되어서 기쁩니다. ¹4월 1일부터 RFC 연간 회원권을 구입하는 모든 직원은 정가에서 15퍼센트를 할인받게 됩니다.
회원 양식은 우리 회사 웹사이트의 기업 제휴 페이지에서 다운로드할 수 있으며 RFC 지점에 직접 제출해야 합니다. ²가장 가까운 RFC 시설은 스틸스 가에 있는데 우리 본사에서 불과 2km 떨어져 있으며 두 번째 지점은 윈슬로우 웨스트 가 42번지에 있습니다.
이번 기회를 이용하기 바랍니다.

질 켄덜
인사과 직원

어휘 colleague 동료 corporate 기업의 regular price 정가 drop 갖다 주다, 내리다 headquarters 본사 take advantage of ~을 이용하다

1 이메일을 쓴 이유는?
(A) 새로운 헬스클럽의 개업을 알리기 위해
(B) 직원 혜택을 설명하기 위해

해설 주제/목적
첫 번째 단락에서 4월 1일부터 RFC 연간 회원권을 구입하는 모든 직원은 정가에서 15퍼센트를 할인받게 된다(Beginning on April 1, all staff members ~ will receive 15 percent off the regular price)며 직원들을 위한 혜택을 안내하고 있으므로 (B)가 정답이다.

2 레야톤 피트니스에 대해 언급된 것은?
(A) 비용이 최근에 인상되었다.
(B) 지점이 한 군데 이상이다.

해설 Not/True
두 번째 단락에서 가장 가까운 RFC 시설은 스틸스 가에 있고, 두 번째 지점은 윈슬로우 웨스트 가 42번지에 있다(The closest RFC facility is located on Stiles Street ~ a second location is at 42 West Avenue in Winslow)고 했으므로 (B)가 정답이다.

[3-4] 편지

코빈 씨께,

저희 기록을 보니 〈투데이즈 트렌드〉 ³6월호를 끝으로 귀하의 구독이 종료될 예정인데 아직 갱신을 안 하셨습니다. 귀하의 갱신을 장려하고자 〈투데이즈 트렌드〉를 할인된 가격으로 제공해 드리고자 합니다. ⁴귀하께서는 현재 호당 3달러를 지불하고 있습니다. 앞으로 6개월간 호당 2.25달러에 드리겠습니다. 즉 구독을 갱신하시면 7월부터 12월까지 총 4.5달러를 할인받으시는 겁니다.
월요일부터 금요일은 오전 9시부터 오후 5시 사이에, 토요일은 오전 10시부터 오후 3시 사이에 사무실 전화 888-555-3214번으로 연락해 주십시오. 일요일은 휴무입니다. 그럼 앞으로도 계속 서비스를 제공해 드릴 수 있기를 고대하겠습니다.

마샤 클레민스
영업이사

어휘 issue (간행물의) 호 renew 갱신하다 subscription 구독(료) reduced 할인된 save 구하다, 절약하다

3 코빈 씨의 현재 구독은 언제 끝날 것인가?
(A) 6월   (B) 12월

해설 세부 사항
첫 번째 단락에서 6월호를 끝으로 코빈 씨의 구독이 종료될 예정(the June issue of Today's Trends will be your last)이라고 했으므로 (A)가 정답이다.

4 코빈 씨가 현재 지불하는 월 구독료는?
(A) 2.25달러   (B) 3달러

해설 세부 사항
첫 번째 단락에서 코빈 씨가 현재 호당 3달러를 지불한다(You are currently paying $3.00 per issue)고 했으므로 (B)가 정답이다.

Paraphrasing 지문의 per issue → 질문의 per month

ETS 실전문제   본책 p.256

1 (C)	2 (A)	3 (C)	4 (D)	5 (A)	6 (B)
7 (D)	8 (A)	9 (B)	10 (D)	11 (A)	12 (A)
13 (D)	14 (A)	15 (C)	16 (B)	17 (C)	18 (C)
19 (B)	20 (A)	21 (D)			

[1-2] 이메일

²수신: 마에데 나세리
발신: 프란체스카 라미레즈
날짜: 6월 18일
제목: 다가오는 콘퍼런스

안녕하세요, 마에데 씨.

²지금쯤 서울 사무소에 적응하셨기를 바랍니다. 이곳 시드니에 있는 저희는 당신이 그립지만, 다음 달에 싱가포르에서 열리는 젊은 엔지니어들을 위한 콘퍼런스(7월 17일-20일)에서 뵐 수 있다면 기쁠 겁니다. ¹마지막 날에 반나절 동안 자유 시간이 있을 것이라고 일정표에 나와 있는데 다른 계획이 없으시면 그 시간에 우리가 시내에서 뭔가 하면 재미있을 거라고 생각했습니다.

아마 기억하시겠지만, 도쿄에서 열린 작년 콘퍼런스에서, 우리는 오후 자유 시간을 미술 전시회와 함께 보냈습니다. 올해는 마리나 베이의 자전거 투어나 주 차이나 구역에서 음식 투어, 또는 싱가포르의 역사적인 건축 양식 투어를 할 수도 있습니다. 저는 음식 투어에 가장 관심이 많지만, 이 활동들 중 어느 것이든 기꺼이 참여할 것입니다. 시간 있으실 때, 7월 20일에 함께 시간을 보내기를 원하시는지, 그리고 어느 활동을 원하시는지 제게 알려 주시기 바랍니다.

곧 이야기 나눌 수 있기를 바라며,

프란체스카 라미레즈, 엔지니어 테크니션
라크로쉐 토목 공학 그룹

어휘 upcoming 다가오는, 곧 있을 indicate 나타내다, 가리키다 recall 기억해 내다, 상기하다 exhibit 전시(회) district 구역, 지구 historical 역사적인 architecture 건축 양식, 건축학 participate in ~에 참여하다

1 이메일의 목적은?
(A) 투어 예약을 확인해 주려고
(B) 콘퍼런스 시간을 추천하려고
(C) 동료와 계획을 세우려고
(D) 도시에 관한 정보를 요청하려고

해설 **주제/목적**
첫 번째 단락에서 콘퍼런스 일정표에 마지막 날에 자유 시간이 있음을 언급하면서 함께 시내에서 뭔가 하면 재미있을 거라고 생각했다(The schedule indicates that there will be a free half-day on the last day, and I thought it would be fun for us to do something in town ~)고 밝힌 뒤로 구체적으로 무엇을 할지 이야기하고 있으므로 (C)가 정답이다.

어휘 confirm 확인해 주다 session (특정 활동을 위한) 시간

2 이메일에서 나세리 씨에 대해 언급하는 것은?
(A) 전에 시드니에서 근무했었다.
(B) 자전거 투어보다 음식 투어를 선호한다.
(C) 처음으로 콘퍼런스에 참석할 예정이다.
(D) 7월 17일에 서울에 갈 예정이다.

해설 **Not/True**
나세리 씨는 이메일의 수신자인데, 첫 번째 단락에 나세리 씨가 서울 사무소에 적응했기를 바란다는 말과 함께, 시드니에 근무하는 사람들이 나세리 씨를 그리워하고 있다(We miss you here in Sydney ~)는 말이 있으므로, 나세리 씨가 시드니에서 근무했었는데 서울로 근무지를 옮겼음을 알 수 있다. 따라서 (A)가 정답이다.

[3-4] 편지

〈월간 포레스트 리빙〉

편집자께,

최근에 실린 '잊힌 종'이라는 기사에서, 필자는 난디미 전나무가 북미에서 자라지 않는다고 언급합니다. 하지만 **3**미국의 버지니아 헤리티지 식물원과 캐나다 브리티시컬럼비아주 이스트 샌즈 보호 구역에 이 특이한 나무의 표본이 있다는 것을 독자들에게 알려 드리고 싶습니다. 저는 세계에서 가장 희귀한 나무들을 보호하는 것을 목표로 하는 연구 활동에 지난 20년을 바쳐 왔는데, 난디미 전나무는 그중 하나이죠. **4**제가 언급한 두 기관 모두 이러한 노력을 함께하는 협력 단체 역할을 하고 있습니다. 기사에서 명확하게 야생에서 자라는 나무를 언급하고 있다는 건 알지만, 그래도 독자들이 알 수 있도록 이 나무가 의도적으로 재배되고 있는 장소를 언급하는 것이 중요하다고 생각합니다.

산제이 리거

어휘 contain 포함하다 specimens 표본 unusual 특이한, 이례적인 dedicate A to B (시간, 노력 등) A를 B에 바치다 initiative 활동, 계획 aimed at ~을 목표로 하는 safeguard 보호하다 rare 희귀한 organization 기관, 단체 serve as ~의 역할을 하다 refer to ~을 언급하다, 가리키다 explicitly 명확하게 intentionally 의도적으로 cultivate 재배하다

3 편지의 목적은?
(A) 독자들에게 특정 나무 종을 심도록 장려하려고
(B) 어떤 나무 종이 멸종 위기에 처한 이유를 설명하려고
(C) 어떤 나무 종이 어디에서 발견될 수 있는지에 관한 정보를 공유하려고
(D) 야생에서 나무를 식별하는 것에 대한 조언을 제공하려고

해설 **주제/목적**
초반부에 두 곳을 언급하면서, 그곳들에 이 특이한 나무의 표본이 있다는 것을 독자들에게 알려 주고 싶다(I want to bring to your readers' attention that ~ both contain specimens of this unusual tree)고 했으므로 (C)가 정답이다.

어휘 plant 심다 particular 특정한 species (동식물의) 종 endangered 멸종 위기에 처한 identify 식별하다, 확인하다

Paraphrasing 지문의 ~ contain specimens of this unusual tree → 정답의 where a species of tree can be found

4 리거 씨가 자신에 대해 언급하는 것은?
(A) 브리티시컬럼비아주에 살고 있다.
(B) 특이한 발견을 했다.
(C) 연구 초점을 바꿨다.
(D) 환경 보호 단체와 일하고 있다.

해설 **Not/True**
후반부에서 자신이 언급한 두 기관 모두 희귀 나무를 보호하기 위한 노력을 함께하는 협력 단체 역할을 하고 있다(~ both of the organizations I have mentioned serve as partners in these efforts)고 언급했으므로 (D)가 정답이다.

어휘 discovery 발견(물) conservation 보호, 보존

[5-6] 이메일

수신: 전 직원
발신: 주드 그로딘
날짜: 5월 30일
제목: 주드 그로딘의 메시지

직원 여러분,

5윌트라우트 하드웨어가 올가을에 체인점 기회를 제공할 것임을 시사하는 몇몇 최근 보도에 대해 말씀드리고 싶습니다. 우리는 실제로 체인점 운영에 대한 가능성을 고려하고 있습니다. 이러한 사업 결정을 내리는 데에는 분명 혜택이 있는데, 그 주된 한 가지는 **6**체인점 운영이 우리에게 훨씬 더 짧은 기간에 더 적은 운영비로

더 폭넓은 고객층을 끌어들일 수 있게 해 준다는 점입니다. 이러한 방식으로 우리의 영역을 확장한다는 아이디어는 매력적입니다.

그렇기는 하지만, 경영진은 현재 사업 모델을 그대로 유지하기로 결정했습니다. 일상적인 운영에 있어 일관성을 유지하고 통제된 방식으로 브랜드 정체성을 계속해서 형성해 나가는 것이 중요합니다. 이는 새로운 월트라우트 하드웨어 지점이 외부 투자자가 아닌 우리 회사에 의해 전적으로 소유되고 관리될 것임을 의미합니다.

어떤 질문이나 우려 사항이든 있으시면 언제든지 제게 연락 주십시오.

주드 그로딘
CEO, 월트라우트 하드웨어

어휘 address (문제 등을) 다루다 franchise 체인점; 체인점 운영권을 주다 opportunity 기회 indeed 실제로, 사실 consider 고려하다 incentive 혜택, 보상(책) attract 끌어들이다 extensive 폭넓은 customer base 고객층 reach 영역, 범위 appealing 매력적인 that being said 그렇기는 하지만, 말이 나온 김에 consistency 일관성 day-to-day 일상적인 identity 정체성 controlled 통제된 wholly 전적으로, 완전히 own 소유하다 investor 투자자

5 이메일의 목적은?
(A) 잘못된 정보를 바로잡으려고
(B) 회사 지도자들을 칭찬하려고
(C) 잘못된 투자 결정에 대한 이유를 설명하려고
(D) 직원회의에서 논의된 주제를 요약하려고

해설 주제/목적
첫 번째 단락에 월트라우트 하드웨어가 체인점 기회를 제공할 것임을 시사하는 몇몇 최근 보도에 대해 말하고 싶다(I want to address some recent reports that have suggested Wiltrout Hardware will offer franchise opportunities ~)고 한 후, 실제로 고려는 했었지만, 현재 사업 모델을 그대로 유지한다는 이야기가 이어지고 있다. 이는 체인점 운영과 관련된 잘못된 정보를 바로잡는 것이므로 (A)가 정답이다.

어휘 correct 바로잡다, 정정하다 praise 칭찬하다 investment 투자(금) summarize 요약하다

6 이메일에 따르면, 체인점 운영이 월트라우트 하드웨어에게 무엇을 할 수 있게 해 줄 것인가?
(A) 제품 선택 범위 확장하기
(B) 더 많은 고객을 신속히 확보하기
(C) 더 많은 승진 기회 제공하기
(D) 업계 선두 주자 되기

해설 세부 사항
첫 번째 단락에서 체인점 운영이 훨씬 더 짧은 기간에 더 적은 운영비로 더 폭넓은 고객층을 끌어들일 수 있게 해 준다(~ franchising would allow us to attract a more extensive customer base in a much shorter period of time ~)는 점을 언급하고 있으므로 (B)가 정답이다.

어휘 selection 선택(할 수 있는 것들) gain 얻다 career advancement 승진

Paraphrasing 지문의 attract a more extensive customer base in a much shorter period of time → 정답의 Gain more customers quickly

[7-9] 이메일

수신: board_of_directors@rasp.com
발신: mwatson@eppm.com
날짜: 11월 21일
제목: 회신: 건물 관리를 위한 제안 요청

이사회 임원 여러분께,

7 이스트 퍼시픽 건물 관리 회사(EPPM)가 레지던스 앳 선라이즈 피어에 제공할 수 있는 서비스와 관련해 월요일에 저희 제안을 발표할 수 있게 해 주셔서 감사합니다. 이 지역에서 손꼽히는 건물 관리 업체로서, 저희 EPPM은 레지던스 앳 선라이즈 피어가 순조롭게 운영되고 아주 멋지게 보이도록 유지하는 데 필요할 수 있는 모든 지원을 제공해 드릴 준비가 잘 되어 있습니다.

모든 지역 사회는 뚜렷이 다르며, 저희 서비스는 아주 다양한 요구를 처리할 수 있습니다. **9** 최고 수준의 지원을 제공하기 위해, 저희는 "모든 상황에 적용되는" 관리 방식을 이용할 수는 없다는 것을 알고 있습니다. 이러한 이유로 인해, 여러분의 건물이 지닌 특정 요구 사항에 저희 서비스를 맞춥니다.

저희 EPPM을 차별화하는 한 가지는 **8** 건물 관리 모바일 앱인 시티 스퀘어를 이용하는 것입니다. 이 앱은 저희가 여러분의 팀과 협업하고, 이웃 업체들과 교류하며, 더 큰 지역 사회의 행사에 관해 최신 정보를 알 수 있게 도움을 줍니다.

다시 한 번, 이번 주 초에 저희 제안을 발표할 수 있는 기회를 주신 것에 대해 감사드립니다. 즐거운 시간이었습니다. 저희 회사와 관련해 추가 질문이 있으시면 알려 주시기 바랍니다.

마렉 왓슨, 부이사
이스트 퍼시픽 건물 관리 회사

어휘 proposal 제안(서) property 건물, 부동산 leading 손꼽히는, 선도적인 be equipped to ~할 준비가 되어 있다, ~할 수 있게 갖춰져 있다 smoothly 순조롭게 distinct 뚜렷이 다른 a wide variety of 아주 다양한 realize 알게 되다, 깨닫다 function 기능하다 one-size-fits-all 모든 상황에 적용되는, 두루 통용되는 set A apart A를 차별화하다 collaborate with ~와 협업하다 connect with ~와 교류하다 neighboring 이웃의, 인근의 up-to-date 최신의 opportunity 기회

7 이메일의 목적은?
(A) 지역 행사들을 홍보하려고
(B) 사업을 위한 제휴 업체를 찾으려고
(C) 한 판매업체에 계약 연장을 제안하려고
(D) 사업 발표에 대해 후속 조치를 취하려고

해설 주제/목적
첫 번째 단락에서 월요일에 제안을 발표할 수 있게 해 준 것에 대해 감사의 인사(Thank you for allowing East Pacific Property Management (EPPM) to present our proposal on Monday ~)를 전하면서 회사의 운영 방식 등

과 관련해 이야기하고 있다. 따라서 제안을 발표한 후에 보내는 이메일임을 알 수 있으므로 (D)가 정답이다.

어휘 vendor 판매업체, 판매업자   contract 계약(서)
extension 연장, 확장   follow up on ~에 대한 후속 조치를 취하다

8 시티 스퀘어가 무엇인가?
(A) 스마트폰 애플리케이션
(B) 정부 기관
(C) 재무 소프트웨어 프로그램
(D) 건물 관리 회사

해설 **세부 사항**
세 번째 단락에서 시티 스퀘어가 건물 관리 모바일 앱(a property management mobile app)이라고 설명하고 있으므로 (A)가 정답이다.

어휘 organization 기관, 단체   financial 재무의, 재정의

Paraphrasing 지문의 mobile app → 정답의 smartphone application

9 [1], [2], [3], [4]로 표시된 곳 중에 다음 문장이 들어가기에 가장 적합한 곳은?
"이러한 이유로 인해, 여러분의 건물이 지닌 특정 요구 사항에 저희 서비스를 맞춥니다."
(A) [1]   (B) [2]   (C) [3]   (D) [4]

해설 **문장 삽입**
주어진 문장은 앞서 언급된 것이 이유임을 밝히는 For this reason과 함께 건물이 지닌 특정 요구 사항에 서비스를 맞춘다는 의미를 지니고 있으므로, 앞 문장에 그 이유가 될 만한 것이 언급되어야 한다. [2] 앞에 언급된 "모든 상황에 적용되는" 관리 방식을 이용할 수 없다는 걸 안다(we realize that we cannot function using a "one-size-fits-all" management style)는 것이 요구 사항에 서비스를 맞추는 이유가 될 수 있으므로 (B)가 정답이다.

어휘 customize (주문에 따라) 맞추다, 주문 제작하다

[10-13] 이메일

발신: office@chibagrandhotel.com
수신: erik.carlsen@gowmail.com
제목: 최근 귀하의 치바 그랜드 투숙
날짜: 4월 18일

칼슨 씨께,

10/11 호텔 경영진 요청으로 4월 8일부터 12일까지 치바 그랜드 호텔에서 투숙하신 것과 관련하여 몇 분간 의견을 공유해 주실 수 있는지 여쭤보고자 메일을 드립니다. 저희 호텔의 인상에 대해 알고 싶습니다. 편의 시설에 얼마나 만족하셨는지요? 머무시는 동안 즐거우셨습니까? 기대에 미치지 못한 점이 있었는지요? 개선해야 할 여지가 있다면 알려 주십시오. 저희는 고객의 완전한 만족을 위해 오롯이 전념하고 있습니다!

12 www.chibagrand.com/yourstay에서 종합 만족도 설문지를 작성하셔서 직접 의견을 공유해 주십시오. 저희가 귀하의 전체적인 경험을 요약할 수 있도록 목록에 있는 모든 부분에 응답해 주시기 바랍니다. **13** 아울러 4월 30일까지 의견을 주시면 치바 그랜드 500달러 추첨 행사에 응모됩니다. 감사합니다.

카나 히로타
치바 그랜드 호텔

어휘 management 경영진   regarding ~에 관해
impression 인상   amenities 편의 시설   expectation 기대
room for ~의 여지   improvement 개선, 향상
be committed to ~에 전념하다, 헌신하다   satisfaction 만족   response 응답   summary 요약   overall 전체적인
sweepstake (상금을 건) 경주, 내기

10 이메일을 쓴 이유는?
(A) 좋지 못한 서비스에 대해 사과하려고
(B) 납부 내역 요약서를 전달하려고
(C) 고객에게 변경 사항에 대해 알리려고
(D) 고객 만족도에 대해 물어보려고

해설 **주제/목적**
첫 번째 단락에서 치바 그랜드 호텔에서 투숙한 것과 관련하여 의견을 공유해 줄 수 있는지 물어보기 위해 이메일을 보낸다(I am writing to ask if you would ~ share feedback with us regarding your April 8-12 stay)고 했으므로 (D)가 정답이다.

어휘 apologize for ~에 대해 사과하다   inquire 묻다

11 칼슨 씨는 호텔에 언제 도착했는가?
(A) 4월 8일
(B) 4월 12일
(C) 4월 18일
(D) 4월 30일

해설 **세부 사항**
첫 번째 단락에서 4월 8일에서 12일까지의 투숙한 것(your April 8-12 stay)과 관련한 피드백을 요청했으므로, 칼슨 씨가 4월 8일에 호텔에 도착했다는 것을 알 수 있다. 따라서 (A)가 정답이다.

12 이메일에 따르면, 온라인 주소에서 무엇을 찾을 수 있는가?
(A) 설문 양식
(B) 호텔로 찾아가는 길 안내
(C) 비용 세부 목록
(D) 호텔 시설 설명

해설 **세부 사항**
두 번째 단락에서 온라인 주소를 제시하며 종합 만족도 설문지(Total Satisfaction Survey)를 작성해 달라고 요청했으므로 (A)가 정답이다.

어휘 questionnaire 설문지   directions 길 안내   detailed 자세한   expense 비용, 경비   description 설명

Paraphrasing 지문의 Total Satisfaction Survey → 정답의 A questionnaire form

13 히로타 씨는 칼슨 씨에게 무엇을 제안하는가?
(A) 전액 환불
(B) 가이드 투어
(C) 향후 방문 시 할인
(D) 당첨 기회

해설 **세부 사항**
두 번째 단락에서 4월 30일까지 의견을 주면 치바 그랜드 500달러 추첨 행사에 응모된다(you will be entered into the $500 Reward Chiba Grand Sweepstakes)고 했으므로 (D)가 정답이다.

[14-17] 이메일

수신: 재커리 케네디 〈zkennedy@sandiahealth.org〉
발신: 지나 워커 〈g.walker@whiteoakmedtechs.com〉
날짜: 10월 29일
제목: 예약

케네디 박사님께,

14 저희 화이트 오크 메디컬 테크놀로지는 의료 제품 라인에 최근 추가된 제품을 알리게 되어 자랑스럽습니다. 최근 개발된 전문가용 체온계는 정확한 측정과 무선 작동의 편리함을 결합한 **14** 최첨단 기술을 활용합니다. 이 기기는 완전한 디지털 판독과 의료 시설 내 모든 곳에서 **15** 온라인 기록 시스템에 체온계를 연결해 주는 블루투스 기능을 특징으로 하고 있습니다. 동반되는 앱을 이용해, **17** 사무실 직원들이 간단한 클릭 한 번으로 결과를 환자의 개별 차트에 바로 복사할 수 있습니다. 이는 수동으로 데이터 입력 시 발생할 수 있는 오류 가능성을 없애 줍니다.

저희 직원이 다음 주에 귀하의 지역을 방문할 예정이며, 귀하의 사무실에서 시연도 해 드리겠습니다. 이 기간이 괜찮으시면, **16** 다음 주 중에서 선호하시는 날짜와 시간을 이 이메일로 보내 주시기 바랍니다. 더 늦은 날짜를 선호하시면, 저에게 직접 전화 주시면, 더 편리한 시간으로 일정을 잡아 드릴 수 있습니다.

지나 워커
화이트 오크 메디컬 테크놀로지
863-555-0111

어휘 addition 추가(되는 것) thermometer 체온계 utilize 활용하다 state-of-the-art 최첨단의 combine A with B A와 B를 결합하다 accurate 정확한 measurement 측정 feature 특징으로 하다 readout 판독, 해독 functionality 기능(성) accompany 동반되다 representative 직원 arrange 일정을 잡다, 조치하다 demonstration 시연(회) work for (일정 등이) ~에게 괜찮다 appointment 예약, 약속

14 이메일의 목적은?
(A) 혁신적인 기기를 홍보하려고
(B) 교체 기기를 요청하려고
(C) 제품 주문을 확인해 주려고
(D) 제품의 결함을 알리려고

해설 **주제/목적**
첫 번째 단락에서 화이트 오크 메디컬 테크놀로지의 의료 제품 라인에 최근 추가된 제품을 알리게 되어 자랑스럽다(We at White Oak Medical Technologies are proud to announce the latest addition to our line of medical products)고 하고, 최첨단 기술을 활용하는 체온계(Our recently developed professional thermometer utilizes state-of-the-art technology ~)의 기능을 설명하고 있다. 이는 최첨단 기술을 사용한 기기를 홍보하는 것이므로 (A)가 정답이다.

어휘 innovative 혁신적인 replacement 교체(품) advise of ~을 알리다 flaw 결함, 흠

> **Paraphrasing** 지문의 thermometer utilizes state-of-the-art technology → 정답의 an innovative device

15 체온계에 대해 언급된 것은?
(A) 매일 데이터를 입력해야 한다.
(B) 제조업체의 베스트셀러 제품이다.
(C) 온라인 시스템에 연결될 수 있다.
(D) 환자를 위한 가정용 버전이 있다.

해설 **Not/True**
첫 번째 단락에서 온라인 기록 시스템에 체온계를 연결해 주는 블루투스 기능(Bluetooth functionality that connects the thermometer to a medical facility's online recordkeeping system)을 한 가지 특징으로 언급하고 있으므로 (C)가 정답이다.

어휘 at-home 가정용의, 집에서 하는

16 이메일에 따르면, 케네디 박사가 왜 워커 씨에게 전화할 수도 있겠는가?
(A) 환자의 차트를 요청하기 위해
(B) 다음 주 이후에 시연 일정을 잡기 위해
(C) 대량 주문 할인에 관해 더 알아보기 위해
(D) 제품 라인에 관해 질문하기 위해

해설 **세부 사항**
마지막 단락에서 다음 주 중에서 선호하는 날짜와 시간을 알려 달라고 요청하면서 더 늦은 날짜를 선호하면 워커 씨에게 직접 전화하면 더 편리한 시간으로 일정을 잡아 줄 수 있다(~ please reply to this e-mail with your preferred day and time next week. If you prefer a later date, please call me directly, and I can arrange an appointment that is more convenient for you)고 알리고 있다. 따라서 다음 주 이후로 시연 일정을 잡으려는 경우에 워커 씨에게 전화할 것으로 볼 수 있으므로 (B)가 정답이다.

어휘 bulk 대량의

17 [1], [2], [3], [4]로 표시된 곳 중에서 다음 문장이 들어가기에 가장 적합한 위치는?

"이는 수동으로 데이터 입력 시 발생할 수 있는 오류 가능성을 없애 줍니다."

(A) [1]   (B) [2]   (C) [3]   (D) [4]

해설 **문장 삽입**
주어진 문장에서 이것(This)이 수동으로 데이터를 입력하면 생길 수 있는 오류 가능성을 없애 준다고 했으므로, 주어진 문장 앞에는 오류 가능성을 없애 주는 This가 가리키는 것이 있

어야 한다. 간단한 클릭 한 번으로 결과를 환자의 개별 차트에 바로 복사하는 기능이 This로 가리키기에 적절하므로 이것이 언급된 문장 뒤인 (C)가 정답이다.

어휘 eliminate 없애다, 제거하다   arise 발생하다, 떠오르다

[18-21] 편지

애니타 신용 조합
SE 메인 가 528번지
포틀랜드, OR 97201

2월 1일

권대호
W 루스벨트 가 4246번지
²⁰타이거드, OR 97224

권 씨께,

저희 애니타 신용 조합은 뛰어난 고객 서비스를 제공해 드리기 위해 지속적으로 애쓰고 있습니다. 은행 운영 개선을 위한 노력의 일환으로, 회원분께 더 나은 서비스를 제공할 것이라 생각하는 새로운 진전 사항들을 알려 드리게 되어 기쁩니다.

¹⁹ ⁽ᴬ⁾포틀랜드 시내의 단 한 곳의 지점에서 30년을 보낸 끝에, ¹⁹ ⁽ᴰ⁾저희는 시설 네트워크를 포함하는 새로운 사업 모델로 전환할 것입니다. 저희는 이 결정이 저희 고객들뿐만 아니라 직원들에게도 유익할 것이라 생각합니다. ¹⁸6월부터 신규 지점들이 타이거드와 그리셤, 비버튼, 그리고 윌슨빌에 문을 열게 됩니다. 더 많은 지점들과 함께, ²⁰애니타 신용 조합은 회원들의 지역 사회에서 직접 서비스를 제공해 드릴 수 있을 것이며, 직원들은 각자의 집과 더 가까운 곳에서 근무할 수 있습니다. 이러한 변화는 저희 신용 조합의 운영비는 줄이고 사업 운영은 개선해 줄 것입니다.

신규 지점을 여는 것뿐만 아니라, ²¹포틀랜드 시내에 있는 저희 본사를 위한 새로운 장소를 찾기 위해 사무용 공간들도 검토하고 있습니다. 저희는 현 임대 계약이 종료되는 내년에 파이낸셜 스퀘어 복합 건물을 떠날 것입니다. 새 본사가 어디에 위치하든 상관없이, 저희 애니타 신용 조합에게 기대하시는 ¹⁹ ⁽ᶜ⁾훌륭한 서비스와 편리한 영업시간은 동일하게 제공할 것입니다.

프리앙카 굽타
사장, 애니타 신용 조합

어휘 constantly 지속적으로   strive 애쓰다   stellar 뛰어난   commitment 헌신, 전념   operation 운영, 영업   development 진전(된 사항), 발전, 개발   shift to ~로 전환하다, ~로 바꾸다   incorporate 포함하다, 통합하다   reduce 줄이다, 감소시키다   assess 검토하다, 평가하다   headquarters 본사   convenient 편리한

18 편지의 목적은?
(A) 은행 계좌 개설을 확인해 주려고
(B) 신임 은행장을 소개하려고
(C) 새 은행 지점들을 알리려고
(D) 은행 계좌 내역서를 제공하려고

해설 주제/목적

두 번째 단락에서 새로운 사업 모델로의 전환을 언급하면서, 6월부터 신규 지점들이 문을 여는 지역들(Starting in June, new branches will open in Tigard, Gresham, Beaverton, and Wilsonville)을 소개하고 있으므로 (C)가 정답이다.

어휘 statement 내역(서), 명세(서)

19 편지에서 애니타 신용 조합에 대해 언급되지 않은 것은?
(A) 현재의 위치에 30년 동안 본사를 두고 있었다.
(B) 이제 직원들에게 재택근무를 할 수 있게 해 준다.
(C) 영업시간을 동일하게 유지한다.
(D) 새로운 사업 모델을 시행한다.

해설 Not/True

두 번째 단락에서 포틀랜드 시내에 위치한 단 한 곳의 지점에서 30년을 보낸(After 30 years in a single branch in downtown Portland) 사실을 언급하는 부분에서 (A)를, 같은 단락에서 새로운 사업 모델로 전환한다(we will shift to a new business model)고 알리는 부분에서 (D)를, 그리고 세 번째 단락에서 편리한 영업시간을 동일하게 유지할 것(it will offer the same convenient hours ~)이라고 밝히는 부분에서 (C)를 각각 확인할 수 있다. 하지만 직원들의 재택근무 허용과 관련된 정보는 제시되어 있지 않으므로 (B)가 정답이다.

어휘 be headquartered at ~에 본사를 두다   implement 시행하다

> **Paraphrasing** 지문의 30 years in a single branch → 보기 (A)의 has been headquartered at its current location for 30 years
> 지문의 will shift to → 보기 (D)의 is implementing
> 지문의 will offer the same convenient hours → 보기 (C)의 is keeping the same business operating hours

20 권 씨가 어떤 신규 지점을 방문할 것 같은가?
(A) 타이거드   (B) 그리셤
(C) 비버튼   (D) 윌슨빌

해설 추론/암시

두 번째 단락에 회원들의 지역 사회에서 직접 서비스를 제공할 수 있을 것(~ Anita Credit Union will be able to serve members directly in their communities ~)이라고 했으며, 상단의 주소에 권 씨가 거주하는 지역이 Tigard로 쓰여 있으므로 (A)가 정답이다.

21 [1], [2], [3], [4]로 표시된 곳 중에 다음 문장이 들어가기에 가장 적합한 곳은?
"저희는 현 임대 계약이 종료되는 내년에 파이낸셜 스퀘어 복합 건물을 떠날 것입니다."
(A) [1]   (B) [2]   (C) [3]   **(D) [4]**

해설 문장 삽입

주어진 문장은 이전 계획을 알리는 내용이다. 따라서 새로운 본사를 위한 사무용 공간들을 검토하고 있다고 알리는 문장 뒤에 위치한 [4]에 들어가 본사 이전 계획에 관해 부연하는 흐름이 되어야 자연스러우므로 (D)가 정답이다.

어휘 complex 복합 건물, 복합 단지   lease 임대 계약(서)

UNIT 18 회람 / 공지 / 광고 / 기사

지문 구성과 독해 전략 ········· 본책 p. 264

터너 베이(7월 11일)—리버런 콤플렉스가 올해의 리본 오브 엑설런스를 수상했다. 리본은 지역 회사들을 소개하는 웹사이트인 에버트레일에서 매년 수여한다.

수상 자격이 되기 위해서는, 기업은 별 4개 만점의 평가 척도에서 평균 별 3.5개를 받아야 한다. 평가 지수는 품질 및 고객 서비스에 대한 기업의 헌신도를 나타낸다. 이전 및 현재 수상자에는 터너 베이 전역의 호텔과 명소, 음식점들이 포함되어 있다. 이번에 리버런은 이 상을 3년 연속으로 수상한 것이다.

"저희 리버런 직원들은 이 영광을 얻게 돼 감격스럽습니다."라고 루시아 베리오스 대변인이 말했다. "6년 전 개장한 이래 저희는 가족들에게 신나는 놀이기구와 건강에 좋은 음식을 제공하기 위해 열심히 일했습니다. 저희는 과학 전시장이 특히 자랑스러운데, 모든 연령대의 고객들을 교육시키고 즐거움을 주는 게임 및 쌍방향 체험을 제공하고 있습니다."

어휘 award 수여하다; 상 showcase 소개하다 qualify for ~의 자격이 되다 enterprise 기업 average 평균 rating scale 평가 척도 attraction 관광 명소 consecutive 연속의 ride 놀이기구 interactive 양방향의, 상호적인

Q1 기사에 의하면, 에버트레일 웹사이트는 어떤 일을 하는가?
(A) 호텔 예약에 할인을 제공한다.
(B) 경치를 즐기는 기차 여행을 설명한다.
(C) 터너 베이에서 제작된 제품을 판매한다.
(D) 지역 업체들을 평가한다.

어휘 describe 설명하다 scenic 경치가 좋은 evaluate 평가하다

Q2 [1], [2], [3], [4]로 표시된 곳 중에서 다음 문장이 들어가기에 가장 적합한 곳은?

"평가 지수는 품질 및 고객 서비스에 대한 기업의 헌신도를 나타낸다."

(A) [1] **(B) [2]** (C) [3] (D) [4]

어휘 dedication 헌신(도)

ETS 유형연습 ········· 본책 p. 265

1 (A) 2 (A) 3 (A) 4 (A)

[1-2] 광고

스프링 파운틴 클린
50년 이상 고급 재료로 만들어 온 스프링 파운틴 클린의 비누는 온몸을 상쾌하게 해 줍니다.

애프터눈 스트롤
¹레몬 및 오렌지의 상쾌한 향으로 에너지 넘치는 기분을 느껴 보세요.

사우스 씨즈
정향나무와 생강의 따뜻한 향을 즐겨 보세요.

²저희 웹사이트 www.springfountainclean.com을 방문하셔서 천연 원료만으로 만든 비누와 샴푸, 그리고 보습제 등 전체 제품을 확인해 보세요.

어휘 ingredient 성분, 재료 scent 향, 향기 savor (맛, 향 등을) 즐기다, 음미하다

1 어느 비누 종류가 과일 향을 특징으로 하는가?
(A) 애프터눈 스트롤 (B) 사우스 씨즈

해설 세부 사항
애프터눈 스트롤이 레몬과 오렌지의 상쾌한 향(the fresh scents of lemon and orange)을 지니고 있는 것으로 소개되어 있으므로 (A)가 정답이다.

어휘 feature 특징으로 하다

> **Paraphrasing** 지문의 the fresh scents of lemon and orange → 질문의 features the smell of fruit

2 광고에 따르면, 스프링 파운틴 클린의 웹사이트에서 찾을 수 있는 것은?
(A) 스프링 파운틴 클린의 모든 제품 정보
(B) 스프링 파운틴 클린 비누 할인 쿠폰

해설 세부 사항
마지막 단락에 스프링 파운틴 클린의 웹사이트에서 천연 원료만으로 만든 비누와 샴푸, 그리고 보습제 등 전체 제품을 확인해 보라(Visit our Web site at www.springfountainclean.com to see our full line of all-natural soaps, shampoos, and moisturizers)고 나와 있으므로 (A)가 정답이다.

> **Paraphrasing** 지문의 our full line → 정답의 all Spring Fountain Clean products

[3-4] 공지

클럽 임시 휴업

빅 박스 피트니스가 ³새로운 모습으로 단장하는 동안 6월 5일부터 9일까지 5일간 문을 닫을 것입니다. 6월 10일에 다시 문을 열 때, ³체육관과 탈의실 곳곳에서 페인트칠을 새로 한 것과 식물, 그리고 기타 장식물들을 보실 수 있을 것입니다. 저희는 또한 댄스 스튜디오 바닥도 새로 손볼 예정입니다. ⁴이 기간 중에, 클럽 회원들께서는 더비 애비뉴 800번지에 있는 브리가둔 피트니스를 무료로 이용하실 수 있을 것입니다. 이 시설을 이용하시려면, 도착 시 유효한 빅 박스 피트니스 회원 카드를 제시하셔야 할 것입니다.

어휘 temporarily 임시로, 일시적으로 freshen up ~을 새롭게 하다 appearance 외관, 겉모습 decoration 장식(물) refinish 다시 손보다 have access to ~을 이용할 수 있다 complimentary 무료의 valid 유효한

3 빅 박스 피트니스에 대해 언급된 것은?
(A) 인테리어를 새롭게 하고 있다.
(B) 신규 회원에게 할인을 제공하고 있다.

해설 **Not/True**
초반부에서 새로운 모습으로 단장한다(we freshen up our appearance)는 사실과 함께 체육관과 탈의실 곳곳에서 페인트칠을 새로 한 것과 식물, 그리고 기타 장식들을 볼 수 있을 것(you can expect to see new paint, plants, and other decorations ~)이라고 했으므로 (A)가 정답이다.

> **Paraphrasing** 지문의 freshen up our appearance → 정답의 updating its interior

4 빅 박스 피트니스 회원들은 무엇을 하도록 권장되는가?
(A) 다른 피트니스 클럽 방문하기
(B) 새 피트니스 강좌에 등록하기

해설 **세부 사항**
후반부에 피트니스 시설을 손보는 기간 중에는 더비 애비뉴 800번지에 있는 브리가둔 피트니스를 무료로 이용할 수 있다(During this time, club members will have complimentary access to Brigadoon Fitness ~)고 알리고 있으므로 (A)가 정답이다.

> **Paraphrasing** 지문의 have complimentary access to Brigadoon Fitness → 정답의 Visit a different fitness club

ETS 실전문제 본책 p.266

1 (D)	2 (C)	3 (D)	4 (C)	5 (D)	6 (B)
7 (B)	8 (C)	9 (D)	10 (A)	11 (B)	12 (B)
13 (D)	14 (B)	15 (D)	16 (D)	17 (C)	18 (B)

[1-2] 기사

에반브리지(10월 27일) — 목요일 저녁에 **1 에반브리지 시 의회는 8대 1로 표결해 휴스턴 필드 소유주들이 제안한 야구 경기장에 500개의 좌석을 추가하는 야심 찬 공사 프로젝트를 승인했다.**
2 일부 에반브리지 주민들은 이 프로젝트가 교통 혼잡 문제를 야기할 것이라는 우려의 목소리를 냈지만, 의회는 좌석 수를 늘리면 더 많은 타지 스포츠 팬들이 경기를 관람할 수 있을 것이라고 설명했다. 시는 세수가 증가할 것이고, 그것은 새로운 버스 노선 추가 같은 계획들에 자금을 지원하는 데 도움이 될 것이다. 이 계획은 또한 휴스턴 필드가 입장권 가격을 올리는 것을 막아줄 것이라고 경기장 소유주들은 주장했다.

어휘 council 의회 vote 표결하다, 투표하다 approve 승인하다 ambitious 야심 찬 resident 주민 voice 목소리를 내다 traffic 교통(량), 차량들 congestion 혼잡 point out 주목하다, 지적하다 tax revenue 세입 fund 자금을 제공하다 initiative 계획 route 경로, 노선 claim 주장하다

1 시 의회는 휴스턴 필드 소유주들이 무엇을 할 수 있게 허용해 주었는가?
(A) 입장권 가격 인상하기
(B) 더 많은 경기 개최하기
(C) 더 넓은 주차 공간 짓기
(D) 좌석 수용 규모 확대하기

해설 **세부 사항**
첫 번째 단락에서 에반브리지 시 의회가 표결을 통해 휴스턴 필드 소유주들이 제안한 야구 경기장에 500개의 좌석을 추가하는 공사 프로젝트를 승인했다(the Evanbridge City Council voted eight to one to approve ~ would add 500 seats to the baseball stadium)고 밝히고 있다. 이는 좌석 수용 규모를 늘리는 것을 승인했다는 뜻이므로 (D)가 정답이다.

어휘 raise 인상하다, 올리다 capacity 수용 규모, 수용력

> **Paraphrasing** 지문의 approve → 질문의 allowed
> 지문의 add 500 seats to the baseball stadium → 정답의 Expand the seating capacity

2 일부 사람들은 왜 해당 계획에 대해 불만을 표현했는가?
(A) 부동산 가치를 떨어뜨릴 것이라고 생각했다.
(B) 대중교통에 들어갈 자금을 줄어들게 할 것이라고 생각했다.
(C) 교통량이 너무 많아질 것이라고 생각했다.
(D) 경기장을 방문객에게 덜 매력적이게 만들 것이라고 생각했다.

해설 **세부 사항**
두 번째 단락에 일부 에반브리지 주민들이 해당 프로젝트가 교통 혼잡 문제를 야기할 것이라는 우려의 목소리를 냈다(some Evanbridge residents voiced concerns that the project would lead to traffic congestion problems)고 언급되어 있으므로 (C)가 정답이다.

어휘 property 부동산, 건물 value 가치, 값어치
take A away from B B에서 A를 덜어내다, A를 B에서 벗어나게 하다 attractive 매력적인

> **Paraphrasing** 지문의 lead to traffic congestion problems → 정답의 create too much traffic

[3-4] 공지

RDX 직원 여러분께,

3 우리 탕비실에 있는 커피메이커가 제대로 작동하지 않는 것을 알고 있습니다. 공급업체에서 주말까지 기술자를 보내 이 기계를 수리하는 일정을 잡아 두었습니다.

3, 4 당분간, 전기 주전자를 이용해 물을 끓이고 가루 위에 부어 커피를 만드시기 바랍니다. 그 후 커피를 보온 유리병에 부어 따뜻하게 유지할 수 있습니다. 가장 효율적인 과정은 아니지만, 그렇게 하면 될 것입니다. **4 누구든 사무실에 처음 도착하시는 분께서 모두를 위해 커피를 만들어 주시기를 요청하고자 합니다.** 오늘 아침에는 제가 기꺼이 처리하겠지만, 우리가 각자 돌아가면서 하게 되기를 바랍니다.

시마 굽타

어휘 kitchenette 탕비실, 작은 주방　function 작동하다, 기능하다　properly 제대로, 적절히　supplier 공급업체, 공급업자　pour (액체를) 붓다, 따르다　grinds (갈아 놓은) 가루　thermal carafe 보온 유리병　efficient 효율적인　pot 주전자　see to ~을 처리하다　take a turn (순서대로) 돌아가면서 하다

3　공지의 목적은?
(A) 직원들에게 업무 공간 위험 요소에 대해 주의를 주기 위해
(B) 새 기기에 관해 직원들에게 의견을 요청하기 위해
(C) 직원들에게 회사 정책을 상기시키기 위해
(D) 직원들에게 임시 해결책에 관해 설명하기 위해

해설　**주제/목적**
첫 번째 단락에서 커피메이커가 제대로 작동하지 않는다(the coffeemaker in our kitchenette is not functioning properly)는 문제를 알린 것과 관련해, 두 번째 단락에서 당분간 전기 주전자를 이용하도록(For the time being, please use the electric kettle to boil water) 요청하면서 그 이용 방식 등을 설명하고 있으므로 (D)가 정답이다.

어휘　hazard 위험 (요소)　solicit 요청하다, 간청하다　feedback 의견　appliance 기기　instruct 설명하다, 지시하다　temporary 임시의, 일시적인　solution 해결책

Paraphrasing 지문의 For the time being, please use the electric kettle → 정답의 a temporary solution

4　굽타 씨가 누구일 것 같은가?
(A) IT 전문가
(B) 커피 공급업자
(C) 사무실 관리자
(D) 수리 기사

해설　**추론/암시**
두 번째 단락에서 문제 해결 방법을 언급하고 먼저 오는 사무실 직원들에게 커피를 만들어 달라고 요청(I would ask that whoever arrives in the office first make a pot of coffee for everyone)하고 있으므로 관리자 역할을 하는 사람일 것으로 추론할 수 있다. 따라서 (C)가 정답이다.

[5-7] 광고

두 달 동안 반값으로 푸에블로넷 프로를 즐겨 보세요

⁵푸에블로넷 프로에서 여러분 분야의 전문가들과 교류하는 것으로 구직 활동에 새로운 활력도 불어넣고 두 달 동안 정가의 50퍼센트 할인 혜택도 누려 보시기 바랍니다. 수백 만 명의 푸에블로넷 프로 이용자들에 합류하고 다음번 꿈의 직장으로 향하는 길의 역할을 할 계정을 만드세요.

열린 소통을 즐겨 보세요. 업무 배경, 지식, 경험을 간략하게 설명하는 프로필을 설정하세요. 여러분의 직업 관련 인맥을 확장하는 데 도움을 줄 수 있는 적합한 사람들에게 연락하세요. ⁷매달 최대 스무 명의 다른 이용자들에게 직접 메시지를 보낼 수 있습니다. 하지만 동료 전문가들과의 교류는 거기서 끝나지 않습니다. ⁶지난 30일 동안 여러분의 프로필을 살펴본 모든 푸에블로넷 프로 이용자들을 확인할 수도 있습니다.

일과 관련된 깨달음을 얻으세요. 여러분 분야의 트렌드를 주도하는 회사들에 관한 최신 정보를 얻고 여러분의 기술이 그곳의 요구 사항에 어떻게 어울리는지 확인하세요. 푸에블로넷 프로 이용자로서, 여러분의 능력에 맞는 일자리를 추천받을 수 있습니다. 심지어 여러분의 프로필이 다른 지원자들의 프로필과 어떻게 비교되는지 알아볼 수도 있습니다. 게다가, 여러분의 정보는 더 많은 구직 면접 자리를 얻는 데 도움을 줄 수 있는 채용 담당자들의 눈에 띄게 될 것입니다.

전문적으로 성장하십시오. 여러분의 경력을 발전시키기 위해 가장 수요가 많은 최신 기술을 습득하십시오. 푸에블로넷 프로를 이용하면, 푸에블로넷 전문 라이브러리에서 1만 개 이상의 강좌를 이용할 수 있으며, 이 자료들을 활용해 다음 면접을 대비할 수 있습니다.

이 한시적인 특가 행사는 1월 15일에 종료됩니다. 지금 바로 시작하여 앞으로 두 달 동안 단지 월 14.99달러로 푸에블로넷 프로를 이용해 보세요! 더 많은 정보는 pueblonetpro.com을 방문하세요.

어휘　reinvigorate 새로운 활력을 불어넣다　connect with ~와 교류하다　account 계정　serve as ~의 역할을 하다　outline 개괄적으로 설명하다　insight 깨우침, 통찰(력)　up-to-date 최신의　match up with ~에 어울리다　fit 적합하다, 알맞다　compare to ~와 비교되다　applicant 지원자　recruiter 채용 담당자　in demand 수요가 있는　advance 발전시키다　have access to ~을 이용할 수 있다, ~에 접근할 수 있다　resource 자료, 자원　limited-time 한시적인　take advantage of ~을 이용하다

5　광고의 대상은 누구인가?
(A) 인재 채용 담당자들
(B) 마케팅 전문가들
(C) 취업 코치들
(D) 구직자들

해설　**세부 사항**
첫 번째 단락에서 푸에블로넷 프로를 이용해 분야별 전문가들과 교류함으로써 구직 활동에 새로운 활력도 불어넣으라(Reinvigorate your job search by connecting with professionals in your field ~)고 알리는 부분을 통해 구직자들이 대상임을 알 수 있다. 따라서 (D)가 정답이다.

6　푸에블로넷 프로에 대해 언급된 것은?
(A) 한시적으로 무료로 사용할 수 있다.
(B) 사용자가 누가 자신의 프로필을 봤는지 확인할 수 있다.
(C) 사용자가 매달 무제한으로 사람들과 연락할 수 있다.
(D) 사용자에게 무료 강좌를 제공하는 대학교 목록을 포함한다.

해설　**Not/True**
두 번째 단락에 지난 30일 동안 프로필을 살펴본 모든 푸에블로넷 프로 이용자들을 확인할 수 있다(You can also see all the Pueblonet Pro users who have viewed your profile over the past 30 days)는 특징이 언급되어 있으므로 (B)가 정답이다.

어휘　available 이용 가능한　at no charge 무료로　allow 할 수 있게 해 주다, 허용하다　unlimited 무제한의　feature 특별히 포함하다, 특징으로 하다

> **Paraphrasing** 지문의 see all the Pueblonet Pro users who have viewed your profile → 정답의 allows users to see who has viewed their profile

7 [1], [2], [3], [4]로 표시된 곳 중에서 다음 문장이 들어가기에 가장 적합한 곳은?

"하지만 동료 전문가들과의 교류는 거기서 끝나지 않습니다."
(A) [1]   **(B) [2]**   (C) [3]   (D) [4]

해설 문장 삽입

주어진 문장은 동료 전문가들과의 교류가 거기서 끝나지 않는다는 의미이므로, 전문가들과의 교류가 언급되는 문장 뒤에 위치해야 한다. 따라서 매달 최대 스무 명의 다른 이용자들에게 직접 메시지를 보낼 수 있다(You can send direct messages to up to twenty other users ~)고 밝히는 문장 뒤에 위치해 추가적인 접근 방법이 있음을 언급하는 흐름이 되는 것이 자연스럽다. 따라서 (B)가 정답이다.

어휘 fellow 동료의, 같은 처지의

[8-10] 회람

수신: 전 직원
발신: 켄 노무라
날짜: 3월 18일
제목: 출장 정책

FPJ 언리미티드는 회사 업무 수행을 위해 직원이 출장을 가야 할 필요성을 알고 있습니다. 직원의 안전을 보장하고 출장 비용을 합리적으로 유지하기 위해, 직원은 출장을 떠나기 전에 출장 승인 양식을 제출해야 합니다. **10**양식 내의 모든 영역은 반드시 작성되어야 합니다. 여기에는 출장 목적과 출장 날짜, 목적지가 포함됩니다.

8부서장이 출장을 승인하고 나면, 해당 직원은 회사의 출장 포털에 로그인해 항공편과 숙소를 선택할 수 있습니다. 오직 승인된 항공사와 파트너 호텔들만 출장 포털에 나타납니다. 회사 업무로 출장을 떠나는 직원들은 기재되어 있지 않은 업체를 통해 출장 준비를 할 수 없습니다.

9예약 과정을 간소화하기 위해, 빈번히 출장을 떠나시는 분들은 포털 내에서 선호하는 출장 시간대와 좌석 선택 정보를 표기해 프로필을 작성할 것을 권합니다. 궁금한 점이 있으시면 소속 부서장님께 연락하시기 바랍니다.

어휘 recognize 인식하다, 알아보다   performance 수행(능력), 실시   ensure 보장하다, 반드시 ~하도록 하다   reasonable 합리적인   authorization 승인, 인가   undertake 시작하다, 착수하다   grant approval 승인하다   accommodation 숙소, 숙박 시설   make an arrangement 조치하다, 마련하다   unlisted 기재되지 않은   streamline 간소화하다   booking 예약   process 과정   frequent 빈번한, 잦은   indicate 표기하다, 나타내다   preferred 선호하는

8 회람에 따르면, 누가 직원 출장 요청을 승인해 줄 수 있는가?
(A) 출장 포털 관리자   (B) 출장 동행자
(C) 부서장   (D) 인사부장

해설 세부 사항

두 번째 단락에서 소속 부서장이 출장을 승인한다(After the employee's manager has granted travel approval ~)고 했으므로 (C)가 정답이다.

어휘 administrator 관리자, 행정 담당자

9 출장용 프로필에 대해 언급된 것은?
(A) 새로 고용된 직원에 의해 만들어져야 한다.
(B) 출장 준비를 할 때 시간을 절약해 줄 수 있다.
(C) 출장이 승인될 수 있기 전에 만들어져야 한다.
(D) 회사의 출장 포털에서 새로운 요소이다.

해설 Not/True

세 번째 단락에서 예약 과정을 간소화하기 위해 프로필을 작성할 것을 권한다(To streamline the booking process, it is recommended that frequent travelers should complete a profile ~)고 했다. 어떤 과정을 간소화하는 것은 결국 시간을 절약하는 것과 같으므로 (B)가 정답이다.

어휘 element 요소

> **Paraphrasing** 지문의 streamline → 정답의 save time

10 [1], [2], [3], [4]로 표시된 곳 중에 다음 문장이 들어가기에 가장 적합한 곳은?

"여기에는 출장 목적과 출장 날짜, 목적지가 포함됩니다."
(A) [1]   (B) [2]   (C) [3]   (D) [4]

해설 문장 삽입

주어진 문장은 앞서 제시된 복수 명사를 지칭하는 대명사 These와 함께 출장 목적과 출장 날짜, 목적지를 포함한다는 의미를 나타낸다. 따라서 복수 명사 All fields를 언급해 모든 영역이 작성되어야 한다고 알리는 문장 뒤에 위치한 [1]에 삽입되어 All fields에 해당하는 구체적인 영역을 밝히는 흐름이 되어야 자연스러우므로 (A)가 정답이다.

어휘 include 포함하다   destination 목적지, 도착지

[11-14] 회람

회람

수신: 전 직원
발신: 인사부
날짜: 7월 2일
제목: 기업 교육 프로그램

11 회사 내에서 승진에 관심 있는 직원들은 기업 교육 프로그램에 참여할 것을 권장합니다. 랜던 인더스트리즈는 오랫동안 이 프로그램에 자부심을 가지고 있습니다. 교육 프로그램의 새로운 주기가 시작되는 9월 1일에 몇 가지 업데이트가 적용될 것입니다.

먼저, 다음 신규 과정을 발표하게 되어 기쁩니다: 서면 커뮤니케이션 개선, **12**철강 업계의 혁신적 실천 사례, 동기 부여와 직원 성과

더욱이, 처음으로 브룩스톤 대학교 경영 대학의 교수진이 교육 과정을 이끌게 됩니다. 직원들의 의견에 따라, 이 과정들은 온라인으로 열리지 않을 것이며, 대신 **13**모든 수업이 정규 근무 시간 후에 현장에서 진행될 것입니다.

이 프로그램의 과정들은 랜넌 인더스트리즈의 모든 직원에게 열려 있지만, 관심 있는 직원은 어느 과정이 자신의 필요와 관심사에 가장 14적합할지 소속 부서장님과 상담할 것을 권합니다.

www.lannoneindustries.com/training을 방문하여 9월의 모든 교육 과정을 확인하고, 각 수업이 무엇을 다룰 것인지 더 살펴보고, 이 프로그램 참여가 여러분의 경력을 어떻게 향상시켜 줄 것인지 알아보세요.

어휘 corporate 기업의   advancement 승진   participate in ~에 참여하다   pride oneself on ~을 자랑으로 여기다   initiative 계획, 운동   take effect 적용되다   following 다음의   improve 개선하다   innovative 혁신적인   practice 관행, 실천 사례   motivation 동기 부여   session (특정 활동을 하는) 시간   occur 일어나다, 발생하다   on-site 현장에서   consult 상담하다   be suited to ~에 적합하다   cover (주제 등) 다루다   discover 알아내다   enhance 향상시키다, 강화하다

11 회람의 목적은?
(A) 직원들에게 대학 학위를 취득하도록 장려하는 것
(B) 직원들에게 회사 프로그램에 관해 알리는 것
(C) 직원들이 교육 프로그램 업데이트를 받을 수 있는 방법을 명시하는 것
(D) 직원들에게 이력서를 업데이트하도록 상기시키는 것

해설 주제/목적
첫 번째 단락에서 회사 내에서 승진에 관심 있는 직원들은 기업 교육 프로그램에 참여할 것을 권장한다(Employees ~ are encouraged to participate in the corporate training program)고 밝히면서 해당 프로그램에 관해 설명하고 있으므로 (B)가 정답이다.

어휘 obtain 얻다, 획득하다   degree 학위   specify 명시하다

12 랜넌 인더스트리즈에 대해 사실일 것 같은 것은?
(A) 사업을 한 지 오래되지 않았다.
(B) 철강 생산에 관여하고 있다.
(C) 대단히 수익성이 좋다.
(D) 직원들에게 초과 근무하기를 기대한다.

해설 추론/암시
두 번째 단락에서 직원 교육 프로그램의 주제 중 하나로 철강 업계의 혁신적 실천 사례(Innovative Practices in the Steel Industry)가 있으므로 철강 생산과 관련된 회사인 것으로 볼 수 있다. 따라서 (B)가 정답이다.

어휘 be involved in ~에 관여하다   profitable 수익성이 좋은

13 9월 1일에 시작하는 과정에 대해 언급된 것은?
(A) 부서장들이 가르칠 것이다.
(B) 직원이 아닌 사람들에게도 공개될 것이다.
(C) 오직 온라인으로만 제공될 것이다.
(D) 랜넌 인더스트리즈에서 열릴 것이다.

해설 Not/True
세 번째 단락에서 모든 수업이 정규 근무 시간 후에 현장에서 진행될 것(~ all sessions will occur on-site after regular work hours)이라고 알리고 있으므로 (D)가 정답이다.

어휘 exclusively 오로지, 독점적으로

14 네 번째 단락, 세 번째 줄에 쓰인 단어 "suited"와 의미가 가장 가까운 것은?
(A) 옷을 입은   **(B) 적절한**
(C) 권장되는   (D) 준비된

해설 동의어 찾기
suited를 포함한 부분은 '그들의 필요와 관심사에 가장 적합할지(may be best suited to their needs and interests)'라는 의미로 해석될 수 있으므로 '적절한'이라는 의미의 (B) appropriate이 정답이다.

[15-18] 기사

곧 다가오는 해산물 축제

오션 시티(4월 7일) — 연례 OC 해산물 축제가 오션 시티 선착장 근처의 그린스톤 공원에 위치한 평소 장소에서 5월 10일부터 5월 14일까지 개최될 것이다. 하지만 15축제 주최 책임자 데비 하노버 씨는 올해 축제가 해산물 이상으로 훨씬 더 많은 것을 특징으로 할 것이라고 말한다.

"여러 미술가들을 초청했고, 15이분들이 바다를 주제로 한 그림과 기타 미술 작품들을 전시하고 판매할 것입니다"라고 하노버 씨가 말한다. "축제 참석자들은 요금을 내고 자신의 15초상화나 캐리커처를 16그려 달라고 할 수도 있을 겁니다."

유명 케이준 요리사인 알렉스 부르크가 뉴올리언스에서 방문할 예정이다. 이 요리사는 두 권의 요리책을 출간했으며, 자신의 온라인 채널을 아주 인기 있게 만들어 준 17새우 요리와 게 요리를 제공하기 위해 처음으로 이 지역을 방문한다.

18하노버 씨는 올해 행사의 광고 예산이 작년보다 20퍼센트 더 늘었고 결과가 긍정적이라고 특별히 언급했다. "많은 호텔과 모텔들이 그 주말에 예약되었습니다"라고 하노버 씨가 말했다. "참석을 원하는 분들은 미리 계획을 세우기를 권합니다."

어휘 annual 연례적인, 해마다의   take place 개최되다   feature 특징으로 하다   themed 주제로 한   attendee 참석자   portrait 초상화   caricature 캐리커처   renowned 유명한   serve (음식 등을) 제공하다   note 특별히 언급하다, 주목하다   budget 예산   positive 긍정적인   reserve 예약하다

15 하노버 씨에 대해 암시된 것은?
(A) 오션 시티 선착장을 소유하고 있다.
(B) 바다를 주제로 한 미술품을 수집한다.
(C) 뉴올리언스를 방문한 적이 있다.
(D) 행사에 여러 활동을 추가했다.

해설 추론/암시
첫 단락에 데비 하노버 씨가 올해 축제가 해산물 이상으로 훨씬 더 많은 것을 특징으로 할 것이라고 말했다(~ Debbie Hannover says that this year's festival will feature much more than seafood)고 언급되어 있고, 두 번째 단락에는 미술 작품 전시 및 판매(~ display and sell their ocean-themed paintings and other works of art)와 초상화와 캐리커처 그리기(~ have their portraits or caricatures drawn) 등이 언급되어 있다. 이를 통해 하노버 씨가 행사에 여러 활동을 추가했음을 추론할 수 있으므로 (D)가 정답이다.

어휘 own 소유하다 collect 수집하다, 모으다

16 두 번째 단락, 여섯 번째 줄에 쓰인 "drawn"과 의미가 가장 가까운 것은?
(A) 연주된, 재생된
(B) 당겨진, 끌린
(C) 이끌리는, 매혹된
(D) 그려진

해설 **동의어 찾기**
drawn을 포함한 부분은 '축제 참석자들은 초상화와 캐리커처를 그려 달라고 할 수도 있을 것이다(Festival attendees will also be able to have their portraits or caricatures drawn ~)'라는 의미로 해석된다. 따라서 (D) sketched가 정답이다.

17 기사에 따르면, 부르크 씨가 축제에서 무엇을 할 것인가?
(A) 자신의 온라인 채널을 위한 영상 만들기
(B) 자신의 요리책 판매하기
(C) 참석자들을 위해 음식 준비하기
(D) 요리 콘테스트에서 심사하기

해설 **세부 사항**
세 번째 단락에서 요리사 부르크 씨가 새우 요리와 게 요리를 제공하기 위해(to serve the shrimp and crab dishes) 축제에 방문한다고 알리고 있으므로 (C)가 정답이다.

어휘 judge 심사하다, 판단하다

> **Paraphrasing** 지문의 serve the shrimp and crab dishes
> → 정답의 Prepare food

18 하노버 씨가 올해 축제 광고에 대해 암시하는 것은?
(A) 텔레비전 광고 방송을 포함한다.
(B) 폭넓은 사람들에게 다가가고 있다.
(C) 일부는 지역 예술가들이 제작했다.
(D) 호텔 소유주들이 만족하지 못한다.

해설 **추론/암시**
네 번째 단락에 하노버 씨는 올해 행사의 광고 예산이 작년보다 20퍼센트 더 늘었고 결과가 긍정적이라고 특별히 언급했다(Ms. Hannover notes that the advertising budget for this year's event is 20 percent larger than last year's, with positive results)고 했다. 광고 예산을 늘린 결과가 긍정적이라는 말은 광고가 효과적이라는 것을 의미하므로 광고가 많은 사람들에게 도달되고 있다고 추론할 수 있다. 따라서 (B)가 정답이다.

어휘 include 포함하다 commercial 광고 (방송)
reach 다가가다, 이르다 audience 사람들, 시청자들, 청중
local 지역의, 현지의 be satisfied with ~에 만족하다

UNIT 19 메시지 / 웹페이지 / 기타

지문 구성과 독해 전략 ······ 본책 p.272

> 안나 리치 [오전 9시 2분]
> 지난달 어디에서 차를 수리하셨어요?
>
> 보니 그린 [오전 9시 5분]
> 린덴 가에 있는 막스 오토모티브에서요. 차에 문제가 있나요?
>
> 안나 리치 [오전 9시 6분]
> 아니요. 직장 동료인 케빈 피터스 씨와 커피숍에서 이야기하는 중이에요. 그가 차를 수리받아야 한대요.
>
> 보니 그린 [오전 9시 8분]
> 케빈한테 막스가 좋았다고 이야기해 주세요. 거기는 부품 가격도 괜찮은 것으로 구해줬고 인건비도 적당했어요.
>
> 안나 리치 [오전 9시 9분]
> 고마워요. 제가 전해 줄게요.

어휘 charge 청구하다 reasonable 적당한 pass on 전하다

Q1 리치 씨는 왜 그린 씨에게 연락했겠는가?
(A) 추천을 원한다.
(B) 어떤 장소로 가는 길을 알아야 한다.
(C) 커피를 마시고 싶다.
(D) 차를 수리해야 한다.

어휘 directions 길 안내

Q2 오전 9시 9분에 리치 씨가 "제가 전해 줄게요"라고 쓸 때 무엇을 의미할 것 같은가?
(A) 출근하는 길에 그린 씨를 차에 태울 것이다.
(B) 다른 수리점을 찾아볼 것이다.
(C) 피터스 씨와 정보를 공유할 것이다.
(D) 피터스 씨에게 돈을 가져다줄 것이다.

어휘 share 공유하다

ETS 유형연습
본책 p.273

1 (B) **2** (A) **3** (A) **4** (B)

[1-2] 웹페이지

https://www.travelwrangler.com/tips-and-advice

팁과 조언

트래블 랭글러 직원 작성

[1] 수수료를 지불하지 않고 여러분의 여행 계획을 마지막 순간에 변경하시거나 취소하실 수 있도록 확실히 해 두는 것이 현명합니다. 따라서 저희 사이트를 이용해 항공권과 호텔 객실, 여행 패키지를 예약하실 때, 선택하길 원하시는 곳의 변경 및 취소 정책을 살펴보실 것을 권해 드립니다.

²9월 한 달 동안, 선카르 호텔 체인이 숙박 기간과 상관없이 모든 객실을 10퍼센트 할인해 드린다는 점에 유의하세요. 선카르 고객 보상 프로그램의 신규 회원도 할인 혜택을 받으실 수 있습니다.

늘 그렇듯이, 앞으로의 여행 준비를 위해 저희 서비스를 이용해 주시는 모든 고객 여러분께 감사드립니다.

> **어휘** ensure 확실히 해 두다, 반드시 ~하도록 하다 last-minute 마지막 순간의 cancellation 취소 accordingly 따라서, 그에 따라 reservation 예약 selection 선택 (가능한 것들) note 유의하다, 주목하다 available 이용 가능한 loyalty program 고객 보상 프로그램 arrange 준비하다, 조치하다

1 웹사이트 정보가 누구를 대상으로 할 것 같은가?
(A) 항공사 관계자 (B) 여행객

해설 **추론/암시**
첫 번째 단락에 수수료를 지불하지 않고 여행 계획을 마지막 순간에 변경 또는 취소할 수 있게 해 두어야 한다(It is always wise to ensure that you can make last-minute changes or cancellations to your travel plans ~)고 언급한 뒤로 항공권 예약 등 여행 준비와 할인 정보 등을 설명하고 있으므로 (B)가 정답이다.

2 선카르 호텔 체인에 대해 언급되는 것은?
(A) 한시적으로 객실 할인을 제공한다.
(B) 최근에 고객 정책을 변경했다.

해설 **Not / True**
두 번째 단락에 9월 한 달 동안, 선카르 호텔 체인이 숙박 기간과 상관없이 모든 객실을 10퍼센트 할인한다(~ for the month of September, the Suncarr Hotels chain is offering a 10% discount on any room for any length of stay)고 쓰여 있으므로 (A)가 정답이다.

> **Paraphrasing** 지문의 for the month of September → 정답의 for a limited time

[3-4] 라벨

사모라 마살라 믹스는 육류, 생선, 채소에 풍미를 더하는 데 완벽한 다용도 무염 혼합물입니다. ³요리할 때 메인 요리에 티스푼으로 한 스푼 넣거나, 코코넛 밀크나 토마토 페이스트, 요거트 또는 퓌레로 만든 채소를 추가해 식사에 곁들일 감칠맛 나는 소스를 만들어 보세요. 이것들은 단지 저희가 소금을 넣지 않고도 풍미를 더하는 방법 중 일부에 불과합니다.

저희는 여러분께서 사모사 마살라 믹스를 어떻게 활용하시는지 보고 싶습니다. ⁴hello@samoramasalamix.com으로 조리법과 요리하신 음식의 사진을 보내 주세요. 저희가 매달 소셜 미디어에 가장 마음에 드는 다섯 가지를 게시할 것입니다.

> **어휘** all-purpose 다용도의, 만능의 salt-free 무염의 flavor 풍미, 맛 create 만들어 내다 delectable 감칠맛 나는 accompany 곁들이다, 동반하다 pureed 퓌레로 만든 greens 채소 spice up 양념하다, 풍미를 더하다 recipe 조리법 creation 창작(물) post 게시하다

3 라벨에 어떤 정보가 제공되는가?
(A) 제품 이용에 대한 아이디어
(B) 성분 목록

해설 **세부 사항**
첫 번째 단락에 제품명과 함께 요리할 때 메인 요리에 티스푼으로 한 스푼 넣거나, 식사에 곁들일 감칠맛 나는 소스를 만들어 보라(Add a teaspoon to your main dish while cooking, or create a delectable sauce ~)고 제품 이용 방법과 관련된 정보가 쓰여 있으므로 (A)가 정답이다.

> **어휘** ingredient (음식의) 성분, 재료

> **Paraphrasing** 지문의 Add a teaspoon to your main dish / create a delectable sauce → 정답의 Ideas for using a product

4 사모라 마살라 믹스 제조사가 매달 무엇을 할 것인가?
(A) 새로운 맛 출시
(B) 고객 의견 온라인 공유

해설 **세부 사항**
두 번째 단락에 이메일로 조리법과 요리한 음식 사진을 보내 달라고 요청하면서 매달 소셜 미디어에 가장 마음에 드는 다섯 가지를 게시할 것(Send your recipe and a picture of your creation ~ We will post five of our favorites on social media every month)이라고 알리고 있으므로 (B)가 정답이다.

> **어휘** release 출시하다, 발매하다

ETS 실전문제

1 (D)	2 (B)	3 (C)	4 (A)	5 (C)	6 (D)
7 (B)	8 (D)	9 (B)	10 (A)	11 (D)	12 (B)
13 (D)	14 (C)	15 (C)	16 (D)	17 (C)	18 (C)
19 (A)					

[1-2] 온라인 채팅

타마라 수실로 (오전 9시 4분) 안녕하세요. ¹제 은행 계좌 중 하나를 해지하고 그 자금을 제 저축 계좌로 옮기고 싶습니다. 그렇게 하도록 도와주실 수 있으세요?

그렉 해먼 (오전 9시 5분) 네, 그 절차를 시작해 드릴 수는 있지만, 우선 지점장님께서 이체를 승인하실 수 있도록 필요한 몇몇 서류를 작성하셔야 합니다. 계좌를 개설하는 데 사용하신 것과 동일한 이메일 주소를 여전히 사용하고 계신가요?

타마라 수실로 (오전 9시 6분) 네.

그렉 해먼 (오전 9시 7분) 보안상의 이유로, 그 이메일을 확인해 주시겠습니까?

타마라 수실로 (오전 9시 7분) t.susilo24@emailcloud.com일 겁니다.

그렉 해먼 (오전 9시 9분) 다 됐습니다. ²제가 이메일 첨부 파일로 해당 서류를 보내 드릴 수 있습니다. 그렇게 해도 괜찮으신가요?

타마라 수실로 (오전 9시 10분) 네.

어휘 account 계좌, 계정 fund 자금 process 과정 complete 완료하다 branch 지점, 지사 approve 승인하다 transfer 이체, 이전 set up 설치하다, 설정하다 verify 확인해 주다, 인증하다 attachment 첨부(된 것) work for (일정, 계획 등이) ~에게 괜찮다

1 수실로 씨가 무엇을 하고 싶어 하는가?
(A) 은행 지점장과 이야기하기
(B) 기술적인 문제 보고하기
(C) 계좌 개설하기
(D) 돈 이체하기

해설 세부 사항
수실로 씨가 오전 9시 4분 메시지에서 자신의 은행 계좌 중 하나를 해지하고 그 자금을 자신의 저축 계좌로 옮기고 싶다(I want to close one of my accounts at the bank and move the funds to my savings account)고 알리고 있으므로 (D)가 정답이다.

Paraphrasing 지문의 move the funds to my savings account → 정답의 Transfer money

2 오전 9시 9분에 해먼 씨가 "그렇게 해도 괜찮으신가요?"라고 쓸 때 무엇을 의미할 것 같은가?
(A) 수실로 씨의 컴퓨터가 제대로 작동하고 있는지 알기를 원한다.
(B) 수실로 씨가 서류의 전달 방식을 확인해 주기를 원한다.
(C) 수실로 씨와의 회의 일정을 잡기를 원한다.
(D) 거리 주소를 확인하기를 원한다.

해설 의도 파악
해먼 씨가 오전 9시 9분 메시지에서 이메일 첨부 파일로 해당 서류를 보내 줄 수 있다(I can get the documents to you by e-mail as an attachment)고 말하면서 그렇게 해도 괜찮은지(Does that work for you?) 묻고 있다. 이는 이메일 첨부 파일로 서류를 전달하는 것이 괜찮은지 확인해 달라는 뜻이므로 (B)가 정답이다.

어휘 function 기능하다 properly 제대로, 적절히 confirm 확인해 주다 method 방법

[3-4] 소셜 미디어 게시물

러켓 가든 서플라이의 저희 팀이 고구마 모종을 묶느라 바쁜 시간을 보냈습니다!

³고구마 모종을 사전 주문하시면서 지역 내에서 주문품을 받아 가시겠다고 표시하셨다면, 내일(6월 5일 일요일)부터 저희 매장에 방문하시기 바랍니다. 땅에 빨리 심을 수 있도록 가능한 한 빨리 해당 모종을 받아 가시기를 권해 드립니다. 주문품 배송을 선택하신 분들은, 저희가 6월 6일 월요일에 발송할 예정이라는 점에 유의하시기 바랍니다. 주문품의 도착 계획을 세우실 수 있도록 배송 추적 번호가 포함된 저희의 메시지를 이메일에서 확인해 보시기 바랍니다. 살아 있는 식물이 담겨 있으므로 여러분의 우편함에 너무 오래 방치해 두지 마시기 바랍니다. ⁴저희가 모든 주문품을 준비하는 모습이 담긴 동영상을 www.luckettgardensupply.com/blog/0602에서 보실 수 있습니다.

어휘 bundle 다발로 꾸리다 seedling 모종, 묘목 preorder 사전 주문하다 indicate 표기하다, 나타내다 pick up 가져가다, 가져오다 locally 지역 내에서, 지역적으로 tracking number 추적 번호 contain 담고 있다 clip 동영상

3 게시물의 목적은?
(A) 계절 농장 작업자를 모집하려고
(B) 배송 지연에 대해 사과하려고
(C) 제품이 이용 가능하다고 알리려고
(D) 농장 매장의 개장을 기념하려고

해설 주제/목적
초반부에서 고구마 모종을 사전 주문하면서 주문품을 받아가겠다고 표시한 경우에 내일부터 매장에 방문하라(If you preordered our sweet potato seedlings and indicated that you would pick up your order locally, you may come to our store starting tomorrow ~)고 알리고 있다. 이는 주문한 제품이 이용 가능하다는 사실을 알리는 것이므로 (C)가 정답이다.

어휘 recruit 모집하다 apologize for ~에 대해 사과하다 delay 지연, 지체 available 이용 가능한 celebrate 기념하다, 축하하다

4 게시물에 따르면, 고객들이 웹페이지에서 할 수 있는 것은?
(A) 짧은 영상 시청하기
(B) 특별 요청하기
(C) 나무 심기 설명 참고하기
(D) 업데이트된 배송 정책 확인하기

해설 세부 사항
후반부에서 모든 주문품을 준비하는 모습이 담긴 동영상을 볼 수 있는 웹페이지 주소(You can watch a clip of us preparing all the orders at www.luckettgardensupply.com/blog/0602)를 언급하고 있으므로 (A)가 정답이다.

어휘 consult (자료 등) 참고하다, (사람) 상담하다 instructions 설명(서), 안내(서) planting 나무 심기

Paraphrasing 지문의 a clip → 정답의 a short video

[5-7] 초대장

⁵성공적인 25주년을 축하하는 자리에 함께해 주세요!

아주 멋진 여정이었으며, 베이커스빌 인더스트리즈의 일원이 되어 주셔서 감사합니다.
우리가 이 기념비적인 순간을 축하하는 동료들과 함께하는 자리에 여러분과 여러분의 손님을 정중히 초대합니다.
저녁 식사와 디저트가 제공될 것입니다.

5, 6 (B), 6 (C) 5월 8일 토요일 오후 7시부터 오후 10시
페어햄튼 리조트 콘퍼런스 센터
6 (A) 콘퍼런스 플라자 8801, 레드우드 베이

⁷(650) 555-0174번이나 mfine@bakersvilleindustries.com 으로 4월 2일까지 매들린 파인 씨에게 답변해 주시기 바랍니다.

어휘 celebrate 기념하다, 축하하다   cordially 정중히
colleague 동료 (직원)   milestone 기념비적인 것, 중대 사건, 중요 단계   respond 답변하다, 대응하다

5. 초대장에 따르면, 5월 8일에 무슨 일이 있을 것인가?
(A) 회사가 매각될 것이다.
(B) 콘퍼런스 센터가 확장될 것이다.
(C) 업체가 기념일을 축하할 것이다.
(D) 임원이 은퇴 기념 파티를 할 것이다.

해설 세부 사항
상단의 제목에 25주년을 기념한다(we celebrate 25 successful years)고 쓰여 있고, 중반부에 그 행사 날짜가 5월 8일로 기재되어 있으므로 (C)가 정답이다.

어휘 expand 확장되다, 확대되다   anniversary (해마다 돌아오는) 기념일   retirement 은퇴

Paraphrasing 지문의 celebrate 25 successful years → 정답의 celebrate an anniversary

6. 초대장에 포함되지 않은 것은?
(A) 행사장 주소
(B) 행사 날짜
(C) 행사 시간
(D) 연사 이름

해설 Not / True
두 번째 단락에 5월 8일 토요일 오후 7시부터 오후 10시 (Saturday, May 8, from 7:00 P.M. to 10:00 P.M.)라고 행사 날짜와 시간이 제시되어 있고, 콘퍼런스 플라자 8801, 레드우드 베이(8801 Conference Plaza, Redwood Bay)라고 행사장 주소도 나와 있다. 따라서 언급되지 않은 (D)가 정답이다.

어휘 venue 행사장

7. 파인 씨는 누구일 것 같은가?
(A) 비즈니스 뉴스를 다루는 기자
(B) 베이커스빌 인더스트리즈 직원
(C) 콘퍼런스 센터 행정 업무 담당자
(D) 레드우드 베이 시 관계자

해설 추론 / 암시
이 초대장은 베이커스빌 인더스트리즈 기념행사의 초대장인데, 마지막 부분에 매들린 파인 씨에게 답변해 주기 바란다 (Please respond by April 2 to Madeline Fine ~)는 내용이 있으므로 파인 씨가 베이커스빌 인더스트리즈 직원이라는 것을 알 수 있다. 따라서 (B)가 정답이다.

어휘 cover (주제 등을) 다루다   administrator 행정 담당자   official 관계자, 당국자

[8-11] 엽서

콘래드 석세스 부동산
⁹**파니타 콘래드, 소유주**
셰릴 피터, 중개인
⁹**짐 타일러, 보조 중개인**
웬츠 가 1178
새스커툰, 서스캐처원, S7K 1J6
306-880-9339

⁸여러분의 부동산 성공이 저희의 최우선 순위입니다. 저희가 주택 매입이나 주택 매각을 즐거운 경험으로 만들어 드리겠습니다.
- ¹⁰저희는 49년 동안 가족이 운영해 온 업체입니다.
- 저희는 여러분이 살고 싶어 하시는 곳의 지역 사회와 학교, 레스토랑, 공원, 그리고 여러 가지 기회들에 대한 통찰을 제공해 드릴 수 있습니다.
- 저희는 처음부터 끝까지 모든 것을 처리해 드립니다.
- ¹¹저희는 무료로 시장 비교 분석 서비스를 제공해 드립니다.
- 저희는 서스캐처원 내 10대 업체로 선정되었습니다.

현 거주자
브랜드 가 21243
새스커툰, 서스캐처원, S7K 1J6

어휘 property 부동산, 건물   real estate 부동산   priority 우선순위   family-owned 가족이 운영하는   insight 통찰력   opportunity 기회   handle 처리하다, 다루다   comparative 비교의   analysis 분석   vote 투표로 선정하다   current 현재의   resident 거주자

8. 엽서의 목적은?
(A) 지역의 새 거주자를 환영하려고
(B) 성장하는 업체를 위해 잠재 영업사원들을 모집하려고
(C) 새로운 업체의 공석을 알리려고
(D) 부동산 회사의 서비스를 홍보하려고

해설 주제 / 목적
사람들의 부동산 성공이 최우선 순위임을 밝히면서 주택 매입이나 주택 매각을 즐거운 경험으로 만들어 주겠다(Your real estate success is our top priority. Let us make buying or selling a home a pleasant experience)고 언급하고 있다. 이는 부동산 업체가 자사의 서비스를 홍보하는 것이므로 (D)가 정답이다.

어휘 neighborhood 지역, 인근, 이웃   recruit 모집하다   potential 잠재적인   promote 홍보하다

9. 타일러 씨에 대해 사실일 것 같은 것은?
(A) 여러 부동산을 소유하고 있다.
(B) 콘래드 씨에 의해 고용되었다.
(C) 새 집으로 이사하는 것에 대해 생각하고 있다.
(D) 브랜드 로드에 거주하고 있다.

해설 추론 / 암시
상단에 타일러 씨는 보조 중개인(Jim Tyler, Associate Broker)으로, 콘래드 씨는 소유주(Panita Conrad, Owner)로 표기되어 있으므로 타일러 씨가 콘래드 씨에 의해 고용된 직원임을 알 수 있다. 따라서 (B)가 정답이다.

어휘 own 소유하다   employ 고용하다

211

10 콘래드 석세스 부동산에 대해 언급된 것은?
(A) 가족이 운영하는 업체이다.
(B) 서스캐처원의 여러 다른 도시로 확장하고 있다.
(C) 최근 새스커툰으로 이전했다.
(D) 새스커툰에서 최고의 업체로 지명되었다.

해설 Not / True
중반부에 49년 동안 가족이 운영해 온 업체(We have been a family-owned business for 49 years)라는 정보가 제시되어 있으므로 (A)가 정답이다.

어휘 expand 확장하다, 확대하다 relocate 이전하다 name 지명하다

11 엽서에 따르면, 무엇이 무료로 제공되는가?
(A) 해당 지역의 상세 지도
(B) 초기 상담 서비스
(C) 소기업 운영에 관한 강연 초대장
(D) 지역 부동산 시장에 대한 비교 연구

해설 세부 사항
후반부에 무료 시장 비교 분석 서비스를 제공해 준다(We provide a free comparative market analysis)는 특징이 소개되어 있으므로 (D)가 정답이다.

어휘 at no charge 무료로 detailed 상세한

> **Paraphrasing** 지문의 free → 질문의 at no charge
> 지문의 comparative market analysis → 정답의 comparative study of the area's property market

[12-15] 문자 메시지

> 카를로 트루히요 (오전 8시 19분)
> 안녕하세요. 사무실로 오고 계시는 중인가요? ¹³에코 페인츠의 새라 우 씨의 전화를 막 받았어요. ¹⁴에코 사의 가을 마케팅 캠페인을 논의하기 위해 오전 10시에 만나길 원하세요.
>
> 제인 윌리엄스 (오전 8시 21분)
> 뜻밖이네요! 그래도 그분에게 발표할 초안은 있을지도 몰라요. 그건 그렇고, 저는 이미 사무실에 와 있어요.
>
> 제프리 반스 (오전 8시 22분)
> 저는 아직 기차입니다.
>
> 카를로 트루히요 (오전 8시 24분)
> 있습니다. 사실, 제가 전체 발표를 다 준비를 해 두었어요. 어쨌든, 그분과 회의할 때 갓 나온 커피와 건강에 좋은 간식이 있었으면 합니다. ¹²,¹⁵제프리 씨, 오시는 길에 과일 한 접시를 구입해 주시겠어요?
>
> 제인 윌리엄스 (오전 8시 27분)
> 원체스터역 옆에 있는 모닝 딜라이트 델리에 보통 썰어 놓은 과일이 있어요.
>
> 제프리 반스 (오전 8시 28분)
> 맞습니다, 제인 씨. 그리고 ¹⁵제 기차가 곧 도착할 겁니다. 제가 처리할게요.
>
> 카를로 트루히요 (오전 8시 30분)
> 잘됐네요! 우 씨에게 좋은 인상을 남겨야 합니다.

> 제프리 반스 (오전 8시 58분)
> 성공입니다! 10분 후에 사무실에 도착할 겁니다.

어휘 on one's way to ~로 가는 길인 unexpected 뜻밖의, 예기치 못한 outline 초안, 개요 present 발표하다, 제시하다 by the way 그건 그렇고, 그런데 usually 보통, 일반적으로 take care of ~을 처리하다 make a good impression 좋은 인상을 남기다

12 트루히요 씨가 팀원들에게 메시지를 쓴 한 가지 이유는?
(A) 슬라이드 준비를 요청하기 위해
(B) 심부름할 사람을 찾기 위해
(C) 프로젝트에 관한 소식을 요청하기 위해
(D) 회사에 지각하는 것을 사과하기 위해

해설 주제 / 목적
트루히요 씨가 8시 24분 메시지에서 제프리 씨에게 회의에 관해 이야기하면서 오는 길에 과일 한 접시를 구입해 달라(Jeffrey, could you pick up a fruit platter on the way in?)고 요청했으므로 (B)가 정답이다.

어휘 run an errand 심부름하다 apologize for ~에 대해 사과하다

13 우 씨가 누구일 것 같은가?
(A) 구직 지원자
(B) 잘 알려진 미술가
(C) 모닝 딜라이트 영업사원
(D) 에코 페인츠 직원

해설 추론 / 암시
트루히요 씨가 8시 19분 메시지에서 에코 페인츠의 새라 우 씨가 전화했다(I just got a call from Sarah Wu at Eco Paints)고 했으므로 (D)가 정답이다.

어휘 applicant 지원자, 신청자 well-known 잘 알려진 associate 직원, 동료, 동업자

14 문자 메시지에 따르면, 오전 10시에 아마 무슨 일이 있을 것인가?
(A) 트루히요 씨가 과일을 구입할 것이다.
(B) 트루히요 씨가 사무실로 출발할 것이다.
(C) 고객과의 회의가 시작될 것이다.
(D) 편의점이 문을 열 것이다.

해설 추론 / 암시
트루히요 씨가 8시 19분 메시지에서 새라 우 씨가 가을 마케팅 캠페인을 논의하기 위해 오전 10시에 만나길 원한다(She wants to meet at 10 A.M. to discuss Eco's fall marketing campaign)고 했고, 그 이후 회의 준비에 대한 메시지가 이어지고 있으므로 (C)가 정답이다.

15 오전 8시 58분에, 반스 씨가 "성공입니다"라고 쓸 때 암시하는 것은?
(A) 우 씨에게 좋은 인상을 남겼다.
(B) 제때 사무실에 도착했다.
(C) 간식을 구입했다.
(D) 분실한 캠페인 초안을 찾았다.

해설 **의도 파악**

트루히요 씨가 8시 24분 메시지에서 제프리 씨에게 오는 길에 과일 한 접시를 구입해 달라(Jeffrey, could you pick up a fruit platter on the way in?)고 요청한 것과 관련해, 반스 씨가 8시 28분 메시지에서 그 일을 처리하겠다(I'll take care of it)고 대답한 후에 "성공입니다"라고 알리는 상황이다. 이는 과일을 구입하는 데 성공했다는 뜻이므로 (C)가 정답이다.

어휘 on time 제때 locate 위치를 찾다 missing 분실한, 빠진, 없는

[16-19] 패키지 삽입지

뭄바이 푸드 라즈말라이 – 전통 인도 디저트

16 제공량: 12인분
순 중량: 850그램
17(A) 냉동 보관
이용 기한 6월 10일

우유와 크림, 코티지 치즈, 설탕, 그리고 향신료들의 독특한 조합으로 가족을 기쁘게 해 주세요. 라즈말라이는 솜씨 있게 조리된 다음, 얇게 썬 피스타치오로 장식되는 달콤한 요리입니다. 모든 음식에 우아함을 더해주며, **17(B) 휴일과 축제에 이상적입니다.**

이용 안내:
상자에서 꺼내 음식 제공용 접시에 놓으세요. **18 전자레인지로 5분간 해동하세요. 10분 동안 그대로 두었다가 제공하십시오.**
개봉 후에는 냉장 보관을 하시기를 바라며, 4일 이내에 소비하십시오. 재냉동하지 마십시오.

17(D) 성분: 우유, 크림, 코티지 치즈, 설탕, 레몬 주스, 카르다몸, 장미수, 그리고 피스타치오

19 스코틀랜드 애버딘 생산
영국 런던 콜카타 산업 유통

어휘 traditional 전통적인 serving 1인당 제공량, 1인분 net weight (식품 용기의 무게를 뺀) 순 중량 unique 녹녹한, 특별한 combination 조합 skillfully 솜씨 있게 decorate 장식하다 addition 추가(되는 것) ideal 이상적인 directions 설명, 안내 remove 꺼내다, 제거하다 microwave 전자레인지에 조리하다 defrost 해동 refrigerate 냉장 보관을 하다 consume 소비하다 refreeze 재냉동하다 ingredient (식품의) 성분, 재료 distribute 유통하다, 배포하다

16 패키지 삽입지에 따르면, 한 상자가 몇 명의 저녁 식사 손님에게 적합할 것인가?
(A) 6명   (B) 8명
(C) 10명   (D) 12명

해설 **세부 사항**
상단에 제공량이 12인분(Servings: 12)으로 표기되어 있으므로 (D)가 정답이다.

어휘 be suitable for ~에 적합하다, ~에 어울리다

17 뭄바이 푸드의 라즈말라이에 대해 암시되지 않은 것은?
(A) 상점 냉동식품 코너에서 찾을 수 있다.
(B) 기념행사에서 제공하기 적합한 요리이다.
(C) 최고의 새로운 디저트로 콘테스트에서 우승했다.
(D) 유제품을 포함하고 있다.

해설 **Not/True**
상단에 '냉동 보관(Keep frozen)'이라는 문구에서 (A)를, 첫 번째 단락의 '휴일과 축제에 이상적이다(is ideal for holidays and festivals)'라는 특징에서 (B)를, 그리고 하단 성분 부분에 '우유, 크림, 치즈(Ingredients: milk, cream, cottage cheese, ~)' 등이 표기된 부분에서 (D)를 확인할 수 있다. 하지만 콘테스트 우승과 관련된 정보는 제시되어 있지 않으므로 (C)가 정답이다.

어휘 appropriate 적합한 serve (음식 등을) 제공하다 celebration 기념행사, 축하 행사 contain 포함하다

> **Paraphrasing** 지문의 holidays and festivals → 보기 (B)의 celebrations
> 지문의 milk, cream, cottage cheese → 보기 (D)의 milk products

18 해당 제품은 전자레인지에서 꺼낸 후에 얼마나 빨리 제공할 준비가 되는가?
(A) 즉시   (B) 5분 후에
(C) 10분 후에   (D) 다음 날에

해설 **세부 사항**
이용 안내에 전자레인지로 5분간 해동한 후, 10분 동안 그대로 두었다가 제공하라(Microwave on the defrost setting for five minutes. Let sit for ten minutes before serving)고 알리고 있으므로 (C)가 정답이다.

어휘 following 다음의, 아래의

19 해당 제품이 어디에서 제조되는가?
(A) 애버딘에서   (B) 콜카타에서
(C) 런던에서   (D) 뭄바이에서

해설 **세부 사항**
하단에 스코틀랜드 애버딘 생산(Produced in Aberdeen, Scotland)으로 표기되어 있으므로 (A)가 정답이다.

> **Paraphrasing** 지문의 Produced → 질문의 manufactured

UNIT 20 복수 지문

지문 구성과 독해 전략 ········· 본책 p.280

중요 공지:

카터스 팜 프레시가 지난주 자사의 채소 통조림(420그램/14.5온스 사이즈) 여러 상자가 잘못된 라벨이 붙여진 채 지역 상점들에 배송됐다고 알렸습니다. 라벨이 잘못된 통조림은 제품 코드가 G7780 또는 G7781로 찍혀 있습니다.

환불을 받으시려면 9월 12일까지 구입하신 상점에 제품을 반품하시기를 바랍니다. 제조업체 정책에 따라 반품 상품과 함께 원본 영수증을 제출해야 합니다.

어휘 announce 알리다, 발표하다 incorrect 부정확한, 맞지 않는 mislabeled 라벨이 잘못 붙여진 purchase 구입 manufacturer 제조사 policy 정책 original 원본의, 원래의 submit 제출하다

델가도 씨께,

귀하의 매장에서 보낸 옥수수 통조림 배송을 받았습니다. 2주 후에 우편으로 67.5달러 수표를 받으실 겁니다. 이는 귀하의 고객들이 라벨이 잘못된 통조림을 반품했을 때 환불된 금액을 충당할 수 있을 것입니다. 논의했던 바와 같이, 여기에는 영수증이 없는 고객에게 환불해 주신 7.5달러가 포함되어 있습니다.

귀하와 귀하의 고객에게 불편을 드려 죄송합니다.

카렌 우
카터스 팜 프레시 고객 서비스 담당자

어휘 shipment 배송품 in the amount of ~의 금액으로 include 포함하다 apologize for ~에 대해 사과하다 inconvenience 불편 patron 고객

Q 우 씨에 대해 암시된 것은?
(A) 통조림 제품을 추가로 받기를 기대한다.
(B) 원래 약속했던 것보다 늦게 수표를 보낼 것이다.
(C) 정책에 예외를 뒀다.
(D) 델가도 씨와 만날 예정이다.

어휘 additional 추가의 goods 상품 originally 원래 make an exception 예외를 두다, 특별 취급하다

ETS 유형연습   본책 p.281

1 (B) **2** (A)

광고 + 후기

비 데어 가전 기기 수리
세인트-데니스 가 839번지, 몬트리올, 퀘벡 H9R 3J4
514-555-0148

다음은 가전 기기 수리가 필요할 때 저희에게 전화 주셔야 하는 몇 가지 아주 중요한 이유입니다.

1번: 저렴한 가격. 시에서 최저가를 보장합니다.
2번: 친절하고, 유니폼을 갖춰 입은 기술자들
3번: **²3대에 걸쳐 가족이 소유해 온 지역 기업입니다.**
4번: 신속하고, 수준 높은 서비스. **¹당일 서비스를 제공하기 위해 모든 노력을 기울입니다.**
5번: 대형 가전 기기 현장 수리와 소형 가전 기기 매장 내 접수
6번: 대형 창고에 많은 물품을 보유하고 있으므로 부품 대기 시간이 없습니다.

어휘 appliance 가전 기기 affordable (가격이) 알맞은, 저렴한 guarantee 보장하다 uniformed 유니폼을 갖춰 입은 family-owned 가족이 소유한 generation 세대 quality 수준 높은, 질 좋은 on-site 현장의 drop-off (사물) 갖다 놓기, (사람) 내려 주기

---

https://www.repairservicesreviews.net

수리 서비스 후기: 비 데어 가전 기기 수리

저는 최근에 저희 집에 있는 물이 새는 냉장고를 고치기 위해 다섯 곳의 다른 수리 서비스 업체에 전화했습니다. 그 모든 곳에 메시지를 남겼습니다. 오직 한 곳만 제게 10분 내에 다시 전화를 주었습니다. 그곳이 바로 비 데어 가전 기기 수리 회사였습니다. 제가 이 업체에 대해 전혀 들어 본 적이 없기는 했지만, **¹당장 문제가 처리되기를 원했기 때문에**, 기회를 잡기로 결정했습니다. **²소유주이신 코발치크 씨**께서 즉시 그 과정을 시작해 주셨습니다. 수리 기사께서 그날 오후에 도착하셨습니다. 그는 신속히 문제를 진단할 수 있었고, 1시간 내로 문제를 수리해 주셨습니다. 믿음이 가고 의지할 수 있으면서 여러분을 계속 기다리게 하지 않을 서비스 업체가 필요하시면 비 데어 가전 기기 수리 회사에 전화해 보시기를 진심으로 추천합니다!

– 랄프 더갠, 6월 4일

어휘 leaking (물, 가스 등이) 새는, 누출되는 attend to ~을 처리하다 immediately 즉시 set A in motion A를 시작하다 process 과정 diagnose 진단하다 trusted 믿음이 가는 reliable 의지할 수 있는, 신뢰할 수 있는

---

1 광고에 기재된 어떤 이유가 더갠 씨에게 가장 매력적이었을 것 같은가?
(A) 3번 **(B) 4번**

해설 연계

후기의 초반부에 더갠 씨는 당장 문제가 처리되기 원했다(I wanted to have the problem attended to right away)는 말과 함께 신속히 문제를 진단해 수리했다는 내용이 있다. 이는 광고의 4번 항목에서 '당일 서비스를 제공하기 위해 모든 노력을 기울인다(We make every effort to provide same-day service)'고 알리는 것과 같은 맥락이므로 (B)가 정답이다.

어휘 appealing to ~에게 매력적인

2 코발치크 씨에 대해 어떤 결론을 내릴 수 있는가?
(A) 가족 기업의 3세대 소유주이다.
(B) 평생 동안 몬트리올에 거주해 왔다.

해설 연계

후기의 중반부에서 코발치크 씨가 소유주(Ms. Kowalczyk, the owner)라고 언급하고 있는데, 광고의 3번 항목에서 3대에 걸쳐 가족이 소유해 온 지역 기업(We have been a family-owned, local business for three generations)이라고 쓰여 있어 코발치크 씨가 그 가족 기업의 3세대 소유주임을 알 수 있으므로 (A)가 정답이다.

어휘 third-generation 3세대의

ETS 실전문제

본책 p.282

1 (B)	2 (A)	3 (A)	4 (D)	5 (D)	6 (B)
7 (D)	8 (A)	9 (D)	10 (A)	11 (C)	12 (C)
13 (A)	14 (D)	15 (B)	16 (B)	17 (C)	18 (D)
19 (C)	20 (D)	21 (B)	22 (D)	23 (C)	24 (A)
25 (B)	26 (C)	27 (A)	28 (D)	29 (D)	30 (D)

[1-5] 안내 책자 + 이메일

앨로이 어드벤처와 함께하는 콜롬비아 당일 여행

콜롬비아에서 가장 아름다운 풍경을 볼 수 있는 재미있고 사교적인 방법을 찾고 계신가요? **1** 앨로이 어드벤처가 매주 매력적인 작은 마을 제리코로 향하는 당일 여행을 제공해 드립니다.

매주 토요일에 영어를 구사하는 현지 전문가가 북적대는 메델린에서 제리코의 진기한 조약돌 거리까지 버스 한 대의 일일 여행객들을 **4** 인솔합니다. **2(B), 2(D)** 제리코에 도착한 후, 해당 그룹은 커피 농장까지 하이킹하고 맛있는 점심을 즐길 것입니다. **2(C)** 이 그룹은 그 후 제리코로 돌아가 이 마을의 주요 장소들을 둘러볼 것입니다. 상세 정보는 아래에 기재되어 있습니다.

• 오전 7시 메델린의 터미널 버스 정류장에서 출발; 오후 8시 복귀
• 총 도보 시간: 3시간; 이동 거리: 9킬로미터
• 견고한 등산화, 자외선 차단제, 물, 그리고 간식 적극 권장
• 점심 식사 포함. 다음 중 하나를 고르세요.
 (1) 닭고기를 곁들인 파스타, (2) 소고기 샌드위치, (3) 해산물 스튜, 또는 (4) **5** 채식 타코
• 비용(교통비 포함): 1인당 10만 콜롬비아 페소

페드로 라라 씨에게 plara@alroyadventures.com으로 이메일을 보내 자리를 예약하세요. 여행 1회당 최대 참가 인원이 20명이라는 점에 유의하시기 바랍니다.

어휘 charming 매력적인 local 현지의, 지역의 a busload of 버스 한 대의 bustling 북적대는 quaint 신기한 plantation 농장 explore 둘러보다, 답사하다 sturdy 견고한, 튼튼한 include 포함하다 reserve 예약하다 spot 자리, 장소 maximum 최대, 최고 participant 참가자

수신: 페드로 라라 ⟨plara@alroyadventures.com⟩
발신: 라다 굽타 ⟨rgupta@sunmail.com⟩
날짜: 3월 11일
제목: 예약 문의

라라 씨께,

제 남편과 저는 이번 주 토요일인 3월 15일에 귀사의 단체 하이킹에 참가하고 싶습니다. **3** 저희는 한동안 제리코를 방문하기를 원해 왔으며, 귀사의 여행은 사람들을 만나기 아주 좋은 방법인 것처럼 보이기도 합니다!

교통편에 관한 질문이 하나 있습니다. **3** 저희는 자동차가 있어서 따로 운전해서 가고 싶습니다. 버스가 승객을 그 마을의 중앙 광장에 내려 주는 것으로 알고 있습니다. 그곳에서 오전 10시에 만날 수 있을 겁니다. 하이킹 후에는, 직접 운전해서 메델린으로 돌아갈 겁니다. 저희는 기꺼이 전체 가격을 지불하겠습니다. 이 요청을 수용해 주실 수 있으신가요? 그러시다면, **5** 저희는 둘 모두 점심 식사로 채식을 선호합니다.

대단히 감사합니다.

라다 굽타

어휘 reservation 예약 inquiry 문의 outing 짧은 여행, 야유회 separately 따로, 분리해서 square 광장 accommodate 수용하다

---

1 앨로이 어드벤처가 무엇인가?
(A) 캠핑장 (B) 여행사
(C) 놀이공원 (D) 스포츠 용품 매장

해설 세부 사항

안내 책자 첫 번째 단락에 앨로이 어드벤처가 매력적인 작은 마을 제리코로 향하는 당일 여행을 제공한다(Alroy Adventures offers weekly day trips to the charming small town of Jerico)는 내용이 언급되어 있으므로 (B)가 정답이다.

2 광고되는 행사의 일부로 언급되지 않은 것은?
(A) 호텔 체크인하기
(B) 식사하기
(C) 작은 마을을 걸어 다니기
(D) 커피가 재배되는 곳 방문하기

해설 Not / True

안내 책자 두 번째 단락에 해당 그룹은 커피 농장까지 하이킹하고 맛있는 점심을 즐긴다(the group will hike to a coffee plantation and enjoy a delicious lunch)고 쓰여 있는 부분에서 (B)와 (D)를, 그리고 제리코로 돌아가 그 마을의 주요 장소들을 둘러본다(The group will then return to Jerico to explore the town's main sites)고 알리는 부분에서 (C)를 확인할 수 있다. 따라서 언급되지 않은 (A)가 정답이다.

Paraphrasing 지문의 hike to a coffee plantation → 보기 (D)의 Visiting a place where coffee is grown
지문의 enjoy a delicious lunch → 보기 (B)의 Eating a meal
지문의 return to Jerico to explore the town's main sites → 보기 (C)의 Walking around a small town

3 굽타 씨는 그룹을 어디에서 만나고 싶어 하는가?
(A) 제리코에서 (B) 메델린에서
(C) 공항에서 (D) 농장에서

해설 세부 사항

이메일의 첫 번째 단락에서 제리코로 여행을 가고 싶어 한다(We have wanted to visit Jerico for a while now ~)고 알리고 있고, 두 번째 단락에서 따로 자동차를 운전해 가서 그곳에서 만나고 싶다(We have a car and would prefer to drive separately. ~ We could meet you there ~)는 뜻을 밝히고 있다. 따라서 (A)가 정답이다.

4 안내 책자에서 두 번째 단락 첫 번째 줄에 쓰인 단어 "leads"와 의미가 가장 가까운 것은?
(A) 진행하다   (B) 영향을 미치다
(C) 열다   (D) 이끌다

해설 **동의어 찾기**
leads를 포함한 문장은 '북적대는 메델린에서 제리코의 진기한 조약돌 거리까지 여행객들을 인솔한다(leads a busload of day trippers from bustling Medellin to the quaint cobblestone streets of Jerico)'와 같은 의미로 해석할 수 있으며, 여기서 leads는 '이끌다, 인솔하다'라는 뜻으로 쓰였다. 따라서 (D) guides가 정답이다.

5 굽타 씨와 남편은 3월 15일에 점심 식사로 무엇을 원하는가?
(A) 파스타   (B) 샌드위치
(C) 스튜   (D) 타코

해설 **연계**
이메일 두 번째 단락에 둘 모두 점심 식사로 채식을 선호한다(we would both prefer the vegetarian option for lunch) 쓰여 있는데, 안내 책자 중반부에 있는 채식 타코(vegetarian tacos)가 그에 해당하는 음식이므로 (D)가 정답이다.

[6-10] 구인 공고 + 회람

엑서소스 LLC와 함께하는 인턴십

엑서소스는 전문 운동선수와 아마추어 운동선수 모두를 위한 영양 프로그램 설계에서 피트니스 업계를 선도하는 빠르게 성장하고 있는 회사입니다. 모든 프로그램은 과학적으로 **6**뒷받침됩니다. 저희는 영양학을 이용해 운동 능력을 개선하고, 회복 시간을 단축시키며, **7**스포츠 관련 부상을 피하거나 치료하는 방법을 운동선수들에게 가르쳐 드립니다. 저희 헌신적인 마케팅팀은 저희 코치들과 영양사들, 그리고 의료 전문가들이 스키 타기와 달리기, 자전거 타기, 그리고 수영하기 등과 같은 다양한 경기장 속 운동선수들에게 다가갈 수 있도록 돕습니다.

8저희는 현재 마케팅 전공 학사 학위 프로그램에 등록되어 있으면서 빠른 속도로 진행되는 전문적인 환경에서 인턴십 활동을 하는 것에 관심이 있는 대학생을 찾고 있습니다. 합격한 지원자는 반드시 세부 사항에 대한 뛰어난 주의력, 다른 사람들과 교류할 수 있는 능력, 그리고 뛰어난 말하기 및 쓰기 의사소통 능력을 소유하고 있어야 합니다. 한 가지 이상의 스포츠 또는 건강 관련 활동을 지속적으로 해온 것은 확실한 가산점이 됩니다.

지원하시려면, https://www.exersource.com/jobs/marketing_internship을 방문하시기 바랍니다.

어휘 nutrition 영양(학)   athlete 운동선수   back 뒷받침하다   improve 개선하다   performance 수행 (능력), 실력   shorten 단축하다   recovery 회복   avoid 피하다   heal 치료하다, 치유하다   related 관련된   injury 부상   dedicated 헌신적인   nutritionist 영양사   reach 다가가다, 이르다   arena 경기장, 활동 무대   enrolled in ~에 등록된   undergraduate degree 학사 학위   fast-paced 빠른 속도로 진행되는   applicant 지원자, 신청자   possess 소유하다   attention 주의(력)   detail 세부 요소   ongoing 지속적인   commitment 참여, 헌신   definite 분명한

회람

10수신: 인사부
발신: 리앤 타운슬리
참조: 에반 펭
날짜: 5월 2일
제목: 인턴직 관련 소식

이틀 전에, 에반 펭 씨와 제가 14명의 인턴직 지원자들의 면접을 완료했습니다. 어제, 저희가 각 지원자에 대한 메모 내용을 비교했으며, 실비아 토레스 씨가 이 직책에 대한 최선의 선택이라는 결론을 내렸습니다. **8**토레스 씨는 앤던 대학교에 다니고 있으며, 인턴십의 모든 기준을 충족하고 있습니다. 이분은 논리 정연하고, 상냥하며, 아주 체계적입니다. **9**이분의 교수님들께서 이분을 위해 열정적인 추천서를 제출했습니다. 이것이 특히 이분을 나머지 지원자들과 차별화해 주는 것입니다. 더욱이, 토레스 씨는 학교 육상팀의 일원입니다.

토레스 씨의 신입 직원 입사 서류를 준비해 주시기 바랍니다. **10**여러분과 함께하는 이분의 오리엔테이션은 5월 9일 오전으로 예정되어야 합니다. 펭 씨와 제가 이분을 환영하기 위해 나머지 저희 팀원들과 함께 참석할 것입니다.

어휘 compare 비교하다   candidate 지원자, 후보자   conclude 결론을 내리다   criteria 기준   articulate 논리 정연한   agreeable 상냥한   well-organized 아주 체계적인   enthusiastic 열정적인   on one's behalf ~을 위해, ~을 대신해   in particular 특히   set A apart from B A를 B와 차별화하다   furthermore 더욱이, 게다가   present 참석한, 출석한

6 구인 공고에서 첫 번째 단락 세 번째 줄에 쓰인 단어 "backed"와 의미가 가장 가까운 것은?
(A) 반전된, 반대의
(B) 뒷받침된, 지지된
(C) 실험된
(D) 지연된, 지체된

해설 **동의어 찾기**
backed를 포함한 부분은 '과학적으로 뒷받침되다(are scientifically backed)'와 같은 의미로 해석할 수 있으므로 (B) supported가 정답이다.

7 엑서소스의 한 가지 목표는?
(A) 스포츠 장비를 디자인하는 것
(B) 스포츠팀들이 운동선수를 모집하도록 돕는 것
(C) 판매용 건강 식품을 준비하는 것
(D) 운동선수 부상을 방지하도록 돕는 것

해설 **세부 사항**
구인 공고의 첫 번째 단락에서 스포츠 관련 부상을 피하거나 치료하는 방법을 운동선수들에게 가르쳐 준다(We teach athletes how to ~ and avoid or heal sports-related injuries)고 언급하고 있으므로 (D)가 정답이다.

어휘 equipment 장비   recruit 모집하다   prevent 방지하다, 막다   injury 부상

Paraphrasing 지문의 avoid ~ sports-related injuries → 정답의 help prevent injuries

8 토레스 씨에 대해 사실일 것 같은 것은?
(A) 마케팅을 공부하고 있다.
(B) 신임 관리자이다.
(C) 전문 수영 선수이다.
(D) 자전거팀 코치이다.

해설 연계
회람의 첫 번째 단락에서 토레스 씨가 인턴십의 모든 기준을 충족한다(Ms. Torres ~ meets all the criteria for the internship)고 알리고 있다. 구인 공고의 두 번째 단락에서 현재 마케팅 전공 학사 학위 프로그램에 등록되어 있는 대학생을 찾고 있다(We seek a student currently enrolled in an undergraduate degree program in marketing ~)고 밝히고 있으므로 토레스 씨가 마케팅을 전공하는 학생임을 알 수 있다. 따라서 (A)가 정답이다.

9 타운슬리 씨에 따르면, 다른 지원자들보다 토렌스 씨가 선택된 주된 이유는?
(A) 아주 체계적이다.
(B) 지역 대학교에 다닌다.
(C) 가장 숙련된 지원자였다.
(D) 강력한 추천을 받았다.

해설 세부 사항
회람의 첫 번째 단락에서 학교 교수님들이 열정적인 추천서를 제출한 것이 나머지 지원자들과 특히 차별화해 주는 부분(Her professors submitted enthusiastic recommendations on her behalf. This, in particular, set her apart from the other candidates)이라고 강조하고 있으므로 (D)가 정답이다.

어휘 skilled 숙련된, 능숙한

Paraphrasing 지문의 enthusiastic → 정답의 strong

10 인사부가 할 것으로 예상되는 것은?
(A) 신입 직원 오리엔테이션 계획하기
(B) 앤던 대학교에 연락하기
(C) 펭 씨를 새로운 팀으로 전근시키기
(D) 2차 면접 일정 잡기

해설 세부 사항
회람 상단에 수신이 인사부(To: Human Resources)로 표기되어 있고, 두 번째 단락에서 신입 사원 입사 서류 준비를 부탁하며, 오리엔테이션이 5월 9일 오전으로 예정되어야 한다(Her orientation with you should be scheduled for the morning of May 9)고 알리고 있으므로 (A)가 정답이다.

어휘 transfer 전근시키다

[11-15] 웹페이지 + 후기

https://www.bavarianouterwear.com/about

| 홈 | 소개 | 제품 | 연락처 |

설립자인 마빈 프리지 씨는 성공적인 회계사로 일하던 중 본인의 진정한 열정이 스노보드와 스키 같은 겨울 스포츠에 있음을 깨닫고 진로를 변경했습니다. 바바리안 산악 지대에 있는 한 마을을 방문하던 중, 프리지 씨는 한 스키 스웨터에 주목했는데, 이것으로 인해 전통적인 스타일이면서 현대적이고 친환경적인 섬유로 만들어진 스웨터가 있으면 좋겠다는 생각을 하게 되었습니다. 프리지 씨가 본인의 아이디어를 함께 스키를 타는 애덤 패터슨 씨와 공유했을 때, 두 분은 스포츠 의류 회사를 시작하기로 결정했습니다. 그들이 생산한 첫 번째 의류는 프리지 씨께서 독일에서 발견했던 스키 스웨터의 현대적인 버전이었습니다. 이는, 실제로, **13** 회사에서 지금껏 제조해 온 유일한 스키 스웨터 모델입니다.

바바리안 아우터웨어는 스키와 하이킹, 그리고 등산을 포함하는 다양한 퍼포먼스 스포츠용 의류를 제공합니다. 수석 디자이너 크리스텐 쿡 씨는 전통적인 디자인과 현대적인 섬유를 면밀히 연구합니다. **11** 쿡 씨는 또한 신제품에 대한 영감을 얻기 위해 전 세계를 여행합니다. **12** 회사 설립자들은 지난 10년 동안 회사의 일일 운영에 계속 관여해 오고 있으며, 패터슨 씨는 인쇄물 카탈로그와 웹사이트를 위한 제품 설명을 계속 작성하고 있습니다.

어휘 founder 설립자, 창립자 accountant 회계사 discover 발견하다 passion 열정 traditional 전통적인 contemporary 현대적인, 동시대의 eco-friendly 친환경적인 fabric 섬유, 직물 fellow 동료의, 같은 처지의 launch 시작하다, 출시하다 garment 의류, 의복 spot 발견하다, 찾다 apparel 의류, 복장 a variety of 다양한 include 포함하다 inspiration 영감 involved in ~에 관여하는, ~에 참여하는 day-to-day 매일의 operation 운영, 가동 description 설명, 묘사

후기: 바바리안 아우터웨어 스키 스웨터

저는 **13** 한 달 전에 바바리안 아우터웨어에서 구입한 스키 스웨터에 대해 복잡한 심정입니다. 이 스웨터가 몸에 잘 맞고 스키를 타는 동안 따뜻하게 해줘서 마음에 듭니다. 이 스웨터의 박음질과 세부적인 강조 요소들이 매력적이게 만들어 줍니다. 저를 실망시킨 점은 소재의 품질입니다. 웹페이지의 제품 설명을 보고 피부에 닿는 느낌이 부드러울 것이라 생각했습니다. 실제로는, **14** 소재가 다소 거칠고 부드럽지 않습니다. **15** 긴 하루 동안 제 학생들을 가르치고 나면, 불편해집니다.

— 에이미 슐츠

어휘 mixed feelings 복잡한 심정 appreciate 진가를 인정하다, 감사하다 fit 잘 맞다, 어울리다 stitching 박음질, 바느질 detailed 세부적인, 상세한 accent 강조 요소 attractive 매력적인 disappoint 실망시키다 quality 품질, 질 material 소재, 재료 rather 다소, 오히려 rough 거친 coarse 거친 instruct 가르치다 uncomfortable 불편한

11 웹페이지에서 쿡 씨에 대해 언급하는 것은?
(A) 막 승진되었다.
(B) 전통적인 섬유를 이용하는 것을 선호한다.
(C) 업무로 인해 주기적으로 여행한다.
(D) 웹사이트를 디자인했다.

해설 Not/True

웹페이지의 두 번째 단락에 쿡 씨가 신제품에 대한 영감을 얻기 위해 전 세계를 여행한다(Ms. Cook also travels the globe to find inspiration for new products)고 언급하고 있으므로 (C)가 정답이다.

어휘 promote 승진시키다 regularly 주기적으로, 규칙적으로

> **Paraphrasing** 지문의 travels the globe to find inspiration for new products → 정답의 regularly travels in her work

12 웹페이지에서 바바리안 아우터웨어에 대해 암시하는 것은?
(A) 본사가 독일에 있다.
(B) 오직 오프라인 매장에서만 제품이 판매된다.
(C) 10년 전에 설립되었다.
(D) 프로 운동선수들에게 인기 있다.

해설 추론/암시

웹페이지의 두 번째 단락에 회사 설립자들이 지난 10년 동안 회사의 일일 운영에 계속 관여해 오고 있다(The company founders have stayed involved in the day-to-day operation of the company for the past ten years)는 내용이 제시되어 있어 회사가 10년 전에 설립된 것으로 볼 수 있으므로 (C)가 정답이다.

어휘 headquarters 본사 physical 물리적인 found 설립하다

13 슐츠 씨가 구입한 제품에 대해 사실일 것 같은 것은?
(A) 바바리안 아우터웨어가 회사를 시작한 이후로 제조해 오고 있는 것과 동일 제품이다.
(B) 더 이상 바바리안 아우터웨어에서 제조되지 않을 것이다.
(C) 할인 대상이다.
(D) 쉽게 손상될 수 있다.

해설 연계

후기 초반부에 한 달 전에 바바리안 아우터웨어에서 구입한 스키 스웨터(the ski sweater that I purchased from Bavarian Outerwear)라고 쓰여 있다. 이 제품과 관련해, 웹페이지의 첫 번째 단락에서 바바리안 아우터웨어는 지금까지 단 하나의 스키 스웨터 모델만 제조해 왔다(the only model of ski sweater the company has ever manufactured)고 알리고 있으므로 (A)가 정답이다.

어휘 be eligible for ~에 대한 대상이다, ~에 대한 자격이 있다

14 후기에 따르면, 제품이 어떻게 개선될 수도 있는가?
(A) 가격을 내림으로써
(B) 여러 다른 색상으로 제공함으로써
(C) 더 큰 사이즈를 이용할 수 있게 만듦으로써
(D) 더 부드러운 소재로 생산함으로써

해설 세부 사항

후기 후반부에 소재가 다소 거칠고 부드럽지 않다(the material is rather rough and coarse)는 단점을 언급하고 있으므로 (D)가 정답이다.

어휘 improve 개선하다 lower 내리다, 낮추다 available 이용 가능한

15 슐츠 씨가 누구일 것 같은가?
(A) 의류 수입업자
(B) 스키 강사
(C) 그래픽 디자이너
(D) 패션 잡지 기자

해설 추론/암시

후기 후반부에 스키복 소재가 안 좋다며, 스키복을 입고 하루 종일 학생들을 가르치고 나면 불편하다(After a long day of instructing my students, it becomes uncomfortable)는 말이 있으므로 스키 강사인 것으로 볼 수 있다. 따라서 (B)가 정답이다.

[16-20] 웹페이지 + 전자 티켓 + 이메일

> https://book-a-train.co.uk/fares
>
> **요금 유형별 예정 시간표**
> **통근자 요금**은 일반적인 통근 시간대에 적용됩니다.
> - 월요일부터 금요일, 오전 6시부터 오전 9시
> - 월요일부터 금요일, 오후 4시부터 오후 7시
>
> **오프 피크 요금**은 붐비지 않는 통근 시간대에만 적용됩니다.
> - 월요일부터 금요일, 오전 9시부터 오전 11시
> - **16** 월요일부터 금요일, 오후 2시부터 오후 4시
> - 월요일부터 금요일, 오후 7시부터 오후 9시
>
> **17 슈퍼 오프 피크 요금**은 평일 중 가장 덜 붐비는 시간대에 적용됩니다.
> - **17** 월요일부터 금요일, 오전 11시부터 오후 2시
> - 월요일부터 금요일, 오후 9시부터 오전 6시
>
> **스탠더드 요금**은 토요일과 일요일, 그리고 공휴일에 하루 종일 적용됩니다.

어휘 fare (교통) 요금 commuter 통근자 apply 적용되다 traditional 일반적인, 전통적인 off-peak 붐비는 시간 외의, 한산한 때의(= nonpeak)

> **Book-a-train.co.uk 전자 티켓**   요금: 24.30파운드
> 승객 숫자: 1명
> 티켓 유형: **17** 슈퍼 오프 피크 사우스베이 노선
> **19** 날짜: 11월 17일   **17** 유효 기한: 11월 17일 오후 2시
> 경로:
> 출발
> 노얼드 센트럴 역
> **18** 도착   경유
> 쉔크스빌   클락스빌

어휘 valid 유효한 route 경로, 노선 via ~을 경유하여, ~을 통해

수신: customercare@book-a-train.co.uk
발신: 롤라 툰지 〈lolatunji@sunmail.co.uk〉
19전송 시간: 11월 17일 화요일 오후 4시 55분
제목: 환불 요청
첨부: 전자 티켓

안녕하세요,

귀사의 열차에서 제가 경험한 문제와 관련해 이메일을 씁니다. 제가 오후 1시 약속 시간에 맞춰 목적지에 도착할 수 있도록 첨부해 드린 전자 티켓을 구입해 오전 11시 15분 열차를 탈 계획이었습니다. 하지만 **20**제가 승강장에 갔을 때, 오전 10시 45분 열차가 여전히 그곳에 있었습니다. 보아 하니, 기술적인 문제로 인해 지연된 것 같았습니다. 저는 그것이 오전 11시 15분 열차라고 생각해 그 열차에 탑승했습니다. 놀랍게도, 이 열차는 오전 11시 5분에 출발했고, 차장이 객차를 지나가면서 티켓을 확인했을 때, 제 전자 티켓을 받아주지 않았습니다. 그분은 클락스빌에 있는 다음 정거장에서 하차하거나 오프 피크 요금으로 추가 8파운드를 지불해야 한다고 말했습니다.

저는 제 약속 시간을 놓치는 위험을 감수하고 싶지 않았기 때문에, 마지못해 추가 요금을 지불했습니다. 저는 이것이 공평하다고 생각하지 않습니다. 오전 10시 45분 열차는 11시가 지나서 역에서 출발했습니다. 그때는, 슈퍼 오프 피크 요금이 적용되는 시간이었습니다. 저는 제 슈퍼 오프 피크 티켓을 사용할 수 있었어야 했습니다. 저는 8파운드를 환불받아야 한다고 생각합니다.

롤라 툰지

어휘 refund 환불(금) encounter 맞닥뜨리다, 직면하다 attach 첨부하다 catch (교통편을) 타다 destination 목적지 appointment 약속, 예약 apparently 보아 하니, 분명히 conductor (기차의) 차장 accept 받아들이다 additional 추가적인 risk 위험을 감수하다 reluctantly 마지못해 in effect 발효 중인, 시행 중인 owe 빚지다

16 웹페이지에 따르면, 월요일 오후 2시 30분에는 어떤 요금이 적용되는가?
(A) 통근자 (B) 오프 피크
(C) 슈퍼 오프 피크 (D) 스탠더드

해설 세부 사항

월요일 오후 2시 30분은 웹페이지의 '오프 피크 요금' 설명에 표기된 '월요일부터 금요일, 오후 2시부터 오후 4시(Monday to Friday from 2:00 P.M. to 4:00 P.M.)'의 시간대에 해당하므로 (B)가 정답이다.

17 몇 시에 툰지 씨의 전자 티켓이 유효하게 되었는가?
(A) 오전 10시 (B) 오전 10시 45분
(C) 오전 11시 (D) 오전 11시 5분

해설 연계

전자 티켓에 유형이 슈퍼 오프 피크(Ticket type: Super off-peak-Southbay Line)로, 유효 기한이 오후 2시까지(Valid Until: 2:00 P.M. on 17 November)로 쓰여 있다. 웹페이지 슈퍼 오프 피크 요금 설명에 적용 시간이 오전 11시부터 오후 2시(Monday to Friday from 11:00 A.M. to 2:00 P.M.)로 나와 있으므로 (C)가 정답이다.

18 전자 티켓에 따르면, 툰지 씨의 목적지가 어디였는가?
(A) 사우스베이 (B) 노얼드
(C) 클락스빌 (D) 쉔크스빌

해설 세부 사항

전자 티켓 하단에 도착지(To)가 SCHENCKSVILLE로 표기되어 있으므로 (D)가 정답이다.

19 툰지 씨가 언제 이메일을 보냈는가?
(A) 열차에 탑승하기 전에
(B) 열차에 탑승해 있는 동안에
(C) 열차 이용 당일 나중에
(D) 열차 이용 며칠 후에

해설 연계

이메일 상단에 전송 시간이 11월 17일 오후 4시 55분(Sent: Tuesday, 17 November, 4:55 P.M.)인데, 전자 티켓에 날짜와 유효 기한이 11월 17일 오후 2시까지(Valid Until: 2:00 P.M. on 17 November)로 나와 있으므로, 열차 이용 당일에 이메일을 보냈다는 것을 알 수 있다. 따라서 (C)가 정답이다.

어휘 aboard ~에 탑승한

20 툰지 씨가 어떤 문제를 언급하는가?
(A) 다른 유형의 티켓을 구입했다.
(B) 예상했던 것보다 열차 시간이 길었다.
(C) 약속 시간에 늦었다.
(D) 실수로 다른 열차에 탑승했다.

해설 세부 사항

이메일 첫 번째 단락에 툰지 씨가 승강장에 갔을 때 오전 10시 45분 열차가 여전히 그곳에 있었고, 그것을 자신이 타려던 오전 11시 15분 열차라고 생각해 탑승했다(But when I got to the platform, the 10:45 A.M. train was still there. ~ I boarded the train thinking it was the 11:15 A.M. train)고 언급되어 있으므로 (D)가 정답이다.

어휘 mistakenly 실수로, 잘못하여

Paraphrasing 지문의 boarded the train thinking it was the 11:15 A.M. train → 정답의 mistakenly boarded the wrong train

[21-25] 웹페이지 + 이메일 + 이메일

https://www.leaseallproperties.com/properties/29182

| 홈 | 소개 | 건물 | 건물 담당 직원 |

건물 29182

21서프사이드 해변에서 단지 몇 걸음 떨어져 있는 이 주택은 완벽한 휴가 장소입니다. 네 개의 침실과 세 개의 욕실이 있는 이 공유 숙박 시설에는 모든 것이 갖춰진 주방과 거실, 일광욕실, 그리고 푸른 파도가 보이는 아름다운 경관을 포함합니다. 최소 5박의 숙박이 필수입니다. **22**7박 이상으로 숙박하시는 고객들께서는 무료 1박 서비스를 받습니다.

편의 시설:

- 주방: 오븐과 레인지, 은식기, 접시, 그리고 조리용품 포함

- 욕실: 타월 및 다양한 세면도구 포함
- 세탁: 이용 가능한 세탁 설비 없음
- 주차: 구내 무료 주차, 이용 가능한 차고 없음
- 지역 행사 쿠폰

어휘 property 건물, 부동산 getaway 휴가(지) vacation rental 공유 숙박 시설 include 포함하다 minimum 최소한의 amenities 편의 시설 supplies 용품, 물품 toiletries 세면도구 on-site 구내의, 부지 내의

수신: ⟨info@leaseallproperties.com⟩
발신: 나탈리아 코왈스키 ⟨kowalskinatalia9@quamail.com⟩
날짜: 6월 9일 금요일
제목: 건물 29182

안녕하세요,

일주일 후부터 서프사이드 해변 대여 주택에서 숙박하는 것을 예약했습니다.

23 편의 시설 목록에 이용할 수 있는 세탁기와 건조기가 없다고 나와 있는데, 웹사이트에 있는 사진에는 세탁기와 건조기가 보입니다. 명확히 설명해 주시겠습니까?

제 여동생과 여동생 가족이 제가 도착하기 하루 전에 비행기로 그 마을에 도착할 것입니다. 제가 도착하기 전에 그들이 그 주택에 들어가는 데 어떤 문제라도 있을까요? 예약할 때 제공한 이용객 숫자에는 이미 포함되어 있습니다.

22 처음에는 5박을 예약했는데, 지금은 웹페이지에 기재된 혜택을 이용하고자 합니다. 저희 숙박 기간을 일주일로 연장할 수 있을까요?

나탈리아 코왈스키

어휘 rental 대여 indicate 나타내다, 가리키다 clarify 명확히 설명하다 originally 처음에, 원래 take advantage of ~을 이용하다 list 기재하다, 목록에 올리다 extend 연장하다

수신: 나탈리아 코왈스키 ⟨kowalskinatalia9@quamail.com⟩
발신: ⟨info@leaseallproperties.com⟩
날짜: 6월 9일 금요일
제목: 회신: 건물 29182
첨부: 할인 코드

안녕하세요, 코왈스키 씨.

이메일 보내 주셔서 감사합니다. 귀하의 질문에 답변해 드리게 되어 기쁩니다.

안타깝게도, **23** 언급하신 제품들은 수리되어야 하기 때문에, 이용하실 수 없을 것입니다. 저희가 웹사이트에서 해당 사진을 삭제할 수 없었습니다. 혼란을 드려 죄송합니다.

귀하께서는 출입문 비밀번호를 이용해 해당 주택에 출입하는 것에 대한 안내 사항을 담은 소개 이메일을 이미 받으셨어야 합니다. 이는 도착하시는 날에 전자식 출입문 비밀번호를 받기 위해 건물 담당 직원에게 전화하라는 내용이 담겨 있습니다. (비밀번호는 각 예약 후에 변경됩니다.) **24** 그 이메일을 여동생 분께 전달해 주세요.

유감스럽게도, **25** 해당 주택은 귀하의 방문 직후에 개조 공사가 예정되어 있으므로, 이번에는 귀하의 숙박을 연장해 드릴 수 없습니다. 귀하의 거래에 대해 감사의 뜻을 전해 드리기 위해, 나중에 저희를 통해 예약하시는 모든 일주일 기간의 숙박에 대해 무료 1박을 하실 수 있는 할인 코드를 첨부해 드렸습니다.

추가 질문이 있으시면 제게 연락 주십시오.

앨런 로즈
리스 올 프라퍼티즈

어휘 unfortunately 안타깝게도, 유감스럽게도 unavailable 이용할 수 없는 remove 없애다, 제거하다 confusion 혼란, 혼동 introduction 소개 instruction 안내, 설명 forward 전달하다, 회송하다 regrettably 유감스럽게도 renovation 개조, 보수 immediately after ~ 직후에 extend 연장하다 appreciation 감사(의 뜻)

---

21 웹페이지에 따르면, 해당 대여 건물에 대해 사실인 것은?
(A) 레스토랑 옆에 있다.
(B) 바다 근처에 있다.
(C) 최대 2명을 수용할 수 있다.
(D) 주차용 차고가 있다.

해설 Not/True

웹페이지의 초반부에 서프사이드 해변에서 단지 몇 걸음 떨어져 있다(Just steps away from Surfside Beach)고 나와 있으므로 (B)가 정답이다.

어휘 accommodate 수용하다 up to 최대 ~의

> **Paraphrasing** 지문의 Just steps away from Surfside Beach → 정답의 near the ocean

22 코왈스키 씨가 왜 대여 주택 숙박 연장을 요청하는가?
(A) 행사 입장권을 이용하기 위해
(B) 여동생의 방문을 수용하기 위해
(C) 지역 행사 쿠폰을 얻기 위해
(D) 무료 추가 1박 서비스를 받기 위해

해설 연계

첫 번째 이메일의 마지막 단락에 원래 5박으로 예약했는데 웹페이지에 기재된 혜택을 이용하고 싶다면서 숙박 기간을 일주일 전체로 연장할 수 있는지(~ I would like to take advantage of the offer listed on your Web page. Can we extend our stay to a full week?) 묻고 있다. 이는 웹페이지의 첫 번째 단락에서 언급하는 7박 이상 숙박하면 무료 1박 서비스를 받는 것(Guests who stay seven or more nights receive a free night)을 의미하므로 (D)가 정답이다.

23 로즈 씨에 따르면, 무엇이 수리를 필요로 하는가?
(A) 일광욕실
(B) 차고 출입문
(C) 세탁기와 건조기
(D) 오븐과 레인지

해설 **연계**
두 번째 이메일의 두 번째 단락에 로즈 씨는 코왈스키 씨가 언급한 제품들이 수리되어야 해서 이용할 수 없다(~ the items you mention need to be repaired, so they will be unavailable for use)고 했는데, 첫 번째 이메일에서 코왈스키 씨가 언급한 제품들은 세탁기와 건조기(~ there will not be a washer and dryer to use, ~)이므로 (C)가 정답이다.

24 코왈스키 씨는 무엇을 하라는 안내를 받는가?
(A) 이메일을 여동생에게 전달하기
(B) 건물 담당 직원에게 이메일 보내기
(C) 출입문 비밀번호 만들기
(D) 예약 변경하기

해설 **세부 사항**
두 번째 이메일의 세 번째 단락에 로즈 씨가 코왈스키 씨에게 출입문 비밀번호와 관련해 설명하면서 해당 이메일을 여동생에게 전달하라(You can go ahead and forward that e-mail to your sister)고 알리고 있으므로 (A)가 정답이다.

어휘 be instructed to ~하라는 안내를 받다 create 만들어 내다

25 로즈 씨가 대여 건물에 대해 코왈스키 씨에게 말하는 것은?
(A) 코왈스키 씨에게 할인된 요금으로 대여되었다.
(B) 개조 공사를 할 예정이다.
(C) 이전의 손님들로부터 좋은 평가를 받았다.
(D) 회사 웹사이트를 위해 사진 촬영되고 있다.

해설 **세부 사항**
두 번째 이메일의 네 번째 단락에서 해당 주택에 대해 코왈스키 씨의 방문 직후에 개조 공사가 예정되어 있다(~ the house is scheduled for renovations immediately after your visit ~)고 밝히고 있으므로 (B)가 정답이다.

어휘 rent 대여하다 at a discounted rate 할인된 요금으로 undergo 거치다, 겪다 previous 이전의, 과거의

Paraphrasing 지문의 is scheduled for renovations →
정답의 is scheduled to undergo renovations

[26-30] 이메일 + 이메일 + 주문서

수신: 타이론 맥키
발신: 레지나 프랭크
날짜: 10월 30일
제목: 주문 요청

맥키 씨께,

개조된 창고의 3층에 있는 새 사무실을 재배정받았는데, 그 공간에 전기 콘센트가 거의 없다시피 합니다. 동시에 노트북 컴퓨터와 모니터의 플러그를 꽂으면서 전화기를 충전할 수 없습니다. **29 쉽게 이용할 수 있도록 책상 위에 놓아둘 수 있는 승인된 멀티탭 옵션이 있을까요?** USB 포트가 있는 장치라면 이상적일 것입니다.

추가로, 접수 담당자의 탁상용 스탠드 코드가 사무실에 있는 어떤 콘센트에도 닿지 않습니다. 이는 3층 공간이 자연광이 부족하기 때문에 아주 중요한 문제입니다. 최소 1개의 연장 코드와 가능하다면

2개 이상의 다른 길이로 된 것이 필요할 겁니다. 마지막으로, **26 저희 금속 세공팀은 실내 고정식 전동 공구들을 연결할 고암페어 멀티탭이 3개 필요하며, 30 전동 세척팀은 야외 세척대에서 이용하기 적합한 멀티탭이 1개 필요합니다.**

감사합니다.

26 레지나 프랭크, 생산팀 관리

어휘 reassign 재배치하다, 재배정하다 converted 개조된 power outlet 전기 콘센트 plug in ~의 플러그를 꽂다 charge 충전하다 approve 승인하다 multi-outlet 다수의 콘센트로 구성된 access 이용, 접근 ideal 이상적인 receptionist 접수 담당자 reach 닿다, 이르다 critical 아주 중요한, 중대한 issue 사안, 문제 lack 부족 extension cord 연장 코드 metalworking 금속 세공 high-amperage 고암페어 power strip 멀티탭 connect 연결하다 fixed 고정된 power-washing 전동 세척 suitable for ~에 적합한, ~에 어울리는

수신: 레지나 프랭크
발신: 타이론 맥키
28 날짜: 11월 2일
제목: 회신: 주문 요청
첨부: 일렉트로-셀 주문서

프랭크 씨께,

27 귀하 및 귀하의 팀에 전력 공급용 콘센트가 충분히 있지 않다는 이메일을 받았습니다. 최근에 구매부에서 그러한 용품을 위해 판매업체 일렉트로-셀을 선택했습니다. 제공해 주신 정보를 바탕으로 볼 때, 이곳의 제품들이 귀하의 요구 사항에 부합할 것이라 생각합니다. **27 우리 회사 인트라넷 사이트의 구매부 페이지에서 이곳의 카탈로그를 다운로드하신 다음, 거기에 있는 제품들 중에서 선택하시기 바랍니다.** 섹션 1에는 다목적 연장 코드들이 있습니다. 섹션 2에는 서지 보호 장치들이 기재되어 있습니다. 섹션 3은 산업용 멀티탭을 위한 것입니다. 그리고 **29 섹션 4는 탁상용 멀티탭을 위한 것입니다.**

이 이메일에 귀하께서 선택하신 것들을 적어서 제게 돌려보내 주실 수 있는 편집 가능한 주문서를 첨부해 드렸습니다. 이 양식에 반드시 제품 번호와 제품 설명, 개당 가격, 그리고 각 제품의 주문 수량을 포함해 주시기를 바랍니다. **28 작성하신 양식을 11월 4일 수요일 오후 3시까지 제게 보내 주시면, 주문하신 것들이 주말쯤 발송될 것이며, 다음 주 주중에 배송품이 도착할 것으로 예상하실 수 있습니다.**

질문이 있으시면 제게 알려 주십시오.

타이론 맥키, 구매부장

어휘 supply 공급 select 선택하다 vendor 판매업체 supplies 용품, 물품 based on ~을 바탕으로 (볼 때) serve one's needs 요구 사항에 부합하다 all-purpose 다목적의 surge protector 서지 보호기 power center 멀티탭, 멀티 콘센트 editable 편집 가능한 fill out 작성하다 include 포함하다 description 설명 price per unit 개당 가격 midweek 주중

221

일렉트로-셀 산업용 전동 용품 주문서			
제품 번호	제품 설명	개당 가격	수량
APC-114	흰색 1구 콘센트 연장 코드, 코드 길이 8피트	12달러	2
APC-116	검은색 2구 콘센트 연장 코드, 코드 길이 12피트	15달러	2
IPS-202	노란색 4구 멀티탭, 고압페어 및 서지 보호, 실내에서만 사용, 코드 길이 10피트	32달러	3
30 IPS-198	검은색 4구 멀티탭, 고압페어 및 서지 보호, 방수 및 30 야외용, 코드 길이 10피트	35달러	1
DPC-45	회색 USB 포트 2개 포함 3구 탁상용 멀티탭, 코드 길이 12피트	41달러	1

어휘 waterproof 방수의   rate ~ 등급의, ~으로 지정된

26 프랭크 씨가 첫 번째 이메일에서 암시하는 것은?
(A) 전에 2층에 사무실이 있었다.
(B) 좀처럼 작업장을 방문하지 않는다.
(C) 제조 담당 직원들을 관리한다.
(D) 자신의 노트북 컴퓨터를 수리받아야 한다.

해설 추론/암시

첫 번째 이메일의 두 번째 단락에서 프랭크 씨가 금속 세공팀을 자신의 금속 세공팀(my metalworking team needs ~)이라고 말하며 필요한 것을 설명하고 있고, 이메일 하단에 이름과 함께 생산팀 관리(Production Team Management)라고 적혀 있으므로 제조 업무 담당 부서를 관리하는 사람인 것으로 볼 수 있다. 따라서 (C)가 정답이다.

어휘 used to 전에 ~했다, ~하곤 했다   rarely 좀처럼 ~ 않다
supervise 관리하다, 감독하다   manufacturing 제조

Paraphrasing 지문의 Production Team Management → 정답의 supervises a manufacturing staff

27 두 번째 이메일의 목적은?
(A) 전원 콘센트 선택에 도움이 되는 정보를 제공하려고
(B) 구매품 청구서 발급 과정을 설명하려고
(C) 기업 안전 정책을 설명하려고
(D) 사무용 장비 할인 행사를 홍보하려고

해설 주제/목적

두 번째 이메일의 첫 번째 단락에서 상대방이 콘센트 문제와 관련해 보낸 이메일(I received your e-mail about not having enough power supply outlets ~)을 언급하면서 회사 인트라넷 사이트의 구매부 페이지에서 카탈로그를 다운로드하고 거기에서 제품들을 선택하라(Please download their catalog from the purchasing department's page on our company intranet site and choose from the products ~)고 한 후 각 세션을 설명하고 있다. 이는 콘센트 선택에 도움이 되는 정보를 제공하는 것이므로 (A)가 정답이다.

어휘 process 과정   bill 청구서를 발급하다   describe 설명하다
corporate 기업의   policy 정책, 방침   promote 홍보하다

28 맥키 씨가 프랭크 씨에게 무엇을 하도록 제안하는가?
(A) 새 전동 용품 판매업체 선택하기
(B) 앞으로 이틀 내에 주문하기
(C) 회사의 인트라넷 사이트 업데이트하기
(D) 추가 사무직원 고용하기

해설 세부 사항

두 번째 이메일의 두 번째 단락에서 작성한 양식을 11월 4일 수요일 오후 3시까지 보내면(If you send me your completed form by 3:00 P.M. on Wednesday, November 4, ~) 주말쯤 발송된다고 했는데, 상단의 이메일 작성 날짜가 11월 2일(Date: November 2)로 쓰여 있어 이틀 내로 주문할 것을 제안하고 있다는 것을 알 수 있다. 따라서 (B)가 정답이다.

29 일렉트로-셀 카탈로그의 어떤 섹션이 프랭크 씨가 사무실에 필요한 제품을 포함하고 있는가?
(A) 섹션 1   (B) 섹션 2
(C) 섹션 3   (D) 섹션 4

해설 연계

첫 번째 이메일의 첫 번째 단락에서 프랭크 씨가 책상 위에 놓아둘 수 있는 멀티탭(Is there an approved multi-outlet power option that can sit on the top of my desk for easy access?)에 관해 문의하고 있는데, 두 번째 지문의 첫 번째 단락에서 섹션 4가 탁상용 멀티탭을 위한 것(Section 4 is for desktop power centers)이라고 했으므로 (D)가 정답이다.

30 프랭크 씨가 누구를 위해 제품 IPS-198을 주문하는 것 같은가?
(A) 자신을 위해
(B) 접수 담당자를 위해
(C) 실내 금속 세공 작업자들을 위해
(D) 전동 세척 담당자들을 위해

해설 연계

주문서에서 IPS-198에 해당하는 제품의 특징 중 하나가 야외용(outdoor rated)인데, 첫 번째 이메일의 두 번째 단락에서 전동 세척팀은 야외 세척대에서 이용하기 적합한 멀티탭이 1개 필요하다(the power-washing team needs one strip suitable for use at their outdoor cleaning station)고 했으므로 (D)가 정답이다.

ETS ACTUAL TEST

본책 p.294

147 (D)	148 (B)	149 (B)	150 (C)	151 (C)
152 (A)	153 (A)	154 (C)	155 (C)	156 (A)
157 (C)	158 (B)	159 (C)	160 (A)	161 (B)
162 (C)	163 (A)	164 (C)	165 (B)	166 (B)
167 (D)	168 (D)	169 (D)	170 (D)	171 (C)
172 (D)	173 (A)	174 (D)	175 (D)	176 (B)
177 (D)	178 (C)	179 (B)	180 (C)	181 (D)
182 (A)	183 (D)	184 (D)	185 (D)	186 (A)
187 (D)	188 (C)	189 (A)	190 (D)	191 (D)
192 (C)	193 (D)	194 (B)	195 (C)	196 (A)
197 (B)	198 (C)	199 (C)	200 (D)	

[147-148] 영수증

스탠타르 브라더스
지역 최고의 미술 및 취미 용품 매장

매장 번호: 7   **147** 매장 위치: 메인 가 6번지, 도버, 오하이오
147 고객: 줄리아 레스턴   판매 날짜/시간: 7월 7일 오전 10시 27분

수량: 1	설명: 스탠타르 나무 페인트붓 세트	가격: 40.00달러
		−30% 재고 정리 세일
	고객 할인액:	12.00달러
	총액:	28.00달러
	현금 결제액:	28.00달러

147 저희 도버 지점에서 쇼핑해 주셔서 감사합니다. www.stanntarbrothers.com 또는 10곳의 저희 지점 중 어디서나 미술 및 취미와 관련해 필요하신 모든 것을 쇼핑해 보십시오. **148** 7월은 종이 공예의 달입니다. 전 지점에서 열리는 무료 워크숍에 참여해 보세요. **148** 매달 새로운 종류의 워크숍을 진행합니다. 더 많은 정보는 저희 웹사이트를 방문하시기 바랍니다.

어휘 region 지역   leading 으뜸가는, 선도적인   quantity 수량   description 설명, 묘사   clearance sale 재고 정리 세일   savings 할인액, 절약한 금액   craft 공예(품)   feature 특징으로 하다

147 레스턴 씨에 대해 언급된 것은?
  (A) 유명 미술가이다.
  (B) 친구를 위해 미술 용품을 구입했다.
  (C) 신용카드로 결제했다.
  (D) 도버 매장에서 제품을 구입했다.

해설 Not/True
영수증 상단 고객 란에서 레스턴 씨 이름을 확인할 수 있고, 매장 위치 란에 도버(Store location: 6 Main Street, Dover, Ohio)라고 쓰여 있다. 또한, 하단에도 도버 지점에서 쇼핑해 주셔서 감사하다(Thank you for shopping at our Dover store)고 쓰여 있으므로 (D)가 정답이다.

148 8월에 무슨 일이 있을 것 같은가?
  (A) 레스턴 씨가 종이 공예를 배울 것이다.
  (B) 새 워크숍 주제가 있을 것이다.
  (C) 재고 정리 세일이 종료될 것이다.
  (D) 스탠타르 브라더스가 새 매장을 열 것이다.

해설 추론/암시
영수증의 하단에서 7월은 종이 공예의 달(July is paper craft month)이라는 정보와 함께 매달 새로운 종류의 워크숍을 진행한다(Each month features a new type of workshop)고 알리고 있다. 따라서 8월에 새로운 주제로 워크숍이 진행된다는 것을 알 수 있으므로 (B)가 정답이다.

어휘 theme 주제

> **Paraphrasing** 지문의 a new type of workshop → 정답의 a new workshop theme

[149-150] 웹페이지

https://www.yourprivateguide.co.uk

| 홈 | 투어 | 연락처 | 예약 |

밀포드 시 경유 투어

긴 경유 시간 동안 환승 항공편을 기다리면서 공항에 앉아 계시는 것에 지치셨나요?

유어 프라이빗 가이드가 여러분과 여러분의 일행에게 밀포드 시 맞춤형 투어를 제공해 드릴 수 있습니다. **149** 저희 투어는 공항에서 시작되고 종료되며, 3~8시간 동안 지속됩니다. 이는 관광을 즐기기를 원하시지만 시간이 제한적인 분들께 안성맞춤입니다. 일정표는 관심사와 가능한 시간을 바탕으로 여러분과 여러분의 일행을 위해 만들어질 것입니다. **150** 투어를 위해, 아이버슨 공원, 댄포스 미술관, 웨스트사이드 항구, 역사적인 에머리 존스 하우스 등과 같은 인기 명소들 중에서 선택해 보세요. 모든 투어가 전용 투어이므로 다른 누구도 여러분의 그룹에 합류하지 않는다는 점에 유의하십시오.

이용 가능 여부와 요금은 예약 페이지를 방문하시기 바랍니다.

어휘 layover 경유   connecting 연결편의   private 개인의, 전용의   personalized 맞춤 제공되는   last 지속되다   sights 관광(지)   limited 제한적인   itinerary 일정(표)   based on ~을 바탕으로   interest 관심(사)   available 이용 가능한   rate 요금

149 투어에 대해 언급된 것은?
  (A) 최근에 인기를 얻게 되었다.
  (B) 공항에서 시작된다.
  (C) 유사 투어들보다 덜 비싸다.
  (D) 준비된 점심 식사를 포함한다.

해설 Not/True
중반부에 투어가 공항에서 시작되고 종료된다(Our tours start and end at the airport ~)고 알리고 있으므로 (B)가 정답이다.

어휘 popularity 인기   include 포함하다

> **Paraphrasing** 지문의 start → 정답의 begins

150 댄포스 미술관에 대해 언급된 것은?
(A) 역사적인 건물 내에 자리 잡고 있다.
(B) 밀포드 시에서 가장 많이 방문하는 관광지이다.
(C) 투어의 일부로 선택될 수 있다.
(D) 그 미술관의 모든 곳을 방문하는 데 3시간이 걸린다.

해설 **Not/True**
중반부에서 투어를 위해 선택할 수 있는 인기 장소들 중 하나로 댄포스 미술관(For your tour, choose from popular sites like Iverson Park, the Danforth Museum of Art, ~)이 포함되어 있으므로 (C)가 정답이다.

어휘 **house** 공간을 제공하다, 수용하다

> **Paraphrasing** 지문의 For your tour, choose from → 정답의 can be selected as part of a tour

[151-152] 문자 메시지

켄 라이샤르트 (오전 10시 4분)
안녕하세요, 펭 씨. 오늘 2시 약속을 상기시켜 드리려고요. **151** 상담 시간 중에, 어떤 종류의 식물을 원하시는지 이야기하면서 제가 귀하의 건물 곳곳을 둘러볼 예정입니다. 그럼 저와 저희 팀이 귀하의 프로젝트를 더 잘 이해하는 데 도움이 될 겁니다.

칼라 펭 (오전 10시 5분)
좋아요. 제가 안내해 드리겠습니다.

켄 라이샤르트 (오전 10시 6분)
그리고, **152** 기회가 되시면, 새로운 테라스에 대한 선호도와 관련해 제가 보내 드린 설문지를 작성해 주시기 바랍니다.

칼라 펭 (오전 10시 7분)
제가 훨씬 앞서 있네요. **152** 받은 메일함을 확인해 보세요.

켄 라이샤르트 (오전 10시 8분)
아주 좋습니다. 오늘 오후에 뵙겠습니다.

어휘 **reminder** (메시지 등의) 상기시키는 것 **appointment** 약속, 예약 **consultation** 상담 **property** 건물, 부동산 **crew** 작업 팀, 조 **get a better understanding of** ~을 더 잘 이해하다 **questionnaire** 설문지 **concerning** ~와 관련해 **preference** 선호 (사항) **patio** 테라스 **be way ahead of** ~보다 훨씬 앞서 있다

151 라이샤르트 씨가 누구일 것 같은가?
(A) 공장 관리자
(B) 부동산 중개인
(C) 전문 조경업자
(D) 시장 조사 분석가

해설 **추론/암시**
라이샤르트 씨가 오전 10시 4분 메시지에서 상담 시간 중에 상대방이 어떤 종류의 식물을 원하는지 이야기도 하고 건물도 둘러볼 것(~ I'll be looking around your property while we discuss what kinds of plants you would like)이라고 언급하고 있으므로, 전문 조경업자임을 알 수 있다. 따라서 (C)가 정답이다.

152 오전 10시 7분에 펭 씨가 "제가 훨씬 앞서 있네요"라고 쓸 때 무엇을 의미할 것 같은가?
(A) 이미 일부 정보를 제공했다.
(B) 테라스에서 몇몇 식물을 제거했다.
(C) 이미 라이샤르트 씨에게 상담 비용을 지불했다.
(D) 라이샤르트 씨보다 앞서 해당 부지에 도착했다.

해설 **의도 파악**
앞선 메시지에서 라이샤르트 씨가 자신이 보낸 설문지를 작성해 달라(please complete the questionnaire ~)고 요청하자, '제가 훨씬 앞서 있네요(I'm way ahead of you)'라고 대답하면서 받은 메일함을 확인해 보라(Check your inbox)고 말하고 있다. 설문지를 이미 작성해 이메일로 보냈다는 의미이므로 (A)가 정답이다.

어휘 **remove** 제거하다, 없애다 **site** 부지, 현장

[153-154] 쿠폰

패리스 배관
수도 문제가 있으신가요? 저희가 도와드리겠습니다!

연말 특가: 주택용 온수기 설치 100달러 할인!
- 11월 15일부터 12월 31일까지 완료되는 작업에 한해 유효함
- **153** 다른 특가 제공 서비스와 결합될 수 없음
- 설치비에는 기존 기기의 제거 및 처리 포함
- 온수기 별도 판매
- 럼버턴 지역만 해당

설치 작업이 시작되기까지 최대 2주가 걸릴 수 있기 때문에 **154** 11월 1일과 12월 15일 사이에 203-555-0129번으로 전화하여 설치 일정을 잡으세요.

어휘 **plumbing** 배관 **woe** 문제, 고민거리 **residential** 주택의, 주거지의 **installation** 설치 **offer** 제공(되는 것) **good** 유효한 **combine A with B** A를 B와 결합하다 **removal** 제거, 없앰 **disposal** 처리, 처분 **unit** 기기 한 대 **separately** 별도로, 분리되어

153 쿠폰에 대해 언급된 것은?
(A) 다른 할인 제공 서비스와 함께 이용될 수 없다.
(B) 모든 상업 고객들에 의해 이용될 수 있다.
(C) 여러 도시에서 유효하다.
(D) 오래된 온수기 처리 비용을 포함하지 않는다.

해설 **Not/True**
두 번째 항목에 다른 특가 제공 서비스와 결합될 수 없다(Cannot be combined with other special offers)고 언급되어 있으므로 (A)가 정답이다.

어휘 **commercial** 상업의 **valid** 유효한 **cover** 포함하다

154 고객이 설치 일정을 잡기 위해 전화할 수 있는 마지막 날이 언제인가?
(A) 11월 1일
(B) 11월 15일
(C) 12월 15일
(D) 12월 31일

해설 **세부 사항**

마지막 단락에 11월 1일과 12월 15일 사이에 전화해서 설치 일정을 잡으라고(Call 203-555-0129 between November 1 and December 15 to schedule your installation, ~) 당부하면서 그 이유를 설명하고 있으므로 (C)가 정답이다.

[155-157] 기사

조수 에너지로 자동차 동력 공급

시사이드(5월 1일) – 에너지 제공업체 코스트 파워가 조력 에너지를 유일한 동력 공급원으로 이용할 자동차 충전소를 설치할 계획이다.

코스트 파워는 최근 시사이드 앞바다에 파도 에너지를 전기로 변환할 부유식 터빈 건설을 완료했다. **155**이 터빈들은 주로 전기 자동차로 바꾸는 운전자가 증가함에 따라 증가하는 이 지역의 전기 수요를 충족하기 위해 설치되었다.

첫 번째 조력 에너지 충전소들이 이달 말까지 시사이드의 여러 해변 근처에 있는 주차장에 **156**배치될 것이다. **157**12월까지 이 회사는 시사이드와 인근 마을 전역에 추가 조력 에너지 충전소를 설치할 계획이다. 많은 곳에서, 이 새로운 충전소들이 기존의 연료 기반 충전소들 옆에 세워질 것이며, 기존의 충전소들은 나중에 조력 에너지로 변경될 수 있다.

어휘 tide 조수 charging station 충전소 tidal 조수의 source 공급원, 원천 floating 떠 있는 convert A into B A를 B로 전환하다 primarily 주로 switch 바꾸다 additional 추가적인 surrounding 인근의, 주변의 existing 기존의 fuel-powered 연료 기반의

155 기사에 따르면, 부유식 터빈을 건설하기로 결정한 이유는?
(A) 터빈을 건설할 육지 공간의 부족
(B) 지역 내 더 많은 일자리 필요
(C) 전기로 동력을 얻는 자동차 수의 증가
(D) 해안 지역을 따라 빠르게 늘어나는 인구

해설 **세부 사항**

두 번째 단락에서 전기 자동차로 바꾸는 운전자가 증가함에 따라 증가하는 이 지역의 전기 수요를 충족하기 위해 설치되었다(The turbines were installed primarily to meet the region's rising electrical needs as more drivers switch to electric vehicles)고 터빈 설치 목적을 언급하고 있으므로 (C)가 정답이다.

어휘 lack 부족 increase 증가 population 인구

> **Paraphrasing** 지문의 more drivers switch to electric vehicles → 정답의 An increase in the number of cars powered by electricity

156 세 번째 단락 두 번째 줄에 쓰인 단어 "placed"와 의미가 가장 가까운 것은?
(A) 놓인   (B) 보인
(C) 주문된   (D) 입력된

해설 **동의어 찾기**

동사 will be placed 뒤에 장소 전치사구가 쓰여 있어 충전소들이 설치되거나 놓인다는 의미를 나타내는 것으로 볼 수 있으므로 (A) put이 정답이다.

157 코스트 파워는 12월까지 무엇을 할 계획인가?
(A) 주차장마다 태양열 전지판을 설치하는 것
(B) 연료 기반의 모든 충전소를 없애는 것
(C) 시사이드 근처의 마을들에 조력 에너지 충전소를 짓는 것
(D) 충전소들을 연료 발전에서 조력 발전으로 전환하는 것

해설 **세부 사항**

세 번째 단락에 12월까지 이 회사는 시사이드와 인근 마을 전역에 추가 조력 에너지 충전소를 설치할 계획(By December, the company plans to install additional tidal charging stations throughout Seaside and the surrounding towns)이라고 했으므로 (C)가 정답이다.

어휘 remove 없애다, 제거하다

> **Paraphrasing** 지문의 install additional tidal charging stations throughout Seaside and the surrounding towns → 정답의 Construct tidal charging stations in towns near Seaside

[158-160] 공지

컨비 밸리 재배자 박람회

5년 차를 맞이해, 컨비 밸리 재배자 박람회가 10월 12일부터 14일까지 루이즈 콘퍼런스 센터에서 다시 열립니다. 경험의 정도가 다양한 유기농 재배 애호가 수백 명이 이 행사에 참석할 것으로 예상됩니다. **158**이 분야에 새로 들어온 사람들은 많은 강의들이 막 시작하는 사람들에게 정보를 제공하고 도와주는 것에 의도적으로 맞춰진다는 점을 알게 될 것입니다.

159등록비는 3일간의 행사 전체에 대해 95달러입니다. 등록은 10월 5일 금요일까지 가능할 것입니다. 또는, 사람들이 박람회 중 어느 날이든 행사장에 도착해 **159**당일 입장료로 45달러를 지불할 수 있습니다. **159**유효한 신분증을 지참한 대학생의 경우, 전체 행사 입장료는 50달러, 하루 입장료는 20달러가 될 것입니다.

일요일 오후에 아주 특별한 마지막 시간이 있을 것이며, 최고의 전문가들로 구성된 패널이 현장에서 참석자들의 질문에 실시간으로 답변해 줄 것입니다. **160**참석자들이 시식할 수 있도록 지역에서 재배한 아주 다양한 유기농 과일과 채소로 만든 간식이 제공될 것입니다.

어휘 grower 재배자 organic-farming 유기 농업 enthusiast 애호가, 열성적인 팬 newcomer 초보자, 신입 appreciate 감사하다 session (특정 활동을 하는) 시간 be geared toward ~에 맞춰지다, ~에 맞게 조정되다 intentionally 의도적으로 registration 등록 entire 전체의 alternatively 또는, 그렇지 않으면 venue 행사장 admission 입장(료) valid 유효한 on hand 현장에 있는, 참석한 respond 답변하다 attendee 참석자 a wide variety of 아주 다양한 locally 지역적으로 sample 시식하다

158 박람회의 많은 시간이 어떤 그룹의 사람들에게 가장 큰 도움이 될 것인가?
(A) 요리사와 음식을 준비하는 직원들
(B) 경험이 많지 않은 농부들
(C) 새 농업용 장비를 개발하는 제조사들
(D) 식품 유통 회사의 관리자들

해설 세부 사항
첫 번째 단락에서 이 분야에 새로 들어온 사람들은 많은 강의들이 막 시작하는 사람들에게 정보를 제공하고 도와주는 것에 의도적으로 맞춰진다는 점을 알게 될 것(Newcomers to the field will appreciate that many sessions will be intentionally geared toward informing and assisting those who are just starting out)이라고 했으므로 (B)가 정답이다.

어휘 limited 많지 않은, 한정된   equipment 장비
distribution 유통, 배포, 배부

> **Paraphrasing** 지문의 Newcomers to the field → 정답의 with limited experience

159 공지에 따르면, 박람회에 대해 사실인 것은?
(A) 올해 더 넓은 행사장에서 개최될 것이다.
(B) 주로 자원봉사자들에 의해 진행될 것이다.
(C) 학생들이 할인된 가격으로 참석할 수 있을 것이다.
(D) 전문가들이 요금을 받고 개별 상담을 제공할 수 있을 것이다.

해설 Not / True
두 번째 단락에서 3일 전체 등록비가 95달러($95 for the entire three-day event), 일일 입장료가 45달러($45 for a single day's admission)라고 언급한 다음, 유효한 신분증을 지참한 대학생들은 3일 전체 등록비가 50달러, 또는 하루 입장료가 20달러(~ the fees will be $50 for the entire event or $20 for one day)라고 설명하고 있다. 대학생들이 할인된 가격으로 참석할 수 있다는 뜻이므로 (C)가 정답이다.

어휘 primarily 주로   volunteer 자원봉사자   individual 개별적인, 개인의

160 박람회의 마지막 행사에 대해 언급된 것은?
(A) 참석자들에게 여러 가지 음식들을 맛볼 기회를 제공할 것이다.
(B) 이용 가능한 가장 큰 방에서 개최될 것이다.
(C) 시상식을 포함할 것이다.
(D) 참석하는 데 20달러의 추가 비용이 들 것이다.

해설 Not / True
세 번째 단락에서 마지막 행사를 설명하면서 참석자들이 시식할 수 있는 아주 다양한 간식이 제공될 것(Snacks will also be provided in the form of a wide variety of locally grown organic fruits and vegetables for attendees to sample)이라고 했으므로 (A)가 정답이다.

어휘 awards ceremony 시상식   cost 비용이 들다

> **Paraphrasing** 지문의 provided in the form of a wide variety of locally grown organic fruits and vegetables for attendees to sample → 정답의 give attendees a chance to taste different foods

[161-163] 웹페이지

---
https://www.homelivingweekly.com

순조롭게 준비하세요

새 거주지에 공공 서비스를 설치하는 일은 때때로 너무 힘들어 보일 수 있습니다. **163** 최근까지, 새 집으로 이사했을 때, 공공 서비스를 받을 수 있는 유일한 방법은 각 공공 서비스 회사에 개별적으로 연락하는 것이었습니다. 다행스럽게도, 지금은 새로 이사 온 주민이 유틸리 커넥트 솔루션즈에 단 한 번 전화하는 것으로 전기와 인터넷, 가스, 기타 가정용 서비스들을 설치하는 것이 가능합니다. 주거용 서비스 지원 분야에서 가장 오래된 회사인 유틸리 커넥트는 "더 쉬운 이사"를 모토로 삼고 있습니다. **161** 이 회사는 현재 어떤 경쟁사들보다 더 넓은 지역을 커버하고 있으며, 남부 및 남서부 지역에서 가장 인기 있는 곳입니다.

유틸리 커넥트 솔루션즈와의 전화 통화는 담당 직원이 선택 가능한 다양한 공공 서비스 제공업체를 설명하고 각각의 월간 요금을 비교해 주기 때문에 일반적으로 한 시간 넘게 지속됩니다. 또한, 이 회사를 이용하는 것에 대한 요금이 없으며, 직원들이 발신인의 동의 없이 어떤 서비스도 주문하지 않습니다.

162 새로 이사 온 주민은 흔히 작업팀이 집에 필요한 장비를 설치할 날짜와 시간을 잡는 것을 어려워하기 때문에, 유틸리 커넥트 솔루션즈는 자동화된 일정 관리 소프트웨어를 이용해 이 과정이 더욱 순조롭게 진행되도록 만듭니다. 이 애플리케이션을 통해 모든 예약을 한 곳에서 집중 관리하는 것은 예약들을 추적하는 것을 더욱 쉽게 만들어 주기도 합니다. 회사 설립자 조 시뇨리니 씨는 말합니다. "저희 유틸리 커넥트의 목표는 무엇보다도 새로 이사 온 주민들의 시간과 노력을 절약시켜 드리는 것입니다."

어휘 get set up 준비되다, 설치되다   obtain 받다, 얻다
utility services (전기, 수도 등의) 공공 서비스   individually 개별적으로   fortunately 다행히   resident 주민   establish 설립하다, 확립하다   assistance 지원, 도움   motto 모토, 좌우명   cover 포함하다, 다루다   geographic 지리적인
typically 일반적으로   representative 직원, 대표자   charge 청구 요금   approval 동의, 승인   crew (함께 작업하는) 팀, 조
automated 자동화된   process 과정   centralize 중앙 집중하다   via ~을 통해   track 추적하다   save 아끼다

161 웹페이지에서 유틸리 커넥트 솔루션즈에 대해 언급하는 것은?
(A) 신입 직원을 고용할 계획이다.
(B) 경쟁사들보다 더 넓은 지역에 서비스를 제공한다.
(C) 최근에 소유권자를 변경했다.
(D) 국제 배송 회사 한 곳에 의해 운영된다.

해설 Not / True
첫 번째 단락에 유틸리 커넥트 솔루션즈가 현재 어떤 경쟁사들보다 더 넓은 지역을 커버하고 있다(The company currently covers a larger geographic area than any of its rivals ~)고 했으므로 (B)가 정답이다.

어휘 competitor 경쟁사, 경쟁자   ownership 소유권(자)
operate 운영하다, 가동하다

> **Paraphrasing** 지문의 covers a larger geographic area than any of its rivals → 정답의 serves a larger area than its competitors

162 웹페이지에 따르면, 새로 이사 온 주민들이 흔히 직면하는 문제는?
(A) 서비스 요금제에 대한 세부 정보가 제대로 전달되지 않음
(B) 예기치 못한 공공요금 인상
(C) 설치 방문 일정을 잡는 것의 어려움
(D) 고객 서비스 직원과 이야기하기까지의 긴 대기 시간

해설 **세부 사항**
세 번째 단락에서 새로 이사 온 주민은 흔히 작업팀이 집에 필요한 장비를 설치할 날짜와 시간을 잡는 것을 어려워한다(Because new residents often find it difficult to schedule dates and times for crews to install needed equipment in a home ~)고 했으므로 (C)가 정답이다.

어휘 communicate (정보 등을) 전달하다, 소통하다   details 세부 사항   unexpected 예기치 못한

> **Paraphrasing** 지문의 new residents often find it difficult → 질문의 a problem that new residents often face
> 지문의 schedule dates and times for crews to install needed equipment → 정답의 scheduling installation visits

163 [1], [2], [3], [4]로 표시된 곳 중에 다음 문장이 들어가기에 가장 적합한 곳은?

"새 거주지에 공공 서비스를 설치하는 일은 때때로 너무 힘들어 보일 수 있습니다."

(A) [1]   (B) [2]   (C) [3]   (D) [4]

해설 **문장 삽입**
주어진 문장은 새 거주지에 공공 서비스를 설치하는 일이 때때로 너무 힘들어 보일 수 있다는 의미이므로, 공공 서비스를 받을 수 있는 유일한 방법은 각 공공 서비스 회사에 개별적으로 연락하는 것이었다(~ the only way to obtain utility services was to contact each utility company individually)고 공공 서비스 설치가 힘들어 보일 수 있는 이유를 언급하는 문장 앞에 들어가는 것 자연스럽다. 따라서 (A)가 정답이다.

어휘 residence 거주지   overwhelming 압도적인

[164-167] 기사

탄탄한 입지를 구축하는 브래드 바이크

렉스퍼드 (4월 24일) – 지난주 도시 내 자전거 이용자들에게 좋은 소식이 전해졌다. ¹⁶⁴시 의회가 지역 내 자전거 공유 업체인 브래드 바이크에 시내 곳곳에 총 120대의 자전거를 포함해 12곳의 대여소를 추가로 설치하는 새로운 계약을 주는 안을 승인했다.

이 프로그램은 3년 전에 8곳의 대여소로 시작했다. 이 프로그램으로 주민들과 관광객들은 다양한 대여소에서 자전거를 1시간 또는 하루 종일 대여할 수 있다. ¹⁶⁵자전거 이용객들은 자신의 휴대폰 앱을 이용해 자전거 잠금을 해제하고 반납한다.

브래드 바이크는 매일 자전거를 이용하는 사람들에게 월간 및 연간 회원권을 제공한다. 가끔씩만 자전거를 타는 사람들을 위해 이용할 때마다 결제하는 요금제도 있다.

¹⁶⁶"우리는 대도시가 아닙니다"라고 시 의회의 애니타 헨더슨 의장이 말했다. "여러 더 큰 도시에서 이런 프로그램이 인기를 얻고 있다는 보고서가 있긴 했지만, 우리는 이곳에서 효과가 있을지 불확실했죠."

실제로, 초기의 시범 운영 프로그램이 아주 좋은 효과를 냈다. 처음부터, ¹⁶⁷주민들은 시에서 대중교통이 잘 연결되어 있지 않은 여러 지역으로 가기 위해 대여 자전거를 이용했다. 운영 첫 해부터 3년 차까지, 회원은 250퍼센트 증가했으며, 1회성 대여는 거의 세 배가 되었다.

12곳의 추가 대여소가 시 전역에 걸쳐 분포되면, 전에는 서비스되지 않았던 지역들에도 자전거 공유 서비스가 제공될 것이다. 브래드 바이크의 네트워크가 확대되면 렉스퍼드 대부분의 지역에 접근성을 높여 줄 것이다.

어휘 council 의회   approve 승인하다   award 수여하다, 주다   docking station 대여소   resident 주민   rent 대여하다   entire 전체의   annual 연간의, 해마다의   pay-per-ride 탈 때마다 결제하는   occasional 때때로 하는, 가끔의   gain 얻다   popularity 인기   uncertain 불확실한   initial 초기의, 처음의   outset 처음, 시작   connect 연결하다   operation 운영, 가동   triple 세 배가 되다   distribute 분포시키다   previously 이전에, 과거에   service 서비스를 제공하다   access 접근, 이용   neighbourhood 지역, 인근, 이웃

164 기사의 주제는?
(A) 자전거 안전을 개선하기 위한 노력
(B) 새로운 도로 공사 프로젝트
(C) 인기 있는 프로그램의 확대
(D) 시의 여러 관광 명소에 대한 투자

해설 **주제/목적**
첫 단락에 시 의회가 지역 내 자전거 공유 업체인 브래드 바이크에 시내 곳곳에 12곳의 대여소를 추가로 설치하는 새로운 계약을 주는 안을 승인했다(The city council approved plans ~ to install an additional twelve docking stations, with 120 bicycles total, around the city)고 했고, 이 프로그램이 초기에 8곳의 대여소로 시작했다는 내용이 있으므로 (C)가 정답이다.

어휘 improve 개선하다, 향상시키다   expansion 확대, 확장   investment 투자(금)   attraction 명소, 인기 장소

> **Paraphrasing** 지문의 install an additional twelve docking stations → 정답의 expansion

165 기사에 따르면, 브래드 바이크에서 대여하기 위해 필요한 것은?
(A) 신용카드   (B) 휴대폰
(C) 활성화 코드   (D) 사진이 부착된 신분증

해설 **세부 사항**

두 번째 단락에 자전거 이용객이 휴대폰 앱을 이용해 자전거 잠금을 해제하고 반납한다(Riders unlock and return the bicycles using an app on their phones)고 했으므로 (B)가 정답이다.

166 헨더슨 씨는 왜 브래드 바이크의 계획이 렉스퍼드에서 성공할 것으로 확신하지 못했는가?
(A) 도시를 방문하는 관광객들이 거의 없기 때문에
(B) 도시가 상대적으로 작기 때문에
(C) 오직 몇몇 자전거 대여소만 이용 가능했기 때문에
(D) 많은 주민들이 자가용으로 운전하는 것을 선호하기 때문에

해설 **세부 사항**

네 번째 단락에 애니타 헨더슨 의장이 대도시가 아니라는 점과 함께 여러 더 큰 도시에서 같은 프로그램이 인기를 얻고 있다는 보고서가 있긴 했지만 자신의 도시에서는 효과가 있을지 불확실하다("We are just not a large city," said Anita Henderson, ~ we were uncertain it would work here.")고 인터뷰한 내용이 쓰여 있으므로 (B)가 정답이다.

어휘 relatively 상대적으로, 비교적

> Paraphrasing 지문의 not a large city → 정답의 the city is relatively small

167 기사에서 브래드 바이크에 대해 암시된 것은?
(A) 현재 렉스퍼드에서 12곳의 자전거 대여소를 유지하고 있다.
(B) 헨더슨 씨에 의해 설립되었다.
(C) 여러 다른 도시에도 서비스를 추가할 계획이다.
(D) 대중교통이 서비스하지 않는 지역에 서비스를 제공한다.

해설 **추론/암시**

다섯 번째 단락에서 주민들은 시에서 대중교통이 잘 연결되어 있지 않은 여러 지역으로 가기 위해 대여 자전거를 이용했다 (~ residents used the rental bicycles to reach areas of the city that are not well connected to public transportation)고 했으므로 (D)가 정답이다.

어휘 currently 현재   maintain 유지하다   found 설립하다

[168-171] 보고서 발췌문

> 광범위한 전기 자동차 사용을 가로막는 장벽
> **168교통국, 에너지 효율에 관한 특별 위원회**
>
> 개요
>
> 플러그인 전기 자동차(PEVs)는 대기 질 개선에서 화석 연료 의존도 감소까지 많은 이점을 제공합니다. **169미국에서는 현재 PEVs가 해외 여러 국가들보다 인기가 낮습니다.** 소비자들의 PEVs 구매를 막는 것으로 알려진 요소에는 170 (A)**높은 구매가**와 170 (B)**제한적인 주행 거리**, 그리고 170 (C)**배터리 충전용 시설의 부족**이 포함됩니다.
> 에너지 효율에 관한 특별 위원회는 PEVs의 판매를 장려할 수 있는 방법을 밝혀 내는 임무를 맡았습니다. 171**여러 주에서 실시된 연구**

에 따르면 리베이트 제공 같은 금전적 보상책이 특정 유형의 PEVs의 판매를 장려하는 효과적인 방법이라고 합니다. 실제로 현재 사용 가능한 PEVs는 네 가지 유형이 있습니다. 차량 이용을 막는 장벽이 다양하므로, 이 보고서는 각 유형을 별도의 섹션에서 다룰 것입니다.

어휘 barrier 장벽, 장애물   widespread 광범위한
committee 위원회   efficiency 효율(성)   abstract 개요, 초록   benefit 이점, 혜택   improve 개선하다   reduce 감소시키다   reliance 의존(도)   discourage 단념시키다, 막다   range 거리, 범위   scarcity 부족   charge 충전하다   be tasked with ~하는 임무를 맡다   identify 밝혀 내다   incentive 보상(책)   rebate 리베이트, 할인   effective 효과적인   treat 다루다   separate 분리된, 별도의

168 보고서 작성자는 누구일 것 같은가?
(A) 자동차 제조 회사
(B) 배터리 제조사
(C) 에너지 생산 회사
(D) 정부 기관

해설 **추론/암시**

상단에 제목과 함께 교통국에 속한 특별 위원회(Office of Transportation, Special Committee on Energy Efficiency)가 제시되어 있으므로 (D)가 정답이다.

> Paraphrasing 지문의 Office of Transportation, Special Committee on Energy Efficiency → 정답의 A government agency

169 미국 내 PEVs의 판매량에 대해 언급된 것은?
(A) 꾸준한 속도로 증가하고 있다.
(B) 일반적으로 다른 국가들보다 낮다.
(C) 리베이트 제공에 영향을 받지 않았다.
(D) 현재 화석 연료로 움직이는 차량의 평균 판매량을 초과한다.

해설 **Not/True**

첫 번째 단락에 미국에서는 현재 PEVs가 해외 여러 국가들보다 인기가 낮다(In the United States, PEVs are currently less popular than they are in several countries overseas)고 언급되어 있으므로 (B)가 정답이다.

어휘 steady 꾸준한   rate 비율, 속도   generally 일반적으로   unaffected 영향을 받지 않은   exceed 초과하다   fossil fuel-powered 화석 연료로 움직이는

> Paraphrasing 지문의 less popular than they are in several countries overseas → 정답의 lower than they are in some other countries

170 소비자들의 PEVs 구매를 막는 요소로 언급되지 않은 것은?
(A) 높은 비용   (B) 제한적인 주행 거리
(C) 충전 시설의 부족 (D) 배터리 불량 빈도

해설 **Not / True**
첫 번째 단락에 소비자들이 PEVs를 구입하지 못하게 막는 요소로 높은 구매가(high purchase price)와 제한적인 주행 거리(limited driving range), 그리고 배터리 충전용 시설의 부족(the scarcity of facilities for charging their batteries)이 제시되어 있으므로 언급되지 않은 (D)가 정답이다.

어휘 lack 부족 frequency 빈도, 잦음 malfunction 불량, 오작동

> **Paraphrasing** 지문의 high purchase price → 보기 (A)의 high cost
> 지문의 scarcity of facilities for charging their batteries → 보기 (C)의 lack of charging facilities

171 [1], [2], [3], [4]로 표시된 곳 중에서 다음 문장이 들어가기에 가장 적합한 곳은?

"실제로 현재 사용 가능한 PEVs는 네 가지 유형이 있습니다."

(A) [1]   (B) [2]   (C) [3]   (D) [4]

해설 **문장 삽입**
주어진 문장은 현재 사용 가능한 PEVs는 네 가지 유형이라는 의미이다. 따라서 금전적 보상책이 특정 유형의 PEVs의 판매를 장려하는 효과적인 방법(financial incentives ~ are an effective way to do this for certain types of PEVs)이라며, PEVs 유형을 언급하는 문장 뒤에서 네 가지가 있다고 알리는 흐름이 되는 것이 자연스러우므로 (C)가 정답이다.

어휘 in fact 실제로, 사실

[172-175] 온라인 채팅

로빈 도엘 (오전 11시) **172, 173** 소티포 투자사의 조시 피터스 씨가 방금 문자를 보내 오늘 회의를 3시로 미룰 수 있는지 물었어요. 두 분은 괜찮으세요?

안드레 올리에나 (오전 11시 2분) 저는 문제없어요. 우리는 밀러 룸을 예약해야 해요. 그곳이 그때 비어 있는지 확인해 보셨나요? 안 하셨으면, 제가 할 수 있어요.

로빈 도엘 (오전 11시 3분) 아뇨, 잊고 있었어요. 확인해 주실 수 있다면, 도움이 될 겁니다.

수마타 싱 (오전 11시 3분) **173** 저는 다른 고객과의 회의가 3시 30분에 시작해요. 소티포와의 회의는 첫 30분 동안만 참석할 수 있겠네요. **174** 그래서 아마 제가 먼저 발표해야 할 것 같은데, 어떻게 생각하세요?

안드레 올리에나 (오전 11시 4분) 네, 지금 바로 확인해 볼게요.

로빈 도엘 (오전 11시 5분) 그렇네요. 약 10분의 시간이 필요할 거라고 하셨죠?

수마타 싱 (오전 11시 6분) 네. 그리고 질문 시간도요.

안드레 올리에나 (오전 11시 10분) 밀러 룸이 그때 잡혀 있긴 하지만, **175** 벤튼 룸이 비어 있습니다. 예약할까요?

로빈 도엘 (오전 11시 11분) **175** 벤튼도 괜찮을 거예요, 감사합니다. 제가 피터스 씨에게 알려 드릴게요.

안드레 올리에나 (오전 11시 12분) 좋습니다. 그곳에서 3시에 뵙죠.

어휘 work for (일정 등이) ~에게 괜찮다 make sense 타당하다, 의미가 통하다 occupied (공간 등이) 점유된, 이용 중인

172 도엘 씨는 처음에 왜 동료 직원들에게 연락하는가?
(A) 한 가지 목표가 달성되었음을 확인해 주기 위해
(B) 회의 내용 요약을 요청하기 위해
(C) 회의 장소를 확인해 주기 위해
(D) 회의 시간 참석 가능 여부에 관해 묻기 위해

해설 **주제/목적**
첫 번째 메시지에서 도엘 씨가 소티포 투자사의 조시 피터스 씨가 방금 문자를 보내 오늘 회의를 3시로 미룰 수 있는지 물었다고 알리면서 나머지 두 사람에게 괜찮은지(Josie Peters from Sotifo Investments just texted to ask whether we could push today's meeting to 3:00. Does that work for you two?) 묻고 있으므로 (D)가 정답이다.

어휘 summarize 요약하다 availability 시간이 있는지 여부

173 피터스 씨가 누구일 것 같은가?
(A) 도엘 씨의 고객
(B) 도엘 씨의 친구
(C) 도엘 씨의 비서
(D) 도엘 씨의 상사

해설 **추론/암시**
첫 번째 메시지에서 도엘 씨가 소티포 투자사의 조시 피터스 씨와 갖는 회의(Josie Peters from Sotifo Investments just texted to ask whether we could push today's meeting ~)를 언급했고, 오전 11시 3분에는 수마타 싱이 또 다른 고객과의 회의가 있다(I have another client meeting ~)고 했으므로, 피터스 씨도 고객임을 추론할 수 있다. 따라서 (A)가 정답이다.

174 오전 11시 5분에, 도엘 씨가 "그렇네요"라고 쓸 때 무엇을 의미하는 것 같은가?
(A) 싱 씨의 발표가 짧아져야 한다.
(B) 밀러 룸이 회의에 적합하다.
(C) 회의실이 반드시 프로젝터를 갖추고 있어야 한다.
(D) 싱 씨가 회의에서 첫 번째 발표자여야 한다.

해설 **의도 파악**
오전 11시 3분 메시지에서 싱 씨가 자신이 발표를 먼저 해야 할 것 같다고 알리면서 동의를 구하자(I should probably do my presentation first, don't you think?), 도엘 씨가 '그렇다(Makes sense)'는 말로 동의를 나타내는 것이므로 (D)가 정답이다.

어휘 shorten 짧게 하다, 단축하다 appropriate 적합한 be equipped with ~을 갖추고 있다

175 올리에나 씨가 곧이어 무엇을 할 것 같은가?
(A) 피터스 씨에게 전화하기
(B) 벤튼 룸 예약하기
(C) 소티포 투자와의 회의에 참석하기
(D) 밀러 룸이 이용 가능한지 파악하기

해설 추론/암시

오전 11시 10분 메시지에서 올리에나 씨가 벤튼 룸이 비어 있다며 그곳을 예약할지(the Benton Room is free. Should I book it?) 묻는 것에 대해 도엘 씨가 벤튼도 좋을 것(Benton will be fine)이라고 대답했으므로 (B)가 정답이다.

어휘 reserve 예약하다 find out 파악하다, 알아내다

[176-180] 회람 + 이메일

회람	
수신:	라일리 레스토랑 직원
178발신:	크리스토퍼 델가도
날짜:	12월 10일
제목:	추가 교대 근무

연휴가 다가오고 있고, **176, 178**이는 연중 가장 바쁜 시기이므로, 나머지 매니저님들과 저는 12월 24일과 26일에 초과 근무를 할 정리 담당자와 서빙 담당자를 찾고 있습니다. 다음 교대 근무 중 언제라도 근무하실 수 있는지 제게 알려 주시기 바랍니다.

- **177**교대 근무 1 (서빙 담당자): 12월 24일 토요일 오전 10시부터 오후 5시까지
- **177, 179**교대 근무 2 (정리 담당자): 12월 24일 토요일 오전 11시부터 오후 5시까지
- **177**교대 근무 3 (서빙 담당자): 12월 24일 토요일 오후 4시부터 오후 11시까지
- **177**교대 근무 4 (정리 담당자): 12월 24일 토요일 오후 5시부터 오후 10시까지
- 교대 근무 5 (서빙 담당자): 12월 26일 월요일 오후 4시부터 오후 10시까지

어휘 extra 추가의, 여분의 shift 교대 근무(조) look for ~을 찾다 busser (식당의) 테이블 정리 담당자 following 다음의, 아래의

수신: 크리스토퍼 델가도
발신: 애널리 브라운
날짜: 12월 11일
제목: 회신: 추가 교대 근무

크리스토퍼 씨께,

179저는 12월 24일 더 이른 시간대에 정리 담당자로 근무할 수 있습니다. 주간 일정을 관리하시니, 제가 보통 토요일에는 근무하지 않는다는 것을 알고 계실 텐데요. 하지만 라일리 레스토랑이 12월 25일에 문을 닫을 것이기 때문에, 기꺼이 추가 근무를 하겠습니다.

그리고 **180**10개월 전에 제가 일을 시작했을 때 지급해 주신 정리 담당자용 반팔 셔츠가 마모의 흔적이 보입니다. 제게 주실 새 유니폼 셔츠가 있나요? 제 다음 교대 근무 중에 받아갈 수 있습니다.

감사합니다.

애널리 브라운

어휘 maintain (일정 등) 관리하다, 유지하다 take on ~을 맡아서 하다 issue 지급하다 sign 흔적, 징후 wear and tear 마모, 닳음

---

176 라일리 레스토랑 매니저들이 왜 직원들에게 추가 교대 근무를 할 수 있는지 묻는가?
(A) 새 서빙 담당자를 교육하는 데 도움이 필요하다.
(B) 레스토랑이 바쁜 시기이다.
(C) 레스토랑이 식사 공간을 더 추가한다.
(D) 일부 직원들이 그때 휴가를 떠날 것이다.

해설 세부 사항

회람의 첫 번째 단락에서 연중 가장 바쁜 시기이기 때문에 초과 근무할 사람들을 찾고 있다(~ it is our busiest time of year, so the other managers and I are looking for bussers and servers ~)고 했으므로 (B)가 정답이다.

어휘 add 추가하다 on vacation 휴가 중인

177 회람에서 서빙 담당자들에 대해 언급하는 것은?
(A) 12월 10일에 회의에 참석할 것이다.
(B) 매주 더 긴 시간을 근무해야 할 것이다.
(C) 연휴 근무 시 정리 담당자들보다 1시간 더 일찍 교대 근무를 시작할 것이다.
(D) 연휴 기간에 더 많은 시급을 벌 것이다.

해설 Not/True

회람의 두 번째 단락에 교대 근무 1과 3에 서빙 담당자들의 교대 근무 시작 시간이 오전 10시와 오후 4시로 표기되어 있는데, 교대 근무 2와 4에 정리 담당자들의 교대 근무 시작 시간은 오전 11시와 오후 5시로 표기되어 있다. 서빙 담당자들이 각각 1시간씩 더 일찍 시작하는 것이므로 (C)가 정답이다.

178 델가도 씨에 대해 언급된 것은?
(A) 오전 10시에 근무를 시작한다.
(B) 12월 25일에 근무할 예정이다.
(C) 라일리 레스토랑에 있는 여러 매니저 중 한 명이다.
(D) 10개월 전에 일을 시작했다.

해설 Not/True

회람 상단의 발신인 항목에서 델가도 씨의 이름을 찾을 수 있고, 회람 첫 번째 단락에서 나머지 다른 매니저들과 자신이 초과 근무할 직원을 찾고 있다(the other managers and I are looking for bussers and servers)고 밝히고 있어 여러 매니저들 중 한 사람인 것으로 볼 수 있으므로 (C)가 정답이다.

179 브라운 씨가 초과 근무가 가능한 시간은?
(A) 교대 근무 1　　**(B) 교대 근무 2**
(C) 교대 근무 3　　(D) 교대 근무 4

해설 연계

이메일의 첫 번째 단락에 12월 24일 더 이른 시간대에 정리 담당자로 근무할 수 있다(I am available to work as a busser for the earlier shift on December 24)고 했다. 회람의 두 번째 단락에서 12월 24일 정리 담당자 근무는 오전 11시에 시작하는 것과 오후 5시에 시작하는 것이 있는데 이른 것은 오전에 시작하는 Shift 2이므로 (B)가 정답이다.

180 브라운 씨에 대해 언급된 것은?
(A) 흔히 토요일마다 근무한다.
(B) 델가도 씨의 회람을 읽지 못했다.
(C) 누가 라일리 레스토랑의 근무 일정표를 만드는지 알지 못한다.
(D) 근무복을 교체하고 싶어 한다.

해설 Not/True
이메일 두 번째 단락에서 10개월 전에 일을 시작했을 때 지급한 정리 담당자용 반팔 셔츠가 마모의 흔적이 보인다며 새 유니폼 셔츠가 있는지(the short-sleeved busser shirt ~ is showing signs of wear and tear. Do you have a new uniform shirt for me?) 묻고 있으므로 (D)가 정답이다.

어휘 replace 교체하다   clothing 의류

> **Paraphrasing** 지문의 the short-sleeved busser shirt → 정답의 a workplace clothing item

[181-185] 이메일 + 온라인 양식

수신: 로라 트랜 〈ltran@shorelinehealthcenter.org〉
발신: 리처드 보니 〈rbonney@aventinas.org〉
날짜: 6월 2일
제목: 추천서 요청

안녕하세요, 트랜 씨.

저희가 최근에 찰스 새너 씨의 면접을 진행했으며, 이분은 어벤티너스 진료소의 건강 교육 진행 부책임자 직책에 고려되고 있습니다. **181, 183**이분께서 귀하를 패밀리 피트니스 프로그램의 직속상관이자 전문가 추천인으로 **182**기재했습니다. 부디 잠시 시간 내셔서 www.aventinas.org/hrreference/390B에서 설문지를 작성해 주시기 바랍니다. 의견을 주셔서 대단히 감사합니다.

리처드 보니
인사부장, 어벤티너스 진료소

어휘 reference 추천서, 추천인   under consideration 고려되고 있는   coordinator 진행 책임자, 조정 담당자   supervisor 상사, 책임자   fill out 작성하다   questionnaire 설문지   input 의견 (제공)

다음 후보자께서 귀하를 추천인으로 기재했습니다: 찰스 새너
구인 목록: 건강 교육 진행 부책임자, 어벤티너스 진료소

이 지원자와 함께 일한 경험에 대해 말씀해 주시기 바랍니다.

1. 지원자가 귀사에서 어떤 역할을 맡았나요? 얼마나 오래 근무했나요?
184새너 씨는 1월부터 쇼어라인 건강 센터에서 제 직원으로 근무해 오고 있습니다. 현재 제 관리하에 인턴사원으로 일주일에 25시간 근무하고 있으며, **183**생활 습관 조정을 위해 담당 의사가 의뢰한 고객들을 상담합니다.

2. 해당 지원자의 가장 뛰어난 장점이 무엇이라고 생각하시나요?
185모든 계층 및 연령대의 고객과 잘 소통합니다. 긍정적이면서 격려하는 태도를 지니고 있으며, 환자 의견 설문 조사에서 지속적으로 높은 평가를 받고 있습니다.

3. 이 지원자에게 우려되는 문제가 있었나요?
이메일 메시지는 지속적으로 즉각 답변하지는 않지만, 문자 메시지는 곧바로 답장합니다.

4. 기회가 된다면 이 지원자를 다시 고용하시겠습니까?
의심의 여지가 없습니다. 안타깝게도, 저희 센터에는 공석인 정규직 일자리가 없습니다. 그렇지 않다면, 저희는 고용할 겁니다. 아직 전문적인 경험이 많지는 않지만, 지역 사회 보건 분야에 대해 폭넓은 지식을 지니고 있습니다. 어떤 업무를 맡겨도 뛰어나게 처리할 것이라고 굳게 믿습니다.

어휘 capacity 지위, 역할, 능력   direction 관리, 감독   counsel 상담하다   refer 소개하다, 추천하다   medical practitioner (개업한) 의사   adjustment 조정, 조절   consider 생각하다, 여기다   strength 장점, 강점   connect with ~와 소통하다, ~와 교류하다   demographic 인구 통계(상)의, 인구 통계학적인   positive 긍정적인   encouraging 격려하는   manner 태도   consistently 지속적으로   rating 평가, 등급   responsive 즉각 대답하는   arise 생기다, 발생하다   without question 의심의 여지없이   otherwise 그렇지 않으면, 그 외에는   firmly 굳게   excel at ~에서 뛰어나다   task 업무

181 이메일의 목적은?
(A) 설문지 수정을 제안하려고
(B) 직무를 설명하려고
(C) 구직 기회를 홍보하려고
(D) 한 직원에 관한 의견을 요청하려고

해설 주제/목적
이메일에서 면접을 본 찰스 새너 씨가 이메일 수신인인 로라 트랜 씨를 상사이자 추천인으로 기재한 사실과 함께 온라인에서 설문지를 작성하도록 요청(He has listed you as his direct supervisor in the Family Fitness Program and as a professional reference. Kindly take a few moments to fill out the questionnaire ~)하고 있으므로 (D)가 정답이다.

어휘 propose 제안하다   revision 수정, 정정   describe 설명하다   responsibility 책무, 책임(감)

182 이메일의 첫 번째 단락 두 번째 줄에 쓰인 단어 "listed"와 의미가 가장 가까운 것은?
(A) 확인했다
(B) 기울었다
(C) 계획했다
(D) 낭독했다

해설 동의어 찾기
listed를 포함한 부분은 '귀하를 직속상관으로 기재했다(He has listed you as his direct supervisor ~)'는 의미이다. 여기서 listed는 '기재했다'라는 뜻으로 쓰였는데, 수신자를 직속상관으로 기재했다는 말은 수신자가 직속상관임을 확인해 주었다는 의미이므로 '(신분을) 확인하다'와 같은 의미의 identify의 과거분사형인 (A) identified가 정답이다.

183 패밀리 피트니스 프로그램에서 새너 씨의 역할은 무엇인가?
(A) 새로운 건강 관리 담당 의사들을 교육한다.
(B) 건강 센터의 기술을 관리한다.
(C) 예약 일정을 잡는다.
(D) 건강 관련 문제들에 관해 고객들을 교육한다.

해설 연계

이메일에 새너 씨가 트랜 씨를 패밀리 피트니스 프로그램의 직속상관으로 기재했다(He has listed you as his direct supervisor in the Family Fitness Program ~)고 했고, 트랜 씨가 새너 씨에 대해 답변한 온라인 양식의 1번 항목에 새너 씨가 생활 습관 조정을 위해 담당 의사가 의뢰한 고객들을 상담한다(counseling clients who were referred by their medical practitioners for lifestyle adjustments)고 했다. 따라서 건강 문제와 관련해 환자들을 교육하는 일을 하는 것으로 볼 수 있으므로 (D)가 정답이다.

184 트랜 씨에 대해 암시된 것은?
(A) 최근에 인턴 프로그램을 끝마쳤다.
(B) 쇼어라인 건강 센터에서 근무한다.
(C) 인사 분야에서 근무한다.
(D) 새너 씨를 위해 구직 면접을 주선했다.

해설 추론/암시

트랜 씨가 작성한 온라인 양식 1번 답변에 새너 씨가 쇼어라인 건강 센터에서 1월부터 본인 밑에서 근무해 오고 있다(Mr. Sanna has been working for me at the Shoreline Health Center ~)고 했으므로 (B)가 정답이다.

어휘 arrange 마련하다, 조치하다

185 온라인 양식에서 새너 씨의 장점 중 하나로 언급하는 것은?
(A) 이메일에 대해 제때 답변하는 것
(B) 고객들과 긍정적으로 교류하는 것
(C) 서류를 제때 제출하는 것
(D) 필요할 때 추가 업무를 맡는 것

해설 세부 사항

온라인 양식 2번 답변에 새너 씨가 모든 계층 및 연령대의 고객과 잘 소통하고, 긍정적이면서 격려하는 태도를 지니고 있다(He connects well with clients from every demographic and age group. He is positive ~)고 했으므로 (B)가 정답이다.

어휘 in a timely fashion 제때, 적절한 시점에 interact with ~와 교류하다 on time 제때 take on ~을 맡다

> **Paraphrasing** 지문의 connects well with clients / positive → 정답의 Interacting positively with clients

---

[186-190] 우편 엽서 + 견적서 + 웹페이지

라이트 월드 윈도우즈
페어뷰 길 81번지
이리, PA 16506

라이트 월드 윈도우즈와 함께 비용을 절약하세요

186 외풍이 심한 창문을 교체하는 것은 에너지 요금을 낮춰 주고, 곤충 문제를 줄여 주며, 여러분의 집이 주는 즐거움을 향상시킬 수 있습니다. 저희 라이트 월드 윈도우즈에서는 영업사원들과 공인 기술자들이 여러분을 가족처럼 대해 드립니다. 저희는 여러분의 프로젝트를 디자인하고 설치하면서 그 과정의 모든 단계를 여러분과 함께합니다. **187** 오늘 저희에게 연락 주셔서 무료 비용 견적서를 받아 보세요. **188** 11월 한 달간 이 엽서를 저희 지역 담당 직원에게 보여 주시고, 창문 구매 및 설치 비용을 20% 할인받으세요.

멜리나 해러웨이
레블스 길 198번지
이리, PA 16506

어휘 drafty 외풍이 심한 lower 낮추다, 내리다 bill 고지서, 청구서 insect 곤충 improve 향상시키다, 개선하다 certified 공인된, 자격증이 있는 treat 대하다, 다루다 install 설치하다 estimate 견적(서) present 제시하다, 보여 주다 representative 직원, 대표자

견적서
날짜: 11월 10일

소유주
멜리나 해러웨이
814-555-0128
melharaway@mailcrate.com

188 영업사원
존 랜크포드
814-555-0155
lankford@lwwindows.com

라이트 월드 윈도우즈가 레블스 길 198번지, 이리, PA 16506에 위치한 주택의 작업을 위해 인력과 장비, 자재, 그리고 철거/청소 서비스를 제공할 것입니다. 모든 창문은 25년 품질 보증 서비스를 포함합니다. 가격은 이 견적서 발급 날짜로부터 30일 동안 유효합니다.

수량	창문 선택	제품당 가격	총액
6	시리즈 1500 내리닫이창 (**190** 가격은 저희 가격 일치 보증제를 반영합니다)	380달러	2,280달러
2	미닫이창	350달러	700달러
1	전망창	450달러	450달러
	설치 및 처리 수수료		175달러
	프로젝트 소계		3,605달러
	188 20% 할인		-721달러
	총계		2,884달러

상기 조건이 수용 가능하실 경우, 아래에 서명하시고 이 문서를 담당 영업직원에게 돌려보내 주시기 바랍니다. 기술자가 귀하께 전화 드려서 저희 설치 작업 일정에 추가해 드릴 것입니다.

고객 서명: _____ 날짜: _____

어휘 labor 인력, 노동력 equipment 장비 material 자재, 소재 demolition 철거 come with ~을 포함하다 warranty 품질 보증(서) good 유효한 double-hung 내리닫이의 reflect 반영하다 price match guarantee 가격 일치 보증제 setup 설치, 설정, 준비 disposal 처리, 처분 acceptable 수용 가능한, 만족스러운

---

https://www.lwwindows.com/guarantee

저희 가격 일치 보증제

저희 라이트 월드 윈도우즈에서는 최고의 가격으로 최고의 제품을 전해 드릴 수 있으리라 확신합니다. 그것이 바로 저희가 특별 가격 일치 보증제를 제공하는 이유입니다. **189, 190** 저희 가격을 능가하는 다른 창문 회사의 견적서를 보여 주시면, 해당 프로젝트가 동일 사양을 충족한다면, 그 가격에 맞춰 드리겠습니다.

라이트 월드 윈도우즈에서 쇼핑하시면, 창문을 언제나 최저가로 구입하실 것입니다. 이 제공 서비스에 관한 더 많은 상세 정보는 여러분의 담당 영업직원에게 연락하시기 바랍니다.

어휘 be confident that ~임을 확신하다 beat 능가하다, 이기다 provided ~한다면 specifications 사양

186 엽서에 따르면, 주택 소유주가 왜 창문 교체를 고려해 봐야 하는가?
(A) 에너지 요금을 줄이기 위해
(B) 현대적인 모습을 만들어 내기 위해
(C) 주택 가치를 높이기 위해
(D) 집에 빛이 더 많이 들어오도록 하기 위해

해설 세부 사항
엽서 초반부에 외풍이 심한 창문을 교체하면 에너지 요금을 낮출 수 있다(Replacing drafty windows can lower your energy bills ~)고 했으므로 (A)가 정답이다.

어휘 value 가치, 값어치

Paraphrasing 지문의 lower → 정답의 reduce

187 엽서에서 라이트 월드 윈도우즈에 대해 언급된 것은?
(A) 곤충으로 인한 피해를 검사할 수 있다.
(B) 무료로 견적서를 제공해 준다.
(C) 가족 소유의 업체이다.
(D) 11월에 문을 닫을 것이다.

해설 Not/True
엽서 중반부에 오늘 연락하여 무료 비용 견적서를 받아 보라(Contact us today for a free cost estimate)고 했으므로 (B)가 정답이다.

어휘 inspect 검사하다, 점검하다 at no cost 무료로

Paraphrasing 지문의 free → 정답의 at no cost

188 해러웨이 씨가 어떻게 견적서에서 20퍼센트 할인을 받았는가?
(A) 재방문 고객 할인을 요청함으로써
(B) 가족 구성원을 잠재 고객으로 소개함으로써
(C) 엽서를 랜크포드 씨에게 제공함으로써
(D) 웹페이지에서 쿠폰을 다운로드함으로써

해설 연계
엽서 후반부에 엽서를 지역 담당 직원에게 제시하여 창문 구매 및 설치 비용을 20% 할인받으라(Present this postcard to one of our local representatives to receive 20% off ~)고 했다. 견적서의 오른쪽 상단에 해러웨이 씨의 담당 영업직원 이름이 존 랜크포드(Sales Representative Jon Lankford)로 쓰여 있어, 이 사람에게 엽서를 제시했다는 것을 알 수 있으므로 (C)가 정답이다.

어휘 ask for ~을 요청하다 repeat customer 재방문 고객 refer 소개하다, 추천하다 potential 잠재적인

189 웹페이지에 무엇이 설명되어 있는가?
(A) 가격 경쟁이 어떻게 고객에게 유익한지
(B) 영업직원에게 어떻게 연락하는지
(C) 창문이 얼마나 자주 교체되어야 하는지
(D) 고객이 어떻게 창문을 더 오래 지속되게 만들 수 있는지

해설 세부 사항
웹페이지 첫 번째 단락에 가격 일치 보증제를 언급하면서 자사의 가격을 능가하는 다른 창문 회사의 견적서를 보여 주면, 그 가격에 맞춰 준다(If you show us a cost estimate from another window company that beats our price, we will match it, ~)고 했다. 이는 가격 경쟁이 고객에게 어떻게 유리한지를 나타내므로 (A)가 정답이다.

어휘 competitive 경쟁적인, 경쟁력 있는 benefit 유익하다

190 해러웨이 씨에 대해 결론 내릴 수 있는 것은?
(A) 작은 업체를 소유하고 있다.
(B) 새로운 집을 짓고 있다.
(C) 새 창문에 대한 주문 사항을 여러 차례 변경했다.
(D) 한 곳이 넘는 회사에 견적서를 요청했다.

해설 연계
견적서의 표에 표기된 첫 번째 창문 설명에 가격이 가격 일치 보증제를 반영한다(price reflects our Price Match Guarantee)고 했는데, 이에 대해 웹페이지 첫 번째 단락에 자사의 가격을 능가하는 다른 창문 회사의 견적서를 보여 주면, 그 가격에 맞춰 준다(If you show us a cost estimate from another window company that beats our price, we will match it, ~)고 언급하고 있어 다른 곳에서도 견적서를 받은 것을 알 수 있으므로 (D)가 정답이다.

어휘 own 소유하다 revise 변경하다, 수정하다

[191-195] 주문서 + 이메일 + 이메일

애스터 출장 요리 주문서

행사 날짜: 6월 10일 손님: 30명
시간: 오후 6시 30분부터 장소: 써니뷰 커뮤니티 센터
     오후 8시 30분까지
191목적: 트리폴드 출판사의 연례 직원 감사 저녁 만찬

뷔페 메뉴
- **192 (A)**애피타이저: 바비큐 윙, 알싸한 고기 완자, 튀긴 애호박
- 샐러드: 이탈리안 비네그레트 또는 요거트 허브 드레싱을 곁들인 **192 (B)**여러 재료를 섞은 샐러드
- 주 요리 선택
  주 요리 1: 신선한 채소와 현미를 곁들이 마늘 치킨
  주 요리 2: 신선한 바질을 곁들인 **192 (D)**채식 파스타 프리마베라
- 디저트: 초콜릿 쉬폰 파이
- 음료: 물, 탄산음료, 커피, 각종 차

연락 담당자: 트리폴드 출판사, 배은미, Eun-Mi.Pae@trifoldpublishers.com

메모: 단순하면서도 우아한 테이블 장식이 이용 가능하며, 식탁보 선택도 마찬가지입니다. 긴 직사각형 테이블용 하얀색 리넨 또는 **194** 원형 테이블용 하늘색 리넨

어휘 catering 출장 요리 제공(업) annual 연례적인 appreciation 감사(의 뜻) beverage 음료 assorted 각종의, 갖가지의 tasteful 우아한, 멋있는 decoration 장식(물) linen 리넨 제품 rectangular 직사각형의 circular 원형의

수신: Eun-Mi.Pae@trifoldpublishers.com
발신: jim@astorcatering.com
날짜: 6월 5일
제목: 참석자 및 질문

안녕하세요, 은미 씨.

정확한 참석자 수에 관한 음성 메시지를 막 받았습니다. **193**팀들의 손님을 고려하여 숫자를 30명에서 60명으로 조정했습니다. 추가 식사 비용은 최종 청구서에 추가될 것입니다.

커뮤니티 센터에는 긴 직사각형 테이블과 원형 테이블이 있습니다. 이 정도 규모의 그룹에는 원형 테이블을 추천해 드리는데, 식사 중에 대화를 나누기 더 좋기 때문입니다. 정확한 식탁보를 가져갈 수 있도록 제게 알려 주시기 바랍니다. 커뮤니티 센터에 선택하실 것을 알려 주셔야 합니다.

또한, **195**라즈베리가 지금 제철이기 때문에, 지역 내 과일 공급업체로부터 물량을 막 받았습니다. 현재 선택하신 디저트 대신 신선한 라즈베리가 토핑된 아이스크림 케이크에 관심이 있으실까요? 비용은 동일할 것입니다.

짐 애스터

어휘 attendee 참석자 correct 정확한, 알맞은 adjust 조정하다, 조절하다 account for ~을 고려하다, ~을 설명하다 opportunity 기회 in season 제철인 batch (한 회분의) 물량 supplier 공급업체 selection 선택(한 것)

수신: jim@astorcatering.com
발신: Eun-Mi.Pae@trifoldpublishers.com
날짜: 6월 5일
제목: 회신: 참석자 및 질문

안녕하세요, 짐 씨.

식사 인원수를 조정해 주셔서 대단히 감사합니다. 주문했을 때 정확한 총 인원을 간과한 점에 대해 사과드립니다. 추가 비용은 문제가 되지 않을 것입니다. 이 행사는 회사에 매우 중요한 행사이기 때문에 예산은 많이 잡혀 있습니다.

귀하의 제안에 따라, **194**오늘 오후에 커뮤니티 센터에 저희가 원형 테이블을 이용할 생각이라고 알리겠습니다.

195최근 계속 이어지고 있는 따뜻한 날씨 때문에 제안해 주신 디저트가 특히 상쾌할 것 같네요. 그걸로 선택하겠습니다. 아주 유연하게 대처해 주셔서 감사합니다.

어휘 apologize for ~에 대해 사과하다 overlook 간과하다 expense (지출) 비용 budget 예산 follow 따르다 suggestion 제안, 의견 intend ~할 생각이다 sound ~한 것 같다, ~하게 들리다 refreshing 상쾌하게 하는, 신선한 flexible 유연한, 탄력적인

---

191 트리폴드 출판사가 왜 저녁 만찬 행사를 계획하고 있는가?
(A) 은퇴를 기념하기 위해
(B) 신입 직원들을 환영하기 위해
(C) 최근의 사업 성공을 축하하기 위해
(D) 직원들에게 감사하기 위해

해설 세부 사항

주문서 상단에 행사 개최 목적이 '트리폴드 출판사의 연례 직원 감사 저녁 만찬(Purpose: Trifold Publishers' Annual Employee Appreciation Dinner)'이라고 쓰여 있으므로 (D)가 정답이다.

어휘 celebrate 기념하다, 축하하다 retirement 은퇴하다

Paraphrasing 지문의 Appreciation → 정답의 thank

192 주문서에 기재된 뷔페 메뉴에 포함되지 않은 것은?
(A) 애피타이저
(B) 여러 재료를 섞은 샐러드
(C) 빵과 버터
(D) 채식 식사 메뉴

해설 Not/True

주문서의 중반부에 Appetizers와 Mixed salad, 그리고 Vegetarian pasta primavera가 쓰여 있어 (A), (B), (D)를 각각 확인할 수 있다. 하지만 빵과 버터는 제시되어 있지 않으므로 (C)가 정답이다.

193 첫 번째 이메일에 따르면, 예상 손님 수는 왜 조정되었는가?
(A) 일부 직원들이 참석할 수 없다.
(B) 회사가 최근에 직원을 추가로 고용했다.
(C) 회사가 일부 중요 고객들을 초대하기로 결정했다.
(D) 직원들의 손님들이 계산되지 않았다.

해설 세부 사항

첫 번째 이메일의 첫 번째 단락에 팀원들의 손님을 고려하여 숫자를 30명에서 60명으로 조정했다(We have adjusted the number from 30 to 60 to account for your team members' guests)고 했으므로 그 손님들이 누락되었다는 것을 알 수 있다. 따라서 (D)가 정답이다.

194 애스터 출장 요리가 행사를 위해 제공할 식탁보와 관련해 암시된 것은?

(A) 직사각형이다.
(B) 하늘색 리넨이다.
(C) 행사 전날에 전달될 것이다.
(D) 반납되기 전에 반드시 세탁되어야 한다.

해설 연계

주문서 하단 메모에 식탁보 선택에 대해 긴 직사각형 테이블용 하얀색 리넨 식탁보와 원형 테이블용 하늘색 리넨 식탁보(~ as are a choice of tablecloths: white linen for long, rectangular tables or light-blue linen tablecloths for circular tables)가 언급되는데, 두 번째 이메일의 두 번째 단락에 커뮤니티 센터에 원형 테이블을 이용할 생각이라고 알리겠다(~ we intend to use the circular tables)고 했으므로 원형 테이블용 하늘색 식탁보를 쓸 것임을 알 수 있다. 따라서 (B)가 정답이다.

195 행사용 디저트에 대해 언급된 것은?

(A) 고객들 사이에서 인기 있는 선택지이다.
(B) 계절 과일을 특징으로 할 것이다.
(C) 따뜻하게 제공될 것이다.
(D) 다른 디저트를 선택하는 것보다 더 많은 비용이 든다.

해설 연계

첫 번째 이메일의 세 번째 단락에서 짐 씨가 라즈베리가 지금 제철이라는 말과 함께 신선한 라즈베리가 토핑된 아이스크림 케이크를 제안한 것(Also, raspberries are now in season, ~ Would you be interested in ice-cream cake with fresh raspberry topping ~)과 관련해, 두 번째 이메일의 세 번째 단락에서 그걸 선택하겠다(Let's go with that selection)고 했으므로 (B)가 정답이다.

어휘 feature 특징으로 하다   serve (음식 등) 제공하다

[196-200] 일정표 + 트럭 패널 + 이메일

로일랜드 트럭 수송
3월 21일 일정표

출발	기사	차량	경로
196 오전 5시	버트 페이버	트럭 3882	캔자스 위치타 출발, 헤이스빌 도착 (3번 왕복)
오전 6시	**198** 로즈 메이컨	트럭 2711	**198** 캔자스 위치타 출발, 오클라호마 털사 도착 (1번 왕복)
오전 7시 30분	에밀리 최	트럭 2889	캔자스 위치타 출발, 인디애나 사우스 벤드 도착 (1번 왕복)
오전 8시	**197** 이언 오티즈	트럭 6007	캔자스 위치타 출발, 미주리 스프링필드 도착 (1번 왕복)

어휘 vehicle 차량   route 경로, 노선   round trip 왕복 이동

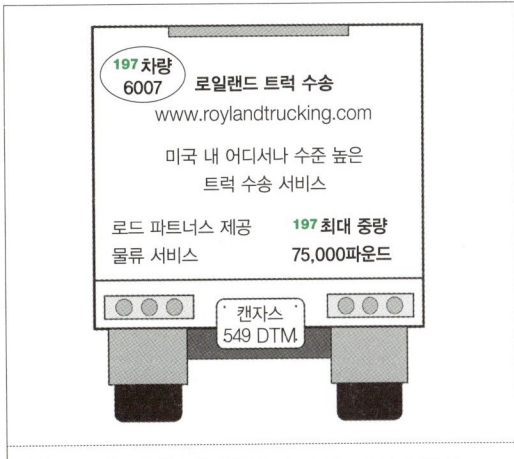

어휘 quality 수준 높은, 양질의   logistics 물류 (서비스)   maximum 최대의

수신: 테드 심즈 〈t.simms@roylandtrucking.com〉
발신: 코피 스탱글 〈kofi@amail.com〉
날짜: 3월 22일
제목: 채용
첨부: 스탱글_이력서

심즈 씨께,

198 어제 이른 아침에 위치타 바로 외곽에 위치한 고속도로 휴게소에서 귀사의 기사들 중 한 분인 로즈 메이컨 씨를 만났습니다. 그분께서 귀사를 높이 평가하면서 제게 귀하께 연락해 볼 것을 권했습니다. **200** 저는 포키토 트럭 수송 사에서 8년 동안 근무해 왔으며, 완벽한 운행 기록을 보유하고 있습니다. 안타깝게도, 포키토 사에는 현재 야간 운행 기회만 있는데, 저는 주간 근무를 선호합니다.

199 첨부해 드린 것은 제 이력서이며, 개인 추천서와 전문가 추천서를 모두 포함하고 있습니다. 귀사와 함께할 기회와 관련해 이야기 나눠 볼 수 있기를 고대합니다.

코피 스탱글

어휘 employment 채용, 고용   résumé 이력서
speak highly of ~을 높이 평가하다   attach 첨부하다

196 3월 21일에 페이버 씨가 언제 처음 캔자스 위치타에서 출발했는가?

(A) 오전 5시에
(B) 오전 6시에
(C) 오전 7시 30분에
(D) 오전 8시에

해설 세부 사항

일정표 첫 번째 줄에 페이버 씨의 이름과 함께 출발 시간이 5:00 A.M.으로 표기되어 있으므로 (A)가 정답이다.

197 오티즈 씨가 3월 21일에 운행한 트럭에 대해 언급된 것은?

(A) 로일랜드 트럭 수송 회사의 최신 차량이다.
(B) 최대 75,000파운드의 화물을 수송할 수 있다.
(C) 최근에 정기 점검을 받았다.
(D) 캔자스 지역 내 배송에만 이용된다.

해설 **연계**
일정표 마지막 줄에 오티즈 씨의 이름과 함께 차량 번호가 Truck 6007로 표기되어 있는데, 트럭 패널 상단의 차량 번호가 6007이고 하단에 최대 중량이 75,000파운드(Maximum Weight 75,000 Pounds)로 나와 있으므로 (B)가 정답이다.

어휘 load 짐, 화물 up to 최대 ~의 undergo 거치다, 겪다 maintenance 정비, 유지 관리

> **Paraphrasing** 지문의 Maximum Weight 75,000 Pounds
> → 정답의 It can carry loads up to 75,000 pounds

198 휴게소에서 스탱글 씨와 이야기한 기사와 관련해 결론 내릴 수 있는 것은?
(A) 헤이스빌에 살고 있다.
(B) 최 씨를 교육하는 데 도움을 주었다.
(C) 오클라호마로 이동하고 있었다.
(D) 8년 동안 트럭 기사였다.

해설 **연계**
이메일 첫 번째 단락에 휴게소에서 로즈 메이컨 씨를 만났다(I met one of your drivers, Rose Macon ~)고 했는데, 일정표 두 번째 줄에 로즈 메이컨 씨의 도착지가 오클라호마의 털사(Wichita, Kansas, to Tulsa, Oklahoma)로 나와 있으므로 (C)가 정답이다.

199 심즈 씨가 로일랜드 트럭 수송 회사의 어느 부서에서 근무하고 있을 것 같은가?
(A) 일정 관리   (B) 구매
(C) 인사   (D) 차량 정비

해설 **추론/암시**
이메일 두 번째 단락에 스탱글 씨가 자신의 이력서를 첨부했다고 알리며, 심즈 씨의 회사에서 근무할 기회와 관련해 이야기하기를 고대한다(Attached is my résumé, ~ I look forward to speaking with you about opportunities with your company)고 언급하고 있다. 따라서 직원 채용과 관련된 업무를 담당하는 부서인 (C)가 정답이다.

200 스탱글 씨가 이메일에서 암시하는 것은?
(A) 위치타 근처에 집을 소유하고 있다.
(B) 심즈 씨에게 전화로 연락하려 했다.
(C) 포키토 트럭 수송 회사에서 자신의 일정에 만족하고 있다.
(D) 과속 벌금을 부과받은 적이 없다.

해설 **추론/암시**
이메일 첫 번째 단락에 완벽한 운행 기록을 보유하고 있다(~ have a perfect driving record)고 했으므로 (D)가 정답이다.

어휘 be satisfied with ~에 만족하다 fine 벌금을 부과하다

> **Paraphrasing** 지문의 have a perfect driving record
> → 정답의 has never been fined for driving too fast

YBM

ETS 토익 단기공략 750+

실전 모의고사

LISTENING TEST

In the Listening test, you will be asked to demonstrate how well you understand spoken English. The entire Listening test will last approximately 45 minutes. There are four parts, and directions are given for each part. You must mark your answers on the separate answer sheet. Do not write your answers in your test book.

PART 1

Directions: For each question in this part, you will hear four statements about a picture in your test book. When you hear the statements, you must select the one statement that best describes what you see in the picture. Then find the number of the question on your answer sheet and mark your answer. The statements will not be printed in your test book and will be spoken only one time.

Statement (C), "They're sitting at a table," is the best description of the picture, so you should select answer (C) and mark it on your answer sheet.

1.

2.

GO ON TO THE NEXT PAGE

3.

4.

5.

6.

PART 2

Directions: You will hear a question or statement and three responses spoken in English. They will not be printed in your test book and will be spoken only one time. Select the best response to the question or statement and mark the letter (A), (B), or (C) on your answer sheet.

7. Mark your answer on your answer sheet.
8. Mark your answer on your answer sheet.
9. Mark your answer on your answer sheet.
10. Mark your answer on your answer sheet.
11. Mark your answer on your answer sheet.
12. Mark your answer on your answer sheet.
13. Mark your answer on your answer sheet.
14. Mark your answer on your answer sheet.
15. Mark your answer on your answer sheet.
16. Mark your answer on your answer sheet.
17. Mark your answer on your answer sheet.
18. Mark your answer on your answer sheet.
19. Mark your answer on your answer sheet.
20. Mark your answer on your answer sheet.
21. Mark your answer on your answer sheet.
22. Mark your answer on your answer sheet.
23. Mark your answer on your answer sheet.
24. Mark your answer on your answer sheet.
25. Mark your answer on your answer sheet.
26. Mark your answer on your answer sheet.
27. Mark your answer on your answer sheet.
28. Mark your answer on your answer sheet.
29. Mark your answer on your answer sheet.
30. Mark your answer on your answer sheet.
31. Mark your answer on your answer sheet.

PART 3

Directions: You will hear some conversations between two or more people. You will be asked to answer three questions about what the speakers say in each conversation. Select the best response to each question and mark the letter (A), (B), (C), or (D) on your answer sheet. The conversations will not be printed in your test book and will be spoken only one time.

32. According to the man, what helped to attract new customers?
    (A) Lowering the price of a service
    (B) Increasing online advertising
    (C) Partnering with another business
    (D) Offering a loyalty program

33. What does the woman think they should do?
    (A) Hire more employees
    (B) Open a new branch
    (C) Expand a building
    (D) Upgrade some facilities

34. What will the woman do next?
    (A) Create a job posting
    (B) Schedule a meeting
    (C) Write a contract
    (D) Check a budget

35. Which department does the man most likely work in?
    (A) Finance
    (B) Quality control
    (C) Marketing
    (D) Technical support

36. Why does the man say he is excited?
    (A) A product received good reviews.
    (B) A survey was completed early.
    (C) Some instructions are easy to understand.
    (D) Some parts have become cheaper.

37. According to the woman, what has helped the company?
    (A) The hiring of more workers
    (B) A change in regulations
    (C) Strategic promotion overseas
    (D) Funding from the government

38. What kind of items does the woman's business repair?
    (A) Watches
    (B) Rare books
    (C) Furniture
    (D) Musical instruments

39. What does the woman want to know about an object?
    (A) Its color
    (B) Its manufacturer
    (C) Its age
    (D) Its materials

40. What is the man surprised about?
    (A) A task will be time-consuming.
    (B) A price is higher than expected.
    (C) Some work can start immediately.
    (D) Some services are no longer available.

41. What industry do the women work in?
    (A) Architecture
    (B) Pharmaceuticals
    (C) Finance
    (D) Publishing

42. What does the man inquire about?
    (A) The leader of an orientation
    (B) The start date of a position
    (C) The time of a meeting
    (D) The size of a team

43. What will the man probably do next?
    (A) Select a password
    (B) Take an office tour
    (C) Edit some paperwork
    (D) Learn about some rules

GO ON TO THE NEXT PAGE

44. What is the man having trouble doing?
   (A) Charging a laptop
   (B) Visiting a Web site
   (C) Accessing an account
   (D) Keeping a screen on

45. Why does the man say, "Sandra and Tim called me this morning"?
   (A) To verify a plan for an employee meeting
   (B) To point out others with the same problem
   (C) To explain that a team is short-staffed
   (D) To suggest getting assistance from coworkers

46. What does the woman plan to do next?
   (A) Write a memo to the staff
   (B) File a complaint with a manager
   (C) Bring the man some equipment
   (D) Create some new security badges

47. What kind of service does the speakers' business offer?
   (A) Event catering
   (B) Park tours
   (C) Commercial cleaning
   (D) Boat rentals

48. What resource do the speakers check?
   (A) A company brochure
   (B) A timetable
   (C) A seating chart
   (D) A city report

49. What does the man suggest doing?
   (A) Looking into less expensive options
   (B) Requesting a loan from a bank
   (C) Gathering some feedback from customers
   (D) Researching where to list items for sale

50. Who most likely is the woman?
   (A) A corporate recruiter
   (B) A dance instructor
   (C) A festival organizer
   (D) A news reporter

51. What did Haruka Tagami do last year?
   (A) She accepted a new job.
   (B) She started her own business.
   (C) She won a competition.
   (D) She assisted with an event.

52. What does the woman recommend that the men do?
   (A) Track their progress
   (B) Upgrade their equipment
   (C) Change their diet
   (D) Watch some professionals

53. What are the speakers mainly discussing?
   (A) Renovating a town hall
   (B) Building a public parking lot
   (C) Extending a biking trail
   (D) Adding a carpool lane

54. What problem does the woman tell the man about?
   (A) A change is bad for the environment.
   (B) There is limited space for a project.
   (C) The city does not have enough funds.
   (D) Residents have rejected a proposal.

55. What does the man offer to do?
   (A) Approve a design
   (B) Contact an expert
   (C) Research a business
   (D) Visit a site

56. What field do the speakers work in?

    (A) Publishing
    (B) Transportation
    (C) Medicine
    (D) Architecture

57. What does the woman say she must do?

    (A) Follow up with a client
    (B) Prepare for a business trip
    (C) Place an order for supplies
    (D) Lead an orientation session

58. Why does the man say, "They didn't request any changes"?

    (A) To complain about a team
    (B) To explain why a task is finished
    (C) To reassure the woman
    (D) To thank the woman for her help

59. Why did the woman want to visit the store?

    (A) She read about the business in a magazine.
    (B) She heard an advertisement about it.
    (C) She received a coupon in the mail.
    (D) She saw a product display while passing by.

60. What does the man mention about a product?

    (A) It is very durable.
    (B) It has several color options.
    (C) It is easy to clean.
    (D) It comes with a warranty.

61. According to the man, what is included in the price?

    (A) Delivery
    (B) A cleaning product
    (C) Installation
    (D) A design consultation

Crowfield	5 km
Lombard	35 km
Blackwell	46 km
Provo	71 km

62. What kind of event will the speakers attend?

    (A) A fund-raiser
    (B) A grand opening
    (C) A farmers market
    (D) A job fair

63. What does the man think attendees will be interested in?

    (A) A signing bonus
    (B) A company's reputation
    (C) A free sample
    (D) An information packet

64. Look at the graphic. What is the speakers' destination?

    (A) Crowfield
    (B) Lombard
    (C) Blackwell
    (D) Provo

GO ON TO THE NEXT PAGE

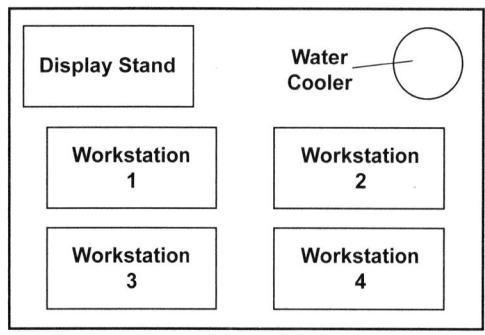

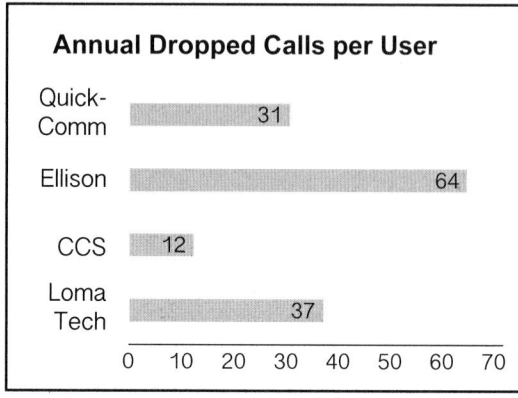

65. Who most likely is the man?
   (A) A sales representative
   (B) A building inspector
   (C) A job candidate
   (D) A delivery person

66. What does the woman plan to do in five minutes?
   (A) Make an announcement
   (B) Attend a meeting online
   (C) Check some product catalogs
   (D) Sign a form on someone's behalf

67. Look at the graphic. Which workstation will the man go to?
   (A) Workstation 1
   (B) Workstation 2
   (C) Workstation 3
   (D) Workstation 4

68. Where most likely do the speakers work?
   (A) At an Internet service provider
   (B) At an electronics firm
   (C) At a television studio
   (D) At an insurance company

69. Look at the graphic. Which company does the man refer to?
   (A) Quick-Comm
   (B) Ellison
   (C) CCS
   (D) Loma Tech

70. What will the man probably do next?
   (A) Inspect some company equipment
   (B) Write a summary of a report
   (C) Print out some customer comments
   (D) Contact company representatives

PART 4

Directions: You will hear some talks given by a single speaker. You will be asked to answer three questions about what the speaker says in each talk. Select the best response to each question and mark the letter (A), (B), (C), or (D) on your answer sheet. The talks will not be printed in your test book and will be spoken only one time.

71. What type of product is being advertised?
    (A) Soft drinks
    (B) Bread
    (C) Chocolate
    (D) Ice cream

72. What does the speaker say is available for free?
    (A) A recipe book
    (B) A product sample
    (C) A factory tour
    (D) A reusable bag

73. According to the speaker, what can the listeners do on a Web site?
    (A) Make a suggestion
    (B) View a price list
    (C) Review a service
    (D) Download a coupon

74. Where most likely is the announcement being made?
    (A) At a real estate firm
    (B) At a dental office
    (C) At a fitness center
    (D) At a hotel lobby

75. Why does the speaker say, "There is a laptop at the reception desk"?
    (A) To promote a product
    (B) To offer a solution
    (C) To report a lost item
    (D) To show a video

76. What does the speaker remind some of the listeners to do?
    (A) Display a parking pass
    (B) Update their insurance policy
    (C) Pick up a pamphlet
    (D) Sign a document

77. Who most likely are the listeners?
    (A) Construction workers
    (B) Bank tellers
    (C) Sales clerks
    (D) Board members

78. What change does the speaker tell the listeners about?
    (A) A work shift will be longer.
    (B) A grand opening has been delayed.
    (C) A deadline has been extended.
    (D) A team will be divided into two.

79. What are the listeners encouraged to do after the meeting?
    (A) Discuss safety concerns
    (B) Share transportation
    (C) Express a preference
    (D) Reserve hotel accommodations

80. What is the workshop about?
    (A) Business communication skills
    (B) Marketing on the Internet
    (C) Sustainable business practices
    (D) Preventing staff turnover

81. What did Tae-hyun Lee recently do?
    (A) He met with politicians.
    (B) He was nominated for an award.
    (C) He wrote a magazine article.
    (D) He launched a new business.

82. What does the speaker instruct the listeners to do?
    (A) Make sure to stay until the end
    (B) Check their contact information
    (C) Complete a form before a session
    (D) Browse Mr. Lee's Web site

GO ON TO THE NEXT PAGE

83. What is the broadcast about?
   (A) Footwear for runners
   (B) Tips for getting in shape
   (C) A sporting event
   (D) Competitions around the world

84. Why does the speaker say, "the only requirement is completing a form"?
   (A) To make a complaint
   (B) To correct an assumption
   (C) To suggest a change
   (D) To encourage participation

85. What did Brandon Roark do last week?
   (A) He sponsored a product.
   (B) He changed his job.
   (C) He traveled abroad.
   (D) He suffered an injury.

86. Where does the speaker work?
   (A) At an appliance store
   (B) At a gardening shop
   (C) At a post office
   (D) At a clothing manufacturer

87. Why is the speaker calling?
   (A) To request an overdue payment
   (B) To apologize for a delay
   (C) To renew a product warranty
   (D) To confirm an installation date

88. What will be sent to the listener?
   (A) A sales receipt
   (B) A set of instructions
   (C) A survey form
   (D) An access code

89. What is the speaker mainly discussing?
   (A) A training seminar
   (B) A visit from a client
   (C) A new company policy
   (D) A corporate merger

90. What are the listeners asked to do?
   (A) Make sure their work areas are organized
   (B) Arrive at the office early for a meeting
   (C) Report any overtime hours they have worked
   (D) E-mail questions about an event to the speaker

91. What does the speaker say about a meal?
   (A) Its start time will remain the same.
   (B) It will be held at a new location.
   (C) Its attendees should report allergies.
   (D) It has been postponed to the following month.

92. Where is the announcement being made?
   (A) At a sports arena
   (B) At a theater
   (C) At a travel agency
   (D) At a museum

93. Why does the speaker say, "we have a beautiful display of artwork in the entrance area"?
   (A) To justify the cost of admission
   (B) To indicate where to use some coupons
   (C) To suggest an activity to pass the time
   (D) To explain why a section is off limits

94. Why should the listeners save their tickets?
   (A) To present them upon reentry to an area
   (B) To exchange them for a beverage
   (C) To participate in a prize drawing
   (D) To qualify for a price reduction

Flowers	Plot Location	Pattern
Daisies	Left rear	Rows
Bluebells	Right rear	Circles
Lavender	Left front	Clusters
Marigolds	Right front	Spirals

95. According to the speaker, why should the listeners be cautious near a wall?

   (A) Some plants have damaged it.
   (B) It has historical value.
   (C) It was recently painted.
   (D) There are animals on the other side.

96. Look at the graphic. Which section of the plot will be planted first?

   (A) The left rear
   (B) The right rear
   (C) The left front
   (D) The right front

97. According to the speaker, what should the listeners do tomorrow?

   (A) Collect their paychecks
   (B) Bring protective gear
   (C) Label some chemicals
   (D) Return broken machinery

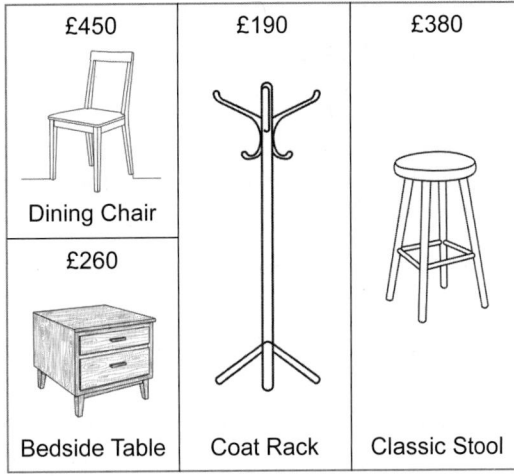

98. What is the purpose of the meeting with the listeners?

   (A) To announce changes in production processes
   (B) To present an investment opportunity
   (C) To explain an assembly procedure
   (D) To request assistance with packaging

99. Who most likely is Esther Sutton?

   (A) A product designer
   (B) A safety inspector
   (C) A company founder
   (D) A financial advisor

100. Look at the graphic. Which product does the speaker point out to the listeners?

   (A) The dining chair
   (B) The bedside table
   (C) The coat rack
   (D) The classic stool

This is the end of the Listening test. Turn to Part 5 in your test book.

GO ON TO THE NEXT PAGE

13

READING TEST

In the Reading test, you will read a variety of texts and answer several different types of reading comprehension questions. The entire Reading test will last 75 minutes. There are three parts, and directions are given for each part. You are encouraged to answer as many questions as possible within the time allowed.

You must mark your answers on the separate answer sheet. Do not write your answers in your test book.

PART 5

Directions: A word or phrase is missing in each of the sentences below. Four answer choices are given below each sentence. Select the best answer to complete the sentence. Then mark the letter (A), (B), (C), or (D) on your answer sheet.

101. To support local artists, the gallery showcased their work ------- the year.
    (A) along
    (B) past
    (C) throughout
    (D) between

102. Businessperson Joseph Delorenzo published an introductory book with ------- advice for aspiring entrepreneurs.
    (A) clinical
    (B) capable
    (C) practical
    (D) exact

103. For the company anniversary party, Ms. Hendricks designed the invitations -------.
    (A) she
    (B) her
    (C) hers
    (D) herself

104. Owing to prior commitments, the coach is not accepting ------- for interviews.
    (A) request
    (B) requested
    (C) requests
    (D) to request

105. Tenants at Carlyle Apartments should remember to close their doors -------.
    (A) softly
    (B) softer
    (C) softened
    (D) softens

106. ------- the severe storm, there was no damage to the fence built by Warren Construction.
    (A) Toward
    (B) Among
    (C) Despite
    (D) Unless

107. Advertise your business on the ------- cover of *Fitness World Monthly* to improve brand awareness.
    (A) great
    (B) side
    (C) popular
    (D) back

108. We must determine which logo design ------- our company's values going forward.
    (A) reflector
    (B) reflecting
    (C) reflects
    (D) reflected

109. Expanding our business into international markets was a ------- game changer.
(A) completely
(B) completes
(C) complete
(D) completeness

110. The software engineers decided to work overtime ------- miss the deadline.
(A) given that
(B) rather than
(C) meanwhile
(D) regarding

111. The ------- of customer service calls that are coming into the call center vastly exceeds the team's current capacity.
(A) reason
(B) volume
(C) distance
(D) statistic

112. ------- the parade, members of community organizations will pass out candy and stickers to spectators.
(A) Whereas
(B) During
(C) Typically
(D) Ongoing

113. After the power outage, affected customers were apologized to -------.
(A) randomly
(B) publicly
(C) hardly
(D) periodically

114. The building's foundation ------- with steel beams to withstand natural disasters.
(A) are reinforced
(B) will be reinforcing
(C) has been reinforced
(D) was reinforcing

115. The company implemented changes based on extremely ------- evidence of inefficiencies.
(A) strongest
(B) strong
(C) strongly
(D) strengths

116. Zander Industries faced ------- for the serious mishandling of the product recall.
(A) persuasion
(B) criticism
(C) hesitation
(D) prominence

117. To speed up the hiring process, use several sites to advertise the ------- position in the accounting department.
(A) elegant
(B) vacant
(C) successive
(D) discontinued

118. Employee attendance needs to be tracked precisely to ensure proper payroll, so it is important to keep an accurate -------.
(A) records
(B) recorded
(C) record
(D) is recorded

119. Within a few years, Ms. Cohen went from being an intern at the radio station to ------- it.
(A) ran
(B) running
(C) runner
(D) be running

120. ------- regular maintenance, the new printer requires quarterly inspections for optimal performance.
(A) Since
(B) In fact
(C) Subsequently
(D) Apart from

121. Bayou Enterprises will ------- the overnight accommodations for the representatives of Axem, the new software firm.
    (A) strain
    (B) commit
    (C) resign
    (D) arrange

122. Denson Publishing's magazines feature ------- work from its team of talented writers.
    (A) collect
    (B) collective
    (C) collectively
    (D) collection

123. Additional support is provided for those ------- are struggling to meet their performance targets.
    (A) everybody
    (B) who
    (C) whenever
    (D) you

124. Due to staff shortages in the busiest season, the vacation policy will require -------.
    (A) evaluate
    (B) evaluated
    (C) evaluates
    (D) evaluation

125. At the year-end banquet, attendees will be ------- to a delicious buffet.
    (A) influenced
    (B) submitted
    (C) treated
    (D) converted

126. Thank you for so ------- donating to the restoration of the historic chapel downtown.
    (A) generous
    (B) generosity
    (C) being generous
    (D) generously

127. Market analysts are observing a ------- toward outsourcing administrative tasks.
    (A) burden
    (B) trend
    (C) routine
    (D) behavior

128. The bottled tea contained an ------- high level of artificial ingredients.
    (A) impartially
    (B) unacceptably
    (C) optionally
    (D) entirely

129. We ------- Kirk Railway conductors to share their suggestions for service improvements.
    (A) invite
    (B) treat
    (C) ensure
    (D) adopt

130. Oliverio Bank's smartphone application allows users to check their accounts around the clock, -------, at the touch of a button.
    (A) everyone
    (B) anybody
    (C) everything
    (D) anywhere

PART 6

Directions: Read the texts that follow. A word, phrase, or sentence is missing in parts of each text. Four answer choices for each question are given below the text. Select the best answer to complete the text. Then mark the letter (A), (B), (C), or (D) on your answer sheet.

Questions 131-134 refer to the following memo.

To: All Management Staff
From: Manako Komatsu
Subject: Fleet expansion
Date: 10 January

Owing to your hard work, we have experienced another successful year of vehicle rentals and have a surplus in the budget. So, we will purchase more vehicles for our fleet. ------- . The new 131. vehicles ------- able to drive at least thirty-five miles per gallon. In addition, many customers have 132. expressed the need for help in ------- . So, we must purchase separate GPS-enabled devices that 133. direct drivers to their destinations. ------- , these can be purchased in bulk for a reasonable price. 134.

131. (A) Some drivers prefer to use their own auto insurance.
 (B) Further training may prevent these errors in the future.
 (C) Matching the rates of our competitors was a wise decision.
 (D) We are prioritizing small, fuel-efficient vehicles.

132. (A) could have been
 (B) should be
 (C) have been
 (D) to be

133. (A) financing
 (B) navigating
 (C) consulting
 (D) investing

134. (A) As an example
 (B) As a consequence
 (C) On a positive note
 (D) In contrast

Questions 135-138 refer to the following letter.

March 8

Violet Calloway
791 Flannigan Street
Kent, WA 98042

Dear Ms. Calloway,

I am writing to confirm that I would like to ------- my lease for unit 304 in Garza Towers. I am
                                              135.
pleased with the building and its amenities, so I plan to stay here for another year.

I know that you carry out a property inspection annually, and this would be a good time to do so
anyway. The drain in the bathroom sink needs addressing, ------- the flooring in the kitchen, which
                                                          136.
is starting to peel away.

------- . Therefore, I can be available at almost any time to let work crews enter the property.
137.

Please e-mail me at amberpoole@odenton.com to indicate ------- of this message and let me
                                                        138.
know the next steps.

Sincerely,

Amber Poole

135. (A) observe
     (B) terminate
     (C) impact
     (D) extend

136. (A) as soon as
     (B) along with
     (C) except for
     (D) regardless of

137. (A) My job is entirely remote, so I am at home most of the day.
     (B) I am pleased to have an assigned parking spot so close.
     (C) The noise from other tenants can be very distracting at times.
     (D) A two-bedroom unit would better suit my preferences these days.

138. (A) recommendation
     (B) permission
     (C) acknowledgment
     (D) commitment

Questions 139-142 refer to the following e-mail.

To: l.burgess@burgesselectric.com
From: pulvera@jsadvertising.com
Date: June 8
Subject: Advertising your business

Dear Mr. Burgess,

As an independent contractor, you understand how ------- word-of-mouth advertising can be. 139.
Customers who are satisfied with your electrician services are likely to tell friends and family members about you. ------- , personal referrals can only get you so far. That is why it is important 140.
to continue advertising online and in traditional newspapers. If you are looking for advertising solutions but ------- by the options, we can help. ------- . 141. 142.

Contact us at 555-0894 at your convenience for a free consultation with a member of our team.

Sincerely,
Alba Pulver

139. (A) confirmed
(B) delicate
(C) impressed
(D) effective

140. (A) Likewise
(B) Nevertheless
(C) Instead
(D) Consequently

141. (A) had overwhelmed
(B) overwhelming
(C) are overwhelmed
(D) to overwhelm

142. (A) Furthermore, some information on social media may be incorrect.
(B) Over the years, our staff size has nearly doubled.
(C) Best of all, our in-house designers can create the ad for you.
(D) We appreciate your kind comments regarding our service.

Questions 143-146 refer to the following article.

The pharmaceutical industry is undergoing rapid advancements, particularly in the field of biotechnology. These developments have -------- implications for patient care, as new treatments are becoming more effective and personalized. Improved research -------- faster drug development and approval processes. Experts suggest that these -------- will significantly enhance the quality of healthcare. -------- .

143. (A) annual
 (B) considerate
 (C) wider
 (D) convenient

144. (A) enabling
 (B) enable
 (C) enabler
 (D) enables

145. (A) innovations
 (B) innovated
 (C) innovate
 (D) innovates

146. (A) The journal's article outlines similar preferences.
 (B) Indeed, better patient outcomes and high satisfaction ratings are expected.
 (C) Physicians are trained at a variety of institutions.
 (D) In fact, the age of a patient will affect his or her needs.

PART 7

Directions: In this part you will read a selection of texts, such as magazine and newspaper articles, e-mails, and instant messages. Each text or set of texts is followed by several questions. Select the best answer for each question and mark the letter (A), (B), (C), or (D) on your answer sheet.

Questions 147-148 refer to the following coupon.

LIMITED-TIME OFFER

Before September 1, buy any three packages of Trailz nuts ($2.99 each) and get a fourth one free! Mix and match for the combination of nuts you prefer.

Trailz package options:

- 40 grams of roasted pecans
- 50 grams of crushed walnuts
- 60 grams of raw almonds
- 150 grams of spicy peanuts

---

147. How many packages of nuts must be paid for if the coupon is used?

(A) One
(B) Two
(C) Three
(D) Four

148. What is true about the largest package of Trailz nuts?

(A) Its product is crushed.
(B) Its product is raw.
(C) Its product is roasted.
(D) Its product is spicy.

GO ON TO THE NEXT PAGE

Questions 149-151 refer to the following information.

Welcome to the Nexus!

Our lobby has casual seating, where you can wait for the rest of your party while using our free Wi-Fi. Purchase beverages and light snacks at our café, which is open before and after shows as well as during intermission, when applicable. There you can also turn in or inquire about lost items.

Those with premium seats can also access our VIP lounge, a quiet and elegant space with complimentary drinks, gourmet snacks, and a live feed of the stage. The theater's upper floor has an outdoor balcony with stunning views of the city's skyline.

At the box office, you can pick up an audio guide to learn about the theater's history and tour the building at your own pace. We also have private rooms available for rent. Speak to a staff member at the box office to book one or to find out more about rates.

We hope you have a great time here at the Nexus!

149. For whom is the information most likely intended?

(A) Stage performers
(B) Construction workers
(C) Audience members
(D) Theater staff

150. Where should people bring lost items?

(A) To the VIP lounge
(B) To the lobby
(C) To the box office
(D) To the café

151. According to the information, what are visitors NOT able to do on their own?

(A) Learn about room rates
(B) Get access to the Internet
(C) Take an audio tour
(D) Enjoy scenic views

Questions 152-153 refer to the following Web page.

Alterations

At Addison, we're pleased to offer a complimentary alteration service to ensure that your jeans fit perfectly. Our expert tailors are dedicated to providing a personalized fit by adjusting the length of your jeans to match your measurements and preferences. We understand the importance of quick service, so most alterations are completed within 48 hours, allowing you to enjoy your favorite jeans without delay. This service applies to any pair of Addison jeans, new or old.

For your convenience, you can drop off your jeans at any of our participating stores without advance notice. We will text or call you when your jeans are ready for pickup. Take advantage of this free service today and experience a fresh look. We know that it will help you feel great!

---

152. What is NOT indicated about the alteration service?

(A) It requires in-person pickup.
(B) It will not incur a fee.
(C) It is for Addison jeans only.
(D) It is guaranteed within 48 hours.

153. What is suggested about Addison?

(A) It can custom dye jeans.
(B) It has more than one branch.
(C) It offers bulk discounts.
(D) It is currently hiring tailors.

Questions 154-156 refer to the following announcement.

Take charge of your health!

— [1] —. On Friday, November 15, the Whitby Clinic is sponsoring a Health and Wellness Fair at the Westborough Community Center. The clinic's staff will lead a variety of activities and talks throughout the day. Attendees can get their blood pressure and cholesterol level checked and get screened for vision and hearing issues. Louise Cantrell will lead exercise classes at 10 A.M., 1 P.M., and 3 P.M. as well as give stretching demonstrations. — [2] —. Kenneth Reynolds will give a talk on nutrition and healthy eating habits. Younger attendees can enjoy fun and educational activities, including face painting and a mini obstacle course, in the Kids Zone. — [3] —. Those with food allergies should speak to an event volunteer.

There is no fee for attending the event. — [4] —. However, the event organizers ask that you bring canned goods to donate, which will be given to the nonprofit group Help at Home. Free parking is available on site.

154. What is indicated about Kenneth Reynolds?

(A) He will conduct vision screening tests.
(B) He is an employee of the Whitby Clinic.
(C) He attended the fair last year.
(D) He will help to set up the Kids Zone.

155. What is true about the event?

(A) It takes place over the course of two days.
(B) Its tickets are available online and at the door.
(C) It includes collecting food items for a charity.
(D) Its location is a local medical facility.

156. In which of the positions marked [1], [2], [3], and [4] does the following sentence best belong?

"A variety of healthy refreshments will be served."

(A) [1]
(B) [2]
(C) [3]
(D) [4]

Questions 157-158 refer to the following packing slip.

Thank you for your purchase of a custom-printed mug from Boca Print, included in this shipment. This twelve-ounce ceramic mug features your unique design. Unlike our competitors, who use vinyl cutouts, we transfer the dye directly onto the mug using heat to embed it into the mug, not just have it resting on the surface. This ensures that the vibrant and precise details will remain even after regular washing.

We love to see how our customers are using our products in their everyday lives. Upload a photo of your product on our social media site to get a chance to win a $100 voucher! You will be entered automatically.

157. What does the packing slip indicate about Boca Print's printing process?

(A) It can take up to twelve days.
(B) Its materials should be handled with care.
(C) It is not used by other businesses.
(D) Its cost varies depending on the mug's size.

158. Why is the purchaser encouraged to upload a photograph?

(A) To be eligible for an upcoming prize drawing
(B) To compare the real colors to a sample
(C) To prove that a design does not match a request
(D) To help the company to train its employees

Questions 159-161 refer to the following letter.

Melrose Supermarket
191 Telford Street
LEEDS, LS1 2AL

Donna Crayton
26 Circle Way
HOWDEN, DN14 7EN

Dear Ms. Crayton,

Earn more than 3,000 loyalty points with just one trip to Melrose Supermarket! You'll be credited with 2,000 points automatically when you enroll in the Melrose Supermarket Loyalty Program. Upon your first purchase, you'll be awarded 1,000 points on top of those you earn for that purchase. As a loyalty program member, you'll earn 2 points for every dollar spent at our store. And every month, you can earn double points on featured products, up to 2,500 points. Members can exchange their points for Melrose Supermarket vouchers or vouchers offered by our partners. They'll also be informed of special sales events ahead of time. Don't miss this amazing opportunity! Sign up today at www.melrosesupermarket.net.

All the best,

Marlena Estrada

Marlena Estrada
Loyalty Program Manager, Melrose Supermarket

159. How many loyalty points can Ms. Crayton receive immediately when she signs up for a program?
    (A) 1,000
    (B) 2,000
    (C) 2,500
    (D) 3,000

160. What is true about members of the Melrose Supermarket Loyalty Program?
    (A) They can earn points by patronizing partner businesses.
    (B) They will get coupons for featured products each month.
    (C) They will be notified about certain sales in advance.
    (D) They can exchange their points anytime for cash.

161. The word "miss" in paragraph 1, line 9, is closest in meaning to
    (A) pass up
    (B) fail
    (C) wish for
    (D) misunderstand

Questions 162-163 refer to the following text-message chain.

Cassandra Velez (9:43 A.M.)
Hi, Brian. Could you see if Mr. Yi is waiting in the lobby?

Brian Sloan (9:44 A.M.)
Of course. I'll take a look.

Cassandra Velez (9:45 A.M.)
Thank you. No one is picking up at the front desk, and I'm running late.

Brian Sloan (9:49 A.M.)
He's not there yet. Should I ask the receptionist to tell Mr. Yi you'll be late?

Cassandra Velez (9:50 A.M.)
That's okay. I'm almost there. I'm on the bus, just one stop away. I don't have my car today.

Brian Sloan (9:51 A.M.)
That reminds me! You got a call from Stephen Boone. You can stop by anytime today for pickup.

Cassandra Velez (9:52 A.M.)
Great! The vehicle repairs took longer than I expected, but I'm glad he finished them. I'll be in the office shortly.

Brian Sloan (9:53 A.M.)
See you soon.

162. At 9:44 A.M., what does Mr. Sloan most likely mean when he writes, "I'll take a look"?

(A) He will find out about a schedule change.
(B) He will check an area for Mr. Yi.
(C) He will proofread a report for Ms. Velez.
(D) He will make sure the lobby is tidy.

163. What is suggested about Mr. Boone?

(A) He is an auto mechanic.
(B) He will visit Ms. Velez's office.
(C) He is late for a meeting.
(D) He has picked up some documents.

Questions 164-167 refer to the following article.

AUGUSTA (March 10)—While online stores have made it more difficult for physical retail stores to stay in business, customers still prefer to see some types of products for themselves. — [1] —. This may be a contributing factor in the success of the recently opened Craft Haven store, located at 208 11th Avenue. The store offers a wide variety of yarn and fabric, which many shoppers want to see and touch in person to check the weight and texture. Beads, scrapbooking supplies, and painting kits are also sold. — [2] —. The decorations in the entrance area of the shop include pictures of craft projects completed by customers, a growing showcase of the creativity and talent within the community.

For craft enthusiasts, there are monthly project competitions. — [3] —. Craft Haven also hosts weekly crafting classes for beginners and experts alike as well as other special events. — [4] —.

"We want Craft Haven to be a place where people can come together, learn, and express themselves through crafting," says owner Ada Lawson.

Craft Haven is open daily from 9 A.M. to 7 P.M.

164. Why was the article written?

(A) To announce a change in ownership
(B) To promote a craft fair
(C) To highlight a new business
(D) To introduce a crafting club

165. What is indicated about the entryway?

(A) It displays samples of products.
(B) It has tables for giving demonstrations.
(C) It has been painted by Ms. Lawson.
(D) It features images of people's projects.

166. What is NOT indicated about Craft Haven?

(A) It offers classes for all levels.
(B) It can mix custom paint colors.
(C) Its inventory includes cloth.
(D) Its customers want to feel some products.

167. In which of the positions marked [1], [2], [3], and [4] does the following sentence best belong?

"The next one will be a watercolor demonstration by artist Sophie Gale."

(A) [1]
(B) [2]
(C) [3]
(D) [4]

Questions 168-171 refer to the following press release.

FOR IMMEDIATE RELEASE
CONTACT: Joel Campbell, jcampbell@elmsfordfinance.com

Elmsford Finance to Provide Retirement Advice

EAST POINT, GEORGIA (September 9) —Elmsford Finance, a market leader in financial planning services, announces that it will open registration on September 12 for a free retirement planning webinar on September 25 at 2:00 P.M. Eastern Standard Time. The webinar will be hosted by Allison Torres, an expert in the field, who will cover investment options, tax planning, maximizing government benefits, and how to work out how much is needed for retirement. For anyone unable to attend the event live, a video recording of the webinar will be posted on the company's Web site the following day. It will be available for download for 30 days, though we encourage live participation in order to ask questions. Last year, over five hundred participants gained valuable insights during the debut event, prompting Elmsford Finance to offer this informative session once again.

Elmsford Finance Retirement Planning Webinar
Date: September 25
Time: 2:00 P.M. Eastern Standard Time
Registration Page: www.webinarmax.com/248601

Please note that the webinar is for informational purposes only and does not constitute financial advice, as circumstances may vary. Consult a qualified financial advisor for personalized guidance tailored to your individual retirement planning needs.

168. Why was the press release written?

(A) To advertise a new retirement investment package
(B) To provide information about a learning opportunity
(C) To announce a change to an event's registration procedure
(D) To gather feedback about a company's performance

169. When can people download a recording of an event?

(A) On September 9
(B) On September 25
(C) On September 26
(D) On October 25

170. The phrase "work out" in paragraph 1, line 5, is closest in meaning to

(A) calculate
(B) exercise
(C) apply
(D) practice

171. What is true about Elmsford Finance's upcoming event?

(A) It includes a nominal registration fee.
(B) It is expected to reach full capacity.
(C) It is being held for the second time.
(D) It is expected to have five hundred attendees.

GO ON TO THE NEXT PAGE

Questions 172-175 refer to the following text-message chain.

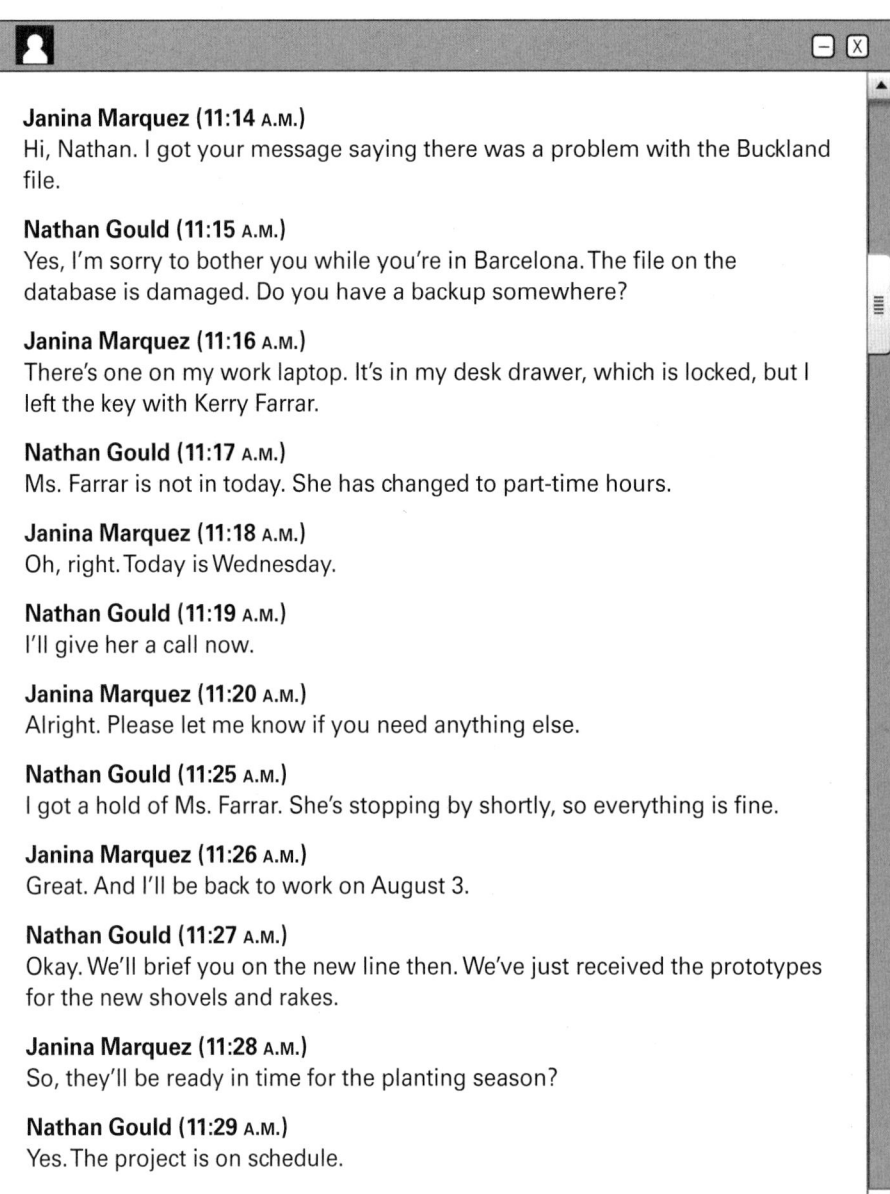

Janina Marquez (11:14 A.M.)
Hi, Nathan. I got your message saying there was a problem with the Buckland file.

Nathan Gould (11:15 A.M.)
Yes, I'm sorry to bother you while you're in Barcelona. The file on the database is damaged. Do you have a backup somewhere?

Janina Marquez (11:16 A.M.)
There's one on my work laptop. It's in my desk drawer, which is locked, but I left the key with Kerry Farrar.

Nathan Gould (11:17 A.M.)
Ms. Farrar is not in today. She has changed to part-time hours.

Janina Marquez (11:18 A.M.)
Oh, right. Today is Wednesday.

Nathan Gould (11:19 A.M.)
I'll give her a call now.

Janina Marquez (11:20 A.M.)
Alright. Please let me know if you need anything else.

Nathan Gould (11:25 A.M.)
I got a hold of Ms. Farrar. She's stopping by shortly, so everything is fine.

Janina Marquez (11:26 A.M.)
Great. And I'll be back to work on August 3.

Nathan Gould (11:27 A.M.)
Okay. We'll brief you on the new line then. We've just received the prototypes for the new shovels and rakes.

Janina Marquez (11:28 A.M.)
So, they'll be ready in time for the planting season?

Nathan Gould (11:29 A.M.)
Yes. The project is on schedule.

172. What is suggested about Barcelona?
    (A) The Buckland headquarters is located there.
    (B) Ms. Marquez will set up an office there.
    (C) Mr. Gould has transferred from there.
    (D) Ms. Marquez is taking a vacation there.

173. What is suggested about Ms. Farrar?
    (A) She is not scheduled to work on Wednesdays.
    (B) She will meet Mr. Gould later today.
    (C) She plans to make a copy of a key.
    (D) She is working as Ms. Marquez's assistant.

174. At 11:25 A.M., what does Mr. Gould mean when he writes, "everything is fine"?
    (A) Ms. Farrar has agreed to cover a shift.
    (B) Ms. Marquez will be able to access a laptop.
    (C) A deadline for a file has been changed.
    (D) Some instructions can be understood.

175. What kinds of items does the writers' company most likely sell?
    (A) Laboratory devices
    (B) Cooking equipment
    (C) Gardening tools
    (D) Sporting goods

GO ON TO THE NEXT PAGE

Questions 176-180 refer to the following memo and e-mail.

Bauman Insurance Company
MEMO

From: Lillian Hale
To: All Bauman Insurance Company Staff
Date: July 30
Subject: Office Painting

Starting from Thursday, the interior walls of our building will be painted, with the communal areas also used by Starkey Logistics—hallways and restrooms—to be completed over the weekend. The schedule is as follows:

Dates	Department	Contact
August 2–3	Marketing & Sales	Priya Desai
August 4–5	(Shared Areas)	Lillian Hale
August 6–7	Human Resources	Theresa Wiley
August 8–9	Finance	Youngmin Park
August 10–11	Information Technology	Colin Thorpe

While your department is being painted, you will work in one of the conference rooms temporarily. You will have to save your files in the shared folder on the company server or to an external hard drive so you can access them from a laptop. Be sure to add password protection to any files that are saved on the company server. Should you have any questions, please e-mail the contact person indicated for your specific department.

From:	Shawn Mitchell <s.mitchell@baumanins.com>
To:	Theresa Wiley <t.wiley@baumanins.com>
Date:	July 31
Subject:	Office painting

Ms. Wiley,

As I am very sensitive to paint fumes, which give me a headache even with minimal exposure, I'm wondering if it would be possible to work from home while the office painting is being carried out.

I don't have any meetings scheduled for the proposed dates, so I don't think this adjustment will negatively affect the team. Please let me know if this is possible.

Thank you,

Shawn Mitchell

176. What is suggested about Bauman Insurance Company?
    (A) It has recently moved to a new site.
    (B) It shares its building with another company.
    (C) Its employees can take extra time off in August.
    (D) Its building has been purchased by a new investor.

177. What does Ms. Hale instruct some employees to do?
    (A) Place their belongings in a box
    (B) Restrict access to their files
    (C) Upgrade some computer software
    (D) Return company laptops promptly

178. Who will handle inquiries for members of the finance team?
    (A) Ms. Hale
    (B) Ms. Wiley
    (C) Mr. Park
    (D) Mr. Thorpe

179. What is the purpose of the e-mail?
    (A) To ask to work from another location
    (B) To suggest an alternative paint product
    (C) To report a scheduling conflict
    (D) To explain an issue with a device

180. In what department does Mr. Mitchell most likely work?
    (A) Marketing & Sales
    (B) Human Resources
    (C) Finance
    (D) Information Technology

Questions 181-185 refer to the following e-mails.

E-Mail message

To: mbakshi@hauerco.com
From: r.chittum@veltrisecurity.com
Date: October 20
Subject: Follow-up

Dear Ms. Bakshi,

I'd like to follow up on your interest in a security system from Veltri Security. During our discussion, I forgot to mention that, as part of the external security of your office building's parking lot, we can also construct fencing and gates to control access to the area. From what I saw today at the premises, security could be improved greatly with the addition of such barriers. Our service will provide you with high-definition cameras throughout the building and parking lot as well as lights equipped with motion sensors. We will also install smart locks at the main entrances, which can be controlled and monitored remotely. I understand that you have already budgeted for the basic package but that you will speak to your company's budget committee on October 28 to request the approval of additional funds. I look forward to discussing your options further once you have finalized your budget.

Sincerely,

Ralph Chittum

E-Mail message

To: r.chittum@veltrisecurity.com
From: mbakshi@hauerco.com
Date: October 25
Subject: RE: Follow-up

Dear Mr. Chittum,

Thank you for taking the time to inform me about the various packages for security services. Your company has an excellent reputation, and I am confident that you are the right firm for this task.

Initially, we thought we would need your services only at our Davidson site. As you mentioned, we have yet to determine the level of security we can commit to. Moreover, we expect our needs to develop over time. Nevertheless, what I can confirm is that the management team has decided that the security services should be extended to our Clarksville site as well. I will contact you again next week, when I have further details. Once everything is finalized, I hope we can draw up a contract as quickly as possible. I appreciate your patience in this matter.

Sincerely,

Maya Bakshi

181. What does the first e-mail indicate about Mr. Chittum?

(A) He visited Ms. Bakshi's business location.
(B) He had to postpone a meeting with Ms. Bakshi.
(C) He previously sold Ms. Bakshi a security system.
(D) He had a phone conversation with Ms. Bakshi.

182. In the first e-mail, what is NOT mentioned as part of a service by Mr. Chittum?

(A) Setting up security cameras
(B) Adding special locks
(C) Installing motion-activated lights
(D) Reviewing video footage

183. What is the purpose of Ms. Bakshi's e-mail?

(A) To confirm the terms of an agreement
(B) To report a change in circumstances
(C) To extend a deadline for a contract
(D) To explain a breach in security

184. In the second e-mail, the word "develop" in paragraph 2, line 3, is closest in meaning to

(A) thrive
(B) invent
(C) evolve
(D) spread

185. What is suggested about Ms. Bakshi?

(A) She initially only wanted outdoor security.
(B) She wants to explore offers from other firms.
(C) She has not addressed a committee yet.
(D) She will transfer to the Clarksville branch.

Questions 186-190 refer to the following job advertisement, e-mail, and calendar.

Join the dynamic team at Keane Realty!

Keane Realty, Bailey City's largest real estate agency, is seeking a licensed real estate agent. Strong communication skills are essential. In addition, a reliable personal vehicle is required, as the job involves visiting properties around Bailey City. You must be available on Saturdays, Sundays, and weekday evenings. Job duties include:

– conducting property tours and open house events for prospective buyers

– assisting clients with property listings, including investigating property values in the target neighborhood

– negotiating purchase agreements and closing sales efficiently

To:	Declan Coe <coedec@eserve.com>
From:	Tomo Daisaki <tomo@keanerealty.com>
Date:	February 5
Subject:	Next steps
Attachment:	📎 property_description.doc

Dear Mr. Coe,

We are pleased to inform you that you have passed the screening phase for the real estate agent position here at Keane Realty. For the next stage of the hiring process, we ask that you write a sample listing for a property. Attached you will find the necessary pictures and information for your reference. Please send this back to me by February 12.

We would also like to invite you to participate in an initial interview, which can be done by phone or video call on February 16. Please let me know which one you would prefer.

I look forward to hearing from you,

Tomo Daisaki

Week of February 7

Name: Declan Coe

7 Sunday	8 Monday	9 Tuesday	10 Wednesday	11 Thursday	12 Friday	13 Saturday
One hour of company research	Dental appointment at 11:00 A.M.	Begin sample listing	Submit sample listing		Book rental van	Lunch with Reggie

186. What is indicated about the real estate agent position?

    (A) It involves managing others.
    (B) It comes with a company vehicle.
    (C) It includes on-the-job training.
    (D) It requires local traveling.

187. What is mentioned as a duty in the job advertisement?

    (A) Taking pictures of homes
    (B) Researching property prices
    (C) Filing building permits
    (D) Assessing loan applications

188. What does Ms. Daisaki offer to Mr. Coe?

    (A) A choice of interview methods
    (B) A bonus for signing a contract
    (C) A letter of recommendation
    (D) An update to a staff directory

189. What is suggested about Mr. Coe?

    (A) He has at least three years of experience.
    (B) He submitted a letter of recommendation.
    (C) He is available to work on the weekend.
    (D) He has a friend working at Keane Realty.

190. When does Mr. Coe plan to complete a required writing sample?

    (A) On the day of the deadline
    (B) The day before the deadline
    (C) Two days before the deadline
    (D) Three days before the deadline

GO ON TO THE NEXT PAGE

Questions 191-195 refer to the following e-mails and article.

From	Felicia Arner <arnerf@siroccoinc.net>
To	Huan Wang <wangh@siroccoinc.net>
Date	March 26
Subject	Report
Attachment	env.impact_vigo.doc

Dear Mr. Wang,

I'm pleased to send you the environmental impact report regarding the Vigo site for our newest wind farm. Fortunately, it only calls for very minor adjustments to our blueprints. That means we're still on schedule to connect the site to the power grid on October 1. If you have any questions, please e-mail me anytime.

Sincerely,

Felicia Arner

---

http://www.energy-watch.com

Sirocco Inc., an emerging player in the renewable energy sector with its home office in Cadiz, has added another wind farm to its operations following its success in Maceda.

The newest site, located in Vigo, passed all safety tests and was connected to the grid on September 12. The wind farm has forty-two turbines, giving it the capacity to generate approximately 110 megawatts of energy. The project was supervised by Sirocco's Head Construction Manager, Terrance Calvert, who is retiring now that it is finished.

A spokesperson for Sirocco Inc. said that the company's next farm, which is being designed by Senior Engineer Mikel Arroyo of Ortiz Engineering, will be built in Padroso. Sirocco plans to commence initial site preparations there shortly and is inviting prospective investors to tour the location.

More information is available at www.siroccoinc.net.

From	Sergio Moreno <moreno.s@siroccoinc.net>
To	Beatriz Torrente <beatriz_torrente@cpinvestments.com>
Date	December 10
Subject	Visit to Padroso
Attachment	dec12_7493.doc

Dear Ms. Torrente,

We are excited about your upcoming visit to the Padroso site. The land-clearing stage has already begun, and our team will be available to answer your questions. Our company has booked you a room at the Plata Hotel, and you can check in on December 12 anytime after 2 P.M. Everything has been paid for, and you can find the booking and confirmation details in the attached document. If I can assist you in any other way, please let me know.

Warmest regards,

Sergio Moreno
Head Construction Manager, Sirocco Inc.

191. In the first e-mail, what is suggested about the environmental impact report?

(A) It was due on March 26.
(B) It did not significantly impact the design.
(C) It must be reviewed annually.
(D) It failed to include an important section.

192. What can be inferred about the Vigo site?

(A) It got connected to the grid early.
(B) Its permit was initially rejected.
(C) It is generating more energy than expected.
(D) It is larger than the site at Maceda.

193. According to the article, where is the Sirocco Inc. headquarters located?

(A) In Padroso
(B) In Vigo
(C) In Cadiz
(D) In Maceda

194. What is true about Mr. Moreno?

(A) He met with Mr. Arroyo.
(B) He worked on the Vigo project.
(C) He visited Ms. Torrente's office.
(D) He took over Mr. Calvert's role.

195. What did Mr. Moreno send along with the e-mail?

(A) A map of some land
(B) A list of employees
(C) Reservation information
(D) His travel itinerary

GO ON TO THE NEXT PAGE

Questions 196-200 refer to the following review, Web page, and e-mail.

---

https://www.baxterfitness.com/reviews/2154

Does the Job

I've been using my Baxter treadmill for a few months, and it's been a great experience so far. I thought it was reasonably priced, considering the numerous features and the sturdy components. It's great that I can fold up the treadmill and keep it between my dresser and the wall, so it's out of the way when not in use. The treadmill has excellent cushioning, so the impact on my joints is minimal. The incline option helps to create a challenging workout. I also like the fact that I can play music from my phone through its speakers. However, this isn't ideal because the machine is really loud when in operation, so I still use my headphones often. Overall, I would recommend this treadmill.

— Jerry Linden, April 22

---

https://www.baxterfitness.com/treadmill_models

Get in shape with help from Baxter Fitness! You can enjoy the benefits of walking, running, and jogging right in your own home with one of our state-of-the-art treadmills. Choose the model that fits your needs and budget.

Pace — $650, recommended for those on a budget
- Maximum speed: 10 mph
- Belt size: 18" x 50"
- Lightweight aluminum frame

Stride — $950, recommended for beginners
- Maximum speed: 12 mph
- Belt size: 20" x 52"
- Built-in speakers

Tempo — $1250, recommended for intermediate runners
- Maximum speed: 12 mph
- Belt size: 22" x 55"
- (198-3) 3 incline positions
- Built-in speakers

Dura-max — $1500, recommended for advanced runners
- Maximum speed: 16 mph
- Belt size: 22" x 60"
- 5 incline positions
- Heart-rate monitoring
- 15 pre-set workout programs

Baxter Guarantee: If you have any issues with your treadmill within the first 12 months of purchase, we will send a technician to repair it at no charge.

All of our treadmills are easy to assemble and come with clear instructions. We also have videos showing you each step.

```
======================== E-Mail message ========================
From:     mahichetti@baxterfitness.com
To:       j.linden@vennemail.com
Date:     April 16
Subject:  Treadmill review
```

Dear Mr. Linden,

Thank you for sharing your feedback about your Baxter treadmill. It is always useful to us to hear from our customers, as this gives us the opportunity to make improvements to future models. I'm pleased that, overall, you are happy with the equipment, but I wonder if your particular treadmill is in need of maintenance. I see on your account that you are still eligible for our free service from a technician. If you would like to book this service, please e-mail me with a range of times and dates that suit your schedule. Additionally, we would like to give you a free rubber treadmill mat, which will reduce vibration and protect your floor. This can be mailed to you or brought by the technician. I look forward to hearing from you soon.

Warmest regards,

Mahi Chetti
Customer Service Manager, Baxter Fitness

---

196. In the review, what does Mr. Linden indicate about his treadmill?

(A) It uses little electricity.
(B) It came with additional components.
(C) It can be stored easily.
(D) It has a removable cushion.

197. What aspect of the treadmill does Mr. Linden think could be better?

(A) The noise level
(B) The lack of safety
(C) The unusual shape
(D) The slow speed

198. What treadmill model does Mr. Linden most likely have?

(A) Pace
(B) Stride
(C) Tempo
(D) Dura-max

199. On the Web page, what is suggested about Baxter Fitness's treadmills?

(A) They are endorsed by professional athletes.
(B) They have the same belt size.
(C) They require assembly after delivery.
(D) They can be exchanged for a refund.

200. What can be inferred about Mr. Linden's treadmill?

(A) It was purchased less than a year ago.
(B) It was part of a product recall.
(C) It came with a rubber mat.
(D) It is probably missing a wire.

Stop! This is the end of the test. If you finish before time is called, you may go back to Parts 5, 6, and 7 and check your work.

Answer Key

750⁺

1 (D)	2 (B)	3 (A)	4 (D)	5 (C)	6 (C)	7 (B)	8 (C)	9 (C)	10 (B)
11 (C)	12 (C)	13 (C)	14 (C)	15 (B)	16 (A)	17 (C)	18 (C)	19 (B)	20 (A)
21 (A)	22 (A)	23 (B)	24 (C)	25 (C)	26 (B)	27 (C)	28 (B)	29 (C)	30 (B)
31 (A)	32 (C)	33 (A)	34 (D)	35 (C)	36 (A)	37 (B)	38 (A)	39 (D)	40 (C)
41 (B)	42 (D)	43 (D)	44 (D)	45 (B)	46 (C)	47 (D)	48 (D)	49 (A)	50 (B)
51 (C)	52 (A)	53 (C)	54 (B)	55 (B)	56 (D)	57 (A)	58 (C)	59 (B)	60 (A)
61 (B)	62 (D)	63 (A)	64 (B)	65 (D)	66 (B)	67 (B)	68 (C)	69 (B)	70 (D)
71 (D)	72 (B)	73 (A)	74 (B)	75 (B)	76 (A)	77 (A)	78 (D)	79 (C)	80 (C)
81 (A)	82 (B)	83 (C)	84 (B)	85 (D)	86 (A)	87 (D)	88 (B)	89 (B)	90 (A)
91 (A)	92 (B)	93 (C)	94 (D)	95 (B)	96 (D)	97 (B)	98 (B)	99 (A)	100 (D)
101 (C)	102 (C)	103 (D)	104 (C)	105 (A)	106 (C)	107 (D)	108 (C)	109 (C)	110 (B)
111 (B)	112 (B)	113 (B)	114 (C)	115 (B)	116 (B)	117 (B)	118 (C)	119 (B)	120 (D)
121 (D)	122 (B)	123 (B)	124 (D)	125 (C)	126 (D)	127 (B)	128 (B)	129 (A)	130 (D)
131 (D)	132 (B)	133 (B)	134 (C)	135 (D)	136 (B)	137 (A)	138 (C)	139 (D)	140 (B)
141 (C)	142 (C)	143 (C)	144 (D)	145 (A)	146 (B)	147 (C)	148 (D)	149 (C)	150 (D)
151 (A)	152 (D)	153 (B)	154 (B)	155 (C)	156 (C)	157 (C)	158 (A)	159 (B)	160 (C)
161 (A)	162 (B)	163 (A)	164 (C)	165 (D)	166 (B)	167 (D)	168 (B)	169 (C)	170 (A)
171 (C)	172 (D)	173 (A)	174 (B)	175 (C)	176 (B)	177 (B)	178 (C)	179 (A)	180 (B)
181 (A)	182 (D)	183 (B)	184 (C)	185 (C)	186 (D)	187 (B)	188 (A)	189 (C)	190 (C)
191 (B)	192 (A)	193 (C)	194 (D)	195 (C)	196 (C)	197 (A)	198 (C)	199 (C)	200 (A)

ANSWER SHEET

실전 모의고사

LISTENING (Part I ~ IV)

READING (Part V ~ VII)

ANSWER SHEET

실전 모의고사

수험번호

응시일자 : 20   년   월   일

성명 / 한글 / 한자 / 영자

LISTENING (Part I ~ IV)

READING (Part V ~ VII)